Autodesk Maya 2027 Basics Guide

Kelly L. Murdock

SDC PUBLICATIONS

SDC Publications
P.O. Box 1334
Mission, KS 66222
913-262-2664
www.SDCpublications.com
Publisher: Stephen Schroff

ISBN-13: 978-1-63057-808-4
ISBN-10: 1-63057-808-8

Printed and bound in the United States of America.

Credits

Acquisitions Editor
Stephen Schroff

Project Editor
Karla Werner

Website/Cover Design
Zach Werner

Copy Editor
Megan Kemper

Dedication

To all the talented artists out there. May your creativity never run dry.

Acknowledgments

I would like to acknowledge several individuals who have been such a huge help on this project. First of all, Stephen Schroff, who has been great as my point contact, and Zach Werner, who has patiently managed the project.

I'd also like to thank my editors. I'd also like to thank all the people at SDC Publications who work behind the scenes to create such great titles.

Thanks to all the wonderful people at Autodesk who have really stepped up their efforts to support me in this project. And thanks to the great development team at Alias for creating such a great software package.

I'd always be remiss if I didn't thank my family, without whose support I'd never get to the end of a book. To Angela, for infinite patience. To Eric and Thomas, for many much-needed interruptions.

About the Author

Kelly L. Murdock has a background in engineering, specializing in computer graphics and a PhD in Instructional Design. This background has led him to many interesting experiences, including using high-end CAD workstations for product design and analysis, working on several large-scale visualization projects, creating 3D models for several blockbuster movies, working as a freelance 3D artist and designer, 3D programming, and a chance to write several high-profile computer graphics books.

Kelly's book credits include multiple editions covering both 3ds Max and Maya. He's also written books on Lightwave, 3D Poser, Illustrator, Anime Studio and co-authored five editions of the *Adobe Creative Suite Bible.* Other credits include the *Adobe Atmosphere Bible, gmax Bible, 3d Graphics and VRML 2.0, Master Visually HTML and XHTML,* and *JavaScript Visual Blueprints*. He's even written a 3D Game Animation for Dummies book.

In his spare time, Kelly enjoys playing and collecting video games.

Table of Contents at a Glance

Introduction

Writing computer books is always a journey. Maya is a different paradigm with an amazing amount of power. In writing this book, I approached the software as a beginner and was careful to explain points that are potential stumbling blocks.

Writing this book was actually like writing two books at once. The unique format is split into concepts and objectives. The concept sections explain the features and the 'why' behind it and the objective sections show you with an example 'how' to complete a task.

As you read through this title, be aware that Maya is a very complex piece of software and this book didn't have the space to cover every aspect of the software, so instead I focused on the main features and topics that are relevant to beginners. The coverage is enough to get you up and running, but you'll want to do some exploring along the way to flesh out your skill with the software.

Kelly L. Murdock

Contents

Chapter 1
Learning the Maya Interface

IN THIS CHAPTER

1.1 Work with menus.

1.2 Use the Status Line buttons.

1.3 Access the Shelf.

1.4 Explore the Channel Box and Layer Editor.

1.5 Identify the animation controls, the Command Line, and the Help Line.

1.6 Use the Toolbox buttons.

1.7 Discover the marking menus.

1.8 Get Help

Maya is a program, created by Autodesk, used to model, animate, and render 3D scenes. 3D scenes created with Maya have appeared in movies, television, advertisements, games, product visualizations, and on the Web. With Maya, you can create and animate your own 3D scenes and render them as still images or as animation sequences.

Several versions of Maya exist and the difference between them lies in the features that are included in each. The commercial version of Maya includes everything you need to create and render 3D scenes and animations. Maya is also available in the Media and Entertainment Collection, which pairs it with other Autodesk products including Arnold, Mudbox and 3ds Max. Student versions are also available at a reduced cost.

At first glance, the Maya interface can be a little daunting, with buttons, controls, and parameters everywhere, but if you look closer, you'll realize that all of the controls are grouped into logical sets. Becoming familiar with these various sets of controls makes the interface much easier to work with.

Along the top edge of the interface are the menus and a toolbar of buttons called the **Status Line**. The menus will change depending on the mode that you're working in. Below the Status Line is a tabbed row of buttons. This row of buttons is called the **Shelf**, and it offers a convenient way to group sets of commands together. To the right of the interface is a panel of parameters called the **Channel Box**. These parameters, known as attributes, will change as different objects are selected. Under the Channel Box is the **Layer Editor**.

Along the bottom of the interface are the Time Slider, the Range Slider, and the animation controls, which are used to specify and move between the different frames of an animation sequence; also at the bottom are the **Command Line**, for entering textual commands, and the **Help Line**. Finally, the horizontal column of buttons to the left of the interface is known as the **Toolbox buttons**. These buttons are used to select and transform scene objects.

A key concept that you need to understand as you begin to work with the interface is that there are several ways to access the same command. For example, you can create a sphere using the Create, Polygon Primitives, Sphere menu command or by using the Polygon Sphere button in the Poly Modeling shelf. This design is intentional, allowing beginners an intuitive method for accessing a command, and giving advanced users an access method that lets them work quicker as they learn the shortcuts.

One of the quickest ways to access advanced-user commands is with the pop-up menus. These context-specific menus appear when you right-click in the interface. Another quick way to access commands is with keyboard shortcuts, known as **hotkeys**.

Maya gives users the option to customize the interface. Using the customization features, you can create a custom set of command icons, define keyboard shortcuts, and even alter menus. Many of the customization options are included in the Windows, Settings/Preferences menu.

There are several help features in Maya that can be used to quickly find a specific command. These include the Help menu, the Search feature and Autodesk Assistant.

Lesson 1.1: Work with Menus

The main menu commands are the first place you should look for commands when you're new to Maya. The commands are listed as text, making them easier to find until you learn what the various buttons do. Each menu can include several submenus. Submenus are identified by a small, right-pointing arrow at the right end of the menu.

Changing Menu Sets

The menus are dynamic and change depending on the **menu set** that is selected. You can change between the menu sets using the drop-down list that is to the very left of the Status Line, as shown in Figure 1-1. The options include Modeling, Rigging, Animation, FX, Rendering and an option to Customize the menu set drop-down list.

Tip

Each of the menu sets has an associated hotkey. These hotkeys are F2 for Modeling, F3 for Rigging, F4 for Animation, F5 for FX, and F6 for Rendering.

The first six menu commands: File, Edit, Create, Select, Modify, Display, and Window, are available in all menu sets. The remaining menus will change as the menu set is changed.

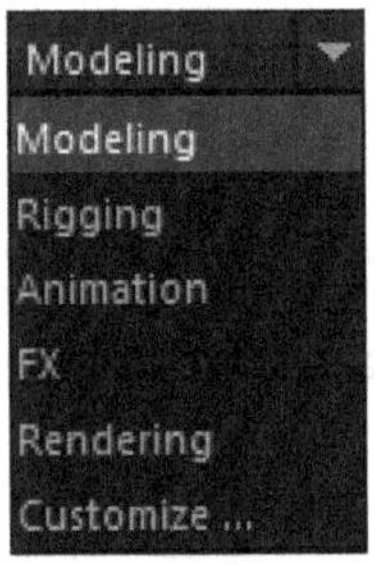

FIGURE 1-1

Menu set selection list

Viewing Keyboard Hotkeys

Several menu commands have a keyboard hotkey listed to the right of the menu, as shown in Figure 1-2. Pressing these hotkeys on the keyboard executes the command. Hotkeys provide a quick and easy way to execute a command, and learning to use them will make you much more efficient. You can customize hotkeys using the Hotkey Editor, which you open with the Windows, Settings/Preferences, Hotkey Editor menu command.

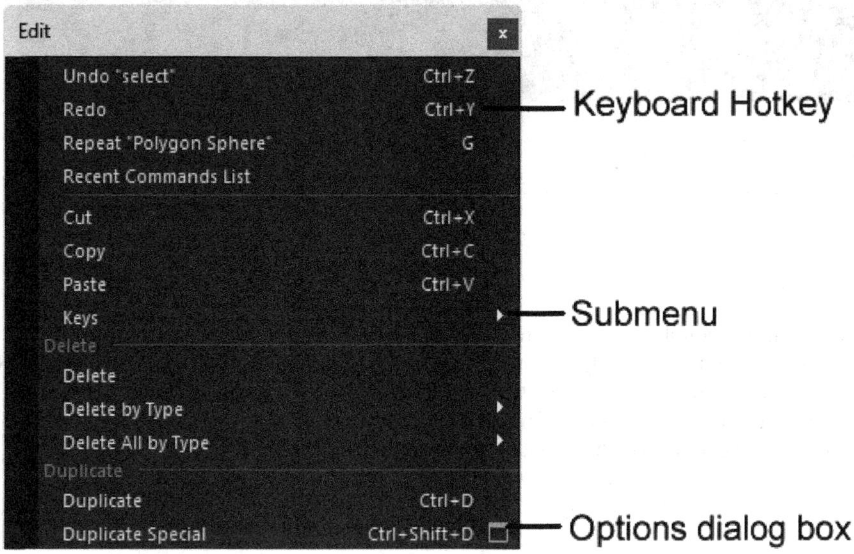

FIGURE 1-2

Hotkeys and option dialog boxes are displayed in the menus

Accessing Option Dialog Boxes

Several menus also include a small box icon to the right of the menu, also shown in Figure 1-2. These box icons will open an Options dialog box for the selected command. These Options dialog boxes, such as the Group Options dialog box shown in Figure 1-3, include parameters that you can change. Clicking the operation name button, such as Group, runs the command with the given parameters. The Close button closes the Options dialog box without applying any changes. Options dialog boxes also include Apply buttons that let you apply the command with the given parameters without closing the dialog box. Using the Apply button, you can execute the command many times without having to reopen the dialog box. The **option dialog box** values are persistent. Any values that are changed will maintain their setting the next time the command is used. You can reset an options dialog box to its default values using the Edit, Reset Settings menu command in the dialog box menu.

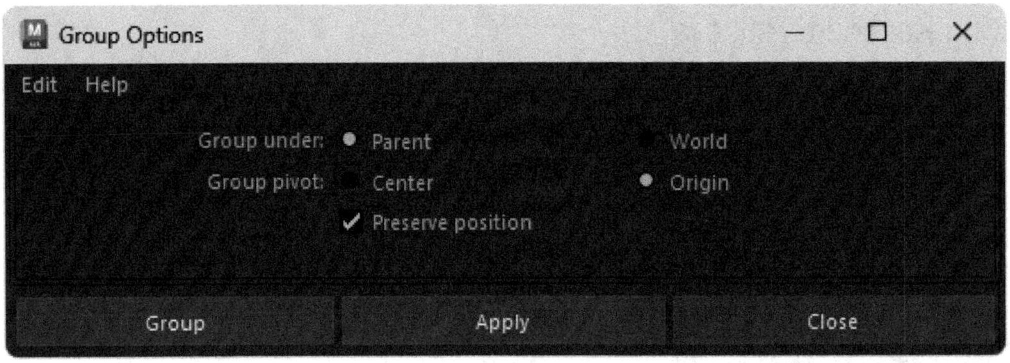

FIGURE 1-3

The Group Options dialog box

Using Tear-Off Menus

At the very top of most menus is a double line called the **tear-off menu**. Clicking on this line makes the menu a tear-off menu and displays it as a separate panel, like the one shown in Figure 1-4, that you can move about by dragging on its title bar. Tear-off menus are convenient because they make the menu commands accessible with one click, but you need the space to leave the tear-off menu open without covering something else. You can close an opened tear-off menu by clicking on the X button in the upper right corner.

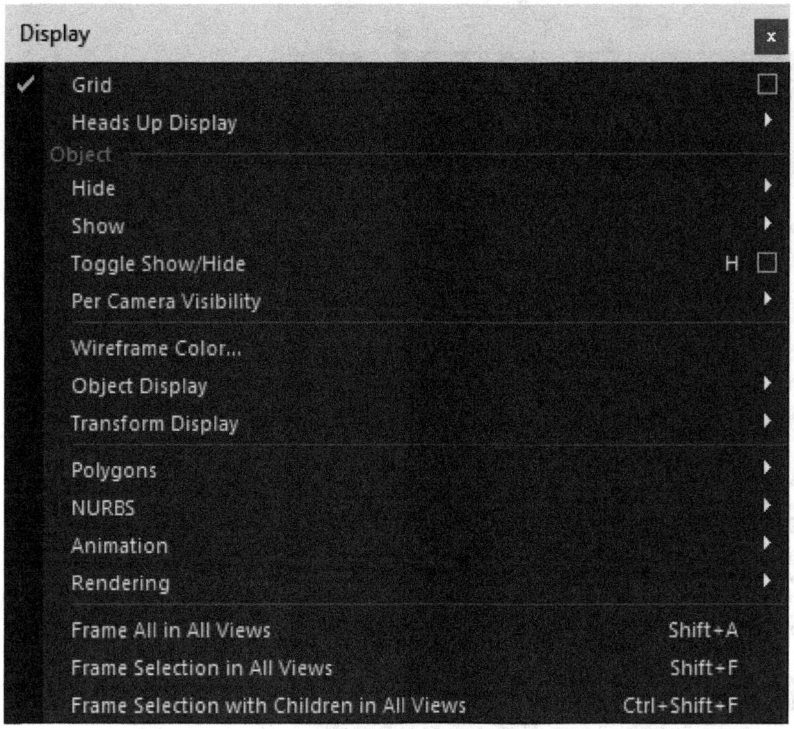

FIGURE 1-4

Tear-off menu

Understanding Tools versus Actions

If you peruse the menus, you'll see many commands that end in the word *Tool*. Tools, when selected, are active until another tool is selected, but actions are only executed once. The last tool used is displayed at the bottom of the **Toolbox** for easy re-selection. Double-clicking a tool's button will open the Tool Settings dialog box, as shown for the Move tool in Figure 1-5. You can also open the Tool Settings using the Show/Hide Tool Settings button at the right end of the Status Line. Tool settings are also persistent and can be reset using the Reset Tool button at the top of the Tool Settings interface.

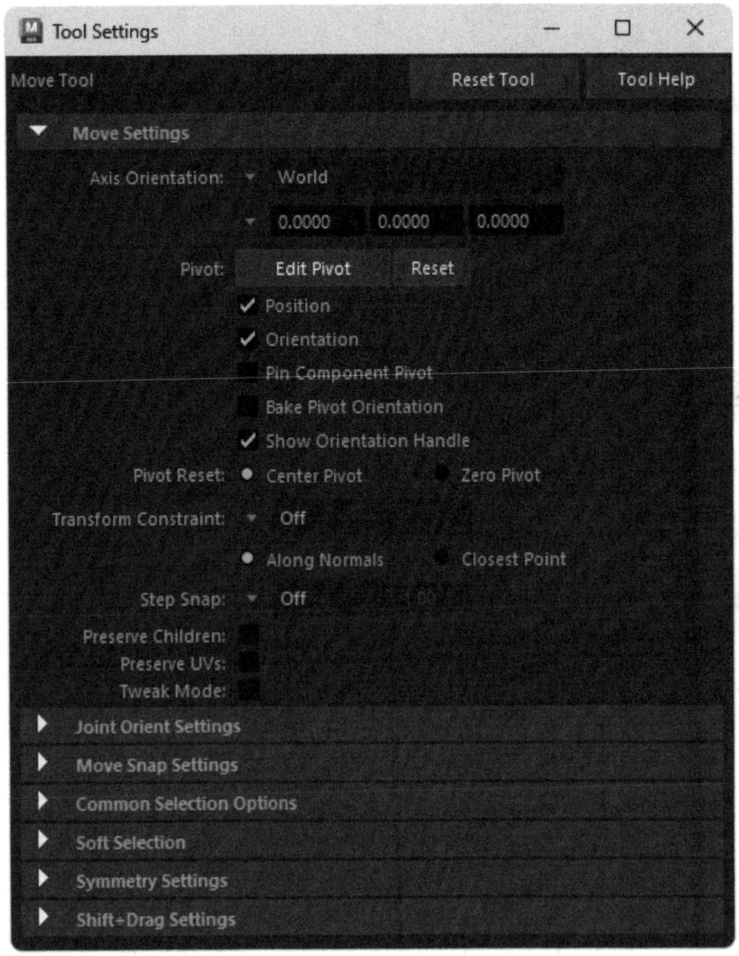

FIGURE 1-5

Tool Settings for the Move tool

Lesson 1.1-Tutorial 1: Use a Menu Command to Create a Polygon Sphere

1. Click on the Create menu, and then select the Polygon Primitives submenu and click on the Options icon to the right of the Sphere menu to open the Polygon Sphere Options dialog box.
2. In the Polygon Sphere Options dialog box, click the Apply button.

    A single sphere object will appear at the origin in the view panel.
3. Click the Close button to exit the dialog box.
4. Click on the Create menu, and then select the Polygon Primitives submenu and click on the Cone menu command. A cone object is added to the scene overlapping the sphere.
5. Press the 5 key to see the objects as shaded objects, then press the F key to frame the objects. The objects resemble a simple crystal ball, as shown in Figure 1-6.
6. Select File, Save Scene As and save the file as **Crystal ball.mb**.

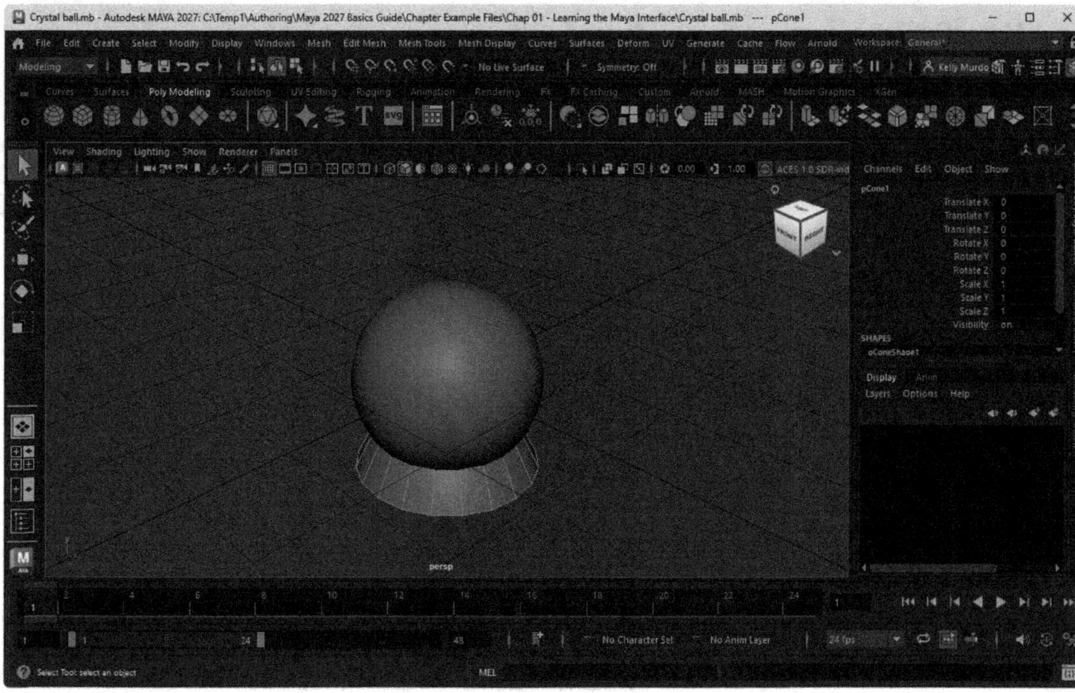

FIGURE 1-6

A simple crystal ball created with sphere and cone objects

Lesson 1.2: Use the Status Line Buttons

Directly below the menus are a long row of buttons that are collectively known as the Status Line. These buttons are constant and cannot be changed, but you can hide them. The buttons are divided into groups that are separated by a dividing bar. Clicking on the dividing bar to the left of each group will hide and unhide the buttons. These button groups include, from left to right, the Menu Set list, File buttons, the Selection Mode menu, Selection Mode buttons, Selection Mask buttons, Snapping buttons, Enable Symmetry option, History buttons, Rendering buttons, the Transform fields, and the Show/Hide Editors buttons, as shown in Figure 1-7. Most of these button groups are presented and discussed in the lesson that corresponds to their features.

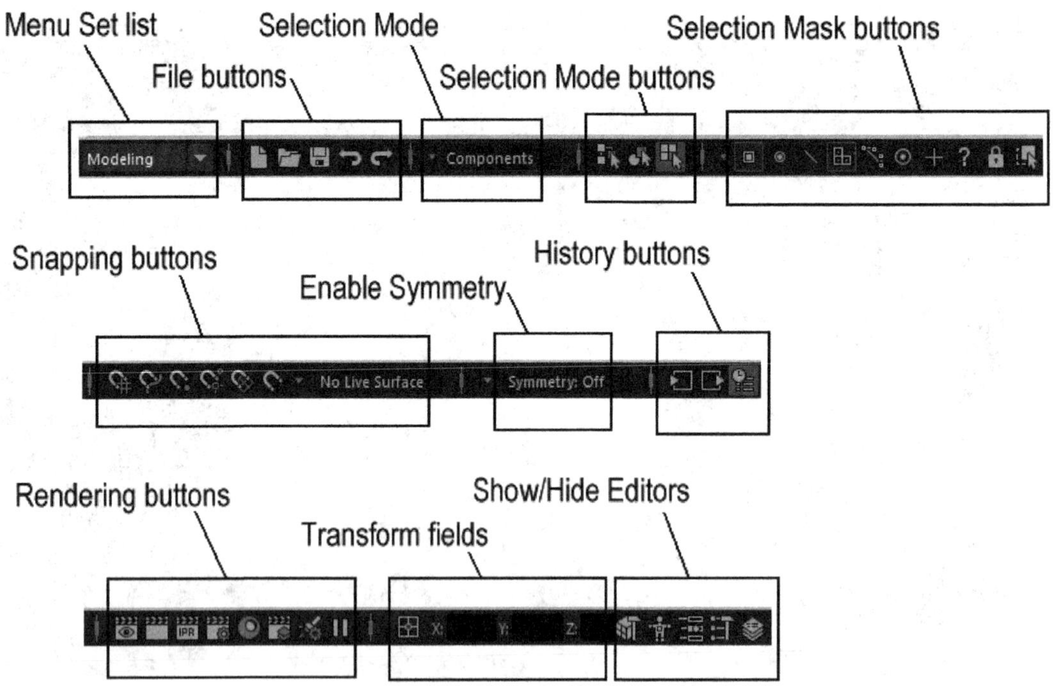

FIGURE 1-7

Status Line groups

Using Pop-up Help

When you first begin to use the Status Line buttons, it can be tricky to know which button does what, but you can view the button's title as a **Pop-up Help** by holding the mouse cursor over the top of the button, as shown in Figure 1-8. Pop-up Help is available for all buttons in the entire interface.

Note

If Pop-up Help starts to get annoying, you can disable it or set its Display Time using the Interface, Help panel in the Preferences dialog box opened with the Window, Settings/Preferences, Preferences menu command.

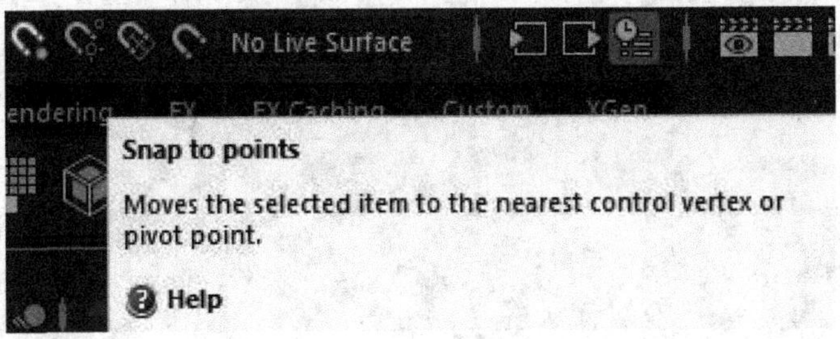

FIGURE 1-8

Pop-up Help

Watching for Cursor Clues

Another helpful visual clue is that the cursor changes when it is over any interface button that has an available right-click pop-up menu. This new cursor displays a small menu icon under the cursor arrow, like the one shown in Figure 1-9. When this icon appears, you can right-click to access an additional menu of options. The cursor also changes when certain tools are used.

FIGURE 1-9

Cursor indicating a right-click pop-up menu

Expanding and Collapsing Icon Button Groups

Each button group in the Status Line is divided by a vertical line with a small rectangle through its center. This divider is called the Show/Hide Bar, and if you click on it, all buttons included in that section will be hidden. Click again to make the buttons reappear. Figure 1-10 shows several collapsed and expanded button sets.

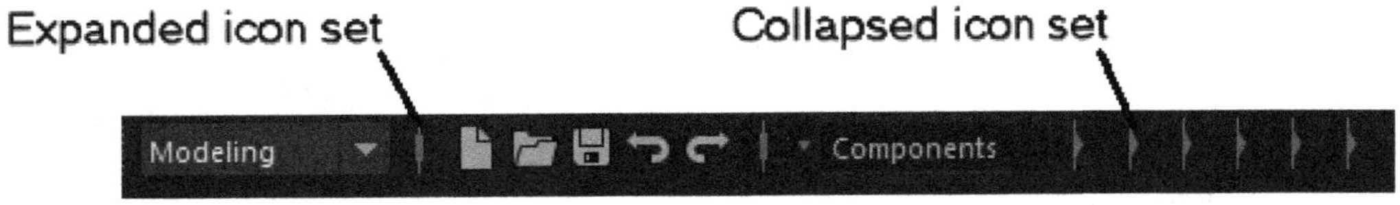

FIGURE 1-10

Expanded and collapsed button sets

Opening and Saving a Scene

To the right of the Menu Set selection list is a set of buttons that you can use to create a new scene, open an existing scene, or save the current scene. Both the Open and Save buttons will open a file dialog box, as shown in Figure 1-11, in which you can select the directory and file name. When saved, the file name will appear on the title bar.

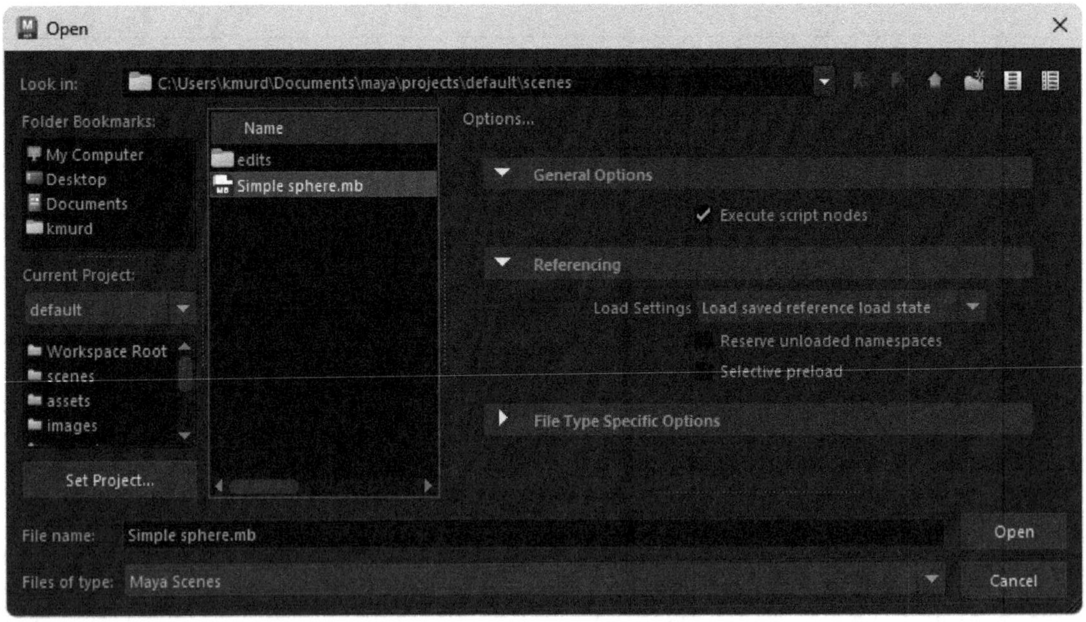

FIGURE 1-11

File dialog box for Windows

Using the Home Screen

By default, the Maya Home Screen, shown in Figure 1-12, appears when Maya is first loaded. This Home Screen has a lot of useful information, but perhaps the most useful is the list of recently opened files and any crash recovery files. Recently opened files can be immediately opened by simply selecting them in the Home Screen.

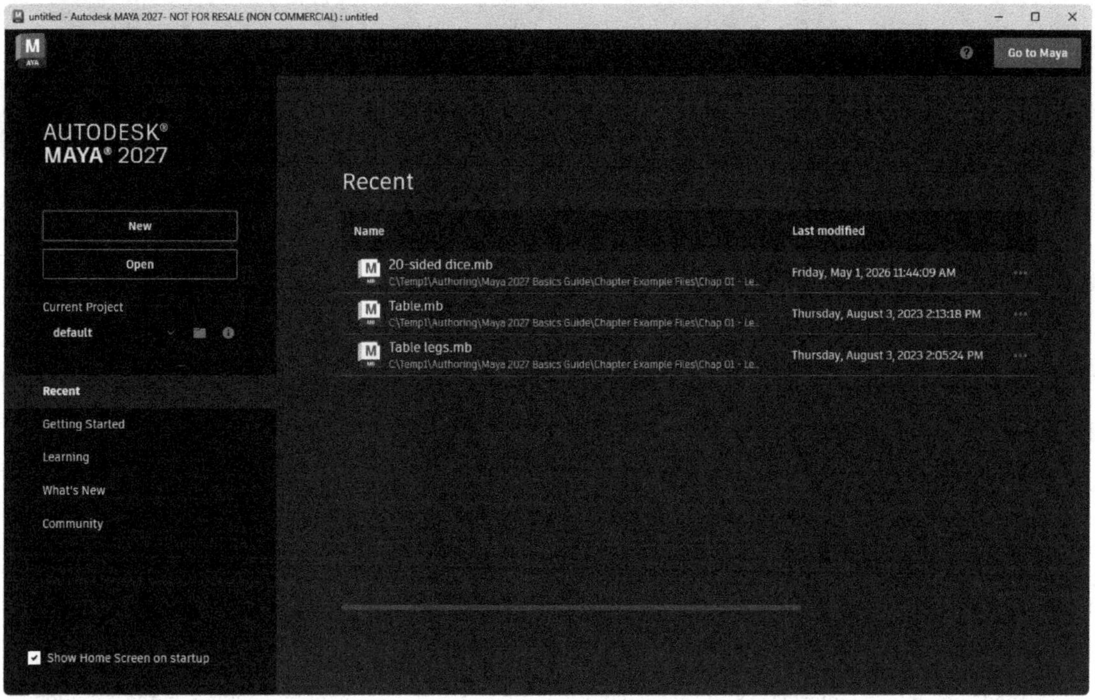

FIGURE 1-12

Maya Home Screen

You can move back and forth between the Maya interface and the Home Screen using the Home icon in the upper left corner of the interface on the menu bar and the Go to Maya button in the upper right corner of the Home Screen.

The Home Screen also includes options to open a new blank scene, open an existing file, set a current project, view tutorial videos or access the Community pages.

Opening Editors

At the right side of the Status Line are several Sidebar buttons, shown in Figure 1-13, that don't belong to a button group and that are always visible. These Sidebar buttons are used to show and hide dialog boxes and sidebar panels that appear to the right of the view panel. The main ones to focus on right now are the Attribute Editor, Tool Settings, and Channel Box. There are also buttons for accessing the Modeling Toolkit and the Character Controls. The Attribute Editor lists all the attributes for the selected object, the Tool Settings will list all the configurable settings for the selected tool, and the Channel Box is a subset of attributes that can be animated, known as being *keyable*.

Note

In the Interface, UI Elements panel of the Preferences dialog box, you can select to have each of the editors open as a separate window instead of within the main window.

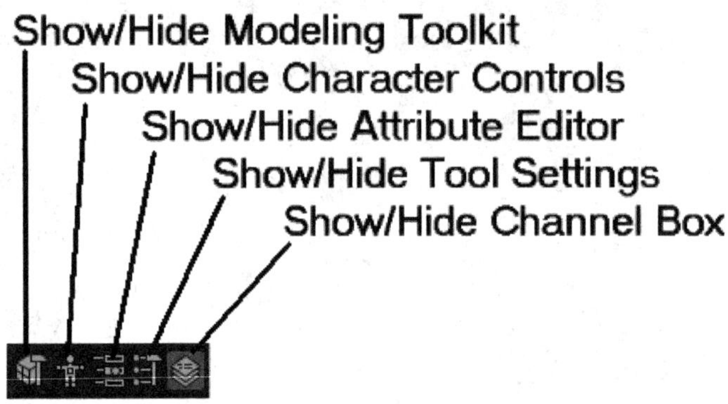

FIGURE 1-13

Sidebar buttons

Showing and Hiding Interface Elements

You can also make any interface element into a floating toolbar by clicking on the dotted double line at the top (or to the left) of the interface element, as shown for the Status Line in Figure 1-14, and dragging it away from the interface. If you drag the element back on top of the interface, a blue line will appear where it will be dropped back into the interface. You can also close or hide a floating element by clicking on the X button in the upper right corner of the element. Use the Windows, UI Elements menu command to make any hidden interface elements visible again.

FIGURE 1-14

Hide interface element bar

Lesson 1.2-Tutorial 1: Open a File

1. Move the mouse over the Status Line buttons at the left end until the Pop-up Help reads *Open a scene*.
2. Click on this button.

   A file dialog box appears, similar to the one shown in Figure 1-11.
3. Locate the chapter 1 directory where the Skateboard.mb file is located.
4. Click on the Skateboard.mb file name and click the Open button.

   The saved file is then loaded into Maya, as shown in Figure 1-15.

Note

```
Before Maya opens a file, it gives you a chance to
save the current file.
```

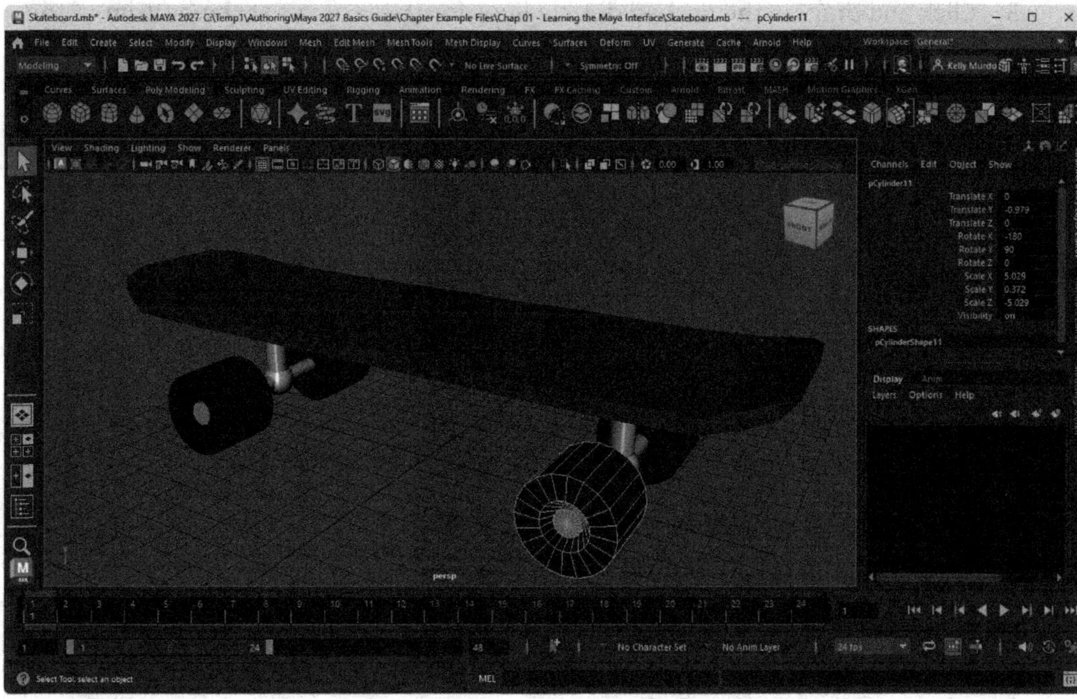

FIGURE 1-15

Opened skateboard file

Lesson 1.2-Tutorial 2: Save a File

1. Click on the Create menu, and then select the Polygon Primitives submenu and click on the Sphere menu to add a sphere to the skateboard scene.
2. Move the mouse over the Status Line buttons at the left end until the Pop-up Help reads *Save the current scene*.
3. Click on this button.

   This file is automatically saved replacing the existing file. When saved, the file name appears in the title bar.

Note

`You can save the scenes with a new file name using the File, Save As menu command.`

Lesson 1.2-Tutorial 3: Maximize the Workspace Interface

1. Click and drag on the dotted double line on the left end of the Status Line and move it away from the interface.

   The Status Line becomes a floating control.
2. Click and drag the dashed double lines for the Shelf, and the Toolbox to make each of these interface elements floating controls.

3. Click and drag on the dashed double lines for the controls at the bottom of the interface to make them floating also. Then close all the floating controls.

   All interface elements will now be floating, maximizing the Workspace, as shown in Figure 1-16.

Tip

`A quicker way to maximize the Workspace is with the Windows, UI Elements, Hide All UI Elements menu command.`

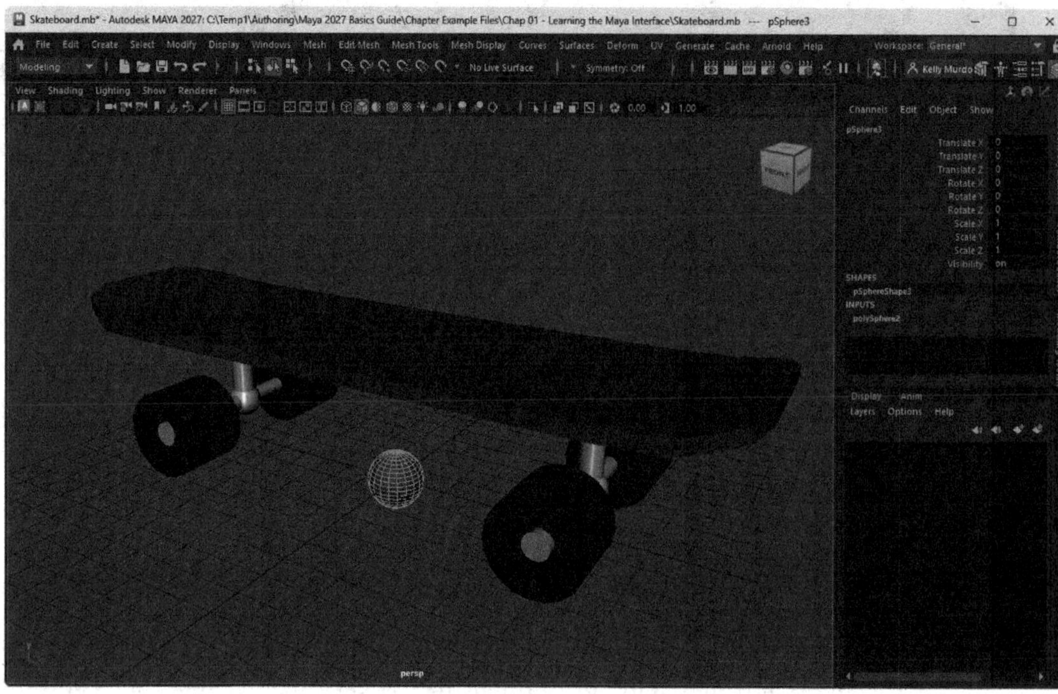

FIGURE 1-16

A maximized Workspace interface

4. Select the Windows, Workspaces, Reset Workspace to Factory Default menu command.

   All the standard interface elements reappear.

Lesson 1.3: Access the Shelf

The Shelf is like a toolbar on steroids. It includes several tabbed panels of buttons. To select a different set of buttons, just click on one of the tabs and the buttons in its set will appear. Figure 1-17 shows the buttons for the Poly Modeling tab.

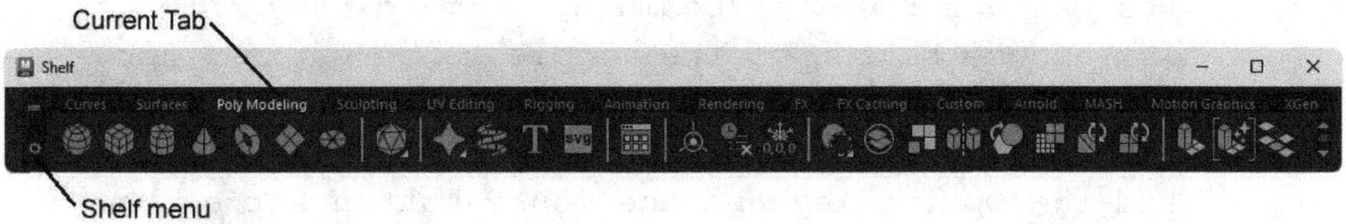

FIGURE 1-17

The Shelf

Using the Shelf Menu

At the left end of the Shelf are two menu icons. The top one looks like a mini-tab and you can use it to select a Shelf tab from a menu. The bottom menu icon is a round star. You can use it to hide all of the Shelf tabs, open the Shelf Editor, create and delete shelves, load a custom shelf, and save all shelves. You can save some interface space by hiding the Shelf tabs. To do this, select Shelf Tabs menu command from the Shelf menu to toggle the option off.

Creating and Deleting Shelves

The Shelf menu can also be used to create and delete shelves. The New Shelf menu command will open a simple dialog box, as shown in Figure 1-18, in which you can name the new shelf. The new empty shelf will then appear at the right end of the tabs. Selecting the Delete Shelf menu command will delete the currently selected shelf.

FIGURE 1-18

Create New Shelf dialog box

Adding Icons and Menu Commands to a Shelf

You can add buttons from any shelf to another shelf by selecting the button and dragging it with the middle mouse button onto the tab of the shelf that you wish to add it to. Menu commands can also be added to the current shelf by clicking on the menu command with the Ctrl/Command and Shift keys held down. You can delete a shelf by selecting it and choosing the Delete Shelf menu from the Shelf menu.

Note

Maya uses all three mouse buttons. If you are using a two-button mouse with a scroll wheel, the scroll wheel acts as the middle mouse button. If your two-button mouse doesn't have a scroll wheel, you can use the Ctrl/Command (command) key and the left mouse button as the middle mouse button. For a Macintosh one-button mouse, the command key and the mouse button act as the middle mouse button and the Option key and the mouse button act as the right mouse button.

Adding Layouts and Scripts to a Shelf

You can add custom layouts to a shelf. Just pick the shelf you want to hold the custom layout and then choose Panel Editor from the Panels menu, located at the top of the view panel. In the Layouts tab, shown in Figure 1-19, select the custom layout that you want to add to the current shelf and click the Add To Shelf button. You can drag scripts from the Script Editor with the middle mouse button and drop them into a shelf. Scripts appear on the Shelf as a button labeled 'MEL', which stands for Maya Embedded Language, Maya's scripting language. More on scripting is covered in Chapter 16, "Using MEL Scripting."

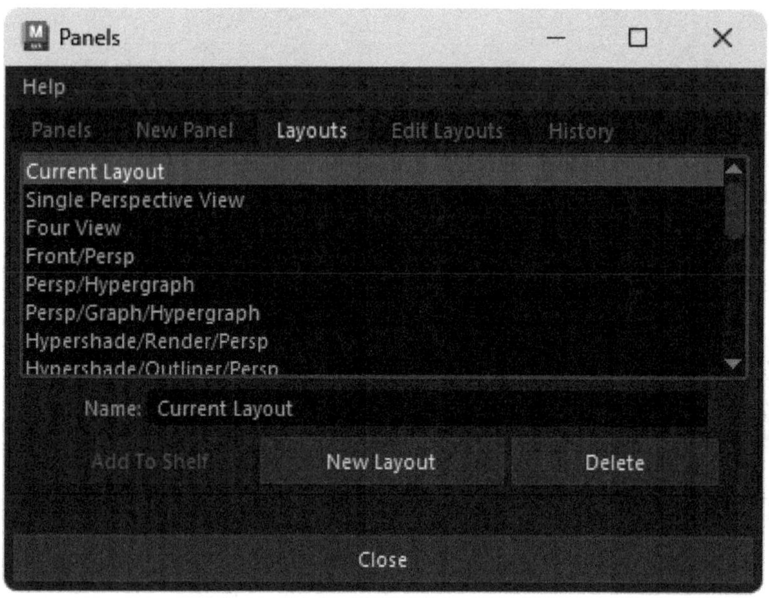

FIGURE 1-19

Panel Editor

Using the Shelf Editor

The Shelves menu includes an option that will open the Shelf Editor dialog box. Using this editor, shown in Figure 1-20, you can reorder and rename the tabs and shelves, edit the icons within each shelf, and change the settings for the shelves.

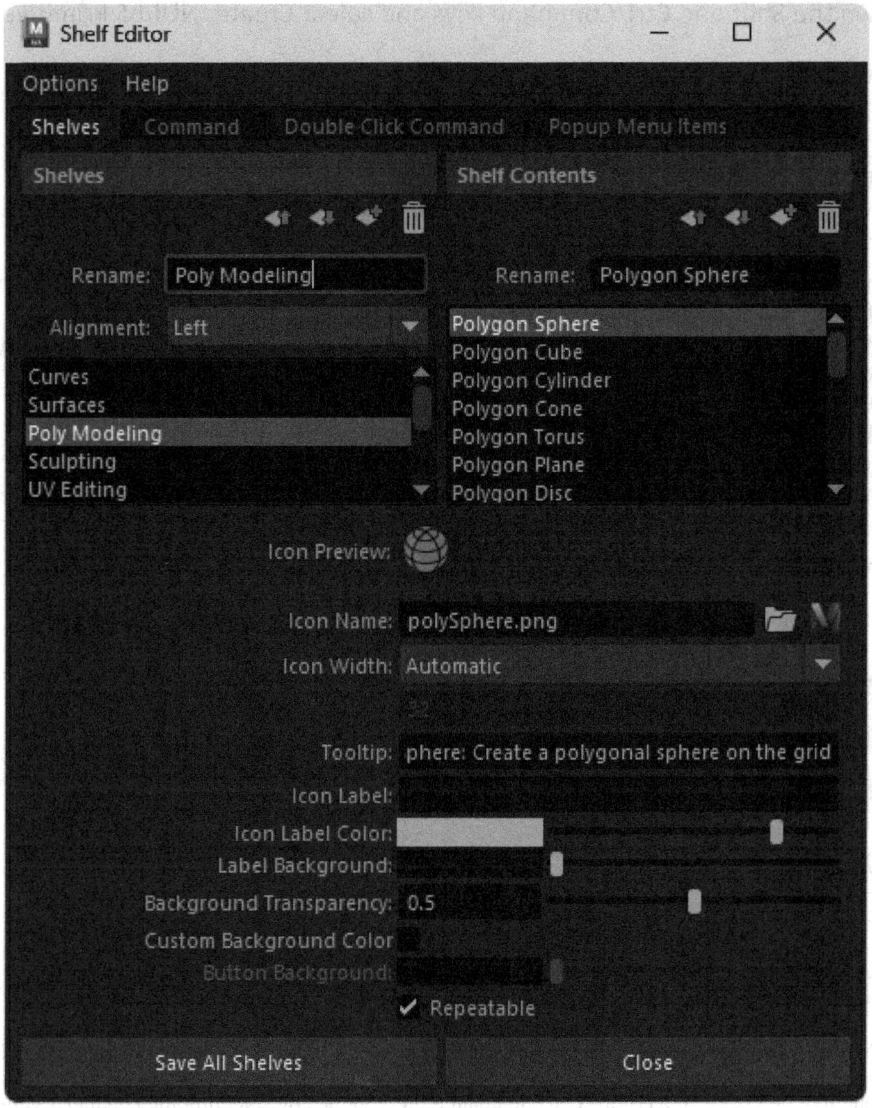

FIGURE 1-20

Shelf Editor

Lesson 1.3-Tutorial 1: Create a New Shelf

1. Click on the Shelf menu and select New Shelf.

   The Create New Shelf dialog box appears.
2. Type the name **MyShelf** for the new shelf and click OK.

   A new tab with the typed name appears at the right end of the Shelf.

Lesson 1.3-Tutorial 2: Populate a New Shelf

1. Select the MyShelf tab to make it active.

2. Hold down the Shift and Ctrl/Command keys and select Create, NURBS Primitives, Sphere.

   A sphere icon is added to the new shelf.
3. Repeat Step 2 with other primitive objects found in the Create menu.

   Each of the selected menu commands appears on the new shelf, as shown in Figure 1-20.
4. Select the Panels, Panel Editor panel menu command.

   The Panel Editor dialog box appears.
5. Select the Layout tab and choose the Four View option. Then, click the Add to Shelf button and then the Close button.

   When the Four View option is selected, the view window changes to show four separate views. After clicking the Add to Shelf button, a new icon appears in the current shelf.
6. Locate the Move tool in the Toolbox and drag the icon with the middle mouse button to the new shelf.

   Dragging an icon with the middle mouse button adds the icon to the current shelf. Figure 1-21 shows the new shelf.
7. Select Save All Shelves from the Shelf menu.

FIGURE 1-21

A custom shelf of menu commands

Lesson 1.4: Explore the Channel Box and Layer Editor

When an object is selected, its keyable attributes (or channels) appear within the Channel Box, shown in Figure 1-22, to the right of the interface. Each attribute has a value associated with it. These values are often numbers, but they can be a state like on or off, or a color. You can change these values by selecting the channel's value, entering a different value, and pressing the Enter key.

Tip

Drag on the left edge of the Channel Box to increase or decrease the Channel Box width. You can make the Channel Box a floating panel by dragging its tab away from the interface.

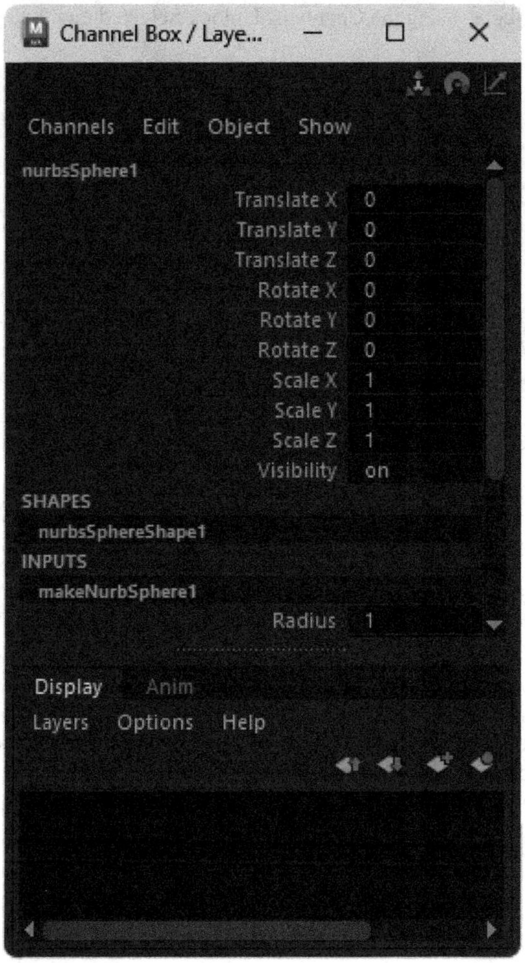

FIGURE 1-22

The Channel Box

Selecting Attributes

You can select a single attribute by clicking on its title. When selected, the attribute title will be highlighted. Holding down the Ctrl/Command key while clicking on several attributes will allow you to select multiple attributes at once; you can also drag the mouse over several attributes to select them.

Changing Attributes with the Mouse

You can interactively change attribute values by selecting an attribute in the Channel Box and then dragging with the middle mouse button in the view panel.

Locking Attributes

Locked attributes cannot be changed. You can lock an attribute by selecting it and choosing the Lock Selected menu command from the Channels menu. Locked attributes will have a gray rectangle to the left of the channel value, as shown in Figure 1-23. Unlock any locked attributes using the Channels, Unlock Selected menu command.

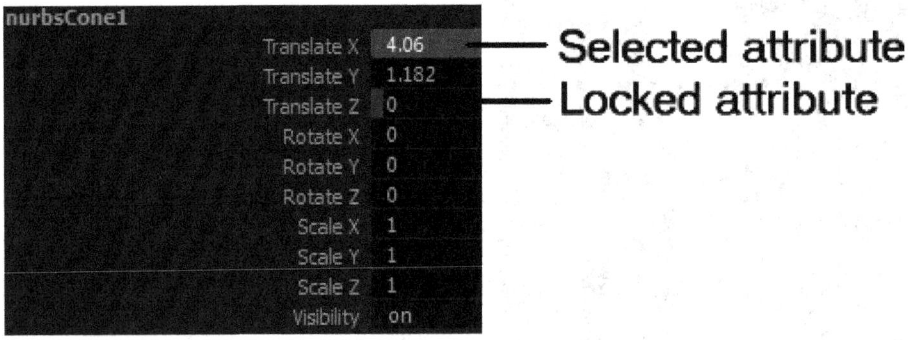

FIGURE 1-23

Locked attributes in the Channel Box

Adding and Deleting Layers

The Layer Editor, shown in Figure 1-24, divides the scene elements up into layers, making them easy to show and hide. For example, you could place all the background objects on one layer and the main characters on another layer; then to work on the main characters, simply enable that layer and you don't have to worry about the background objects getting in the way. Clicking the Create a New Layer button in the Layer Editor creates a new layer. You can give each layer a name, display type, playback option and color. Delete layers using the Layers menu. Deleting a layer does not delete its objects. At the top of the Layer Editor are tabs for working with both Display and Animation layers.

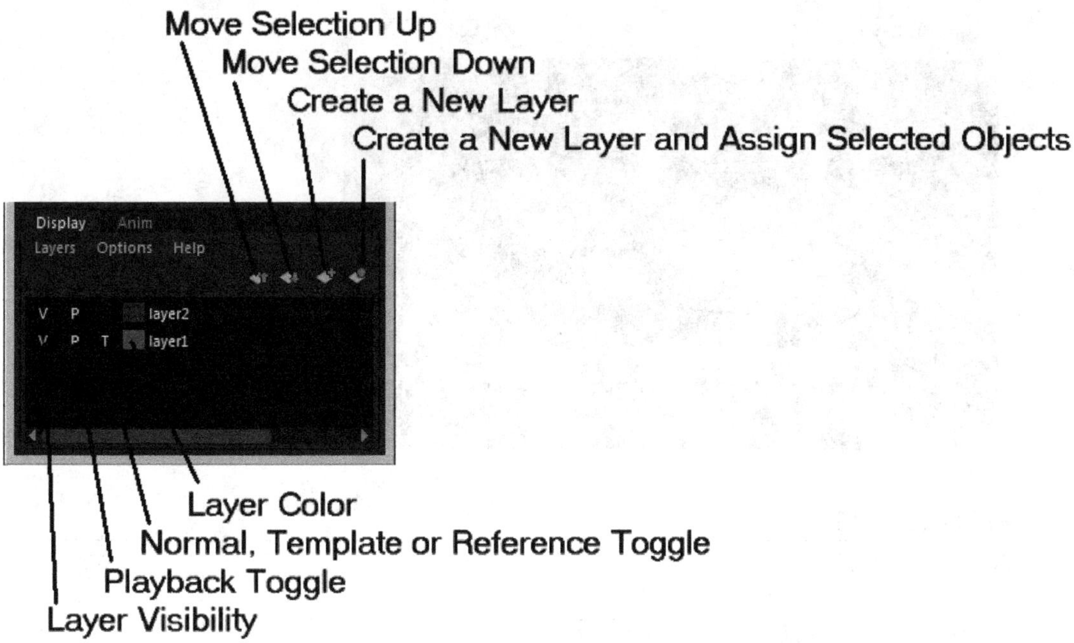

FIGURE 1-24

Layer Editor

Adding Objects to a Layer

You can add selected objects to a layer by right clicking on that layer and selecting Add Selected Objects from the pop-up menu. You can also use the Layers menu to select all objects in a layer and to remove objects from a layer. Objects assume the layer color when viewed as wireframe and unselected.

Hiding All Layer Objects

You can hide Layer objects by clicking the first column in the Layer Editor. This column sets the visibility for the layer objects and is a simple toggle button that you can turn on or off. The letter *V* appears when the layer objects are visible, and the column is empty when the layer objects are hidden. The second column toggles the playback of the layer objects on or off. The letter 'P' appears when playback is enabled.

Freezing All Layer Objects

The third column can be set to Normal, Template or Reference. The letter *T* appears in this column when the layer is a template. Template layers cannot be selected or moved while they are templates. References are proxy objects that stand in for complex objects. The fourth column is the layer color. Double-clicking on this column (or on the layer name) opens the Edit Layer dialog box, shown in Figure 1-25, where you can select a new color, change the layer's attributes, or change the layer's name.

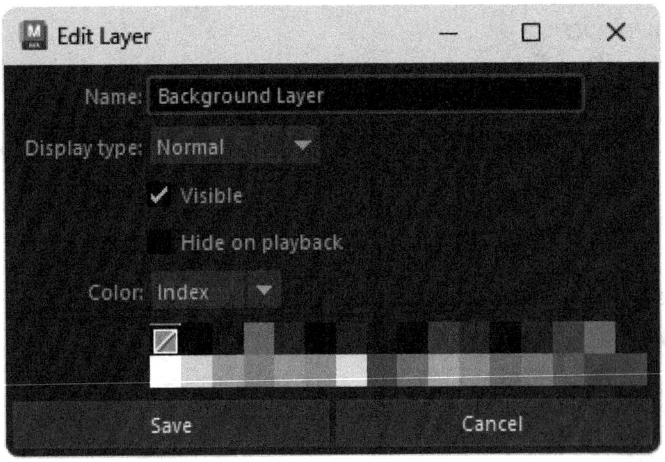

FIGURE 1-25

Edit Layer dialog box

Lesson 1.4-Tutorial 1: Change Channel Box Attributes

1. Select File, Open Scene. Locate and open the Translated Rocket.mb file.

   This file includes a simple rocket centered about the grid origin. All attributes for the rocket object are displayed in the Channel Box.

2. Select the Select, All menu command.

   This selects all the objects that make up the rocket.

3. Enter a 5 in the Translate X attribute and press the Enter key.

   The rocket object is moved five units along the X-axis.

4. Click on the Translate Y attribute in the Channel Box and drag upward in the Workspace with the middle mouse button.

   The rocket object is moved along the Y-axis a distance equal to the amount that the mouse was dragged and the attribute value is changed, as shown in Figure 1-26.

5. Select File, Save Scene As and save the file as **Translated rocket.mb**.

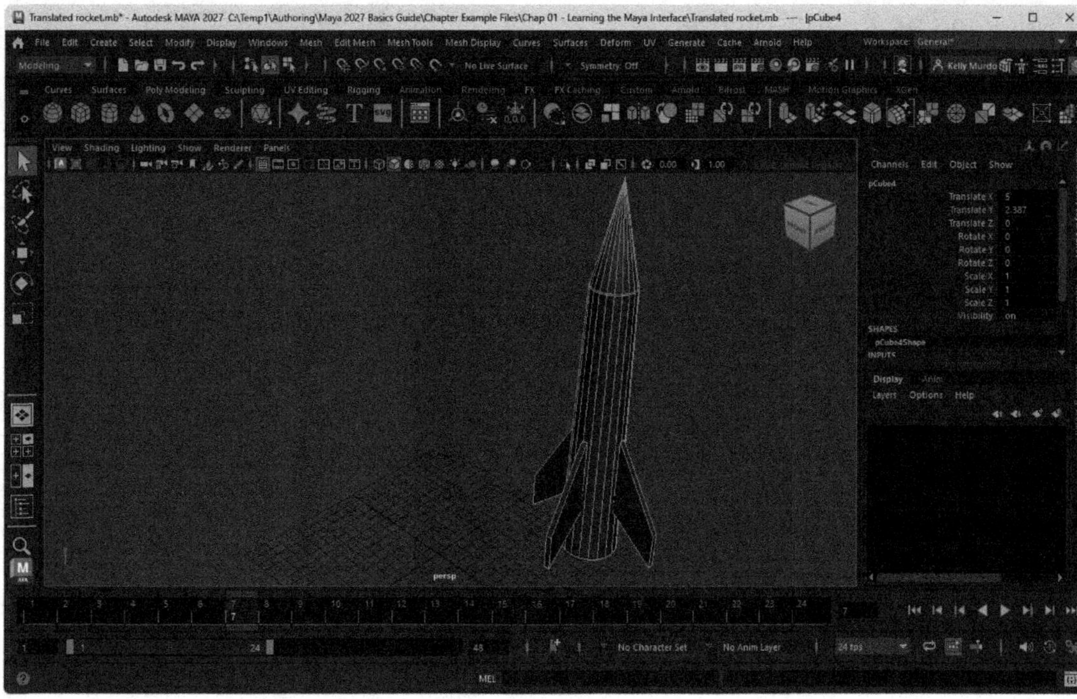

FIGURE 1-26

Translated rocket

Lesson 1.4-Tutorial 2: Create and Rename a New Layer

1. Click the Create a new layer button in the Layer Editor.

   A new layer appears in the Layer Editor.
2. Double-click on the layer to open the Edit Layer dialog box.
3. Type in a name for the new layer and click the Save button.

Lesson 1.4-Tutorial 3: Add Objects to a New Layer

1. Select Create, Polygon Primitives, Sphere to create a sphere object.
2. In the Layer Editor, right click on the new layer and select Add Selected Objects from the pop-up menu.

   The sphere object is added to the new layer.
3. In the Layer Editor, click on the first column in which the V is displayed.

   All objects on the layer are hidden.

Lesson 1.5: Identify the Animation Controls, the Command Line, and the Help Line

At the bottom of the interface are several interface controls that are used to move through the various animation frames. Below these is a Command Line where you can type in commands to be executed. At the very bottom of the interface is a Help Line where context-specific information is displayed.

Selecting an Animation Frame

All current animation frames are displayed on the Time Slider at the bottom of the interface, as shown in Figure 1-27. You move between the different frames by dragging the gray time marker or by entering the frame number in the field to the right of the Time Slider.

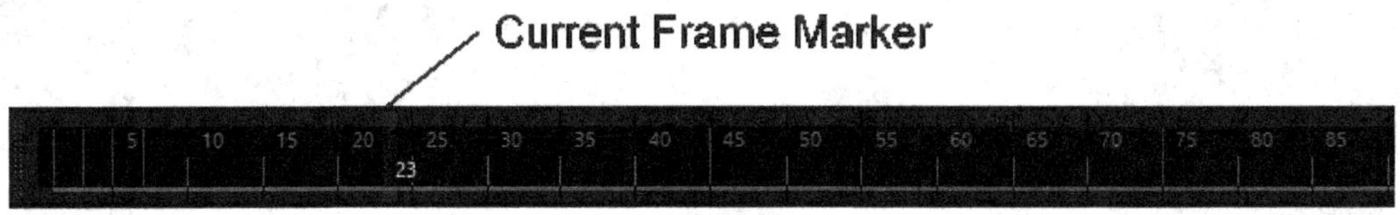

FIGURE 1-27

Time Slider

Setting an Animation Range

Below the Time Slider is the Range Slider, as shown in Figure 1-28. Using this slider, you can focus on a specific range of animation frames. The total number of frames selected in the Range Slider are shown in the Time Slider. The Time Slider changes as the Range Slider is moved. You can extend the total number of animation frames by increasing the Last Frame of Total Animation value to the right of the Range Slider.

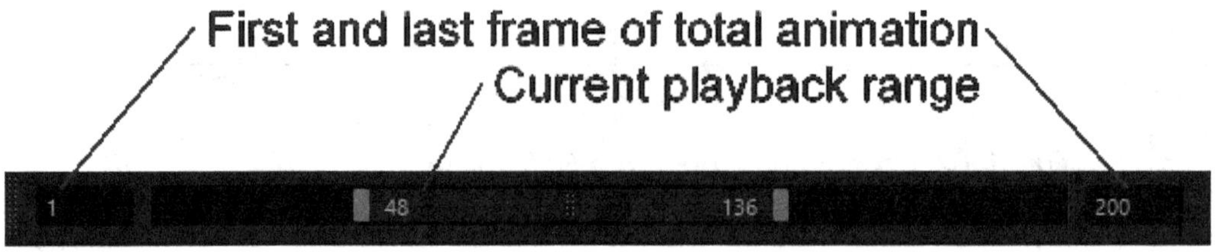

FIGURE 1-28

Range Slider

Playing an Animation

To the right of the animation frame value are several controls for playing, rewinding, and moving through the animation frames, as shown in Figure 1-29. Using these buttons, you can jump to the animation start (or end), step back (or forward) one frame, step back (or forward) one key, or play the animation forward (or backward).

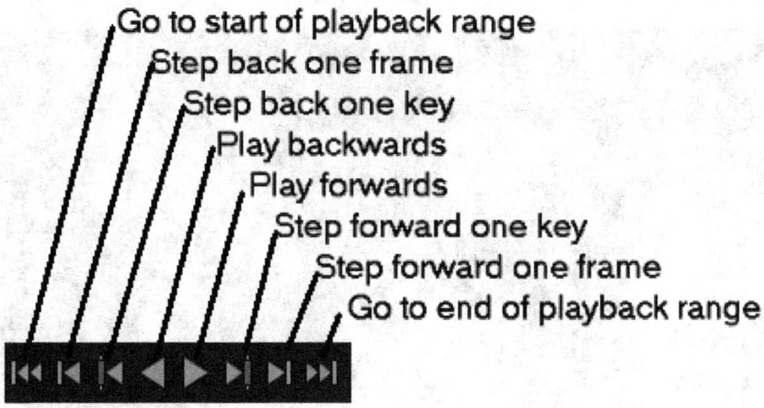

FIGURE 1-29

Animation controls

Accessing the Animation Preferences

Beneath the Go to End button is a button, shown in Figure 1-30, that will open the Preferences dialog box, as shown in Figure 1-31. This dialog box includes all of the preferences for Maya, but when it is opened using this button the Time Slider category is selected, allowing you to change the animation preferences.

FIGURE 1-30

Animation Preferences button

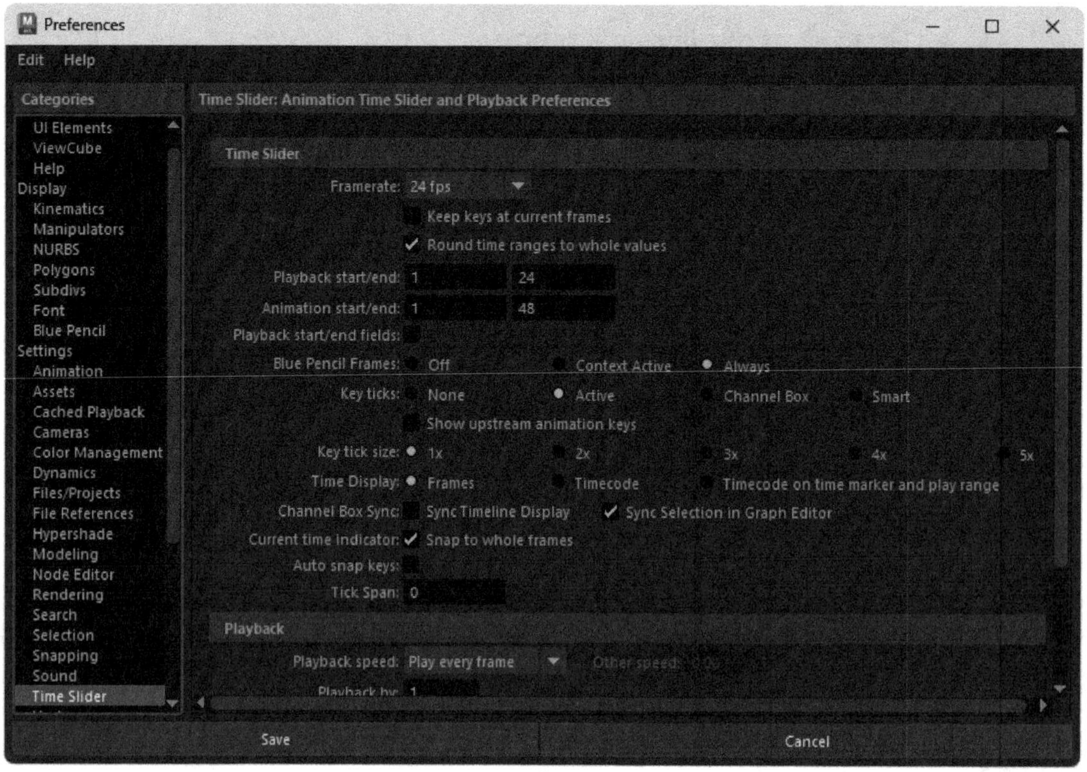

FIGURE 1-31

Preferences dialog box

Using the Command Line

In the Command Line, you can enter textual commands to be executed. All commands should end with a semicolon. The results of these commands are displayed in the dark-colored Results line to the right of the Command Line. To the right of the Results line is the Script Editor button, shown in Figure 1-32, that opens the Script Editor, where you can enter more detailed scripts. More on the Script Editor is covered in Chapter 16, "Using MEL Scripting."

Tip

All commands that are entered into the Command Line are saved in a buffer. Using the Up and Down Arrow keys, you can scroll back and forth through the existing commands. Pressing the Enter key executes the listed command.

FIGURE 1-32

Script Editor button

Viewing the Help Line

At the very bottom of the interface is the Help Line, as shown in Figure 1-33. Within this line, Maya lists instructions that it expects to happen next based on the selected tool or mode. If you're stuck on what to do next, take a look at the Help Line.

FIGURE 1-33

Help Line

Lesson 1.5-Tutorial 1: Play an Animation

1. Select File, Open Scene and open the Billiard balls.mb file.
   This file includes a simple animated scene.
2. Click on the time marker in the Time Slider and drag it to the left.
   The objects in the scene will move as the frames are increased. A frame of the animation sequence is shown in Figure 1-34.

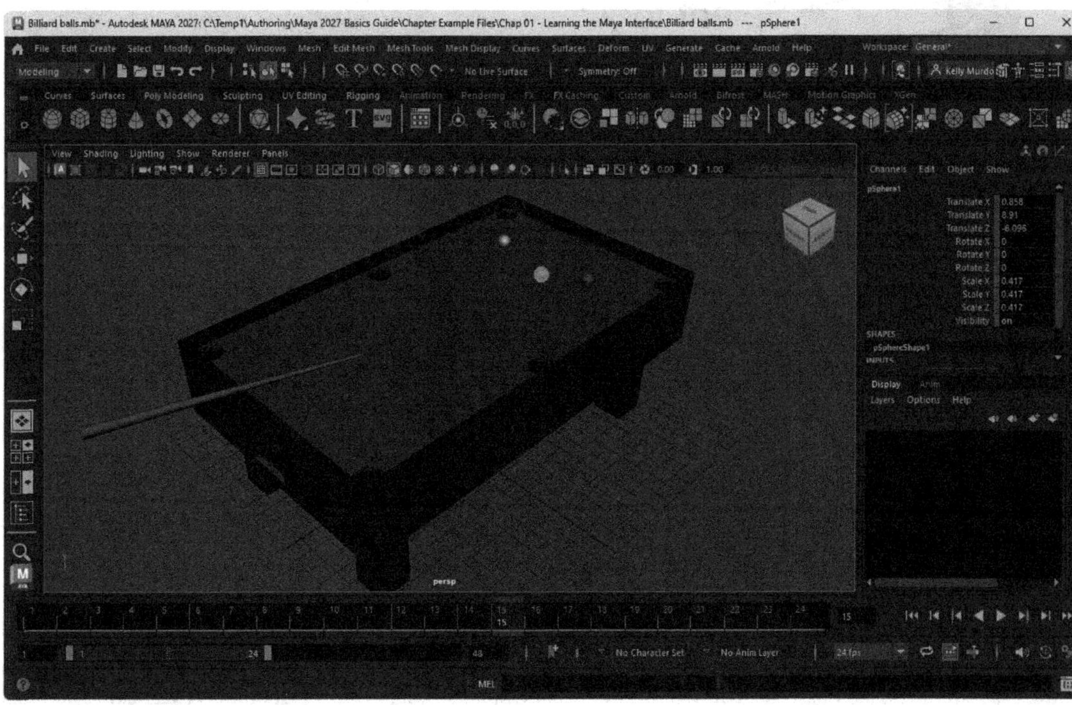

FIGURE 1-34

Animated billiard table

3. Click the Play Forwards button.
   The entire animation sequence will play over and over.
4. Click the Stop button to pause the animation.

Lesson 1.5-Tutorial 2: Enter a Command

1. Select Create, Polygon Primitives, Sphere to create a sphere object.
2. Click on the view panel away from the sphere to deselect it.
3. In the Command Line, type **select pSphere1;** and press the Enter key.
   The sphere object is selected.
4. In the Command Line, type, **move -z 10;**.
   The sphere is moved ten units along the z-axis.
5. Select File, Save Scene As and save the file as **Command line sphere.mb**.

Lesson 1.6: Use the Toolbox

On the left side of the interface is a column of buttons collectively known as the Toolbox, as shown in Figure 1-35.

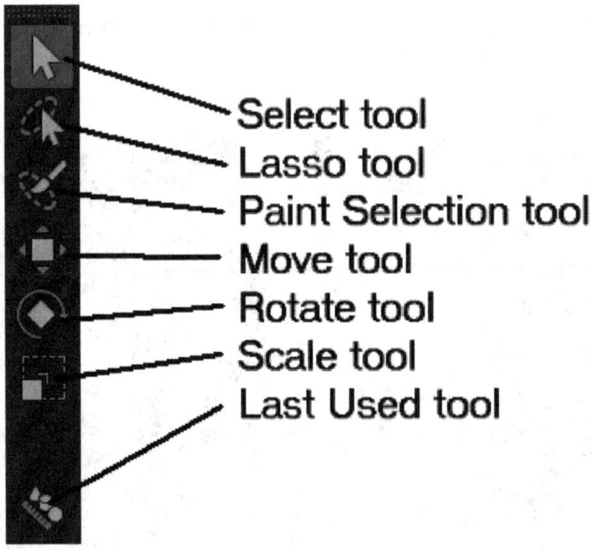

FIGURE 1-35
Toolbox

Selecting Objects

The first three buttons in the Toolbox are used to select objects in the scene. These are the Select Objects tool, the Lasso tool and the Paint Selection tool. The Select Object tool lets you select objects by clicking on objects or by dragging a rectangular border. The Lasso tool lets you drag a freehand outline over the object you want to select. The Paint Selection tool lets you drag or paint over components (such as vertices) to select them.

Holding down the Shift key while clicking on objects with the Select Objects tool will add objects to the selection set. All selected objects will appear white except for the last object selected, which will appear light green. This light green object is known as the *key object*. More details on selecting objects are covered in Chapter 4, "Working with Objects."

Using the Transform Tools

The Toolbox also includes the Move, Rotate, and Scale tools. When any of these tools are selected, a manipulator will appear at the center (pivot point) of the selected object. With these tools, you can transform the selected object. The manipulator lets you transform the tool along a single axis or within a single plane, as shown for the Move tool in Figure 1-36. You can also click on the transform values displayed on the Status Line or in the Channel Box and enter new values using the keyboard.

Tip

```
Once a transform handle on one of the transform
tools is selected, it turns yellow. You can then
drag the selected handle using the middle mouse
button.
```

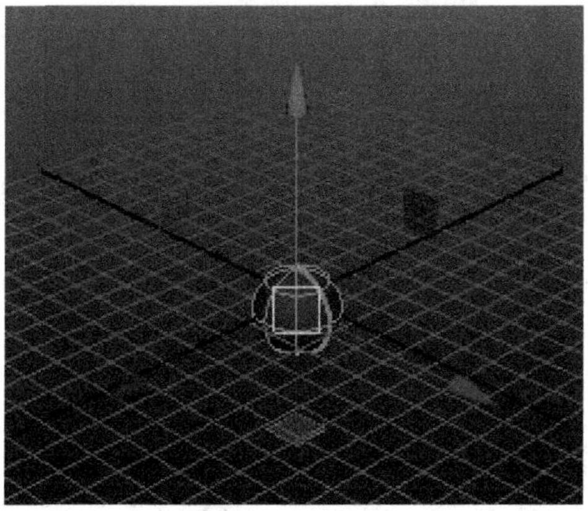

FIGURE 1-36

Manipulator controls for the Move tool

Understanding Manipulators

Each of the transform manipulators has color-coded components that will let you constrain a transform to a single axis—red is for the X-axis, green is for the Y-axis, and blue is for the Z-axis, as shown in Figure 1-37. The selected manipulator axis will turn yellow and dragging will transform the object along the selected axis.

Tip

```
The Hotkeys for the transform tools are q for
Select Object, w for Move, e for Rotate, and r for
Scale.
```

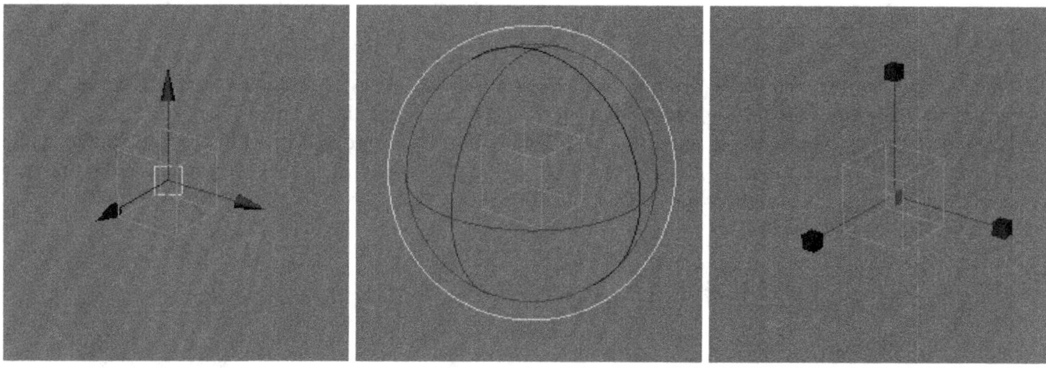

Move Manipulator Rotate Manipulator Scale Manipulator

FIGURE 1-37

Transform Manipulators

There are many other manipulators besides the transform manipulators. For example, when a spotlight object is selected, you can enable a manipulator that lets you alter its light properties such as its falloff cone, direction and intensity by dragging in the view.

Beneath the Scale tool button in the Toolbox is another button that holds the last tool that was used. Remember that any menu item or button that includes the word *Tool* in its name will remain active until another tool is selected and will appear at the bottom of the Toolbox.

Note

The last slot in the Toolbox is reserved for tools selected from the menus. The Toolbox tools will not occupy this slot.

Lesson 1.6-Tutorial 1: Select Objects

1. Open the Table parts.mb file.

   This file includes five box objects that are used to make a table.

2. Click on the Select tool and click on one of the cube objects.

   The selected cube in the scene turns light green and its attributes appear in the Channel Box.

3. Hold down the Shift key and click on the other cubes in the scene.

   All cubes in the scene are selected and the last cube clicked on will be light green.

4. With all 4 cubes selected, enter a value of 6 in the Scale Y attribute in the Channel Box.

   All cubes in the scene are scaled along their Y-axis to create the legs of a table, as shown in Figure 1-38.

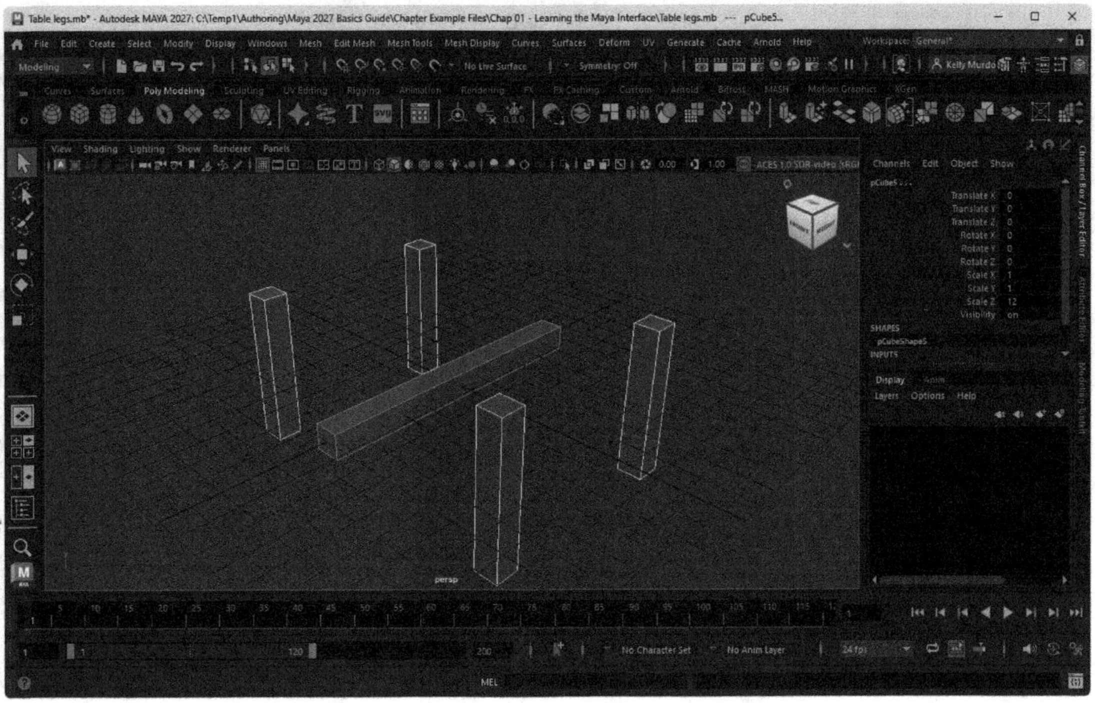

FIGURE 1-38

Selected objects

Lesson 1.6-Tutorial 2: Transform an Object

1. Open the Table legs.mb file again.
2. Click on the Select tool and click on the stretched box object in the center of the scene.
3. Click the Move tool in the Toolbox and drag the green (Y-axis) upward until it is above the four leg objects.

   The box object moves upward in the scene.
4. Click the Scale tool in the Toolbox and drag the red (X-axis) to the right until it covers the four leg objects to create a table.

   The box object is elongated along the X-axis, as shown in Figure 1-39.
5. Select File, Save Scene As and save the file as **Table.mb**.

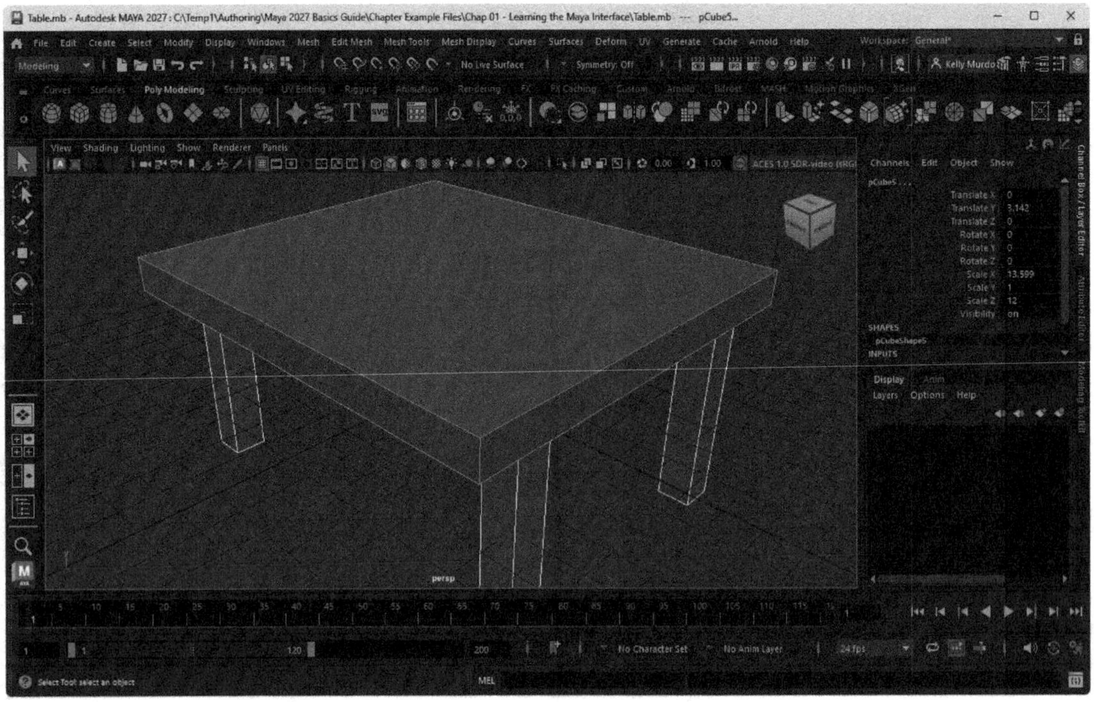

FIGURE 1-39

Transformed objects

Lesson 1.7: Discover the Marking Menus

Once you get used to the menu commands, you can learn to work faster using the hidden marking menus. These menus will pop-up different commands when you right-click on objects in the scene.

Accessing the Marking Menus

For quick access to many common commands, you can open a **marking menu** by right-clicking in the view panel and holding the mouse button down until the menu appears. You can then move the cursor between the different menu options and release the mouse button to select the desired menu command. Figure 1-40 shows the marking menu for a polygon sphere object.

Tip

You can access a marking menu of selection options by holding down the q key while clicking in the view panel. You can access other custom marking menus in a similar manner such as Move Tool options (w), Rotate Tool options (e), Scale Tool options (r), and Polygon Brush options (o).

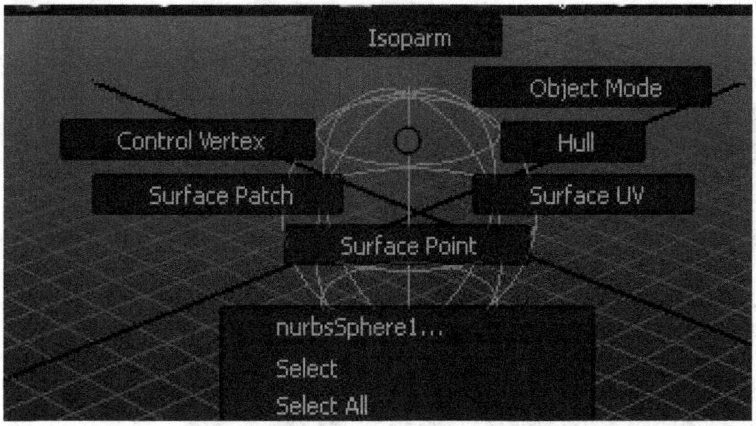

FIGURE 1-40

Marking menu

Customizing Marking Menus

You can alter the contents of a marking menu, assign a hotkey to a marking menu, or add a marking menu to the **Hotbox** using the Marking Menu Settings dialog box, shown in Figure 1-41. You access this dialog box using the Windows, Settings/Preferences, Marking Menu Editor menu command.

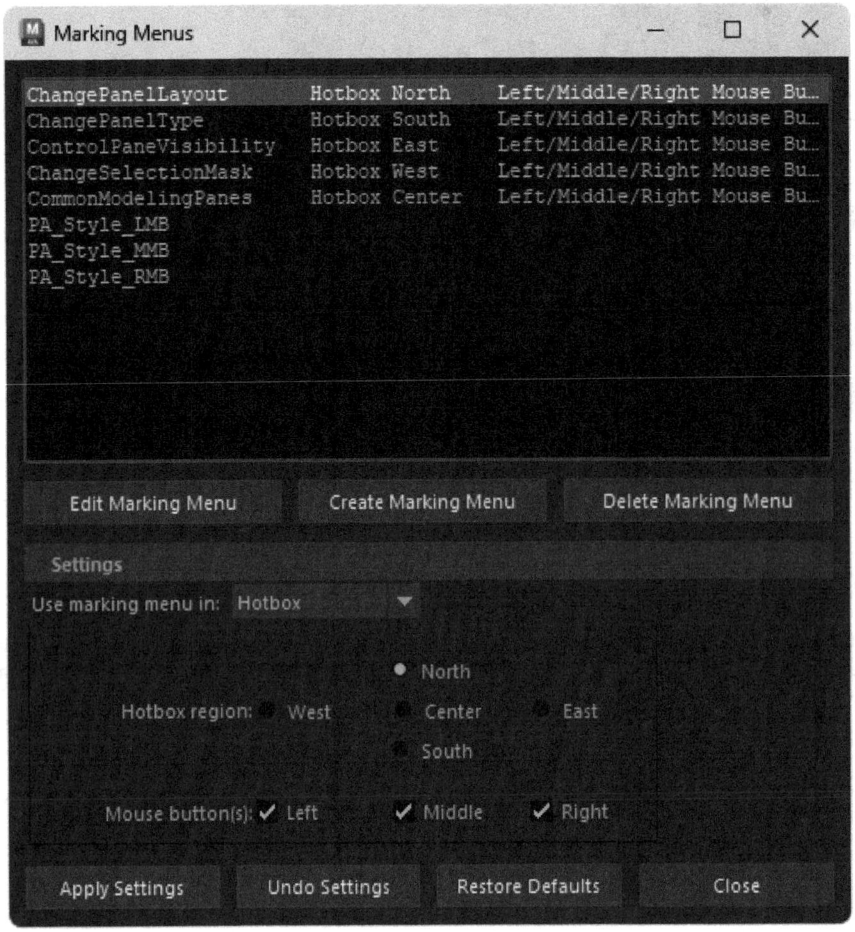

FIGURE 1-41

Marking Menus Settings dialog box

Using the Hotbox

The Hotbox, shown in Figure 1-42, is a complete set of customizable menus that you can access by pressing and holding the Spacebar. Using the Hotbox Controls option in the Hotbox, you can select which menu commands appear in the Hotbox.

FIGURE 1-42

Hotbox

Customizing the Hotbox

If you select the Hotbox Controls option from the Hotbox, you can select which menu sets to include in the Hotbox. You can also select to Show or Hide all menus.

Lesson 1.7-Tutorial 1: Access a Marking Menu

1. Select Create, Polygon Primitives, Sphere to create a sphere object.
2. Click on the view panel away from the sphere to deselect it.
3. Right-click on the sphere and choose Select from the pop-up marking menu.

   The sphere object is selected.

Lesson 1.7-Tutorial 2: Use the Hotbox

1. Move the cursor to the center of the view panel and press and hold the Spacebar.

   The Hotbox appears centered around where the cursor is located, as shown in Figure 1-43.
2. Drag the cursor to the Create button and select the Polygon Primitives, Sphere command.

   The sphere object appears in the view panel.
3. Release the Spacebar.

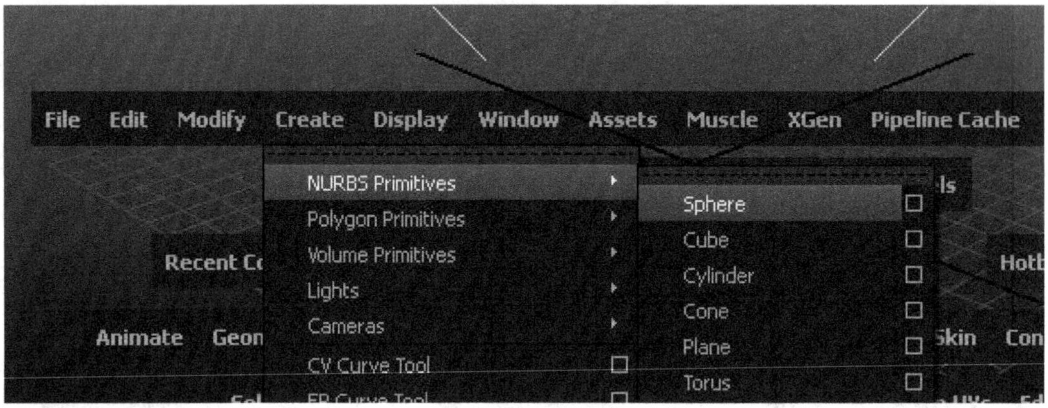

FIGURE 1-43

The Hotbox

Lesson 1.8: Get Help

Maya is a complex piece of software with tons of features, and it is easy to get lost when looking for a specific command. To help navigate all these features, there are several resources to try out including the Help menu, The Search box and Autodesk Assistant.

Accessing the Help menu

At the very right end of the menu is a Help menu. Included in this menu are commands to access the Maya Help documents with the F1 key. These help files open within a web browser, as shown in Figure 1-44. There are also options to take a Quick Tour, view Interactive Tutorials and link to the YouTube Learning Channel. The Scripting Reference command includes help files for MEL and Python. You can also give feedback on Maya to Autodesk directly.

Tip

At the bottom of the Toolbox and Layout buttons is a Maya logo button. This button opens the Maya Help files in a web browser.

FIGURE 1-44

The Maya help files

Searching Commands, Tools and Scene Objects

Underneath the layout buttons is a Search button with a magnifying glass icon. You can open this Search text field by clicking on this icon, selecting Search from the Help menu, or by pressing the Command/Ctrl + F key. If you open the pop-up menu under the Search icon, you can choose from Search (for tools and commands), Select (for selecting scene objects), MEL (for searching or running MEL commands), and Python (for searching or running Python commands).At the right end of the Search field is a Filter icon that can be used to filter the search list to specific topics such as Animation, Modeling, Curves, etc.

If you type into the Search field, Maya will present a list of all the commands or tools that match the entered text. For example, if you enter 'extrude' in the Search field, Maya presents a list of commands to extrude curves, to extrude components and the Wedge command, as shown in Figure 1-45. If you select the extrude components command from the Search list, the Edit Mesh, Extrude command is automatically selected just as if you selected it from the menu and you can use it right away. Also, notice that the Search feature does context searching and will find something similar to what you requested without matching the exact text such as the Wedge command in the above example.

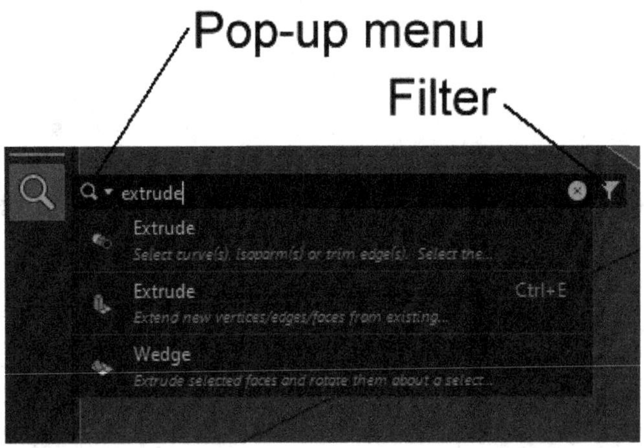

FIGURE 1-45

Search tools and commands

If you select the Select option from the pop-up menu, then any scene objects that match the typed text are immediately selected. This provides another quick way to select objects without having to open the Outliner.

The MEL and Python search options let you search for specific scripting commands and if you select a command from the search list, the command is automatically executed.

Using Autodesk Assistant

At the bottom of Help menu is a command to access the Autodesk Assistant. This feature opens a dialog box, shown in Figure 1-46, where you can use an AI assistant to get specific step-by-step commands on performing a specific task. For example, if I ask the assistant how to "lathe a curve over 180 degrees," it gives me the specific steps to do this. It also gives me steps to edit the sweep angle after creation, the Maya and Python scripts to do the same, and links to the help pages for more information.

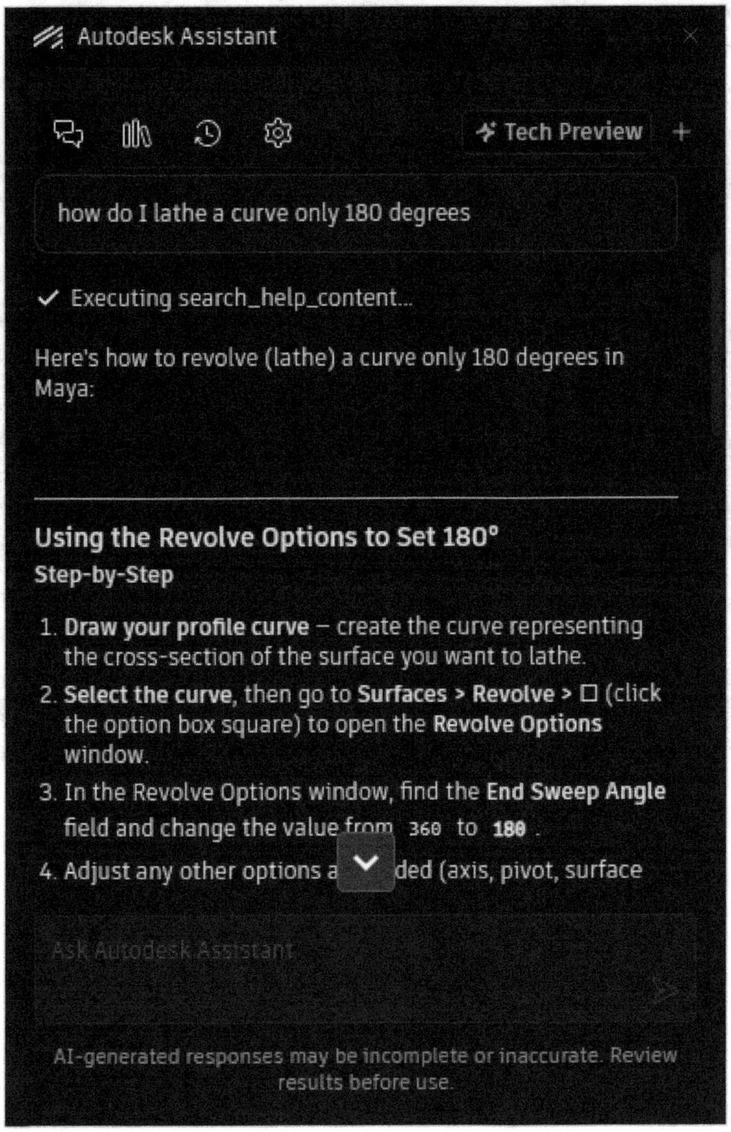

FIGURE 1-46

Autodesk Assistant gives step-by-step commands for specific tasks.

Lesson 1.8-Tutorial 1: Search for a Command

1. Select the File, Open Scene menu command and select the Billiard balls.mb file to open.

   A perspective view of the billiard table object is displayed.

2. Underneath the Quick Layout buttons, click on the Search button. In the Search field that appears, type Blue Pencil.

   A list of commands appears.

3. Select the first option in the list and press Enter.

   The Blue Pencil mode is selected then its toolbar appears.

4. Mark up the scene with the Blue Pencil tools, as shown in Figure 1-47.
5. Select File, Save Scene As and name the new scene **Billiard balls with notes**.

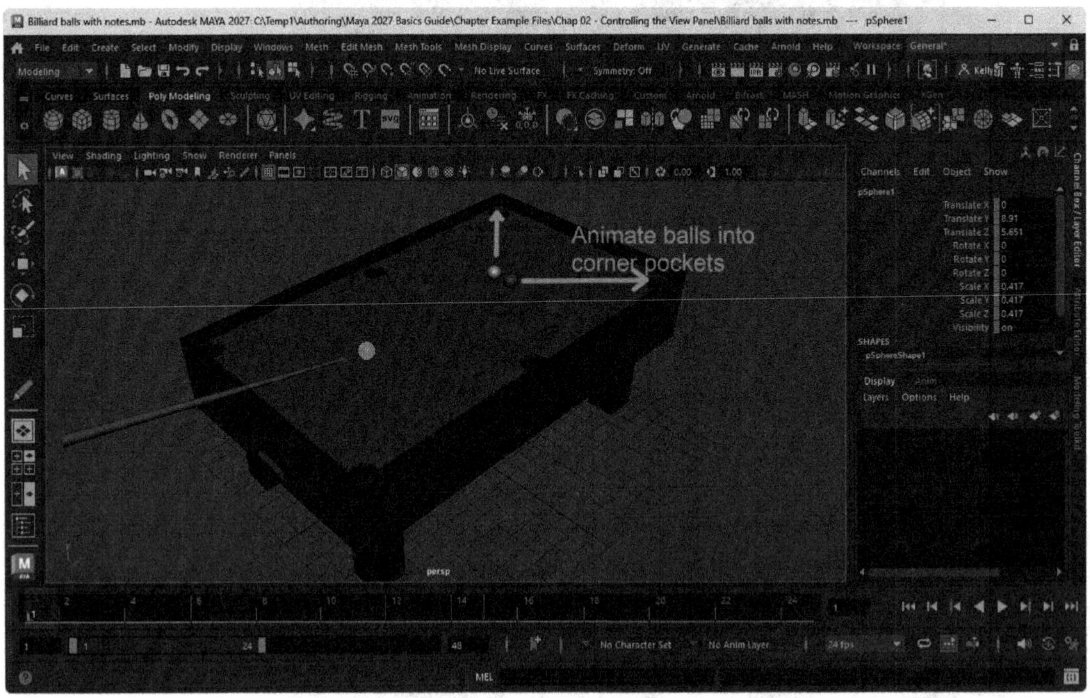

FIGURE 1-47

Billiard balls scene with notes

Lesson 1.8-Tutorial 2: Use Autodesk Assistant

1. Select the Help, Autodesk Assistant menu command.

    The Autodesk Assistant dialog box opens.

2. In the Ask Autodesk Assistant text box type in the question, "**How do I create a 20-sided dice?**"

    A list of commands appears.

3. Locate and copy the MEL Script text, then paste this script into the MEL field at the bottom of the Maya interface and press the Enter key.

    A 20-sided object appears in the View panel.

4. Press the F key to frame the selected object.

    The object's size fills the View panel, as shown in Figure 1-48.

5. Select File, Save Scene As and name the new scene **20-sided dice**.

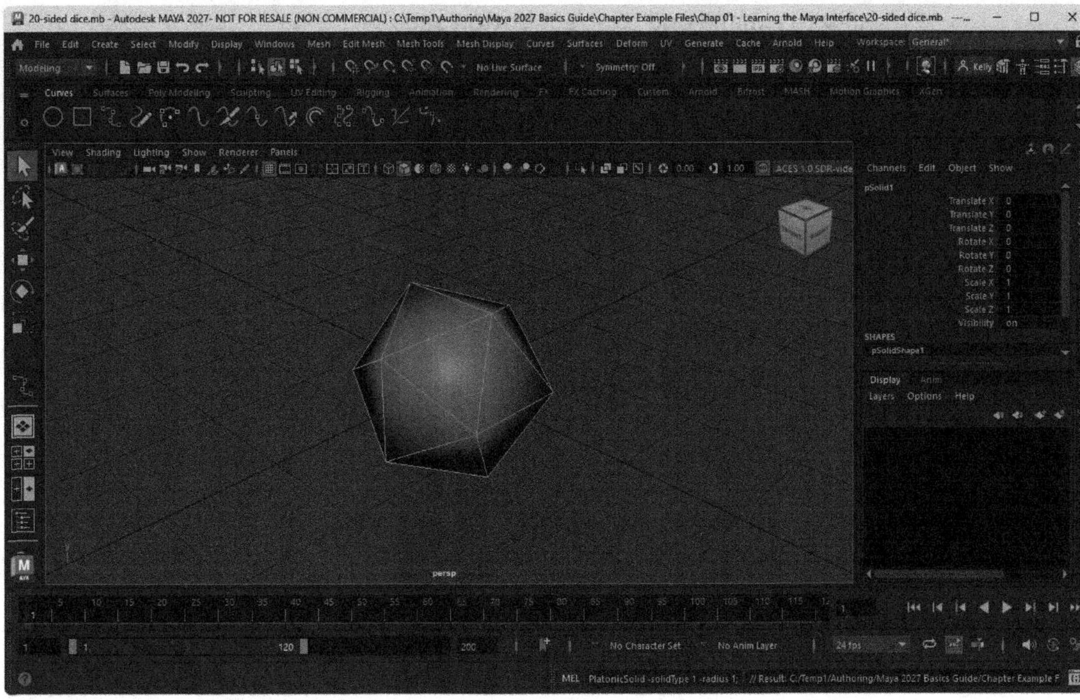

FIGURE 1-48

20-sided dice created with Autodesk Assistant

Chapter Summary

This chapter takes you through a tour of the Maya interface, covering the basic interface elements, including the menus, the Status Line buttons, the Shelf, the Channel Box, the Layer Editor, the Animation Controls, the Command Line, the Help Line, and the Toolbox buttons. This chapter also explains how to work with these various interface elements and presents the marking menus and the Hotbox as other ways to work with the interface. The chapter concludes with some ideas on resources for getting help.

What You Have Learned

In this chapter, you learned

* How to switch between the different menu sets.
* How to use keyboard hotkeys.
* How to access option dialog boxes from menus.
* How to tear off menus.
* The difference between tools and actions.
* How to use pop-up help to identify buttons.
* How to identify a change in the cursor denoting right-click menus.

* How to expand and contract button sets.
* How to open and save scene files.
* How to show and hide the different interface elements.
* How to use the Shelf.
* How to add and delete items from a Shelf.
* How to use parameters in the Channel Box.
* How to use the Layer Editor.
* How to work with the animation controls.
* How to use the Command and Help Lines.
* How to select and transform objects using the Toolbox tools.
* How to use and customize the marking menus and the Hotbox.
* How to search for commands, tools and scene objects.
* How to use the AI-powered Autodesk Assistant.

Key Terms From This Chapter

* **Menu set.** A dynamic set of menu options selected from a drop-down list at the top left of the interface.
* **Hotkey.** A keyboard shortcut that executes a command when pressed.
* **Option dialog box.** A dialog box with additional options opened using the icon found to the right of specific menu options.
* **Tear-off menu.** A panel of menu options that is removed to float freely from the interface.
* **Status Line.** A set of toolbar icons located at the top of the interface.
* **Pop-up help.** A small text title that appears when the cursor is held over the top of an icon.
* **Shelf.** A customizable set of buttons organized into separate groups.
* **Channel Box.** A panel of editable parameters that relate to the current selection.
* **Layer.** A selection of objects grouped together into a set that can be easily selected.
* **Animation controls.** A set of buttons used to control animation frames.

* **Command Line.** A text field where you can enter text commands.

* **Help Line.** A text field that presents the next action that is expected.

* **Toolbox.** A set of selection and transformation icons located to the left of the interface.

* **Marking menu.** A dynamic set of menus accessible by right-clicking on an object.

* **Hotbox.** A comprehensive set of menu options accessible by pressing the Spacebar.

* **Autodesk Assistant**. An AI-powered help resource that lets you use normal language statements to get step-by-step instructions for completing a task.

Chapter 2

Controlling the View Panel

IN THIS CHAPTER

The **View panel** is where you'll do most of your work. It is the large central panel in the middle of the interface that shows the scene objects. It is also called the viewport. Each View panel also includes a menu of options, called the Panel menu, that you can use to control what is displayed.

The objects displayed in the view panel are determined by a hidden camera that is pointing at the scene. You can change the view that is shown in the view panel by moving, zooming, and rotating this hidden camera. Do so by using the Camera tools that are found in the View panel menu or by holding down the Alt/Option key and dragging and using various mouse button combinations to rotate, zoom, and pan the view.

Additional information can be added to the scene using the Heads Up Display feature. You can also annotate the current scene with several drawing features called the Blue Pencil tools. These are used to add notes that are independent of the scene objects.

In addition to changing the view, you can also select to view the scene objects using different **wireframe** resolutions or as a shaded, or textured view. Each option shows the scene objects in more or less quality. By changing the quality of the object being displayed, you can control how quickly the entire scene is updated. For some complex scenes, you may want to set a low-quality setting so you can work on the timing of an animation or you may want to set the quality high to see how the texture wraps around an object.

The View panel menu also includes commands that let you frame a selected object, move between the various views, and show or hide specific object types. Various other interfaces, such as the **Outliner**, **Hypergraph,** and Visor are useful interfaces for working with objects. You can display these interfaces also within a view panel.

Beneath the Toolbox buttons are several buttons used to change the viewport layout. These buttons, known as the **Quick Layout buttons**, are used to switch between a single perspective view and two or four views at a time.

Lesson 2.1: Change the View

The first thing to learn when dealing with view panels is how to change the view. Changing the view panels lets you see the specific area that you want to work on. All the view panel controls have easy-to-use hotkeys associated with them for quick access.

Using the Tumble, Track, Dolly, and Camera Tools

You can accomplish most view changes using the Alt/Option key and the mouse buttons. To **tumble** (or rotate) the camera, hold down the Alt/Option key while dragging with the left mouse button. To **track** (or pan) the camera, hold down the Alt/Option key and drag with the middle mouse button. To **dolly** (or zoom) in and out of the scene, hold down the Alt/Option key and drag with the right mouse button.

Tip

For each of these modes, the mouse cursor changes to match the various modes, as shown in Figure 2-1.

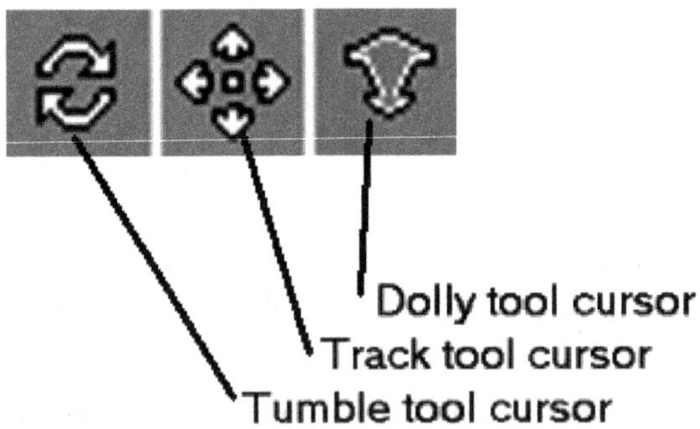

FIGURE 2-1

Tumble, track, and dolly cursors

You can also zoom in on a specific area by dragging over the rectangular area that you want to zoom in on with the Ctrl/Command and Alt/Option keys held down. If you drag from left to right, you'll zoom in; dragging from right to left causes the view to zoom out.

Tip

You can also zoom in and out of the view by scrubbing the mouse's scroll wheel.

You can also change the view using one of the additional camera tools. These tools are accessed from the View, Camera Tools panel menu. The Camera Tools panel menu includes the Tumble, Track, Dolly and Zoom tools that are the same as those accessed with the Alt/Option key held down, but it also includes some additional tools, including the Roll, Azimuth Elevation, Yaw-Pitch, Fly and Walk tools. The Roll tool spins the scene about its center point. The Azimuth Elevation tool raises or lowers the camera relative to the ground plane. The Yaw-Pitch tool rotates the entire scene about the camera instead of rotating the camera about the scene like the Rotate tool. The Fly tool lets the entire scene rotate freely about the camera and uses the Ctrl/Command key to move towards and away from objects.

Tip

If you ever get lost when manipulating a camera, you can always return to the default view using the View, Default Home panel menu command.

The Camera Tools panel menu also has a Walk tool. This tool lets you move about the scene using the W (forward), A (backwards), S (strafe left) and D (strafe right) keys and the mouse controls where to look similar to playing a first-person shooter game. Press the Escape key to exit Walk mode again.

Framing an Object

If you want to focus the view on a selected object or objects, use the View, Frame panel menu command (or press the f hotkey). This command zooms and pans the view automatically so the selected object or objects fill the view panel, as shown in Figure 2-2. You can also focus on all the objects in the scene whether they are selected or not with the View, Frame All panel menu command (or by pressing the a hotkey).

Tip

These commands are also found in the Display menu. The hotkey to frame all objects in all views is Shift+A, and the hotkey to frame the selected object in all views is Shift+F.

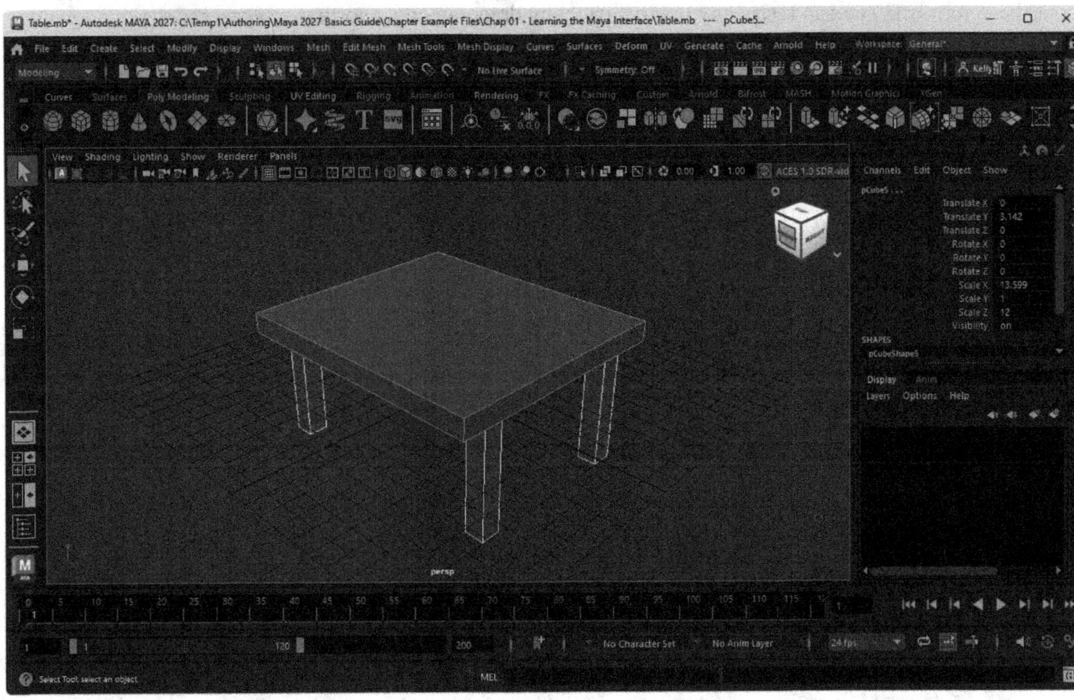

FIGURE 2-2

Framed object

Moving Through Views

You can return to the previous view using the View, Undo View Change (Alt/Option+Z) panel menu command and the View, Redo View Change (Alt/Option+Y) panel menu command moves back to the original view. The hotkeys for these panel menu commands are the [and] keys. You can also bookmark a view using the View, Bookmarks, Edit Bookmarks panel menu command. This opens the Bookmark Editor dialog box, in which you can create, delete and manage your bookmarks. All new bookmarks that you create show up in the View, Bookmarks panel menu. The View, Predefined Bookmarks panel menu also includes several default bookmarks that you may select including Perspective, Front, Top, and so on.

Caution

The Undo View Change (Alt/Option+Z) and the Redo View Change (Alt/Option+Y) commands are different from the standard Undo (Ctrl/Command+Z) and Redo (Ctrl/Command+Y) commands in the Edit menu. One undo is only for view changes and the other is for tool and menu commands.

Tearing Off Panels

If you prefer to work with windowed views that are separate from the interface, you can tear off the panel with the Panels, Tear Off panel menu command. You can also tear off just a copy while leaving the original view panel part of the interface with the Panels, Tear Off Copy panel menu command. Figure 2-3 shows a panel that has been torn-off. You can resize any tear-off panel by dragging on its borders or corners.

Note

When a panel is torn away from the main interface, the Panels panel menu is replaced with a Help menu option.

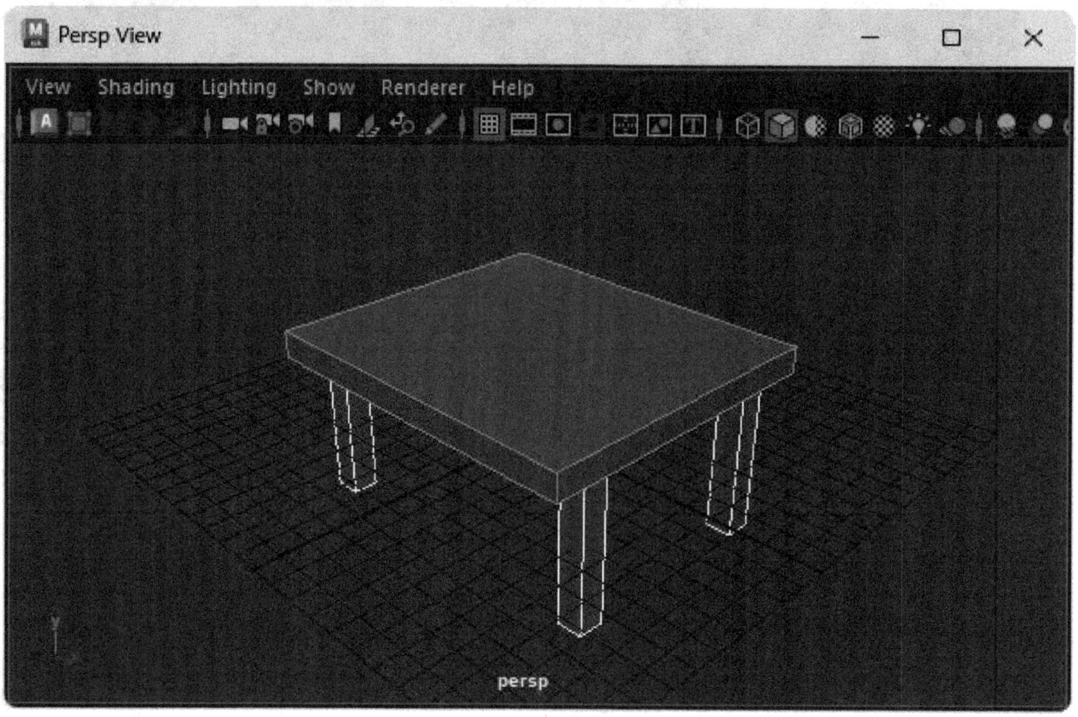

FIGURE 2-3

A tear-off view panel

Using Heads-Up Displays

The Display, Heads Up Display menu includes several options that you can select that overlay information over the active panel. These options include Object Details, Poly Count, Animation Details, Frame Rate, Camera Names, View Axis, Origin Axis and many more. This information is displayed above the existing view, as shown in Figure 2-4.

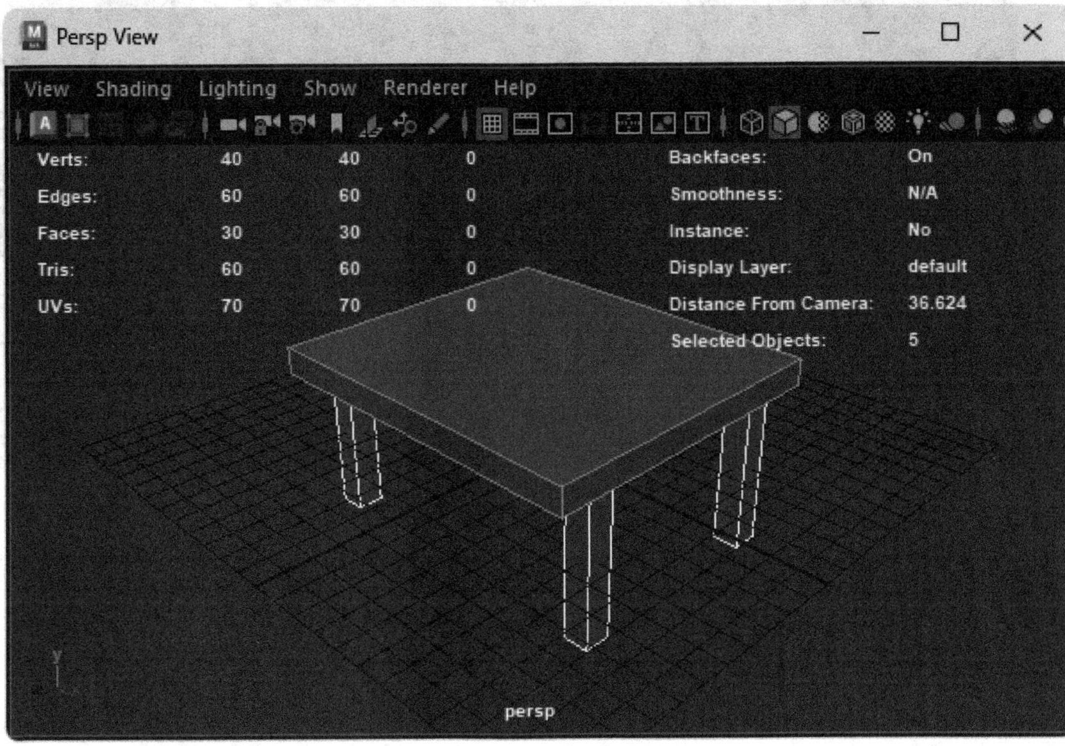

FIGURE 2-4

The Heads-Up Display with Poly Count and Object Details options

Accessing Grids

By default, the wireframe grid is visible in the view panel when you open Maya, but you can toggle this grid on and off if you choose using the Display, Grid menu. If you select the Grid Options, then you can specify the Length and Width of the grid lines, the number of Subdivisions and the display of the grid. These grid lines are not included in the final render and are only there to help you as you navigate the scene.

Opening Other Interfaces Within a Panel

The view panels aren't just used to display scene objects—they may also be used to hold any of Maya's other interfaces or editors including a Render View. Selecting an item from the Panels, Panel panel menu opens the selected interface within the active panel. The list of interfaces that may be opened includes the Outliner, Graph Editor, Dope Sheet, Trax Editor, Hypershade, Render View, and so on. Figure 2-5 shows four view panels with the Outliner, Graph Editor, Render View and Perspective views open.

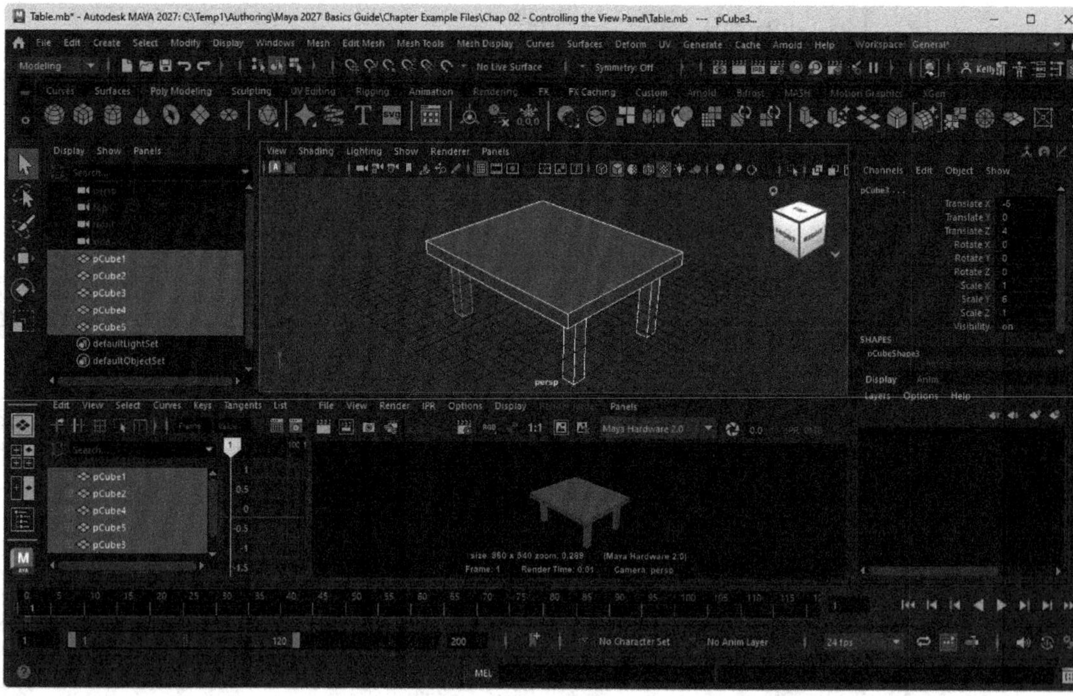

FIGURE 2-5

View panels displaying the Outliner, the Graph Editor, and the Render View interfaces

Annotating with the Blue Pencil tools

If you're working with a scene and you want to make some notes on the current scene without impacting the scene, you can use the Blue Pencil tools. These tools let you mark up a scene using a colored pencil, brush, text, arrows and shapes. At any later time, all the mark up can be instantly removed without altering the scene at all. These tools are really intended to be used in a team setting allowing a technical or art director to give notes to the artists.

To access the Blue Pencil tools, click on the Blue Pencil icon located on the Panel toolbar. This will make the Blue Pencil toolbar available under the Shelf, as shown in Figure 2-6.

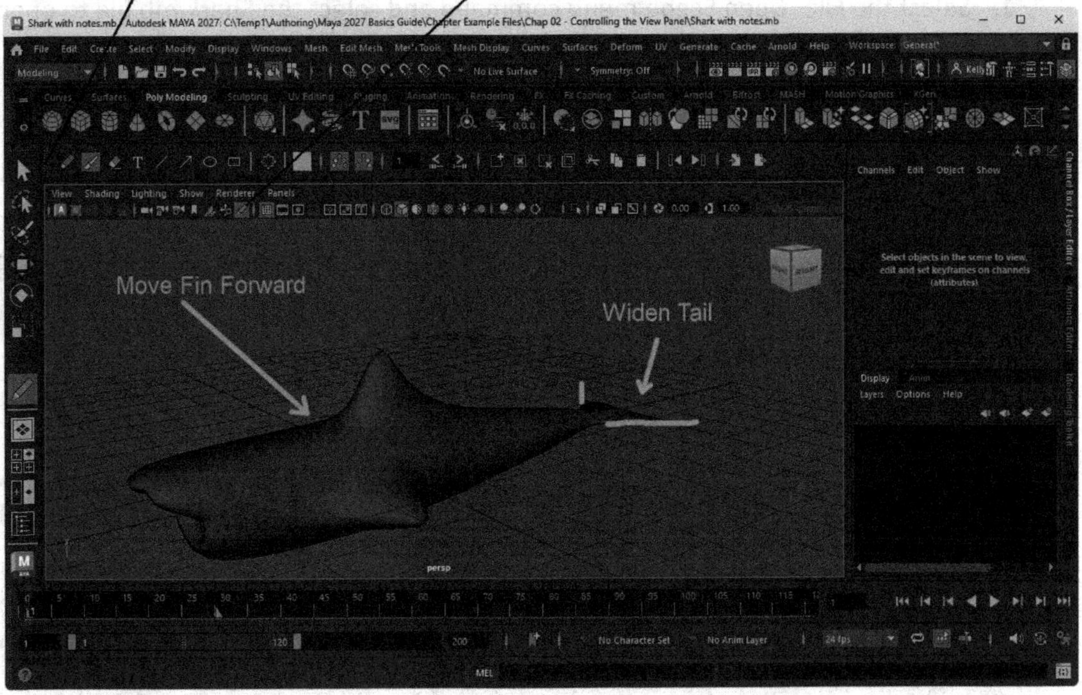

FIGURE 2-6

The Blue Pencil tools let you add notes to the current scene

Within the Blue Pencil toolbar are several useful annotation tools including Pencil, Brush, Eraser, Text, Line, Arrow, Ellipse and Rectangle. If you right click on any of these tools, you can access a pop-up menu of settings. For example, right clicking on the Pencil tool accesses settings for the Size and Opacity. You can also enable the tablet pressure to set the opacity or size. The Brush tool includes an additional setting for Hardness and the Text tool includes settings for Font, Size, and Opacity.

To the right of the various drawing tools is a Transform Mode icon. This button lets you drag a rectangular selection over the drawing notes and after pressing the Enter key, you can move the content within the selection anywhere in the scene. This lets you reposition drawings as needed.

There is also a Color Swatch that you can use to change the color used for all the tools (and it doesn't need to be blue).

Whenever any of the drawing tools are drawn on the scene, a keyframe is added to the Timeline. This appears as a small light blue icon on the Timeline. This enables users to make notes at different points of an animation, and it makes the drawing only visible when that particular frame is selected. However, if you turn on the Ghost Previous and Ghost Next buttons, then the notes will be visible for all frames only shown in a lighter opacity. The next several toolbar buttons let you control how long the current note frame is visible, how they are retimed or moved on the Timeline and cleared and deleted. There are also options to cut, copy and paste frames to different locations on the Timeline.

The final two toolbar icons let you import and export the current frame. Exported frames are saved as a Zip archive file.

Lesson 2.1-Tutorial 1: Change the Object's View

1. Select the File, Open Scene menu command and select the Shark.mb file to open.

   A side view of the shark object is displayed in a single view perspective view panel.

2. Hold down the Alt/Option key and drag in the View panel with the left mouse button. Rotate the shark so that its mouth is visible.

   The shark is rotated about the center of the View panel, as shown in Figure 2-7.

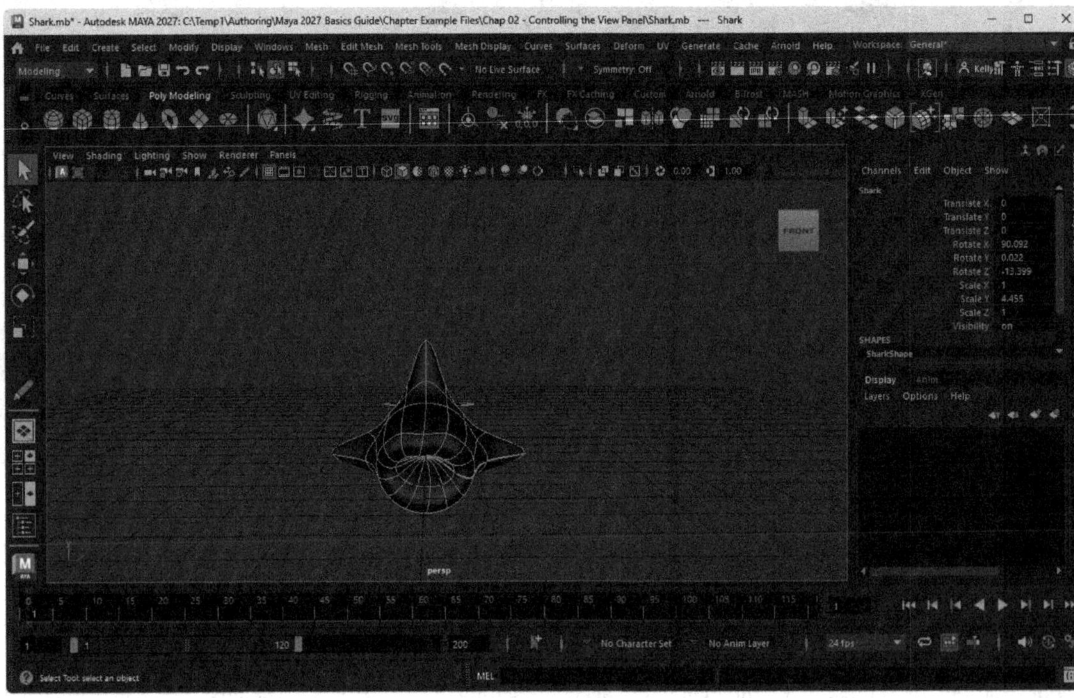

FIGURE 2-7

Rotated view of the shark

3. Hold down the Alt/Option key and drag with the middle mouse button.

   The camera moves in the direction of the mouse, thereby panning the view.

4. Hold down the Alt/Option key and drag with the right mouse button.

   The camera zooms in on the shark, as shown in Figure 2-8.

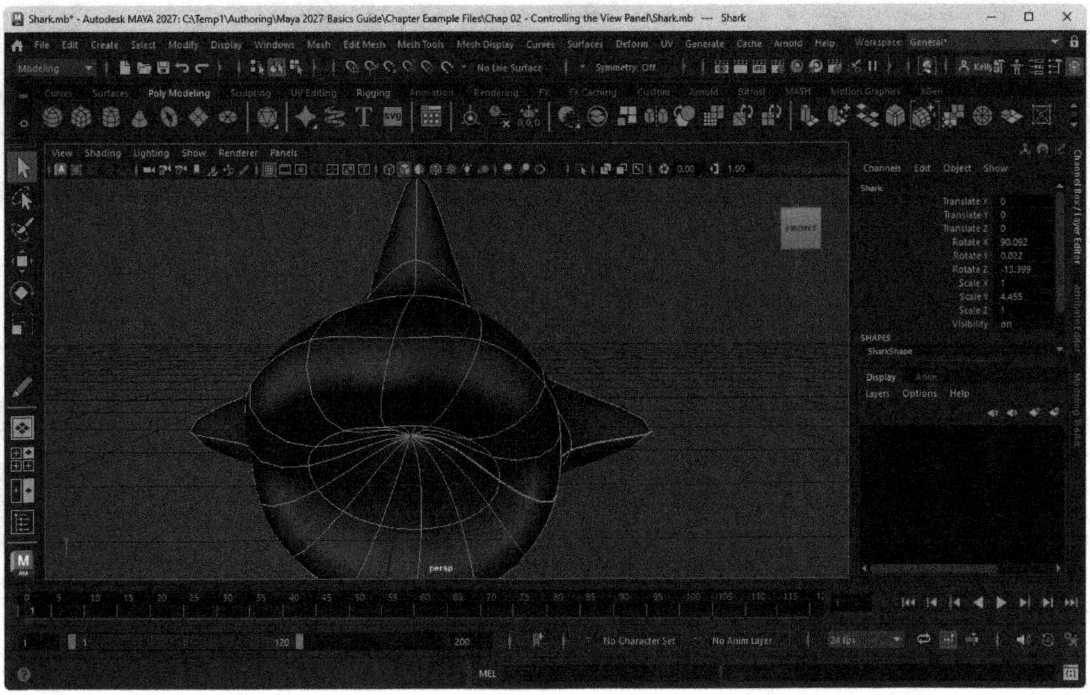

FIGURE 2-8

Zoomed view of the shark

5. After looking at the shark's mouth up close, press the *f* key to frame the shark.

   The camera zooms out until the entire shark is visible in the view panel.
6. Press the [and] keys to move back and forth through the views.
7. Select the Display, Heads Up Display, Object Details menu command.

   Various details about the object are displayed in the upper-right corner of the view panel, as shown in Figure 2-9.

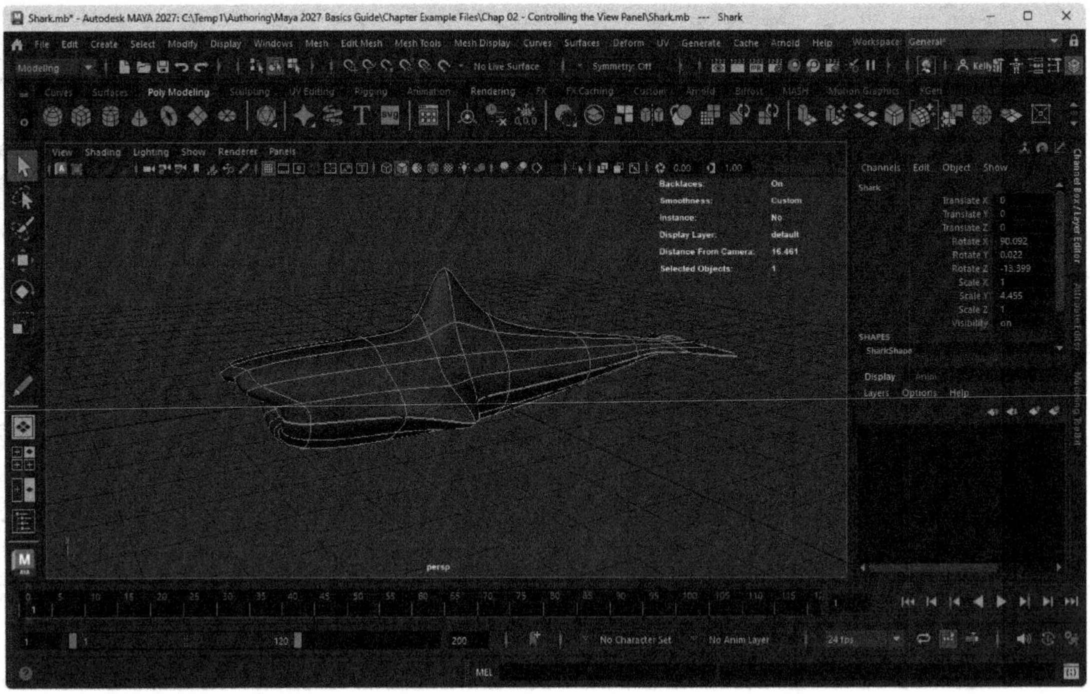

FIGURE 2-9

Shark with Object Details

Lesson 2.1-Tutorial 2: Mark Up the Scene

1. Select the File, Open Scene menu command and select the Table.mb file to open.

   A perspective view of the table object is displayed.

2. Click on the Blue Pencil icon in the Panel toolbar.

   The Blue Pencil toolbar appears underneath the Shelf.

3. Click on the Arrow tool and highlight some areas in the scene.
4. Right click on the Text tool and change the Size setting to 60, then click in the scene and enter some text.

   The table scene with some notes added is displayed in Figure 2-10.

5. Select File, Save Scene As and name the new scene **Table with notes.**

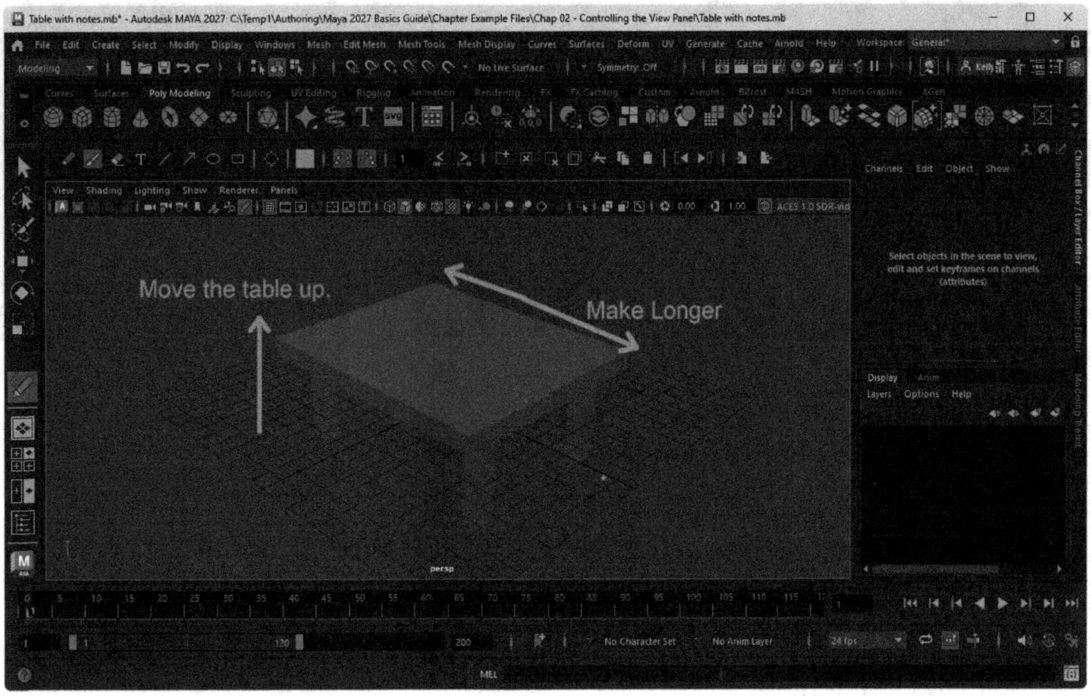

FIGURE 2-10

Table scene with notes

Lesson 2.2: Change Display Options

Complex objects can take a long time to update in the View panels. You can increase the speed at which objects are updated by having the view panels display the objects at a lower **resolution,** or you can view the effect of lighting and texture maps applied to the objects using other display modes.

Changing Resolution

Objects in the scene can be viewed at different quality settings. Low-quality settings show complex scenes in near real-time, whereas high-quality complex scenes may take a while to be viewed.

To view NURBS objects using the Rough setting, press the 1 key. The 2 key gives you a medium representation of the objects, and the 3 key displays the objects using a fine quality setting. Figure 2-11 shows these three levels of resolution.

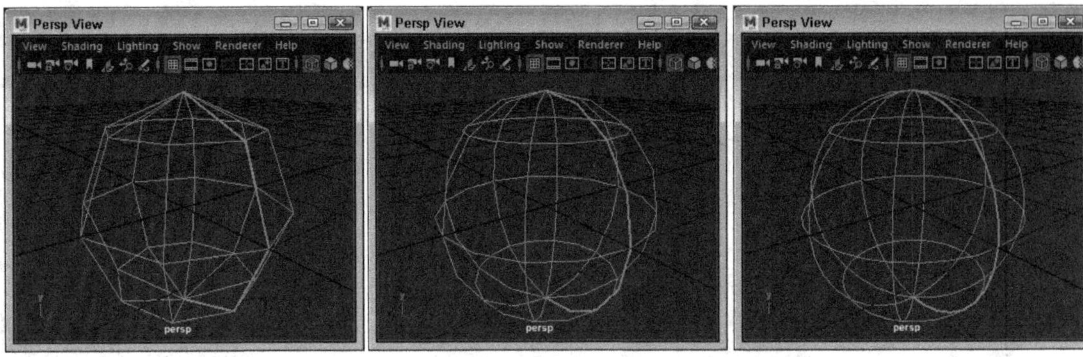

FIGURE 2-11

Rough, Medium, and Fine NURBS spheres

Note

The wireframe resolution settings only have an impact on NURBS objects. Polygon objects are unaffected by these settings.

Changing Shading

Using the options found in the **Shading** panel menu (and several hotkeys), you can change the type of shading that displays the scene objects. The Shading, Wireframe panel menu command (or the 4 key) displays all objects in the scene using a wireframe display method. The Wireframe option only shows the object edges. The Shading, Smooth Shade All panel menu command (or the 5 key) shows all objects using a smooth shaded view. The Shading, Flat Shade All panel menu command shows all objects using a flat shaded view. Flat shading doesn't smooth between adjacent polygons making the object appear blocky. The Shading panel menu also includes a Bounding Box option that shows just a wireframe box that the object would fit in. Figure 2-12 shows a simple sphere as a wireframe, with smooth shading and with flat shading.

FIGURE 2-12

Wireframe, Smooth Shading and Flat Shading

For the smooth and flat shading options, the Shading panel menu also includes commands to apply the smooth or flat shading to only the selected items.

The Shading panel menu includes some additional shading options. The Wireframe on Shaded option displays wireframe edges along with shading; the X-Ray option makes all objects semi-transparent. You can also choose to apply X-Ray to just the joints or just the Active Components.

Tip

At the top of the view panel are icons for changing the shading method and other display settings.

If the Wireframe on Shaded option is enabled on a dense mesh, the wireframe color can easily overpower the shading making the entire mesh appear as the wireframe color. However, if you enable overrides in the Drawing Overrides section of the Attribute Editor for the selected object, you can choose the RGB color and decrease the Opacity of the wireframe color making more of the shading visible.

Displaying Textures

The Shading, Hardware Texturing panel menu command (or the 6 key) displays the objects using a shaded view with textures. Figure 2-13 shows a NURBS sphere displayed with and without textures.

Note

If the scene objects don't have a texture applied, then smooth shaded objects will look the same as texture shaded. Applying textures to objects is covered in Chapter 9, "Assigning Materials and Textures."

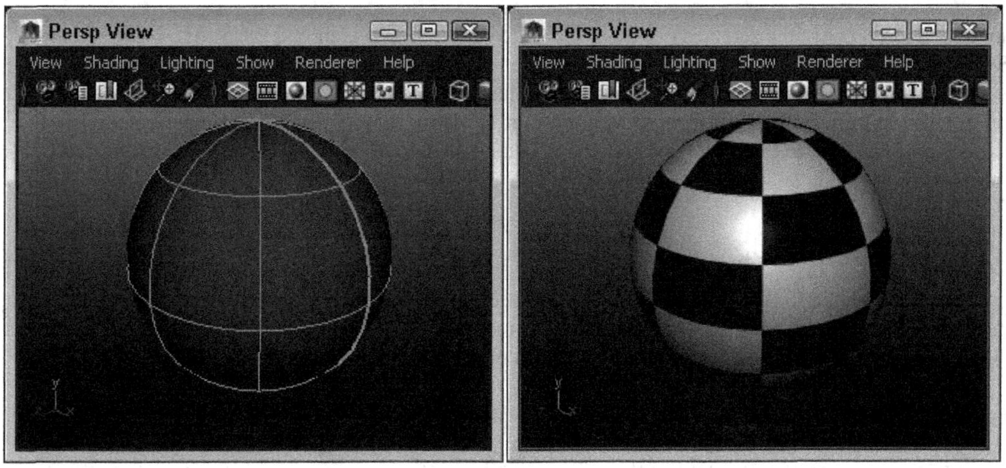

FIGURE 2-13

Textured and non-textured views

Enabling Backface Culling and Improving Wireframes

The Shading, **Backface Culling** panel menu command toggles the display to show only those faces that are facing the viewing camera. All the faces on the backside of the objects are obscured. Figure 2-14 shows a semi-transparent sphere with and without the Backface Culling options enabled.

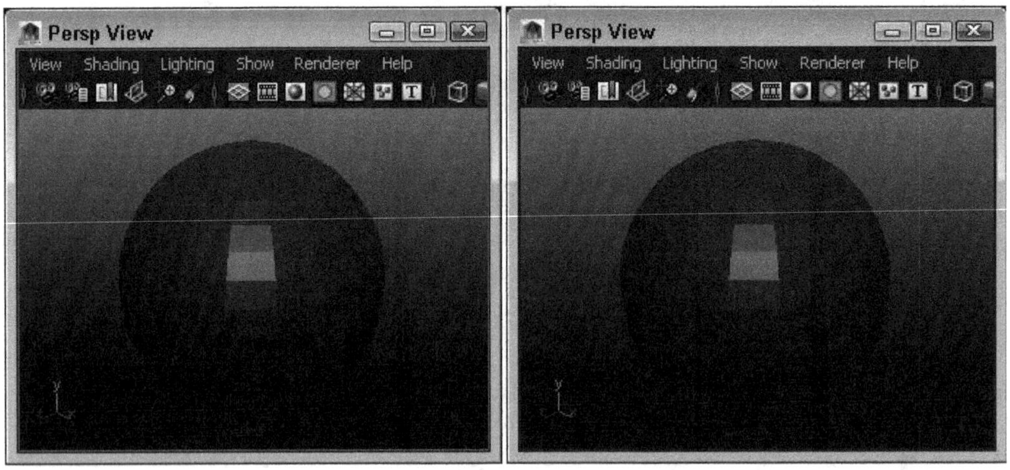

FIGURE 2-14

Backface culling enabled and disabled

The Shading, Smooth Wireframe panel menu command toggles the anti-aliasing of wireframe edges making them much smoother and less jaggy.

Isolating Objects

To change the view so only the selected objects are displayed and framed, choose the Show, Isolate Select, View Selected panel menu command. This command is a toggle option that hides all objects except for those that are selected. Choosing the option again makes all objects reappear. When in isolation mode, the word "Isolate" appears in front of the view title at the bottom of the view panel. The Show, Isolate Select panel menu also includes options to Auto Load New Objects, and Add and Remove Selected Objects, which lets you change which objects are isolated.

Hiding and Showing Objects

As your scene increases in the number of objects, it can become difficult to find specific objects. To help focus on a specific object and to prevent other objects from being accidentally moved, you can use the toggle menus in the Show panel menu to hide and show All objects, no objects or specific object types.

For a more permanent method of hiding objects, you can hide selected objects using the Display, Hide, Hide Selected (Ctrl/Command+h) menu command. In the Display, Hide menu, there are also commands to Hide Unselected Objects (Alt/Option+h), Hide All, and hide only specific geometry types. The Display, Show menu includes similar commands for making objects visible again.

Tip

A more effective way to hide objects is to group scene objects by layers and use the Layer Editor controls to hide all the objects on a specific layer.

Changing Object Name and Color

To help identify objects, you can name the selected object by clicking on the object name that appears in the top of the Channel Box, as shown in Figure 2-15, for the selected object and typing a new name. This name identifies the object in the external interfaces such as the Outliner and the Hypergraph.

Tip

Objects can also be renamed in the Outliner.

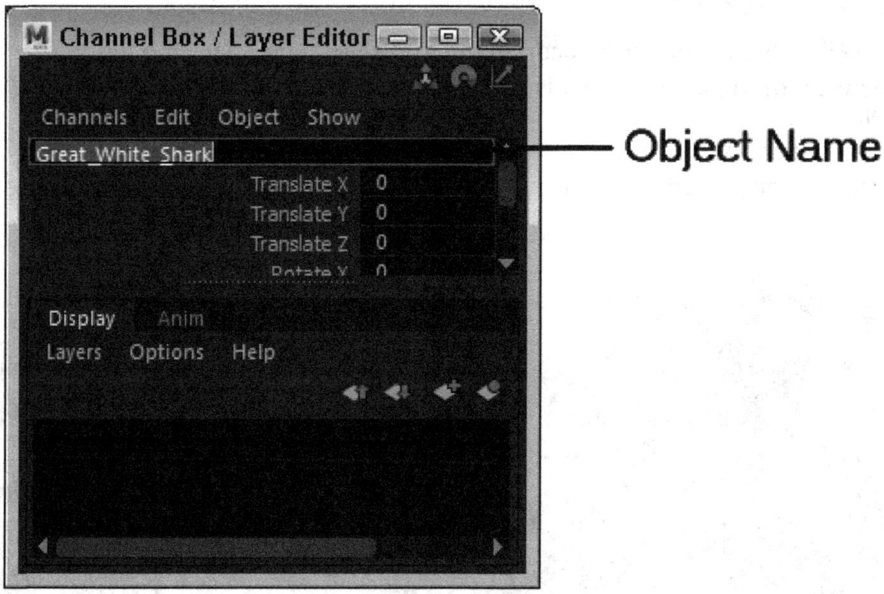

FIGURE 2-15

Object Name in Channel Box

You can also change the object's wireframe color using the Display, Wireframe Color menu command. This opens a simple dialog box, shown in Figure 2-16, in which you can choose from a palette of colors. From the drop-down at the top of the dialog, you can choose from Index colors or RGB colors. Double-clicking on any of the colors opens a Color Selector in which you can customize the color.

Note

Wireframe color is also set by the layer that the object is part of. Layer color is displayed instead of wireframe color if the object is part of a layer.

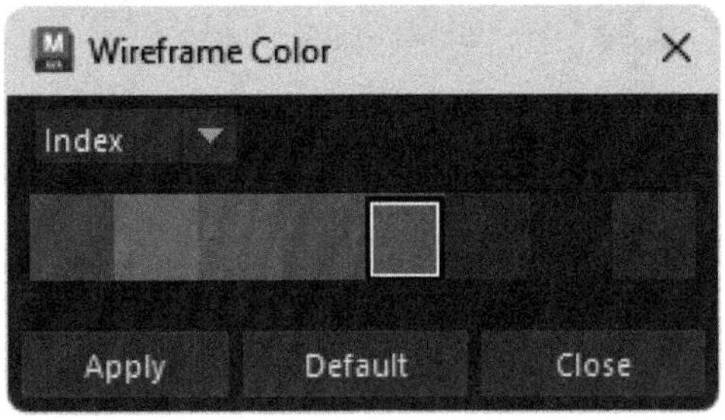

FIGURE 2-16

Changing wireframe color

Lesson 2.2-Tutorial 1: Change the Object's Resolution

1. Select the File, Open Scene menu command and select the Shark.mb file to open.

   A side view of the shark object is displayed in a single view perspective view panel.

2. Press the 1 key on the keyboard.

   The shark is displayed using the lowest resolution setting, as shown in Figure 2-17.

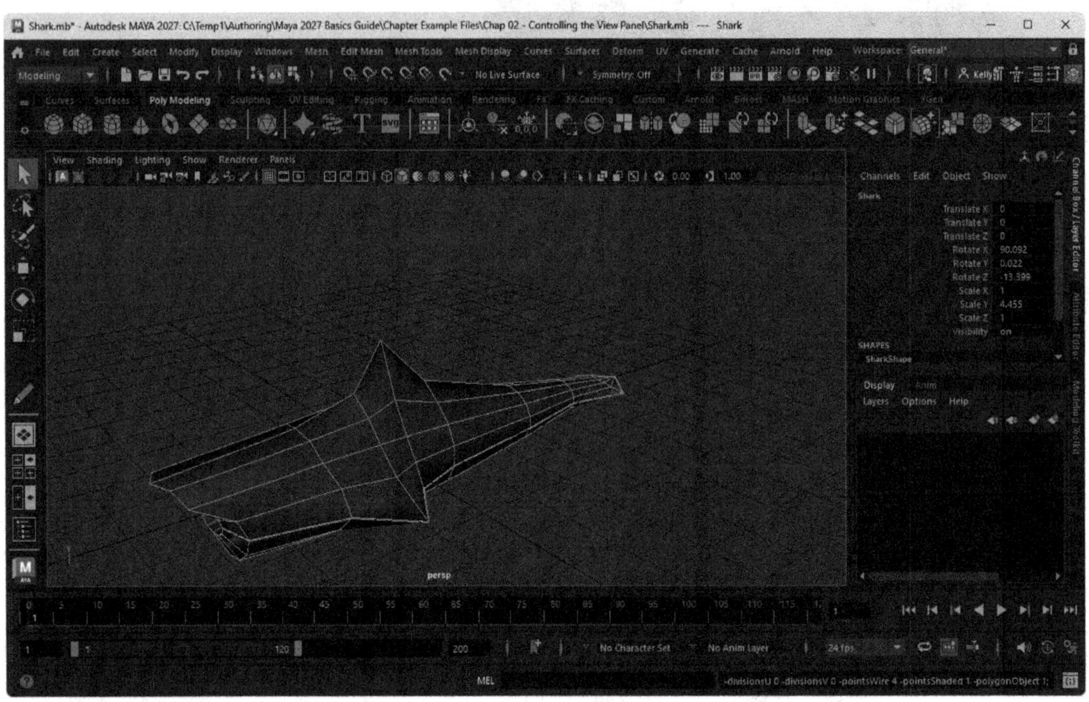

FIGURE 2-17

Shark at the lowest resolution setting

3. Press the 2 key on the keyboard, followed by the 3 key.

   The shark is displayed at the medium and then the high-resolution setting.

4. Press the 4 key to see the shark in wireframe mode, as shown in Figure 2-18, and on the 5 key to see the shark smooth shaded.

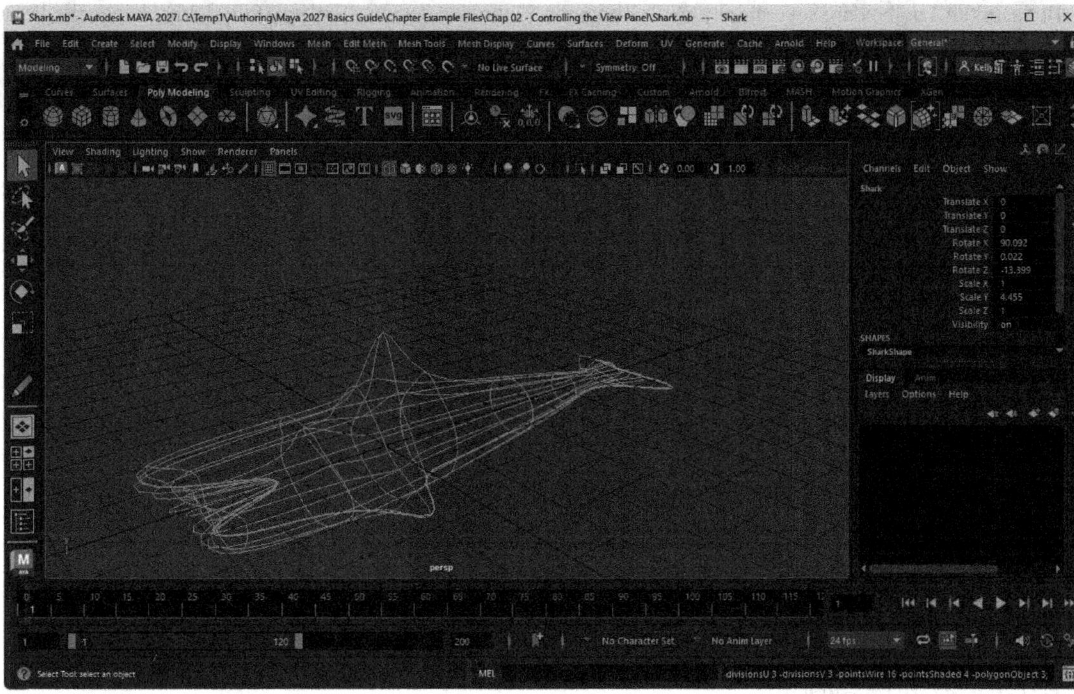

FIGURE 2-18

The wireframe shark

Lesson 2.2-Tutorial 2: Change the Object's Name and Color

1. Select the File, Open Scene menu command and select the Shark.mb file to open.
2. Click on the object's name in the Channel Box and type the name **Great White Shark**.

   The transform and shape nodes for the shark object are changed.
3. Select the Display, Wireframe Color menu command. In the dialog box that opens, double-click on the light blue color. In the Color Chooser that opens, select a bright cyan color and click the Accept button. Then click the Apply button in the Wireframe Color dialog box.
4. Click away from the shark and press the 4 key to see the new color in wireframe view.

   The wireframe shark is now displayed using the new wireframe color.
5. Select File, Save Scene As and name the new scene **Great White Shark**.

Lesson 2.3: Change the Layout

By default, the viewport shows a single perspective view, but you can change the layout to show two or four views at once. The buttons to change the layout are located directly under the Toolbox buttons. Below the Toolbox are several layout buttons known collectively as the Quick Layout buttons.

Switching Layouts

Beneath the Toolbox are several buttons, as shown in Figure 2-19, that allow you to quickly change the layout of the Maya interface. The default layout options include Single Perspective View, Four View, Front/Perspective and Outliner. The Search button opens a text field where you can search for specific commands, tools or even scene objects. The keyboard shortcut for the Search feature is Command/Ctrl + F. The Maya M button at the bottom of the layout buttons opens the help files in a web browser.

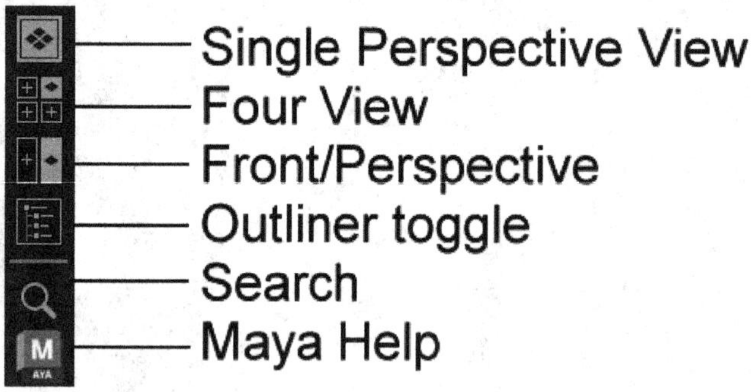

FIGURE 2-19

Quick Layout buttons

Customizing Layouts

You can change the layout that each button opens by right-clicking on the layout buttons and selecting the layout from the pop-up menu. Selecting the Edit Layouts menu command in the right-click pop-up menu opens the Panel Editor.

Resizing and Editing View Panels

When multiple view panels are visible, you can resize the individual panels by dragging the dividers between the panels. Only one view panel can be active at a time.

Tip

Using the Spacebar, you can toggle between making the active view panel fill the entire Workspace and returning to the previous layout. For example, if the Four View layout is selected and the Top view panel is the active view panel, pressing the Spacebar maximizes the Top view panel.

You can use the Panel menu command on the Panels menu to change the view for any panel. You can find the Panels menu at the top of each view panel. The Panels, Panel Editor menu command opens the Panels dialog box, shown in Figure 2-20. With this dialog box in the Edit Layouts tab, you can create a new panel and edit custom layouts.

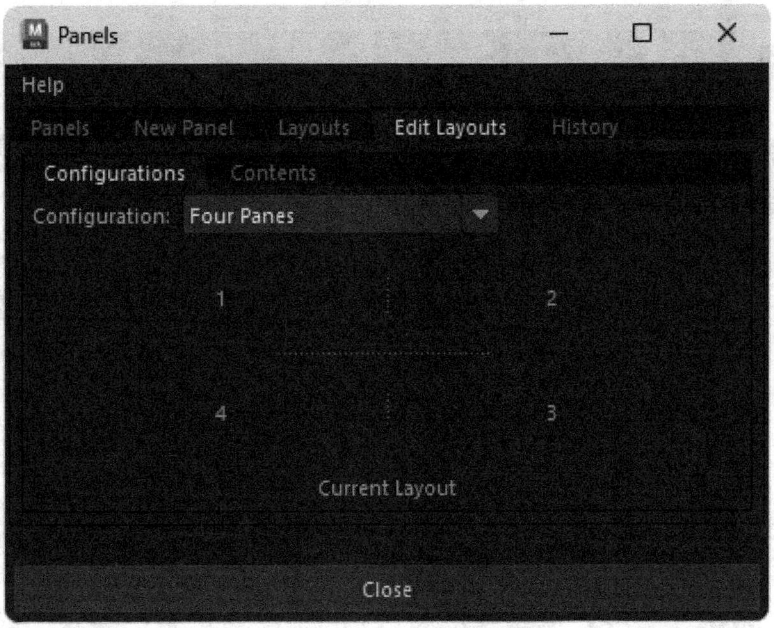

FIGURE 2-20

Panels dialog box

Using the Outliner

The last layout button in the Quick Layout buttons is a button to show/hide the Outliner. The Outliner pane, shown in Figure 2-21, lists all the objects in the current scene by name. When working with small objects, it can often be easier to locate an object by its name than by clicking on it. The Outliner is perfect for locating objects in this manner. Click on the Show/Hide Outliner button and the Outliner appears to the left of the view panel. Any selected object in the scene is also highlighted in the Outliner.

Tip

You can rename an object by clicking on its name at the top of the Channel Box, but you can also use the Outliner to rename objects.

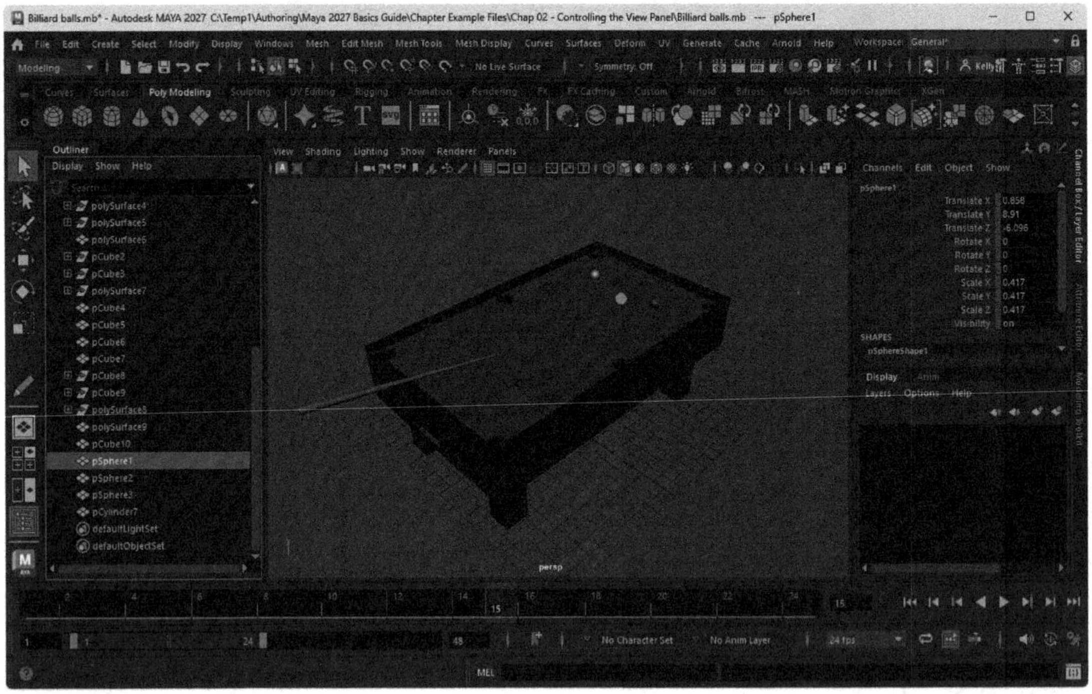

FIGURE 2-21

Outliner pane

Lesson 2.3-Tutorial 1: Change the Interface Layout

1. Click and drag the Show/Hide Channel Box tab at the right end of the view panel away from the interface to make more room for the view panels.
2. Click on the Four Views button in the Quick Layout buttons.

   The layout is changed to show four views, as shown in Figure 2-22.

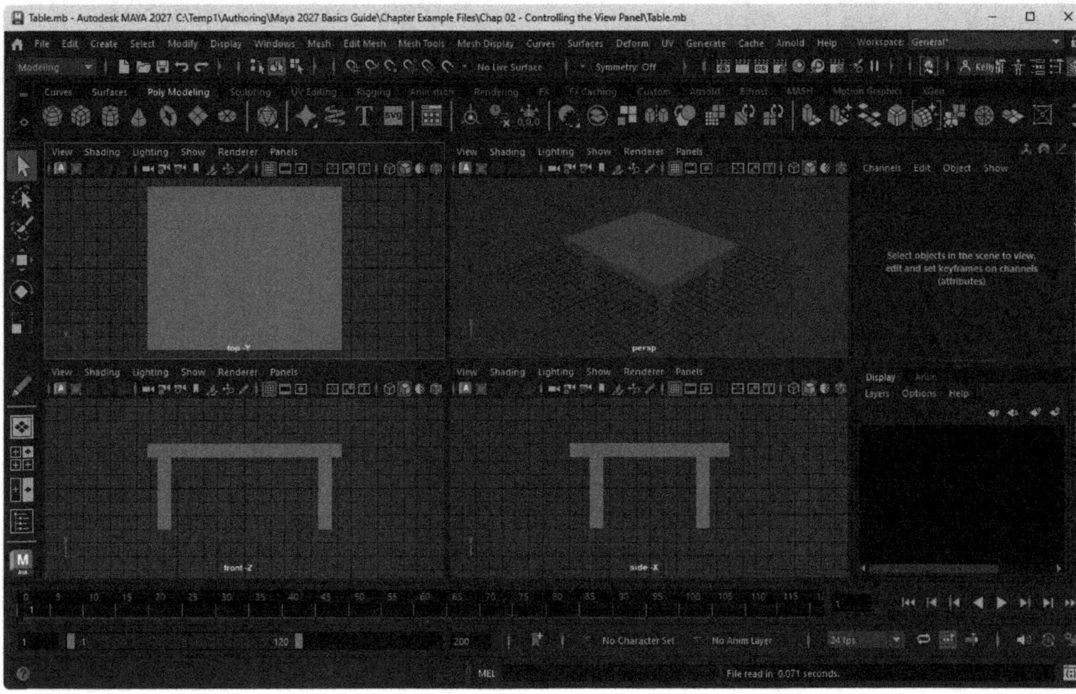

FIGURE 2-22

Four views

Chapter Summary

This chapter covers the view panel and explains how to use the view panel to change the scene view and also how to alter the scene display options. These options give you the chance to switch between different resolutions and views (wireframe, shaded, and textured views). The Quick Layout buttons let you change the viewport layout.

What You Have Learned

In this chapter, you learned

* How to change the view using the various camera tools.
* How to frame an object within the view panel.
* How to move through the various views.
* How to tear off the current view panel.
* How to use the heads-up display options.
* How to open an interface within a view panel.
* How to add notes and text to a scene with the Blue Pencil tools.
* How to change the shading method.
* How to isolate, hide, and show objects.
* How to change an object's name and wireframe color.
* How to switch between the different layouts.

Key Terms From This Chapter

* **View panel.** The central scene window where objects are displayed.
* **Tumble.** The act of rotating a camera to change the view's orientation.
* **Track.** The act of panning the camera to change the view's focal point.
* **Dolly.** The act of zooming the camera to change the view's focus width.
* **Framing.** The process of zooming and panning the camera to focus on the selected object.
* **Heads-Up Display.** A menu command for adding informative text to the view panel.
* **Grid.** A non-rendered series of intersecting lines that marks the origin of the scene coordinate system.
* **Blue Pencil tools.** A set of drawing tools used to annotate scenes with notes.
* **Resolution.** A measure of the detail (or number of elements) used to display scene objects.
* **Shading.** A display method used to show scene objects as solid objects.
* **Wireframe.** A display method that shows scene objects using contour lines.
* **Textures.** Bitmaps images that are wrapped about a scene object.

* **Backface Culling.** A display option that makes object elements located on the backside invisible.

* **Quick Layout buttons.** A set of buttons for changing the interface layout.

Chapter 3
Starting with Primitive Objects

IN THIS CHAPTER

The first task is to get some objects in the scene that you can work with. The quickest way to get objects in the scene is to start with primitive objects. Maya includes several different Polygon and NURBS primitives that you can select from the Create menu or from the Shelf icons. Although these primitives are standard shapes like cubes, spheres and cones, each of them has a load of options that you can use to create a large assortment of different objects.

The options dialog box for each shape is accessed using the Options icon located to the right of the primitive's name in the Create menu. These same options are also available in the Channel Box when the object is selected, so you can change the look of these primitive objects at any time.

Another really helpful primitive tool located in the Create menu is the Type tool. Using this tool, you can create 3D objects from a line of text. The Type tool has a lot of options for customizing the look and shape of the resulting objects.

Further down the Create menu is a section of objects called the Construction Aids. These objects include Construction Planes, Locators and different Measure Tools. These objects are not rendered with the scene but can be invaluable when you need to line up and position other objects.

Another place to look for pre-built objects is in the Content Browser. This browser has a large assortment of different objects that you can start with.

Finally, the internet is full of sites that have models that you can purchase, download and use. The File, Input menu command is used to import these models into Maya.

Lesson 3.1: Use Polygon Primitives

There are a couple of ways to create polygon mesh objects, but the easiest way is to start with a primitive polygon object. Maya includes a large assortment of primitive objects, found in the Create menu. Once created, you can use the editing tools to modify the primitives in an endless number of ways.

Creating Polygon Primitives

The easiest way to create polygon objects is with the Create, **Polygon Primitives** menu command. This menu includes the following polygon primitives: Sphere, Cube, Cylinder, Cone, Torus, Plane, Disc, Platonic Solids (Tetrahedron, Cube, Octahedron, Icosahedron and Dodecahedron), Pyramid, Prism, Pipe, Helix, Gear, and Soccer Ball. A sampling of these primitive objects is shown in Figure 3-1. Each of these polygon primitives has an Options dialog box, such as the Polygon Torus Options shown in Figure 3-2, in which you can enter precise dimensional values such as Radius and Height.

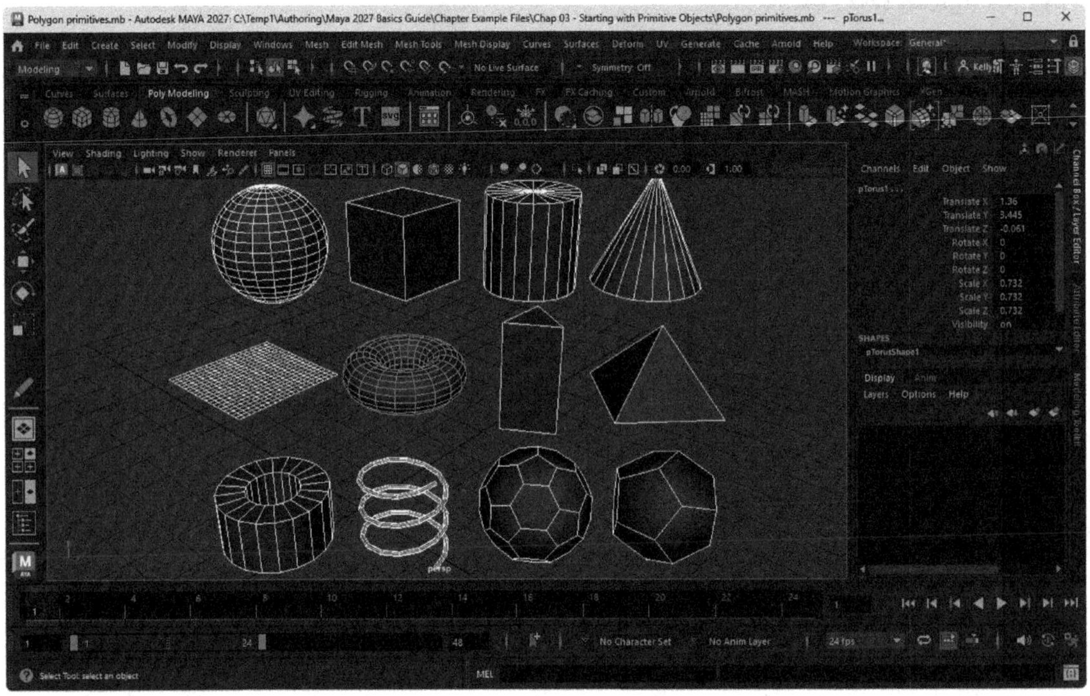

FIGURE 3-1

Polygon primitives

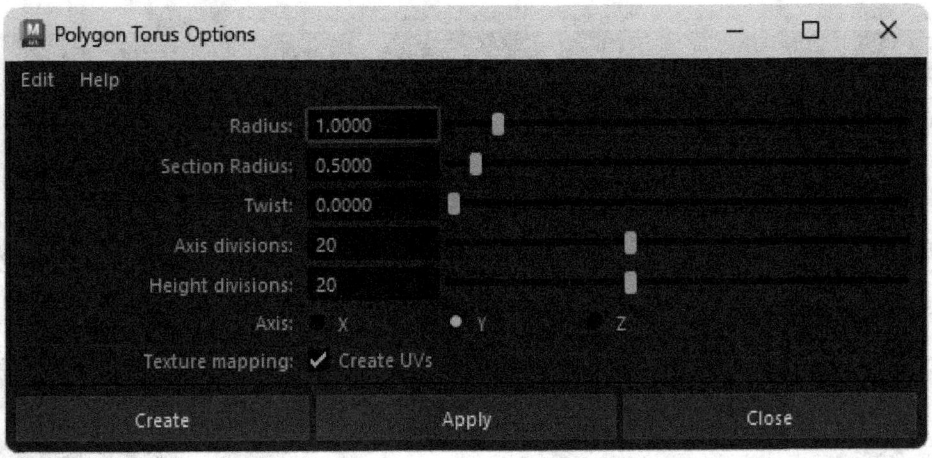

FIGURE 3-2

Polygon torus options

Creating Gears

One of the more advanced polygon primitive objects is the Gear object. Using the Polygon Gear Options dialog box, shown in Figure 3-3, you can create gears with a specified number of sides (or teeth). You can also set the Gear Spacing, Offset and Tip length. Gears can also be built with a Twist and/or a Taper. Figure 3-4 shows a sampling of gears that are possible.

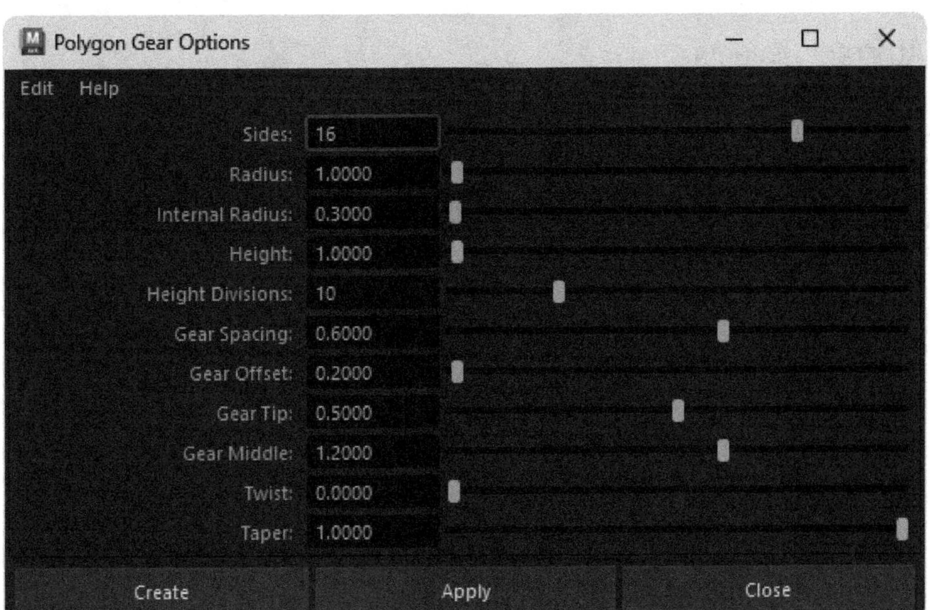

FIGURE 3-3

Polygon gear options

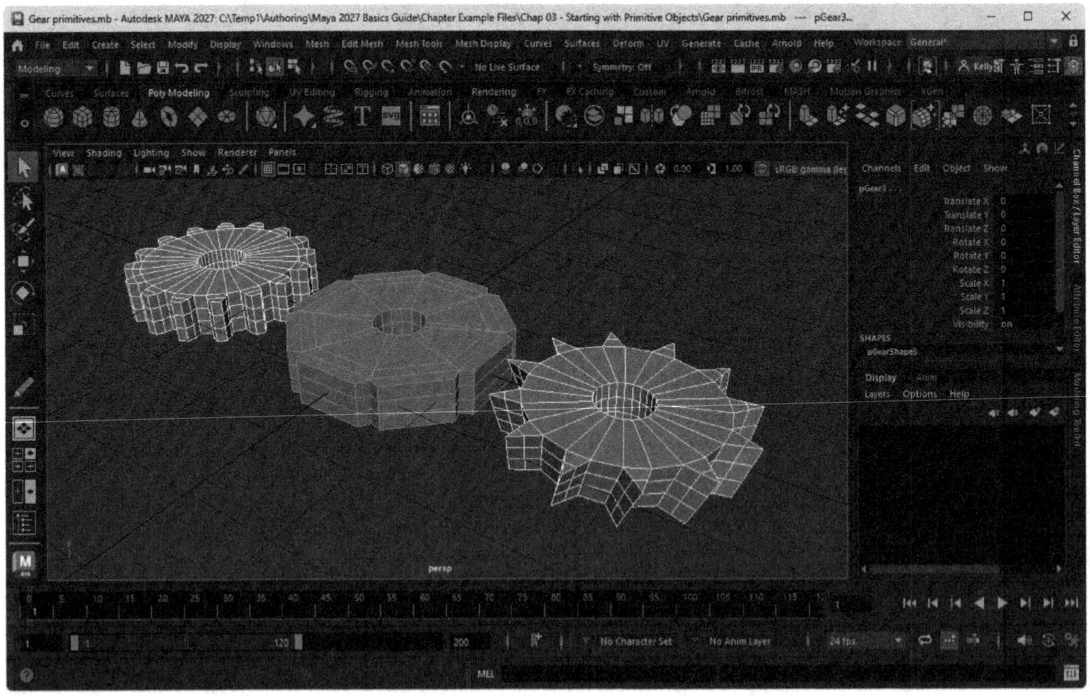

FIGURE 3-4

Polygon gear objects

Creating Abstract Objects

Within the Polygon Primitives menu are three unique primitive object types collectively known as **Super Shapes**. These shapes use advanced mathematic algorithms with a large group of settings to create abstract, complex objects. The three types are Super Ellipse, Spherical Harmonics and Ultra Shape. Each type has multiple vague parameters such as Ultra1 and Harmonics5 that control the look of the object. Perhaps easier is the Random button located in the PolySuperShape node of the Attribute Editor. Figure 3-5 shows several random Super Shape objects.

FIGURE 3-5

Super Shape objects

Lesson 3.1-Tutorial 1: Create Polygon Primitives

1. Create a polygon sphere object using the Create, Polygon Primitives, Sphere menu command.
2. Enter a value of 2.0 for the TranslateY attribute in the Channel Box.
3. Create a polygon cone object using the Create, Polygon Primitives, Cone menu command.
4. Enter a TranslateY value of 0.3, a RotateZ value of 180, and a ScaleY value of 1.5 in the Channel Box.

   These attribute values raise the sphere and position the cone underneath it to resemble an ice cream cone, as shown in Figure 3-6.
5. Select File, Save Scene As and save the file as **Ice cream cone.mb**.

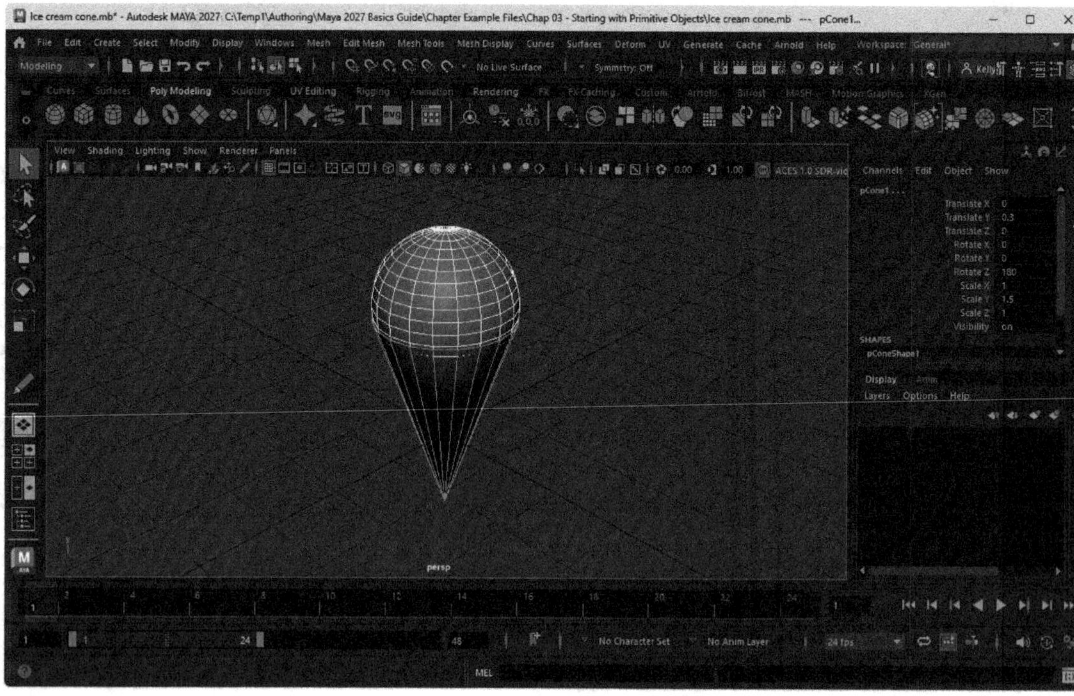

FIGURE 3-6

Ice cream cone made from polygon primitives

Lesson 3.2: Learn the NURBS Primitives

NURBS objects are different from polygon objects in that they are based on curves. This gives them a different set of components. The simplest NURBS surfaces are the primitive objects that can be created using the Create, **NURBS Primitives** menu. The NURBS primitives include the sphere, cube, cylinder, cone, plane, and torus (which is shaped like a doughnut), as shown in Figure 3-7. When selected, the primitive object appears at the grid's origin.

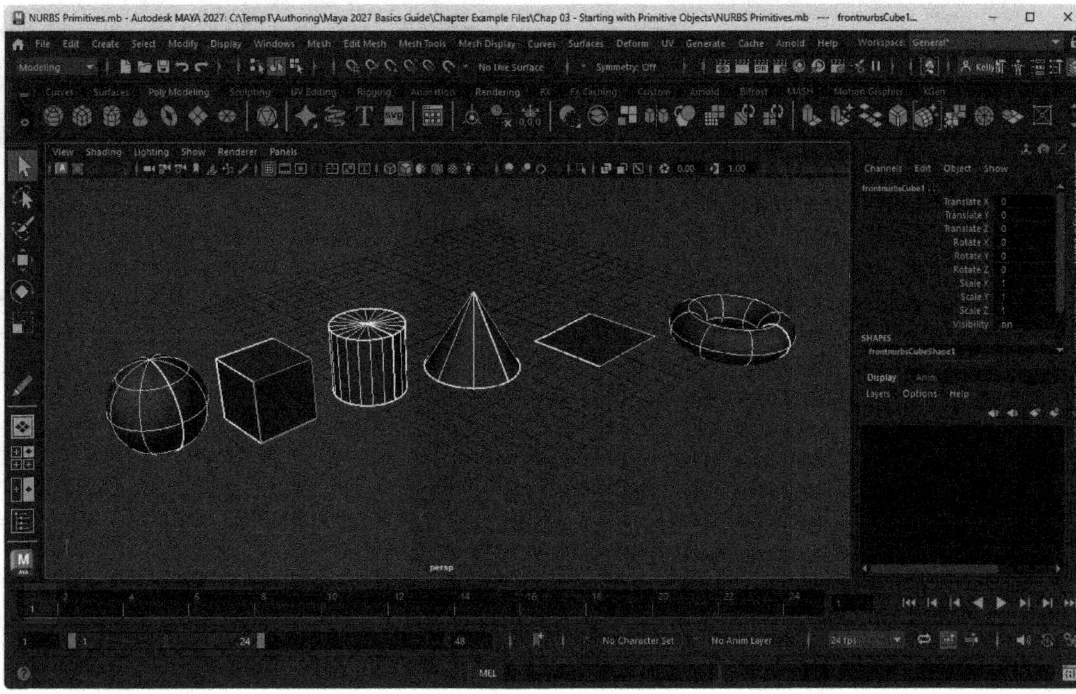

FIGURE 3-7

NURBS primitives

Creating Spheres and Cubes

For the NURBS sphere primitive, you can select the axis about which the sphere is oriented. You can also change the start and end sweep angle values to create a partial sphere, as shown in Figure 3-8, using the Sphere Options dialog box. The Radius value determines the size of the sphere, and the number of sections and spans defines the number of isoparms that are shown in the sphere. The cube NURBS primitive includes similar orientation axis. You can also specify the cube's width, length, and height values and the U and V Patches options set the number of isoparms.

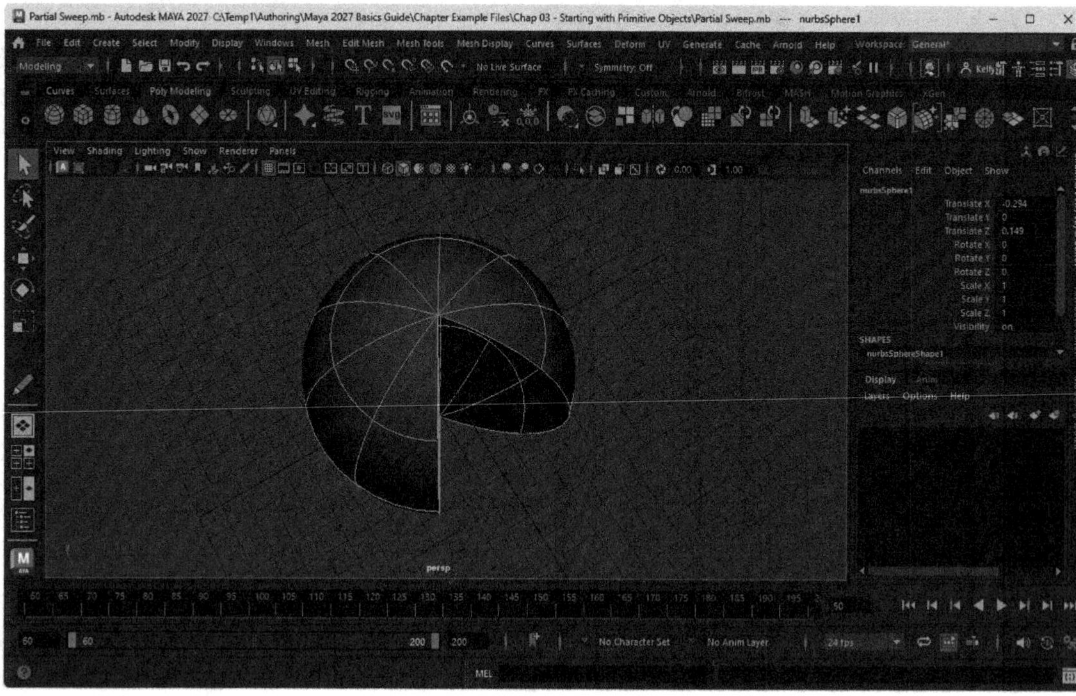

FIGURE 3-8

Partial Sweep NURBS primitives

Creating Cylinders and Cones

The cylinder and cone NURBS primitives include Start and End Sweep Angles settings for creating partial objects. You can also enter radius and height values and whether the object includes a cap on the top, bottom, or both. The number of sections and spans determines the number of patches that make up the object.

Creating a Plane and a Torus

For plane NURBS primitives, you can set the width and length values. For the torus NURBS primitive, you can set start and end sweep angle values, as well as radius and minor radius values. The minor radius value sets the size of the torus cross section.

Inserting Isoparms

The number of **isoparms** is initially set by the value for the number of segments and spans in the Options dialog box, but you can add more patches to a NURBS primitive using the Surfaces, Insert Isoparms menu command. If you select Isoparm display mode from the marking menu, you can drag from an existing isoparm to the location where you want the new isoparm to be located. This location is marked with a yellow dashed line, shown in Figure 3-9. If you apply the Insert Isoparms menu command with the At Selection option enabled, a new isoparm is created. The Between Selections option lets you create new isoparms for the U or V direction for the entire object.

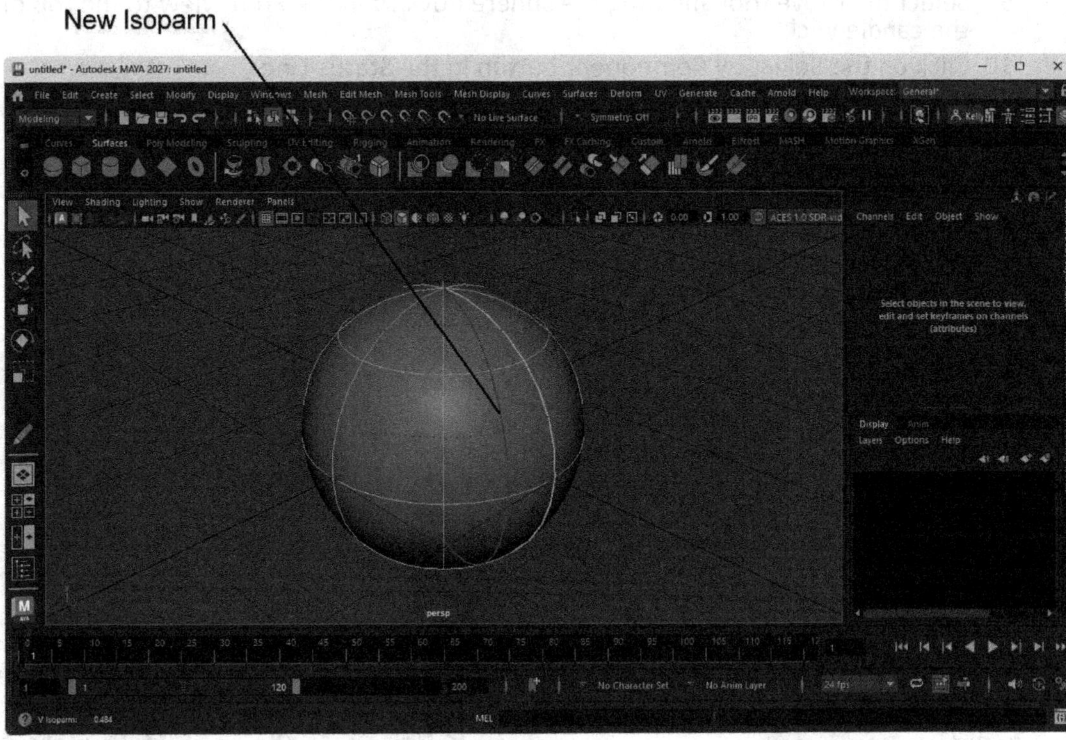

FIGURE 3-9

Inserted isoparm

Lesson 3.2-Tutorial 1: Create a Candle from Primitives

1. Click on the Four Views button in the Quick Layout Buttons.
2. Create a cylinder object using the Create, NURBS Primitives, Cylinder menu command.
3. Click on the Scale tool and drag the green Y-axis manipulator to increase the cylinder's height.
4. Create another cylinder object using the Create, NURBS Primitives, Cylinder menu command.
5. Drag the center handle in the Top view with the Scale tool to reduce the diameter of the cylinder, and then drag the green Y-axis manipulator upward to lengthen the cylinder. Select the Move tool and drag the green Y-axis manipulator to move the small cylinder to the top of the larger cylinder.

   The larger cylinder is for the candle, and the smaller cylinder is the wick.
6. Create another cylinder object using the Create, NURBS Primitives, Cylinder menu command.
7. Drag the center handle in the Top view with the Scale tool to increase the diameter of the cylinder, and then drag the green Y-axis manipulator downward to reduce the cylinder's height. Select the Move tool and drag the green Y-axis manipulator to move the large flat cylinder to the base of the candle to create a base for the candle.
8. Create a sphere object using the Create, NURBS Primitives, Sphere menu command.

9. Select the Move tool and drag the sphere upward in the Front view to the top of the candle wick.
10. Click on the Select by Component button in the Status Line.
11. Drag over all the top CV points in the Front view and move them upward in the Front view using the green Y-axis manipulator.
12. Select the very top CV point on the sphere and drag it up and to the left in the Front view.

    The edited sphere looks like a simple candle flame, as shown in Figure 3-10.
13. Select File, Save Scene As and save the file as **Primitive candle.mb**.

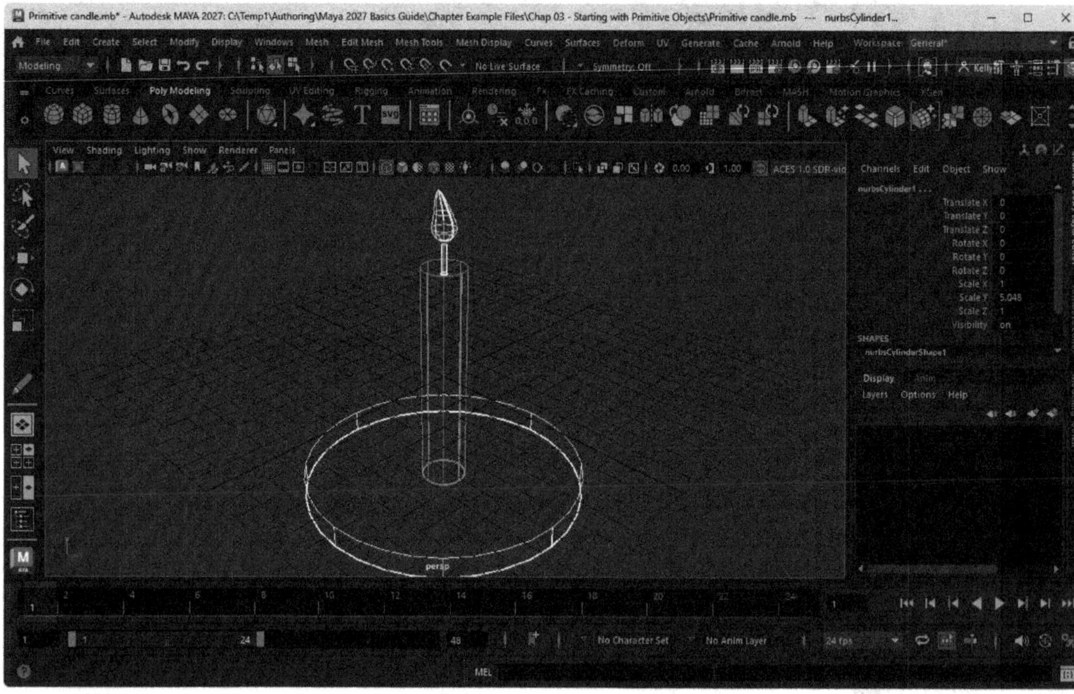

FIGURE 3-10

Primitive candle

Lesson 3.2-Tutorial 2: Add Isoparms

1. Create a cone object using the Create, NURBS Primitives, Cone menu command.
2. Right-click on the cone object and select Isoparms from the pop-up marking menu.
3. Then, click and drag from the bottom circle upward about halfway up the cone.

    A yellow dotted line appears where the new isoparm is located.
4. Select Surfaces, Insert Isoparms.

    A new isoparm is added to the object.
5. Right-click on the cone object and select Isoparms from the pop-up marking menu again.
6. Drag over the bottom circle and the new isoparm to select them both.

    The isoparms turn yellow when selected.
7. Select Surfaces, Insert Isoparms, Options.

8. Select the Between Selections option and set the # Isoparms to Insert value to 5. Then click the Insert button.

    Five new isoparms are created and equally spaced between the two selected isoparms, as shown in Figure 3-11.

9. Select File, Save Scene As and save the file as **New isoparms.mb**.

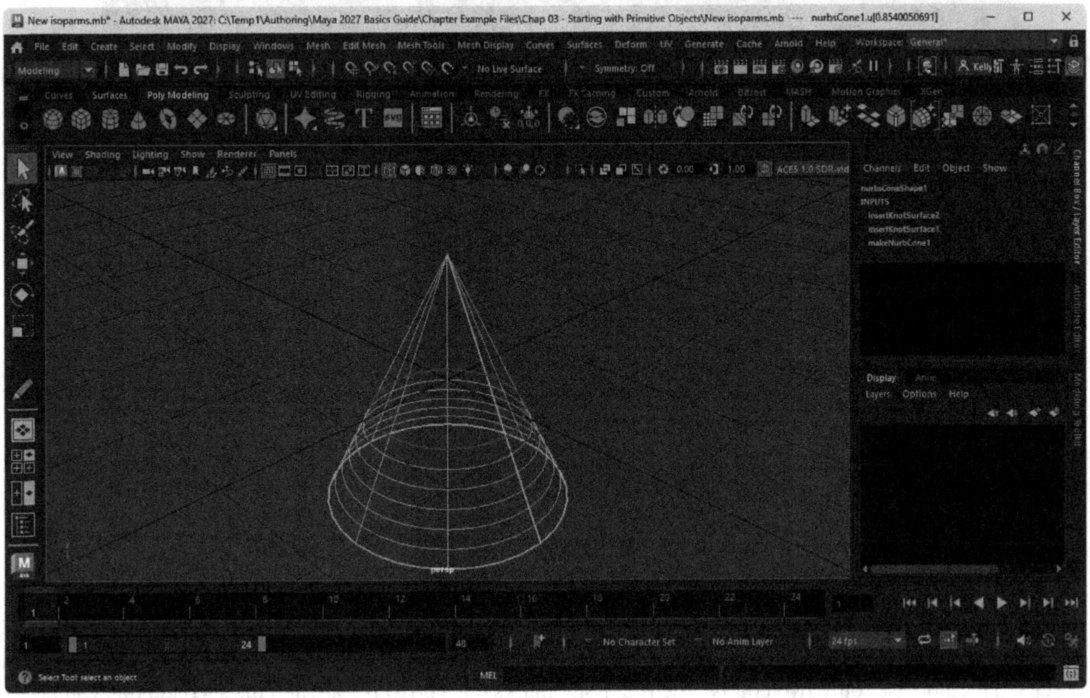

FIGURE 3-11

New isoparms

Lesson 3.3: Draw 2D Primitives

Located within the Create, NURBS menu are two 2D primitive objects for creating a circle and square. There are also two different options for creating 2D arcs found in the Create, Curve Tools menu.

Creating Circles and Squares

At the bottom of the Create, NURBS Primitives menu are two menu commands that you can use to create a perfect circle and a square. These shapes are positioned at the center of the grid. Using the options dialog box (shown in Figure 3-12) for the circle primitive, you can set several options including the axis about which the shape is oriented, the Sweep Angle (for creating partial circles), the Radius, and the number of Sections that make up the shape for the circle. Options for the square primitive include the orientation axis, side lengths, and Spans per Side.

Note

Creating a NURBS square primitive results in four separate straight-line segments that you can select independently.

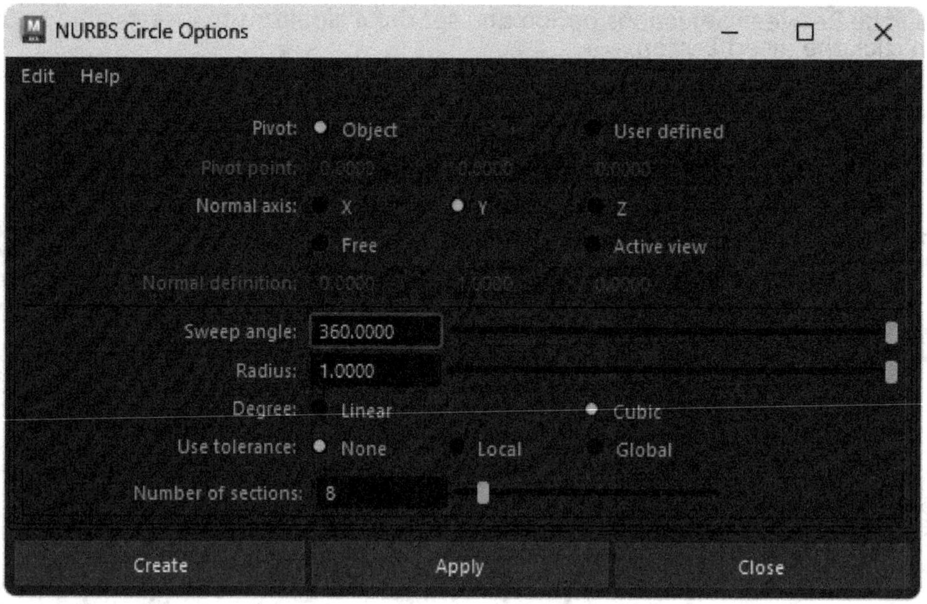

FIGURE 3-12

NURBS Circle Options

Creating Arcs

There are actually two methods for creating arcs found in the Create, Curve Tools menu. One method uses three points. The first and last point mark the endpoints of the arc, and the middle point marks a point on the arc. The second method uses only two points. The first point marks one end of the arc and the second point can be dragged to set the curvature and the second endpoint. Once the arc points are positioned, you can move them by dragging the vertices. Clicking the two-point arc's circle manipulator changes the direction of the arc. Figure 3-13 shows both arc creation methods.

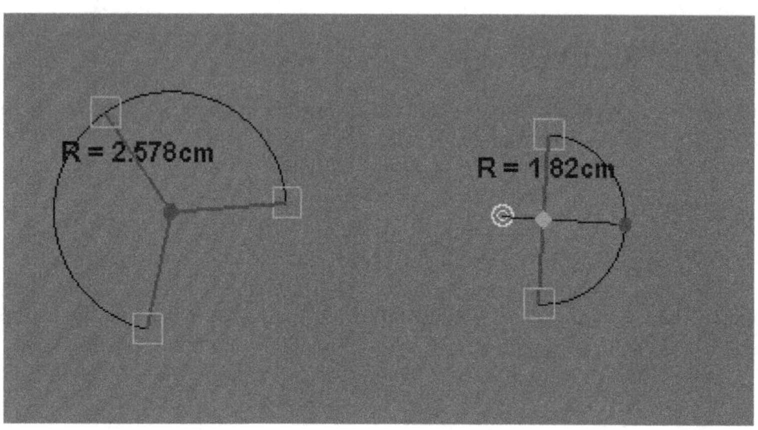

FIGURE 3-13

Three- and two-point circular arcs

Lesson 3.3-Tutorial 1: Create an Eye Using Arcs and Primitive Shapes

1. Click on the Create menu, and then select the NURBS Primitives submenu and click on the icon to the right of the Square menu to open the Options dialog box.
2. In the NURBS Square Options dialog box, select the Y Normal Axis, set the Length of Side 1 and 2 options to 1.0 and click the Create button.

   A simple square shape appears at the origin in the view panel.
3. With the square selected, click on the View, Frame Selected panel menu command or press the f key. Then click on the Four View button in the Quick Layout Buttons and select the Top View panel and press the spacebar to maximize the viewport.
4. In the Status Line, click on the Snap to Points button to enable point snapping.
5. Click on the Create, Curve Tools, Two Point Circular Arc menu command then click on two opposite corners of the square in the Top view panel and press the Enter key. Then select the Two Point Circular Arc tool again and click on the same two opposite corners of the square in the opposite order and press the Enter key again.

   Two circular arcs appear positioned between the opposite corners of the square.
6. Click on the Create menu, and then select the NURBS Primitives submenu and click on the icon to the right of the Circle menu to open the Options dialog box.
7. In the NURBS Circle Options dialog box, select the Y Normal Axis, set the Sweep Angle setting to 360 and the Radius value to 0.25, and then click the Create button.

   A circle appears in the center of the eye.
8. Select all edges of the square object and press the Delete key to delete the square shape. The eye shape is displayed, as seen in Figure 3-14.
9. Select File, Save Scene As and save the file as **Eye shape.mb**.

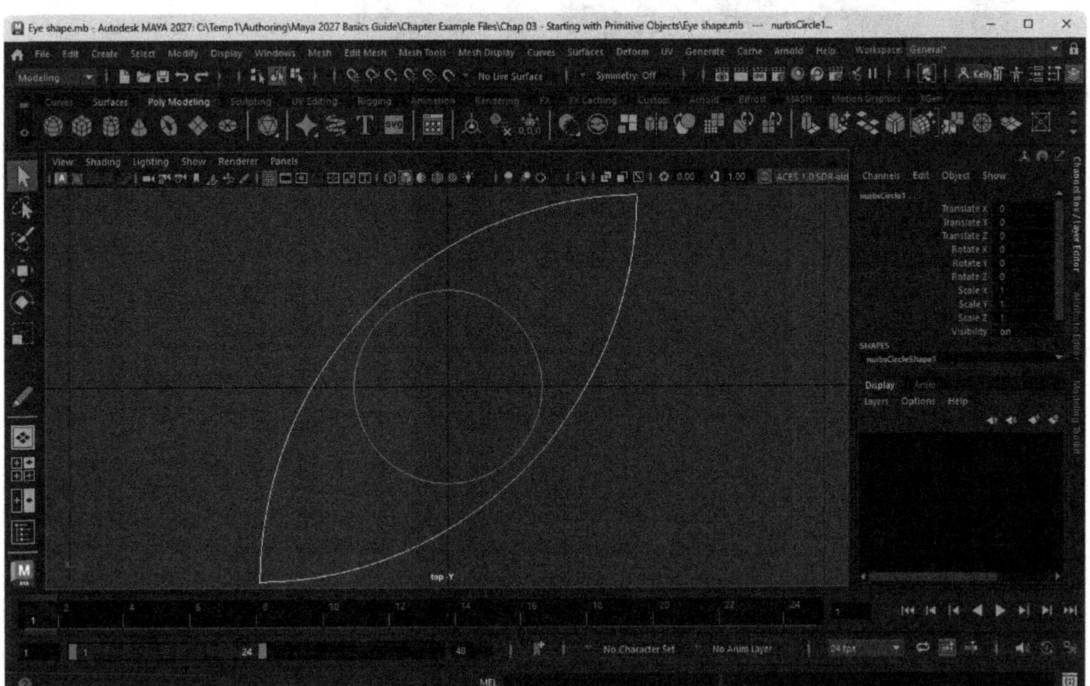

FIGURE 3-14

Eye shape

Lesson 3.4: Create 3D Type

Simple text can be created as extruded mesh objects using the Create, Type menu command. Once created, you can select and alter the text, font, size, tracking, kerning and alignment using the Type1 node in the Attribute Editor, as shown in Figure 3-15. You can also select the font to use from a list of available system fonts. The text characters are automatically extruded, shaded and positioned, but you can change any of these settings using the various attributes in the Channel Box. At the bottom of the Attribute Editor is the Type Manipulator button. Selecting this button lets you choose and edit individual letters in the text.

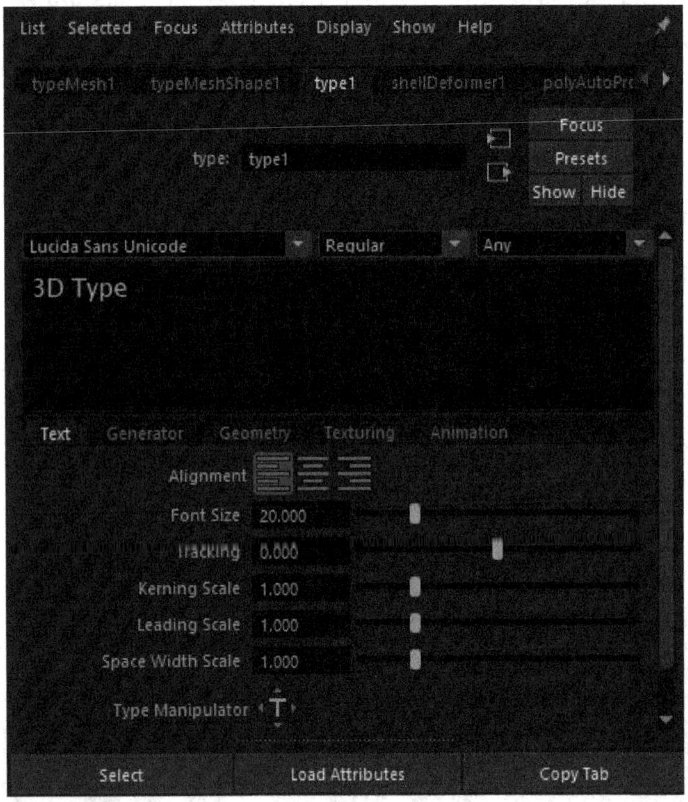

FIGURE 3-15

Type attributes

Generating Text Curves

Within the Attribute Editor for the Type1 node are several tabs for Text, Generator, Geometry, Texturing and Animation. If you look at the bottom of the Mesh Settings section in the Geometry tab, you'll find a button to Create Curves from Type. This button creates 2D curves of the extruded type and can be useful for creating other surfaces.

Changing Extrusion Depth

Also within the Geometry tab are the settings for the Extrusion Distance, Offset and profile. Figure 3-16 shows some text with an extrusion profile selected. You'll need to increase the Offset value to see the extrusion profile applied.

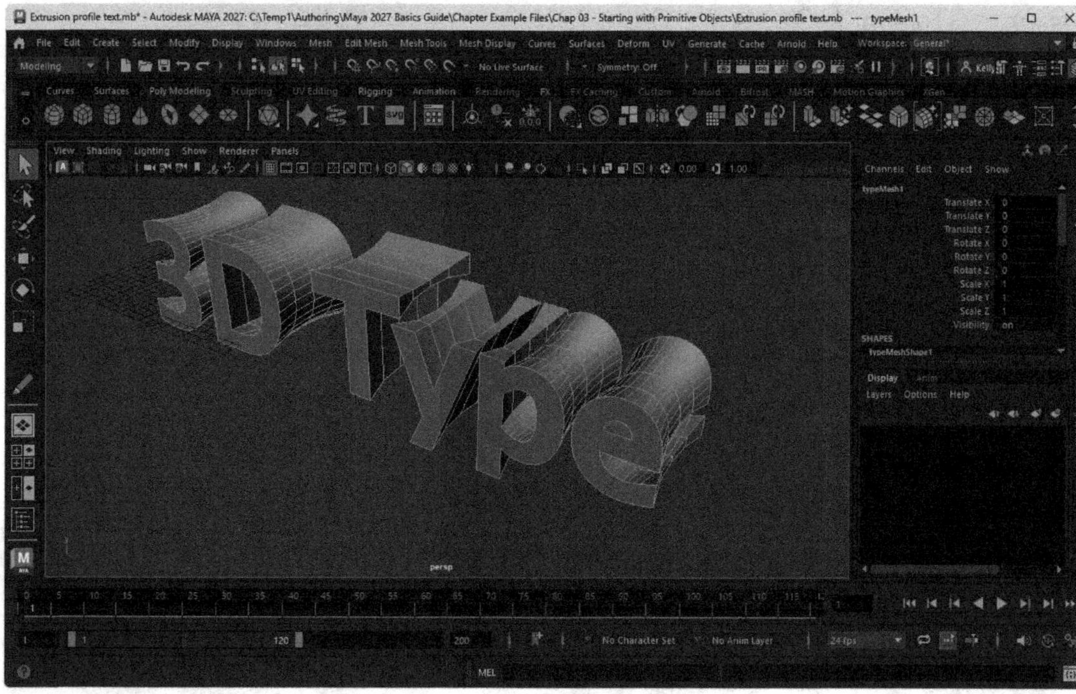

FIGURE 3-16

Text extrusion profile

Creating Beveled Type

Further down in the Geometry tab is settings for applying a bevel to the edge of the type. The available options are shown in Figure 3-17.

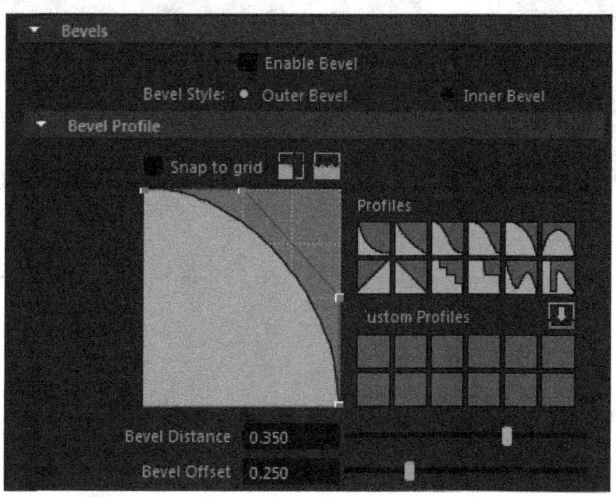

FIGURE 3-17

Bevel options

Lesson 3.4-Tutorial 1: Create and Bevel Text

1. Click on the Four View button from the Quick Layout buttons.
2. Select the Create, Type menu command.

   Some extruded 3D text automatically appears in the view panel and the Attribute Editor opens.
3. At the top of the Attribute Editor, click on the Type1 tab. Enter the word, 'Maya' in the text field.

   The text is updated automatically.

   Click on the Geometry tab in the Attribute Editor under the text field. In the Bevels section, enable the Outer Bevel option. Then select the Enable Outer Bevel option and choose the rounded bevel icon. The text is updated with the selected bevel, as shown in Figure 3-18.
4. Select File, Save Scene As and save the file as **Beveled text.mb**.

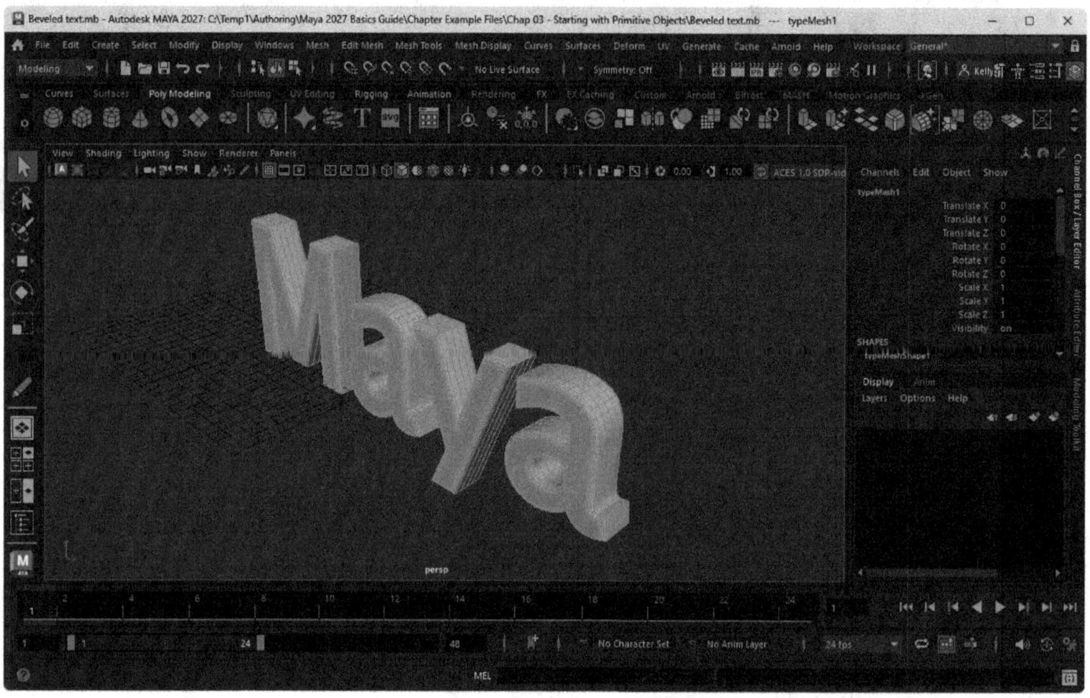

FIGURE 3-18

Beveled text

Lesson 3.4-Tutorial 2: Create a Sign

1. Click on the Four View button and select Top View panel and press the spacebar to maximize the viewport.
2. Select the Create, NURBS Primitives, Circle menu command.

   A circle is created.
3. Create another circle and drag on the center manipulator of Scale tool to increase the size of the new circle larger than the first.
4. Select the Create, Curve Tools, EP Curve Tool menu command. Click outside the outer circle in the upper-right corner and again in the lower-left corner to create a

straight line that runs diagonally through both circles. Press the Enter key to complete the line.

5. Select the Edit, Duplicate menu command. Select the Move tool and drag the center handle until the duplicated line is parallel to the first one.

   The diagonal line is duplicated and offset.

6. Drag over both circles and both intersecting diagonal lines to select them, then select the Curves, Cut, Options menu command. In the Cut Curve Options dialog box, select the At All Intersections option and the Keep All Curve Segments options, then click the Apply button. Select the interior portions of the lines and circles and the edges that extend beyond the circle and press the Delete key to make a 'No' sign.

7. Select the curves that make up the lower inner portion of the sign and choose the Curves, Attach, Option menu command. In the Attach Curves Options dialog box, choose the Connect option and click the Apply button. Then choose the straight line of the top inner portion and choose the Curves, Reverse Direction menu, then attach all the curves of the upper inner portion together with the Attach menu again. Then attach all the curves that make up the outer circle together.

8. Select the outer circle and the two interior pieces to extrude. Select the Surfaces, Extrude, Options menu command. Select the Distance option, choose the Specify option with the Y-axis and enter an Extrude Length value of 0.25. Click the Extrude button.

   The selected curves are extruded.

9. Select the Create, Type menu command. Within the Type1 node in the Attribute Editor, enter the text '2D' and set the Extrude Distance to 0.5.

   Text is added to the scene.

10. Select the text and use the transform tools to rotate, scale and move the text into place within the circle.

    The resulting sign is shown in Figure 3-19.

11. Select File, Save Scene As and save the file as **No 2D sign.mb**.

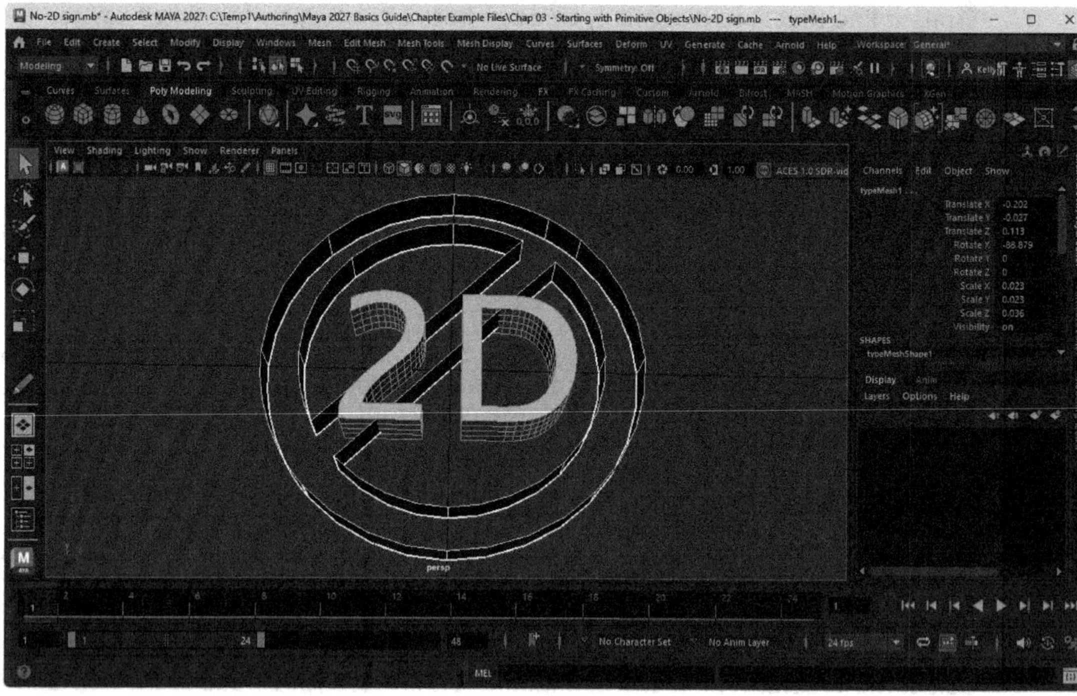

FIGURE 3-19

A simple sign created using curves and text

Lesson 3.5: Use Construction Aid Objects

Sometimes it can be tricky to orient objects in 3D space. For example, the ground plane is a helpful grid that shows where the bottom of the scene is located. It is not rendered with the scene and can be turned on or off. Within the Create menu are several other helpful objects that are not rendered that are called Construction Aids. These objects include a Construction Plane, Free Image Plane, Locator, Annotation and several Measure Tools.

Placing Construction Planes

Just like the ground plane, you can place additional planes around the scene wherever you need them. In the Options dialog box, you can set planes in the YX, YZ, and XZ axes. You can also set the size of these planes. These planes help you to orient the scene origin.

Placing Free Image Planes

The Create, Free Image Planes menu command places an **image plane** in the scene. You can recognize image planes because they have an X through them, as shown in Figure 3-20. The Options for these planes are Width and Height values, but you can use the Move, Rotate and Scale tools to position, orient and scale the planes in any manner. Although image planes by default aren't rendered, you can apply textures to them and use them as backgrounds or use them to project a reference image.

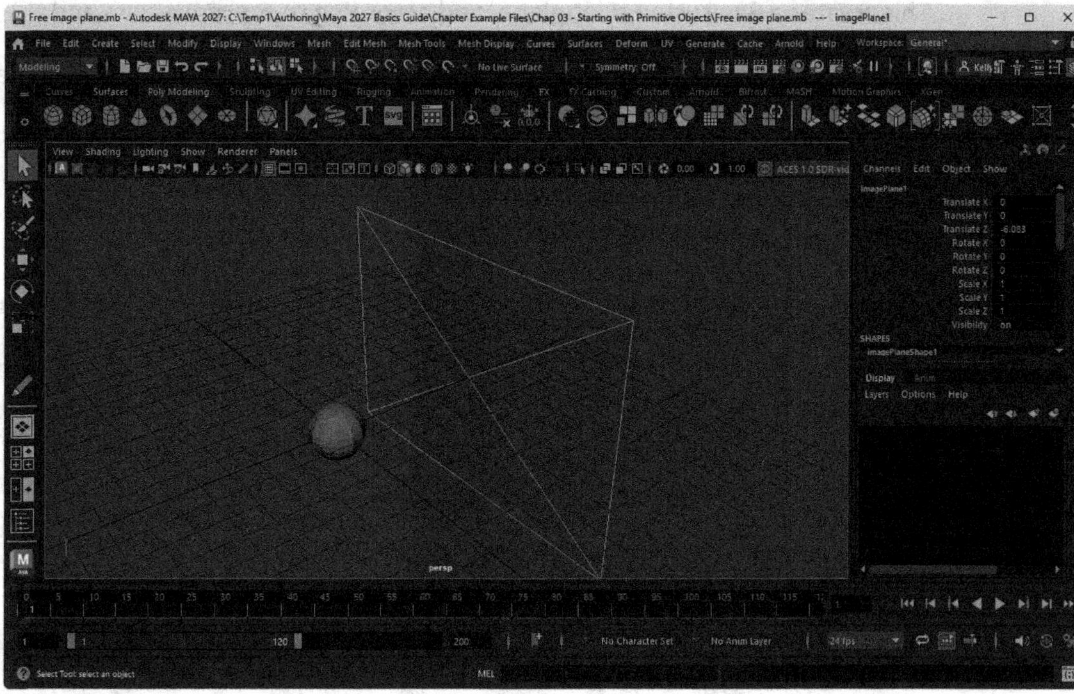

FIGURE 3-20

A simple image plane

Marking position with Locators

A **Locator** object is a simple point in space. These are useful if you want to identify a location that you can find later. For example, you could mark all the places in the scene where you want trees to be positioned using Locator objects and then build the scene without having to worry about the trees. Then at the end, you could use the Modify, Replace Objects to replace all the named Locator objects with trees.

Annotating objects

Selecting the Create, Annotation menu command opens a dialog box where you can type some text. This text then appears in the scene over the selected object. The text isn't rendered but is helpful for identifying objects. Annotation text can be selected and deleted.

Using the Measure Tools

Within the Create, Measure Tools menu are three tools: Distance Tool, Parameter Tool and Arc Length Tool. The Distance Tool lets you click on two points and the distance between them is displayed. The Parameter Tool lets you click and drag over a NURBS surface or along the length of a curve and its parameters or length along the curve is displayed. If you release the mouse, then the values at that spot are displayed. The Arc Length Tool works just like the Parameter tool, except it measures the length of an arc.

Lesson 3.5-Tutorial 1: Test Pythagoras

1. Select the Create, Polygon Primitives, Plane, Options menu command.
2. Set the Width to 3, the Height to 4 and the Divisions both to 3.

This creates a 3x4 rectangular plane, and according to my math class and Pythagoras, the resulting diagonal should be 5.

3. Select the Create, Annotation menu command and enter 'The diagonal should be 5' in the text box.
4. Select the Create, Measure Tools, Distance Tool menu command and click on opposite corners of the plane object.

   The Distance tool displays the result close to 5, as shown in Figure 3-21.
5. Select File, Save Scene As and save the file as **Testing Pythagoras.mb**.

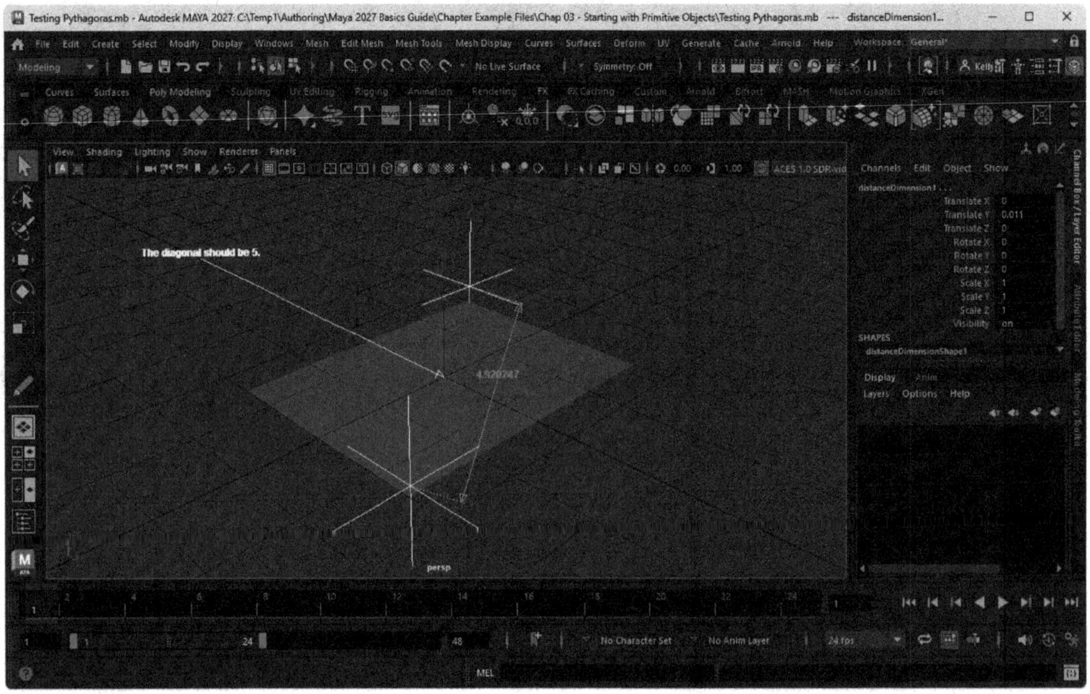

FIGURE 3-21

Using the Distance Tool

Lesson 3.6: Access the Content Browser

Another great place to find objects to work with is in the Content Browser. This browser is opened using the Windows, Content Browser menu command. The browser is filled with all kinds of examples of different features including animation, FX, Lighting, Rendering and Modeling. It is within the Modeling category where you can find an assortment of example meshes.

Browsing the mesh categories

The categories in the Modeling group of the **Content Browser** include animals, bipeds, clothing, props, vehicles and weapons. Each example has a thumbnail of the mesh, as shown in Figure 3-46. When a thumbnail is selected, its detailed information is shown in the Metadata panel. To load a mesh, simply select it and drag and drop it in a viewport window.

Loading meshes from the Content Browser

Once you've decided on the mesh to load, it is easy to get it into Maya. To load a mesh, simply select it and drag and drop it in a viewport window.

Note

```
If you don't see anything in the viewport after
dropping an object, you might need to zoom out to
see the object.
```

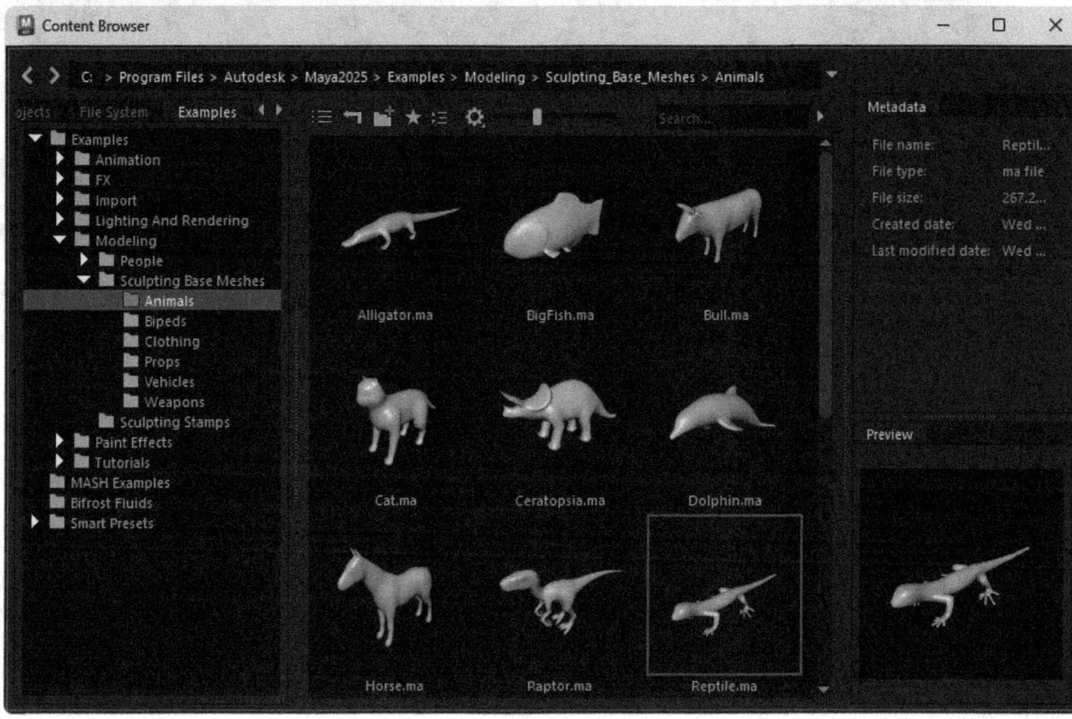

FIGURE 3-22

The Content Browser

Lesson 3.6-Tutorial 1: Load a mesh from the Content Browser

1. Select the Windows, Content Browser menu command.
2. Within the Content Browser, expand the Modeling folder, then expand the Sculpting Base Meshes and the Animals folder.

   All the animal meshes in this folder are shown as thumbnails.
3. Drag and drop the Reptile.ma object in the viewport.
4. Zoom out in the viewport, select the mesh and press the F key.

   The reptile mesh is centered in the viewport, as shown in Figure 3-23.
5. Select File, Save Scene As and save the file as **Reptile.mb**.

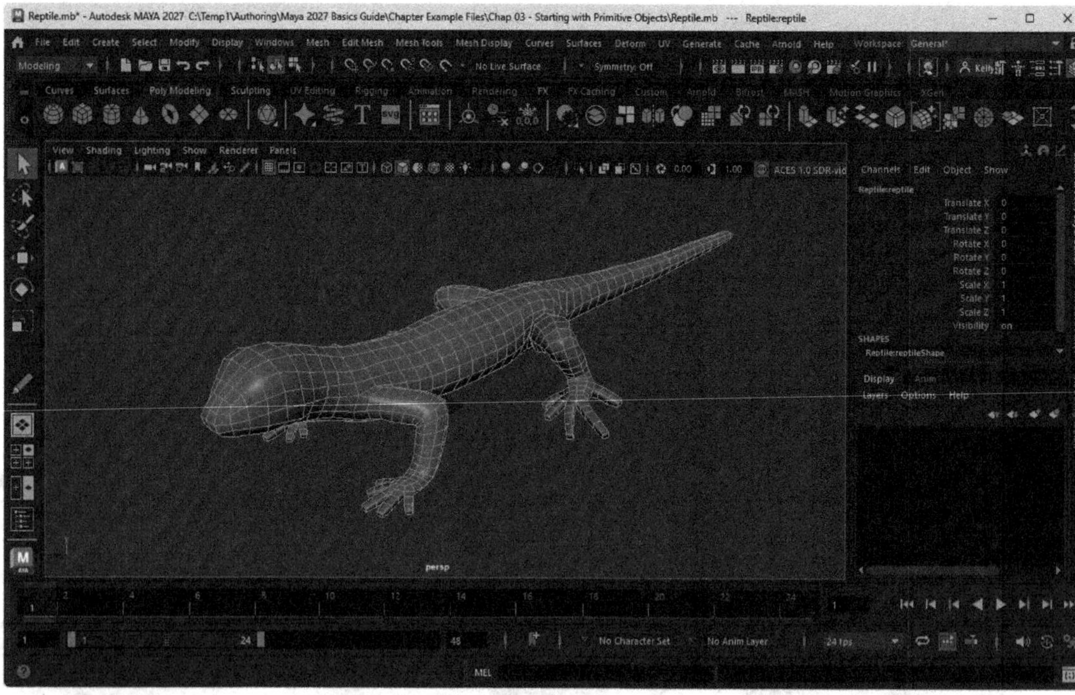

FIGURE 3-23

Reptile mesh loaded from the Content Browser

Lesson 3.7: Import Objects

Another crucial place to get objects is to import them using the File, Import menu command. Maya can input a large number of different formats including OBJ, FBX, and DXF, Maya can also import and work with curves in the Adobe Illustrator (AI), EPS and SVG formats.

Importing 3D meshes

Across the internet are tons of 3d model repositories and almost all of them can be imported into Maya. One of the most popular formats is the OBJ format, but if you are moving meshes between the different Autodesk products, the FBX format is common. Several Computer Aided Design (CAD) packages are also supported including CATIA and ProEngineer.

Caution

If you are downloading 3D meshes from the Internet, make sure you have legal permission to use the mesh in your scene. Reusing copyrighted content without permission could land you in a world of trouble.

Importing 2D

In addition to 3D meshes, Maya can also import and work with 2D content. This can be used as background reference materials or as the start of 3D meshes. Be aware that importing 2D will only get the base curves. Details like the line thickness or fills are usually lost.

Creating 3D meshes from 2D outlines

Within the Create menu are options to create an Adobe Illustrator Object and SVG objects. These commands load in a 2D set of curves and extrude them to create a 3D mesh. For Adobe Illustrator files, you can use the Options dialog box, shown in Figure 3-24, to import just the curves as a 2D object or choose the Bevel option where you can set the Bevel style and Extrude amount.

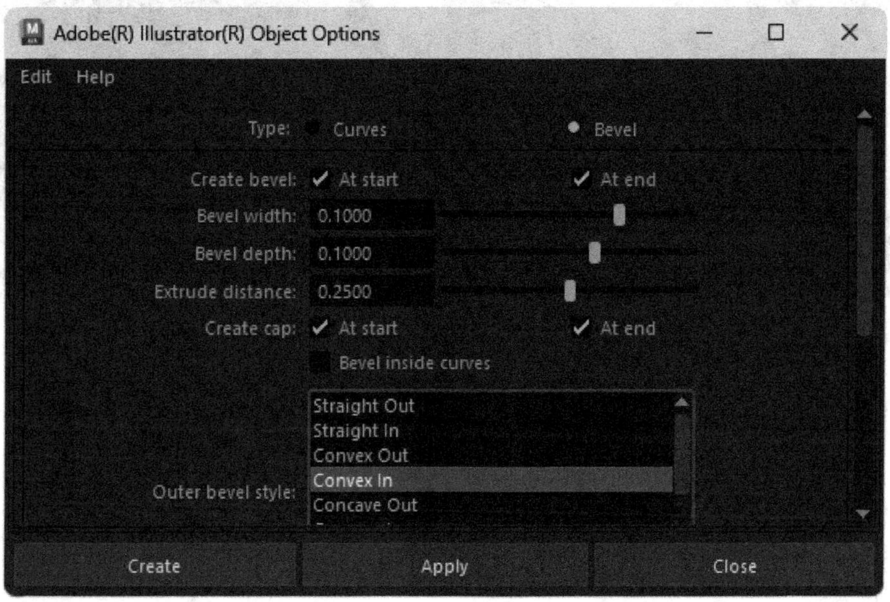

FIGURE 3-24

Adobe Illustrator Object Options dialog box

The Create, SVG menu command creates a proxy object and gives you the option in the Attribute Editor to simply paste in SVG code or load an SVG file using an Import feature. Once loaded, you can use the SVG, Geometry, Texturing and Animation tabs in the Attribute Editor to change all aspects of the SVG object. Within the SVG tab you can set the overall Size of the imported elements and within the Path list all layers in the original file are visible. You can select each layer and set its Position Z Offset and Scale Z to separate and size the layers. The Geometry tab includes features for enabling extrusions and bevels.

Lesson 3.7-Tutorial 1: Import a 3D mesh

1. Select the File, Import menu command.
2. Select the FBX option in the Files of Type drop-down list at the bottom of the Import dialog box. Then locate the **Toy Duck.fbx** file and click the Import button.

   The 3D mesh in the FBX file is loaded into the viewport, as shown in Figure 3-25.
3. Select the imported mesh and press the F key to zoom in on the imported object.
4. Select File, Save Scene As and save the file as **Toy Duck.mb**.

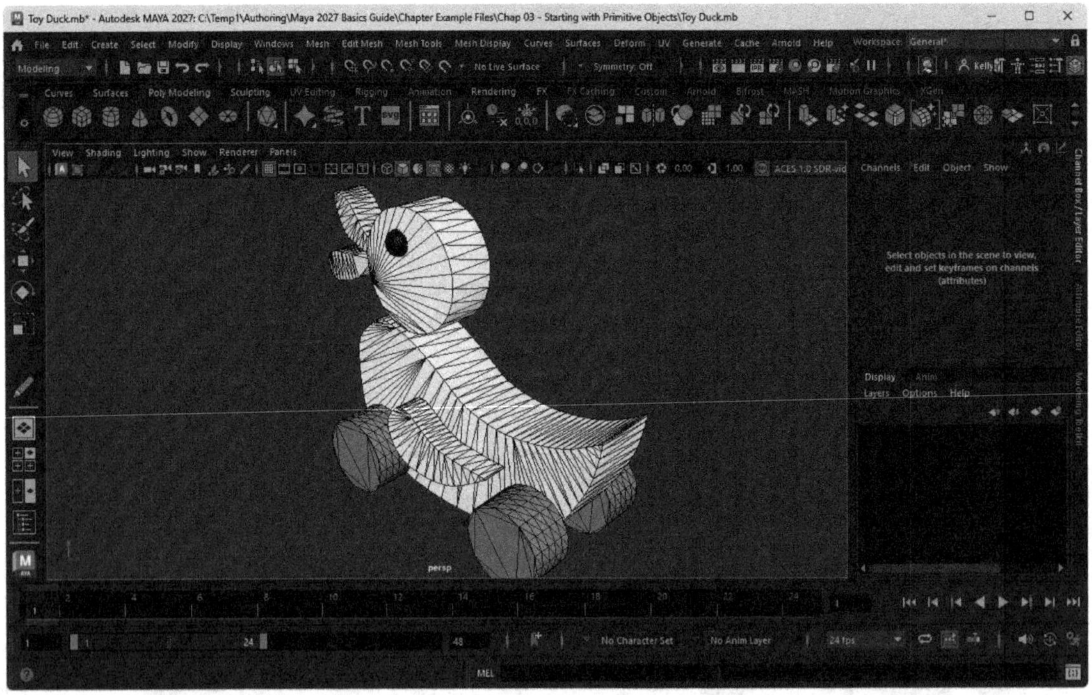

FIGURE 3-25

Imported 3D mesh

Lesson 3.7-Tutorial 2: Import Adobe Illustrator content

1. Select the File, Import menu command.
2. Select the Adobe Illustrator option in the Files of Type drop-down list at the bottom of the Import dialog box. Then locate the **Box It Up Co logo.ai** file and click the Import button.

   The curves in the AI file are loaded into the viewport, as shown in Figure 3-26.
3. Select the imported curves and press the F key to zoom in on the curves.
4. Select File, Save Scene As and save the file as **Box It Up Co logo.mb**.

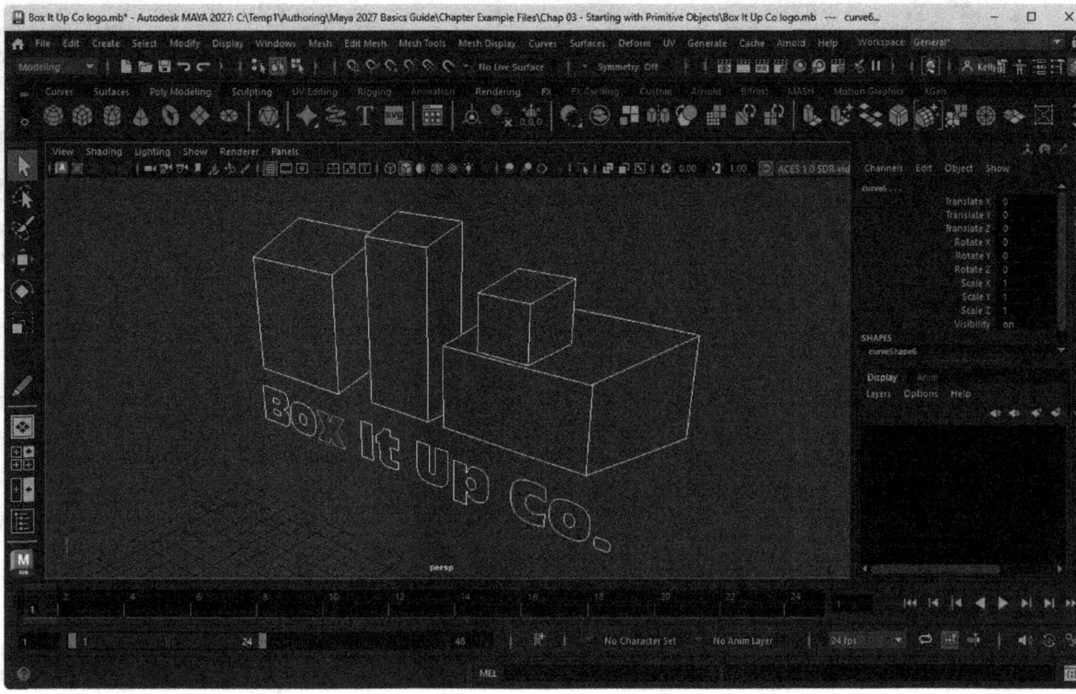

FIGURE 3-26

Imported Adobe Illustrator logo

Lesson 3.7-Tutorial 3: Import SVG content

1. Select the Select, SVG menu command.

   A placeholder appears in the viewport, and the Attribute Editor opens.

2. In the Attribute Editor, click on the Import button, then select and load the **Concentric circles.svg** file.

   The SVG elements are loaded and displayed in the viewport.

3. Within the SVG tab in the Attribute Editor, select each circle layer and drag the Position Z Offset slider to bring each successive layer forward.
4. Within the Geometry tab in the Attribute Editor, click on the Enable Bevel option and set the Bevel Distance to 0.141.

   The imported SVG file has been modified using the Attribute Editor settings, as shown in Figure 3-27.

5. Select File, Save Scene As and save the file as **SVG tower.mb**.

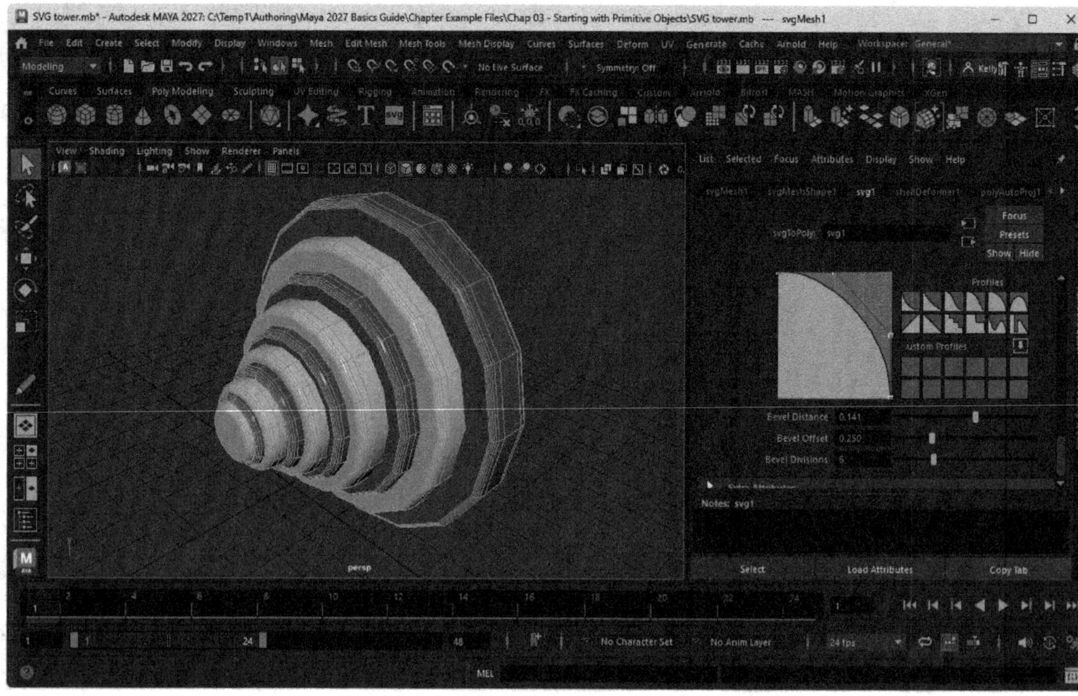

FIGURE 3-27

Imported SVG content

Chapter Summary

This chapter shows how to start modeling by working with primitive objects. Both Polygon and NURBS primitives were presented. Using the various available options, you can modify primitives using simple attributes. Several 2D primitives and arcs were also presented. The Create menu includes several unique objects including the Type command and several construction aid objects. The Type operation is a unique curve operation that lets you create text using a specific font and characters. The construction aid objects let you mark, measure and annotate scene objects. The Content Browser provides another rich resource of examples that you can draw on. Finally, this chapter showed how you can import both 3D meshes and 2D curves.

What You Have Learned

In this chapter, you learned

* How to create polygon primitives.
* How to create NURBS primitives.
* How to insert an isoparm into a model.
* How to create primitive shapes such as circles and squares.
* How to create arcs.
* How to create, extrude and bevel text with the Type tool.
* How to create reference points with construction planes.

* How to use Locators, Annotations and the various Measure Tools.
* How to access the Content Browser.
* How to load meshes from the Content Browser.
* How to import 3D meshes and 2D curves.
* How to extrude and bevel 2D designs into 3D.

Key Terms From This Chapter

* **Polygon Primitives.** A collection of pre-built polygon-based objects.
* **NURBS Primitives.** A collection of pre-built NURBS-based objects.
* **Super Shapes.** A collection of abstract primitive objects.
* **Isoparametric curve.** Representative lines that show the object's surface. Called isoparms for short.
* **Arc.** A curve made up of part of a circle.
* **Extruding.** The process of creating a surface by moving the curve perpendicular to itself.
* **Beveling.** The process of smoothing a surface by adding a face to the surface edges.
* **Construction Plane.** A plane that shows where each axis plane is located.
* **Image Plane.** A background plane where a background texture or image can be loaded.
* **Locator.** A non-rendered marker that identifies a point in space.
* **Content Browser.** An interface that holds examples for all the different Maya features.

Chapter 4

Working with Objects

IN THIS CHAPTER

- 4.1 Select objects.
- 4.2 Select components.
- 4.3 Transform, group, and parent objects.
- 4.4 Snap and align objects.
- 4.5 Understand nodes and attributes.

Now that you are familiar with the interface, the viewport panel and primitive objects, you'll next need to learn to work with objects. Working with objects includes selecting, transforming, and applying commands to selected objects.

Before an object can be transformed or edited, it needs to be selected. Selecting objects is as easy as clicking on the object or dragging over it with the Select Tool, but there are other ways to select objects such as clicking on its name in the Outliner or selecting its node in the Node Editor.

Each object is made up of components, such as vertices, edges and faces, that can be selected and transformed to change the object at a detailed level. Understanding how to work with these components is the key to editing objects. Maya includes a component mode to display and select components, as well as a mode for working with objects.

Objects and components are transformed using the tools found in the Toolbox. These tools let you move, rotate, and scale the selected object or component about a defined pivot point. To facilitate the moving of multiple objects, you can combine multiple selected objects together into a group or a hierarchy of objects using the Group and Parent commands.

The Snap and Align commands make it easy to position objects exactly where you want them. Maya includes options to snap to grid points, to curves or to points. You can even specify that an object is "live" which makes all new objects snap to its surface.

Another way to look at the objects in a scene is to identify each object as a separate node. Each node has attributes associated with it. You can view these nodes in the Node Editor. As nodes are connected, their history is recorded. You can revisit this history to make changes to the scene. Understanding how to edit an object's attributes is the key to editing with precision.

Lesson 4.1: Select Objects

There are several ways to select objects. The easiest is to click on an object with the Select tool (located in the Toolbox), shown in Figure 4-1. You can also select objects by dragging a rectangular outline over the objects that you want to select or to draw an outline around the object with the Lasso tool, shown in Figure 4-2. When dragging an outline or drawing with the Lasso tool, all objects that are at least partially contained within the outline are selected. Selected objects are easy to identify because all their edges are highlighted.

Tip

```
The hotkey for the Select Tool is the Q key.
```

FIGURE 4-1

The Select tool

FIGURE 4-2

The Lasso tool

Selecting Multiple Objects

Holding down the Shift key while clicking on objects allows you to select multiple objects. You can remove selected objects from the current selection set by holding down the Ctrl/Command key while clicking on the object to remove.

Understanding the Key Object

When multiple objects are selected, the last object selected is colored light green, as shown in Figure 4-3. This color indicates the **key object**. Several tools use the key object for certain operations. For example, when rotating multiple objects, the key object's pivot point is used as the rotation center.

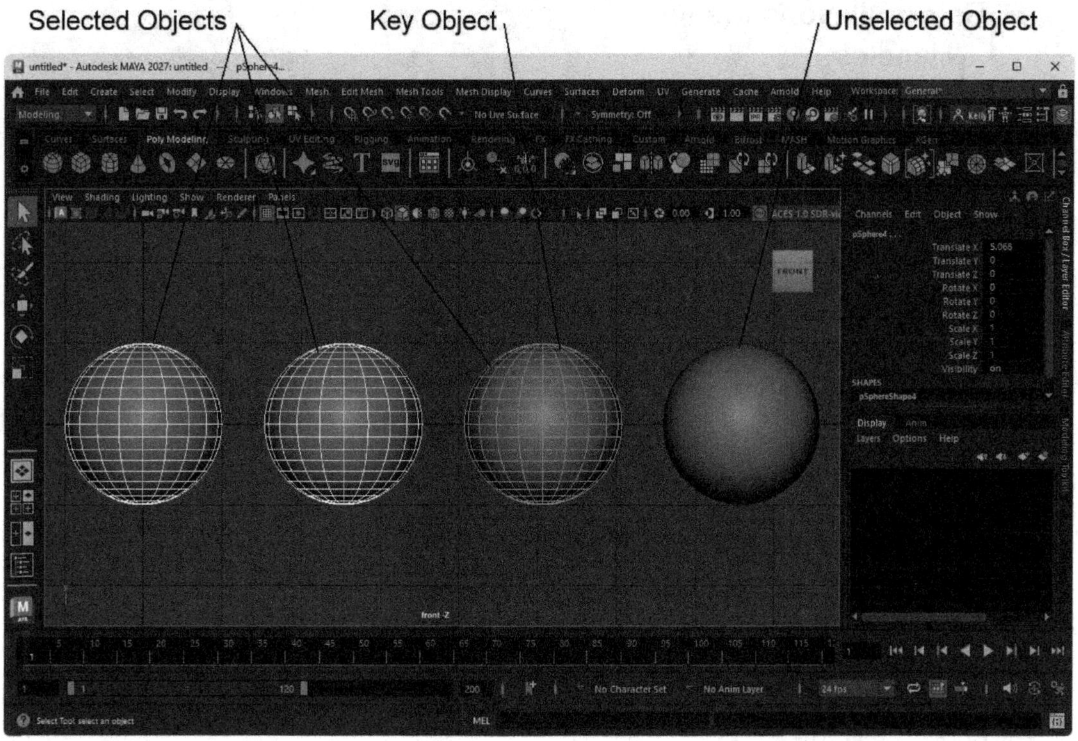

FIGURE 4-3
The key object

Using Selection Masks

If the scene has an assortment of many different types of objects, you can apply a **selection mask** to limit the types of objects that can be selected. The selection masks, shown in Figure 4-4, are located on the Status Line and consist of Handles, Joints, Curves, Surfaces, Deformations, Dynamics, Rendering, and Miscellaneous. Each of these categories include several different types of objects. For example, the Rendering category includes Lights, Cameras and Texture objects. Right clicking on each selection mask icon in the Status Line displays the various objects for each category. They work like this: if you have a complex scene with several light objects, then you can quickly select just the lights by disabling all the selection mask icons except for the Rendering selection mask and selecting the entire scene.

Note

A different set of selection masks are available for component mode, including Points, Parm Points, Lines, Faces, Hulls, Pivots, Handles, and Miscellaneous.

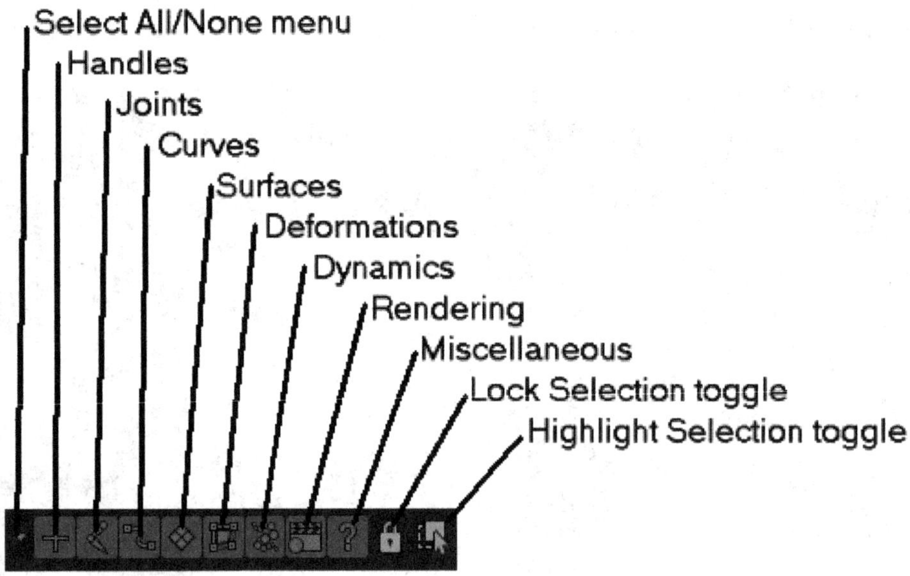

FIGURE 4-4

The selection masks

Selecting by Menu

The Select menu includes several selection commands, including Select All, All by Type, Deselect All, Select Hierarchy, Select Inverse, and Select Similar. The Select Hierarchy selects all objects in the current hierarchy of the selected object. The Select Inverse command deselects the current object and selects all unselected objects. This is a quick way to get everything except the current selected object. The Select Similar command automatically selects all similar objects to the one currently selected. For example, if you select a single light and choose Select Similar, then all lights in the scene will be selected.

Tip

The Select, Deselect All command unselects all objects, but you can also unselect all objects by simply clicking in the viewport away from all other objects.

Saving a Selection Set

A selection set is a grouping of objects and is useful if you want to quickly select a number of objects and remember the selection. You can create a selection set using the Create, Sets, Set menu command. Sets appear in the Outliner for recall.

The Create, Sets, Quick Select Set menu command opens a simple dialog box where you can name the quick select set. These sets are less permanent than those sets listed in the Outliner and are recalled using the Select, Quick Select Set menu.

Lesson 4.1-Tutorial 1: Select Multiple Objects

1. Select the File, Open Scene menu command and select the Box of donuts.mb file to open.

2. Click on the Select tool at the top of the Toolbox.
3. Hold down the Shift key and click on each of the donuts.

    The last donut selected is highlighted light green and all other donuts are white. The light green donut, shown in Figure 4-5, is the key object.

4. Select the Create, Sets, Quick Select Set menu command and name the quick set **Donuts** in the dialog box that appears.

    The selected donuts may now be recalled at any time using the Select, Quick Select Sets, Donuts menu command.

5. Select the File, Save Scene As menu command and save the file as **Selected donuts.**

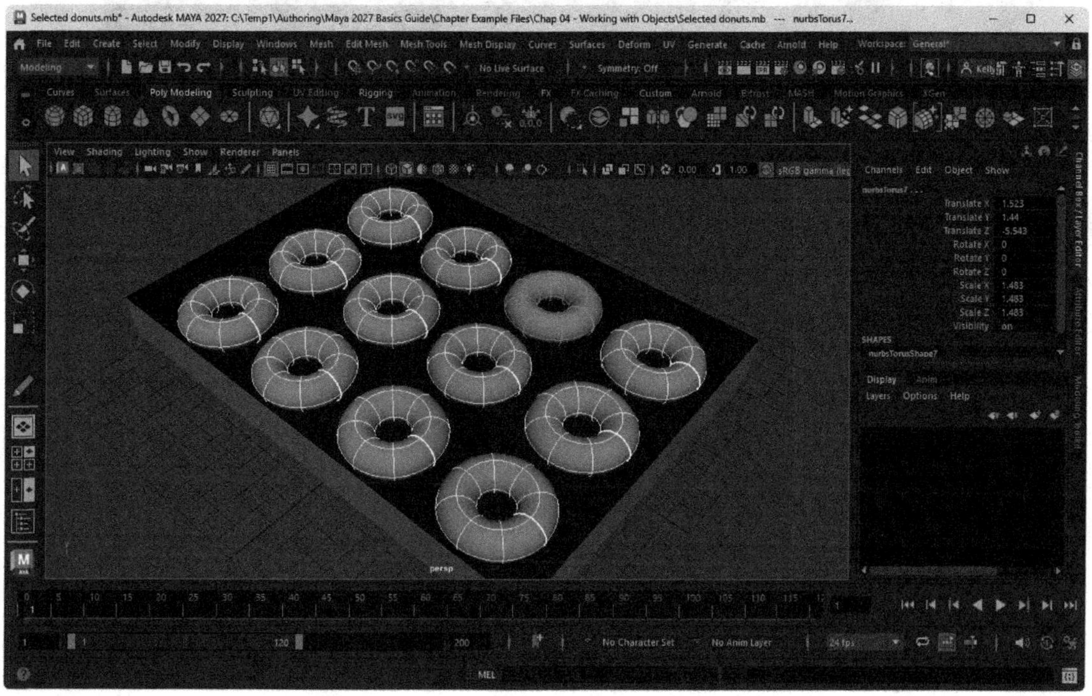

FIGURE 4-5

Selected objects

Lesson 4.2: Select Components

All objects are made of individual components, and the type of components depends on the type of object. For example, polygon objects are made of Vertices, Edges, and Faces and NURBS objects have Control Vertices (CVs), Isoparms, Surface Patches and Hulls. Components can only be selected when Component Mode is enabled. Once enabled, you can select individual components or groups of components and move them as needed to change the shape of the object. Figure 4-6 shows a simple torus with one CV selected and moved. Notice how it drastically changes the shape of the object.

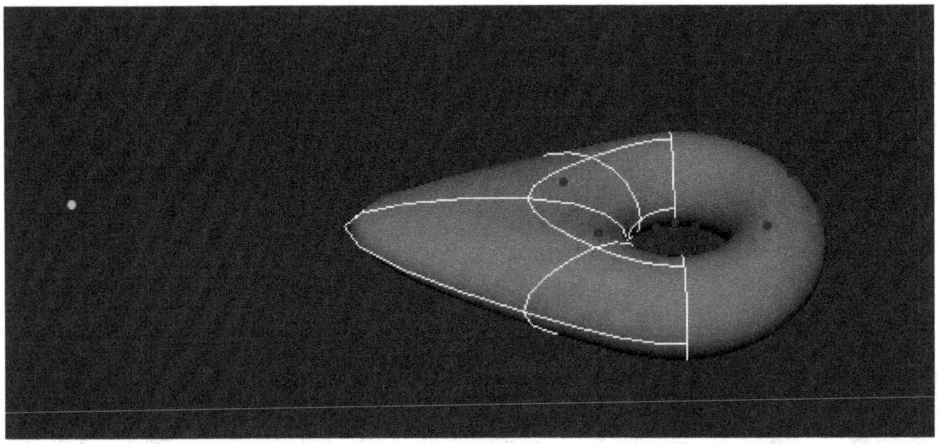

FIGURE 4-6

Torus with a moved component

Switching to Component Mode

If you click on the Select by Component Type button (see Figure 4-7) in the Status Line, the components for the selected object are displayed. You can also use the Select, Object/Component menu command. The default component is to show all vertices or Control Vertices (CVs) as purple dots and as yellow dots when selected. The hotkey to toggle between Object and Component selection modes is F8.

FIGURE 4-7

The Select by Component Type button

The quickest way to access the various component modes is with the right click marking menu, as shown in Figure 4-8. There is also an option to return to Object Mode.

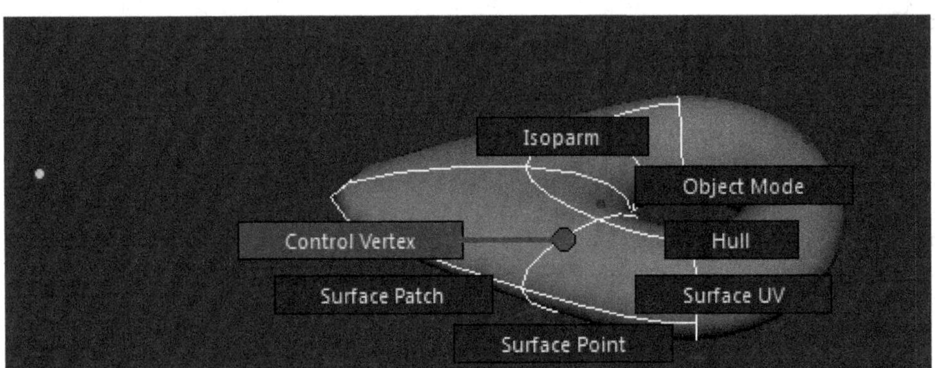

FIGURE 4-8

The right click marking menu shows the various component modes.

Selecting Components

Components are selected just like selecting objects by clicking on a single component or by dragging an outline over the components that you want to select with the Select Tool or the Lasso Tool. You can also select components by dragging over the object with the Paint Selection tool. The selected components are colored yellow, and the unselected components are colored magenta, as shown in Figure 4-9.

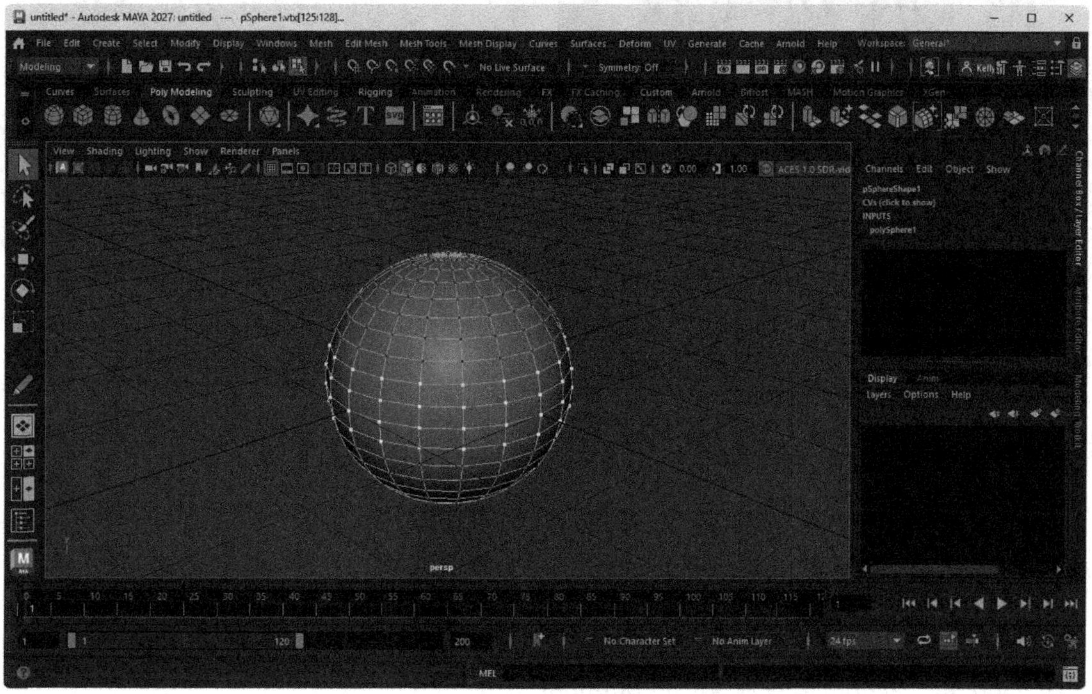

FIGURE 4-9

Selected components are yellow

Growing and Shrinking Selections

If a component is selected, you can use the Select, Grow (>) and Select, Shrink (<) menu commands to increase or decrease the adjacent components around the current ones that are selected. This provides an easy way to select exactly the components that you want. The Select menu also has options to Grow Along Loop and Shrink Along Loop to increase the selected components vertically or horizontally along the edge lines.

Selecting Edges

If the Edge component mode is selected, then you can click on an edge to select it. The selected edge is colored orange and the unselected edges are blue. If a single edge segment is selected, you can use the Select, Contiguous Edges menu command to automatically select the entire length of the edge end to end. This provides a quick way to select an entire **edge loop** that runs all the way around a sphere object, as shown in Figure 4-10.

Tip

Double clicking a single edge component for polygon objects automatically selects the entire edge loop.

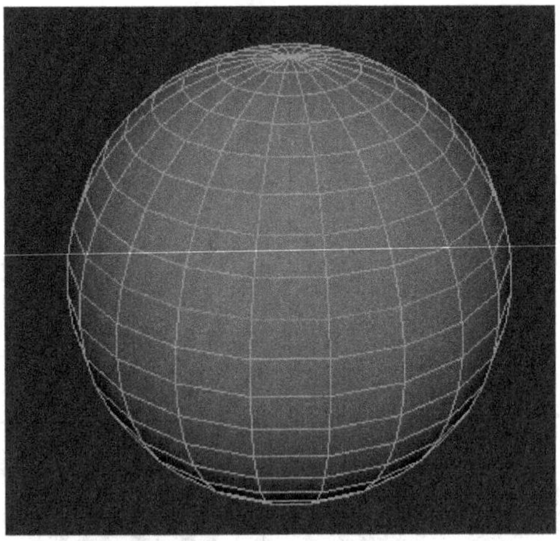

FIGURE 4-10

Selected edge is marked in orange

The Select, Shortest Edge Path Tool menu command selects all edges that make the shortest path between two points that you select. This is a good option for marking seams in the current object.

Lesson 4.2-Tutorial 1: Select Components

1. Select the File, Open Scene menu command and select the Box of donuts.mb file to open.
2. Click on the Lasso tool in the Toolbox and encircle portions of the middle two donuts.
3. Then hold down the Ctrl/Command key and encircle a portion of the underside of the box to deselect it.
4. Click on the Select by Component Type button in the Status Line (or press the F8 key).
5. Hold down the Shift key and encircle the center of both donuts.
6. Press the F key to focus in on the selected donuts.

   The center Control Vertices (CV) points for the selected donuts are selected and are displayed in yellow, as shown in Figure 4-11.
7. Select the File, Save Scene As menu command and save the file as **Selected donut centers**.

FIGURE 4-11

Component mode

Lesson 4.3: Transform, Group, and Parent Objects

Transforming involves positioning and orienting objects in the correct location for the scene. All transformations take place about the object's pivot point.

Understanding Pivot Points

Every object has a pivot point. The pivot point is the point about which the object is transformed. By default the pivot is usually positioned at the center of the object, as shown in Figure 4-12. It is marked by a yellow square at the center of the manipulator. You can reposition an object's pivot point by pressing the Insert key to enter pivot point editing mode. You can then use the transformation tools to move and rotate the pivot point. Press the Insert key again to exit pivot point mode. You can move the pivot to the object's center using the Modify, Center Pivot menu command.

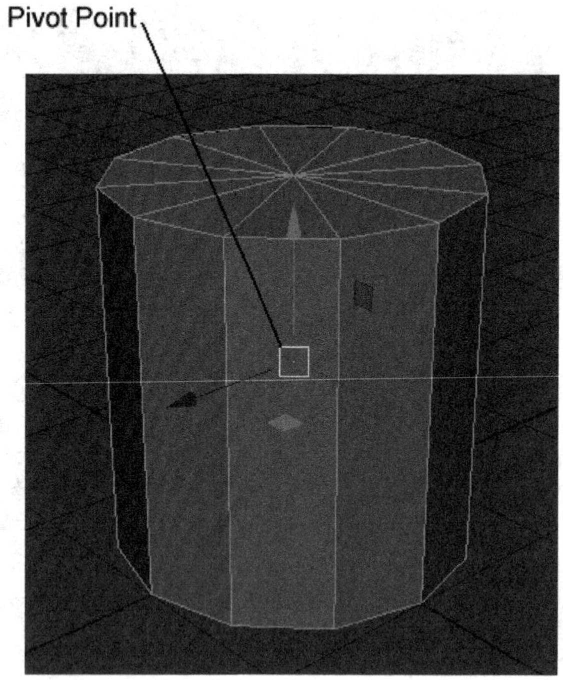

FIGURE 4-12

The pivot point

Transforming Objects Along an Axis

Objects can be transformed using the Move, Rotate, and Scale tools found in the Toolbox. Selecting any of these tools makes a manipulator appear at the pivot point for the selected object. You can constrain the transformation to a single axis by clicking on one of the axis manipulators. The selected constrained axis turns yellow. You can transform along the selected axis by dragging the selected manipulator (or by dragging in any direction in the View panel with the middle mouse button).

Tip

You can also constrain a transform to a single axis by holding down the Shift key and dragging in the direction of the axis arrow with the middle mouse button.

Transforming Objects Within a Plane

You can transform objects within an orthographic view like the Top or Front view in two directions at once using the square handle located at the center of the manipulator. In a Perspective view, you can constrain the transform to a single plane by holding down the Ctrl/Command key while clicking on the axis arrow that points to the plane you want to constrain to. The square manipulator handle aligns to the plane that it is constrained to. Clicking on the square handle with the Ctrl/Command key held down toggles it back to the camera plane. Figure 4-13 shows an object constrained to move in the YZ-plane.

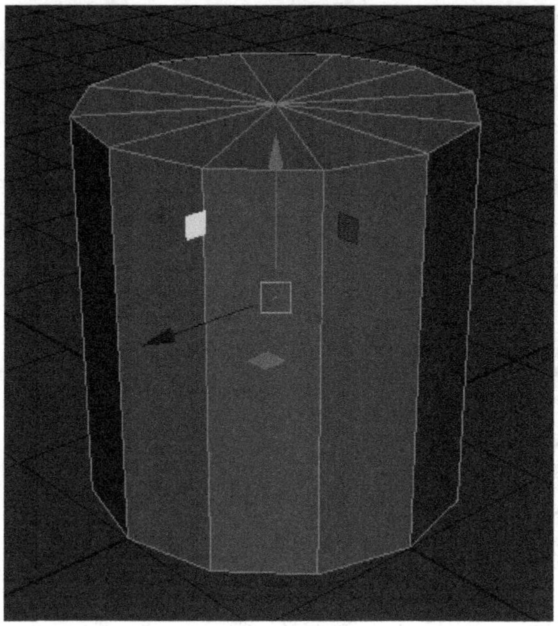

FIGURE 4-13

An object constrained to the YZ-plane.

Constrained Rotations

The Rotate tool(e) also has a manipulator, but it looks and works a little differently than the Move tool (w). The Rotate manipulator, shown in Figure 4-14, includes three circular rings that surround the pivot point that allow you to rotate about each of the axes. There is also a yellow ring that surrounds the entire manipulator that lets you spin the object about its center. If multiple objects are selected, then the pivot point is at the center of the key object.

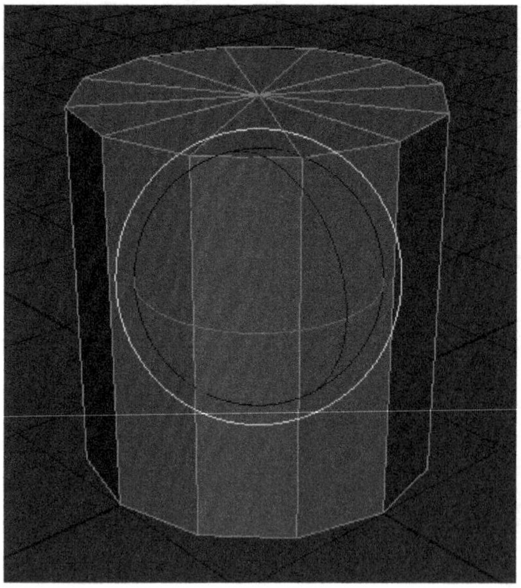

FIGURE 4-14

The Rotate manipulator

Uniform and Non-Uniform Scaling

The Scale tool(r) also has a manipulator that looks similar to the Move tool manipulator except it has small cubes at each axis end instead of arrows, as shown in Figure 4-15. Dragging one of the axis handles will scale the object in both the positive and negative directions about the pivot point. This is called **non-uniform scaling** because it distorts the shape of the object. If you drag on the center handle, then the entire object gets larger. This is **uniform scaling**, and the overall shape of the object doesn't change.

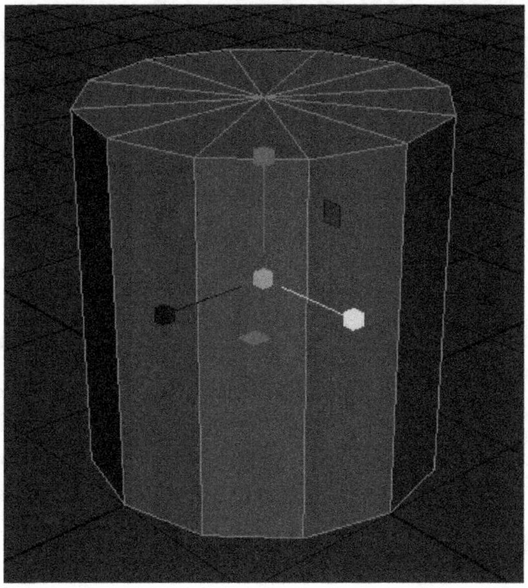

FIGURE 4-15

The Scale manipulator

Grouping Objects Together

When multiple objects are selected together, they are transformed together, but once another object is selected, the grouping is lost. To permanently create a group that can be reselected, use the Edit, Group (Ctrl/Command+g) menu command. This new group shows up as a selectable node in the Outliner, as shown in Figure 4-16. You can dissolve a group using the Edit, Ungroup menu command.

Tip

New groups are simply called group with a number, but you can rename them in the Outliner by double clicking on its name.

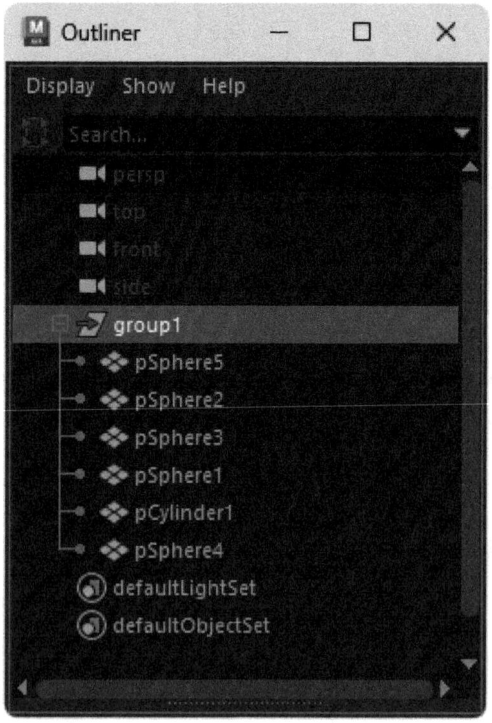

FIGURE 4-16

Groups displayed in the Outliner

Parenting Objects

Another way to combine objects is to parent one object to another. This creates a hierarchy of objects with parent/child relationships. All child objects are transformed along with the parent object, but children objects can move independently of the parent. To create a parent-child link between two objects, select the child object and then select the parent object and use the Edit, Parent (hotkey: P) menu command. The key object (the last-selected object) is the parent object. Use the Edit, Unparent (Shift+P) menu command to break a parent-child link. You can quickly select all parent and child objects included in the hierarchy with the Select, Hierarchy menu command.

Viewing Hierarchy in the Outliner

To view all scene objects by name as a hierarchical list, you can open the Outliner using the Windows, Outliner menu command or with the toggle button at the bottom of the Quick Layout buttons. The Outliner, shown in Figure 4-17, displays all child objects underneath their parents. It also includes hidden objects, such as the hidden view cameras and the default lights. The Outliner is also an easy place to select objects. Dragging and dropping nodes with the middle mouse button lets you re-order the hierarchy creating parent and children objects.

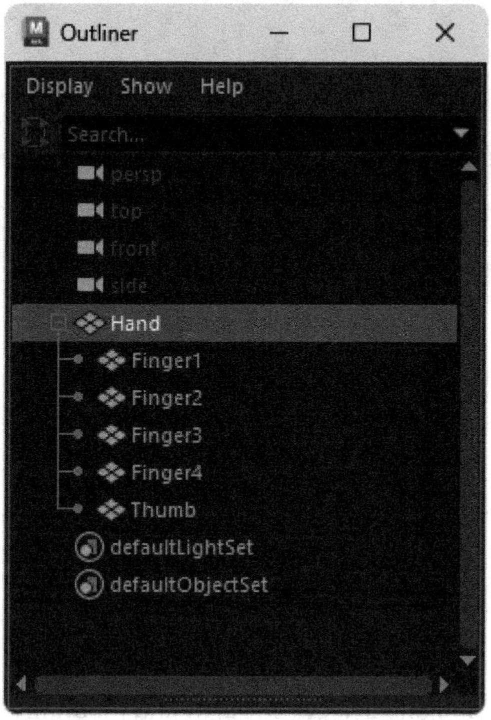

FIGURE 4-17

The Outliner

Using Undo, Redo, and Repeat

You can undo your mistakes using the Edit, Undo menu command (Ctrl/Command+z) and redo using the Edit, Redo menu command (Shift+z). You can also repeat the last command using the Edit, Repeat menu command (hotkey: g). The Edit, Recent Commands menu opens a dialog box (Figure 4-18) that lists the recently executed commands. Using this dialog box, you can selectively choose which actions to undo.

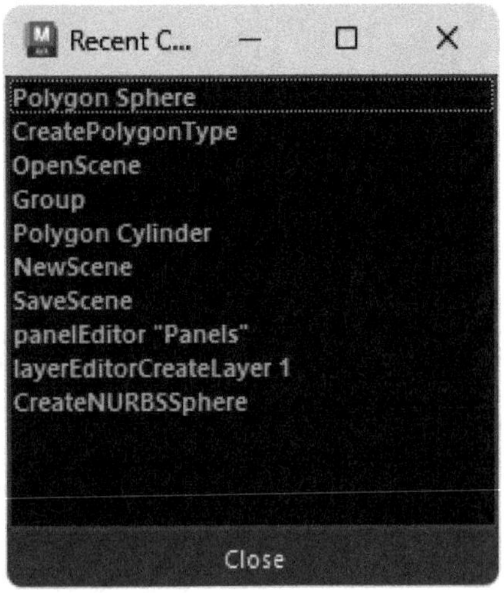

FIGURE 4-18

Recent Commands dialog box.

Lesson 4.3-Tutorial 1: Move Pivot Point

1. Select the File, Open Scene menu command and select the Earth and moon.mb file to open.
2. Click on the smaller sphere object to select it.
3. Click on the Rotate tool in the Toolbox and drag the green Y-axis manipulator handle to rotate the moon object about its center.
4. Click on the Move tool and press the Insert key on the keyboard to enable pivot point mode.
5. Drag the red X-axis manipulator handle to the center of the large sphere and press the Insert key again to exit pivot point mode.
6. Click on the Rotate tool again and drag the green Y-axis handle again.

   This time, the moon rotates around the center Earth object, as shown in Figure 4-19.
7. Select the File, Save Scene As menu command and save the file as **Rotating moon.mb**.

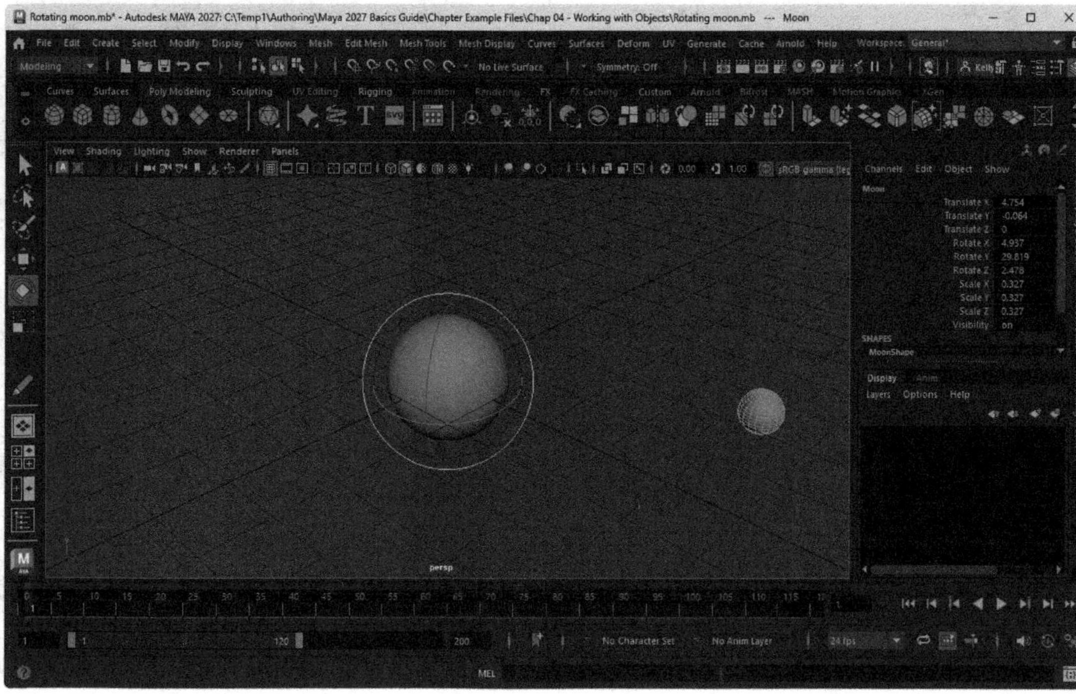

FIGURE 4-19

Moon rotates about the moved pivot point

Lesson 4.3-Tutorial 2: Transform Car Wheels

1. Select the File, Open Scene menu command and select the Car and wheels.mb file to open.
2. Drag over all the wheels in the Top view to select them all.
3. Click on the Rotate tool in the Toolbox and drag the red X-axis manipulator handle to rotate the wheels about their center 90 degrees so they are correctly positioned relative to the car body.
4. Click on the Move tool and select one of the wheels and drag its center manipulator in the Top view panel to align it to the car body. Repeat this step for the other wheels.

   With all the wheels correctly positioned, the car looks as shown in Figure 4-20.
5. Select the File, Save Scene As menu command and save the file as **Car with wheels-aligned.mb**.

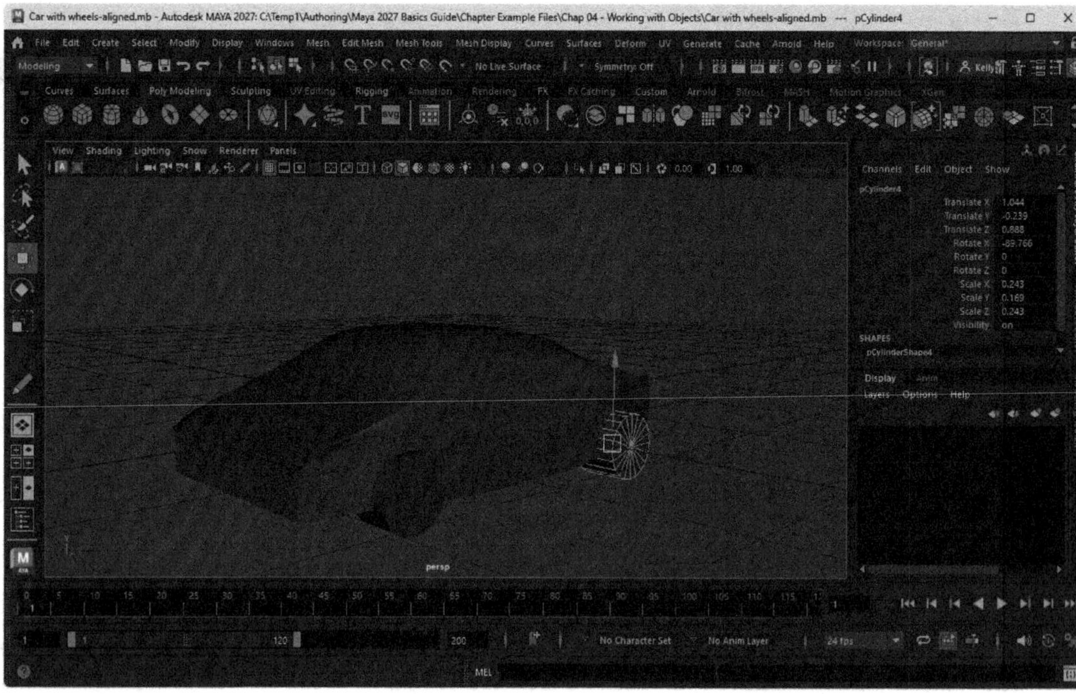

FIGURE 4-20

Car with transformed wheels

Lesson 4.3-Tutorial 3: Parent an Object

1. Select the File, Open Scene menu command and select the Hand and fingers.mb file to open.
2. With the Shift key held down, click on all the fingers and the thumb objects, and then on the hand object.

   With the hand selected last, it becomes the key object.
3. Select the Edit, Parent menu command.

   This command links all the objects together, with the hand object being the parent and fingers being its child, as shown in Figure 4-21.
4. Click on the Move tool and drag the hand object.

   When the parent object is selected and moved, its child objects are also selected and move along with it.
5. Select the File, Save Scene As menu command and save the file as **Parented hand.mb**.

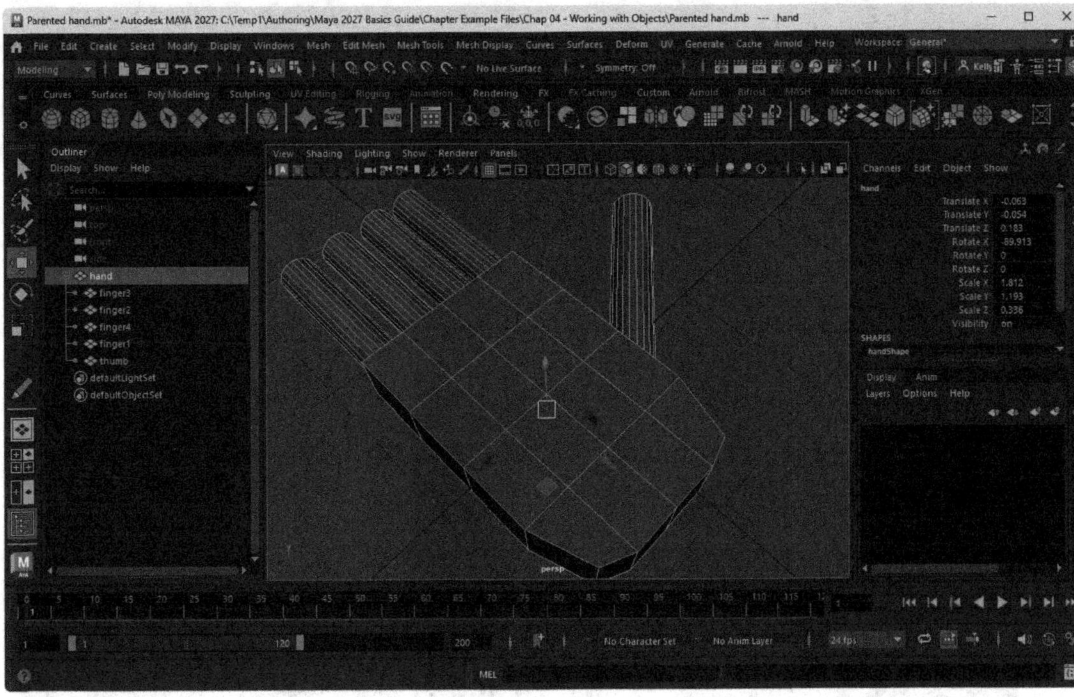

FIGURE 4-21

Parented objects

Lesson 4.4: Snap and Align Objects

Transforming objects leaves you to eyeball the location of the object, but you can precisely position objects using the Snap and Align features. You can tell when a snapping feature is enabled because the center of the manipulator is a circle instead of a square.

Using Grids

When Maya is first started, a default grid is visible in the view panel. The Display, Grid menu command toggles the default grid on and off. There is also a Grid toggle icon button at the top of each view panel. Selecting the Display, Grid, Options menu command opens a dialog box, shown in Figure 4-22, where you can specify the dimensions, color and display options of the default grid. The default grid is useful in snapping objects into place.

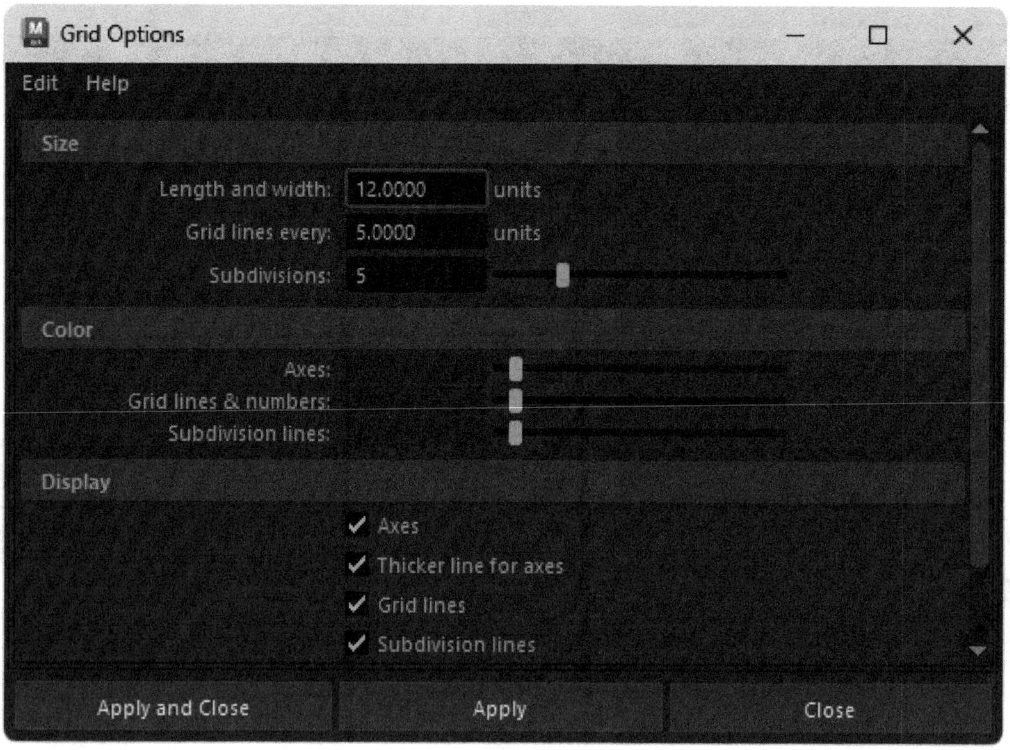

FIGURE 4-22

Grid Options dialog box

Duplicating with Transform

Another common way to precisely position several objects is with the Edit, Duplicate with Transform (Shift+D) menu command. If you create an object, you can use the Edit, Duplicate (Ctrl/Command+d)menu command to create a duplicate of the selected object. With this command, the duplicate object is positioned directly on top of the original object. But, if you create a duplicate object and transform it with the transform tools, the Duplicate with Transform menu command remembers the transform and duplicates the transform while creating the duplicate.

Replacing Objects

You can also replace all selected objects with the key object using the Modify, Replace Objects menu command. This is helpful for placing objects such as trees using simple spheres or Locator objects until the end when you can quickly add all the trees in at once with this command. Using the Replace Objects Options dialog box, you can also select to copy the Rotate and Scale attributes or to use the object's original attributes.

Snapping Objects

With the Move tool selected, you can snap the selected object to a specific grid point, to a curve, to surface points, or to a view plane using the Snap buttons located on the Status Line (see Figure 4-23). Just enable one or more of the snapping buttons and move the object, and it is automatically positioned so that its pivot point is in the same position as the object it is snapped to. You can also snap to a specific point by holding down the middle mouse button and moving the mouse over the snap point with the correct snap mode enabled.

Tip

Holding down the x hotkey, you can enable Grid snapping; holding down the c hotkey, you can enable Curve snapping; and holding down the v hotkey enables Point snapping. These hotkeys work without having the Grid option on the Status Line enabled.

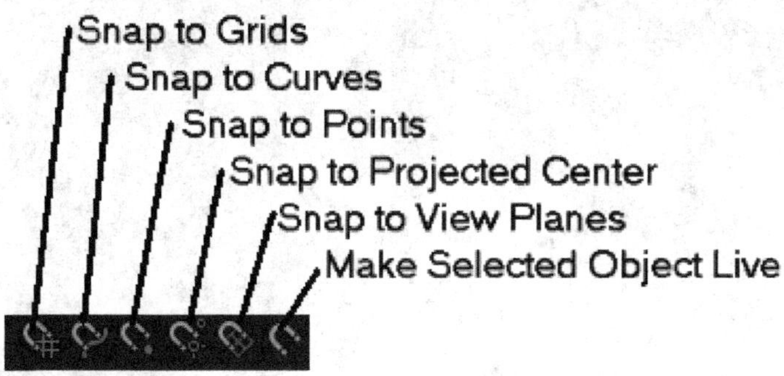

FIGURE 4-23
Snap buttons

Snapping to a Live Object

With the Modify, Make Live menu command, you can designate that the selected object or objects are live. Any new objects that are created or moved with the center Snap manipulator are automatically snapped to the surface of the Live object. The live objector objects are displayed using a dark green color. This allows you to draw curves on the surface of the “live” object. The name of the "live" object is listed in the text field to the right of the Snap to Live button on the Status Line. If you right click on the live object text field you can add or remove objects from the current live selection. You can also use the Live Object button on the Status Line to turn Live Object mode on and off. Selecting the Modify, Make Not Live menu command changes an object back into a normal object.

Aligning Objects

With two or more objects selected, you can use the Modify, Snap Align Objects menu command to align objects by point or object. The Options dialog box for the Align Objects menu command (see Figure 4-24) lets you align the objects by Min, Mid, Max, Dist, or Stack in each of the axes.

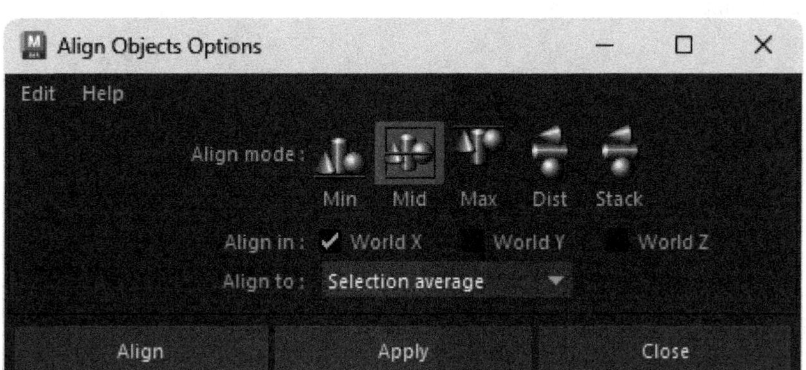

FIGURE 4-24
Align Objects options

The Align tool (also found in the Modify menu) displays several alignment icons (see Figure 4-25) in the view panel. Choosing one of these icons aligns the selected objects. All selected objects are aligned with the key object.

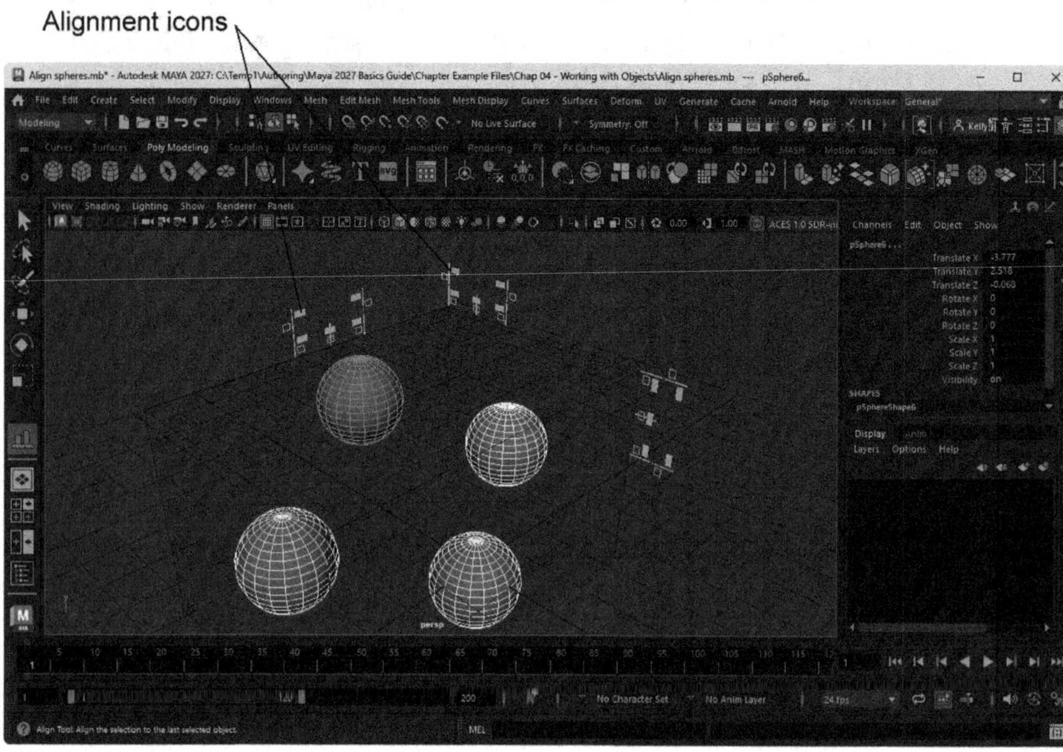

FIGURE 4-25

The Align tool

Aligning Points

Using component mode, you can select one, two or three points on each object that you want to align and use the Modify, Snap Align Objects, Point to Point or 2 Points to 2 Points or 3 Points to 3 Points menu commands to align objects using the selected points.

Caution

> In order to use the point alignment options, the selected points must be roughly the same distance apart.

Snapping Surfaces Together

Another common way to align objects is with the Modify, Snap Together tool. This tool lets you click and drag a cursor over the surface of the selected object. An arrow cursor points away from the surface. Clicking on a second object lets you drag over the surface to locate where the connection is made. A line connects the two surfaces at their designated connection points, as shown in Figure 4-26. Pressing the Enter key completes the snapping.

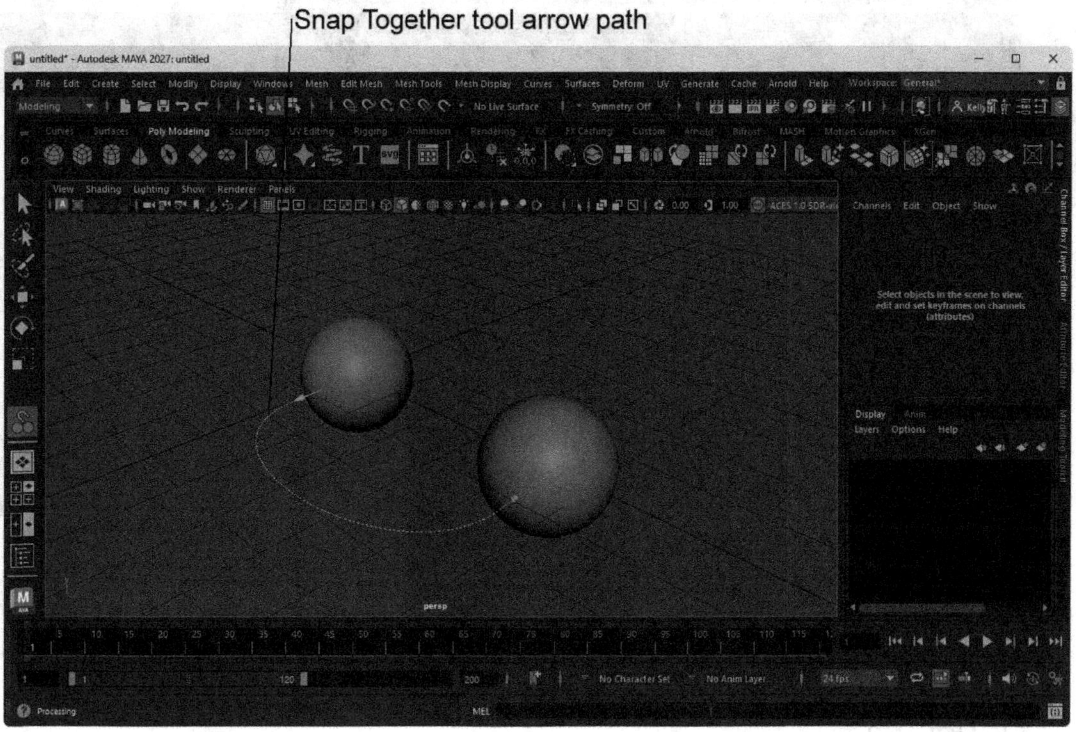

FIGURE 4-26

The line shows the points that are to be connected

Lesson 4.4-Tutorial 1: Snap Objects to Grid Points

1. Select the File, Open Scene menu command and select the Stairs.mb file to open.
2. Click on the single stair object to select it.
3. Click on the Snap to Grids button in the Status Line.
4. Select the Edit, Duplicate menu command (or press the Ctrl/Command+d hotkey) to create a duplicate stair object.

   The duplicate stair object is positioned in the same position as the original stair object.
5. Select the Move tool in the Toolbox and drag the duplicated stair object upward along the Y-axis in the Front view panel and to the right along the negative Z-axis in the Side view panel.

   With the Snap to Grids option enabled, moving the stair object snaps to the nearest grid point. This makes it easy to correctly and precisely align the stairs.
6. With the duplicate stair selected, choose the Edit, Duplicate with Transform menu command several times to create a set of stairs, as shown in Figure 4-27.
7. Select the File, Save Scene As menu command and save the file as **Snapped stairs**.

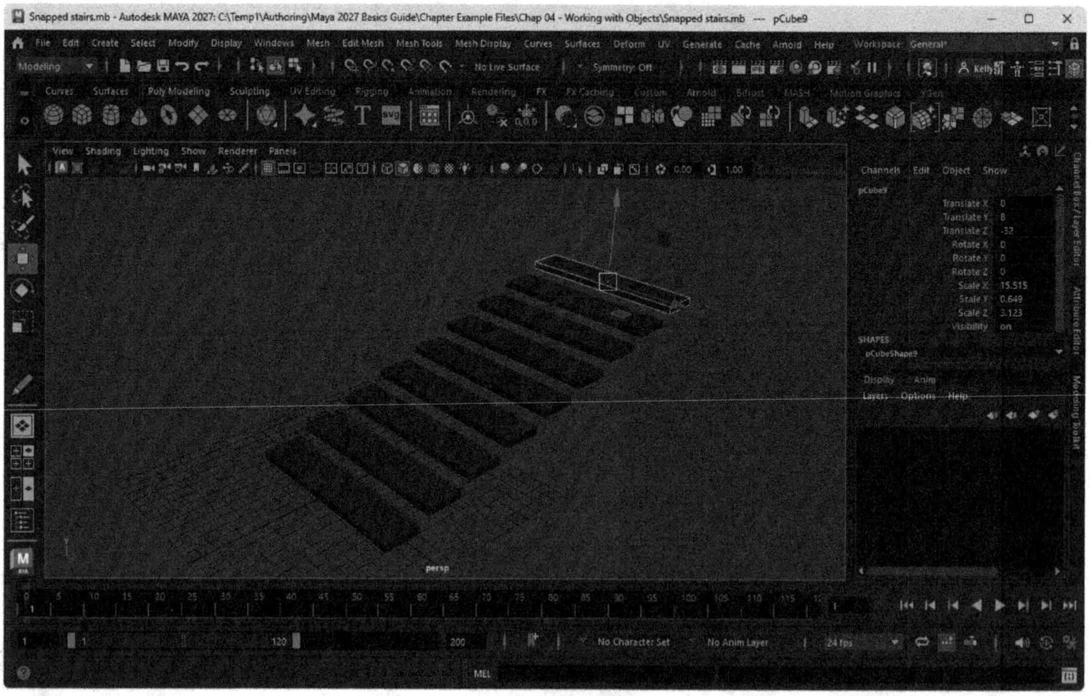

FIGURE 4-27

Snapped stairs

Lesson 4.4-Tutorial 2: Snap to a Curve

1. Select the File, Open Scene menu command and select the Heart necklace.mb file to open.
2. Click on the heart object to select it.
3. Click on the Snap to Curves button in the Status Line.
4. Select the Move tool in the Toolbox.
5. Hold down the C key and click the curve with the middle mouse button and drag the heart object to its correct position on the necklace.

   With the Snap to Curve option enabled, clicking on the curve with the middle mouse button snaps the heart object to the curve, as shown in Figure 4-28.
6. Select the File, Save Scene As menu command and save the file as **Snapped heart necklace**.

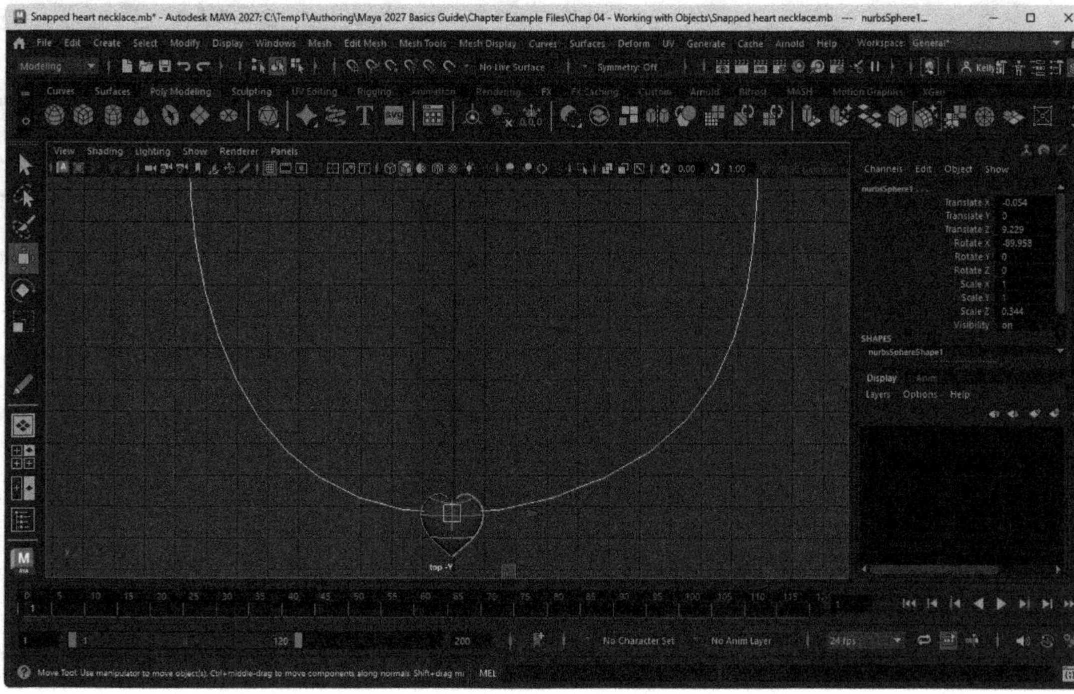

FIGURE 4-28

Heart snapped to a curve

Lesson 4.4-Tutorial 3: Snap to a Live Object

1. Select the File, Open Scene menu command and select the Simple cube.mb file to open.
2. Double click on the Move tool and in the Move Snap Settings rollout, make sure the Vertex option is enabled.
3. Click on the cube object to select it.
4. Select the Modify, Make Live menu command.

   The cube object turns dark green to mark that it is live.
5. Create a sphere object and select it.
6. Select the Move tool in the Toolbox.
7. Drag the center Snap manipulator (it is a yellow circle at the center of the sphere) of the sphere to one of the cube corners. Be careful not to use the manipulator's axis arrows because they will move beyond the cube.

   Because the cube is a live object, the sphere cannot be moved beyond the borders of the cube.
8. Select the Edit, Duplicate menu command and drag the duplicated sphere's Snap manipulator to another of the cube's corners. Repeat this until every corner has a sphere, as shown in Figure 4-29.
9. Click away from all objects to deselect all objects, and then choose the Modify, Make Not Live menu command to return the cube to its original state.
10. Select the File, Save Scene As menu command and save the file as **Cube with snapped spheres**.

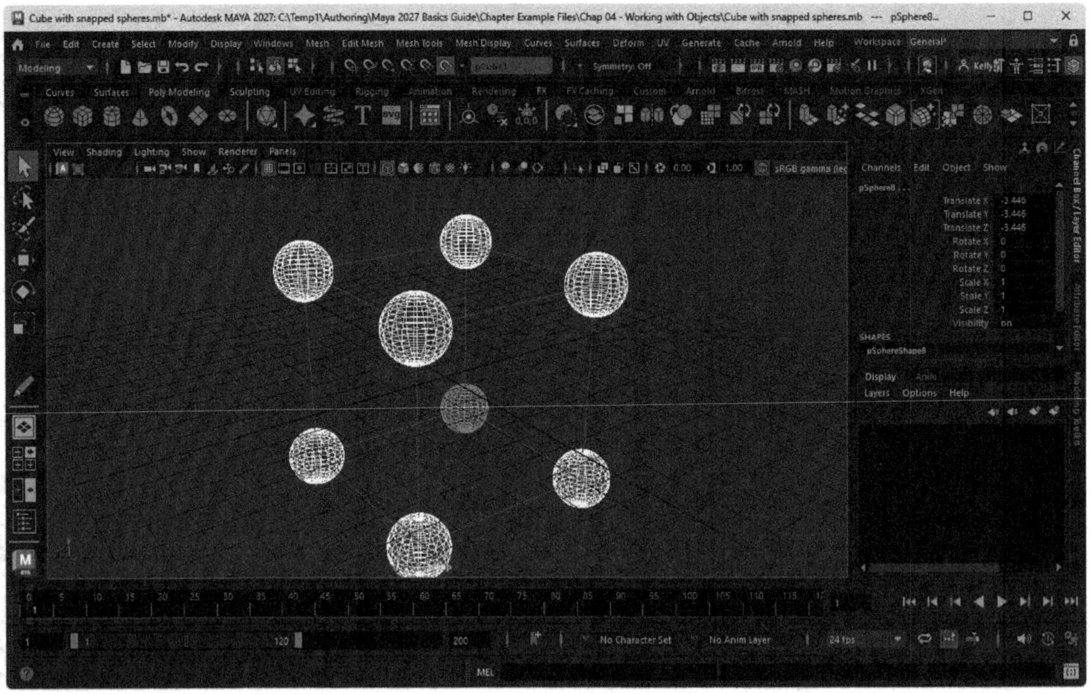

FIGURE 4-29

Spheres snapped to live cube object

Lesson 4.4-Tutorial 4: Align Letters

1. Select the File, Open Scene menu command and select the Stairs letters.mb file to open.
2. Click on the letter "t" to select it, hold down the Shift key and select the letter "s".

   This makes the letter "s" the key object.
3. Select the Modify, Align Tool menu command to enable the Align tool.

   With the Align Tool enabled and two or more objects selected, several light-blue alignment icons appear in the View panel.
4. Click on the Align Top to Bottom icon to align the letter "t" above the letter "s".
5. Repeat steps 2-4 for each pair of letters remaining in the word to create a stairstep effect (see Figure 4-30).
6. Select the File, Save Scene As menu command and save the file as **Staircase letters**.

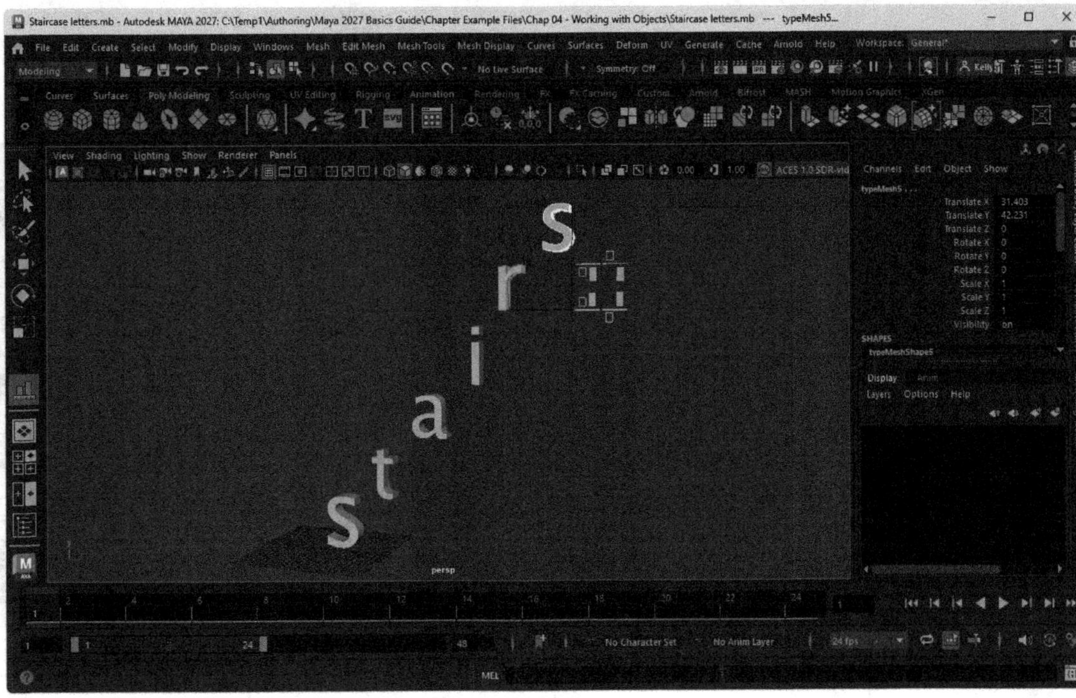

FIGURE 4-30

Aligned letters

Lesson 4.5: Understand Nodes and Attributes

In addition to a visual representation found in the View panel, each object is also represented as a node. Nodes can be viewed using the Node Editor, as shown in Figure 4-31. You can open the Node Editor using the Windows, Node Editor menu command. Each node holds *attributes*, which are the values that determine the properties of the node and its related object. These attributes are also visible in the Attribute Editor and in the Channel Box. Nodes simply provide another way to work with objects that is independent of size.

Note

If no nodes are visible when you open the Node Editor, select a scene object and click on the Input and Output Connections icon button.

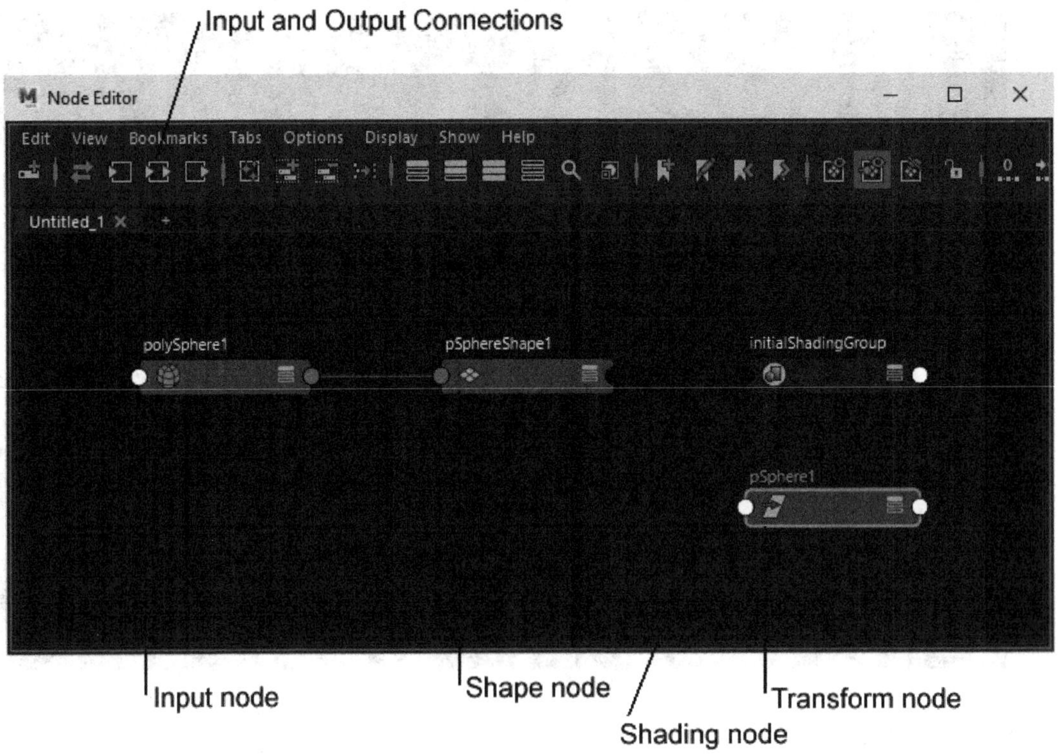

FIGURE 4-31

Node Editor, Simple mode

For a default primitive object, these four nodes are created: an Input node, a Shape node, a Shading node and a Transform node. The Input node holds the primitive attributes like Radius and Subdivisions. This feeds into the Shape node that holds all the component positions, which in turn, feeds into the Shading node that defines how the object is colored. These three nodes are dependent on each other. The Transform node holds the object's position in the scene, and it is separate and not dependent on the other nodes.

Understanding the Various Node Types

Maya includes several different node types. For example, a Transform node holds the scene position, rotation, and scale information and Light node holds information about a light object. Every time an operation is made on an object, a new node holding the attributes of that operation is added. For example, if Mesh, Reduce command is made on a sphere object, a new Reduce node is added, as shown in Figure 4-32. These operations are also listed in the Channel Box under Inputs. A single object, like a sphere or a camera, can be made up of many nodes. Some of these are connected and others stand alone.

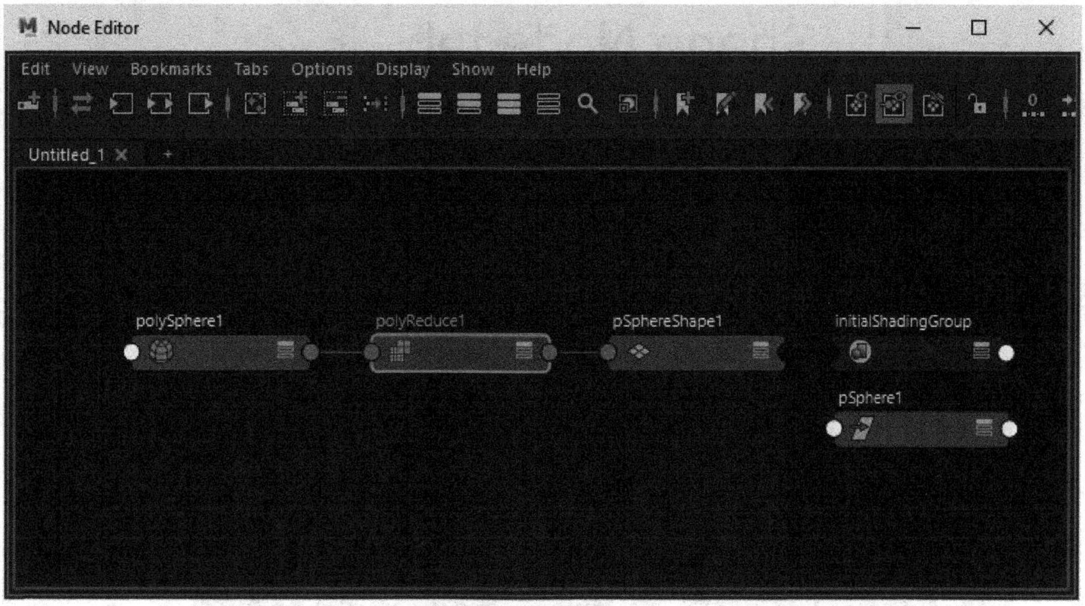

FIGURE 4-32

Sphere object with a Reduce node added

Viewing Nodes in the Attribute Editor

When a node is selected in the Node Editor, it is highlighted green, and its attributes appear in the Attribute Editor. Each node title is also displayed for the selected object as tabs along the top of the Attribute Editor, as shown for a simple sphere in Figure 4-33. The selected node typically matches the selected object, but you can pin the Attribute Editor to a specific node using the Pin Tab button in the upper right corner of the Attribute Editor. This keeps the current node visible regardless of what is selected, and it will remain visible until the Pin Tab button is toggled off.

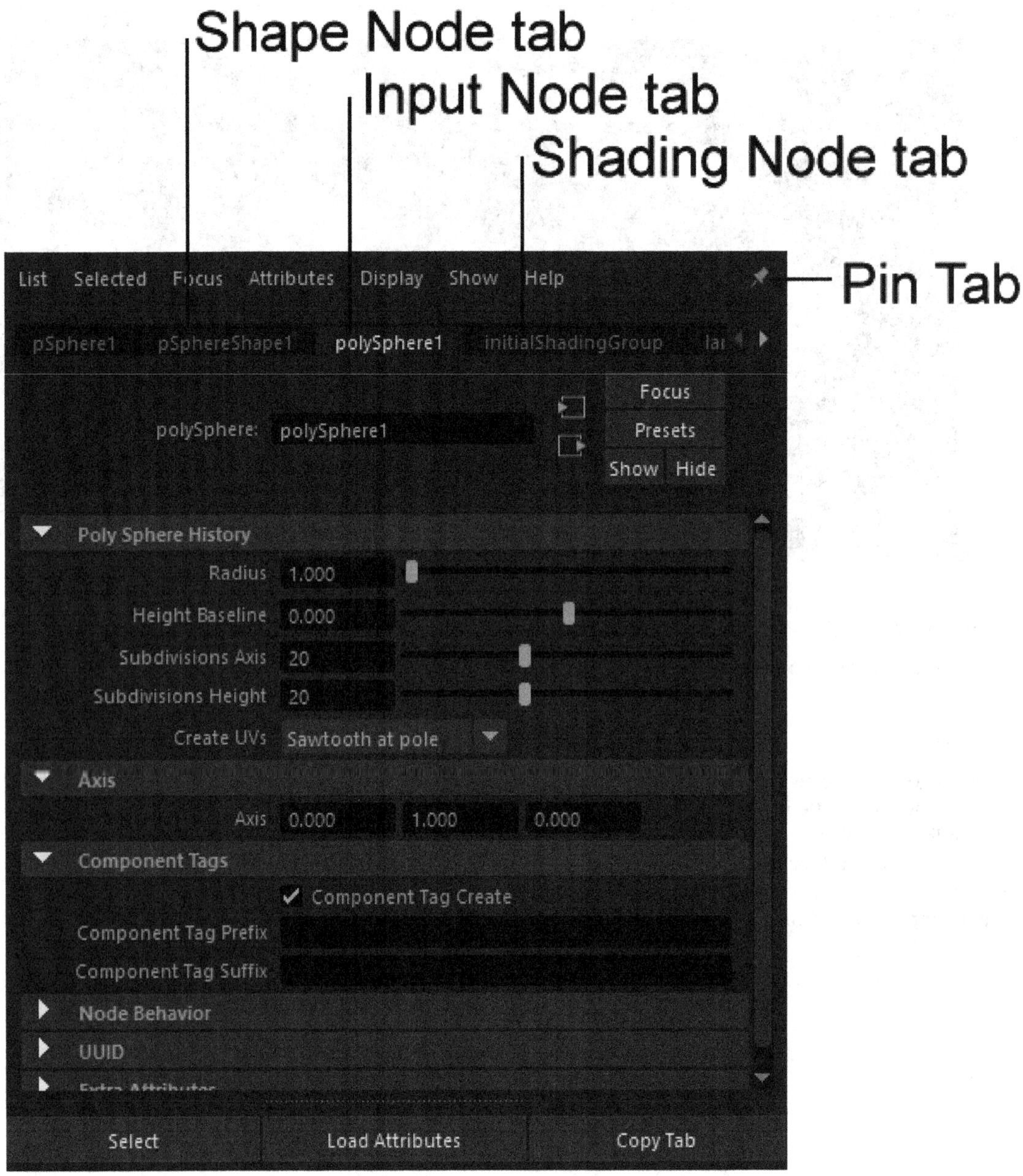

FIGURE 4-33

The Attribute Editor

The Channel Box also shows node names and all its attributes, as shown in Figure 4-34, but these nodes are limited to the selected object.

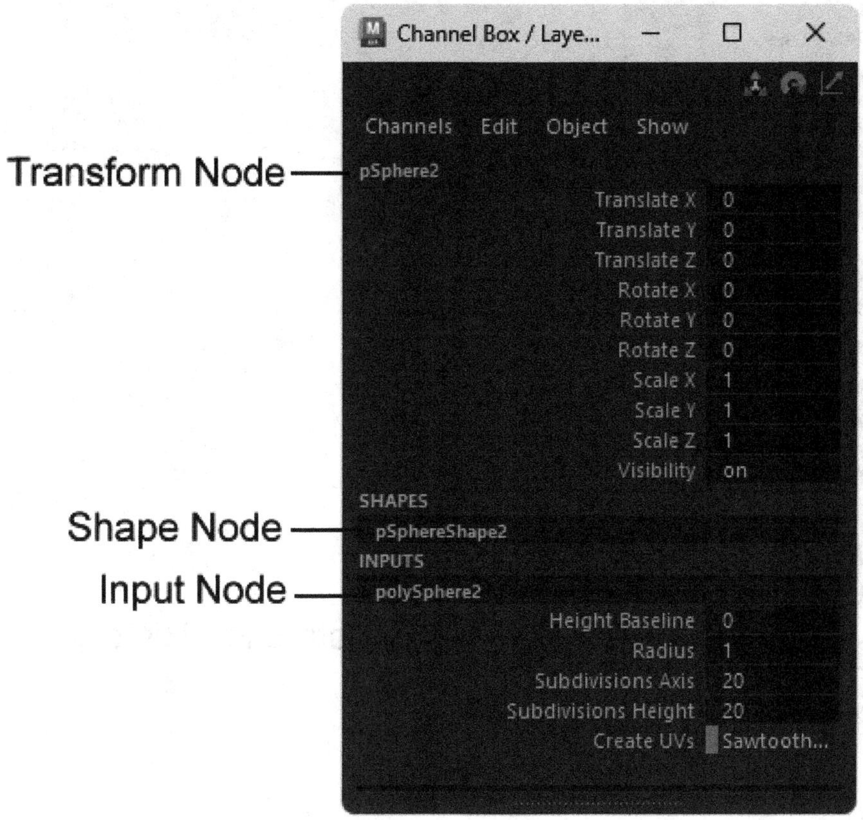

FIGURE 4-34

Channel Box nodes and attributes

Viewing construction history

Any operation that is applied to an object appears in the Inputs section of the Channel Box. If you click on these operation names, then the attributes for that operation are displayed. Accessing these attributes lets you go back and change the parameters of the operation. The operations are listed in the order they are applied to the object with the most recent operations at the top and the oldest operation at the bottom. All operations taken together is called the construction history, as shown in Figure 4-35.

Caution

If you change the attributes on some of the earliest operation nodes, you could change the overall shape of the object.

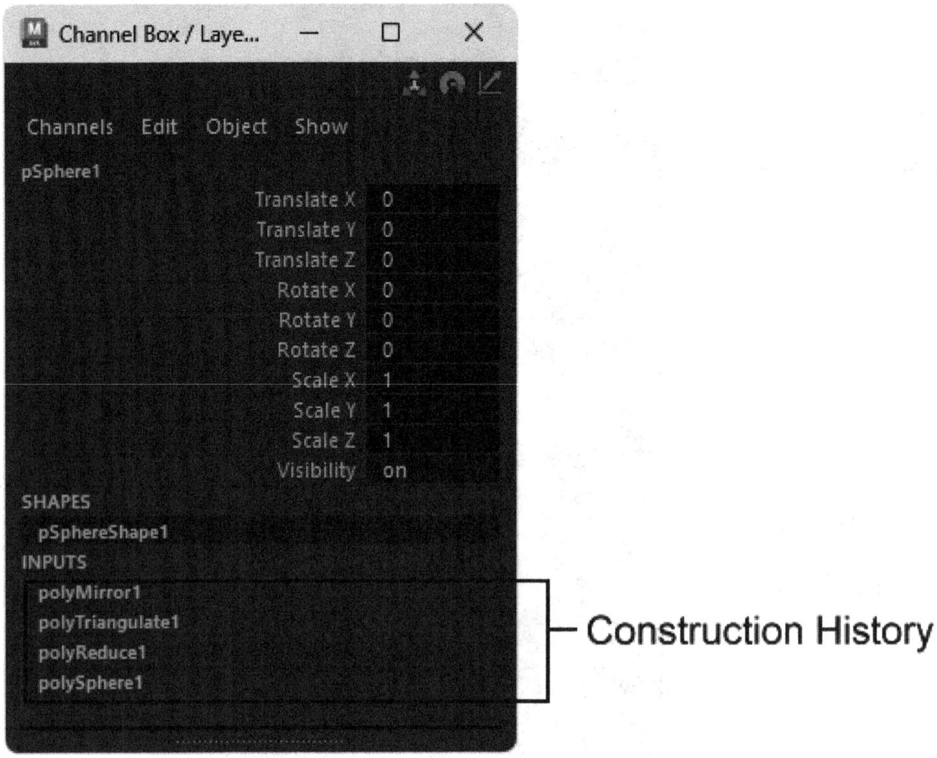

FIGURE 4-35

Construction history

Deleting construction history

Every operation done to an object creates a new node and adds to the Inputs list in the Channel Box. If you look at each of these nodes it tells a story of how the object was created. As you work with objects, the history that is saved adds overhead to the object, which can slow down the system. You can simplify an object by deleting its construction history using the Edit, Delete by Type, History or using the Edit, Delete History command in the Channel Box. This removes all the extraneous nodes resulting in a simplified object.

Caution

It is usually best to delete the construction history when you are sure you won't want to make any more changes to the object.

If you don't want to mess with construction history at all, you can disable the Construction History On and Off button on the Status Line. When disabled, construction history isn't recorded at all, but you also lose the ability to make changes.

Editing Attributes

All the keyable attributes associated with an object can be viewed in the Channel Box, but this is just a subset of the total number of attributes. A complete set of attributes may be viewed in the Attribute Editor. Attributes that have a purple background are controlled by another attribute and cannot be changed. You can change multiple attribute values at the same time by holding down the Shift key and selecting them before changing the value.

Working with Nodes

Selected nodes in the Node Editor can be viewed using Simple (1), Connected (2) or Full Mode (3) with the Edit menu. Simple mode shows each node as a simple rectangle. Connected mode shows just the input and output connections for the node and Full mode shows all attributes in a list for the selected node, as shown in Figure 4-36. You can also toggle through these modes by clicking on the Show Attributes to the right of every node.

Tip

You can use the Alt/Option+middle mouse button and the Alt/Option+right mouse button to pan and zoom with the Node Editor. The mouse scroll wheel can also zoom the Node Editor. You can also use the *f* hotkey to frame the selected nodes.

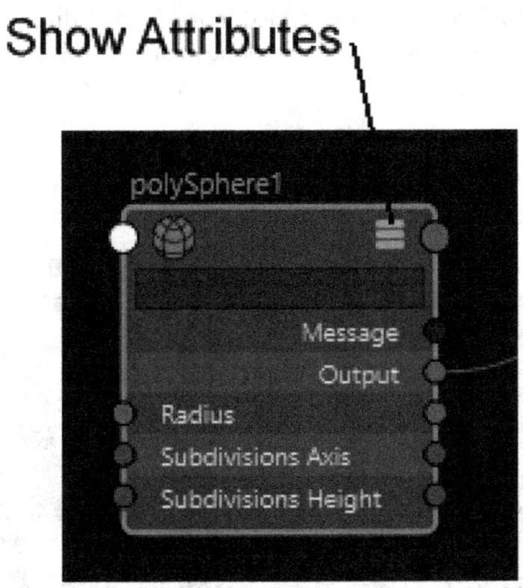

FIGURE 4-36

Node with attributes

Viewing Dependency with Node Editor

Within the Node Editor, the relationships between the different nodes are represented with interconnecting lines. Using the Input and Output Connections buttons, shown in Figure 4-37, you can quickly view any nodes that are upstream and downstream from the selected node. These same buttons can also be found in the Attribute Editor and on the Status Line. The Input and Output Connections button shows all nodes in both directions or the entire tree of nodes of the selected object.

FIGURE 4-37

Input and Output Connections buttons

The real power of the Node Editor is being able to connect attributes between nodes. For example, if you connect the Translate attribute on one object to the Scale attribute on another, then moving the first object will cause the second object to scale like a monster that gets bigger as you get closer.

Adding Nodes

Nodes are added automatically anytime an object is created or a command is executed on an object, but some utility nodes, such as those that work between nodes like a multiplier, need to be added in the Node Editor using the Create Node icon button. This command opens an interface with all the available nodes you can select, as shown in Figure 4-38.

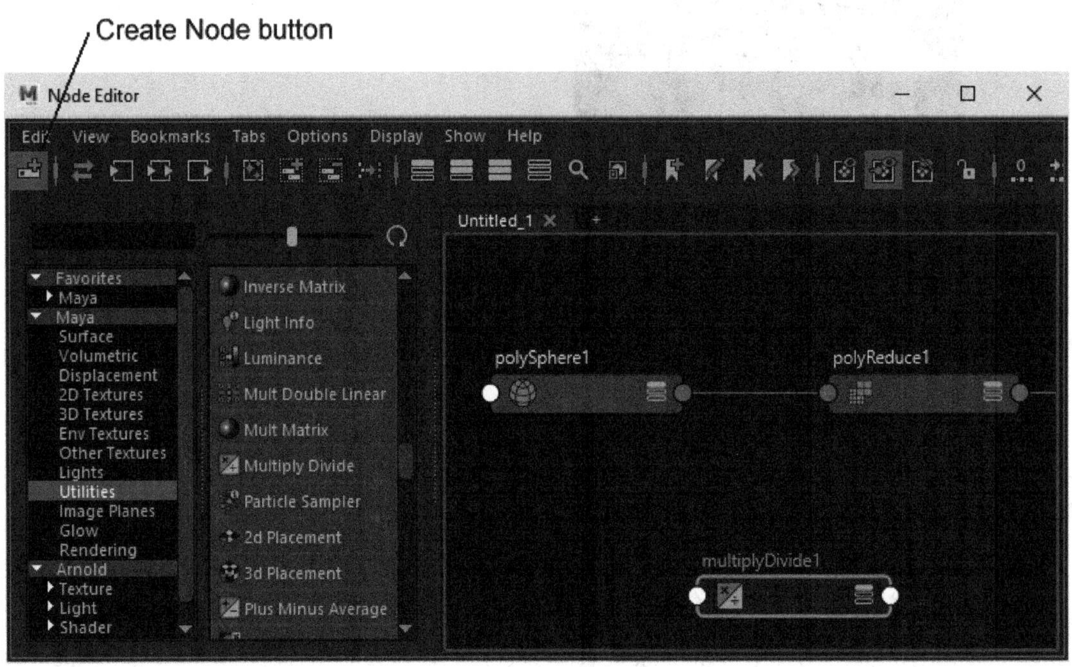

FIGURE 4-38

Create Node button

Connecting Nodes

On the left and right side of the node are input and output ports. The left side is the input and the right side holds the output. To connect two nodes, simply drag from the output of one node to the input of another. This creates a connecting line and feeds the value of the output into the input. For example, in Figure 4-39, the Translate X attribute of the first sphere is connected to the Translate Y attribute of a second sphere. This causes the second sphere to move upward when the first sphere moves in the positive X direction. It also locks (or makes dependent) the Translate Y attribute for the second sphere, which means it cannot be changed.

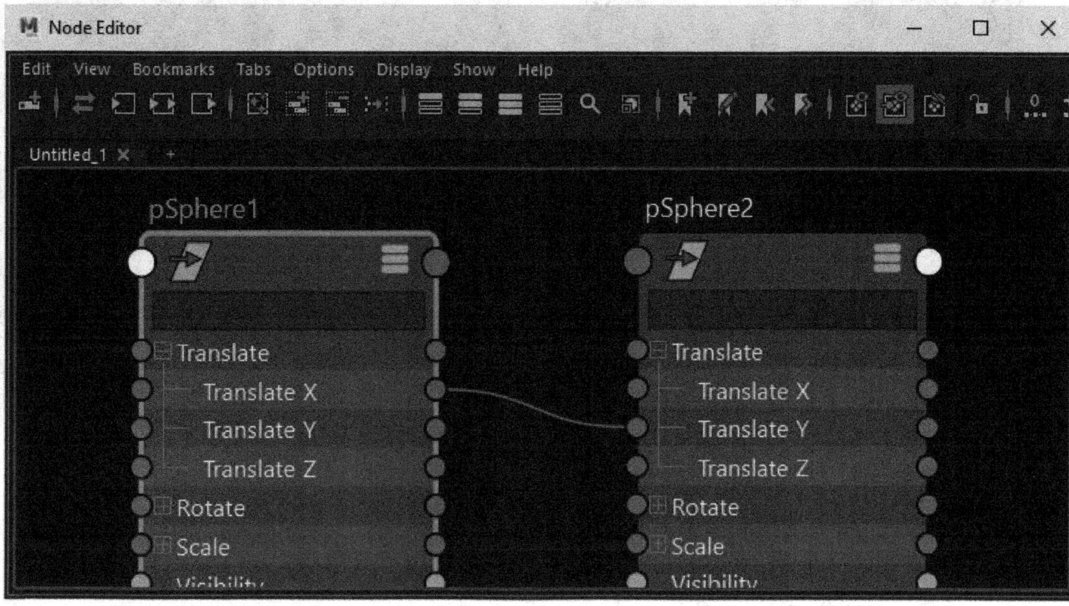

FIGURE 4-39

Connected nodes

Lesson 4.5-Tutorial 1: Explore Dependent Nodes

1. Select the File, Open Scene menu command and select the House shape.mb file to open.
2. Click on the house shape on the left to select it.

   The shape on the left is the curve used to create the extruded shape, which is shown on the right. The curve is light green, and the dependent extrusion is light purple, as shown in Figure 4-40. In the Channel Box, three nodes are visible: the curve object's Transform node, called curve1; the Shape node, called curveShape1; and the Output node, called extrude1. The curve node feeds the extrude output node.

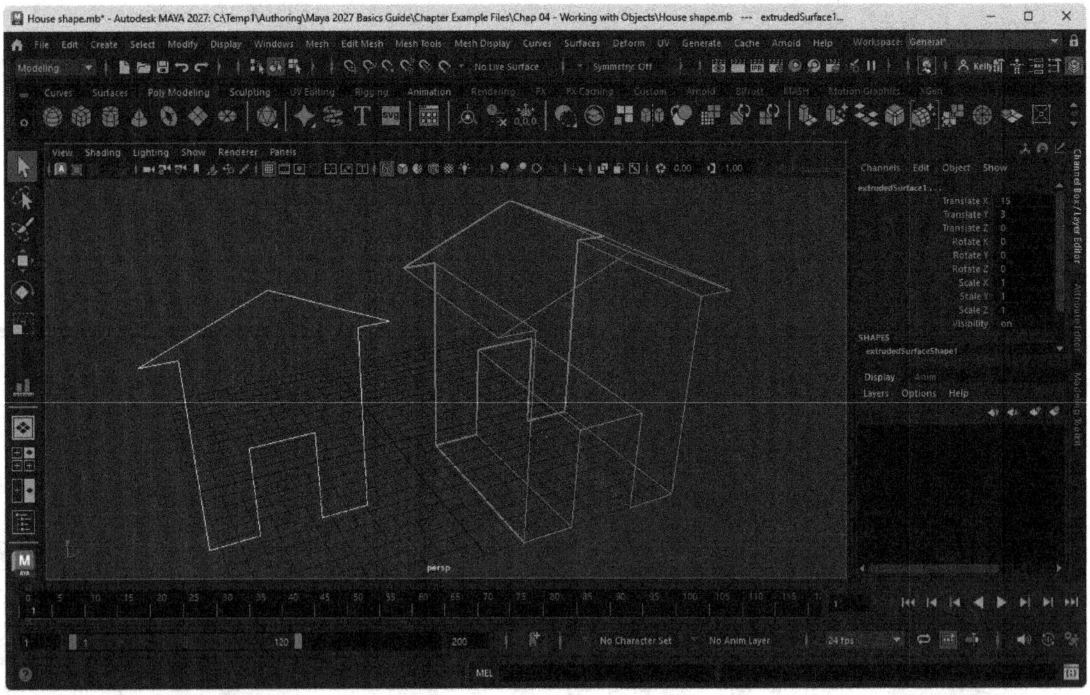

FIGURE 4-40

The extrusion is dependent on the shape.

3. Click on the output node labeled extrude1 in the Channel Box.

   The attributes for this node are displayed.
4. Click on the Select by Component Type button in the Status Line.

   The CVs for the curve are displayed.
5. Select the Move tool in the Toolbox and drag to alter the shape's CVs.

   Changing the curve changes the extruded surface also, as shown in Figure 4-41.
6. Select the File, Save Scene As menu command and save the file as **Modified house shape**.

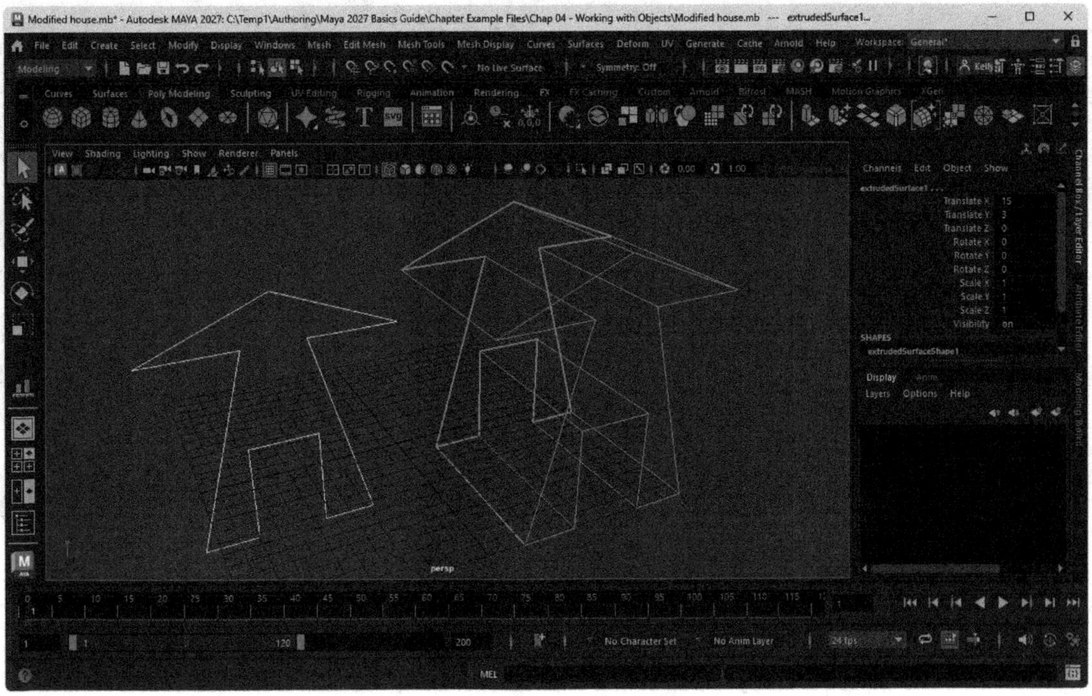

FIGURE 4-41

The modified house

Lesson 4.5-Tutorial 2: Delete Construction History

1. Select the File, Open Scene menu command and select the House shape.mb file to open.
2. Click on the house shape on the right in the Top view panel to select it.
3. Select the Edit, Delete by Type, History menu command.

   The extrusion surface is now independent on the curve on the left.
4. Select the File, Save Scene As menu command and save the file as **Independent house shape**.

Lesson 4.5-Tutorial 3: Building Node Dependency

1. Select the File, Open Scene menu command and select the Shark and net.mb file to open.

   This file has a shark model and a bunch of spheres grouped together named bubbles.
2. Select the shark and the bubble group objects and choose Windows, Node Editor to open the Node Editor.
3. Locate the Shark and Bubbles transform nodes and position them next to one another, then open the attributes for each node. You can hide all the other nodes by selecting them and choosing the Remove Selected Nodes from Graph button.
4. Connect the Output port of the Shark's Translate Z attribute to the Input port of the Plane'sTranslate Y attribute, as shown in Figure 4-42.

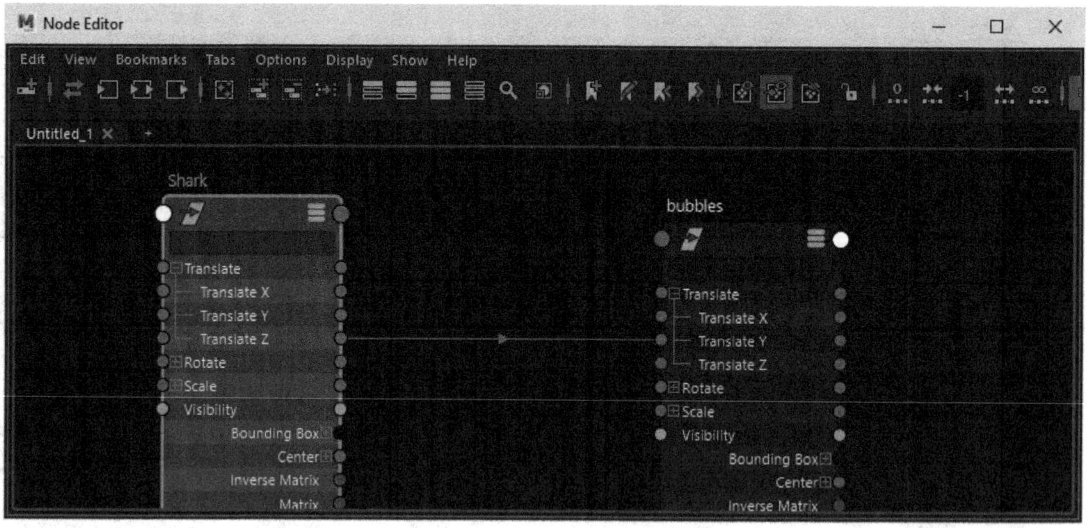

FIGURE 4-42

Two connected nodes in the Node Editor.

5. Select the shark object in the viewport and drag the blue Z handle forward.

   As the shark moves forward, the bubbles move upward, as shown in Figure 4-43.

6. Select the File, Save Scene As menu command and save the file as **Rising bubbles**.

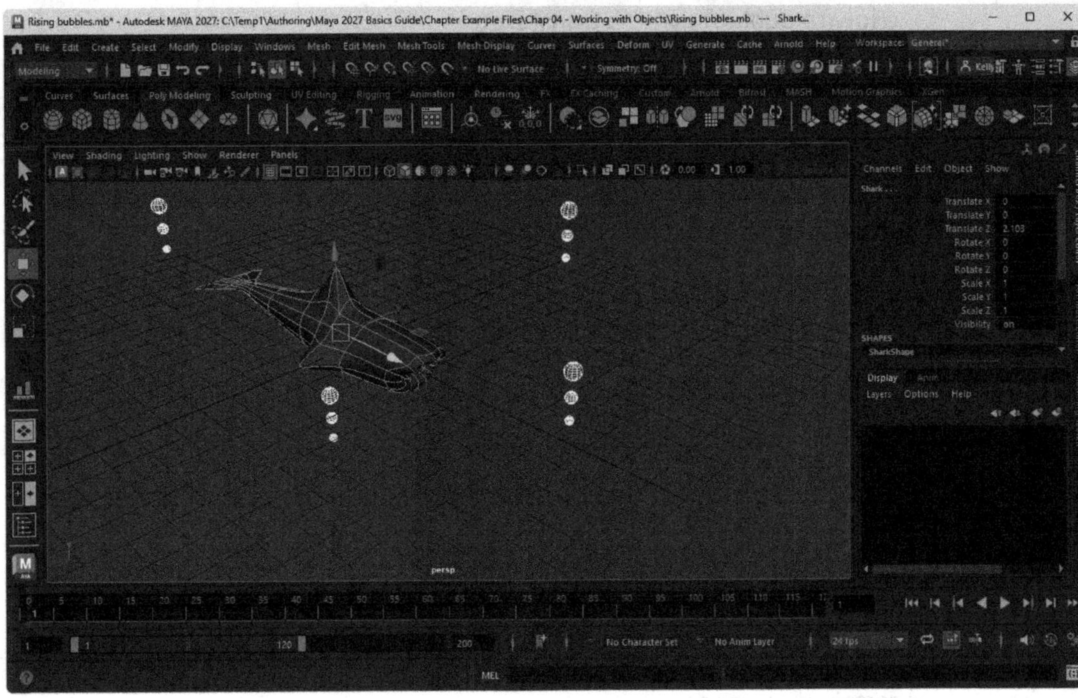

FIGURE 4-43

The bubbles rise as the shark moves forward

Chapter Summary

This chapter covers how to select objects using the Select and Lasso tools. Once you select an object, you can transform and edit it using the Toolbox tools. Components were also introduced, and you learned how to access component mode. You can group several objects and parent them together to create complex objects that move together. The Snap and Align tools control how objects are moved and positioned relative to one another. Finally, the concept of nodes was explained and node representations in the Attribute Editor and the Node Editor were shown along with construction history and connecting nodes.

What You Have Learned

In this chapter, you learned

* How to select objects.
* The importance of the key object.
* How to use selection masks and selection sets.
* How to select object components.
* How to use and move pivot points.
* How to transform objects along an axis or within a plane.
* How to group and parent objects together into hierarchies.

* How to duplicate with a transform.
* How to use grids and snap objects together.
* How to snap to a live object.
* How to align objects.
* How to undo, redo, and repeat commands.
* The various node types.
* How to view nodes in the Attribute Editor and the Node Editor.
* How to edit attributes.
* How to view and delete Construction History.
* How to connect nodes in the Node Editor.

Key Terms From This Chapter

* **Key object.** The last object that is selected. The key object is the base object for certain commands.
* **Selection mask.** A filter that limits the types of objects that can be selected.
* **Selection set.** A selection of objects that are named for quick recall.
* **Components.** The subobjects that make up an entire object. Can include faces, vertices, CVs, and so on.
* **Edge Loop.** The entire length of an edge that runs end to end.
* **Uniform Scaling.** Changing the entire size of an object without changing its shape.
* **Non-Uniform Scaling.** Scaling an object along only one or two axes to change the overall shape of the object.
* **Pivot point.** The point about which the object or objects are rotated.
* **Grouping.** The process of collecting multiple objects together into a named group.
* **Default grid.** An invisible array of points that mark the origin of the scene.
* **Snapping.** The process of automatically moving an object to precisely align with a specific component.
* **Aligning.** The process of moving objects so that certain components have the same position.
* **Node.** A selectable scene container that holds specific attributes.

* **Attributes.** Values that determine the properties of the node.

* **Outliner.** An interface that displays all scene objects as simple nodes.

* **Node Editor.** An interface that shows all scene objects as nodes in a hierarchical display.

* **Construction history.** A list of commands executed to build a scene.

Chapter 5

Creating and Editing Polygon Objects

IN THIS CHAPTER

- **5.1** **Learn normals and manually create polygons.**
- **5.2** **Edit polygons.**
- **5.3** **Use polygon operations.**
- **5.4** **Retopology and smooth polygon edges.**
- **5.5** **Use polygon Booleans and triangulate polygons.**
- **5.6** **Create holes in polygons.**
- **5.7** **Work with edge loops, rings, and borders.**
- **5.8** **Learn the Modeling Toolkit.**
- **5.9** **Model with the Quad Draw Tool.**

Maya can work with several different types of meshes, but polygon meshes have the most features. Polygon surfaces are made from polygons that are positioned edge to edge and smoothed between the edges. You can model anything using polygons, but polygon models make it easier to work with individual faces, making them especially useful for modeling machine parts such as gears.

The components that make up a polygon object include vertices, edges, and faces. Each polygon face also has two sides—one facing inward and one facing outward. A vector called the **normal** extends outward from the outward-facing face. This is the face that is shaded when the polygon is rendered.

Maya includes several polygon primitives, but you can also create polygons manually using the Create Polygon tool. The direction (clockwise or counterclockwise) in which you create a polygon determines the normal's direction.

You can edit polygon objects by moving their components using similar tools that curves and NURBS use. There are also several useful commands found in the Edit Mesh menu that you can use to subdivide, split, cut faces, merge vertices and edges, and delete components. The Edit Mesh menu also includes several polygon operations that you can use to **extrude**, **chamfer**, and **bevel** the polygon components.

Learning to work with normals gives you control over how a polygon object is smoothed and shaded. Boolean operations are used to combine, subtract or find the intersection between two overlapping objects. Triangulation is another aspect of polygon objects that controls how they are rendered. This chapter also covers several methods for creating holes in a polygon surface.

One popular modeling method is to align rows of polygons end to end in constructs called edgeloops. Maya includes selection tools and operations for working with edgeloops, rings and borders.

When modeling with polygon objects, Maya has an advanced panel that places all the necessary tools and commands in a single place. The Modeling Toolkit panel is opened using its button on the right end of the Status Line.

Within the Modeling Toolkit is the Quad Draw tool. This tool lets you work with multiple components at once without switching component modes.

Lesson 5.1: Learn Normals and Manually Create Polygons

Learning to control the normals of a polygon object saves you many headaches down the road. Imagine creating an object, but when you render it, nothing shows up. Misplaced normals might be the problem. This is common when importing objects. Understanding normals is also important as you begin to build polygons by hand. Once you have created a polygon, you can add polygon objects together or detach them.

Understanding Normals

The polygon normal is a hidden vector that defines which side of the polygon should be shaded. For example, a standard cube object would have normals for each face pointing outward to tell the rendering engine that all these faces should be rendered. The opposite sides of each polygon face the interior of the cube and therefore do not need to be rendered.

Determining Normal Direction

When creating a polygon face, the normal is determined by the direction that the vertices are created. Creating vertices in a counterclockwise direction results in an outward pointing normal, and creating vertices in a clockwise direction results in an inward pointing normal. The right-hand rule is an easy way to remember this; just curl the fingers of your right-hand in the direction that the vertices were made and your thumb points in the direction of the resulting normal.

Showing Normals

If some faces on your object aren't displayed in shaded view, you may have some misplaced normals. This is common for imported objects. To see an object's normals, select Display, Polygons, Face Normals. This menu command adds a single vector that extends from the center of each polygon face. Figure 5-1 shows the normals for a polygon sphere. There is also an option to display Vertex Normals.

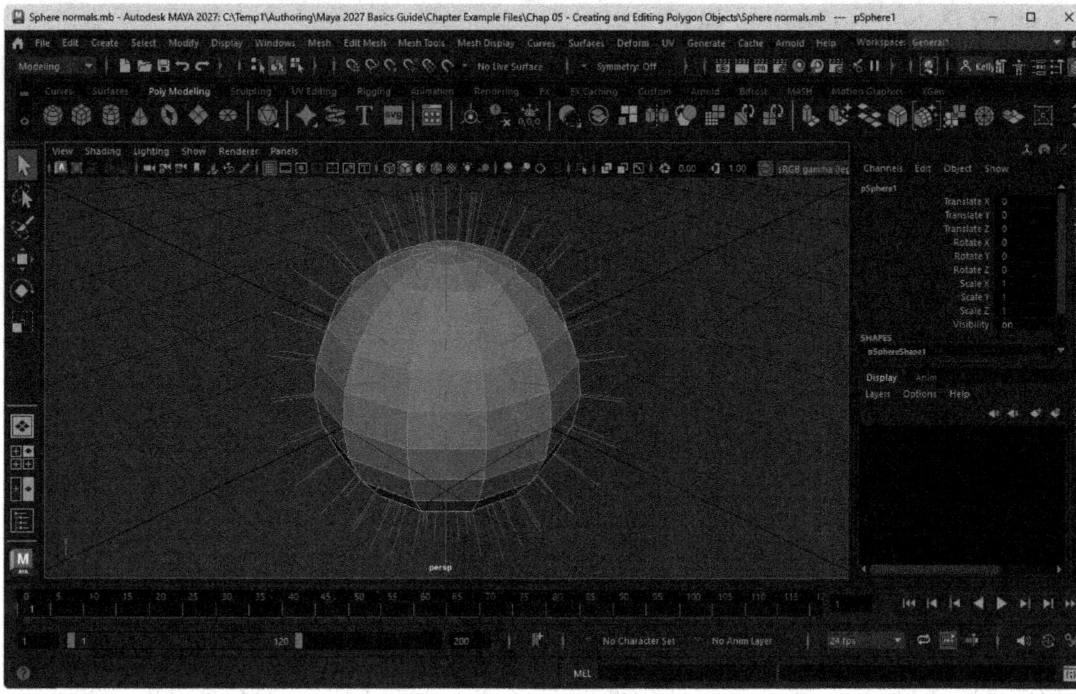

FIGURE 5-1

Normal vectors

Reversing and Controlling Normals

If you select a number of face components, you can reverse their normal direction using the Mesh Display, Reverse menu command. This is useful to repair some polygons on imported objects that are shaded incorrectly. Be aware that reversing all the normals on an object will make it look inside out. Reversing normals is helpful, but it is more likely that you'll want to unify the direction of all of the normals, which you can do using the Mesh Display, Conform menu command. This points all normals in the direction of the majority of the face normals.

Normals define how the light bounces off the surface of an object. Using the Mesh Display, Vertex Normal Edit Tool menu command, you can control the precise direction that the normals point. This is useful to fix some shading anomalies that appear when you render an object. The Mesh Display menu also includes commands to Lock and Unlock Normals.

Softening and Hardening Edges

You can make each selected edge appear hard using the Mesh Display, Soften/Harden menu commands. The Soften Edge command sets the vertex normal on each end of the edge to 180 degrees, which makes the edge appear soft and smooth when rendered. The Harden Edge command sets the vertex normal on each end of the edge to 0 degrees, causing the edge to appear sharp and hard when rendered. Changing the normals with these commands doesn't change the geometry of the object, only how it is rendered.

Using the Vertex Normal Edit Tool

With the Vertex Normal Edit Tool, found in the Mesh Display menu, you can rotate the selected vertices to any direction. This tool places a rotate manipulator that lets you interactively control the vertex normals.

Creating Polygon Objects by Hand

Another way to create polygon objects is with the Mesh Tools, Create Polygon tool. This tool lets you create a series of connected polygons by clicking where the polygon vertices should be located. The polygonal surfaces that are created are *coplanar*, which means that all its vertices are on the same plane. Pressing the Delete key deletes the last vertex. Pressing the Insert key enters a mode in which you can move the last vertex. Press the Insert key again to continue adding vertices. When the polygon is complete, you can press the Enter key to exit the tool or press the Y key to create another polygon.

Tip

It is best to limit polygons to only 3 or 4 vertices. Polygons with more vertices are supported but can cause problems with some polygon editing commands.

Appending to a Polygon

With an existing polygon object selected, you can use the Mesh Tools, Append to Polygon tool. When this tool is selected, the polygon's edges appear thick, as shown in Figure 5-2. Click to select the edge that you want to append to, and then click to position the other vertices that make up the appended polygon. You can use the Delete and Insert keys with this tool, just like with the Create Polygon tool, to delete or edit vertices. When the appended polygon is finished, press the Enter key to exit the tool or the Y key to create more appended polygons. This tool lets you quickly manually build out a custom mesh object with multiple polygons.

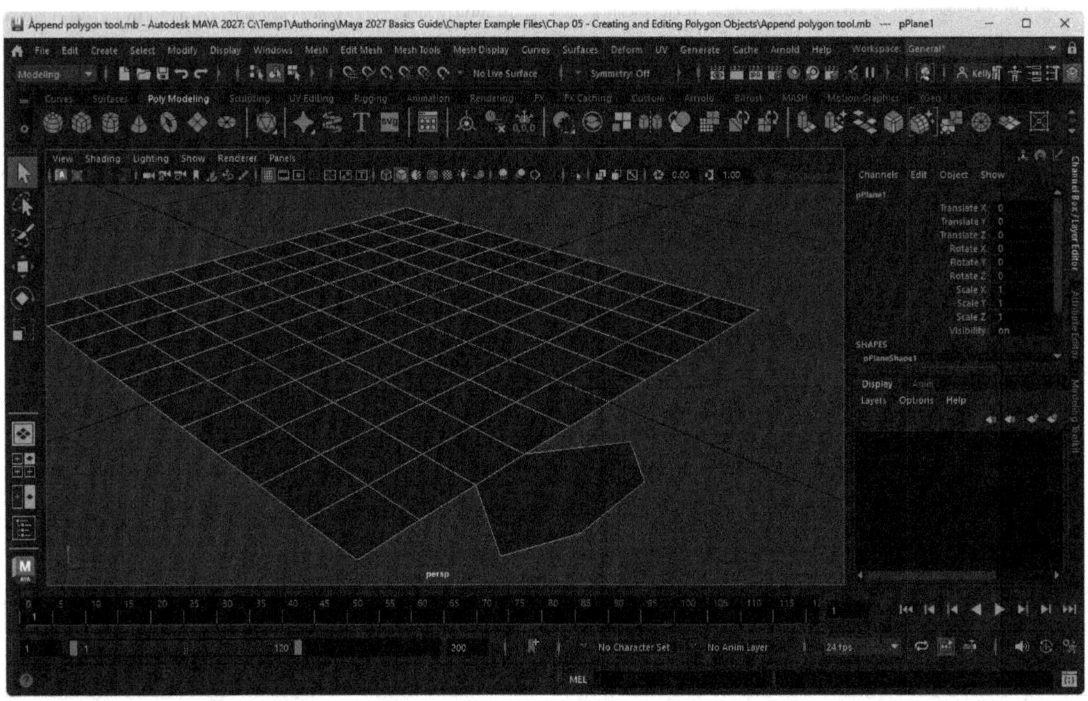

FIGURE 5-2

Append to polygon

Combining Polygons

The Mesh, Combine menu command combines two or more selected polygons together to make a single polygon object. Combined polygons are transformed together. Be aware that combined polygons are not connected edge to edge. Use the Append to Polygon tool to fuse polygons together. You can undo the Combine command with the Mesh, Separate menu command.

Mirroring Polygon Objects

You can quickly create a duplicate copy of the existing polygon object using the Mesh, Mirror menu command. This command only works on objects; it cannot be used on components such as faces, edges, and vertices. The Polygon Mirror Options dialog box lets you specify the mirror direction and whether the mirrored object is merged with the original. Figure 5-3 shows a polygon cone primitive mirrored about its +Y-axis.

Note

```
Use the Cut Geometry option to mirror a portion of
the object. This option places a slicing plane in
the view and mirrors the selected object on each
side of the plane. This is useful for symmetrical
models.
```

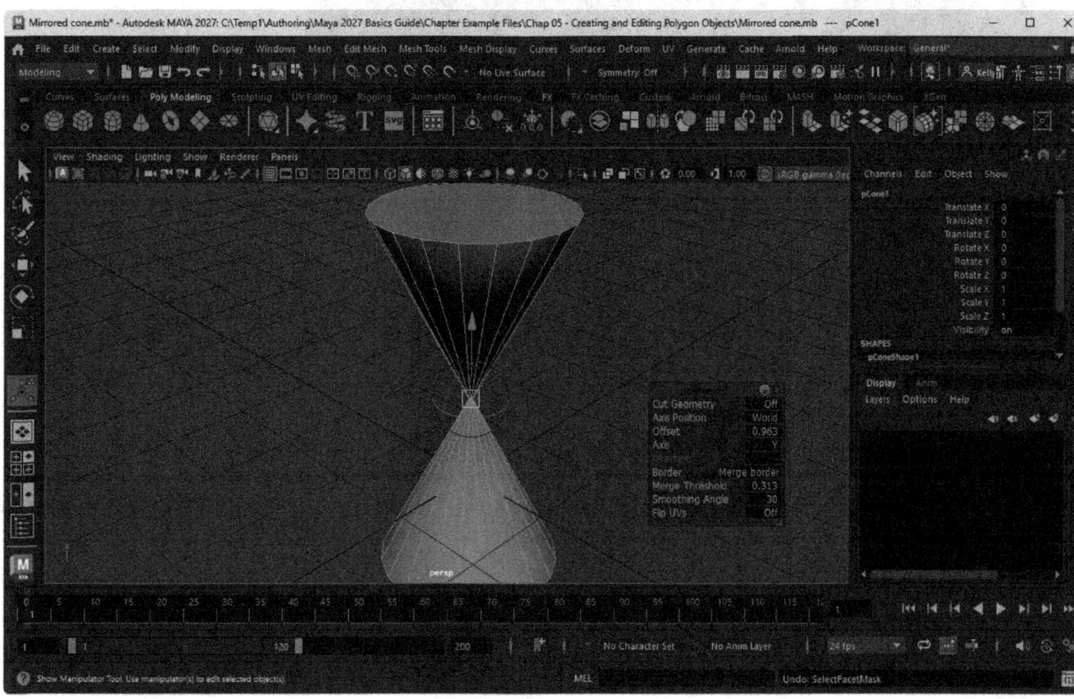

FIGURE 5-3

Mirrored polygon cone primitive

Using In-View Editors

Many of the Polygon Edit features present a small selection of attributes in a small dialog box positioned adjacent to the current object, as shown in Figure 5-4. This dialog box of settings is called an In-View Editor and it provides a quick way to change some of the most common attributes without having to access the Channel Box or the Attribute Editor. Attributes in the In-View Editor can be changed by typing in new values, or by dragging with the middle mouse button just like the Channel Box. The In-View Editor will stay active allowing you to change the settings of the current command until another object is selected or another tool is selected. You can turn off the In-View Editors with the Display, Heads Up Display, In-View Editors menu.

Tip

You can also use the In-View Editor box for newly created polygon primitives by pressing the T hotkey to enable the Show Manipulator Tool.

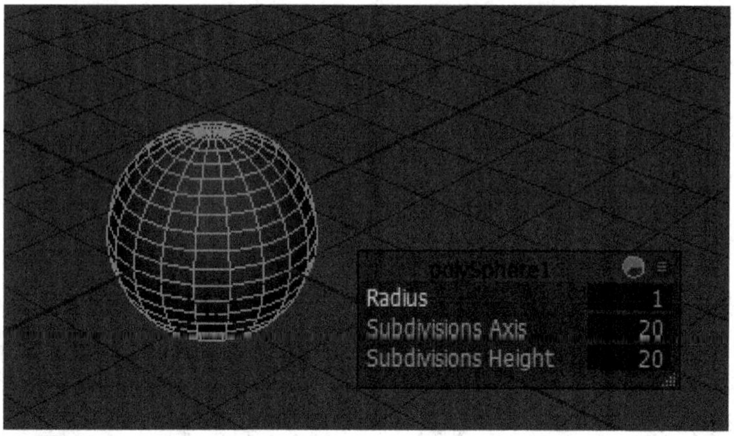

FIGURE 5-4

In-View Editor

Cleaning Up and Reducing Polygons

As you work with polygon objects, there is a good chance that you'll end up with some artifacts that may cause problems, such as non-planar faces, zero-length edges, and so on. You can remove all of these potential problems with the Mesh, Cleanup menu command. If the total number of polygons is too high, you can reduce the number with the Mesh, Reduce menu command. Figure 5-5 shows a polygon sphere primitive that has been reduced once, twice, and three times.

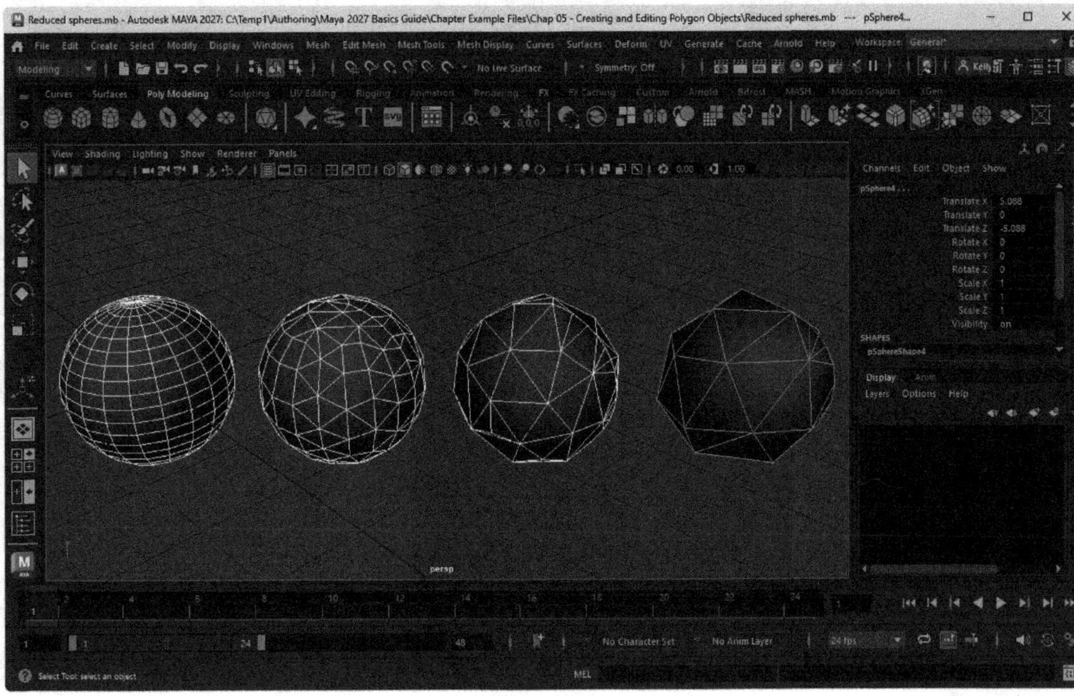

FIGURE 5-5

Reduced sphere primitives

Lesson 5.1-Tutorial 1: Conform Normals

1. Select File, Open Scene and open the Sphere with reversed normals.mb file.
2. Select the sphere and choose the Display, Polygons, Face Normals menu command to display the normals.

   Many of the normals of the sphere are reversed and point inward.
3. With the sphere selected, choose the Mesh Display, Conform menu command.

   The normal for each face is changed to point in the same direction.
4. Select File, Save Scene As and save the file as **Conformed normals.mb**.

Lesson 5.1-Tutorial 2: Create a Polygon

1. Click on the Panel View button from the Quick Layout buttons and select the Top View, then press the space bar to maximize this view.
2. Click the Snap to Grid button in the Status Line.
3. Select the Mesh Tools, Create Polygon menu command.
4. Click symmetrically around the origin five times to create a pentagon shape.
5. Press the Enter key to complete the polygon, as shown in Figure 5-6.
6. Select File, Save Scene As and save the file as **Pentagon.mb**.

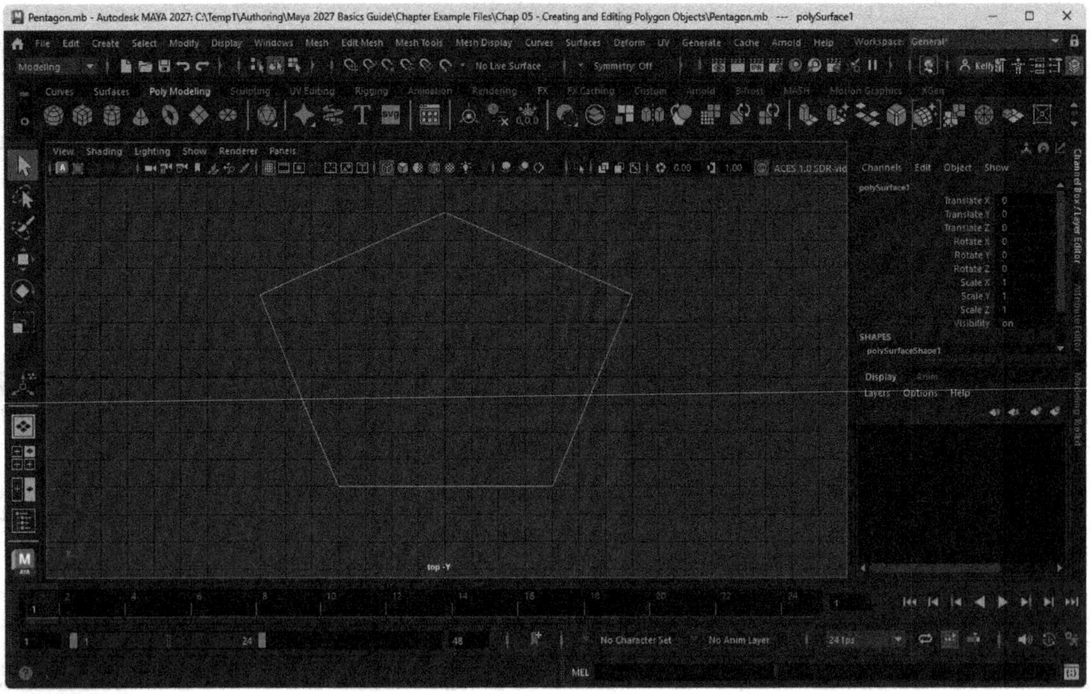

FIGURE 5-6

Manual polygon

Lesson 5.1-Tutorial 3: Append to a Polygon

1. Select the File, Open Scene menu command and open the Pentagon.mb file.
2. With the pentagon shape selected, choose the Mesh Tools, Append to Polygon menu command.

   The lines of the pentagon are thicker.
3. Click on the bottom edge of the pentagon and then click at a point between and under the edge to make the point of a star.
4. Press the Y key to create another attachment.
5. Repeat Steps 3 and 4 for each edge in the pentagon until the star looks like that in Figure 5-7.
6. Select File, Save Scene As and save the file as **Star.mb**.

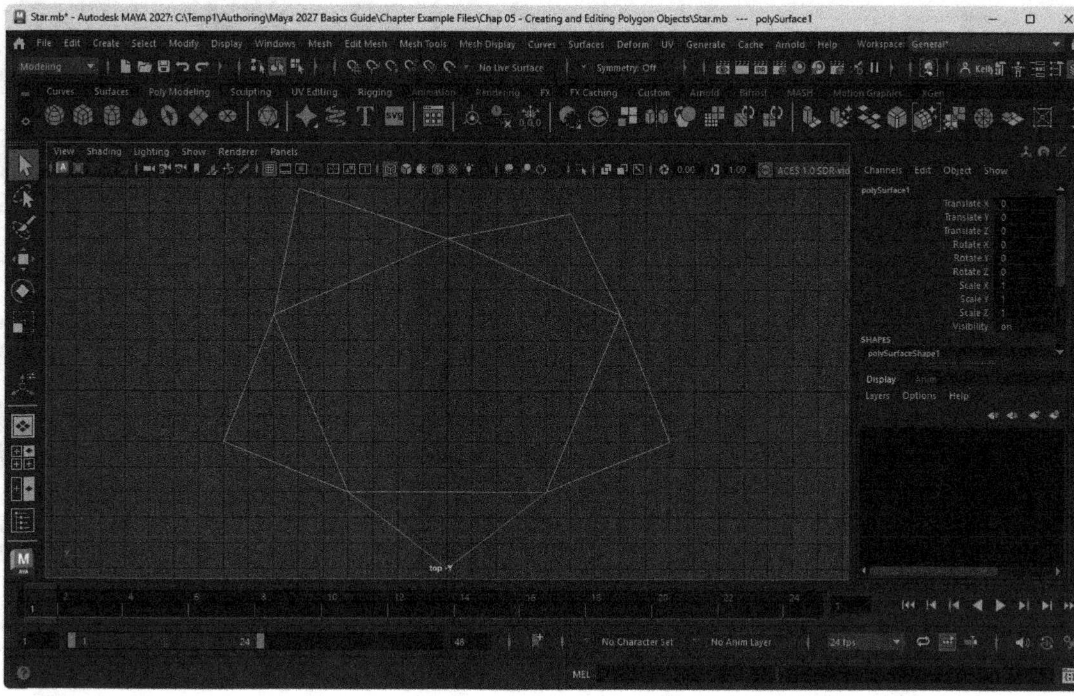

FIGURE 5-7

Polygon star

Lesson 5.1-Tutorial 4: Mirror an Object

1. Select the File, Open Scene menu command and open the Hammer.mb file.
2. Select both parts of the hammer.
3. Select the Mesh, Combine menu command.

   This command combines both hammer parts into a single object.
4. Select the Mesh, Mirror, Options menu command, and in the Polygon Mirror Options dialog box that appears, select the +Z option and click the Mirror button.

   The Mirror Geometry menu command creates a copy of the hammer, as shown in Figure 5-8.
5. Select File, Save Scene As and save the file as **Mirrored hammer.mb**.

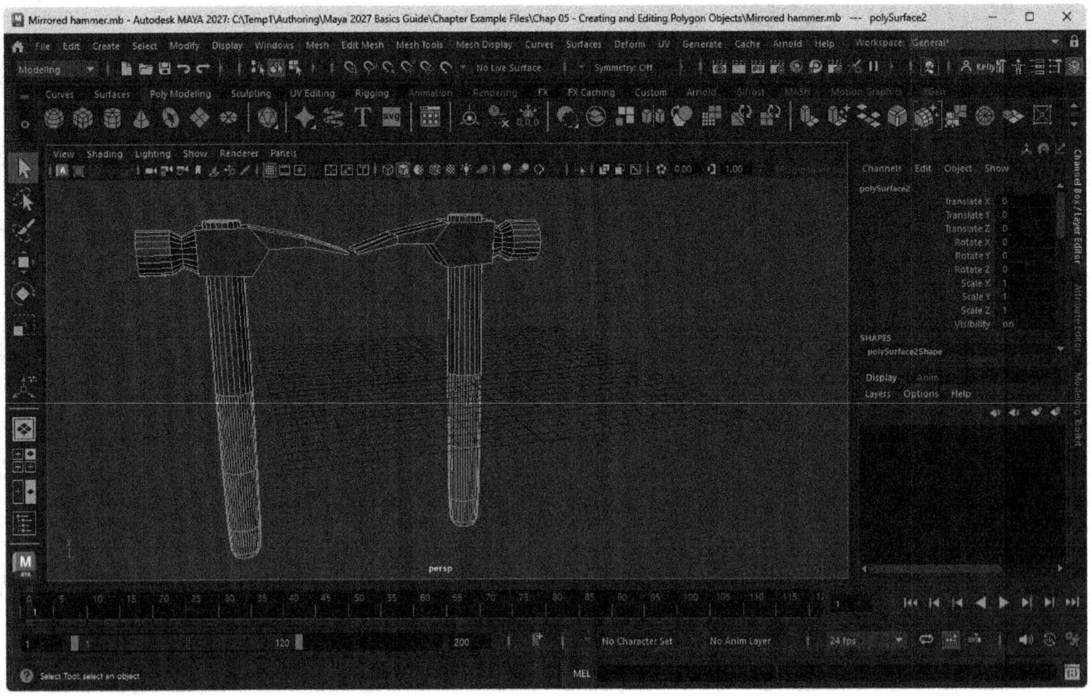

FIGURE 5-8

Mirrored hammer

Lesson 5.2: Edit Polygons

You can edit polygon objects by selecting and transforming their components. In addition to transforming components, the Edit Mesh menu includes many commands for working with polygon components. The Edit Mesh menu groups the menu commands by the components that they work on.

Selecting Polygon Components

When the Select by Components button on the Status Line is enabled, all vertices that make up a polygon are displayed. From the right-click pop-up marking menu, shown in Figure 5-9, you can select to work with vertices, edges, or faces. There is also a Multi option that lets you select different types of components at the same time. Some operations, like the Wedge command, require that you select both a face and an edge component. Holding down the Shift key lets you select several components at once.

The Select menu, shown in Figure 5-10, includes several commands that help you select the exact components to work with. The commands include Grow, Shrink, and Select Contiguous Edges, as well as several commands to convert the current selection between the various component types.

Note

Another common polygon component is UV, which is used to place textures on polygon objects. The UV component is discussed in Chapter 9, "Assigning Materials and Textures."

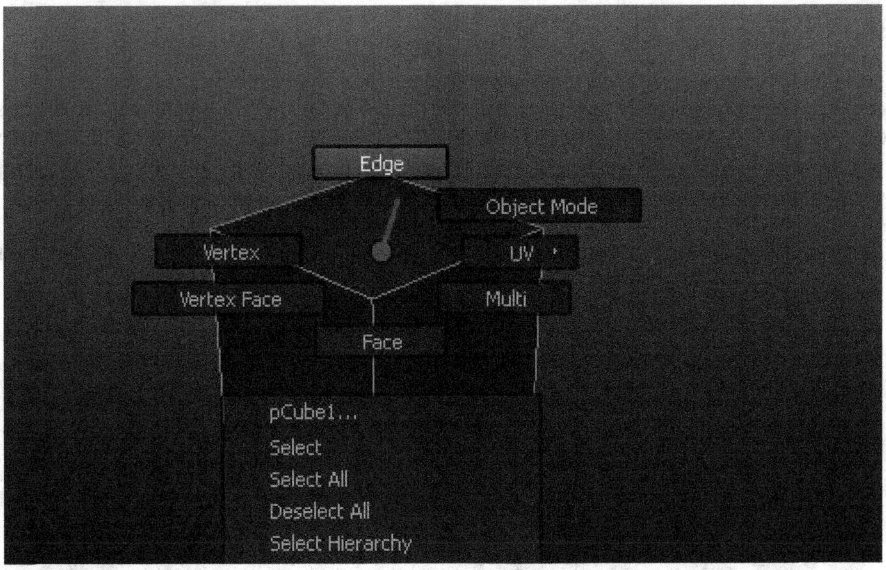

FIGURE 5-9

The polygon marking menu

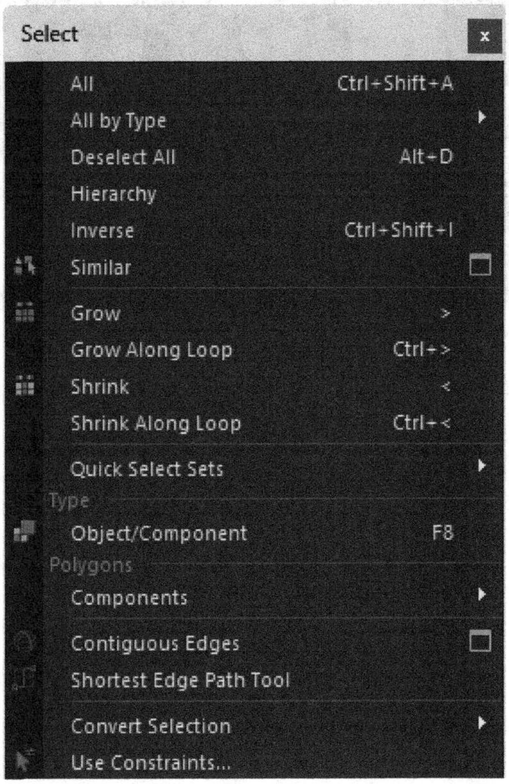

FIGURE 5-10

The Select menu for the Polygons menu set

Subdividing and Splitting Polygon Faces

The real benefit of polygons becomes apparent as many appended polygons are combined to represent a surface. Areas of detail require more polygons than areas of less detail. You can add more polygons to an area by selecting an object's faces or edges and using the Edit Mesh, Add Divisions menu command. This command subdivides all selected faces into Quads or Triangles using the Subdivision Level value. It does this by placing a new vertex in the center of the face and creating a new edge from the midpoint of each existing edge to the center vertex. If an edge is selected, then it is simply divided into several segments by adding more vertices along the edge. Figure 5-11 shows a simple polygon cube that has been duplicated and subdivided to different levels.

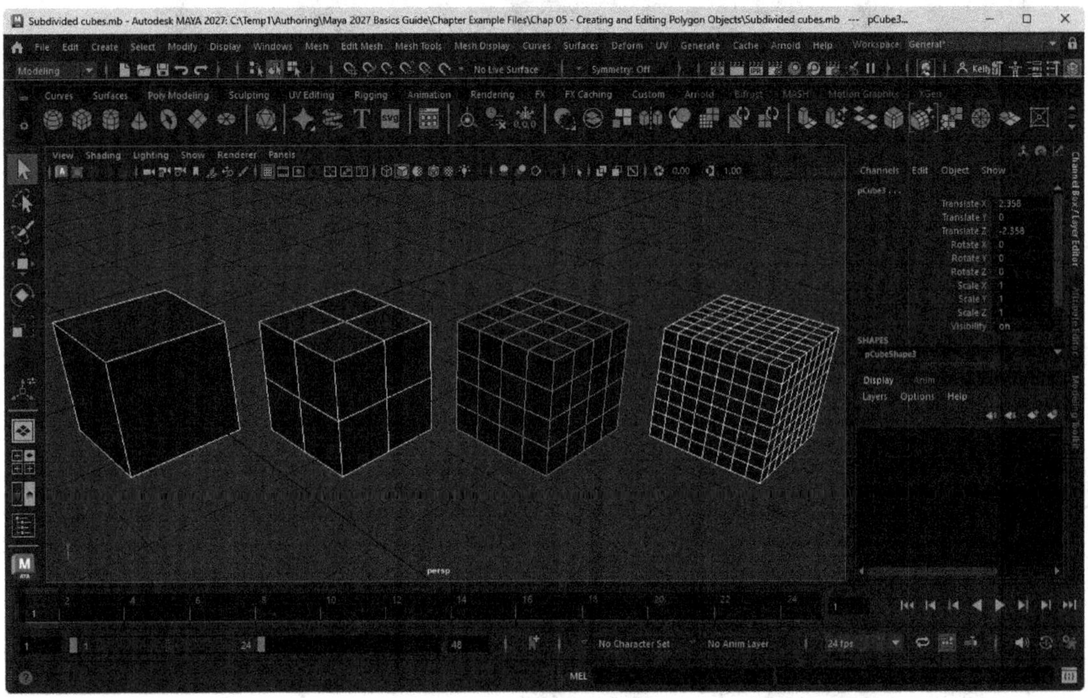

FIGURE 5-11

A subdivided cube

If you want to subdivide a polygon face with more control, you can use the Mesh Tools, Multi-Cut tool. To use this tool, you must first select a polygon object; then click on the edge where you want the split to occur, and then click near a neighboring edge and drag to position exactly where the split is. You can continue to make many splits at a single time by continuing to click near a neighboring edge. Pressing the Delete key deletes the last split point. Pressing the Enter key completes the split operation. Figure 5-12 shows a plane face in the process of being split.

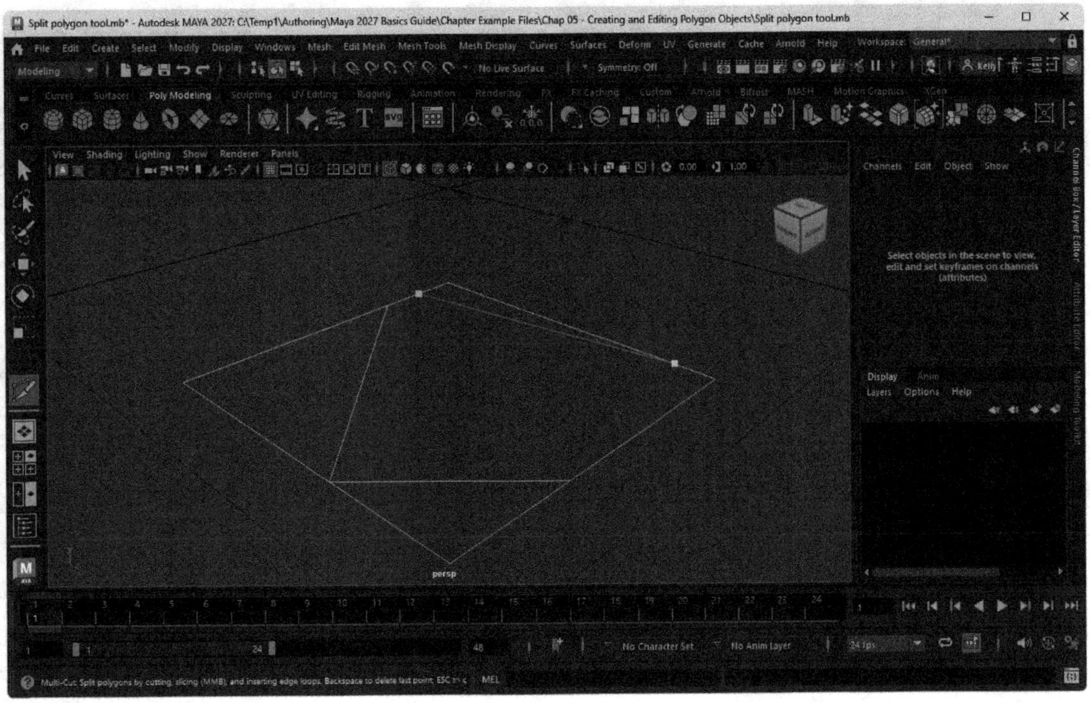

FIGURE 5-12

A split cube face

Cutting Faces

The Mesh Tools, Multi-Cut tool can also be used to cut faces. You'll need to select a polygon object or face to cut before selecting this tool. Once a polygon face or object is selected, you can click at the point where the cut is to be located and drag to the next vertex to create a cut. When you release the mouse, the polygon face is cut where you click, as shown in Figure 5-13.

Tip

```
If you hold down the Shift key while clicking on
an edge, the midpoint of that edge is
automatically selected and highlighted.
```

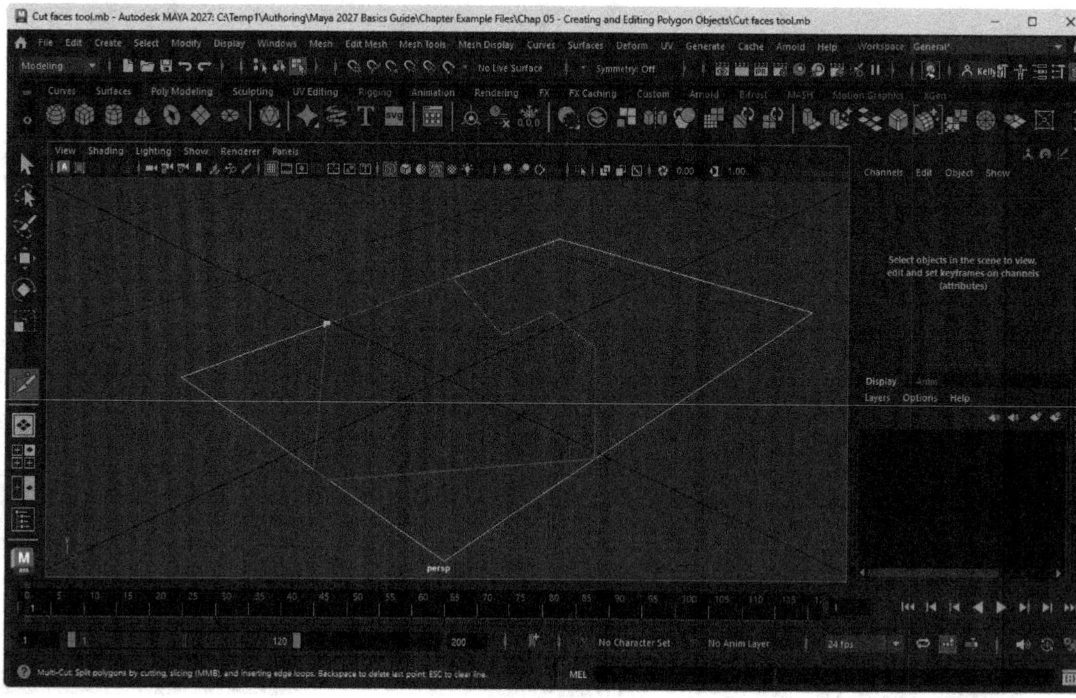

FIGURE 5-13

A cut face

Merging Vertices

You can simplify a polygon by merging its vertices together using the Edit Mesh, Merge tool menu command. The two selected vertices must be within the specified Threshold value and they must belong to two polygons that are combined in the same polygon object. There is also a Merge to Center menu command that merges all the selected vertices to a point located at the center of the selected edges. Figure 5-14 shows four vertices in a plane object that have been merged together with the Merge to Center menu command.

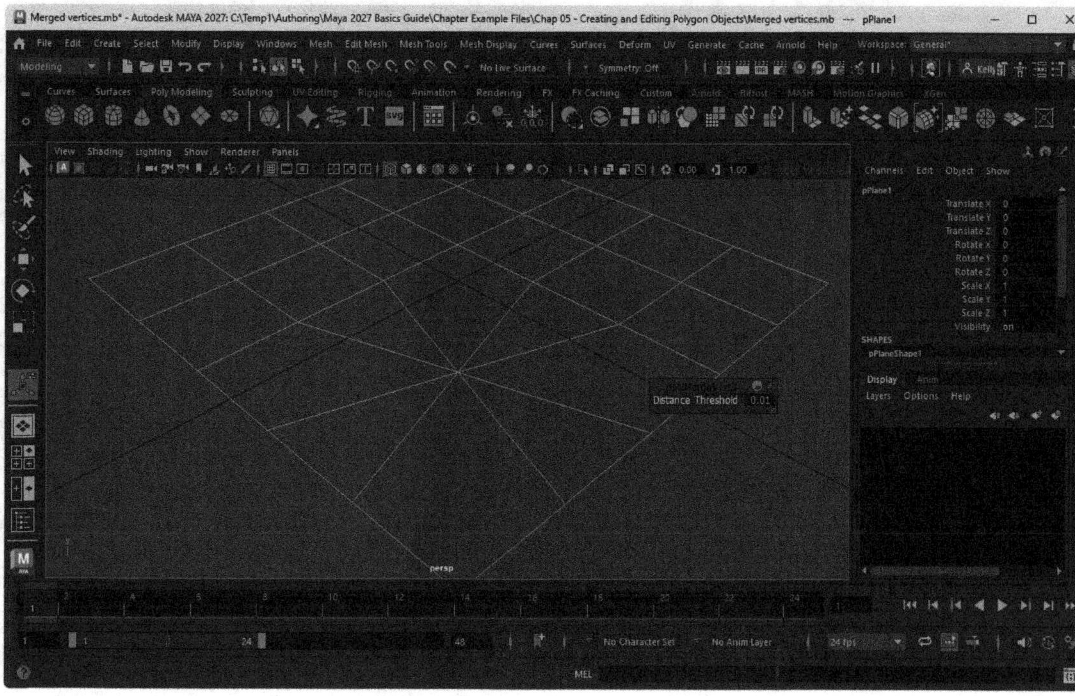

FIGURE 5-14

Merged vertices

Merging and Collapsing Edges

The Edit Mesh, Merge menu command can also be used to merge edges, but they must be within the Threshold value. The Merge to Center menu command works on edges also. Another way to eliminate edges is with the Edit Mesh, Collapse command. The Collapse menu command replaces the selected vertices with a single vertex at its midpoint and connects its adjacent vertices to the new vertex. Figure 5-15 shows two objects where the top edge on the right one has been selected and collapsed.

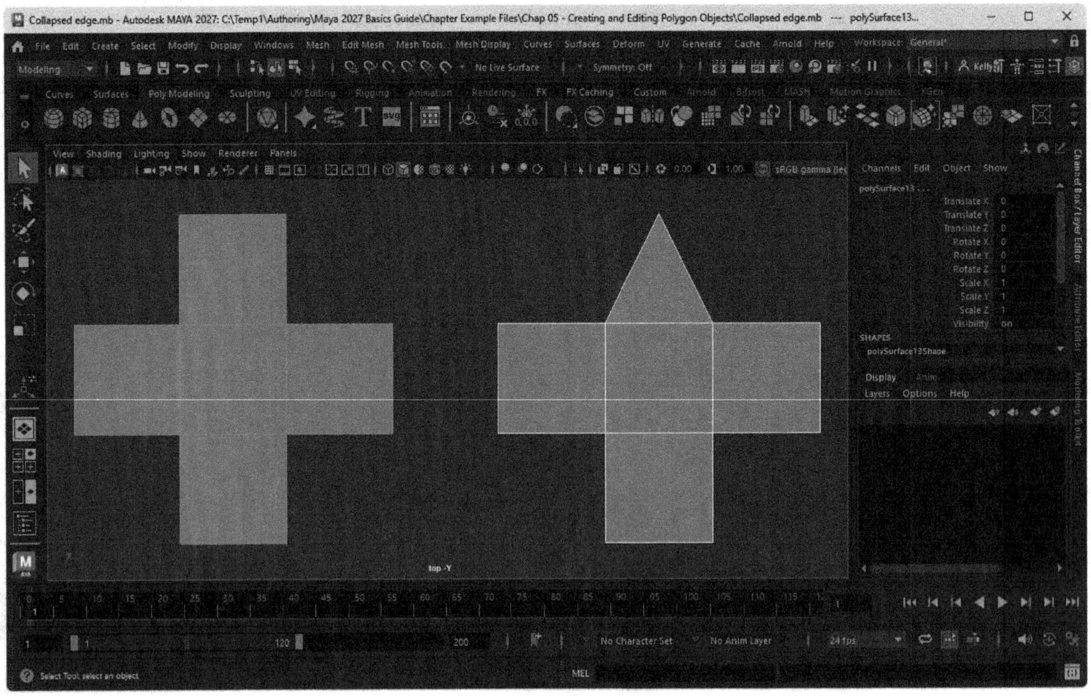

FIGURE 5-15

Merged edges

Bridging Edges

Perhaps the coolest way to connect two edges is with the Edit Mesh, Bridge menu command. This command adds a face between two selected vertices. You can also select options to increase the number of Divisions, the Taper of the new faces and whether it has a Twist to it. Figure 5-16 shows two non-parallel polygons where the middle two edges have been selected and bridged with 4 divisions.

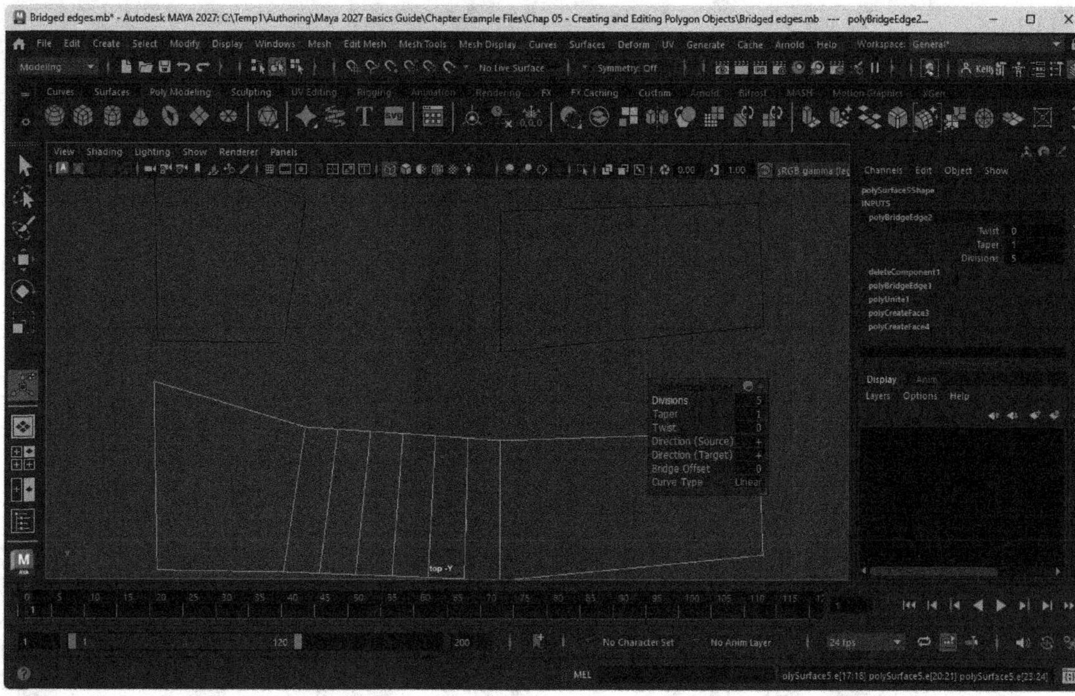

FIGURE 5-16

Bridged edges

Deleting Components

You can select and delete corner vertices and polygon faces with the Delete key, but the Delete key will not work on interior vertices or edges. For those, you can use the Edit Mesh, Delete Edge/Vertex menu command. When an interior vertex is deleted, it also removes the attached edges and when an interior edge is deleted, it also deletes the adjoining vertices. Another method for deleting edges and faces is to select them and use the Edit Mesh, Collapse menu command. This command collapses the selected edges or faces into a single vertex.

Lesson 5.2-Tutorial 1: Create a Mushroom

1. Create a polygon sphere object using the Create, Polygon Primitives, Sphere menu command.
2. Enter a value of 0.5 for the TranslateY value in the Channel Box.
3. Click on the Select by Component Type button in the Status Line, and then right-click and select the Face option from the pop-up marking menu.
4. Drag over the lower half of the sphere in the Front view panel and press the Delete key.
5. Click the Select by Object Type button on the Status Line and choose the Mesh, Fill Hole menu command.

    Half of the sphere faces are deleted, leaving a large open hole. The Fill Hole command replaces the hole with a single polygon.
6. Right-click on the sphere and select Edge from the pop-up marking menu. Then select all of the edges along the bottom of the hemisphere.

Tip

> The easiest way to select all of the bottom edges is to drag over the final row of polygons in the Front view panel and then to hold down the Ctrl/Command key while selecting the final row of faces, leaving just the edges.

7. Select the Scale tool and drag the center handle to reduce the size of the bottom circle. Then move it slightly upward in the Front view panel with the Move tool.
8. Create a polygon cone object using the Create, Polygon Primitives, Cone menu command.
9. Set the ScaleX and ScaleZ values in the Channel Box to 0.25.

   This cone becomes the thin stem for the mushroom, as shown in Figure 5-17.
10. Select File, Save Scene As and save the file as **Mushroom.mb**.

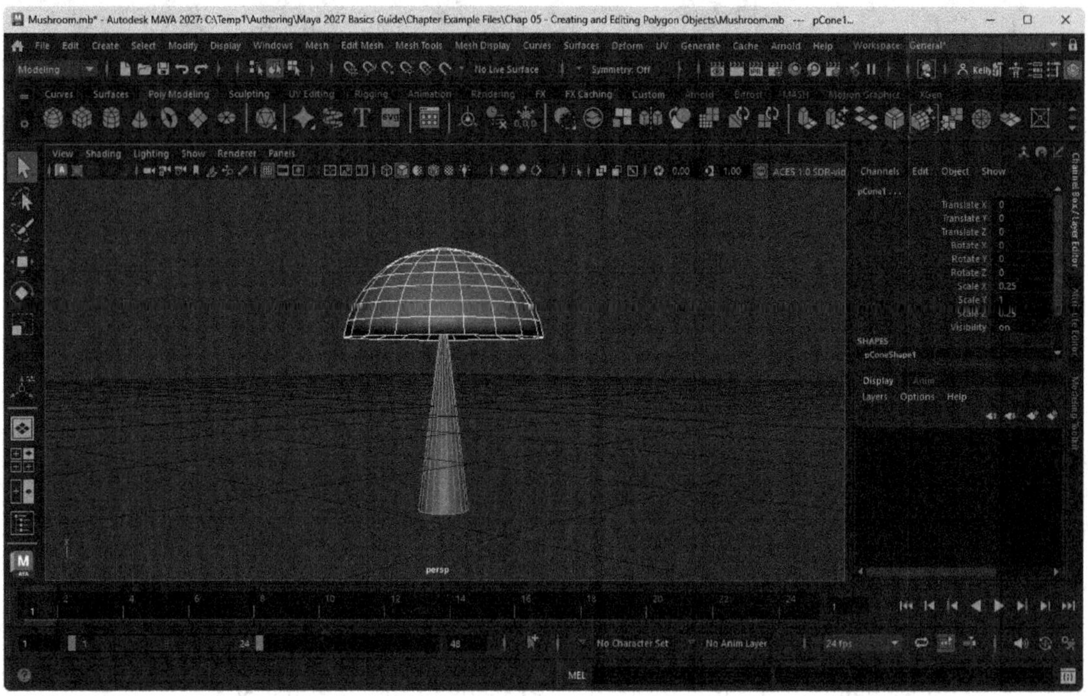

FIGURE 5-17

A polygon mushroom

Lesson 5.2-Tutorial 2: Bridge Edges

1. Select the File, Open Scene menu command and open the Capital M.mb file.

   This file includes shapes at each corner for the letter, 'M'. The shapes are hard to see when not selected, so choose the Select, All menu to see all the objects more clearly.
2. Click on the Select by Component Type button in the Status Line, and then right-click and select the Edge option from the pop-up marking menu.

3. Select the top edge in the lower left square and while holding down the Shift key, also select the bottom left edge in the triangle directly above it. Choose the Edge Mesh, Bridge menu command. Then, set the Divisions to 2 in the In-View Editor box.
4. Select the bottom right edge in the top left triangle and the top left edge in the lower middle triangle while holding down the Shift key, then choose the Edit Mesh, Bridge menu command again.
5. Repeat Steps 3 and 4 for the last two segments of the capital letter, 'M'.

   Figure 5-18 shows the resulting letter.
6. Select File, Save Scene As and save the file as **Bridged capital M.mb**.

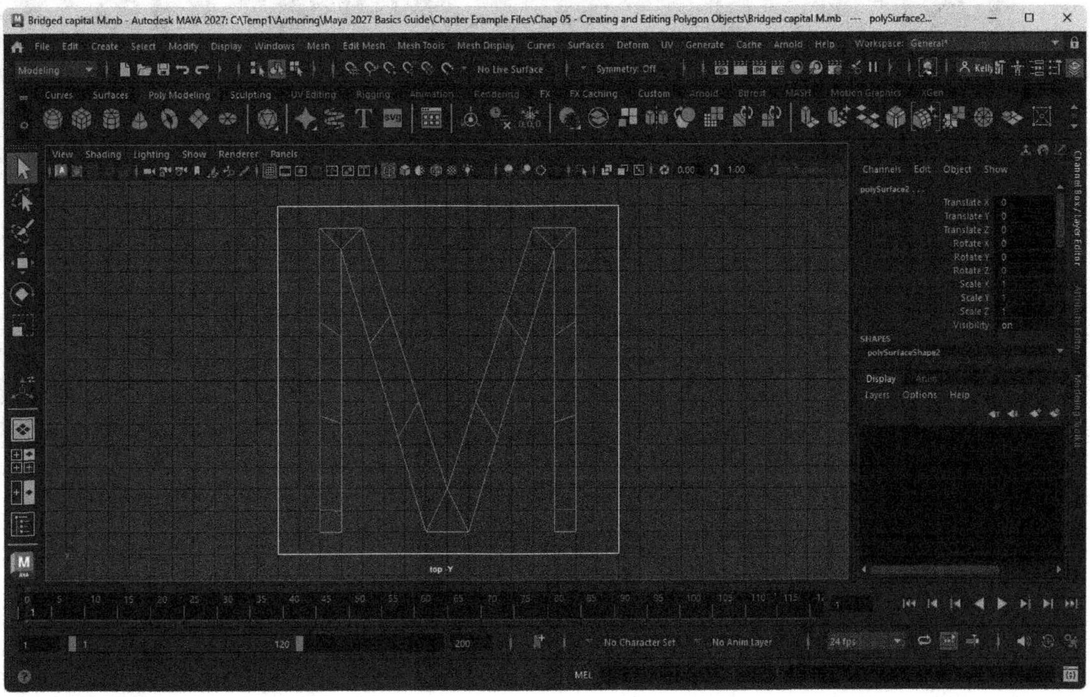

FIGURE 5-18

Letter created with the Bridge command

Lesson 5.2-Tutorial 3: Merge Vertices and Edges

1. Select the File, Open Scene menu command and open the Compass.mb file.
2. Select the top square, right-click, and select Vertex from the pop-up marking menu.
3. Drag over the top two vertices and select the Edit Mesh, Merge to Center menu command.

   This command combines the top two vertices, making the square into a triangle that points away from the center square.
4. Repeat Steps 2 and 3 for all the outer squares.
5. Right-click and select the Object Mode option from the pop-up marking menu. Then, choose all the polygon shapes and choose the Mesh, Combine menu command.
6. Select the Edit Mesh, Merge, Options menu command and set the Threshold value to 6.0, and then click the Apply button.

All of the edges within the Threshold value are merged, as shown in Figure 5-19.

7. Select File, Save Scene As and save the file as **Merged compass.mb**.

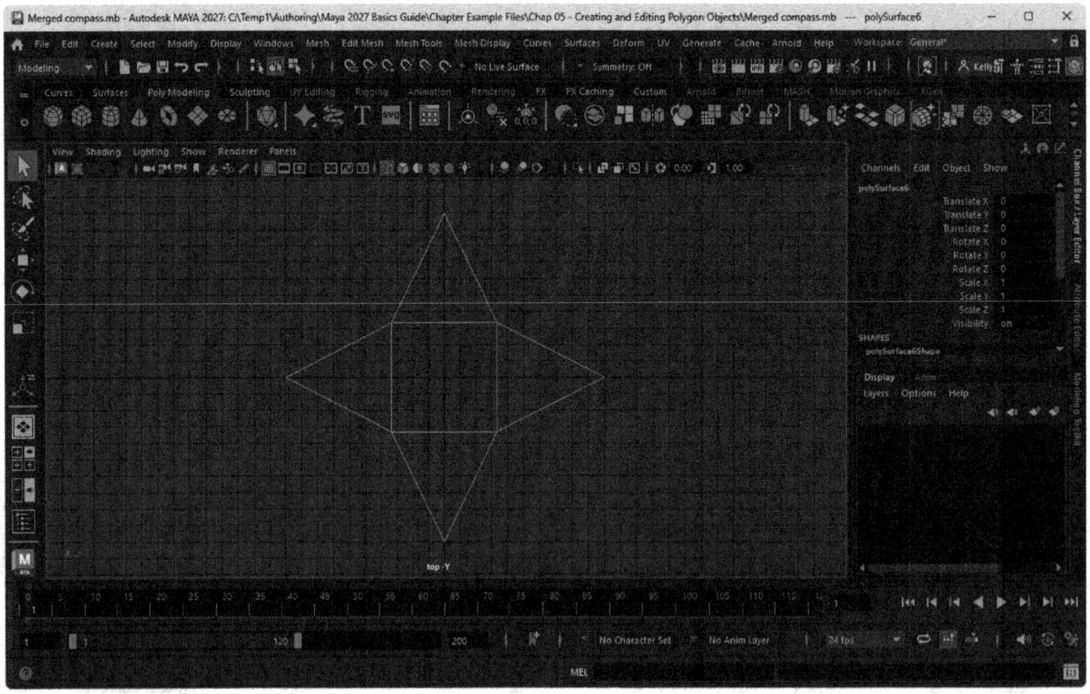

FIGURE 5-19

A merged compass

Lesson 5.3: Use Polygon Operations

With certain polygon components selected, you can use one of the many polygon operations found in the Edit Mesh menu. These operations let you extrude, chamfer, and bevel the selected components.

Tip

When accessing most of the polygon operations found in the Edit Mesh menu, a pop-up options control appears with settings for the operation that you can change without having to open the Options dialog box.

Duplicating Faces

If a polygon face or several faces are selected, you can use the Edit Mesh, Duplicate menu command to create a copy of the selected faces. The Duplicate Faces options dialog box lets you specify an offset value that you can use to offset the copy within the selected face, as shown in Figure 5-20. You can also define the transform values or a direction for the duplicated faces, or you can use the manipulator. The options dialog box also includes a Random setting that you can use to randomize the faces.

Tip

The Edit Mesh, Extract menu command works just like the Duplicate Faces menu command except that a copy isn't made and the selected faces are separated from the object.

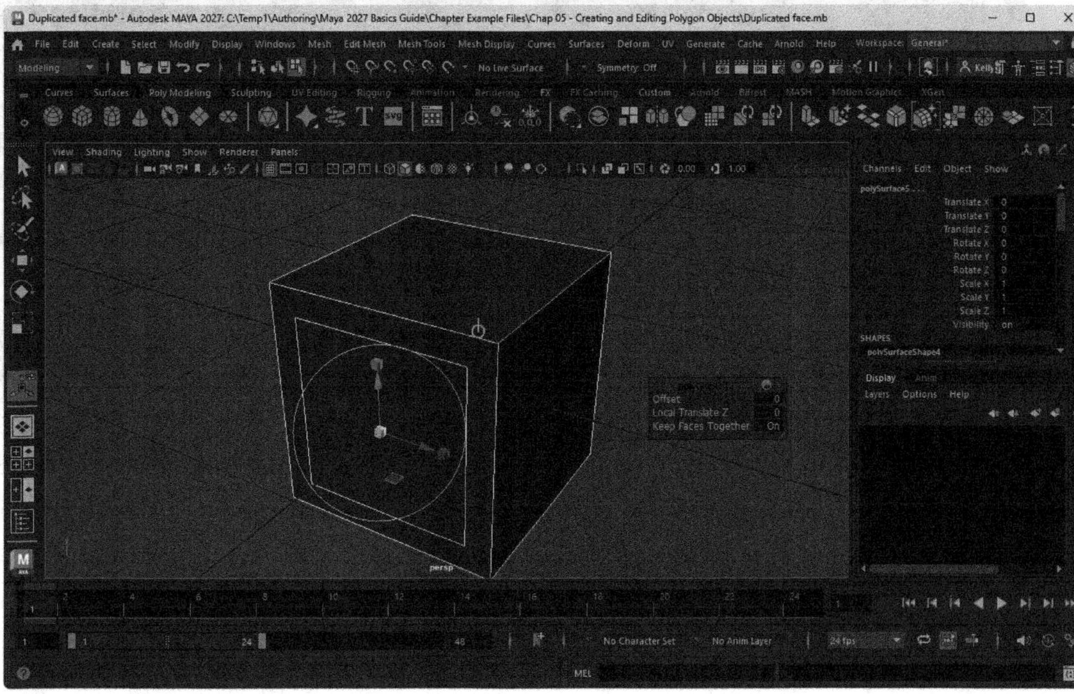

FIGURE 5-20

Duplicated face

Extruding Components

The Edit Mesh, Extrude menu command raises the selected component along its normal a given length and creates new faces that equal a specified width value. This command can be used on vertices, edges and faces. Figure 5-21 shows a single vertex, edge and face of a plane object extruded.

Tip

If the Shift+Drag setting is enabled in the Tool Settings dialog box for the transform tools, then you can extrude the selected component by simply holding down the Shift key while dragging with one of the transform tools.

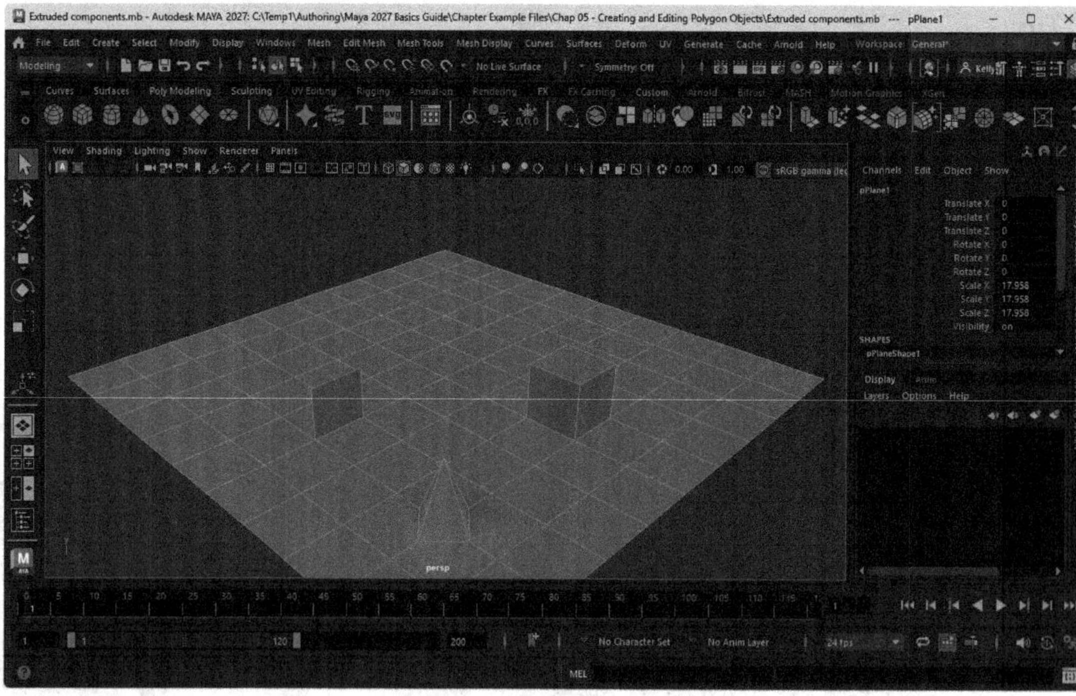

FIGURE 5-21

An extruded vertex, edge and face

Each has options for setting the Length and Width of the extrusion. You can also set the number of Divisions to use. For edges and faces, you can specify Offset, Thickness, Taper, and Twist values. When the Extrude command is applied to a selection of edges or faces, a manipulator appears. With this manipulator, you can move and scale the extruded edge or face. Figure 5-22 shows several extruded faces rising from a plane object with the option to Keep Faces Together turned off and the Taper value set to 0.

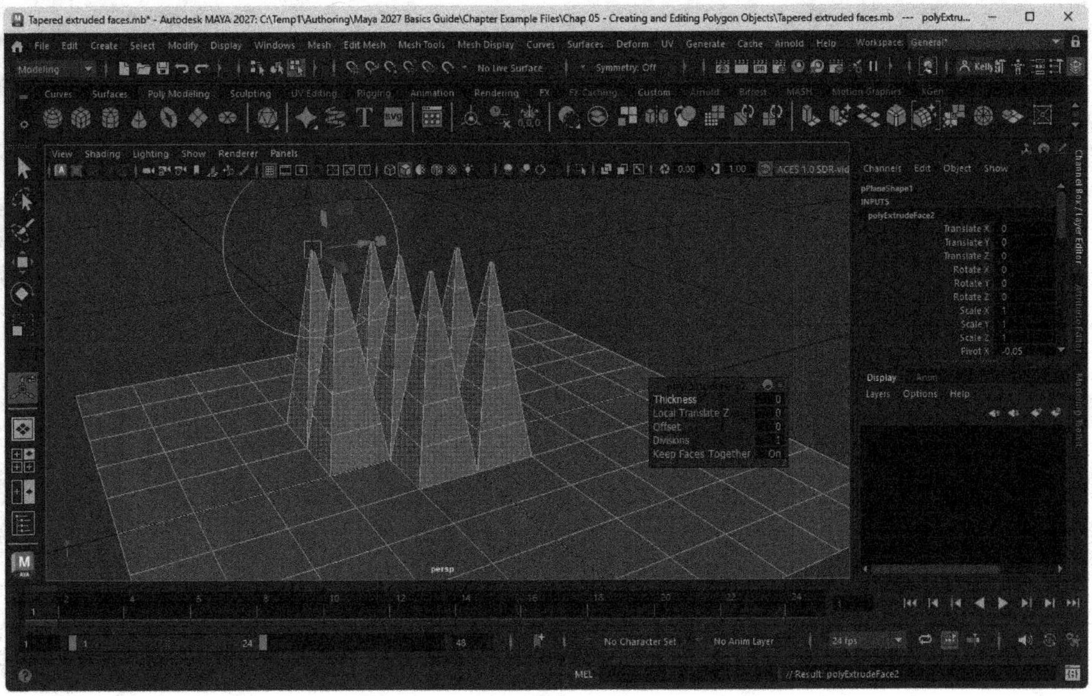

FIGURE 5-22

Several extruded faces tapered independently

Using Smart Extrude

When extruding a polygon face above the surface, new side faces are automatically added to extruded face, but if you push the face into the object, the sides remain causing an indented face, which generally requires some clean up. A cleaner way to extrude is with the Edit Mesh, Smart Extrude menu command. Figure 5-23 shows the two Extrude methods. Notice how the one on the right simply pushed through the object and removed the polygons to make a hole.

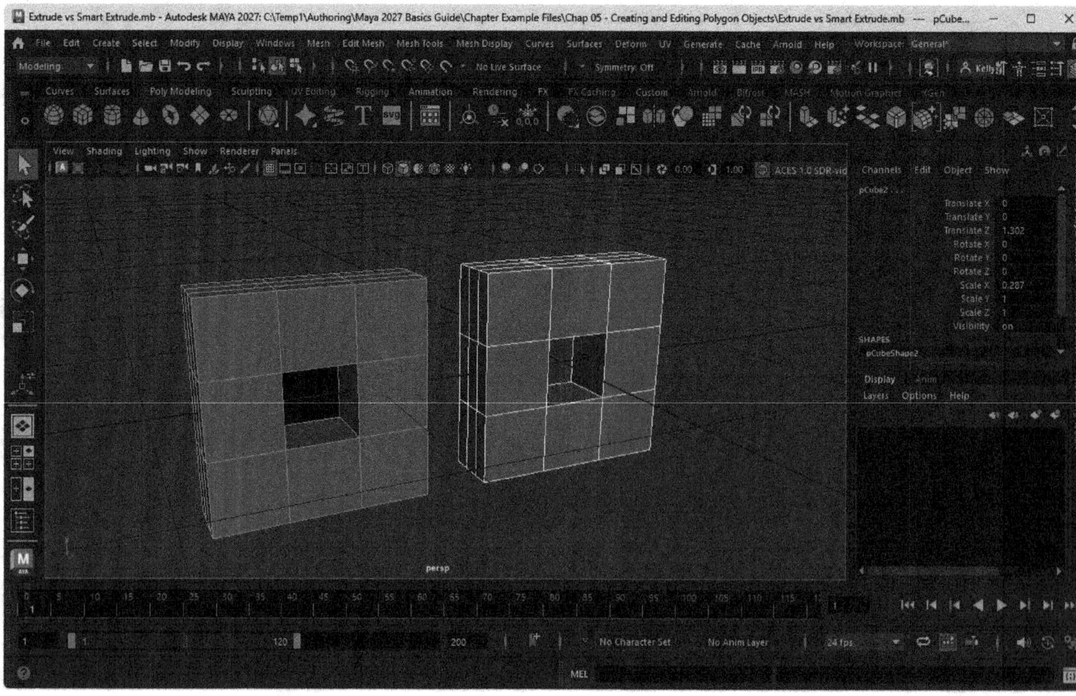

FIGURE 5-23

Standard Extrude (left) versus Smart Extrude (right)

The Smart Extrude feature will only work on face subobject selections. When a face is extruded into another part of the current object, the faces are combined and any extra faces are automatically removed. This provides a quick and easy way to edit an object by pushing and pulling faces in each direction.

Tip

After using the Smart Extrude tool, you can press the G hotkey to reset the tool using the same axes orientation.

Chamfer a Vertex

Chamfering a vertex replaces each vertex with a face and connects the face component with the other adjacent faces. This is useful when you need to round an object. The Edit Mesh, Chamfer Vertices, Options dialog box includes an option to delete the face and to specify the width of the face that is created in place of the vertex. Figure 5-24 shows a cube object with each vertex that has been chamfered.

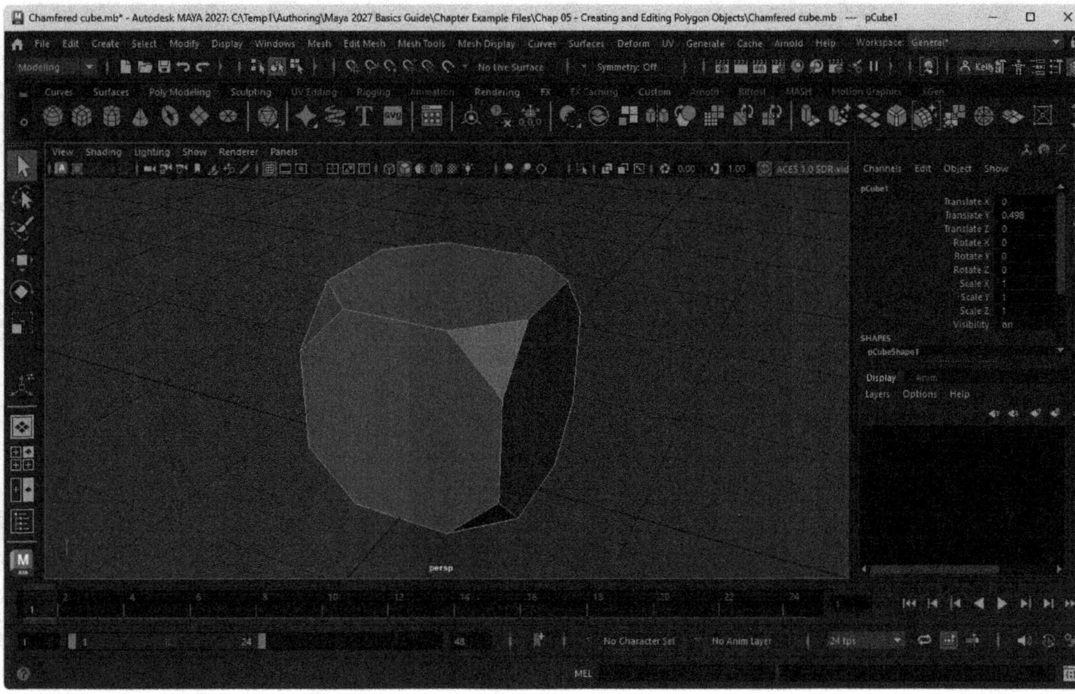

FIGURE 5-24

A chamfered vertex

Beveling an Edge

A bevel operation is similar to a chamfer, except it is applied to edges. You can make an edge into a face with the Edit Mesh, Bevel menu command. In the Bevel Options dialog box, you can specify Width, which is how far away from the edge the faces extend and Segments, which is the number of faces to use to replace the edge. If multiple segments are used to create the bevel, you can have them round the bevel outward with a Depth value of 1 or invert the bevel with a Depth value of -1. Figure 5-25 shows a single edge of a cube object that has been beveled. The left most cube is beveled with a single segment and a Width of 0.5, the second cube is beveled using three segments, the third cube reduces the Width value to 0.1 with a Depth of 1 and the right cube has a Depth value of -1 causing the inverted bevel.

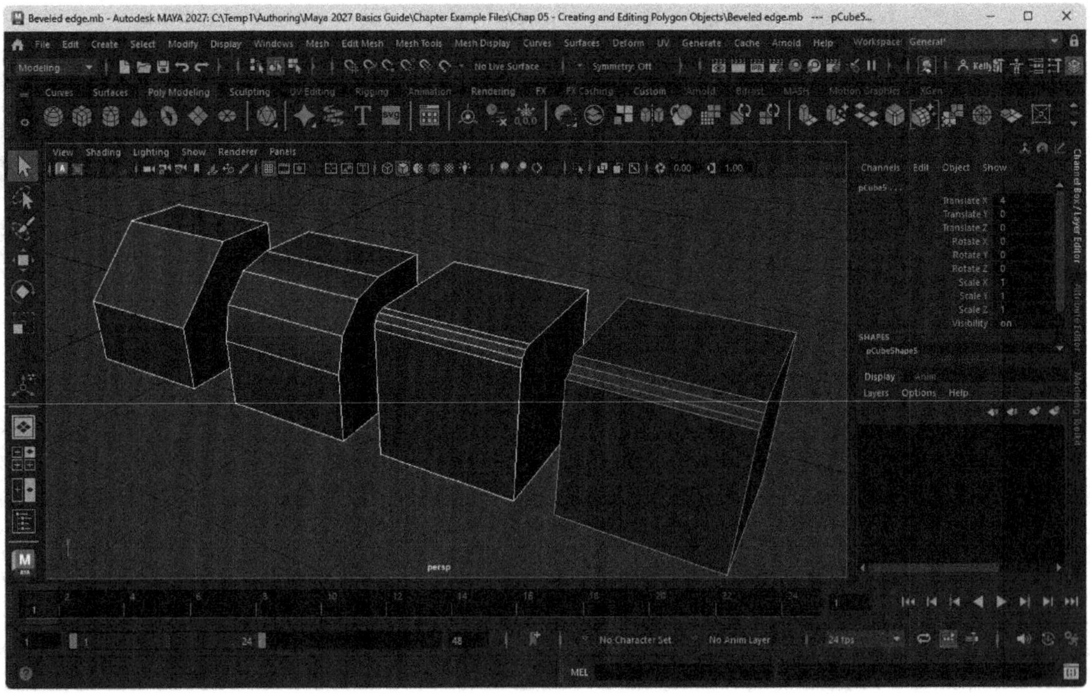

FIGURE 5-25

A beveled edge

If the entire object is selected, then all edges are beveled with the Bevel command, or you can select only those edges that you want to bevel. The Bevel Options dialog box also has an option to bevel only the Hard Edges in the object, or you can specify a Smoothing Angle that only bevels edges that have an angle between adjacent faces that is greater than the defined Smoothing Angle.

Using Smart Bevel

The Edit Mesh, Smart Bevel menu command lets you set the transition Width value between two intersecting surfaces. This results in a smoother result. Smart Bevel is best used following a Boolean operation where object surfaces are combined. Figure 5-26 shows a simple cylinder that has been combined onto the top of a cube with a Smart Bevel. The Width value sets how far from the original edge the bevel extends. The Segments value sets the number of edges to add to the bevel. The Depth value sets how tight the bevel follows the original objects.

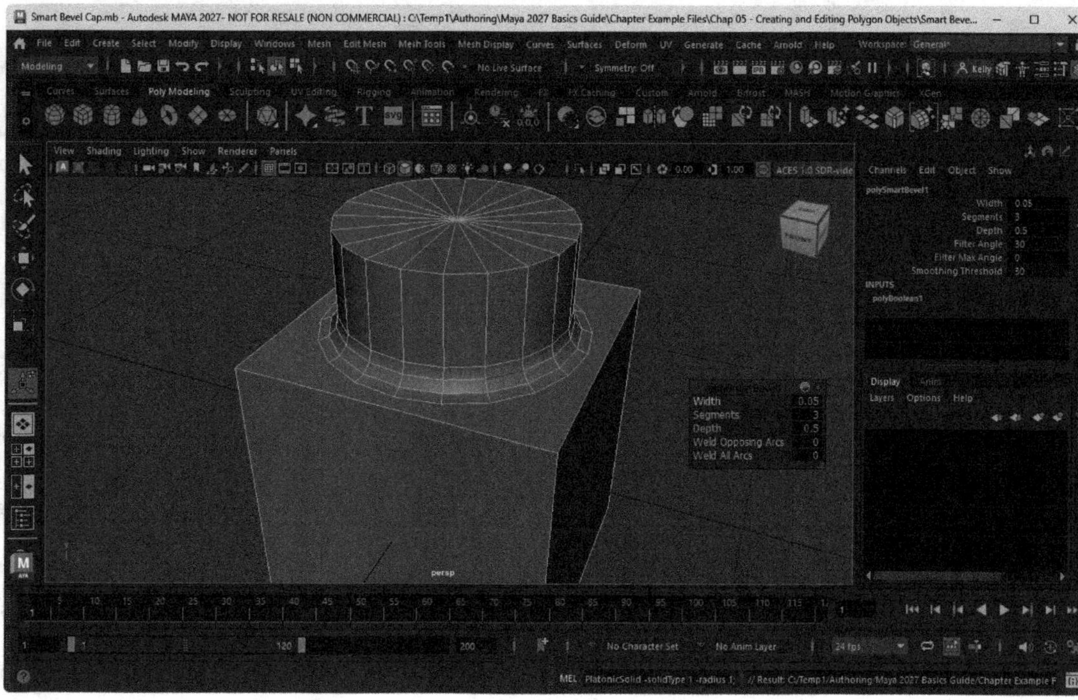

FIGURE 5-26

Smart Bevel provides a smooth transition

Poking a Face

The Edit Mesh, Poke menu command adds a vertex to the center of the selected polygon face and subdivides the face using this new vertex. The vertex is also raised from the surface as if someone poked it from underneath. This operation is similar to the Extrude Vertex menu command, except it is applied to face components. Figure 5-27 shows a single face of a plane object that has been poked.

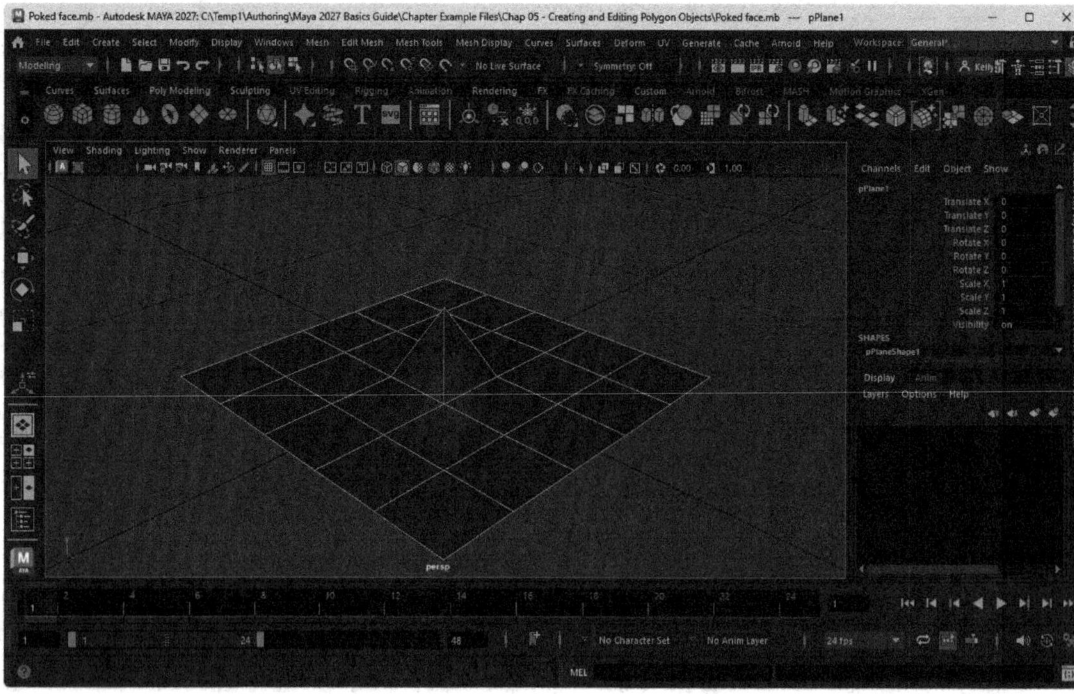

FIGURE 5-27

A poked face

Creating a Wedge

The Edit Mesh, Wedge menu command rotates a selected face using a selected edge, and the rotated face is connected with the series of segmented faces to its original location. This creates a wedge-like effect rising from the surface of the selected face. You can select both a Face and an Edge component by selecting the Multi option in the right click marking menu and hold down the Shift key when selecting. In the Wedge Face Options dialog box, you can select the Wedge Angle and the number of Wedge Divisions. Figure 5-28 shows a wedge rising from a plane object.

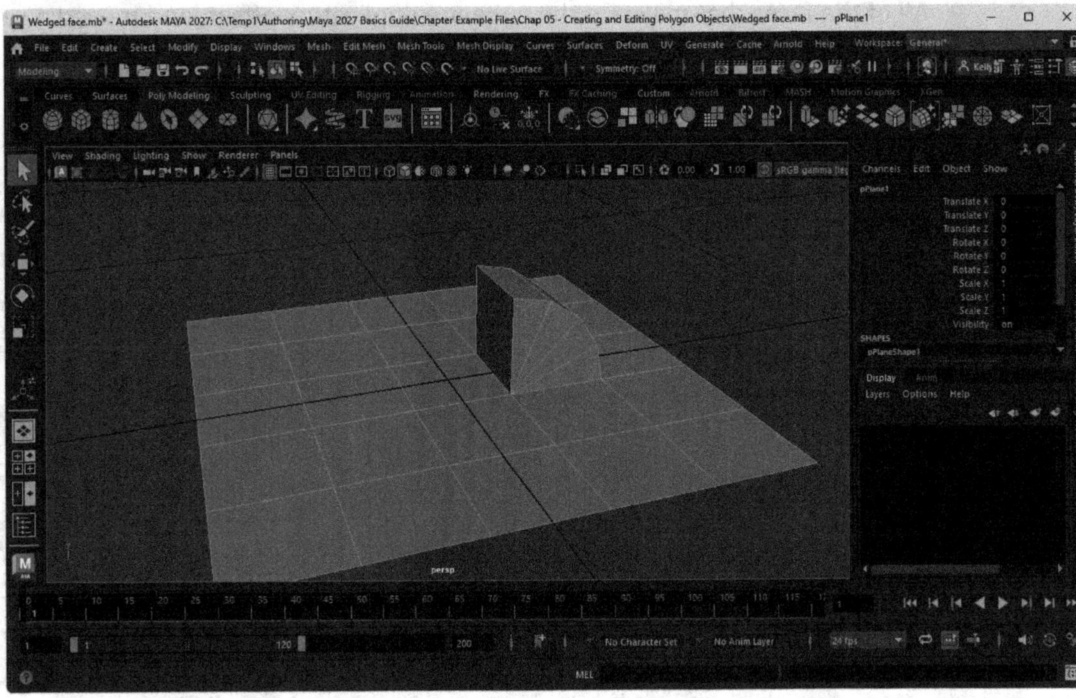

FIGURE 5-28

A wedged face

Using Symmetry

The Symmetry feature lets you model both sides of an object at the same time. You can enable the Symmetry feature, found on the Status Line, for the Object X,Y, Z, the World X, Y, Z or the Topology. The Topology option lets you select an edge in the object about which symmetry edits are applied. Simply select the desired symmetry axis and all edits made to the current object are automatically applied across the selected axis. The selected symmetry option is displayed as text at the top of the view panel. Similar symmetry settings can also be found in the Tool Settings for the transform tools and in the Modeling Toolkit.

Caution

Symmetrical edits will only be made if equal components can be found on either side of the selected axis.

Lesson 5.3-Tutorial 1: Offset Faces

1. Create a polygon cube object using the Create, Polygon Primitives, Cube menu commands.
2. Right-click on the cube object and select the Face option from the pop-up marking menu.
3. Drag over the entire cube to select all its faces.
4. Select the Edit Mesh, Duplicate, Options menu command, and in the Duplicate Face Options dialog box that appears, set the Offset value to 0.1, and the Z-axis Translate value (the third column) to 0.5.
5. Click the Duplicate button.

All of the faces that make up the cube are duplicated, offset, and moved away from the original as if the cube were pulled apart, as shown in Figure 5-29.

6. Select File, Save Scene As and save the file as **Exploded cube.mb**.

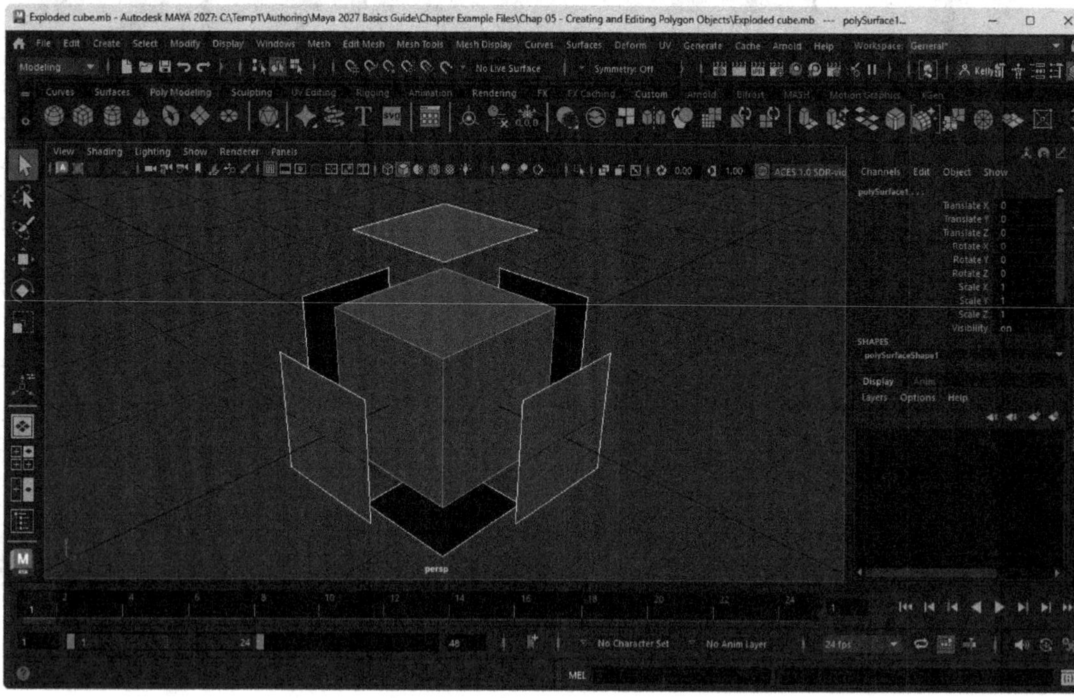

FIGURE 5-29

An exploded cube

Lesson 5.3-Tutorial 2: Extrude Cube Vertices

1. Create a polygon cube object using the Create, Polygon Primitives, Cube menu command.
2. Select Vertex from the right-click pop-up marking menu and drag over the entire cube to select all of its vertices.
3. Select the Edit Mesh, Extrude menu command.

   Each vertex is extruded, creating a star object like the one shown in Figure 5-30.
4. Select File, Save Scene As and save the file as **Extruded vertex star.mb**.

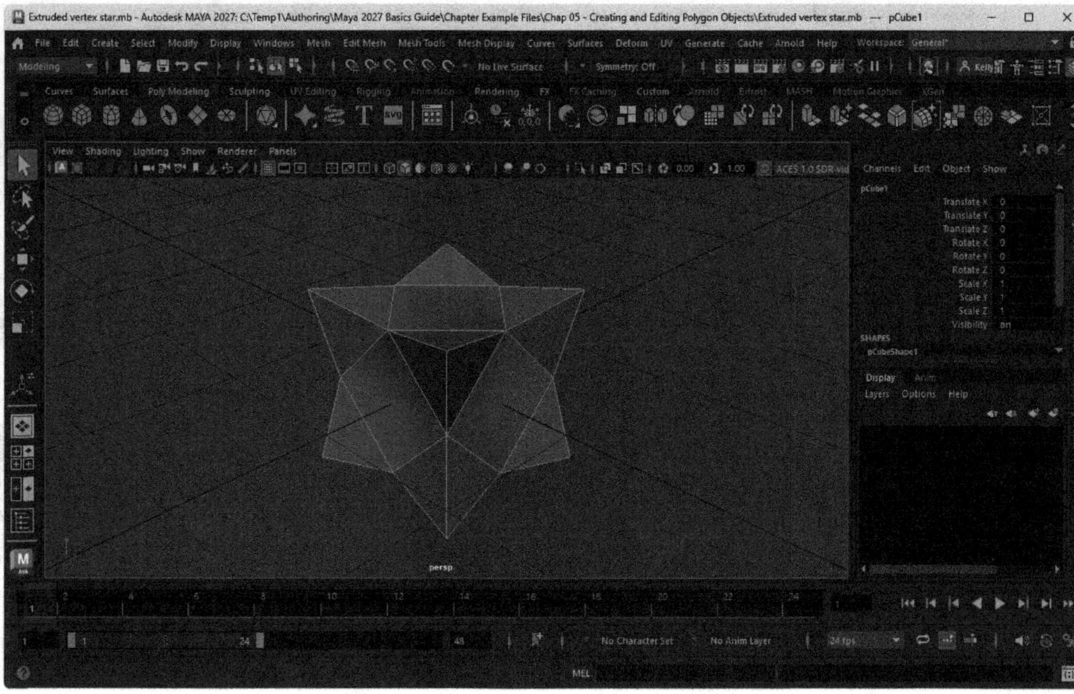

FIGURE 5-30

An extruded vertex star

Lesson 5.3-Tutorial 3: Extrude Cube Edges and Faces

1. Create a polygon cube object using the Create, Polygon Primitives, Cube menu command.
2. With the cube object selected, choose Edit, Duplicate and move the duplicate cube to the right with the Move tool.
3. Right-click on the left cube and select Edge from the right-click pop-up marking menu and drag over the entire cube to select all of its edges.
4. Select the Edit Mesh, Extrude menu command. Select the blue Z-axis and drag it away from the cube object to extrude its edges.
5. Right-click on the right cube and select Face from the right-click pop-up marking menu and drag over the entire cube to select all of its faces.
6. Select the Edit Mesh, Extrude menu command. Select the blue Z-axis and drag it away from the cube object to extrude its faces.

   The cube on the left has extruded edges and the cube on the right has extruded faces. Notice the difference between the two shown in Figure 5-31.
7. Select File, Save Scene As and save the file as **Extruded cube.mb**.

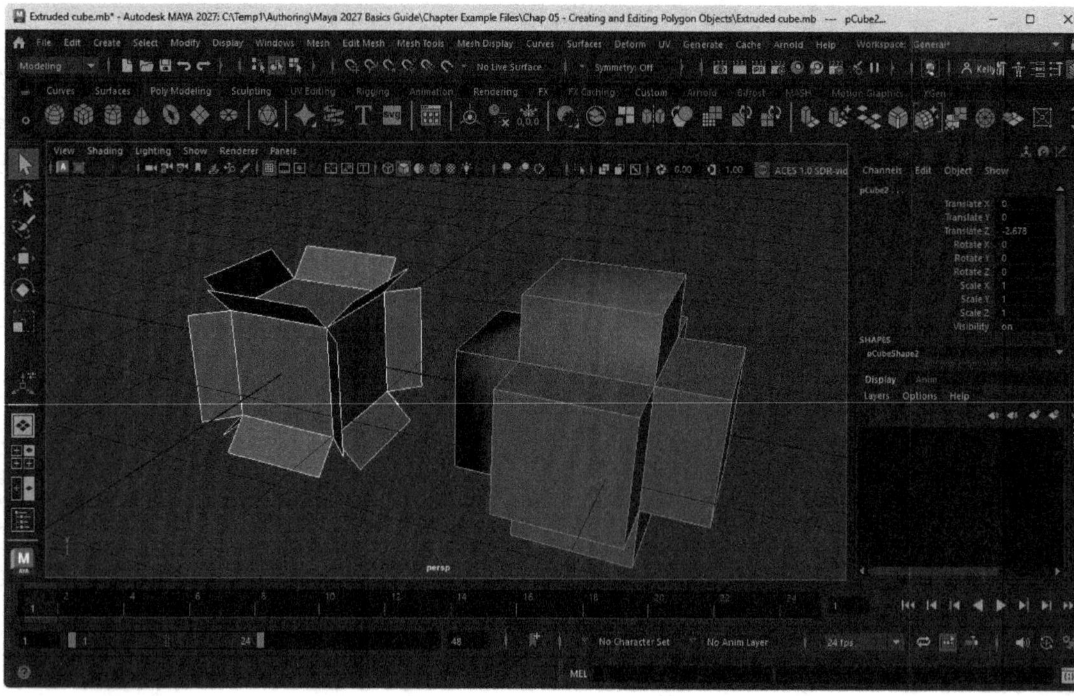

FIGURE 5-31

Extruded cubes

Lesson 5.3-Tutorial 4: Use Smart Extrude

1. Open the Polygon Cube Options dialog box using the Create, Polygon Primitives, Cube, Options menu command. Set the Width and Depth Divisions to 9 and click the Create button.
2. Right-click on the cube and select Face from the right-click pop-up marking menu and select all the top polygon faces that are one face in from the outer edge of the cube with the Shift key held down.
3. Select the Edit Mesh, Smart Extrude menu command.

   A manipulator appears in the center of the cube.
4. Drag the red axis manipulator downward to cut away all the selected polygon faces.
5. Select the center side polygon face on the inner square object, press the G hotkey to reselect the Smart Extrude tool and drag the red axis out towards the outer square. Then, repeat for each of the inner square sides.

   The extruded faces from the inner square are automatically connected to the faces of the outer square.
6. Select the two side faces at one of the corners of the inner square with the Shift key held down, press the G hotkey to reselect the Smart Extrude tool and drag the red axis out towards the outer square. Then, repeat for each of the inner square corners.

   The extruded faces from the inner square are automatically connected to the faces of the outer square.
7. Select the nine center faces with the Shift key held down, press the G hotkey to reselect the Smart Extrude tool and drag the red axis upward.

The resulting tile, as shown in Figure 5-32, is a single object without any interior duplicate faces.

8. Select File, Save Scene As and save the file as **Smart Extrude tile.mb**.

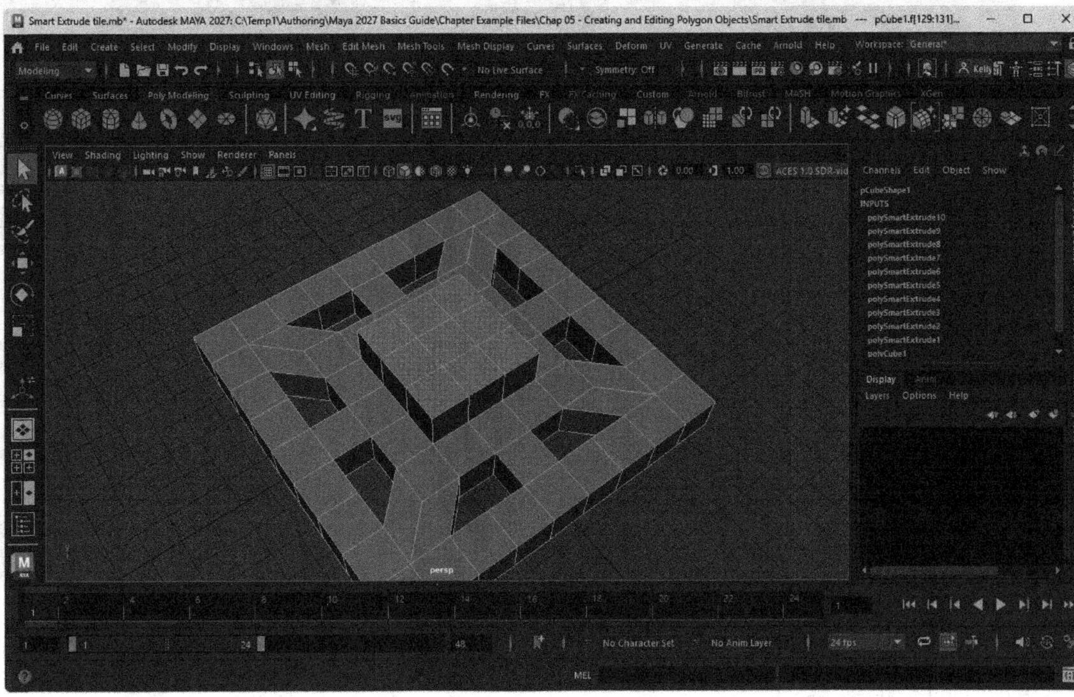

FIGURE 5-32

A chamfered cube

Lesson 5.3-Tutorial 5: Chamfer Vertices

1. Create a polygon cube object using the Create, Polygon Primitives, Cube menu command.
2. Right-click on the cube and select Vertex from the right-click pop-up marking menu and drag over the entire cube to select all of its vertices.
3. Select the Edit Mesh, Chamfer Vertices menu command.

   All vertices on the cube are chamfered, revealing several holes.
4. Drag over the entire cube to select it and choose Mesh, Fill Hole.

   All the chamfered holes are now filled, revealing a cube with octagonal sides, as shown in Figure 5-33.
5. Select File, Save Scene As and save the file as **Chamfered cube.mb**.

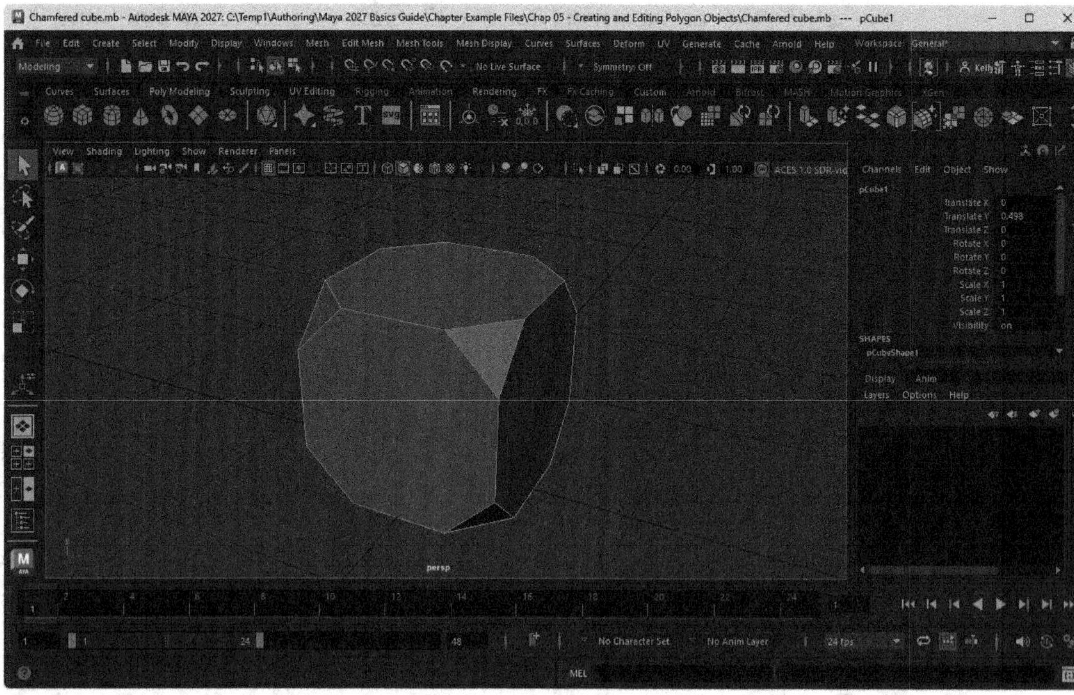

FIGURE 5-33

A chamfered cube

Lesson 5.3-Tutorial 6: Bevel Table Corners

1. Select File, Open Scene and open the Table.mb file.
2. Right-click on the table top and select Edge from the right-click pop-up marking menu, then select the four vertical edges at each of the corners with the Shift key held down.
3. Select the Edit Mesh, Bevel, Options menu command. Set the Width value to 0.1, the Segments to 3, and the Depth to 1, then click the Bevel button.

   The corners of the table top are beveled, as shown in Figure 5-34.
4. Select File, Save Scene As and save the file as **Beveled table.mb**.

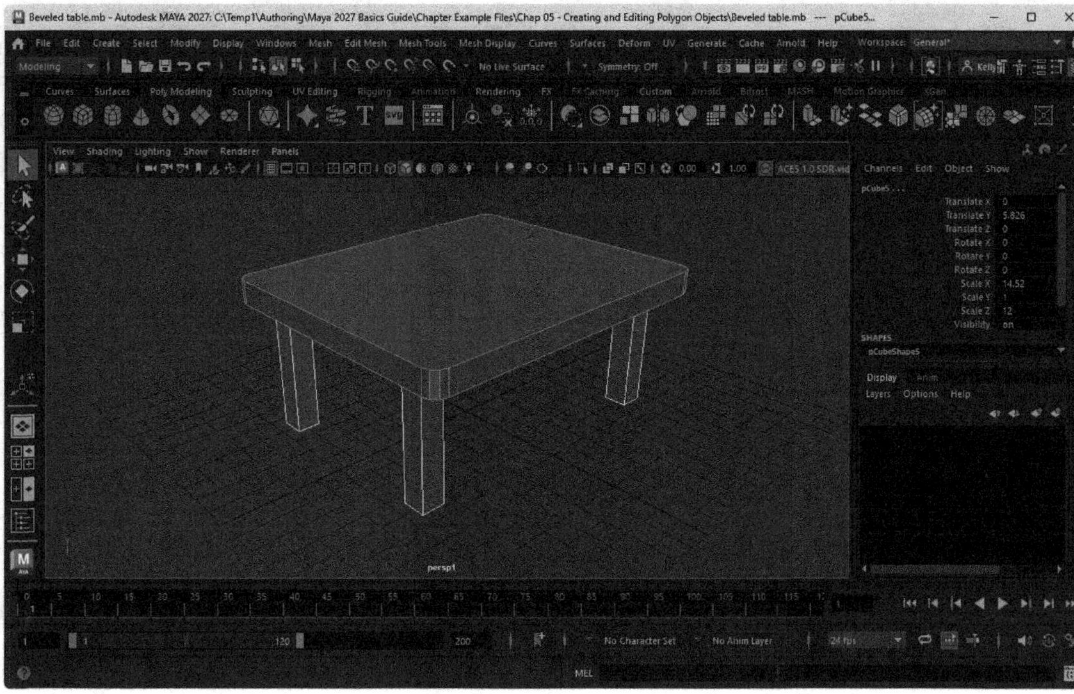

FIGURE 5-34

A beveled table

Lesson 5.3-Tutorial 7: Smart Bevel Connections

1. Select File, Open Scene and open the Dumbell.mb file.
2. Select all three cylinder objects and choose the Mesh, Booleans, Union menu command.

   All three objects are combined into a single object.
3. Right-click on the dumbbell object and select Edge from the right-click pop-up marking menu and select a single edge where the cross member meets the right dumbell.
4. Choose the Select, Contiguous Edges menu command.

   All the edges for the connection are selected.
5. Choose the Edge Mesh, Smart Bevel menu command. In the In-View attributes editor, set the Width to 0.2 and the Segments to 5.
6. Then repeat the Smart Bevel command for the opposite dumbbell.

   The connection has a smooth transition, as shown in Figure 5-35.
7. Select File, Save Scene As and save the file as **Beveled Dumbell.mb**.

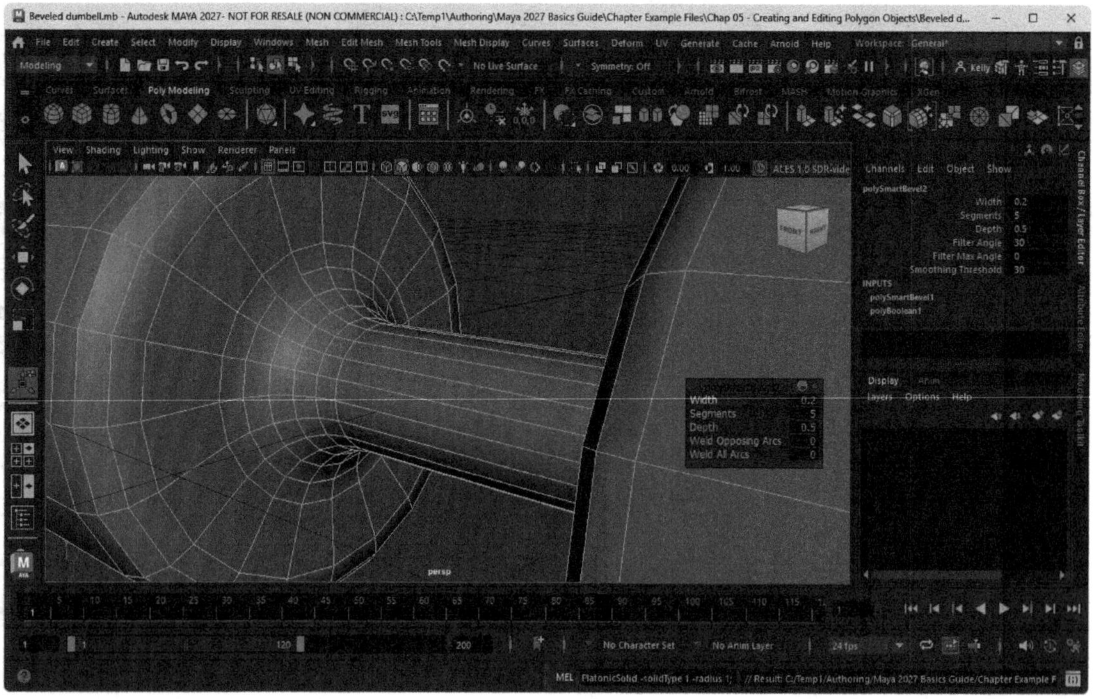

FIGURE 5-35

Transition with Smart Bevel

Lesson 5.3-Tutorial 8: Poke Faces

1. Create a polygon sphere object using the Create, Polygon Primitives, Sphere menu command.
2. Set the Axis Divisions and Height Divisions values in the Channel Box to 10.
3. Right-click on the sphere and select Face from the right-click pop-up marking menu and drag over the entire sphere to select all of its faces.
4. Select the Edit Mesh, Face Poke menu command.
5. A manipulator appears. Drag the blue Z-axis handle to pull the faces away from the sphere center.

   Each face of the sphere is raised like a spike, as shown in Figure 5-36.
6. Select File, Save Scene As and save the file as **Poked sphere.mb**.

FIGURE 5-36

A poked sphere

Lesson 5.3-Tutorial 9: Wedge Faces

1. Create a polygon cube object using the Create, Polygon Primitives, Cube menu command.
2. Right-click on the cube and select Multi from the right-click pop-up marking menu and drag over one of the side faces to select it.

   The Multi selection mode lets you select different component types including faces and edges at the same time.
3. Drag over the lower edge of the selected face with the Shift key held down, so that both the face and edge are selected at the same time.
4. Select the Edit Mesh, Wedge menu command.

   A wedge extends outward from the selected face.
5. Repeat steps 2-4 for the other side faces.

   Each face of the cube extends outward, as shown in Figure 5-37.
6. Select File, Save Scene As and save the file as **Wedged cube.mb**.

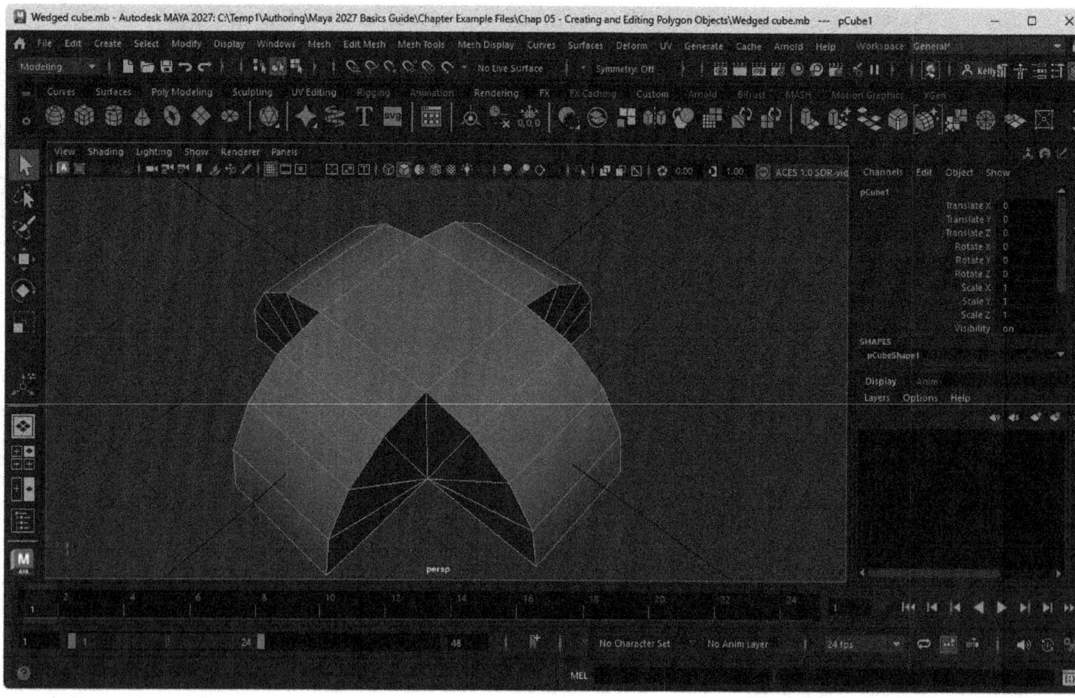

FIGURE 5-37

Wedged cube

Lesson 5.3-Tutorial 10: Symmetrical Editing

1. Create a polygon cube object using the Create, Polygon Primitives, Sphere menu command.
2. On the Status Line, select the Object X option from the Symmetry drop-down list.
3. Right-click on the sphere and select Face from the right-click pop-up marking menu and drag over one of the side faces to select it.
4. Select the Edit Mesh, Extrude menu command.
5. In the pop-up options dialog box, set the Local Translate Z value to 1, the Offset to 0.1 and the Divisions to 5.

   The extrusion is applied to both sides of the sphere, as shown in Figure 5-38.
6. Select File, Save Scene As and save the file as **Symmetrical extrusion.mb**.

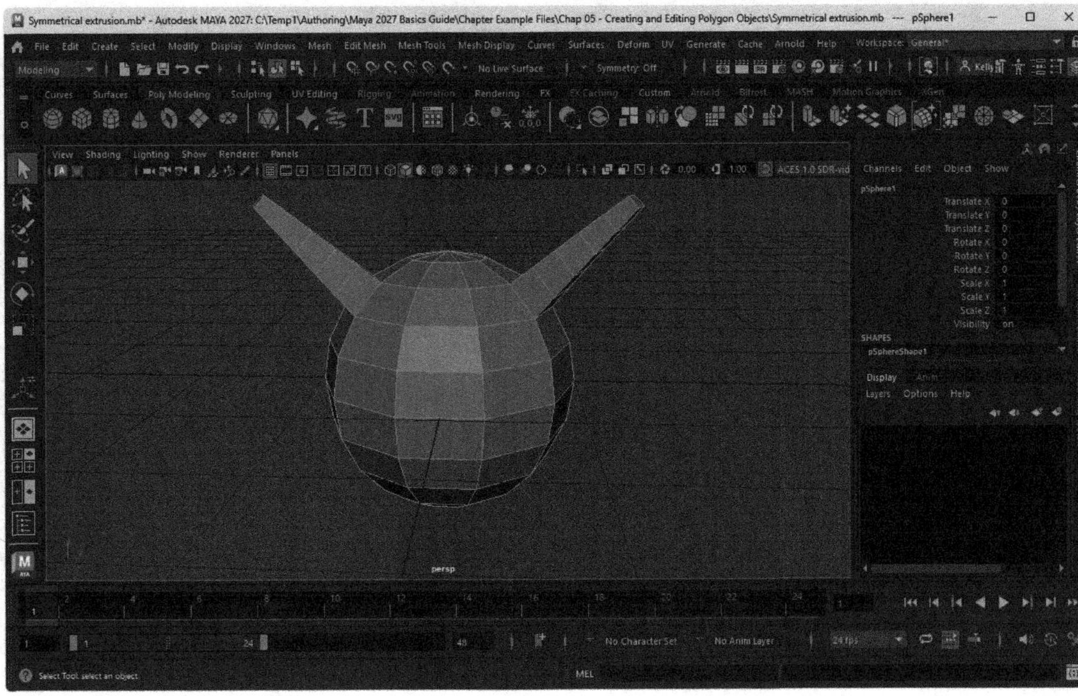

FIGURE 5-38
Symmetrical extrusions

Lesson 5.4: Retopology and Smooth Polygon Edges

The Mesh menu also includes a couple of commands to optimize and smooth the entire object. Retopology is the process of simplifying the topology (or surface) of an object. New hardware is available that scans objects using lasers and photographs. These systems are amazing, but they often result in models that have a huge number of polygons making them difficult to work with in Maya. The Mesh, Retopologize command reduces the overall number of polygons in an object while maintaining its shape and surface.

The Mesh menu also includes a Smooth command. Smoothing a polygon object removes all its hard edges and gives the object a more organic look.

Retopologizing a Mesh

Although the Mesh, Retopologize menu is useful for reducing the number of polygons in an object, it is also useful for cleaning up an object with odd-shaped polygons. For example, if you use a boolean operation to cut a hole into a rectangular slab, the resulting polygons will be odd-shaped to align with the hole, as shown in Figure 5-39. However, the Mesh, Retopologize command can be used to create a new topology for the mesh while maintaining its overall look and shape.

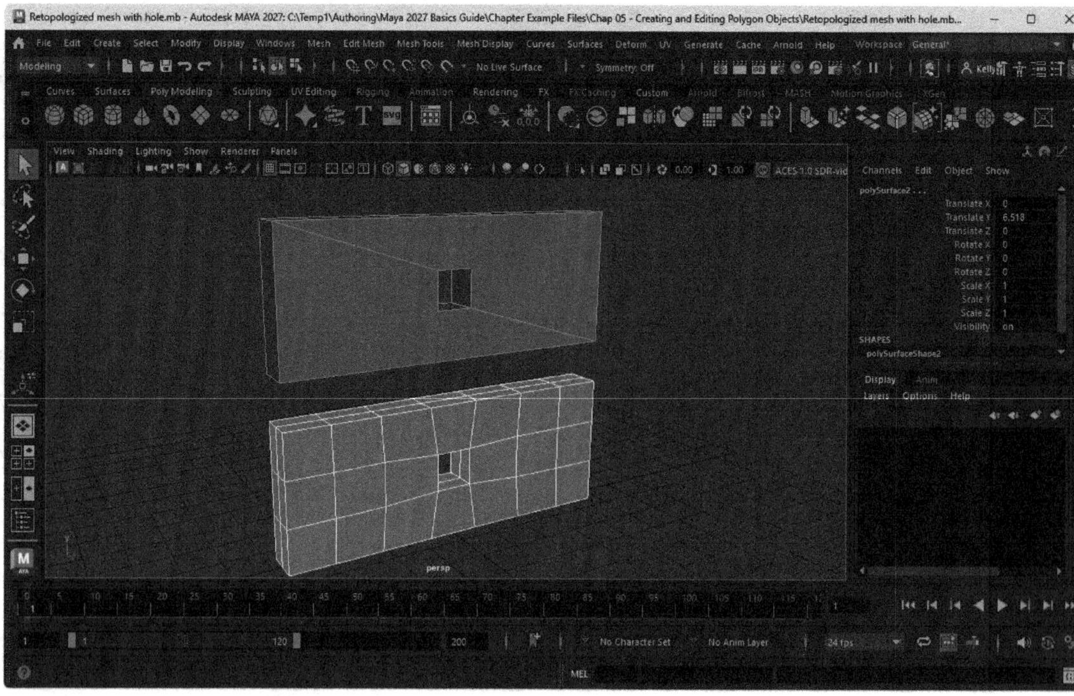

FIGURE 5-39

Using Retopologize will create a new topology while maintaining its shape

The Retopologize command can run into problems if the mesh has problem areas such as zero-length edges and non-planar faces. You can quickly identify and correct many of these potential problems with the Mesh, Cleanup command. The Retopologize Options dialog box also includes options to Scan Mesh for Issues and Preprocess Mesh. Enabling both these options will help produce cleaner, quicker results.

Within the Retopologize Options dialog box are settings to Preprocess Mesh, keep the original mesh, and Preserve Hard Edges. If the Preserve Hard Edges is disabled, then the retopology command will smooth the edges as needed to reduce the total number of polygons. There are also settings for specifying the Target Face Count. This isthe value that you set to reduce large mesh models. There is also a Tolerance (%) value that the algorithm tries to stay within when reducing.

The Retopologize command will try to create four-sided polygons throughout the mesh, but the setting for Topology Regularity gives you control over how tightly this is followed. A value of 0 follows four-sided polygons really tight and 1 is more relaxed. The Face Uniformity sets how different the sizes are between all retopologized polygons. A setting of 0 allows different sizes and a setting of 1 tries to keep them all about the same size. The lower Anisotropy setting determines how much the converted polygons can stretch, while a setting of 1 causes all polygons to be more square.

The Retopologize Options dialog box also includes a Symmetry option that you can enable. By taking advantage of an object's symmetry, you can create a cleaner resulting mesh that is centered about the designated axis. It can also make the Retopologize command run faster since only half of the object needs to be reworked.

Smoothing Polygons with Subdivisions

Although the Mesh Display, Soften Edges doesn't change the geometry of a model, there is a command that smoothes out an object by altering its geometry. To smooth a selection of faces, you can use the Mesh, Smooth menu command. This method subdivides the selected faces depending on the Subdivision Levels value found in the Smooth Options dialog box. Be aware that higher Subdivision Levels values produce a huge number of polygons. Figure 5-40 shows a polygon cone object that has been smoothed with the Mesh, Smooth menu command.

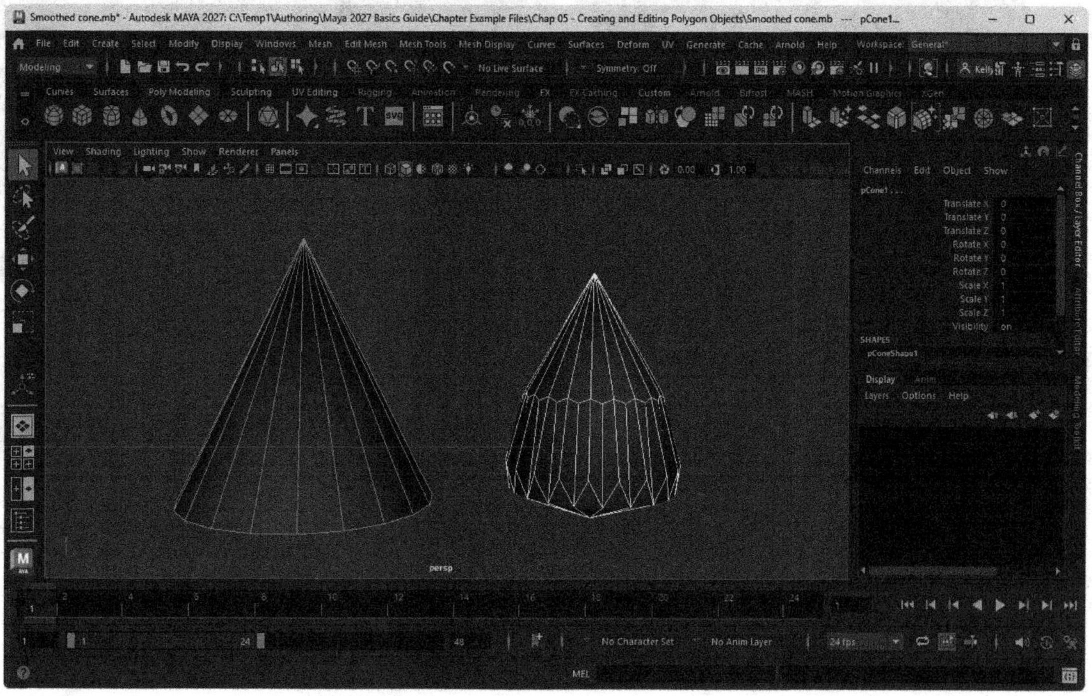

FIGURE 5-40

A smoothed cone

Creating a Smooth Proxy

Smoothing an object can create a dense mesh of polygons that makes it difficult to edit; using the Mesh, Smooth Proxy menu command creates a smooth dense object but leaves the original object in place. Editing the components of the original object changes the smoothed object also. Using a smooth proxy makes it easier to edit the dense smoothed mesh. You can also move and scale the proxy object independent of the smoothed object and in a shaded view; the proxy object is semi-transparent, allowing the smooth object to be seen.

Tip

If the Smooth Proxy object is selected, you can use the Ctrl+~ hotkey to switch between the normal polygon and the smooth proxy display.

Adding a Crease to a Smoothed Polygon

Applying a smooth proxy operation to a polygon model causes the entire surface to be smoothed, but if you want to selectively maintain some hard edges, you can use the Mesh, Smooth Proxy, Crease tool to add a hard crease to the selected edges, as shown in Figure 5-41. To use this tool, choose the tool and select the polygon proxy edges that you want to crease and then drag with the middle mouse button to adjust the crease amount.

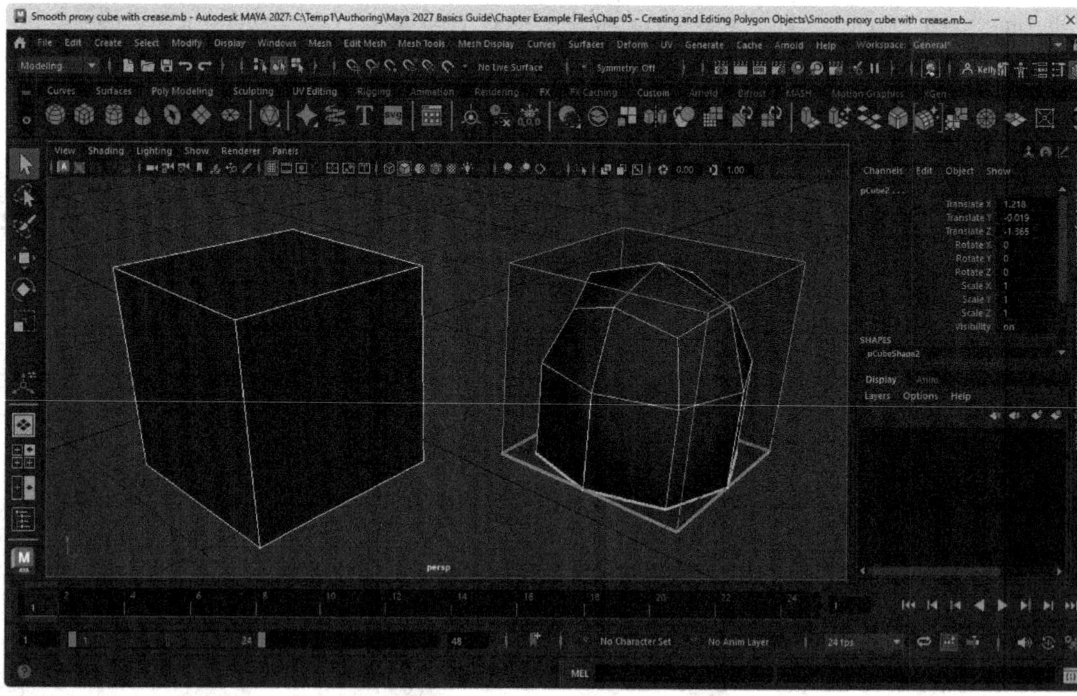

FIGURE 5-41

A smoothed proxy cone with a crease on one end.

Smoothing Polygons with Vertex Averaging

Another way to smooth polygon faces is with the Mesh Display, Average menu command. This command moves the selected vertices to form a smooth surface without adding more polygons to the mesh.

Unsmoothing a Dense Mesh

Sometimes you end up with a dense mesh that has lots of subdivisions. This is common for meshes that have been sculpted, but they result in a mesh that is too complex to work in a game engine. For these cases, you can remove some of the subdivision levels without losing the edits using the Mesh, Unsmooth command. The options include keeping the original and selecting the number of levels to remove.

Lesson 5.4-Tutorial 1: Retopologize Mesh

1. Select File, Open Scene and open the Toy Duck.mb file.
2. Select the Display, Heads Up Display, Poly Count menu command.
3. Select the toy duck on the right and choose the Mesh, Retopologize, Options menu command.
4. Set the Target Face Count to 2500 with a Tolerance of 10%, then click the Retopologize button.

   The resulting toy duck is cleaner and will be easier to work with, as shown in Figure 5-42.
5. Select File, Save Scene As and save the file as **Retopologized duck.mb**.

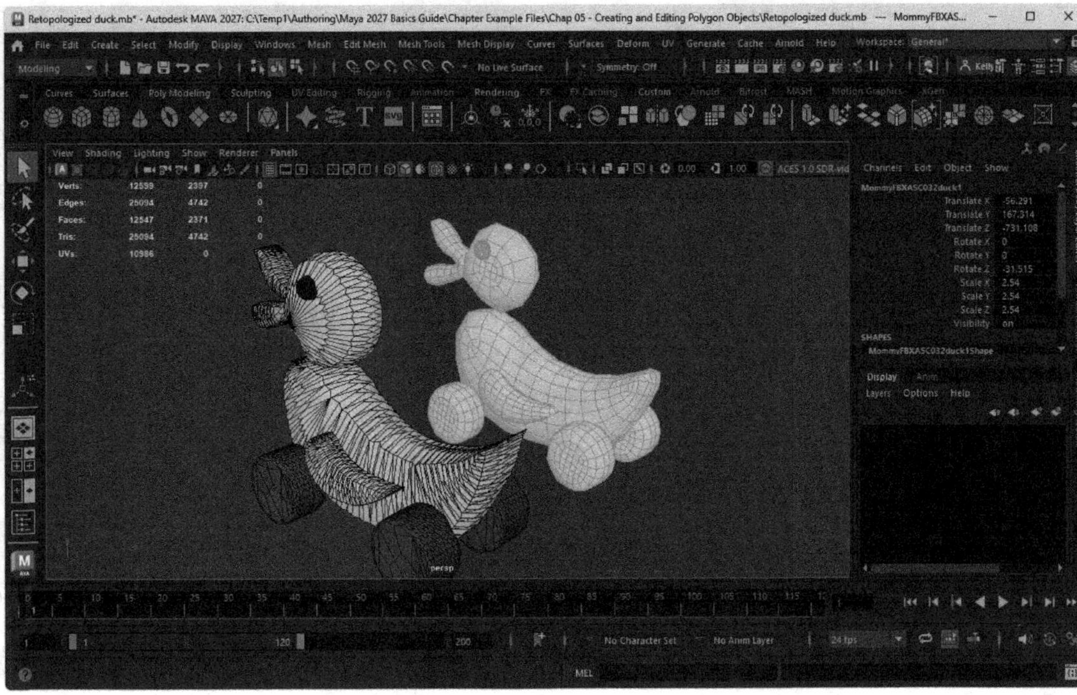

FIGURE 5-42

Reduced polygon duck after retopologizing

Lesson 5.4-Tutorial 2: Smooth Faces

1. Select File, Open Scene and open the Poked sphere.mb file.
2. Right-click on the sphere and select Face from the right-click pop-up marking menu and drag over the entire sphere to select all its faces.
3. Select the Mesh, Smooth menu command.

   Each face is subdivided and smoothed, turning the spikes into bumps, as shown in Figure 5-43.
4. Select File, Save Scene As and save the file as **Bumpy sphere.mb**.

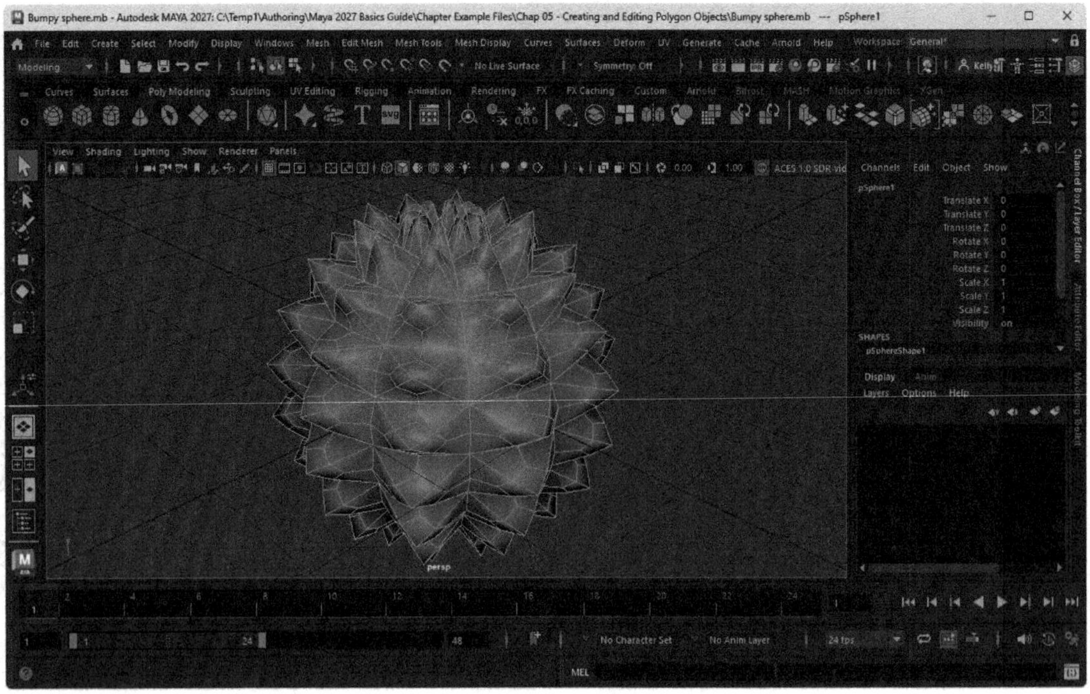

FIGURE 5-43

A bumpy sphere

Lesson 5.4-Tutorial 3: Smooth Proxy Turtle

1. Select File, Open Scene and open the Turtle.mb file.
2. With the turtle object selected, choose the Mesh, Smooth Proxy, Subdiv Proxy menu command.

   The original object remains as a proxy, but a smoothed version appears underneath the original-colored magenta.
3. Move the original object above the smoothed object.
4. Select and drag some of the components of the original object.

   As the components of the original object are moved, the underlying smoothed object is affected, as shown in Figure 5-44.
5. Select File, Save Scene As and save the file as **Smoothed turtle.mb**.

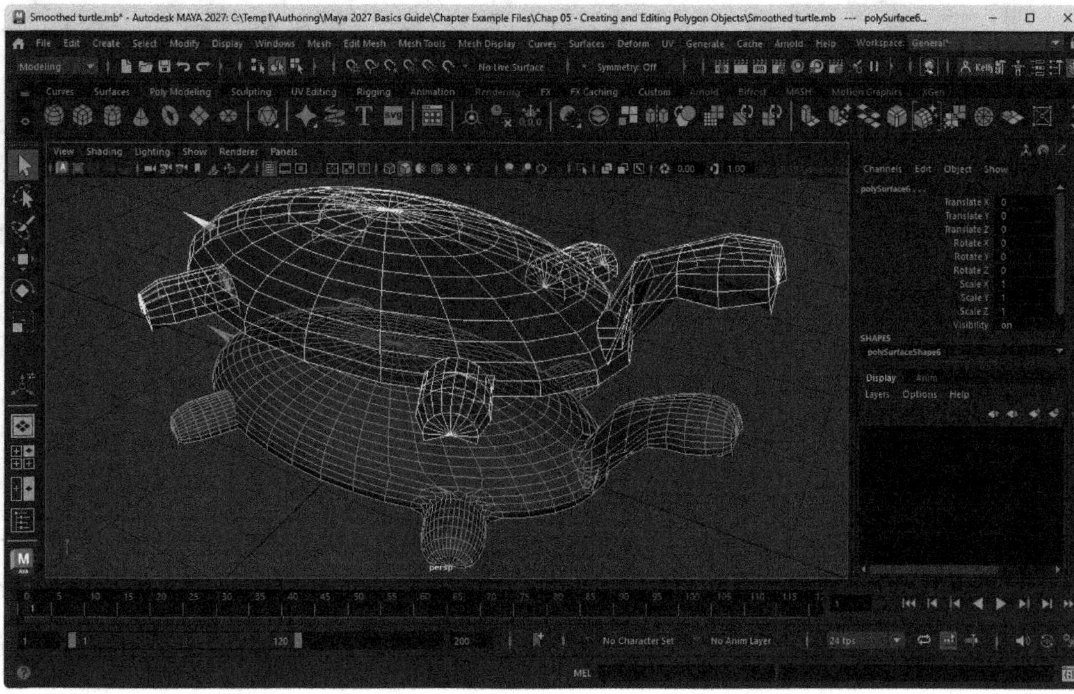

FIGURE 5-44

Smoothed proxy

Lesson 5.4-Tutorial 4: Smooth Faces with Vertex Averaging

1. Create a polygon sphere object using the Create, Polygon Primitives, Sphere menu command.
2. Click on the Four Views button in the Quick Layout Buttons.
3. Click on the Select by Component Type button in the Status Line.
4. Drag over the lower half of the sphere faces in the Front view and press the Delete key.

   Deleting the lower half of the sphere's faces creates a perfect hemisphere.
5. Drag over the last row of faces in the Front view to select them and choose the Edit Mesh, Extrude menu command. Then drag the blue Z-axis manipulator to extrude the selected faces. If the faces are all together, then turn off the Keep Faces Together option to make each face extrude independent of each other.
6. Click on the Select by Object Type button in the Status Line and choose the Mesh, Smooth menu command.

   The object is smoothed and the number of polygons is increased.
7. Select the Mesh Display, Average menu command to apply an additional smoothing.

   The Average Vertices menu command smoothes the object even more without adding to the complexity of the object, as shown in Figure 5-45.
8. Select File, Save Scene As and save the file as **Smoothed sun.mb**.

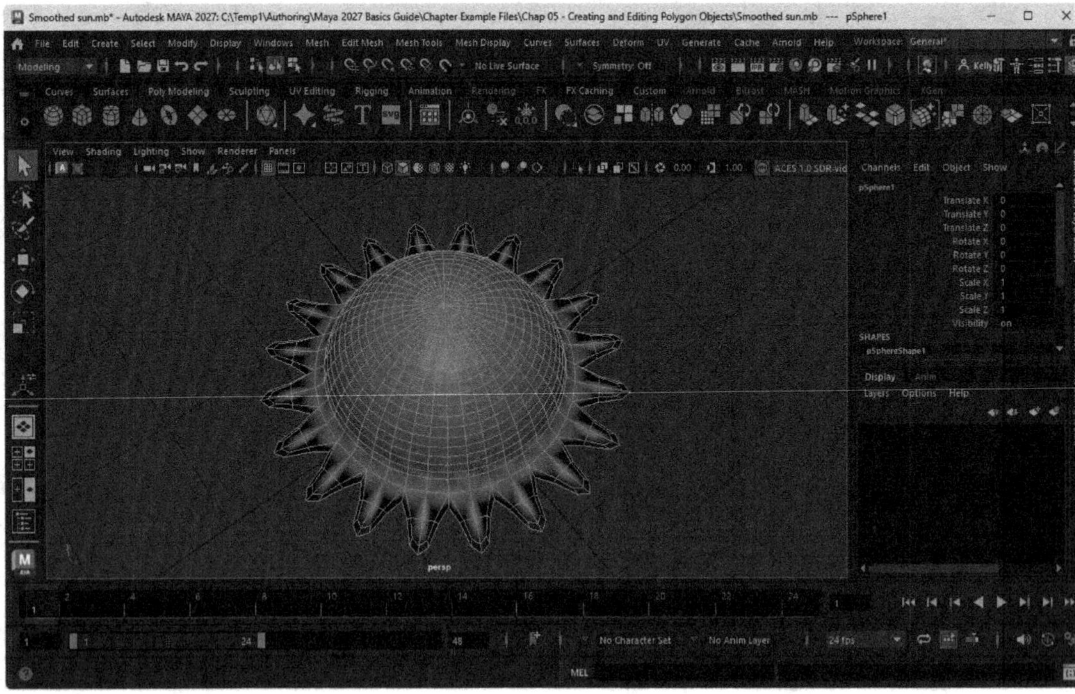

FIGURE 5-45

Smoothed sun

Lesson 5.5: Use Polygon Booleans and Triangulate Polygons

When two polygon surfaces overlap, you can use the Mesh, Booleans menu to compute the Union, Difference (A-B and B-A), or Intersection between the two objects. The menu also includes commands to Slice, Hole Punch, Cut Out and Split Edges. To use any of these commands, just select the two overlapping polygon objects and select the desired command. Figure 5-46 shows the various Boolean operations performed on a polygon cube and a polygon cylinder.

Tip

To produce the smoothest Boolean operations, make sure the surfaces that are being combined have a sufficient number of faces.

FIGURE 5-46

Polygon Boolean operations: Union, Difference (A-B), Difference (B-A), and Intersection

When any of the Boolean operations are used on objects, the objects used to create the boolean, which are called input objects, don't disappear from the scene, but appear as wireframe. They are also included in a list, called the Boolean Stack, in the Attribute Editor. Using the Attribute Editor, you can drag and drop the input objects in the stack to change their order, or you can select the individual input objects by name and use the Transform tools to move, rotate or scale the input object's shape thereby changing the resulting boolean, as shown in Figure 5-47.The Boolean Stack in the Attribute Editor also includes icons to change the Boolean Operation, the Visibility of the input objects, and a toggle to Enable/Disable the boolean.

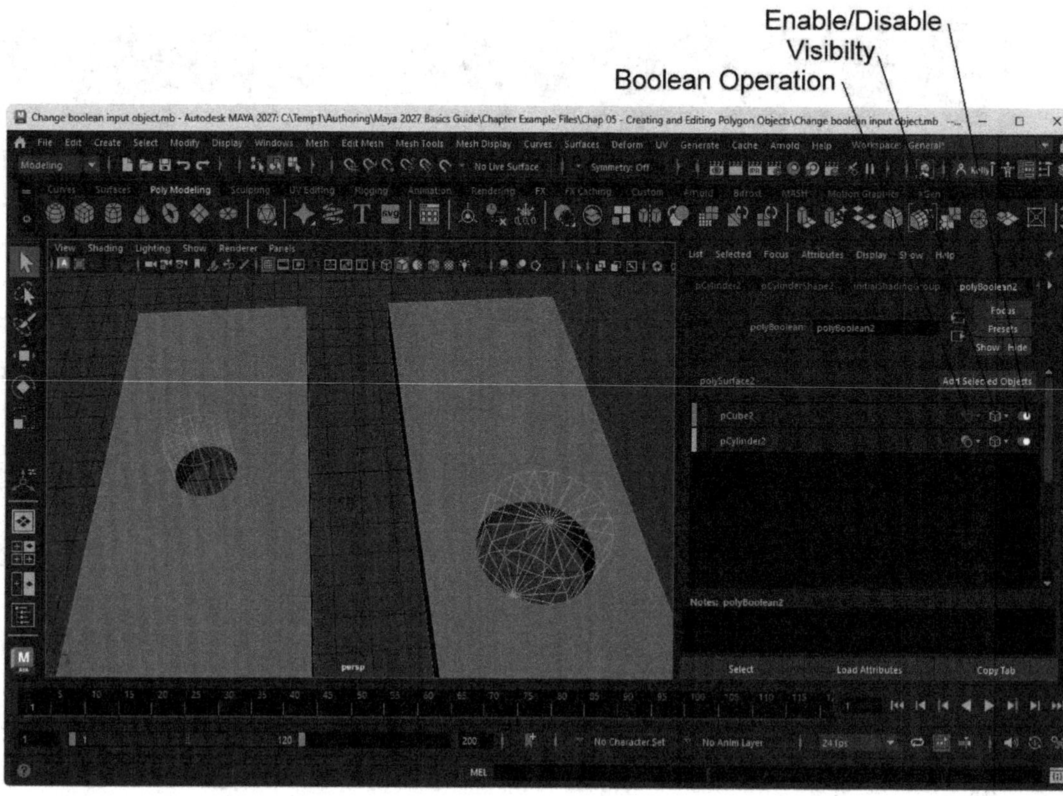

FIGURE 5-47

Selecting an input object lets you change the boolean

Once a boolean is created using one of the Boolean operators, you can add more objects to the Boolean Stack in the Attribute Editor by selecting the object in the Outliner and dragging it with the middle mouse button onto the Stack. You can then select one of the Boolean Operations in the Stack list to have the new input object affect the current boolean object. You can also add more objects to the Stack list by right clicking on objects in the Boolean Stack and choosing to Duplicate as a Copy or Duplicate as an Instance.

Tip

Before adding a new input object to an existing boolean object, make sure the new object overlaps the current boolean object and you may wish to pin the Boolean Stack in place using the Pin icon in the upper right corner of the Attribute Editor.

To remove any of the input objects from the Boolean Stack, simply select it in the scene and press Delete, or right click on the object in the stack and select the Remove option. If you are happy with the results, you can remove the Boolean Stack and all the input objects by selecting Edit, Delete by Type, History.

Combining Polygon Objects

When the Mesh, Booleans, Union menu command is used on two overlapping surfaces, the intersecting lines are removed, and the resulting object acts as a single object.

Finding the Difference Between Objects

The Mesh, Booleans, Difference (A-B) menu command removes the overlapping portion of the second selected object from the first selected object and the Mesh, Booleans, Difference (B-A) does the opposite and removes the overlapping portion from the first object from the second one.

Creating an Intersection Object

The Mesh, Booleans, Intersection menu command removes all but the intersecting portion of the two overlapping surfaces.

Slicing and Punching Holes

The Mesh, Booleans, Slice menu command uses the second object as a knife that cuts the overlapping portion away from the first object, but it leaves two objects behind, the first object with the overlapping section cut away and the intersection portion as a second object. The Punch Hole command also uses the second object like a knife, but it only cuts a hole in the surface of the first object.

Using Cut Out and Split Edges

The Mesh, Booleans, Cut Out menu command is like the intersection command, but it only leaves the overlapping surface. The Split Edges command removes the second object and only leaves the edges where the two objects overlapped on the first object. Examples of these last four boolean commands (Slice, Punch Hole, Cut Out, Split Edge) are shown in Figure 5-48.

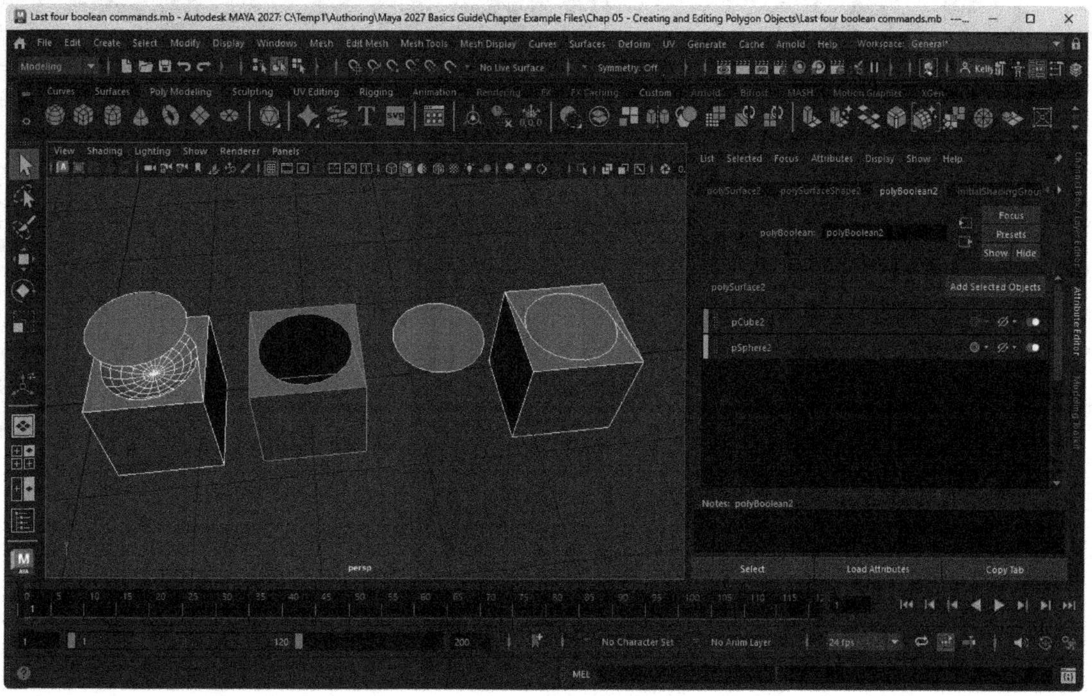

FIGURE 5-48

The last four boolean commands: Slice, Punch Hole, Cut Out and Split Edge

Using Boolean Volumes

When applying booleans, you can change the Geometry Mode from Mesh to Volume in the Boolean Operation Options dialog box. The Volume option treats all combined objects as whole volumetric objects and eliminates all interior edges during the operation. The result is a single object without any holes. The density of the resulting volume is determined by the Voxel Size setting with smaller numbers resulting in more accurate volumes. The Geometry Mode can be set to Volume for Union, Difference, and Intersection boolean operations.

Tip

> Set the Voxel Size to a larger number when starting to get a good approximation of the volume and then lower the Voxel Size setting for the final result.

Figure 5-49 shows two examples of Volume Booleans. The left objects have a Voxel Size setting of 0.5 and the right set has a Voxel Size setting of 0.1. Using the Boolean Stack, you can select individual objects and transform them to refine the overall volume. You can also select and alter components.

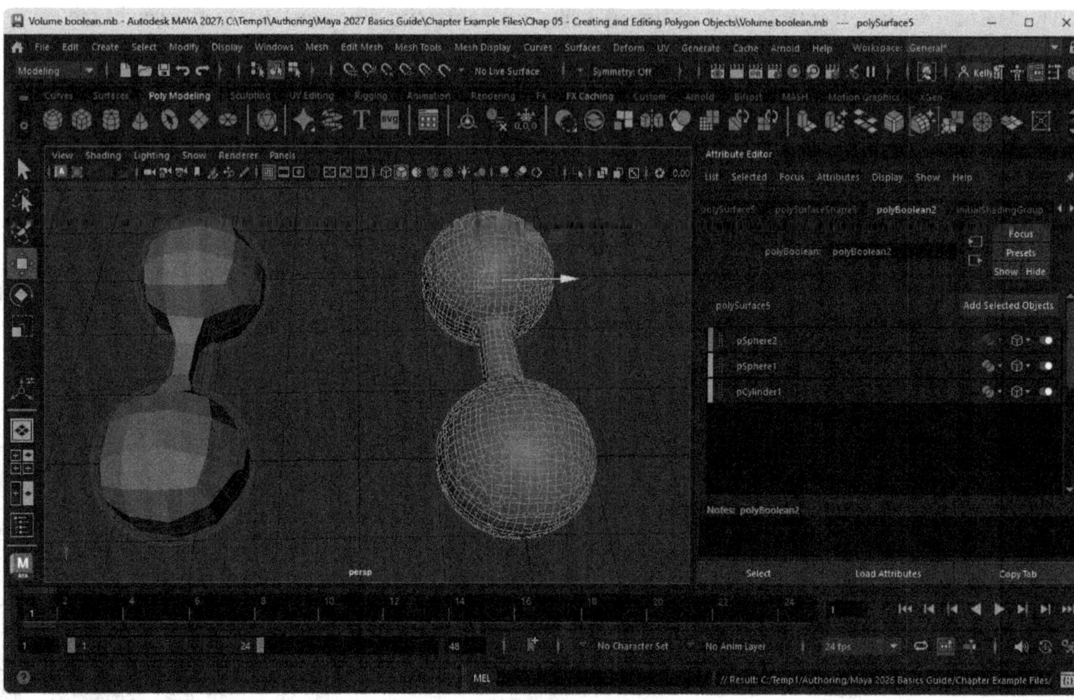

FIGURE 5-49

Volume boolean

Triangulating Polygon Faces

If you create a polygon manually, you can accidentally create a surface that is non-planar. Non-planar surfaces are surfaces that have vertices that aren't on the same plane. This condition can cause problems when they are rendered. The Mesh, Triangulate menu command divides all selected polygon faces into triangles. This ensures that all faces are co-planar. Figure 5-50 shows a simple polygon plane object that has been triangulated.

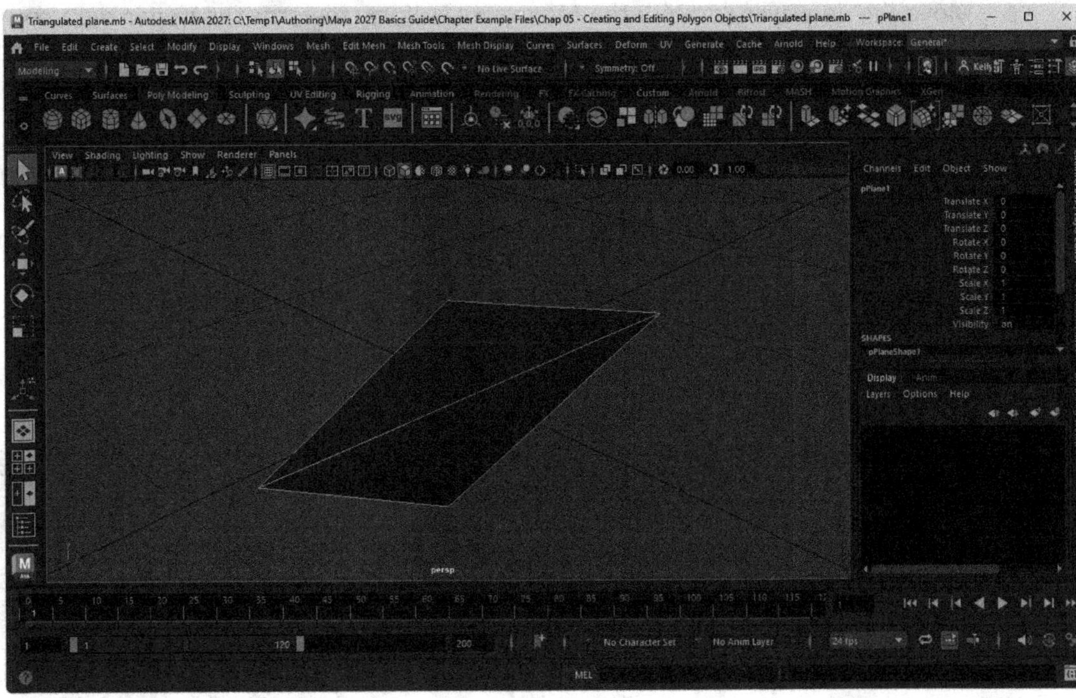

FIGURE 5-50

A triangulated plane object

Switching Polygon Faces to Rectangles

If you prefer to work with rectangles, you can use the Mesh, Quadrangulate menu command. Rectangular faces in modeling are typically called Quads and they are often easier to work with since they line up in easy to use rows and columns. This reduces the number of faces by half.

Flipping Triangle Edges

If you use the Triangulation command and the added edge for a face runs the wrong way, you can flip its direction by selecting the edge and using the Edit Mesh, Flip Triangle Edge menu command. This command cannot be used on border edges, though.

Lesson 5.5-Tutorial 1: Create a Button from Booleans

1. Create a polygon cylinder object using the Create, Polygon Primitives, Cylinder menu command.
2. Click on the polyCylinder1 input node in the Channel Box and change the Radius value to 15, the Height value to 1, and the Subdivision Axis value to 36.
3. Create another cylinder object using the Create, Polygon Primitives, Cylinder menu command.

   The large, flat cylinder is the button and the smaller cylinders are used to cut out the buttonholes using a Booleans operation.
4. Click the Four Views button from the Quick Layout buttons.
5. Change the Radius value for the new cylinder to 1.0.

6. Move the new cylinder with the Move tool halfway towards the upper-right corner of the button.
7. Duplicate the new cylinder object with the Edit, Duplicate menu command (Ctrl/Command+d) and drag the blue Z-axis manipulator to move the duplicate downward in the Top view panel.
8. Select both smaller cylinders, duplicate them, and drag them to the left in the Top view panel using the red X-axis manipulator.
9. Select the button object and then all four of the smaller cylinders, and then choose the Mesh, Booleans, Difference (A-B) menu command.

   The Boolean operation removes the smaller cylinders from the larger button face, as shown in Figure 5-51.
10. Select File, Save Scene As and save the file as **Boolean button.mb**.

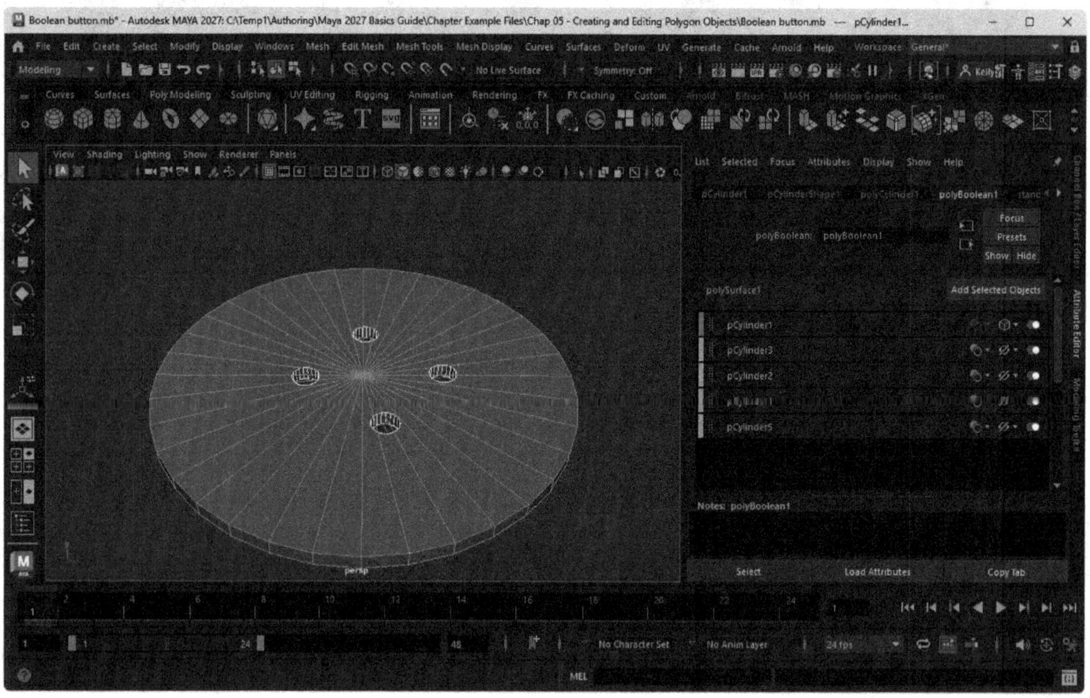

FIGURE 5-51

A Boolean button

Lesson 5.5-Tutorial 2: Change Boolean

1. Select File, Open Scene and open the Spatula-3 holes.mb file.

   This file has a simple spatula model with three holes created using the boolean difference (A-B) operation.
2. Select the spatula head and choose the PolyBoolean1 node in the Attribute Editor, then click on the Pin Tab button in the upper right corner of the Attribute Editor to keep it from changing.
3. Select the pCube5 input object in the Boolean Stack and choose the Edit, Duplicate menu command.

   This duplicates the input object and creates a new object named pCube6.

4. Select the Windows, Outliner menu command to open the Outliner, then locate the pCube6 object name and drag with the middle mouse button to an open area in the Boolean Stack.

   The new input object is added to the Boolean Stack.
5. Click on the Boolean Operation button in the stack and choose the Difference (A-B) option.
6. Select each of the input objects in the Boolean Stack and reposition them with the Move tool so they are regularly spaced.

   The spatula now has four holes instead of three, as shown in Figure 5-52.
7. Select File, Save Scene As and save the file as **Spatula-4 holes.mb**.

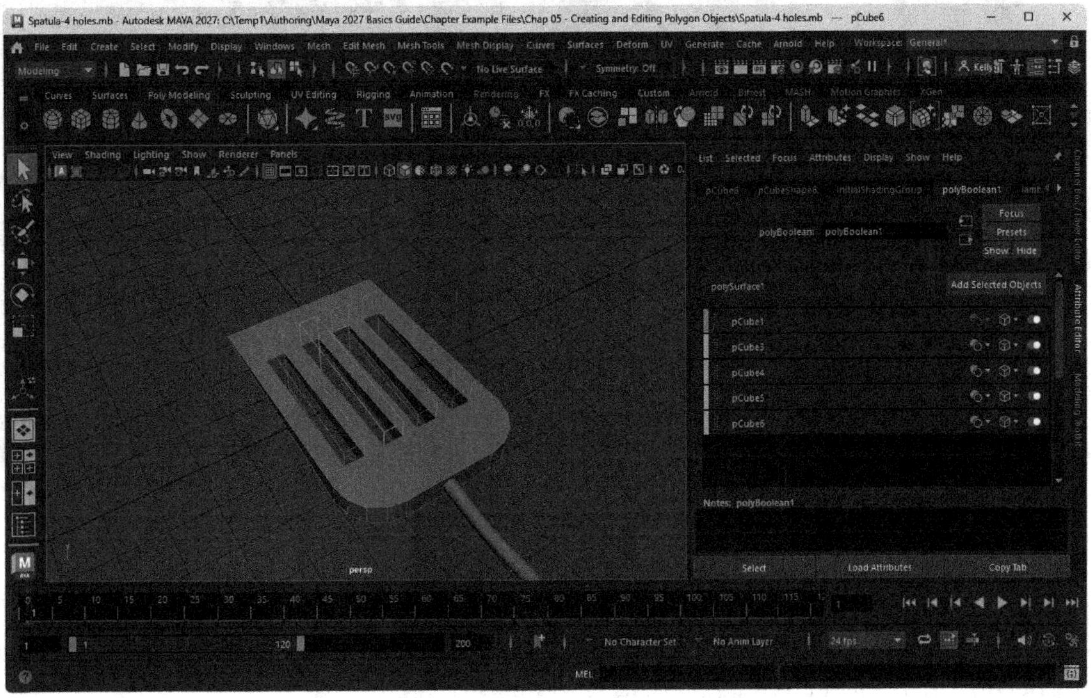

FIGURE 5-52

A Spatula with four holes

Lesson 5.5-Tutorial 3: Organic Modeling with Volume Booleans

1. In the panel menu, select the Panels, Orthographic, Side setting to see the Side view.
2. Select the Create, Curve Tools, CV Curve Tool and draw a single straight line from the grid origin to the top of the viewport with 4 CV points. Press Enter to complete the line. Then, draw two lines extending from the straight line outward and curving upward on either side of the main line to form the branches of a cactus plant.
3. Switch back to the Perspective view, select the main line and choose the Create, Sweep Mesh menu command. In the Attribute Editor, select the Circle option and enable the Cap option. Then repeat this command for the other two side curves.
4. Select all three cylinder objects and choose the Mesh, Boolean, Union, Options menu command. In the Union Operation, Options dialog box, set the Geometry Mode to Volume, the Voxel Size to 0.5, and click the Apply and Close button.

5. Select the Mesh, Smooth command to increase the density of the cactus plant.

   This resulting volume mesh is shown in Figure 5-53.
6. Select File, Save Scene As and save the file as **Cactus volume boolean.mb**.

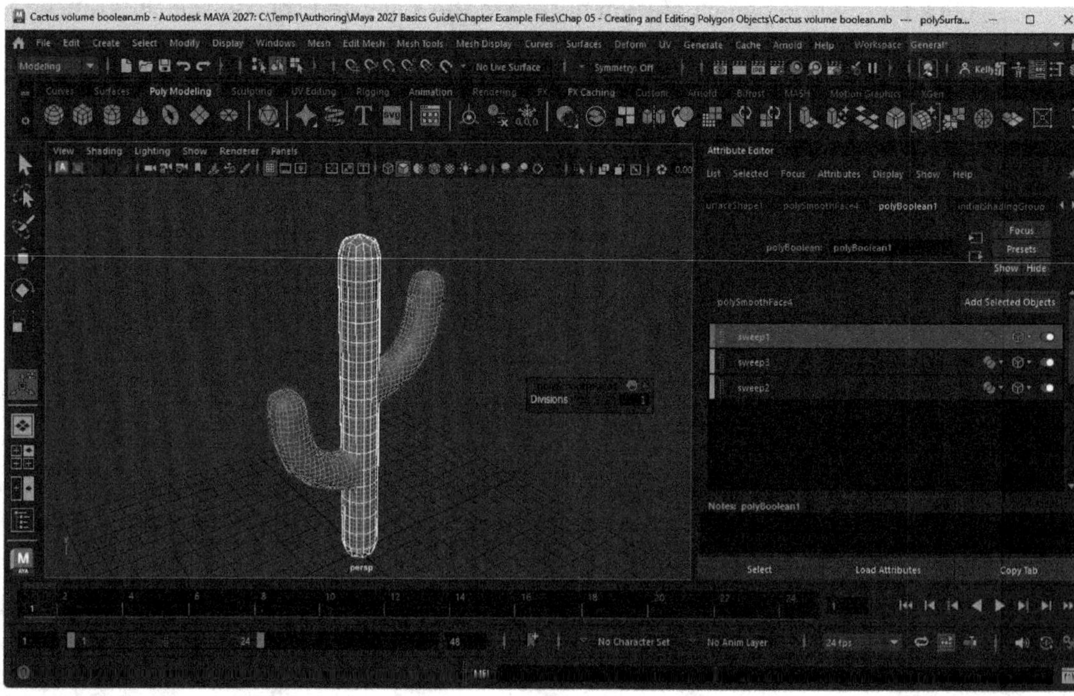

FIGURE 5-53

A cactus volume boolean

Lesson 5.5-Tutorial 4: Triangulate Non-Planar Polygons

1. Create a polygon plane object using the Create, Polygon Primitives, Plane menu command.
2. Click on the polyPlane1 input node in the Channel Box and change the Subdivision Width and Subdivision Height values to 1.
3. Right-click on the plane object and select Vertex from the pop-up marking menu.
4. Select and move the right vertex upward with the Move tool.
5. Select and move the left vertex downward with the Move tool.

   This movement makes the plane object non-planar.
6. Select the entire plane object and choose Mesh, Triangulate.
7. Right-click on the plane object and select Edge from the pop-up marking menu.
8. Select the center triangulated edge and choose Edit Mesh, Flip Triangle Edge.

   The center triangulated edge is flipped to run between the opposite two vertices, as shown in Figure 5-54.
9. Select File, Save Scene As and save the file as **Triangulated plane object.mb**.

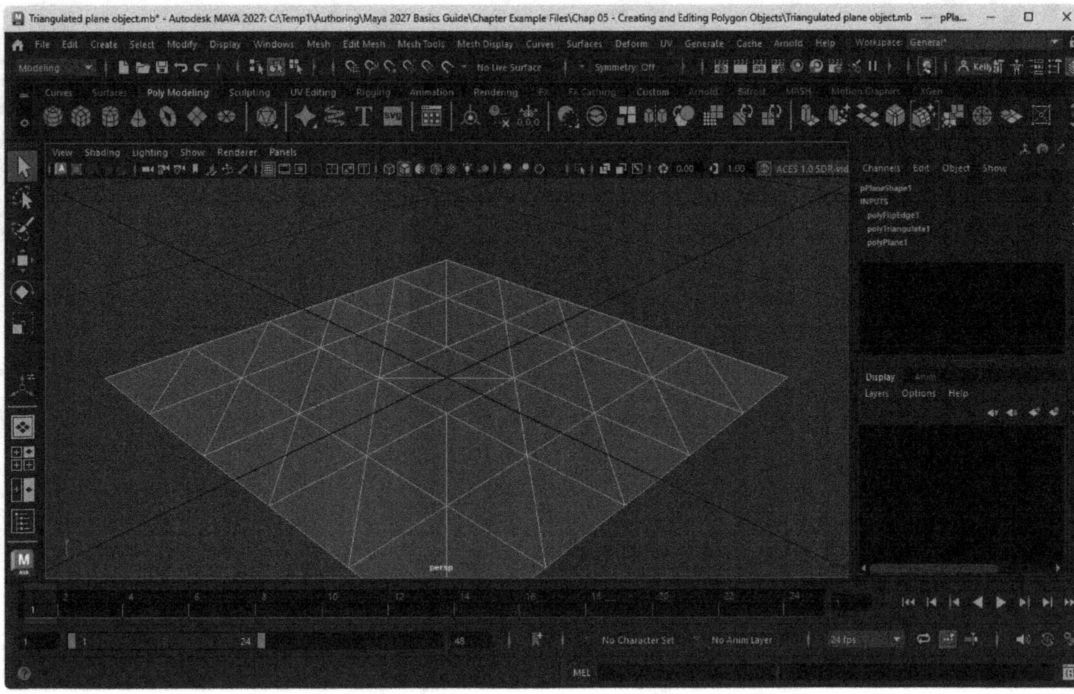

FIGURE 5-54

A triangulated plane

Lesson 5.6: Create Holes in Polygons

There are several ways to create a hole in a polygon object. Perhaps the easiest is to just select and delete a polygon face component. Be aware that deleting a polygon face makes the interior of the polygon object visible.

Detaching a Vertex

The Edit Mesh menu also includes a Detach menu command. When this command is used on a selected vertex, it creates a separate vertex for each edge coming into the selected vertex. These vertices can then be selected independently and moved away from the others to create a hole in the geometry. Figure 5-55 shows a single vertex that has been detached. Each detached vertex has then been moved away from its original position.

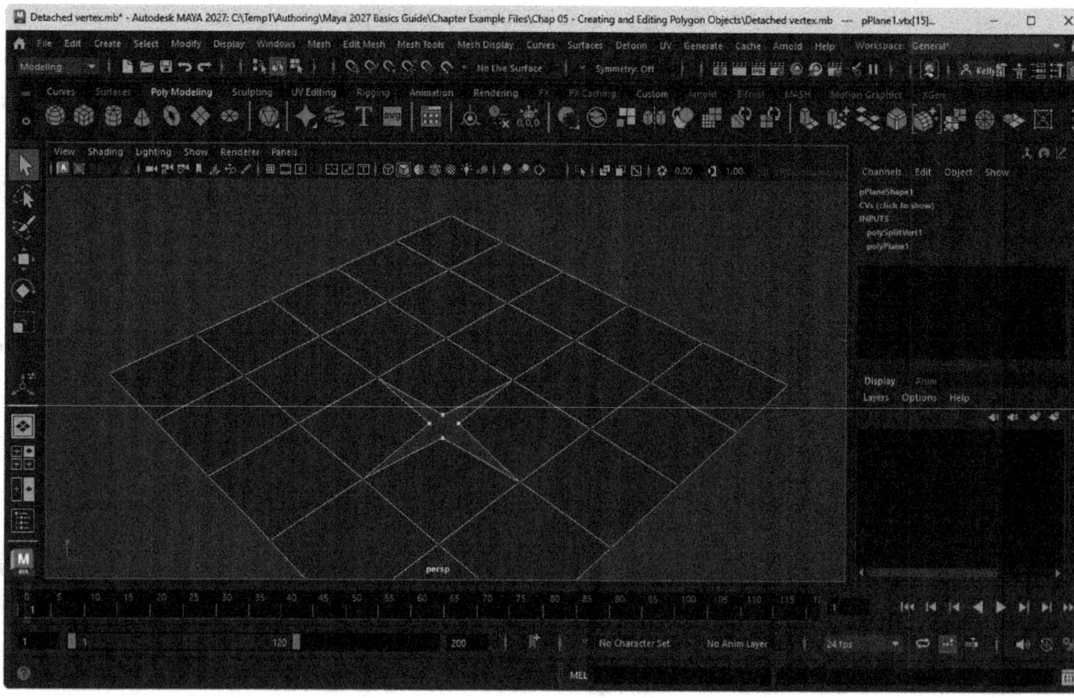

FIGURE 5-55

A detached vertex

Detaching Faces

If a polygon face or several faces are selected, you can use the Edit Mesh, Detach menu command to separate the selected faces from the polygon object. The detached faces can then be moved using the transform tools. Edges can also be detached, but they can only be moved separate from one another if a row of edges is detached or if one of the edges touches an open border. Figure 5-56 shows a plane object with several extracted faces.

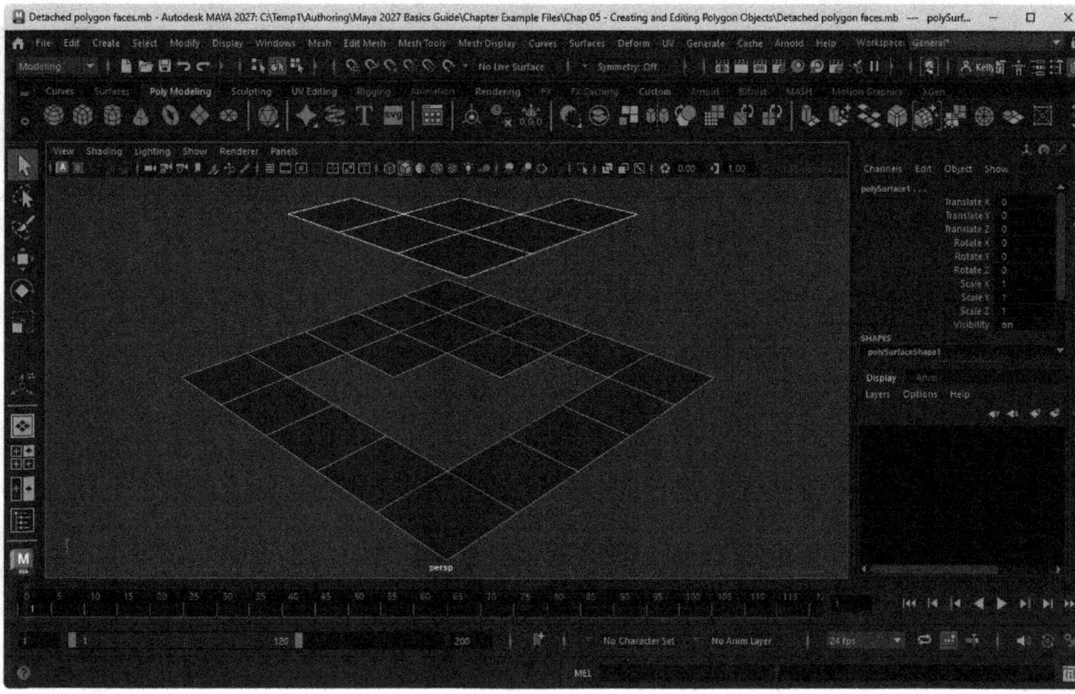

FIGURE 5-56

Extracted faces

Using the Make Hole Tool

Use the Mesh Tools, Make Hole tool to create a hole within a single polygon object's face. The face used to make the hole must be part of the polygon object and it must project within a single face on the object. In Component mode, select the Make Hole tool and click on the face that receives the hole and then on the face that makes the hole and then press the Enter key. If the face to make the hole is positioned away from the other face, new polygons are created to meet the hole. The Tool Options dialog box includes several merge modes, including Project First, Project Middle, or Project Second. Figure 5-57 shows one plane object cutting a hole into another one.

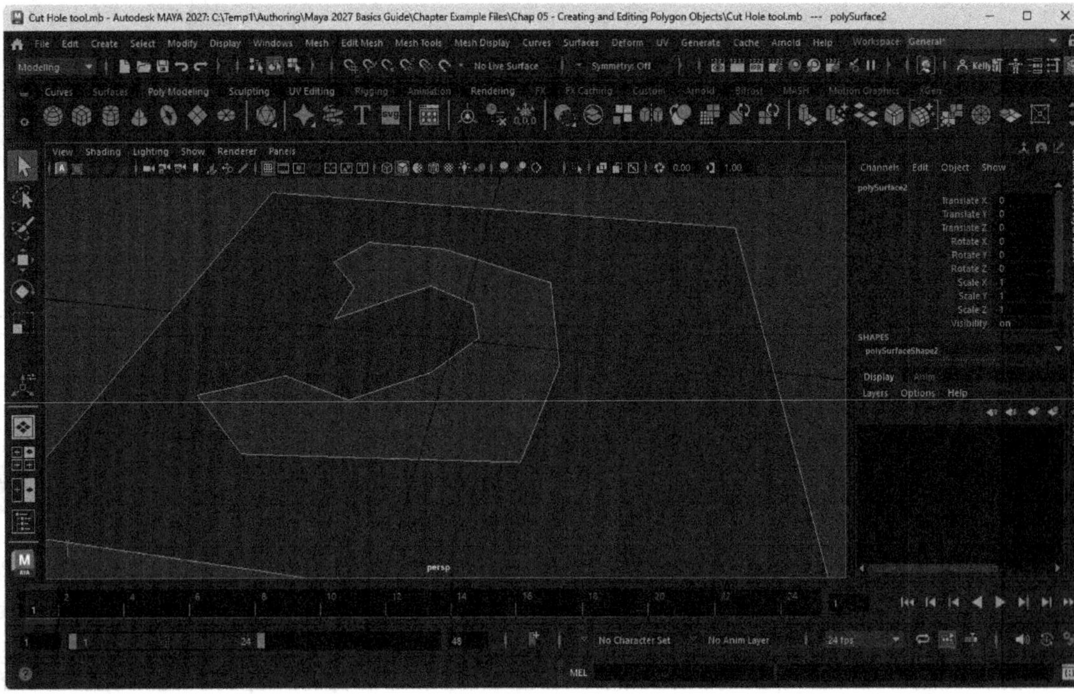

FIGURE 5-57

Creating a hole

Filling Holes

To fill a hole that may have been created by deleting a face, you can use the Mesh, Fill Hole command. This command patches all holes in the current object.

Tip

Using the Fill Holes command likely fills the hole with a non-planar polygon. You can fix this with the Mesh, Cleanup menu command or by selecting the new polygon and using the Mesh, Triangulate or Quadrangulate commands.

Lesson 5.6-Tutorial 1: Add Holes to a Cube

1. Create a polygon cube object using the Create, Polygon Primitives, Cube menu command.
2. Right-click on the cube object and select Face from the pop-up marking menu. Then drag over the entire cube to select all of its faces.
3. Select the Edit Mesh, Duplicate, Options menu command to open the Duplicate Face Options dialog box.
4. Set the Offset value to 0.2 and click the Duplicate button. Then, drag with the blue Z-axis manipulator to pull the offset face outward.

The Duplicate Faces menu command creates and moves a slightly smaller duplicate face away from the center of the cube. These faces will be used to create holes in the cube.

5. With all objects selected in Object mode, choose the Mesh, Combine menu command.
6. Select the Mesh Tools, Make Hole Tool menu command.
7. In Component mode, click on the cube face and then on its matching duplicated face while holding down the Shift key and press the Enter key.

   A hole is cut in the underlying cube, but the hole won't be visible until you make the view panel shaded using the 5 key.
8. Repeat Step 6 and 7 for each cube face.

   The final cube is shown in Figure 5-58.
9. Select File, Save Scene As and save the file as **Cube with holes.mb**.

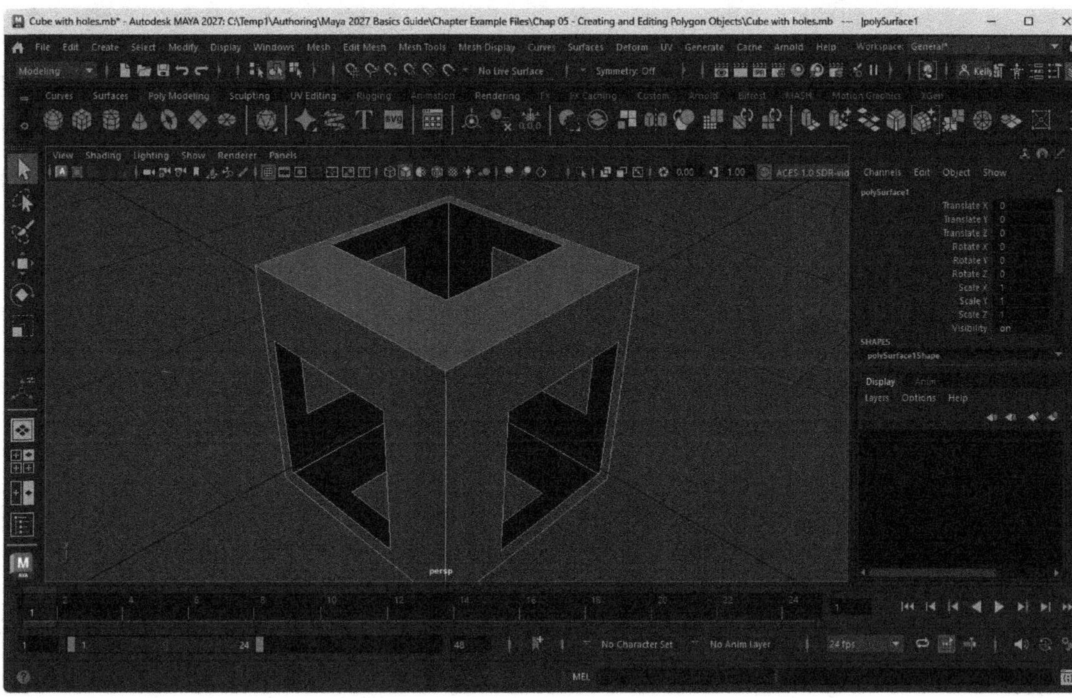

FIGURE 5-58

Cube with holes

Lesson 5.7: Work with Edge Loops, Rings, and Borders

For many models, the capability to select edge loops, rings, and borders is helpful. For example, cutting a hole in a torso and selecting the border edge enables you to quickly extrude those edges to create an arm. An edge loop is a group of edges that are aligned end to end, an edge ring is a group of edges that are aligned parallel to one another in a column, and a border includes the edges that surround a hole in the polygon model, as shown in Figure 5-59.

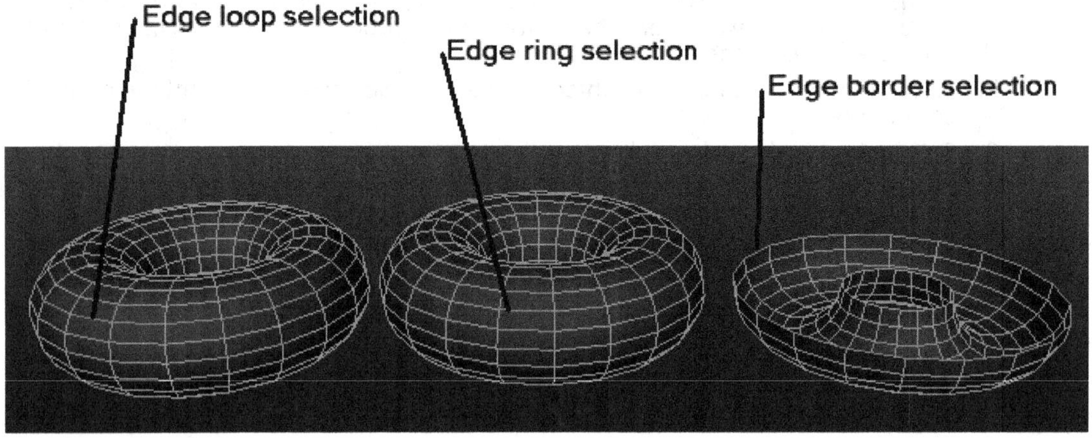

FIGURE 5-59

Edge loop, ring, and border selections

Selecting Edge Loops, Rings, and Borders

When working with polygon objects, you can select an edge loop by simply double clicking on an edge in Edge component mode. Edge rings are selected by selecting a single edge and using the Select, Convert Selection, To Edge Ring menu command.

Converting Selections

Using the Select, Convert Selection options, you can convert an existing selection of components to the desired selection, including edge loops, edge rings, face paths, and contained faces and edges.

Using the Insert Loop Tool

The Mesh Tools, Insert Edge Loop tool is used to quickly create another edge loop next to the selected edge. Selecting this tool and dragging from an edge makes duplicate edge loops appear. These duplicate edges appear as dashed lines, as shown in Figure 5-60, and you can drag to move them closer or further from the selected edge. Releasing the mouse button places the new duplicate edge loop. The Mesh Tools, Offset Edge Loop menu command places two new edge loops on either side of the current edge loop selection.

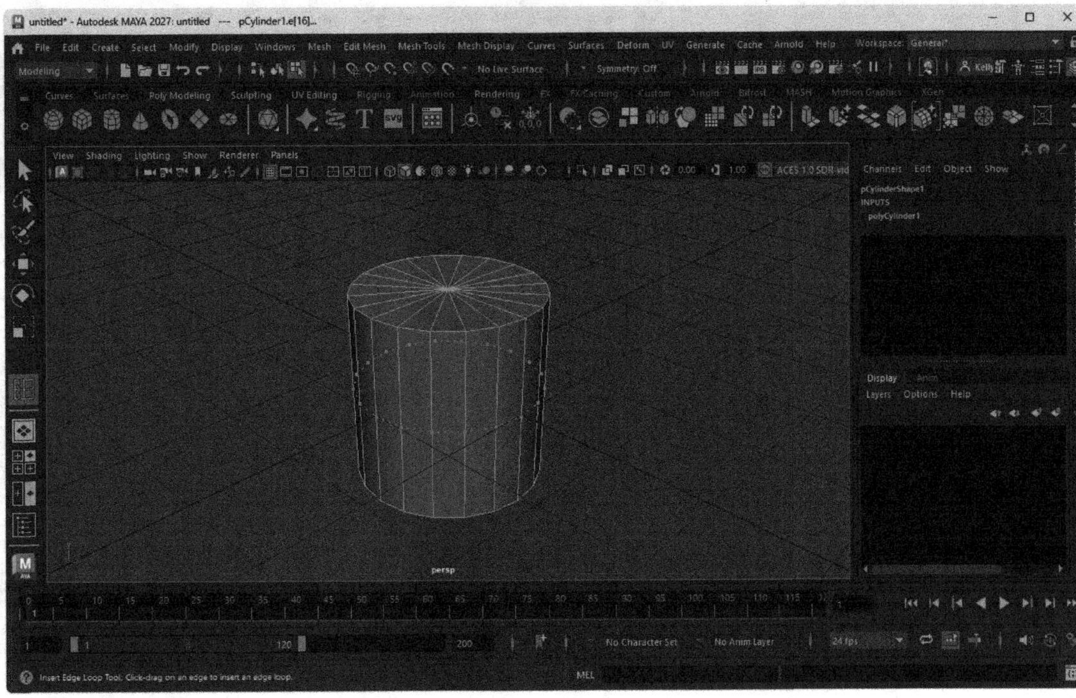

FIGURE 5-60

Duplicate edge loops

Creating Custom Edge Loops

Within the Tool Settings dialog box for the Insert Edge Loops tool is an option to Auto Complete. If this option is disabled, then you can create your own custom edge loop by marking the edges to include and then pressing the Enter key when completed. The edges you select need to be adjacent to the current edge for this to work. Figure 5-61 shows an edge loop that follows just such a unique path. If the Press Enter option in the Offset Edge Loop Options dialog box is enabled, then you can simply select an edge to be surrounded with an edge loop and press Enter to complete it.

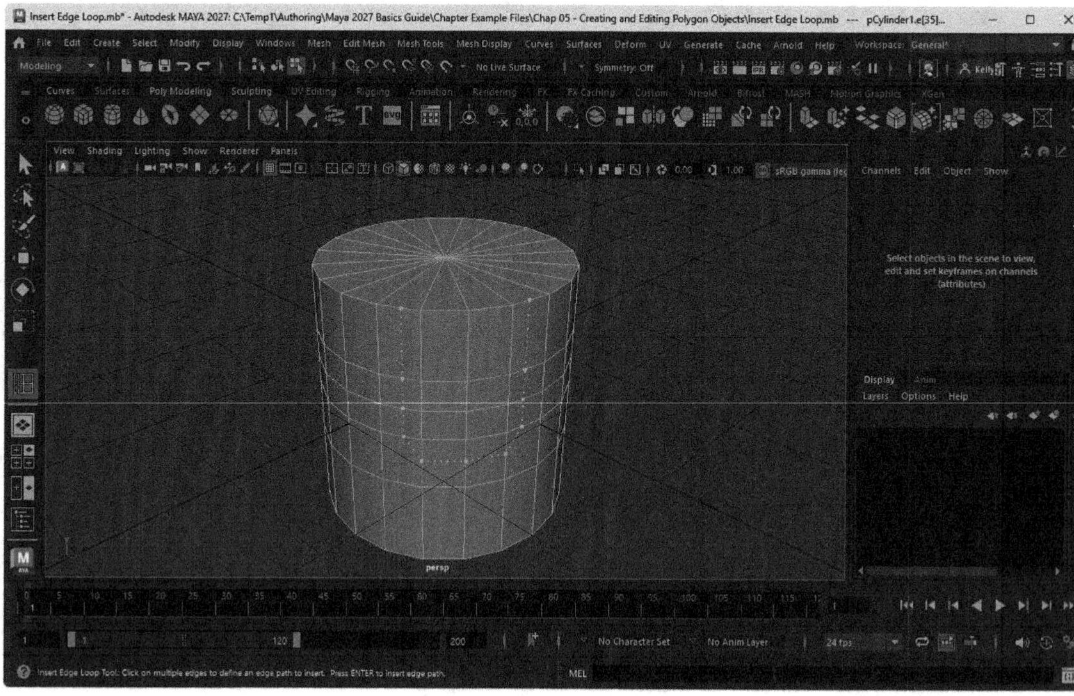

FIGURE 5-61

Customized edge ring

Lesson 5.7-Tutorial 1: Add Edge Loops to a Face

1. Select File, Open Scene and open the Simple face.mb file.

   This face was created using Subdivision Surfaces and converted to polygons. The Sculpt Geometry tool was then used to indent the eyes and nose.

2. Select the Mesh Tools, Offset Edge Loop Tool, Option menu command.
3. In the Offset Edge Loop Options dialog box, disable the Tool Completion option by choosing the Press Enter option and click the Enter Tool and Close button.
4. Select the single horizontal edge in the center of the eye socket and press the Enter key to make the edge loop. Repeat for the opposite eye.

   The Duplicate Edge Loop tool adds two radial edge loops surrounding the eyes.

5. Select the Mesh Tools, Insert Edge Loop, Option menu command.

   The Tool Settings window opens to the right of the view panel.

6. Disable the Auto Complete option in the Tool Settings window.
7. Click on several horizontal edges that run along the right side of the nose. Then select several vertical edges under the nose and some more horizontal edges that run along the left side of the nose.

   A simple edge ring is added that surrounds the nose.

8. Select the Mesh Tools, Offset Edge Loop Tool, Option menu command again. This time, enable the Auto Complete option and click the Enter Tool and Close button.
9. Click on the new edge ring that surrounds the nose and drag to create two new edge rings that are positioned close to the existing edge ring.

   The face with its new edge loops and rings is shown in Figure 5-62.

10. Select File, Save Scene As and save the file as **Edge loop face.mb**.

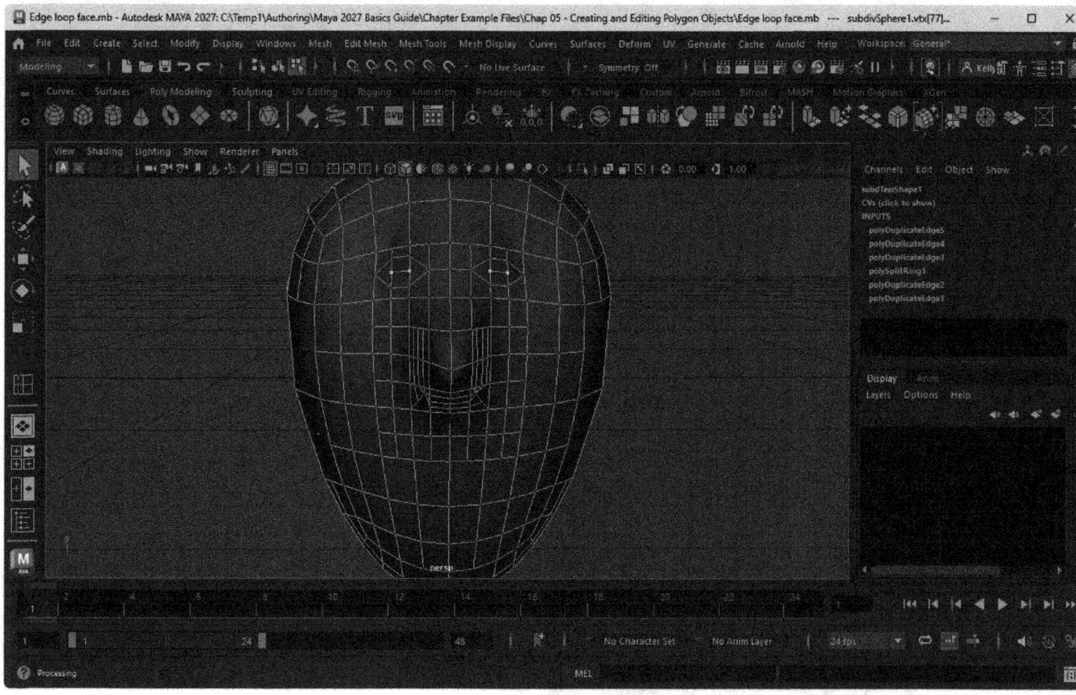

FIGURE 5-62

Face with edge loops

Lesson 5.8: Learn the Modeling Toolkit

All of the key polygon modeling tools and commands are located together in the Modeling Toolkit, shown in Figure 5-63. You can open this panel using its button at the right end of the Status Line next to the Attribute Editor button.

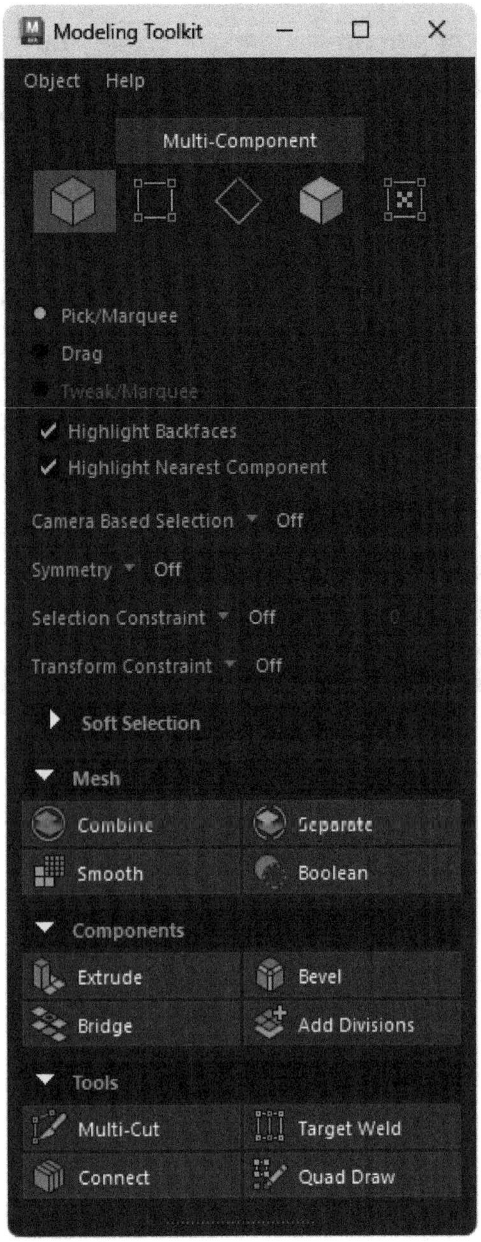

FIGURE 5-63

Modeling Toolkit panel

Selecting Components

The top section of the Modeling Toolkit includes buttons for selecting components. The buttons are for selecting Objects, Vertices, Edges, Faces and UVs. Whichever mode is current is highlighted blue. The Multi-Component button lets you choose Vertices, Edges and Faces all at once. Underneath these component modes are several selection options.

Tip

If you Ctrl/Command click on a component mode, then the current selection is converted to the clicked on component mode.

Setting Constraints

The Selection Constraints make it easier to select specific types of selections. If the Angle constraint is enabled, then only those components within the specified angle threshold can be selected. This limits the components to the desired ones. Other Selection Constraints include Border, Edge Loop, Edge Ring and Shell. For the Transform Constraints you can choose Edge Slide and Surface Slide. These limit the movement of the selected component to be only along the edge or across the surface of the object. This prevents the component from being moved off the surface of the object and maintains its smoothness.

Using Soft Selection

If you select a single component like a vertex and move it, only that vertex moves causing a disjointed surface where that vertex was moved. However, if you enable Soft Select in the Modeling Toolkit, then all the vertices surrounding the selected one are also moved, but to a less extent and it gets less as the distance from the selected vertex increases. This lets you select a central vertex, like the one shown in Figure 5-64, and move them all together in a smooth result. You can also set the gradient of the surrounding components as desired.

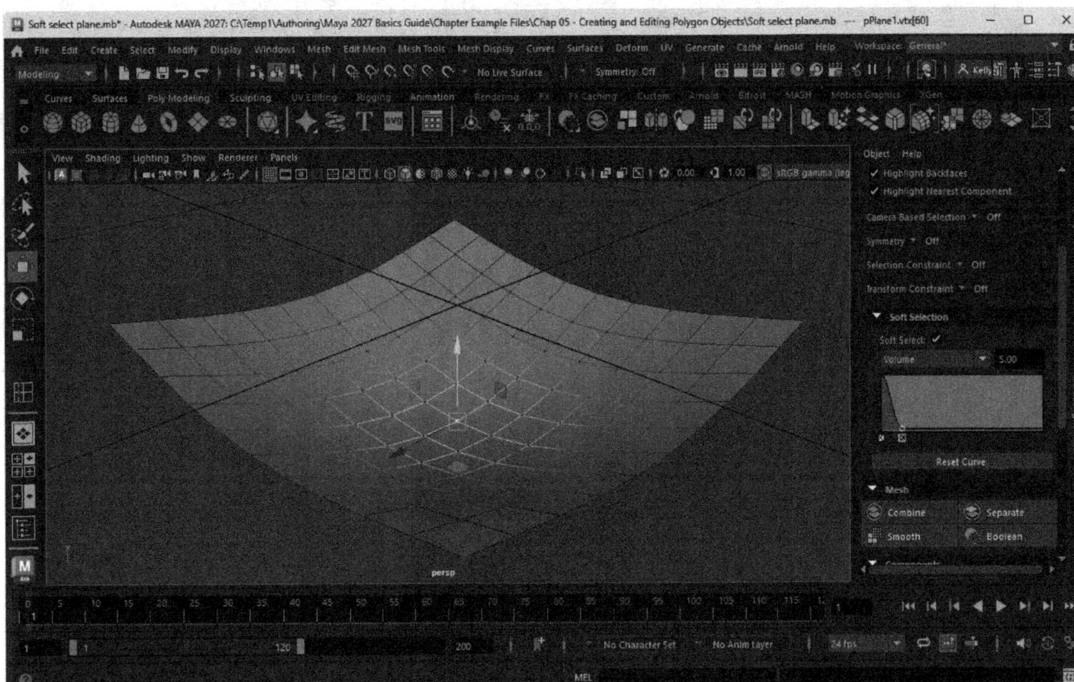

FIGURE 5-64

Soft Selection

Using Polygon Tools

The next section of the Modeling Toolkit includes many of the main polygon commands and tools. They are divided in the tools that apply to the entire Mesh including Combine, Separate, Smooth and Boolean. The Components tools are Extrude, Bevel, Bridge and Add Divisions and the Tools section has Multi-Cut, Target Weld, Connect and Quad Draw. There is also a section at the bottom of the Modeling Toolkit where you can add your own favorite tools.

Using the Target Weld Tool

The Target Weld tool is useful for quickly reducing the number of vertices and edges in a model. Select the Target Weld button in the Modeling Toolkit and click on a vertex or edge to weld, then drag to any nearby vertex or edge and the target will be highlighted. Click again on the mouse to weld the selected component to its target. This works regardless of the distance between the two components. Figure 5-65 shows two vertices being welded and the right sphere shows the results. This tool is also found in the Mesh Tools, Target Weld menu.

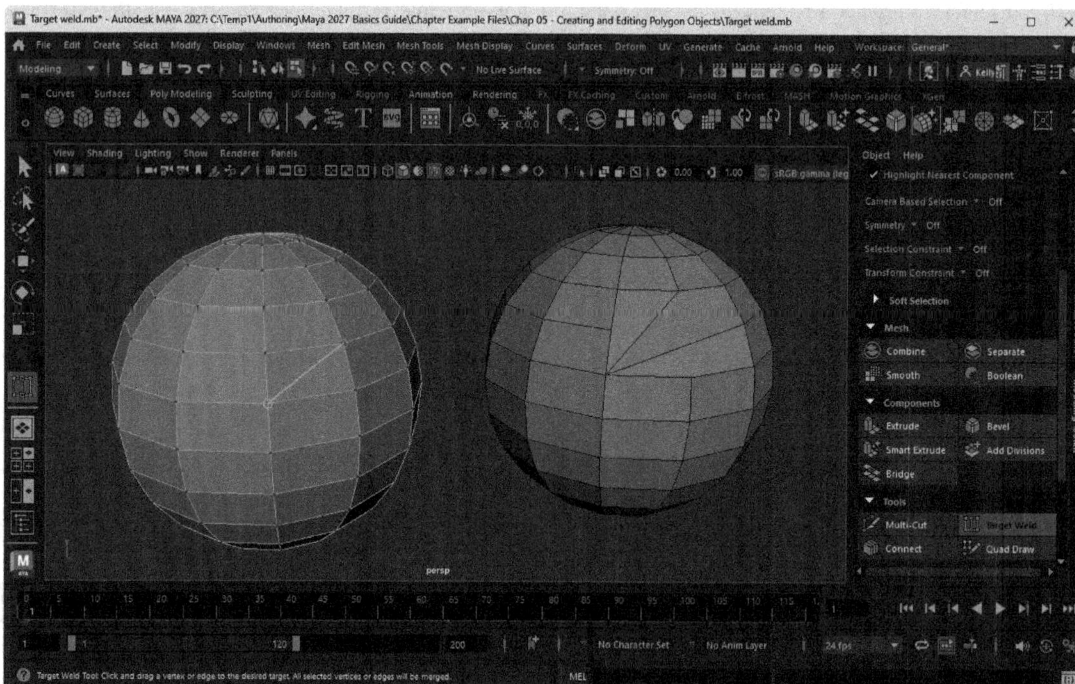

FIGURE 5-65

Target Weld

Making Shapes with the Connect Tool

The Connect tool can subdivide components interactively as you click on them creating a shape on the polygon object. This provides a quick and easy way to cut holes in an object. To use this tool, select it in the Modeling Toolkit or from the Mesh Tools, Connect menu, then click on the polygon faces that you want divided in half. You can continue to select polygons with the Shift key held down until the path is correct. Press the Enter key to apply the change. Clicking on edges with the Connect tool subdivides the entire edge ring. You can also use it on Vertices. Within the Connect Options are settings for Slide, number of Segments, and Pinch. If you drag on the path with the middle mouse button, you can increase the number of Segments, as shown in Figure 5-66.

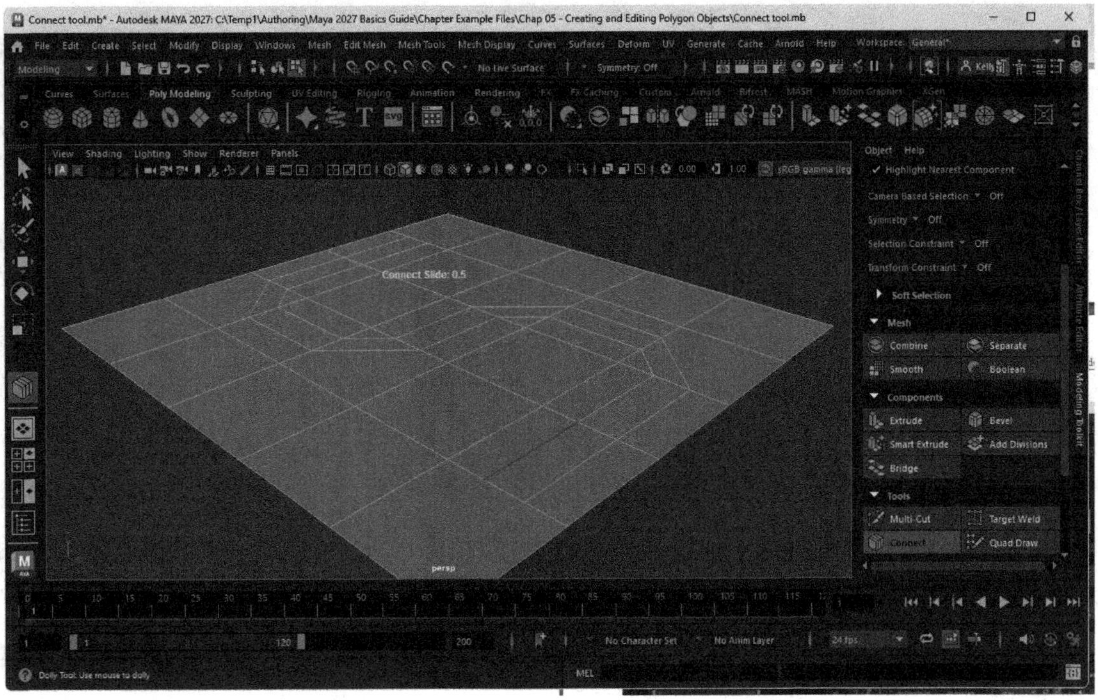

FIGURE 5-66

Connect tool path

Lesson 5.8-Tutorial 1: Modeling with Constraints and Soft Select

1. Create a polygon sphere object using the Create, Polygon Primitives, Sphere menu command.
2. Click on the Modeling Toolkit button at the right end of the Status Line.
3. Select the Edge Component mode and set the Selection Constraint to Edge Loop, then click on an edge at the middle of the sphere.
4. Enable the Soft Select option and choose the Surface option with a value of 0.25.
5. Select the Scale Tool in the toolbox and drag outward.

   The saucer looking object is created, as shown in Figure 5-67.
6. Select File, Save Scene As and save the file as **Flying Saucer.mb**.

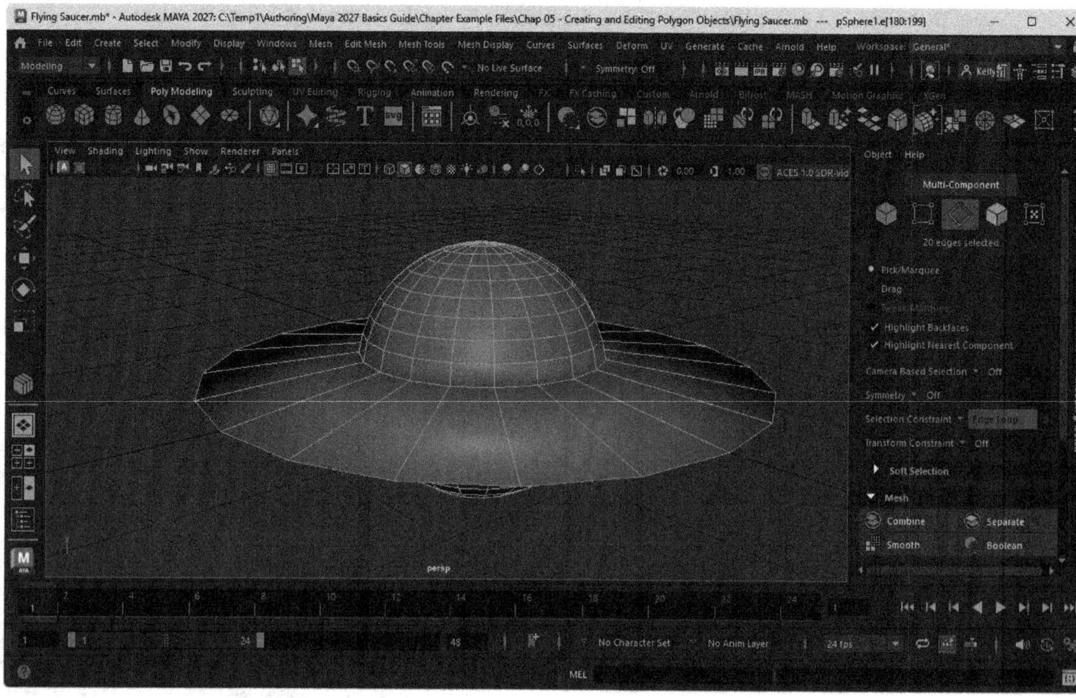

FIGURE 5-67

Flying Saucer

Lesson 5.8-Tutorial 2: Adding Arms to a Torso

1. Select File, Open Scene and open the Torso.mb file.

   This file includes a simple polygon cube object with multiple divisions.
2. In the Symmetry drop-down list in the Status Line, select the Object X symmetry option. This will build arms on both sides of the torso at the same time.
3. Click on the Modeling Toolkit button at the right end of the Status Line.
4. Select the Face Component mode and click on the Connect tool, then with the Shift key held down select the top row of faces along the side of the torso and continue around in a circle to mark the hole for the arm.
5. Select all the interior faces with the Shift key held down where the arm goes and press the Delete key to remove those faces.
6. Select the Edge Component mode and double click on one of the arm hole edges to select the entire border.
7. Click on the Extrusion tool and drag outward away from the torso to create the arm. In the Channel Box, set the number of Divisions to 5, as shown in Figure 5-68.
8. Select File, Save Scene As and save the file as **Torso with arms.mb**.

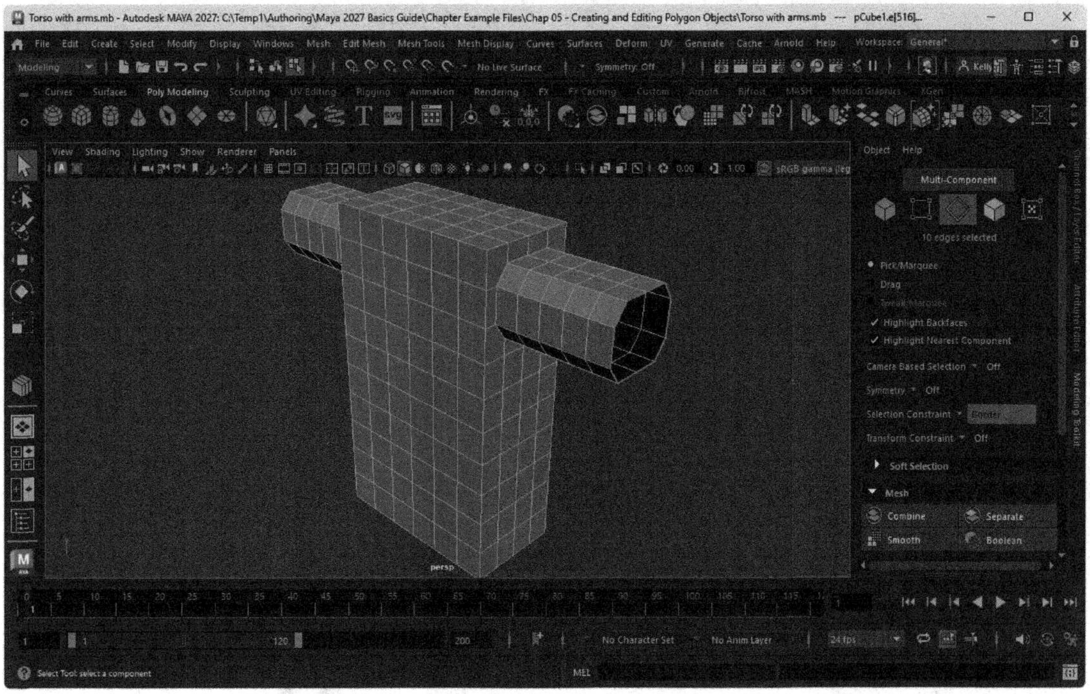

FIGURE 5-68

Torso with arms

Lesson 5.9: Model with the Quad Draw Tool

The last tool available in the Modeling Toolkit is the Quad Draw tool. The Quad Draw tool is the huge timesaver for modeling in Maya. It allows you to create and attach polygons, move components, insert edge loops, extend boundary edges, relax the mesh and more in one tool. The gotcha is that you need to learn a whole bunch of hotkeys. You can access a list of the available hotkeys for the Quad Draw tool in the Tool Settings dialog box, shown in Figure 5-69.

Note

The Quad Draw tool can only be used if a polygon mesh object is selected or a Live object is selected.

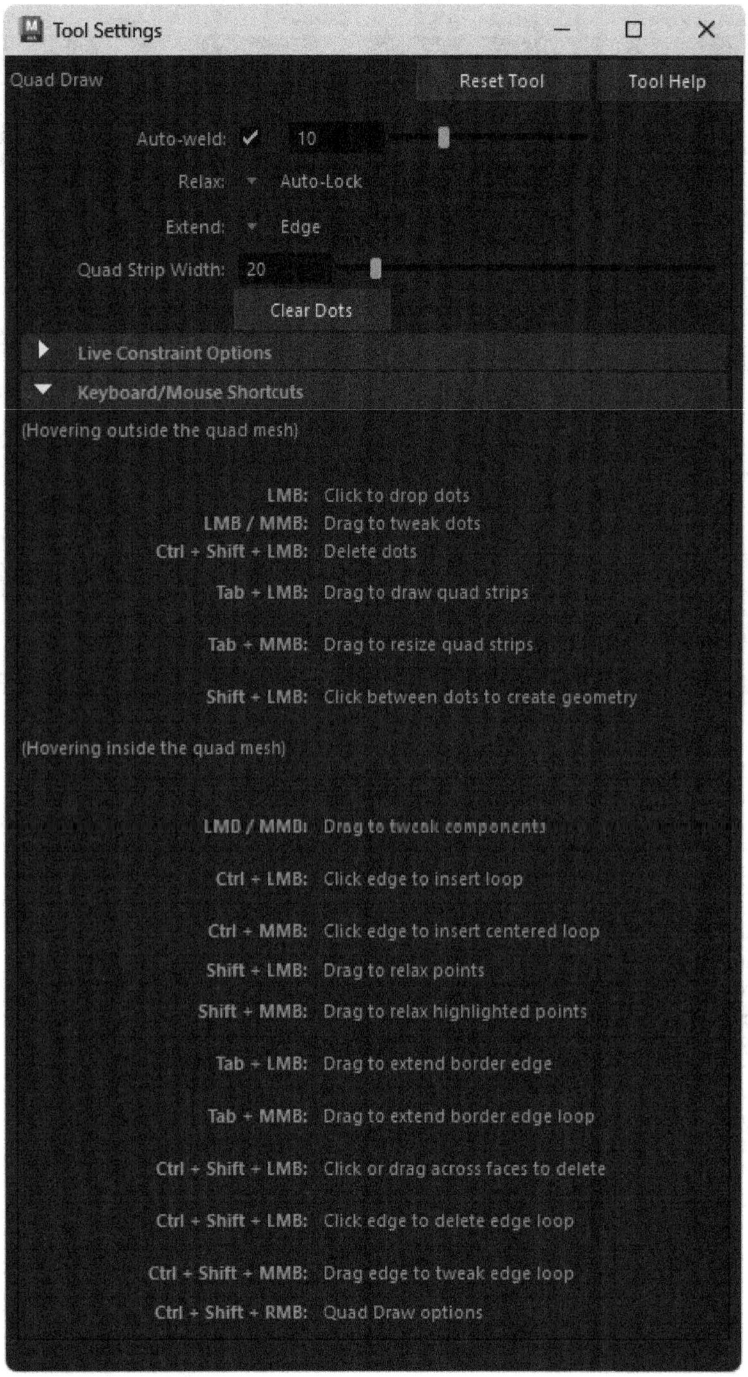

FIGURE 5-69

Hotkeys for the Quad Draw tool

Creating Polygons with the Quad Draw Tool

Creating polygons with the Quad Draw tool is a two-step process. First, you need to place all the vertices. This is done by simply clicking in an open space away from any other polygons. Placed vertices can be snapped to grid points or to the surface of a Live object. Placed vertices can be moved by dragging them to a new location. If you misplace a vertex, you can quickly delete it by clicking on it with the Ctrl/Command and Shift keys held down.

Once the necessary vertices are placed, you can hold down the Shift key and move the cursor in-between the placed vertices; a sample polygon appears, as shown in Figure 5-70. If you move about the vertices, other sample polygons appear connecting the vertices in different ways. The sample polygons also connect to the original mesh object. Click to create the sample polygon. Moving to other vertices, you can quickly create multiple attached polygons.

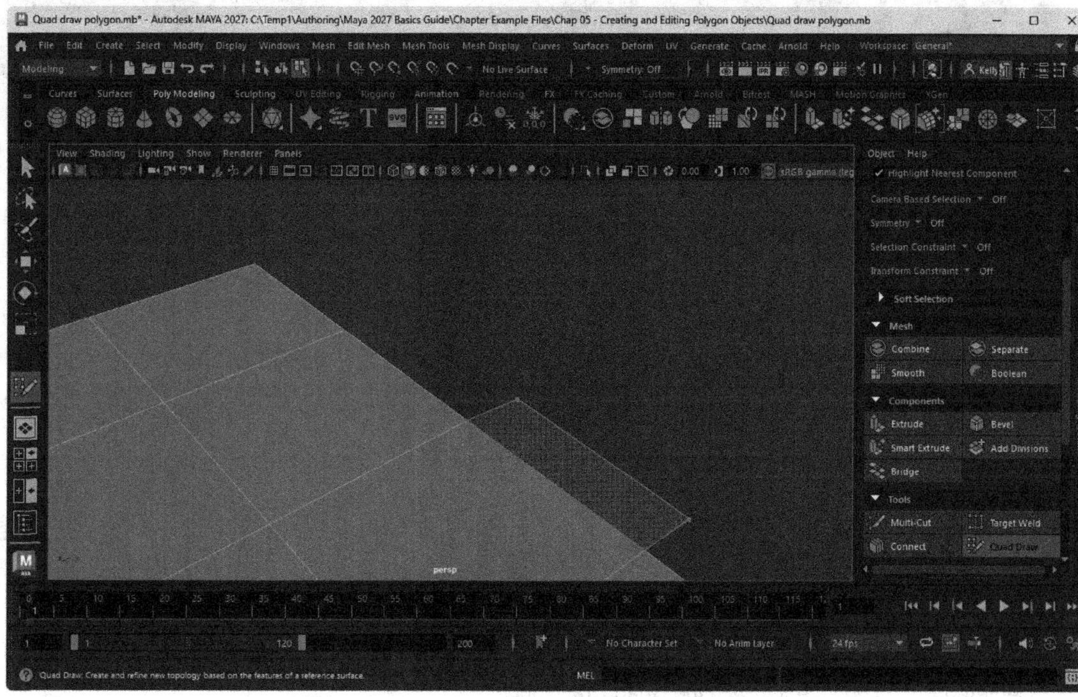

FIGURE 5-70

Sample polygon created with the Quad Draw tool

Moving Components with the Quad Draw Tool

When moving the Quad Draw tool over the surface of the polygon object, the component directly underneath the cursor turns red. While red, you can click and drag the selected component to move it. This lets you quickly make tweaks to the mesh object by moving its components. All components are accessible without having to switch between the various component modes.

Relaxing Components with the Quad Draw Tool

Another way to move components with the Relax mode. Dragging over the interior components with the Shift key held down will slowly move the tight components away from each other. This is helpful if you make some wild moves or if you just need to generally smooth out a rough area. Drag with the Shift key and the middle mouse button to relax the highlighted points only.

Adding Edge Loops with the Quad Draw Tool

An Edge Loop is a row of continuous edges running end to end for the length of the polygon object. You can quickly create a new Edge Loop by holding down the Ctrl/Command key and clicking on an interior edge in the polygon object with the Quad Draw tool. The Edge Loop will run perpendicular to the edge you click on. Holding down the Ctrl/Command key and clicking on an edge with the middle mouse button will center the Edge loop within the polygon, as shown in Figure 5-71.

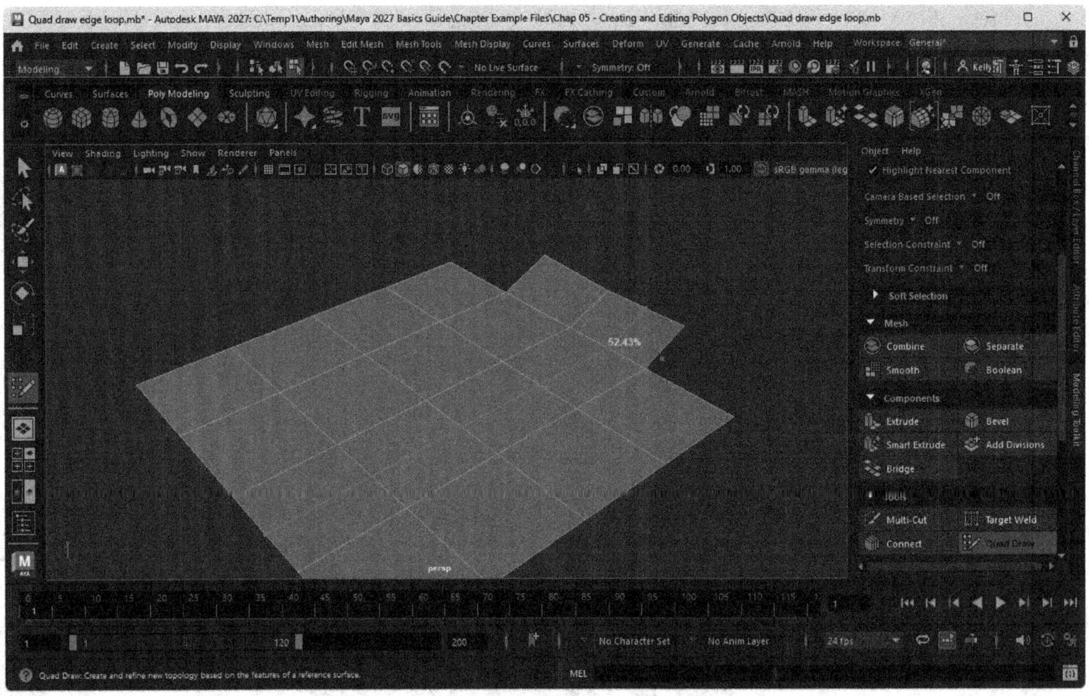

FIGURE 5-71

Centered Edge Loop created with the Quad Draw tool

Extending Edges with the Quad Draw Tool

Holding down the Tab key and dragging an edge away from the polygon object extends the edge. Before releasing the mouse, you can position the new edge by moving the mouse. If you drag with the middle mouse button, then the entire edge loop is created and moved away from the mesh object. Figure 5-72 shows a new edge created in this manner.

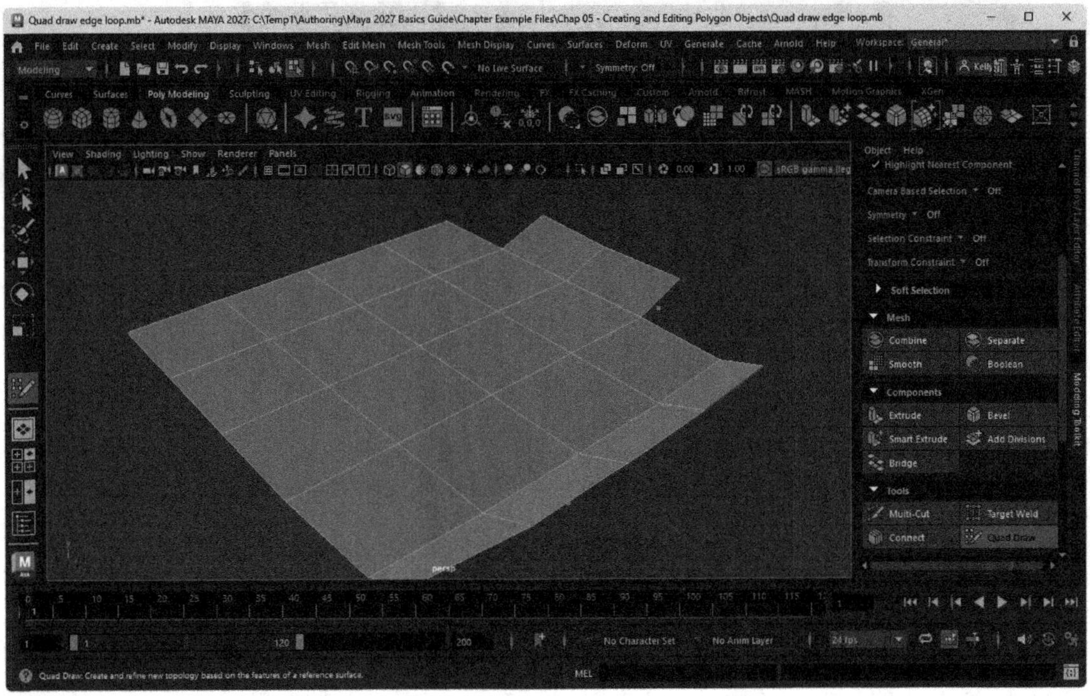

FIGURE 5-72

New Edge Loop extended with the Quad Draw tool

Deleting Components with the Quad Draw Tool

Clicking on an interior face or edge with the Ctrl/Command and Shift keys held down lets you delete the selected component. For edges, the entire Edge Loop is deleted. The Ctrl/Command and Shift key with the middle mouse button lets you reposition the selected edge loop.

Accessing the Quad Draw Tool Options

If you right click with the Ctrl/Command and Shift keys held down, then a marking menu, shown in Figure 5-73, appears. Using these options, you can Clear Dots, Soften/Harden Edges, access the Multi-Cut Tool, Auto-Weld, and set the Relax and Extend options.

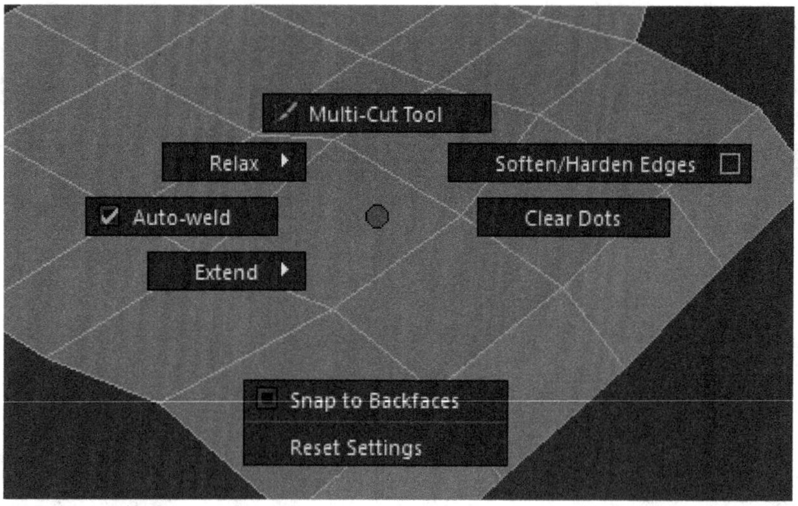

FIGURE 5-73

The Quad Draw tool options

Lesson 5.9-Tutorial 1: Adding Arms to a Torso

1. Select File, Open Scene and open the Torso with arms.mb file.

   This file includes a simple polygon cube object with arms extruding on either side.

2. In the Symmetry drop-down list in the Status Line, select the Object X symmetry option. This will apply changes to both sides of the torso at the same time.
3. Click on the Modeling Toolkit button at the right end of the Status Line.
4. Select the Quad Draw tool, hold down the Ctrl/Command and Shift key and click on the corner edge loop above the shoulder.
5. Select and drag the edge where torso meets the arm and move it towards the arm to soften the connection to the arm. Then, do the same on the rear side of the torso.
6. Select and delete the hard edges around the neck and on both vertical sides of the torso by clicking on the edges with the Ctrl/Command and Shift keys.
7. Select and pull the two faces outward when the chest is located to give the upper torso some shape.
8. Select and drag inward the faces and edges around the waist to give it some shape. Then hold down the Shift key and drag over the waist area to relax the components to make it smooth. The results are shown in Figure 5-74.
9. Select File, Save Scene As and save the file as **Smoother torso with arms.mb**.

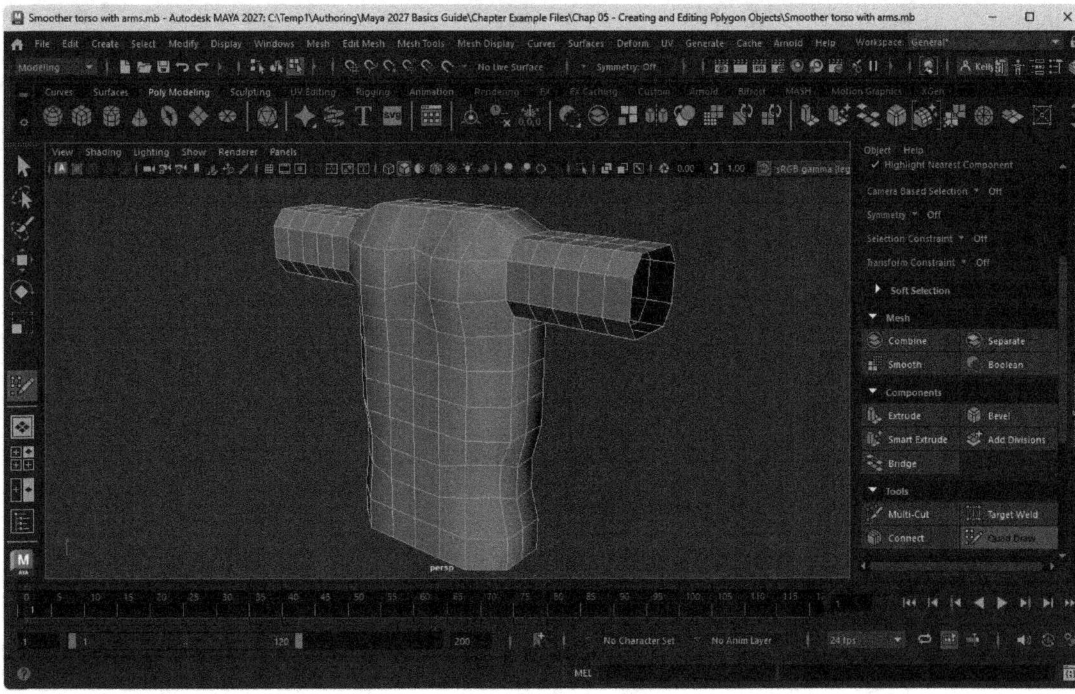

FIGURE 5-74

Smoother torso with arms

Chapter Summary

This chapter covers modeling with polygons. All polygon modeling commands are found in the Mesh, Edit Mesh, Mesh Tools and Mesh Display menus. Maya includes several default polygon primitive objects as well as a Create Polygon tool that you can use to create custom polygons. Normals determine which side of a polygon gets shaded. You can edit polygons by moving their vertex, face, or edge components. There are also numerous polygon operations for working with polygon components, including extrude, chamfer, bevel, Smart Bevel, and merge. Boolean operations provide a way to combine polygon objects using union, difference, and intersection methods. There are also tools for making holes in polygons and tools for working with edge loops. The Modeling Toolkit conveniently places all the necessary tools for working with polygons in one panel. For tweaking polygon objects, the Quad Draw tool uses hotkeys for working with all components at once.

What You Have Learned

In this chapter, you learned

* How to display and reverse face normals.
* How to soften and harden normals.
* How to create a custom polygon with the Create Polygon tool.
* How to append polygons with the Append to Polygon tool.
* How to clean up and reduce a polygon object.
* How to select the various polygon components.
* How to duplicate and offset a polygon face.
* How to subdivide a polygon face.
* How to split and cut a polygon face.
* How to merge vertices and edges and delete components.
* How to enable symmetrical editing.
* How to retopologize a mesh.
* How to smooth polygons and use a smooth proxy.
* How to add creases to a smooth proxy.
* How to use Booleans.
* How to change and add more objects to a Boolean.
* How to triangulate polygons.
* How to split a vertex.
* How to extract faces.
* How to use the Make Holes tool.
* How to fill existing polygon holes.
* How to select edge loops, edge rings, and borders.
* How to create edge loops and edge rings.
* How to access the Modeling Toolkit.
* How to use selection and transform constraints.
* How to make a soft selection.
* How to access the Quad Draw tool.
* How to use the Quad Draw tool to work with components.

Key Terms From This Chapter

* **Polygon.** A co-planar surface created from three or more linear edges.
* **Normal.** A vector extending perpendicular from the surface of a polygon used to determine the polygon's inner and outer faces.
* **Appending.** The process of attaching a polygon to an existing polygon.
* **In-View Editor.** A small dialog box of attributes that appears next to the object being edited in lieu of the Channel Box.
* **Reduce.** An operation that reduces the total number of polygons in a model.
* **Cleanup.** An operation that removes potential trouble parts of a polygon model such as unattached vertices.
* **Subdividing.** An operation for splitting all polygon faces into two or more faces.
* **Extruding.** An operation that moves the selected component perpendicular from its current position.
* **Chamfer.** An operation that replaces the selected vertices with polygon faces.
* **Bevel.** An operation that replaces an edge with a polygon face.
* **Smart Bevel.** A bevel operation that creates a smooth transition between overlapping objects and are combined using the Boolean operation.
* **Poking.** An operation that adds a vertex to the center of the selected face and attaches edges to the new vertex.
* **Wedge.** A model structure created by rotating a face about an edge and connecting it to the original face's position.
* **Retopology.** The process of simplifying the topology (or surface) of an object resulting in fewer and more regularly aligned polygons.
* **Smooth proxy.** A smoothed copy of an original polygon object.
* **Booleans.** A set of operations for combining two polygon objects together using a union, difference, or intersection.
* **Input object.** An object used in a boolean operation.
* **Boolean Stack.** A list in the Attribute Editor of all the objects used in a Boolean operation.
* **Edge loop.** A series of edges that run end to end across the surface of a polygon object.

* **Edge ring.** A series of parallel edges that run across the surface of a polygon object.

* **Border.** A series of edges that line a polygon hole.

* **Modeling Toolkit.** A panel of commands placed together for working with polygon objects.

* **Quad Draw tool.** A tool found in the Modeling Toolkit that lets you move and work with all components at once.

Chapter 6
Working with NURBS Surfaces

IN THIS CHAPTER

- 6.1 Edit NURBS surfaces.
- 6.2 Apply surface operators.
- 6.3 Trim NURBS surfaces.
- 6.4 Use Boolean tools.
- 6.5 Stitch surfaces together.
- 6.6 Convert objects.

NURBS is an acronym for *Non-Uniform Rational B-Spline*. These splines are mathematically defined lines that you can manipulate to form unique shapes. A *NURBS surface* is a solid object created from NURBS curves. NURBS surfaces are useful for modeling organic objects like flowers and trees where the surfaces flow into one another.

NURBS surfaces, like NURBS curves, can be edited by moving their control vertices (CVs). You can also display hulls for the NURBS surfaces to see how the various CVs are connected. Using the right-click marking menu, you can select to see all the components that make up a NURBS surface.

Another common component for NURBS surfaces is an **isoparametric curve**(isoparms, for short). *Isoparms* are representative lines that show the object surface. The direction of an isoparm is defined using the U and V coordinate system with U-direction isoparms running horizontally and V-direction isoparms running vertically.

At the Rough resolution (enabled by pressing the 1 key) the number of isoparms is greatly reduced, but at the Fine resolution (enabled by pressing the 3 key), many additional isoparms are shown. New isoparms can be created easily by dragging from an existing isoparm to mark the location of the new isoparm. Marked isoparms can be made permanent using the Surfaces, Insert Isoparms menu command.

The area between the Isoparms is called a *patch*. Each patch face has two sides. The side that is rendered is determined by the direction of a hidden vector that is called the *normal*. It extends perpendicular to the patch face.

NURBS surfaces can be created using the Create, NURBS Primitives menu or by using one of the Surfaces menu commands on a NURBS curve. Once the NURBS surface is created you can use the operations found in the Surfaces menu to work with it.

Some of the operations found in the Surfaces menu let you attach and detach, align, open and close, extend, offset and fillet surfaces. These operations all require that one or more surfaces are selected before they can be used. The Help Line explains exactly what must be selected to use an operation.

The Surfaces menu also includes several tools and commands that may be used to edit NURBS surfaces including the **Surface Editing tool**, the Sculpt Geometry tool, and the Break and Smooth Tangent commands. The Surface Editing tool lets you click on a surface location and move it with a manipulator or change its tangent. The Sculpt Geometry tool lets you push, pull, and smooth a surface using an interactively changeable brush. Breaking tangents lets you create hard edges on NURBS surfaces.

Trimming is the process of adding holes to NURBS surfaces. This is accomplished by marking the area to trim with a NURBS curve. These curves must be attached to the surface by projecting it onto the surface, marking an intersection between another surface or by drawing on a live object.

Booleans offer a way to combine, subtract, and extract an intersecting volume between two overlapping NURBS surfaces.

Stitching NURBS surfaces together attaches the surfaces so that moving one causes the other to move with it. Maya lets you stitch objects by points, edges or using a Global Stitch command.

You can also convert between the various modeling types using the Modify, Convert menu. This menu allows you to convert between NURBS, polygons, and subdivision surfaces.

Lesson 6.1: Edit NURBS Surfaces

Once a NURBS surface is created, you can edit its surface directly by selecting and transforming its components. Transforming the object's CVs edits the basic shape of these primitives. To see an object's CVs, click the Select by Component Type button in the Status Line (or press the F8 key); select the primitive's CVs by right-clicking on the object and selecting Control Vertices from the marking menu. The selected CVs can then be transformed using the Move, Rotate, and Scale tools.

Selecting Components

NURBS surfaces can have as many times the number of CVs as a NURBS curve, as shown in Figure 6-1, which can make it tricky to select the exact CVs you want. To help resolve this problem, you can use the commands in the Select menu. The Select menu includes the Grow, Shrink, Select CV Selection Boundary, and Surface Border commands. These commands can really be helpful as you select NURBS surface components to edit.

Tip

With a CV selected, you can use the arrow keys to select the adjacent CV.

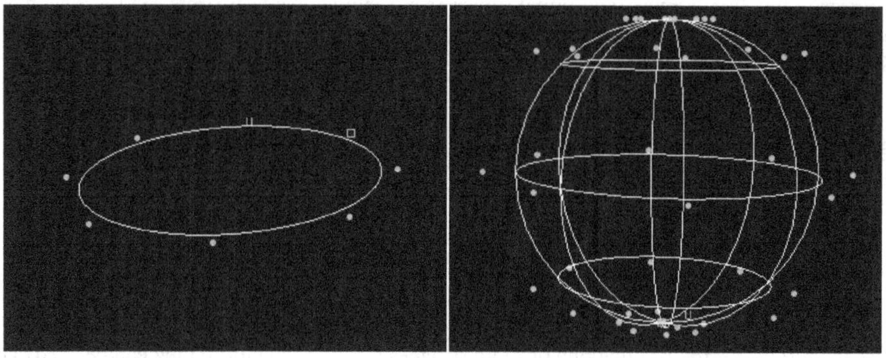

Circle: 8 CVs NURBS Sphere: 40 CVs

FIGURE 6-1

Circle CVs vs. Sphere CVs

Using the Surface Editing Tool

With the Surfaces, Surface Editing, Surface Editing tool selected, you can click on any point of the surface and a set of manipulators appears (as shown in Figure 6-2) that let you move the selected point. Dragging the Point Position handle moves the point and dragging the Slide Along Curve manipulator with the middle mouse button slides the Point Position handle along the isoparm. Clicking the Tangent Direction toggle switches between a U-align, V-align, and normal-aligned tangent. The Tangent Direction handle can also be manipulated to change the surface point's tangent. Clicking on one of the dotted axis lines aligns the tangent to that axis.

Note

When editing with the Surface Editing tool, you can only select isoparm intersection points when viewing the object in wireframe view, but in Full Shading view, you can select any visible point on the object surface.

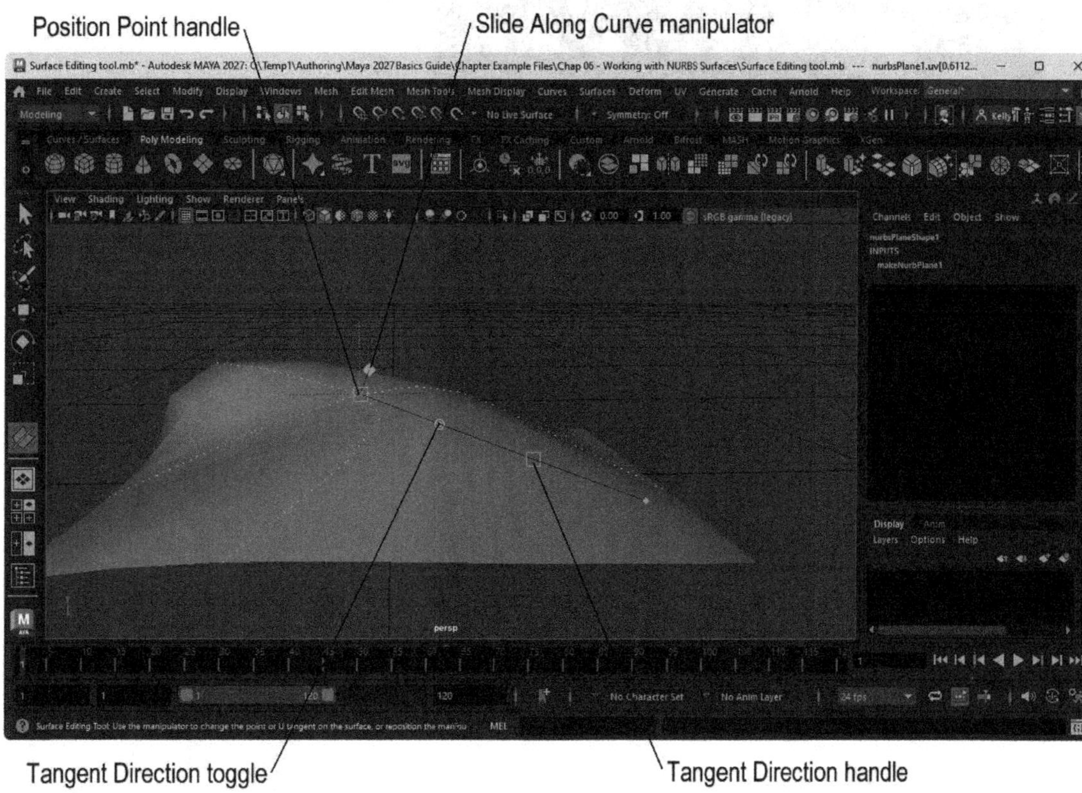

FIGURE 6-2

Surface Editing tool

Using the Sculpt Geometry Tool

The Sculpt Geometry tool, available in the Surfaces menu, lets you push, pull, smooth, and erase surface CVs. Using the Tool Settings dialog box, shown in Figure 6-3, you can select the radius, opacity, and shape of the sculpt tool. When selected, a red manipulator shows you the size of the brush radius and an arrow pointing away from the radial circle shows how far the brush moves the surface. You can then paint on the surface of an object to deform the surface.

Tip

You can interactively change the brush radius by dragging with the b key held down; you can change the brush distance by dragging with the m key held down.

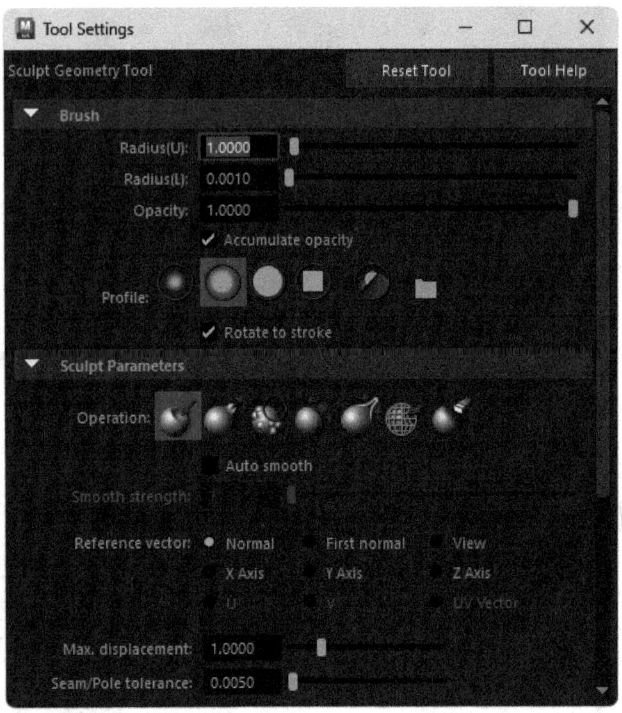

FIGURE 6-3

Sculpt Geometry tool options

Simplifying Surfaces

The Surfaces, Rebuild menu command reduces the complexity of a surface. This option offers several different rebuild options and you can rebuild only the U or V direction.

Breaking and Smoothing Tangents

By default, NURBS surfaces are smooth across their surface because the tangent points between all the CVs are aligned, but if you want to create a hard edge, you can break the tangent for a selected isoparm using the Surfaces, Surface Editing, Break Tangents menu command. The Surfaces, Surface Editing, Smooth Tangents menu command may be used to smooth an isoparm that has been broken.

Lesson 6.1-Tutorial 1: Edit NURBS Components

1. Create a plane object using the Create, NURBS Primitives, Plane menu command.
2. Click on the Select by Component Type button in the Status Line (or press the F8 key).
3. Select the Move tool, hold down the Shift key and select the CVs at opposite corners of the plane object.
4. Then drag the two CVs upward using the green Y-axis manipulator.

   The surface of the plane object bends to follow the CVs' movements.
5. Hold down the Shift key and select the other two opposite corner CVs.
6. Drag these two CVs downward using the green Y-axis manipulator.
7. Press the 5 key to see this surface shaded, as shown in Figure 6-4.
8. Select File, Save Scene As and save the file as **Bent plane object.mb**.

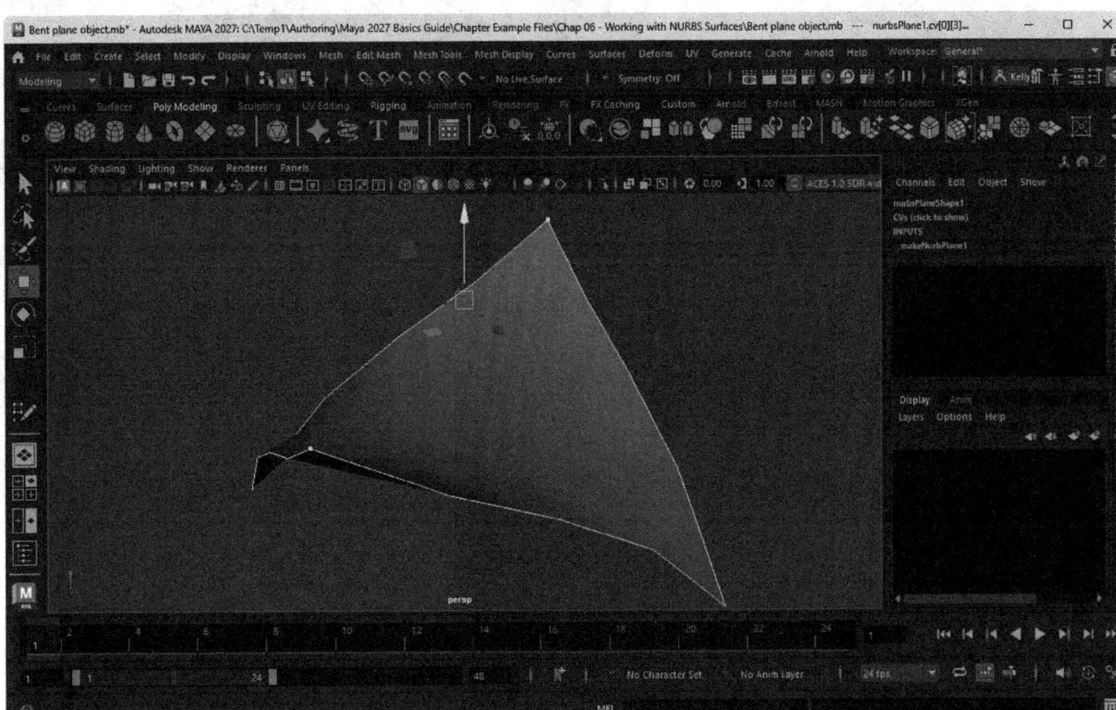

FIGURE 6-4

Bent plane object

Lesson 6.1-Tutorial 2: Use the Surface Editing Tool

1. Create a sphere object using the Create, NURBS Primitives, Sphere menu command.

2. Click on the Panel View button from the Quick Layout buttons and select the Top View panel and press the spacebar to maximize the viewport.
3. Select the Surfaces, Surface Editing, Surface Editing Tool menu command.
4. Click on the left edge of the sphere and drag the Point Position handle to the left to elongate the sphere.
5. Then select and drag the Tangent Distance handle until it is on top of the Point Position handle.
6. Repeat Steps 4 and 5 for the right side of the sphere.
7. Click the Model View button again and select the Perspective view. Then press the 5 key to see the object shaded.

    The sphere object looks like a football, as shown in Figure 6-5.
8. Select File, Save Scene As and save the file as **Football.mb**.

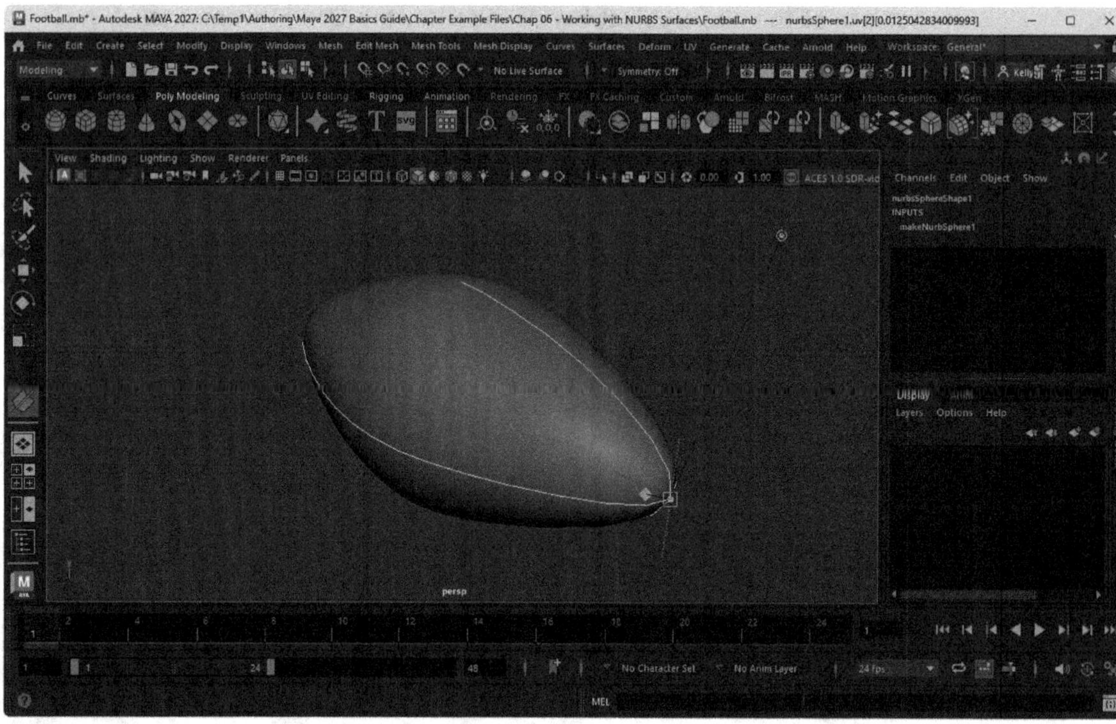

FIGURE 6-5

A football object

Lesson 6.1-Tutorial 3: Use the Sculpt Geometry Tool

1. Select the Create, NURBS Primitives, Cylinder, Options menu command to open the NURBS Cylinder Options dialog box. Set the Radius value to 5, the Height to 15, the Number of Sections to 20 and the Number of Spans to 10. Select the Both option for Caps and click the Create button.
2. Press the f key to zoom in on the selected plane object.
3. Select the Surfaces, Sculpt Geometry Tool menu command. Double-click on the tool in the Toolbox and select the Pull option from the Tool Settings panel.

4. Hold down the 'b' key and drag the tool radius to around 2.0. Then hold down the 'm' key and drag the Max Displacement value to around 2.0.

   Moving the cursor over the cylinder surface shows the size of the Radius and an arrow pointing out from the surface shows the Max Displacement.

5. Move the sculpt cursor to the side of the cylinder and drag several times to pull a section away from the surface. This pulled section is the character's nose.
6. Rotate the view until the pulled area is directly in front of the view. Select the Push option in the Tool Settings panel and drag below the pulled area to create a mouth.
7. Hold down the 'b' key and drag to set the Radius to about 1.0, and then drag in two places above the nose area to create some eye sockets.
8. Select the Create, NURBS Primitives, Sphere menu command and position the sphere in one of the eye sockets with the Move tool.
9. With the sphere still selected, choose the Edit, Duplicate menu command and move the duplicate sphere to the other eye socket.

   The simple character face object is shown in Figure 6-6.

10. Select File, Save Scene As and save the file as **Sculpted face.mb**.

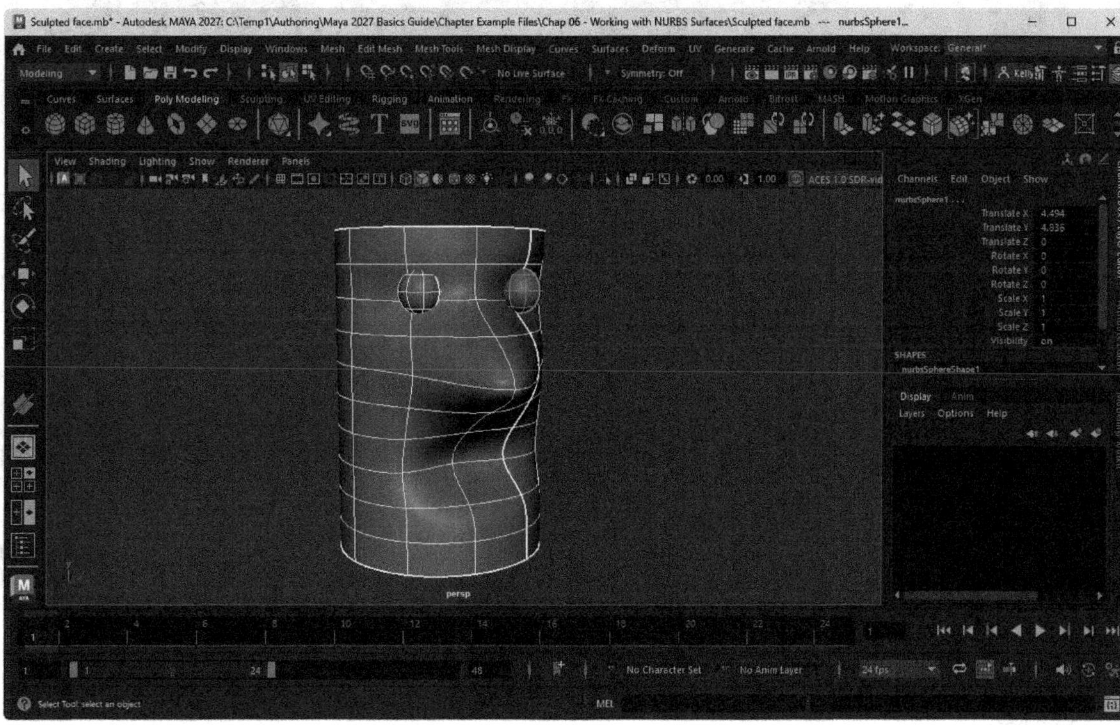

FIGURE 6-6

Sculpted face

Lesson 6.1-Tutorial 4: Create a Hard Edge

1. Create a sphere object using the Create, NURBS Primitives, Sphere menu command.
2. Right-click on the sphere and select Isoparm from the pop-up marking menu.
3. Drag over one of the vertical running isoparms to select it.

4. With an isoparm selected, choose the Surfaces, Surface Editing, Break Tangent menu twice.
5. Right-click on the sphere and select Control Vertex from the pop-up marking menu.
6. Select the center CV that lies on the previously selected isoparm and drag it away from the center of the sphere.
7. Press the 5 key to see the object shaded.

   With the tangent broken for the given isoparm, extra CVs have been added to the object that make the selected isoparm a hard edge.
8. Select the Create, NURBS Primitives, Sphere menu command and position the sphere as one of the eyes with the Move tool.
9. With the sphere still selected, choose the Edit, Duplicate menu command and move the duplicate sphere to the other eye position, as shown in Figure 6-7.
10. Select File, Save Scene As and save the file as **Bird head.mb**.

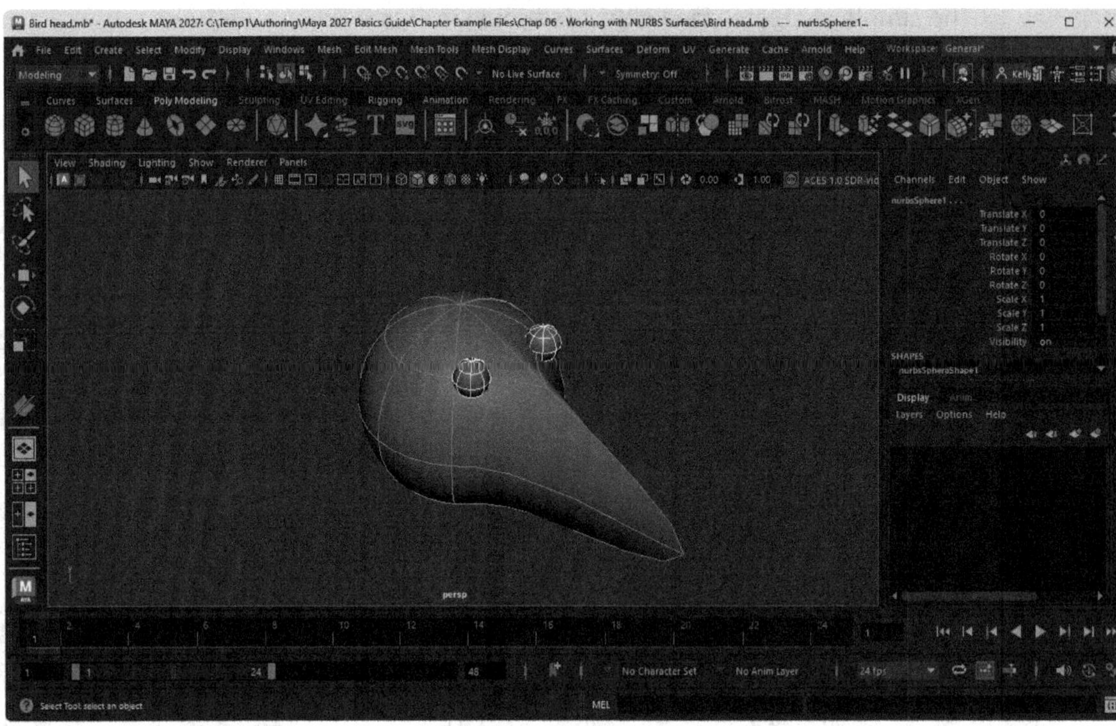

FIGURE 6-7

Bird head

Lesson 6.2: Apply Surface Operators

The Surfaces menu includes many actions that can be used to combine, align, offset, and blend NURBS surfaces. Most of these menu commands also have an options dialog box available.

Attaching and Detaching Surfaces

Two selected surfaces can be attached to one another using the Surfaces, Attach menu command. The Connect option stretches to attach the closest edge of the last-selected NURBS surface to the other surface, but the Blend option stretches both patches equally, as shown in Figure 6-8. If you select an isoparm, you can use the Surfaces, Detach menu command to detach the isoparm and the patches that are attached to it from the original object.

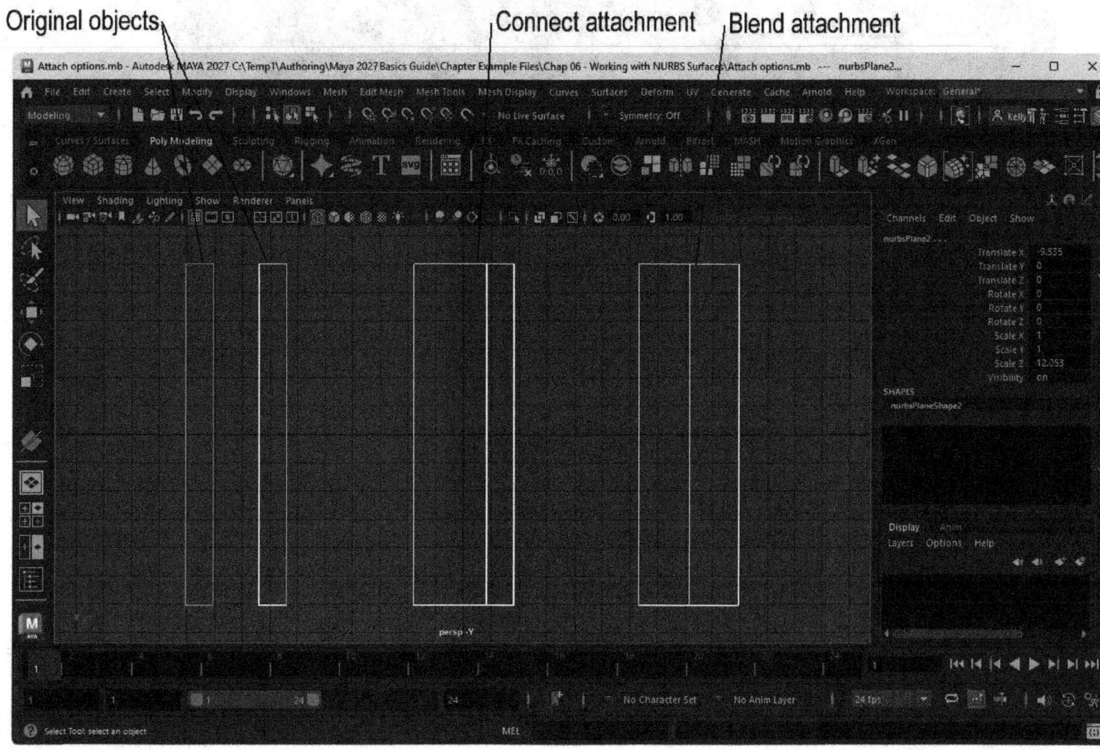

FIGURE 6-8

Attach options

Aligning Surfaces

With the isoparms on two surfaces selected, you can align the surfaces to each other. The Align Surfaces Options dialog box, shown in Figure 6-9, lets you choose to align a curve's position, tangent, or curvature. When the Position option is selected, you can select which surface to move: first, second, or both (which moves both surfaces halfway). With the Tangent or Curvature options selected, you can select to modify the tangents along the edge of either surface or both.

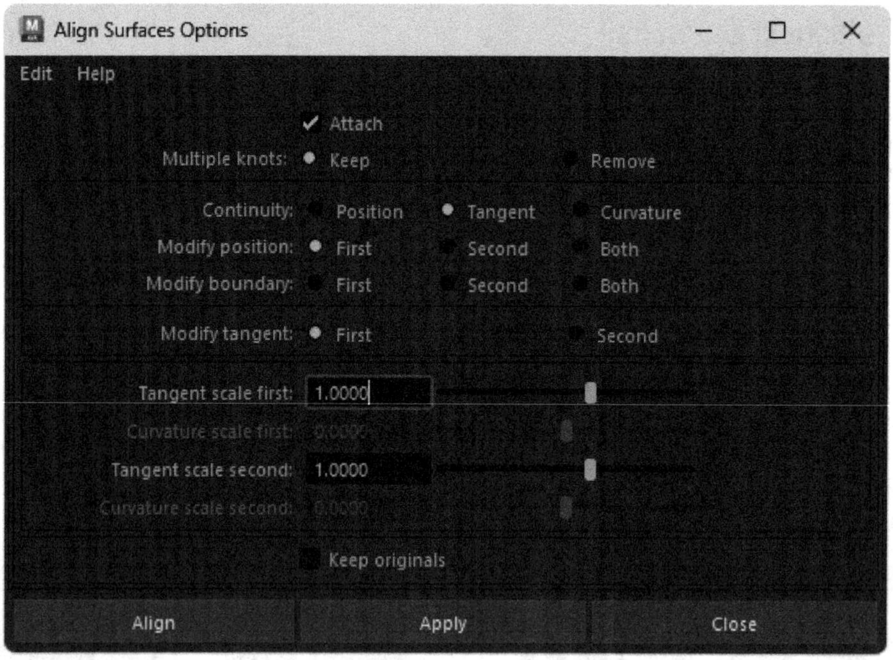

FIGURE 6-9

Align Surfaces options

Closing and Opening NURBS Surfaces

The Surfaces, Open/Close menu command creates a closed surface from an open surface and vice versa. In the Open/Close Options dialog box, you can select to close the surface along the U, V or both directions, as shown in Figure 6-10. You can also select to ignore the existing shape, preserve the existing surface, or blend the existing surface.

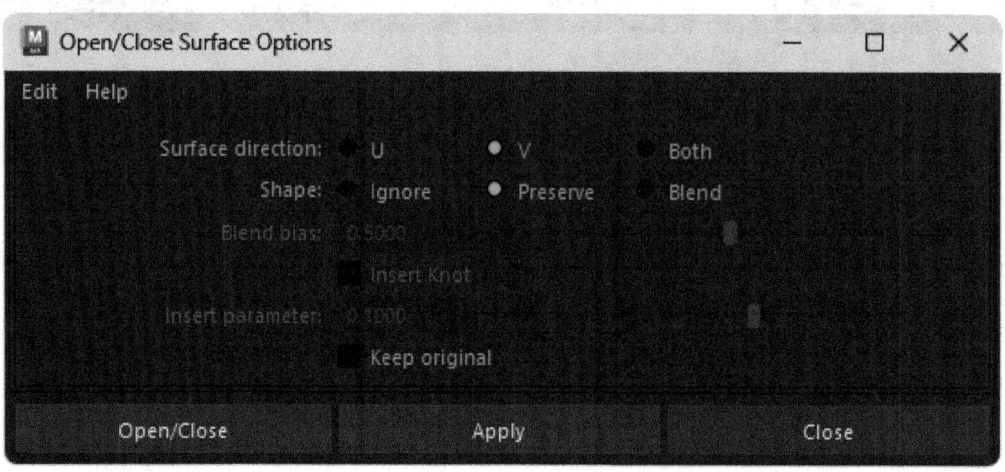

FIGURE 6-10

Open/Close Surface options

Extending Surfaces

With a NURBS surface selected, you can extend its open edges using the Surfaces, Extend menu command. From the options dialog box, you can select to extend the surface based on tangents or an extrapolation of the existing points. You can specify the distance to extend and the side (start, end, or both) and direction (U, V, or both). The Join to Original option makes the extensions part of the original surface.

Offsetting a Surface

Using the Edit, Duplicate command you can create a copy of a surface and then move it an offset distance or you can use the Surfaces, Offset to do the same operation in one action. The options dialog box lets you specify the offset distance. Figure 6-11 shows a simple sphere that has been offset, forming a large sphere that encompasses the first.

Tip

> You can also duplicate only a portion of an object using the Surfaces, Duplicate NURBS Patch menu command. This command only duplicates the selected NURBS patches.

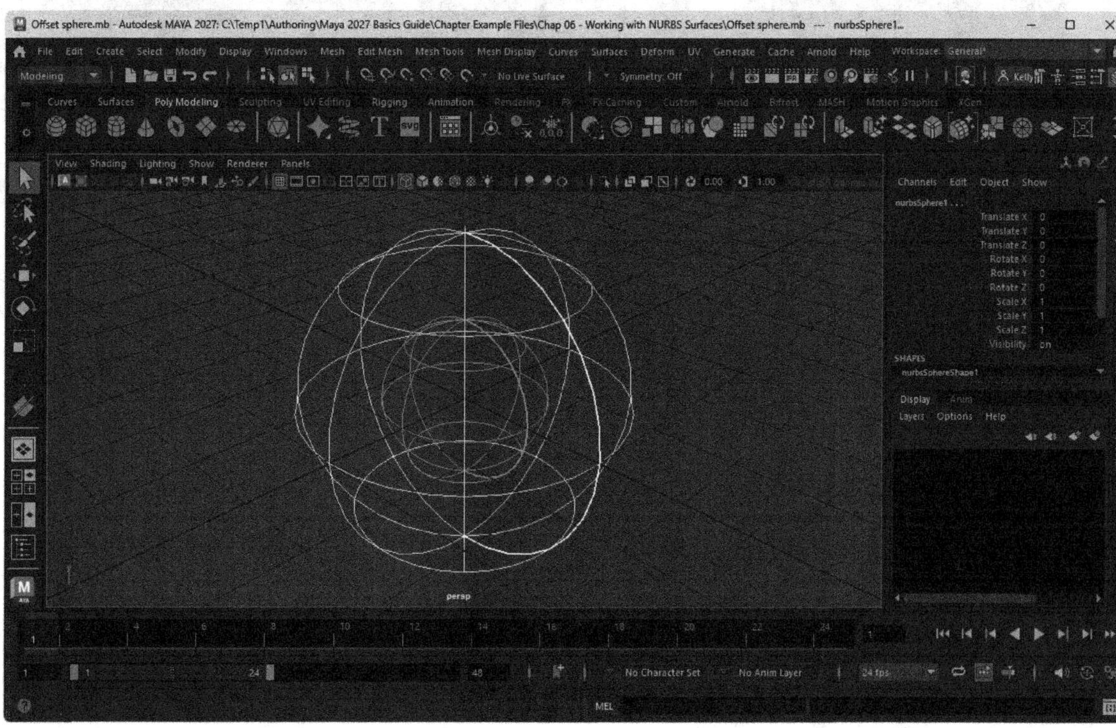

FIGURE 6-11

Offset sphere

Filleting Surfaces

If two surfaces intersect, you can create a **fillet** that smoothes the intersecting edges. The Surfaces, Surface Fillet menu offers three fillet options: Circular Fillet, Freeform Fillet, and the Fillet Blend tool. The Circular Fillet option can be used to round the edges of two overlapping surfaces. The Freeform Fillet option uses a selected isoparm or anon-surface curve to mark where the fillet starts and ends. Figure 6-12 shows a fillet formed by selecting the isoparms on two intersecting plane objects.

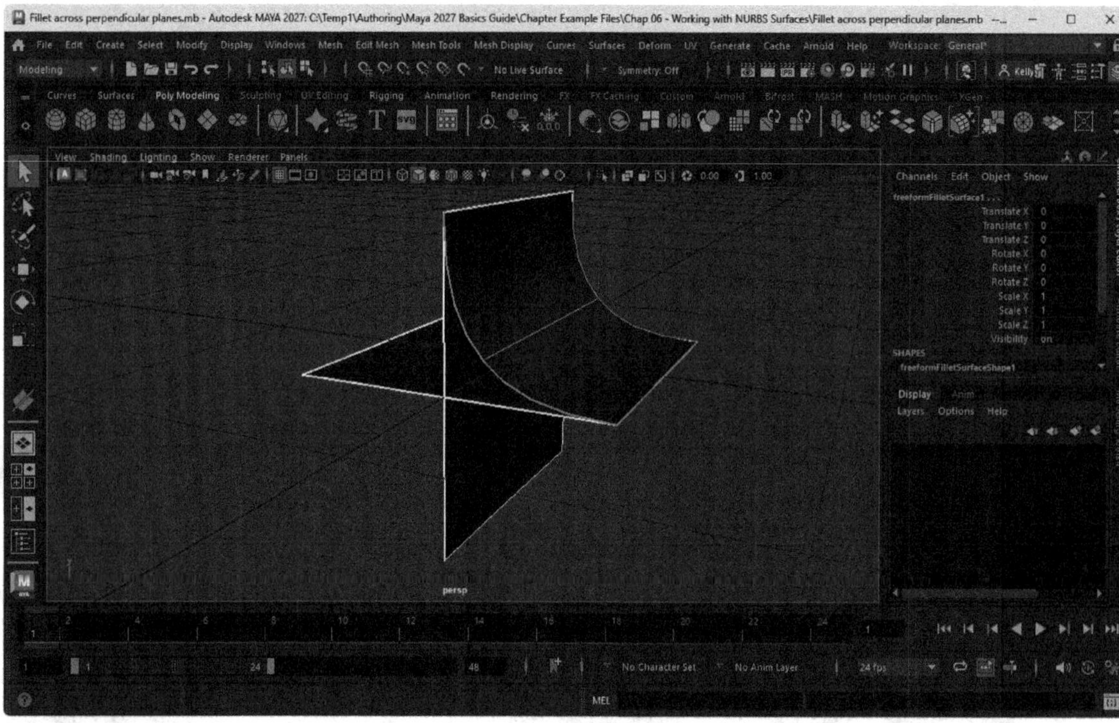

FIGURE 6-12

Freeform fillet

Blending Surfaces

Two surfaces can be blended together using the Surfaces, Surface Fillet, Fillet Blend tool. To use this tool, select two surfaces and choose the Fillet Blend tool menu command. The Help Line asks you to click on the isoparms for the first surface and press Enter, and then click on the isoparms for the second surface and press Enter to complete the blend. Figure 6-13 shows two torus objects blended together.

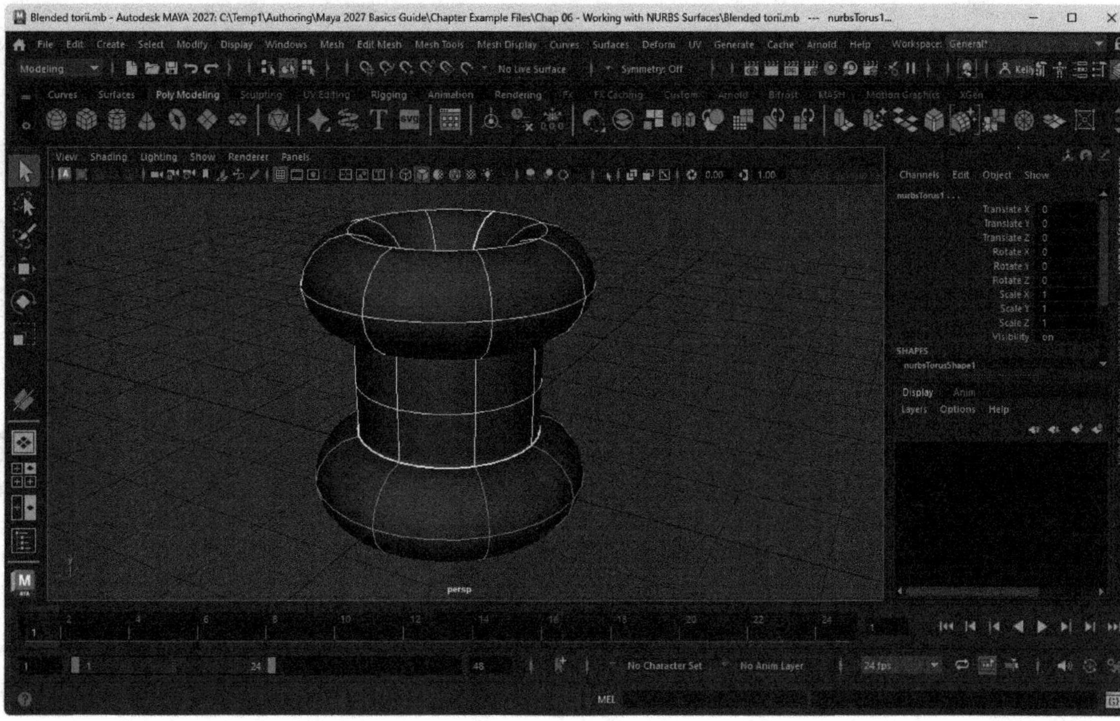

FIGURE 6-13

Blended torus objects

Lesson 6.2-Tutorial 1: Attach Surfaces

1. Select the Create, Curve Tools, EP Curve Tool menu command and click several times in the view panel to create a simple NURBS curve. Press the Enter key to exit Curve Create mode.
2. Extrude the NURBS curve with the Surfaces, Extrude, Options menu command. Select the Distance option in the Extrude Options dialog box with an extrude length of 1.0, and then click the Extrude button.
3. Duplicate the extruded curve surface with the Edit, Duplicate menu command.
4. Drag the duplicated extruded surface upward with the Move tool.
5. Select both extruded surfaces and select the Surfaces, Attach menu command.
6. Repeat Steps 3-5 two more times.

   The surface based off the NURBS curves has been created, as shown in Figure 6-14.
7. Select File, Save Scene As and save the file as **Attached NURBS surface.mb**.

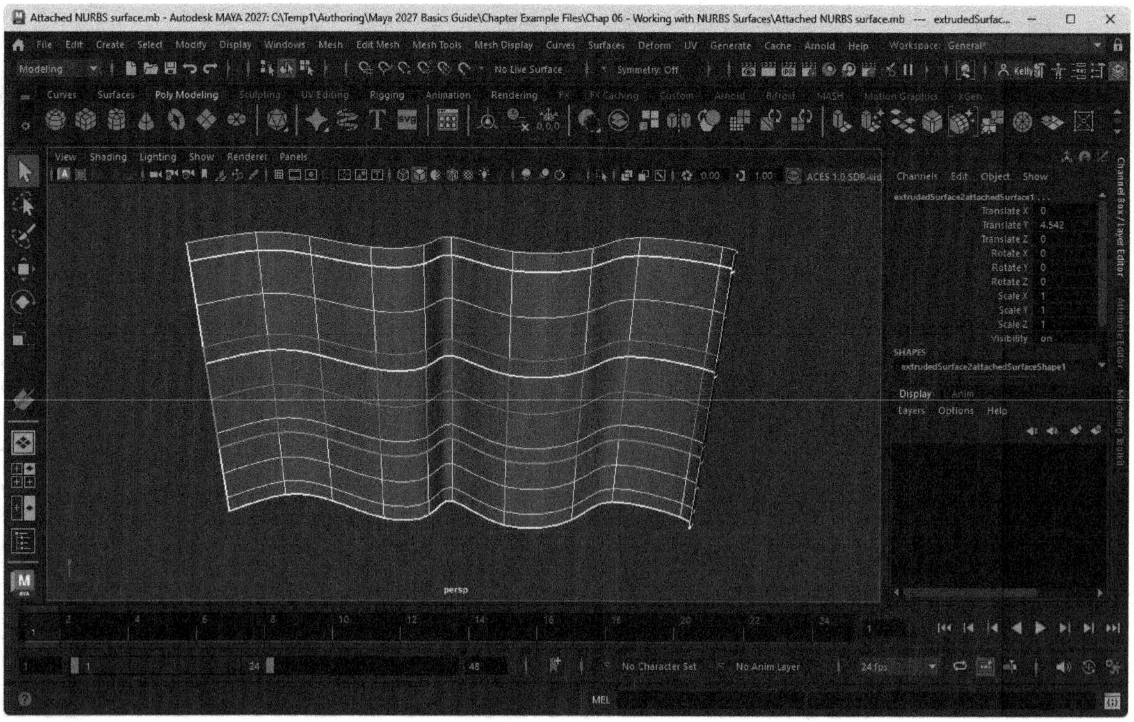

FIGURE 6-14
Attached surface

Lesson 6.2-Tutorial 2: Detach Surfaces

1. Create a sphere object using the Create, NURBS Primitives, Sphere menu command.
2. Right-click on the sphere and select the Isoparm option from the pop-up marking menu.
3. Hold down the Shift key and select each isoparm that runs from the top to the bottom of the sphere.
4. Select the Surfaces, Detach menu command.
5. Select the Move tool and move each separate slice away from the center of the sphere.

   The Detach Surfaces menu command can be used to separate the sphere object into separate slices, as shown in Figure 6-15.
6. Select File, Save Scene As and save the file as **Segmented sphere.mb**.

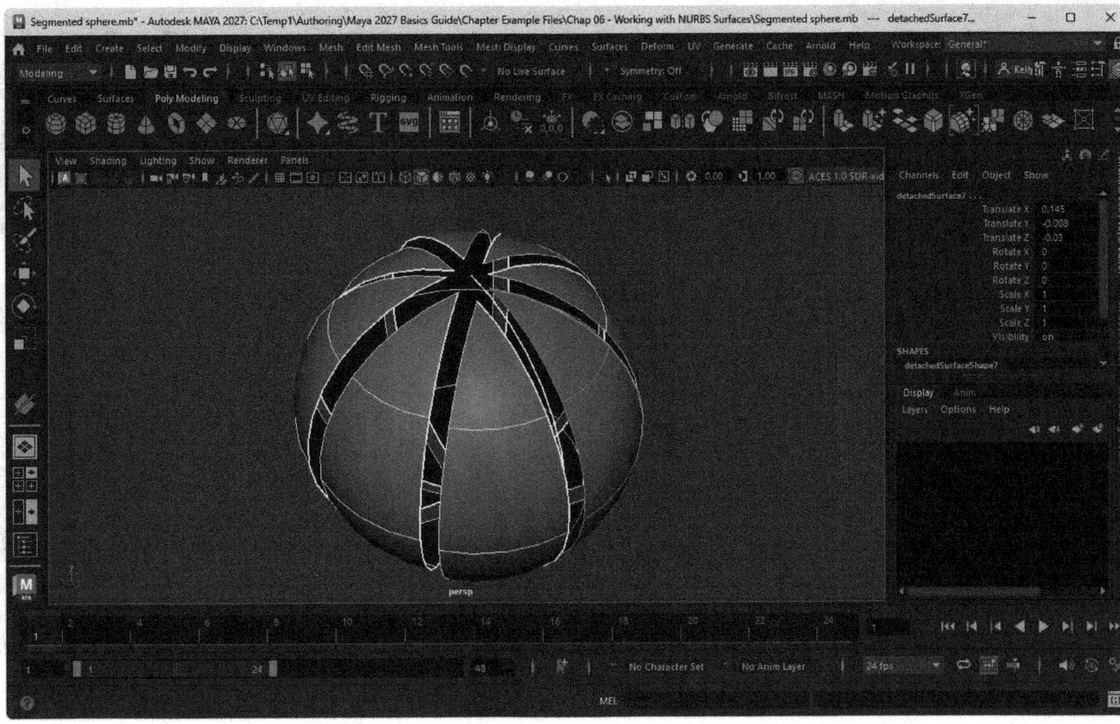

FIGURE 6-15

Segmented sphere

Lesson 6.2-Tutorial 3: Open and Close a Surface

1. Create a torus object using the Create, NURBS Primitives, Torus menu command.
2. Select the Surfaces, Open/Close Surfaces menu command.

   Since the torus object is already a closed object, the Open/Close Surfaces menu command creates an open surface by removing a section of the object.
3. Select the Surfaces, Open/Close menu command again.

   This time the torus is an open object, so the open surfaces are closed to resemble a flattened tire, as shown in Figure 6-16.
4. Select File, Save Scene As and save the file as **Flat tire.mb**.

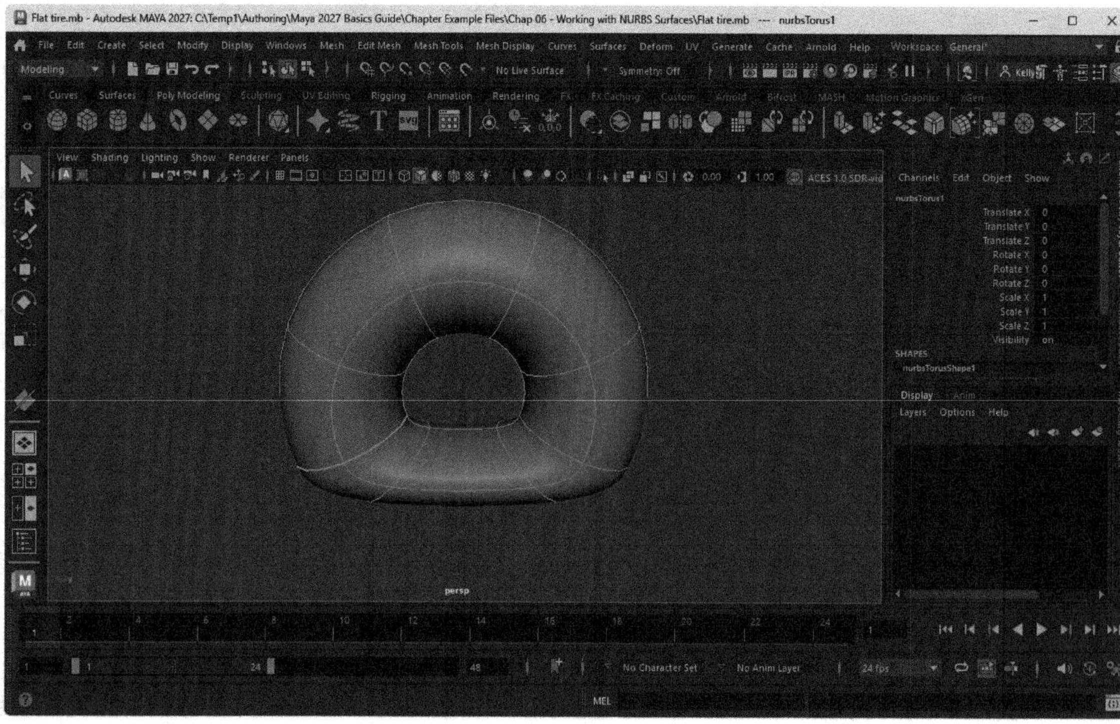

FIGURE 6-16

A closed torus surface

Lesson 6.2-Tutorial 4: Offset Surface

1. Create a cylinder object using the Create, NURBS Primitives, Cylinder menu command.
2. With the cylinder object selected, choose the Surfaces, Offset menu command six times.

   The surface is offset a distance of 1.0 from the original, as shown in Figure 6-17.
3. Select File, Save Scene As and save the file as **Offset cylinders.mb**.

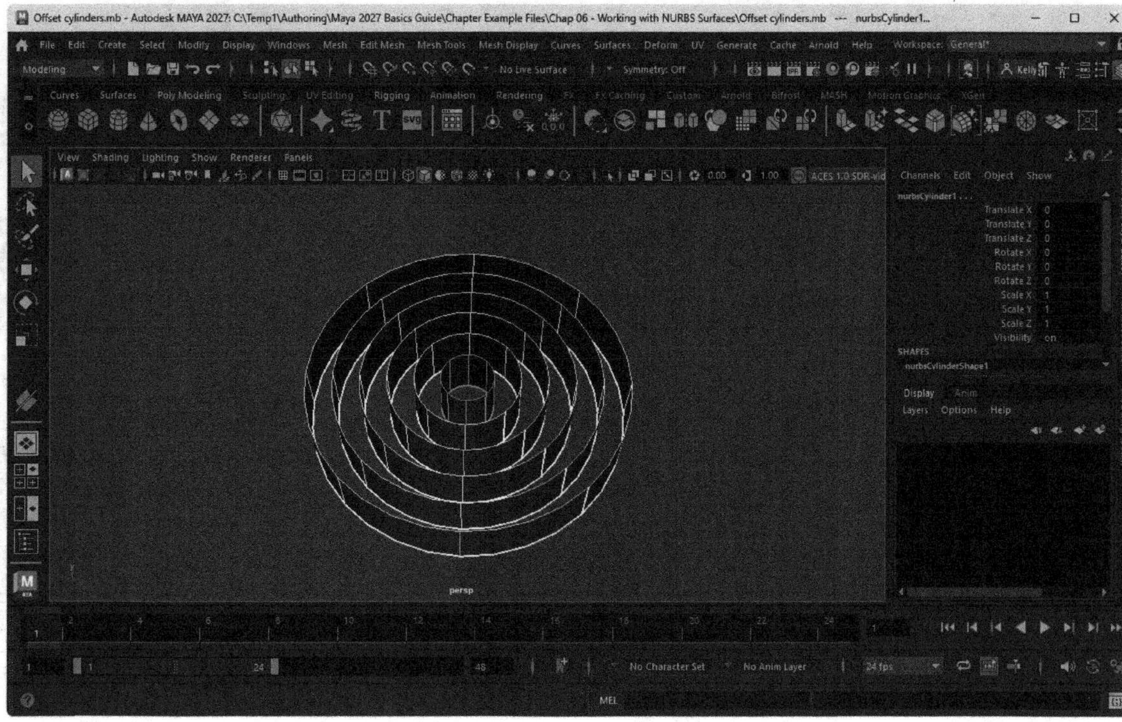

FIGURE 6-17

Offset cylinders

Lesson 6.2-Tutorial 5: Add a Circular Fillet

1. Create a cube object using the Create, NURBS Primitives, Cube menu command.
2. Hold down the Shift key and select the top and front surfaces of the cube.
3. Select the Surfaces, Surface Fillet, Circular Fillet, Options menu command.
4. Set the Radius value to –0.25 and click the Apply button.

   The corner between the two adjacent cube surfaces is rounded.
5. Select the front and bottom surfaces of the cube and repeat Step 4.
6. Repeat Step 4 again for the bottom and back and back and top surfaces.

   The cube has been rounded around the entire cube, as shown in Figure 6-18.
7. Select File, Save Scene As and save the file as **Cube with filleted corners.mb**.

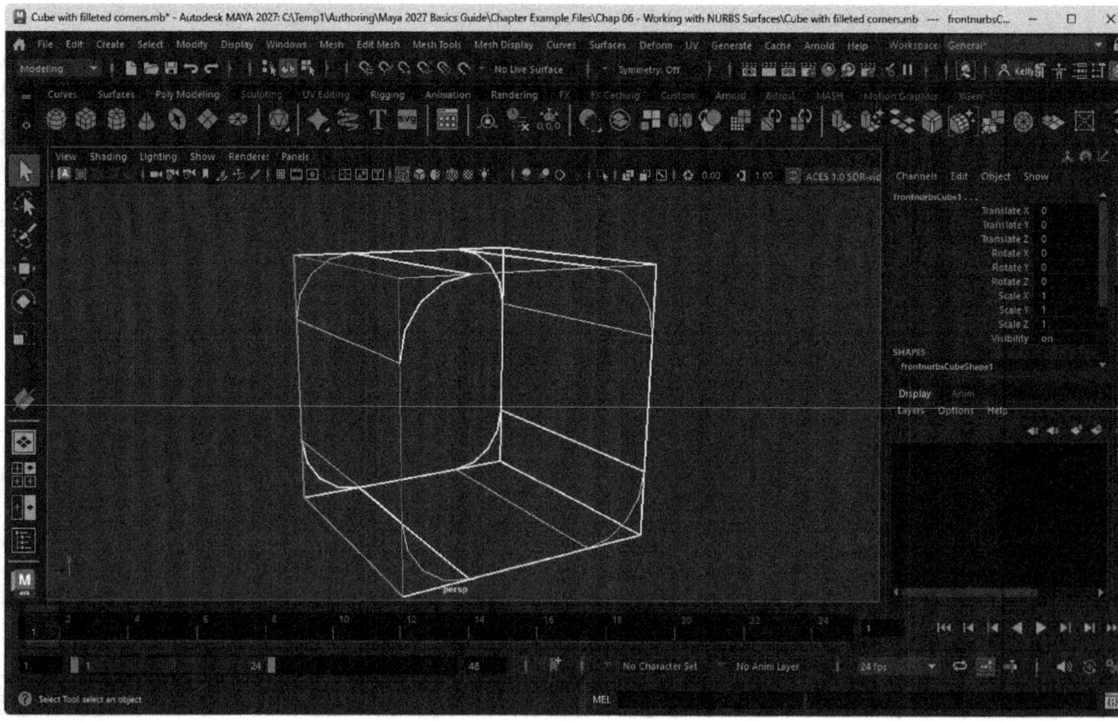

FIGURE 6-18

Cube with filleted corners

Lesson 6.2-Tutorial 6: Blend Two Surfaces

1. Create a cylinder object using the Create, NURBS Primitives, Cylinder menu command.
2. Select Edit, Duplicate to create a duplicate cylinder.
3. Click on the Move tool and move the duplicate cylinder upward and a little to the right. Then rotate it slightly in the Front view panel with the Rotate Tool.
4. With both objects selected, select the Surfaces, Surface Fillet, Fillet Blend Tool menu command.

   With the Fillet Blend tool active, the cursor changes and the Help Line gives instructions.
5. In the Front view panel, click on the bottom5 edge of the top cylinder object and press the Enter key.
6. Then click on the top edge of the bottom cylinder object and press the Enter key again.

   The two cylinders are blended together to create a new object. The blended objects look like a finger joint, as shown in Figure 6-19, and moving either of the cylinders causes the blend to move also.
7. Select File, Save Scene As and save the file as **Blended cylinders.mb**.

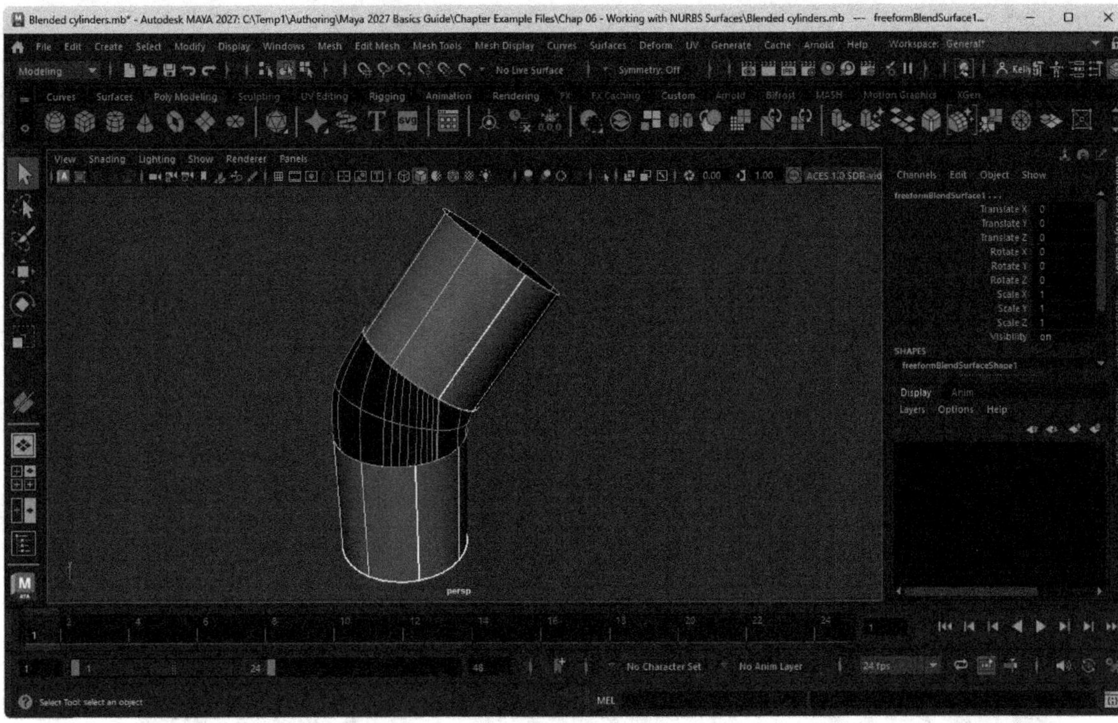

FIGURE 6-19

Blended cylinder

Lesson 6.3: Trim NURBS Surfaces

Mathematically speaking, NURBS surfaces do not contain any holes, but you can simulate a hole or a partial NURBS Surface by trimming the surface. The trimmed portion still exists, but it is hidden and is not displayed. Before a NURBS surface can be trimmed, it must have a curve on its surface that defines the trimming borders. These curves can be drawn on a surface when the surface is "live" or they can be projected onto the surface.

Drawing Curves on a NURBS Surface

A selected NURBS surface can be made "live" by clicking on the Make Object Live button in the Status Line. The button looks like a magnet, as shown in Figure 6-20. The live object is displayed using dark green lines. Once live, you can use any of the curve drawing tools found in the Create menu and the resulting curve is snapped to the surface of the live object. Click on the Make Object Live button again to exit Live mode.

FIGURE 6-20

Make Live toggle button

Projecting Curves onto a NURBS Surface

In addition to drawing a curve on a NURBS surface, you can also project an existing curve onto a surface. To do this, select both the curve and the receiving object and select the Surfaces, Project Curve On Surface menu command. Using the Project Curve on Surface Options dialog box, shown in Figure 6-21, you can select to project the curve using the Active view or using the Surface normal. Once projected, you can change the position of the curve using the manipulator that appears.

Caution

Be aware that projecting a curve onto a solid NURBS object projects it onto both sides of the object.

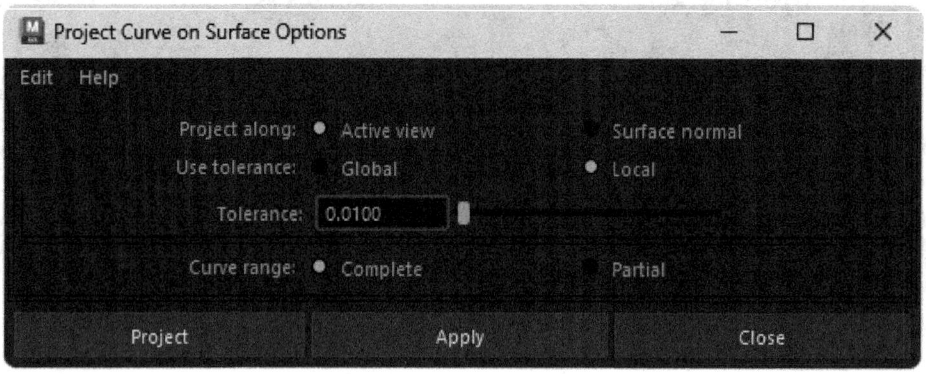

FIGURE 6-21

Project Curve on Surface options

Marking Intersecting Surfaces

A final way to draw a curve on a surface is to mark where two surfaces intersect. If two selected surfaces intersect, you can use the Surfaces, Intersect menu command to create a curve that marks the intersecting section. Figure 6-22 shows the intersections between two cylinders. In the Intersect Surfaces options dialog box, you can create intersecting curves based on the first surface or both surfaces. The created curve can be placed on the surface or free of the objects. You can also set a tolerance value.

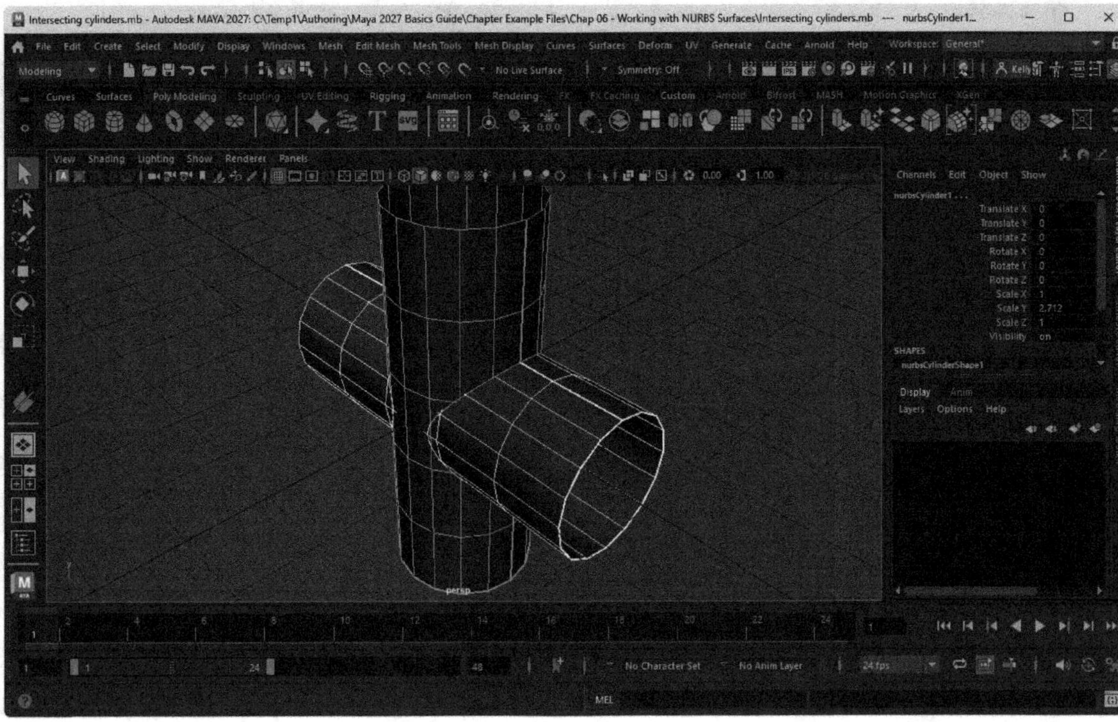

FIGURE 6-22
Intersecting surfaces

Trimming a Surface

A selected NURBS surface with a curve on its surface can be trimmed using the Surfaces, Trim tool. The Trim tool displays all surface isoparms as dashed lines, as shown in Figure 6-23. You can then click on the isoparms to keep as part of the object. Pressing the Enter key causes the unselected areas to be trimmed. The options dialog box includes an option to discard the section that you click on. A trimmed area can be undone using the Surfaces, Untrim menu command.

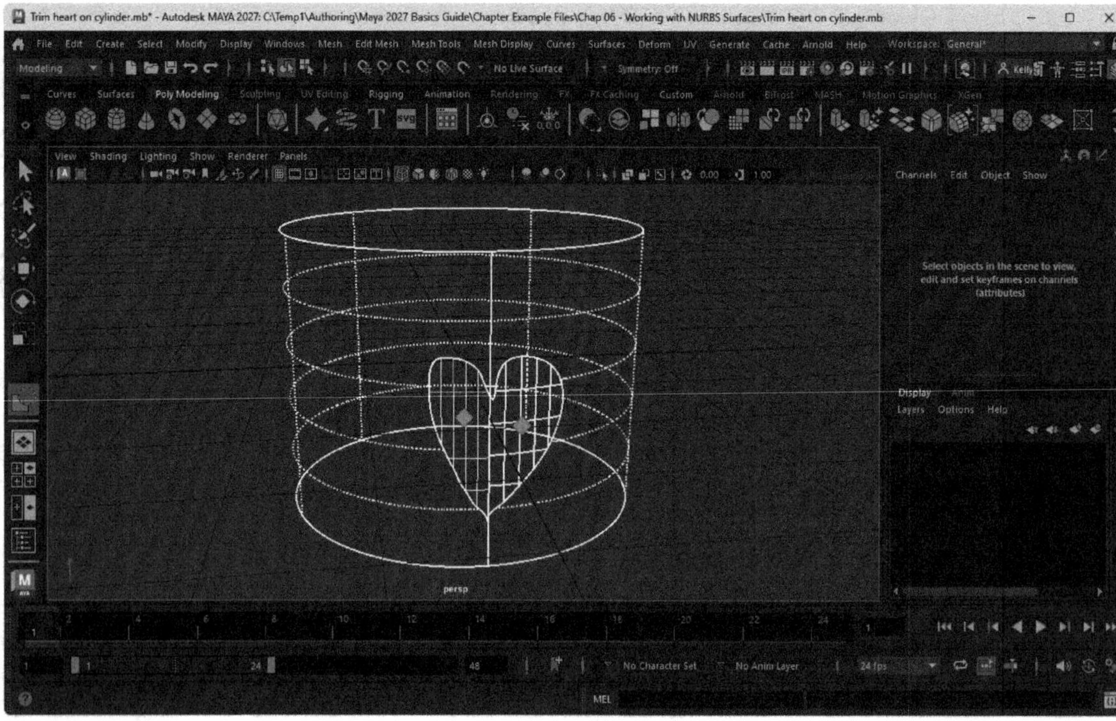

FIGURE 6-23

The Trim tool

Lesson 6.3-Tutorial 1: Draw and Trim a Surface

1. Create a sphere object using the Create, NURBS Primitives, Sphere menu command.
2. Click the Make the Selected Object Live button in the Status Line.

   The sphere object appears dark green in the view panel.
3. Select the Create, Curve Tools, EP Curve Tool and click on the sphere object to create an 'S' shape, but don't finish the shape. Press the Enter key to create the curve.
4. Select Curves, Open/Close to close the curve.
5. Click on the Make the Selected Object Live button in the Status Line again to exit Live mode.
6. Drag over the sphere object to select both the sphere and the drawn curve.
7. Select Surfaces, Trim Tool.

   All interior lines that make up the shape and the sphere are displayed as dashed lines.
8. Click on the sphere lines outside the shape and press the Enter key.
9. Press the 5 key to shade the object.

   The shape is trimmed from the sphere object, as shown in Figure 6-24.
10. Select File, Save Scene As and save the file as **Trimmed sphere.mb**.

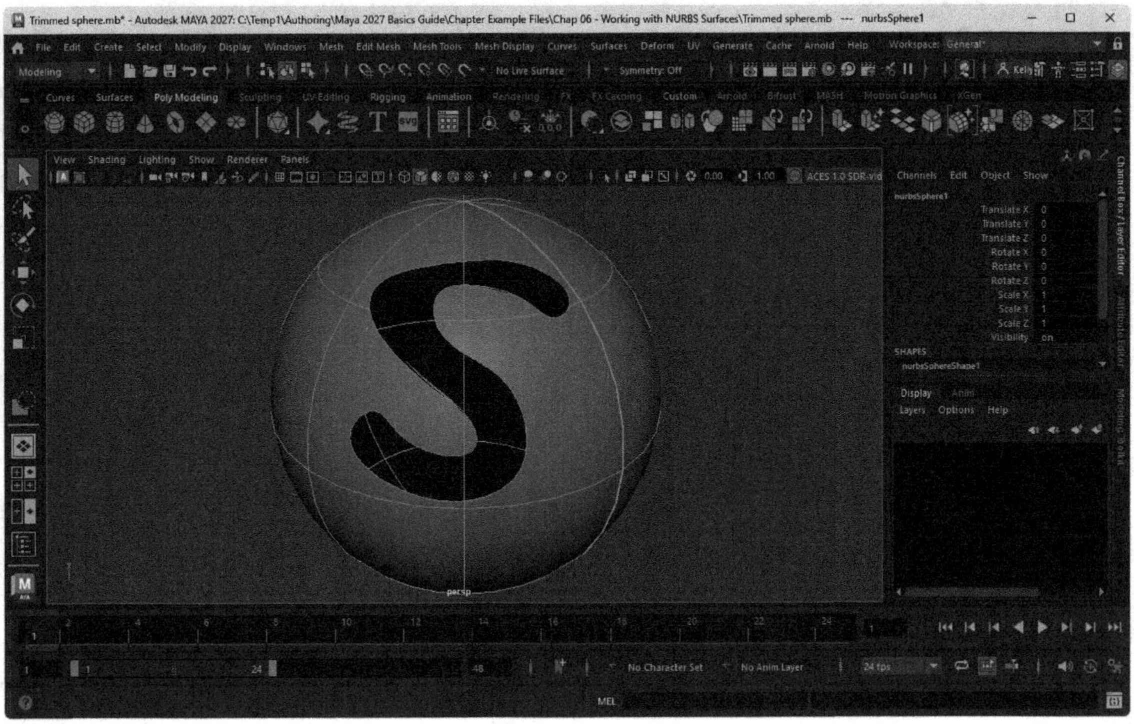

FIGURE 6-24

Trimmed sphere

Lesson 6.3-Tutorial 2: Project and Trim a Curve

1. Create a cube object using the Create, NURBS Primitives, Cube menu command.
2. Create a circle object using the Create, NURBS Primitives, Circle menu command.
3. Select the Move tool and drag the circle object upward using the green Y-axis until the circle is above the cube.
4. Select the circle and the cube objects in the Top view panel.
5. Choose the Surfaces, Project Curve on Surface menu command.

   A manipulator appears that lets you precisely position the location of the projected curve.
6. Select the cube object and choose the Surfaces, Trim Tool menu command.

   All interior lines that make up the shape and the cylinder are displayed as dashed lines.
7. Click on the cube lines outside the circle and press the Enter key.
8. Press the 5 key to shade the object.

   The circle is trimmed from the cube object, as shown in Figure 6-25.
9. Select File, Save Scene As and save the file as **Trimmed cube.mb**.

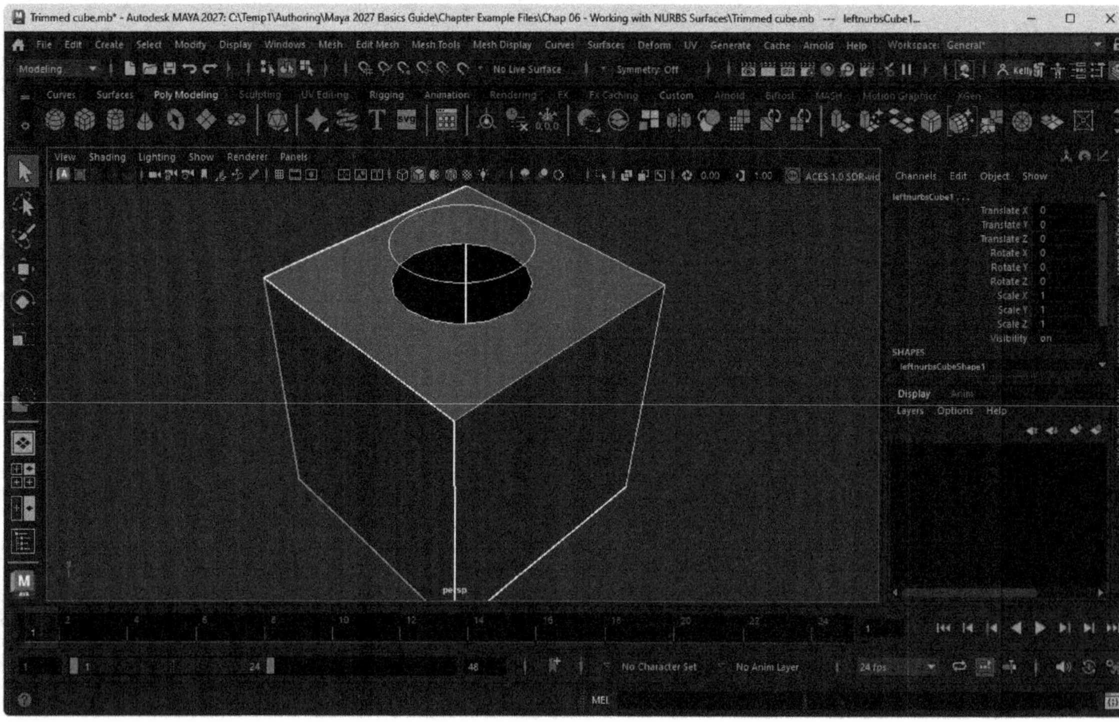

FIGURE 6-25

The trimmed cube

Lesson 6.4: Use Boolean Tools

When NURBS surfaces overlap, you can use the Surfaces, Booleans menu to access one of three tools that can be used to add, subtract, or locate the intersection between the two objects. With any of these tools selected, you can click to select the first object or objects and then press the Enter key before clicking to select the second object or objects. The options dialog box (shown for the Union tool in Figure 6-26) for each of these tools lets you delete the inputs and exit the tool on completion.

Caution

The Boolean tools can only work on two NURBS surfaces at once.

FIGURE 6-26
NURBS Boolean Union options

Combining Surfaces with the Union Tool

When the Union tool is used on two overlapping surfaces, the intersecting lines are removed and the resulting object acts as a single object.

Removing Surface Parts with the Difference Tool

The Difference tool removes an overlapping portion of the second selected object from the first selected object. The order in which the objects are selected is important. Reversing the selection order changes the result.

Creating a Surface Intersection with the Intersect Tool

The Intersect Tool removes all but the intersecting portion of the two overlapping surfaces.

Lesson 6.4-Tutorial 1: Create Boolean Union Surfaces

1. Select File, Open Scene and open the file named Boolean.mb.
2. Select the Surfaces, Booleans, Union Tool menu command.
3. Then select the sphere object and press the Enter key.
4. Click on one of the cylinder objects and press the Enter key again to union the objects together. Then click away from the objects to deselect all objects.
5. Repeat Steps 2-4 for the other two cylinders.

   The final object is shown in Figure 6-27.
6. Select File, Save Scene As and save the file as **Boolean union.mb.**

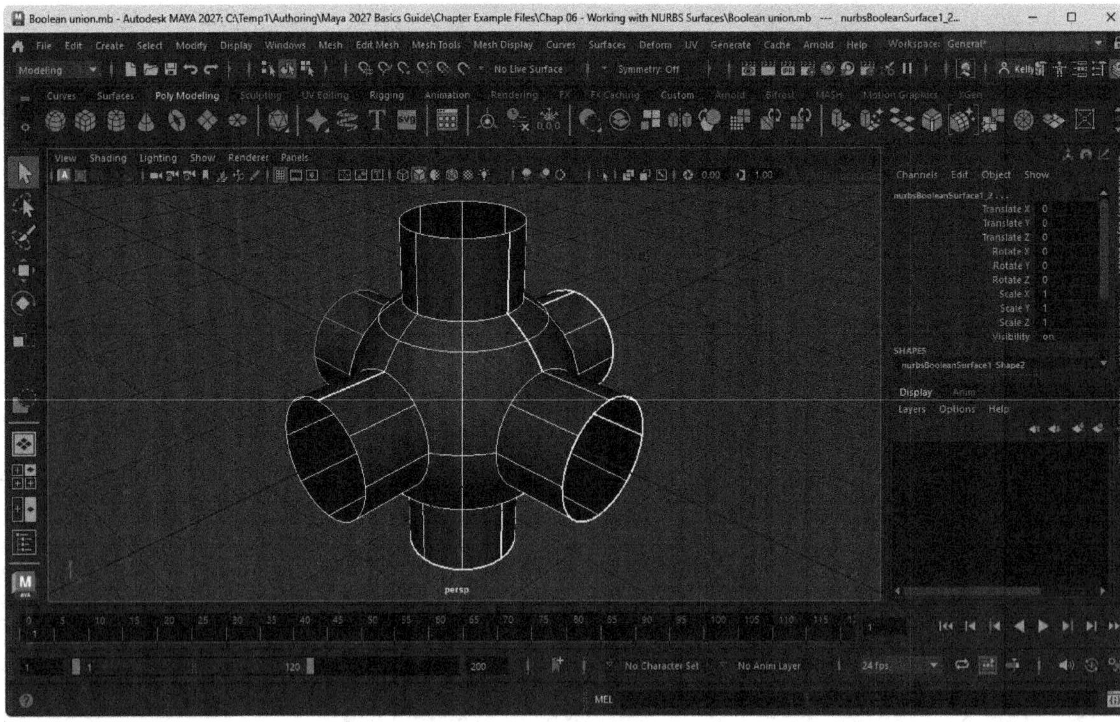

FIGURE 6-27

A Boolean union

Lesson 6.4-Tutorial 2: Create Boolean Difference Surfaces

1. Select File, Open Scene and open the file named Boolean.mb.
2. Select the Surfaces, Booleans, Difference Tool menu command.
3. Select the sphere object and press the Enter key.
4. Click on one of the cylinder objects and press the Enter key again to subtract one object from the other. Then click away from the objects to deselect all objects.
5. Repeat Steps 2-4 for the other two cylinders.

   The final object is shown in Figure 6-28.
6. Select File, Save Scene As and save the file as **Boolean subtract.mb**.

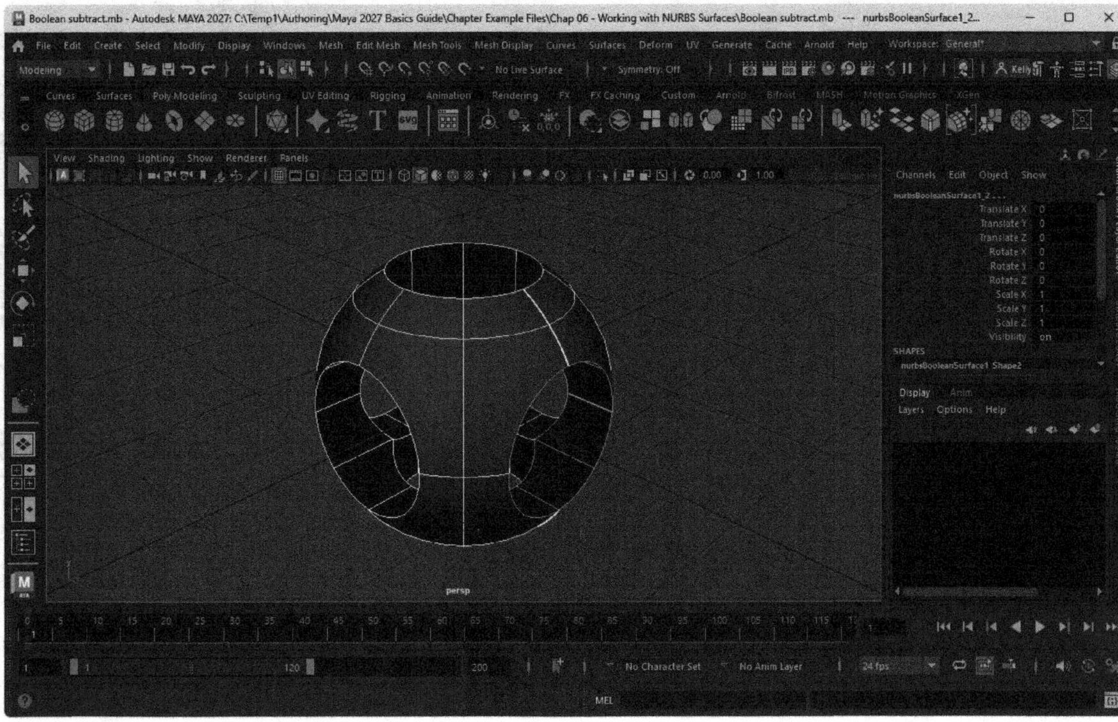

FIGURE 6-28

A Boolean subtract

Lesson 6.4-Tutorial 3: Create Boolean Intersect Surfaces

1. Select File, Open Scene and open the file named Boolean.mb.
2. Select the Surfaces, Booleans, Intersect Tool menu command.
3. Then select the sphere object and press the Enter key.
4. Click on one of the cylinder objects and press the Enter key again to intersect one object from the other. Then click away from the objects to deselect all objects.
5. Repeat Steps 2-4 for the other two cylinders.

   The final object is shown in Figure 6-29.
6. Select File, Save Scene As and save the file as **Boolean intersect.mb**.

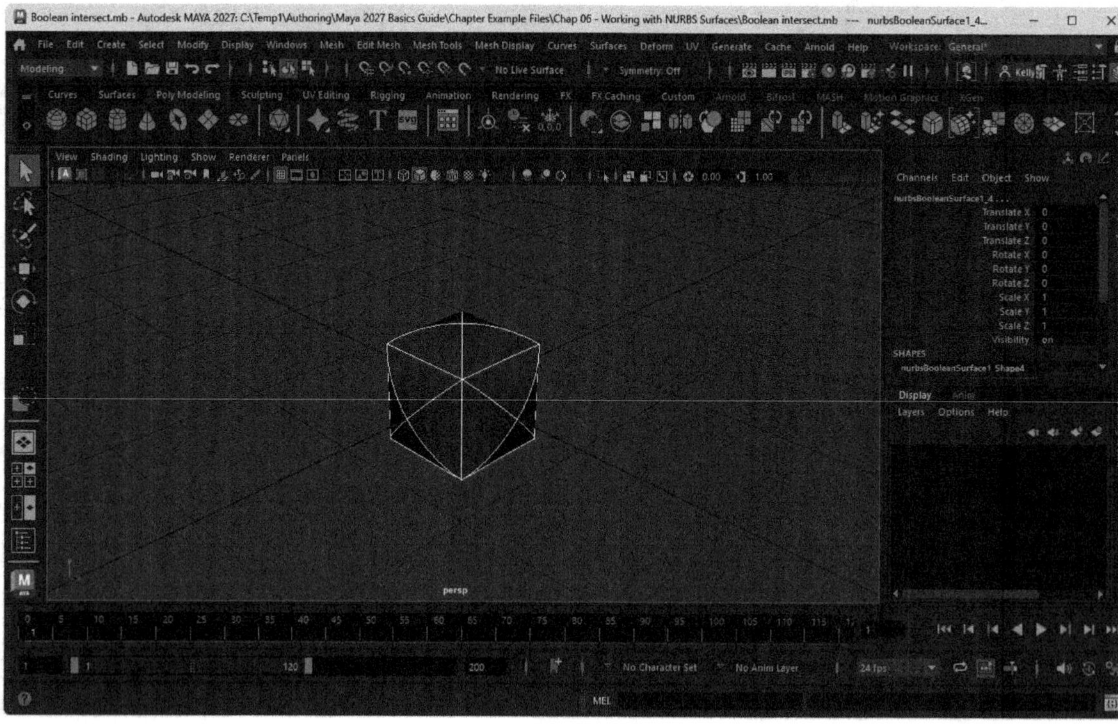

FIGURE 6-29

A Boolean intersect

Lesson 6.5: Stitch Surfaces Together

In addition to the Attach command, another common way to combine two surfaces is with the Surfaces, Stitch menu commands. There are several different ways to stitch surfaces, including using the Stitch Surface Points command, the Stitch Edges tool, and Global Stitch. Figure 6-30 shows the effect of moving a row of stitched plane objects away from their stitched neighbors.

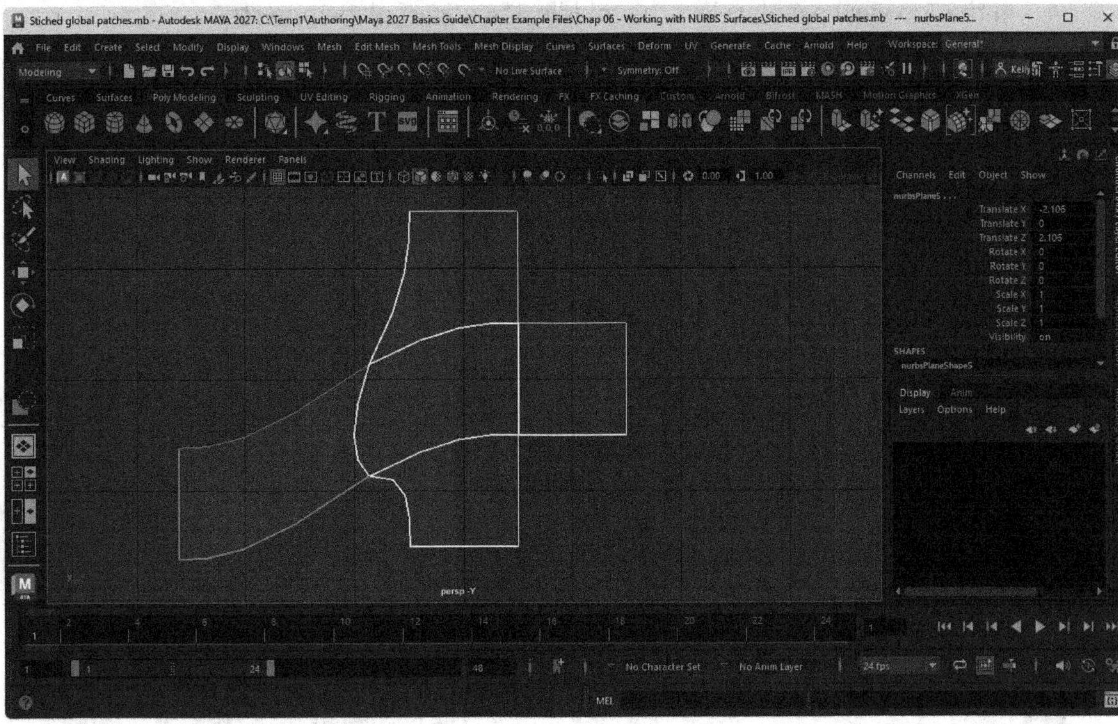

FIGURE 6-30
Stitched edges

Applying Global Stitch

When several surfaces are placed next to one another as you are modeling an object, they can be independently moved, causing gaps in your model. To prevent this, you can stitch the individual objects together using the Surfaces, Stitch, Global Stitch menu command. This creates an attachment between the objects so that moving one causes the other to move with it, even though they are separate objects.

Stitching Surface Points Together

If two CVs are selected, you can use the Surfaces, Stitch, Stitch Surface Points menu command to connect the two points together. This moves the two points to the same location.

Stitching Surface Edges Together

It is more common to stitch entire edges than to stitch individual points. NURBS edges can be stitched using the Surfaces, Stitch, Stitch Edges tool. This tool instructs you to select a boundary edge isoparm line and then a second boundary isoparm that is moved to the location of the first isoparm edge.

Lesson 6.5-Tutorial 1: Apply Global Stitch

1. Select File, Open Scene and open the file named 6*6 planes.mb.

   This scene has an array of 6 by 6 plane objects positioned next to each other.
2. Select the Select All menu command.
3. Then select the Surfaces, Stitch, Global Stitch menu command.

4. In the Top view panel, select the middle 4*4 grid of plane objects.
5. With the Move tool, drag the selected plane objects upward in the Front view panel.
6. In the Top view panel, select the middle 2*2 grid of plane objects.
7. With the Move tool, drag the selected plane objects upward even further in the Front view panel.

   For the resulting hill-shaped object, shown in Figure 6-31, the unselected plane objects move along with their adjacent plane objects because they are stitched together.
8. Select File, Save Scene As and save the file as **Global stitch.mb**.

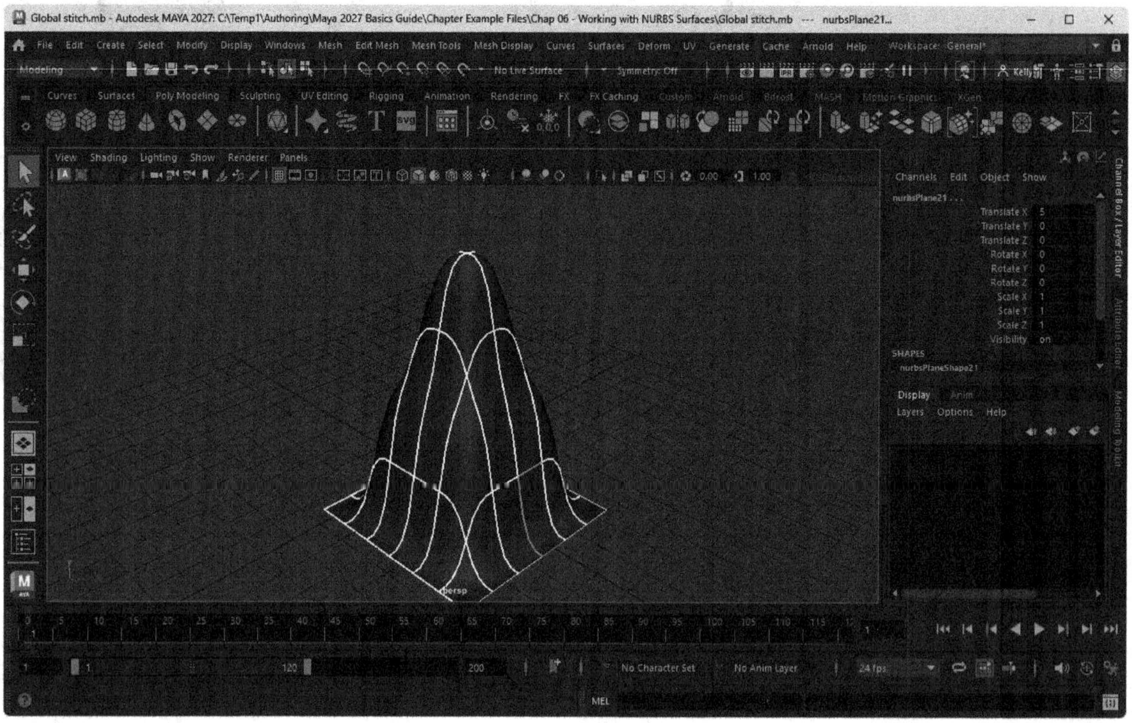

FIGURE 6-31

Global stitch

Lesson 6.6: Convert Objects

Each of the various modeling types includes several advantages. You can switch between the various object types using the Modify, Convert menu selections. Using these menu commands, you can convert NURBS objects to polygons and subdivision surfaces, polygons to subdivision surfaces, and subdivision surfaces to NURBS and polygons.

Note

```
You can't convert polygon objects directly to NURBS,
but you can convert them to subdivision surfaces and
then back to NURBS.
```

Converting NURBS to Polygons

You can convert NURBS objects to polygons using the Modify, Convert, NURBS to Polygons menu command. Using this command creates a converted polygon object on top of the existing NURBS object. The Convert NURBS to Polygons Options dialog box, shown in Figure 6-32, lets you select to use triangles or quads for the converted polygon object. You can also select the tessellation method. The options include General, where you can specify the number of U and V spans; Count, where you can specify the number of polygons; Standard Fit, which lets Maya calculate the best conversion parameters; and Control Points, which simply uses the NURBS CVs as polygon vertices.

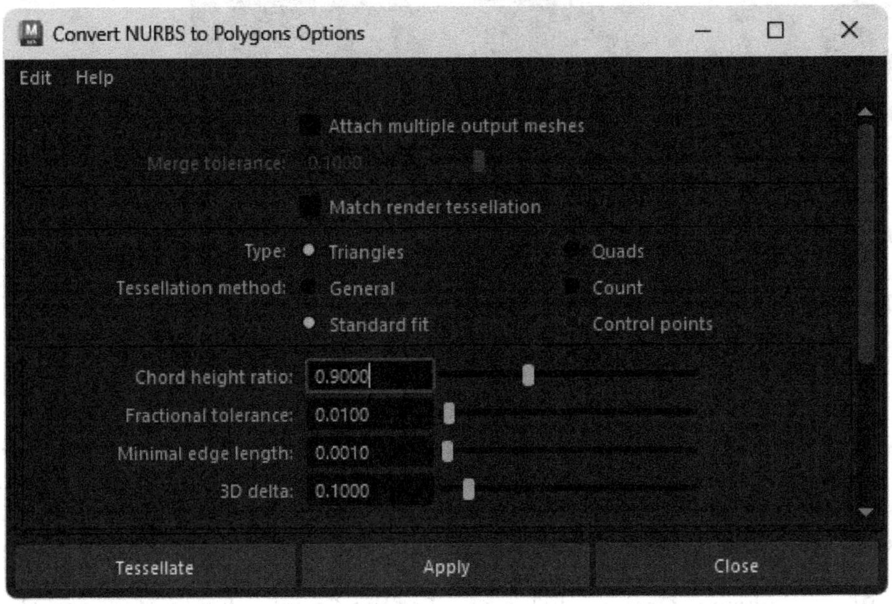

FIGURE 6-32

Convert NURBS to Polygons Options

Converting to Subdivision Surfaces

NURBS objects and polygon objects can both be converted to subdivision surfaces using the Modify, Convert, NURBS to Subdiv, and Polygons to Subdiv menu commands. All converted components make up the base (Level 0) level for the subdivision surface. The Options dialog box for these commands includes Maximum Base Mesh Faces and the Maximum Edges Per Vertex settings. Some complex geometries cannot be converted, such as when three polygon faces share an edge or adjacent faces have opposite-pointing normals. You should use the Mesh, Cleanup command prior to converting if you are having trouble.

Converting Subdivision Surfaces to NURBS and Polygons

You can convert subdivision surfaces to NURBS and polygon objects using the Modify, Convert, Subdiv to NURBS and Subdiv to Polygons menu commands. Subdivision surfaces that are converted to NURBS split the separate levels with different resolutions into separate NURBS objects. You can fix this with the Surfaces, Attach and Surfaces, Stitch, Global Stitch commands. This makes the converted NURBS surface act as a single object. The Convert Subdiv to Polygons Options box offers four tessellation methods: Uniform, Adaptive, Polygon Count, and Vertices, as shown in Figure 6-33.

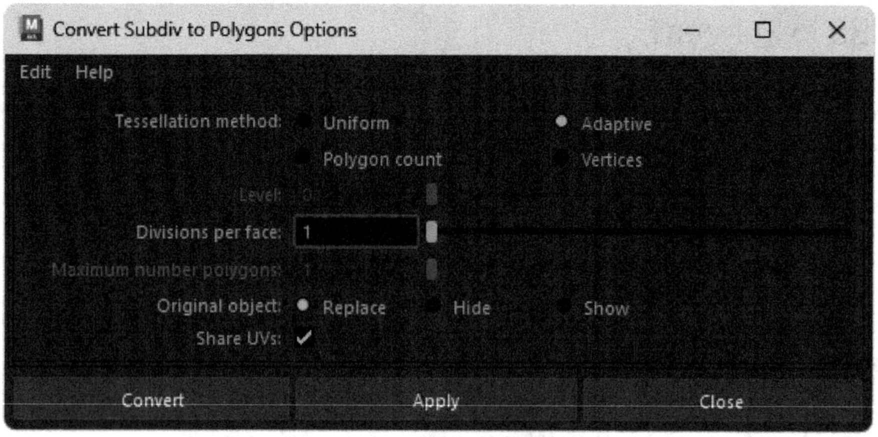

FIGURE 6-33

Convert Subdiv to Polygons option

Lesson 6.6-Tutorial 1: Convert NURBS to Polygons

1. Create a NURBS sphere object using the Create, NURBS Primitives, Sphere menu command.
2. Select the Modify, Convert, NURBS to Polygons, Options menu command.
3. In the Convert NURBS to Polygons Options dialog box, select the Quads option and the General tessellation method. Then set the Number of U and V parameters to 10 each and click the Apply button.
4. Move the converted sphere below the original.
5. Select the original NURBS sphere and select the Count tessellation method in the Convert NURBS to Polygons Options dialog box. Set the Count value to 1000 and click the Apply button.
6. Move this converted sphere next to the other converted sphere.
7. Repeat Steps 5 and 6 for the Standard Fit and Control Points tessellation methods in the Convert NURBS to Polygons Options dialog box.

   The converted spheres all have a different number of polygons, as shown in Figure 6-34.
8. Select File, Save Scene As and save the file as **Converted NURBS spheres.mb**.

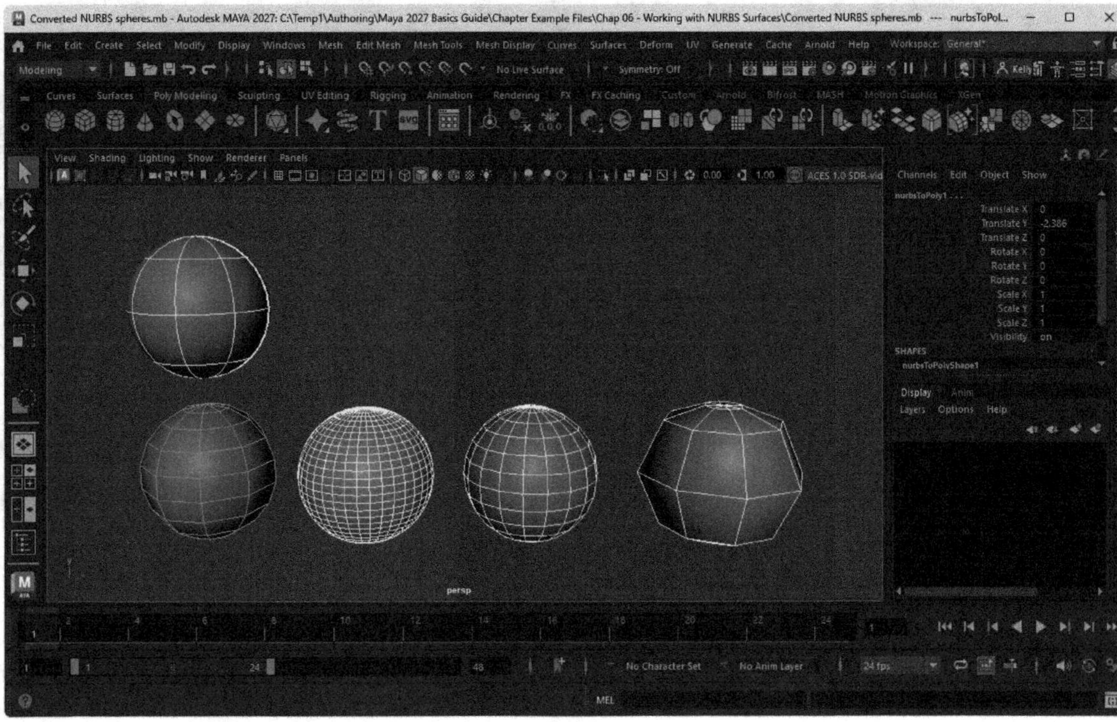

FIGURE 6-34

Converted NURBS spheres

Lesson 6.6-Tutorial 2: Convert NURBS to Polygons and Back

1. Create a NURBS cube object using the Create, NURBS Primitives, Cube menu command.
2. Select the Modify, Convert, NURBS to Polygons menu command.
3. With the cube selected, choose the Modify, Convert, Polygons to Subdiv menu command.
4. Select the Modify, Convert, Subdiv to NURBS menu command.

   Overusing the convert commands can result in some undesirable anomalies, as shown in Figure 6-35.
5. Select File, Save Scene As and save the file as **Overconverted cube.mb**.

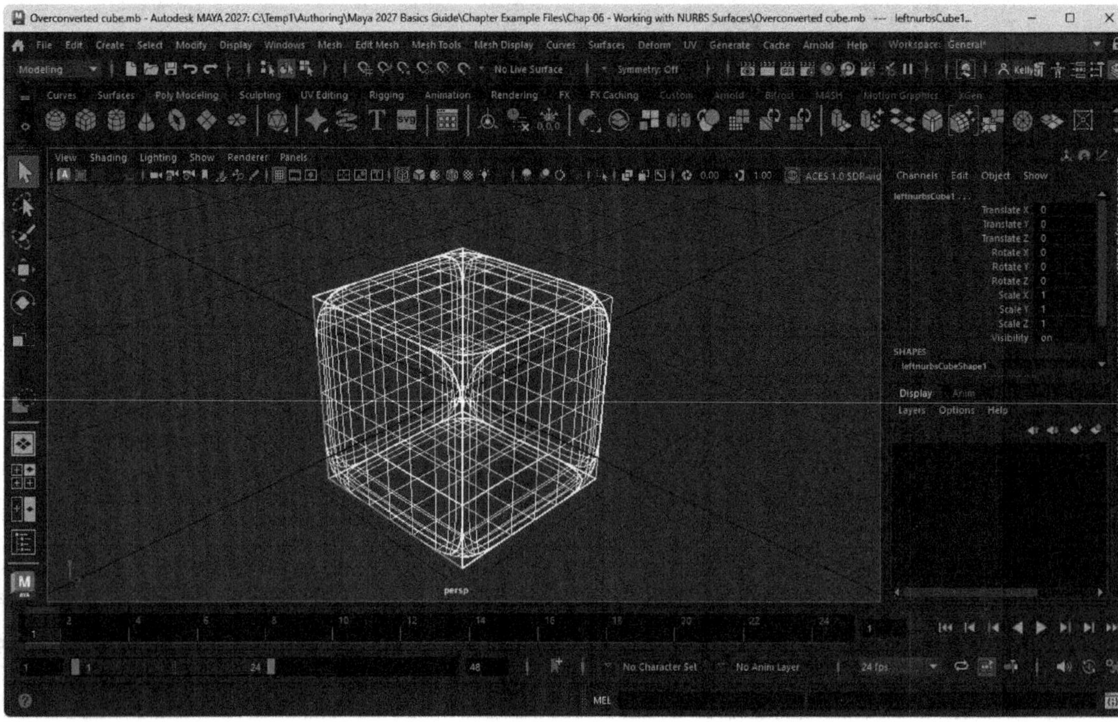

FIGURE 6-35

Overconverted cube

Chapter Summary

This chapter covers modeling with NURBS surfaces. NURBS is an acronym for Non-Uniform Rational B-Splines. NURBS are great for modeling organic models such as plants, trees, and other objects that flow smoothly from part to part. NURBS are created from curves that line each patch and can be edited by moving the object's CVs or Control Vertices. This chapter also covers editing NURBS components and applying surface operators such as attaching, filleting, trimming, and blending several objects together. Another way to combine two or more NURBS objects is with the Boolean operations. Stitching NURBS patches together makes them move together when adjacent patches are moved. The Convert commands let you change the selected object between the various modeling types.

What You Have Learned

In this chapter, you learned

* How to select NURBS components.
* How to use the Surface Editing and the Sculpt Geometry tools.
* How to work with tangents.
* How to attach, detach, and align NURBS surfaces.
* How to open, close, and extend NURBS surfaces.
* How to use NURBS operators such as offsetting, filleting, and blending.

* How to draw a curve on a NURBS surface and use it to trim an area.
* How to project a curve on a NURBS surface and use it to trim an area.
* How to use the Union, Difference, and Intersection Boolean tools.
* How to stitch multiple NURBS patches together.
* How to convert between NURBS, polygon, and subdivision surfaces.

Key Terms From This Chapter

* **NURBS.** A 3D surface created from curves that define its area. An acronym that stands for Non-Uniform Rational B-Spline.
* **Torus.** A circular primitive object with a circular cross section, shaped like a doughnut.
* **Isoparametric curve.** Representative lines that show the object's surface. Called isoparms for short.
* **NURBS patch.** The surface area that lies in between isoparms.
* **Surface Editing tool.** A tool that uses a manipulator to edit the surface curvature.
* **Sculpt Geometry tool.** A tool used to push and pull on an object's surface.
* **Filleting.** The process of smoothing the corner between two adjacent faces.
* **Trimming.** The process of cutting holes into a NURBS surface.
* **Boolean.** Operations used to combine surfaces by adding, subtracting, or intersecting two or more objects.
* **Stitching.** The process of attaching adjacent patches together so they move without creating holes.
* **Convert.** A series of commands that lets you change one modeling type such as NURBS to another modeling type such as a subdivision surface.

Chapter 7
Drawing and Editing Curves

IN THIS CHAPTER

- 7.1 Create curves.
- 7.2 Edit curve details.
- 7.3 Modify curves.
- 7.4 Apply curve operators.
- 7.5 Create sweep meshes.
- 7.6 Create simple surfaces from curves.

The first step when starting out modeling is to learn to work with curves. Curves aren't rendered, but they form the basis of all NURBS surfaces and learning to work with them gives you an advantage as you begin to model NURBS surfaces. Understanding how to create surfaces from curves is an essential part of NURBS modeling.

To understand curves in Maya, you need to understand the curve components. Each Maya curve consists of several control vertices (**CVs**) that define its curvature. The first CV is displayed as a small square. All other CVs are marked as dots. The order of the CVs is significant, as the curve is used to make a surface. You can see the CVs that make up a curve by selecting Component mode or by selecting Control Vertex from the right-click marking menu.

The control vertices are often easier to see if the curve's hulls are displayed. A **hull** is a line that connects two adjacent CVs. You can display all hulls for a curve using the marking menu.

Maya curves also include edit points. Edit points are positioned on the curve's path and are displayed as a small x. Each edit point is linked to a CV, and moving the edit point moves the CVs and vice versa. Moving CVs offers more control than moving edit points. You can view a curve's edit points using the marking menu.

Maya includes primitive 2D shapes like circle and square and tools for creating arcs, but most of the curves you create will be freehand. Maya allows several different ways to create curves. The **CV Curve tool** creates a curve by positioning the CVs, the **EP Curve tool** creates curves when you click on the location of the edit points that lie on the curve's path, and the Pencil Curve tool lets you draw curves in the view panel. There is also a Bezier Curve tool that places points with tangent handles. Moving these tangent handles lets you change the curvature around the point. All of these tools are located in the Create, Curve Tools menu.

Outlined text is another special class of curves that you can create and edit.

Once curves are created, you can edit the curves by selecting and moving the individual CVs and edit points. You can also edit curves using commands like Combine, Align, Close, Reverse, and Simplify. These commands and more are found in the Curves menu, which is part of the Modeling menu set. Learning to use the Curves commands is another vital step in preparing curves to be turned into surfaces.

You can use selected curves to create surfaces using a number of different techniques, including Revolve, Loft, Extrude, and Bevel. These commands are located in the Surfaces menu.

Lesson 7.1: Create Curves

Maya includes several tools that may be used to create curves, and there are also some curve primitives available in the Create menu. Each of these tools work by placing points or vertices and having Maya compute the curve lines that are drawn between these points.

Creating Smooth Curves

In Maya, you can create smooth curves by positioning the curve's control vertices (CVs) with the Create, Curve Tools, CV Curve tool or by positioning the curve's edit points with the Create, Curve Tools, EP Curve tool. The difference between these two tools is that the curve passes through all vertices of a curve created with the EP Curve tool and the curve only passes through the end vertices of a curve created with the CV Curve tool. After clicking to place the vertices, you can press the Enter key or click on the Select tool to end the curve. Figure 7-1 shows an example of each of these curves.

Tip

Pressing the Insert key while placing vertices allows you to move the last placed vertex. Pressing the Insert key again lets you continue adding vertices. Pressing the Delete key deletes the last-created vertex.

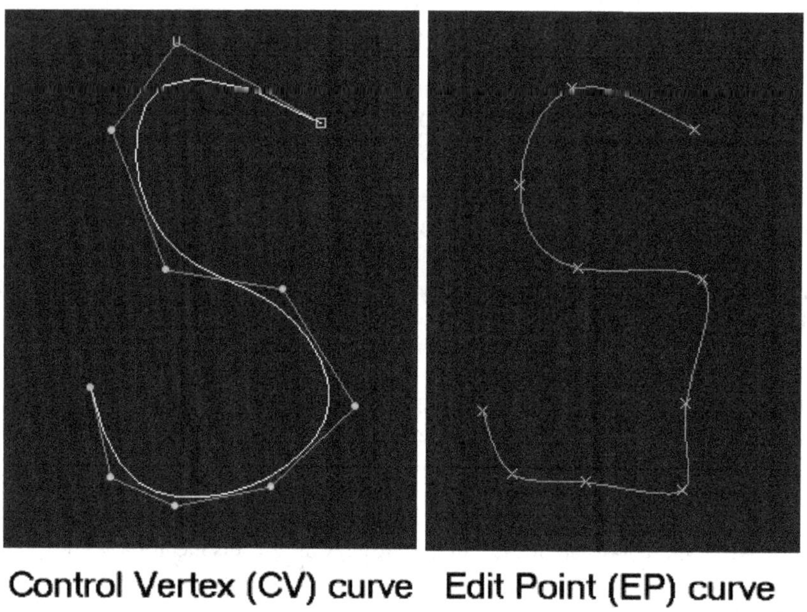

FIGURE 7-1

CV and EP curves

Creating Straight Line Curves

In the Options dialog box for the CV and EP Curve tools, you can select the degree of the curve. Selecting the 1 Linear option causes all curve spans to be straight lines. Higher degree values require more CVs before a span is created. Figure 7-2 shows the various **curve degrees**.

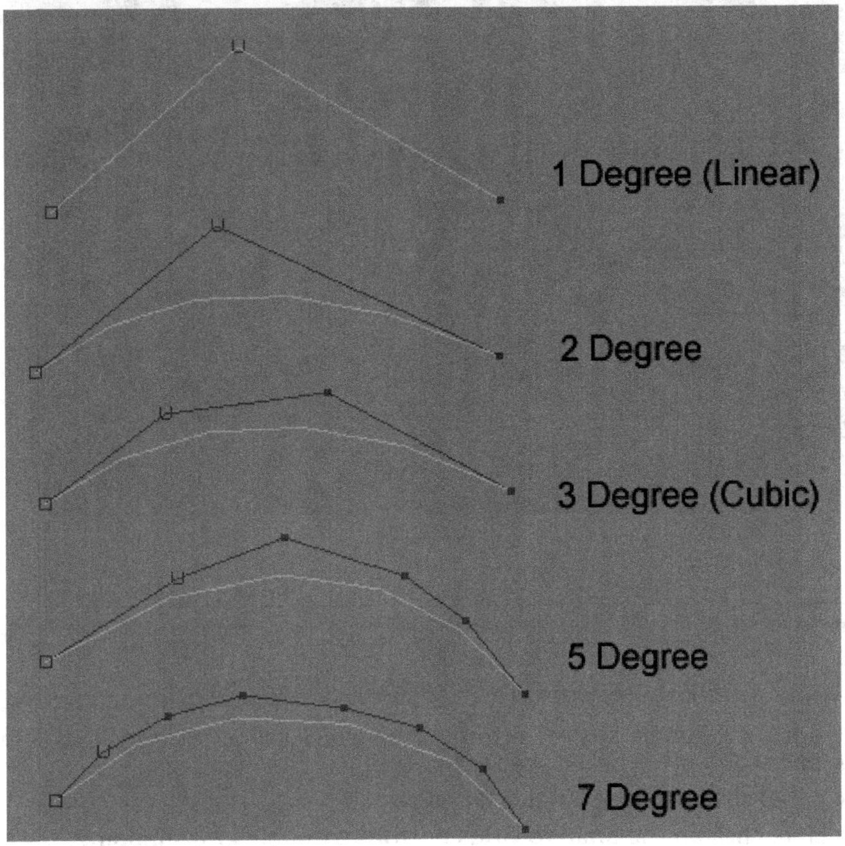

FIGURE 7-2

Curve degrees

Drawing Freehand Curves

You can draw freehand curves using the Pencil Curve tool, which is also found in the Create, Curve Tools menu. This automatically creates a curve with as many vertices as it takes to represent the drawn curve. Clicking the Select by Component Type button on the Status Line shows all the vertices for the selected curve and using the right-click marking menu lets you display the Control Vertices or Edit Points that make up the curve.

Simplifying and Smoothing Curves

Freehand curves can result in a large number of vertices. You can reduce the total number of vertices used to represent a curve with the Curves, Rebuild menu command. The Rebuild Curve Options dialog box, shown in Figure 7-3, includes several options for defining what the reduced curve should look like. Selected curves can also be smoothed using the Curves, Smooth command. This provides a way to quickly improve the smoothness of a hand-drawn curve. The Smooth Curve Options dialog box includes a Smoothness value that determines how aggressively the curve is smoothed.

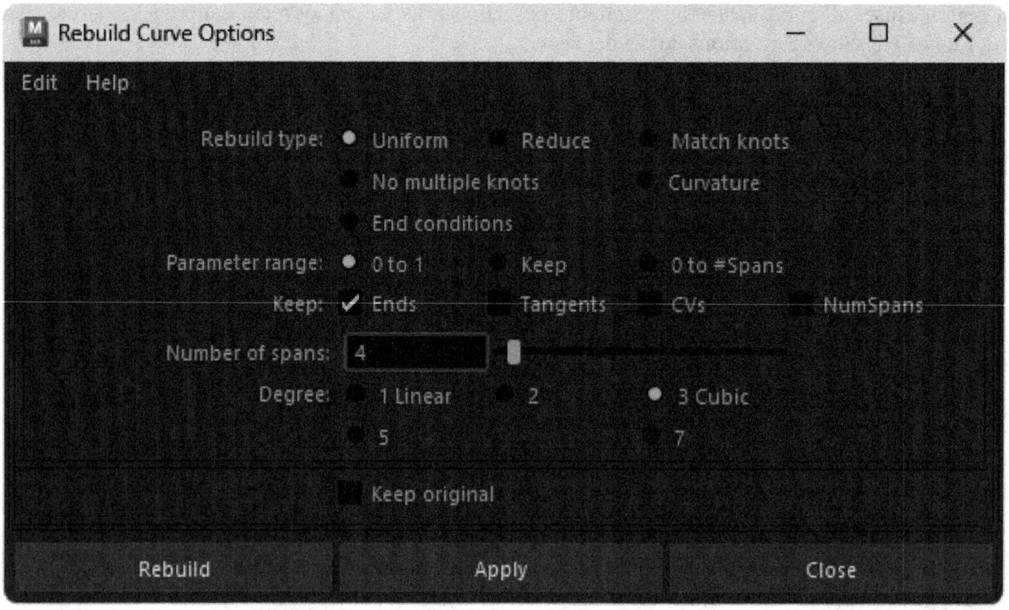

FIGURE 7-3

Rebuild Curve Options

Lesson 7.1-Tutorial 1: Draw and Compare CV, EP, and Freehand Curves

1. Click on the Four View button at the bottom of the Quick Layout Buttons and select the Top View panel and press the spacebar to maximize the viewport.

   The view panel changes to show the Top view.

2. In the Status Line, click on the Snap to Grids button to enable grid snapping.
3. Select Create, Curve Tools, CV Curve Tool and click on grid intersection points in a zig-zag pattern.
4. Select Create, Curve Tools, EP Curve Tool and click on grid intersection points beneath the CV Curve in the same zig-zag pattern.

   Notice how the curve created with the CV Curve tool winds between the placed points and the second curve has the line run through the grid snap points.

5. Select Create, Curve Tools, Pencil Curve Tool and draw the same zig-zag pattern beneath the other two curves.

   Notice how the Pencil Curve tool doesn't snap to the grid and is freehand. Figure 7-4 shows the resulting curves.

6. Select File, Save Scene As and save the file as **Wavy zig-zag lines.mb**.

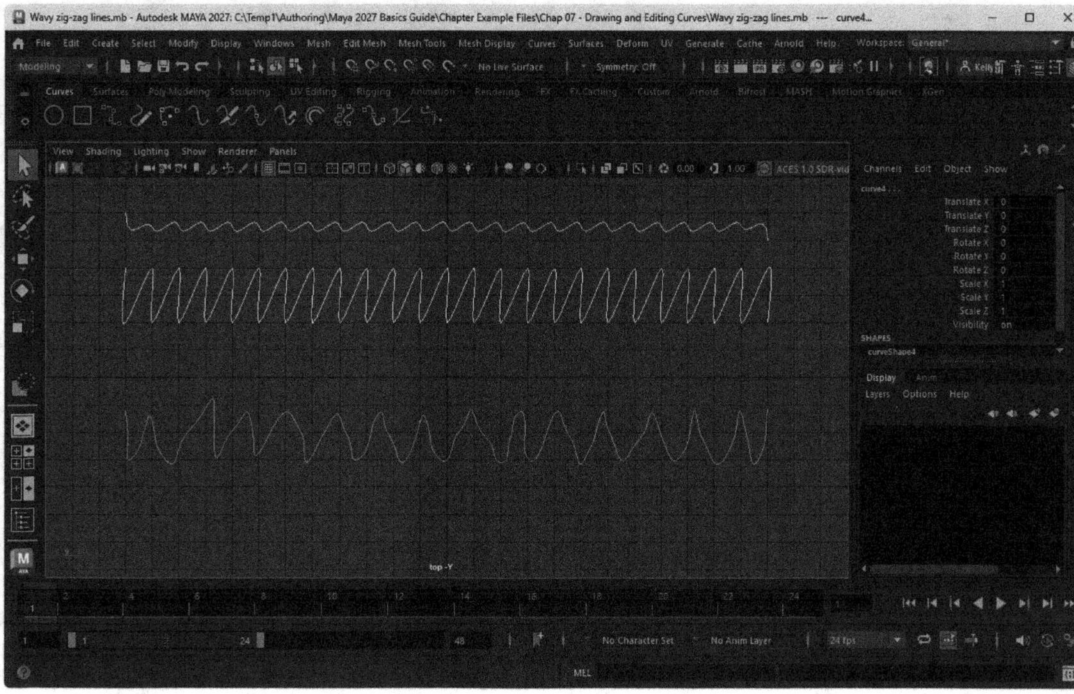

FIGURE 7-4

CV, EP and Freehand curves

Lesson 7.1-Tutorial 2: Simplify Freehand Curves

1. Click on the Four View button at the bottom of the Quick Layout Buttons and select the Top View panel and press the spacebar to maximize the viewport.

   The view panel changes to show the Top view.

2. Select Create, Curve Tools, Pencil Curve Tool and draw a freehand spiral in the center of the Top panel.
3. Click on the Show or Hide the Attribute Editor button on the right end of the Status Line to display the Attribute Editor. Look at the number of spans for the freehand spiral.

   A single span is the distance between each edit point. It defines the complexity of the curve and is related to the number of CVs. Figure 7-5 shows the freehand spiral.

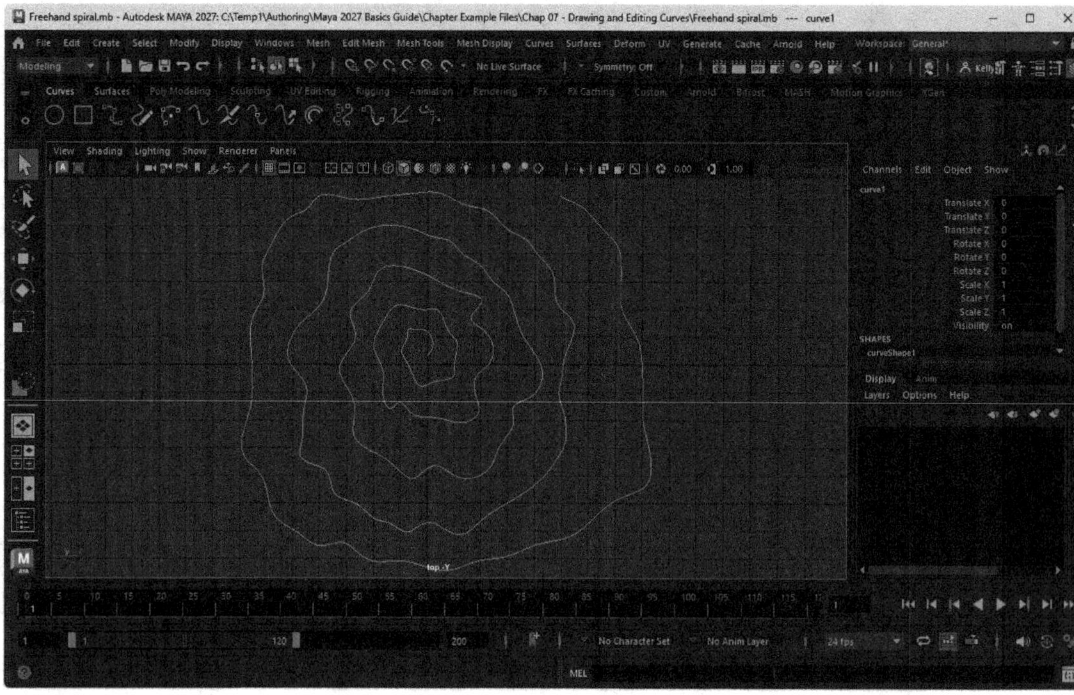

FIGURE 7-5

The freehand spiral

4. Open the options dialog box for Curves, Rebuild. Set the number of spans to half its original value and click the Apply button.

   The curve is significantly reduced and simplified, as shown in Figure 7-6.

5. Continue to decrease the number of spans in the options dialog box by half and click the Apply button again until the curve is simplified as much as it can be without changing its shape.

Note

If you've reduced the curve too much, you can use the Edit, Undo menu command to return the curve to its previous state.

6. Select File, Save Scene As and save the file as **Rebuilt freehand spiral.mb**.

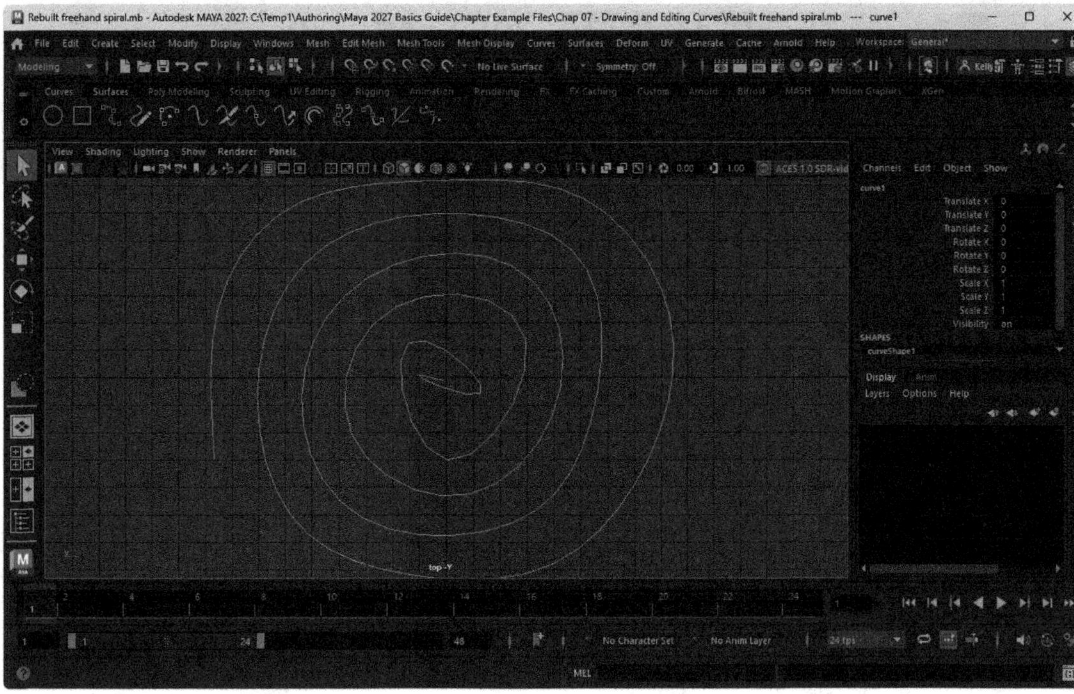

FIGURE 7-6

Rebuilt freehand spiral

Lesson 7.2: Edit Curve Details

There are two methods for editing curve details. One method is to use component mode and to move the CVs or edit points. This alters the curvature of the curve around the vertex. An easy way to select CVs or edit points is to right-click and select the component type that you want to move from the marking menu. Components can only be moved in Component mode, which is available on the Status Line.

Note

The Rotate and Scale tools can be used when multiple vertices are selected, but they have no effect when a single vertex is selected.

Using the Edit Curve Tool

Another method for editing curves is to use the Edit Curve tool, found in the Curves menu. This tool places a manipulator, shown in Figure 7-7, on the curve that lets you select any position on the curve and move it regardless of its vertices. With the Edit Curve tool, simply click anywhere on the curve and the manipulator will appear. The Slide Along Curve handle lets you drag the manipulator along the length of the curve to position it exactly where you want it. If you drag the Point Position handle, the curve point where the manipulator is located moves.

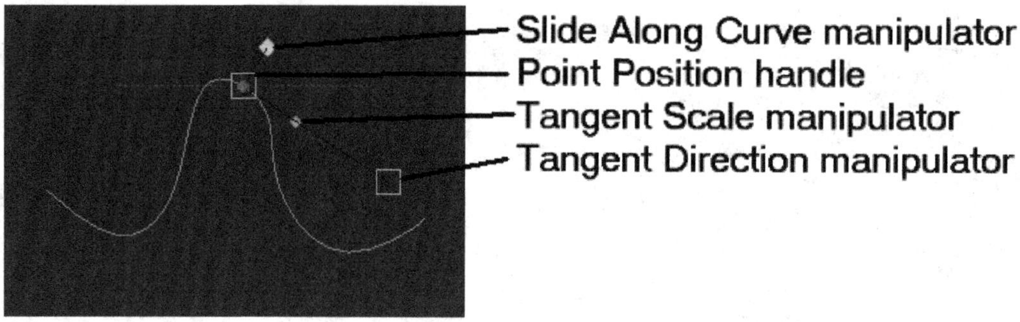

FIGURE 7-7

The Edit Curve manipulator

Altering Tangents

The Edit Curve tool also makes the point's Tangent Direction handle selectable. This tangent determines the direction that the curve flows into and out of the selected point. It is identified as a light blue square connected by a black line. Figure 7-8 shows the effect of dragging the Tangent Direction handle. Notice how the curve around the selected point bends. Clicking on one of the dotted axes aligns the tangent with that axis. The Tangent Scale manipulator controls how sharp the curve is at that point.

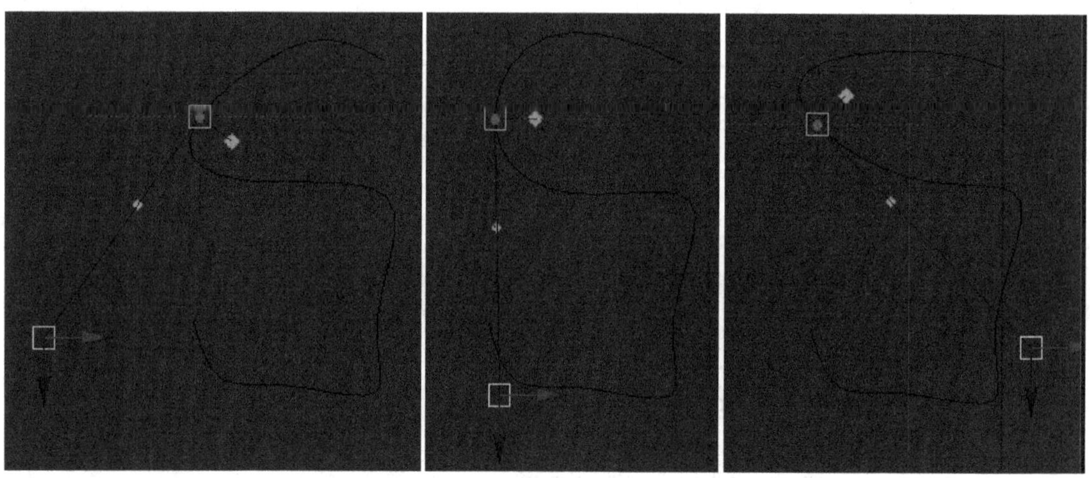

FIGURE 7-8

Changing tangent direction

Adding Sharp Points to a Curve

To add a sharp point to a curve, you can slide the Tangent Scale handle close to the selected point with the Edit Curves tool or you can stack several vertices on top of each other. Vertices may be stacked on a selected Edit Point using the Curves, Insert Knot menu command. The Insert Knot Options dialog box lets you select to add another additional point on top of the selected Edit Point or in between the selected Edit Points. When two knots are added to the same point, the CV is placed on top of the Edit Point causing a sharp corner in the curve, as shown in Figure 7-9.

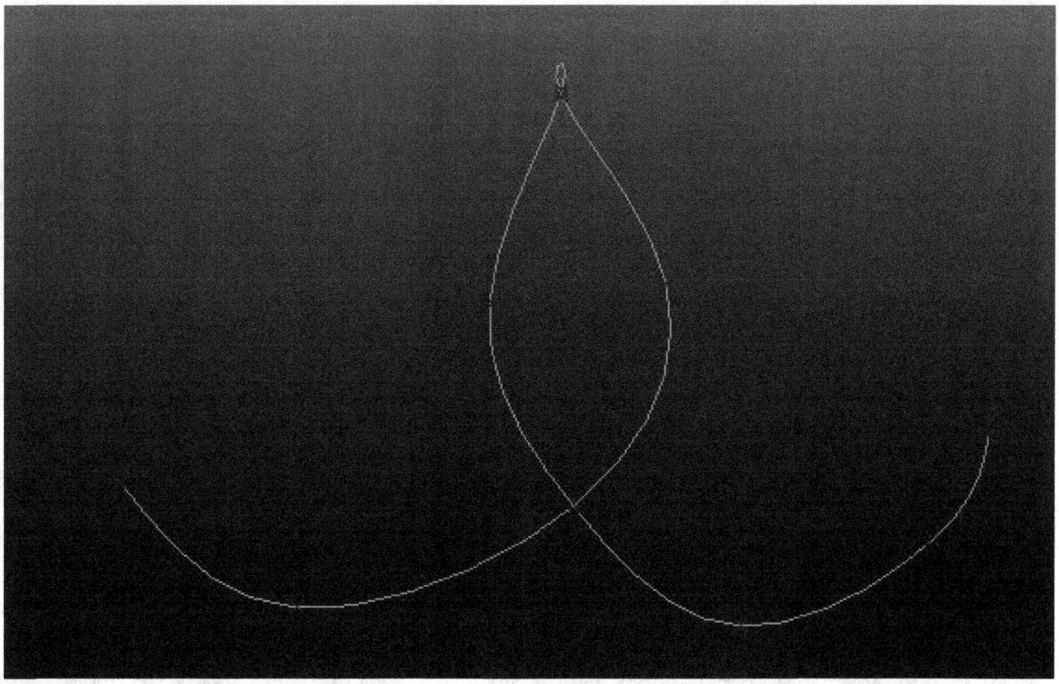

FIGURE 7-9

Duplicated Edit Points make sharp corners

Adding Points to the End of a Curve

You can add vertices to the end of an open curve using the Curves, Add Points Tool. If a curve is selected, clicking with the Add Points Tool adds a new CV to the end of the curve.

Note

You can also add points to the end of a curve with the Curves, Extend, Extend Curve menu command. The Options dialog box for Extend Curve allows you to extend the curve's start, end or both a specified distance or to a specific point's location.

Closing and Opening Curves

Closed curves are curves whose last vertex is attached to the first, making it a complete loop. A circle is a good example of a closed curve. Several 3D operations require that a curve be closed. You can automatically close an open curve using the Curves, Open/Close menu command. Closed curves can be made open by using the same command. Figure 7-10 shows the curve in the previous figure that has been closed with the Open/Close Curves menu command.

Note

With a closed curve, it can be difficult to select the beginning or ending CV point. The Select menu

```
includes commands for selecting all CVs, First CV
on Curve and Last CV on Curve.
```

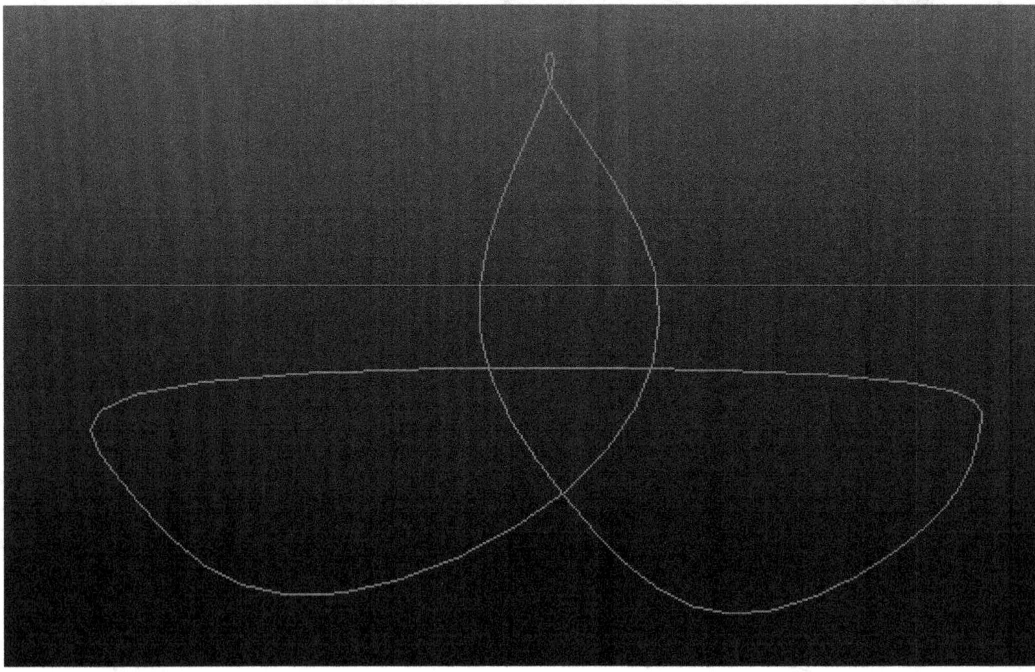

FIGURE 7-10

Closed curve

Lesson 7.2-Tutorial 1: Create and Edit a Star Shape

1. Click on the Four View button from the Quick Layout Buttons and select the Top View panel and press the spacebar to maximize the viewport.

   The view panel changes to show the Top view.
2. Open the Options dialog box for the Create, Curve Tools, EP Curve tool and select the 1 Linear Curve Degree option.

   The option creates straight lines.
3. In the Status Line, click on the Snap to Grids button to enable grid snapping.
4. Click in the Top panel to create 11 vertices for a star. Then press the Enter key to exit the EP Curve tool.
5. In the Status Line, click the Select by Component button and make sure the Points selection mask button is selected.

   The curve's CVs should be displayed, as shown in Figure 7-11.
6. Select the Move tool in the Toolbox and drag over the CV that you want to move and then drag it to its new location.
7. Select File, Save Scene As and save the file as **Star.mb**.

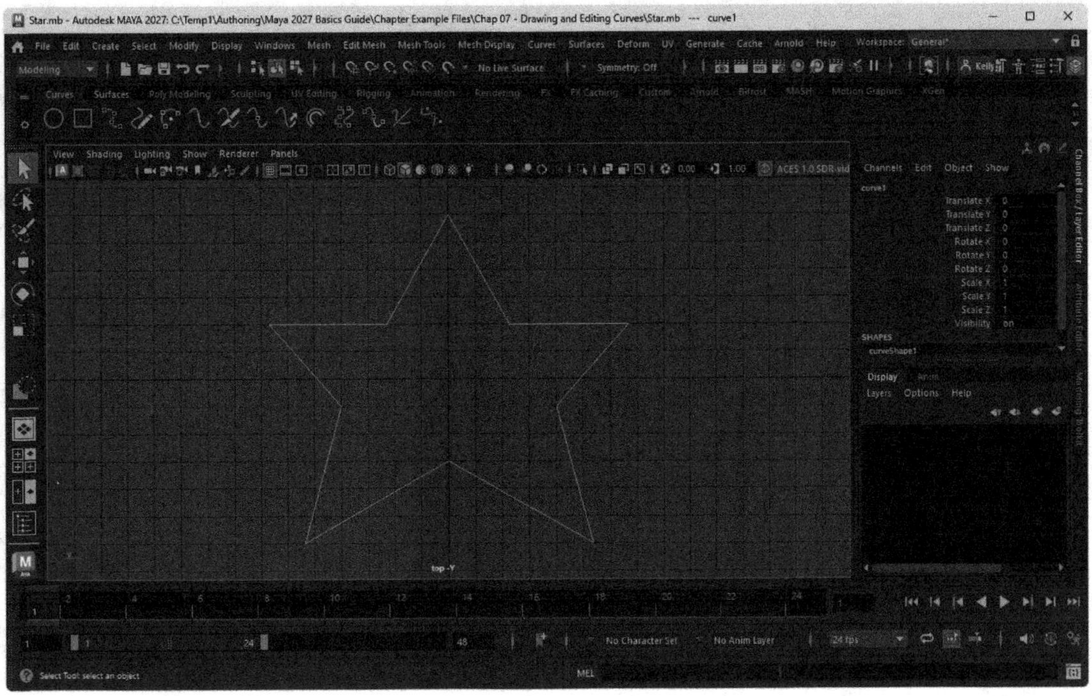

FIGURE 7-11

Star shape

Lesson 7.2-Tutorial 2: Use the Edit Curve Tool

1. Select the File, Open menu command and open the Tulip curve.mb file.
2. Select the Curves, Edit Curve tool menu command and click on the upper-right corner of the curve.

   The Edit Curve manipulator appears, allowing you to drag the selected point to modify the curve.
3. Drag the upper-right portion of the curve outward to make it symmetrical with the left side of the curve.
4. Click with the Edit Curve tool on the center point, and then drag the center handle downward.
5. Click and drag on the Point Position handle to slide the manipulator to the very bottom of the curve and then click on the red horizontal axis to align the tangent with this axis.

   With the tangent manipulator aligned with an axis, the curve is symmetrical, as shown in Figure 7-12.
6. Select File, Save Scene As and save the file as **New tulip curve.mb**.

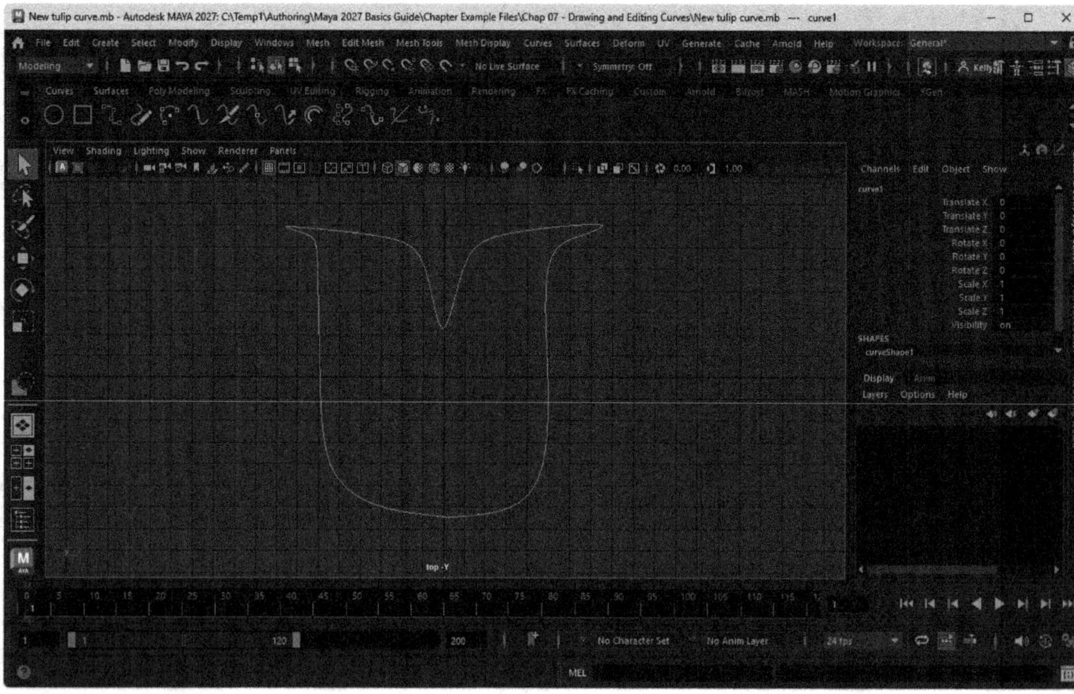

FIGURE 7-12

Tulip shape

Lesson 7.2-Tutorial 3: Create Sharp Points

1. Click on the Four View button from the Quick Layout Buttons and select the Top View panel and press the spacebar to maximize the viewport.

   The view panel changes to show the Top view.

2. Click on the Snap to Grids button in the Status Line to enable grid snapping.
3. Select the Create, Curve Tools, EP Curve tool and click five times to create a closed square, and then press the Enter key to exit the tool.

   The closed curve now looks like a rounded square with one sharp corner where the first and last point are located.

4. Click the Select by Component button on the Status Line to display the curve's CVs.
5. Right-click on the curve and select the Edit Points pop-up menu command to display the curve's Edit Points.
6. Hold down the Shift key and select the three rounded corner Edit Points and choose the Curves, Insert Knot menu command. Then select the same corner points again and apply the Curves, Insert Knot menu command again.

   The second time a new knot is added to the Edit Point, the CV is added on top of the Edit Point.

7. Select all four corner Edit Points and CVs together and then click on the Scale tool button and drag from the center manipulator outward.

   With the added knots, each corner becomes a sharp point, as shown in Figure 7-13.

8. Select File, Save Scene As and save the file as **Sharp corner square.mb**.

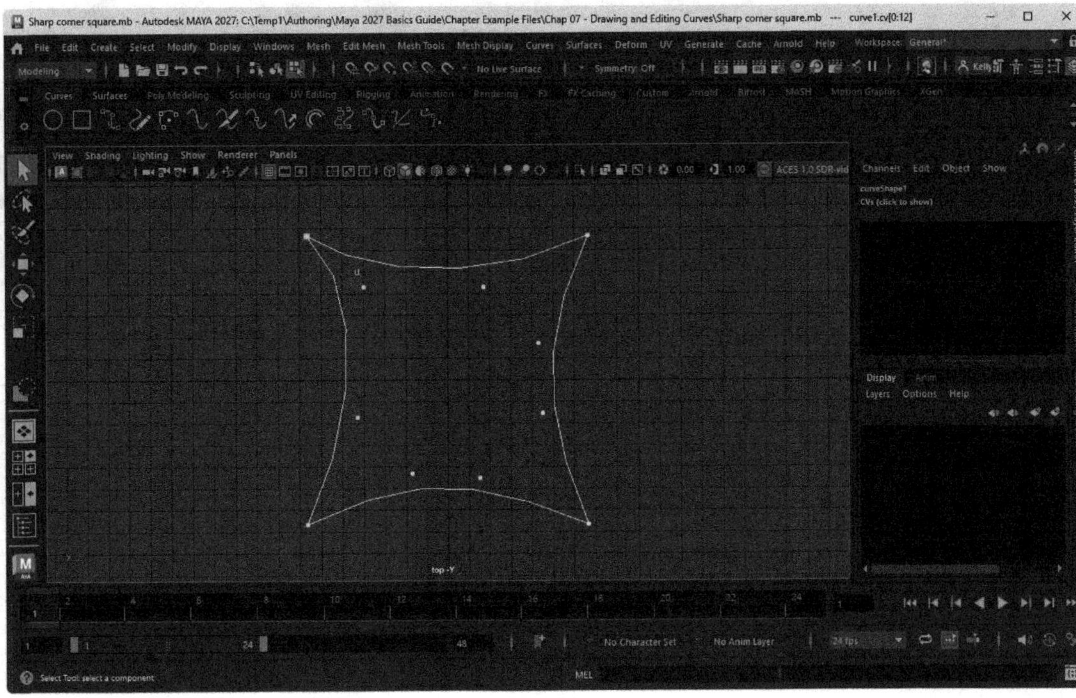

FIGURE 7-13

Sharp points from double knots

Lesson 7.2-Tutorial 4: Close a Curve

1. Click on the Four View button from the Quick Layout Buttons and select the Top View panel and press the spacebar to maximize the viewport.

   The view panel changes to show the Top view.

2. Click on the Snap to Grids button in the Status Line to enable grid snapping.
3. Select the Create, Curve Tools, EP Curve tool and click in the view panel to create an open shape. Press the Enter key when done.
4. With the curve selected, choose the Curves, Open/Close menu command.

   Another line segment is added to the curve that joins the first and last points while maintaining the curvature of the curve, as shown in Figure 7-14.

5. Select File, Save Scene As and save the file as **Closed curve.mb**.

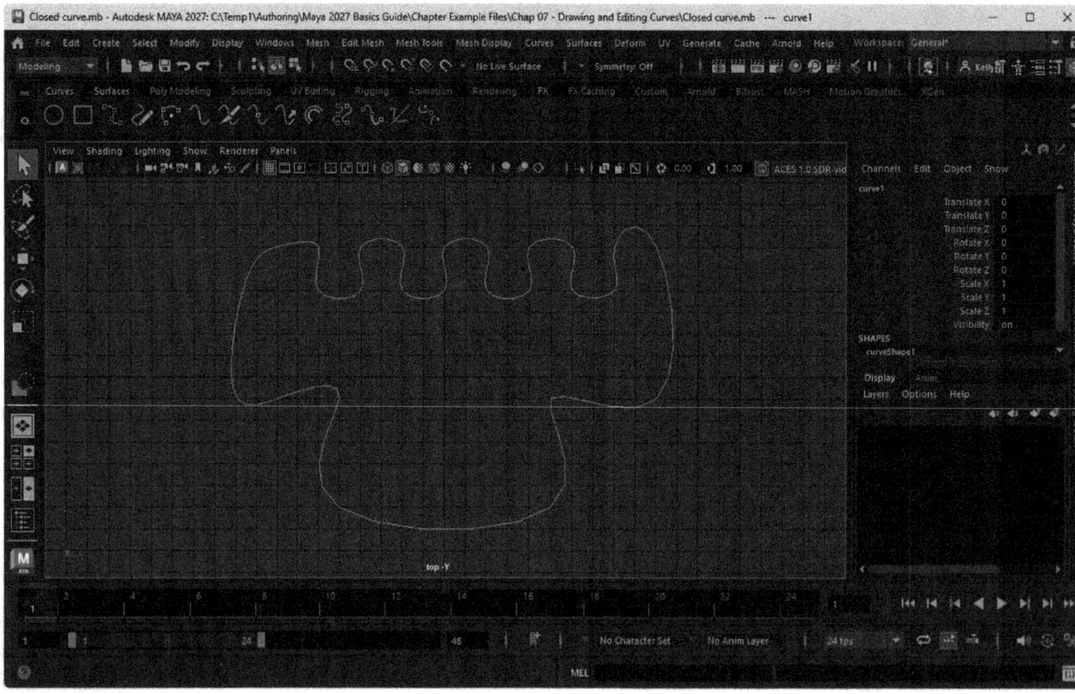

FIGURE 7-14

Closed curve

Lesson 7.3: Modify Curves

In addition to editing curves, the Curves menu also includes several preset commands for modifying curves in many unique ways such as Straighten, Smooth, Curl, Bend and Scale Curvature.

Locking Length

At any time during the curve modification process, you can select the Curves, Lock Length menu command. This command causes the length of the curve to be set and locked, so it won't change as modification commands are applied. There is also an Unlock Length command from removing the lock.

Straightening Curves

Curves drawn with the Pencil Curve tool aren't always the straightest curves, but you can straighten them easily with the Curves, Straighten menu command. The direction of the straightened curve follows the initial direction of the first point.

Smoothing Curves

The Curves, Smooth menu command (found in the Modify section of the Curves menu near the top) gradually reduces the curvature of a curve by reducing it to a straight line. This is different than the Curves, Smooth menu command (located in the Edit section of the Curves menu near the bottom), which removes abrupt changes in the curve while maintaining its curvature. Figure 7-15 shows a freehand curve (on top) that has been smoothed once (middle curve) and twice (bottom curve).

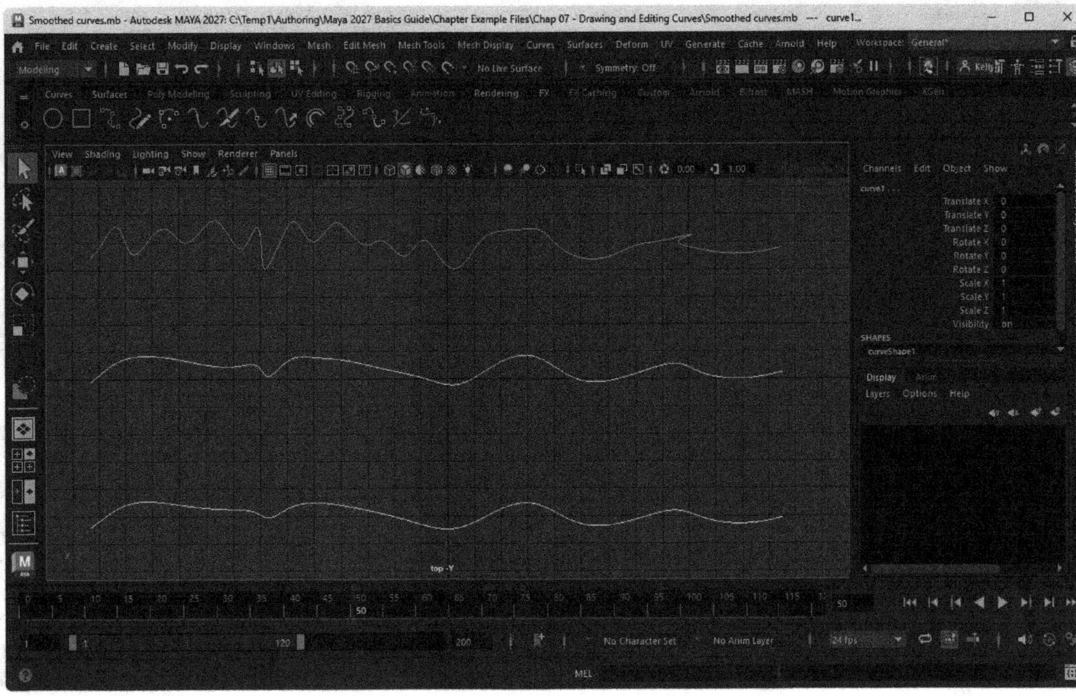

FIGURE 7-15

Smoothed curves

Curling and Bending Curves

The Curves, Curl menu command moves the CVs relative to one another to cause the curve to curl about itself creating several loops in the curve. The Curves, Bend menu command is similar to the Curl command, except all CVs move together to bend the entire curve together and the Curl command causes loops to appear in several places along the curve. Figure 7-16 shows the Curl (right) and Bend (left) commands multiple times to a curve.

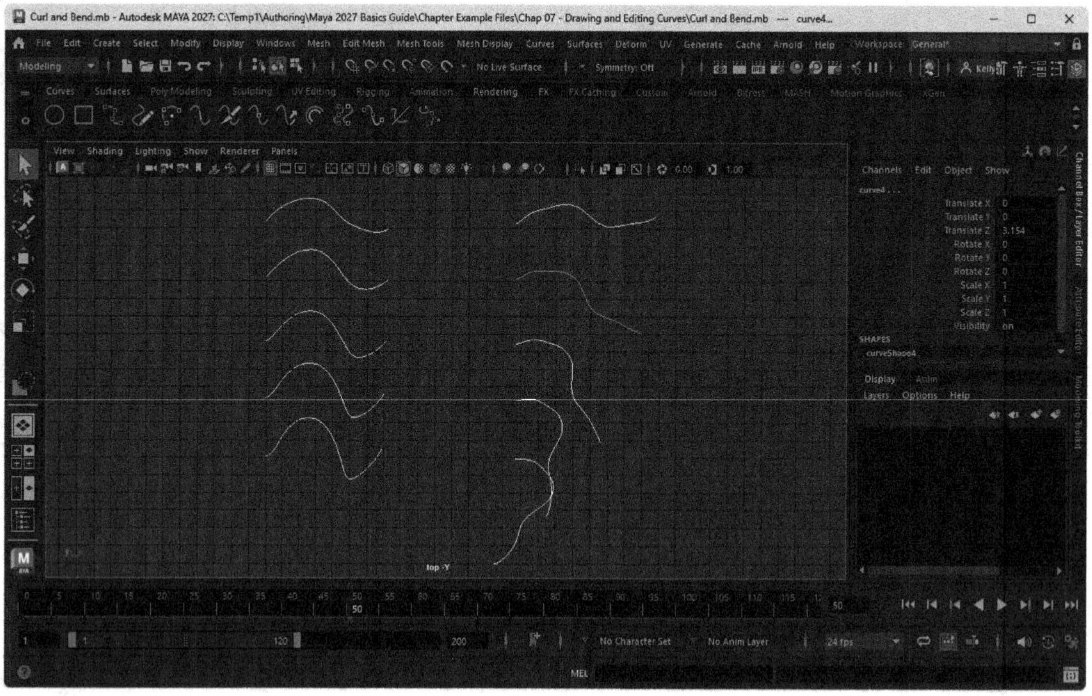

FIGURE 7-16

Curled and bent modified curves

Scaling Curvature

The Curves, Scale Curvature menu command modifies a curve by exaggerating the curve. If the curve includes lots of curves, this command scales the entire curve using the first curve it finds. A Scale Factor lower than 1.0 removes some of the curvature from the curve.

Lesson 7.3-Tutorial 1: Curl a Curve

1. Click on the Four View button from the Quick Layout Buttons and select the Top View panel and press the spacebar to maximize the viewport.

   The view panel changes to show the Top view.
2. Select the Create, Curve Tools, Pencil Curve tool menu command and draw a curve across the top of the view panel.
3. With the curve selected, choose the Edit, Duplicate menu command and drag the duplicate curve downward slightly.
4. With the duplicate curve selected, select the Edit, Duplicate with Transform menu command multiple times or press the Shift+D keyboard shortcut multiple times.

   Duplicating the curves multiple times creates multiple parallel aligned curves, as shown in Figure 7-17.

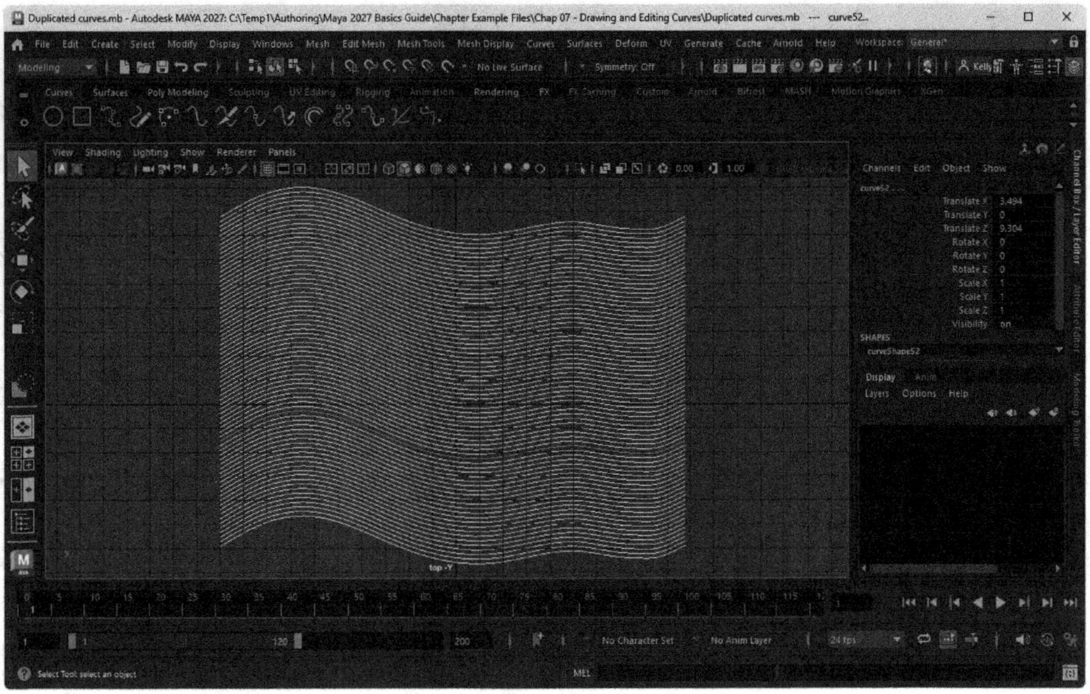

FIGURE 7-17

Parallel curves

5. Select the Select, All menu command to select all the curves.
6. With all the curves selected, choose the Curves, Smooth menu command.

   The Smooth menu command removes the harshness that comes from drawing a freehand curve.
7. Select the Curves, Curl menu command multiple times.

   The Curl menu command adds some bumps to the parallel lines, as shown in Figure 7-18.
8. Select File, Save Scene As and save the file as **Curled curves.mb**.

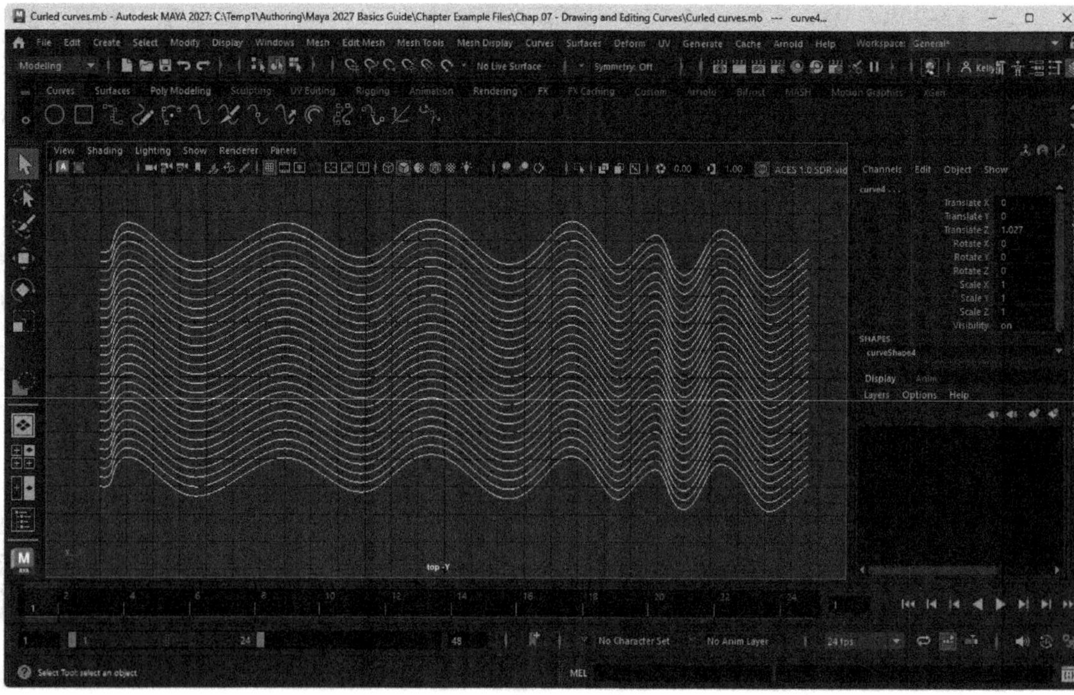

FIGURE 7-18

Curled curves

Lesson 7.4: Apply Curve Operators

In the Curves menu, shown in Figure 7-19, you'll find several operations that can be used to edit curves in unique ways. Many of these operators require that more than one curve is selected. If you're having trouble with the curve operator, check out the Help Line for information on which curve is expected to be selected.

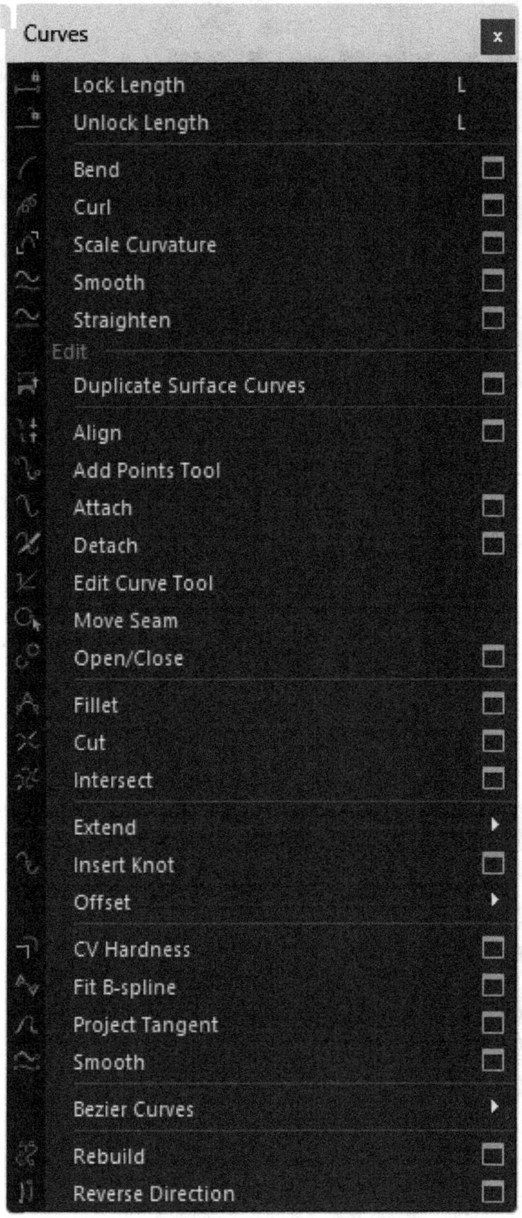

FIGURE 7-19

The Curves menu

Attaching Curves

If two curves are selected, you can connect the closest ends of each curve together using the Curves, Attach menu command. The Attach Curves Options dialog box, shown in Figure 7-20, includes options to connect or blend the two curves. The Connect option joins the curves with a minimal change in the curvature of the original curves, and Blend smoothes the two curves together based on the Blend Bias value. If you keep the original curves, changes made to the original curves are also applied to the combined curve.

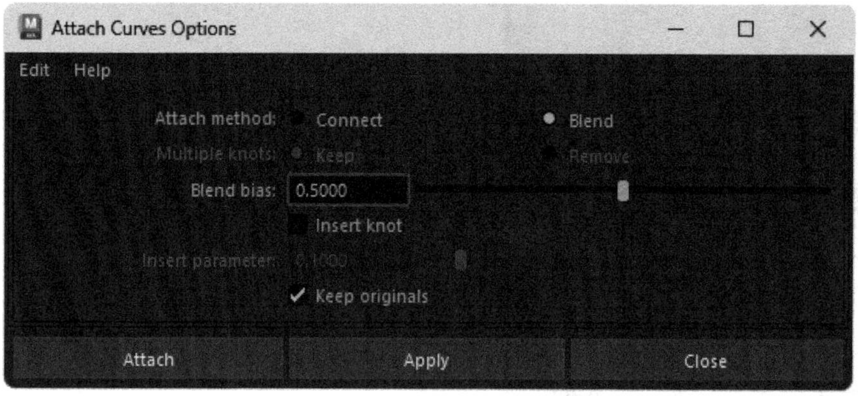

FIGURE 7-20

Attach Curves options

Aligning Curves

With two curves selected, you can align the curves. The Align Curves Options dialog box, shown in Figure 7-21, lets you choose to align a curve's position, tangent, or curvature. When the Position option is selected, you can select which curve to move—the first, second, or both (which moves both curves halfway). With the Tangent or Curvature options selected, you can select to modify the tangent of either curve or both.

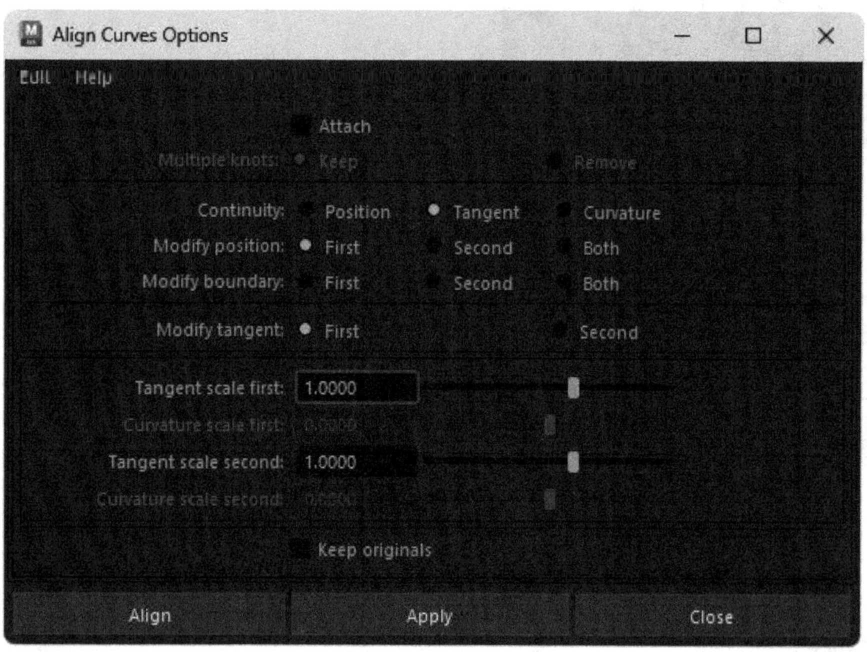

FIGURE 7-21

Align Curves Options

Detaching and Cutting Curves

You can split a curve into two separate curves by selecting an edit point where the cut is made and using the Curves, Detach menu command. If several edit points are selected, the curve is subdivided into a separate curve for each selected edit point which marks a cut. If two intersecting curves are selected, the Curves, Cut menu command can be used to cut the curves where they intersect. The Options dialog box includes an option to use only the last curve to cut the other curves. You can also select to keep the longest segment, all curve segments, or the segments with curve points.

Finding Curve Intersections

The Curves, Intersect menu command finds and marks in the active view the intersections between two curves. In the Intersect Curves Options dialog box, you can specify a tolerance that finds all curve intersections within the given Tolerance value.

Offsetting Curves

An **offset curve** is a curve that is created by moving all of the curve vertices perpendicular a given distance from their current positions. This can be done to a selected curve using the Curves, Offset, Offset Curve menu command. Using the Offset Curve Options dialog box, shown in Figure 7-22, you can adjust the offset value. A Positive value offsets the curve on the right and a negative value offsets the curve on the left. The Loop Cutting and Cutting Radius options can be used to change tight details from becoming loops and sharp points.

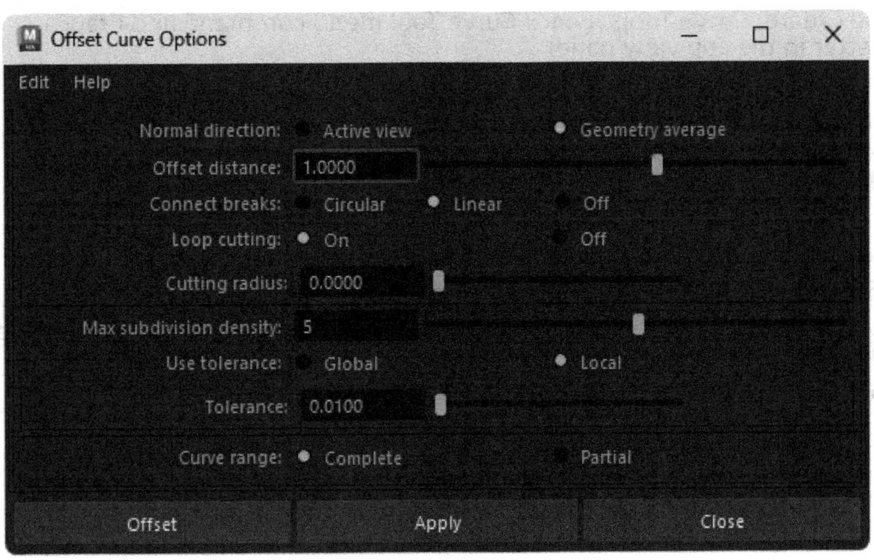

FIGURE 7-22

Offset Curve Options

Filleting Curves

A **fillet** rounds the intersection between two curves. For example, if two sides of a square are selected, using the Curves, Fillet menu command creates a new curve that rounds the corner. In the Fillet Curve Options dialog box, shown in Figure 7-23, you can select to trim, join, and keep the original curve. The Radius value determines how much roundness to apply.

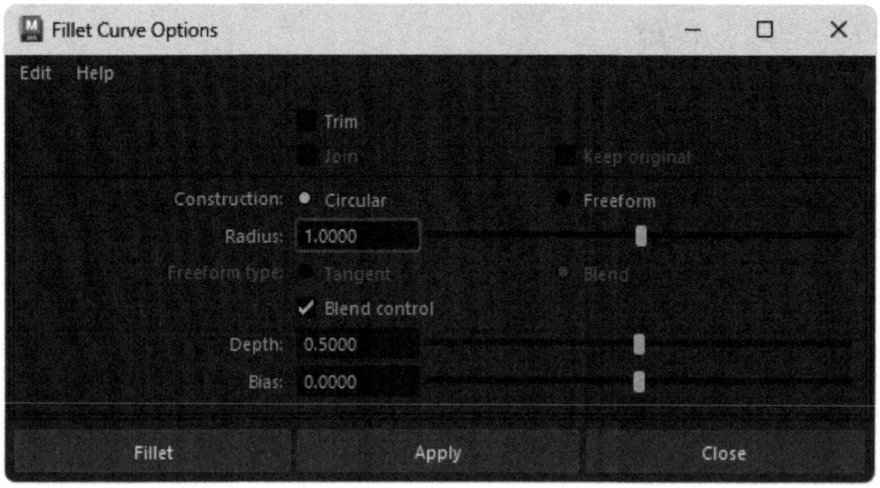

FIGURE 7-23

Fillet Curve options

Lesson 7.4-Tutorial 1: Connect Cursive Letters

1. Select the Create, Curve Tools, Pencil Curve Tool menu command and draw a cursive letter in the Top view panel.
2. Draw another cursive letter that is separate from the first in the Top view panel.
3. Continue to draw individual cursive letters until all letters for the word are complete.
4. Select all letters and choose the Curves, Smooth menu command.
5. Select the first two letters and choose the Curves, Attach menu command.

   The curves that make up the two separate letters are combined into one.
6. Repeat Step 5 with the remaining letters. Figure 7-24 shows the results.

   The Attach Curves menu command combines all the separate curves into one, but in the following figure, you can still see parts of the original curves.
7. Select File, Save Scene As and save the file as **Cursive word.mb**.

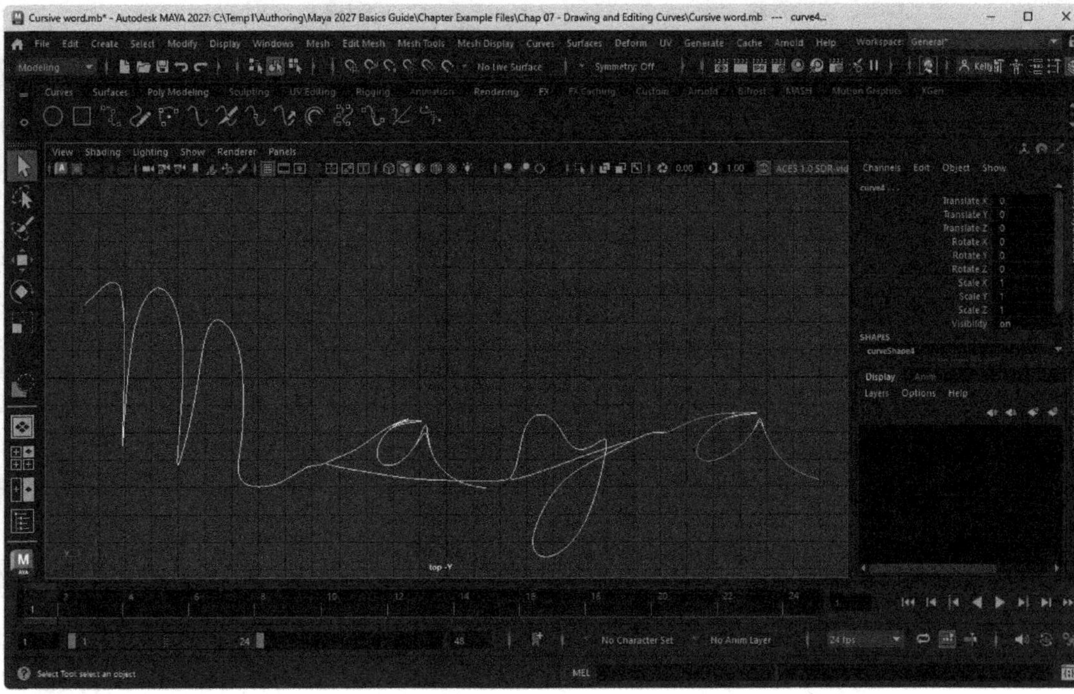

FIGURE 7-24

Attached cursive letters

Lesson 7.4-Tutorial 2: Align Flower Petals

1. Select the Create, Curve Tools, Pencil Curve Tool menu command and draw several disconnected flower petals in the Top view panel.
2. Select all petals and choose the Curves, Smooth menu command.
3. Select a flower petal curve and with the Shift key held down, select the next adjacent flower petal curve.
4. Select the Curves, Align, Options dialog box menu command.
5. In the Align Curves Options dialog box, enable the Attach option and click the Apply button.

   The non-key selected flower petal curve is connected to the other.
6. Hold down the Shift key and select the next adjacent flower petal curve and press the Apply button again.
7. Repeat Step 5 until all of the flower petal curves are part of the same curve.
8. Select Curves, Open/Close to complete the curve.

   The petal curves are now combined and connected into a single curve, as shown in Figure 7-25.
9. Select File, Save Scene As and save the file as **Aligned flower petals.mb**.

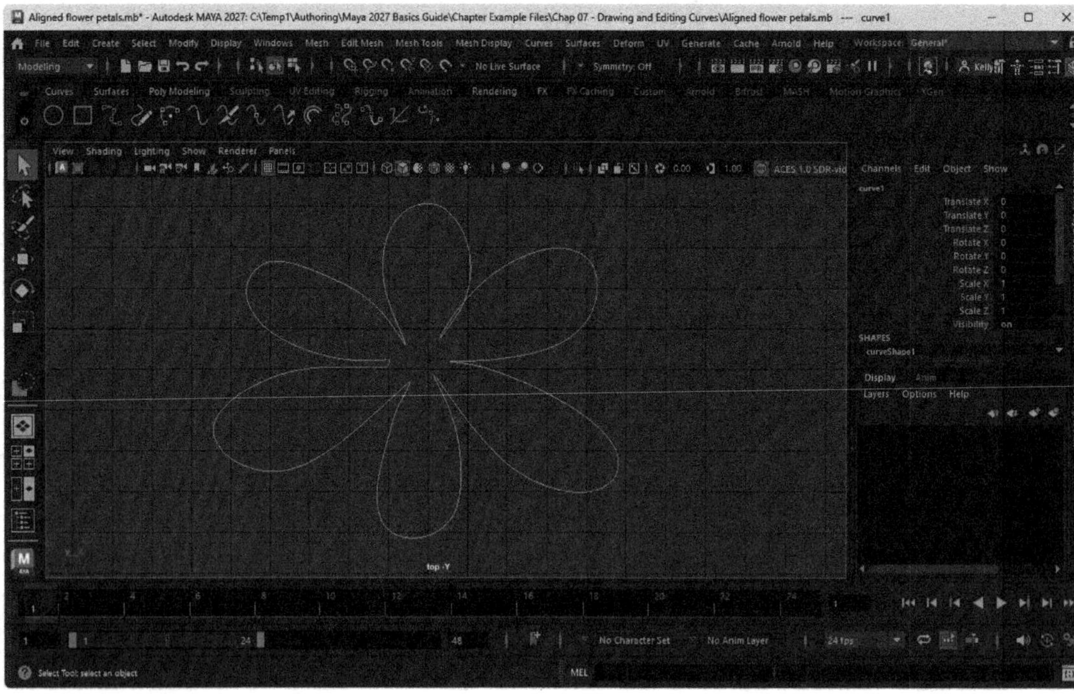

FIGURE 7-25

Aligned flower petal curves

Lesson 7.4-Tutorial 3: Offset Curves

1. Select the Create, Curve Tools, Pencil Curve Tool menu command and draw a single line with several smooth bumps in the Top view panel.
2. With the curve selected, choose the Curves, Offset, Offset Curve, Options menu command. Then click the Apply button.

   Another curve appears that is offset from the first.
3. In the Offset Curve Options dialog box, set the Offset Distance value to 0.5 and then click the Apply button again.
4. Repeat Step 3 with Offset Distance values of 0.25 and 0.12.
5. Select the original curve again and enter an Offset Distance value of –1 and click the Apply button.
6. Repeat Step 3 again with the Offset Distance values of –0.5, -0.25, and –0.12.

   The resulting offset curves look like a river, as shown in Figure 7-26.
7. Select File, Save Scene As and save the file as **Offset river.mb**.

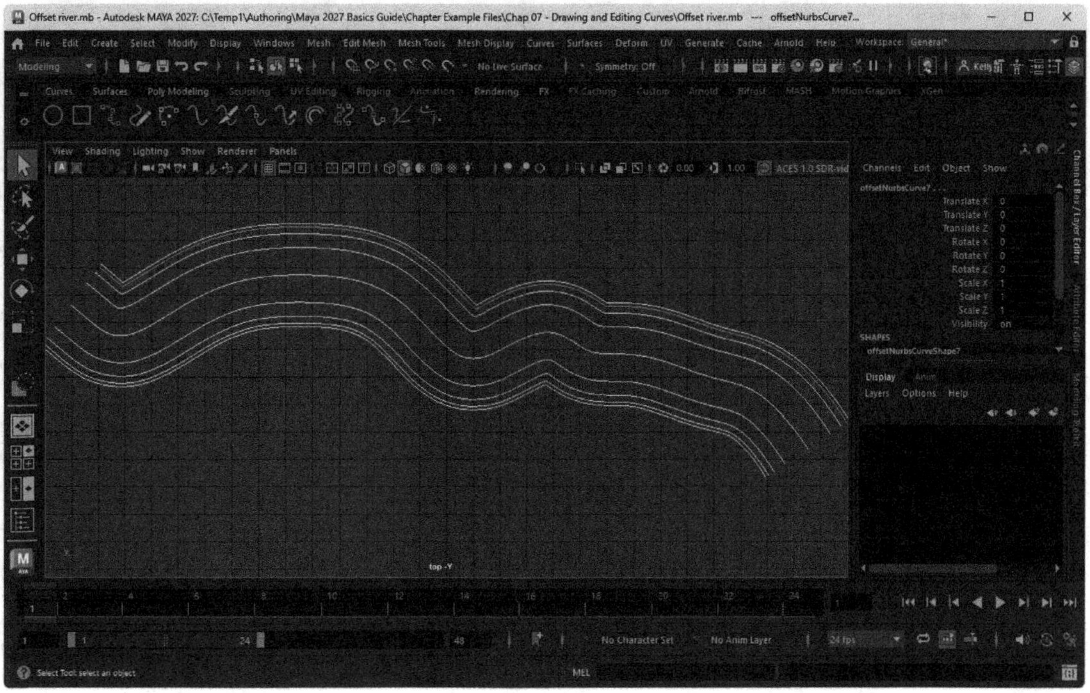

FIGURE 7-26

Offset river curves

Lesson 7.4-Tutorial 4: Fillet Curves

1. Select the Create, NURBS Primitives, Square menu command to create a square in the Top view panel.
2. Drag over one of the square corners to select two of its edges.
3. Select the Curves, Fillet, Options menu command. Enable the Trim option, set the Radius value to 0.1, and click the Apply button.

   A fillet is applied to the two edges, rounding the corner of the square.
4. Drag over another corner to select two more edges and click the Apply button again.
5. Repeat Step 4 with the remaining two corners. Figure 7-27 shows the results.
6. Select File, Save Scene As and save the file as **Rounded square.mb**.

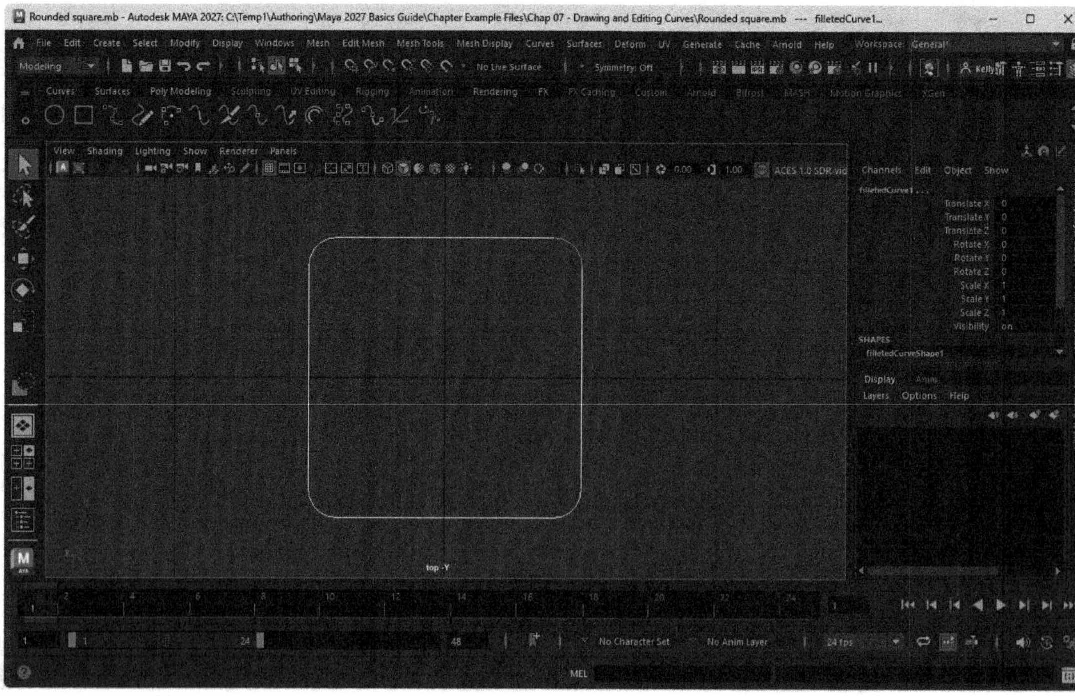

FIGURE 7-27

A rounded square

Lesson 7.5: Create Sweep Mesh Objects

The easiest way to create a 3D object from a curve is with the Sweep Mesh object. You can find this feature in the Create menu. To use it simply select the curve and choose the Create, **Sweep Mesh** menu command. This sweeps a circular cross-section along the length of the curve, as shown in Figure 7-28.

Tip

If no curve is selected, the Create, Sweep Mesh menu command will create a single straight sweep object.

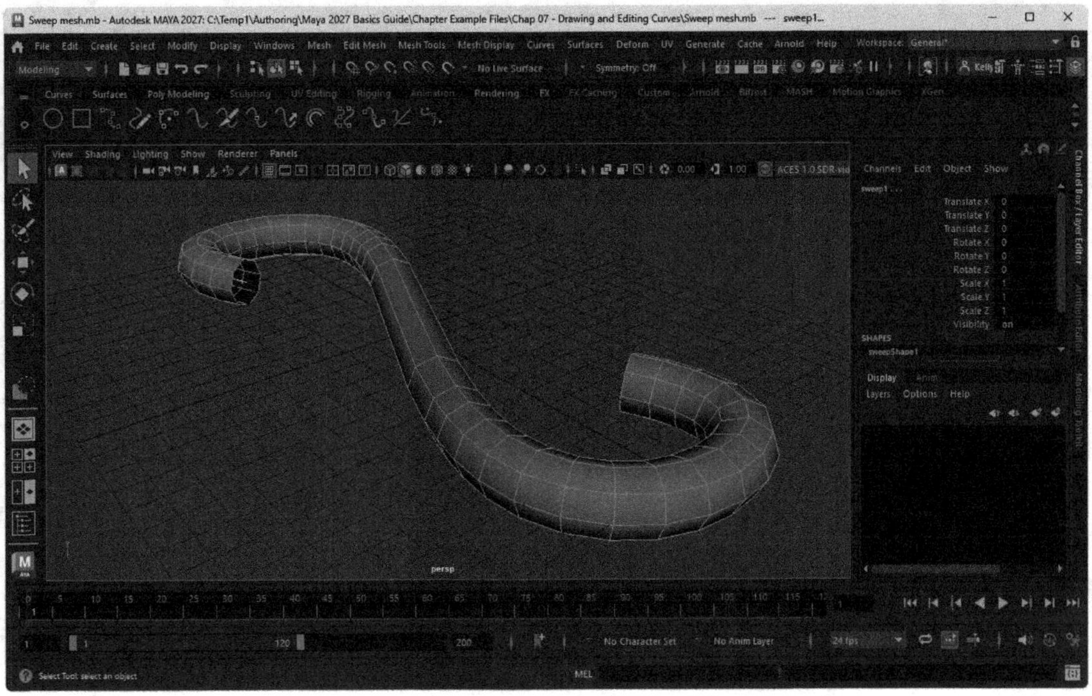

FIGURE 7-28

A Sweep Mesh object

Changing the cross-section

Sweep Mesh objects are made circular by default, but if you visit the Attribute Editor with the object selected, you can change the sweep profile. Several presets are available including Poly, Rectangle, Line, Arc, Wave and Custom. For the Poly profile, you can also choose between a Circle and Star types. The Star type has every other vertex indented. The Custom profile option lets you select another curve as the sweep profile.

Creating a group of sweeps

Beneath the Sweep Profile settings is the Distribution section. If you choose to enable the Distribution option, then a single sweep profile becomes multiple. You can choose to group these multiple sweeps around the center (Radial), in a box shape (Square) or in a straight line (Linear). You can also set the number of sweeps, their size and rotation. Figure 7-29 shows a sweep with a Distribution of 5.

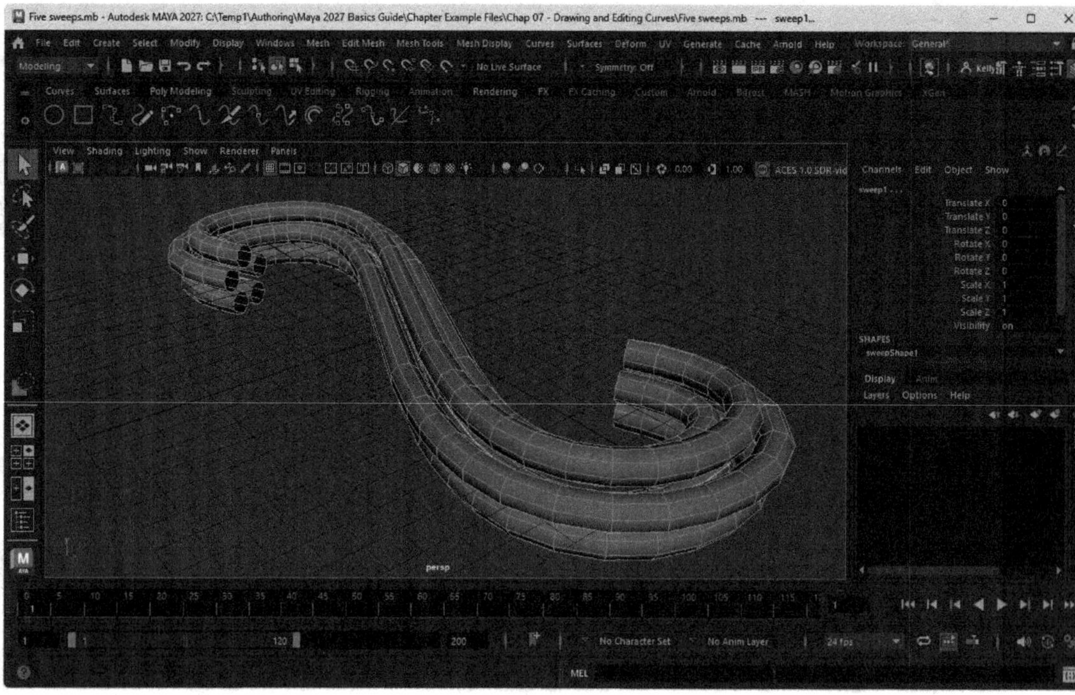

FIGURE 7-29

A group of five Sweep Mesh objects

Adding twist and taper

Within the Transformation section are settings to set **Twist** and **Taper** values. There are also options to Scale and Rotate the sweep as a unit.

Optimizing a sweep mesh

The Sweep Mesh object is only going to be as smooth as the original curve. If you have a lot of tight bends in the curve, the sweep will exaggerate those bends. However, if you look into the Interpolation section of the Attribute Editor, you can see options to set the Precision, the number of Steps from Start to End, the number of Steps from EP to EP, or the Distance between each connected cross-section. For each of these options, you can also enable the Optimize option which places more cross-sections in curvy areas and less in straight areas.

Applying to multiple curves

If you select multiple curves, you can use the Sweep Mesh Options dialog box to apply all the same settings to all the selected curves (One node for multiple curves) or apply different settings for each selected curve (One node for each curve). If this second option is selected, each independent node can be selected within the Attribute Editor for each curve.

Lesson 7.5-Tutorial 1: Sweep a bugle

1. Select File, Open Scene and open the Bugle curve.mb file.

   This file has a curve to represent a bugle.

2. Select the curve and choose the Create, Sweep Mesh menu command.

   A circular cross-section is added along the length of the curve.

3. In the Attribute Editor, open the Transformation section and set the Scale Profile to 1.0 and the Taper value to 2.0.
4. Then adjust the Taper Curve so it flares at the end of the bugle, as shown in Figure 7-30.
5. Select File, Save Scene As and save the file as **Bugle mesh.mb**.

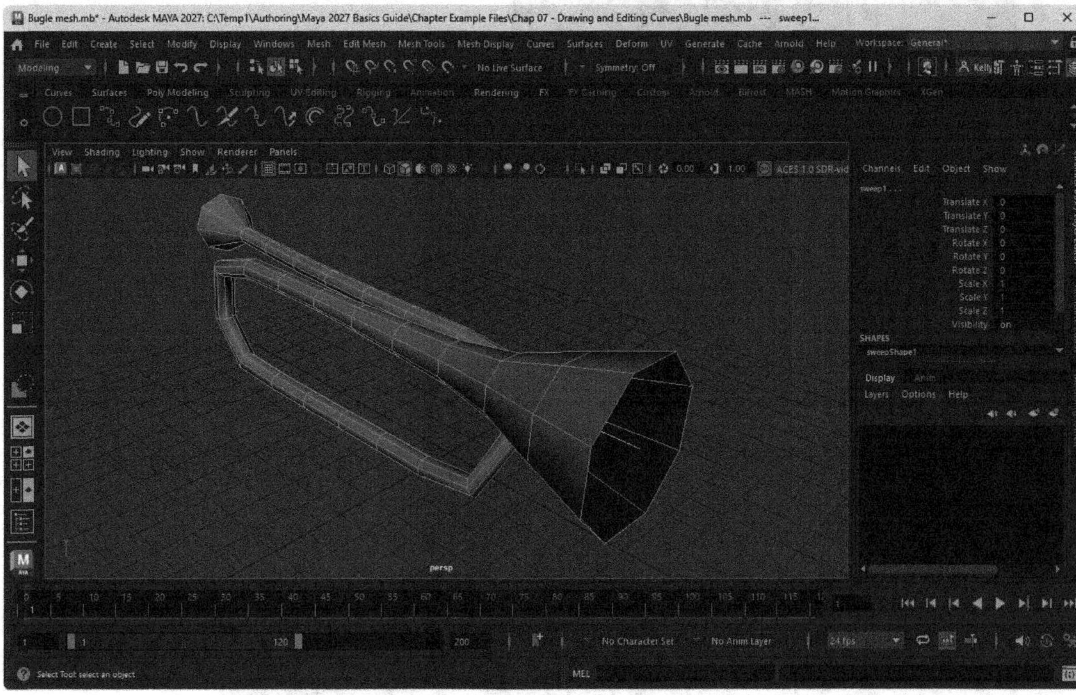

FIGURE 7-30

Sweeped bugle

Lesson 7.6: Create Simple Surfaces from Curves

The top of the Surfaces menu, shown in Figure 7-31, includes many options for turning a selected curve into a surface. For all surfaces, you can select in the Options dialog box what the geometry is output as. The options include NURBS, Polygons, or Bezier curves. The Surfaces menu also includes many commands for editing existing surfaces. These will be covered in the next chapter.

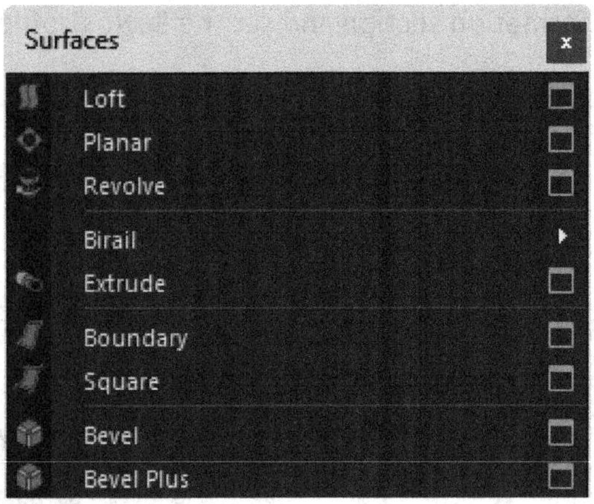

FIGURE 7-31

The Surfaces menu

Revolving a Curve

A curve can be revolved around an axis to form a circular symmetrical object using the Surfaces, Revolve menu command. The Revolve Options dialog box, shown in Figure 7-32, can be used to select which axis is used for the revolution. You can also specify a start and end sweep angle to revolve only partially. A revolved curve can be used to create a baseball bat, a wine glass, or any symmetrically round object.

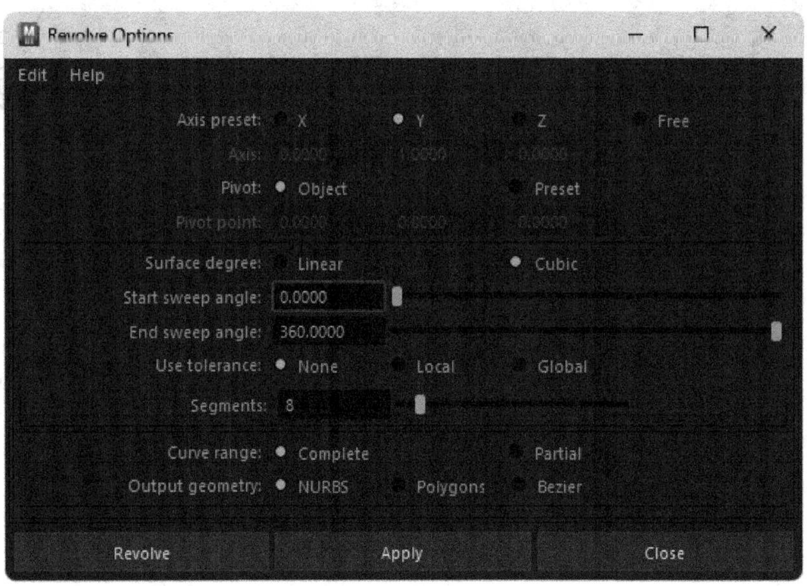

FIGURE 7-32

Revolve options

Lofting a Set of Curves

If the symmetrically round shape you're trying to create has differently shaped cross sections along its length, you can create these using a **loft** operation. The Surfaces, Loft menu command only works if two or more curves are selected. Lines that combine the curves to create a surface are followed in the order they were created.

Caution

> If the curve direction between different lofted cross sections is switched, the resulting lofted surface is twisted. You can fix this by enabling the Auto Reverse option in the Options dialog box or with the Curves, Reverse Direction menu command.

Creating Planar Curves

If you have several intersecting curves that form a closed area or a single closed curve, you can turn them into a planar surface with the Surfaces, Planar menu command.

Creating a Surface from Boundary Curves

Planar surfaces are created from curves that are co-planar, but curves that aren't in the same plane can also be used to create a surface using the Surfaces, Boundary menu command. The curves that define the surface boundary can be ordered automatically or as selected. If the Common End Points option is set to Required, the corner points between curves need to be positioned together, but if the Optional option is selected, the corner points don't need to match.

Extruding Curves

Extruded curves move a cross section curve perpendicular to the plane it resides in to create a surface. This movement can be in a specified direction or a given amount, as shown in Figure 7-33. The extrusion could also be along a profile while maintaining the cross section's orientation (with the Flat option) or along a profile where the cross section is always perpendicular to the profile curve (with the Tube option). You can also specify rotation and scale values, which indicate the amount the cross section is rotated or scaled as it is extruded. To create an extrusion, select the cross section curve first and then the path curve and then select Surfaces, Extrude.

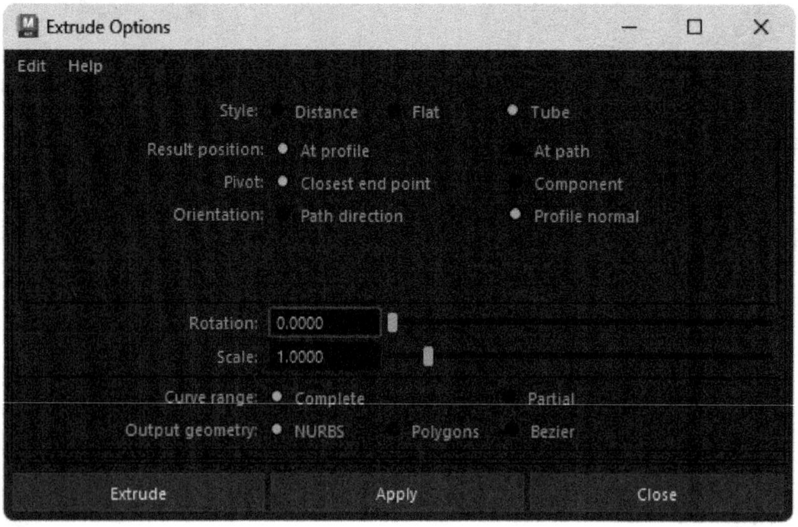

FIGURE 7-33

Extrude options

Using the Birail Tools

A *birail* sweeps a curve (rail1) along a profile to a second curve (rail2). The Surfaces, Birail menu includes three options: Birail 1 Tool, Birail 2 Tool, and Birail 3+ Tool. The difference between them is the number of profile curves that each tool can use. To create a birail surface, create two rail curves and at least one profile curve, select the profile curve and select the Birail tool. The Help Line instructs you to then choose the first rail curve followed by the second rail curve.

Caution

The profile and rail curves must intersect at their corner points in order for the birail operation to work. Use the Snap Points feature in the Status Line to ensure that the points intersect.

Lesson 7.6-Tutorial 1: Revolve a Baseball Bat

1. Click on the Four View button from the Toolbox and select Top View panel and press the spacebar to maximize the viewport.

   The view panel changes to show the Top view.
2. Select Create, Curve Tools, CV Curve Tool and click in the Top panel to create the profile of a baseball bat that extends horizontally.
3. After initially placing the CVs for the curve, click on the Select by Component button (or press F8) in the Status Line and click the Move tool in the Toolbox and move the CVs to where you want them.
4. After moving the CVs, click the Select by Object button in the Status Line. Then, open the Options dialog box for the Surfaces, Revolve menu command, select the X Axis, and click the Apply button. The resulting bat is shown in Figure 7-34.
5. Select File, Save Scene As and save the file as **Revolved baseball bat.mb**.

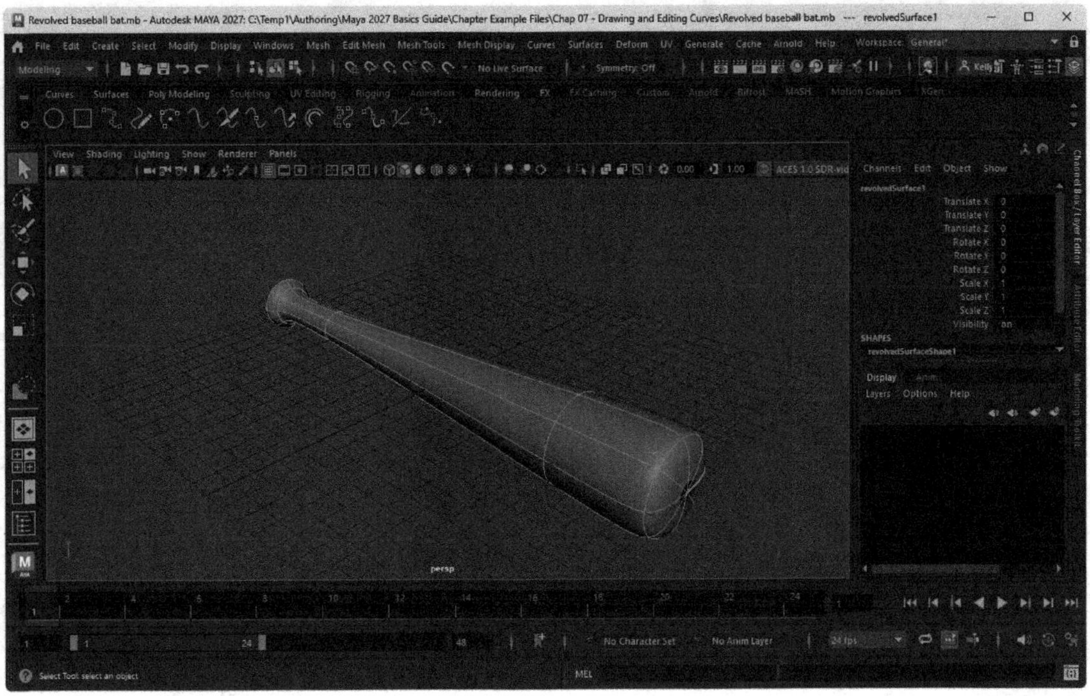

FIGURE 7-34

Revolved baseball bat

Lesson 7.6-Tutorial 2: Loft a Banana

1. Click on the Four View button from the Quick Layout buttons.
2. Select Create, NURBS Primitives, Circle menu command.

   A single circle appears in the view panel at the origin.
3. Select Edit, Duplicate to create a duplicate circle on top of the existing one.
4. Select the Move tool in the Toolbox and drag the duplicated circle in the Front panel upward and slightly to the left.
5. With the duplicated circle still selected, click on the Scale tool in the Toolbox and drag from the center of the circle outward until the circle is about four times the size of the original circle.
6. Select the original circle at the origin and select Edit, Duplicate to create another copy.
7. With the Move tool, drag this second duplicate circle upward twice as far as the first duplicated circle.
8. With the Shift key held down, click on the circles in order from the bottom to the top.
9. Select the Surfaces, Loft menu command.

   All three circles are joined together into a surface, as shown in Figure 7-35.
10. Select File, Save Scene As and save the file as **Lofted banana.mb**.

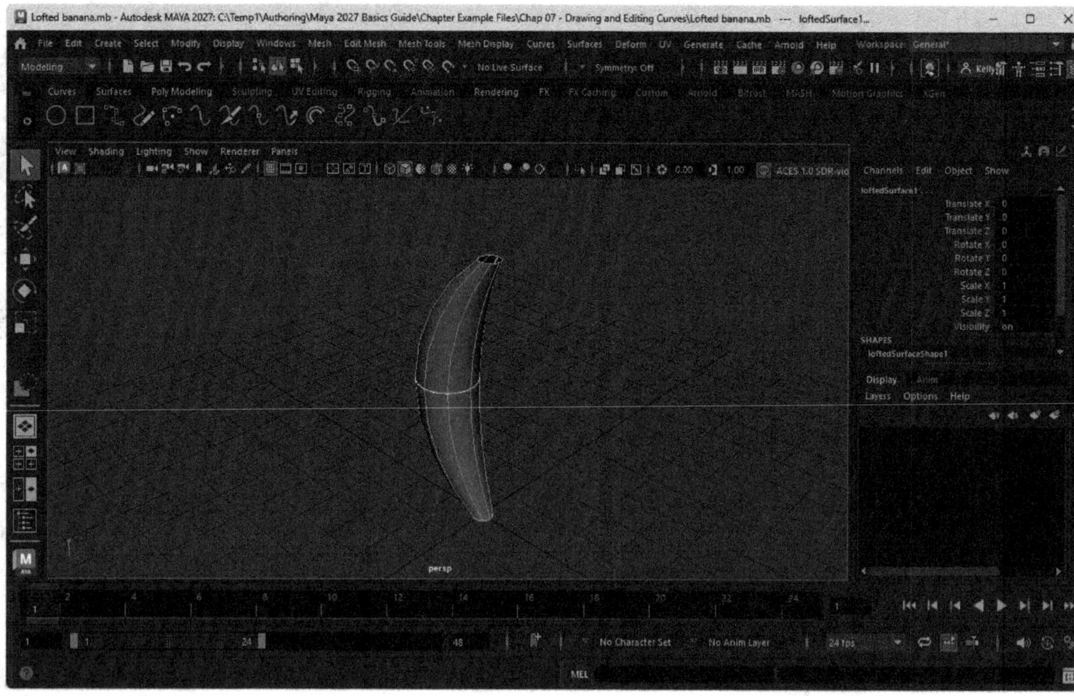

FIGURE 7-35

The lofted banana

Lesson 7.6-Tutorial 3: Create a Planar Surface

1. Click on the Four View button from the Quick Layout buttons and select the Top View panel and press the spacebar to maximize the viewport.
2. Select the Create, Curve Tools, EP Curve Tool menu command. Double-click on this tool in the Toolbox and in the Tool Settings panel that opens, set the Curve Degree to 1 Linear.
3. Enable the Snap to Grids button in the Status Line.
4. Click in the Top view panel to create the outline of a shirt and press the Enter key when finished.
5. With the shirt curve selected, choose the Surfaces, Planar menu command.
6. Press the 5 key to see the shaded surface.

   The shirt curve is filled in, becoming a surface, as shown in Figure 7-36.
7. Select File, Save Scene As and save the file as **Planar shirt.mb**.

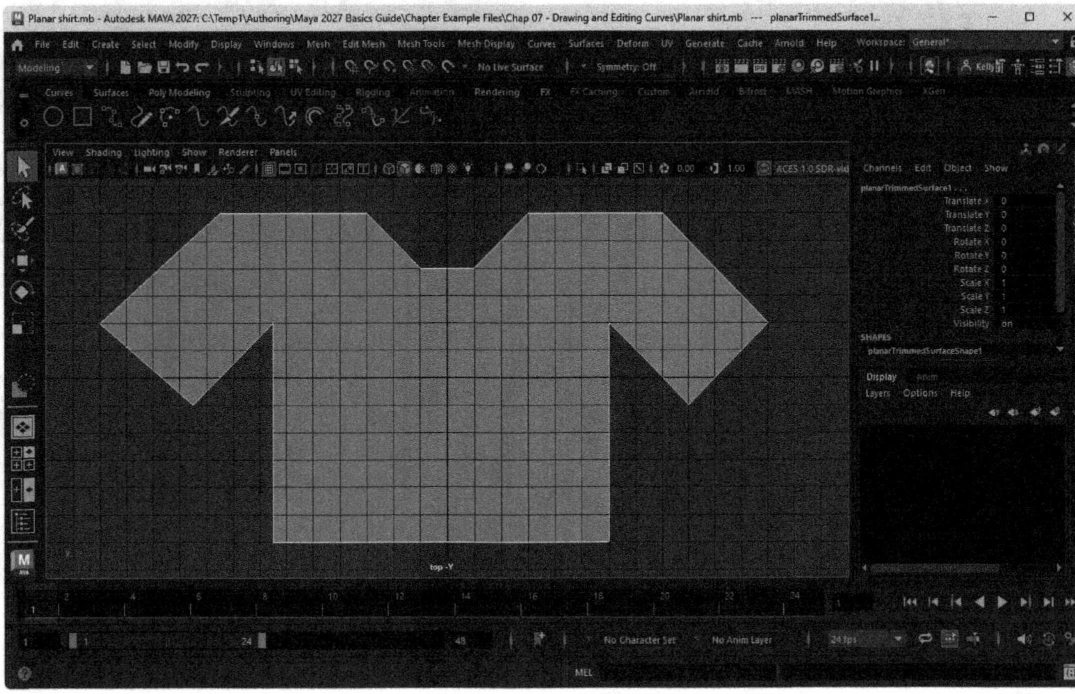

FIGURE 7-36

The planar shirt

Lesson 7.6-Tutorial 4: Extrude a Circle

1. Click on the Four View button from the Quick Layout buttons.
2. Select the Create, NURBS Primitives, Circle menu command.
3. Select the Scale tool and drag the center handle in the Top view panel to increase the circle's size to fill the view panel.
4. Select the Rotate tool in the Toolbox and drag the red X-axis manipulator to rotate the duplicated circle in the Top view panel 90 degrees.
5. Select Edit, Duplicate to create a duplicate circle on top of the existing one.
6. Select the Rotate tool from the Toolbox and drag the blue Z-axis manipulator to rotate the duplicated circle in the Side view panel 90 degrees.
7. Drag over both circles to select them both, and then choose Surfaces, Extrude, Options to open the Extrude Options dialog box.
8. Select the Tube, At Path, Component, and Profile Normal options and set the Scale value to 2.0., and then click the Extrude button.
9. Select the Perspective view panel and press the 5 key to see the shaded surface.

   The circle that is the key object is swept around the path of the other circle with the scale gradually increasing to double its size. Figure 7-37 shows the interesting resulting surface.
10. Select File, Save Scene As and save the file as **Extruded circle.mb**.

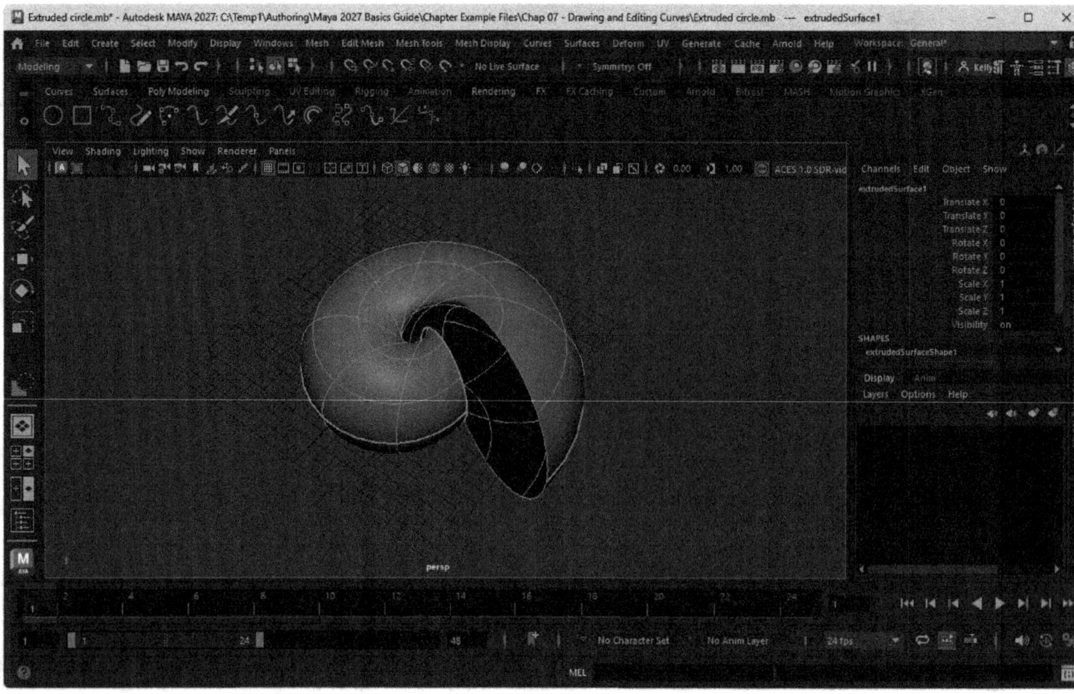

FIGURE 7-37

Extruded scaled circle

Lesson 7.6-Tutorial 5: Create a Birail Surface

1. Click on the Four View button from the Quick Layout buttons.
2. Select the Create, NURBS Primitives, Square menu command.

   A single square made from four straight-line curves appears in the Top view panel at the origin.
3. Select the Scale tool and drag on the center handle to increase the size of the square to fill the view panel.
4. Click on the Select by Component Type button in the Status Line (or press the F8 key).
5. Drag over the middle two CVs in the top and bottom lines.
6. Select the Move tool and drag the CVs upward in the Front view panel.
7. Drag over the middle two CVs in the left and right lines in the Top view panel.
8. Drag downward in the Front view panel.

   The connected curves are displaced so that the adjacent lines curve away from each other.
9. Click away from all the curves to deselect them and click on the Select by Object Type button in the Status Line.
10. Select the Surfaces, Birail, Birail 2 Tool menu command.

    The Help Line displays the order in which the curves need to be clicked.
11. Drag over the left and right lines of the square in the Top view. Then drag over the top and bottom lines in the Top view panel.
12. Press the 3 key to see the new NURBS surface at a higher resolution.

The resulting surface, shown in Figure 7-38, runs along the rails between the profile curves.

13. Select File, Save Scene As and save the file as **Birail surface.mb**.

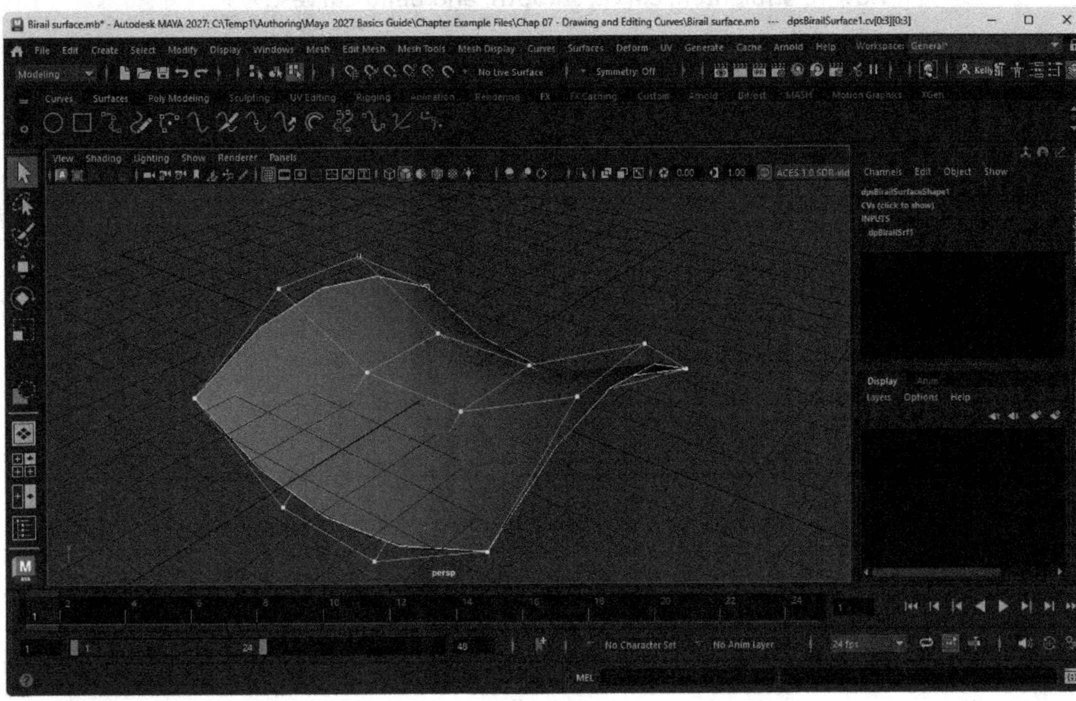

FIGURE 7-38

The birail surface

Chapter Summary

This chapter covers the details of creating and working with curves. 2D curves are an essential modeling construct and are often used to create more complex 3D surfaces. The Create menu includes several ways to draw curves including the CV, EP, and Pencil tools. The Curves menu includes many curve operations for changing the shape of the selected curve. You can also edit a curve by moving its components. The Surfaces menu includes commands for extruding, lofting, revolving, and other commands for creating 3D surfaces from a simple 2D curve.

What You Have Learned

In this chapter, you learned

* How to create primitive shapes such as circles and squares.
* How to create smooth curves, freehand curves, and straight lines.
* How to smooth curves.
* How to use the Edit Curve tool.
* How to change the curve shape by altering its tangents.

* How to add points to a curve.
* How to open and close curves.
* How to straighten, curve, smooth, and bend curves.
* How to attach, detach, align, and cut curves.
* How to find curve intersections.
* How to offset and fillet a selected curve.
* How to create a 3D surface from a curve by revolving, lofting, and extruding curves.
* How to use the birail tools.
* How to create and bevel text with the Type tool.

Key Terms From This Chapter

* **CV.** Control Vertex. A curve component that defines the curvature of the curve.
* **Hull.** A set of straight lines that connects a curve's CV points.
* **CV curve.** A curve created by placing CV points.
* **EP curve.** A curve created by placing points that the curve passes through.
* **Curve degree.** The amount of curve applied to a line.
* **Linear curve.** A curve with a degree of 1, resulting in straight lines.
* **Edit Curve tool.** A tool used to edit the curvature of a curve using handles attached to the curve.
* **Tangent.** A handle that determines the direction and severity of the curvature of a curve.
* **Offset curve.** A duplicated curve that is moved parallel to the selected curve.
* **Sweep Mesh**. An object created by sweeping a given cross-section along the length of a curve.
* **Twist**. When an object twists about itself over the length of the object.
* **Taper**. When an object changes its cross-section diameter over the length of the object.
* **Filleting.** The process of smoothing a corner of a curve.
* **Revolving.** The process of creating a surface by rotating a curve about an axis.

* **Lofting.** The process of creating a surface by connecting several cross sections together.

* **Extruding.** The process of creating a surface by moving the curve perpendicular to itself.

* **Beveling.** The process of smoothing a surface by adding a face to the surface edges.

Chapter 8

Using Deformers

IN THIS CHAPTER

Deformers are like operations in that they can change the look of a surface or curves. There are an assortment of different deformers, and they each change the object in different ways. These deformers can bend, twist, skew and alter the objects.

When a deformer is applied, they also add another node to the object. These nodes can be accessed in the Attribute Editor and the Channel Box, and they provide a set of attributes that you can change after the deformer is applied. For example, you can revisit the degrees to twist an object about its center. Many of these attributes are also keyable, meaning you can animate them by setting keys. Deformers also place a manipulator around the object that provides handles that you can use to change the shape of the object interactively.

All the various deformers are located within the Deform menu. This menu is available when either the Modeling, Rigging or the Animation menu sets are active. Some of the deformers are better suited to animation such as the Blend Shape, Jiggle, and Morph features, but others are really helpful as you model such as the Bend, Flare and Squash deformers.

Lesson 8.1: Use nonlinear deformers

A good place to start with deformers is with the category called nonlinear deformers. This set is in the Deform, Nonlinear menu and includes Bend, Flare, Sine, Squash, Twist and Wave. All of these deformers have attributes associated with them that you can change once the deformer is applied. Most deformers don't show any change to the object when applied, but they will deform once their attributes are changed.

Bending objects

The first of the nonlinear deformers is the Bend deformer. To use this deformer, select an object and choose the Deform, Bend menu command. Initially nothing seems to happen, but if you look closely at the Attribute Editor, you'll see a new Bend node has been added to the object history. Selecting this node in the Attribute Editor makes several new attributes available. The Curvature value defines the amount of bend to apply to the object, and the Low and High Bound values let you remove the upper or lower part of the object from the bend influence. Figure 8-1 shows three cylinder objects with a Curvature value of 100. The left object has the High Bound set to 0 and the right object has the Low Bound set to 0. At the center of each object is a deformer manipulator that has handles that you can use to change the attribute values. You can also move, rotate and scale the deform manipulator to change the effect.

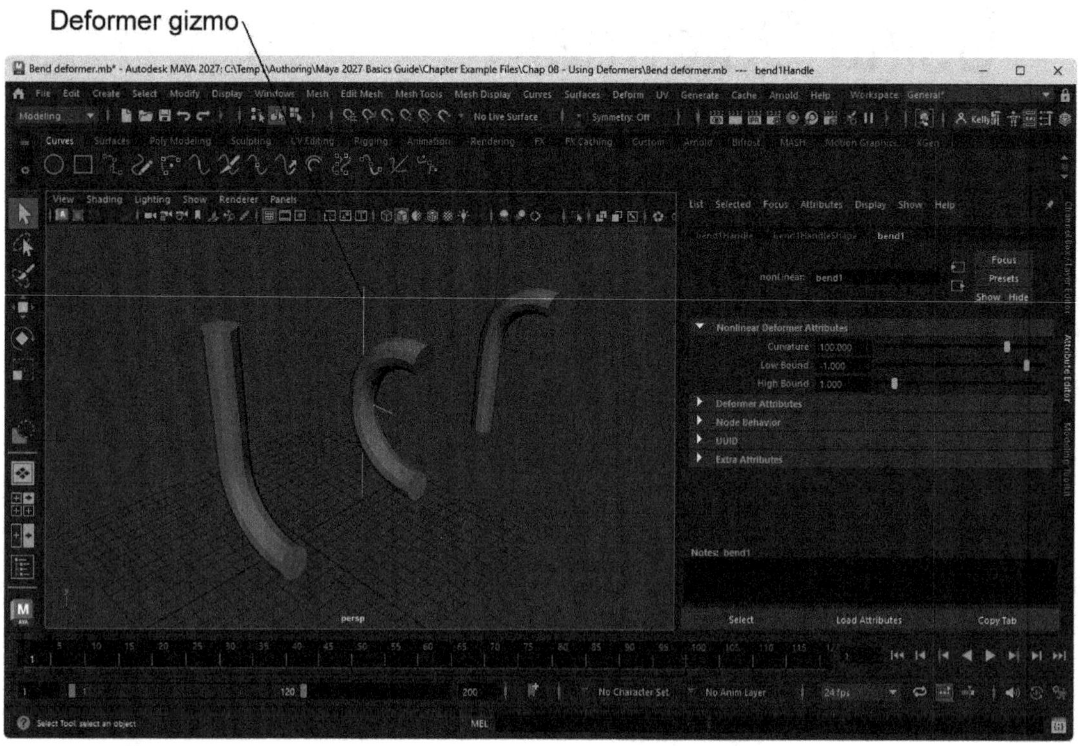

FIGURE 8-1

Cylinders with the Bend deformer.

Flaring objects

The Flare deformer stretches out the top, middle or bottom of an object. The Start Flare attributes change the width in the X or Z directions at one end of the object and the End Flare attributes change the width in the X and Z directions on the other end of the object. You can also set the Start and End Flare values to 0 to make it reduce to a point. The Curve attribute bends inward or outward from the center and you can remove either the high or low end from the deformer's influence. Figure 8-2 shows the Flare deformer applied to three cylinder objects using the Curve attribute. The left object has a Low Bound set to 0 and the right object has a High Bound set to 0.

FIGURE 8-2

Cylinders with the Flare deformer.

Squashing objects

When a rubber ball bounces, it squashes when it hits the ground and then stretches out when it rebounds. The Squash deformer simulates this action with a Factor attribute, as shown in Figure 8-3 over 5 spheres. There is also an Expand value that increases the squash or stretch effect. You can also set a maximum expansion position and to smooth above or below.

Tip

Using the Squash deformer is a great way to animate a soft or rubber-like object hitting the floor.

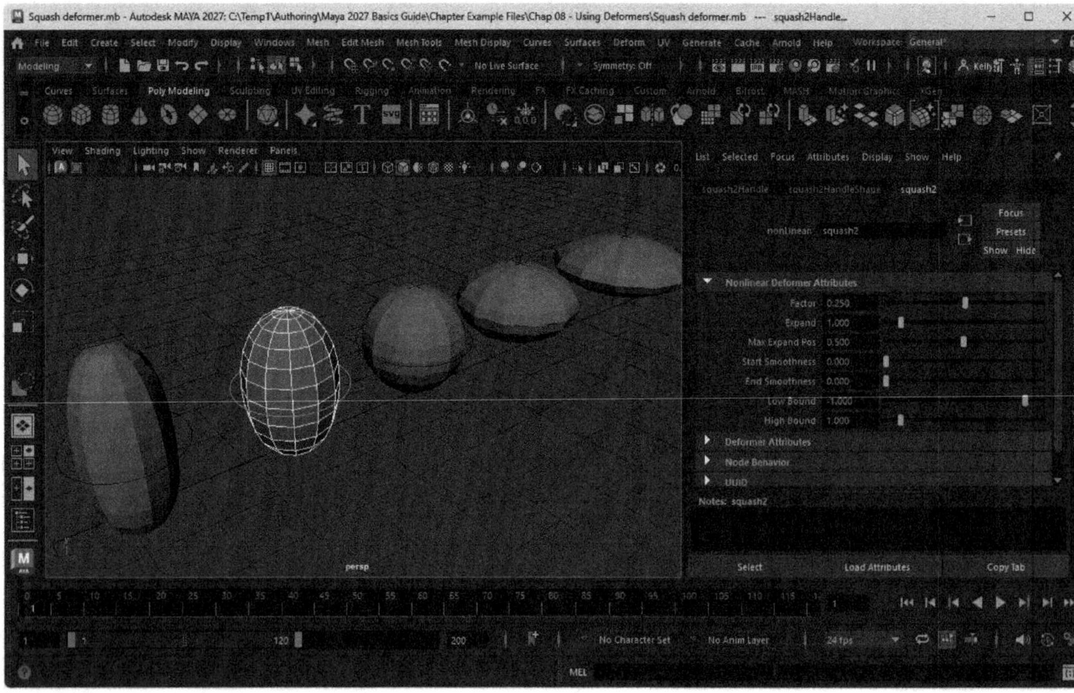

FIGURE 8-3

Spheres with the Squash deformer.

Twisting objects

The Twist deformer lets you set the Start and End Angles for the twist that runs the length of the object. You can also set the Low and High Bounds for the object. Figure 8-4 shows a ladder object that is twisted 300 degrees over its length with low and high bounds set for the right and left objects.

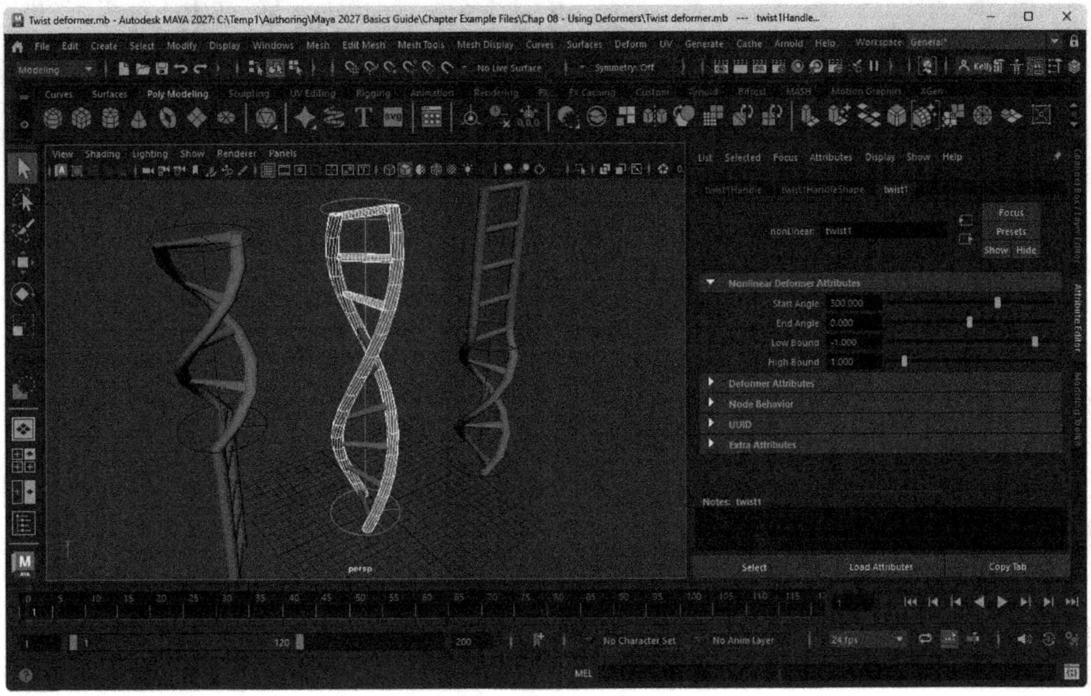

FIGURE 8-4

Ladders with the Twist deformer.

Adding waves

Within the Nonlinear deformers are two wave-based features. The Sine deformer applies a sine wave to long thin objects like an extended cylinder and the Wave deformer works best with flat wide objects like the Plane object, shown in Figure 8-5. For each you can set the Amplitude, Wavelength, Offset and Dropoff.

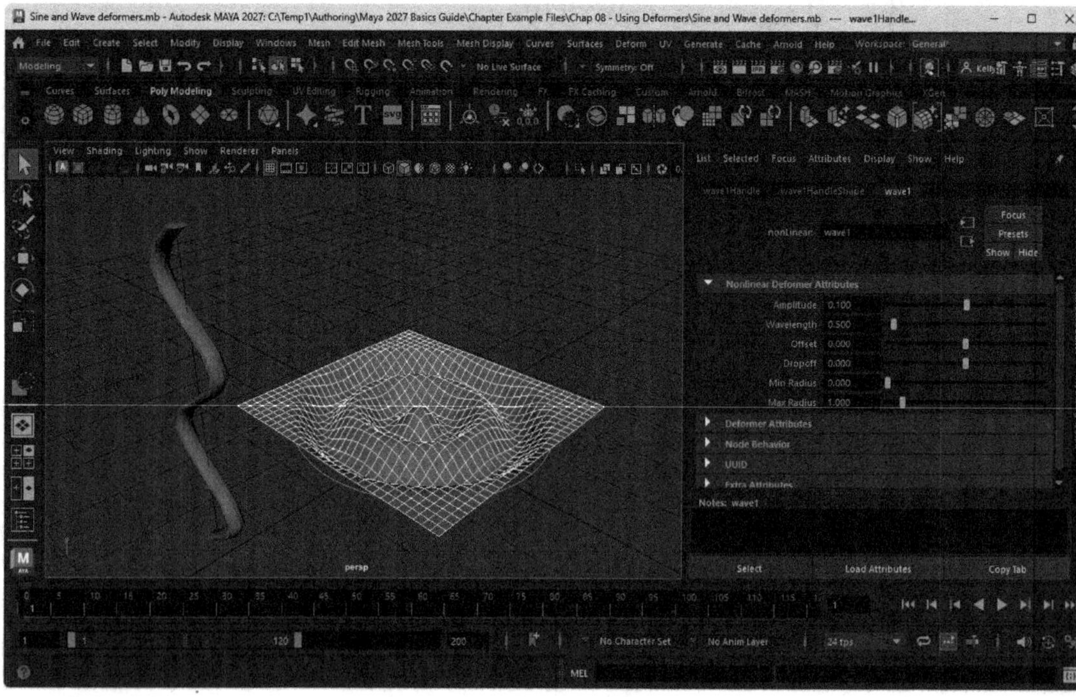

FIGURE 8-5

The Sine and Wave deformers.

Lesson 8.1-Tutorial 1: Bending a hammer

1. Select File, Open Scene and open the Hammer.mb file.
2. Select both parts of the hammer object and choose the Deform, Nonlinear, Bend menu command.

   The Bend deformer is applied to the hammer.
3. Select and increase the Curvature value in the Attribute Editor.

   The Hammer bends to the side.
4. Choose the Edit, Undo command to reset the Curvature value.
5. With the deformer manipulator selected, use the Rotate tool to drag the green manipulator 90 degrees to the left.
6. Change the Curvature value in the Attribute Editor to make the hammer bend forward as shown in Figure 8-6.
7. Select File, Save Scene As and save the file as **Bended hammer.mb**.

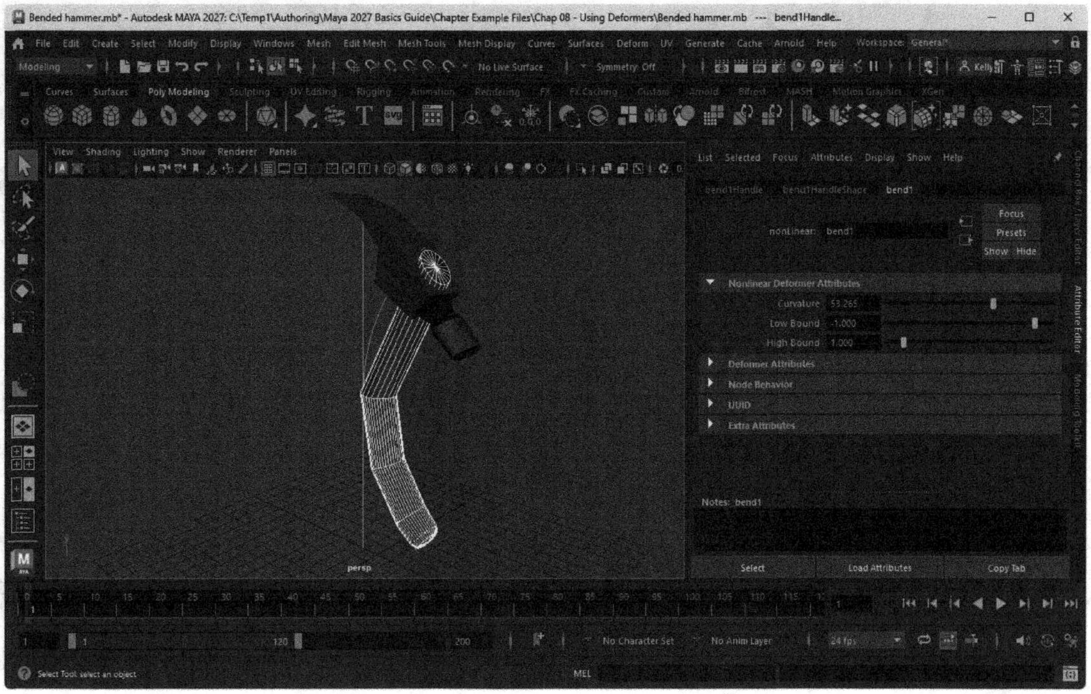

FIGURE 8-6

Hammer with a Bend deformer.

Lesson 8.1-Tutorial 2: Adding a wave to a table

1. Select File, Open Scene and open the Table.mb file.
2. Select the table top object and open the Attribute Editor.

   The table top is a modified cube with only 1 subdivision, which won't deform well.
3. Select and increase the Subdivisions Width and Depth values to 30 in the Attribute Editor.
4. Choose the Deform, Nonlinear, Wave command and set the Amplitude to 0.03 and the Wavelength to 0.3.

   The table top is made wavy, as shown in Figure 8-7.
5. Select File, Save Scene As and save the file as **Wavy table.mb**.

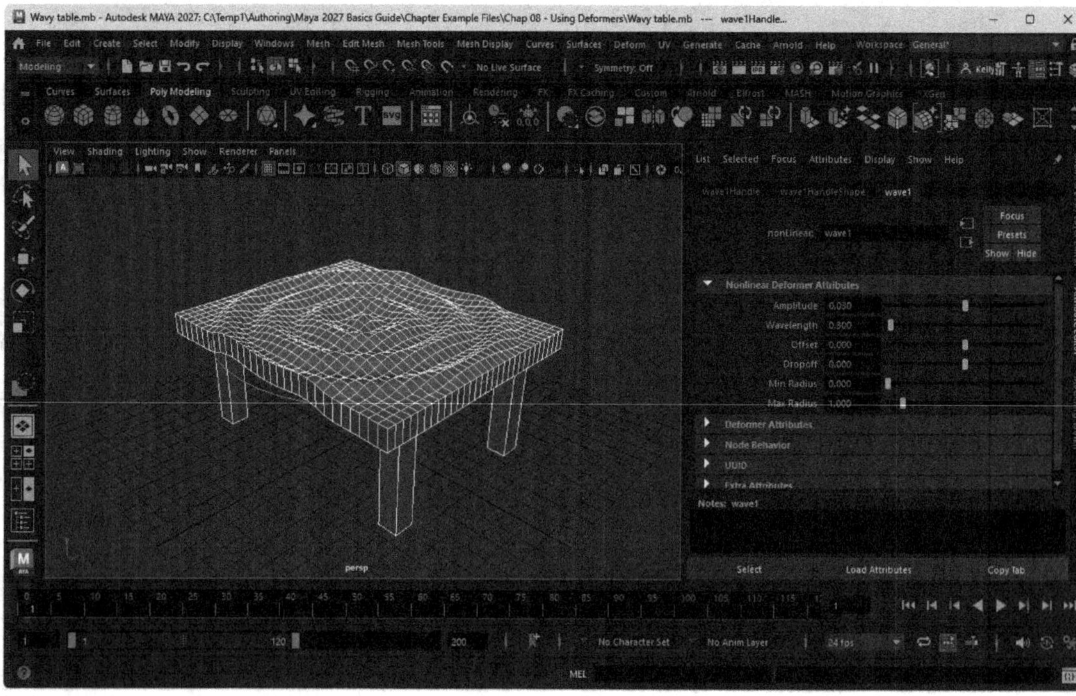

FIGURE 8-7

A wavy table.

Lesson 8.2: Working with Deformers

Now that you've applied some deformers and have a feel for them, there are some important points that make it easier to work with deformers.

Adding object density

When deforming objects, you need to make sure that the object has enough subdivisions to deform. If the number of segments in the object is too few, the deformation will be blocky and unsmooth. For primitive objects, you can revisit the Sections or Division attributes in the Attribute Editor under the node for the object's name and increase the **object's density**. For polygon meshes, you can apply the Edit Mesh, Add Divisions operation. For NURBS surfaces, use the Surfaces, Rebuilt menu command. Figure 8-8 shows three cylinder objects with the Bend deformer applied. The left object has only 4 height divisions and is blocky, the middle object has 12 divisions and is smooth, but the right object has 30 divisions and is the smoothest.

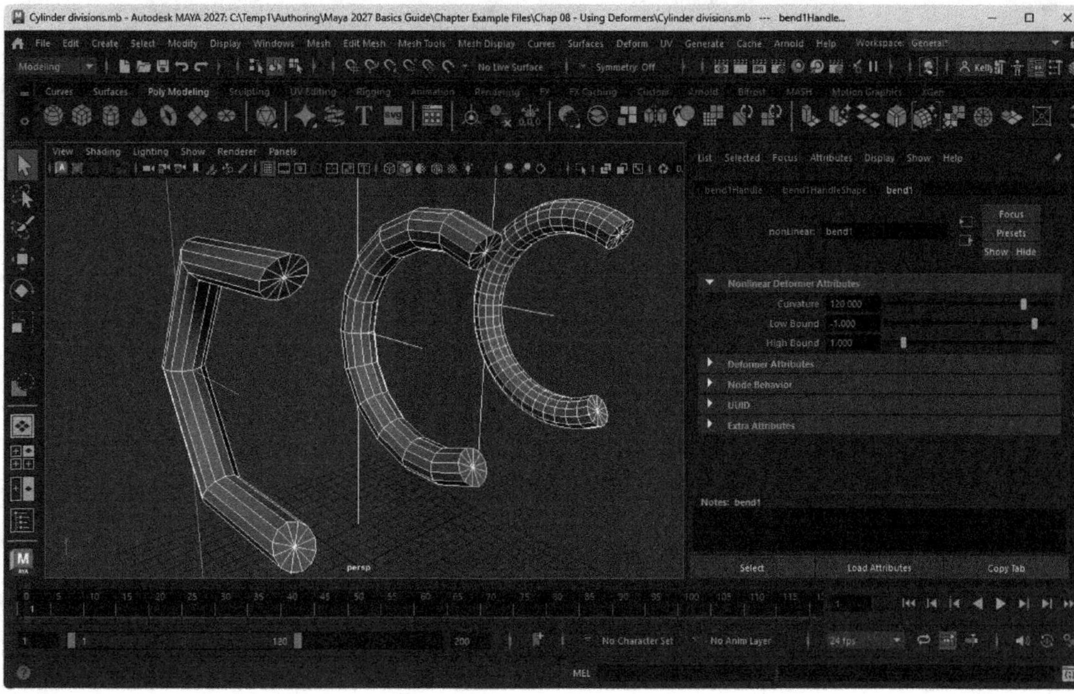

FIGURE 8-8

An object with more divisions deforms smoother.

Using manipulator handles

You can affect the deformer using the values in the Attribute Editor, but you can also interactively change the deformer values by dragging on the manipulator's **handles**. These handles are small light blue squares in the viewport, as shown in Figure 8-9. To make these handles visible, select the Modify, Transformation Tools, Show Manipulator Tool menu command or press the t hotkey.

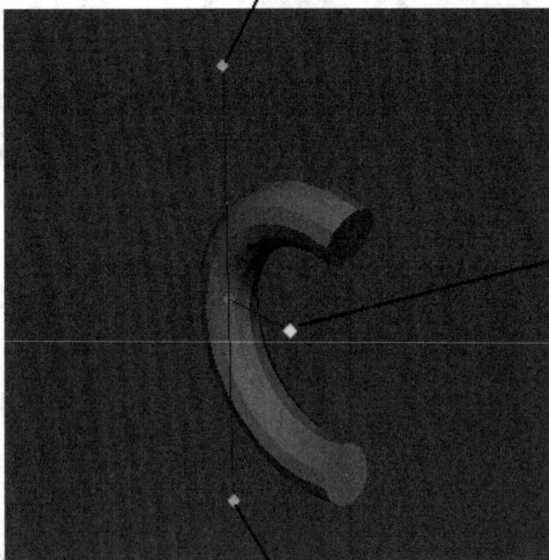

FIGURE 8-9

The deformer handles.

Removing the deformer

If you are unhappy with the deformer and want it to go away, simply select the deformer manipulator and press the Delete key or you could choose its name in the Outliner and press the Delete key. The deformer name is typically something like Bend1Handle. This deletes the deformer and removes its node from the object's history. Deleting a deformer also removes its effects.

Making the changes permanent

If you are happy with the deformation changes to an object, you can simplify it and make the deformations permanent by deleting its history using the Edit, Delete by Type, History menu command.

Transforming the manipulator

If you select the manipulator in the viewport, you can move, rotate or scale the manipulator to get different results. If the deformation is applied about the wrong axis, try resetting its values, transforming the manipulator and then apply the deformation values again.

Applying multiple deformers

A single object can have multiple deformers applied to it and the order that they are applied will have a difference in the final result, but regardless of their application order, you can revisit and manage all the deformers using the Deformation rollout for the object's Shape node in the Attribute Editor. This rollout, shown in Figure 8-10, displays all the deformations applied to the selected object. It also includes toggle switches to turn each deformer on and off, a Count showing the number of vertices in the object before and after the deformer, a column listing the Type of deformer, and column showing any Weights applied. At the top of the rollout are controls for filtering the deformers to display and arrow buttons for moving the selected deformer up or down in the list. All deformers in the list are applied in order from the top to the bottom.

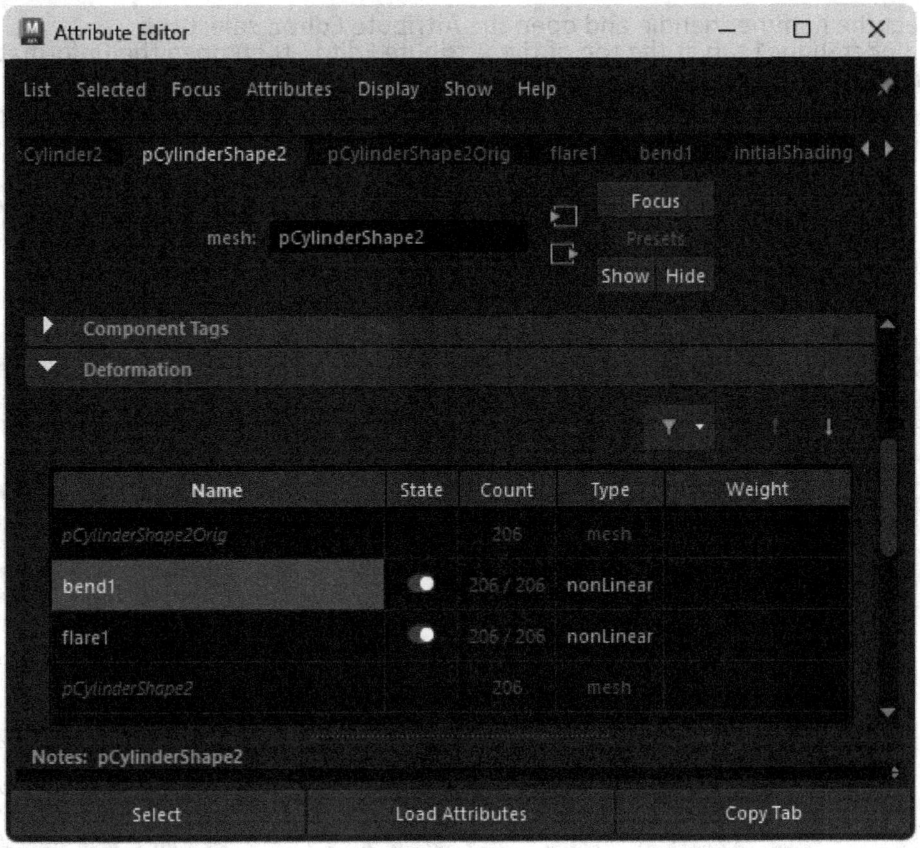

FIGURE 8-10

Deformation rollout in the Attribute Editor

Painting Deformer Weights

If you need more precise control over exactly which areas get moved according to an attribute setting, you can use the Paint **Deformer Weights** feature. This feature is found for the various deformers at the bottom of the Deform menu, but you'll want to select the Options dialog box to access the Tool Settings dialog box where you can choose the different Brush settings. The components that are painted white get the full effect of the attribute value and components painted black get none.

Lesson 8.2-Tutorial 1: Work with Multiple Deformers

1. Select File, Open Scene and open the Bended hammer.mb file.
   This file includes a hammer object with the nonlinear Bend deformer applied to its handle.
2. Select the hammer handle object and choose the PolyCylinder1 node in the Channel Box and set the Subdivisions Height value to 20.
   This will add the necessary polygons to the cylinder to make the deformations smooth
3. Select the Deform, Nonlinear, Flare menu command and set the Start Flare X and Start Flare Z values to 3.

Applying another deformer flattens out the hammer while still keeping the bend.

4. Select the hammer handle and open the Attribute Editor, select the pCylinderShape1 tab at the top of the Attribute Editor, then open the Deformation rollout.
5. Select the Flare1 deformation from the Deformation rollout list and click the Up arrow button at the top of the Deformation rollout to reorder the Flare deformer above the Bend deformer.

   Changing the order causes the Flare deformer to be applied before the Bend deformer which changes the shape of the hammer, as shown in Figure 8-11.
6. Select File, Save Scene As and save the file as **Flared and bended hammer.mb**.

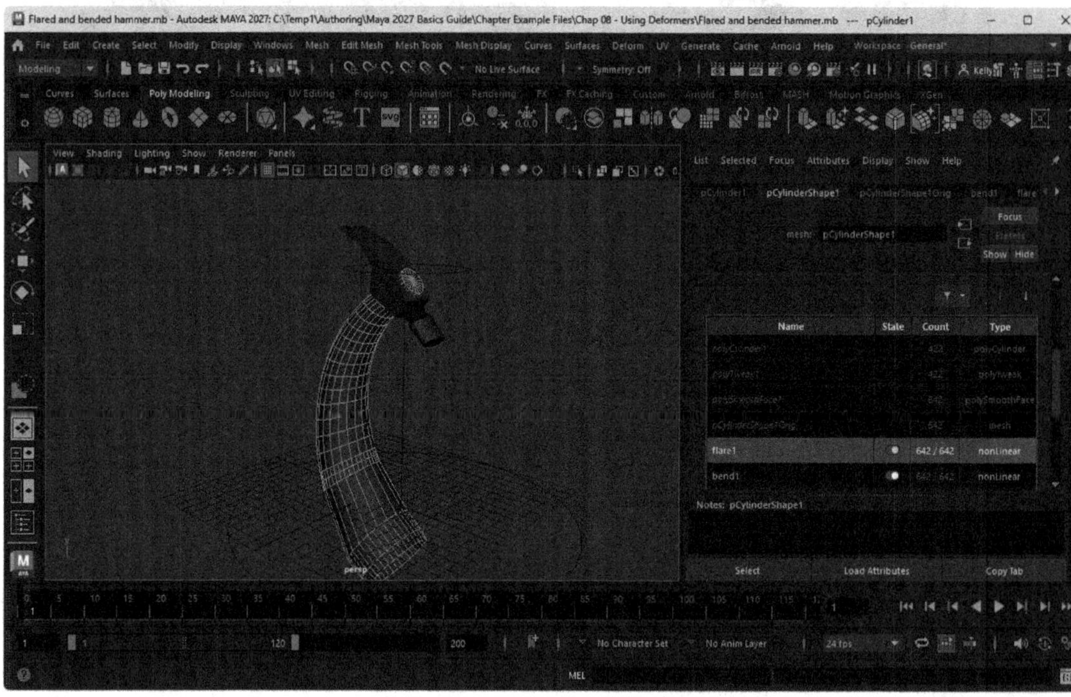

FIGURE 8-11

Hammer with the Flare and Bend deformers applied.

Lesson 8.2-Tutorial 2: Painting Deformer Weights

1. Select File, Open Scene and open the Flared cylinder.mb file.

   This file has a simple cylinder object with the nonlinear Flare deformer applied.
2. Select the cylinder object and choose the Deform, Paint Weights, Nonlinear, Options menu command at the bottom of the menu under the Weights section.

   This opens the Tool Settings dialog box.
3. The flare1.weights should be selected in the Paint Attributes section. Set the Value to 1.0 and the Paint Operation to Add and then paint over every other vertex in the fifth row down from the top. You'll need to rotate the viewport around to get the vertices on the backside.

The vertices that are painted are extended outward away from the center of the object, as shown in Figure 8-12.

4. Select File, Save Scene As and save the file as **Painted weights.mb**.

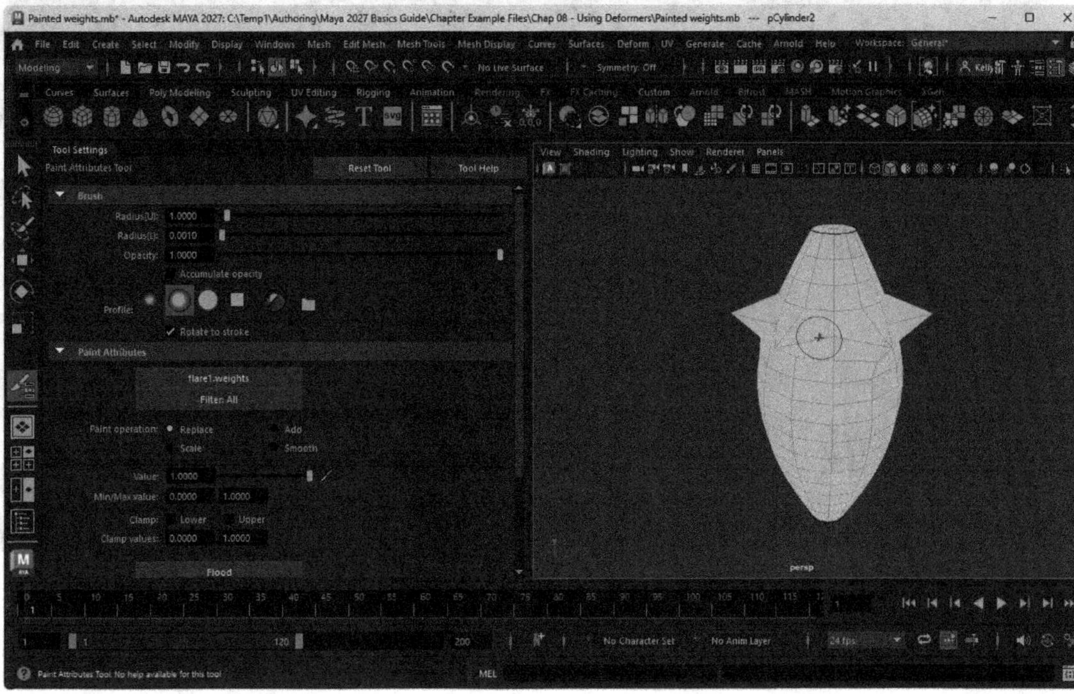

FIGURE 8-12

Painted Deformer Weights.

Lesson 8.3: Modifying with the Lattice and Wire Deformers

Two other unique deformers in the Deform menu are the **Lattice** and **Wire** deformers. These deformers work by surrounding the mesh with a grid-aligned lattice of points or a 2D shape that deforms the mesh under their control.

Using the Lattice deformer

The Scale tool is great for increasing size or scaling along an axis, but if you want to scale just the center a mesh, it doesn't work too well. For these types of deformation, the Lattice deformer is just the trick. This deformer surrounds the model with a 3D grid of lattice points and the model is influenced by these points, so scaling in the center lattice points will scale in just the center of the model, as shown in Figure 8-13.

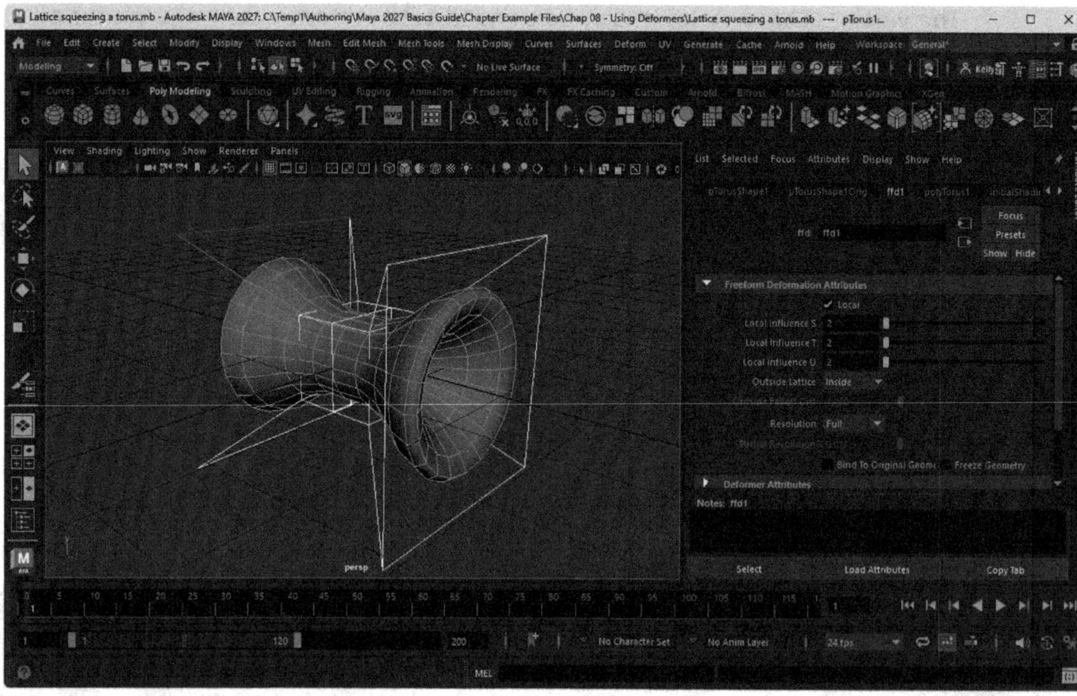

FIGURE 8-13

Lattice deformer.

One of the key options for this deformer is that you can set the number of divisions in the surrounding lattice. This lets you add more divisions in the areas where you need them and keep other areas simple. Divisions can be set for each axis and the lattice surrounding the object will always be box shaped.

Using the Wire deformer

Another similar deformer that controls the objects within it is the Wire deformer. This deformer lets you choose a 2D shape to control the underlying mesh. It works by selecting first the object to be deformed and then the 2D shape positioned near the object. You need to press Enter after each selecting step. The shape will then deform the object when moved, as shown in Figure 8-14.

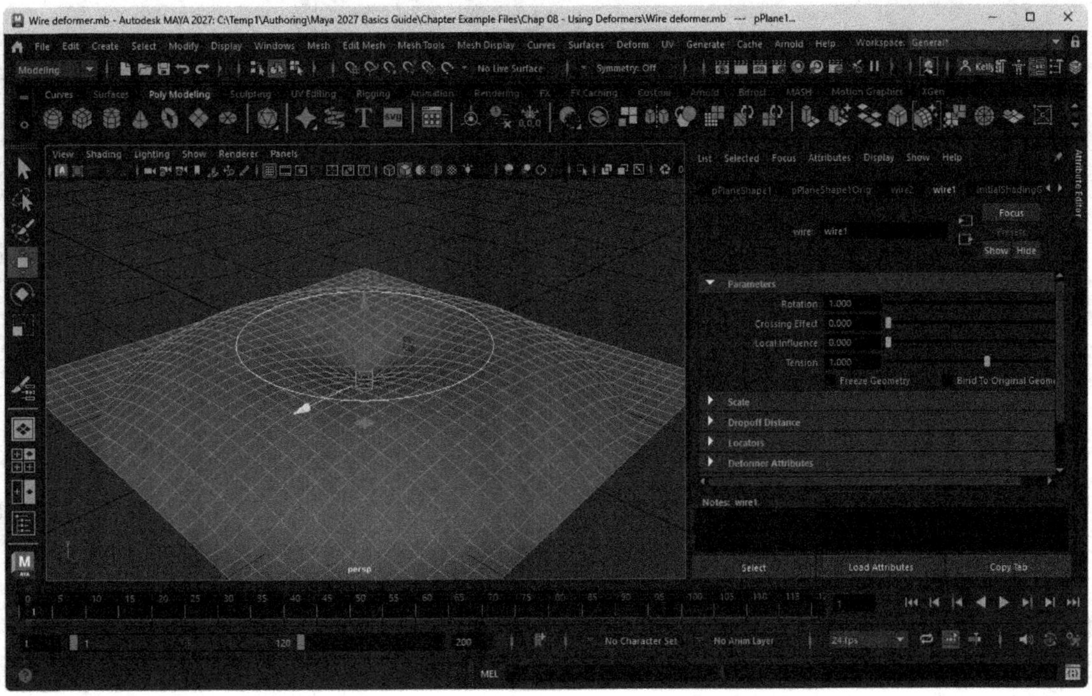

FIGURE 8-14

Wire deformer.

Lesson 8.3-Tutorial 1: Using a Lattice deformer

1. Select File, Open Scene and open the Mushroom.mb file.

   This file has a simple mushroom object, but it looks too perfect. We'll use the Lattice deformer to give it a unique look.

2. Select the mushroom object and choose the Deform, Lattice, Options menu command.

   This opens the Lattice Options dialog box.

3. Set the Divisions for each of the axes to 2, 5 and 2 to create several lattice points along the height of the object, then click the Apply button.
4. Right click on the lattice and choose Lattice Points, then select the two upper right lattice points and drag them up and away from the mushroom. Then scale these two points in to be closer to each other.
5. Select all four vertices that make up the bottom two rows and scale them inward.

   The mushroom is deformed following the lattice to give it a unique look, as shown in Figure 8-15.

6. Select File, Save Scene As and save the file as **Deformed mushroom.mb**.

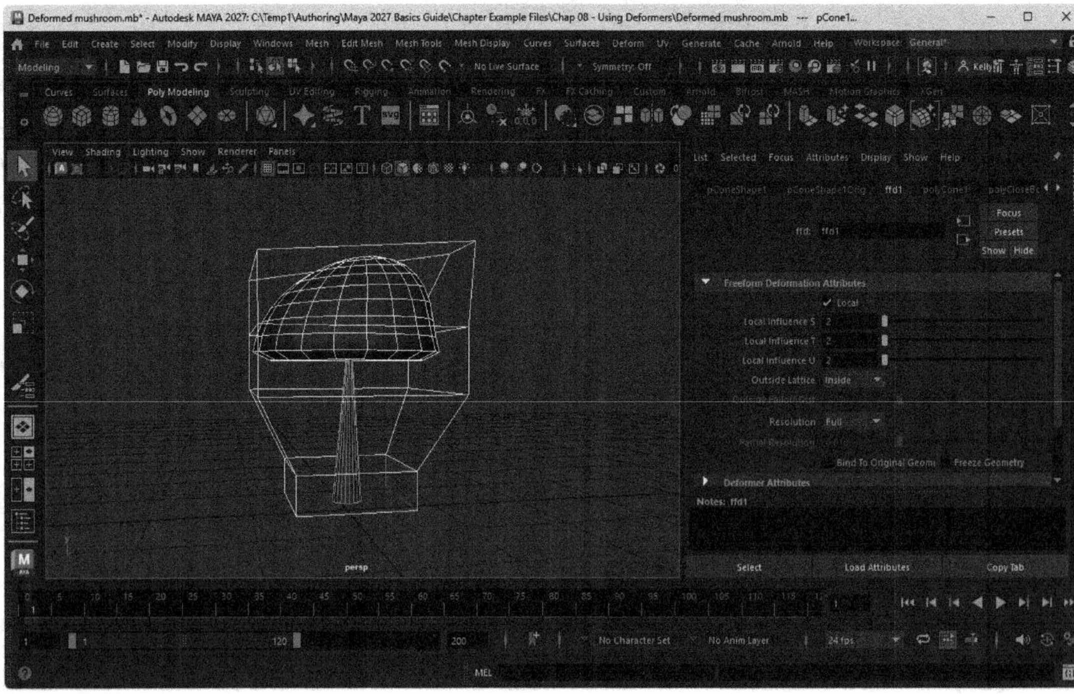

FIGURE 8-15

Lattice deformed mushrooms.

Lesson 8.3-Tutorial 2: Using a Wire deformer

1. Select File, Open Scene and open the Star.mb file.

   This file has a simple star shape.

2. Select the Create, Polygon Primitives, Plane, Options menu command.

   This opens the Polygon Plane Options dialog box.

3. Set the Width and Height Divisions values to 120, then click the Apply button. Then scale up the Plane until it is larger than the Start shape.

   This creates a really dense Plane object.

4. Select the Deform, Wire menu command, then select the Plane object and press the Enter key and finally select the Star shape and press the Enter key again.
5. Choose the Move tool and move the Star shape upward.

   The Plane object is deformed to follow the moving shape, as shown in Figure 8-16.

6. Select File, Save Scene As and save the file as **Wire star.mb**.

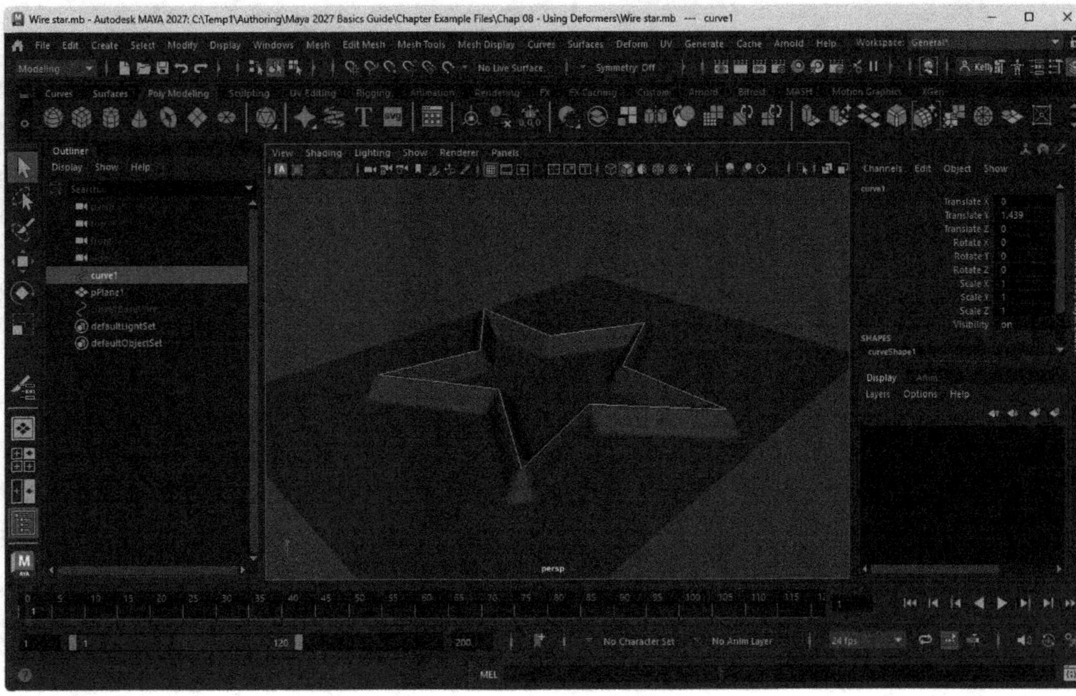

FIGURE 8-16

A Plane object deformed by a Star shape.

Lesson 8.4: Conforming with the ShrinkWrap Deformer

If you need to have one object conform to the surface of another, you can use the **ShrinkWrap deformer**. To use this, simply select the object that will be deformed first and then select the object to deform to next with the Shift key held down so both objects are selected, then choose the Deform, ShrinkWrap menu command.

This deformer causes the deformed object to be smashed flat onto the surface of the second object, as shown on the right in Figure 8-17. Using the Projection attribute, you can set the direction used to move the deforming object. The options include Toward Inner Object, which moves towards the grid center; Toward Center, which moves to the object's center; Parallel to Axes, Vertex Normals or Closest, which moves the points towards the closest point on the second object. You can also set the Offset to move the wrapping object off the surface of its target.

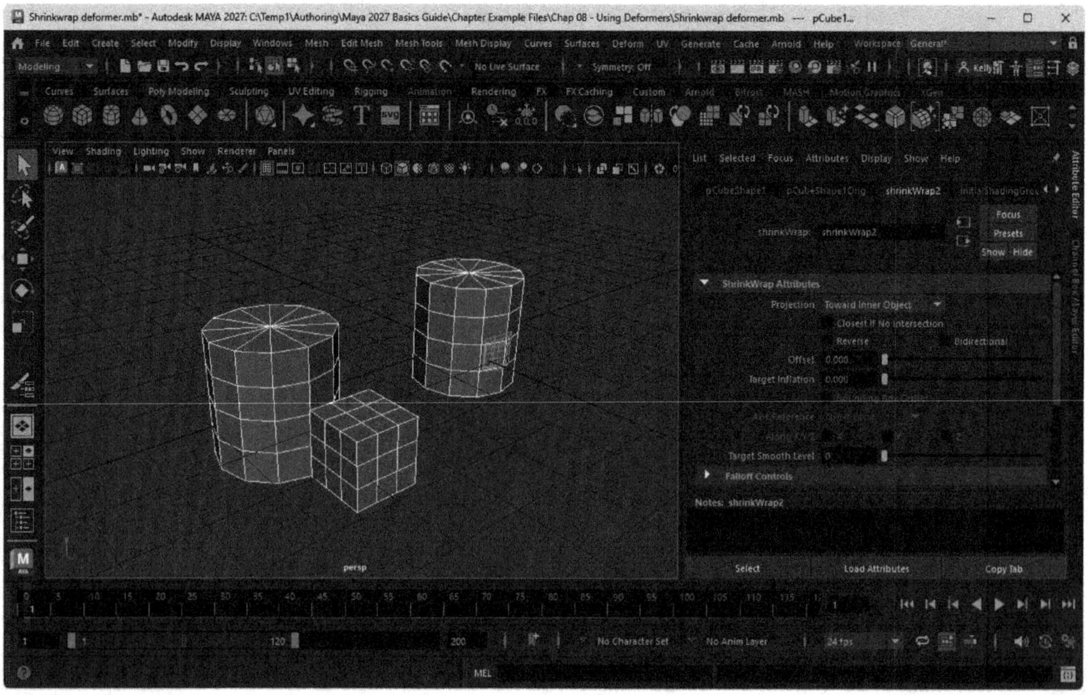

FIGURE 8-17

The ShrinkWrap deformer.

If you only want the lower end of an object to wrap to the target, then you can select the vertices on the lower end of an object before selecting the target object and only those selected points will be wrapped. This is a good way to maintain the original shape of the first object, as shown in Figure 8-18.

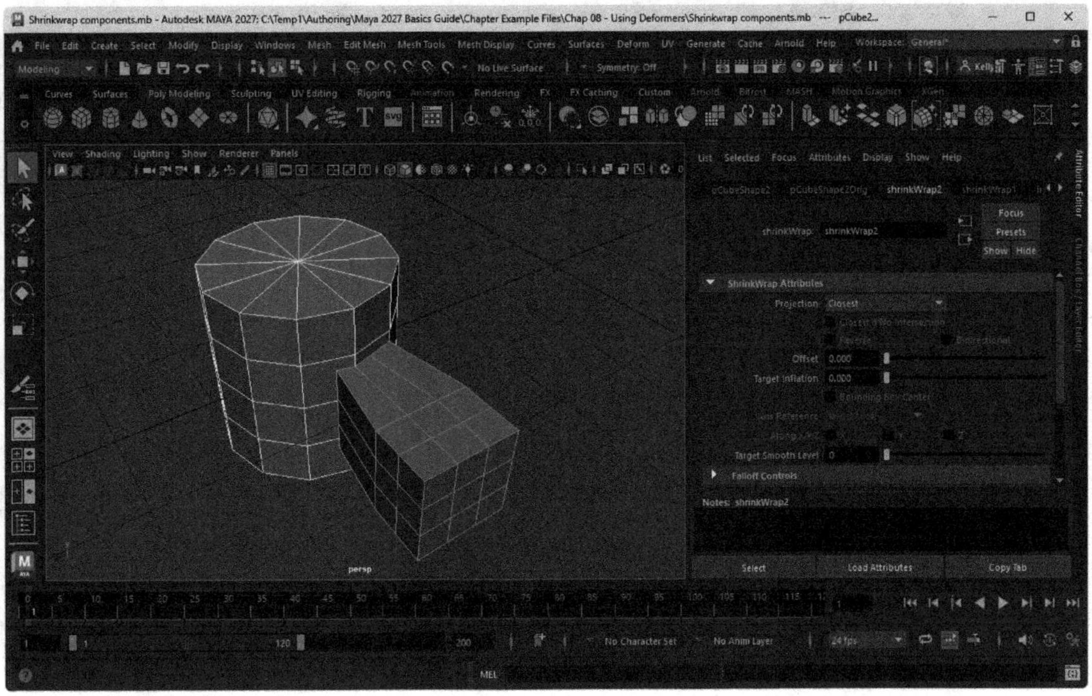

FIGURE 8-18

Using the ShrinkWrap deformer with components.

Lesson 8.4-Tutorial 1: Wrapping a road to a terrain

1. Select File, Open Scene and open the Road over hills.mb file.

   This file has a simple Plane object representing a road positioned over a hilly terrain.

2. Select the road object, hold down the Shift key and select the terrain object.
3. Choose the Deform, ShrinkWrap menu command.
4. Choose the ShrinkWrap node in the Attribute Editor and change the Projection option to Vertex Normals, then increase the Offset to 0.015.

   This projects the road directly below onto the terrain and offsets it slightly above, as shown in Figure 8-17.

5. Choose the Move tool and move the Star shape upward.

   The Plane object is deformed to follow the moving shape, as shown in Figure 8-19.

6. Select File, Save Scene As and save the file as **Road on terrain.mb**.

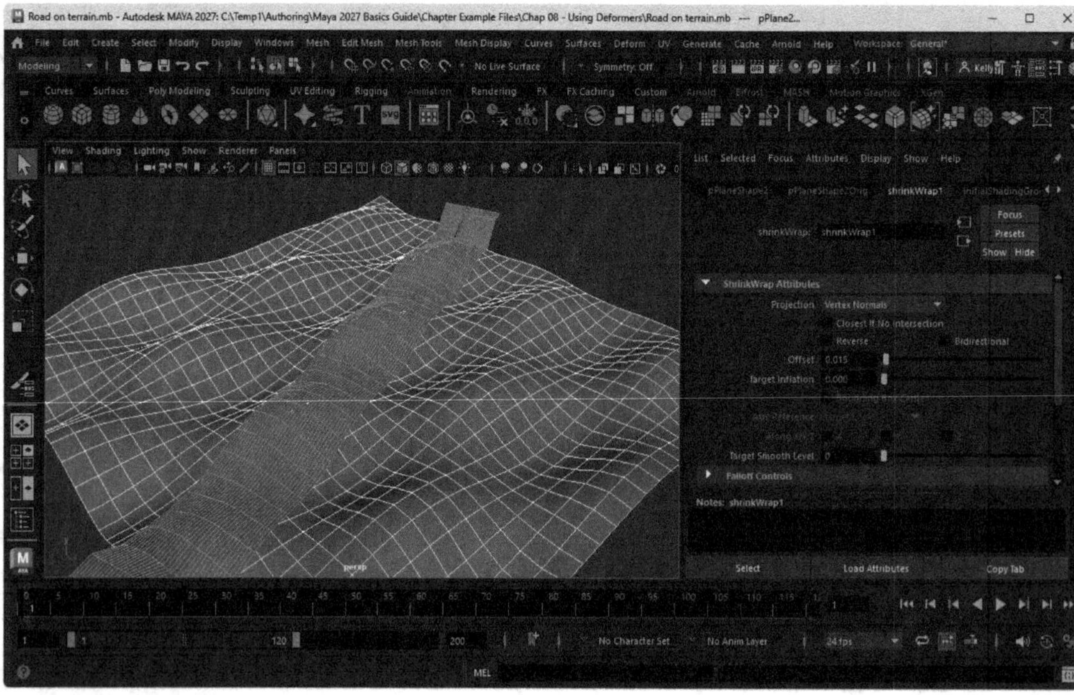

FIGURE 8-19

The ShrinkWrap deformer places the road on the terrain.

Lesson 8.5: Deforming Components

Most deformers can work with both objects and components, but several deformers are designed to work mainly with components including the Cluster, Solidify and Delta Mush deformers. Within the Shape node is a way to name a group of components with the Component Tag feature.

Using Component Tags

Some deformers are applied to selected sets of components. If you painstakingly select a bunch of components and then work with the mesh and later realize you need to remember that component selection, it can be tricky to select them all again. The answer is to create a Component Tag. To do so, simply select the object's Shape node and look for the Component Tags section in the Attribute Editor, as shown in Figure 8-20. Click the Add a New Component Tag button (the plus sign icon) and a new component tag is added to the list. You can double click on its name and rename the tag. To recall the components, just right click on the component tag and select the Select Components option in the pop-up menu.

FIGURE 8-20

Painted Deformer Weights.

Moving component groups with the Cluster deformer

The **Cluster** deformer is used to deform a group of components together. To assign a cluster, first select a group of components, usually vertices, and then use the Deform, Cluster menu command. This places a small letter C at the center of the selected components and adds a Cluster handle node in the Outliner and Attribute Editor. Once selected, you can use the Transform tools to deform the cluster, as shown in Figure 8-21. A benefit of a cluster is that you don't have to reselect all the components each time.

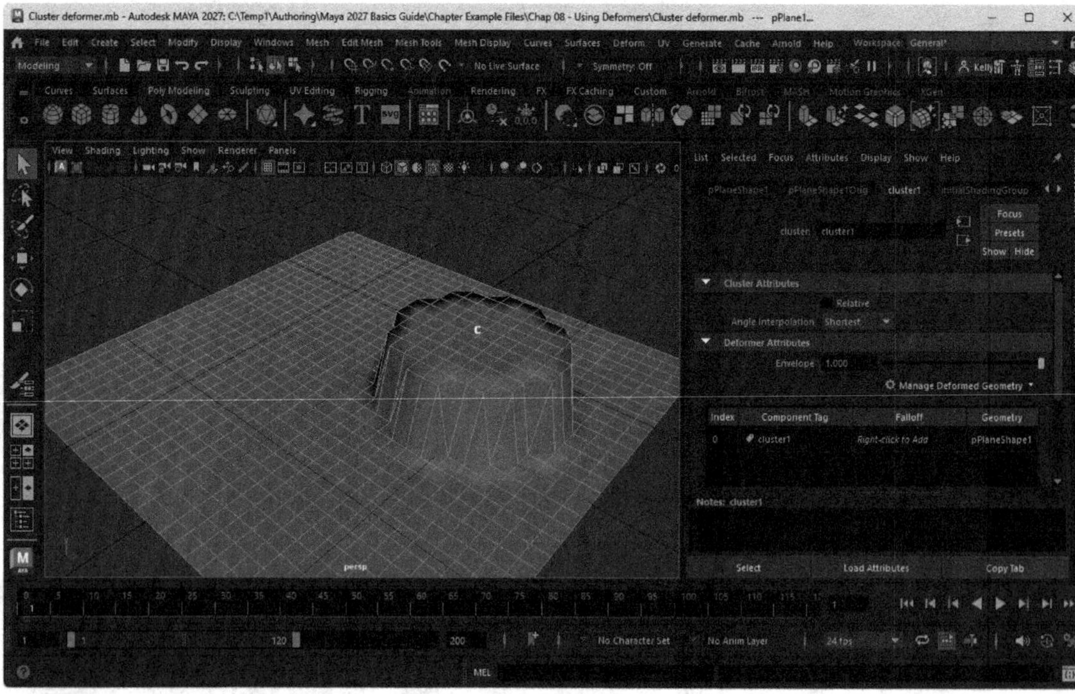

FIGURE 8-21

A Cluster deformer moves a group of vertices.

Preventing movement with the Solidify deformer

If you have details on your model that stick out, like a side mirror on a car or thorns on a rose, they can be badly distorted when the entire object is deformed. Applying the **Solidify** deformer to such components will prevent this bad distortion. To use this deformer, select the components on the object and choose the Deform, Solidify menu command. Make sure you apply the Solidify deformer after the object deformer. Figure 8-22 shows a half a ladder with the Twist deformer applied. Notice how the rungs on the left ladder are flattened as they get further from the center, but the rungs on the right ladder with the Solidify deformer applied stay round.

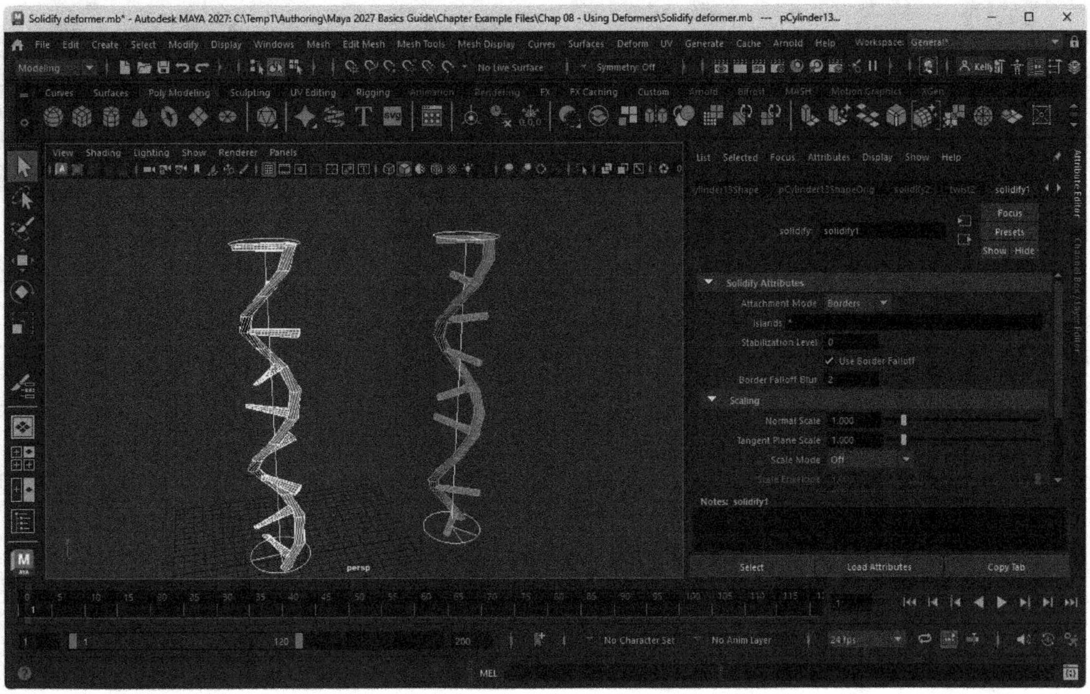

FIGURE 8-22

The Solidify deformer keeps details of a deformed object from distortion.

Smoothing with the Delta Mush deformer

Some deformers can cause wild deformations to an object. If you need to tame some areas, the **Delta Mush** deformer is a good solution. This deformer is applied to components after another deformer has been applied. Simply select the components to smooth out and choose the Deform, Delta Mush menu command. Figure 8-23 shows a Plane object deformed by a Wave deformer and several selected vertices have been smoothed using the Delta Mush deformer.

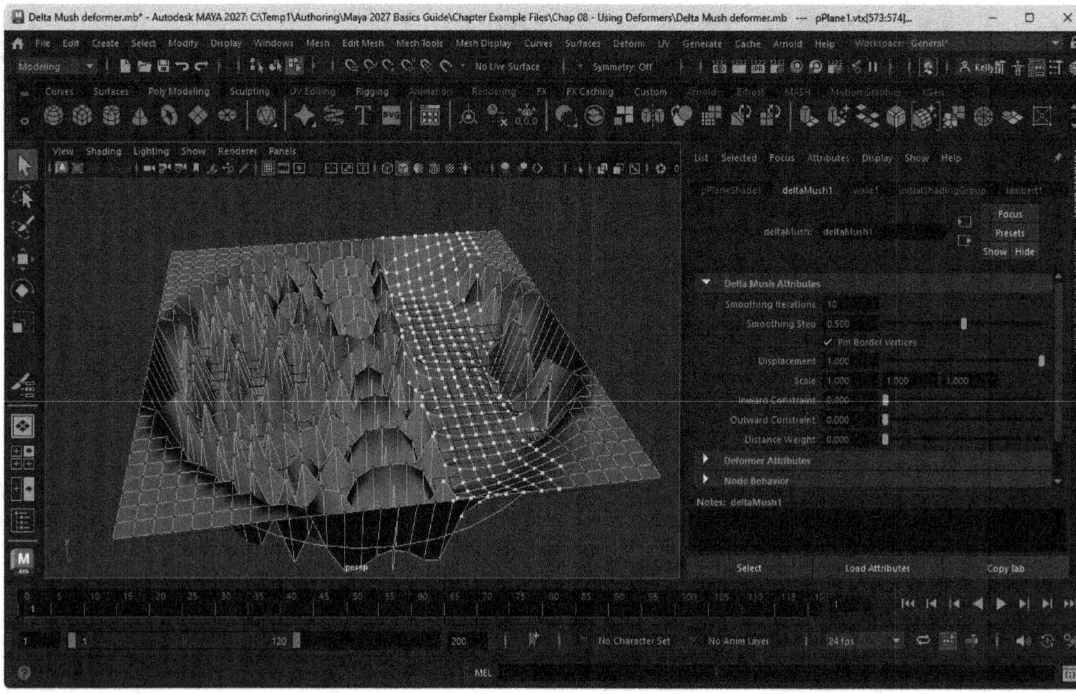

FIGURE 8-23

The Delta Mush deformer.

Lesson 8.5-Tutorial 1: Carving a river through a terrain.

1. Select File, Open Scene and open the Wild terrain.mb file.

   This file has a simple Plane object deformed using a Noise texture.

2. Choose the Paint Selection tool in the Toolbox and drag it over a set of vertices in the viewport to represent a river.
3. Choose the Deform, Delta Mush menu command.
4. With the vertices still selected, select the Move tool and move the components down to create a river.

   The Delta Mush deformer smoothes the selected vertices, as shown in Figure 8-24.

5. Select File, Save Scene As and save the file as **River through terrain.mb**.

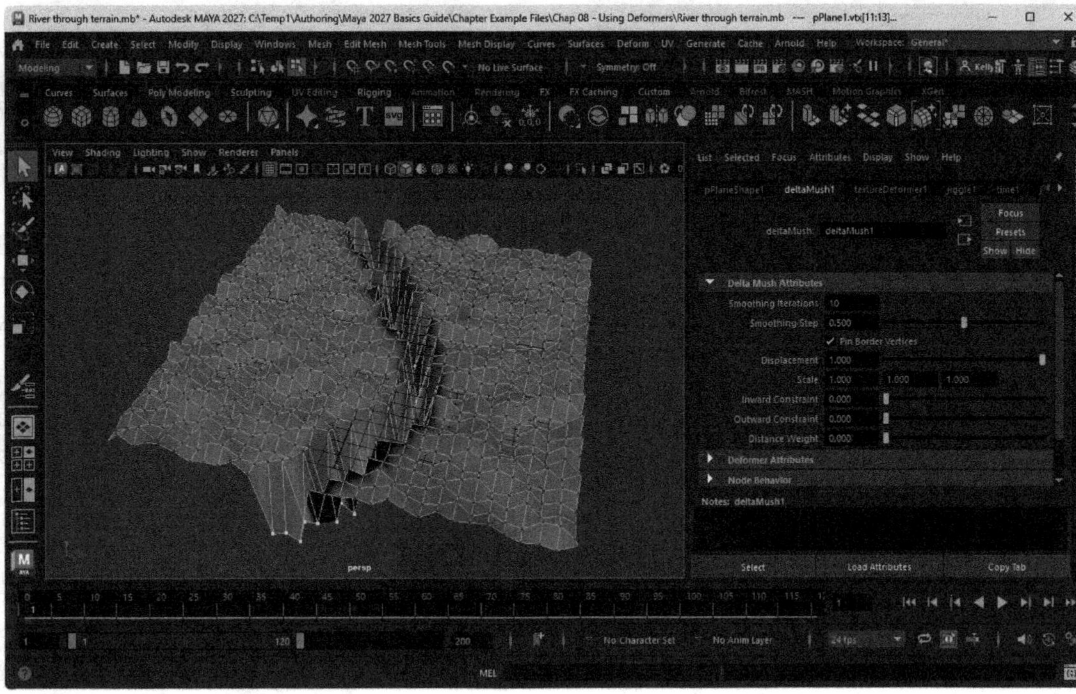

FIGURE 8-24

The Delta Mush deformer smoothes a river path.

Lesson 8.6: Creating Softbody Objects

When editing object components, most objects are rigid and move in straight lines independent of their surrounding components. However, if you think of softbody objects like blankets or a stuffed animal, they move differently. Pushing on the head of a pillow causes the whole pillow to move together. You can create **softbody** motion using the **Tension deformer**. Figure 8-25 shows an example of softbody motion. When selecting and moving the head, the top lizard moves just the selected head components, but the lower lizard stretches the whole neck naturally when the head moves.

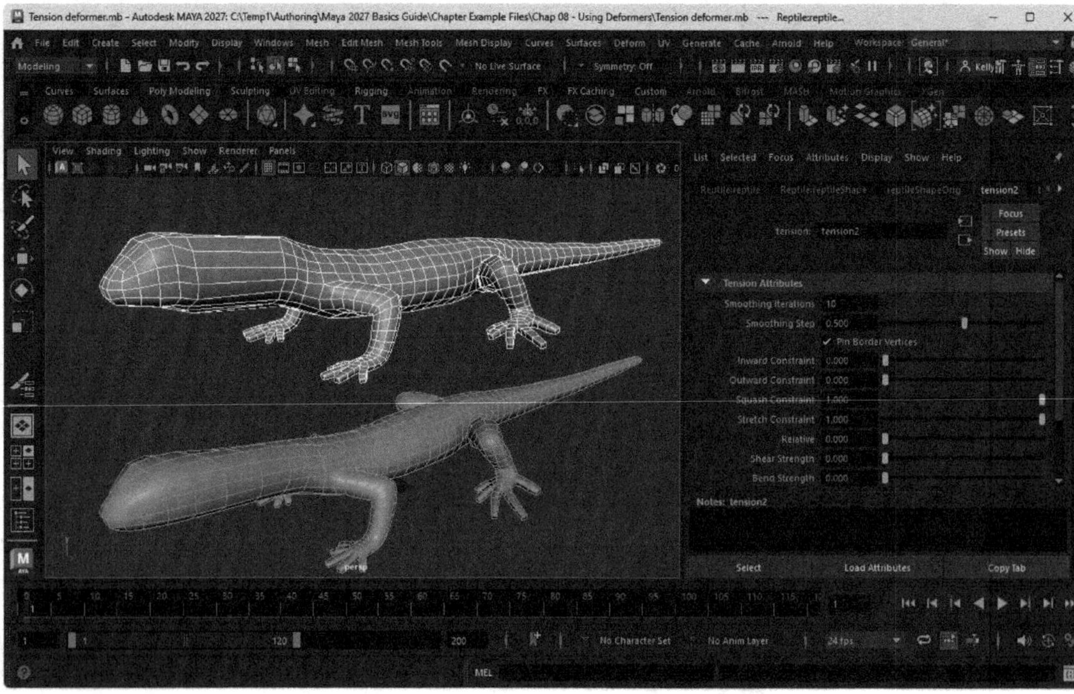

FIGURE 8-25

The Tension deformer creates a softbody.

Lesson 8.6-Tutorial 1: Creating a softbody.

1. Select File, Open Scene and open the Bumpy sphere.mb file.

   This file has an extruded sphere with lots of bumps.

2. With the sphere selected, choose the Deform, Tension menu command.
3. Right click on the sphere and select the Vertex option, then select a move several vertices away from the center.
4. Choose the Deform, Tension menu command again to apply the deformer a second time.

   The sphere vertices move slightly back towards the center.

5. Select a bunch of vertices and move them to see the softbody motion.

   The Tension deformer causes all parts of the object to move together, as shown in Figure 8-26.

6. Select File, Save Scene As and save the file as **Softbody sphere.mb**.

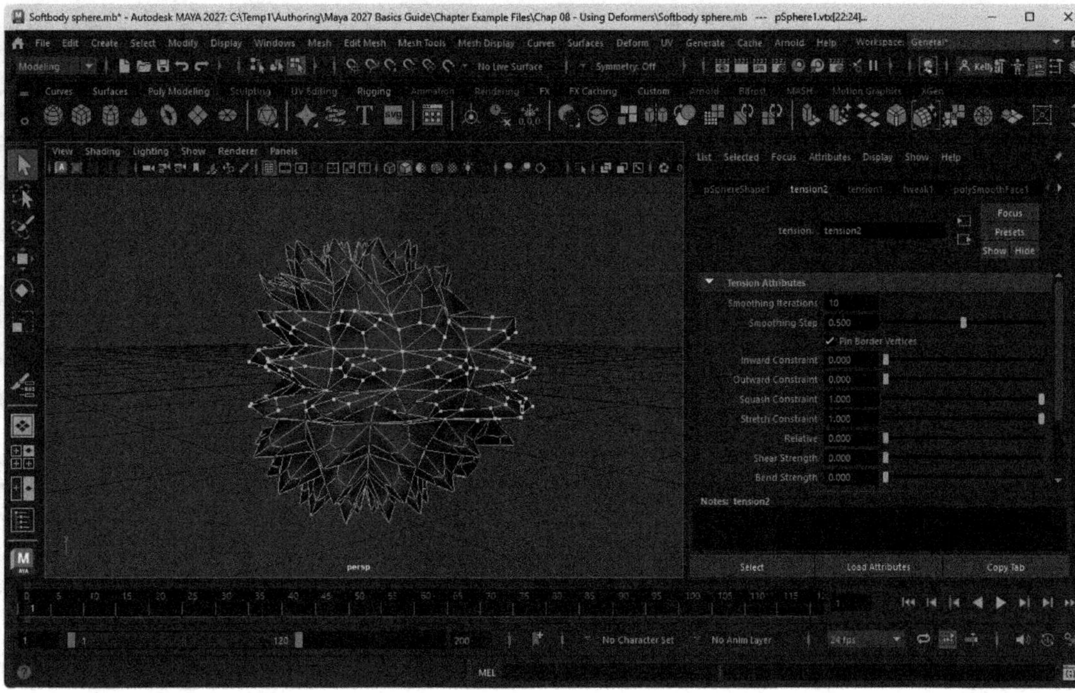

FIGURE 8-26

The Tension deformer creates softbody motion.

Lesson 8.7: Use the Texture deformer

Extruding textures is another great way to deform surfaces. The **Texture deformer** lets you choose a texture to use as the deformation source. Once applied, the Texture deformer lets you select a texture to load. These textures can be one from a file or it can be one of the many procedural textures available in Maya such as Checker, Noise or Fractal. You can also set the Strength and Offset for the loaded texture. Figure 8-27 shows a simple Plane object with a checker texture applied to it.

Tip

Another way to distort objects with textures is to use a displacement map. These are covered in Chapter 9, "Assigning Materials and Textures."

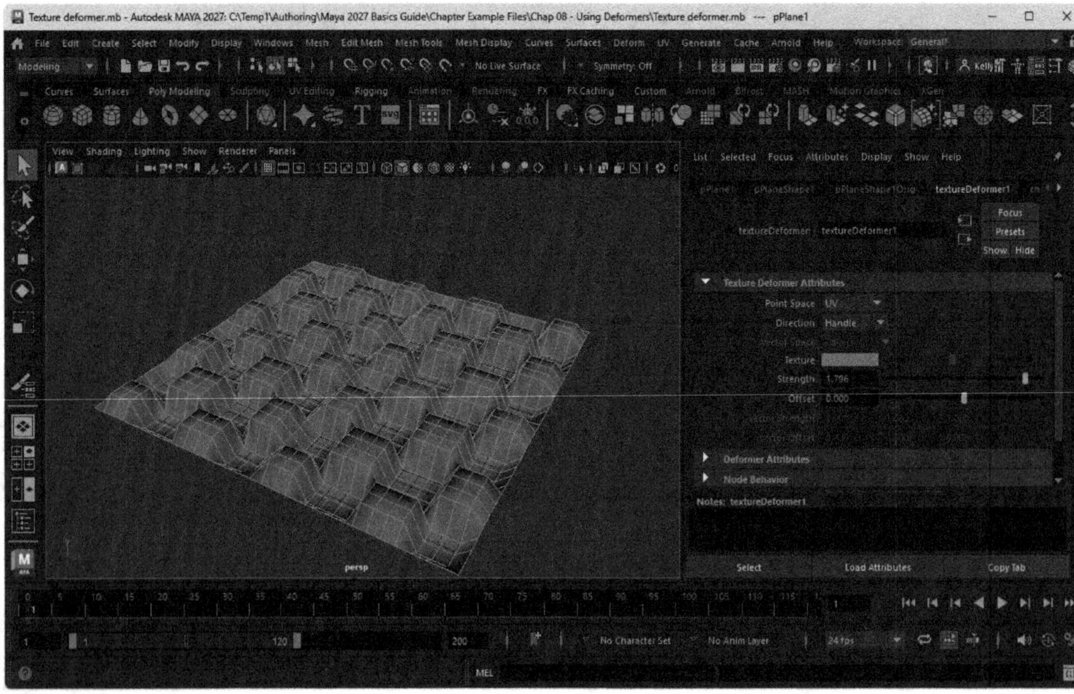

FIGURE 8-27

The Texture deformer with a checker texture loaded.

The key to deforming with textures is in the color luminance. The places in the loaded texture that are white are pushed upward and the places that are black are pushed downward. Gray areas are somewhere between based on whether they are closer to white or black.

Lesson 8.7-Tutorial 1: Deforming with a texture.

1. Select the Create, Polygon Primitives, Plane, Options menu command. In the Polygon Plane Options dialog box, set the Width and Height Divisions values to 300.

   This creates a very dense Plane mesh.

2. With the Plane selected, choose the Deform, Texture menu command. Click on the small map button to the far right of the Texture attribute in the Attribute Editor.

   This opens the Create Render Node dialog box.

3. Select the File option and click on the File button to the right of the Image Name attribute in the Attribute Editor. Select the Tulip logo.tif file from the downloaded files and click Open.

   The Plane object is deformed to match the loaded texture, as shown in Figure 8-28.

4. Select File, Save Scene As and save the file as **Tulip logo deformation.mb**.

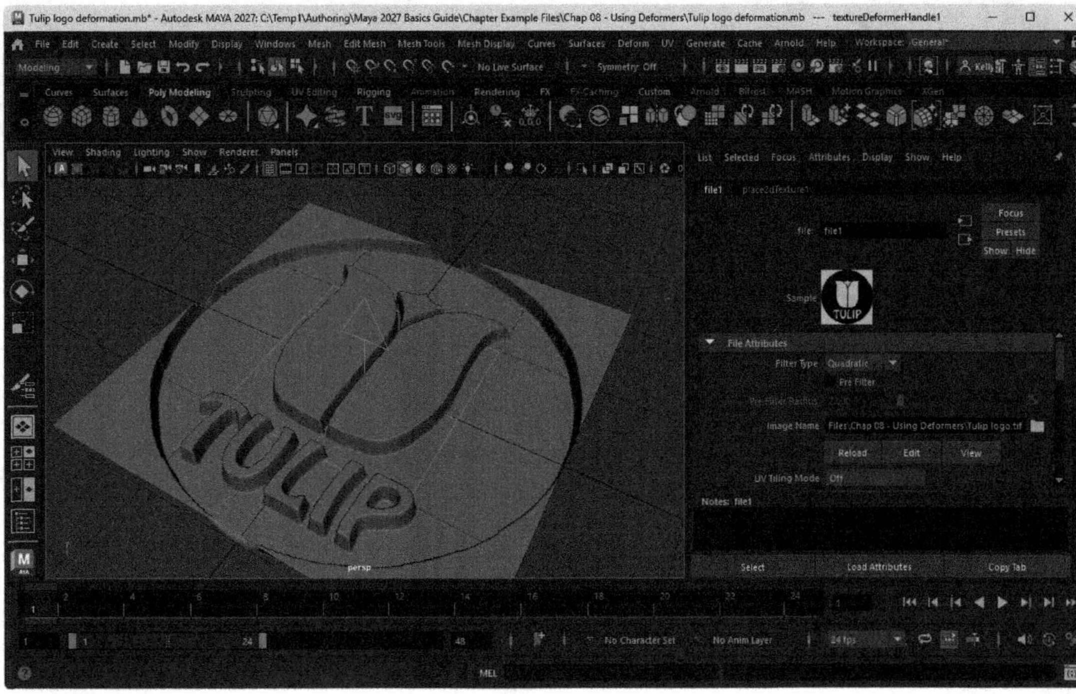

FIGURE 8-28

The logo texture was used to deform this Plane object.

Chapter Summary

This chapter covers several of the available deformers located in the Deform menu. The Deform, Nonlinear menu includes several standard deformers for bending, flaring, squashing, twisting and adding waves to objects. Deformers can be added to entire objects or to individual sets of components. The deformer manipulator makes it easy to work with deformers in the viewport. For a more detailed edition, you can paint weights that control only portions of the deformation.

Influence deformers like Lattice and Wire control the mesh underneath them. The ShrinkWrap deformer lets you match the surface of two different objects to make them seamless. Some deformers are best applied to a set of components like the Cluster, Solidify and Delta Mush deformers. You can also use Component Tags to mark and name a set of components. Using the Tension deformer, you can create a softbody object and finally, the Texture deformer uses loaded textures to deform the surface based on the texture's luminance.

What You Have Learned

In this chapter, you learned

* How to use the various nonlinear deformers.
* How to bend, flare and squash objects.
* How to twist and add waves to objects.
* How to add object density.
* How to use deformer handles and manipulators.
* How to remove a deformer from an object.
* How to make the deformations permanent.
* How to reorder deformers.
* How to paint deformer weights.
* How to use the Lattice and Wire deformers.
* How to wrap one object to another with the ShrinkWrap deformer.
* How to deform components.
* How to mark a group of components with Component Tags.
* How to use the Cluster, Solidify and Delta Mush deformers.
* How to create softbody objects with the Tension deformer.

Key Terms From This Chapter

* **Deformer.** A command that adds a manipulator to an object with attributes that can deform its surface.
* **Object density.** The total number of divisions that make up an object.
* **Handles.** A manipulator part that lets you change attributes by dragging in the viewport.
* **Deformer Weights.** A weight value that is applied to each vertex in an object to set its influence by a specific attribute. These are applied using a paint brush interface.
* **Lattice.** A deformer that surrounds the object with a grid of points that influence the shape of the object contained within it.

* **Wire deformer.** A curve that is attached to a selected set of components under its influence.

* **ShrinkWrap deformer.** A deformer that wraps one object onto the surface of another.

* **Component Tag.** A named and marked set of selected components for easy recall.

* **Cluster.** A group of vertices that moves together.

* **Solidify.** A deformer that removes a set of components from the influence of other deformers.

* **Delta Mush deformer.** A deformer that smoothes out wild distortions.

* **Softbody.** An object whose components move together by maintaining the distance between their adjacent components.

* **Tension deformer.** A deformer that makes objects act like softbody objects.

* **Texture deformer.** A deformer that deforms the surface based on the texture's luminance.

Chapter 9
Assigning Materials and Textures

IN THIS CHAPTER

9.1 Apply materials.

9.2 Use the Hypershade.

9.3 Work with materials.

9.4 Work with textures.

9.5 Position textures.

9.6 Use displacement map.

9.7 Use utilities nodes.

9.8 Paint in 3D.

9.9 Edit UVs.

Modeling geometry is only one aspect of creating a realistic object. Another critical aspect involves dressing objects with the correct materials and textures. Using materials and textures, you can change attributes such as the color, transparency, and shininess of an object.

Materials are often referred to as **shaders** in Maya. Materials control how the light interacts with the object's surface. Material nodes are combined to make up a shading group and can be applied to objects in the scene. A single material can consist of many different rendering nodes. Each node contributes to the final rendering.

Textures are the image files that can act as input nodes for the various material attributes such as color or transparency. For example, a wood material may have a texture node that includes colors, another texture node to define its shininess, and a relief texture node that defines its surface bumps. In addition, each node has several attributes that define its description. You can change node attributes in the Attribute Editor.

You can view all of the details on material and texture nodes in an interface called the **Hypershade**. You can connect nodes together so that the output of one node becomes the input of another. The Connection Editor connects attributes together. You can also drag materials with the middle mouse button from the Hypershade and drop them on objects in the viewports to apply the materials to scene objects.

The Hypershade has access to all the various render nodes using the **Create Bar** and the Work Area is used to view and connect nodes together. All attributes for the selected node are displayed in the Attribute Editor. The available nodes include Surface, 2D and 3D textures, and an assortment of utility render nodes that enable you to do things like control the placement of textures and blend different materials.

You can create effective materials by understanding the differences between all of the various materials and textures. Displacement maps are used to change the geometry of objects by moving its components to match a given texture map, but the results of displacement maps are only visible when rendered. Objects that use displacement maps can be converted to geometry objects using the Modify, Convert menu.

The Texturing menu includes a 3D Paint tool that lets you paint colors using the Artisan and Paint Effect brushes directly on 3D objects. This tool also lets you paint other attributes, such as transparency and **bump maps**.

If a single texture map is applied to a complex object, you can use the UV Editor to define how the texture maps to the object's components. The UV Editor has lots of tools to help make this easy to do. For example, if you create a single texture map with all the sides of a pair of dice, you can use the UV Editor to apply each face to the sides of a cube to texture the dice.

Lesson 9.1: Apply Materials

When an object is first created, a default material is applied to it; this is the Open PBR Shader material. You can see this material using the openPBR shader1 tab in the Attribute Editor, as shown in Figure 9-1. You can replace this default material with a new material and, once it's applied, you can edit the material's attributes—such as Color, Transparency, and Specularity—in the Attribute Editor.

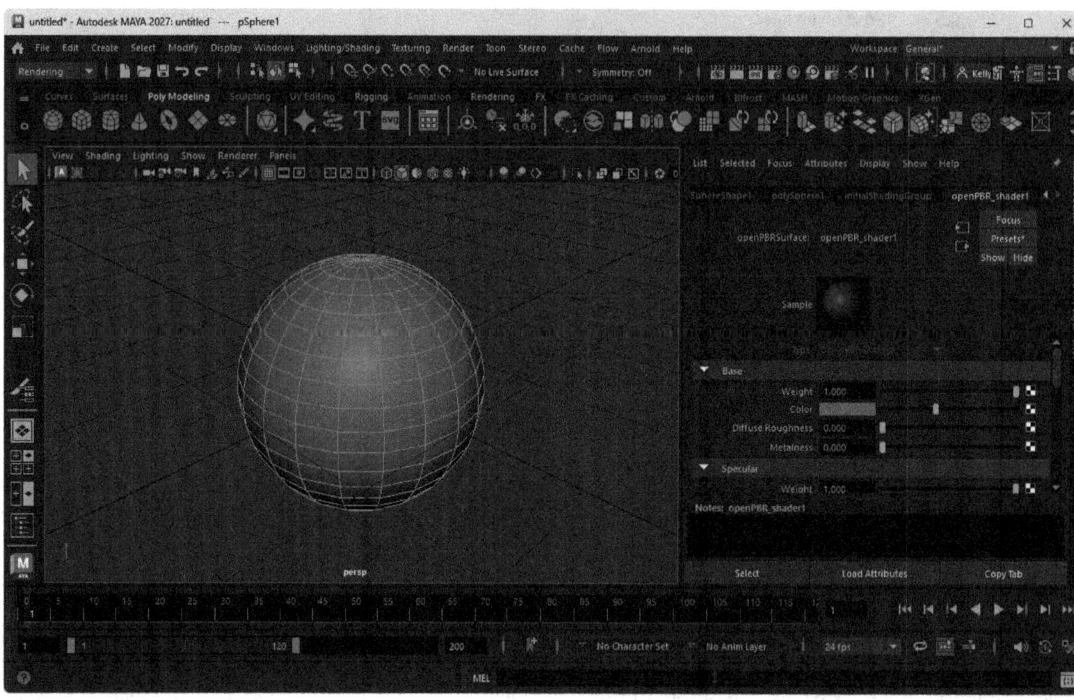

FIGURE 9-1

Default material node

Applying New Materials

When an object is selected in the view panel you can apply a new material to the object using the Lighting/Shading, Assign New Material menu command. The Lighting/Shading menu command is available when the Rendering menu set is selected. This opens a submenu of several material and environment options, as shown in Figure 9-2. Selecting a material from the menu creates a new shading group and material nodes that you can view in the Attribute Editor. You can view the material attributes for the selected object using the Lighting/Shading, Material Attributes menu command.

Note

If the Lighting/Shading, Assign Favorite Material, Automatic Attribute Editor menu command is enabled, assigning a new material automatically opens the Attribute Editor.

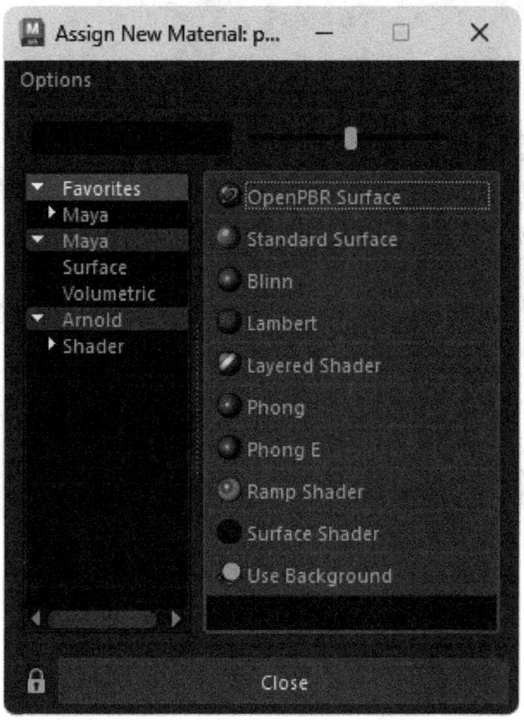

FIGURE 9-2

A sample of the available materials

Applying Open PBR Surface Presets

It is easy to get overwhelmed with materials and shaders, but Maya includes a great shader for getting started called the Open PBR Surface shader. When this shader is applied to an object, you can access a large number of presets using the Presets button near the top of the Attribute Editor when the Open PBR Surface tab is selected. The presets include Brushed Metal, Car Paint, Chrome, Clay, Frosted Glass, Jade, Rubber, Velvet, etc. For each of these presets, you can still change their attributes like color to get just the look you want. Figure 9-3 shows a quick Arnold render of a sphere and plane objects using the Open PBR Surface shader.

Tip

Another benefit of the Open PBR Surface shader is that it will work with any of the selected renderers including Arnold.

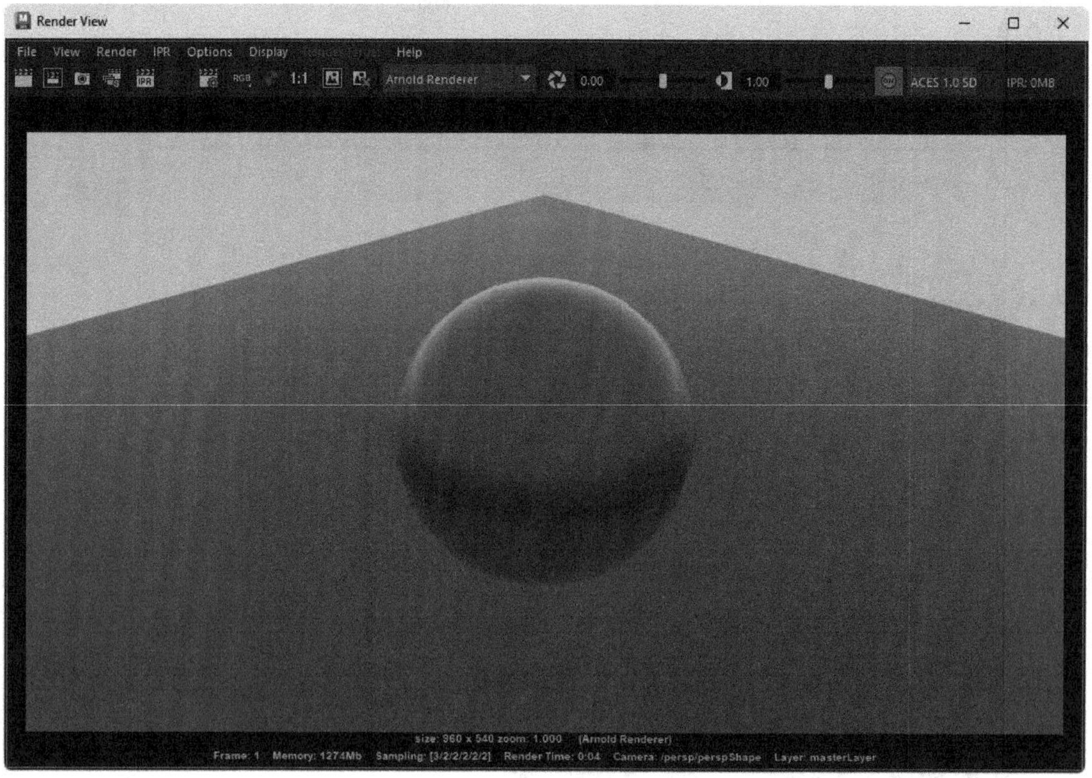

FIGURE 9-3

The Open PBR Surface materials rendered in Arnold

Renaming Materials

Although the material node is named by default using the material name followed by a single-digit number, you can enter a new name for the material in the Attribute Editor by clicking on the name above the Sample. Renaming materials is a good way to easily find them again if you plan on reusing them within the scene.

Applying Existing Materials

Maya keeps track of all the materials applied to different objects in the scene. You can apply an existing material to another object in the scene using the Lighting/Shading, Assign Existing Material menu command, which includes the names of all the currently used materials.

Applying Materials to Selected Faces

When a material is applied to an object, the entire object gets the material, but if you select a polygon face or a NURBS patch, then you can apply any existing materials to only the selected face or patch using the Lighting/Shading, Assign Existing Material menu command. The assign material menus are also available in the right-click marking menu.

Changing Material Attributes

Most of the attributes found in the Attribute Editor for a material node consist of a color swatch, a value slider, and a button to open the Create Render Node dialog box, as shown in Figure 9-4. The color swatch shows the current color that is applied to the attribute. For attributes such as Color, the color represents the actual color that is displayed, but for other attributes, like Transparency, the color represents a value with black being a minimum value and white being the maximum value. Clicking the color swatch opens a Color Chooser in which you can select a new color. The Create Render Node dialog box, shown in Figure 9-5, lets you select textures to replace solid colors. Each texture node has its own set of attributes.

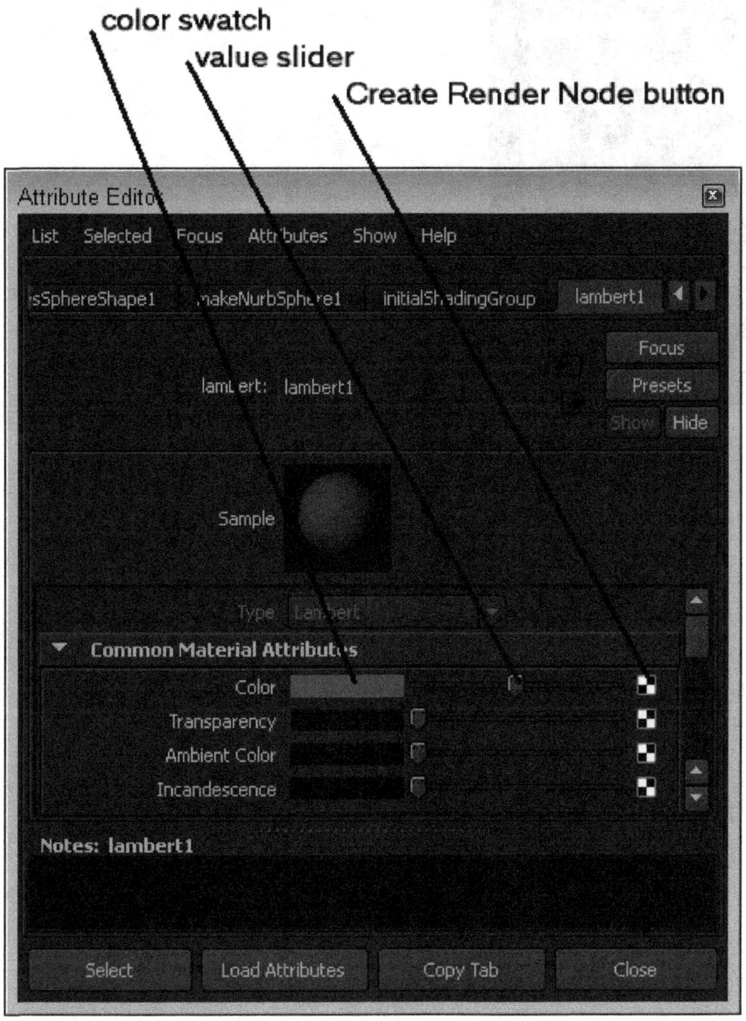

FIGURE 9-4

Material attribute controls

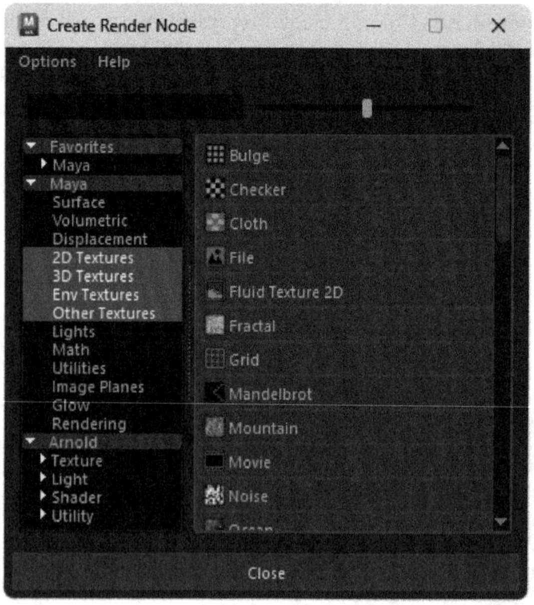

FIGURE 9-5

The Create Render Node dialog box

Moving Between Nodes

If you replace the Color attribute of a material with a texture, the Create Render Node button is also replaced with an Input Connection button. Clicking this button opens attributes for the Input node, which in this case is the texture node. Using the Input and Output Connection buttons (see Figure 9-6), you can move forward and backward through all of the nodes that make up the entire material.

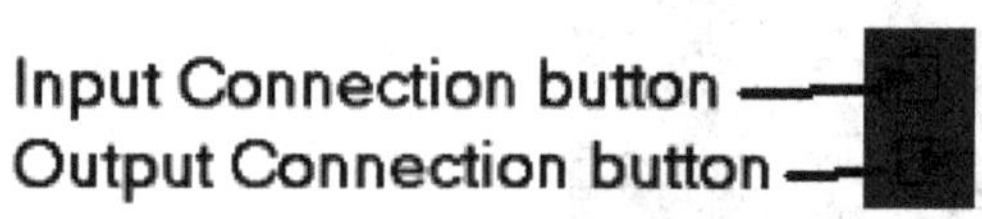

FIGURE 9-6

Input and Output Connection buttons

Rendering Materials

To see a rough view of the material and textures applied to an object, press the 6 key but be aware that the view panel displays only a limited set of material properties, such as color, texture, and transparency. To see all of the material details, such as bump maps, you'll need to render the scene using the Render View interface (shown in Figure 9-7), which you can open using the Windows, Rendering Editors, Render View menu command, or by clicking on the Open Render View button on the Status Line.

FIGURE 9-7

Render View interface

Lesson 9.1-Tutorial 1: Apply a Material

1. Create a sphere object using the Create, NURBS Primitives, Sphere menu command.
2. Click on the Menu Sets drop-down list to the far left of the Status Line and select the Rendering menu set.
3. With the sphere selected, choose the Lighting/Shading, Assign New Material menu command, then double click on the Phong shader in the Assign New Material dialog box.
4. Press the 6 key to enable the view panel to display textures.

   Applying this new material opens the Attribute Editor and displays the material node. The object in the view panel is displayed using this new material.
5. In the Attribute Editor, type the name Shiny red for this material.
6. Click on the color swatch for the Color attribute and choose a red color in the Color Chooser, and then click the Accept button.
7. Select the Windows, Rendering Editors, Render View menu command. In the Render View window that opens, choose the Options, Render Using Maya Software menu command, then click the Render the Current Frame button at the left end of the Render View toolbar.

   Figure 9-8 shows the shiny red material applied to the sphere in the Render View window.
8. Select File, Save Scene As and save the file as Shiny red sphere.mb.

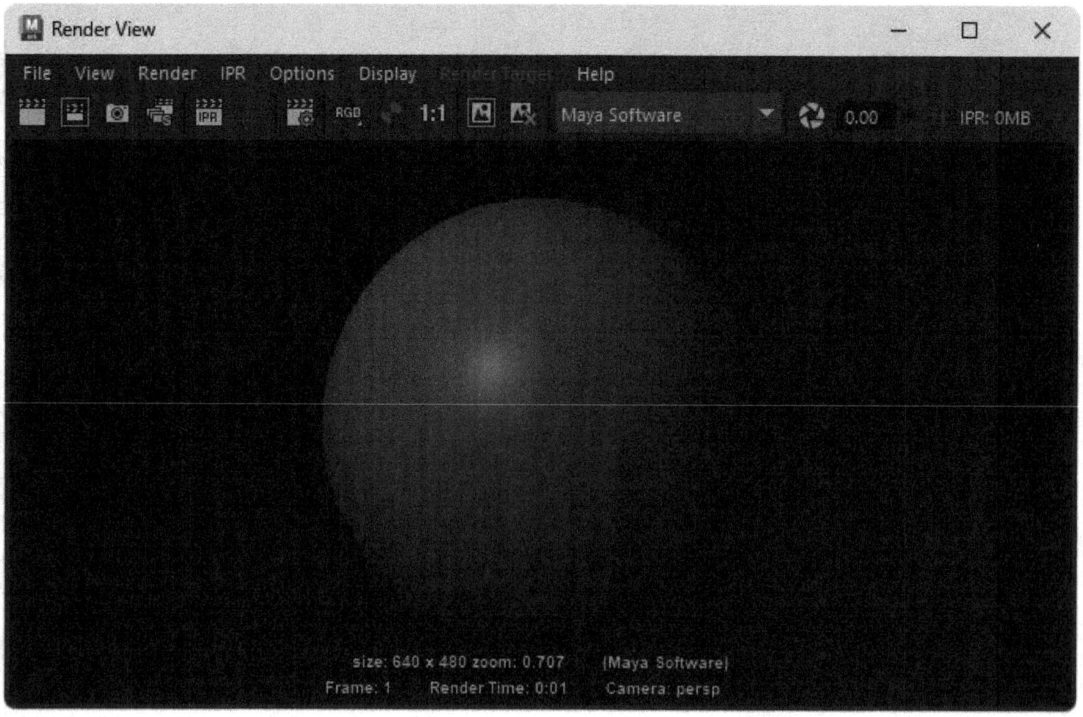

FIGURE 9-8

Shiny red sphere

Lesson 9.1-Tutorial 2: Apply a Material to Face Selection

1. Open the Die.mb file using the File, Open Scene menu command.

   This file includes a simple NURBS cube object and 6 materials named Die Face 1 through Die Face 6.

2. Select one of the faces of the cube, then select the Lighting/Shading, Apply Existing Material, Die Face 1 material.
3. Select another cube face and repeat Step 2 with the Die Face 2 material.
4. Continue to add a different material to each cube face through Die Face 6.

   Figure 9-9 shows the resulting die.

Select File, Save Scene As and save the file as **Die with pips.mb**.

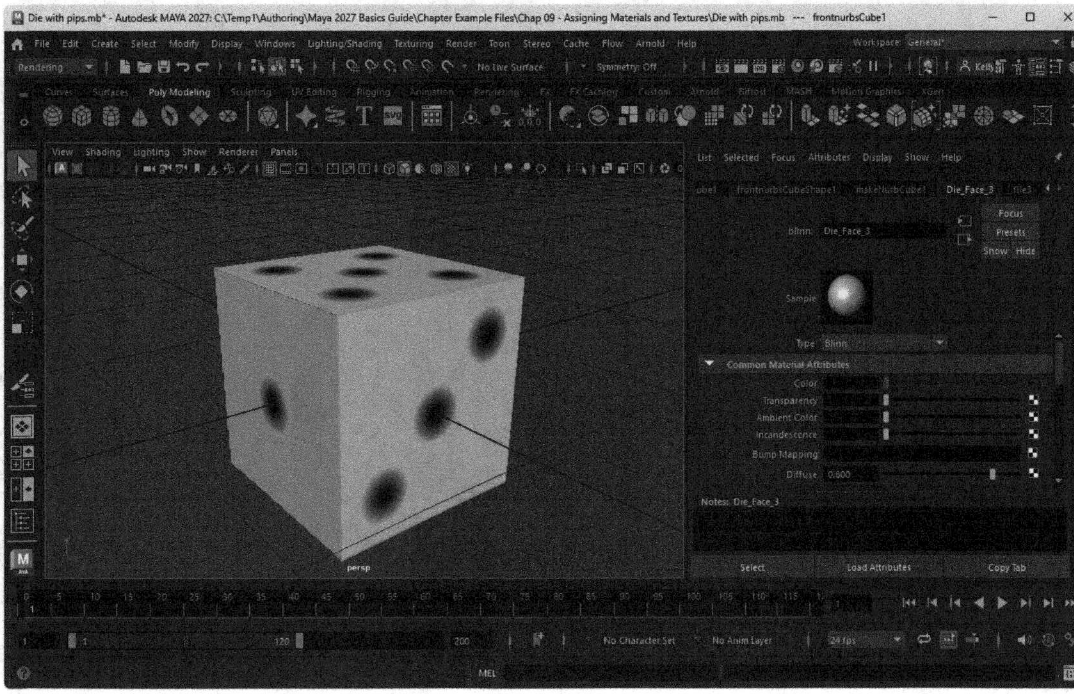

FIGURE 9-9

Cube with different material on each face

Lesson 9.1-Tutorial 3: Apply and Render a Texture

1. Create a sphere object using the Create, NURBS Primitives, Sphere menu command.
2. With the sphere selected, choose the Lighting/Shading, Assign New Material menu command and double click on the Blinn shader in the Assign New Material dialog box to select it. In the Attribute Editor, click on the Create Render Node button for the Color attribute.
3. Select the Checker option in the Create Render Node dialog box.
4. Press the 6 key to enable the view panel to display textures.

   The Create Render Node dialog box automatically closes, and the Checker node is made active in the Attribute Editor.
5. In the Attribute Editor, click on the Go to Output Connection button.

   Clicking the Go to Output button causes the blinn1 node to be selected in the Attribute Editor.
6. Click on the Create Render Node button for the Bump Mapping attribute, and click on the Fractal button in the Create Render Node dialog box.

   Although a bump map has been added to the sphere material, no change is shown in the view panel.
7. Select the Render, Render Current Frame menu command.

   The Render View window opens, as shown in Figure 9-10, and the current view panel is rendered showing the applied bump map.
8. Select File, Save Scene As and save the file as **Checkered bumpy sphere.mb**.

FIGURE 9-10

A rendered checkered sphere

Lesson 9.2: Use the Hypershade

The Hypershade, shown in Figure 9-11, is the interface wherein you can see and work with the entire network of nodes that make up a material. It is useful when you begin to create custom materials. These custom materials can then be applied to objects in the scene directly from the Hypershade. You can access the Hypershade using the Windows, Rendering Editors, Hypershade menu command. The Hypershade interface consists of a menu, a toolbar, and several different panes—the Browser pane, the Create Bar, and the main tabbed view pane. There is also a preview pane and the Attribute Editor. Each pane, except for the main tabbed pane, can be moved and/or closed by pulling it away from the interface. You can bring back closed panes using the Window menu.

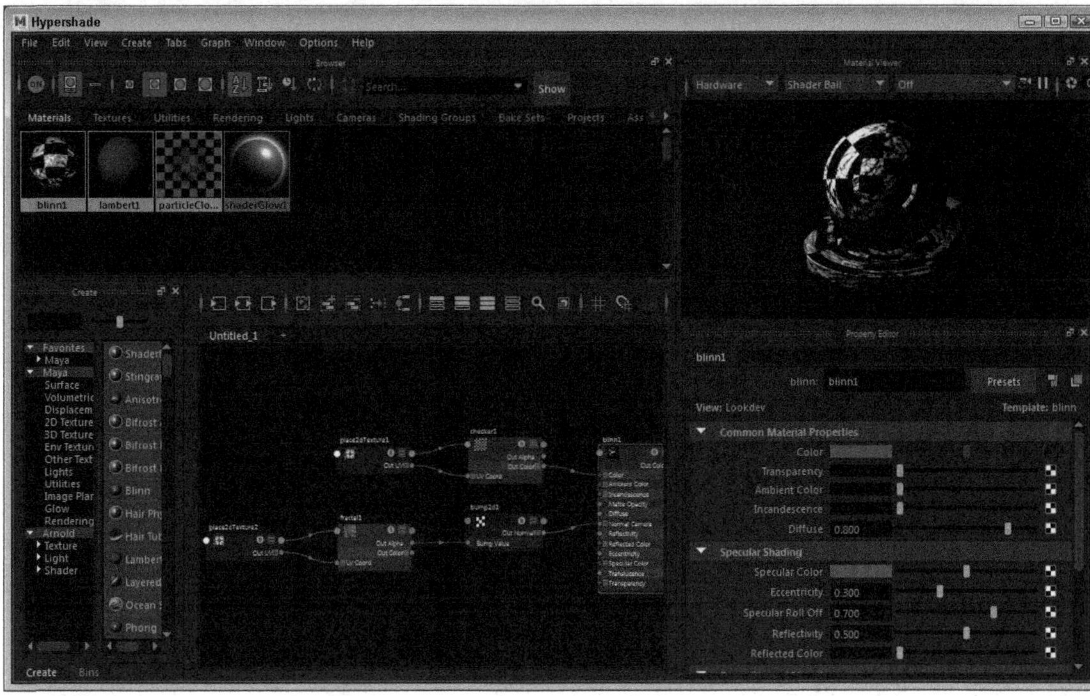

FIGURE 9-11

The Hypershade

Using the Create Bar

The pane on the lower left of the Hypershade is the Create Bar, as shown in Figure 9-12. The Create Bar is the source of available rendering nodes similar to the Create Render Node dialog box. Each of the categories of nodes can be selected using sections that can be expanded and collapsed as needed. Some of the available node categories include Surface, Volumetric, Displacement, 2D and 3D Textures, Lights, Utilities, and Glow. Each category lists and displays a thumbnail for the available nodes.

FIGURE 9-12

The Create Bar

Using the tabbed panes

Clicking on a node in the Create Bar adds the selected node to the Browser pane and the main tabbed view pane in the Hypershade. The Browser pane includes tabs that you can use to view only a specific category of rendering nodes for the current scene, including Materials, Textures, Utilities, Lights, Cameras, Shading Groups, Bake Sets, and Projects. Above the tabs on the upper pane is a text field where you can search for specific nodes. Figure 9-13 shows the Browser pane with the Textures tab selected. This shows all of the textures currently used in the scene. The main tabbed view pane includes a Work Area tab that is used as a scratch pad to connect the various nodes. You can also use the Tabs menu to create new tabs and manage the existing tab sets.

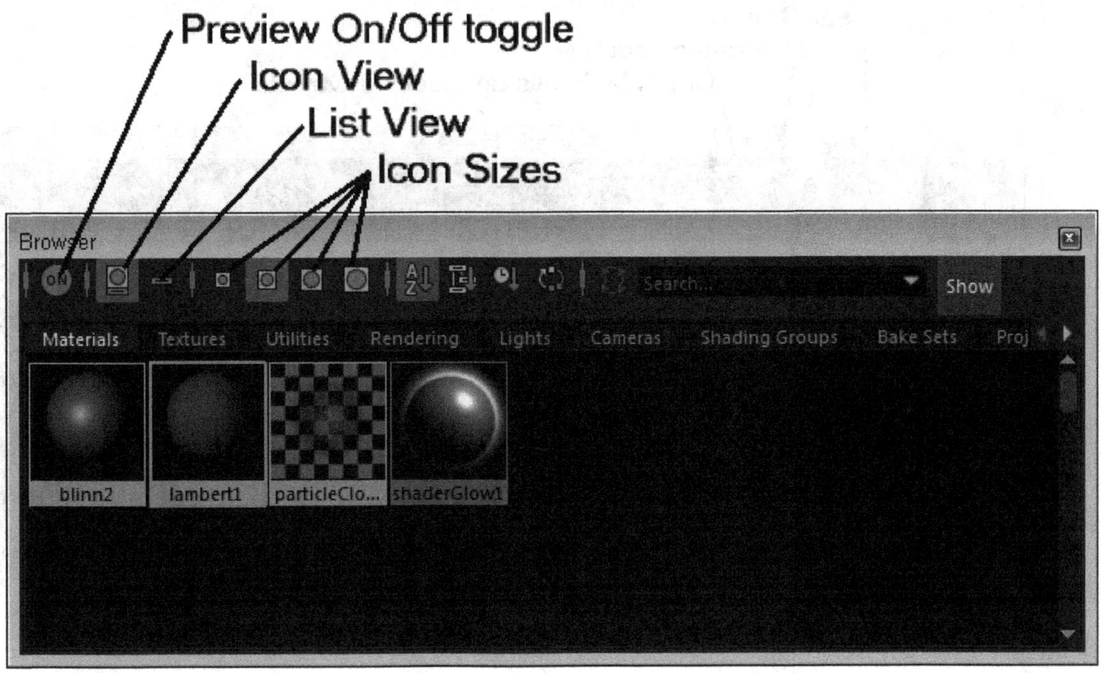

FIGURE 9-13

Browser pane

Using the Work Area

The Work Area tabbed pane, shown in Figure 9-14, is where you'll spend most of your time creating custom materials. You can select nodes within the Work Area by clicking on them; you can also drag over several nodes with the mouse or hold down the Shift key while clicking to select multiple nodes. Selected nodes are highlighted green. You can move selected nodes within the Hypershade by dragging them. You can use the Alt/Option key together with the middle and right mouse buttons to pan and zoom selected nodes within the Hypershade. The Clear Graph toolbar button erases all nodes in the Work Area. The Rearrange Graph toolbar button lines up all nodes within the Work Area pane and the Graph Materials on Selected Objects toolbar button displays the nodes for the selected object.

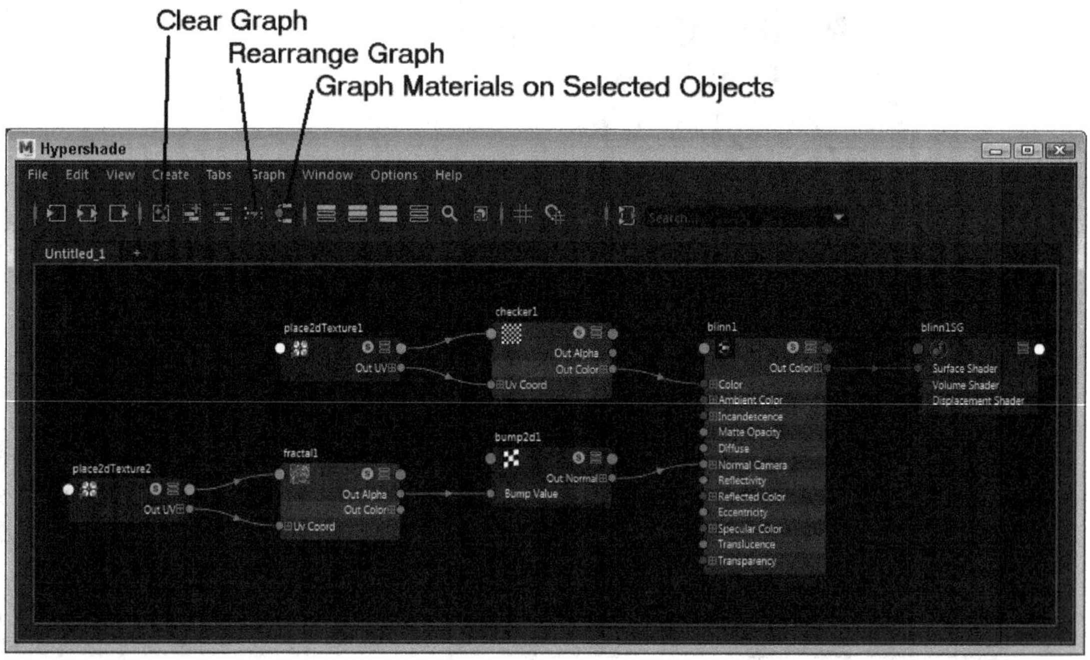

FIGURE 9-14

The Work Area tab

Working with Nodes

Each active node in the Hypershade is represented by a rectangular icon that displays the current settings for the material or texture. These icons are updated as you make changes to the node's attributes. In the upper right corner of each node is a button to expand or contract the number of attributes that are shown. This is used to simplify the nodes or to show all the available attributes. Clicking on the node name lets you rename the node.

Connecting Nodes

Clicking on a node in the Create Bar makes the node appear in the Work Area. You can connect nodes together to create complex materials. These connections are displayed in the Hypershade as arrowed lines. The different colors represent different types of data. Each node has an input port on the top left side of the node and output port on the top right side. There are also ports next to each individual attribute. To connect two nodes, drag from the output port and drop it on the input port for another material node to which you want to connect it. You can also connect nodes by dragging from the input back to the output port. Node attributes can only connect values that are compatible. For example, you cannot connect a color value to a position value. The Hypershade is smart enough to hide all properties that are incompatible when you drag to connect two nodes. If you drag from or drop on the topmost input or output port, a pop-up menu appears (like the one shown in Figure 9-15), from which you can select from several common attributes to use.

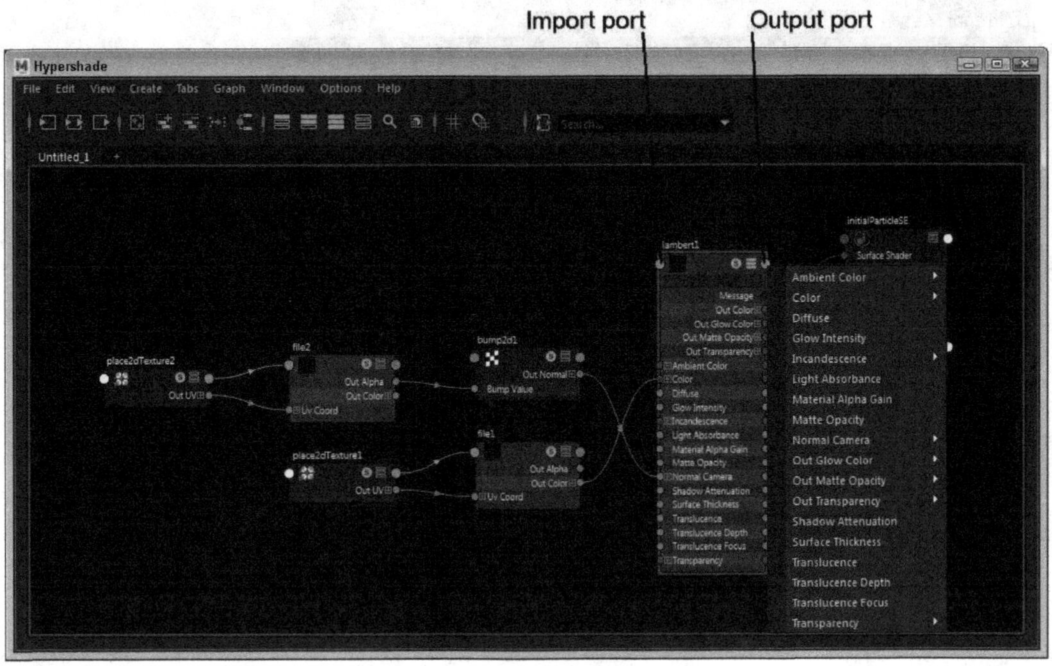

FIGURE 9-15

The Connection pop-up menu

Using the Material Viewer

The Material Viewer, shown in Figure 9-16, lets you see the resulting material applied to an object without having to revisit the viewports. Using the top toolbar, you can change the rendering system, the preview object, and the scene lighting.

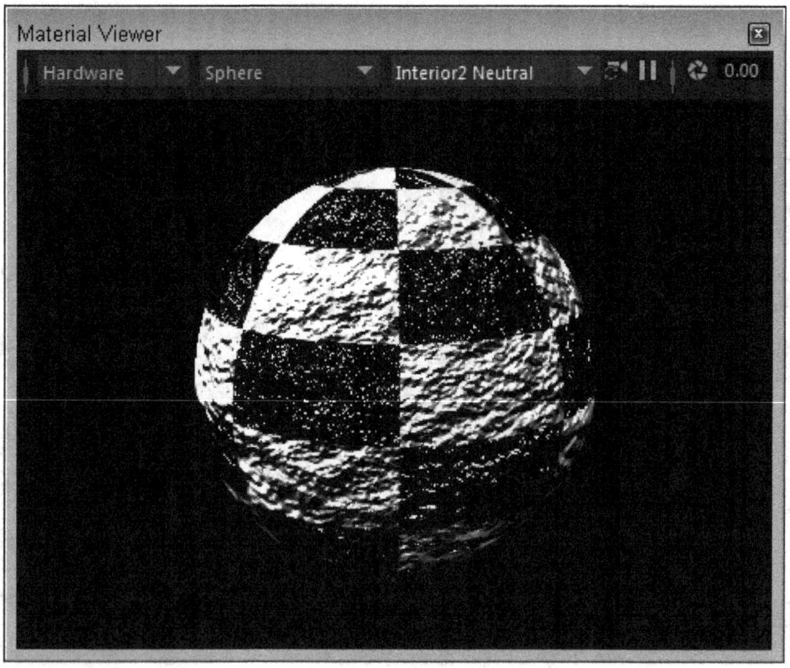

FIGURE 9-16

The Material Viewer

Dragging Materials to Objects

You can apply material nodes in the Hypershade to objects in the view panels by dragging the material icon in the Browser pane with the middle mouse button and dropping it on the object in the view panel that it is to be assigned to. You can also assign materials to the selected object by right-clicking on a material in the Hypershade Browser and selecting Assign Material to Selection from the pop-up menu.

Lesson 9.2-Tutorial 1: Create a Custom Material

1. Create a sphere object using the Create, NURBS Primitives, Sphere menu command.
2. Select the Windows, Rendering Editors, Hypershade menu command to open the Hypershade interface.
3. In the Hypershade's Create Bar, expand the Maya category to see the Surface, 2D Textures and 3D Textures categories.
4. Then locate and click on the Blinn material node, the Grid 2D texture node, and the Crater 3D texture node.

   Each of these nodes appears in the Work Area tab.
5. Drag from the Out Color attribute port in the Crater texture node and drop it on top of the Color input port for the Blinn1 material node. Drag from the Out Color attribute port in the Grid texture node and drop it on top of the Specular Color attribute port in the Blinn1 material node.
6. Click on the Rearrange Graph button on the toolbar to arrange the nodes.
7. Select the sphere object in the view panel, right-click on the Blinn1 material in the Browser pane, and select the Assign Material to Selection from the pop-up menu.

   Figure 9-17 shows the resulting material in the Hypershade's Work Area tab.
8. Select File, Save Scene As and save the file as **Custom material.mb**.

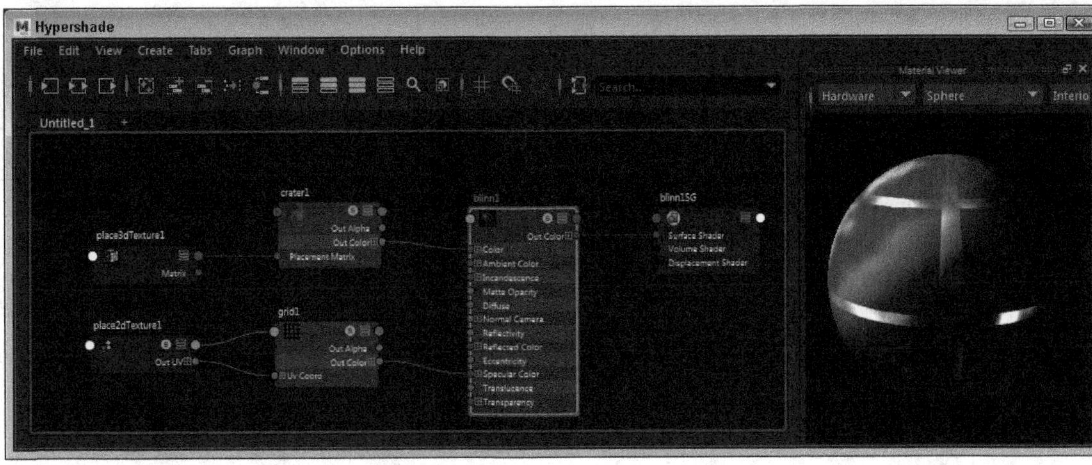

FIGURE 9-17

A Custom material

Lesson 9.2-Tutorial 2: Create a Custom Cloth Material

1. Create a sphere object using the Create, NURBS Primitives, Sphere menu command.
2. Select the Windows, Rendering Editors, Hypershade menu command to open the Hypershade interface.
3. Click on the Lambert material node and the Cloth 2D texture node.

    Each of these nodes appears in the Work Area tab.
4. Drag the Out Color output port in the Cloth1 texture and drop it on top of the Color port in the Lambert2 material node.
5. Drag the Lambert2 material in the Browser pane with the middle mouse button and drop it on top of the sphere in the view panel.

    Figure 9-18 shows the resulting material in the Hypershade's Work Area tab.
6. Select File, Save Scene As and save the file as **Cloth material.mb**.

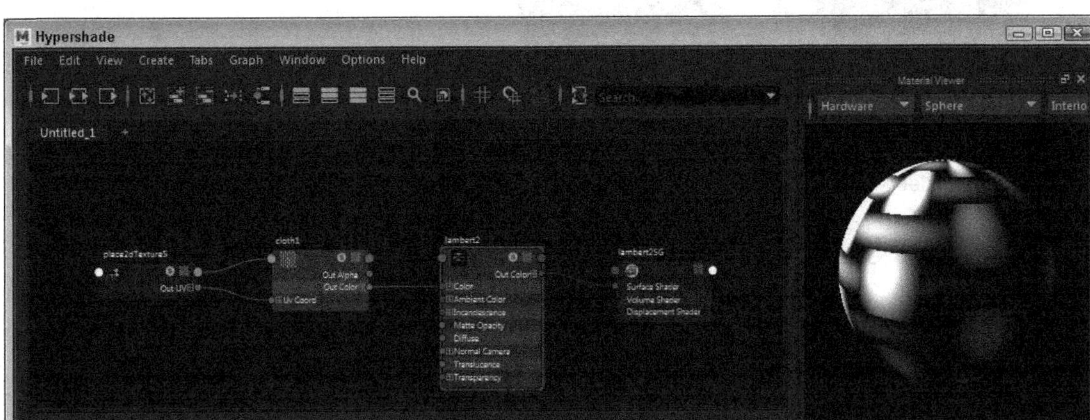

FIGURE 9-18

Another custom material

Lesson 9.3: Work with Materials

The first category in the Hypershade Create Bar is Surface. Each Surface node includes attributes that define such material properties as color and transparency. You can edit these attributes in the Attribute Editor. In addition to the Open PBR Surface materials, Maya also includes support for volumetric and displacement materials. Figure 9-19 shows all the nodes available in the Surface and Volumetric Materials categories.

Note

```
The Create Bar also includes several specialized
materials such as Bifrost and Hair. These
materials work with specialized Maya tools and are
best used with those toolsets.
```

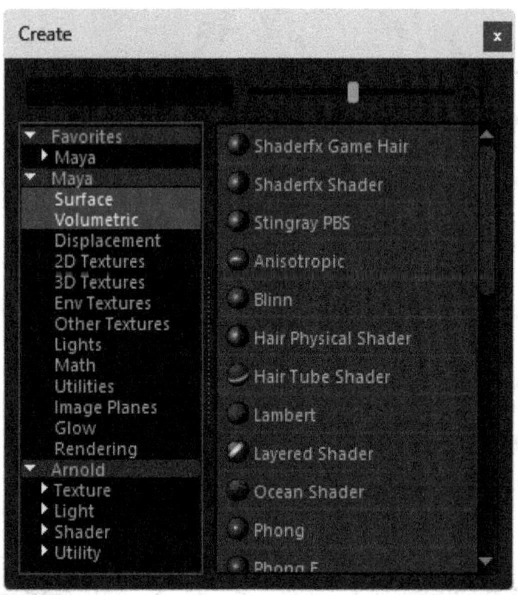

FIGURE 9-19

Material nodes

Learning the Surface Materials

Maya includes the following common surface materials (or shaders):

* **Anisotropic**. This material has elliptical specular highlights.
* **Blinn**. This material has soft circular highlights and is good for metallic surfaces.

* **Lambert**. This material has no highlights and is useful for cloth and non-reflective surfaces.
* **Layered Shader**. This material can combine several shaders into one and allows you to apply several materials to a single object.
* **Phong**. This material includes a hard circular highlight and is good for glass surfaces.
* **Phong E**. This material is similar to the Phong Shader, but it is optimized to render faster.
* **Ramp Shader**. This material gives you control over a gradient ramp.
* **Shading Map**. This material allows you to change the colors that are rendered and can be used to render cartoons.
* **Surface Shader**. This material allows you to connect an attribute to the surface material attributes.
* **Open PBR Surface**. This material is the default shader with many presets and advanced attributes.
* **Standard Surface**. This material is a good general-purpose shader with many presets.
* **Use Background**. This material allows you to alter the shadows and reflections of an object.

A key difference between these different surface materials is how the light is reflected off its surface. This is most evident in the specular highlights.

Changing Material Color

One property that is common for most surface materials is color. You can see the current color for a selected surface material node in the Attribute Editor. Dragging the Color Slider changes the color's brightness, and clicking on the color swatch opens the Color Chooser dialog box, as shown in Figure 9-20, wherein you can select a new color. The Color Chooser can display color values in RGB or HSV. The Color Chooser also includes a Blend rollout, where you can create new colors by blending four corner colors and a Palette rollout by scrolling to the bottom of the Color Chooser dialog box.

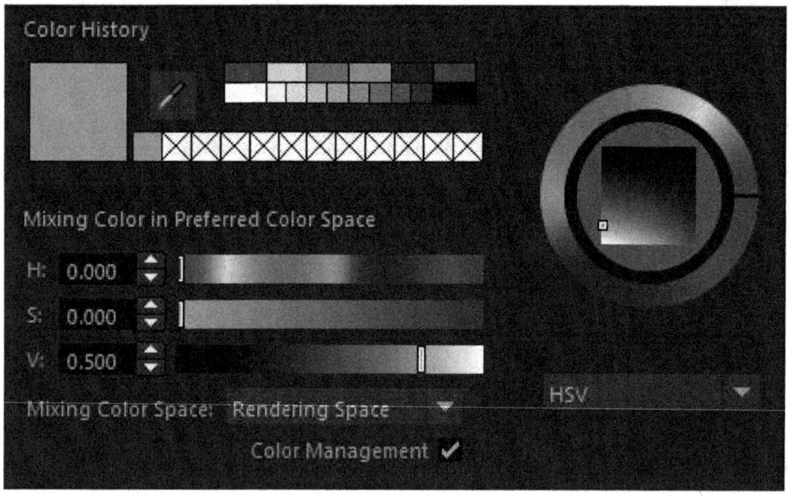

FIGURE 9-20

The Color Chooser

Changing Material Transparency

Another common surface material attribute is transparency. The Transparency attribute includes a color swatch and a slider. Setting the Transparency color to pure black will make an object opaque and setting the color swatch to pure white makes it completely transparent. Any color between black and white will make the material semi-transparent.

Using Other Material Attributes

Surface materials include many other attributes. The following is a small sampling of some of the common material attributes:

* **Type.** Lets you change the material Shader.
* **Ambient Color**. Lightens the material's color but has no effect when black.
* **Incandescence.** Color emitted from the object like a light bulb.
* **Diffuse**. Represents the purity of the color.
* **Translucence**. How much light shows through an object.
* **Specular Color**. The color of the specular highlights.
* **Reflectivity**. Defines how reflective a surface is.
* **Reflected Color**. The color that is reflected by the object.
* **Eccentricity**. Controls the size of the specular highlights.
* **Roughness**. Determines the blurriness of the specular highlights.

Layering Materials

You can use the Layered Shader material to create advanced materials by layering several materials together, as shown in Figure 9-21. To create a layered material, drag to connect the materials that you want onto the Layered Shader node with the middle mouse button and select the Inputmenu option in the pop-up menu. This connects the material as a layer and the material is included in the Attribute Editor. The material at the left in the Attribute Editor is the top-most material, as shown in Figure 9-22, and all materials need to be at least partially transparent in order to see the materials underneath.

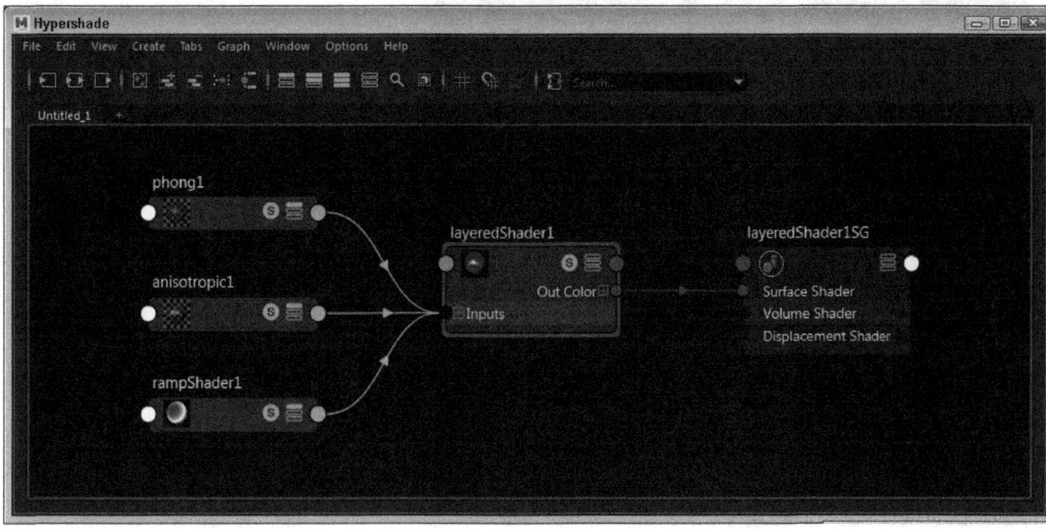

FIGURE 9-21

A layered material

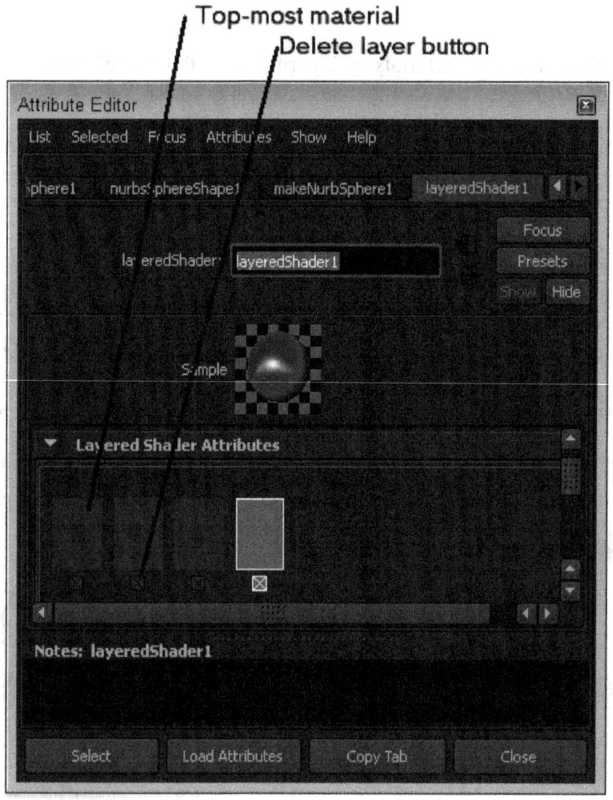

FIGURE 9-22

The Attribute Editor for the Layered Shader

Using the Ramp Shader

The color section for the Ramp Shader material in the Attribute Editor includes a rectangle that represents the gradient ramp, as shown in Figure 9-23. Click on the rectangle at the location where you want to add a new color. A small circle appears above the rectangle, and a small square appears below. If you select the circle, you can change its color by clicking the Selected Color swatch, and if you drag the circle, you can reposition the color. If you click the square, the color is deleted. You can also create gradient maps for the Transparency, Incandescence, Specular Color, Specular Shading, Specular Roll Off, Reflectivity, and Environment attributes.

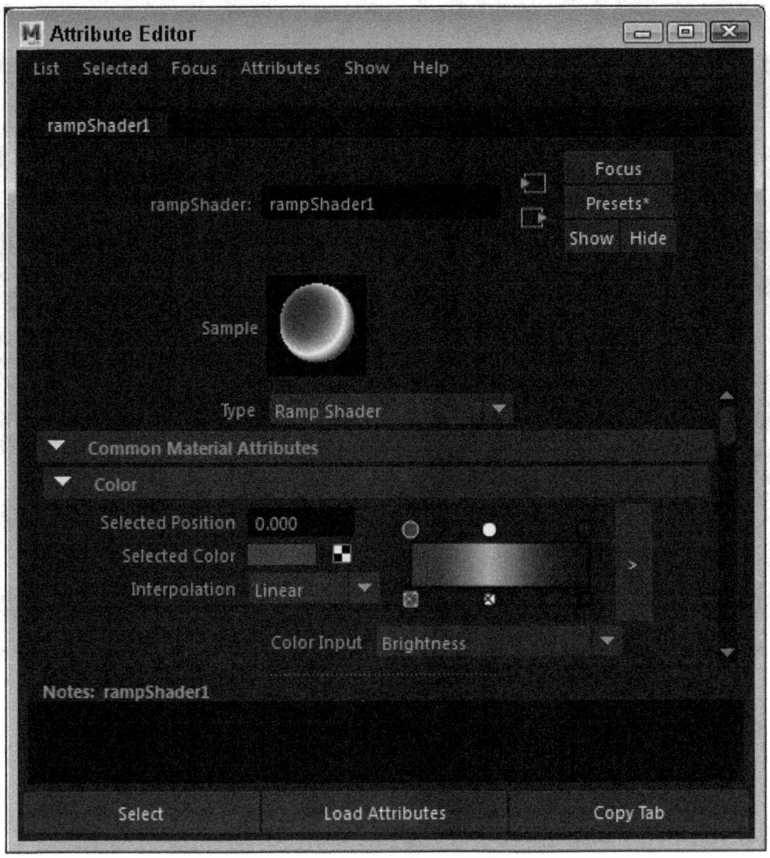

FIGURE 9-23

The Attribute Editor for Ramp Shader

Using the Shading Map

The Shading Map material has attributes for a Color and a Shading Map Color. It uses the Shading Map Color texture to determine the shading for the Color. For example, if you use a Ramp texture as the Shading Map Color, all the bright spots on the object are set to one end of the ramp and the darker spots get the lower part of the ramp, as shown in Figure 9-24.

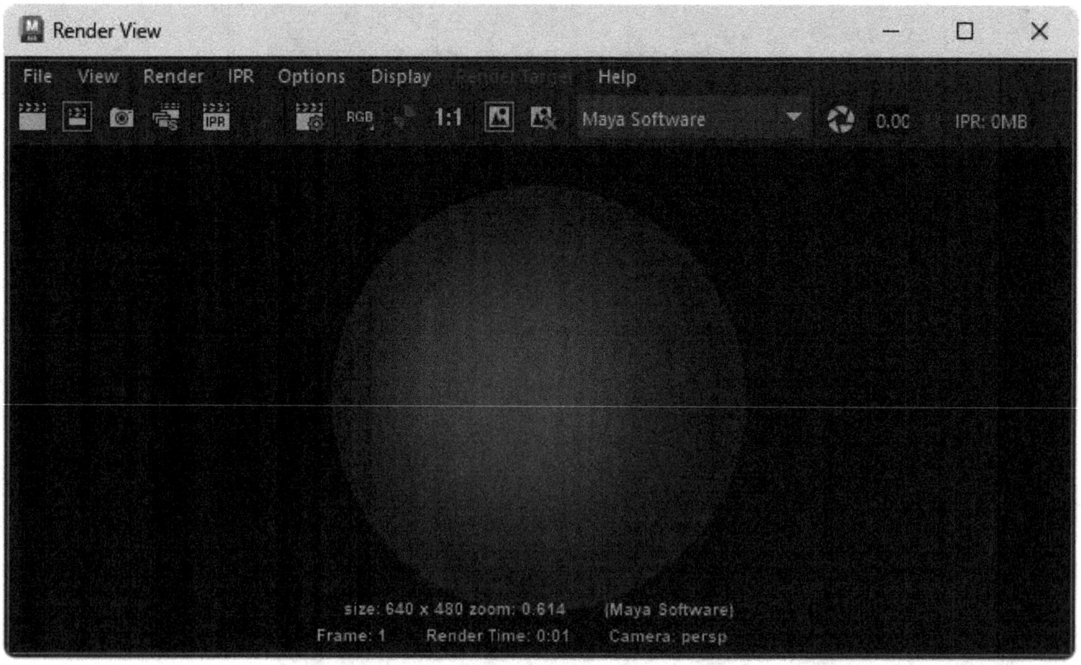

FIGURE 9-24

Shading Map material

Lesson 9.3-Tutorial 1: Change Color and Transparency

1. Create a sphere object using the Create, NURBS Primitives, Sphere menu command.
2. Select the Windows, Rendering Editors, Hypershade menu command to open the Hypershade interface.
3. Click on the Blinn material node in the Create Bar.
4. In the Attribute Editor, click the color swatch for the Color attribute.

   The Color Chooser opens.
5. Drag the color locator dot in the color wheel over to the orange color and drag the brightness slider up towards the top.

   The color in the Attribute Editor and Hypershade is automatically updated.
6. Click the Accept button to close the Color Chooser.
7. Drag the slider for the Transparency attribute to the right.
8. Select the sphere object in the view panel, right-click on the Blinn1 material in the Browser pane of the Hypershade and select Assign Material to Selection from the pop-up menu.

   The sphere object is updated with the orange transparent material in the Render View window, as shown in Figure 9-25.
9. Select File, Save Scene As and save the file as **Orange transparent sphere.mb**.

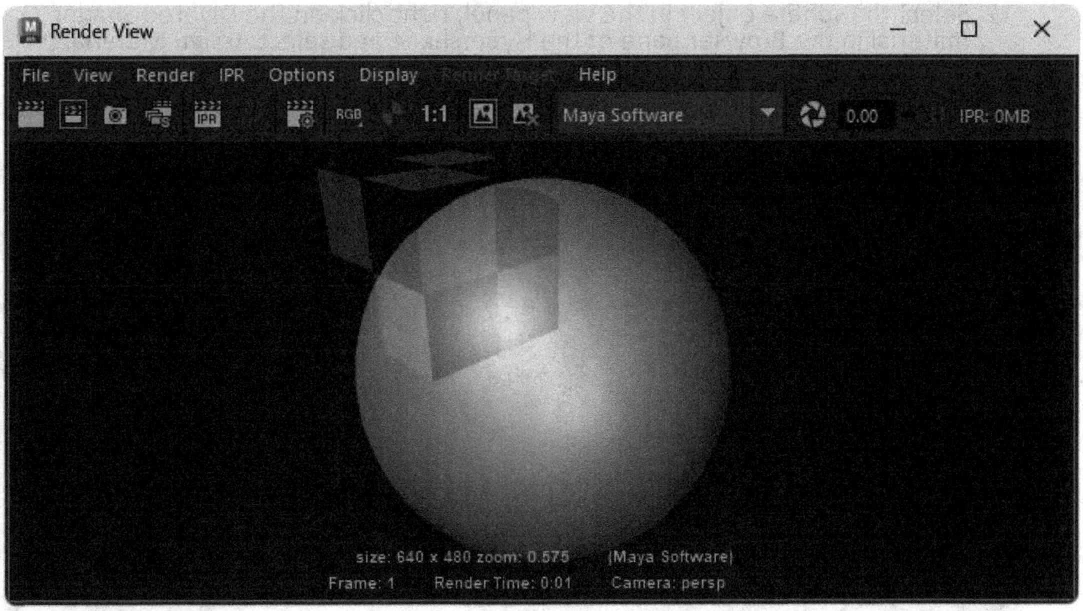

FIGURE 9-25

Orange transparent sphere

Lesson 9.3-Tutorial 2: Layer Materials

1. Create a sphere object using the Create, NURBS Primitives, Sphere menu command.
2. Select the Windows, Rendering Editors, Hypershade menu command to open the Hypershade interface.
3. Click on the Layered Shader material node in the Create Bar.
4. Click to create the Anisotropic material node and drag the Anisotropic Shading Group output port and drop it on the Inputs port for the Layered Shader node in the Work Area.
5. Repeat Step 4 with the Phong and Ramp Shader materials.
6. Click the Rearrange Graph button in the Hypershade toolbar to rearrange the nodes.
7. Select the Layered Shader node and change its Color attribute to black and drag the slider for its Transparency attribute to the right.
8. Select the Anisotropic node and drag its Transparency slider halfway to the right.
9. Select the Phong node, set its Color to a bright purple, and drag the slider for its Transparency attribute halfway to the right.
10. Select the Ramp Shader node and change the Selected Color attribute to red. Click in the middle of the gradient ramp bar and select white and then click on the right end of the gradient ramp bar and select a blue color.
11. Change the Color Input attribute to Brightness.

    The resulting layered material includes an elliptical highlight--compliments of the Anisotropic material--a normal circular highlight from the Phong material, and a gradient ramp of colors from the Ramp Shader material in the Render View window, as shown in Figure 9-26.

12. Select the sphere object in the view panel, right-click on the Layered Shader material in the Browser pane of the Hypershade and select Assign Material to Selection from the pop-up menu.
13. Select File, Save Scene As and save the file as **Layered material with ramp.mb**.

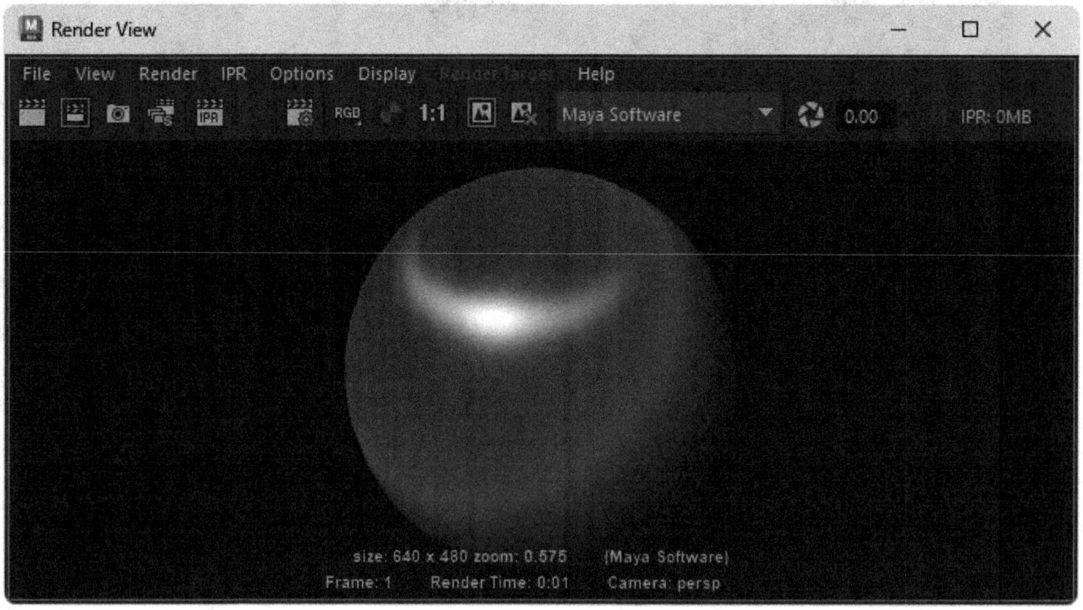

FIGURE 9-26

Layered material with ramp

Lesson 9.3-Tutorial 3: Use a Shading Map

1. Create a sphere object using the Create, NURBS Primitives, Sphere menu command.
2. Select the Windows, Rendering Editors, Hypershade menu command to open the Hypershade interface.
3. Click on the Shading Map material node in the Create Bar.
4. Create a Blinn material node and connect it to the Shading Map node in the Work Area using the Out Color to Color, the Out Glow to Glow Color and the Out Transparency to Transparency.
5. Select the ShadingMap1 node in the Hypershade and in the Attribute Editor, click on the Create Render Node button for the Shading Map Color attribute.
6. In the Create Render Node dialog box, choose the Checker node.
7. Click the Rearrange Graph button in the Hypershade toolbar to rearrange the nodes.
8. Select the Blinn1 node and change its Color attribute to a light purple color.

    The checker texture is used to represent the light purple shading for the Blinn material, as shown in Figure 9-27, creating a set of black and white stripes.
9. Select the sphere object in the view panel, right-click on the Blinn1 material in the Browser pane of the Hypershade and select Assign Material to Selection from the pop-up menu.
10. Select File, Save Scene As and save the file as **Striped sphere.mb**.

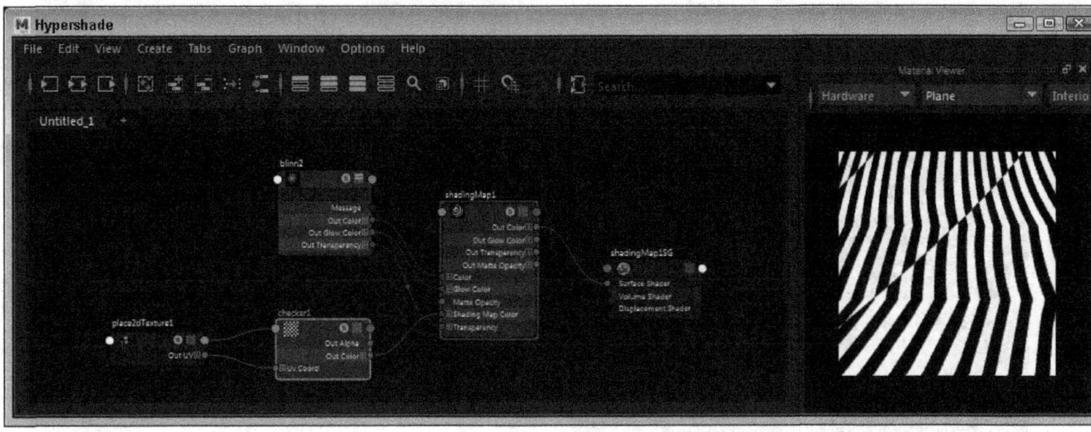

FIGURE 9-27

Material nodes for a striped sphere

Lesson 9.4: Work with Textures

Once a material node is created, you can connect texture nodes to it as inputs to the material's color, bump maps, transparency, specular highlights, and so on. You can apply many textures from the Create Bar, but you can also connect any image file using the File texture node. Texture nodes include several categories: 2D textures, 3D textures, Environment textures, and Others. Figure 9-28 shows the available 2D Texture nodes and Figure 9-29 shows the available 3D Texture nodes.

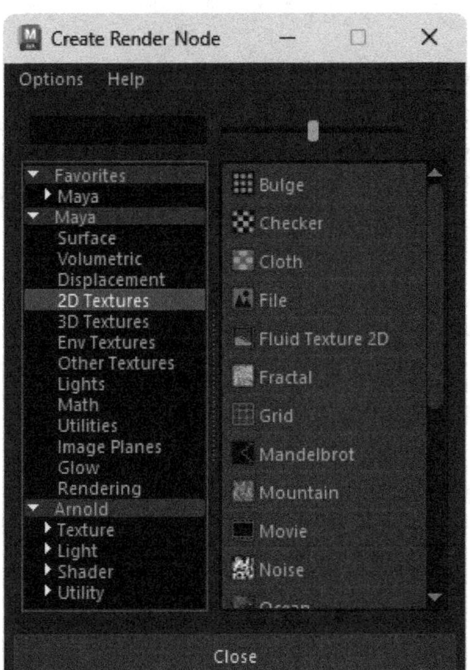

FIGURE 9-28

2D Texture nodes

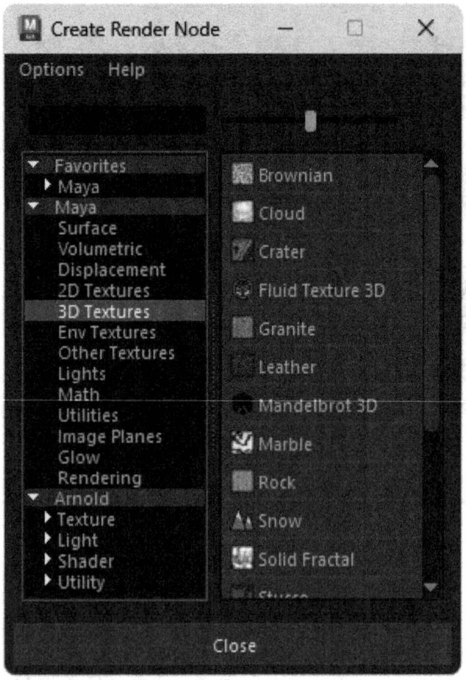

FIGURE 9-29

3D Texture nodes

Connecting Texture Nodes

You can connect textures to materials by dragging them and dropping them on a node attribute in the Work Area or you can simply select the Create Render Node button for an attribute in the Attribute Editor. The pop-up menu that appears lets you select what the texture appears as. The pop-up menu options include many of the common material attributes or you can drag the attribute ports directly.

Applying Textures as Color

When textures are applied as a material's color, the texture image is wrapped around the object. Selecting the texture node displays its attributes in the Attribute Editor. Many texture nodes must be connected with a utility node—for instance, a 2D texture node must be connected to a place2dTexture utility node, as shown in Figure 9-30. These utility nodes let you control the placement on the texture map on the object. When you click on a texture node in the Create Bar, Maya automatically adds and connects the necessary utility nodes in the Work Area.

Tip

If a texture's utility node isn't visible in the Hypershade, select the texture and click the Input Connections button.

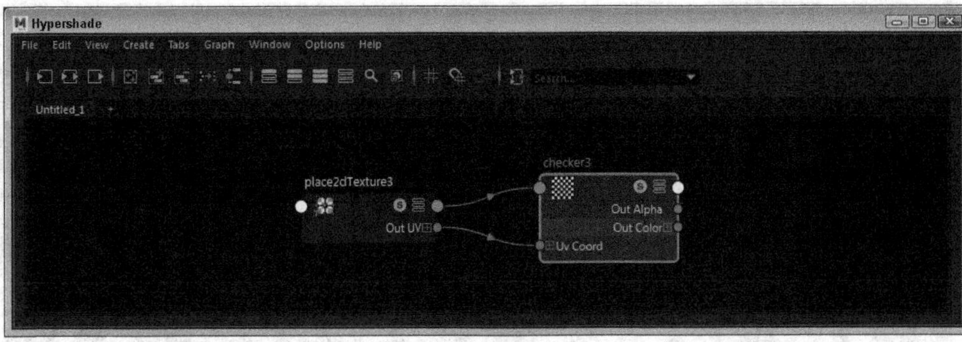

FIGURE 9-30

Texture map and utility node

Mapping Textures to Attributes

Applying a texture to a material attribute like Transparency causes the white areas to become transparent and the black areas to remain opaque, as shown in Figure 9-31. This works the same way for most of the other attributes—including specularity, reflection, and incandescence—as well.

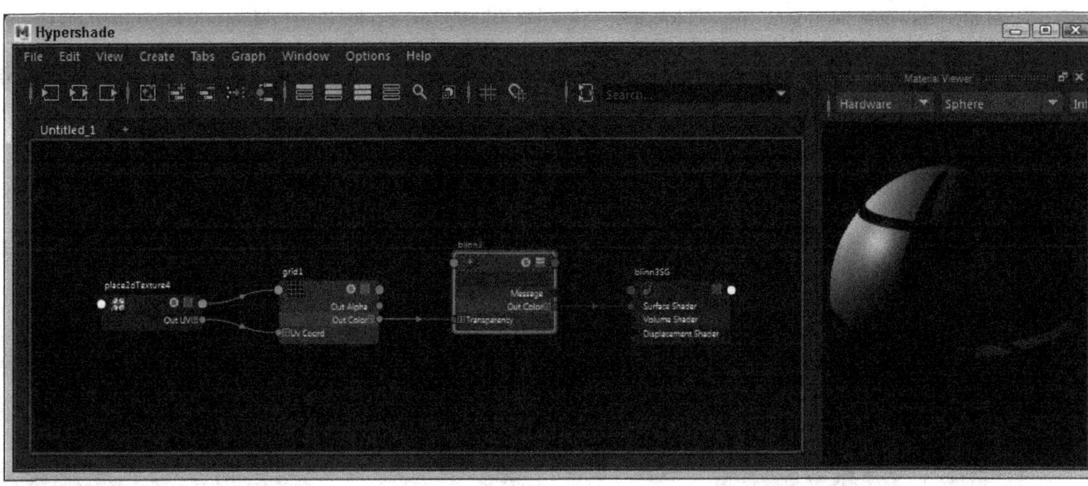

FIGURE 9-31

Texture-controlling transparency

Using Bump Maps

You can use textures to affect the relief of a surface using bump maps. Bump maps cause white textured areas to appear indented and black areas to appear "flat," as shown in Figure 9-32. You can use bump maps to add some relief to an object's surface. Connecting a texture as a bump map automatically adds a utility node that controls the amount of relief. The Bump Depth attribute controls how far the surface is indented and can be a negative value.

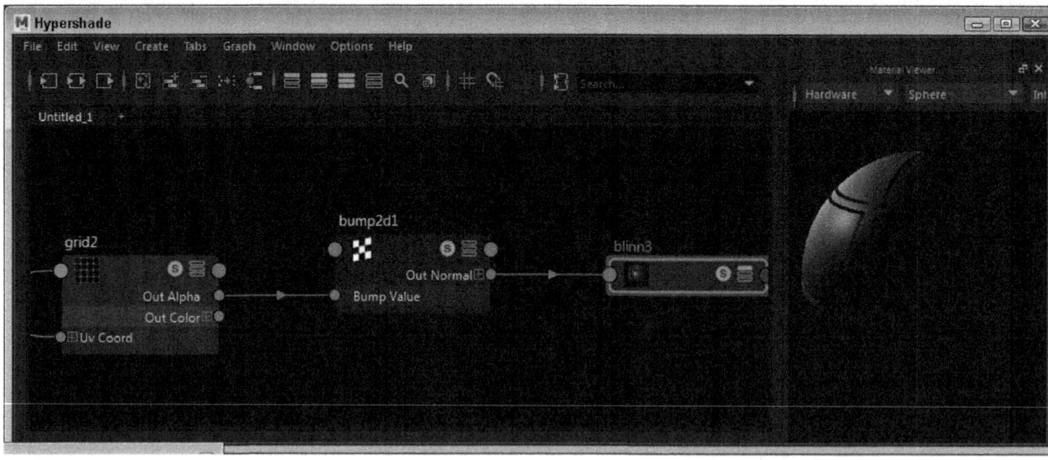

FIGURE 9-32

A Bump map

Loading File Textures

You can also use custom image files as textures with the File texture node. Once this node is connected to a material attribute, you can select it in the Work Area and, in the Attribute Editor, you can click on the File button by the Image Name field. This opens a file dialog box from which you can select the image file to load and use as a texture. Figure 9-33 shows an image of a mountain stream mapped onto the surface of a cube in the Render View window.

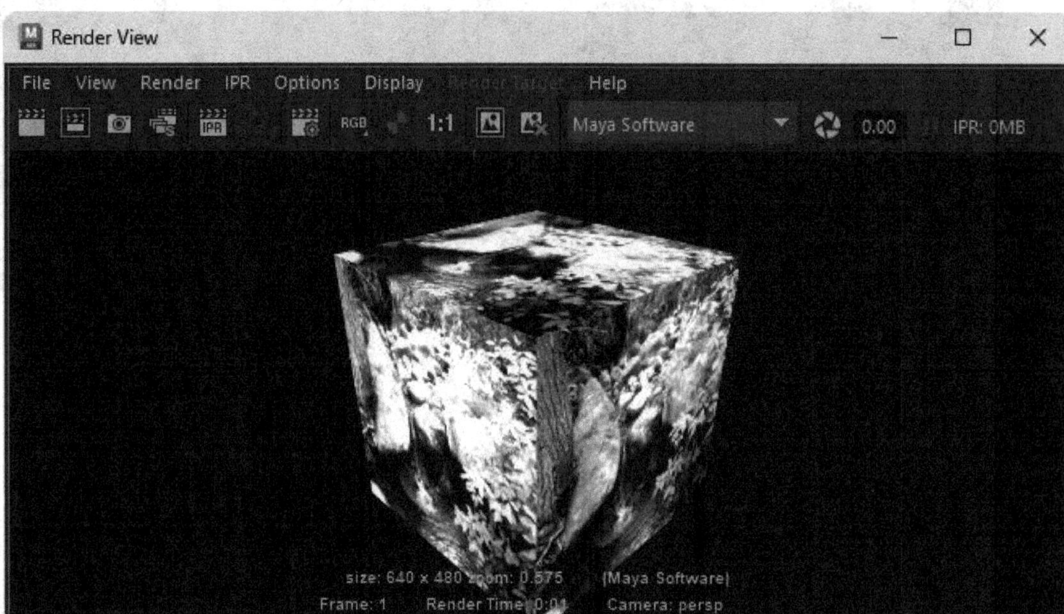

FIGURE 9-33

An image-mapped cube

Layering Textures

You can layer several textures on top of one another using the Layered Texture node found in the Other Textures category, as shown in Figure 9-34. With this node selected, you can drag and drop several textures onto the Layered Texture node with the middle mouse button and select the Input attribute port. Each separate texture is listed within the Attribute Editor. You can change their position by dragging them using the middle mouse button. The Layered Texture node includes an Alpha value that blends between the layered textures, and you can select from many different Blend modes, such as Over, In, Out, Add, Subtract, and Multiply.

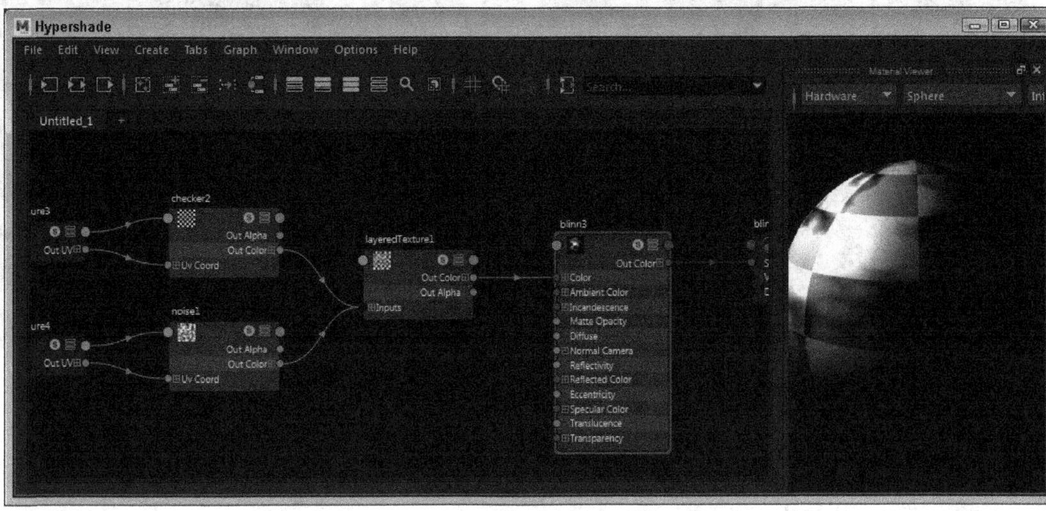

FIGURE 9-34

A layered texture

Lesson 9.4-Tutorial 1: Apply Textures

1. Create a sphere object using the Create, NURBS Primitives, Sphere menu command.
2. Select the Windows, Rendering Editors, Hypershade menu command to open the Hypershade interface.
3. Click on the Blinn material node in the Create Bar.
4. Connect the Out Color port of the Crater texture node to the Color port on the Blinn1 node in the Work Area.
5. Connect the Out Color port of the Grid texture node with the Specular Color port on the Blinn1 node in the Work Area.
6. Connect the Out Normal port on the Bump2D node from the Noise texture node with the Normal Camera port on the Blinn1 node in the Work Area.

   The Blinn1 material is updated.
7. Click on the Rearrange Graph button in the Hypershade toolbar.
8. Select the sphere object in the view panel, right-click on the Blinn1 material in the Browser pane of the Hypershade and select Assign Material to Selection from the pop-up menu.

   The sphere object is updated with the mapped textures in the Render View window, as shown in Figure 9-35.
9. Select File, Save Scene As and save the file as **Texture mapped sphere.mb**.

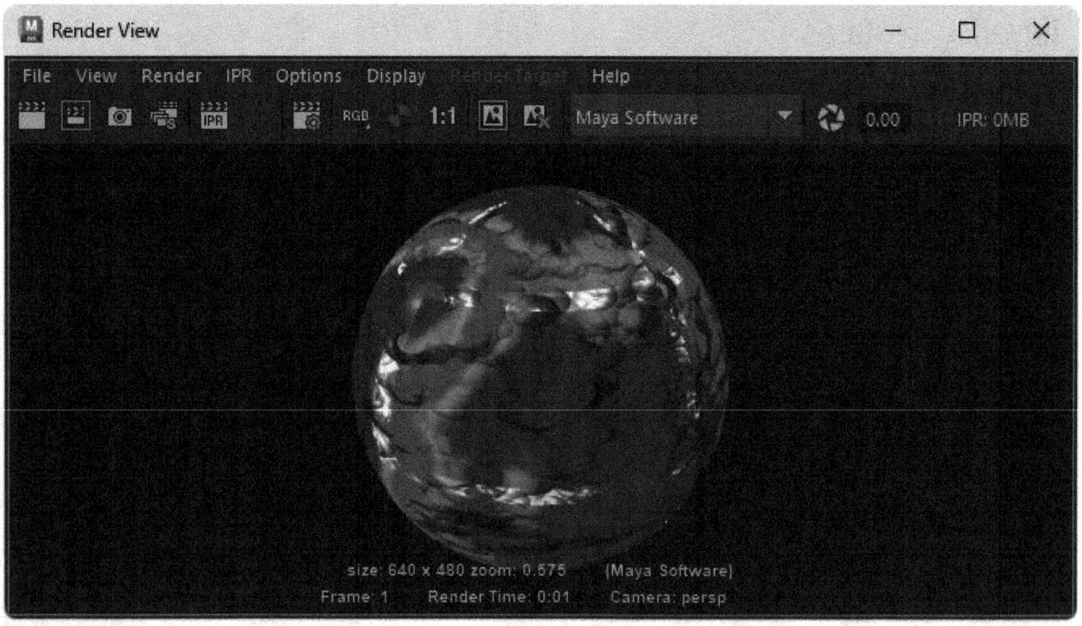

FIGURE 9-35

A texture-mapped sphere

Lesson 9.4-Tutorial 2: Load an Image Texture

1. Create a cube object using the Create, NURBS Primitives, Cube menu command.
2. Select the Windows, Rendering Editors, Hypershade menu command to open the Hypershade interface.
3. Click on the Lambert material node in the Create Bar.
4. Click on the File texture node in the Create Bar. Connect the Out Color port to the Color port on the Lambert1 node in the Work Area.
5. Click on the Load File button in the Attribute Editor and select the Coast from Diamond Head.jpg file and click the Open button.

   The image file is loaded and displayed in the File1 texture node in the Hypershade.
6. Click on the Rearrange Graph button in the Hypershade toolbar.
7. Select the cube object in the view panel, right-click on the Lambert1 material in the Browser pane in the Hypershade and select Assign Material to Selection from the pop-up menu.
8. With the Lambert1 material selected in the Hypershade, drag the Ambient Color attribute halfway toward the right.

   All sides of the cube are wrapped with the image file texture, as shown in the Render View window in Figure 9-36.
9. Select File, Save Scene As and save the file as **Image file cube.mb**.

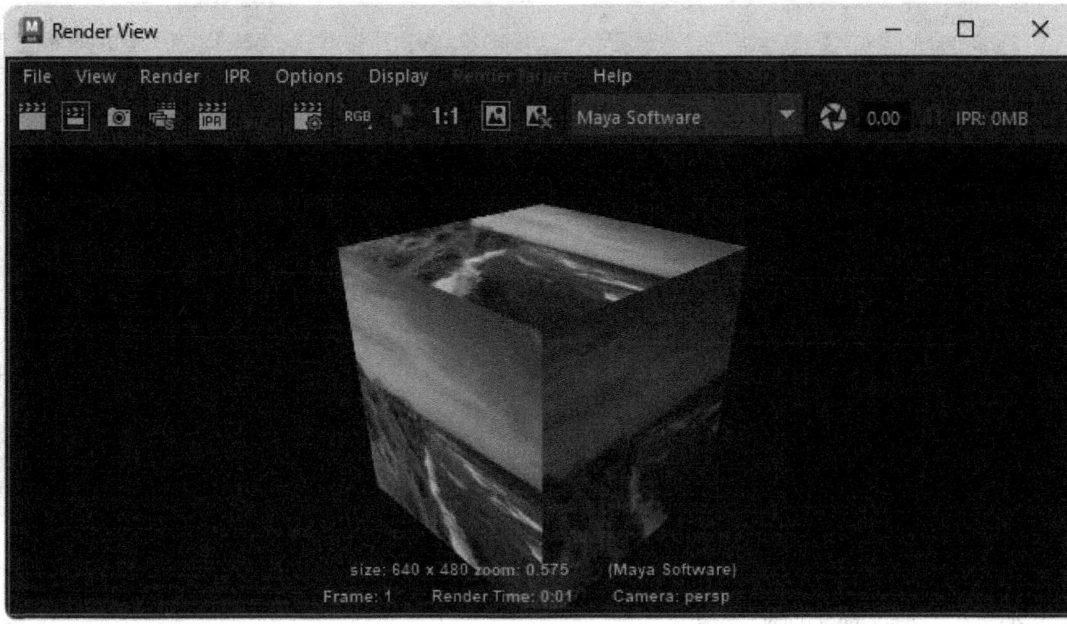

FIGURE 9-36

Image file cube

Lesson 9.5: Position Textures

When textures are applied to a material as colors or bump maps, Maya automatically creates a utility node that includes positional information for the texture. Using the attributes of this utility node, you can control the texture's offset, tiling, rotation, and how often it repeats. The Utilities category in the Create Bar includes utilities for 2D and 3D bump maps and texture placement.

Using Default Mapping

The default mapping method wraps the texture around the object using a spherical shape. To accomplish this default mapping, Maya connects the appropriate 2D or 3D placement utility node, as shown in Figure 9-37, in the Work Area. The attributes of this node control the placement of the texture. The Attribute Editor for this node includes settings for Coverage, translation, rotation, how the texture is mirrored, wrapped and staggered.

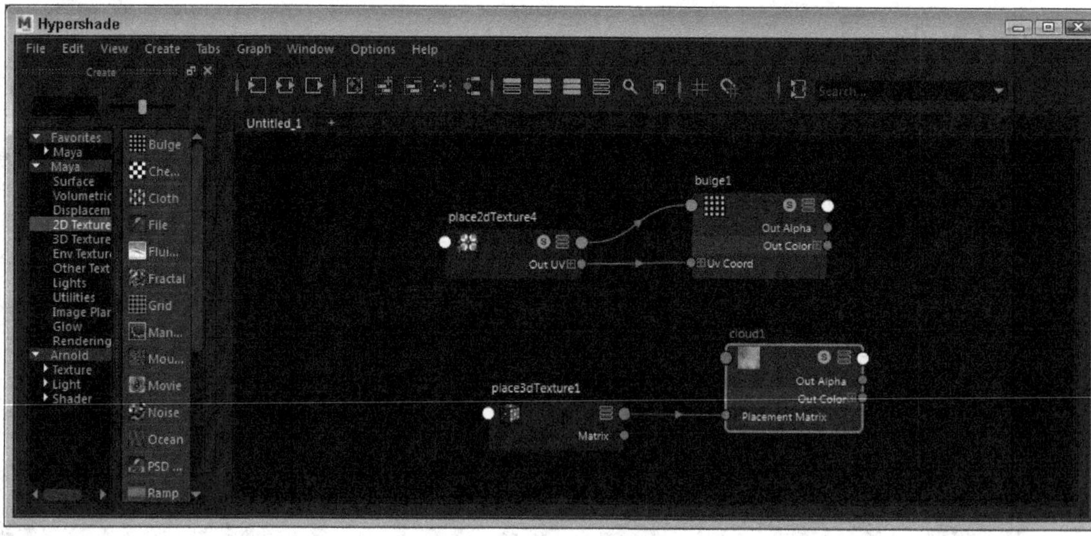

FIGURE 9-37

2D and 3D placement utility nodes

Using Projection Mapping

When the Projection Utility node is connected between a texture and a material, as shown in Figure 9-38, several additional mapping options become available. Projection mapping works like a film projector is casting the texture onto the object. You can also select from several different projection types, including Planar, Spherical, Cylindrical, Ball, Cubic, Tri Planar, Concentric, and Perspective. Each type projects the texture using a different shape. For best results, try to use a mapping type that matches the shape of the object such as Planar for flat planes, Cylindrical for pipes and barrels, and Spherical for balls and globes.

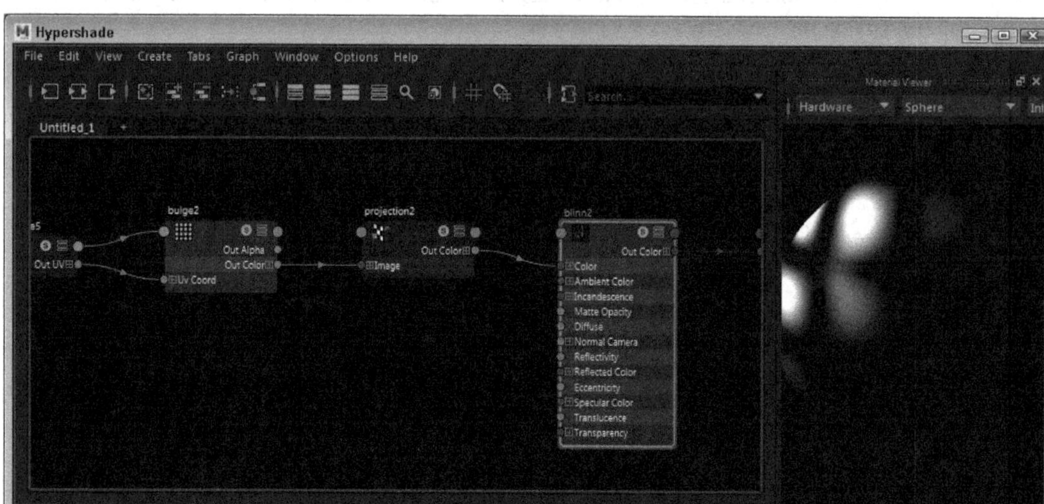

FIGURE 9-38

The Projection utility node

Placing 2D Textures

Once textures have been applied to a NURBS object, you can reposition and reorient the textures using the Texturing, NURBS Texture Placement tool. This tool lets you select a face and change its attribute by dragging with the middle mouse button on the red manipulator handles, as shown in Figure 9-39, within the view panels. Moving the manipulator handles changes the attributes for the 2D Texture Placement node.

Tip

> You can also access the NURBS Texture Placement tool using the Interactive Placement button in the Attribute Editor when the 2D Placement node is selected.

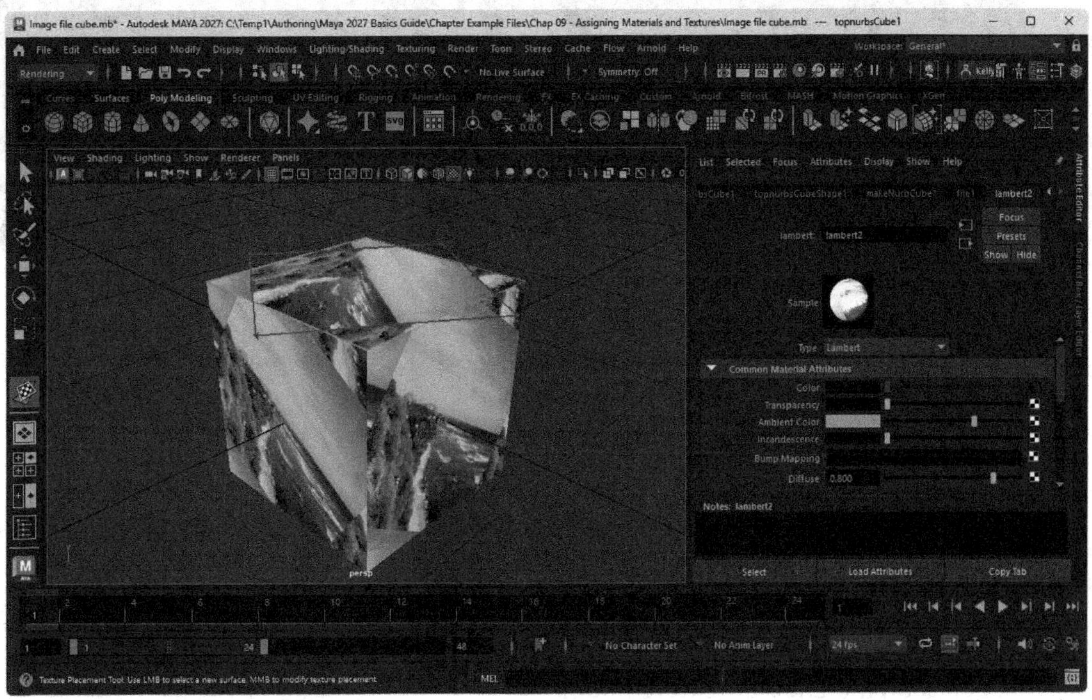

FIGURE 9-39

2D texture placement manipulator

Placing 3D Textures

The 3D Placement utility node includes a button that lets you interactively place the texture by moving a manipulator in the view panels. When this utility node is selected, you can click the Interactive Placement button in the Attribute Editor. This places a manipulator on the surface of the object, as shown in Figure 9-40. Drag the manipulator's handles to position the projected texture. There is also a Fit to BBox button that fits the texture to the object's Bounding Box.

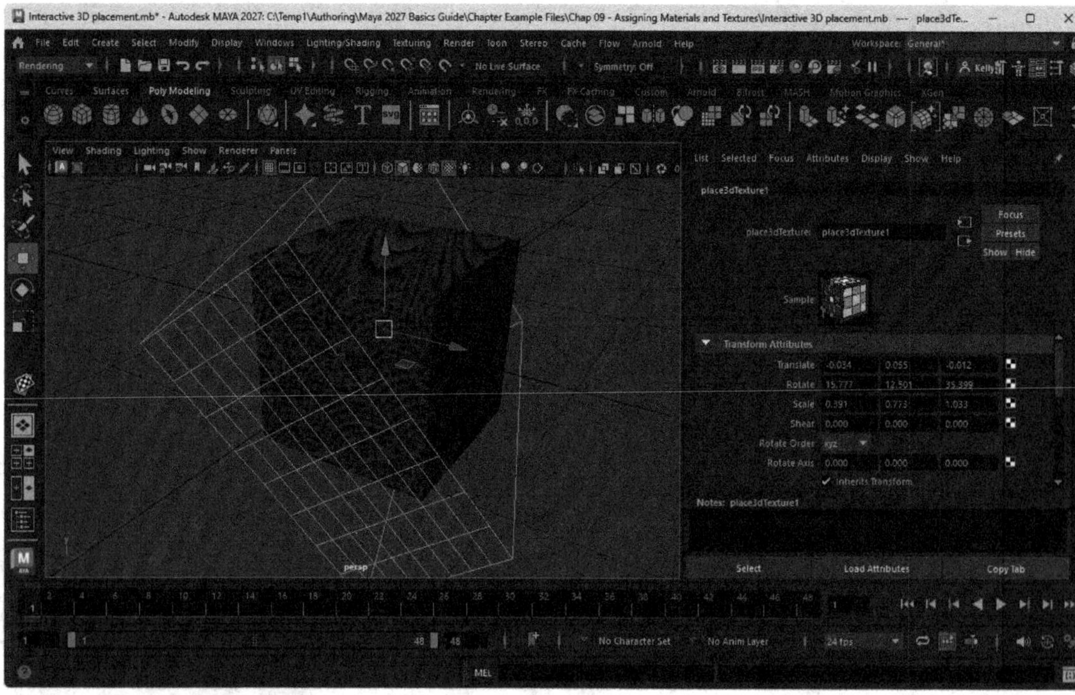

FIGURE 9-40

3D texture placement manipulator

Lesson 9.5-Tutorial 1: Position 2D Textures

1. Create a NURBS cube object using the Create, NURBS Primitives, Cube menu command.
2. Select the Windows, Rendering Editors, Hypershade menu command to open the Hypershade interface.
3. Click on the Blinn material node in the Create Bar.
4. Click on the Create Render Node button for the Color attribute in the Attribute Editor.
5. Click on the Checker texture node.
6. Select the Checker1 texture node in the Attribute Editor and change the Default Color setting in the Color Balance section to red.
7. Click the Rearrange Graph button in the Hypershade toolbar.
8. With the cube selected, right-click on the Blinn1 material in the Browser pane of the Hypershade and select the Assign Material to Selection from the pop-up menu.
9. Select the Texturing, NURBS Texture Placement Tool menu command and click on the top face of the NURBS cube.
10. Drag each edge manipulator handle towards the center of the cube face with the middle mouse button.

    The sample sphere material in the Hypershade colors a portion of the sample sphere red, as shown in Figure 9-41.
11. Select File, Save Scene As and save the file as **Shifted checker map.mb**.

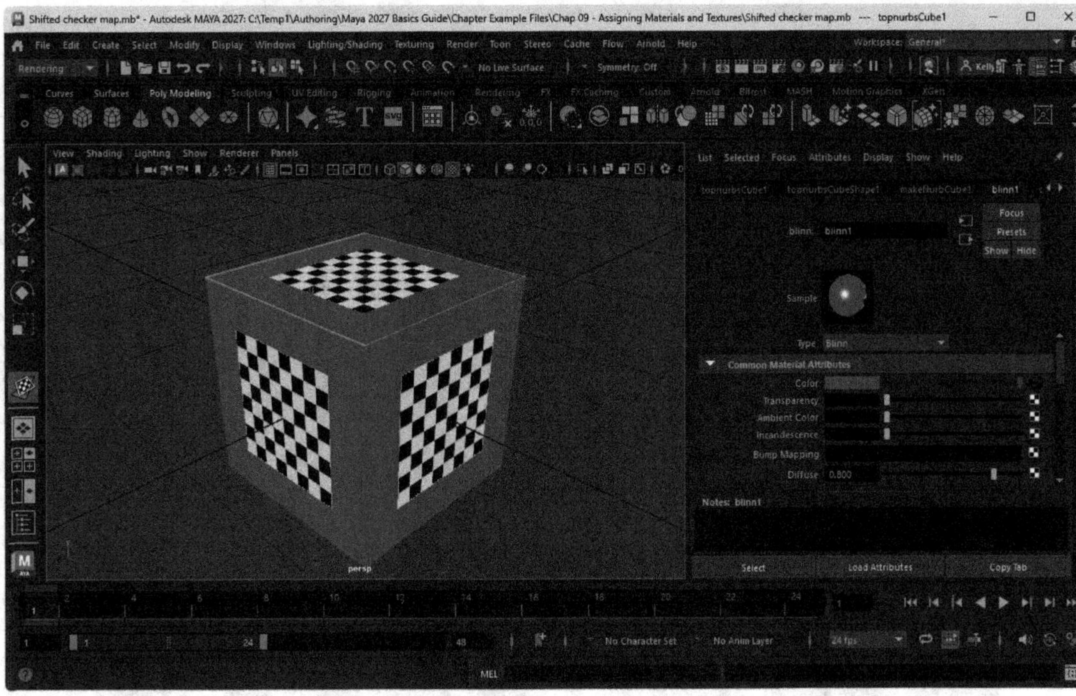

FIGURE 9-41

Shifted texture map

Lesson 9.5-Tutorial 2: Position 3D Textures

1. Create a NURBS sphere object using the Create, NURBS Primitives, Sphere menu command.
2. Select the Windows, Rendering Editors, Hypershade menu command to open the Hypershade interface.
3. Click on the Blinn material node in the Create Bar.
4. Click on the Create Render Node button for the Color attribute in the Attribute Editor.
5. Click on the Marble 3D texture node.
6. With the sphere selected, right-click on the Blinn1 material in the Browser pane of the Hypershade and select the Assign Material to Selection from the pop-up menu.
7. Click the Rearrange Graph button in the Hypershade toolbar.
8. Select the Place3dTexture1 utility node in the Hypershade.
9. Click the Fit to Group BBox button in the Attribute Editor.
10. Drag the light blue circle manipulator to rotate the texture.

    The marbled veins shift in the sample material in the Hypershade, as shown in Figure 9-42.
11. Select File, Save Scene As and save the file as **Marbled sphere.mb**.

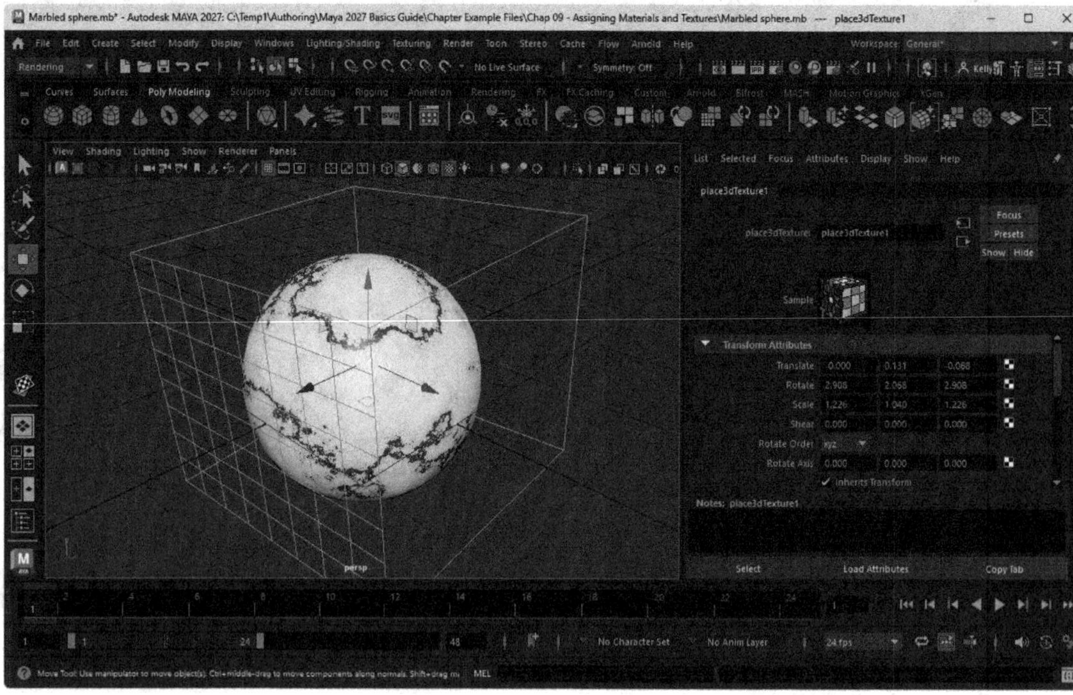

FIGURE 9-42

Marbled sphere

Lesson 9.6: Use Displacement Maps

For adding bumps to an object, there are two methods you can use--Bump maps and Displacement maps. Bump maps are quick and easy, but Displacement maps can change the actual shape of the object.

Bump Maps vs. Displacement Maps

Bump maps were covered earlier in this chapter, but they deserve a side-by-side comparison to Displacement maps since both accomplish the same goal of adding relief to the surface of an object. Bump maps add relief to the surface by simply changing how the normals look when rendered, but they do not change the geometry of the object in any way. They also will not change the way shadows look. Applying a Bump map to a sphere object will maintain the smooth edges of the sphere.

Displacement maps, on the other hand, will change the geometry of the object and will also have an impact on its shadows. Because of the way displacement maps are created, they can take a lot more rendering power and will take much longer to render. It is also important to make sure that the object receiving the displacement map has sufficient components to work with, so remember to subdivide the polygon mesh before applying a displacement map. Figure 9-43 shows the bump map sphere on the left and the displacement map sphere on the right.

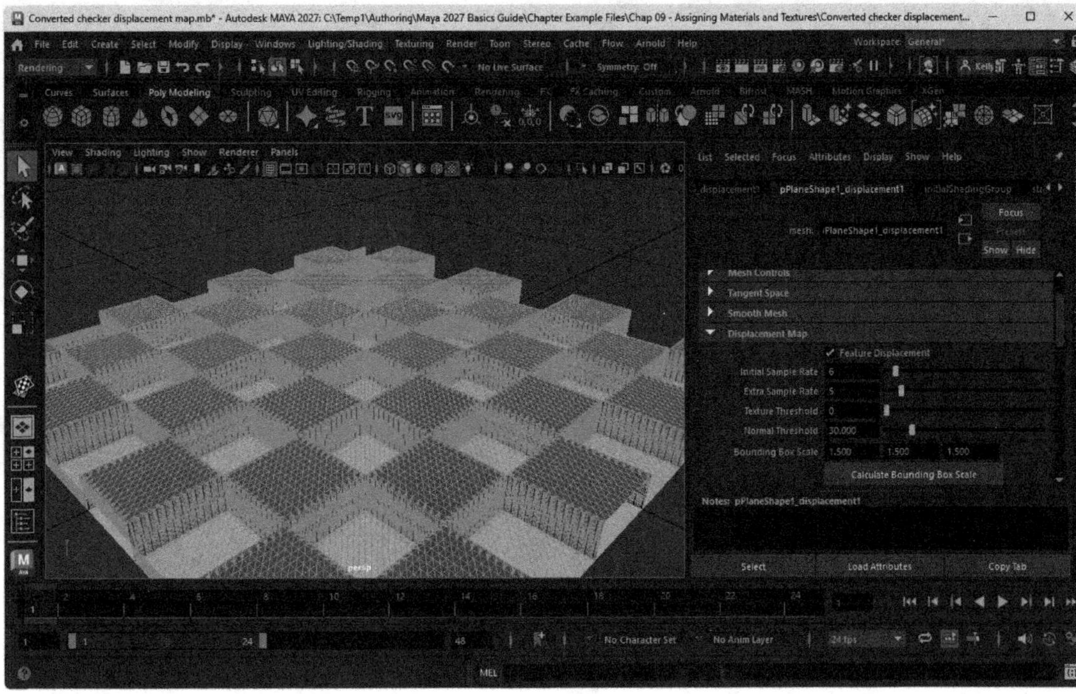

FIGURE 9-48

Converted checker displacement map

Lesson 9.7: Use Utilities Nodes

The Utilities category of the Hypershade includes many utilities that perform specialized functions. For example, the Blend Colors utility lets you blend two different textures or colors together.

Using the General Utilities

The General Utilities category in the Create Bar, shown in Figure 9-49, includes many nodes that are applied automatically when needed, such as the Bump 2d, Bump 3d, and 2d and 3d Placement. It also includes several miscellaneous utilities used to display different colors based on a given situation, such as the Distance Between, Condition, Height Field, Light Info, Multiply, Divide, or Average.

FIGURE 9-49

General utility rendering nodes

Using the Color Utilities

The Color Utilities, shown along with the other Utilities, includes nodes that can alter several color properties of a texture. These utilities include Blend Colors, Clamp, Contrast, Gamma Correct, and more.

Using the Switch Utilities

The Switch Utilities category in the Create Bar includes nodes that can apply different materials to patches in the same object.

Lesson 9.7-Tutorial 1: Blend Colors

1. Create a NURBS sphere object using the Create, NURBS Primitives, Sphere menu command.
2. Select the Windows, Rendering Editors, Hypershade menu command to open the Hypershade interface.
3. Click on the Blinn material node in the Create Bar.
4. Click on the Create Render Node button for the Color attribute in the Attribute Editor.
5. Click on the Blend Colors utility node in the Utilities category.

   The Blend Colors node includes two colors that are blended together to create a purple color. Using this node gives you the ability to set animation keys for the colors. Figure 9-50shows the nodes for this material.
6. Drag the Rock texture from the Create Bar. Connect the out Color port for the Rock1 node to the Color1 for the blendColors1 node. Then, create the Marble texture node from the Create Bar and connect the Out Color port to the Color2 port on the blendColors1 node.

The texture placement nodes are added automatically. You can also blend textures using the Blend Colors node.

7. Click the Rearrange Graph button in the Hypershade toolbar.
8. With the sphere selected, right-click on the Blinn1 material in the Browser pane of the Hypershade and select the Assign Material to Selection from the pop-up menu.
9. Select File, Save Scene As and save the file as **Blended textures.mb**.

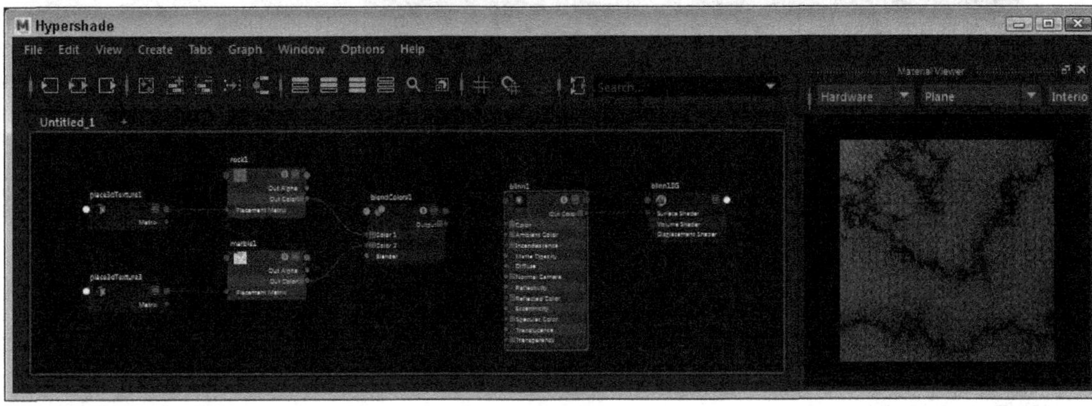

FIGURE 9-50

Blended textures

Lesson 9.8: Paint in 3D

The Texturing, 3D Paint tool lets you paint directly on a 3D surface using several different modes with Artisan or Paint Effects brushes. You can also paint other attributes including bumps, transparency, and specular color. To see the 3D Paint tool settings, click on the Show Tool Settings button on the right end of the Status Line or double click on the 3D Paint icon at the bottom of the Toolbox after it is selected.

Assigning a Paint Texture

Before you can paint on an object, the object must be selected, have a material besides the default applied, and have a paint texture assigned to it. To assign a paint texture to an object, select the Texturing, 3D Paint tool, open the Tool Settings, and click on the Assign/Edit Textures button in the File Textures section. This button opens a simple dialog box, shown in Figure 9-51, where you can specify the dimensions of the paint texture.

Note

`If the brush cursor displays a large red X in the viewport, a paint texture hasn't been assigned to the object, and you won't be able to paint.`

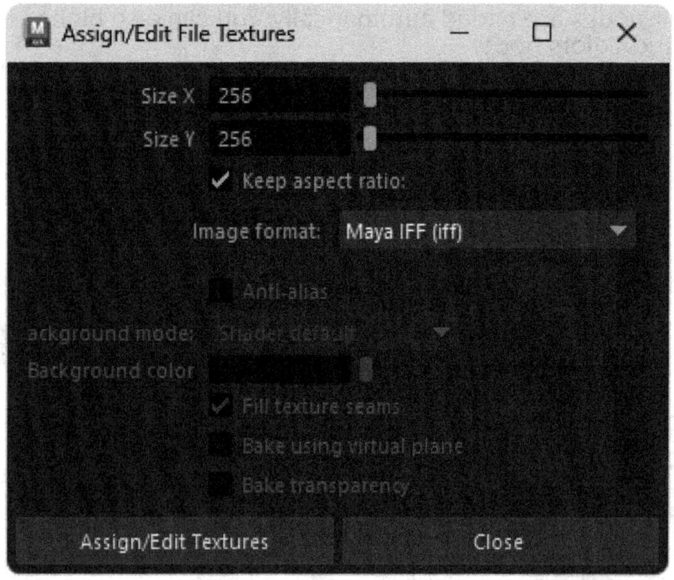

FIGURE 9-51

The Assign/Edit File Textures dialog box

Selecting a Brush

The 3D Paint tool may use any of the Artisan or Paint Effects brushes. You can select these brushes from the Brush section of the Tool Settings panel, from which you can also set the Radius values for the selected brush. Holding down the B key while dragging in the view panel enables you to interactively change the brush radius. Figure 9-52shows a simple paint stroke drawn on a sphere object.

FIGURE 9-52

Paint on an object

Applying Color

To change the paint color, click the Color swatch in the Color section of the Tool Settings panel and select a new color from the Color Chooser. You can also control the opacity of the painted color with the Opacity setting. The Flood Paint button colors the entire object using the Flood Color or colors only the selected components if the Selected option is enabled.

Using Different Paint Operations

Depending on the type of brush that is selected, the selected color can be painted, erased, or cloned with the Artisan brush or painted, smeared and blurred with a Paint Effects brush. These options are located in the Paint Operations section of the Tool Settings panel. This section also allows you to select a Blend mode. Figure 9-53shows a sphere that was painted with one color, and then much of that color was erased using the Erase Paint Operation.

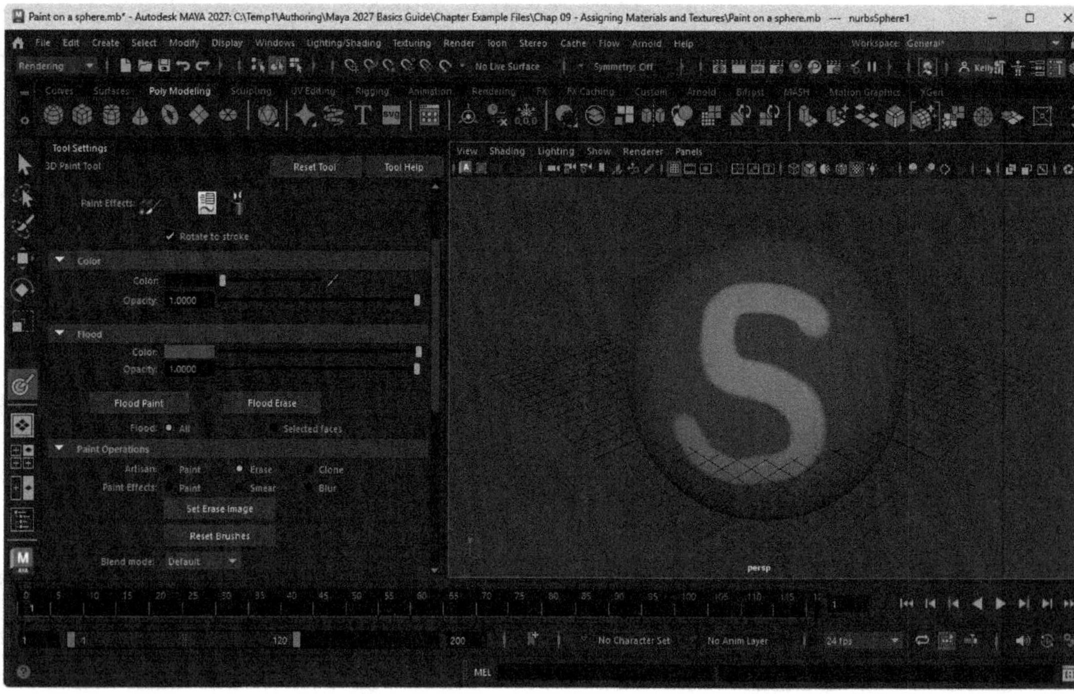

FIGURE 9-53

Erasing paint

Painting Other Attributes

In the File Textures section of the Tool Settings panel, you can choose the attribute to paint. The options include Color, Transparency, Incandescence, Bump Map, Specular Color, Reflectivity, Ambient, Diffuse, Translucence, Reflected Color, and Displacement. Figure 9-54shows a simple sphere with some painted bumps.

Note

You must add a new paint texture to the object with the Assign/New Textures button for each new attribute you paint.

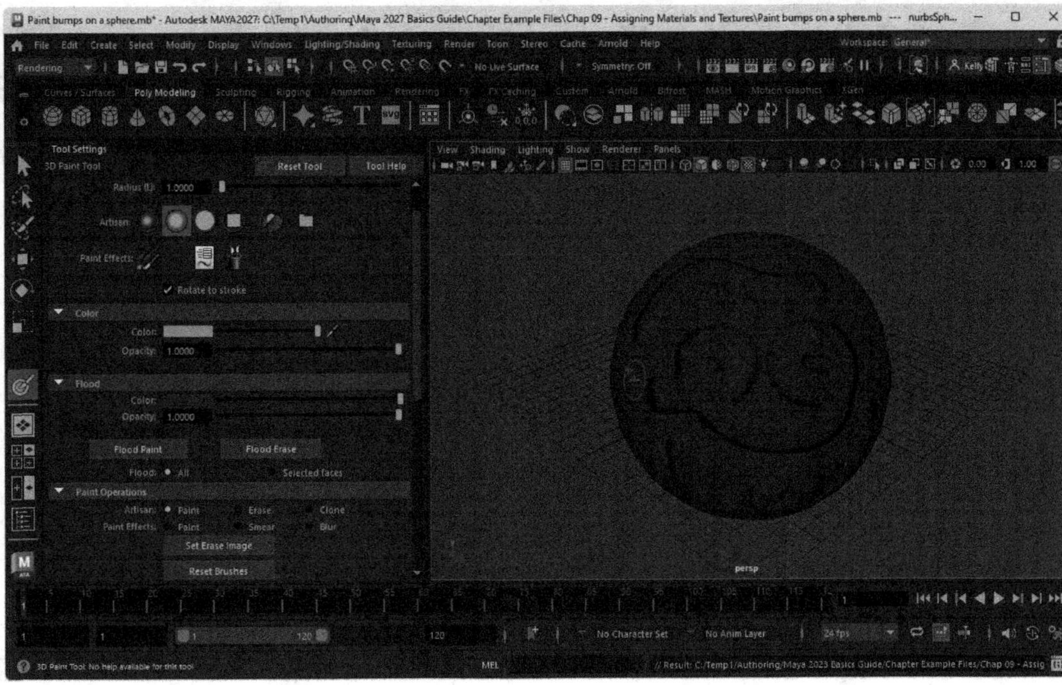

FIGURE 9-54

Painted bump maps

Lesson 9.8-Tutorial 1: Use the 3D Paint Tool

1. Open the Football.mb file using the File, Open Scene menu command.
2. With the football object selected, choose the Lighting/Shading, Assign New Material, Lambert menu command.
3. Click on the Color attribute in the Attribute Editor and select the brown color from the Color Chooser.
4. Select the Texturing, 3D Paint Tool menu command and double click on the 3D Paint tool in the Toolbox to open the Tool Settings panel.
5. In the Tool Settings panel, click on the Assign/Edit Textures button in the File Textures section. In the Assign/Edit Textures dialog box, click the Assign/Edit Textures button.
6. Click on one of the Artisan brushes in the Brush section.
7. In the Color section, click on the Color swatch and select a white color from the Color Chooser.
8. Hold down the B key and drag in the view panel to change the brush radius size.
9. Paint directly on the football to create some threads.

   The white colors painted on the football become part of the texture applied to the football material, as shown in Figure 9-55.
10. Select File, Save Scene As, and save the file as **Painted football.mb**.

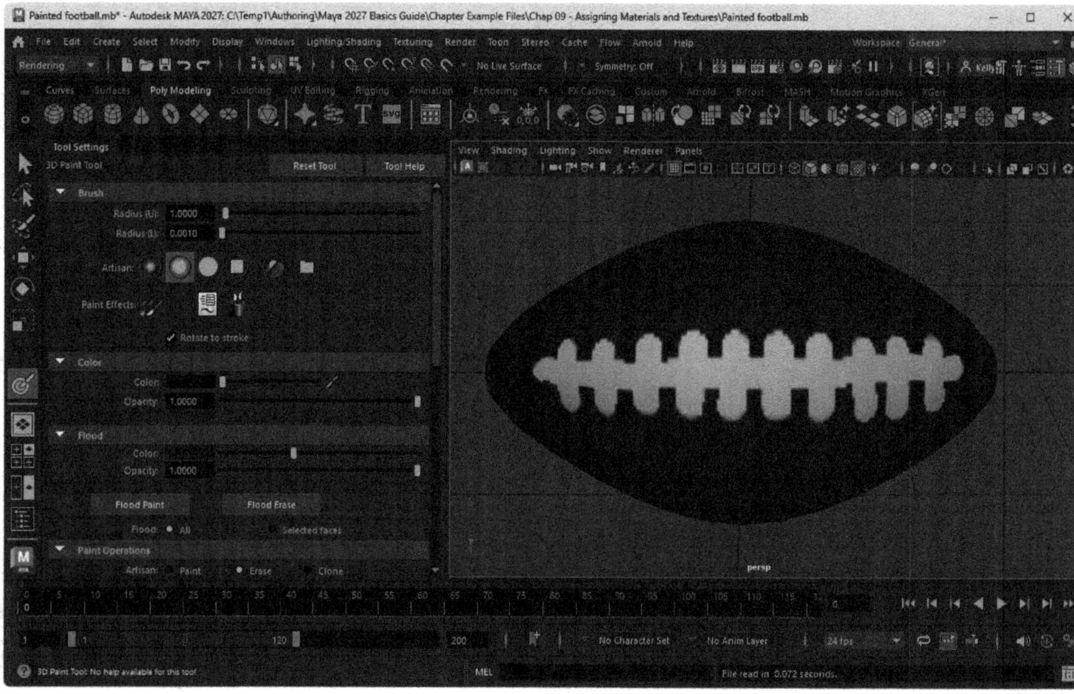

FIGURE 9-55

Football with painted threads

Lesson 9.9: Edit UVs

From what has been covered so far, applying textures to a complex model like a car would require that each separate texture be placed in a separate file, so one texture for the front grill and another the tire rims, and another for the license plate. This could easily result in hundreds of texture files to keep track of. An alternative to this is to place all the textures for a model in a single file and then map each texture to its correct position on the model using UV coordinates.

Understanding UVs

Earlier in the chapter, we learned how applying a texture to an object wraps it about its surface. Now imagine drawing the exact position on each polygon face on the wrapped texture and then unwrapping it again. In the unwrapped texture, you can see each polygon face's position and its location on the unwrapped texture map can be identified using horizontal and vertical coordinates from the upper left corner of the texture image. These coordinates are UV coordinates and they define precisely which part of the applied texture covers each polygon face in the model.

Accessing the UV Editor

Maya has a tool for working with UV coordinates and textures. It is called the UV Editor, and you can open it using the Windows, Modeling Editors, UV Editor menu command or the UV, UV Editor menu. Figure 9-56 shows a mountain stream texture wrapped around a simple cube object. Each face of the cube is shown as a flat square in the UV Editor, and the texture is superimposed over the top. For this object, you can see that only a portion of the nature texture covers the different polygon faces, but using the UV Editor, you can scale and move the polygon faces so that more of the texture is used. The UV menu is found in the Modeling menu set.

Note

You can Pan and Zoom the view in the UV Editor just like the normal viewport with the Alt/Option key and the middle and right mouse buttons.

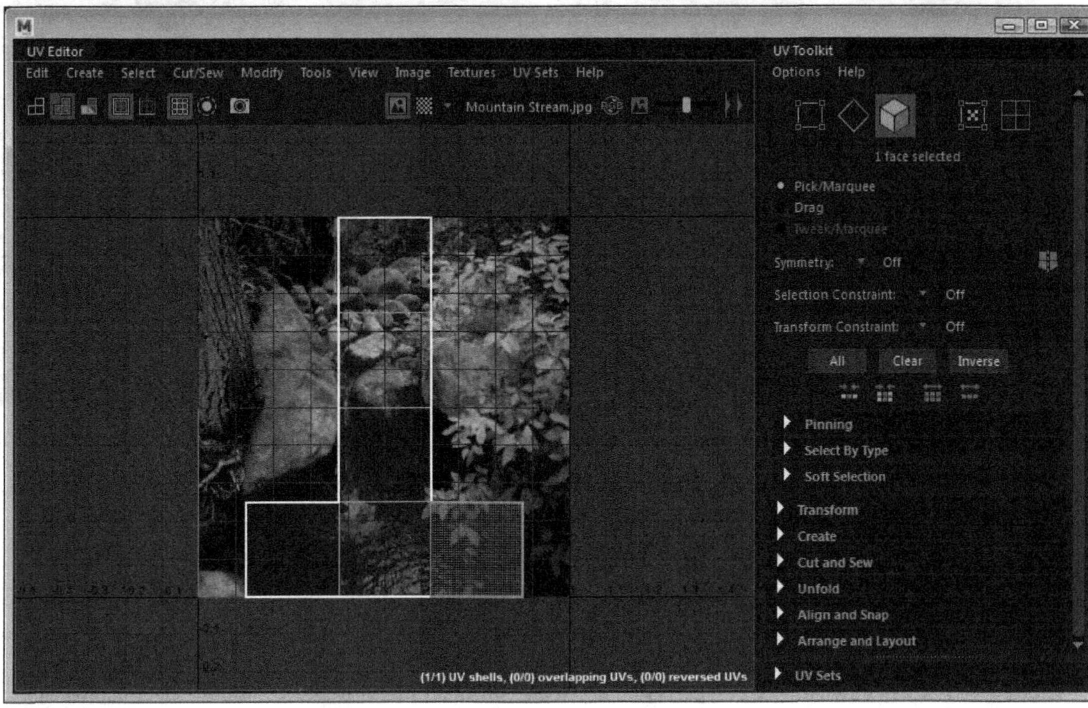

FIGURE 9-56

UV Editor

Selecting and Editing UV Components

You can select the different component modes from the top of the UV Toolkit and from the Select menu. The available components include Vertex, Edge, Face, UV and UV Shell. Within the UV Editor, components are selected and transformed just as they are in the normal viewports by dragging over the component or clicking on it. Holding down the Shift key lets you add to the selection, and the Ctrl/Command key removes from the current selection. Once a component is selected, you can move, rotate and scale it using the normal Toolbox tools. Figure 9-57 shows the same cube that uses more of the texture after several faces have been scaled.

Note

Moving components in the UV Editor only changes how the texture is mapped to the object. It will not change the shape of the object.

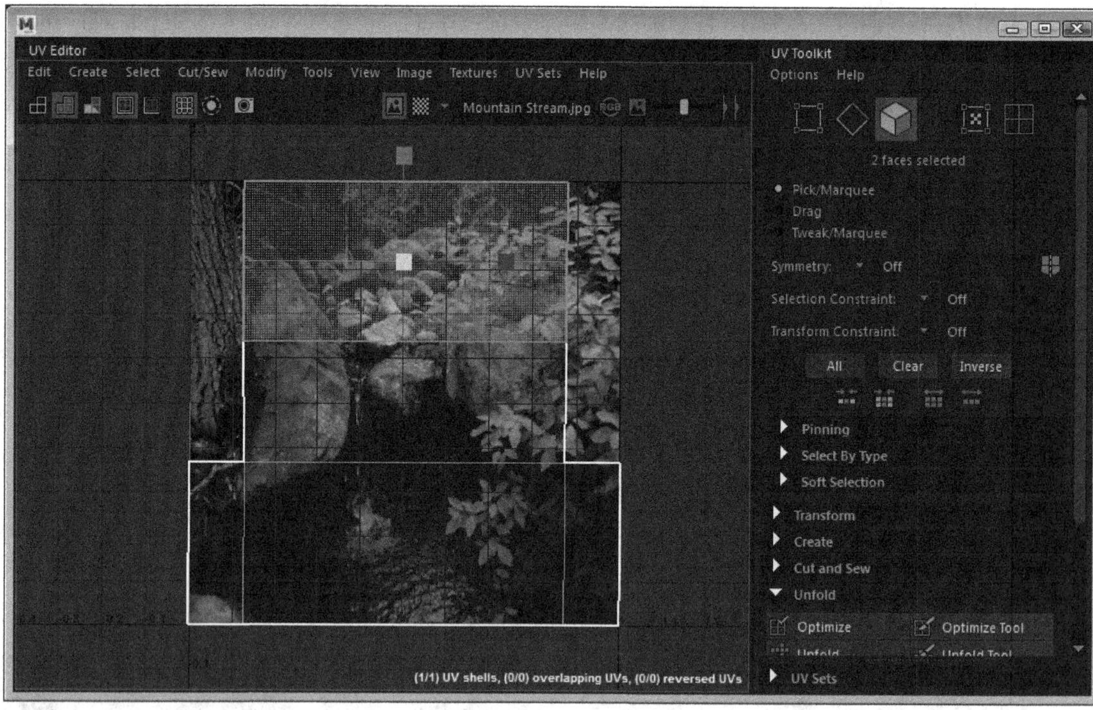

FIGURE 9-57

Scaled cube UVs

Working with UVs and Shells

Selecting a single vertex using Vertex component mode in the UV Editor will highlight several vertices at once. This is because that single vertex is connected to several different faces in the actual object and moving the selected vertex will move all the polygons that it is a part of. Each vertex in the UV Editor also marks a specific UV coordinate on the texture map and if you want to move just a single UV coordinate without all its attached faces, you can select the UV component mode and then move each vertex independent of the others.

If you select a cylinder object and open it in the UV Editor, you will notice that it consists of three separate shapes, a rectangle for the cylinder sides and two circles for the top and bottom caps of the cylinder, as shown in Figure 9-58. Each of these shapes is a UV shell. Maya recognized the cylinder and split the UVs into shapes along the borders. If you select the UV Shell component mode, then you can easily select all the polygon faces that are included in the UV shell and move them into place.

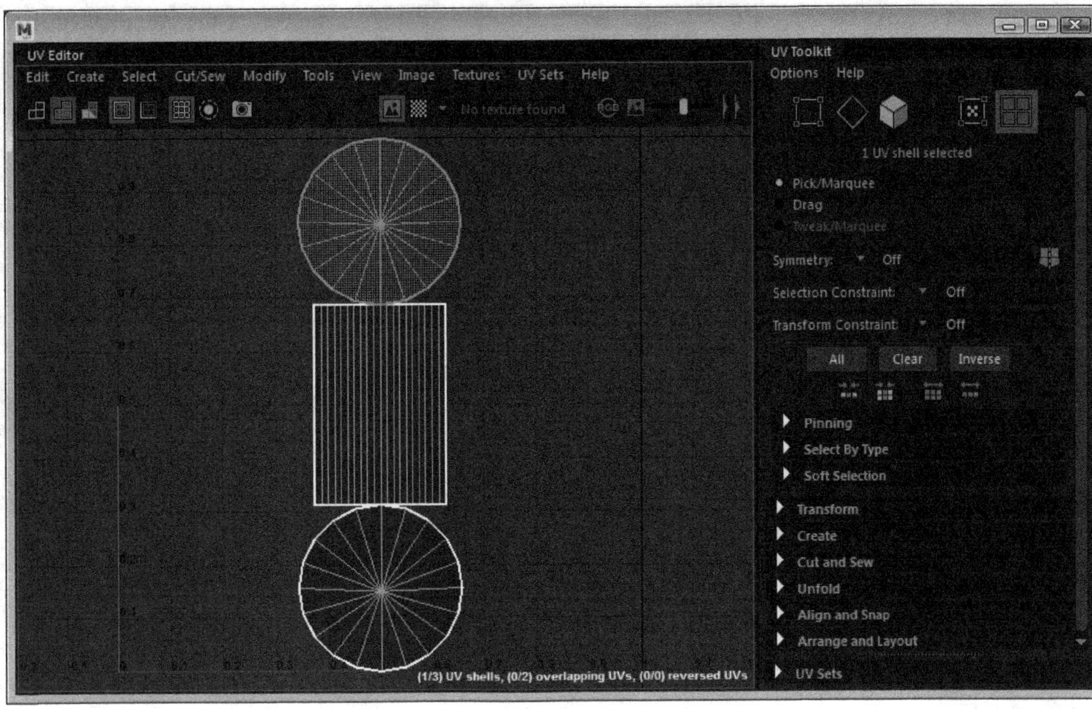

FIGURE 9-58

UV Shells

Selecting several faces and choosing the Cut/Sew, Create UV Shell menu command creates a new UV shell group using the selected faces. This provides a convenient way to divide the model into logical texture groups that are easy to select and move into place.

Using Different Mappings

When an object is opened in the UV Editor, Maya tries its best to expose all the UVs, but often the results are not what you want. Using the Create menu in the UV Editor, you can select a UV shell or a bunch of faces and lay them out in several different ways. The options include Automatic, Camera-based, Normal-based, Cylindrical, Planar, Spherical, Best Plane and Contour Stretch. The Best Plane option creates a planar map based on the selected vertices and the Contour Stretch option pulls four corners in opposite directions to flatten out the selection. Each of these mapping types have lots of options that you can specify. Figure 9-59 shows a sphere with the Automatic mapping method. A separate UV shell was created for each axis surrounding the sphere.

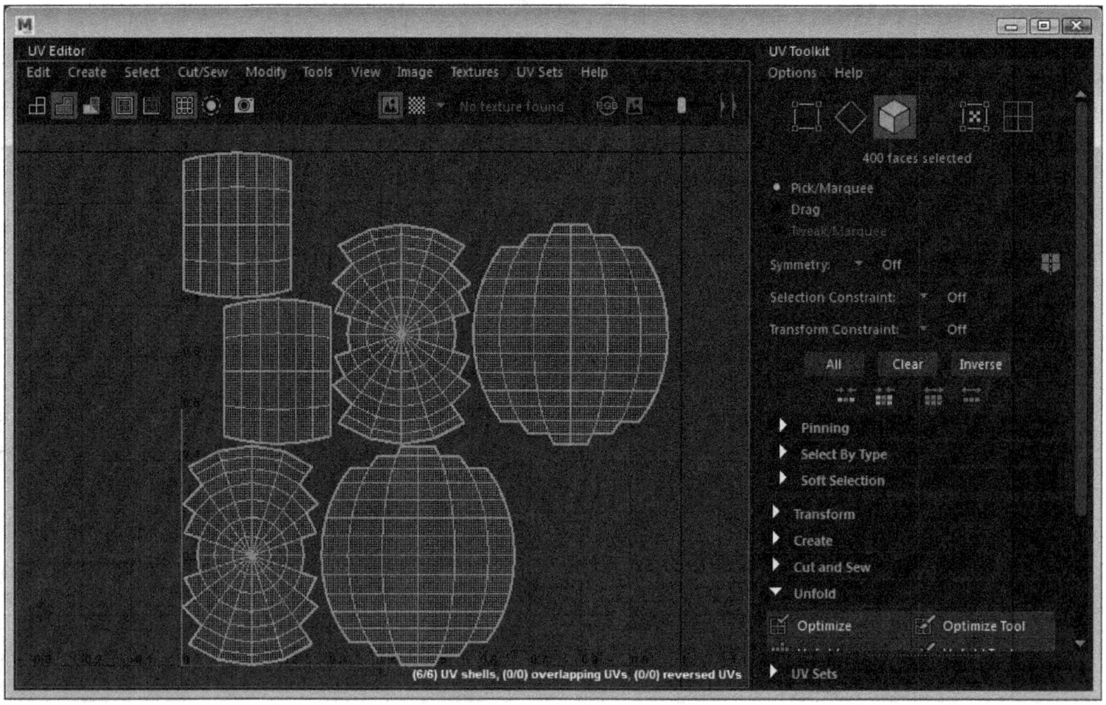

FIGURE 9-59

Sphere with Automatic mapping

Unfolding UV Shells

Textures are projected in 2D and if you project a 2D texture onto a curved 3D object, you can often get some areas where the texture stretches across the face causing a distortion. To counter this distortion, you need to lay the UVs out flat. Within the Unfold category in the UV Toolkit are several tools to flatten out UVs. The Optimize button moves all UVs to be evenly spaced from one another. There is also an Optimize Tool that lets you drag over UVs to move them. The Unfold button unwraps all the UVs so that none are overlapping. There is also an Unwrap tool. The Straighten UVs button aligns all UVs into straight rows and columns. Figure 9-60 shows the sphere from the previous figure after being optimized and straightened.

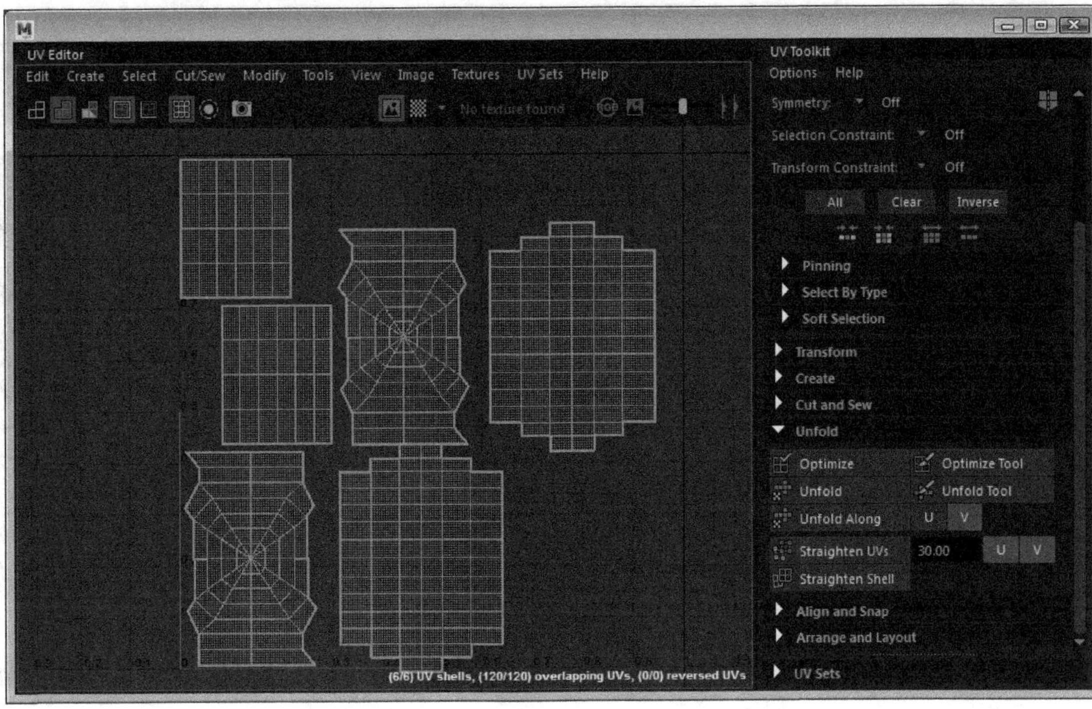

FIGURE 9-60

Sphere after being optimized and straightened

Cutting and Sewing UVs

When a shell is too large to flatten out easily, you can separate it into small sections using the Cut features. Selecting an edge and choosing the Cut/Sew, Cut menu command adds a seam to the object and separates the UV shell into two. There is also a Cut Tool, in the UV Toolkit, that lets you cut edges by dragging over them. The Cut/Sew, Sew menu command will reattach the selected edges to its cut edge, but you'll often want to use the Cut and Move menu command because it moves the shell with the selected edge to its matching border. When an edge is selected, its matching edge is also highlighted. Figure 9-61 shows a UV shell that was moved and sewed to its matching boundary.

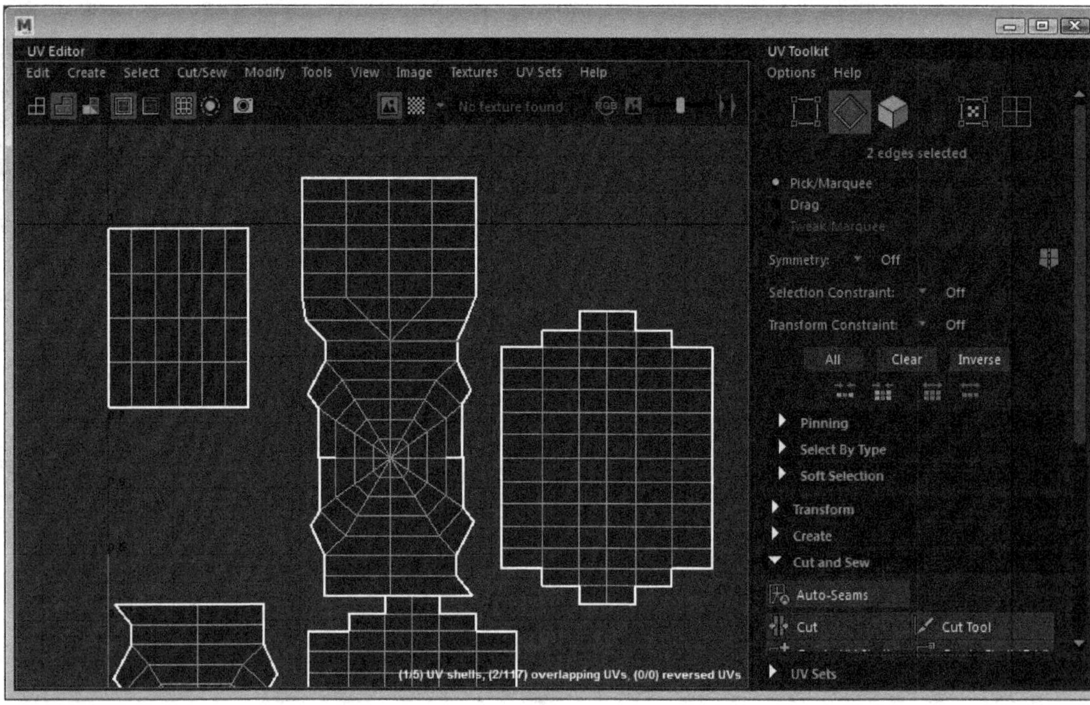

FIGURE 9-61

UV Shell moved and sewed

Arranging UV Shells

When applying a texture to a complex model, you'll want to make the UV shells that represent some areas larger to show more details. For example, the texture on the back of the head doesn't need a lot of detail, but the eyes could use the extra detail. In order to maximize the texture area, you can use the Arrange and Layout category to rearrange the UV shells. There are options to Orient Shells, Stack and Unstack, Stack Similar, Gather and Randomize. The Layout button places all shells end to end to fill the texture area, as shown in Figure 9-62.

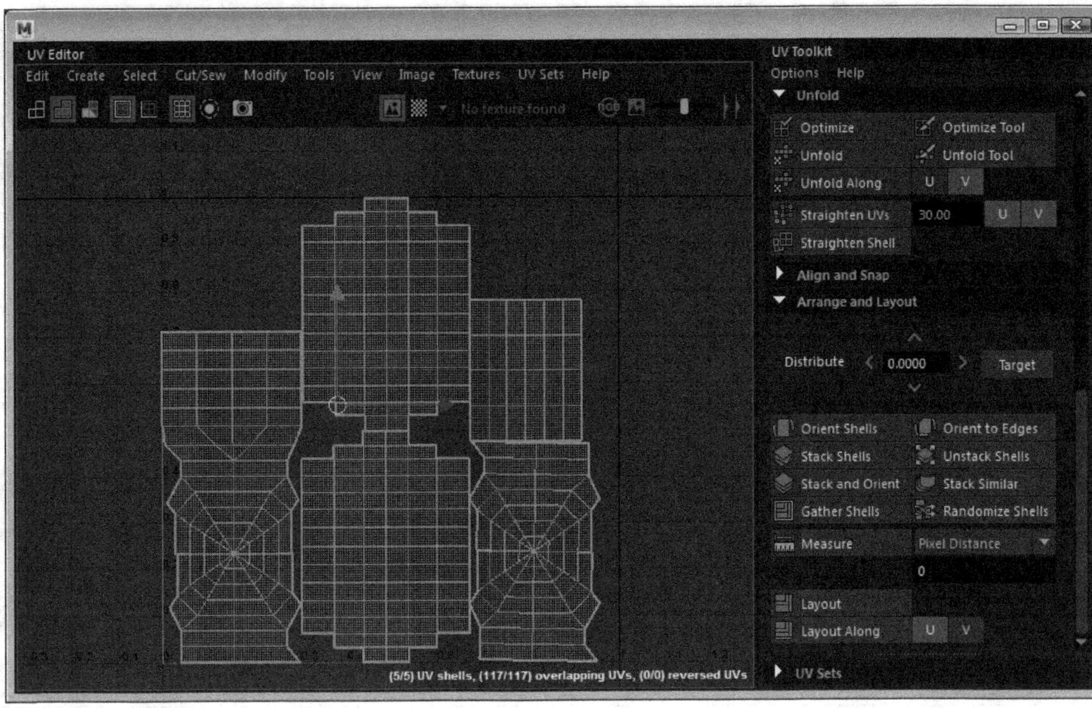

FIGURE 9-62

UV Shells layout

Generating a UV Snapshot

If you layout all your UV shells before creating the texture, you can use the Image, UV Snapshot menu command to create an image of the laid-out UVs. This image can be opened within Photoshop and provides a good guide for drawing the textures.

Lesson 9.9-Tutorial 1: Edit UVs

1. Create a cylinder object using the Create, Polygon Primitives, Cylinder menu command.
2. With the cylinder object selected, choose the Lighting/Shading, Assign New Material menu command and choose the Blinn material.
3. Click on the Create Render Node button for the Color attribute in the Attribute Editor and select the File node. Then click on the File icon in the Image Name attribute and choose the Soda can texture.tif image file.
4. Select the Windows, Modeling Editors, UV Editor menu command.
5. From the top of the UV Toolkit, choose the UV Shell component mode, then drag over the top circle component to select it. With the Scale and Move tools, position the UVs for the top of the cylinder over the top of the soda can texture.
6. Repeat step 5 for the bottom of the soda can.
7. Select the rectangular section of UVs that are for the sides of the cylinder and scale it to fit over the label texture, as shown in Figure 9-63.

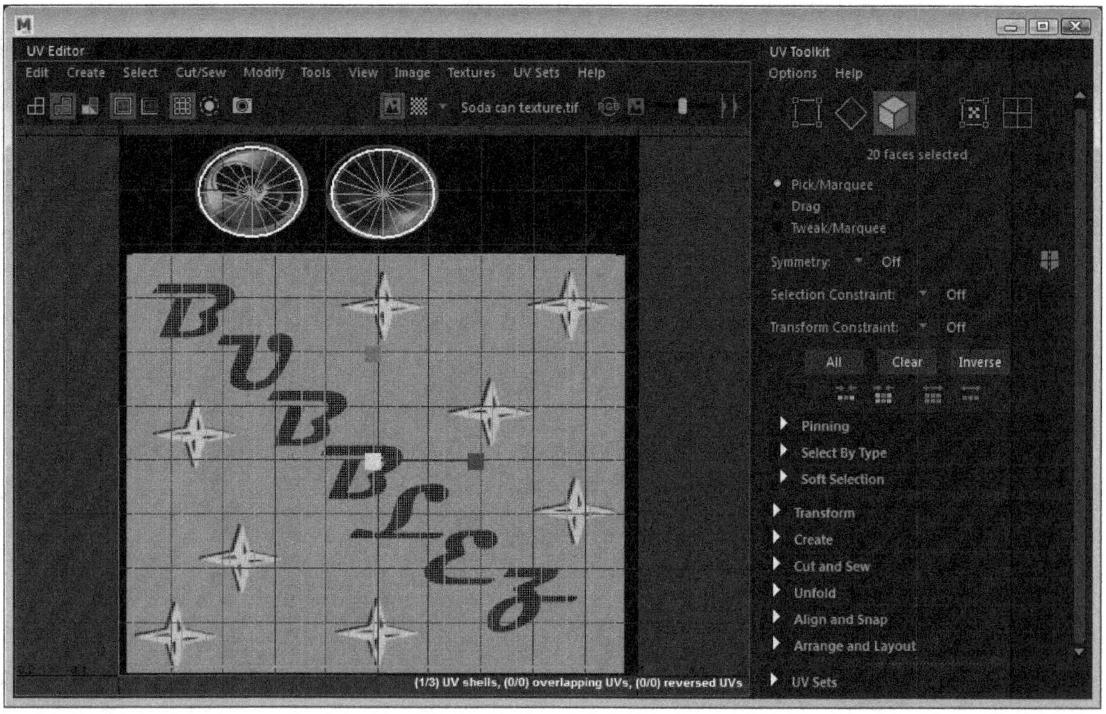

FIGURE 9-63

UVs scaled to match texture

The texture is now correctly positioned about the cylinder, as shown in Figure 9-64.

8. Select File, Save Scene As, and save the file as **Soda can.mb**.

FIGURE 9-64

Soda can with texture

Lesson 9.9-Tutorial 2: Work with UV Shells

1. Open the Dumbbell.mb file using the File, Open Scene menu command.
2. With the dumbbell object selected, choose the Lighting/Shading, Assign New Material menu command and choose the Blinn material.
3. Click on the Create Render Node button for the Color attribute in the Attribute Editor and select the File node. Then click on the File icon in the Image Name attribute and choose the Dumbbell texture.tif image file.
4. Select the Windows, Modeling Editors, UV Editor menu command.
5. From the top of the UV Toolkit, choose the UV Shell component mode, then drag over all the UV shells to select them all. Click on the Layout button in the Arrange and Layout section of the UV Toolkit to separate all the shells. Then, click on the Stack Similar to align all similar shells together.
6. Drag over the UV shell that highlights the center bar of the dumbbell and scale the shell to fit the top portion of the texture.
7. Select the Face component mode and drag over to select the lower third of the circular UV shells without a hole in the middle. Select the Cut/Sew, Create UV Shell menu command to separate this selection from the shell.
8. Scale and move this new selection over the 50 in the texture. Then scale and move all remaining shells to the lower right of the texture over the pure black.

   The resulting textures and UV placements are shown in Figure 9-65 and the resulting dumbbell with textures is shown in Figure 9-66.
9. Select File, Save Scene As, and save the file as **Mapped dumbbell.mb.**

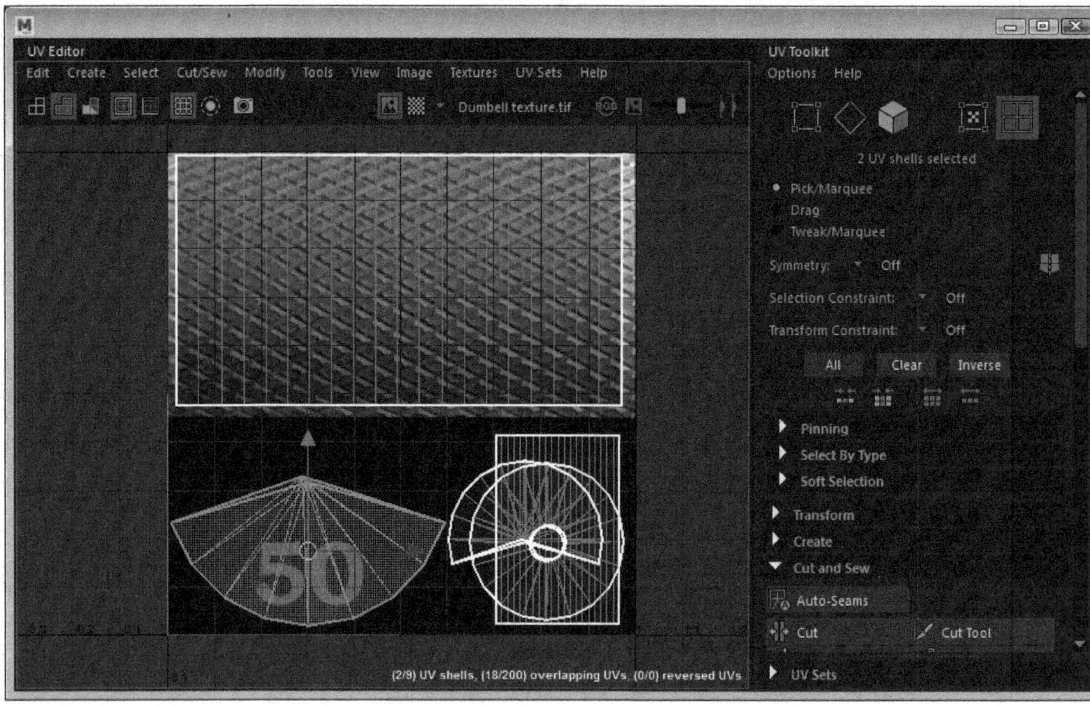

FIGURE 9-65

Placed UV shells

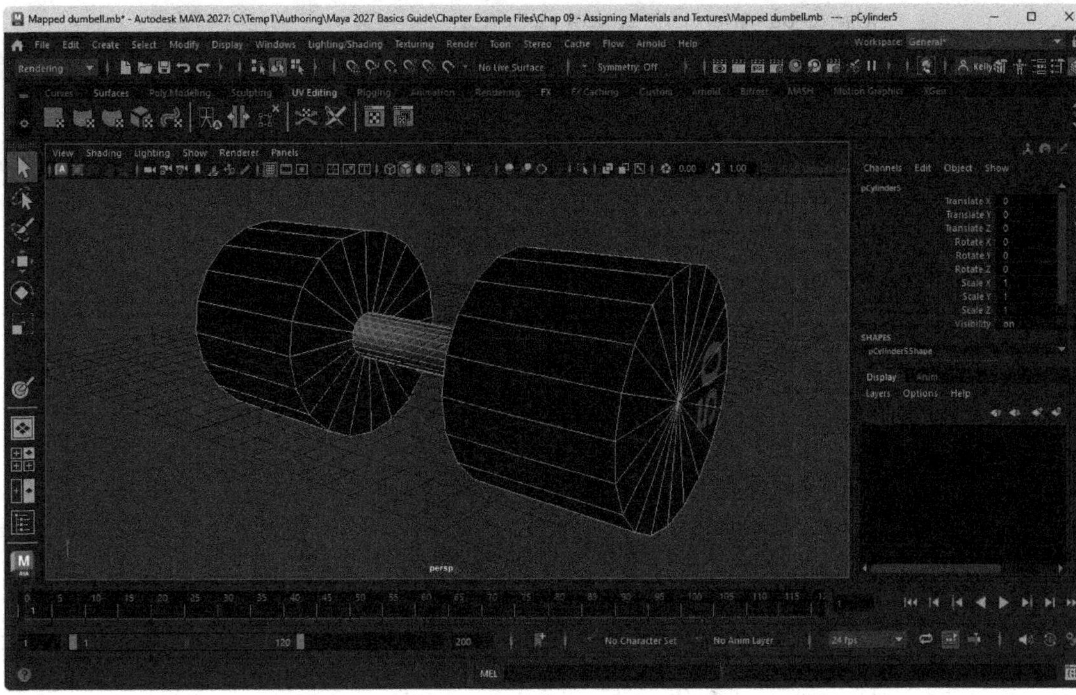

FIGURE 9-66

Dumbbell with texture

Chapter Summary

This chapter covers the basics of creating and applying materials and textures to objects. Materials and textures are defined in the Hypershade interface. This interface lets you connect various nodes to create an endless variety of custom materials. You can also apply textures to objects and position them using various placement utility nodes. Bumps and relief textures are added to materials using the Bump Map attribute and/or Displacement maps. The 3D Paint tool lets you apply paint using a brush directly on the surface of an object in the view panel. Finally, the UV Editor is used to define the precise placement of texture onto different areas of an object.

What You Have Learned

In this chapter, you learned

* How to apply new materials to objects.
* How to apply materials to a selected face.
* How to view and change material attributes.
* How to move between material nodes.
* How to render materials.
* How to use the Hypershade and the Create Bar.
* How to connect nodes in the Hypershade.

* How to use the Connection Editor.
* How to apply materials by dragging them.
* How to use the various surface materials.
* How to change material colors.
* How to change a material's transparency.
* How to use the various material attributes.
* How to layer materials.
* How to use the Ramp Shader and the Shading Map.
* How to connect texture nodes.
* How to map textures to a specific attribute.
* How to add bump maps to an object.
* How to load file textures and layer textures.
* How to use the different mapping methods.
* How to use default and projection mapping.
* How to place 2D and 3D textures.
* How to use displacement maps.
* How to convert displacement maps to objects.
* How to use the various material utility nodes.
* How to assign a paint texture.
* How to use the 3D Paint tool.
* How to access the UV Editor.
* How to select and transform UV components.
* How to unfold UV shells.
* How to cut and sew UVs.
* How to arrange and layout UV shells.

Key Terms From This Chapter

* **Material.** A set of surface properties that are assigned to an object to simulate various object materials.

* **Shader.** A complex set of connected material nodes that define a specific material.

* **Bump map.** A texture that is used to set the relief of a material where dark areas are raised and lighter areas are indented.
* **Hypershade.** An interface where materials and shaders are created.
* **Create Bar.** A selection list in the Hypershade where you can choose from default materials, textures and nodes.
* **Node.** A single set of material attributes that you can connect to other nodes to create a shader.
* **Connection Editor.** An interface for defining the connections between various nodes.
* **Anisotropic.** A material noted for its elliptical specular highlights.
* **Lambert.** A material with no highlights; useful for cloth and non-reflective surfaces.
* **Blinn.** A material with soft, circular highlights; good for metallic surfaces.
* **Phong.** A material with a hard, circular highlight; good for glass surfaces.
* **Texture.** A bitmap file that is wrapped around an object.
* **Mapping.** The method used to wrap a texture around an object.
* **Displacement map.** The image map that is used to modify the geometry of an object.
* **UV coordinate.** A set of values used to define how a texture maps onto an object face.
* **UV shell.** The grouping of UVs that are marked by boundaries making them easy to select.

Chapter 10
Adding Paint Effects

IN THIS CHAPTER

- 10.1 Use the preset brushes.
- 10.2 Create custom brushes.
- 10.3 Paint in 2D.
- 10.4 Paint on 3D objects.
- 10.5 Edit Paint Effects.

Several of Maya's tools let you paint within the scene. These paint features include Paint Textures, Paint Weights, Paint to Select, Paint to Sculpt, and Paint Effects. Of all these paint features, **Paint Effects** is probably the most innovative and exciting. Using the Paint Effects Tool, you can paint brush strokes and objects directly in the view panel, on a 2D canvas, or directly on a 3D object.

Paint Effects are applied using brushes. You can set the attributes—such as the size, color, thickness, and shape of the brush head—of these brushes. You can also select from several styles of brushes, including airbrushes, markers, oils, pencils, pens, and watercolors. In addition to the default preset brushes, you can create and save your own custom brushes.

Dragging a brush in the scene produces a **stroke**. These strokes can be simple strokes like a normal paintbrush would make or a growth stroke, which causes additional strokes to appear and extend from the base stroke. Using growth strokes, you can paint trees and flowers simply by drawing the base stem; Maya adds all the smaller limbs and branches automatically.

All of the Paint Effect brushes are found in the **Content Browser** interface. Brushes contained in the Content Browser include animal furs, clouds, feathers, flowers, glows, hair, and so on.

To apply a Paint Effect, a special panel mode is available called the Paint Effect panel. This panel includes several unique controls for accessing **alpha channels,** taking snapshots and editing the brush settings.

The Generate menu, within the Modeling menu set, also includes several commands for controlling brushes and their settings. Using the Preset Blending command, you can combine the settings of different brushes. The Make Paintable option lets you paint directly on the surface of the selected NURBS object and the **Auto Paint** feature paints on an object using a grid or random strokes.

Lesson 10.1: Use the Preset Brushes

Paint Effects in Maya are fun to play with, thanks to the variety of unique brushes that are available. You can start by playing with the available preset brushes, but you can also change the attributes of a brush to create a custom brush.

Accessing the Paint Effects Panel

If you select a Paint Effects brush using the Generate, Get Brush command, then the Content Browser of available brushes appears. Using these brushes you can draw directly in the viewport or you can switch to a canvas view using the Panels, Panel, Paint Effects, menu in the panel menu. You can also use the Paint, Paint Scene menu to switch back to viewport mode or click on one of the Viewport Layout buttons to exit Paint Scene mode. Figure 10-1 shows Paint Canvas mode with several sample brush effects.

Note

```
The Generate menu is found in the Modeling menu
set.
```

FIGURE 10-1

Paint Canvas mode

Using the Paint Effects Tool

The Paint Effects tool can paint in the view panel in Scene Painting mode whenever a brush is selected using the Generate, Get Brush menu. Using the Tool settings, you can configure the Pressure Mapping values for a graphics tablet.

Using Preset Brushes

Many preset brushes are available. These are all found in the Content Browser, as shown in Figure 10-2. To see the name of each brush, hold the mouse cursor over the top of the icon button and its name appears in the pop-up Help. Some of the sample brushes include Curly Hair, Bubbles, Crystals, Charcoal, Red Oil, Smear, Gold, Water Tube, Neon Blue, and Grass Clump.

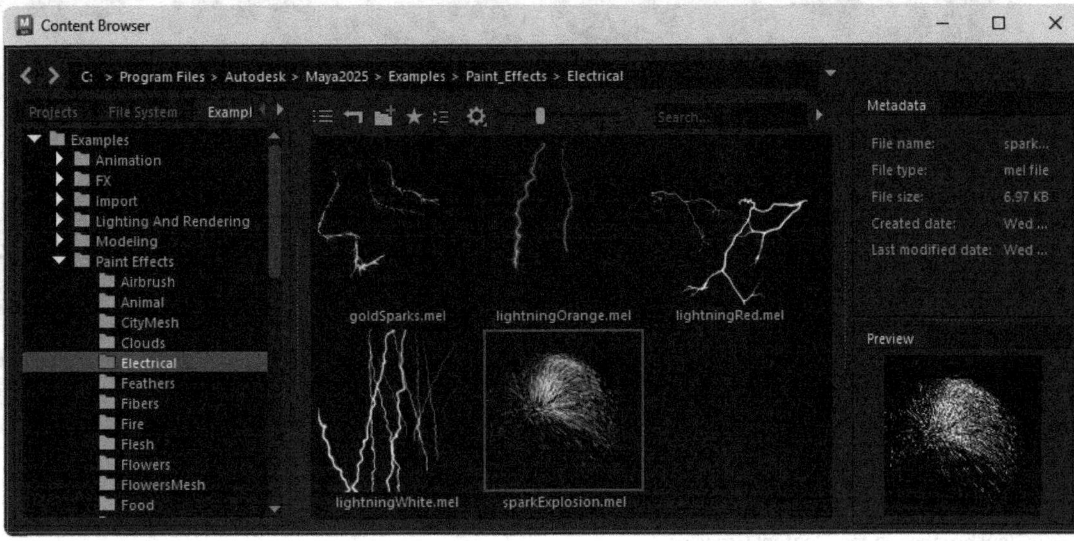

FIGURE 10-2

Paint Effects in the Content Browser

Introducing the Content Browser

The Content Browser includes a categorized look at the folders on your hard drive, as shown again in Figure 10-3. Each folder contains thumbnails of the available content, including brushes. You can open the Content Browser dialog box using the Windows, Content Browser menu command. Sample Paint Effects folders in the Content Browser include categories such as animal, clouds, feathers, flowers, food, fun, galactic, hair, trees, and underwater.

Note

You can also open the Content Browser by selecting the Generate, Get Brush menu command.

FIGURE 10-3

Glow brushes in the Content Browser

Blending Presets

You can blend brush presets together so the shape of one brush is combined with the shading of another brush using the Generate, Preset Blending menu command. To blend two brushes, select the first brush and then open the Brush Preset Blend Options dialog box and choose the percentage of shape and shading to use from the second preset. Then select the second preset. Figure 10-4 shows the shape of the Down Feather brush blended with the shading from the Crystal, Neon Blue, and Lightning brushes.

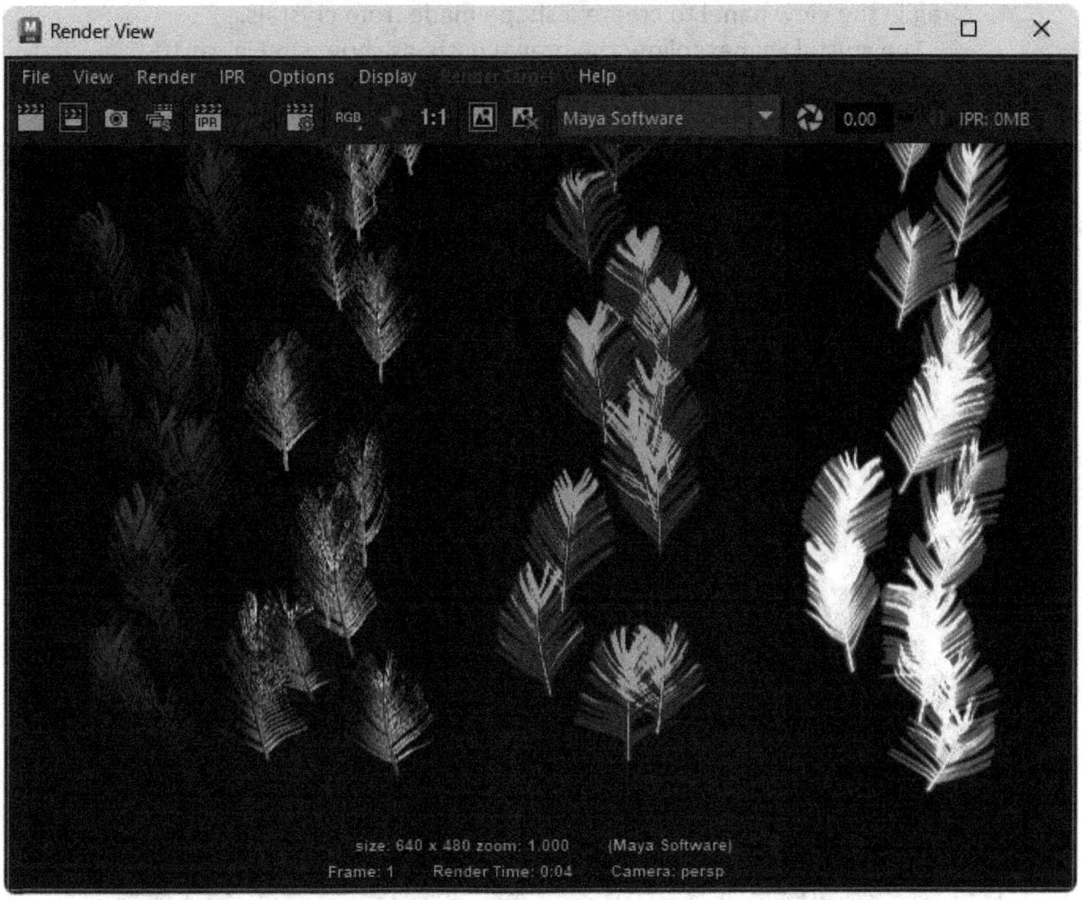

FIGURE 10-4

Blended Paint Effects

Redrawing the View

As you paint in the view panel, some Paint Effects are drawn as wireframe lines in order to save memory. You can set the display value for the selected Paint Effect using the Stroke Refresh panel menu. This menu appears in Scene Painting mode. The options include Off, Wireframe, and Rendered.

Clearing the View

If you want to delete the last-created stroke, you can simply use the Edit, Undo menu command. This clears the strokes in the order they were created. If you want to clear the entire view, you can use the Clear Canvas/Delete All Strokes panel toolbar button. This completely erases all Paint Effects but doesn't delete any objects.

Lesson 10.1-Tutorial 1: Use a Paint Effects Brush

1. Select the Modeling menu set from the drop-down list to the left in the Status Line.
2. Select the Panels, Panel, Paint Effects panel menu command to enter Scene Painting mode.
3. Click on the Crystals Brush icon in the Paint Effects, Fun Mesh category of the Content Browser.

4. Drag in the view panel to create a shape made from crystals.
   The crystal shapes follow the drawn path, as shown in Figure 10-5.
5. Select File, Save Scene As and save the file as **Crystal paint effect.mb**.

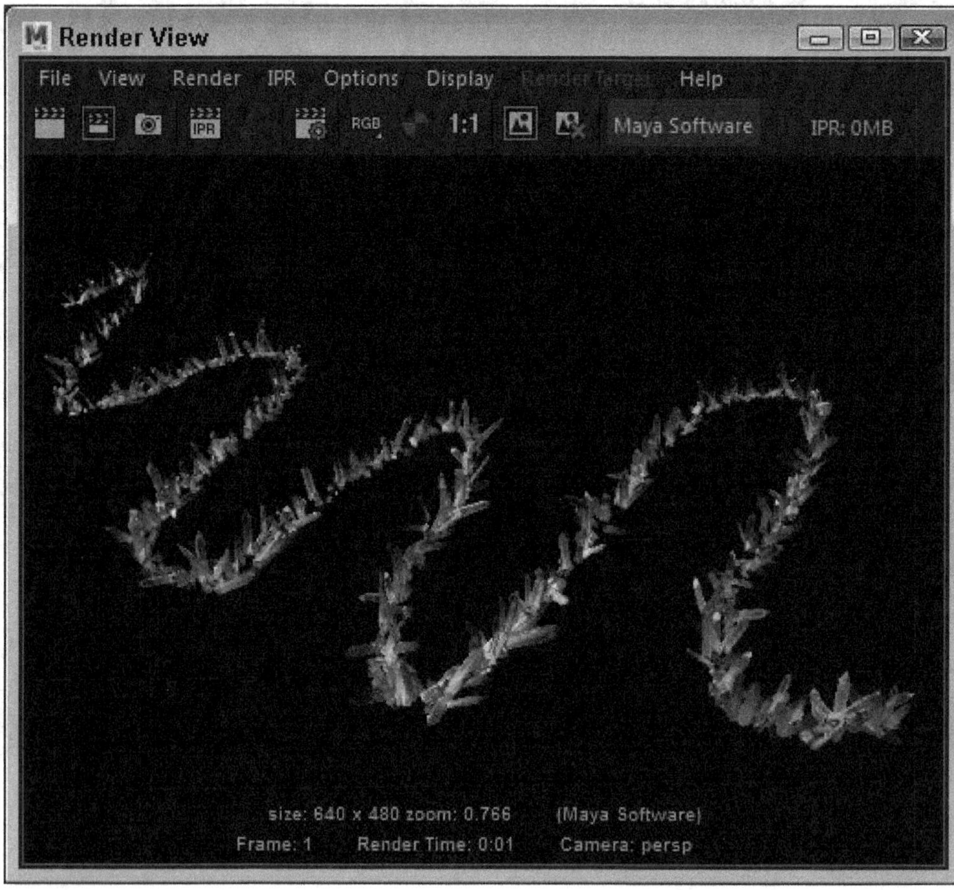

FIGURE 10-5

The Crystal Paint effect

Lesson 10.1-Tutorial 2: Use a Content Browser Brush

1. Select the Panels, Panel, Paint Effects menu command to enter Scene Painting mode.
2. Select the Generate, Get Brush menu command.
   The Content Browser dialog box opens.
3. Click on the Fun folder to the left.
   Thumbnails of the brushes contained within this folder are displayed.
4. Click on the Jumping Springs brush.
5. Drag in the center of the view panel to create a shape and zoom in on the created springs, as shown in Figure 10-6.
6. Select File, Save Scene As and save the file as **Jumping springs.mb**.

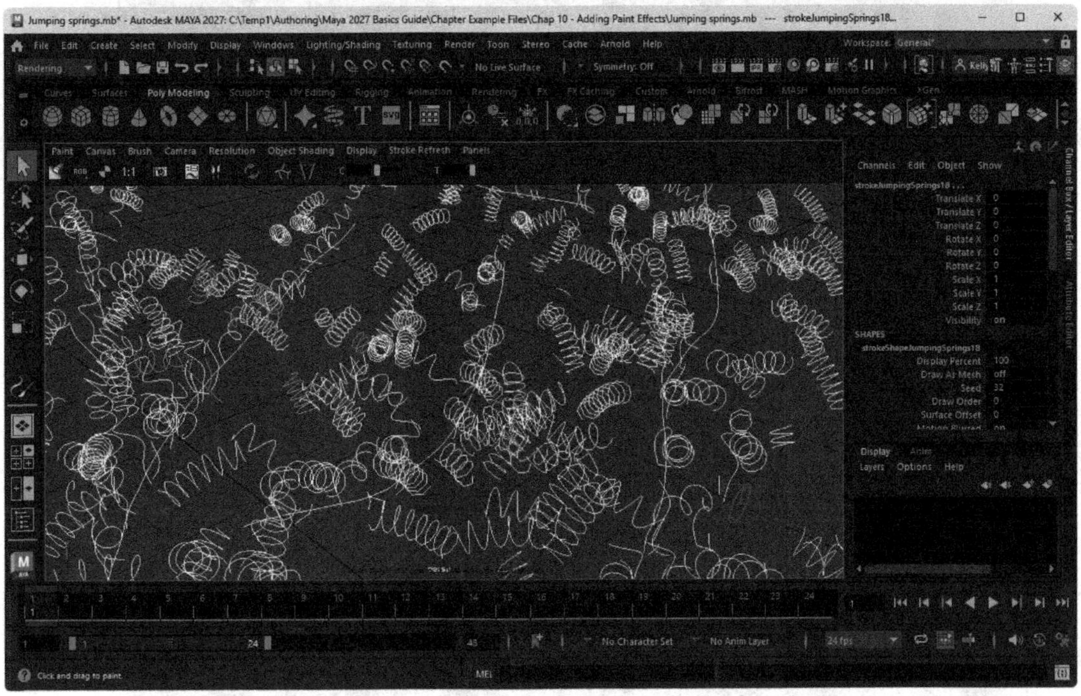

FIGURE 10-6

The Jumping Springs Paint Effect

Lesson 10.1-Tutorial 3: Blend Brushes

1. Select the Panels, Panel, Paint Effects menu command to enter Scene Painting mode.
2. Click on the Crystals Brush icon in the Content Browser.
3. Drag in the view panel to create a shape made from crystals.
4. Select the Generate, Preset Blending, Options menu command.

   The Brush Preset Blend dialog box opens.
5. Enter a Shading value of 100% and a Shape value of 0%.

   This causes the blended brush to use all of the shading attributes of the next-selected brush and none of its shape attributes.
6. Click on the Gold Brush icon in the Paint Effects, Metal category of the Content Browser.
7. Drag next to the existing set of crystals to reveal a set of gold crystals, as shown in Figure 10-7.
8. Select File, Save Scene As and save the file as **Gold crystals.mb**.

FIGURE 10-7

The Blended Paint Effect

Lesson 10.2: Create Custom Brushes

Preset brushes are great for starters, but you'll quickly want to know how to customize the brushes. Every brush pulls from a long list of attributes that you can alter to change the brush. You can save customized brushes for later use.

Changing Template Brush Settings

When a preset brush is selected, the brush settings are copied to the Template Brush Settings dialog box, which holds the global settings for the brush. You can change the template brush settings at any time using the Generate, Template Brush Settings menu command. This opens the Paint Effects Brush Settings dialog box, shown in Figure 10-8, where you can change brush attributes like the size, color, shadows, and glows. You can reset the current brush settings at any time with the Generate, Reset Template Brush menu command.

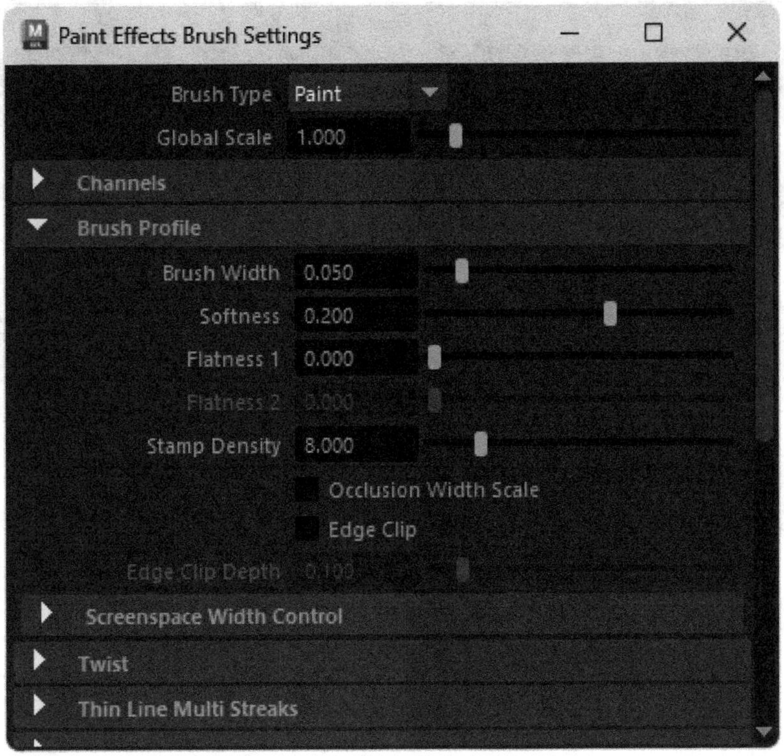

FIGURE 10-8

The Paint Effects Brush Settings dialog box

Using the Various Brush Types

The top of the Paint Effects Brush Settings dialog box includes a drop-down list from which you can select the brush type you want. The available options include Paint, Smear, Blur, Erase, Thin Line, and Mesh. The Paint brush type actually places color and the Erase brush type removes it. The Smear and Blur brush type alters the existing colors with a smear or blur effect. The Thin Line brush type divides the strokes into many thin lines like the Curly Hair brush. The Mesh brush type places random mesh objects about the scene like the Crystals and Tacks brushes. Figure 10-9 shows four brush strokes using the Red Oil brush. The second and third lines were done with the Smear and Blur brush types, and in the bottom line the Erase brush type was used to erase some of the line. Figure 10-10 shows examples of the Thin Line and Mesh brush types.

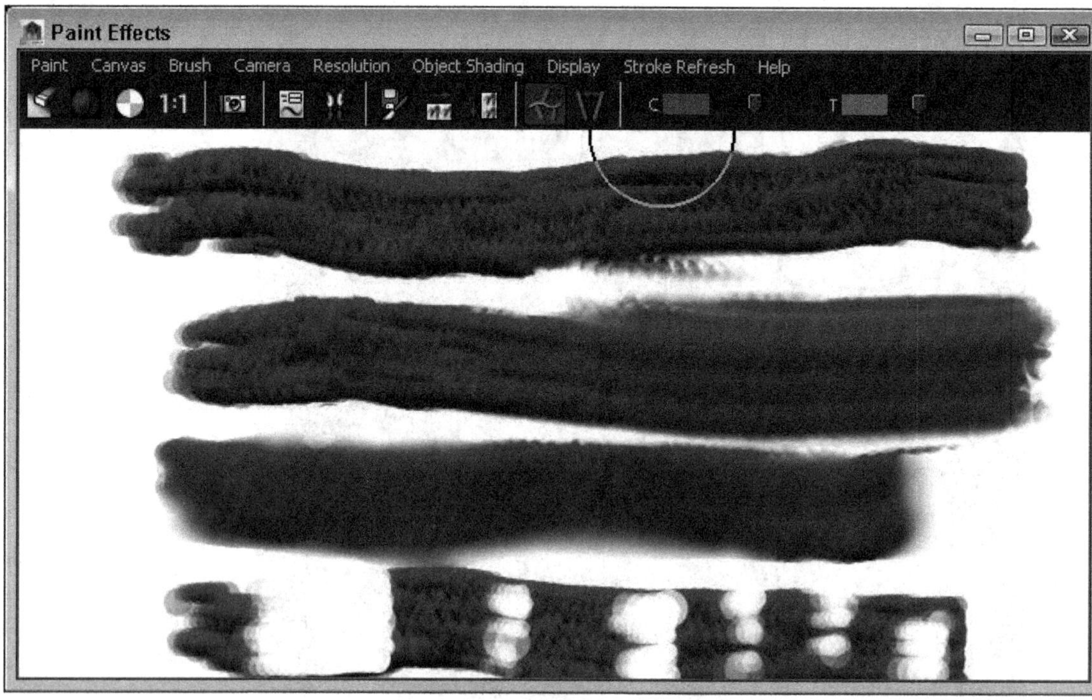

FIGURE 10-9

Brush types

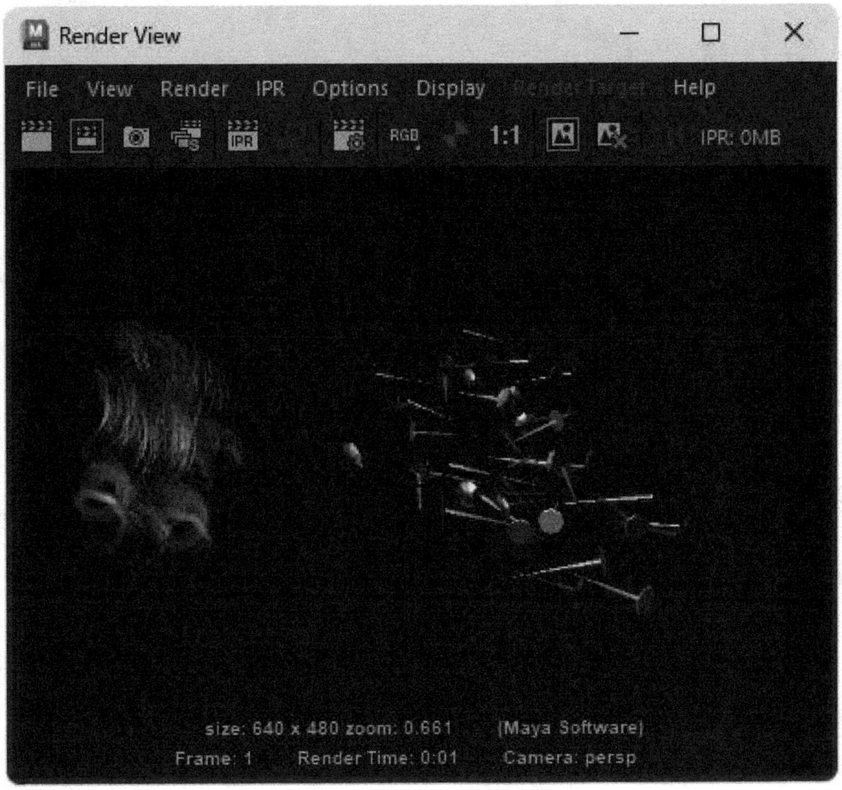

FIGURE 10-10

Curly Hair and Tacks brushes

Changing Brush Size

Use the Global Scale attribute in the Paint Effects Brush Settings dialog box to change the overall size of the brush. This attribute uniformly changes the size of the brush as indicated by the circular (or spherical) cursor that appears in the view panel. In the Brush Profile section, you'll find the Brush Width attribute. This affects the individual brush width, which can increase the size of a single blade of grass or spread the distance between individual brushes, as shown in Figure 10-11. Other attributes in this section include Softness, Flatness, and Stamp Density, which determines the thickness of a stroke.

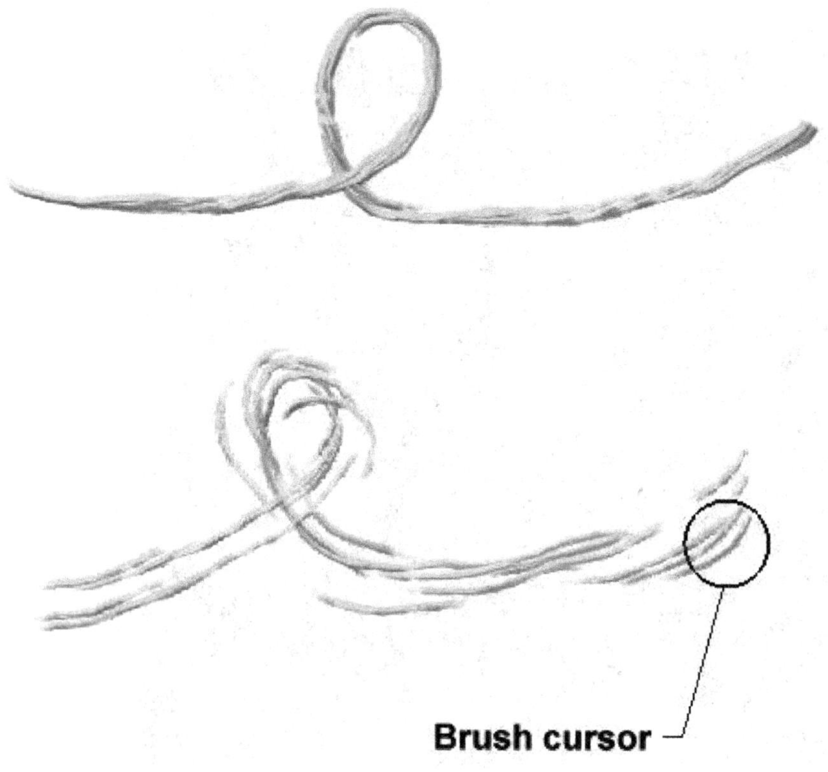

FIGURE 10-11

Increasing brush width

Changing Brush Color

Each of the preset brushes has a color (or colors) that it uses. For example, the Red Oil brush has a red color defined as its primary color. The brushes' colors are found in the Shading section of the Paint Effects Brush Settings dialog box. Clicking on the color swatch lets you choose a new color in the Color Chooser. You can also choose colors for incandescence and transparency. Figure 10-12 shows the Vitamin E brush with several primary colors.

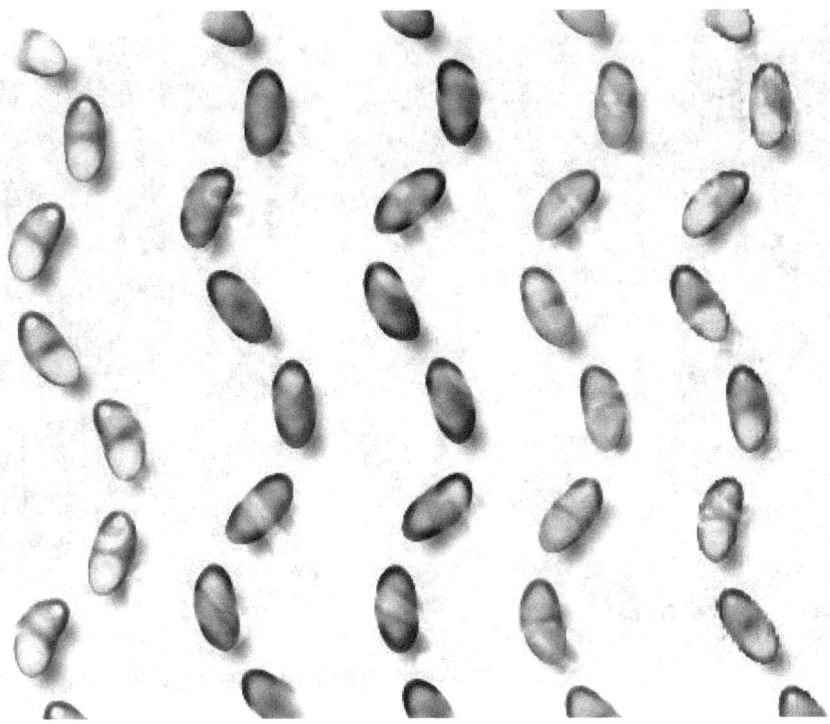

FIGURE 10-12

Changed colors with the Vitamin E brush

Enabling Illumination and Shadows

Using the Illumination section of the Paint Effects Brush Settings dialog box, you can choose whether the Paint Effects have no light cast on them, that the default lights illuminate them, or that real scene lights illuminate them. The Illuminated option lets you specify a Light Direction and you can change the settings for Specular, Specular Power, and Specular Color. The Shadow Effects section includes three options for fake shadows, including None, 2D Offset (which is a simple drop shadow), and 3D Cast. Fake shadows render quickly, but you can also enable real shadows by enabling the Cast Shadows options. Real shadows can take a long time to render. Figure 10-13 shows three lines painted with the Gold brush. The top one has no illumination, the middle one has standard illumination, and the bottom one has a blue specular color.

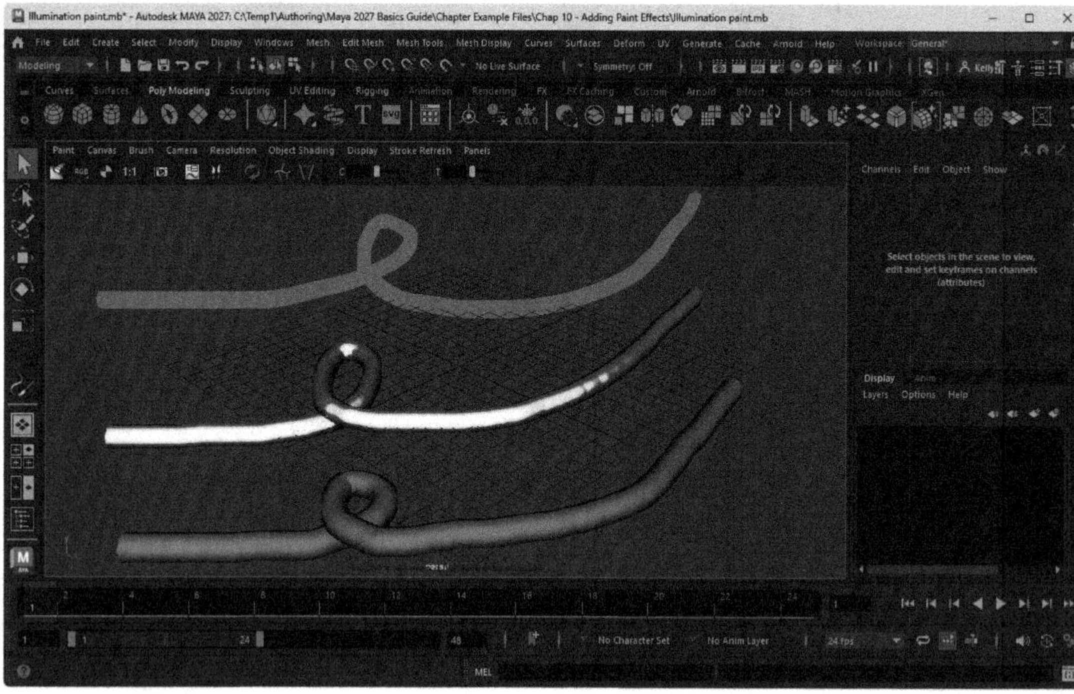

FIGURE 10-13

Altered illumination

Enabling Glows

The Glow section enables you to set the amount of glow that emanates, the glow color, and the glow spread. Several preset brushes use glows, including the Neon Blue, Galaxy, and Lightning brushes. Figure 10-14 shows the Green Snake brush with no glow enabled, with a normal glow enabled, and with a bright green glow enabled.

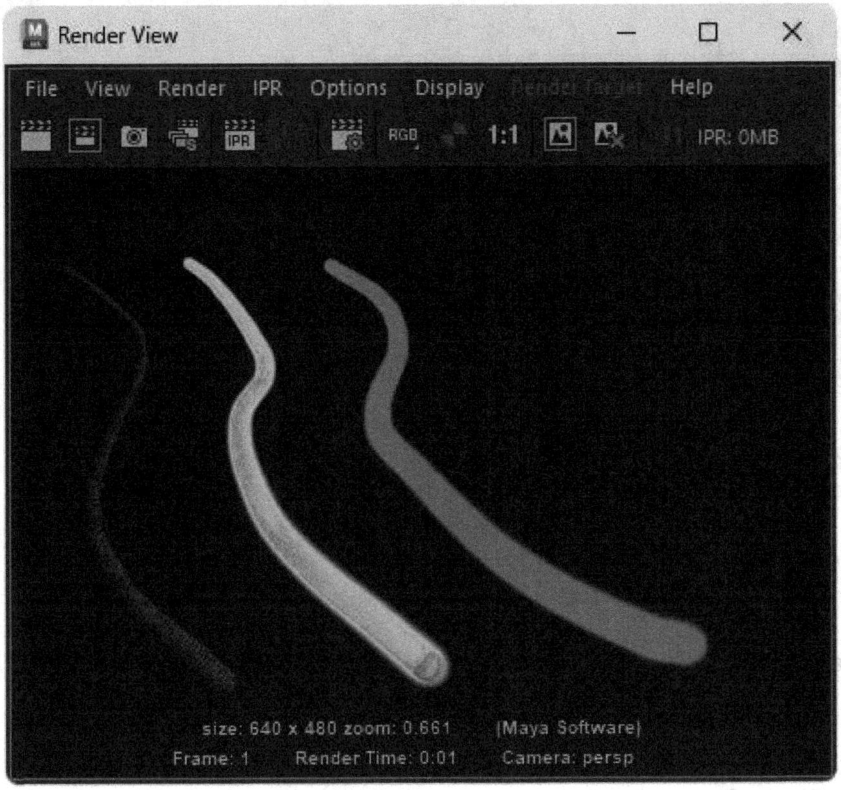

FIGURE 10-14

Enabled glows

Creating and Saving Custom Brushes

If you've tweaked a brush and you like its settings, you can save the custom brush to the Shelf or to the Content Browser using the Generate, Save Brush Preset menu command. This opens a dialog box, shown in Figure 10-15, in which you can name the custom brush and give it a directory.

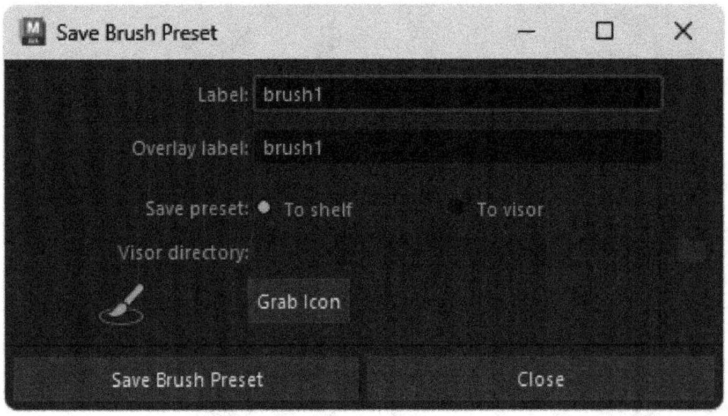

FIGURE 10-15

The Save Brush Preset dialog box

Lesson 10.2-Tutorial 1: Change Brush Size

1. Select the Panels, Panel, Paint Effects menu command to enter Scene Painting mode.
2. Click on the Simple Tree Brush icon in the Paint Effects, Trees section of the Content Browser.
3. Drag in the view panel to create a line of trees.
4. Select the Generate, Template Brush Settings menu command.
5. Change the Global Scale value to 0.5 and draw a parallel line in the view panel.
6. Repeat Step 5 for Global Scale values of 0.75, 1.0, and 1.25.

   The rows of trees gradually get larger as the Global Scale value is increased, as shown in Figure 10-16.
7. Select File, Save Scene As and save the file as **Rows of trees.mb**.

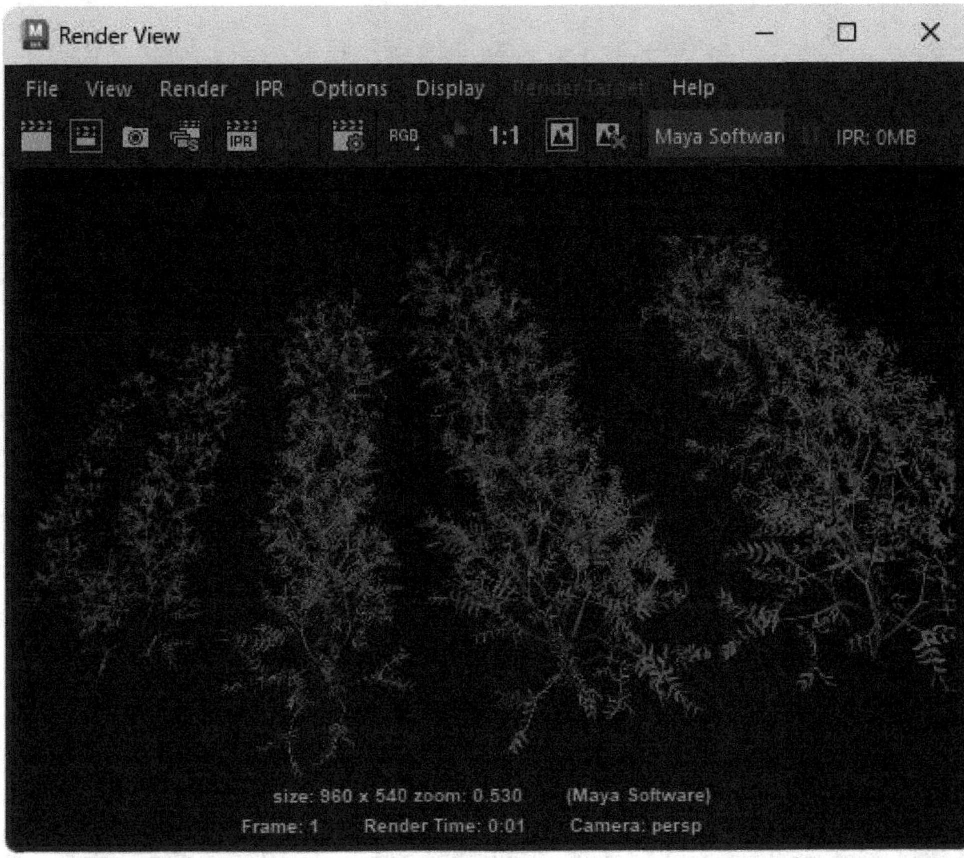

FIGURE 10-16

Rows of trees

Lesson 10.2-Tutorial 2: Change Brush Color

1. Select the Panels, Panel, Paint Effects menu command to enter Scene Painting mode.
2. Click on the Lightning Brush icon in the Paint Effects, Electrical section of the Content Browser.
3. Drag a vertical line in the view panel to create some lightning.
4. Select the Generate, Template Brush Settings menu command.
5. Select the Shading section and click on the Color1 color swatch and change it to blue. Then change the Incandescence1 color to dark blue.
6. Select the Tube Shading section and change the Color2 and Incandescence2 colors to different tints of blue and dark blue.
7. Select the Glow section and change the Glow Color to a light blue color.
8. Drag again in the view panel to create another vertical line parallel to the first.
9. Repeat Steps 5-8 with the colors green, yellow, and red.

   The rows of lightning change from left to right, as shown in Figure 10-17.
10. Select File, Save Scene As and save the file as **Lightning colors.mb**.

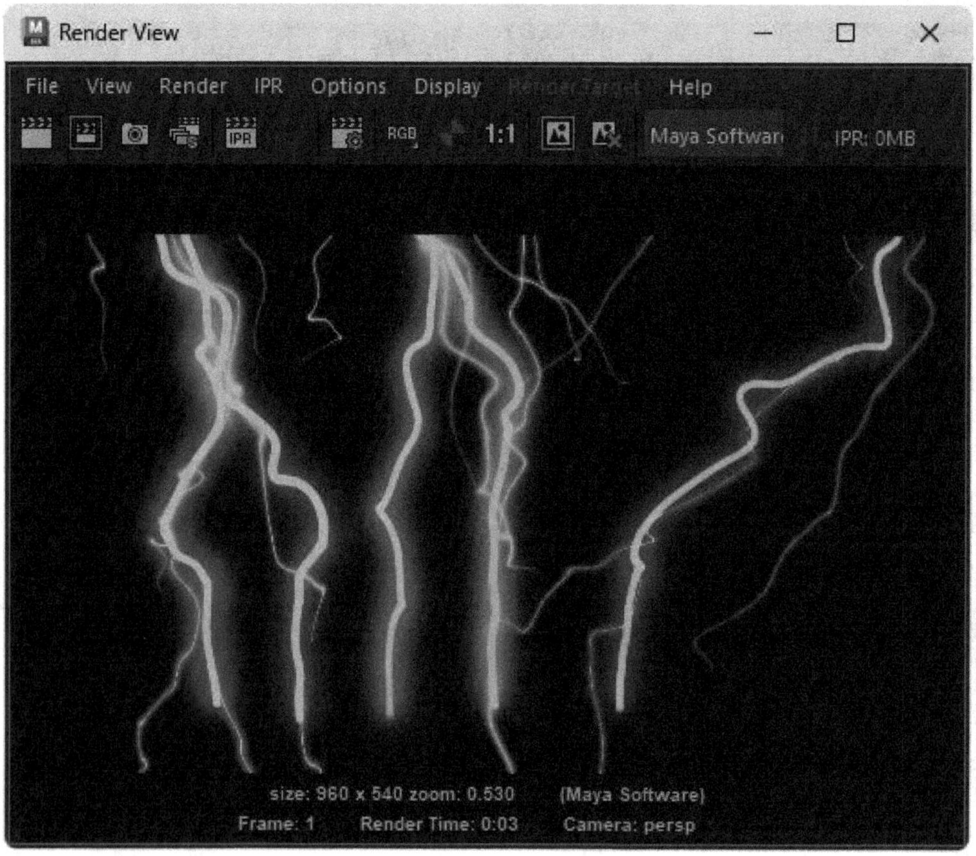

FIGURE 10-17

Lightning colors

Lesson 10.2-Tutorial 3: Add Shadows

1. Create a NURBS plane using the Create, NURBS Primitives, Plane menu command.
2. Select the Display, Frame Selection in All Views menu command (or press the f key) to zoom in on the plane object.
3. Select the Panels, Panel, Paint Effects menu command to enter Scene Painting mode.
4. Click on the Daisy Large Brush icon in the Paint Effects, Flowers section of the Content Browser.
5. Select the Paint Effects, Template Brush Settings menu command.
6. Select the Shadow Effects section, and then select the 3D Cast option in the Fake Shadow drop-down list.
7. Set the Global Scale value to 0.25.
8. Drag with the Paint Effects brush across the plane object.
9. Press the 5 key to see a shaded view of the plane object.

   The Scene Painting view shows several red arrows that cut through the scene. These arrows show the direction of the default lights. Notice how shadows are cast on the plane object, as shown in Figure 10-18.

10. Select File, Save Scene As and save the file as **Daisies with shadows.mb**.

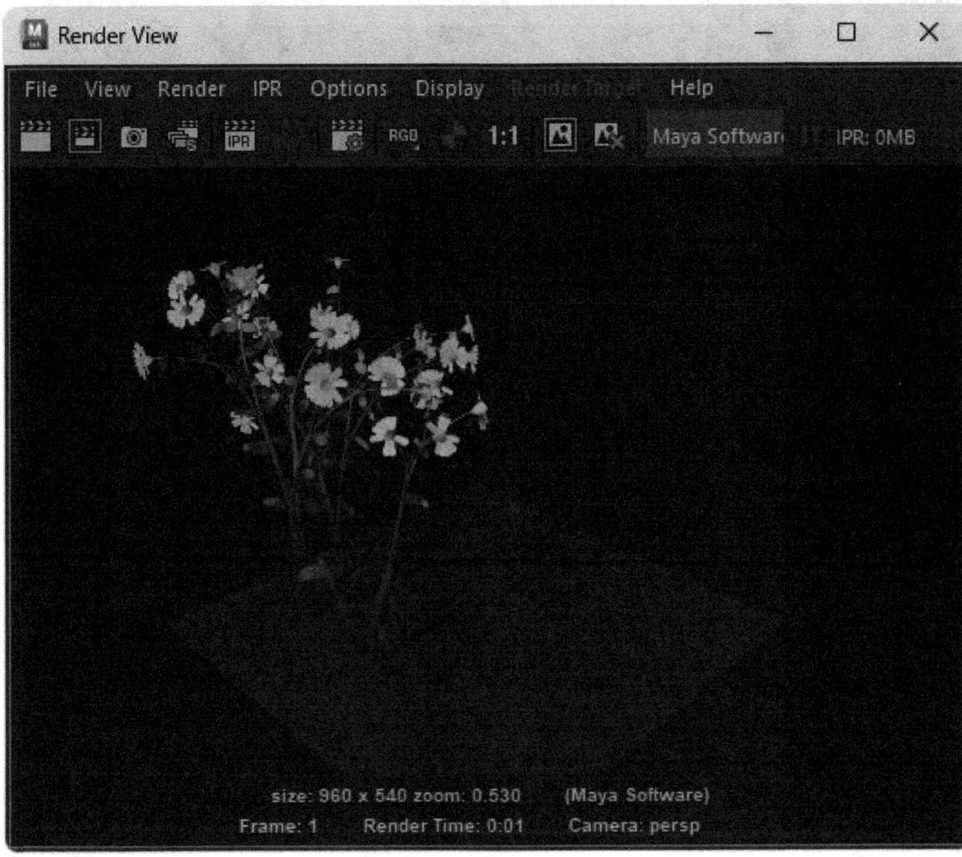

FIGURE 10-18

Cast shadows

Lesson 10.2-Tutorial 4: Add a Glow

1. Select the Panels, Panel, Paint Effects menu command to enter Scene Painting mode.
2. Click on the Orange Pastel Scribble Brush icon in the Paint Effects, Pastels section of the Content Browser.
3. Select the Paint Effects, Template Brush Settings menu command.
4. Change the Global Scale value to 10.0 and, in the Glow section, change the Glow value to 0.5.
5. Drag in the view panel to create a circular pattern.

   The glow effect added to the Orange Pastel Scribble brush makes the brush brighter when it overlaps itself, creating an explosion effect, as shown in Figure 10-19.
6. Select File, Save Scene As and save the file as **Explosion.mb**.

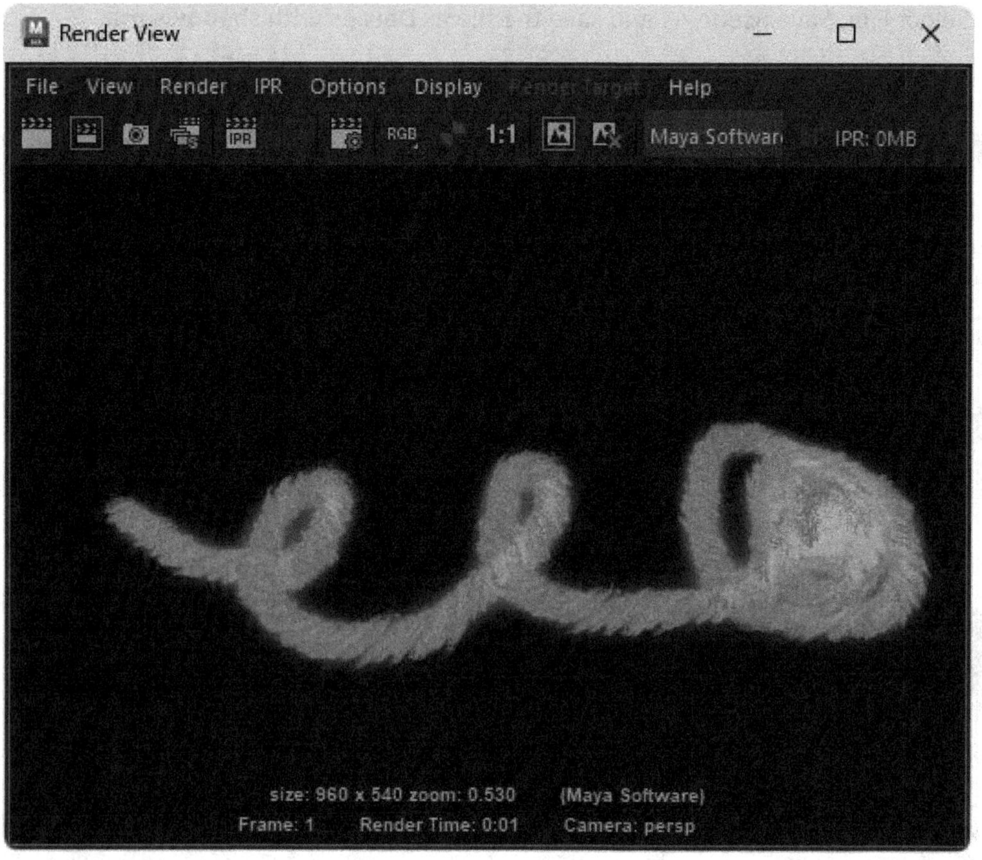

FIGURE 10-19

Explosion effect

Lesson 10.3: Paint in 2D

Sometimes drawing in the view panels with its perspective view isn't what you need. If you use Maya's **Paint Canvas**, you can draw and save images in 2D. The Paint Canvas is easy to identify because it has a white background and the canvas dimensions are displayed at the bottom of the view panel. You can use images you create with the Paint Canvas as textures or backgrounds.

Introducing the Paint Effects Canvas

Once the Paint Effects panel is visible, you can open the paint canvas using the Paint, Paint Canvas menu command. This displays the current view panel as a simple, orthogonal 2D canvas, as shown in Figure 10-20. Paint effects painted to the Paint Effects canvas cannot be edited and need to be saved before you return to the view panel. The Paint, Paint Scene menu command exits out of the paint canvas.

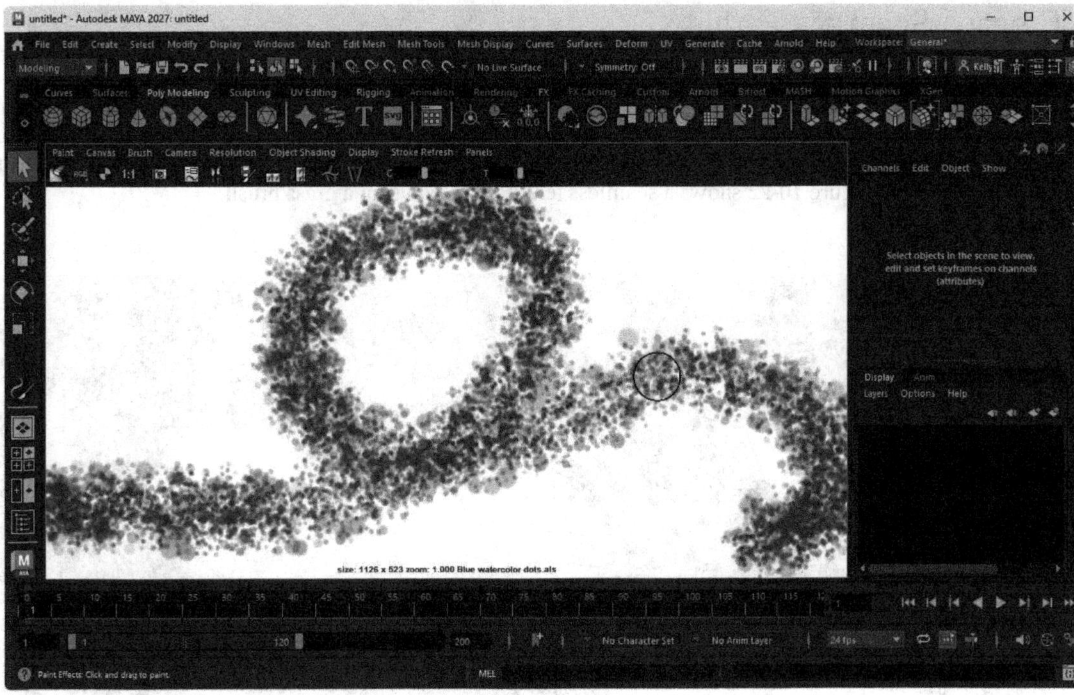

FIGURE 10-20

The Paint canvas

Changing the Canvas Size

The size of the paint canvas, along with its zoom amount, is shown in blue at the bottom of the canvas. The default canvas size is the size of the view panel window in pixels. You can change the size of the canvas using the Canvas, Set Size menu command. This opens a dialog box, shown in Figure 10-21, in which you can enter the new canvas dimensions.

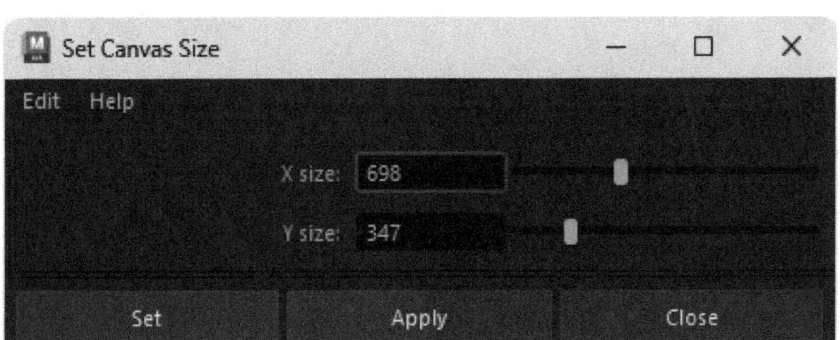

FIGURE 10-21

Set Canvas Size dialog box

Creating Seamless Textures

You can use the Paint Effects canvas to easily create **seamless textures**. Typical textures have seams that appear when they are repeated side by side. A seamless texture has opposite sides that match perfectly so that the seams aren't evident. Enabling the Canvas, Wrap, Horizontally and Canvas, Wrap, Vertically panel menu commands makes any strokes that run off the edge of the canvas continue on the opposite edge, thereby creating a seamless texture. Figure 10-22 shows a seamless texture created using a grass brush.

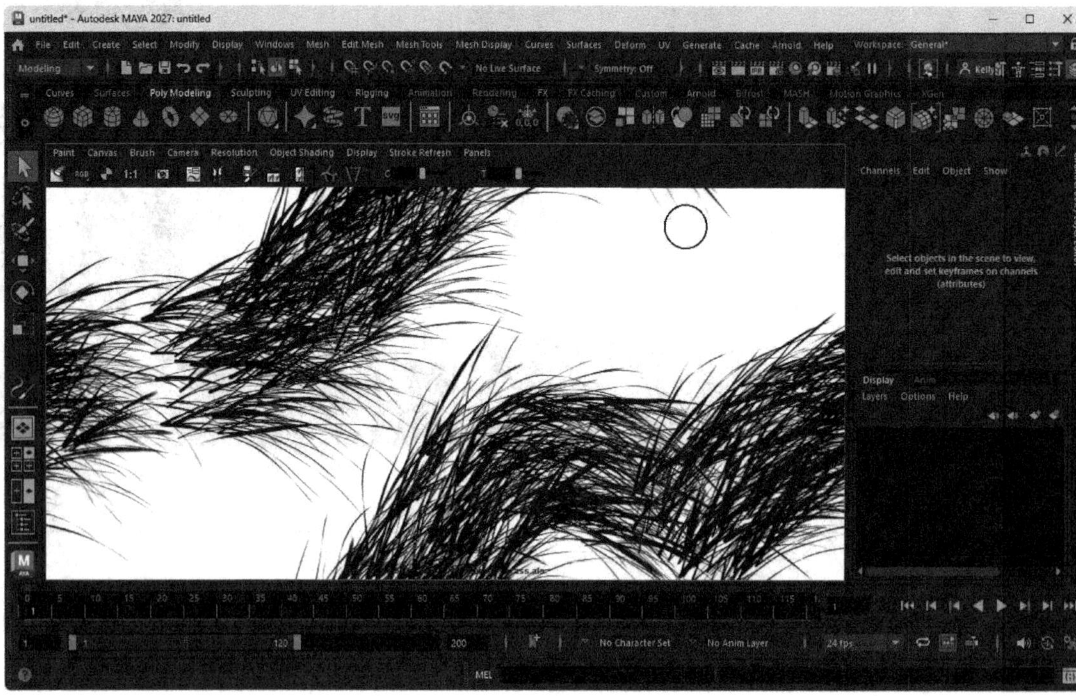

FIGURE 10-22

A seamless texture

Saving Textures

The Paint Effects Canvas lets you save any image drawn in the canvas with the Canvas, Save As menu command. The default image format is the Alias PIX format, but you can save the image in a number of different formats, including Cineon, DDS, EPS, GIF, JPEG, RLA, SGI, and so on. You can also save just a snapshot of the current image with the Paint, Save Snapshot menu command or with the Snapshot toolbar button. There is also a Canvas, Auto Save feature that you can enable.

Undoing the Last Stroke

You can use the normal Undo feature to undo any setting changes, but it cannot undo any brush strokes drawn in the paint canvas. The Canvas, Canvas Undo command undoes the last stroke added to the canvas.

Saving the Alpha Channel

Selecting the Display, Alpha Channel menu command in the panel menu or the Display Alpha Channel toolbar button displays the alpha channel for the canvas image, like the one shown in Figure 10-23. You can use alpha channels to represent transparency and to mask out unwanted areas. For an alpha channel, white areas appear black and black areas appear white. All other colors appear gray depending on their brightness.

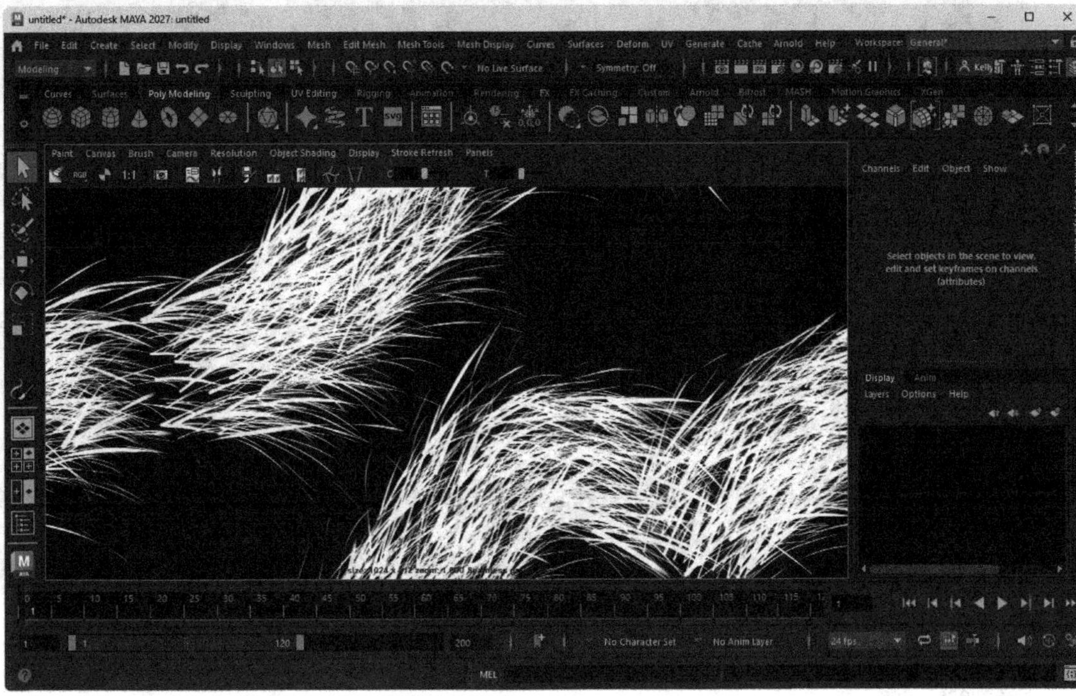

FIGURE 10-23

Canvas alpha channel

Lesson 10.3-Tutorial 1: Create a Seamless Texture

1. Select the Panels, Panel, Paint Effects menu command to enter Scene Painting mode.
2. Select the Paint, Paint Canvas menu command.
3. Select the Canvas, Wrap, Horizontally and the Canvas, Wrap, Vertically panel menu commands.
4. Click on the Vine Gray Bud Brush icon in the Paint Effects, Plants section of the Content Browser.
5. In the paint canvas, drag a diagonal line that moves from one corner of the canvas to the other.

   Notice how the vines that extend from either side of the canvas reappear on the opposite side, as shown in Figure 10-24.
6. Select Canvas, Save As and save the file as **Seamless vines.iff**.

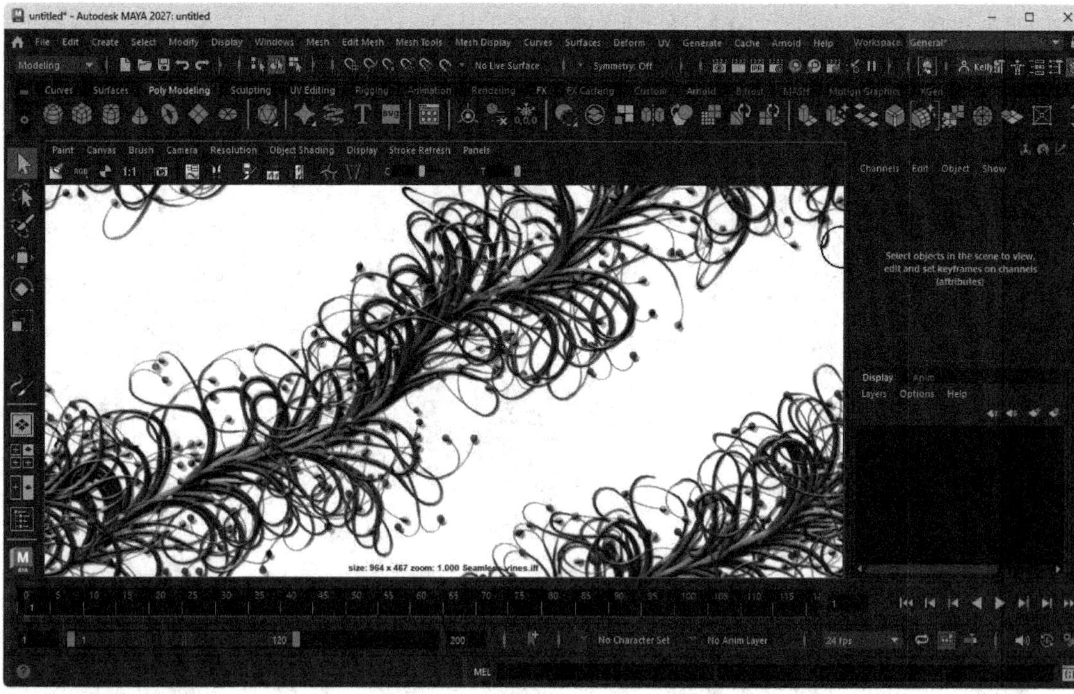

FIGURE 10-24
Seamless vines

Lesson 10.3-Tutorial 2: Save an Image and Alpha Channel

1. Select the Panels, Panel, Paint Effects menu command to enter Scene Painting mode.
2. Select the Paint, Paint Canvas menu command.
3. Click on the Simple Tree Brush icon in the Paint Effects, Trees section of the Content Browser.
4. Drag in the paint canvas to create a simple tree branch.
5. Click on the Flame Curly icon in the Paint Effects, Fire section of the Content Browser.
6. Drag with the Flame brush over the top of the tree branch.

   The resulting image is shown in Figure 10-25.
7. Select Canvas, Save As and save the image as **Burning tree.iff**.
8. Click on the Display Alpha button in the panel toolbar.

   The alpha channel for the image is displayed, as shown in Figure 10-26. Notice how the transparent flames are partially visible.
9. Select Canvas, Save As and save the image as **Burning tree alpha.iff**.

FIGURE 10-25

A burning tree

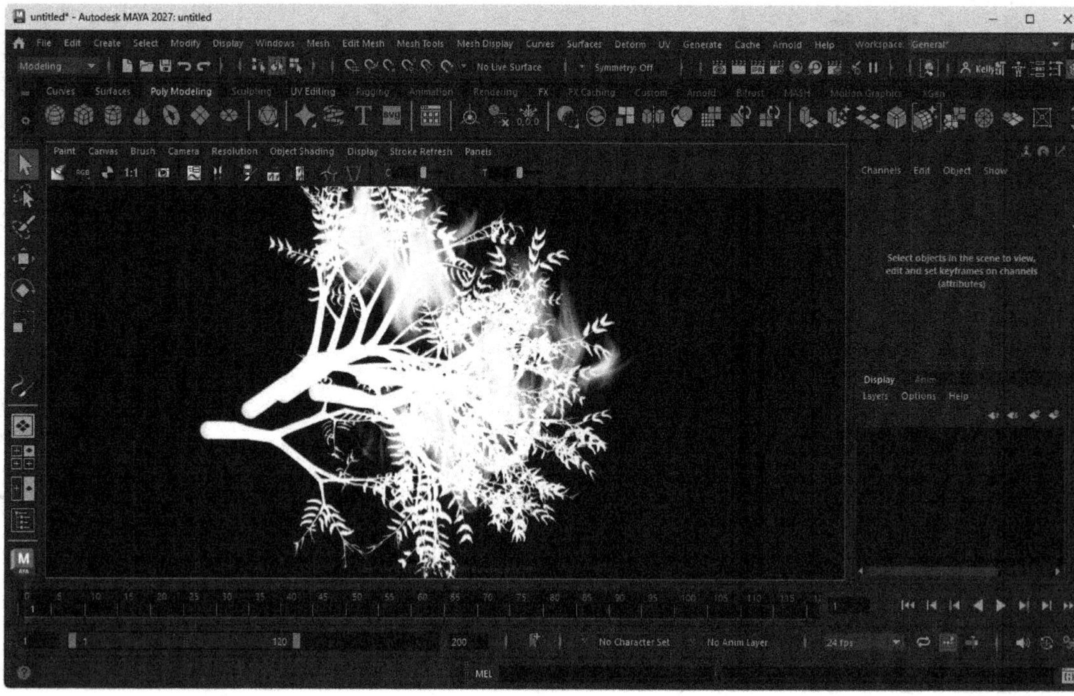

FIGURE 10-26

Alpha channel of the burning tree

Lesson 10.4: Paint on 3D Objects

Painting an image in 2D is fine for creating textures, but Maya also provides a way to paint directly on 3D objects.

Painting in a View Panel

In addition to painting on the Paint Canvas, the default is to paint directly in the scene. To access Paint Scene mode from the paint canvas, you can select the Paint, Paint Scene panel menu command. You can also paint in Modeling mode, but the strokes are only shown in wireframe. Figure 10-27 shows a simple sphere with two Paint Effects trees positioned next to it.

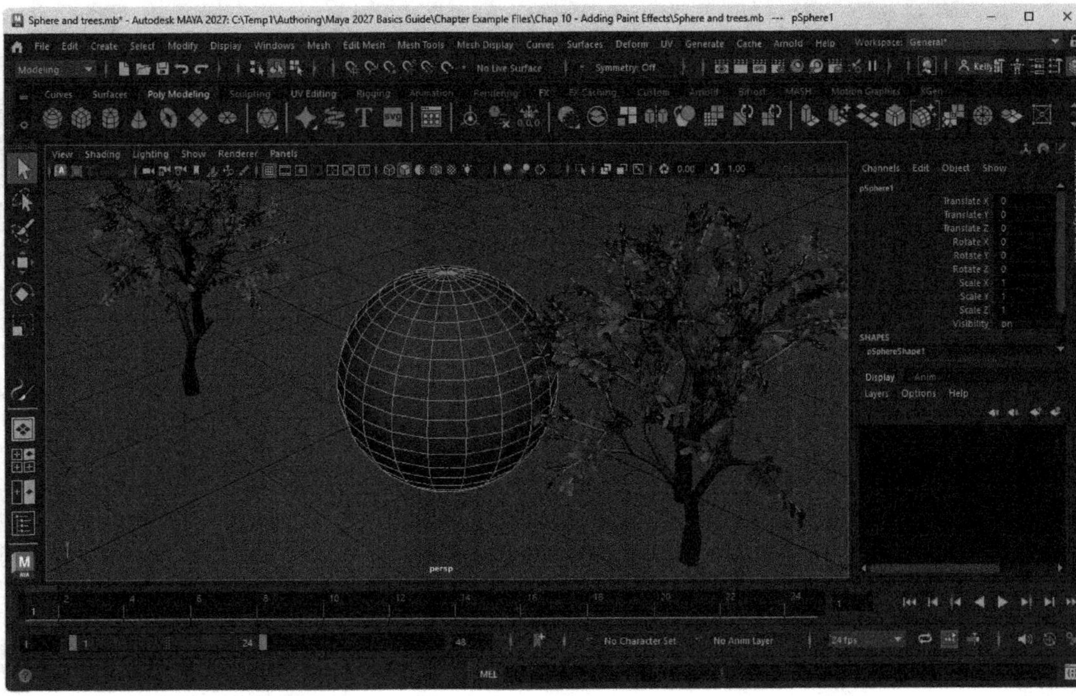

FIGURE 10-27
Combining models and Paint Effects

Painting on Objects

You can make selected objects paintable with the Generate, Make Paintable menu command. This allows you to paint directly on the surface of the object. Paint Effects are painted on the View Plane by default, but you can switch to painting on 3D objects using the Generate, Paint on Paintable Objects menu command. Figure 10-28 shows a NURBS sphere that has been made paintable and covered with the grass Paint Effect.

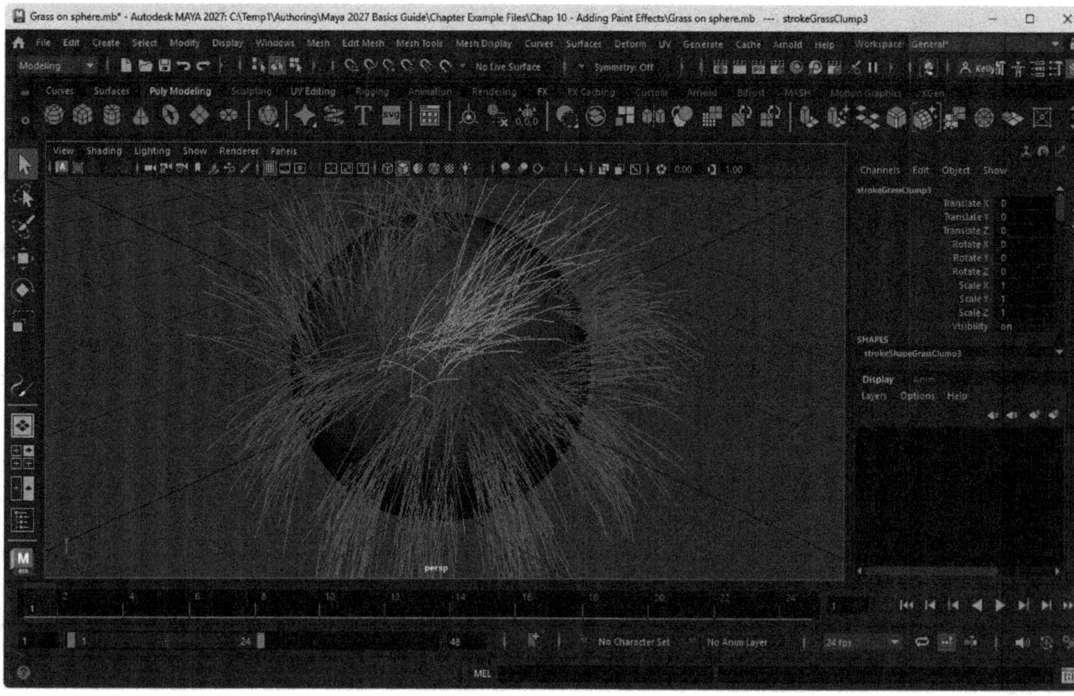

FIGURE 10-28

Paintable object

Auto-Painting an Object

With a NURBS surface selected, you can automatically apply paint strokes to its surface using the Generate, Auto Paint, Paint Grid menu command. The Paint Grid Options dialog box lets you specify the number of spans in U and V to cover. The Auto Paint menu also includes a Random Paint option that randomly paints strokes on the object's surface. Figure 10-29 shows a simple NURBS torus object that has been auto-painted with a Neon Blue brush.

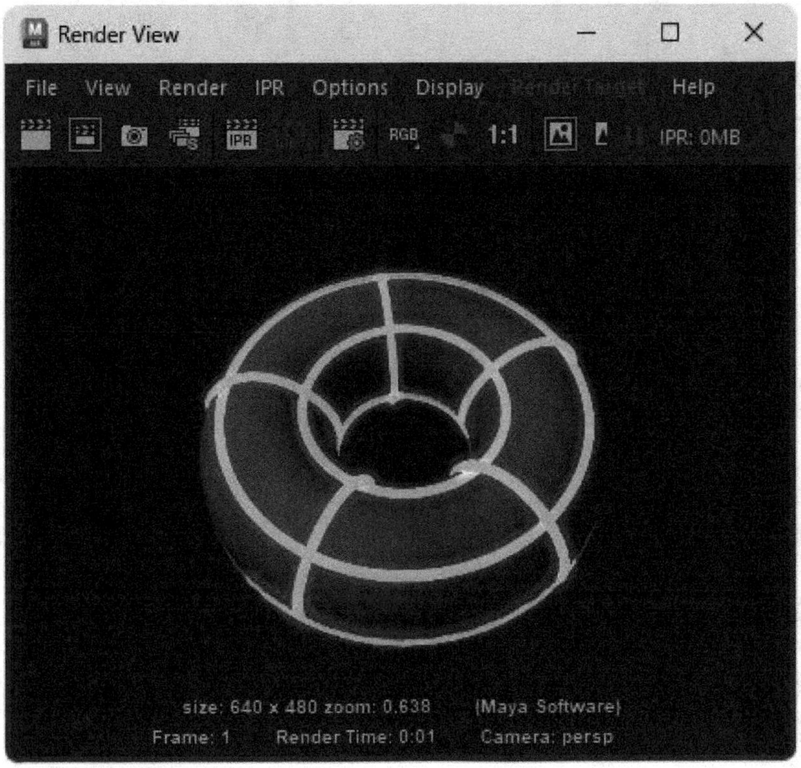

FIGURE 10-29

Auto-painted torus object

Saving Depth as a Grayscale Map

When Paint Effects are drawn in Scene Paint mode, they have a depth value that determines how close or far from the camera they are. You can save this depth information as a grayscale image using the Paint, Save Depth as Grayscale menu command. You can then use depth image maps as textures to control the placement of objects.

Lesson 10.4-Tutorial 1: Paint on Objects

1. Create a NURBS sphere object using the Create, NURBS Primitives, Sphere menu command.
2. With the sphere selected, choose the Generate, Make Paintable menu command.
3. Select the Panels, Panel, Paint Effects menu command to enter Scene Painting mode.
4. Click on the Curly Flame Brush icon in the Paint Effects, Fire section of the Content Browser.
5. Drag over the top of the sphere object.

   The flames from the brush are painted only on the sphere, as shown in Figure 10-30.
6. Select File, Save Scene As and save the file as **Flaming sphere.mb**.

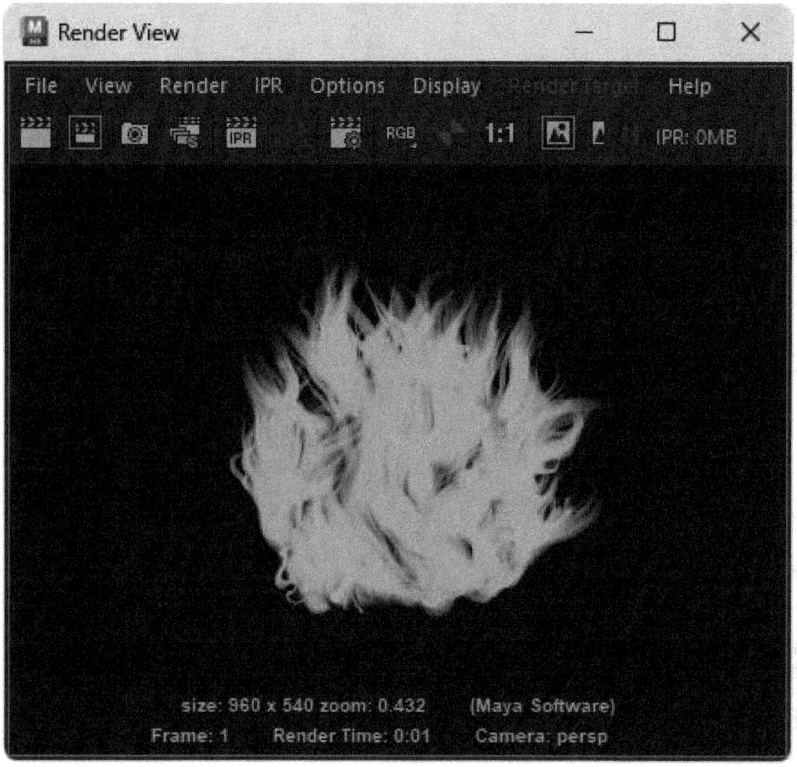

FIGURE 10-30
A flaming sphere

Lesson 10.4-Tutorial 2: Auto-Paint on Objects

1. Create a NURBS sphere object using the Create, NURBS Primitives, Sphere menu command.
2. With the sphere selected, click on the Cumulus Cloud Brush icon in the Paint Effects, Clouds section of the Content Browser.
3. Select the Generate, Auto Paint, Paint Grid menu command.

   Clouds are automatically added to surround the sphere.
4. Select the sphere object again.
5. Click on the Lightning Brush icon in the Paint Effects, Electrical section of the Content Browser.
6. Select the Generate, Auto Paint, Paint Random menu command.
7. Select the Panels, Panel, Paint Effects menu command to enter Scene Painting mode.

   The sphere surrounded with clouds and lightning is displayed, as shown in Figure 10-31.
8. Select File, Save Scene As and save the file as **Cloud and lightning sphere.mb**.

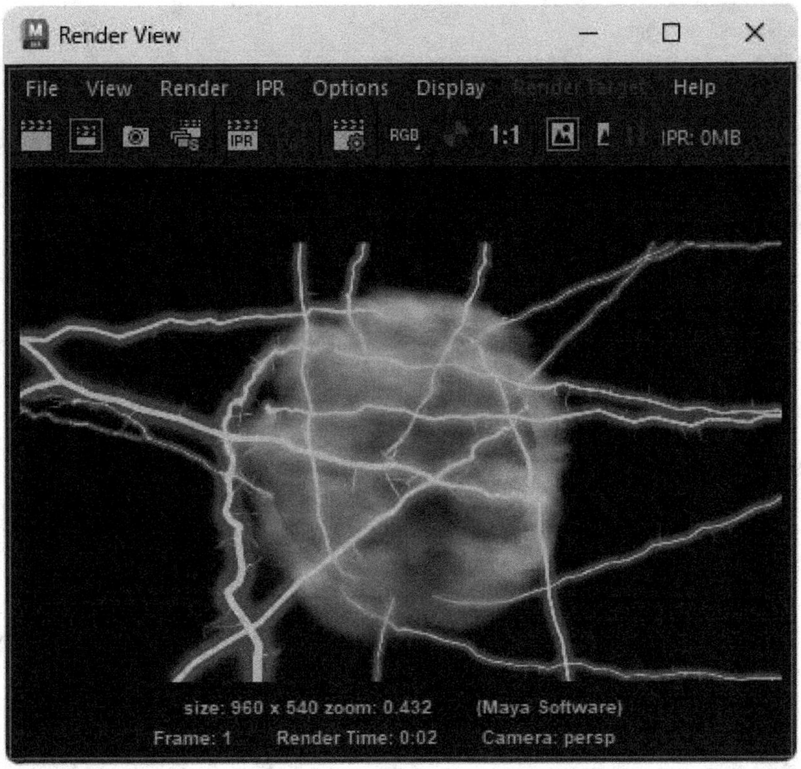

FIGURE 10-31

An auto-painted sphere

Lesson 10.5: Edit Paint Effects

You can edit paint strokes that have been drawn in the Modeling or Scene Painting mode once you select them using the Attribute Editor. Every stroke that is painted includes a tab in the Attribute Editor for the stroke, for the brush, and for the time.

Selecting Strokes

Before you can edit existing strokes, you need to select them. You can select a stroke using the Paint Effects Strokes selection mask by right-clicking on the Curves selection mask in the Status Line, or you can display all strokes as wireframe lines in Scene Painting mode by holding down the Ctrl/Command key. You can also use the Generate, Select Brush/Stroke Names Containing menu command. This opens a dialog box, shown in Figure 10-32, in which you can type the name of the brush or stroke you want to select. Selected strokes appear light green, and their tabs appear in the Attribute Editor. The Edit, Select All by Type, Strokes menu command selects all strokes.

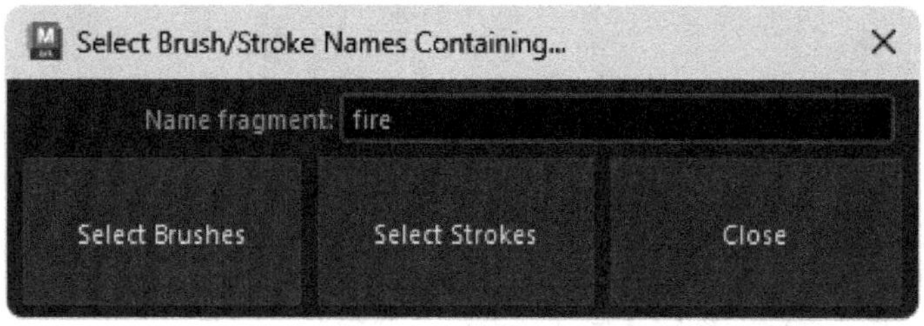

FIGURE 10-32

The Select Brush/Stroke Names Containing dialog box

Editing Strokes

Once a stroke is selected, you can edit its stroke attributes or the brush attributes used to create it using the Attribute Editor or the Channel Box. Changes to the stroke are displayed immediately.

Converting Strokes to Polygons

If you really want to edit Paint Strokes, you can convert them to polygons with the Modify, Convert, Paint Effects to Polygons menu command. There are also options to convert Paint Effects to curves and to NURBS. Figure 10-33 shows a set of crystals created as a Paint Effect that has been converted to polygons.

FIGURE 10-33

Paint Effects converted to polygons

Changing the Default Light

Another way to change the Paint Effects is to edit the default light that they use. In Scene Paint mode, the default light is shown as four dark red arrows that point in the direction that the light is shining. If you hold down the Ctrl/Command key, you can select these light arrows. When selected, their attributes show up in the Attribute Editor, where you can change their light type, color, and intensity. You can also set the light's transform node.

Lesson 10.5-Tutorial 1: Select and Edit Strokes

1. Select the File, Open Scene As menu command, and then locate and open the Curly hair sphere.mb file.

   This file includes a NURBS sphere that has been auto-painted with the Curly Hair brush.
2. Select the Generate, Select Brush/Stroke Names Containing menu command.
3. In the dialog box that appears, type **Hair** and click the Select Brushes button.

   The Curly Hair Brush node appears in the Attribute Editor.
4. Enter a value of 1.25 for the Global Scale.

   The brush used to create the Paint Effect is updated, as shown in Figure 10-34.
5. Select File, Save Scene As and save the file as **Curly hair sphere - short.mb**.

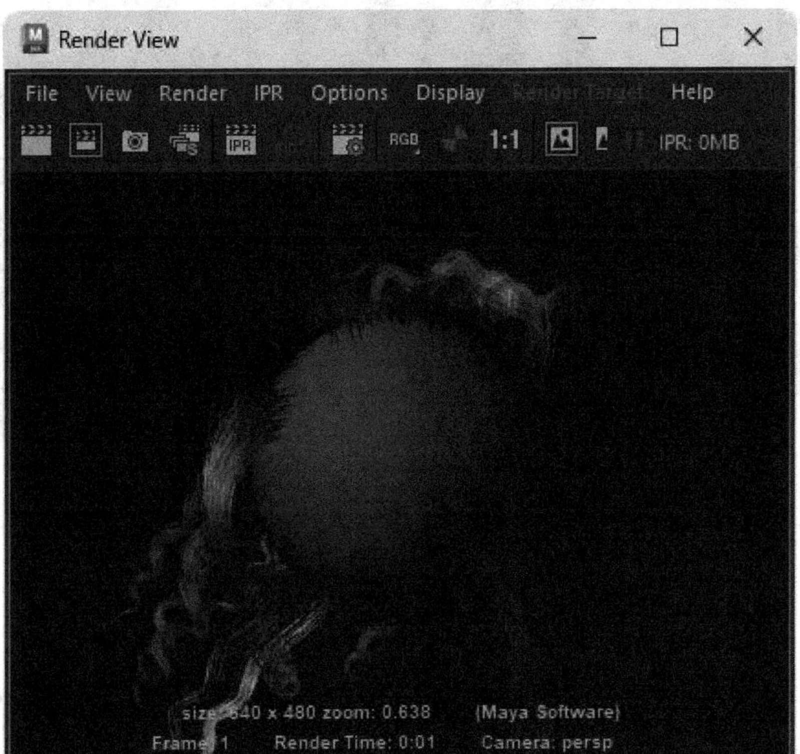

FIGURE 10-34

Edited brush values

Lesson 10.5-Tutorial 2: Convert Paint Effects to Polygons

1. Select the Panels, Panel, Paint Effects menu command to enter Scene Painting mode.
2. Click on the Light Bulb Brush icon in the Paint Effects, Objects Mesh section of the Content Browser.
3. Drag in the view panel to create a bunch of light bulbs.
4. Select the Modify, Convert, Paint Effects to Polygons menu command.

   All the light bulbs are now polygon objects, as shown in Figure 10-35, and you can edit them using the Edit Polygons menu options.
5. Select File, Save Scene As and save the file as **Polygon light bulbs.mb**.

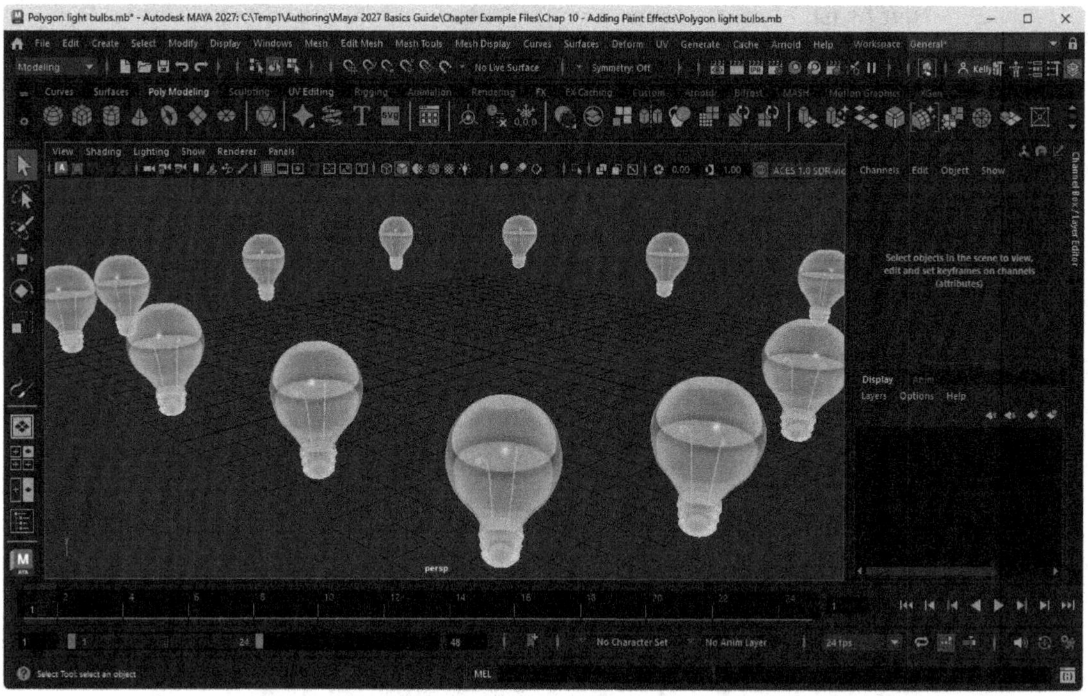

FIGURE 10-35

Polygon light bulbs

Chapter Summary

This chapter covers Maya's innovative Paint Effects feature. Using one of the many preset brushes, you can quickly create Paint Effects such as flowers, trees, clouds, and buildings without having to model and texture objects. In addition to the presets, you can create custom brushes by blending effects of different brushes. The Paint Effects menu and Settings dialog box include many settings for controlling every aspect of the paint strokes, including size, color, glow, illumination, and so on. The Canvas interface lets you paint and save images in 2D, or you can paint directly on 3D objects in the 3D scene. You can convert objects created with Paint Effects into polygon objects.

What You Have Learned

In this chapter, you learned

* How to access the Paint Effects panel.
* How to access the preset brushes found in the Content Browser.
* How to create new brushes by blending existing brushes.
* How to redraw and clear the current view.
* How to change the brush settings.
* How to use the Paint, Smear, Blur, and Erase brushes.
* How to change the brush size and color.
* How to enable brush illumination, glows, and shadows.
* How to create and save custom brushes.
* How to use the Paint Effects canvas.
* How to change the canvas size and enable seamless textures.
* How to save canvas images.
* How to save an alpha channel.
* How to paint on 3D objects.
* How to use the Auto Paint features.
* How to select and edit paint strokes.
* How to convert paint strokes to polygons.

Key Terms From This Chapter

* **Paint Effects.** An innovative Maya feature that lets you paint objects in the scene using brushes.
* **Brush.** An interface element used to create Paint Effects within a scene.
* **Content Browser.** A dialog box that holds presets that can be quickly selected, such as Paint Effects.
* **Stroke.** The resulting lines produced by dragging a brush in the scene.
* **Canvas.** A 2D interface where you can paint and save objects.
* **Seamless texture.** An image that allows strokes drawn on one edge of the canvas to be wrapped to the opposite edge.
* **Alpha channel.** An image that shows the transparency values of the scene as a grayscale image.

* **Auto Paint.** A painting mode that automatically applies strokes to the selected object.

Chapter 11
Using Cameras and Lights

IN THIS CHAPTER

- 11.1 Work with cameras.
- 11.2 Create a background.
- 11.3 Create and position lights.
- 11.4 Change light settings.
- 11.5 Create light effects.

Before moving on to animation and rendering, there are two more object types that you'll need to learn how to create and use—cameras and lights.

You can position cameras anywhere within the scene and then look at the current scene in a unique way through these positioned cameras. A single scene can contain several cameras, and cameras can be animated. Several types of cameras exist. The Camera and Aim camera type includes an Aim point that you can place at the location where the camera should be focused. The Camera, Aim and Up camera type includes two Aim points, one for aiming the camera direction and the other for controlling how the camera twists about its focus axis.

Camera attributes include **Angle of View, Focal Length,** and **Clipping Planes.** You can also set a camera to create a depth-of-field effect, which focuses on a specific point in the scene and blurs all other objects.

You can attach backgrounds to cameras and then render them using an **image plane.** Using this image plane, you can create a background consisting of a solid color, a texture, or a loaded image. Background images are rendered with the scene.

Lights are critical to the success of a scene, and light placement and settings should be well-thought-out in order to convey the appropriate ambience. A typical lighting design includes a main light that provides most of the light for the scene and is used to create shadows, a background light that is positioned behind the main objects, and two or more secondary lights that are positioned in front of and to the sides of the scene objects, providing extra light.

There are several types of lights in Maya, each with its own advantages. They include Spot lights, Point lights, Directional lights, Volume lights, Area lights, and Ambient light. You can position lights using the transform tools and interactively change a light's settings using light manipulators. Attributes include Color, Intensity, and Decay.

You can enable shadows for lights using **depth maps** or **Ray Traced Shadows**. The difference is quality versus render speed. Depth maps are sufficient in most instances, but you might want to use Ray-Traced shadows when the scene requires a crisp, accurate shadow line.

You can also use lights to create a number of effects, including illuminated fog, glows, halos, and light effects.

Lesson 11.1: Work with Cameras

Behind every view panel is a camera that controls what is visible. By creating a custom camera, you can position the camera anywhere in the scene and change its settings.

Creating Cameras

Use the Create menu to create your own custom cameras. The Create, Cameras menu includes three camera types. The standard camera is used most often, but you can link the Camera and Aim camera to a point that can be aimed at a specific point in the scene. The Camera, Aim and Up camera is like the Camera and Aim camera, except it also includes a point for defining the camera's upward position. Figure 11-1 shows the icons for each of these cameras.

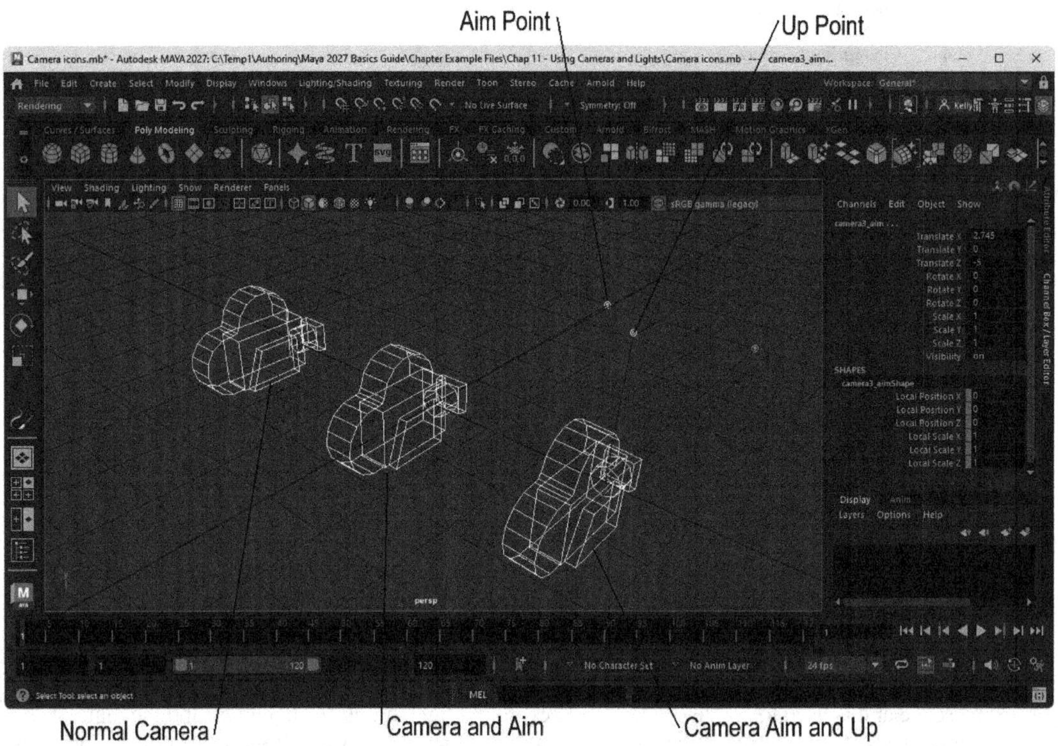

FIGURE 11-1

Camera icons

Changing Camera Settings

With a camera selected, you can change its settings using the Channel Box or the Attribute Editor. Use the View, Camera Attribute Editor panel menu command to get quick access to the current camera's settings, as shown in Figure 11-2. Sample attributes include the Angle of View, Focal Length, and Scale. Use the Near and Far Clip Planes options to set the nearest and farthest objects that the camera can see. When the viewing camera is selected, you can change its attributes and the view is updated.

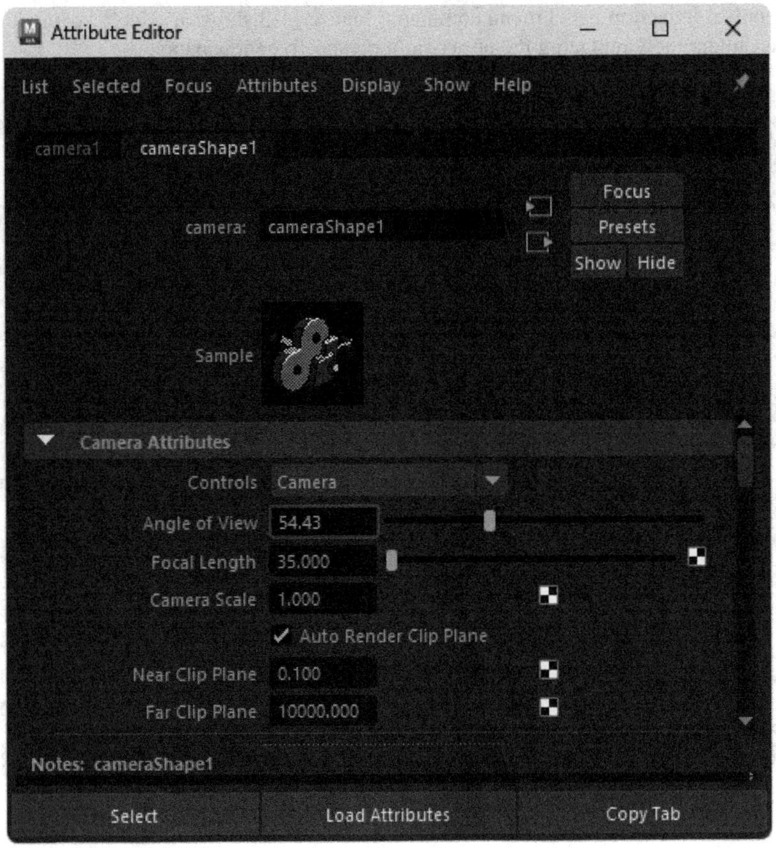

FIGURE 11-2

Camera settings

Selecting a Camera

You can easily select most objects in the scene by simply clicking on them, but the current camera is pointing at the scene, and its icon cannot be clicked on in the current view panel. There are several ways to select the current camera. You can select its icon from a different view panel; open and select it from the Outliner with the Windows, Outliner menu command; or select the View, Select Camera panel menu command.

Positioning Cameras

You can use the standard transform tools on cameras, but the Scale tool only changes the camera's icon size. You can rotate a Camera and Aim type camera by selecting and moving the camera's aim point. The top point of a Camera, Aim and Up type camera can be moved to twirl the camera about its center point. For precise camera positioning, you can always change the camera's transform node attributes in the Channel Box. If you have the camera exactly where you want it, you can prevent it from accidentally being moved with the View, Lock Camera panel menu command.

Looking Through a New Camera

With a camera selected, you can change the view panel so that the scene is seen through the new camera using the Panels, Look Through Selected panel menu command. You can force the current camera to look at a selected object using the View, Look at Selection panel menu command. Figure 11-3 shows a selected camera pointed at several objects and the camera view replacing the upper-right perspective view panel.

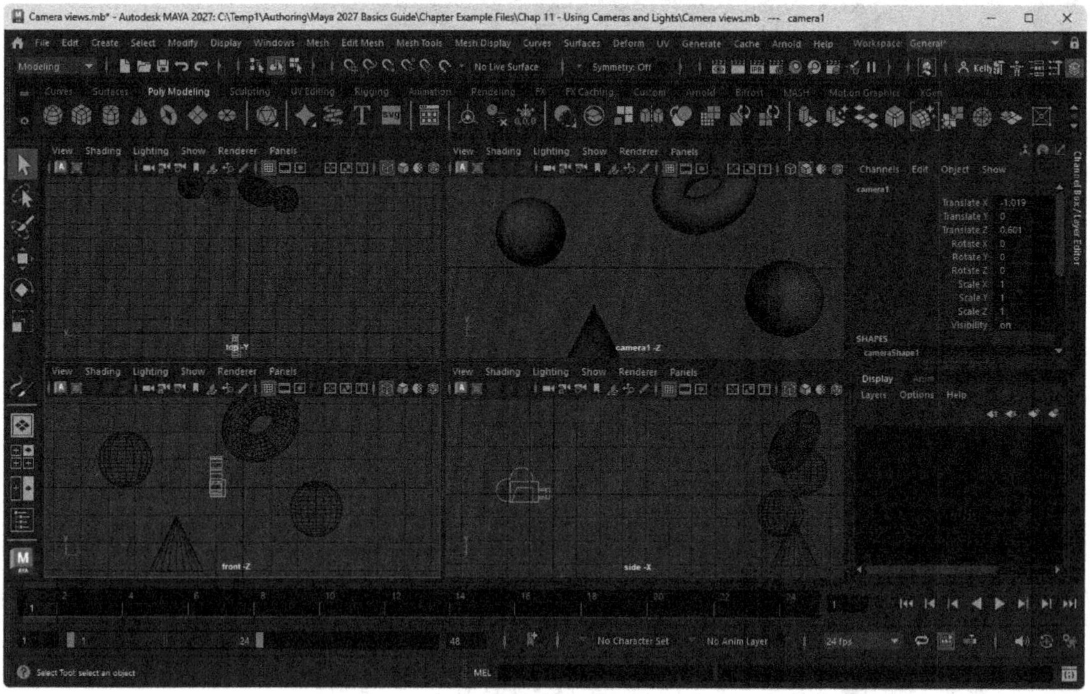

FIGURE 11-3

Camera view

Setting View Guidelines

When you work with a 3D scene, you can enable boundaries that mark the exact areas that appear within the rendered scene, as shown in Figure 11-4. The areas inside the boundaries are called **safe areas**. All areas within the safe-area boundaries are visible when the action or text is output to broadcast TV. The View, Camera Settings panel menu command is where you enable the Safe Action, Safe Title, and Resolution Gate boundary options.

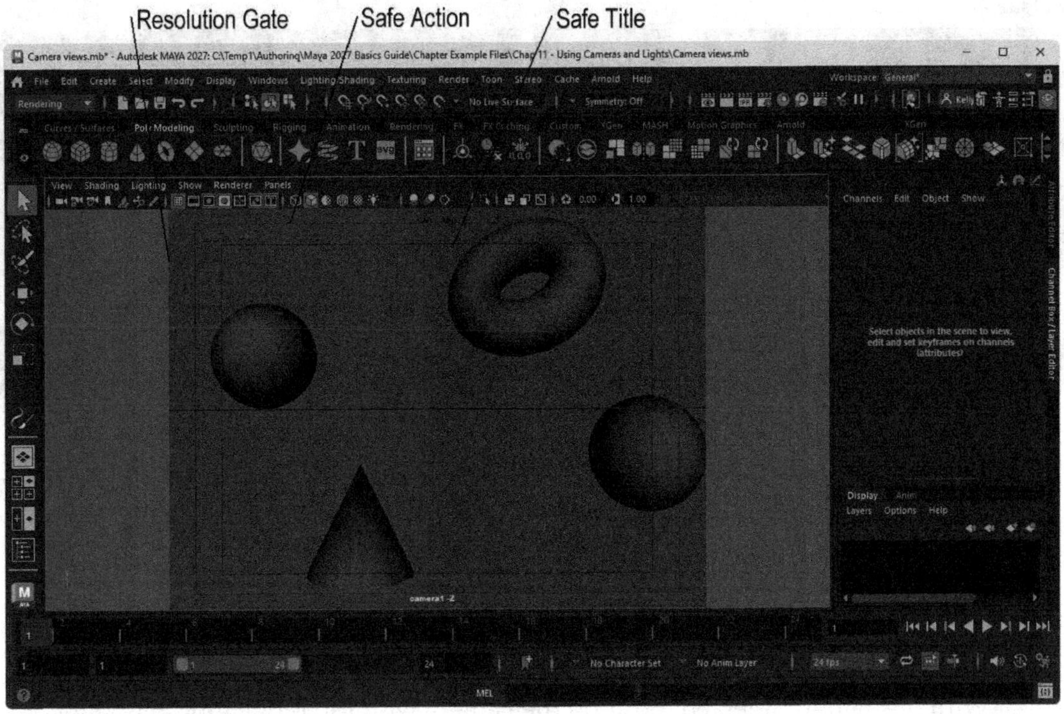

FIGURE 11-4

Safe boundaries

Changing the Depth of Field

You can set scene cameras to focus on a specific point within the scene, making all objects closer or farther from that point gradually blurred. This effect is known as a **depth-of-field** effect. In Maya, you can enable a depth-of-field effect in the Depth of Field section of the Attribute Editor. Once the effect is enabled, you can set attributes such as Focus Distance, which defines where the scene is in focus. Figure 11-5 shows a rendered scene of a row of simple trees with and without the Depth of Field option enabled.

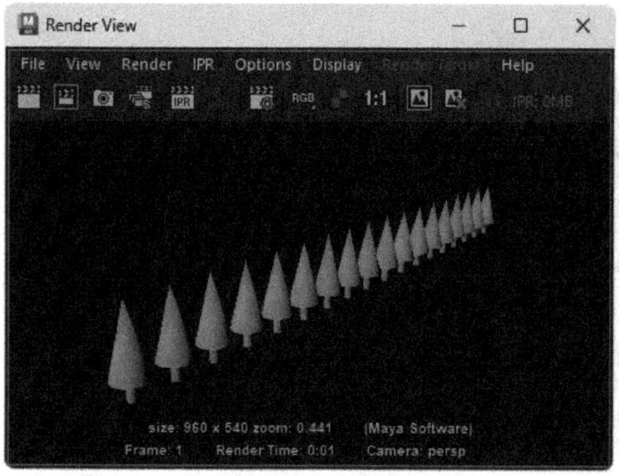

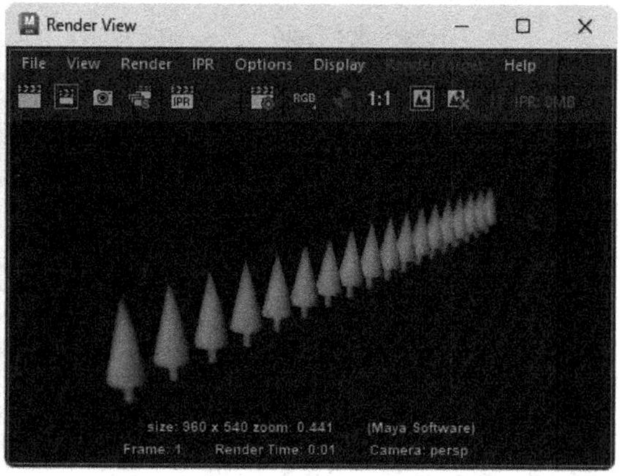

FIGURE 11-5

With and without depth of field

Lesson 11.1-Tutorial 1: Create a Camera

1. Select the File, Open Scene menu command and open the Simple chair.mb file.
2. Select the Create, Cameras, Camera menu command to create a new scene camera.
3. With the camera selected, position the camera with the Move tool so that it is pointing at the chair object.
4. With the camera still selected, choose the Panels, Look Through Selected panel menu command in the Perspective view panel.

   The perspective view is changed to the Camera1 view.
5. While using the other views and looking through the Camera1 view, continue to move and rotate the camera object in the other views until the chair is centered, as shown in Figure 11-6.
6. Select File, Save Scene As and save the file as **Centered chair.mb**.

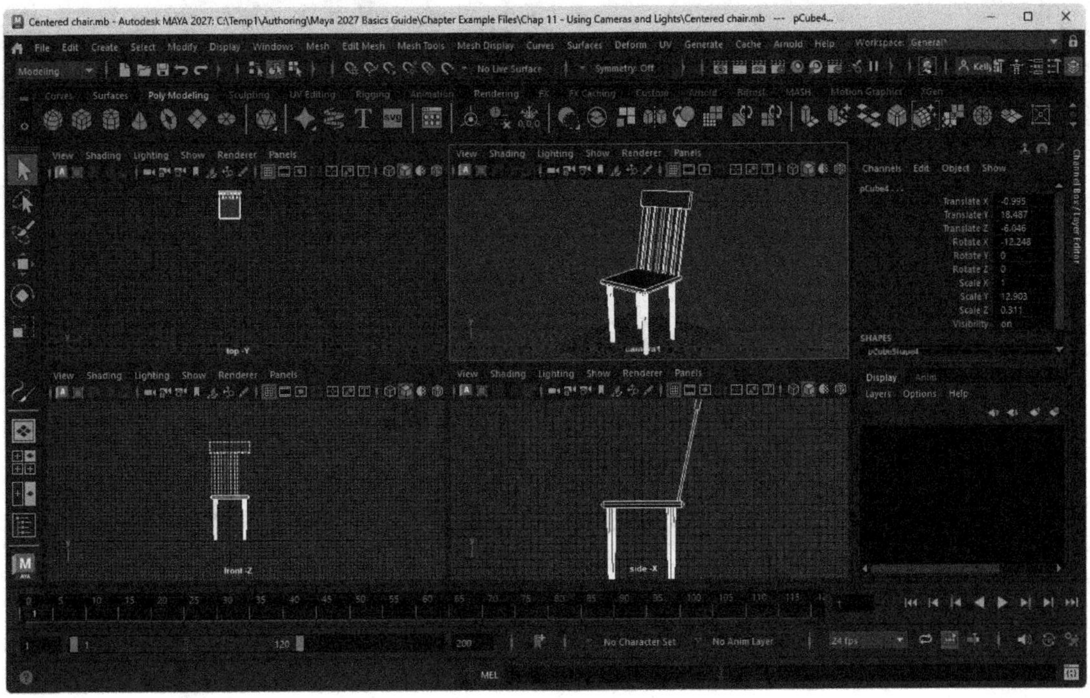

FIGURE 11-6

Centered chair

Lesson 11.1-Tutorial 2: Aim a Camera

1. Select the File, Open Scene menu command and open the Simple chair.mb file.
2. Select the Create, Cameras, Camera and Aim menu command to create a new scene camera.
3. With the camera selected, position the camera with the Move tool so that it is positioned a distance above and away from the chair object.
4. Using one of the other view panels, select the aim point and move it to the center of the chair.
5. Select the camera object again and choose the Panels, Look Through Selected panel menu command for the Perspective view.

   The aim point automatically controls the rotation of the camera so that it is pointing at the aim point, as shown in Figure 11-7.
6. Select File, Save Scene As and save the file as **Aimed chair.mb**.

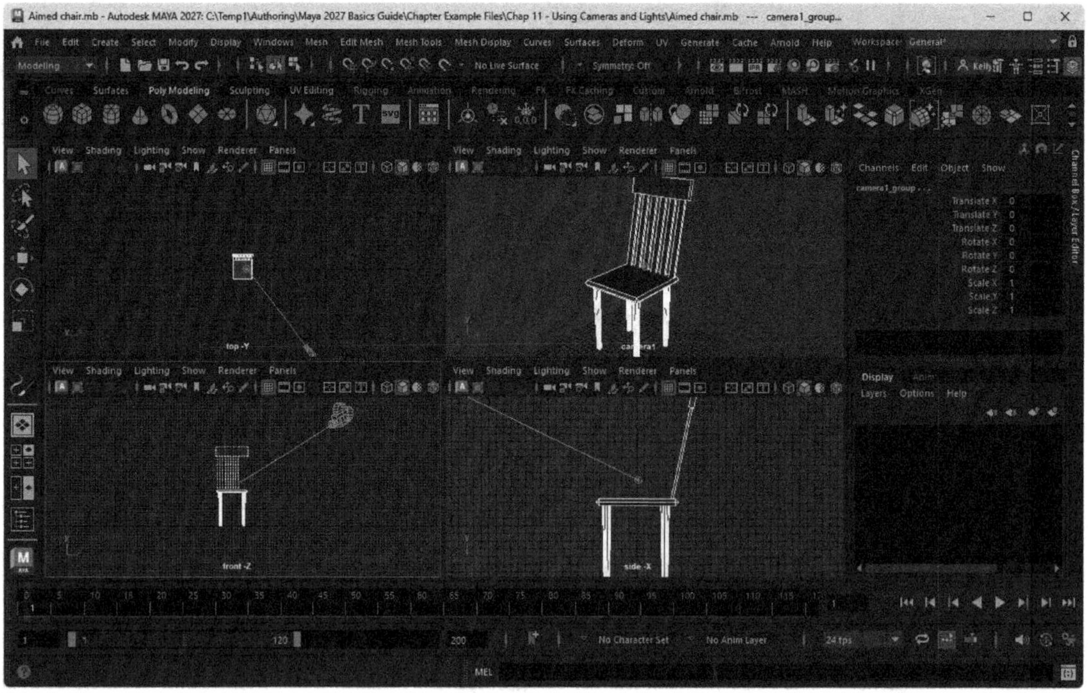

FIGURE 11-7

Aimed camera view

Lesson 11.1-Tutorial 3: Create a Depth-of-Field Effect

1. Select the File, Open Scene menu command and open the Row of chairs.mb file.
2. Select the Create, Cameras, Camera and Aim menu command to create a new scene camera.
3. With the camera selected, position the camera with the Move tool so that it is positioned a distance above and away from the chairs.
4. Select the aim point and move it to the center of the middle chair.
5. Select the camera object again and choose the Panels, Look Through Selected panel menu command for the Perspective view.
6. With the Camera1 view active, select the View, Camera Attribute Editor panel menu command or press the Ctrl/Command+A keys.
7. In the Depth of Field section, enable the Depth of Field option and set the Focus Distance value to be equal to the Focal Length value.
8. In the Environment section of the Attribute Editor, drag the Background Slider towards the right end to make the background light gray.
9. In the Render View dialog box, select the Render, Render, camera1 menu command to render the scene using the camera view.

   By setting the Focus Distance value to be equal to the Focal Length value, the camera focus is at the aim point and all other points are blurry, as shown in Figure 11-8.
10. Select File, Save Scene As and save the file as **Depth of field chairs.mb**.

FIGURE 11-8

Depth-of-field effect

Lesson 11.2: Create a Background

Each camera is linked to an image plane that you can use to provide a scene background. You can set this background to display a solid color, a texture, or an image. The image plane is rendered along with the scene when the camera view is selected.

Setting the Background Color

With the current camera selected, the Background Color attribute can be found in the Environment section of the Attribute Editor, as shown in Figure 11-9. To change the background color, just click on the color swatch and select a new color in the Color Chooser.

FIGURE 11-9

Environment section

Adding an Image Plane

You can add image planes to a camera object and then the image planes hold a texture of an image that acts as the background for the scene. To create an image plane for a camera, you first need to select a camera and click the Create button in the Environment section of the Attribute Editor for the camera node. The image plane appears as a rectangle with an X through it, as shown in Figure 11-10.

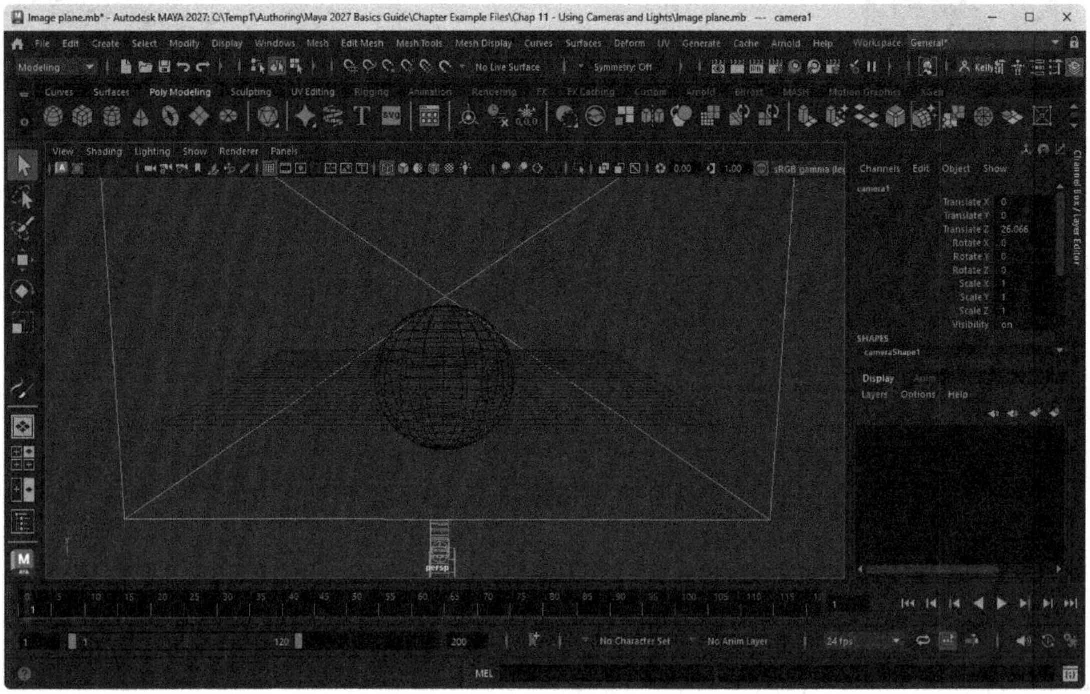

FIGURE 11-10

An image plane

Creating a Textured Background

The Type attribute in the Image Plane Attributes section for the Image Plane node includes two options—Image File and Texture. If you select the Texture option, you can click on the Create Render Node button and select a texture to use for the background. Figure 11-11 uses the Checker render node as a background.

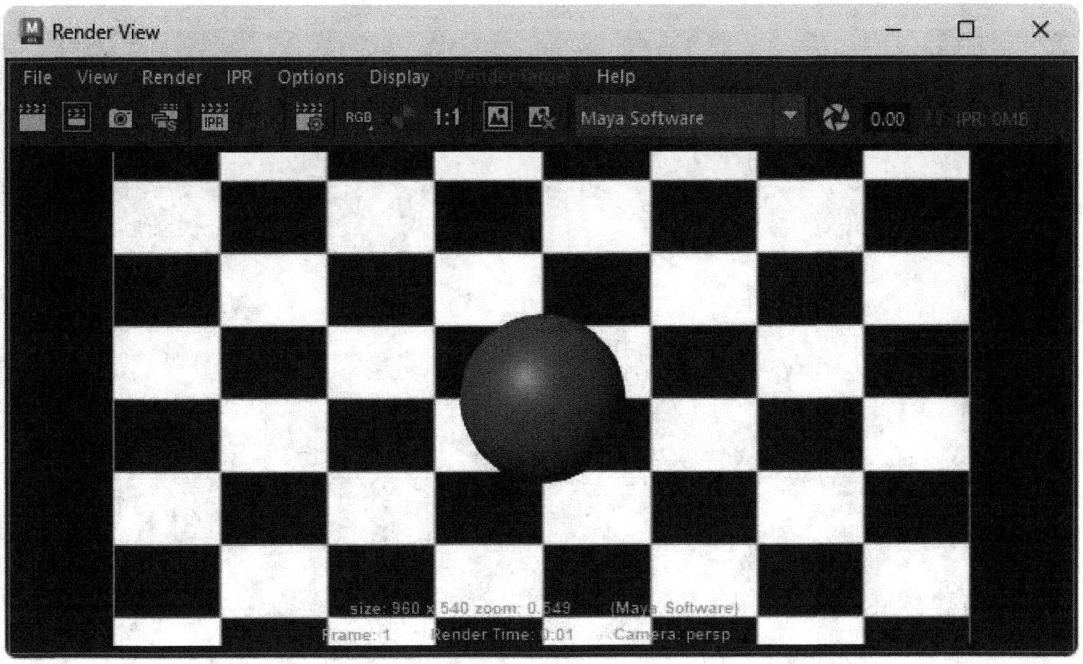

FIGURE 11-11

Texture background

Loading a Background Image

In addition to placing textures on an image plane, you can also select an image to be placed on the image plane. An easier way to load an image for the background is to use the View, Image Plane, Import Image panel menu command. This causes a file dialog box to open from which you can select the image to load. Figure 11-12 shows a rendered scene with an image background.

FIGURE 11-12

Image background

Positioning the Background

Images and textures that are loaded onto the image plane can be positioned using the attributes in the Placement section for the Image Plane node in the Attribute Editor. The Fit drop-down list allows you to select to fit the image using the Fill, Best, Horizontal, Vertical, or To Size options. The Fit to Resolution Gate and Fit to Film Gate buttons automatically fit the background. You can also offset and rotate the background image.

Tip

You can select and access the image plane attributes using the View, Image Plane, Image Plane Attributes panel menu command.

Lesson 11.2-Tutorial 1: Change Background Color

1. Select the File, Open Scene menu command and open the Hot air balloon.mb file.
2. Select the View, Select Camera panel menu command in the Perspective view panel.
3. Click on the Show Attribute Editor button in the Status Line or press the Ctrl/Command+A keys.
4. Click on the Background Color swatch in the Environment section of the Attribute Editor.
5. Select a light blue color in the Color Chooser and click the Accept button.
6. Click the Render the Current Frame button in the Status Line.

   The scene is rendered using the background color, as shown in Figure 11-13.

7. Select File, Save Scene As and save the file as **Background color.mb**.

FIGURE 11-13

Background color

Lesson 11.2-Tutorial 2: Change Background Texture

1. Select the File, Open Scene menu command and open the Hot air balloon.mb file.
2. Select the View, Select Camera panel menu command in the Perspective view panel.
3. Click on the Show Attribute Editor button in the Status Line or press the Ctrl/Command+A keys.
4. Click on the Create button in the Environment section of the Attribute Editor to create an image plane.

   An image plane is added to the current view.
5. Click the Type drop-down list and select Texture.
6. Click the Create Render Node button (which has a small checkered pattern on it) next to the Texture field.

   The Create Render Node dialog box appears.
7. Click the Cloud texture node.
8. Click on the place3dTexture1 node in the Attribute Editor and set all the Scale values to 50.
9. Click the Render the Current Frame button in the Status Line.

   The scene is rendered using the background texture, as shown in Figure 11-14.
10. Select File, Save Scene As and save the file as **Background texture.mb**.

FIGURE 11-14

Background texture

Lesson 11.2-Tutorial 3: Add and Position a Background Image

1. Select the File, Open Scene menu command and open the Hot air balloon.mb file.
2. Select the View, Select Camera panel menu command in the Perspective view panel.
3. Click on the Show Attribute Editor button in the Status Line or press the Ctrl/Command+A keys.
4. Click on the Create button in the Environment section of the Attribute Editor to create an image plane.

   An image plane is added to the current view.
5. Click the Open File button next to the Image Name field.
6. In the File dialog box, locate and open the Coast from Diamond Head.jpg image.
7. In the Placement section, Click the Fit to Resolution Gate button.
8. Click the Render the Current Frame button in the Status Line.

   The scene is rendered using the background image, as shown in Figure 11-15.
9. Select File, Save Scene As and save the file as **Background image.mb**.

FIGURE 11-15

Background image

Lesson 11.3: Create and Position Lights

If you render a scene with only the default lights, the scene might appear flat. Proper use of lights can create ambience for the scene.

Using Default Lights

If no lights are present in a scene, Maya renders the scene using its default lights. Default lights can be enabled using the 5 key and are only meant to help render objects during the modeling phase, before you add any lights. Default lights can be disabled in the Render Options section of the Render Settings dialog box for the Maya Software and Maya Hardware renderers.

Caution

The Arnold Renderer doesn't use default lights and is enabled by default. If you try to render the scene using Arnold before adding any lights, the scene objects will appear black.

Understanding the Light Types

Maya includes several types of lights that you can use. One of the key differences between these light types is the shape of the light source and the direction that the light is cast. The light types include:

- **Ambient light.** Raises the overall light in the scene by increasing the brightness of all objects.
- **Directional light.** Casts light in parallel rays from a cylindrical source.
- **Point light.** Casts light equally in all directions from a single point.
- **Spot light.** Casts light from a cone that can be positioned.
- **Area light.** Casts light equally from a specified area.
- **Volume light.** Casts light within a specified volume.

Figure 11-16 shows each of the light types.

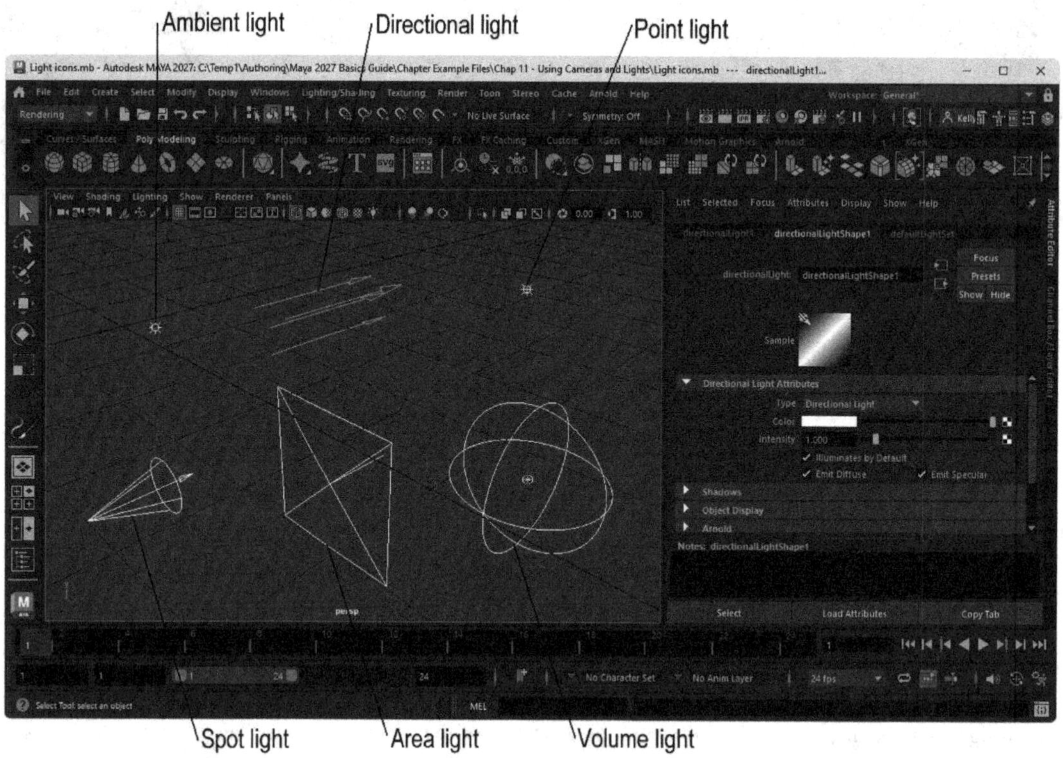

FIGURE 11-16

The Light types

Creating Lights

You can create any light type using the Create, Lights menu. You can also create lights using the Create Bar in the Hypershade. Each light type has an Options dialog box in which you can change settings prior to creating the light.

Manipulating Lights

When lights are created, their icon appears in the view panel. Clicking on the Display, Show, Light Manipulators menu command enables the light manipulator, shown in Figure 11-17. Clicking on the manipulator switches the attributes that can be changed. For all lights (except the Spot light), the first mode lets you change the light and aiming point's position and the second mode lets you set the light's pivot point.

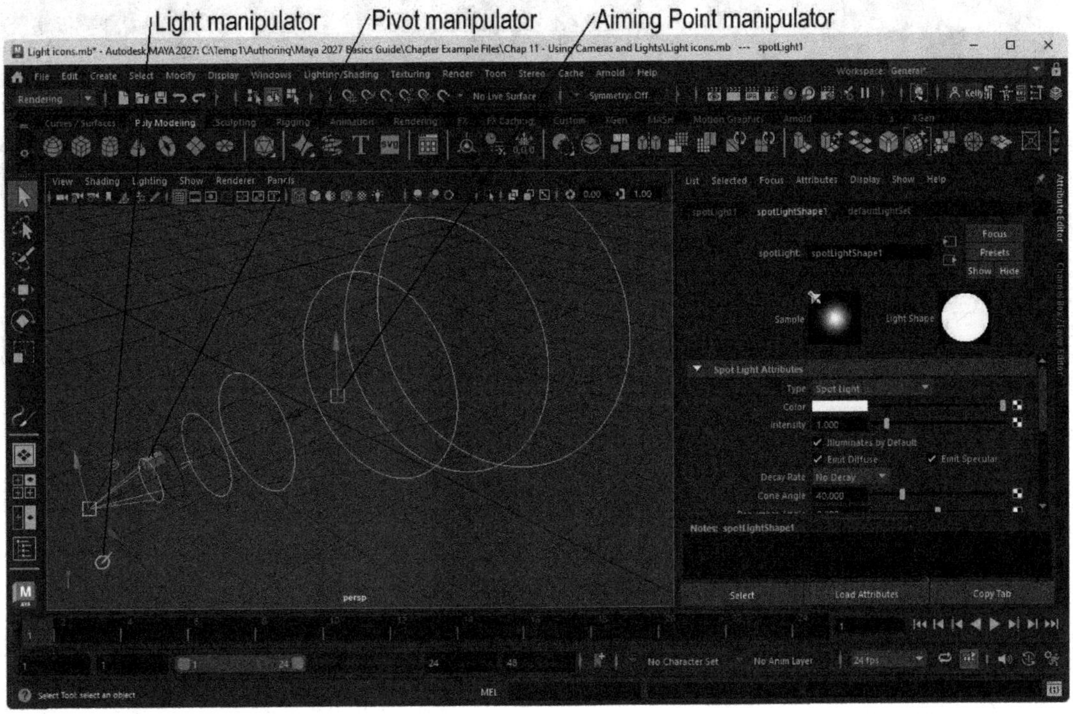

FIGURE 11-17

The light manipulators

Manipulating Spot Lights

Spot lights include many additional attributes that can be changed with the light manipulator. Clicking on the light manipulator switches between attributes for the Cone Radius, the Penumbra Radius, and the Decay. For each of these attributes, you can drag to change its value. Figure 11-18 shows a Spot light with the Decay manipulator enabled.

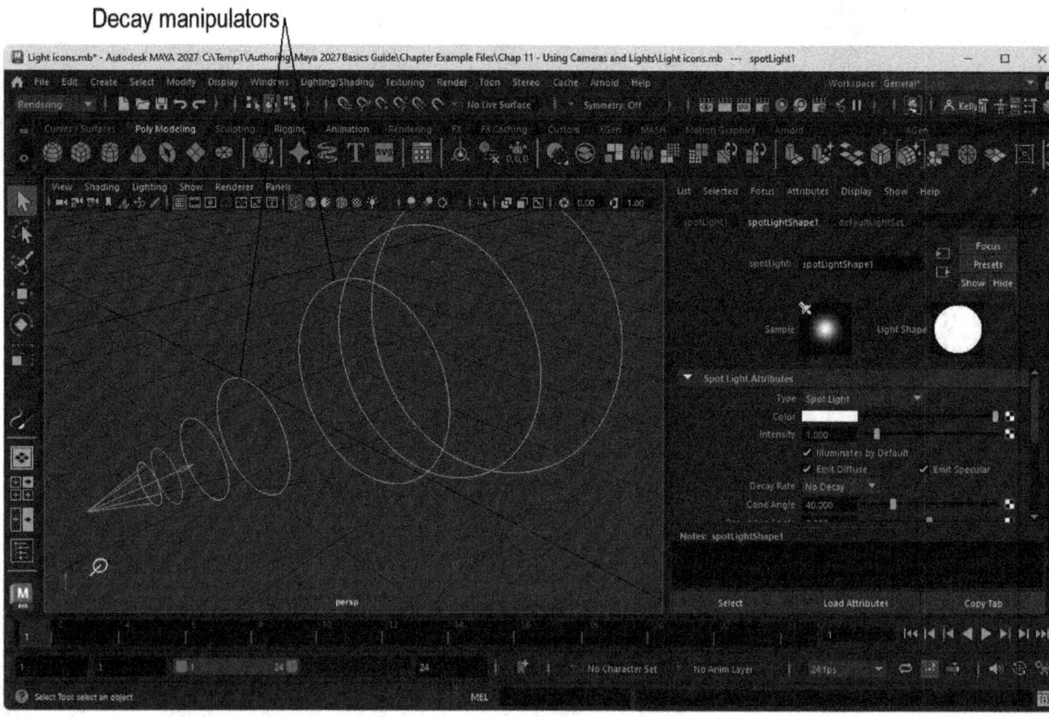

FIGURE 11-18

Decay manipulator

Lesson 11.3-Tutorial 1: Create and Manipulate a Light

1. Select the File, Open Scene menu command and open the Tree.mb file.
2. Select the Create, Lights, Spot Light menu command.

   A light icon is added to the scene at the origin.
3. Select the Scale tool and scale the light icon to increase its size.
4. Click on the Display, Show, Light Manipulator menu command. The default manipulator lets you move the camera and aiming point.
5. With the light selected, change the Intensity value in the Channel Box to 2.0.
6. Select the Perspective view panel and press the 5 key to enable smooth shading, then press the 7 key to see the light effect.
7. Drag in the various views until the light is set a distance above and away from the tree and the aim point is at the tree's base, as shown in Figure 11-19.
8. Click the Render the Current Frame button in the Status Line.

   The rendered scene is displayed using the spot light, as shown in Figure 11-20.
9. Select File, Save Scene As and save the file as **Spot light on tree.mb**.

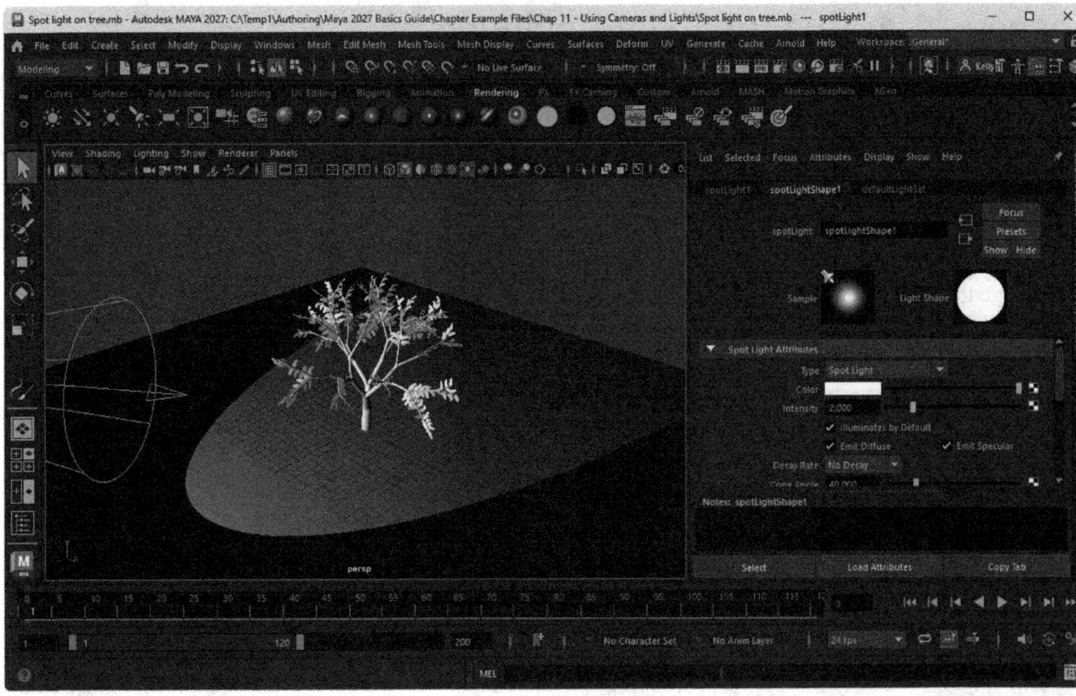

FIGURE 11-19

The Spot light

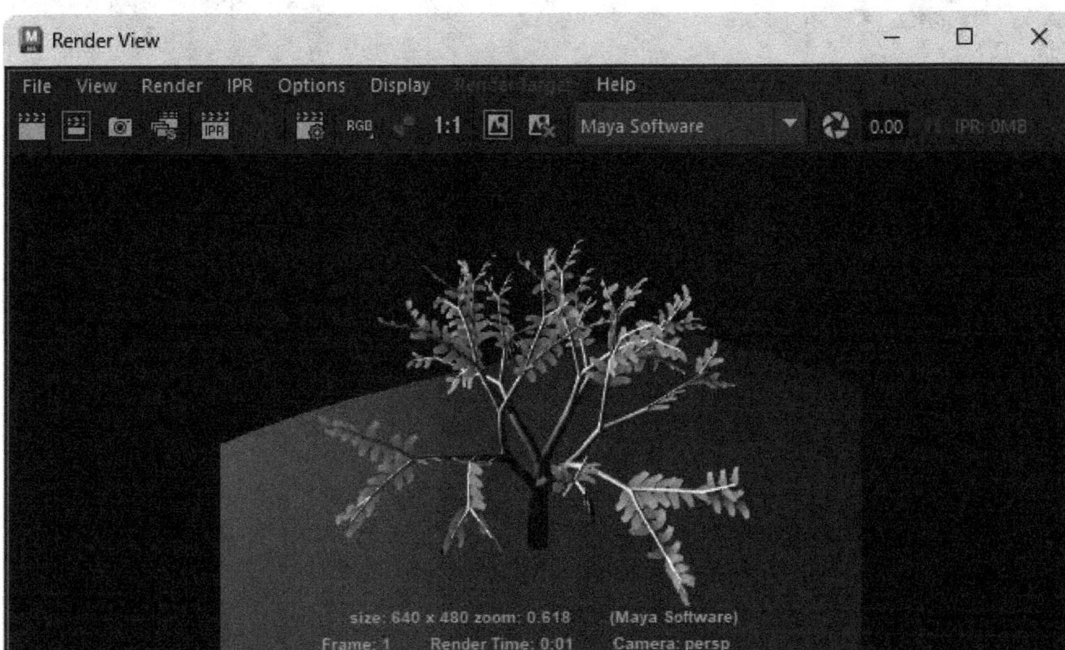

FIGURE 11-20

A rendered Spot light

Lesson 11.4: Change Light Settings

You can access a light's attributes in the Attribute Editor when the light is selected; you can also access these attributes by double-clicking on the light's icon in the Hypershade. Each light includes a Type attribute that you can use to switch between different light types.

Changing Light Color

Although most lights are white, lights can have color. Clicking on the color swatch in the Attribute Editor lets you change the light color in the Color Chooser. Figure 11-21 shows four Spot lights with different colors.

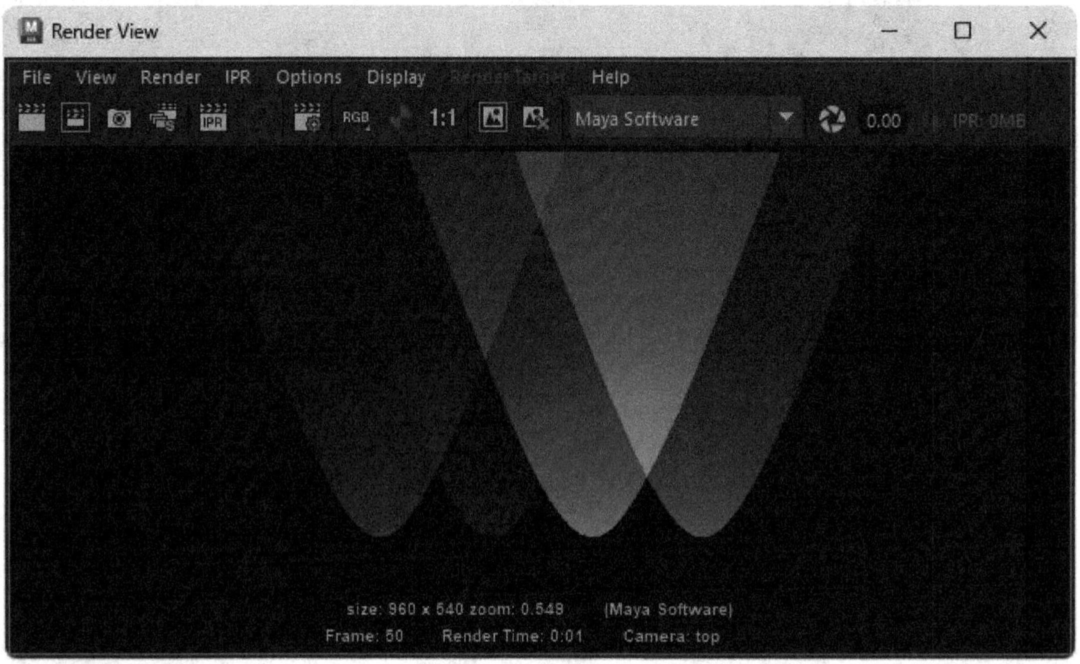

FIGURE 11-21

Colored spot lights

Changing Light Intensity and Decay

The brightness of a light is controlled by its Intensity attribute. For several light types (Area, Point, and Spot), you can select a Decay rate. This attribute defines how quickly the **light intensity** decreases over distance. The options include No Decay, Linear, Quadratic, and Cubic. Figure 11-22 shows each of the Decay types.

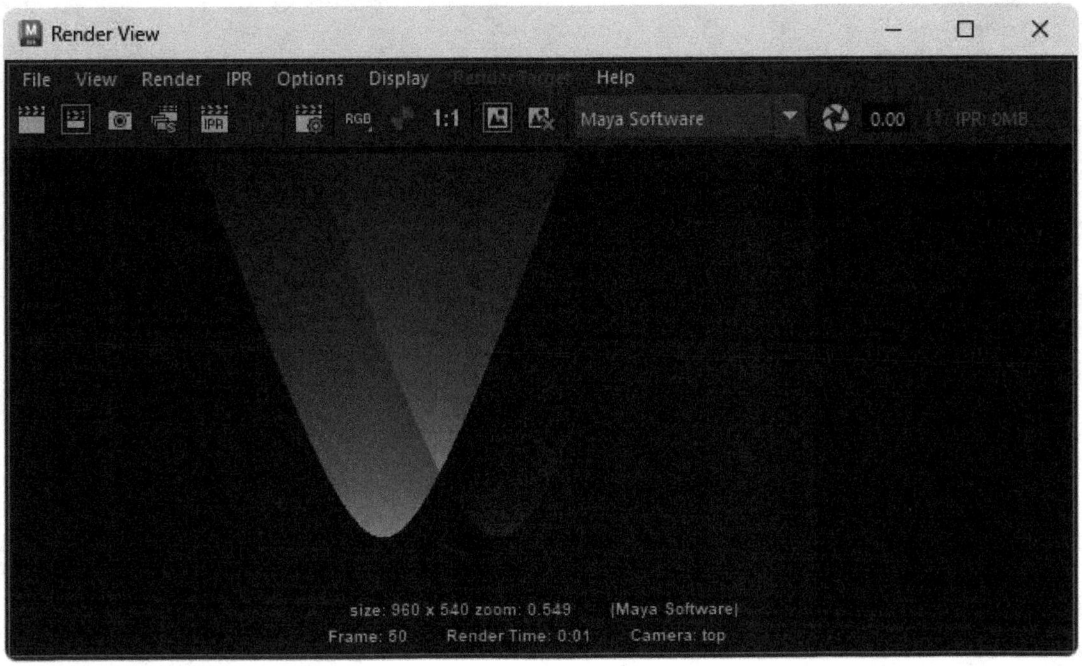

FIGURE 11-22

Decaying lights

Enabling Shadows

Maya includes support for two types of shadows—Depth Map shadows, which render quickly and are less accurate, and Raytraced shadows, which are more accurate but take longer to render. You can enable either shadow type with the Use Depth Map Shadows or the Use Ray Trace Shadows options. Figure 11-23 shows Depth Map shadows cast by a spherical object.

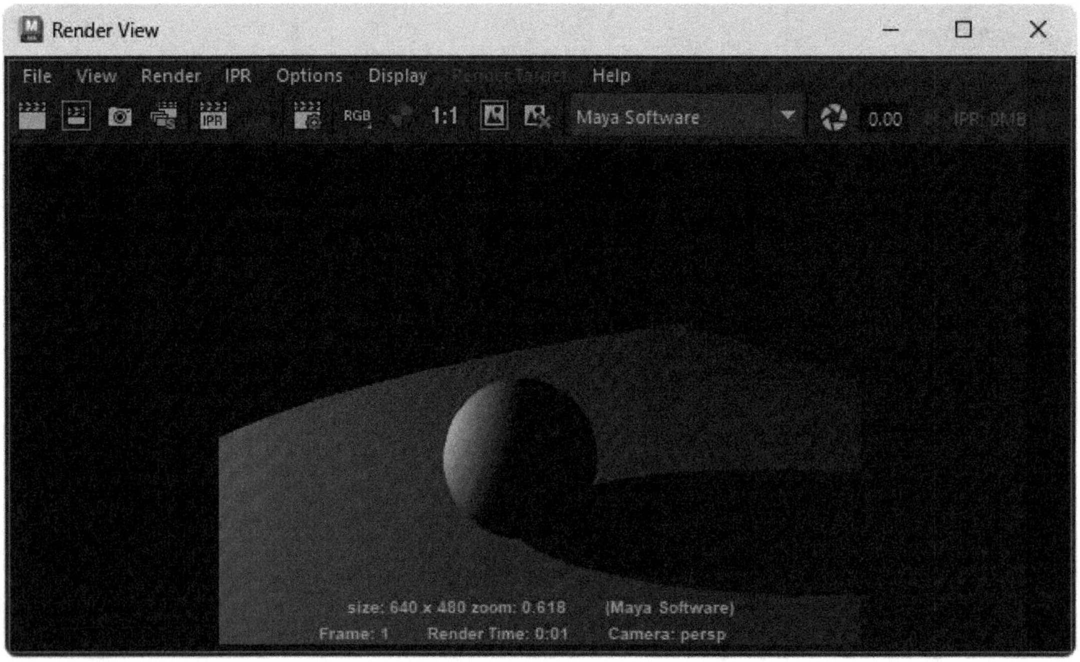

FIGURE 11-23

Depth Map shadows

Viewing All Scene Lights

When a full scene comes together, it can likely include a whole assortment of lights which makes selecting and editing lights difficult. However, Maya includes a handy tool for viewing and editing all the scene lights in a single location. The Light Editor, shown in Figure 11-24, is opened using the Windows, Rendering Editors, Light Editor menu command.

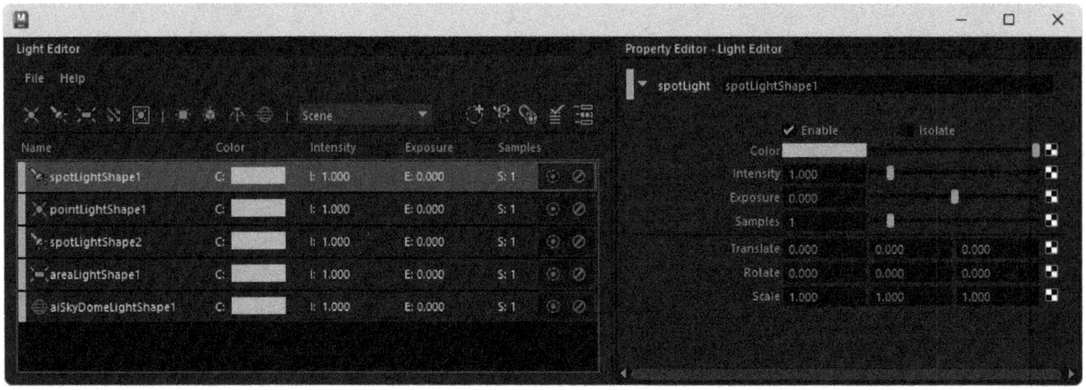

FIGURE 11-24

Light Editor

The Light Editor dialog box shows all scene lights along with controls and attributes that can be edited. This provides a way to quickly see the effect of each individual light in the scene. There are options to

Enable/Disable and Isolate each light. Buttons along the top toolbar let you create new lights of any type including Arnold lights. Sets of lights can also be grouped together and you can also quickly change each light's Color, Intensity, Exposure, Samples, Position, Orientation, and Scale.

Lesson 11.4-Tutorial 1: Change Light Color and Intensity

1. Select the File, Open Scene menu command and open the Spot light on tree.mb file.
2. Select the Spot light object.
3. Click on the Show Attribute Editor button in the Status Line or press the Ctrl/Command+A keys.
4. Click on the Color swatch in the Attribute Editor.
5. Select a bright yellow color from the Color Chooser and click the Accept button.
6. Increase the Intensity value to 3.0.
7. Right-click on the Perspective view panel and click the Render the Current Frame button in the Status Line.

   The scene is rendered using the yellow Spot light, as shown in Figure 11-25.
8. Select File, Save Scene As and save the file as **Yellow spot light on tree.mb**.

FIGURE 11-25

Yellow Spot light

Lesson 11.4-Tutorial 2: Enable Shadows

1. Select the File, Open Scene menu command and open the Spot light on tree.mb file.
2. Select the Spot light object.
3. Click on the Show Attribute Editor button in the Status Line or press the Ctrl/Command+A keys.

4. Click to open the Depth Map Shadow Attributes section in the Attribute Editor.
5. Enable the Use Depth Map Shadows option.
6. Right-click on the Perspective view panel and click the Render the Current Frame button in the Status Line.

   The scene is rendered including shadows, as shown in Figure 11-26.
7. Select File, Save Scene As and save the file as **Shadowed spot light on tree.mb**.

FIGURE 11-26

Spot light and shadows

Lesson 11.5: Create Light Effects

You can add light effects to most lights in a scene using the Light Effects section of the Attribute Editor. These light effects can include fog, glows, halos, and **lens flares**. The key to several of these light effects is the Optical FX render node, found in the Glow section of the Utilities category of the Create Render Node dialog box. This render node includes the necessary settings to add glows, halos, and lens flares to a positioned light.

Note

Light effects aren't available for all light types, such as Ambient and Directional lights.

Creating Light Fog

If you look closely at the Attribute Editor for the selected light, you'll see that you can apply a render node to many attributes, including Color and Intensity. If you open the Light Effects section, you'll find several additional attributes, including Fog and Glow. To create one of the fog effects, you'll need to position the light where you want the illuminated fog to be and then click the Create Render Node button. This automatically adds the Light Fog render node to the light. For the Light Fog node, you can set Fog Color, Type, Radius, and Intensity options. Figure 11-27 shows a Fog light applied to a Point light in front of a sphere.

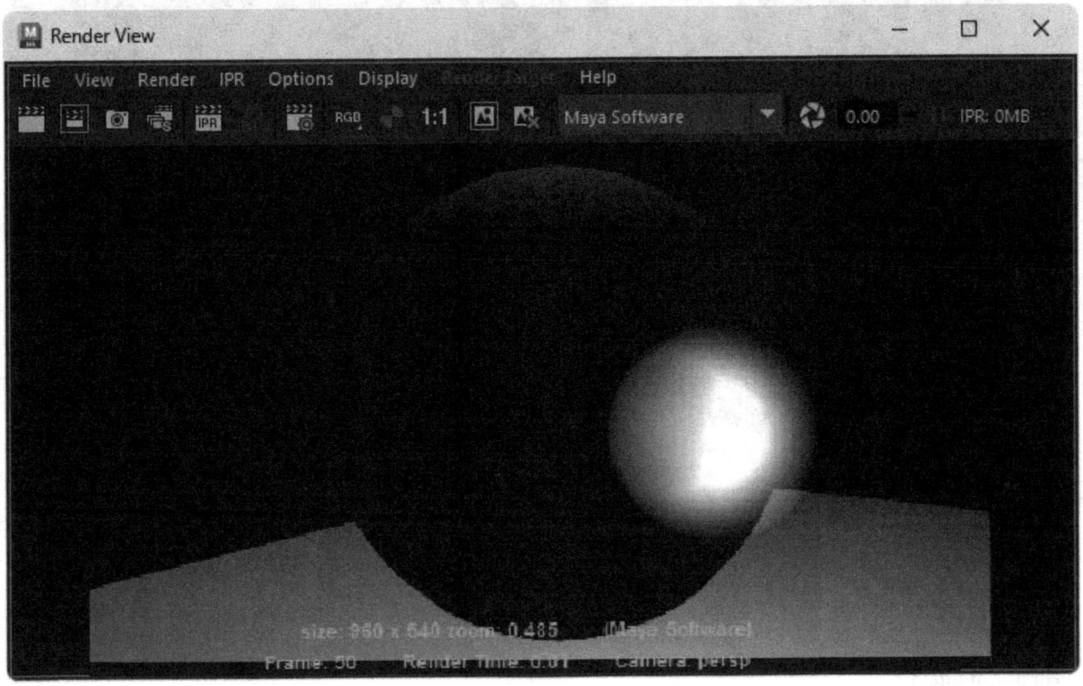

FIGURE 11-27

Fog light effect

Note

```
If the Light Fog effect isn't rendering, then
click the Environment Fog map icon in the Render
Options rollout of the Maya Software tab in the
Render Settings dialog box.
```

Creating Glows and Halos

If you click the Create Render Node button for the Glow attribute, the Optical FX render node is added. The Optical FX render node includes attributes for creating glows and halos. The options for each include None, Linear, Exponential, Ball, Lens Flare, and Rim Halo. You can also set the number of star points, glow and halo colors, spread, and intensity. Figure 11-28 shows a five-point Rim Halo applied using a Point light.

FIGURE 11-28

Halo light effect

Creating Lens Flares

Once you've added a glow or halo effect to a light, you can also enable a lens effect with the Lens Effect option. Lens flares have their own set of attributes, including Flare Color and Intensity. Figure 11-29 shows the same halo with the Lens Flare effect enabled.

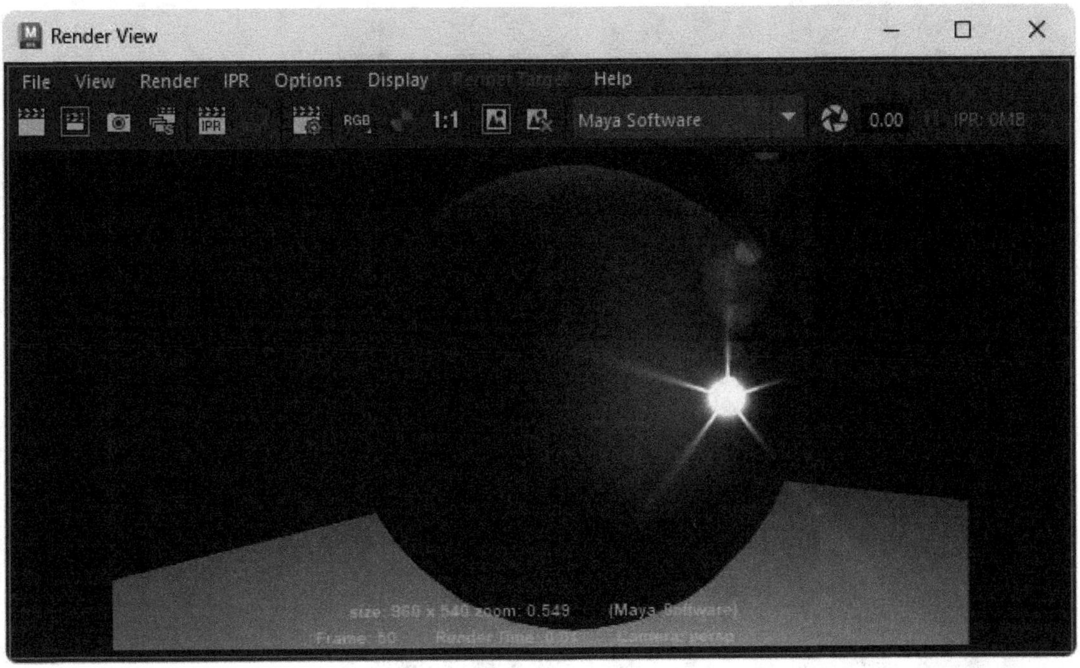

FIGURE 11-29

Lens Flare light effect

Lesson 11.5-Tutorial 1: Enable Light Fog

1. Select the File, Open Scene menu command and open the Background image.mb file.
2. Select the Create, Lights, Point Light menu command.
3. Drag the Point light with the Move tool and position it in front of the balloon object.
4. Click on the Show Attribute Editor button in the Status Line or press the Ctrl/Command+A keys.
5. Open the Light Effects section in the Attribute Editor.
6. Set the Fog Radius value to 3.0.
7. Click on the Create Render Node button to the right of the Light Fog attribute.

   A Light Fog render node is added to the light and its attributes are opened in the Attribute Editor, as shown in Figure 11-30.
8. Right-click on the Perspective view panel and click the Render the Current Frame button in the Status Line.

   The scene is rendered, as shown in Figure 11-31.
9. Select File, Save Scene As and save the file as **Light fog on balloon.mb**.

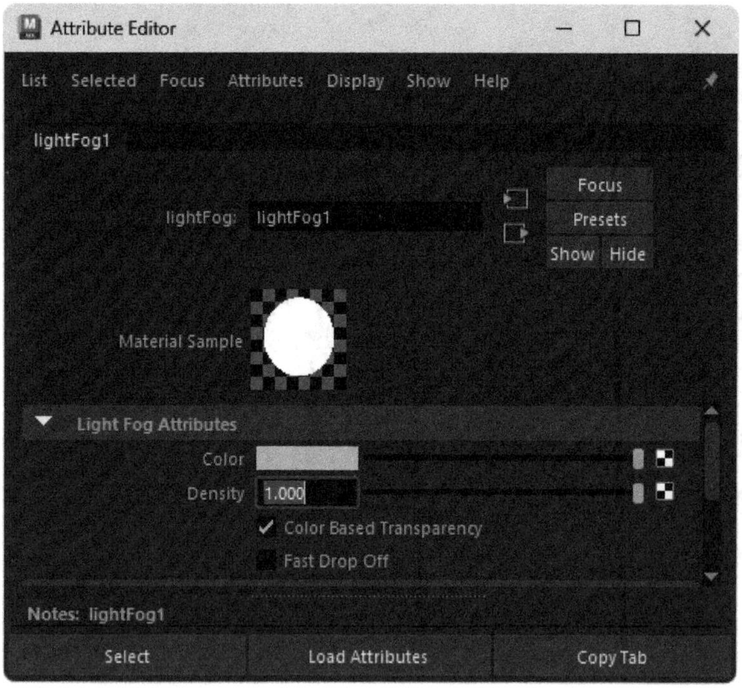

FIGURE 11-30

Light Fog render node

FIGURE 11-31

Fog light on balloon

Lesson 11.5-Tutorial 2: Enable a Halo Light Effect

1. Select the File, Open Scene menu command and open the Background image.mb file.
2. Select the Create, Lights, Point Light menu command.
3. Drag the Point light with the Move tool and position it in front of the balloon object.
4. Click on the Show Attribute Editor button in the Status Line or press the Ctrl/Command+A keys.
5. Open the Light Effects section in the Attribute Editor.
6. Click on the Create Render Node button to the right of the Light Glow attribute.

   An Optical FX render node is added to the light and its attributes open in the Attribute Editor.
7. Enable the Active and Lens Flare options in the Optical FX Attributes section.
8. Right-click on the Perspective view panel and click the Render the Current Frame button in the Status Line.

   The scene is rendered, as shown in Figure 11-32.
9. Select File, Save Scene As and save the file as **Halo effect on balloon.mb**.

FIGURE 11-32

Halo light effect on balloon

Chapter Summary

This chapter covers cameras, background image planes, and lights. Cameras are non-visible objects placed in the scene that set the view of what is to be rendered. There are three camera types, including a camera with an aiming point. Cameras have special effects that you can use, including clipping planes and depth of field. Image planes are objects attached to a camera that hold a background that is rendered with the scene. This background can be a texture or a loaded image.

Lights add illumination and shadow effects to the scene. Of the six available light types, some have specialized features such as the Spot light, which allows you to set the amount of decay over time. You can also use lights to position special effects such as fog, glows, halos, and lens flares.

What You Have Learned

In this chapter, you learned

* How to create, position, and use cameras.
* How to change camera settings.
* How to see a view through the selected camera.
* How to create a depth-of-field effect.
* How to set a background color.
* How to create and use an image plane with a texture or an image.

* How to position a background image on an image plane.
* How to add a light to the scene.
* The different light types.
* How to use the various light manipulators.
* How to change a light's color, intensity, and decay values.
* How to enable shadows.
* How to access the Light Editor.
* How to create light effects such as fog, glows, and halos.
* How to add a lens flare to the scene.

Key Terms From This Chapter

* **Angle of View.** A camera's angle value used to set the width of the scene viewed through the camera. Sets the width of the view area.
* **Focal Length.** A camera setting used to determine where the camera's focus is located.
* **Near and Far Clipping planes.** Near and Far camera planes that define where objects are not visible.
* **Safe area.** A set of camera markings that denote where title and action areas are definitely visible.
* **Depth of Field.** A camera effect where objects farther away from the focus point become gradually blurrier.
* **Image plane.** A background plane where a background texture or image can be loaded.
* **Default lights**. A set of lights that are available by default as part of a new scene.
* **Light decay**. A light property that causes light intensity to gradually diminish.
* **Light intensity**. A value that denotes the power of a light source.
* **Depth map shadow**. A shadowing method created by saving the shadows into a bitmap that is projected onto the scene.
* **Raytrace shadow**s. A shadowing method that computes shadows by following light rays as they move around the scene.

* **Lens flare**. A lighting effect that simulates the effect of pointing a camera at a light source.

Chapter 12
Animating with Keyframes

IN THIS CHAPTER

- 12.1 Set keyframes.
- 12.2 View an animation.
- 12.3 Animate using motion paths.
- 12.4 Edit animation curves.
- 12.5 Control animation timing and adding sound.
- 13.6 Create Multi-Shot Animations

Simple 3D animation is surprisingly easy. Because Maya knows the exact location of objects in the 3D scene, it can quickly and easily interpolate the location of an object as it moves between two different points in space. These locations in space are called **keyframes** and they define intermediate positions of an object along its motion.

You can set keyframes for an object's position, rotation, scale, and any object attribute that is keyable. All keys, once created, are displayed along the **Time Slider** at the bottom of the interface. You can copy and paste these keys to other objects and then shift and scale them as needed.

Once an animation is created, you view it by scrolling through the time frames in the Time Slider. A preview of the animation is shown in the view panel. The Animation Controls are also useful in moving through an animation sequence. If the view panel is having trouble updating the scene fast enough, you can send snapshots of the current scene to a buffer using the **Playblast** feature.

There are several features that make it easier to visualize the animated objects. These features include motion trails, which show the trajectory of the object's motion, and **ghosting**, which shows copies of the animated object as it progresses in its motion.

Besides keyframing, another common way to animate objects is to attach an object to a motion path. The object then follows the path over a given number of frames. This makes it easy to draw a curve that defines exactly where the object moves.

You can also edit animated scenes in the **Graph Editor,** where all object motions and attribute changes are shown as graphed curves and all keys are points. You can edit these curves and points by changing their smoothness and working with their tangents.

Another common editing interface is the **Dope Sheet,** which is useful in synchronizing the timing of different objects. Sound files can be loaded and synched with the animation using the Audio menu.

The **Sequencer** interface is used to combine several shots together from different cameras in the scene. It can also import audio files and export the entire sequencer to Playblast.

Lesson 12.1: Set Keyframes

You can animate using keys by positioning an object at its starting state and setting a key, and then changing it to its ending state and setting another key. Maya then interpolates between the two states for all the times in between the two keys. Keys enable you to create fairly complex animation sequences with a limited number of well-placed keys.

Note

`All animation menu commands are found in the Animation menu set.`

Setting Keys

When an object is in the exact position, you can set a key for the current time using the Key, Set Key menu command. You can also set keys by right-clicking on an attribute in the Attribute Editor or in the Channel Box and selecting Key Selected or Key All Keyable from the pop-up menu. Attributes that have keys set have a red mark to the left of the attribute value in the Channel Box or are shaded red in the Attribute Editor, as shown in Figure 12-1.

Tip

`The S key is the hotkey for setting keys.`

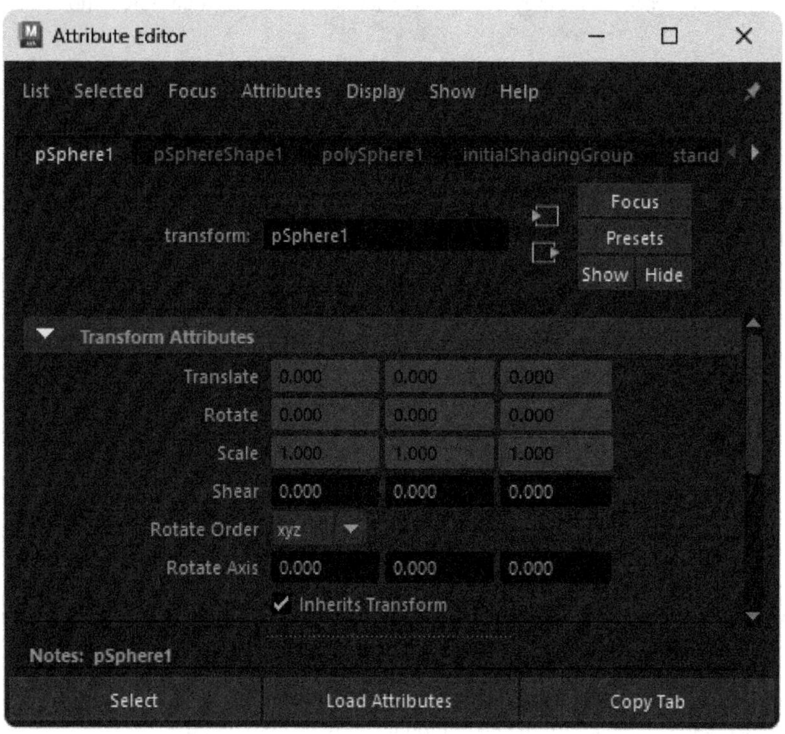

FIGURE 12-1

Keyed attributes

Using Auto Key

You can use **Auto Key** mode to automatically create keys for attributes that already have at least one key. To enable the Auto Key toggle, shown in Figure 12-2, click on the Auto Key button at the right end of the Range Slider. The button turns red when active. Once Auto Key is active, you can select a new time or update an attribute and the key is created automatically without needing to use the Set Keys menu command.

Caution

You need to create a keyframe for the selected object before enabling Auto Key or it won't work.

FIGURE 12-2

The Auto Key button

Selecting Keys

Keys for the selected object appear on the Time Slider as thin red lines. If you click on one of these red lines in the Time Slider, the current time is moved to that time and the key is selected. Selected keys are highlighted, as shown in Figure 12-3. If you hold down the Shift key and drag over several keys, the selected time turns light blue and all of the keys within that segment are selected, as shown in Figure 12-4. Double clicking on the Time Slider, selects all visible frames and keys. You can shift or scale the selected time by dragging on the arrows positioned within and at either end of the selected area.

Tip

Using the Key Tick Size setting in the Time Slider panel of the Preferences dialog box, you can increase the thickness of the keys displayed in the Time Slider.

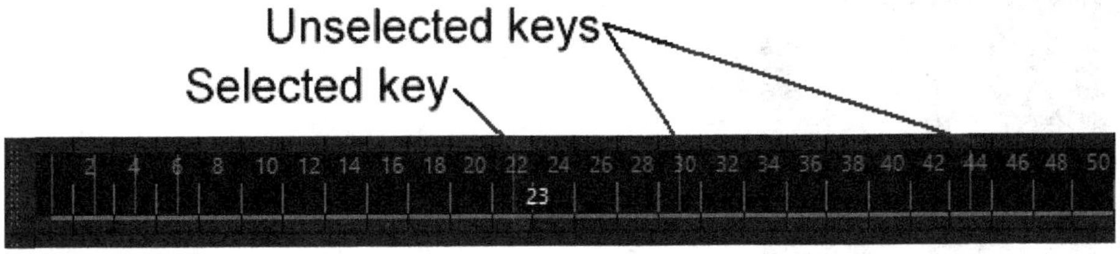

FIGURE 12-3

Time Slider keys

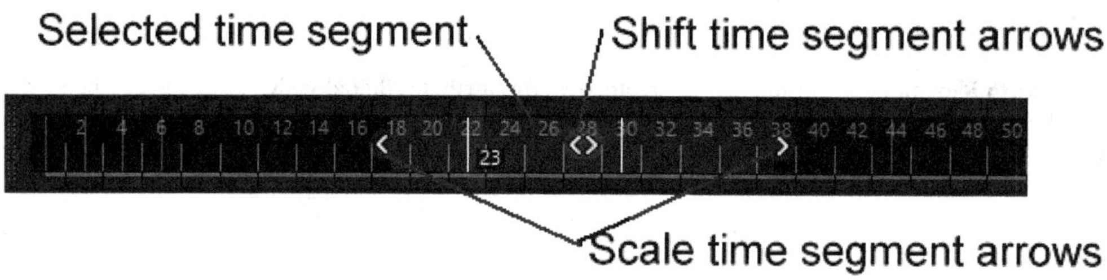

FIGURE 12-4

A selected time segment

Adding Bookmarks to the Time Slider

A time selection lets you work with a region of keys on the Time Slider, but it is only temporary. To make a more permanent selection that is easy to re-select, use the Time Slider Bookmark feature. You can access this feature using the Bookmark icon, shown in Figure 12-5, located to the right of the Range Slider. Clicking the Bookmark icon opens the Create Bookmark dialog box, shown in Figure 12-6. Within this dialog box, you can give the bookmark a name, a color, and a range. The bookmark shows up on the Time Slider in the selected color above the selected range of keys, as shown in Figure 12-7.

FIGURE 12-5

Create Bookmark icon

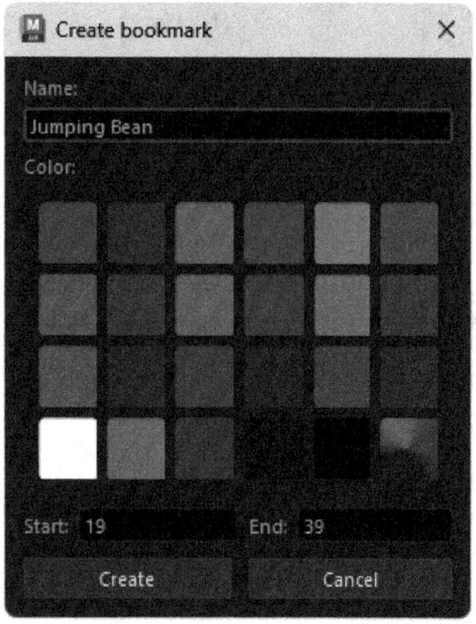

FIGURE 12-6

Create Bookmark dialog box

FIGURE 12-7
Bookmark on Time Slider

If you right click on a bookmark in the Time Slider, you can select to Create, Edit, Frame, Delete, move between adjacent bookmarks, or open the Bookmark Manager.

Copying Keys

You can copy and paste a set of keys for the selected object between files using the Keys Clipboard. To copy the keys to the Clipboard, select the Key, Cut Keys or Key, Copy Keys menu command. The keys stay on the Clipboard as you close the current scene and open a new one. You can paste keys to the selected object using the Key, Paste Keys menu command.

Deleting Keys

The Key, Delete Keys menu command deletes all selected keys for the selected object. Any keys set for unselected objects remain intact.

Snapping Keys

The Key, Snap Keys menu command causes all selected keys to be snapped to their nearest Value or Time. This is especially useful after scaling several selected keys. The Snap Keys Options dialog box, shown in Figure 12-8, lets you select to snap only the selected keys or all keys. You can also select to snap only Times, Values or Both.

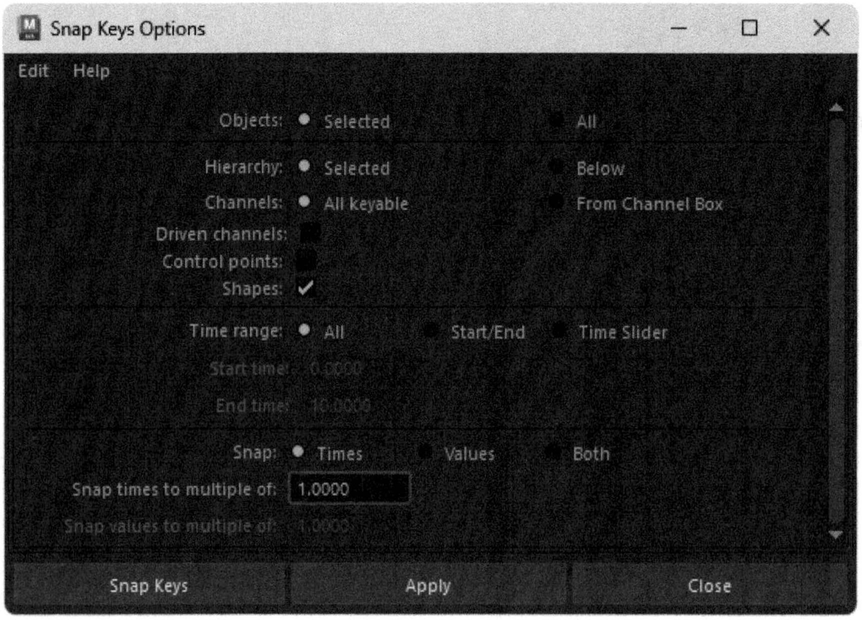

FIGURE 12-8

Snap Keys Options dialog box

Lesson 12.1-Tutorial 1: Set Keys

1. Create a NURBS sphere object using the Create, NURBS Primitives, Sphere menu command.
2. With the Time Slider at frame 1, select the Key, Set Key menu command.

   All transform attributes in the Channel Box are highlighted in red to show that they have keys associated with them.
3. Drag the time in the Time Slider to frame 25.

Note

> If frame 25 isn't visible, drag the right end of the Range Slider until the frame is visible. If the Range doesn't extend to frame 50, enter 50 in the text field to the right of the Range Slider.

4. Change the ScaleX, ScaleY, and ScaleZ attributes in the Channel Box to 5.0.
5. Select the Key, Set Key menu command again.
6. Drag the time in the Time Slider to frame 50.
7. Change the ScaleX, ScaleY, and ScaleZ attributes in the Channel Box back to 1.0.
8. Select the Key, Set Key menu command again.
9. Drag the Time Slider marker back and forth.

   The sphere increases and decreases in size as you drag the Time Slider.
10. Select File, Save Scene As and save the file as **Growing sphere.mb**.

Lesson 12.1-Tutorial 2: Use Auto Key

1. Create a NURBS sphere object using the Create, NURBS Primitives, Sphere menu command.
2. With the Time Slider at frame 1, click on the makeNurbsSphere1 input node in the Channel Box, click on the Start Sweep attribute, and then right-click and select Key Selected from the pop-up menu.
3. Click the Auto Key button in the lower-right corner of the interface.
4. Drag the time in the Time Slider to frame 25.
5. Change the Start Sweep value to 180.
6. Drag the time in the Time Slider to frame 50.
7. Change the Start Sweep value to 359.
8. Drag the Time Slider marker back and forth.

   The sphere slowly disappears as you drag the Time Slider, as shown in Figure 12-9.
9. Select File, Save Scene As and save the file as **Sweeping sphere.mb**.

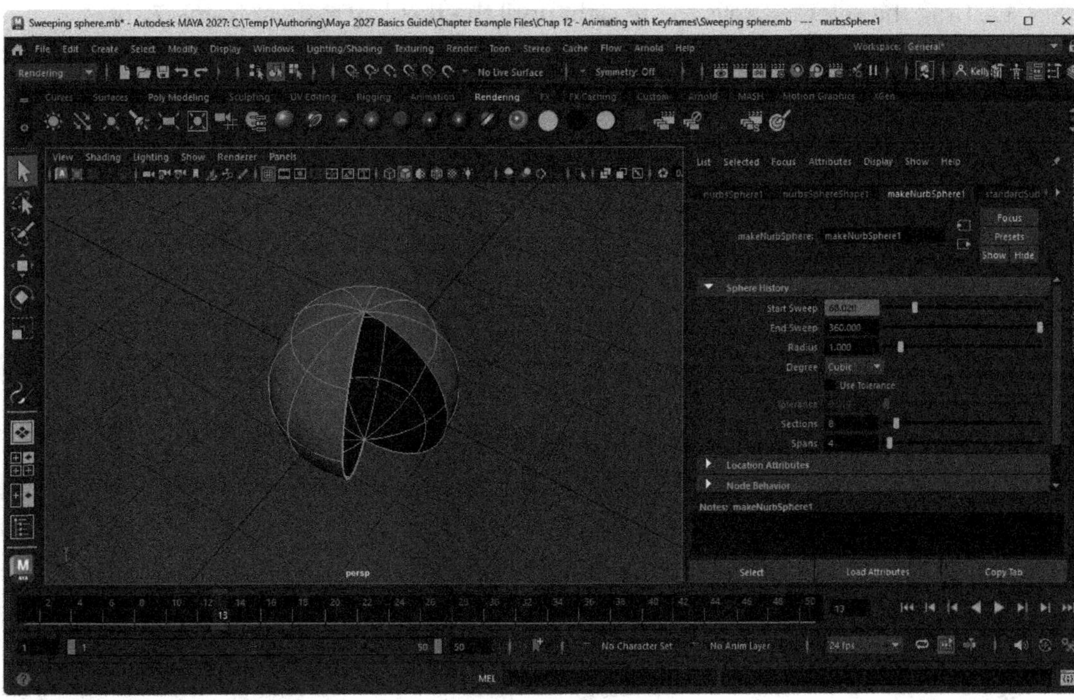

FIGURE 12-9

Sweeping sphere

Lesson 12.1-Tutorial 3: Move Keys

1. Create a NURBS sphere object using the Create, NURBS Primitives, Sphere menu command, and then create a NURBS plane object and scale the plane object to be larger than the sphere.
2. Select the sphere and click on the Select by Component Type button in the Status Line.
3. Drag over all the CVs that make up the lower portion of the sphere in the Front view to select them.

4. Select the Key, Set Key menu command.
5. Drag the time in the Time Slider to frame 3.
6. Drag the CVs upward in the Side view and select the Key, Set Key menu command again.

   This example shows that components as well as objects can be animated. By dragging the lower portion of CVs upward, the sphere is being squashed over three frames.

7. Click on the Select by Object Type button in the Status Line.
8. Select the sphere and move it upward in the Front view and select the Key, Set Key menu command.
9. Drag the Time Slider to frame 10, move the sphere back down to the plane object, and select the Key, Set Key menu command again (or press the s hotkey).

   The sphere is now falling onto the plane object.

10. Click on the Select by Component Type button in the Status Line again.
11. Select the same CVs that were selected earlier and drag over the set keys in the Time Slider with the Shift key held down.
12. Drag the selected keys to the right until the first key rests at frame 7.

    Dragging over the set keys with the Shift key held down turns the selected keys red and displays some arrows that you can use to move or scale the selected keys.

13. Drag the Time Slider marker back and forth.

    The sphere falls to the base plane where it is squashed as it impacts with the plane object, as shown in Figure 12-10.

14. Select File, Save Scene As and save the file as **Falling sphere.mb**.

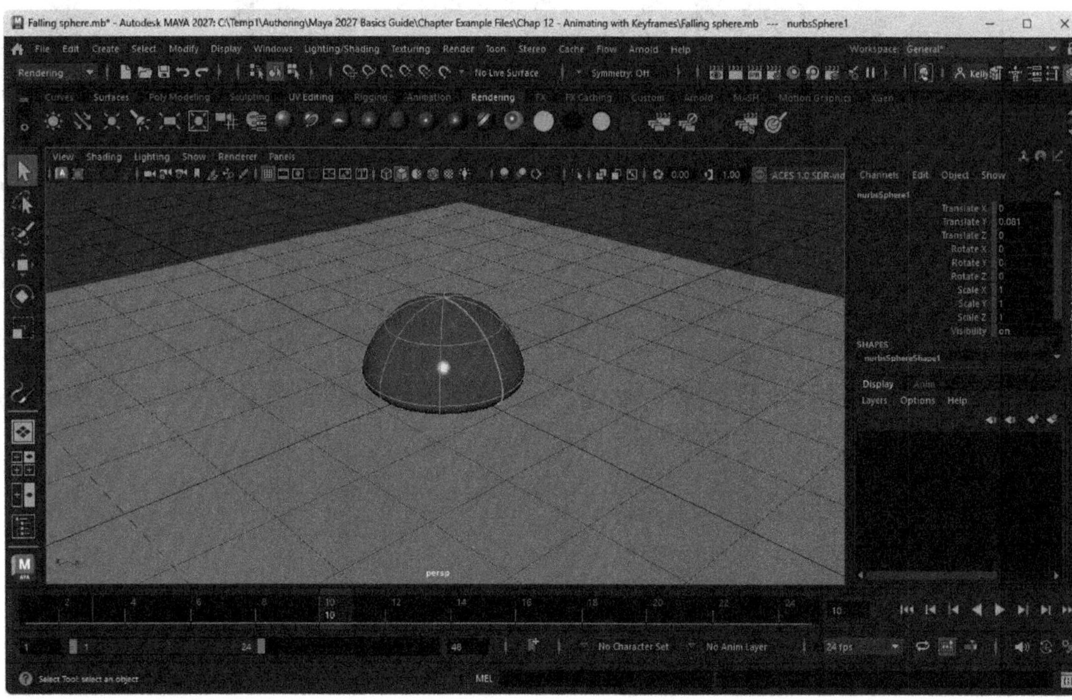

FIGURE 12-10

Animated squashed sphere

Lesson 12.2: View an Animation

Spending a lot of time rendering a final animation only to find out that you've made a mistake can be time consuming and frustrating. Previewing animations can help eliminate mistakes early on.

Previewing Animation

Clicking the Play Forward button in the animation controls (shown in Figure 12-11) at the bottom of the interface cycles through the frames in the active view panel. You can also click on the Play Backwards button to see the animation in reverse. If you select and drag the Time Slider handle, the view panel is updated as you drag between the various frames.

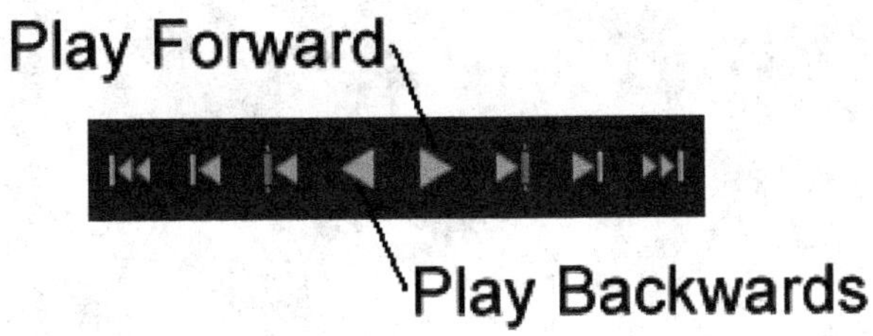

FIGURE 12-11

Animation controls

Setting Frame Rate

Frame Rate is the number of frames that are played per second. It is commonly referred to as fps for frames per second. There is a drop-down list under the Animation Controls where you can set the Frame Rate for the viewport playback. The default is 24 fps, but you can speed up the playback by lowering the fps or slow it down by increasing the fps. Movies use a Frame Rate of 24 fps, television runs at 29.97 fps and high-res video games run at 30 or 60 fps.

Looping an Animation

Beneath the Play Backwards button is a Loop toggle button. This button has 3 states—Once, Oscillate, and Continuous. The Once option plays the animation through once when the Play Forward button is clicked. Oscillate causes the animation to be played repeatedly forward and then backward, and the Continuous option plays the animation forward repeatedly.

Tip

You can also access the Playback Looping options from a pop-up menu by right-clicking on the Time Slider or the Animation Controls.

Accessing Animation Preferences

If you click on the Animation Preferences button, next to the Auto Key button, the Timeline panel of the Preferences dialog box appears, as shown in Figure 12-12. In this dialog box, you can set the number of frames that appear in the Time Slider, the size of the Time Slider and Keys, and default playback speed.

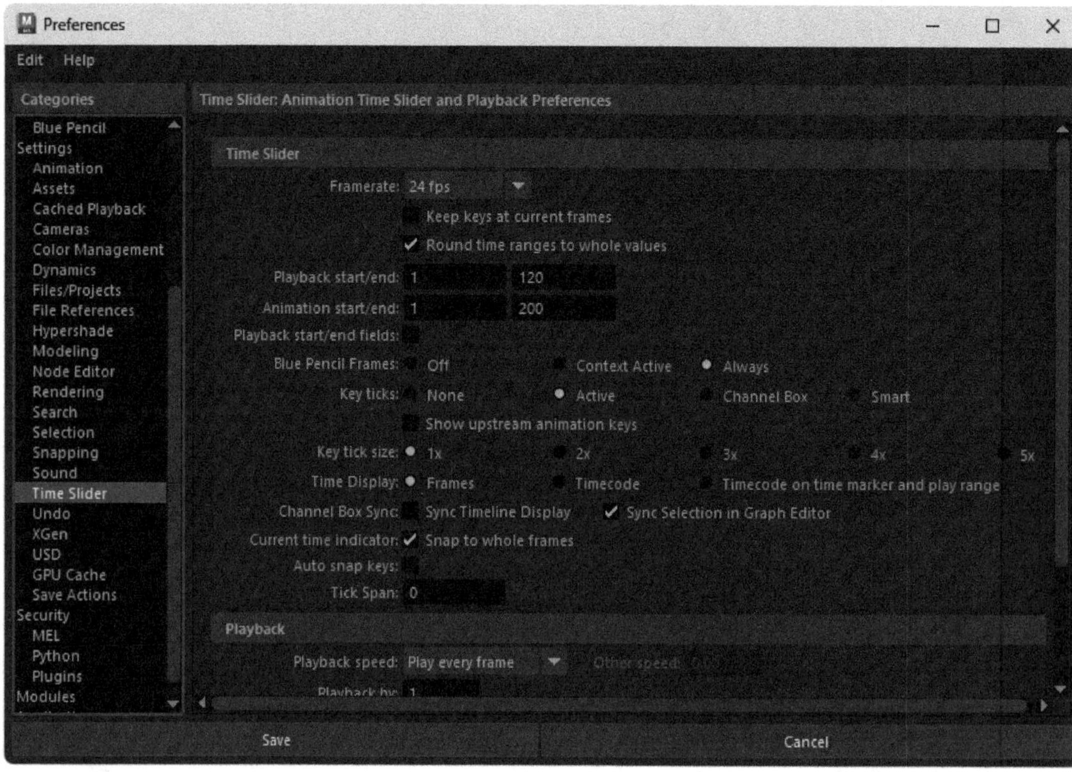

FIGURE 12-12

Animation preferences

Enabling Ghosting

Ghosting is an animation technique in which you see an object's position in the previous and/or coming frames, as shown for the sphere in Figure 12-13. This is helpful when you work on the timing of an object's motion. To enable ghosting, select the Visualize, Ghost Selected menu command. If you need more control over the ghosting options, you can open the Ghosting Editor dialog box, shown in Figure 12-14. Using this dialog box, you can select exactly which frames are ghosted or how many frames before and after the current frame are shown. You can also change the ghost colors and opacity. To disable ghosting, use the Visualize, Unghost Selected or the Visualize, Unghost All menu commands.

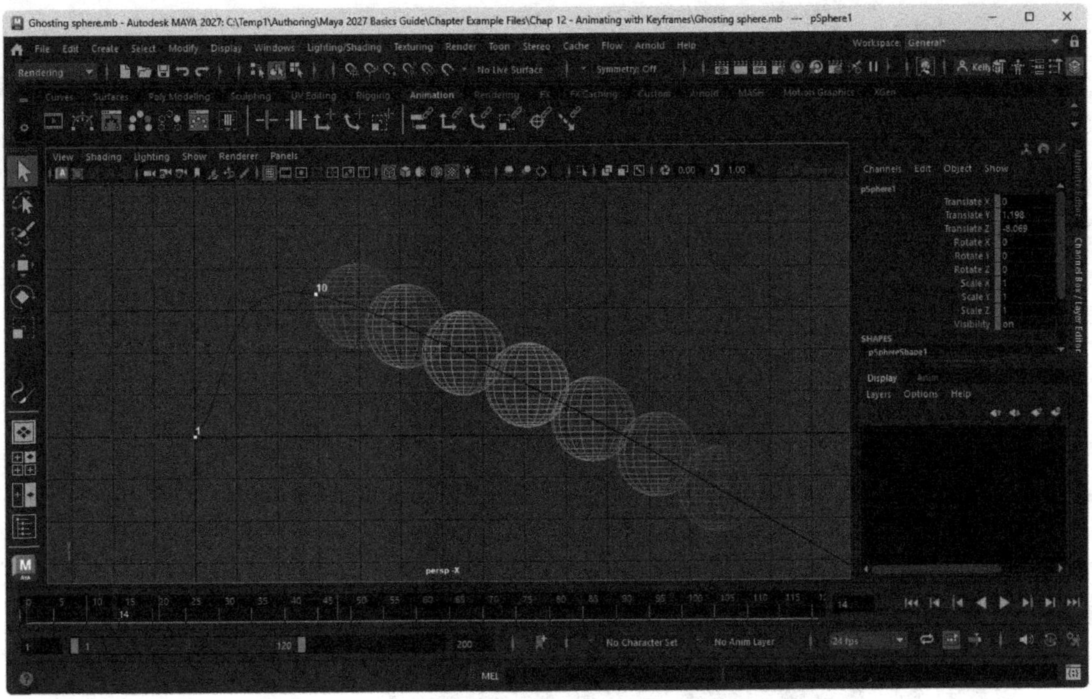

FIGURE 12-13

Ghosted objects

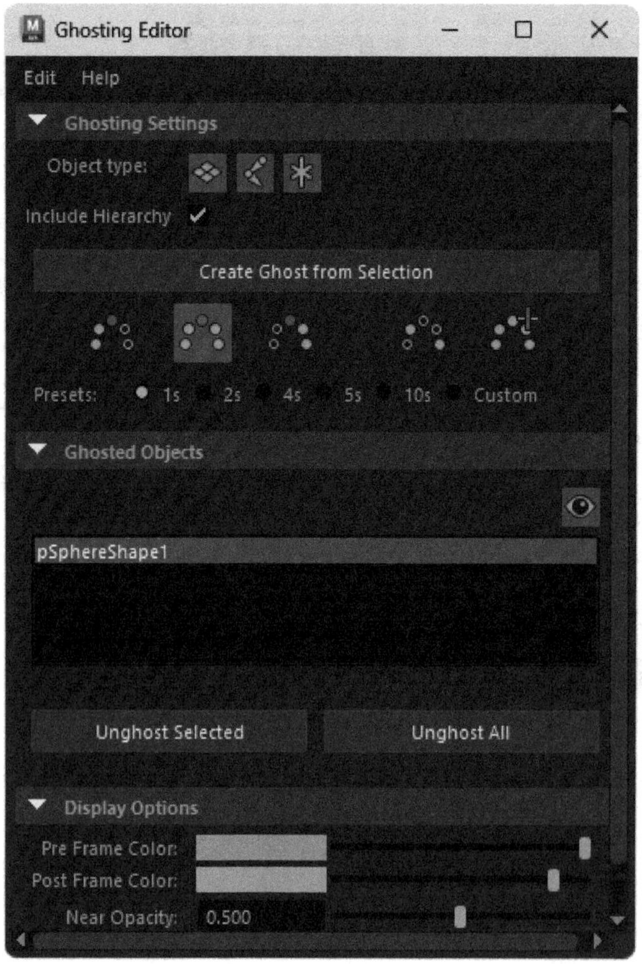

FIGURE 12-14

Ghosting Editor dialog box

Creating Motion Trails

A **motion trail** is the trajectory path that marks the progress of an animated object as it moves between frames, as shown in Figure 12-15. A single animated object can have multiple motion trails attached at different locations. You can also display the frame and key numbers along the motion trail.

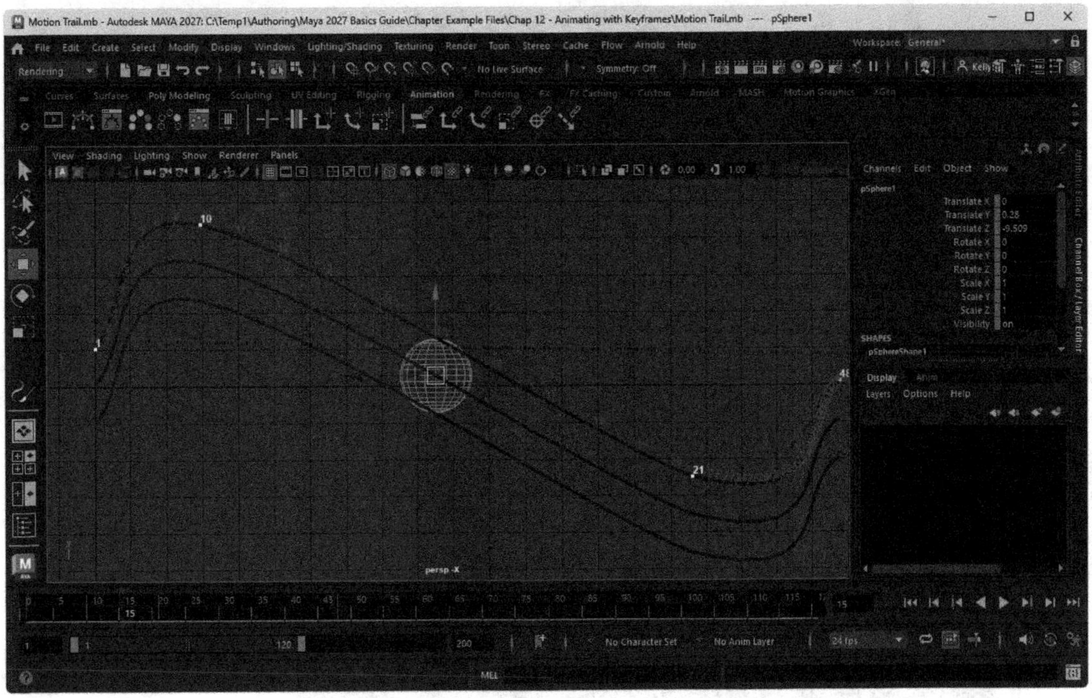

FIGURE 12-15

A motion trail

To create a motion trail and manage its settings, open the Motion Trail Editor dialog box with the Visualize, Motion Trail Editor menu command. In the Motion Trail Editor dialog box, shown in Figure 12-16, create a motion trail by selecting the animated object and clicking the Create Motion Trail button. You can rename each motion trail by double clicking on its name. Created motion trails can be always visible or visible when selected. There is also an X-Ray Draw option that lets the trails show through the object. The various Draw Modes determine how the selected motion trail is colored; Constant displays a single color, Alternating Frames, changes color each frame, Past/Future colors previous frames in one color and future frames in another, and Velocity colors the motion trail differently based on the object's speed.

In the Edit Settings rollout, you can set the Pivot for the selected motion trail or choose the Custom option, which lets you use a Move tool to reposition the location of the selected motion trail. In The Display Settings rollout, you can select to show Key and Frame markers and numbers. You can also set the motion trail thickness and colors.

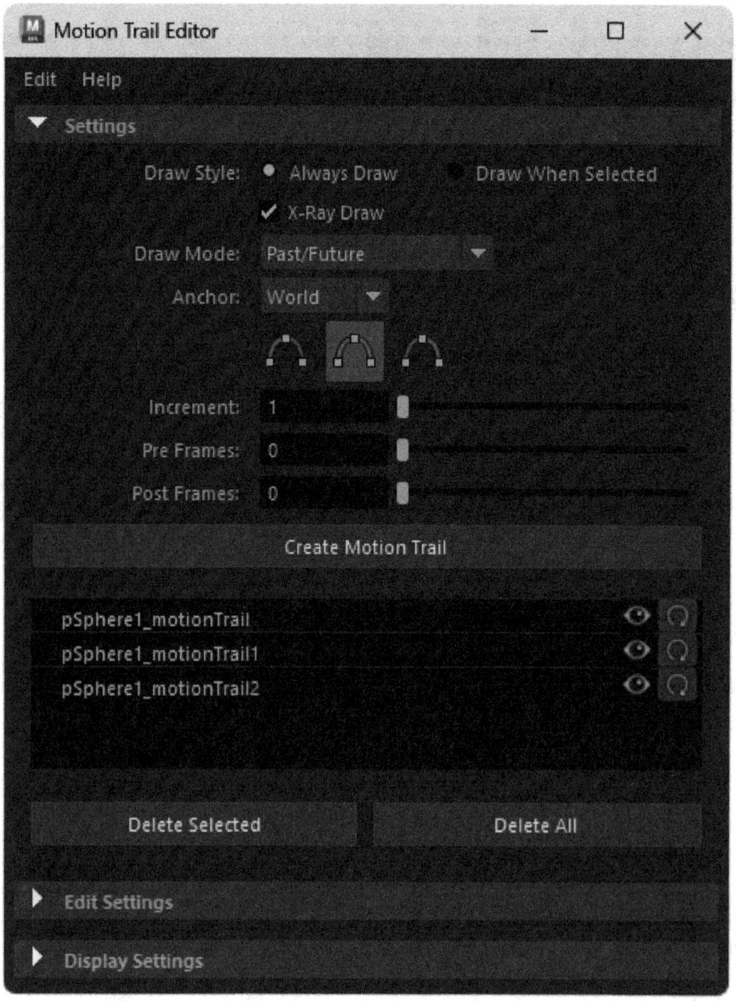

FIGURE 12-16

Motion Trail Editor

Moving Motion Trail Keys

Motion Trails are a great visualization tool to see how objects move through the scene, but they can also be used to change the motion of an object by selecting and moving the Motion Trail keys. When a Motion Trail is visible, any keys associated with the animated object are shown in white. If you drag over these keys, they are selected and you can use the Move tool to drag them to a new location thereby changing the object's animation. Figure 12-17 shows the result after selecting and dragging the key are frame 21 upward.

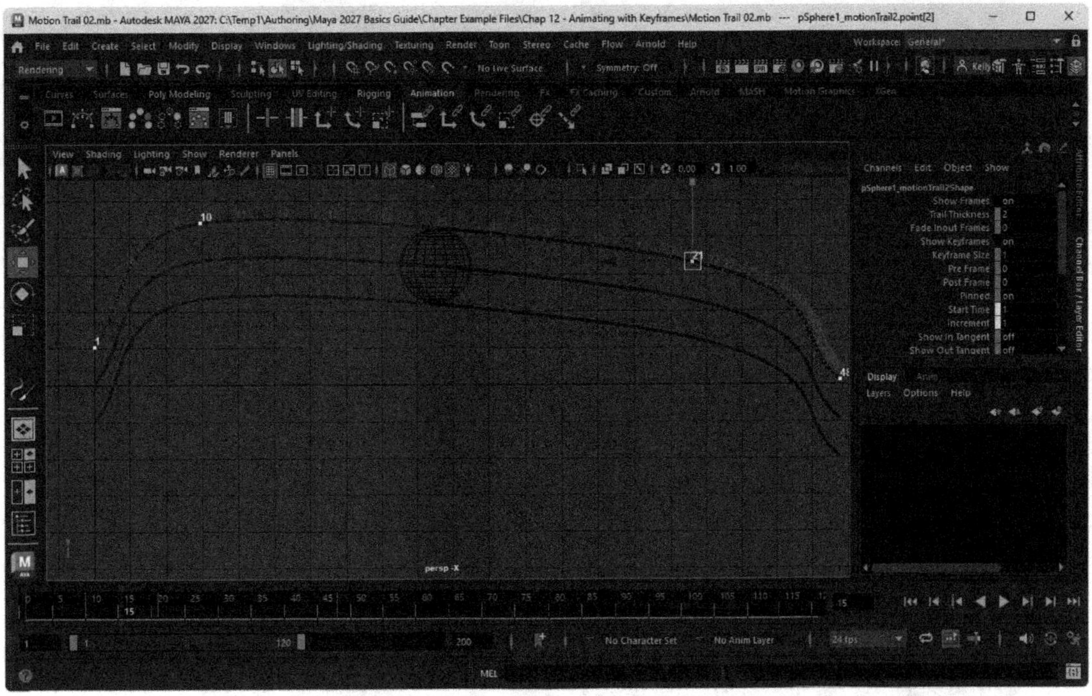

FIGURE 12-17

Motion Trail after dragging a key

Enabling Cached Playback

Cached Playback is a feature that is enabled by default using the toggle button located next to the Looping button under the Animation Controls. When enabled, Maya will save all the animation frames to a cache where it can quickly be recalled and played as needed. If any changes are made to the scene, then Maya automatically updates the cached data. The Cached Playback feature can be disabled using the toggle button.

Using Playblast

The Windows, Playblast menu command captures a screenshot of the active view panel for each frame. These frames are then stitched together to create a preview animation that is played in the default system movie player. The Playblast Options dialog box, shown in Figure 12-18, lets you set the Time Range, Viewer, and Display Size options. You can also select to save the preview to a file. Playblast supports AVI, Webm, and Image formats.

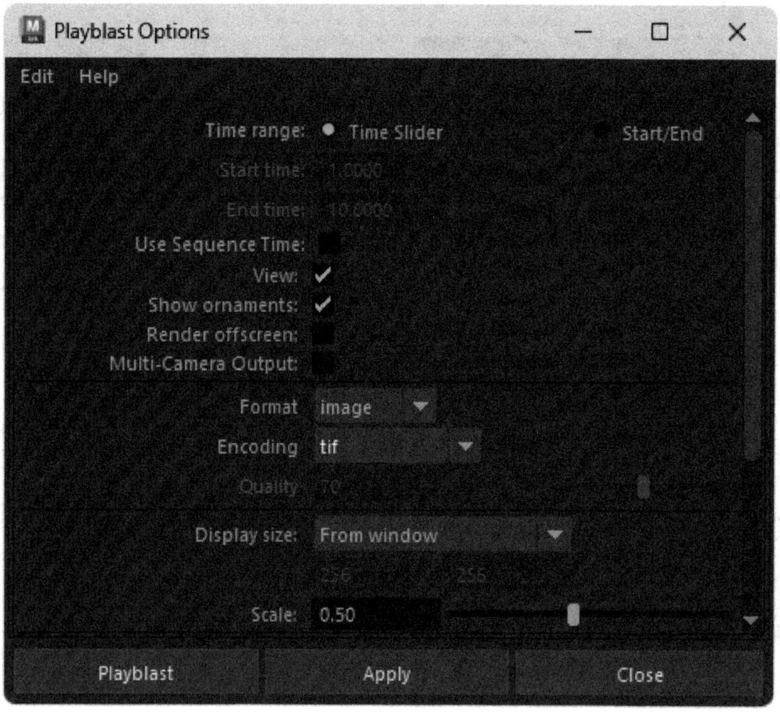

FIGURE 12-18

Playblast Options dialog box

Lesson 12.2-Tutorial 1: Preview an Animation

1. Select the File, Open Scene menu command and locate and open the Simple airplane.mb file.
2. Drag the Time Slider to frame 10.
3. With the airplane selected, choose the Visualize, Open Ghosting Editor menu command.
4. In the Ghosting Editor dialog box, choose the Use Ghosts on Frames that Precede and Follow. Select the Custom Presets and choose 3 Change the Frame Step to 3.
5. In the Animation Controls, press the Play Forward button.

   The animation loops over and over with ghosting enabled, as shown in Figure 12-19.
6. Select File, Save Scene As and save the file as **Airplane with ghost.mb**.

FIGURE 12-19

A ghosted airplane

Lesson 12.2-Tutorial 2: Edit Motion Trail

1. Select the File, Open Scene menu command and locate and open the Buzzing bee.mb file.
2. Select the Key, Set Key menu command (or press the S hotkey), drag the Time Slider to frame 10 and move the bee a short step towards the flower, and set another key.
3. Repeat step 2 seven more times until keys are set for every 10 frames until the bee reaches the flower.
4. Select the Visualize, Motion Trail Editor menu command and click the Create Motion Trail button in the Editor.

   A Motion Trail is displayed in the viewport as a straight line.
5. Drag over the Motion Trail key at frame 10 to select it, then move the key upward towards the top of the viewport. Select and move the Motion Trail key at frame 30 about halfway as far as the previous frame and repeat for frame 50 to make a bumpy path to the flower, as shown in Figure 12-20.
6. In the Animation Controls, press the Play Forward button.

   The animation loops over and over with the bee approaching the flower.
7. Select File, Save Scene As and save the file as **Bee and flower.mb**.

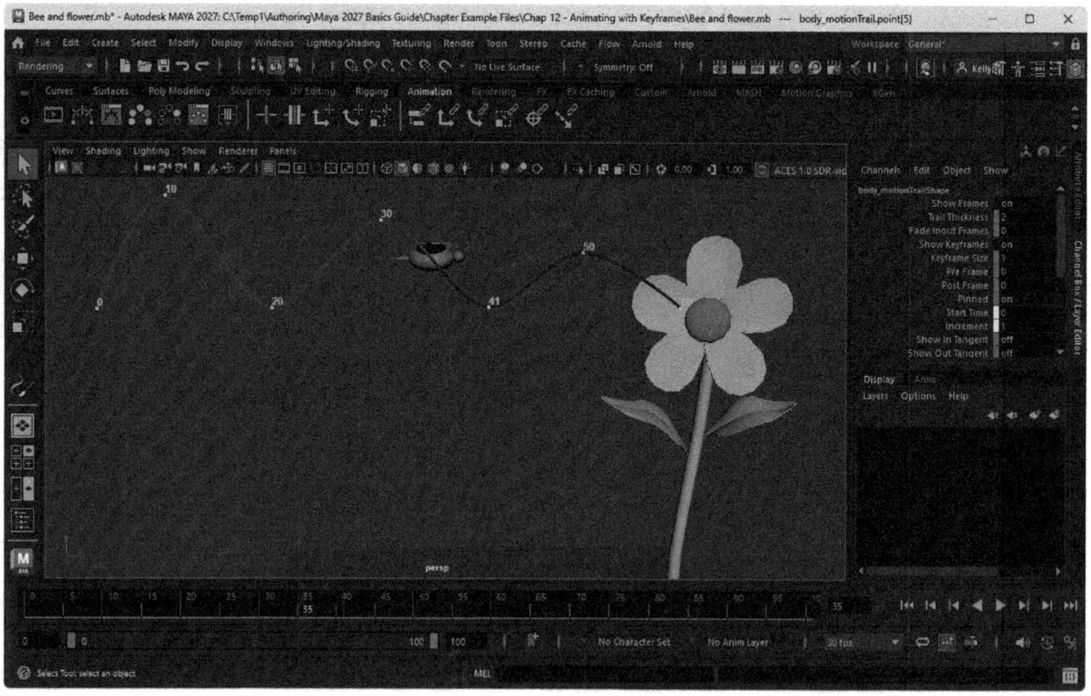

FIGURE 12-20

A bee approaching a flower

Lesson 12.2-Tutorial 3: Use Playblast

1. Select the File, Open Scene menu command, locate and open the Simple airplane.mb file.
2. Select the Windows, Playblast menu command.

   Every frame of the animation is captured in the Playblast buffer and the animated frames are shown in the default system video player, such as the Windows Media Player, as shown in Figure 12-21.

FIGURE 12-21

A Playblastpreview

Lesson 12.3: Animate Using Motion Paths

Keyframing is easy to work with, but sometimes it can be easier to define a path and to have an object follow that path. **Motion paths** are curves that you can use to define how an object should move through the scene.

Creating Motion Path Keys

You can create a motion path by dragging objects about the scene and using the Constrain, Motion Paths, Set Motion Path Key menu command. This command places a motion path key for the selected object for the current time frame. Moving the object to another location and using this command again creates another key, and a curve joining the keys is drawn. Each motion path key acts as a point on the curve. Figure 12-22 shows a sphere following a motion path with several motion path keys.

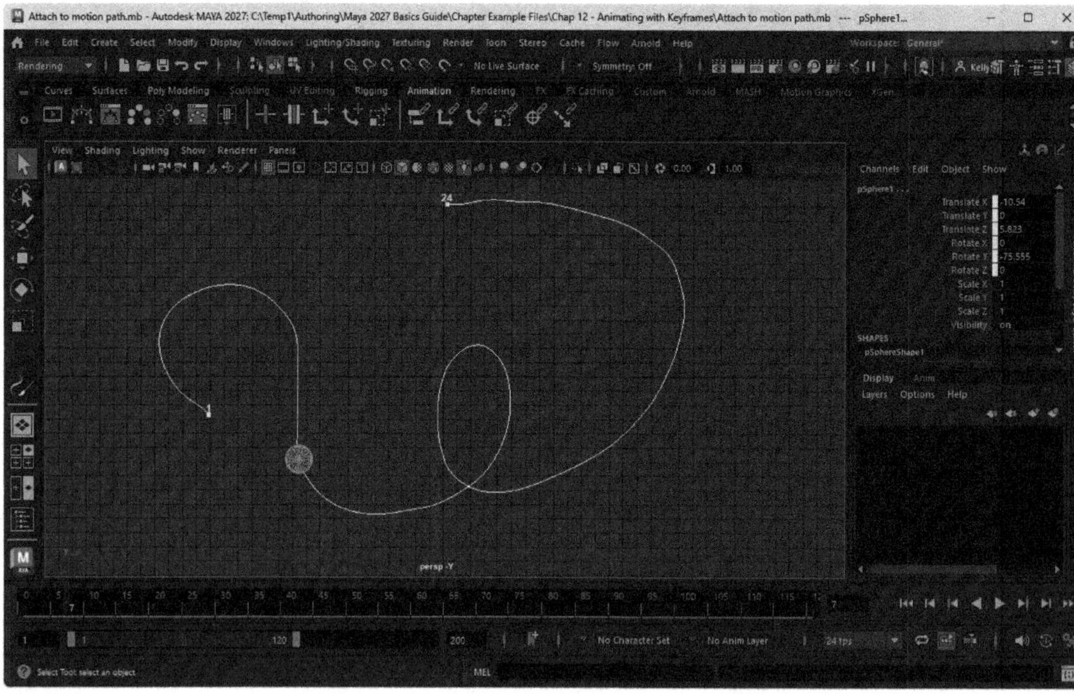

FIGURE 12-22

Motion path keys

Drawing a Motion Path

You can use any NURBS curve as a motion path. By default, the first point on the NURBS curve marks the starting point for the attached object. You can create motion paths using any of the curve creation tools found in the Create menu, including the CV Curve tool, the EP Curve tool, and the Pencil Curve tool.

Attaching an Object to a Motion Path

To attach an object to a motion path, you need to select the object or objects to attach and then select the NURBS path that you want to use for the motion path with the Shift key held down. The motion path curve should always be selected last. Select the Constrain, Motion Paths, Attach to Motion Path menu command. Figure 12-23 shows a NURBS sphere that has been attached to the motion path. Clicking the Play Forward button shows the sphere following the entire path. Within the Attach to Motion Path Options dialog box is a Follow option. If enabled, the selected object will be rotated so that its length is always parallel to the path.

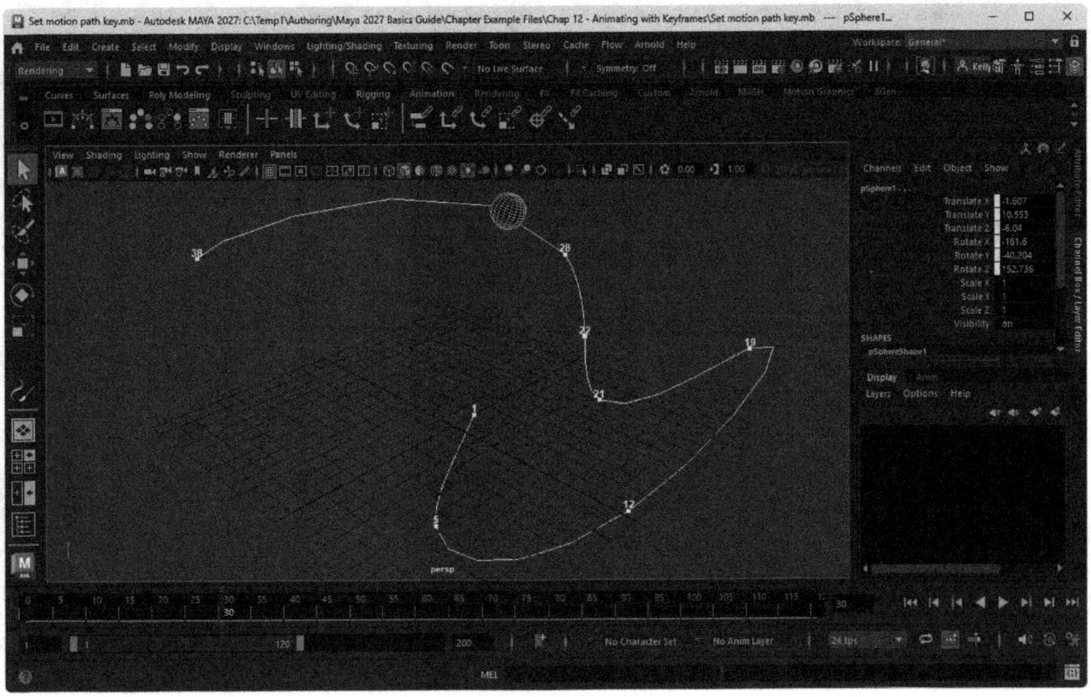

FIGURE 12-23

Attached sphere and motion path

Adjusting an Attached Motion Path

When an object is attached to a motion path, you can move the object along the motion path by dragging the Time Slider. To adjust the attached motion path, you can move the attached object with the Move tool and create a new motion path key with the Constrain, Motion Paths, Set Motion Path Key menu command. Figure 12-24 shows an adjustment made to the existing attached path.

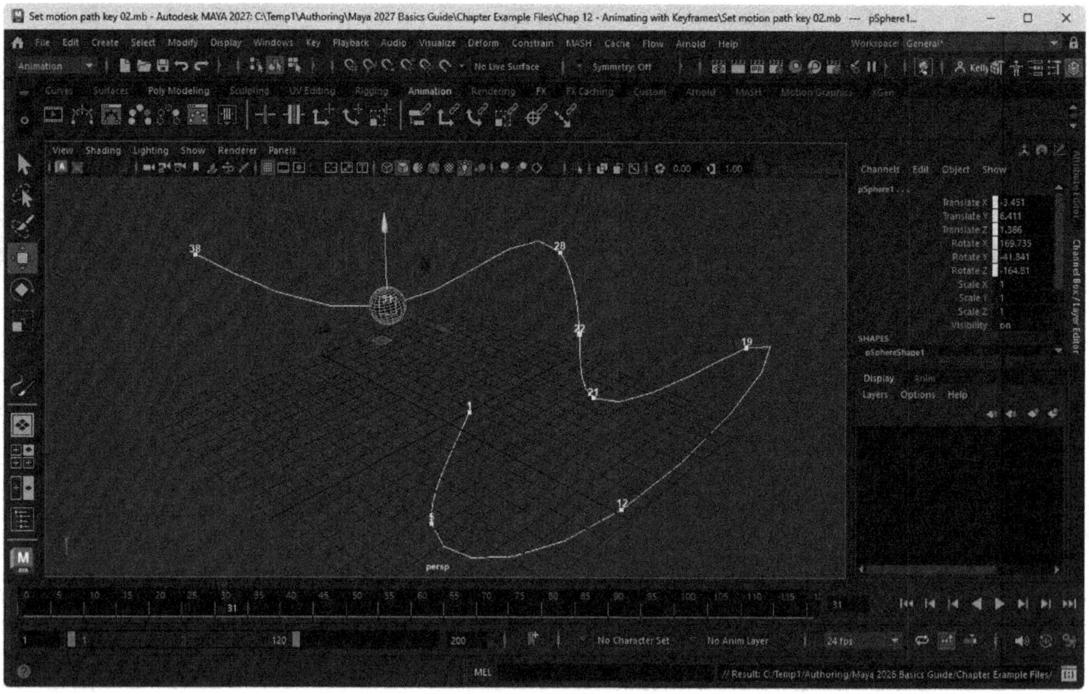

FIGURE 12-24

Adjusted motion path

Deforming an Object as it Follows a Motion Path

If an object follows a motion path, you can select the object and choose the Constrain, Motion Paths, Flow Path Object menu command. This command causes a lattice to appear around the selected object. This lattice deforms as it moves along the motion path such as bending around tight corners. By altering this lattice, you can control how the object deforms as it follows the motion path. Figure 12-25 shows a torus object that follows a motion path with a lattice surrounding it.

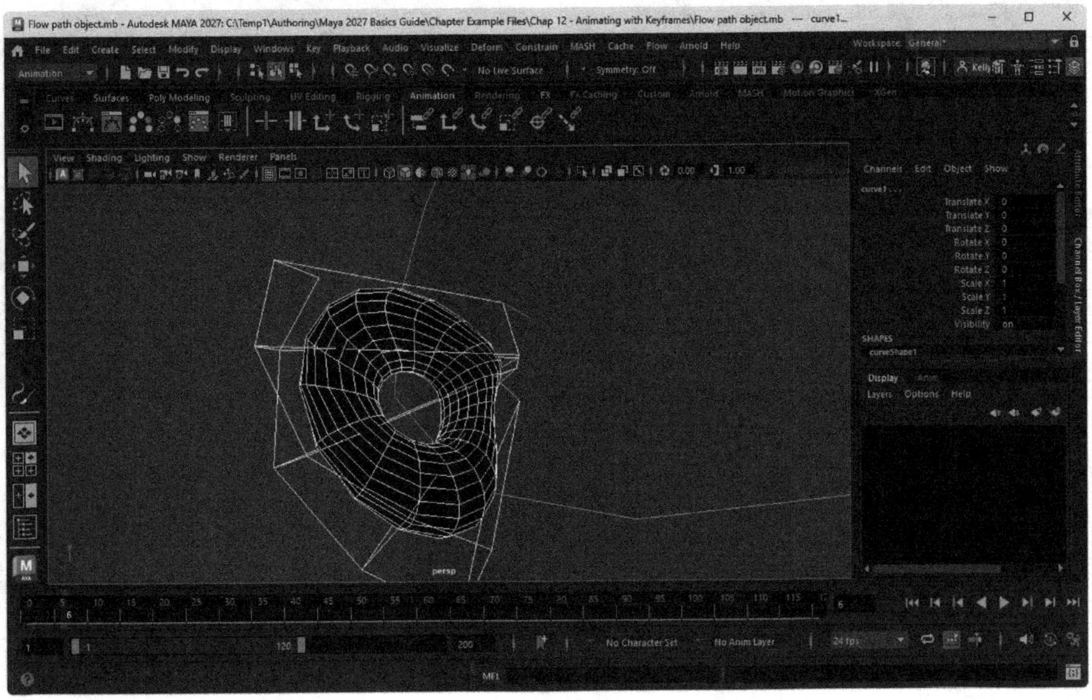

FIGURE 12-25

Deform lattice surrounding an object

Lesson 12.3-Tutorial 1: Create a Motion Path

1. Create a NURBS cone object using the Create, NURBS Primitives, Cone menu command.
2. Select the Constrain, Motion Paths, Set Motion Path Key menu command.
3. Drag the Time Slider to frame 5 and drag the cone away from its current position.
4. Select the Constrain, Motion Paths, Set Motion Path Key menu command again.
5. Repeat steps 3 and 4 several more times.

   Each key acts as a curve point for the motion path.
6. Press the Play Forward button.

   The cone object follows the motion path curve, as shown in Figure 12-26.
7. Select File, Save Scene As and save the file as **Motion path.mb**.

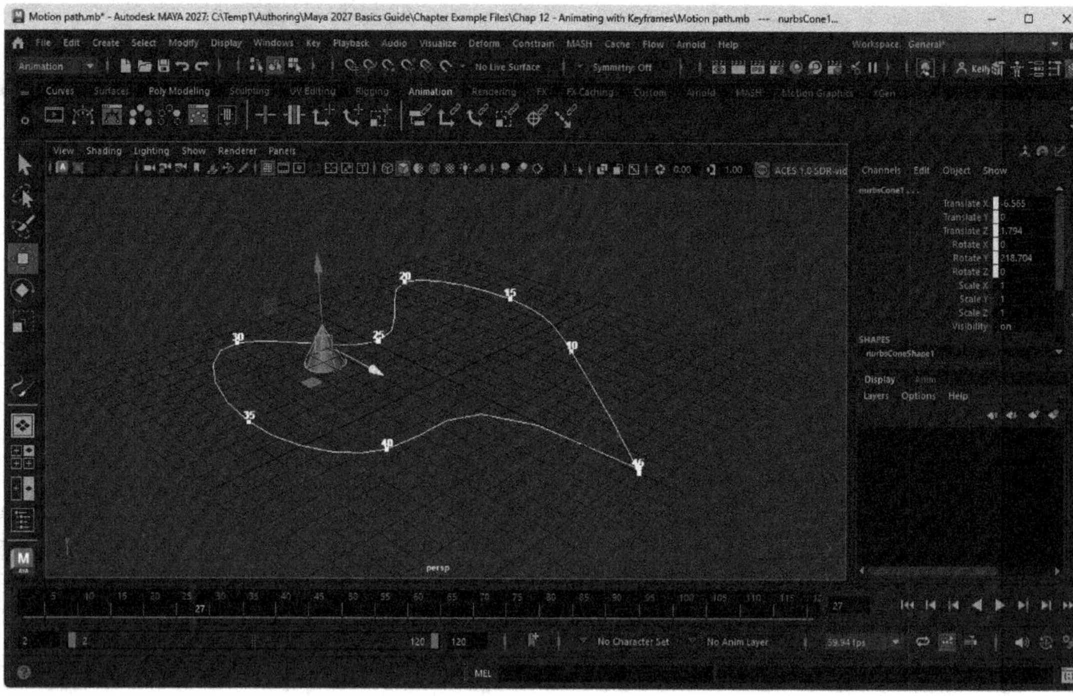

FIGURE 12-26

A motion path created by moving an object

Lesson 12.3-Tutorial 2: Draw a Motion Path and Attach an Object

1. Select the File, Open Scene menu command, locate and open the Shark.mb file.
2. Select the Create, Pencil Curve tool menu command.
3. Draw a path for the shark to follow in the Perspective view panel.
4. Select the shark object, and then hold down the Shift key and select the path curve.
5. Select the Constrain, Motion Paths, Attach to Motion Path, Options menu command.
6. Disable the Follow option in the Attach to Motion Path Options dialog box and click the Attach button.

   The shark object is positioned at the beginning of the path curve.
7. Press the Play Forward button to see the shark follow the path.

   The shark object follows the curve, as shown in Figure 12-27.
8. Select File, Save Scene As and save the file as **Shark on path.mb**.

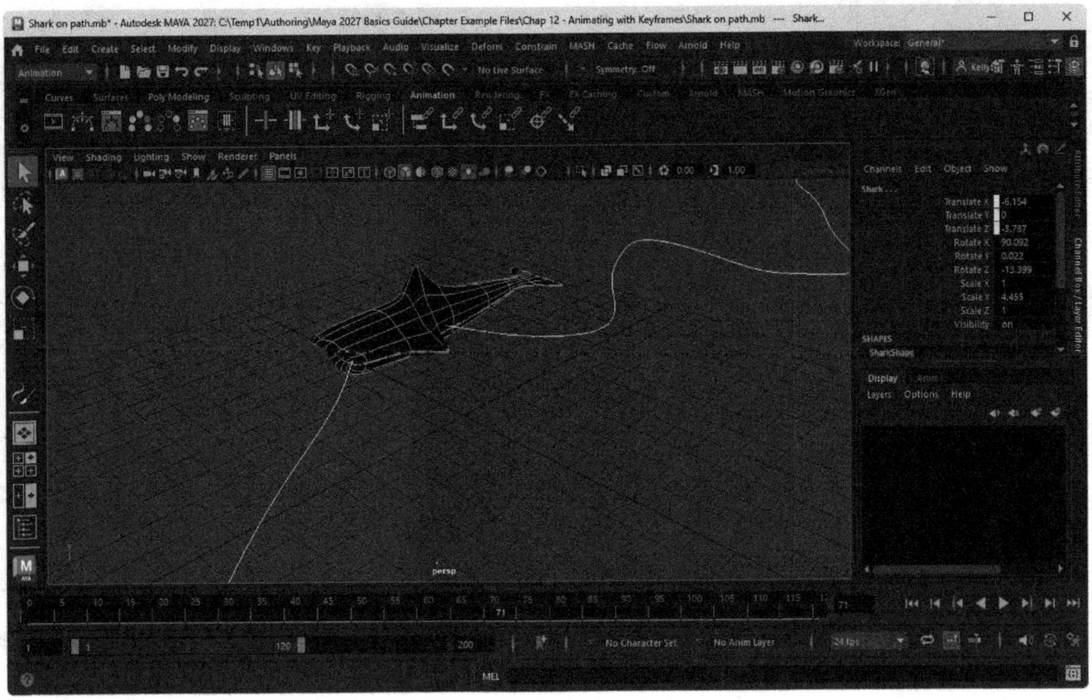

FIGURE 12-27

An animated shark following a path

Lesson 12.4: Edit Animation Curves

Fine-tuning an animation can be tricky using the view panels, but Maya makes all animations available as graphed lines in the Graph Editor. This makes tweaking animation curves easier.

Using the Graph Editor

The Graph Editor, shown in Figure 12-28, shows the change in animated attributes over time as graphed lines. Each key is represented as a point, and the animation curve defines the movement of the attribute between the key points. Open the Graph Editor using the Windows, Animation Editors, Graph Editor menu command. The nodes and keyable attributes are listed in the left pane. If an attribute is selected in the left pane, its animation curves are displayed in the right pane. Using the Shift and Ctrl/Command keys, you can select multiple attributes.

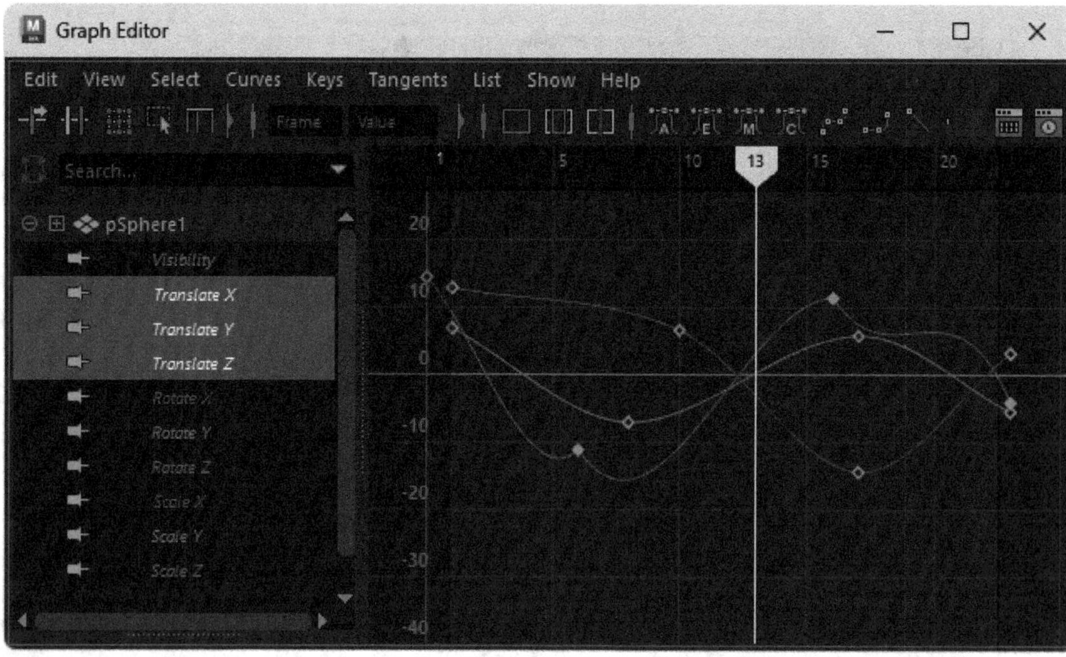

FIGURE 12-28

The Graph Editor

Framing Curves

The Graph Editor includes two buttons on its toolbar, as shown in Figure 12-29, that frame the selected curves. The Frame All button fits all the selected animation curves within the right pane, and the Frame Playback Range shows the entire range of frames for the current scene. These commands also appear in the View menu, along with options to Frame Selection and Center Current Time.

Tip

You can also use the Alt/Option+middle and right mouse buttons to pan and zoom the animation curve pane.

FIGURE 12-29

Frame All (left) and Frame Playback Range (right) buttons

Editing Keys

You can select a key by dragging over it in the right pane. When a key is selected, its key point turns white. A small square appears to the left of the attribute name for each curve that has a selected key, and the key's frame number and value appear in the top toolbar, as shown in Figure 12-30. Using the Shift key, you can select multiple keys at the same time. If the Move Nearest Picked Key tool is selected in the Toolbar, you can move the selected keys by dragging with the middle mouse button. You can enable the Time Snap and Value Snap buttons so that they snap the keys as they move.

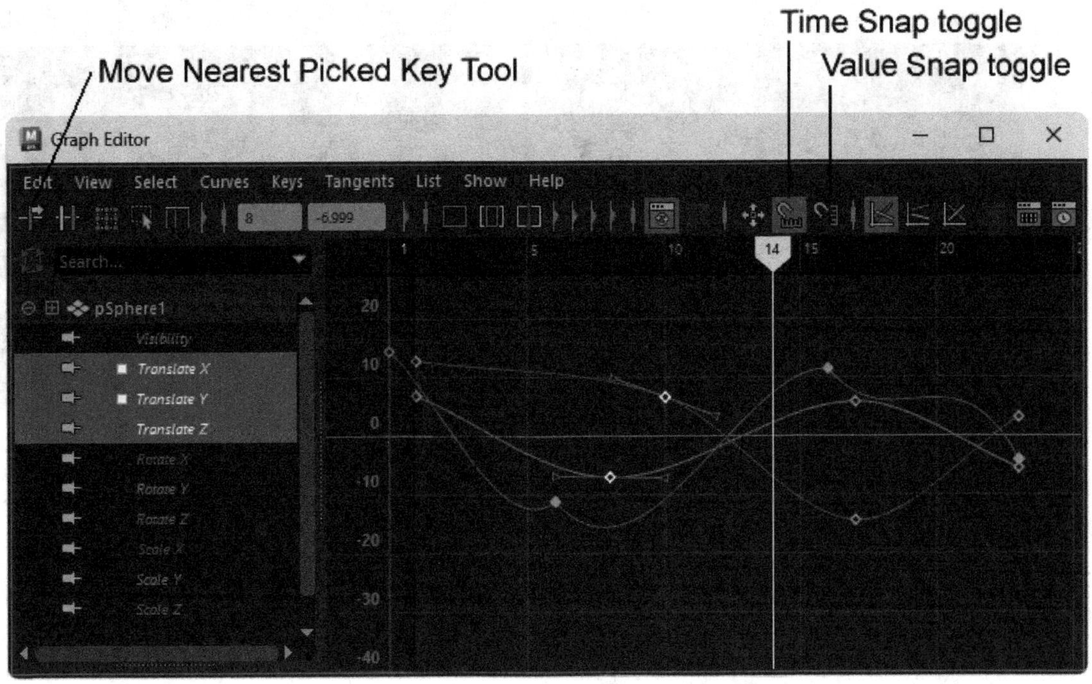

FIGURE 12-30

Selected keys

Adding and Removing Keys

With a curve selected in the Graph Editor, you can add or insert keys to the curve by clicking on the Insert Keys tool button in the Graph Editor toolbar, shown in Figure 12-31. When the Keys, Add Key tool is enabled, you can click on the curve at the location where you want the key.

FIGURE 12-31

Insert Keys button

You can delete a key by selecting it and choosing the Edit, Delete menu command. Within the Keys menu is a Remove Key menu to remove multiple keys at once. The submenu options include removing Unsnapped, Before or After Current Frame, Outside Selected Range, Ripple Delete, and Redundant Keys.

Rescaling Multiple Keys

If multiple keys are selected, you can use the Rescale Tool to move or to change the distance between adjacent frames of keys. When selected, the Rescale Tool surrounds the selected keys with handles that can be used to scale the keys up and/or out. If you need more control over the selected keys, you can use the Lattice Deform Keys tool to move specific areas of the selected keys. Finally, the Retime Tool can be used to increase or decrease the timing between areas of an animation. To use this tool, double click to position a vertical bar, then repeat to place a second vertical bar, as shown in Figure 12-32. You can then drag with the middle mouse button to change the number of frames between the two markers. All other keys remain fixed relative to the retimed area.

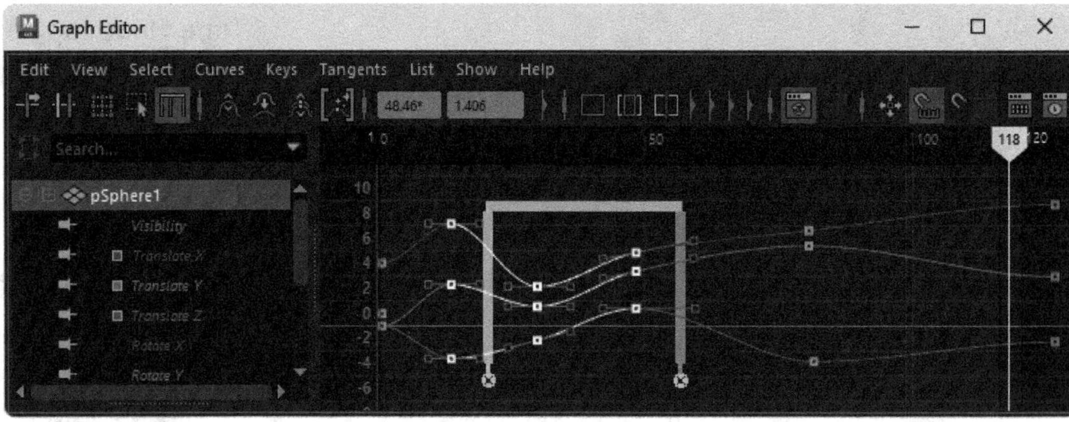

FIGURE 12-32

Markers for the Retime Tool

Reducing and Smoothing Curves

If the animation curves are really crazy with too many keys, jagged sections or outlying peaks, there are several curve editing functions in the Curves menu you can use. Too many keys is a common problem if you load in a motion capture data file. If an animation curve includes too many keys, you can use the Curves, Key Reducer Filter menu command to reduce the total number of keys. Figure 12-33 shows the Key Reducer Filter Options where you can set the Precision value to maintain.

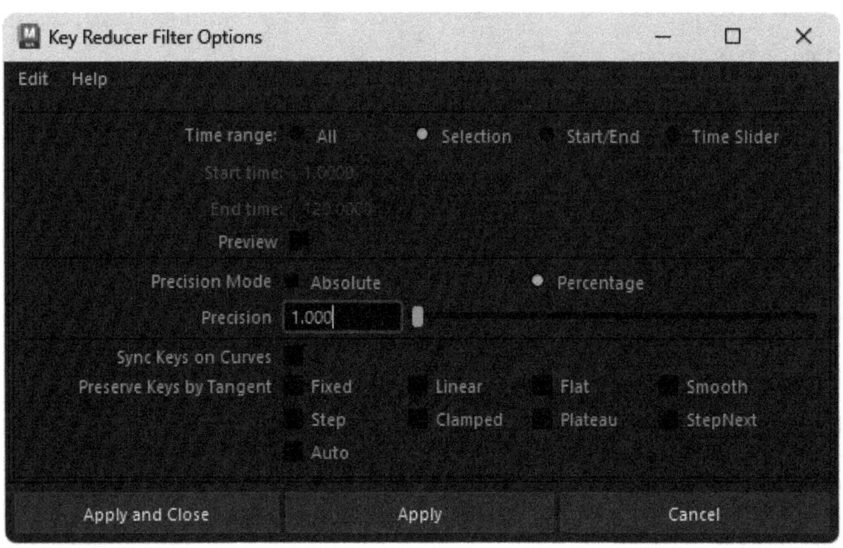

FIGURE 12-33

Key Reducer Filter Options

If the curve is too jagged and the resulting animation shakes, then you can smooth the curve using the Curves, Smooth Filter (Gaussian) menu command. With this feature, you can set which section of the curve to smooth and also a Filter Width value, which sets how aggressively the smooth filter is. This works by averaging the keys for the selected section. There is also a Preview option so you can see the results before they are applied.

The Curves menu also includes a Peak Removal Filter menu that lowers any peaks from the selected range.

Sculpting Curves

If you need to make a lot of smooth changes across the animation curves, you can use the Curve Sculpt tools, located on the Graph Editor toolbar, as shown in Figure 12-34. These three tools use the Maya brush to move all the keys within the brush radius with the greatest effect in the center of the brush radius and gradually reducing the effect towards the brush edge. They include the Grab, Smooth, and Smear tools. The Grab tool moves all the keys within the brush radius, the Smooth tool reduces any peaks, and the Smear tool pushes the keys in the direction of the brush.

FIGURE 12-34

Curve Sculpt buttons

Tip

```
If any of the Curve Sculpt tools are selected, you
can change the Size of the brush by dragging
horizontally with the middle mouse button.
Dragging vertically with the middle mouse button
changes the brush strength value.
```

Setting Infinity Conditions

Even if no keys are set when an object completes its keyed motions, you can set the motion to repeat or loop indefinitely. These are known as *infinity conditions*. You can set the infinity condition before the first key with the Curves, Pre Infinity menu command and the infinity condition for the animation curve after the last key with the Curves, Post Infinity menu command. The options include Cycle, Cycle with Offset, Oscillate, Linear, and Constant. To view the resulting curve effect, select the View, Infinity menu command and the curve motions are shown as dashed lines. Figure 12-35 shows a simple animated sequence with a Cycle Post-Infinity setting.

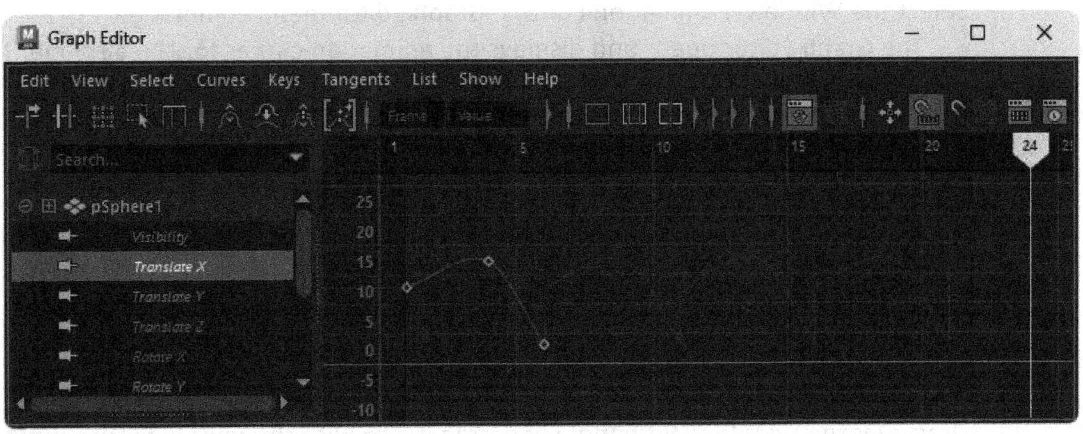

FIGURE 12-35

Pre- and Post-Infinity settings

Working with Tangents

The smoothness of the curve leading to and from the key points is determined by the key's **tangent points**. To see the tangents, select the View, Tangents menu command. Each tangent extends to either side of the key point. You can select and move tangent points using the middle mouse button. Both tangent points are in a straight line by default, but if you select the Tangents, Break Tangents menu command, you can move each tangent handle independently. You can also select several tangent positions from the Tangents menu. The options include Spline, Linear, Clamped, Stepped, Stepped Next, Flat, Fixed, and Plateau. Figure 12-36 shows the Graph Editor with the Tangents visible. Notice how the second selected key has broken tangents resulting in a sharp point.

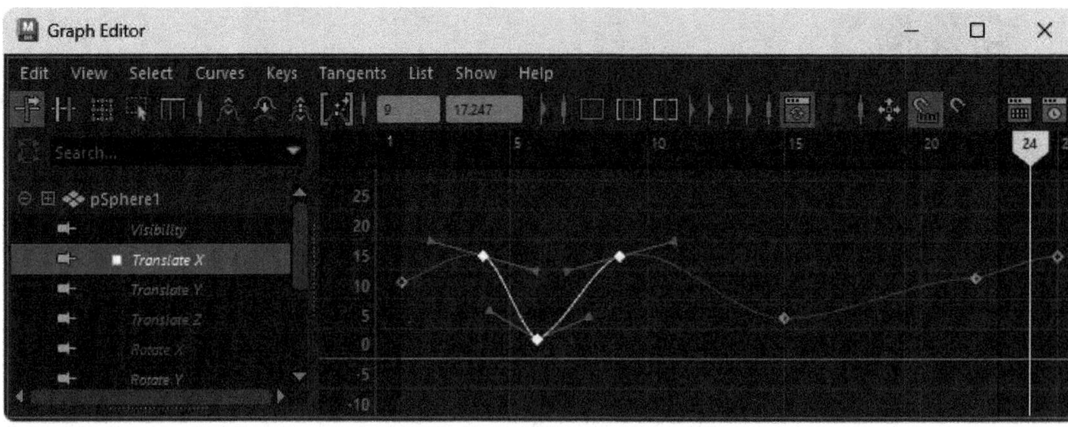

FIGURE 12-36

Graph Editor with tangents

Lesson 12.4-Tutorial 1: Edit Animation Curves

1. Select the File, Open Scene menu command, locate and open the Animated airplane.mb file.
2. Select the airplane object.
3. Select the Windows, Animation Editors, Graph Editor menu command.

    The Graph Editor opens and displays the animation curves for the airplane. The top red curve is the RotateX curve, and the lower red curve is the TranslateX curve, and the straight blue lines are the TranslateZ and ScaleZ curves.
4. Drag over the center key on the RotateX curve to select it.
5. With the Move tool selected, drag the key point upward with the middle mouse button.
6. With the key point still selected, choose the View, Tangents, On Active Keys menu command.
7. Select the Tangents, Break Tangents menu command.

    This makes the tangents for the selected key point visible.
8. Drag over the left tangent handle to select it and drag it with the middle mouse button downward.
9. Drag over the right tangent handle and drag it also with the middle mouse button downward to form a sharp point.

    The animation in the curve editor now resembles Figure 12-37 and the rotating animation of the airplane now happens much quicker.

10. Select File, Save Scene As and save the file as **Curve edited airplane.mb**.

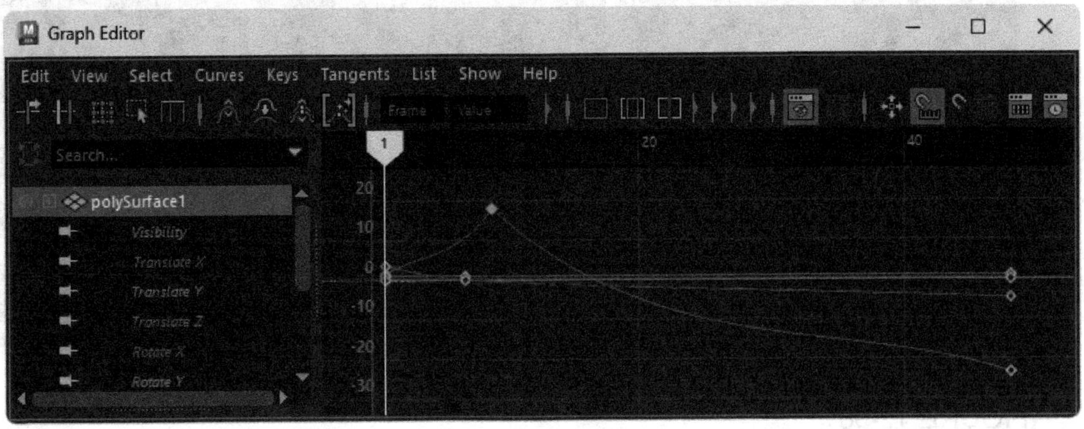

FIGURE 12-37

Curve edited airplane

Lesson 12.4-Tutorial 2: Repeat Motion

1. Select the File, Open Scene menu command, locate and open the Jumping bean.mb file.
2. Select the bean object.
3. Select the Windows, Animation Editors, Graph Editor menu command.
4. Select the View, Infinity menu command.

   The Graph Editor displays dashed lines for the continuing motion of the selected object.
5. Select the Curves, Post Infinity, Cycle with Offset menu command.

   The Graph Editor changes the dashed lines to show the offset motion for the bean object, as shown in Figure 12-38.
6. Click the Play Forward button to see the entire animation.
7. Select File, Save Scene As and save the file as **Repeating jumping bean.mb**.

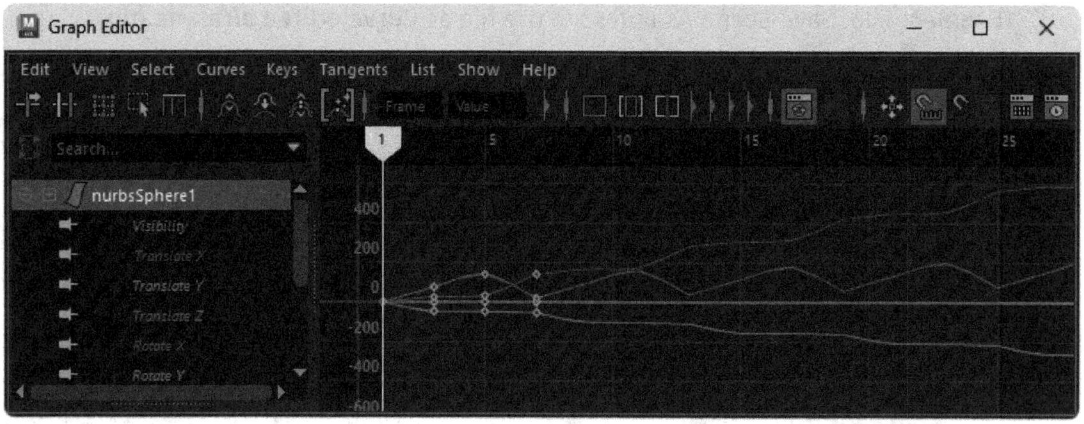

FIGURE 12-38

Repeating motion

Lesson 12.5: Control Animation Timing and Add Sound

The Dope Sheet is helpful when synchronizing several objects within the scene and matching object interactions to an audio file.

Using the Dope Sheet

The Dope Sheet shows all keys as small squares graphed at their location in time. You can select and move these keys using the middle mouse button. All the attributes for the scene objects are listed in a hierarchy over to the left and a Time Slider with the scene frames are shown above the keys. You can use the Framing buttons to show all the keys, just the Playback Range, or to center the display at the current frame. The Dope Sheet, shown in Figure 12-39, is opened using the Windows, Animation Editors, Dope Sheet menu command.

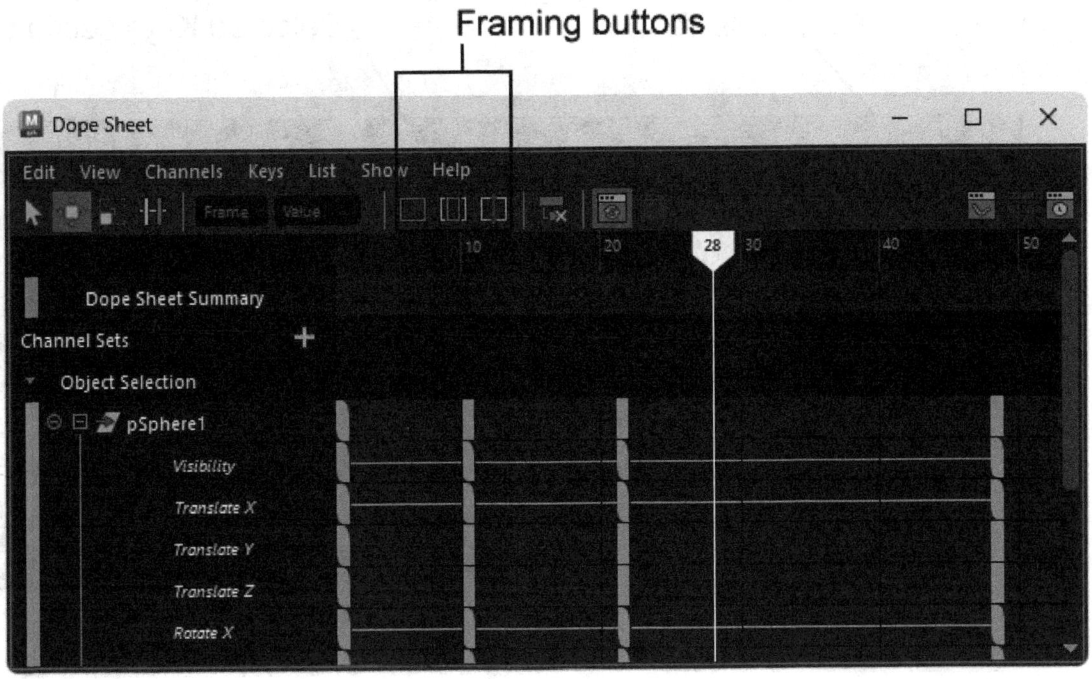

FIGURE 12-39

The Dope Sheet

Within the Dope Sheet Editor, you can pan the current set of keys with the Alt/Option and middle mouse key or zoom the current view with the Alt/Option and right mouse key.

Selecting, Moving, and Scaling Keys

The Select Tool button lets you drag over a section of the Dope Sheet. The keys within the selected area are selected and highlighted in white. Once selected, you can drag the selected keys left or right using the Move Tool or with the middle mouse button. The Scale Tool is used to rescale the distance between the rows of selected keys using the handles displayed at each corner of the selection, as shown in Figure 12-40, or you can drag the center handle to move the selected area to a new position. Changing the distance between rows of keys will affect the speed of the animation with less space causing the animation to play quicker and more space causing the animation to play slower.

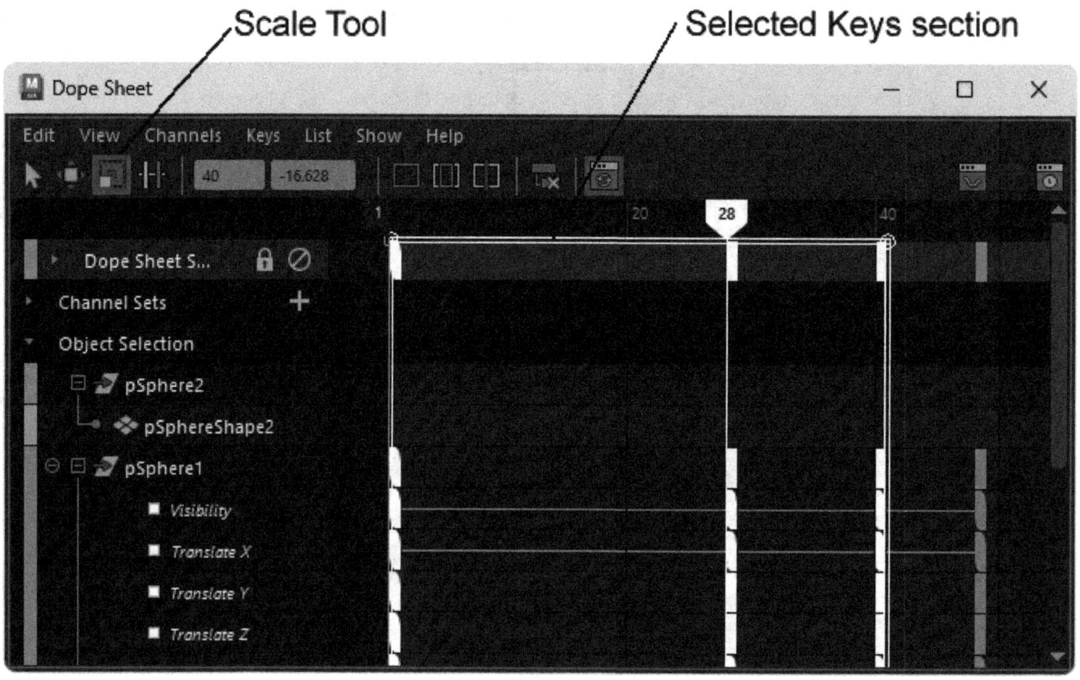

FIGURE 12-40

The Dope Sheet with selected keys

You can also cut and copy the selected keys with the Edit, Cut/Copy menu commands (Ctrl/Command+X and Ctrl/Command +C hotkeys) and paste them in a new location with the Edit, Paste menu command (Ctrl/Command +V hotkey). If keys are pasted in the middle of some keys, all existing keys are automatically shifted to accommodate the pasted keys.

Muting and Locking Keys

To temporarily remove the effect of keys, you can select the Keys, Mute Key menu command or click the Mute button to the right of each attribute. Muted attributes are cross-hatched. The Keys, Unmute Key menu command restores any muted keys. There is also a Lock button next to the Mute button to the right of each attribute. This button lets you lock the attribute so it cannot be changed.

Defining Channel Sets

By default, the Dope Sheet displays all attributes for the selected objects, which can result in a long list of attributes to wade through. Using Channel Sets, located at the top of the Dope Sheet, you can define a smaller set of attributes to keep track of for each selection. Click on the plus sign next to the Channel Sets track to create a new channel set. Double click its name to rename it, then drag and drop any of the attributes with the middle mouse button onto the new channel set name to add an attribute to the set. The Channels menu includes commands to mute and/or lock the entire selected channel. Figure 12-41 shows the Dope Sheet with a new Channel Set created for the animated sphere.

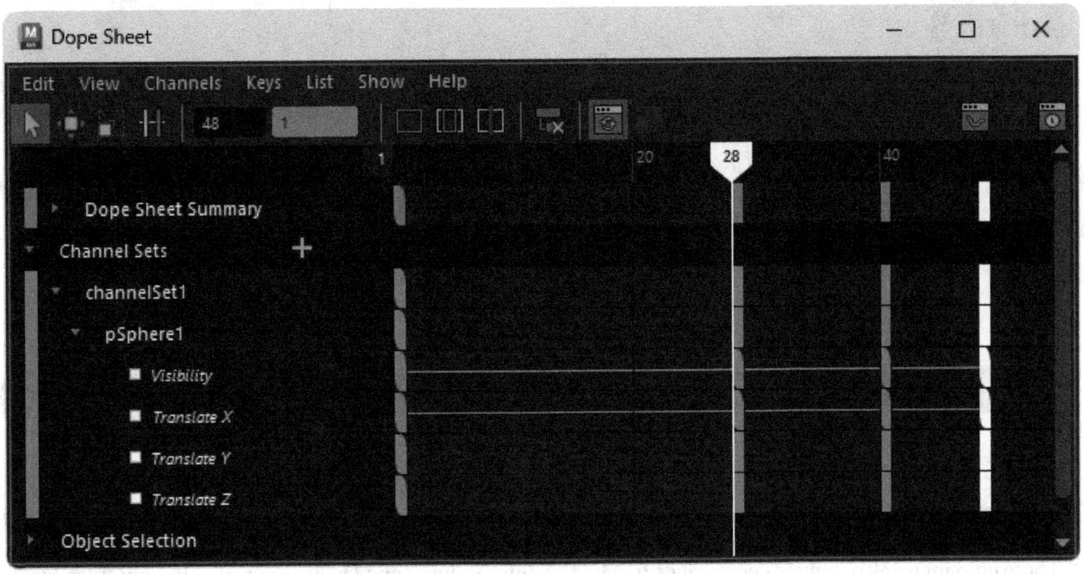

FIGURE 12-41

The Dope Sheet with a defined Channel Set

Inserting Keys

Selecting the Insert Keys Tool lets you click anywhere on the Dope Sheet to create a new key. This new key will automatically assume its current value, which will be interpolated if the key is located between two other keys, but you can change its value using the Frame and Value boxes displayed on the Dope Sheet toolbar. If you zoom in far enough, the key markers will display the key's value, as shown in Figure 12-42. Double click on the key marker to change its value. Selected keys can be deleted with the Delete key or using the Edit, Delete menu.

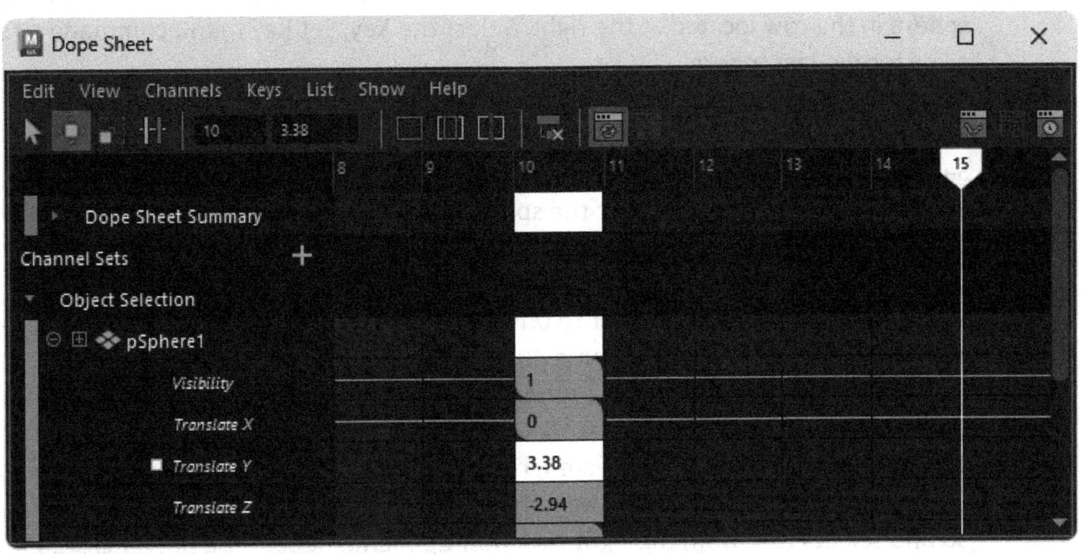

FIGURE 12-42

Display and edit key values

Adding Sound

You can import sound files into Maya using the File, Import or using the Audio, Import Audio menu command. Supported audio files include WAV and AIF formats. Once imported, the waveform of the audio file appears in the Time Slider, where it is easy to synch with the keys. The imported sound file also appears in the Dope Sheet. Figure 12-43 shows the waveform for the imported audio file in the Time Slider.

Tip

Dropping an audio file on the Time Slider automatically imports it.

FIGURE 12-43

An imported sound file

The Audio menu also includes commands to Mute, Adjust Volume and Delete Sounds. All audio files loaded in the scene also are listed in the Audio menu where you can select which ones to use.

Lesson 12.5-Tutorial 1: Use the Dope Sheet

1. Select the File, Open Scene menu command, locate and open the Newtons cradle.mb file.
2. Select the first sphere located at the left. Select the Rotate tool and drag on the blue Z-axis manipulator to rotate the sphere away from the other spheres. Select the Key, Set Key menu command.
3. Drag the Time Slider to frame 10. Rotate the sphere back into place next to the other spheres and choose Key, Set Key menu command to set another key. Select the last sphere in the row located at the right. Select the Key, Set Key menu command to set a key for the last sphere.
4. Drag the Time Slider to frame 20. Rotate the sphere away from the other spheres. Select the Key, Set Key menu command.
5. Select the Windows, Animation Editors, Dope Sheet menu command. The Dope Sheet displays all of the keys for the sphere as rectangles.
6. With the last sphere still selected, click on the Insert Keys Tool in the Dope Sheet toolbar and click on the Dope Sheet where the Rotate Z key aligns with Frame 30, then set the Value in the toolbar to 0.This creates a new key with the same value as the one in the first column in frame 30.
7. In the view panel, select the first sphere object again and expand its channels in the Dope Sheet until the Rotate Z channel is visible.
8. With the Select Tool button selected, right click on the Rotate Z key in the second column and choose Copy from the pop-up menu. Then drag the Time Slider to frame 30 and select Paste from the right click pop-up menu. Repeat the previous step to copy the Rotate Z key from the first column to frame 40. The additional keys cause the spheres to swing back and forth, as shown in Figure 12-44.
9. Click on the Play Animation button to view the resulting animation.

10. Select File, Save Scene As and save the file as **Animated Newtons cradle.mb.**

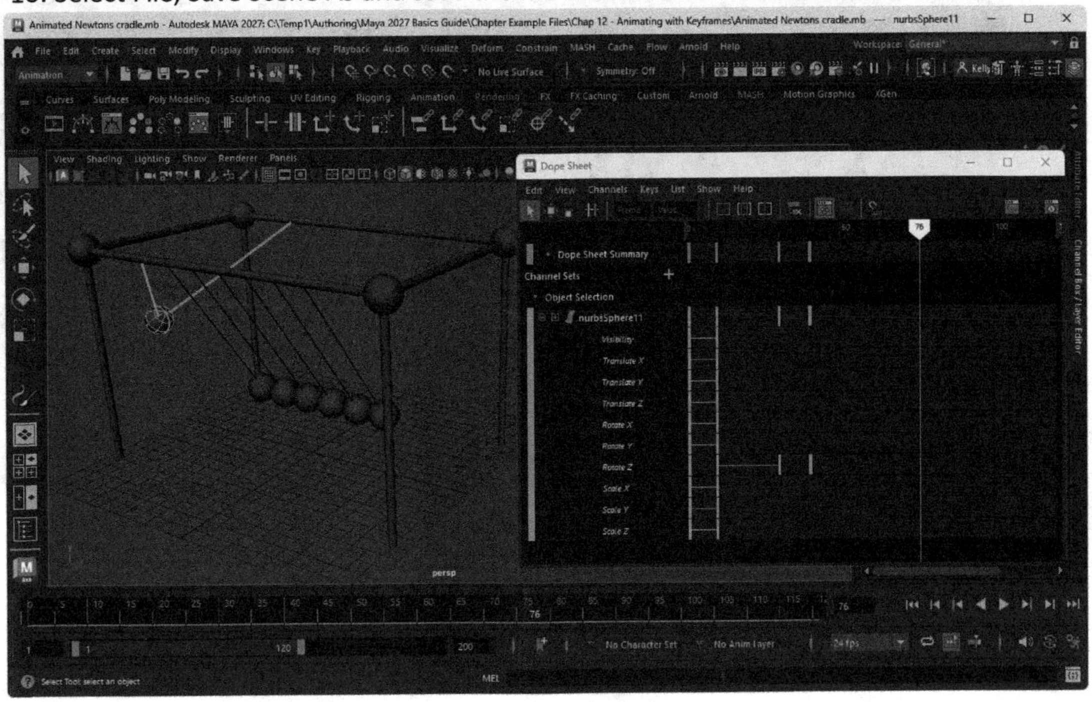

FIGURE 12-44

Animated Newton's cradle

Lesson 12.5-Tutorial 2: Add Sound

1. Select the File, Open Scene menu command, locate and open the Bouncing ball.mb file.
2. Select the File, Import menu command. Locate and import the Boing.wav file.

   The imported audio file appears in the Time Slider.
3. Select the Windows, Animation Editors, Dope Sheet menu command.

   The Dope Sheet displays all of the keys for the sphere as rectangles along with the audio file.
4. Click on the center keys for the NURBS sphere object to select them.
5. Drag them to the right to align them with the sound file.

   The Dope Sheet shows the selected keys aligned with the start of the audio file, as shown in Figure 12-45.
6. Select File, Save Scene As and save the file as **Bouncing ball with sound.mb**.

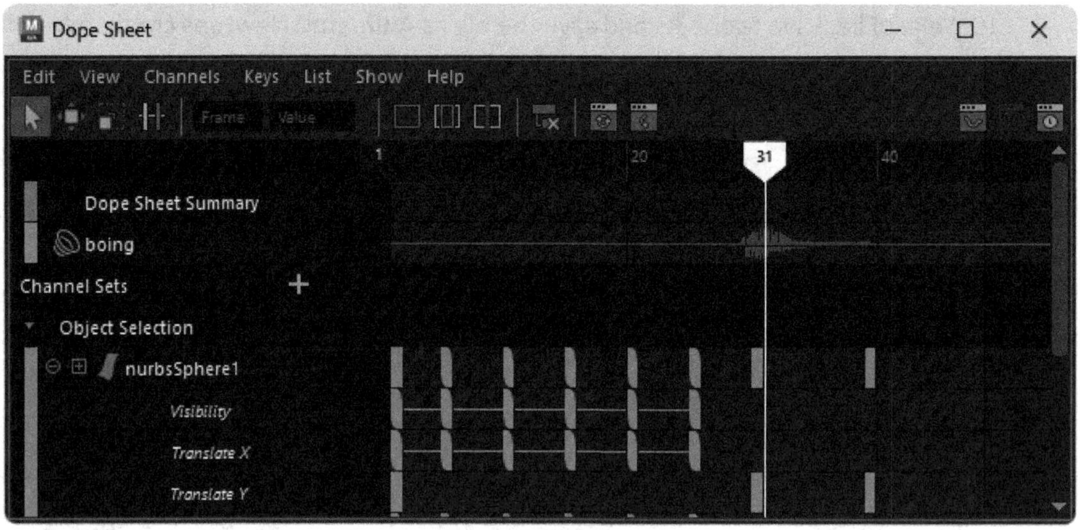

FIGURE 12-45

Added Sound

Lesson 12.6: Create Multi-Shot Animations

The Sequencer is used to create a multi-shot animation using several different cameras in the current scene.

Using the Sequencer

The Sequencer window is opened with the Windows, Animation Editors, Sequencer. This window, shown in Figure 12-46, can be docked to the interface by dragging it to the lower edge of the interface above the Timeline.

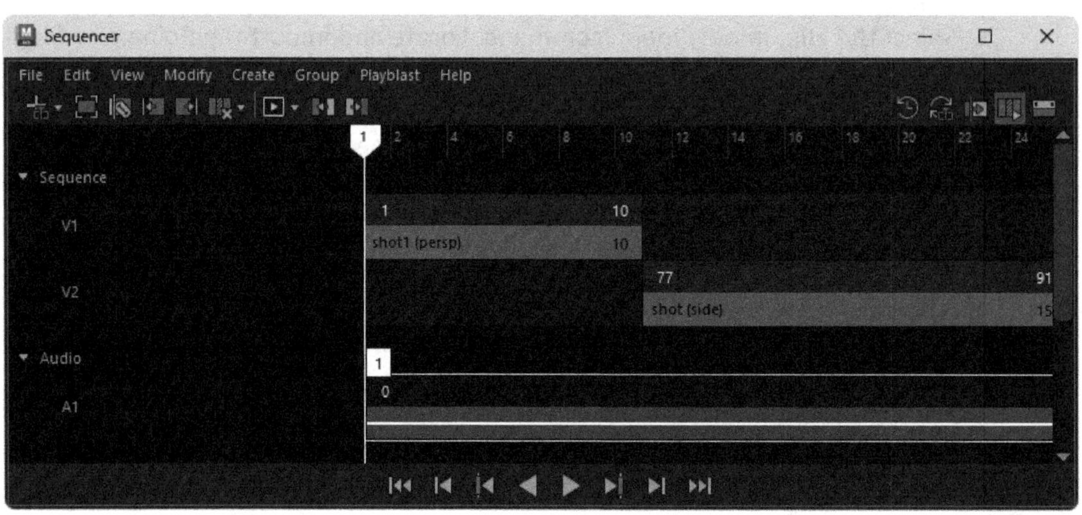

FIGURE 12-46

Sequencer window

Adding Shots

Each shot in the sequence appears as a single rectangle with a label and the camera that is being used. To create a new shot, use the Create, Shot or the Create, Shot from Timeline menu command. The length of the shot's rectangle is set to the number of frames that the shot covers, but you can adjust the start and length of the shot by dragging on its left or right edge. You can also reposition a shot by dragging it to a new location on the Timeline. If you right click on the shot, you can Split, Mute, or Lock the shot. The right click menu also includes options to adjust its label, color, and which camera it uses. If two shots are overlapped, then the top-most shot is used.

Importing Audio

All new shots are added to the top of the Sequencer window, but audio tracks appear below the shots. You can import audio using the File, Import Shot Audio or the File, Import Sequencer Audio menu commands. Each imported audio track shows the waveform of the audio, and it extends for the length of the audio track.

Playing the Entire Sequence

Play controls for the Sequencers are available at the bottom of the window. You can also create a Playblast for the entire sequence using the Playblast menu. When a Playblast is initialized for any shots, a thumbnail of the shots is placed on the shot rectangle.

Lesson 12.6-Tutorial 1: Use Sequencer

1. Select the File, Open Scene menu command, locate and open the Checkers.mb file.
   This file includes a checkerboard of checkers with the first few moves animated.
2. Select the Windows, Animation Editors, Sequencer menu command.
   The Sequencer window opens.
3. Select the Create, Shot, Options menu command. In the Create Shot Options, select **red_camera** as the Shot Camera with frames from 1 to 5 and click the Create Shot button.
4. Create another shot called shot2 with the **black_camera** from frames 6 to 10, then drag this shot to be adjacent to the first shot.
5. Create shot 3 with the **red_camera** from frames 11 to 20 and shot 4 with the **black_camera** from frames 21 to 30. Align all the shots from left to right in the Sequencer window.
6. Hold down the Shift key can select all four shots, then choose the View, Frame All menu command.
7. Select the Playblast, Playblast All Shots menu command.
   A thumbnail is added for each shot, as shown in Figure 12-47.
8. Select File, Save Scene As and save the file as **Checkers sequence.mb**.

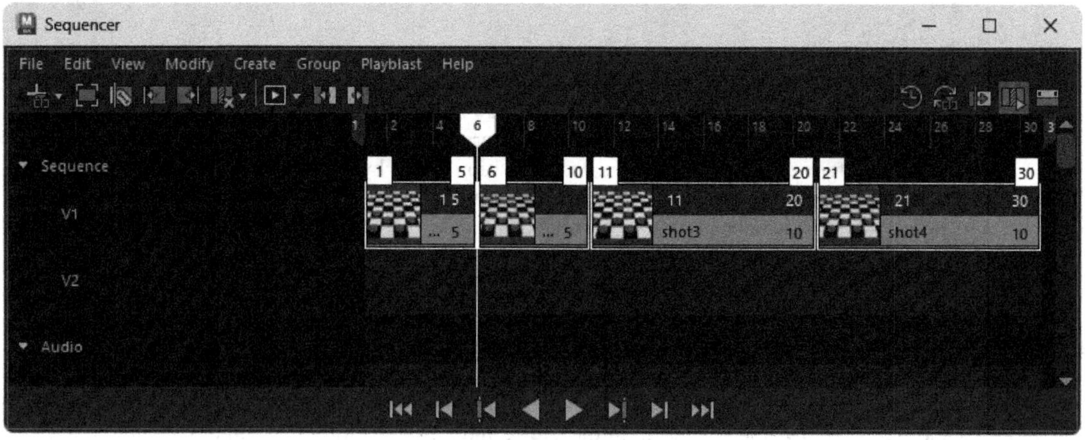

FIGURE 12-47

Checkers sequence

Chapter Summary

This chapter covers the basics of animating scenes using keyframes. Keyframes define the state of scene objects for a given frame of animation. All keys appear on the Time Slider located at the bottom of the interface. You can play back any created animation using the Animation Controls and using the Playblast feature. Animations can also be created using motion paths. To edit animation keys and parameters, you can use the Graph Editor, which displays all keys as points and curves that can be easily edited. The Dope Sheet controls the timing of the animation and provides a way to add sound to an animation. The Sequencer combines several shots into a single animated sequence.

What You Have Learned

In this chapter, you learned

* How to set keyframes.
* How to use the Auto Key mode.
* How to select keys on the Time Slider.
* How to use the Time Slider menu to cut, copy, paste, delete, and snap keys.
* How to preview an animation.
* How to change the Frame Rate.
* How to make an animation loop.
* How to enable ghosting.
* How to display and edit motion trails.
* How to use Playblast.
* How to create a motion path.
* How to attach an object to a motion path.

* How to edit an existing motion path and deform an object following a motion path.
* How to use the Graph Editor.
* How to frame curves in the Graph Editor.
* How to edit and insert keys in the Graph Editor.
* How to smooth and simplify Graph Editor curves.
* How to set Pre- and Post-Infinity conditions.
* How to work with tangents in the Graph Editor.
* How to open and edit keys in the Dope Sheet.
* How to add sound to an animation.
* How to create a multi-shot animation using the Sequencer.

Key Terms From This Chapter

* **Keyframe.** An animation setting that records the state of an object for a given frame.
* **Auto Key.** The mode that automatically creates keys whenever an object moves or a parameter changes.
* **Time Slider.** An interface element that displays all the frames and keys for the current animation.
* **Looping.** A setting that causes an animation to repeatedly play.
* **Frame Rate.** The speed at which an animation plays determined by the number of frames per second (fps).
* **Ghosting.** A setting that makes multiple copies of the animated objects appear at regular intervals along a motion path.
* **Motion trail.** A curve that shows the path of the animated object.
* **Playblast.** A feature that plays the current animation in a separate media player.
* **Motion path.** A created curve that defines the animation path that an object follows.
* **Graph Editor.** An interface that displays all animation actions as graphed curves allowing editing and modification.

* **Infinity conditions.** A setting that enables an animated sequence to repeat indefinitely.

* **Tangents.** Handles that control the curvature of a curve near each key point.

* **Dope Sheet.** An interface used to display and edit the timing of an animation.

* **Sequencer**. An editor used to combine shots from several different cameras into a single animated sequence.

Chapter 13
Working with Characters

IN THIS CHAPTER

- 13.1 Build a skeleton.
- 13.2 Edit joint attributes.
- 13.3 Add Inverse Kinematics.
- 13.4 Skin a character.
- 13.5 Edit a skin.
- 13.6 Create a Quick Rig.
- 13.7 Animate a Quick Rig.
- 13.8 Add hair and fur.

Animating characters is much easier if you take some steps to prepare your character to be animated. This process is called **rigging** and it involves applying constraints to the character so that it moves in a believable fashion without its arm bending backwards.

Part of the rigging process is to create an underlying skeleton that can be animated. The actual character model creates a skin that is positioned over the skeleton. The skin must be bound to the skeleton before the skeleton can control the skin.

Skeletons are created using Joint objects. Using the Create Joints command, you can click on the locations where the joints are to be located. Each new joint is attached in a hierarchical structure to the other joints. Each joint also has attributes that you can set using the Attribute Editor. One of these attributes lets you set limits to the joint's movement. By limiting the motion of the skeleton's joints, you can control how the character moves.

Another way to control a skeleton's movement is with **Inverse Kinematics** (IK). Inverse Kinematics enables you to animate the character by placing its hands and feet and letting the rest of the body follow.

When the skin is created, it then needs to be bound to a skeleton. Once the skeleton is bound to a skin, you can control the skin by moving the various joints and bones of the skeleton.

You can also edit and deform a character's skin by using Influence objects and by painting skin weights.

For human-shaped characters, a complete rig can automatically be created using the Quick Rig feature. Rigs can then easily be animated using imported motion capture data files. The MotionMaker Editor can automatically create motion paths for biped, dog, and horse rigs. Motions created using the MotionMaker Editor can be retargeted to other rigs using the Character Controls panel.

Adding hair and fur to a character increases the realism of the character.

Lesson 13.1: Build a Skeleton

A character's skeleton consists of all the underlying bones and joints that are necessary to animate a character. A skeleton consists of bones, which are rectangular boxes that narrow from its parent joint to its child joint and joints; these joints are spheres at either end of the bone, as shown in Figure 13-1. The joints of the skeleton are connected to one another using parenting. Each skeleton can have only one root, which is the top-most parent.

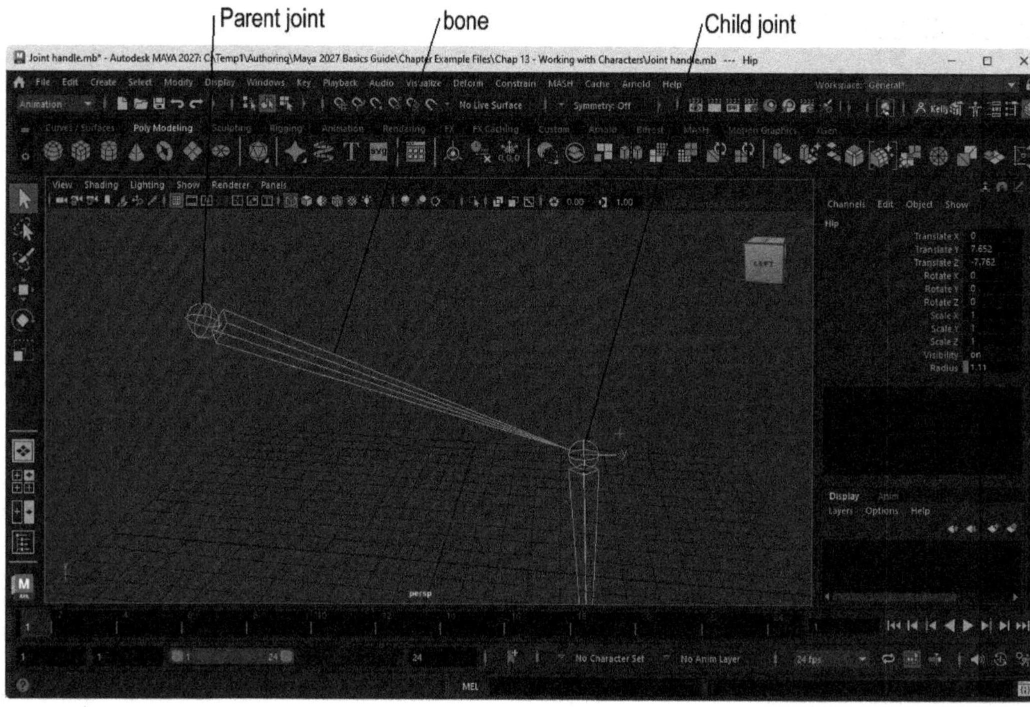

FIGURE 13-1

Bone and joints

Creating Joints

You can use the Skeleton, Create Joint tool menu command to create new bones and joints. Click in the view panel where the parent joint is and click again where the child joint is. A bone connects the two joints. You can then click again to create an attached bone and joint. When you've completed the entire joint chain, press the Enter key. When a joint is selected, all of its children bones and joints are automatically selected. When creating joints, pressing the Delete key deletes the last bone and joint, the Insert key lets you move the last created joint, and the middle mouse button lets you reposition the last joint.

Note

The Skeleton menu is part of the Rigging menu set.

Inserting a Joint

Once you have created a joint chain, you can insert an attached joint chain using the Skeleton, Insert Joint menu command. With this command, click on the joint that you want to share and drag to create a new joint. To enable your characters to have more motion, split a long bone into several smaller ones, like the one in Figure 13-2.

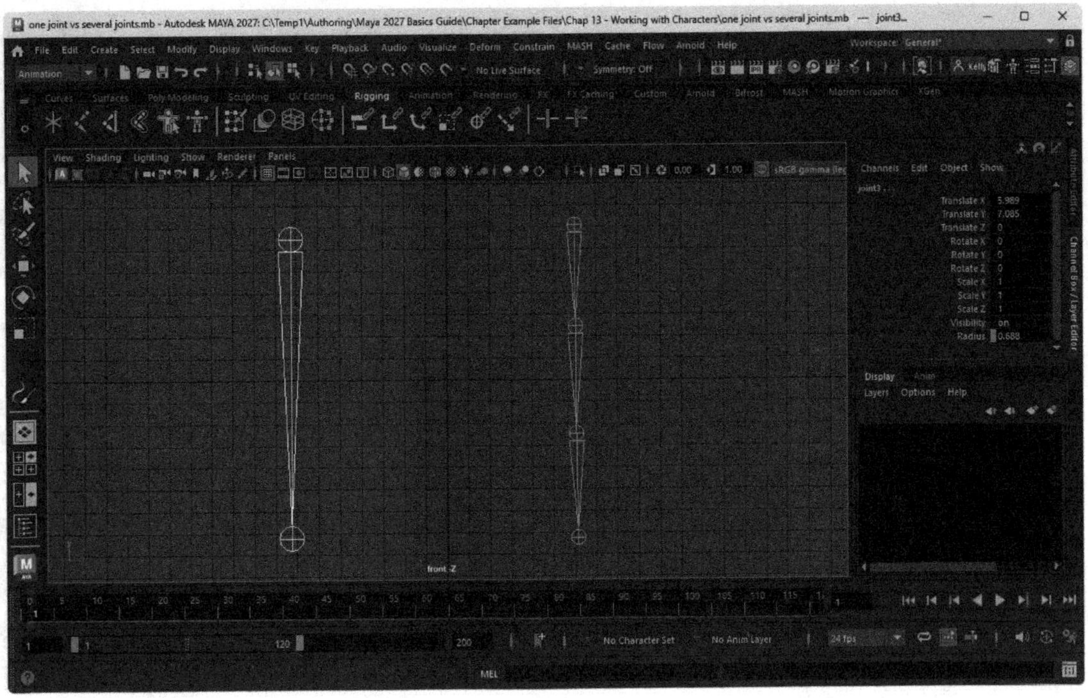

FIGURE 13-2

Inserting joints

Connecting a Joint Chain

You can connect a selected joint chain with a root joint to a selected joint in another chain with the Skeleton, Connect Joint menu command. To use this tool, select the root joint on one chain, hold down the Shift key, select the joint of another chain, and select the menu command. The Connect Joint Options dialog box includes two modes. The Connect Joint mode moves and aligns the root joint chain to the other chain, and the Parent Joint mode leaves both joints in place, creating a bone that connects the two joints. Figure 13-3 shows a skeleton before and after a chain has been connected.

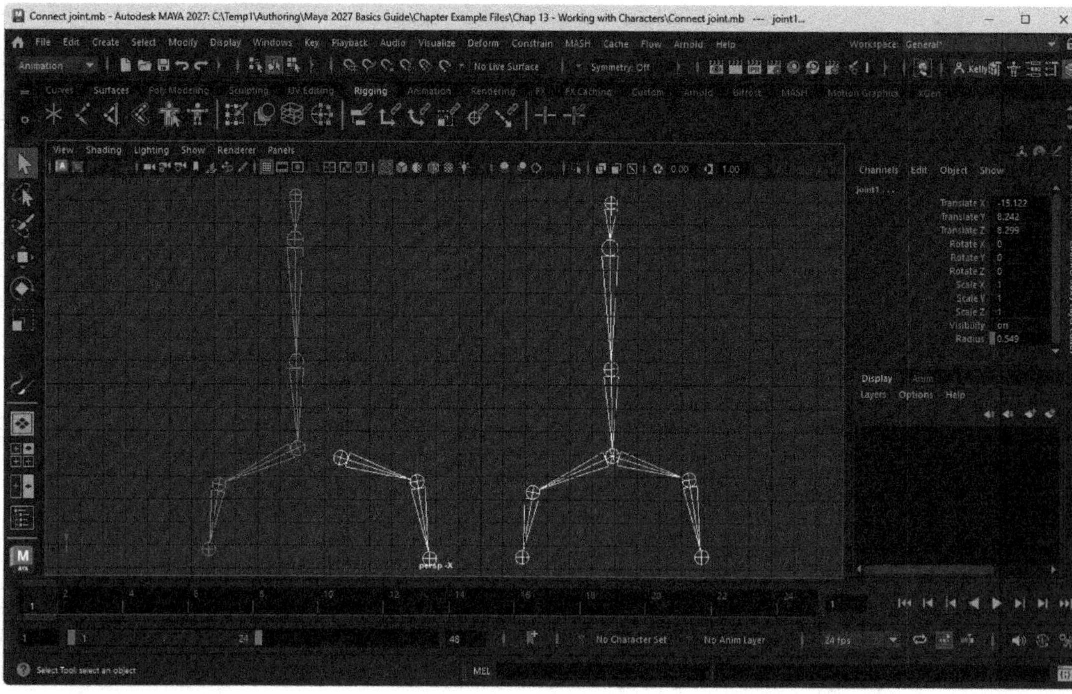

FIGURE 13-3

Connected chain

Removing and Disconnecting Joints

You can remove a joint from a joint chain with the Skeleton, Remove Joint menu command, and a joint can be disconnected from a joint chain with the Skeleton, Disconnect Joint menu command. Root joints cannot be disconnected or removed, but you can delete the entire joint chain, including the root joint, with the Delete key.

Mirroring Joints

Many characters have a regular symmetry that you can quickly duplicate with the Skeleton, Mirror Joints menu command. To mirror a joint chain, you need to select one joint away from where it is connected. The Mirror Joint Options dialog box, shown in Figure 13-4, lets you choose the plane about which the mirror takes place.

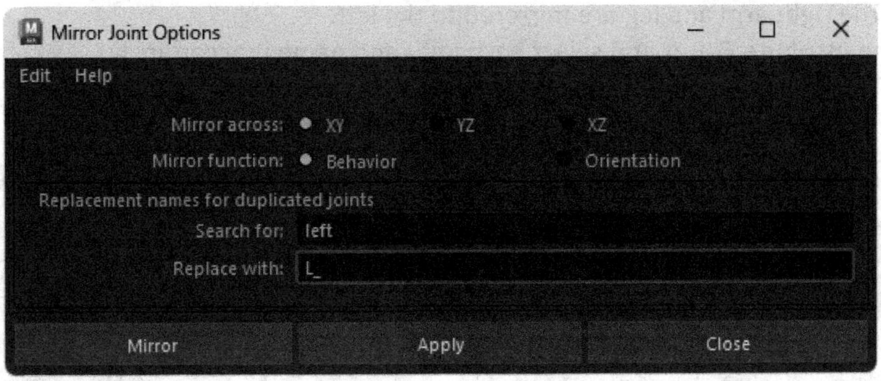

FIGURE 13-4

Mirror Joint Options dialog box

Resetting the Root Joint

Although it may seem natural to have a skeleton start with the head joint, the pelvis is actually the best joint to be the root for human characters. If you've created your skeleton with the head as the root, you can reset it to the pelvis root joint with the Skeleton, Reroot Skeleton menu command.

Naming Joints

When joints are created with the Create Joint menu, they are given the name "joint" followed by a number. If you don't name joints when created, it can become confusing to locate the correct joint later as you animate. Using the Joint attribute located at the top of the Attribute Editor, you can name the various joints.

Tip

```
Looking at the skeleton hierarchy in the Windows,
Outliner gives you a chance to double check all
the joint connections.
```

Lesson 13.1-Tutorial 1: Create a Skeleton

1. Select the Panels, Orthographic, Front panel menu command to display the front view panel.
2. Select the Skeleton, Joint Tool menu command.

Click at the top of the Front view panel and again to create a head joint, then a little below the head to create the neck joint, then click again further down to create a pelvis joint. Then, click to the right of the pelvis joint to create the hip joint. Continue clicking down to create joints for the knee, foot and toe joints.

3. Press the Enter key to end Joint Creation mode.
4. Select the center pelvis joint and choose the Skeleton, Reroot Skeleton menu command.

    This command flips the head joint and makes the pelvis the root for the skeleton.

5. Select the Skeleton, Insert Joint menu command and drag from the neck joint out to the right to create shoulder, elbow, and wrist joints.
6. Select the joint between the right shoulder and elbow joints, and then choose the Skeleton, Mirror Joint, Options menu command. Select the YZ option and click the Apply button. Then repeat this step for the right hip and knee joints.

The right arm and leg are mirrored to the left.

7. Open the Attribute Editor and select each joint and name it accordingly.

   The completed simple skeleton is shown in Figure 13-5.

8. Select File, Save Scene As and save the file as **Simple skeleton.mb**.

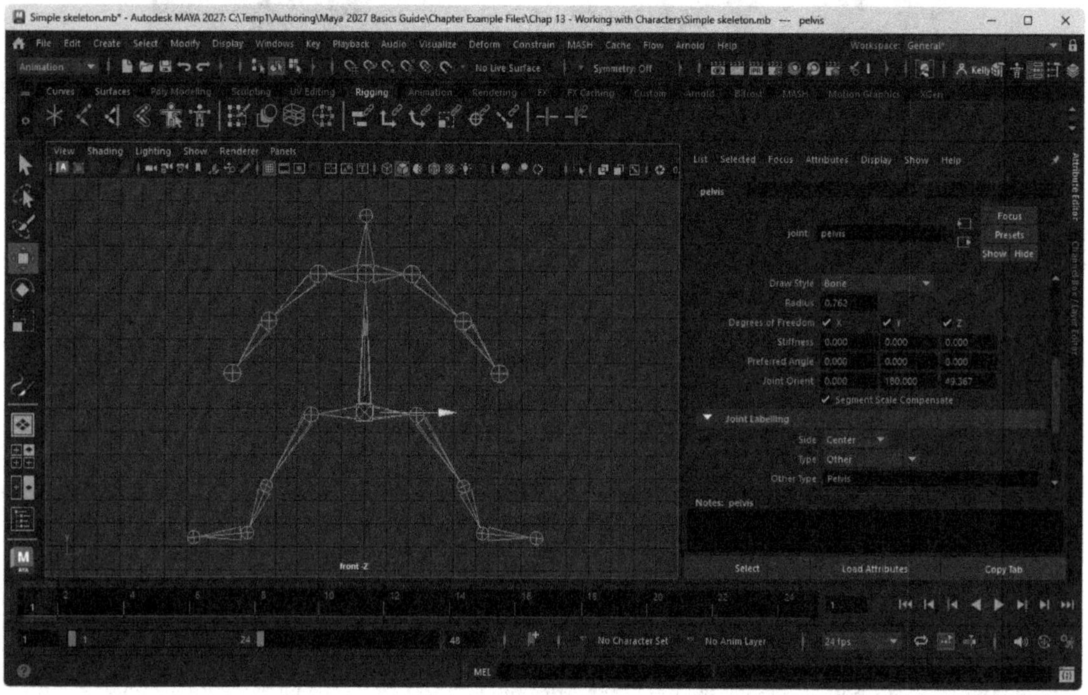

FIGURE 13-5

Simple skeleton

Lesson 13.1-Tutorial 2: Add a Tail to the Skeleton

1. Select the File, Open Scene menu command then locate and open the **Simple skeleton**.mb file.
2. Use the Panels, Perspective, Persp panel menu command to change to the Perspective view and rotate the view until the side view is visible.
3. Select the Skeleton, Insert Joint menu command.
4. Drag from the Pelvis joint away to the back of the skeleton to create a new tail joint. Continue dragging out to create three bones. Press the Enter key to complete the chain. Move the tail bones into position behind the skeleton.
5. In the Attribute Editor, name the joints for the tail.

   The tail joint chain is connected to the skeleton, as shown in Figure 13-6. You can see the final skeleton hierarchy in the Outliner, shown in Figure 13-7.

6. Select File, Save Scene As and save the file as **Skeleton with tail.mb**.

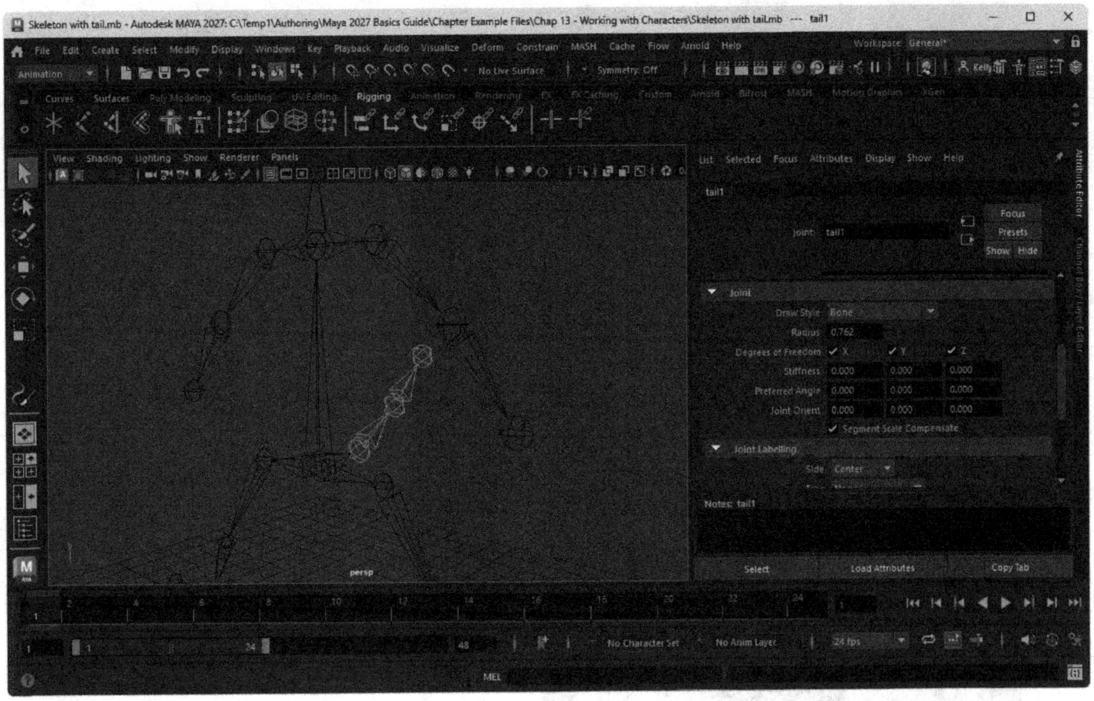

FIGURE 13-6

Skeleton with tail

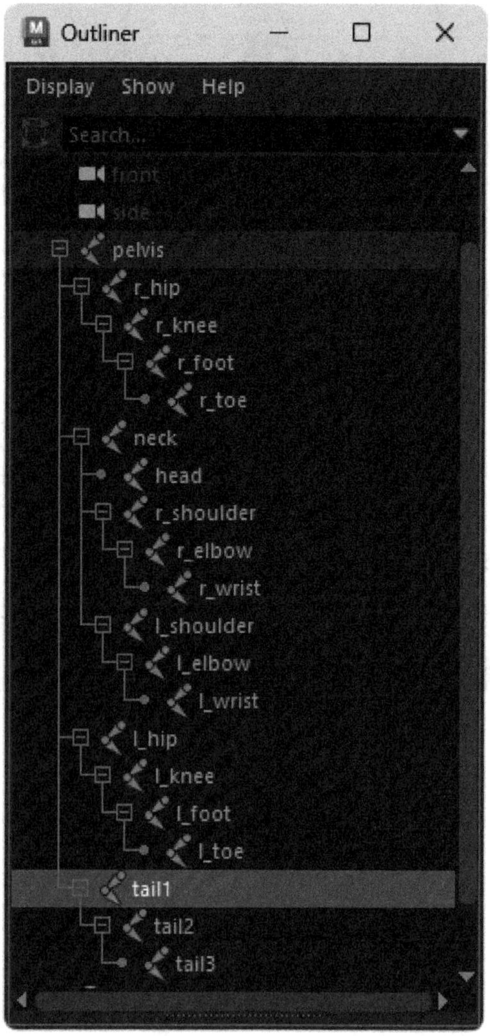

FIGURE 13-7

Skeleton hierarchy shown in the Outliner

Lesson 13.2: Edit Joint Attributes

Once you have created a rough skeleton, you can select the individual joints and define limits on how they can be moved and rotated. Applying correct limits helps ensure that your character moves in a realistic manner as it is being animated.

Inheriting Transforms

By default, all child joints move along with their parent. However, you can disable this action and have each joint move independently of its parent by disabling the Inherits Transform check box in the Transform Attributes on the Attribute Editor.

Orienting Joints

The Joint section of the Attribute Editor includes check boxes for specifying the degrees of freedom about which the joint can move. If any of these check boxes are disabled, the joint cannot rotate about the disabled axis. This section also lets you set the orientation for the joint, which is the angle that the bone points away from the joint. Preferred angle is the angle where the joint is most comfortable, and the stiffness defines how much force is required to move the joint from its preferred angle. You can return the selected joint to its preferred angle at any time with the Skeleton, Assume Preferred Angle menu command.

Labeling Joints

Each joint can be labeled, which is useful in locating joints as you animate. To label a joint, select it and choose a label from the Type drop-down list in the Joint Labeling section of the Attribute Editor or you can use the Skeleton, Joint Labeling, Add Joint Label menu options. The options in the Type list include all the major body parts, or you can select Other and type in your own. The Side marks the left or right side in parentheses. Enable the Draw Label check box to make the label appear in the view panel, as shown in Figure 13-8.

Note

Labeling joints is different from naming joints. The Joint name located at the top of the Attribute Editor identifies the object in the Outliner and the Joint Label identifies the joint in the viewport using labels. Both are important.

Tip

All joint labels are color-coordinated, based on their side.

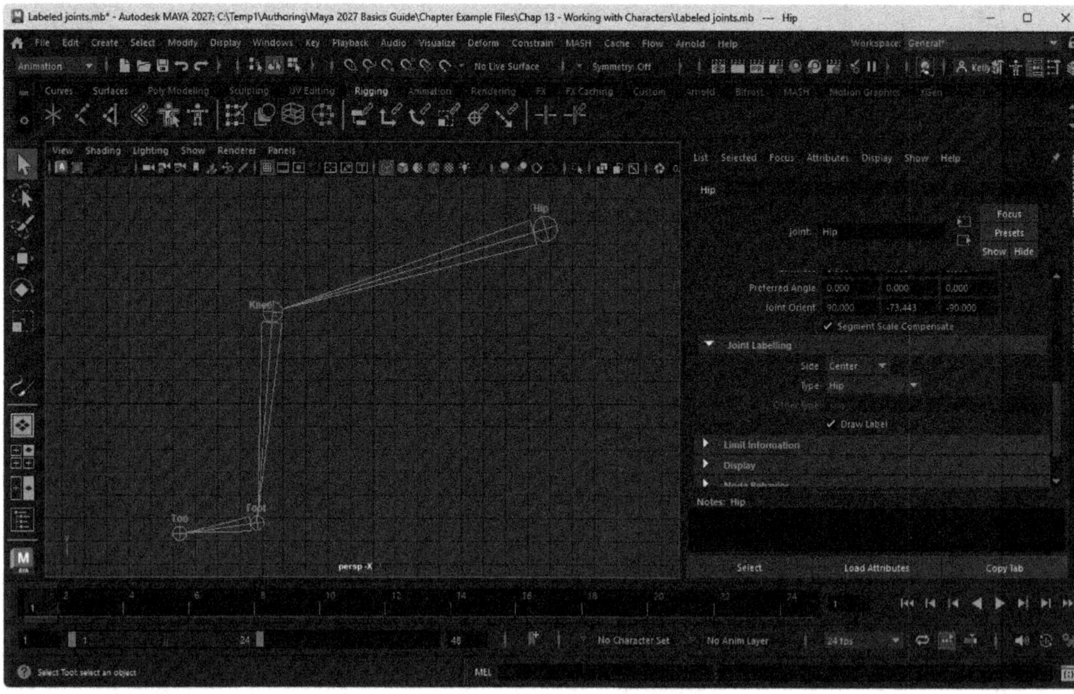

FIGURE 13-8

Labeled joints

Showing and Hiding Labels

Labels are useful in finding joints, but with many labels, they can get in the way. You can show and hide all labels using the Skeleton, Joint Labeling, Show/Hide All Labels menu command. The Skeleton, Joint Labeling, Toggle Selected Labels menu command shows or hides the labels for the selected joints. You can also rename all joints based on the labels or create labels based on the joint names with commands in the Skeleton, Joint Labeling menu.

Tip

Using the Custom Font Size setting in the Display, Font section of the Preferences dialog box, you can increase the size of the joint labels.

Limiting Joints

The Limit Information section of the Attribute Editor (shown in Figure 13-9) lets you specify the translate, rotate and scale limits of the selected joint. For example, a knee joint can rotate forward to 90 degrees and backward about 75 degrees along the z-axis, but limiting its rotation for the X and Y axes keeps your animated character from having awkward bent legs by accident. For each dimension and transformation, you deselect its check box to keep its motion unlimited, or enable its limit and type in a value for its Maximum and Minimum limit values. Once limits are imposed, you can test them in the view panel by transforming the joint.

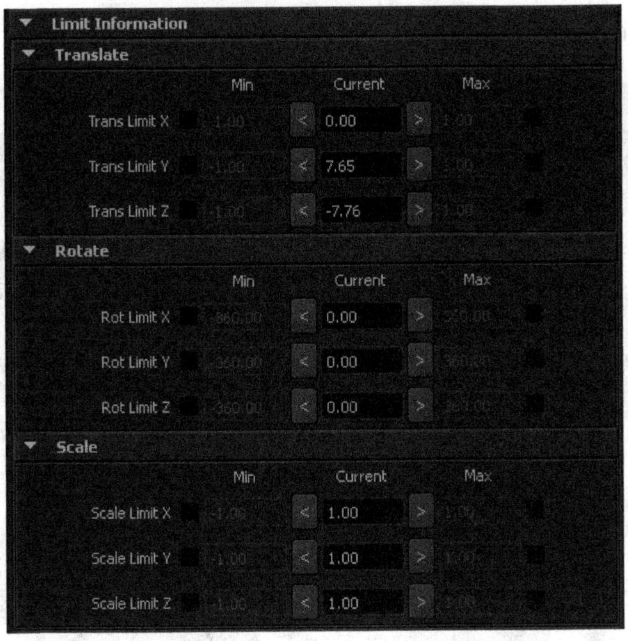

FIGURE 13-9
Limit Information

Displaying Joints

The Display section of the Attribute Editor lets you display a handle for the joint and move the handle away from the actual joint. Having a joint positioned away from the joint is helpful once you begin to animate the skeleton with a skin applied. Display Local Axis is also helpful. It displays axes around the joint as a quick reference. You can also set the default manipulator that appears when the joint is selected and the visibility of the joint and its children. Figure 13-10 shows a joint with the handle positioned away from the joint and the Local Axis option enabled.

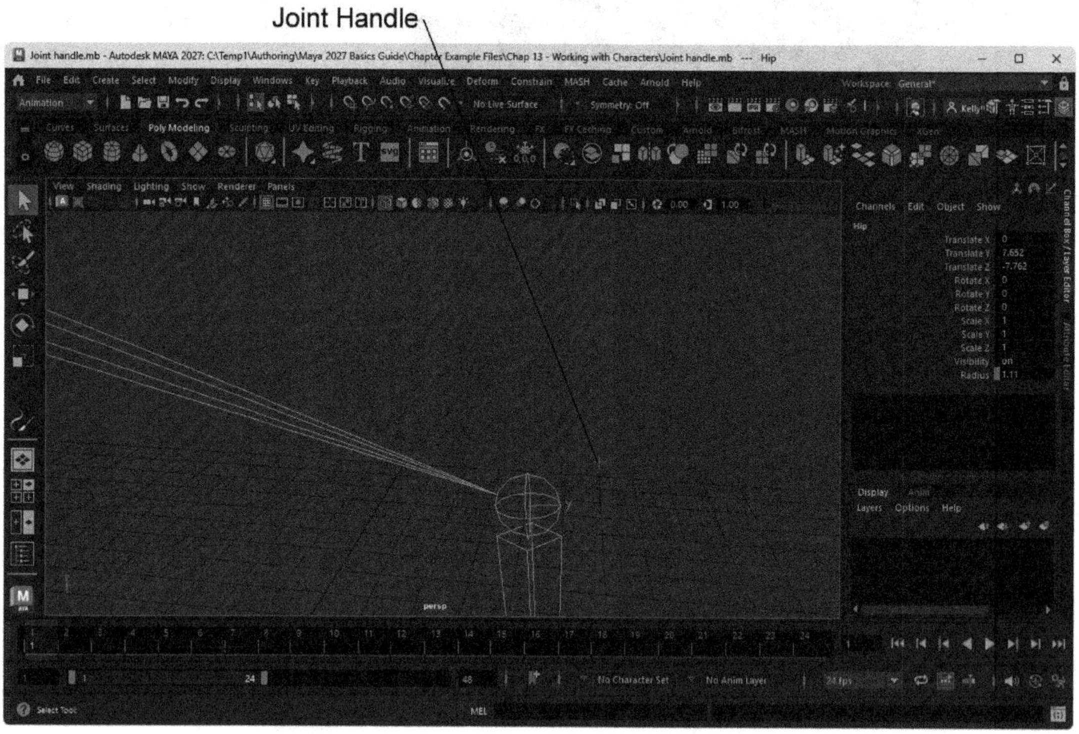

FIGURE 13-10

Joint handle

Lesson 13.2-Tutorial 1: Label Joints

1. Select the File, Open Scene menu command, and then locate and open the Simple skeleton.mb file.
2. Select the head joint and open the Attributes Editor.
3. In the Joint Labeling section, select the Head option from the Type list and select Center from the Side list. Then, enable the Draw Label option.
4. Repeat Step 3 for the remaining joints.

   With the Draw Label option enabled, the text label appears for each labeled joint, as shown in Figure 13-11.
5. Select File, Save Scene As, and save the file as **Labeled skeleton.mb**.

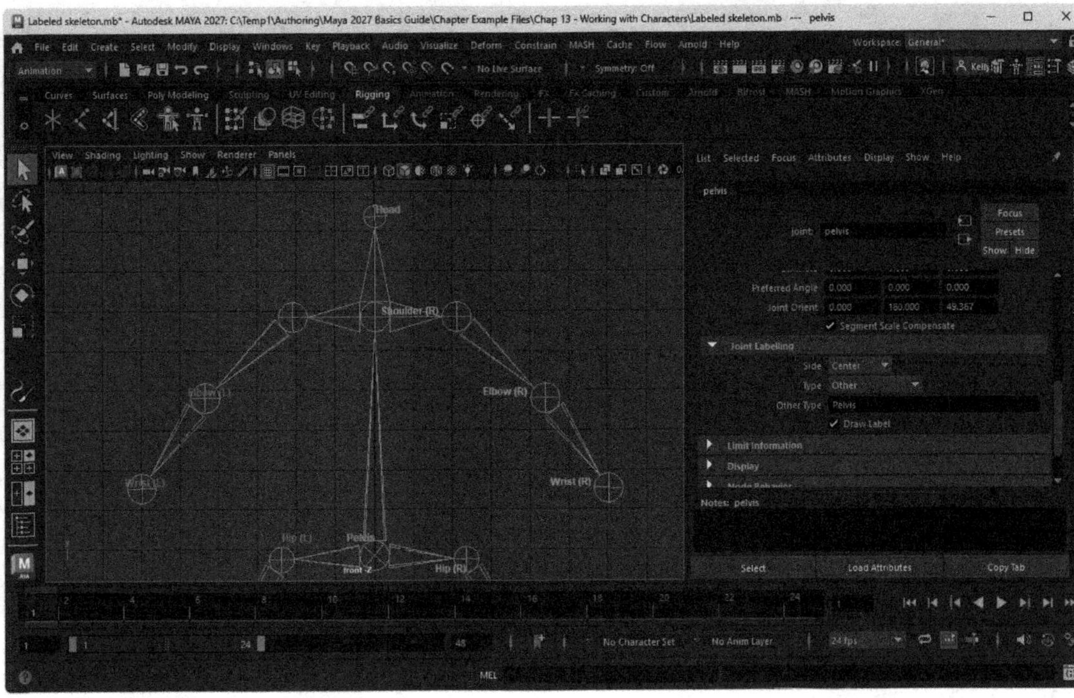

FIGURE 13-11

Labeled skeleton

Lesson 13.2-Tutorial 2: Limit Joint Motion

1. Select the Skeleton, Create Joint menu command and click in the Front view to create a simple three-bone set of joints to represent an arm.
2. Select the elbow joint and open the Attributes Editor.
3. In the Limit Information section, enable the Minimum and Maximum Rotation Limit options for the z-axis.
4. Set the Minimum limit value to –90 and the Maximum limit value to 75.
5. Select the Rotate tool from the Toolbox and drag the blue z-axis manipulator to test the limits.

   With the limits enabled, the joint stops moving once a limit is reached, as shown in Figure 13-12.
6. Select File, Save Scene As, and save the file as **Limited arm.mb**.

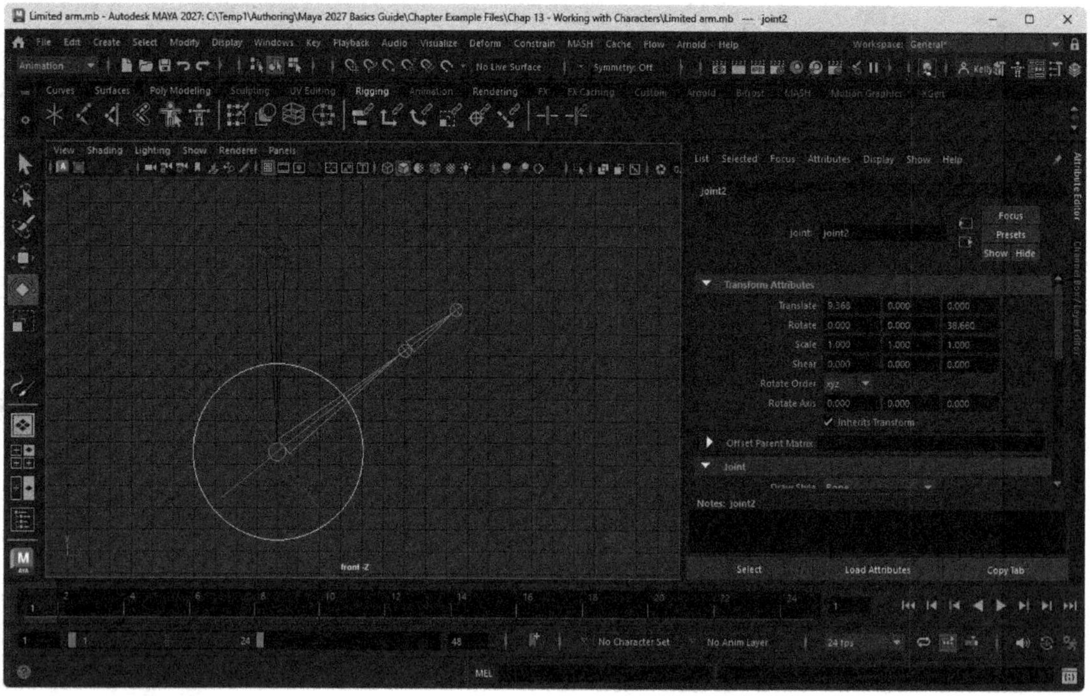

FIGURE 13-12

Limited arm movement

Lesson 13.3: Add Inverse Kinematics

Inverse Kinematics (IK) is a feature that you can add to a skeleton that lets the child object control the motions of its parent object. Normal hierarchical motion is to move the child along with the parent. This motion is called **Forward Kinematics** (FK), but as characters walk and move, it is easier to animate a character by dragging their feet into position rather than by positioning their feet by rotating their upper leg. IK allows you to control a character's legs and arms by moving its hands and feet. FK lets you control a character's feet and hands by dragging its legs and arms.

Using the Create IK Handle Command

You can use the Skeleton, Create IK Handle menu command to add IK to a skeleton. To do so, just select the tool and click on the parent joint followed by the last child joint in the limb. For example, to set up IK for the elbow, you'd select the shoulder joint and then the wrist joint. This overlays a light green triangle for the limb and adds an IK handle to the last joint, as shown in Figure 13-13. If you move this handle, the bones follow naturally.

Tip

All skeleton bones that have an IK solution applied to them appear light brown when unselected.

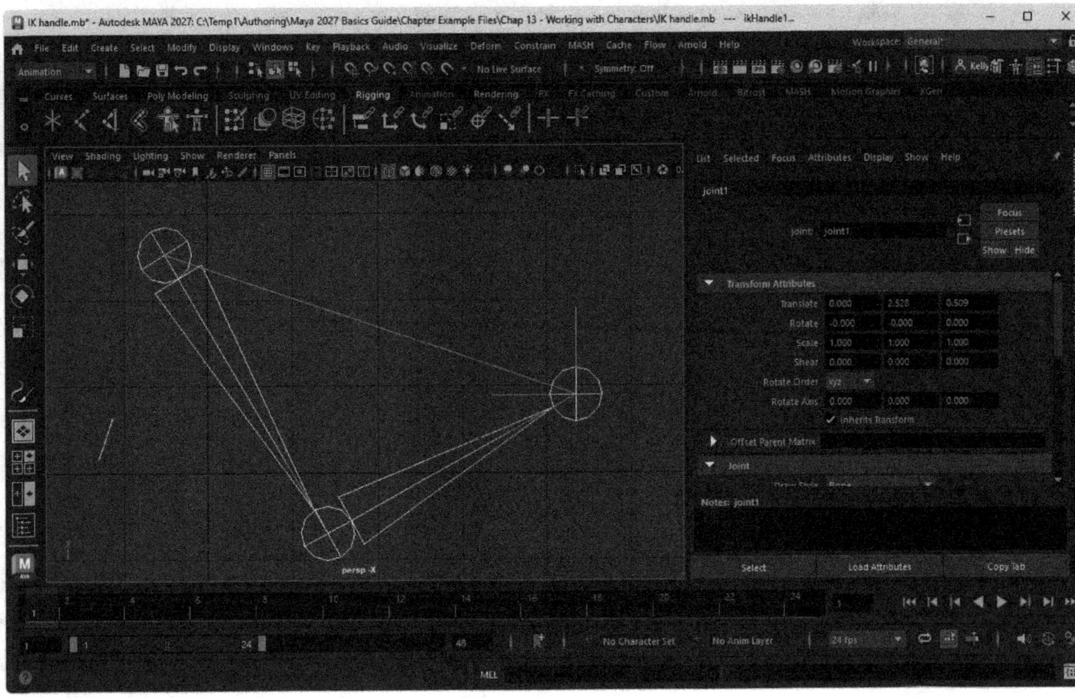

FIGURE 13-13

IK handle

Using the Create IK Spline Handle Command

In addition to the Create IK Handle command, the Skeleton menu includes a second type of IK that you can apply to spline objects. This type of IK, called the IK Spline Handle, is useful for tails that are made from many bones in a straight line. It is applied to a joint chain the same way as the IK Handle is—by selecting the first and last joints in the chain. The command creates a NURBS curve that runs along the joint chain. Selecting and moving this curve's CV components causes the joint chain to move as well. Figure 13-14 shows a joint chain with an IK spline solution.

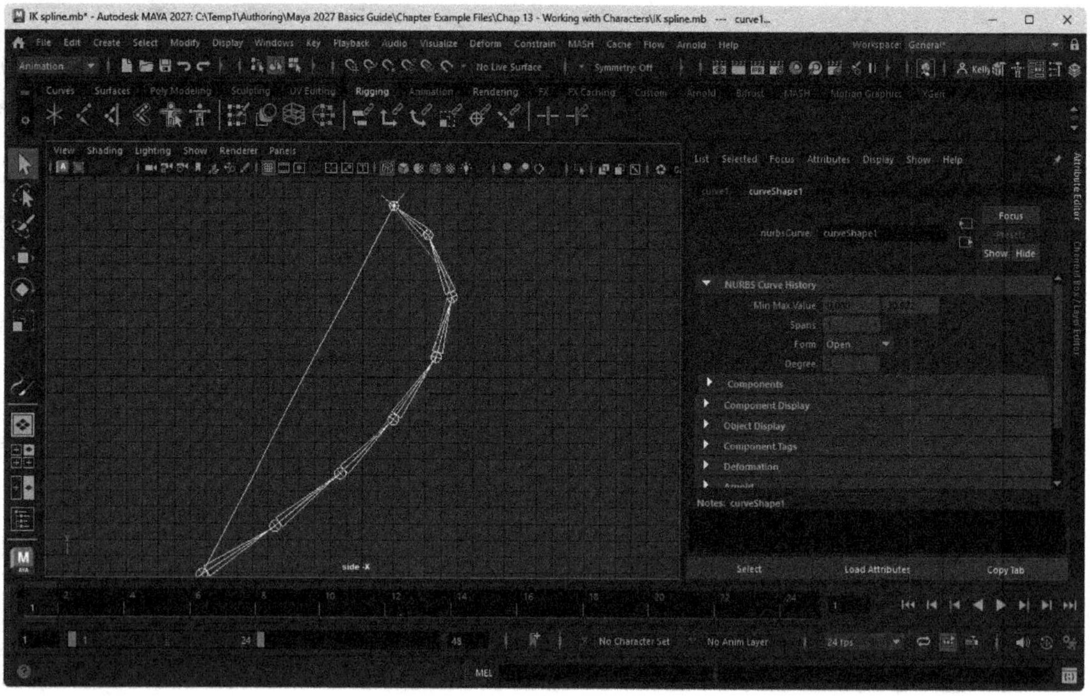

FIGURE 13-14

IK spline

Posing the IK Handles

With the IK handle selected, you can use the transform tools to move the joint into place. Sometimes when posing the IK handles, it can become difficult to see where joints should be located with the skeleton in the way. To move an IK handle without having the skeleton follow, simply select the Skeleton, Disable Selected IK Handles menu command. Then the Skeleton, Enabled Selected IK Handles menu command snaps the skeleton to the handle's location. You can also control the Roll and Twist. The IK Handle includes a pole vector to indicate the Preferred Angle, as shown in Figure 13-15. The Set Preferred Angle and Assume Preferred Angle commands are used to set and return to the set orientation.

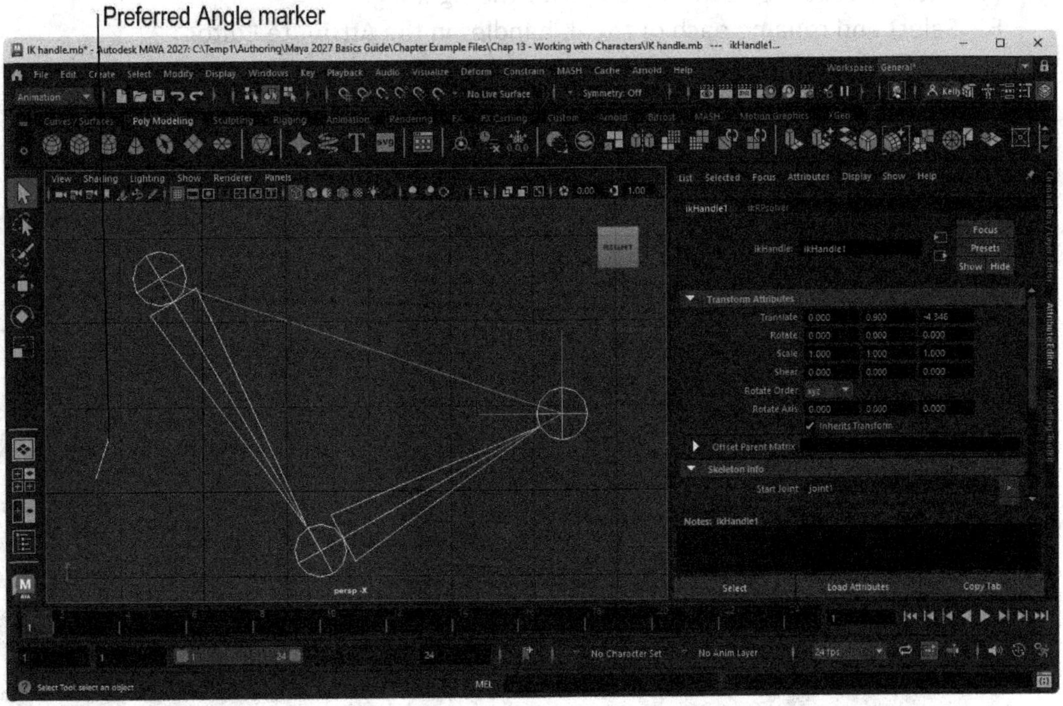

FIGURE 13-15

Roll and Twist manipulators

Switching Between FK and IK

As you animate, there may be times when you'll want to use Forward Kinematics to animate your character. With the IK handle selected, you can find the IK Blend attribute in the IK Solver Attributes section of the Attribute Editor; setting this attribute to 0.0 makes the control of the skeleton limb revert to FK. A setting of 1.0 uses the IK solution and anything in between blends between the two solutions.

Lesson 13.3-Tutorial 1: Add IK to a Skeleton

1. Select the File, Open Scene menu command then locate and open the Skeleton with tail.mb file.
2. Select the Skeleton, Create IK Handle menu command.
3. Click on the left shoulder joint and again on the left wrist joint. Then, repeat this step for the right arm.

   IK handles are created for each arm that move the two arm bones together when the IK handle located at the wrist is moved.
4. Select the Skeleton, Create IK Handle menu command again and select the left hip joint and the left foot joint. Set the Twist value in the IK Solver Attributes rollout to 180.

   Changing the Twist value reorients the joint so the foot moves backward instead of forward.
5. Then, use the Create IK Handle command again to create another IK chain from the left knee joint to the left toe joint to enable the foot to pivot about the ankle.
6. Select the left hip joint and rotate it around so the leg is pointing forward.

7. Then, repeat the last three steps for the right leg.
8. Select and rename each of the IK handles in the Attribute Editor.

   IK handles are created for each wrist, foot, and toe that move the both bones in the IK chain as the IK handle is moved. The right arm IK chain is shown in Figure 13-16.
9. Select File, Save Scene As and save the file as **Simple IK.mb**.

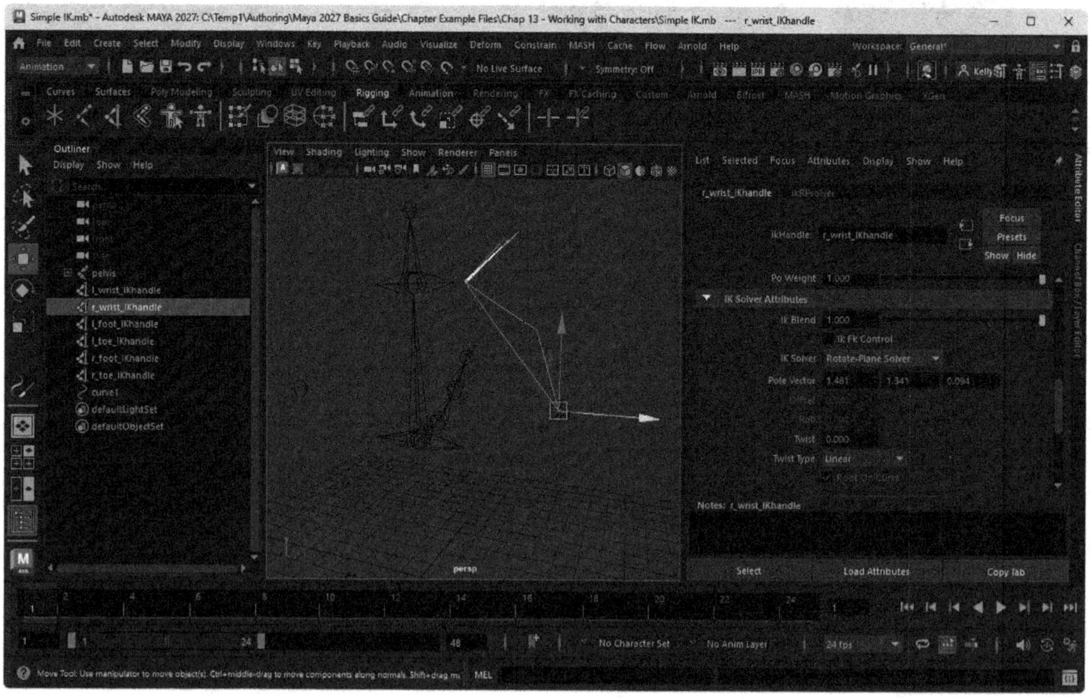

FIGURE 13-16

Simple IK

Lesson 13.3-Tutorial 2: Add IK Spline to the Skeleton Tail

1. Select the File, Open Scene menu command, then locate and open the Simple IK.mb file.
2. Select the Window, Outliner menu command to open the Outliner. Click on pelvis joint and then on tail1 in the Outliner to expand them.
3. Select the Skeleton, Create IK Spline Handle menu command.
4. Click on the pelvis joint in the Outliner and then on the tail3 joint in the view panel.

   This creates a NURBS curve that you can edit to control the tail's position, as shown in Figure 13-17.
5. Select the new IK handle and name it in the Attribute Editor.
6. Select File, Save Scene As and save the file as **Spline IK.mb**.

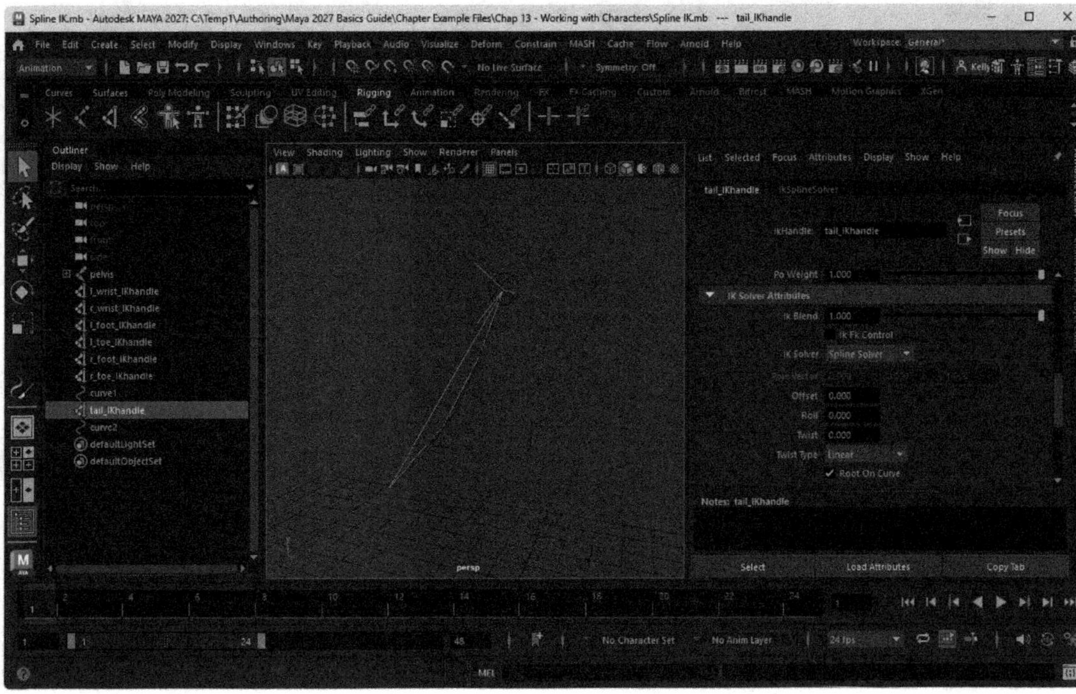

FIGURE 13-17

Simple IK spline

Lesson 13.4: Skin a Character

Skinning a character involves adding a surface to a skeleton hierarchy. This skin is bound to the skeleton and moves as the underlying skeleton is moved. You can bind skin to a skeleton using the Skin, Bind Skin menu command. Skinning displaces the skin around the joints and deforms the skin in order to maintain a smooth appearance.

Note

The Skin menu is also part of the Rigging menu set.

Creating Effective Skin

As you create a skin surface, remember that the skin only deforms and bends to the extent of the resolution of the skin surface, so when you create a skin object make sure that the number of spans and the number of sections is sufficient. Figure 13-18 shows two skeletons with smooth cylinder skins at different resolutions. The skin on the right deforms better than its counterpart on the left with minimal resolution.

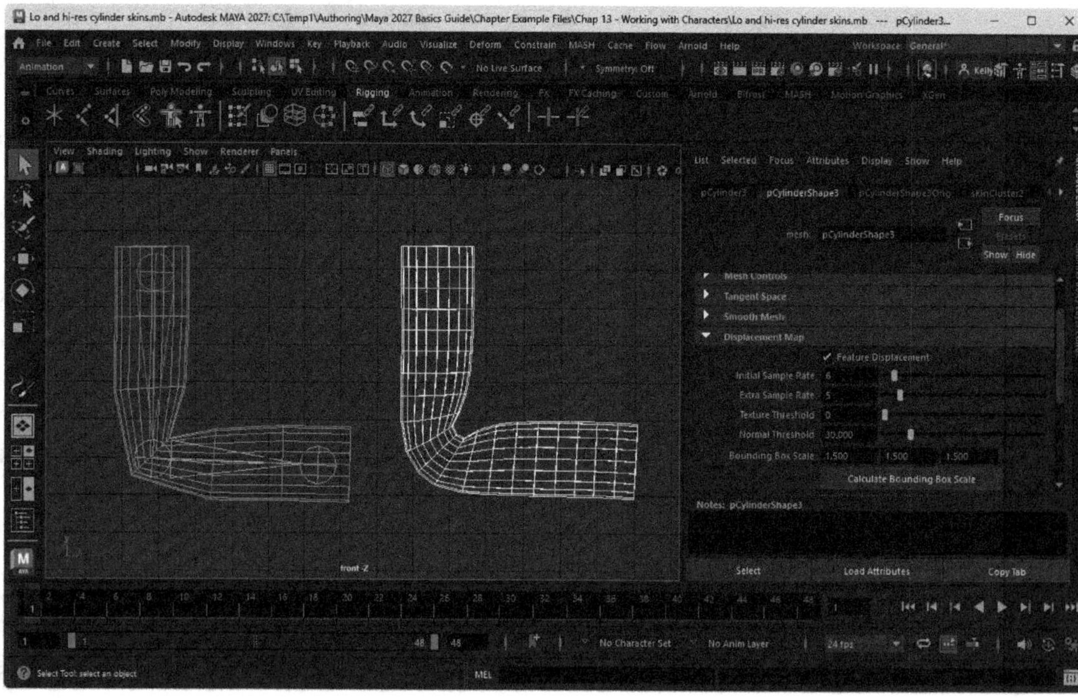

FIGURE 13-18

Skins require sufficient resolution

Positioning a Skeleton

Once the skin and the skeleton are created, you'll want to move the skeleton so that it lies in the center of the skin. Be sure to check all views for alignment. For the final rendered scene, you can hide the skeleton using the Display, Hide, Hide Kinematics, All menu command.

Using X-Ray Mode

The Shading panel menu includes a mode that makes it easy to align skeletal joints and skin. The Shading, X-Ray mode makes all objects semi-transparent so that you can see through the skin model to align the joints. There is also an X-Ray Joints option that keeps the shading on all objects, but lets you see the joints underneath.

Binding Skin

With a skin and a skeleton created and aligned, you can create a smooth skin binding between the skin and the skeleton using the Skin, Bind Skin menu command. The skin must be selected first and then the skeleton. Make sure to select the root joint for the skeleton to get the entire hierarchy. Once the skeleton and skin are bound, you can deform the skin by moving and rotating the underlying skeleton bones and joints. Figure 13-19 shows a simple cylinder that has been bound to a two-bone skeleton. The Shading, X-Ray Joints option has been enabled. Notice also that all the transform values in the Channel Box for the selected skin are locked because the underlying skeleton controls them.

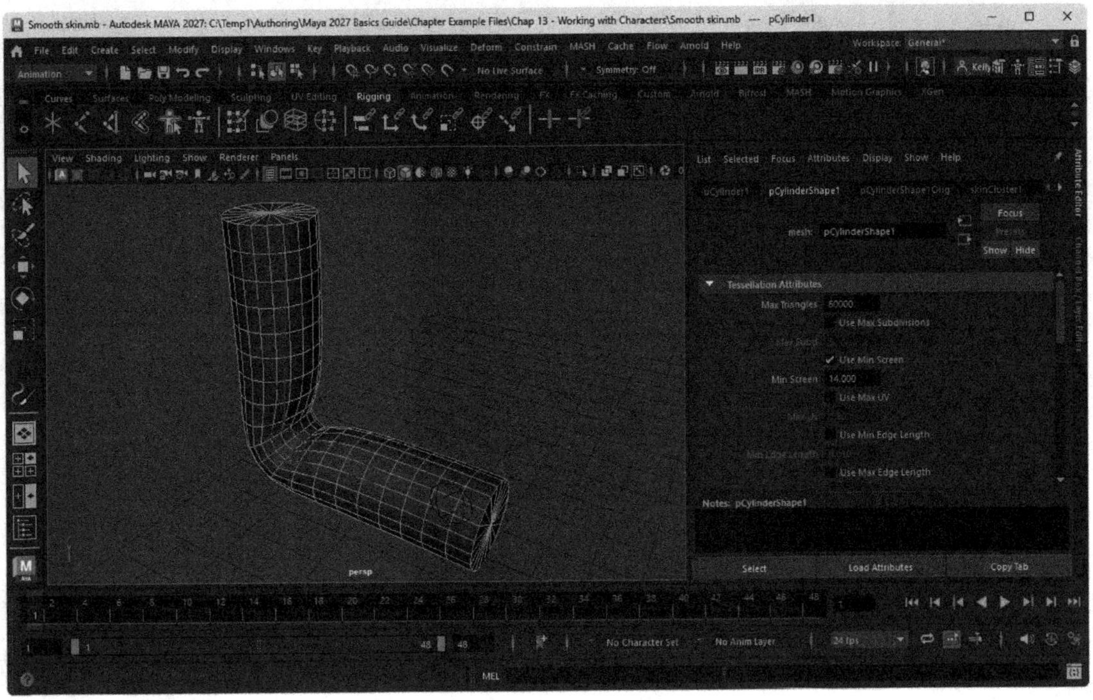

FIGURE 13-19

Smooth skin

Binding Interactive Skin

The Bind Skin option makes its best guess for matching the skin to the bones, but if you want more control over how the areas of the skin match to the bones, you can use the Skin, Interactive Bind Skin menu command. This option surrounds each bone with a capsule-shaped manipulator that you can move and scale to control each bone's influence. Figure 13-20 shows the manipulator for the Interactive Bind Skin. Drag on the red circle to expand the size of one end of the capsule, drag on the blue lines to scale the length and the green ends will lengthen or shorten the manipulator. Using this bind type lets you edit the capsules later with the Interactive Bind Skin tool, covered later in this chapter.

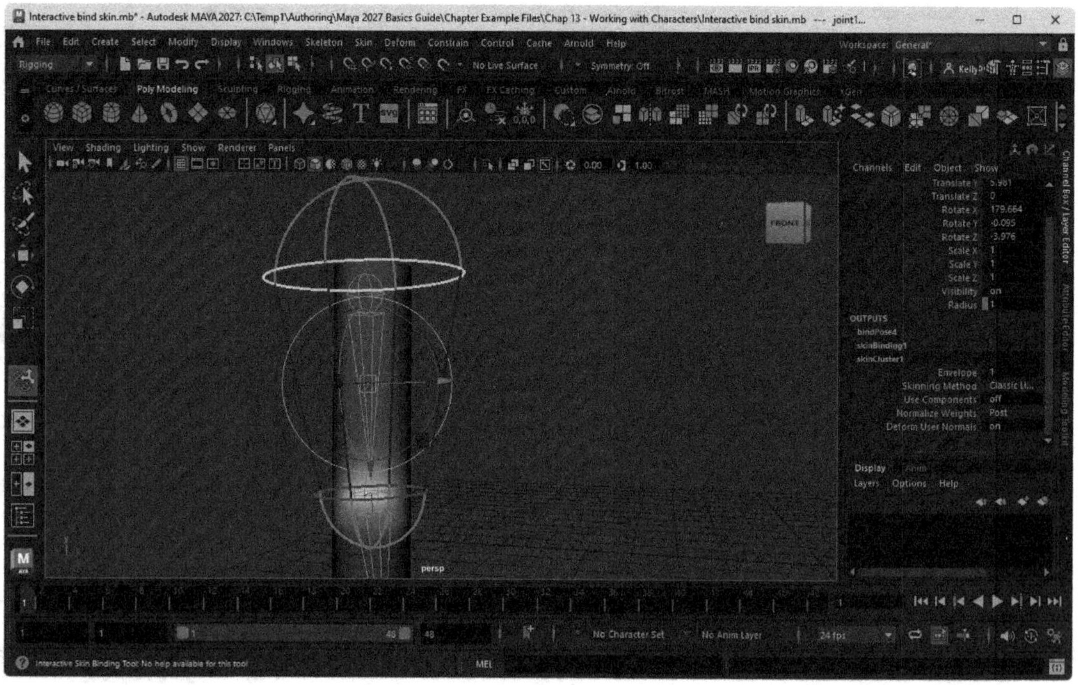

FIGURE 13-20

Interactive bind skin

Returning to Default Pose

You can reset the position of your skin and skeleton at any time to its original pose that was used before the binding took place using the Skin, Go to Bind Pose menu command.

Unbinding Skin

You can use the Skin, Unbind Skin menu command to detach the selected skin object from its skeleton. This removes any deformations that were applied to the skin by moving the skeleton and returns the skin to its shape before it was bound to the skeleton.

Animating Joints

Once a character is skinned and rigged, you can animate it by moving the various joints and IK handles and setting animation keys.

Lesson 13.4-Tutorial 1: Position a Skin

1. Select the File, Open Scene menu command, then locate and open the Sample IK.mb file.
2. Select the File, Import menu command, and then locate and import the Simple skin.mb file.

   The skin object is imported into the file with the IK skeleton. This skin was created by overlaying scaled spheres on the skeleton, and then combining them all into a single mesh object.
3. Enable the Shading, X-Ray Joints option in the panel menu to see the joints.

4. Scale the skin object to a size that roughly covers the skeleton object.
5. Click the Four Views button from the Quick Layout Buttons.
6. Select and move each joint to where it lies along the center of the skin objects in all views.

Tip

```
When moving the foot joint, be careful that you
don't select the IK effector, or else all the IK
joints will move.
```

Figure 13-21 shows the front view panel with the skin positioned over the skeleton.

7. Select File, Save Scene As and save the file as **Positioned skin.mb**.

Note

```
This example is a backward workflow. Typically,
you will model the character skin first and then
fit the skeleton to fit the character skin.
```

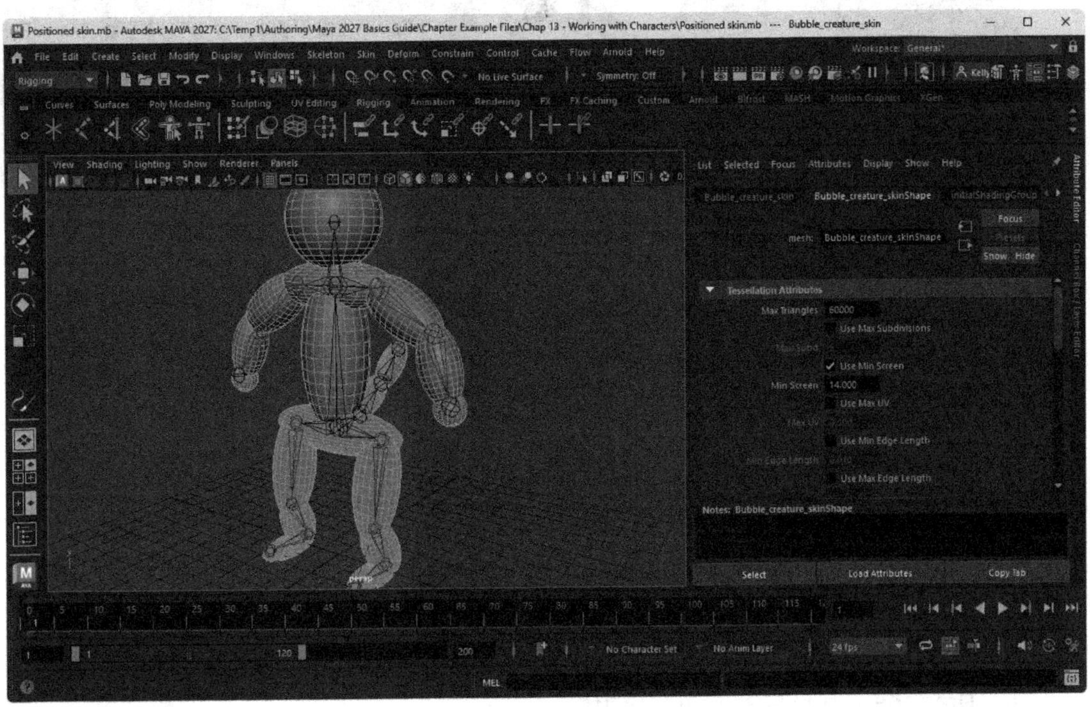

FIGURE 13-21

Positioned skin

Lesson 13.4-Tutorial 2: Bind Skin

1. Select the File, Open Scene menu command, then locate and open the Positioned skin.mb file.

2. Select the skeleton object, hold down the Shift key, and select the skin object.
3. Select the Skin, Bind Skin menu command.
   The skin is now bound to the skeleton, as shown in Figure 13-22.
4. Select File, Save Scene As and save the file as **Bound skin.mb**.

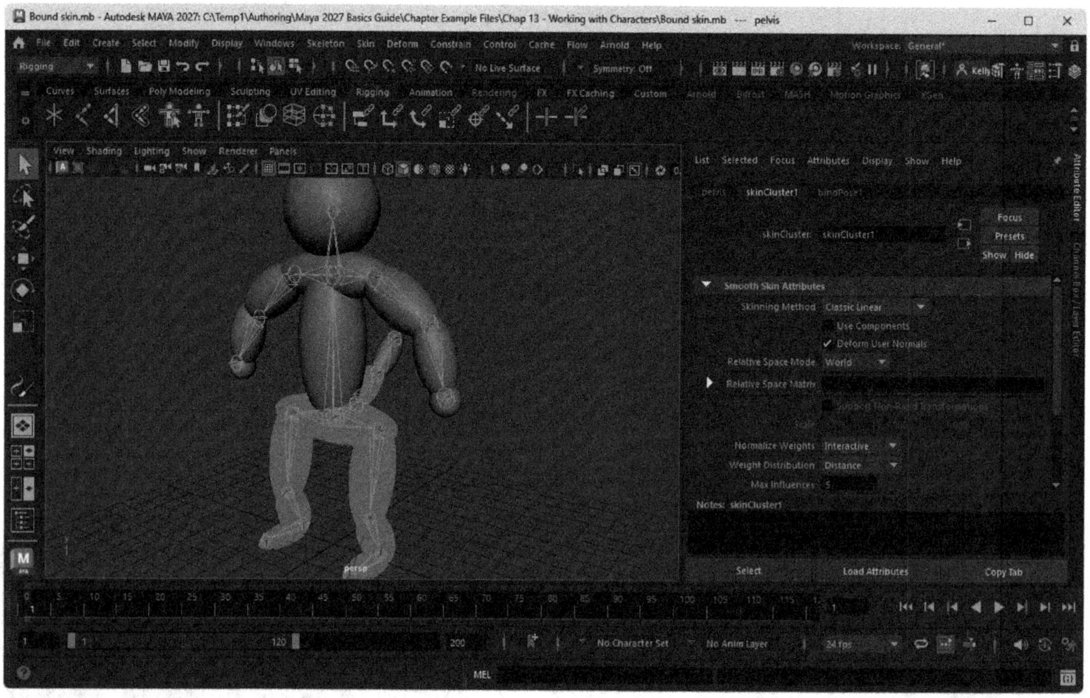

FIGURE 13-22

Bound skin

Lesson 13.4-Tutorial 3: Create a Walk Cycle

1. Select the File, Open Scene menu command, then locate and open the Bound skin.mb file.
2. Rotate the view to the side of the character.
3. Select and set keys for all of the various IK handles with the Key, Set Key menu command or by pressing the S hotkey and then enable the Auto Key button.
4. Select the right foot IK handle and move it backwards about 10 degrees, then select the right toe IK handle and move it until the foot is flat to the ground. Then select the left foot IK handle and move it forward about 10 degrees and position the left toe IK handle so the foot is flat to the ground. Finally, move the left wrist IK handle forward and the right wrist IK handle backwards.
5. Drag the Time Slider to frame 10.
6. Select the right foot IK handle and move it forward to where the left foot is, then select the right toe IK handle and move it until the foot is flat to the ground. Then select the left foot IK handle and move it backwards to where the right foot was in frame 1 and position the left toe IK handle so the foot is flat to the ground. Finally, move the left wrist IK handle backwards and the right wrist IK handle forwards to be opposite of the feet.
7. In the Outliner, select all the IK handle objects and choose the Windows, Animation Editors, Dope Sheet menu command. Click on the keys in Frame 1 to select them

all, then choose the Edit, Copy menu command. Drag the Time Slider to Frame 20 and choose the Edit, Paste menu command.

8. Drag the Time Slider to see the walking cycle.

   One frame of the animation is shown in Figure 13-23.

9. Select File, Save Scene As, and save the file as **Walk cycle.mb**.

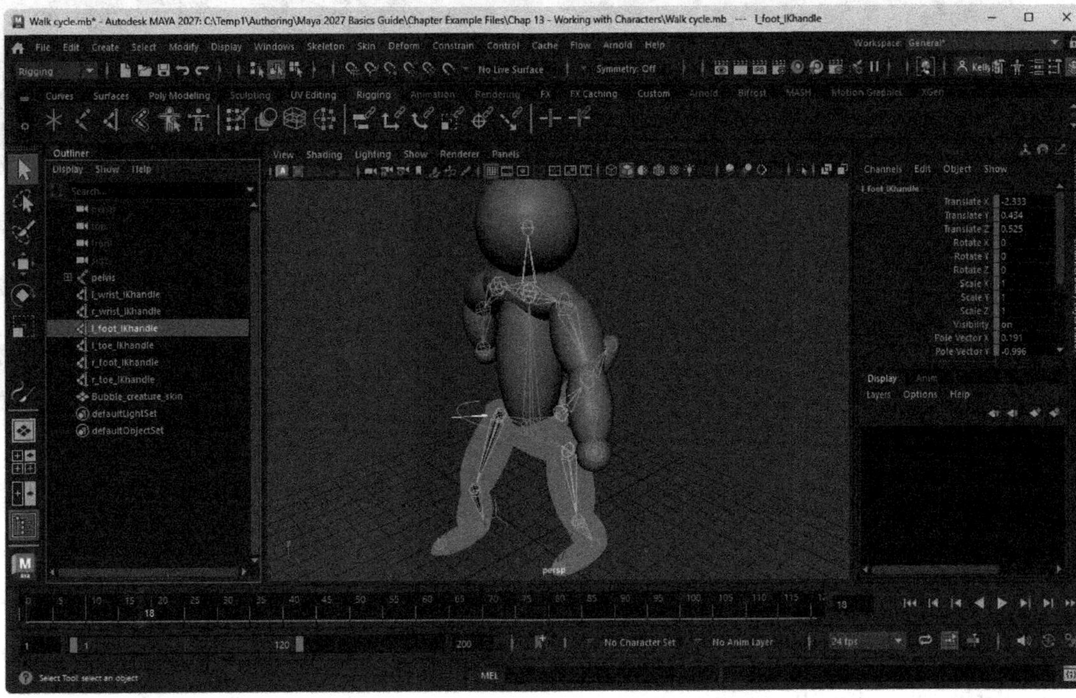

FIGURE 13-23

Animated character

Lesson 13.5: Edit a Skin

With a skin bound to a skeleton, you can control its movement using the skeleton, but as you begin to animate the character, you may notice some places where the skin isn't moving the way you'd like. To fix these problems, you may need to edit the skin. Maya provides several ways to edit skins, including influence objects and skin weights.

Adding Influence Objects

An influence object is a NURBS or polygon object that is placed near a skin object that pushes or pulls all nearby skin points to it. To add an influence object to a skin, select the skeleton and use the Skin, Go to the Bind Pose menu command, and then select the skin object, followed by the object that you want to use as the influence object and choose the Skin, Edit Influences, Add Influence menu command. Once an influence object is added to a skin, you can change the amount of skin deformation by moving the skin object closer to the influence object or by moving the influence object closer to the skin. Figure 13-24 shows an arm skin with a bulging muscle determined by the sphere influence object. You can remove influence objects using the Skin, Edit Influences, Remove Influence menu command.

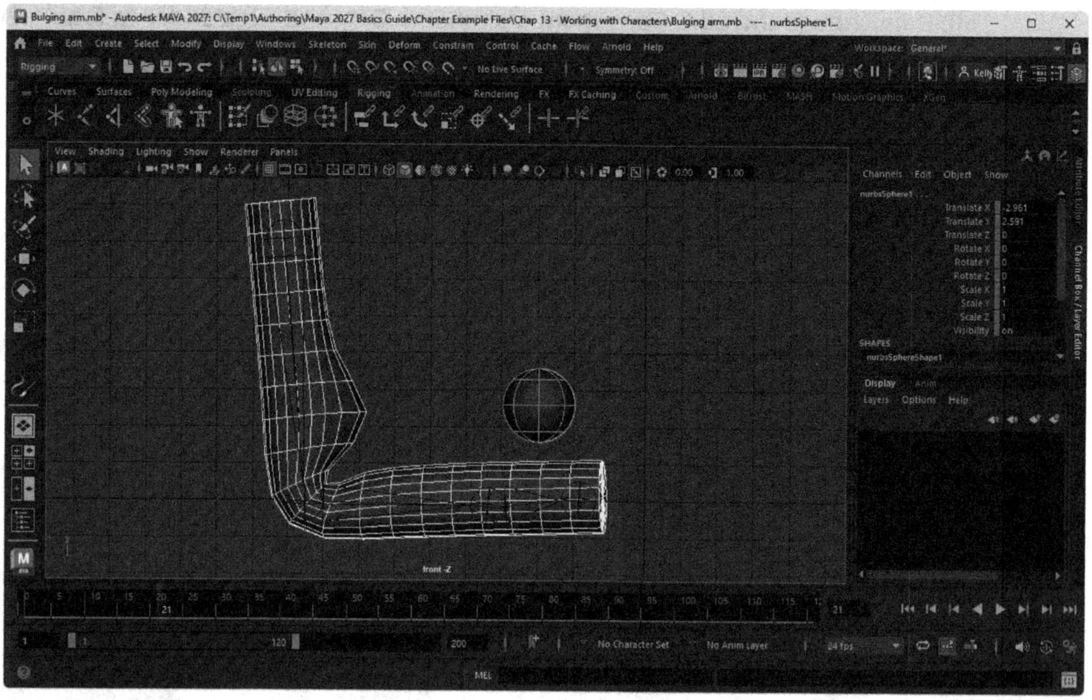

FIGURE 13-24

Influence object

Understanding Skin Weights

Another way to edit a skin is with skin weights. Each selected joint has an influence over the skin vertices that surround it. By changing this weighting, you can determine whether the skin is affected by the joint. A good example of this is the movement of a character's head. If the head skin is much larger than the bone that is used to control it, moving the head only moves those skin points near the top of the head and the neck where it is close to the bone, causing the character's head to remain stationary except for its neck and top. To fix this problem, you can set all vertices on the head to be affected by the head joint. You can view the weights for each selected skin vertex and each nearby joint in the Component Editor (shown in Figure 13-25), which you open using the Windows, General Editors, Component Editor.

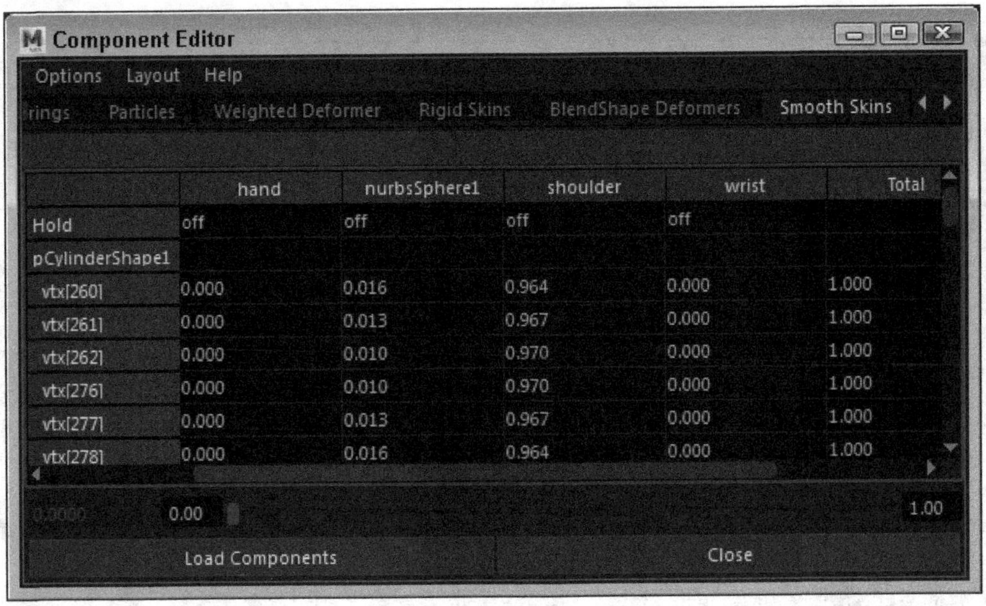

FIGURE 13-25

Component Editor

Using the Interactive Bind Skin Tool

Each vertex in the skin mesh moves according to its Skin Weight value. A Skin Weight of 1 means that the vertex and the portion of the skin around it moves 100 percent with the underlying bone. For sections around the middle and end of the bone, this is what you want, but for sections near the joint, you'll want a Skin Weight value of 50 percent or less. This causes the vertices to move only half the way, creating a smoother deformation. Using the Interactive Bind Skin Tool on skins that are bound using the Interactive Bind Skin command, you can set the Skin Weights around a bone by moving the manipulator lines that surround it, as shown in Figure 13-26. If you enable shaded mode, then you can see the Skin Weights as colors with red being 100 percent, yellow being 50 percent and green being 0.

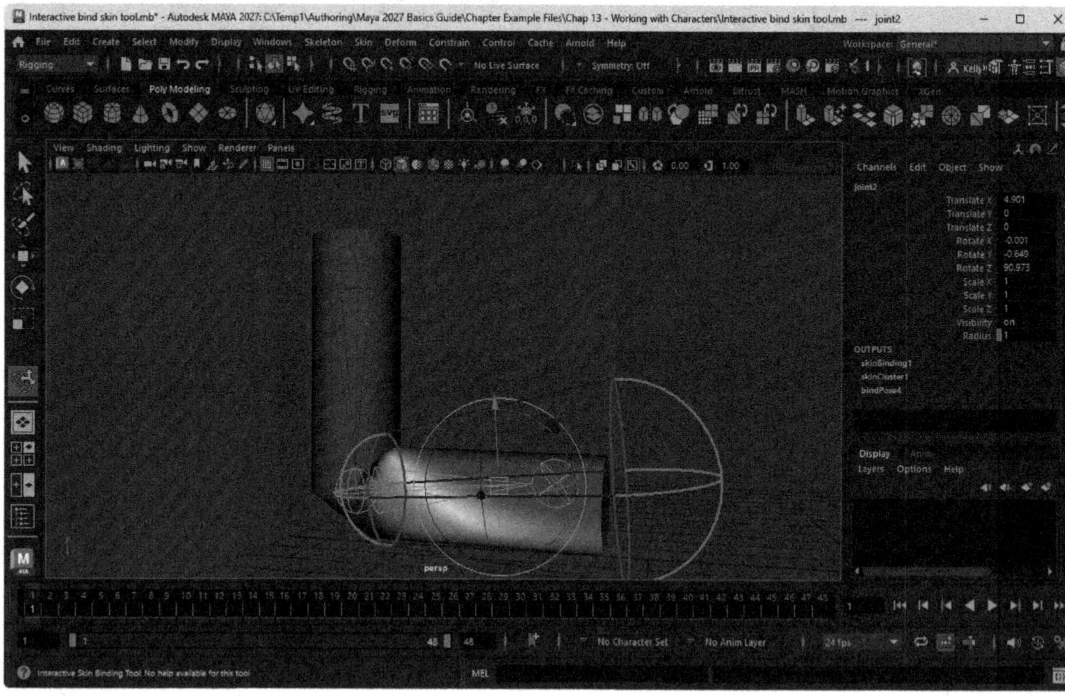

FIGURE 13-26

Interactive Bind Skin Tool

Painting and Smoothing Skin Weights

For more control over the Skin Weights, the Paint Skin Weights Tool lets you use brushes to paint the influence value. The Skin Weight values are shown as a black to white gradient that interactively changes as you paint. The settings for the Paint Skin Weights Tool are in the Tool Settings panel, as shown in Figure 13-27. The Skin menu also has a Smooth Skin Weights menu command that automatically smoothes the weights values within a given tolerance.

Note

The Paint Skin Weights tool works on skin objects bound with the Bind Skin and the Interactive Bind Skin commands.

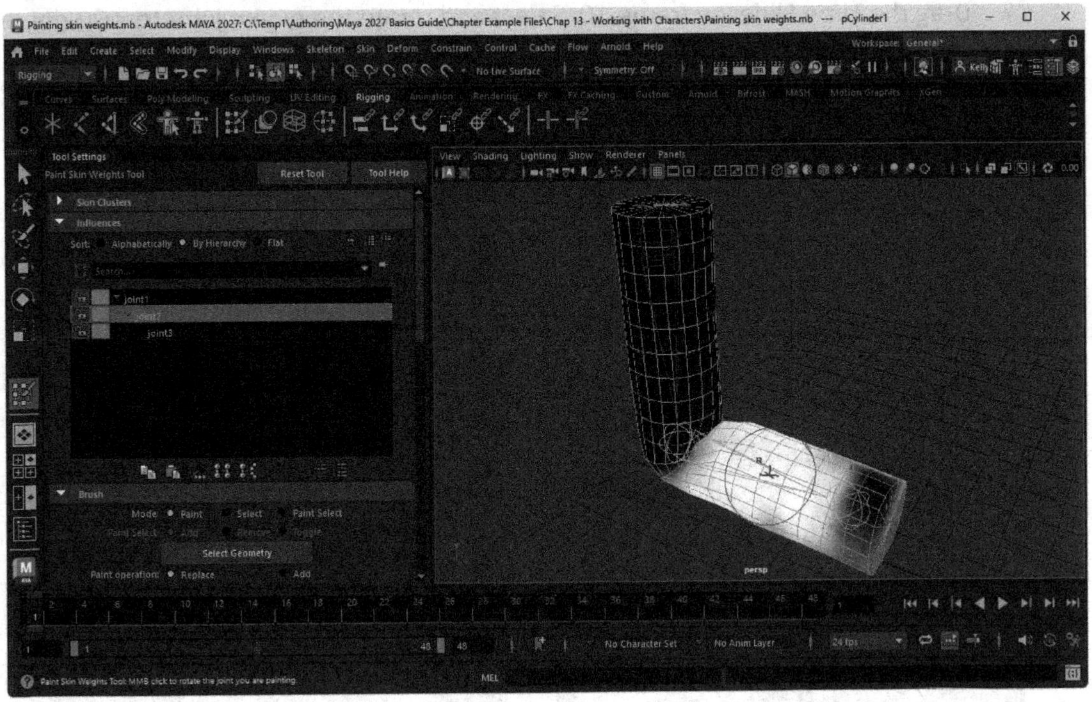

FIGURE 13-27

Painting skin weights

Mirroring Skin Weights

If your character has symmetry and you've correctly set all the skin weights for one half of the body, then the Skin, Mirror Skin Weights menu command lets you copy the weights to the other side of the body.

Resetting Skin Weights

If painting weights causes more problems, you can always return the skin weights to their default settings with the Skin, Reset Weights to Default menu command.

Lesson 13.5-Tutorial 1: Add Influence Object

1. Select the File, Open Scene menu command, and then locate and open the Arm chain.mb file.
2. Select the Create, NURBS Primitives, Sphere menu command to create a sphere object. Move the sphere close to the upper arm.
3. Select the skeleton and choose the Skin, Go to Bind Pose menu command.

   The skeleton and skin return to the pose that they were in when the skin was bound to the skeleton.
4. Select the skin object, hold down the Shift key, and select the sphere object.
5. Choose the Skin, Edit Influences, Add Influence menu command.

   The sphere is now set to influence the skin points closest to it.
6. Select the elbow joint and press the S key to set an animation key. Then select the sphere object and press the S key again. Then click on the Auto Key button.

7. Drag the Time Slider to frame 10. Select and rotate the elbow joint to a 90-degree bend and drag the sphere object to the right.
8. Drag the Time Slider back and forth.

   The upper arm muscle bulges as the arm is bent, as shown in Figure 13-28.
9. Select File, Save Scene As, and save the file as **Bulging arm.mb**.

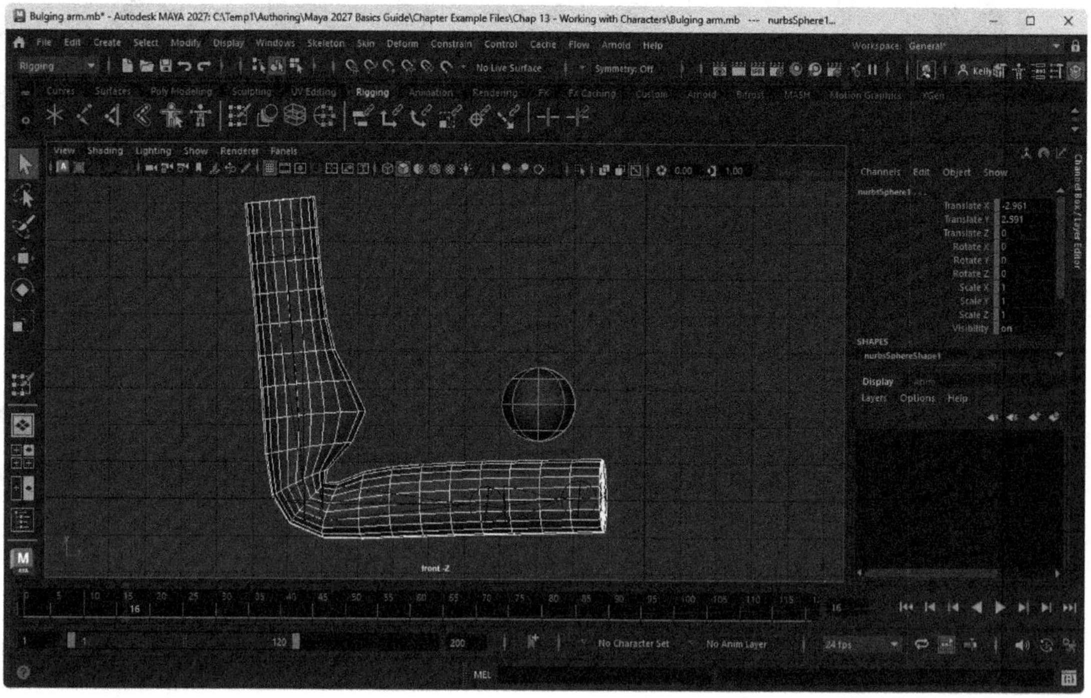

FIGURE 13-28

Bulging arm movement

Lesson 13.5-Tutorial 2: Paint Weights

1. Select the File, Open Scene menu command, and then locate and open the Arm chain.mb file.
2. Select the skin object and choose the Skin, Paint Skin Weights menu command. Double-click on the Paint Skin Weights tool in the Toolbox to open the Tool Settings panel.
3. Press the 5 key to see the objects in shaded view.

   Each of the skin bones are listed in the Tool Settings panel, and the weights for the selected joint are displayed in black and white in the view panel.
4. In the Tool Settings panel, select the elbow joint and set the Radius(U) value in the Stroke panel to 0.25.
5. Click on the eyedropper button in the Tool Settings panel and select the weight value above the elbow joint where the arm is still at full width, and then paint the vertices above the elbow where the arm starts to deform.

   The elbow has a more realistic line where the skin folds instead of the deep bend that was there before, as shown in Figure 13-29.
6. Select File, Save Scene As, and save the file as **Painted weights.mb**.

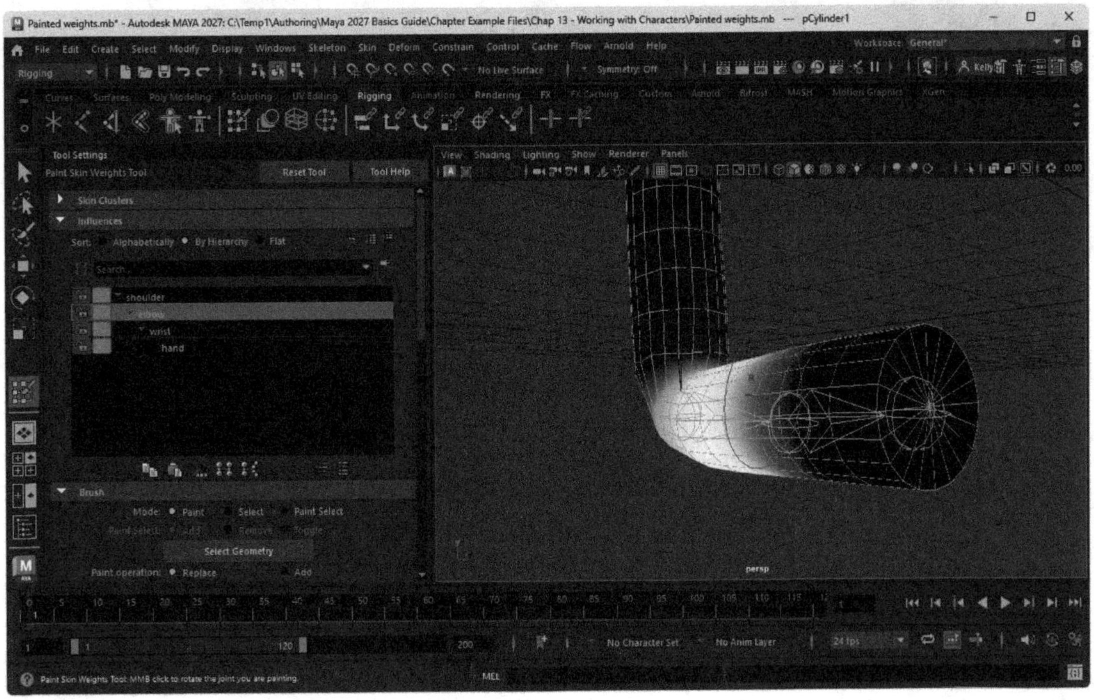

FIGURE 13-29

Painted weights

Lesson 13.6: Create a Quick Rig

Now that you know how to manually create a skeleton and bind it to a skin, Maya has a way to automatically complete the rigging for a biped character using its Quick Rig feature. Within the Skeleton menu is a Quick Rig command that automatically adds a skeleton and all the rigging to a character. This can be done using the One-Click option or a Step-by-Step process that gives you more control over the created rig.

Creating a Rig with One-Click

When the Skeleton, Quick Rig menu command is selected, the Quick Rig dialog box opens, as shown in Figure 13-30. If you select the One-Click option and click the Auto-Rig button, then a complete skeleton hierarchy for the biped character is created.

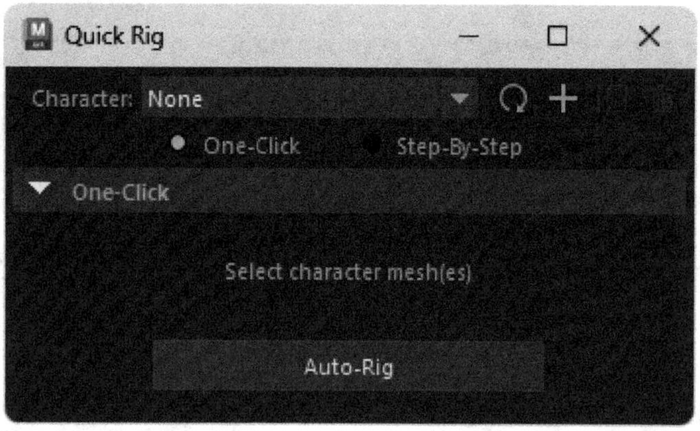

FIGURE 13-30

One-Click Quick Rig

Creating a Step-by-Step Rig

If the Step-by-Step option for the Quick Rig is selected, then you have more control over each step of the rig creation, as shown in Figure 13-31. The first step is to select the character geometry. The next step is to place the guides that are used to determine where the joints are placed. There are several options for setting the guides based on the type of geometry that is being used. The third step lets you manually reposition any of the guides. The fourth step creates the skeleton and control rig, and the last step binds the skin to the skeleton.

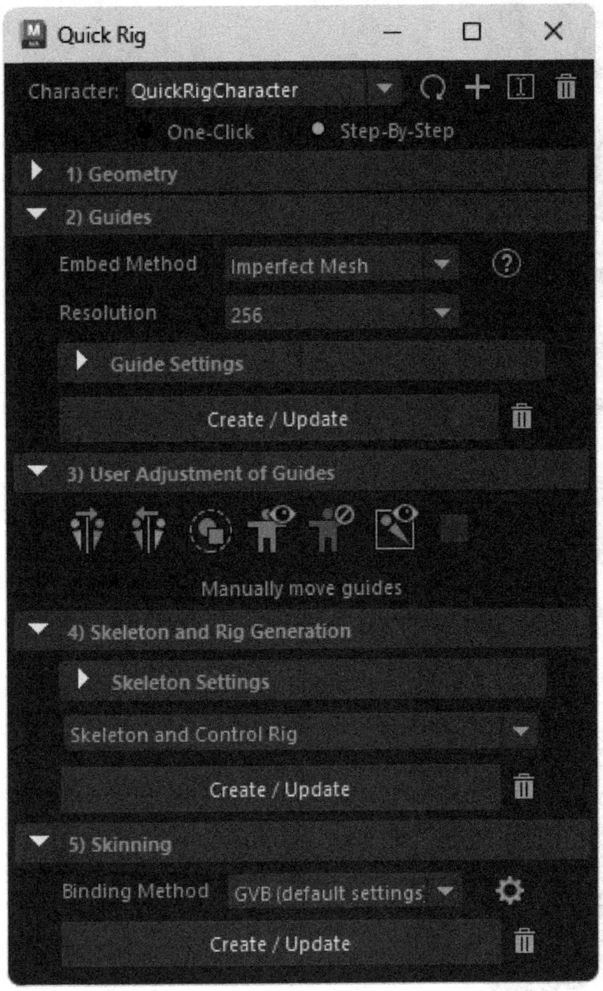

FIGURE 13-31

Step-by-Step Quick Rig

Controlling the Human IK Rig

Once the Quick Rig is created, the Human IK dialog box appears, as shown in Figure 13-32. You can also open this dialog box using the button at the right end of the Status Line by clicking on the Character Controls button. This control panel has easy selection points for all the major skeleton joints. Simply click on the joint and it is automatically selected within the viewports. Then you can easily animate the character using the Toolbox tools.

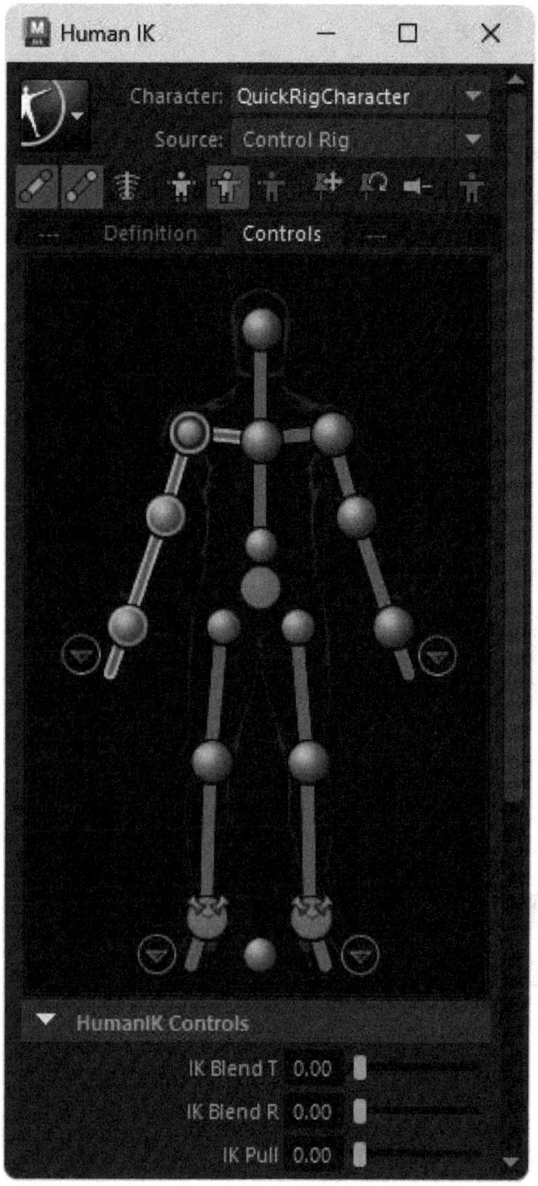

FIGURE 13-32

Character Control Tool

Lesson 13.6-Tutorial 1: Create a Quick Rig

1. Select the File, Open Scene menu command, then locate and open the Simple Skin.mb file.
2. Select the skin mesh and choose the Skeleton, Quick Rig menu command.

   The Quick Rig panel appears.
3. Select the One-Click option and click the Auto-Rig button.
4. Open the Character Control Tool panel using the Status Line button at the right end of the Status Line.

5. Select the left shoulder joint and rotate the shoulder using the Rotate tool.
   The left arm rotates under the control of the skeleton rig.
   Figure 13-33 shows the resulting Quick-Rig skeleton.
6. Select File, Save Scene As and save the file as **Quick Rig.mb**.

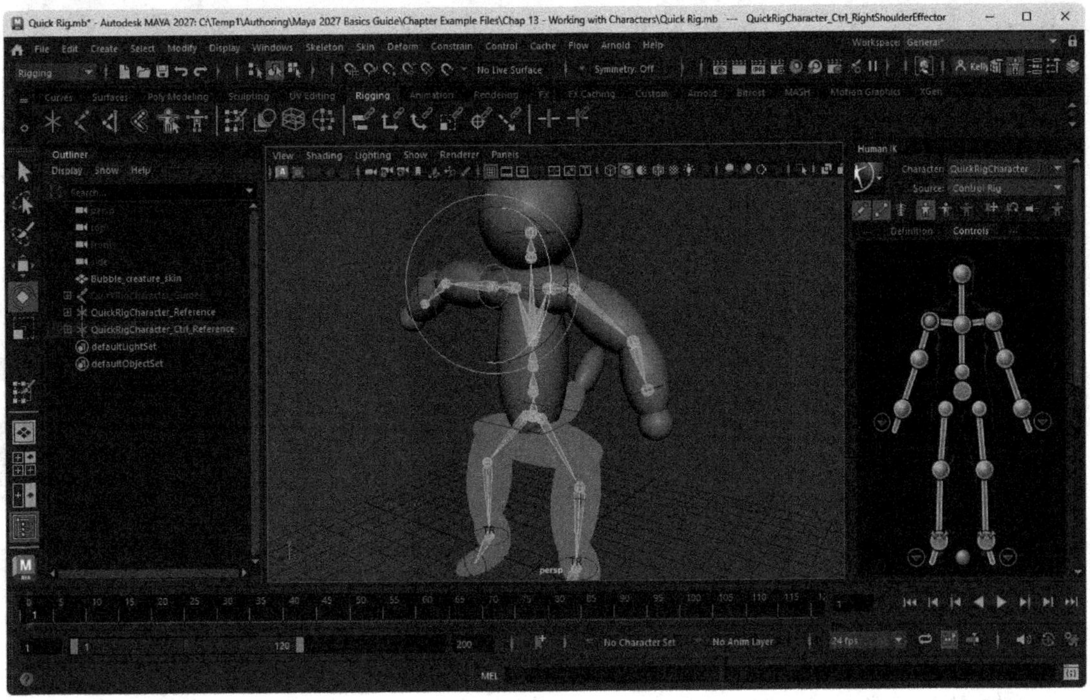

FIGURE 13-33

Positioned skin

Lesson 13.7: Animate a Quick Rig

Once a Quick Rig is applied to a character, you can use Motion Capture data to automatically animate the character. Maya includes another animation tool to quickly animate characters. This tool is the MotionMaker Editor.

Animating with Motion Capture data

One of the major benefits of using a standard human rig is that many repositories include libraries of motion capture data. With a rig added to a skinned model, it is easy to have the character move using the motion capture data. First, simply load the motion capture file using the File, Import menu command. These files usually use the FBX format. Once loaded, the file will appear as a rigged skeleton in the viewport. You can click the Play Animation button to see its motion. To apply the motion to the defined rig, open the Human IK panel and set the Source drop-down list to the loaded motion capture set. The character will then move using the motion capture data. You might need to clean up the skin mesh if it doesn't match the motion capture data exactly.

Note

The Windows, Content Browser holds several good example skins and motion capture examples.

Defining Motion with the MotionMaker Editor

The MotionMaker Editor is located in the Windows, Animation Editors menu. This editor, shown in Figure 13-34, includes a simple window that matches the Timeline. It also includes default rigs for male and female bipeds, a dog, and a horse. Selecting one of these rigs from the Create menu adds the rig to the current scene. Beneath the character rig is a Path Locator object. By positioning and setting keys for the Path Locator, you can define the path that the rig will follow. After clicking the Generate Motion button, the rig will automatically follow the path with realistic steps, body and arm motion. Along the motion path, you can also add specific Actions such as jumps for the rig to follow.

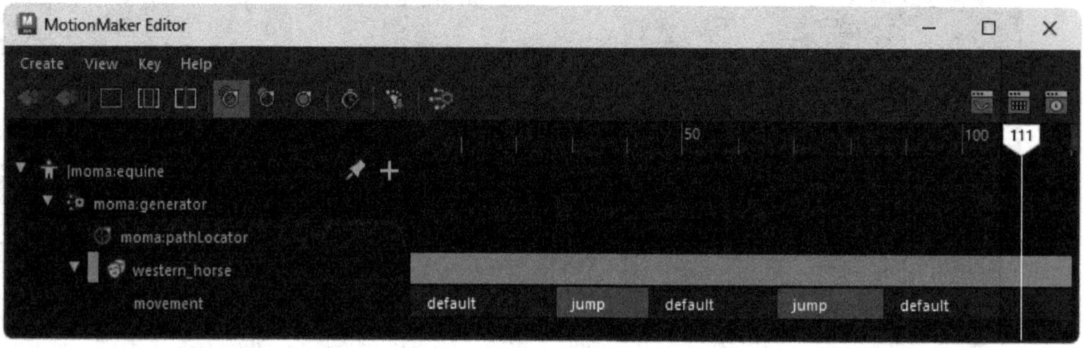

FIGURE 13-34

MotionMaker Editor

Retargeting MotionMaker Movements to Another Rig

Once you've created a desired motion using the default rig in the MotionMaker Editor, you can easily retarget the motion onto another rig with the Character Control panel. Simply load the new rig and select it as the Character in the Character Control panel and choose the MotionMaker default motion as the Source. This causes the new character rig to use the motion defined by the MotionMaker editor. Be sure to hide the default MotionMaker character before continuing.

Lesson 13.7-Tutorial 1: Animate with Motion Capture

1. Select the Windows, Content Browser menu command to open the Content Browser window. Under the Examples, Modeling, Sculpting Base Meshes, Bipeds folder, drag and drop the Monster Wolf Man character into the viewport. Then locate the Pointing.fbx file in the Examples, Animation, Motion Capture, FBX folder and drop it also in the viewport.
2. Select the skin mesh and choose the Skeleton, Quick Rig menu command.

   The Quick Rig panel appears.
3. Select the One-Click option and click the Auto-Rig button.
4. Open the Character Control Tool panel using the Status Line button at the right end of the Status Line. Select the Source drop-down list and choose the Pointing option to apply the motion capture to the new rig.
5. Click the Play Animation button to see the character move using the motion capture data, as shown in Figure 13-35.

6. Open the Outliner, select the Pointing Reference node and choose the Display, Hide, Hide Selection to hide the motion capture skeleton.
7. Select File, Save Scene As and save the file as **Pointing wolfman.mb**.

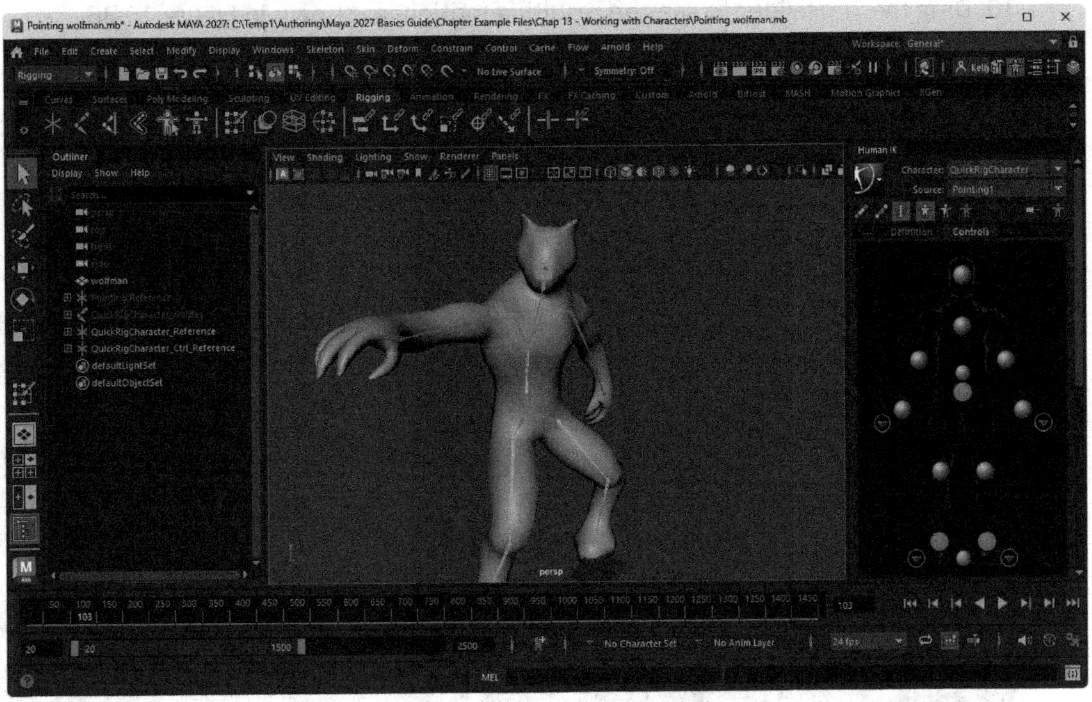

FIGURE 13-35

Posed character using motion capture

Lesson 13.7-Tutorial 2: Define Motion in the MotionMaker Editor

1. Select the File, Open Scene menu command, and then locate and open the **Barrel race course.mb** file.
2. Select Windows, Animation Editors, MotionMaker Editor to open the MotionMaker Editor window.
3. Choose the Create, adsk_biped menu option to create a human rig in the MotionMaker Editor window.
4. Select the human rig and the Path Selector objects and move them to the right end of the barrel course.
5. Press the S key to create a key at frame 1, then drag the Timeline to frame 120 and move the just the Path Locator object to the left end of the course, and press the S key to create another key.
6. Click the Generate Motion button in the MotionMaker Editor window to generate the motion between the two set frames.

   MotionMaker computes the human motion and snaps the rig to the end position.
7. Select the Visualize, Motion Trail Editor menu command and with the Path Locator selected, press the Create Motion Trail button.
8. Drag the Timeslider back to the point where the runner passes the third barrel. Select the Path Locator object and press the S key to create another key, then

select and move the Motion Trail key point to an outside point beyond the third barrel object. Repeat this step for the remaining two barrels.

9. Click the Generate Motion button again in the MotionMaker Editor window to generate the new motion path.
10. Drag the Timeslider to see the resulting motion, as shown in Figure 13-36.
11. Select File, Save Scene As and save the file as **Barrel race motion.mb**.

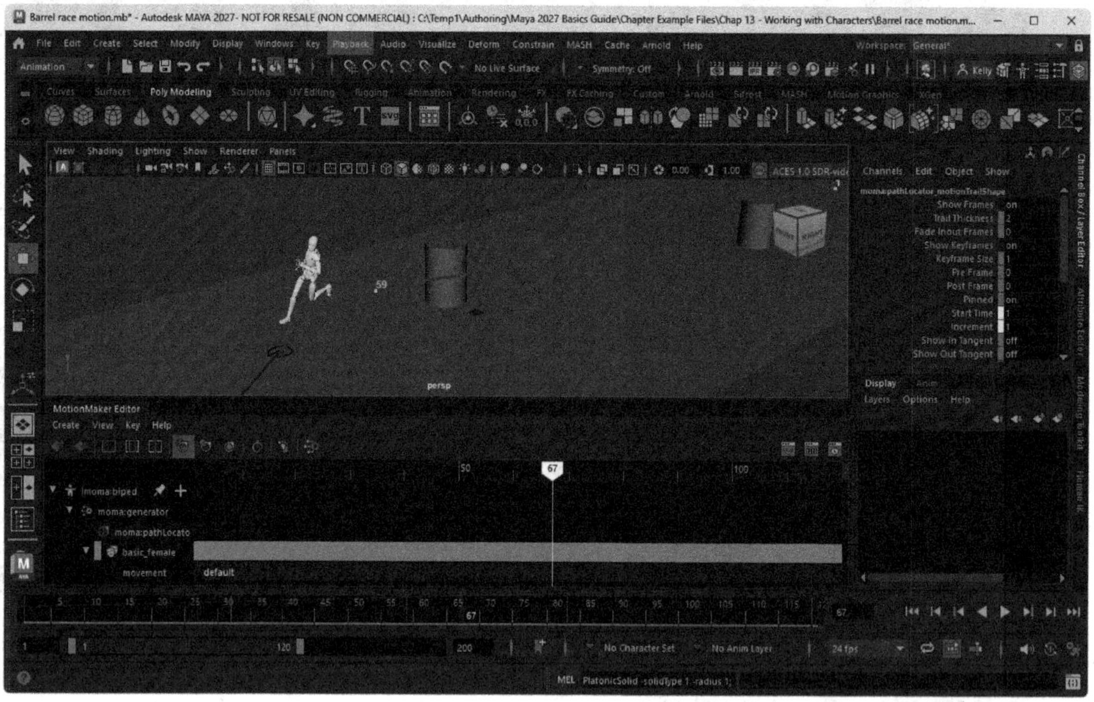

FIGURE 13-36

Runner motion created using MotionMaker

Lesson 13.7-Tutorial 3: Retarget Motion to Another Rig

1. Select the File, Open Scene menu command, and then locate and open the **Barrel race motion.mb** file.
2. Select File, Import menu command and choose the **Pointing Wolfman.mb** from the chapter 13 folder.

   The file with 2500 frames loads as shown on the Timeline.
3. Underneath the Timeline, set the total number of frames to 120.
4. Open the Character Controls panel and choose the **Pointing_Wolfman character** in the Character drop-down list and the **moma:Standard Biped** from the Source drop-down list.

   The Wolfman mesh now runs along with the default biped character.
5. Open the Outliner and select the **moma:biped** character. Delete the key in the Timeline at frame 1. In the Channel Box, set the Visibility attribute to off.
6. Drag the Timeslider to see the resulting motion, as shown in Figure 13-37.
7. Select File, Save Scene As and save the file as **Barrel race wolfman.mb**.

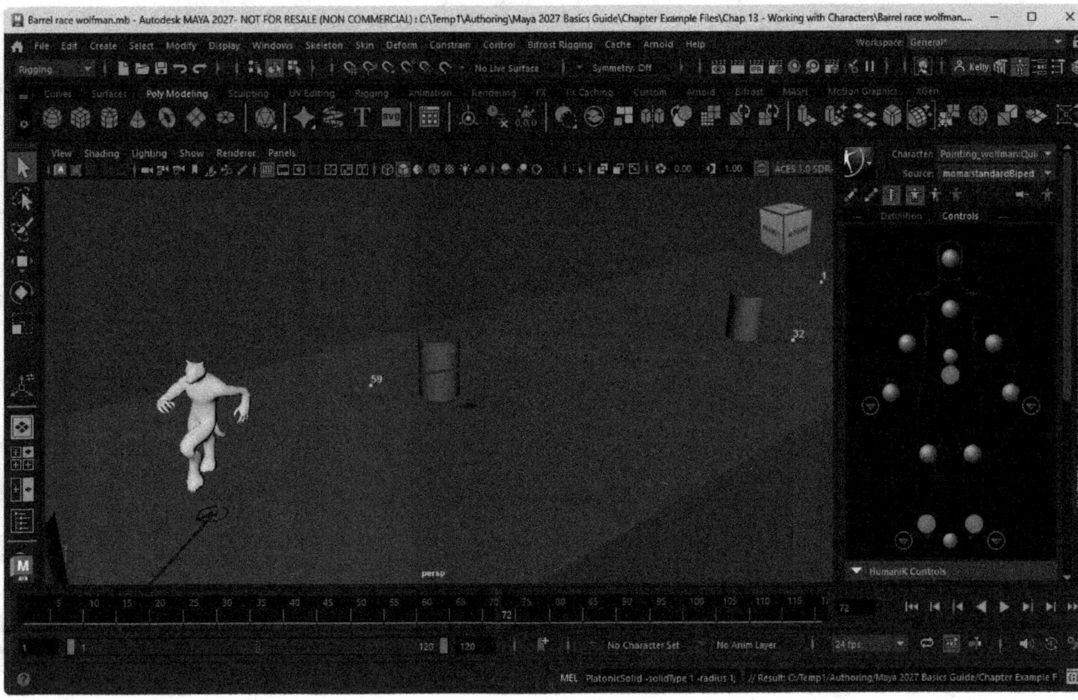

FIGURE 13-37

Biped motion switched to Wolfman rig

Lesson 13.8: Add Hair and Fur

Adding hair and fur to characters can do a lot to increase the realism of the character. Hair and fur are tricky because they deal with so many follicles that if they were treated as regular geometry objects, they would grind the processor to a halt. Hair instead is a separate system, much like particles, that together act together. They are also dealt with in a unique way when it comes to rendering by rendering the geometry first and then adding the hair.

Adding preset hair to an object

The easiest way to add hair and fur to a selected object is to choose one of the hair examples. These examples have all the attributes already set to creating a unique hair look. Several hair presets are available in the Content Browser, which is accessed using the nHair, Get Hair Example menu command. Figure 13-38 shows the Curly Short example applied to a sphere object.

Note

```
The nHair menu is in the FX menu set.
```

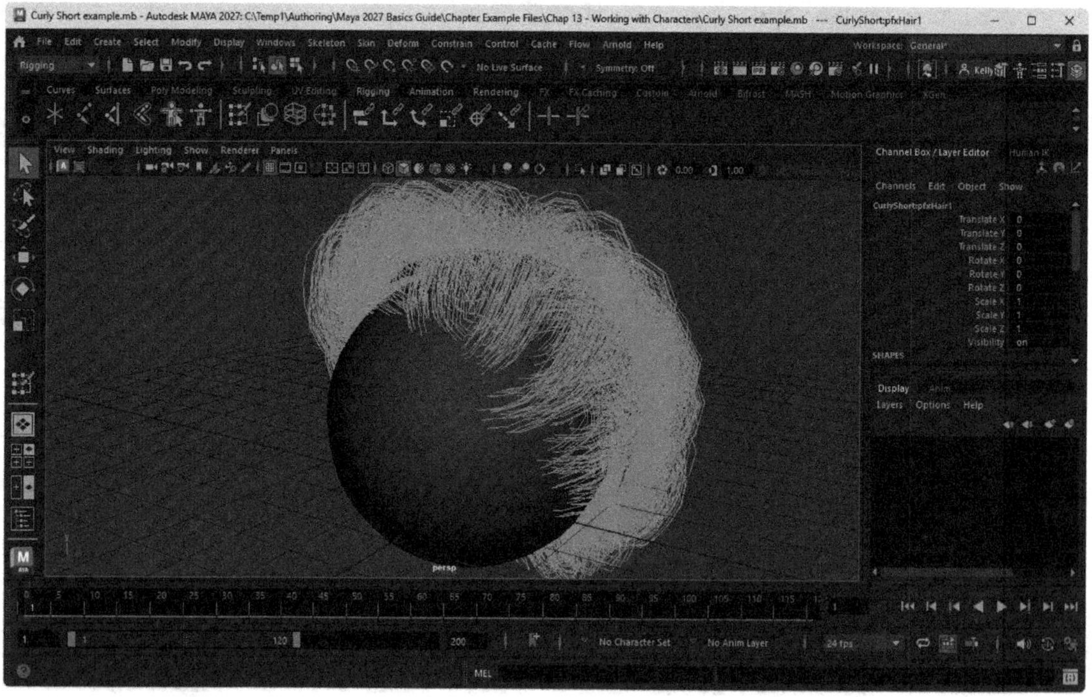

FIGURE 13-38

Curly Short hair example

Creating hair

Hair can be created on the selected object using the nHair, Create Hair menu command. This adds groups of hair to regular hair points around the surface of the object. If you open the Create Hair Options dialog box, there are options to Output hair as Paint Effects, NURBS Curves or a combination of both. You can also specify the Points Per Hair and the Length of the new hairs. Figure 13-39 shows a simple sphere with new hairs created using the Create Hair tool. Notice how the hairs all point out straight from the surface when first created.

FIGURE 13-39

Creating hair

Style hair

Once hair is added to an object, you can use several tools in the nHair menu to style the hair. The Scale Hair Tool lets you drag in the view panel to change the hair's length. The Paint Hair Follicles tool lets you paint hair on the surface of the object using the configurable Artisan brushes. The Paint Hair Follicles Settings dialog box includes modes for painting and deleting hairs. The Paint Hair Textures tool includes options for painting baldness, color and specularity.

Making hair dynamic

Another property that you can set for hair is whether the hair is dynamic or static. Dynamic hair can be simulated to droop under the effects of gravity. To cause dynamic hair to fall naturally, select the nCache, Create New Cache, nObject menu command. This causes the hair to fall naturally about the object it is attached to over the available range of frames. Figure 13-40 shows hair dynamically moved about the sphere object.

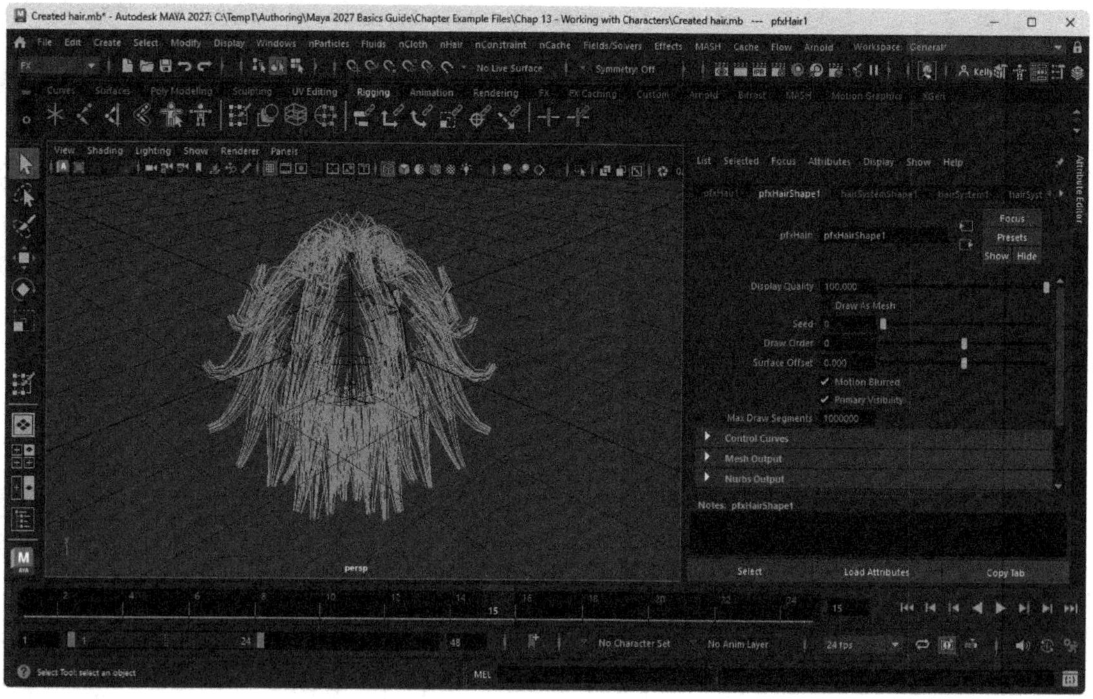

FIGURE 13-40

Dynamic hair

Creating and editing hair attributes

The look of the hair can be changed by altering the many different attributes that are available in the Attribute Editor including the Base and Tip Color, Opacity, Curl, Scraggle and Clumping. All of these attributes are located in the hair System Shape tab in the Attribute Editor. Figure 13-41 shows some clumpy curly hair on a sphere.

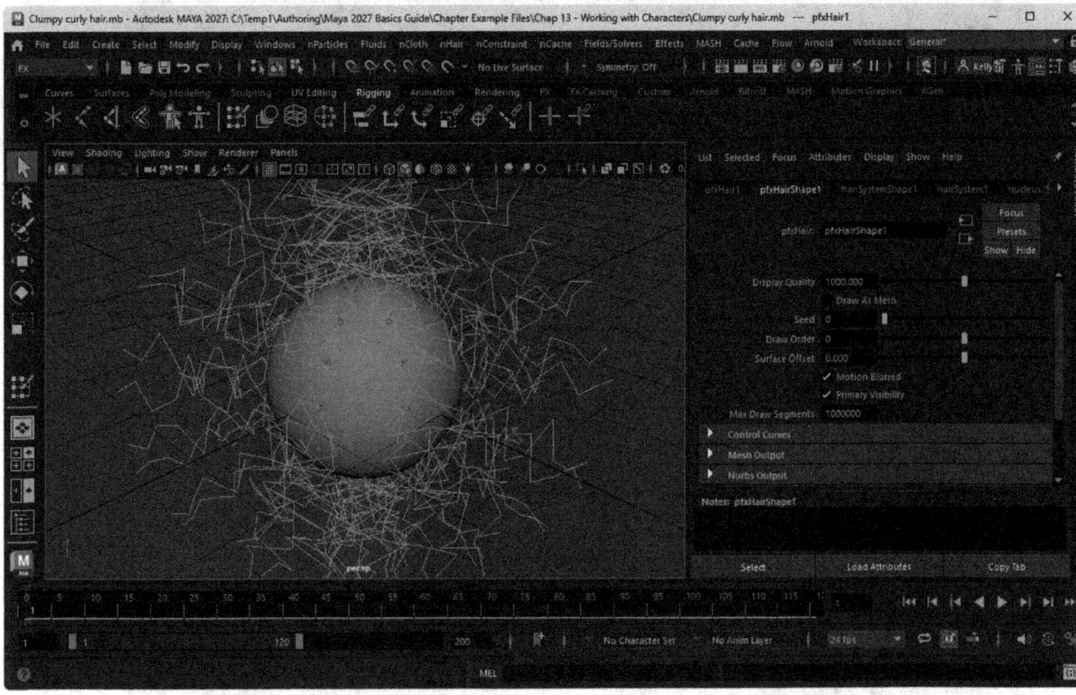

FIGURE 13-41

Clumpy Curly hair

Rendering hair and fur

When hair and fur is displayed in the view panel, only a fraction of the total number of hairs are displayed. These hairs are only guides, but when the final hair system is rendered, the total number of hairs are interpolated between the displayed guides. To render the final object with hair, click on the Render Current Frame button on the Status Line. Figure 13-42 shows the sphere with the Clumpy Curly hair applied to it.

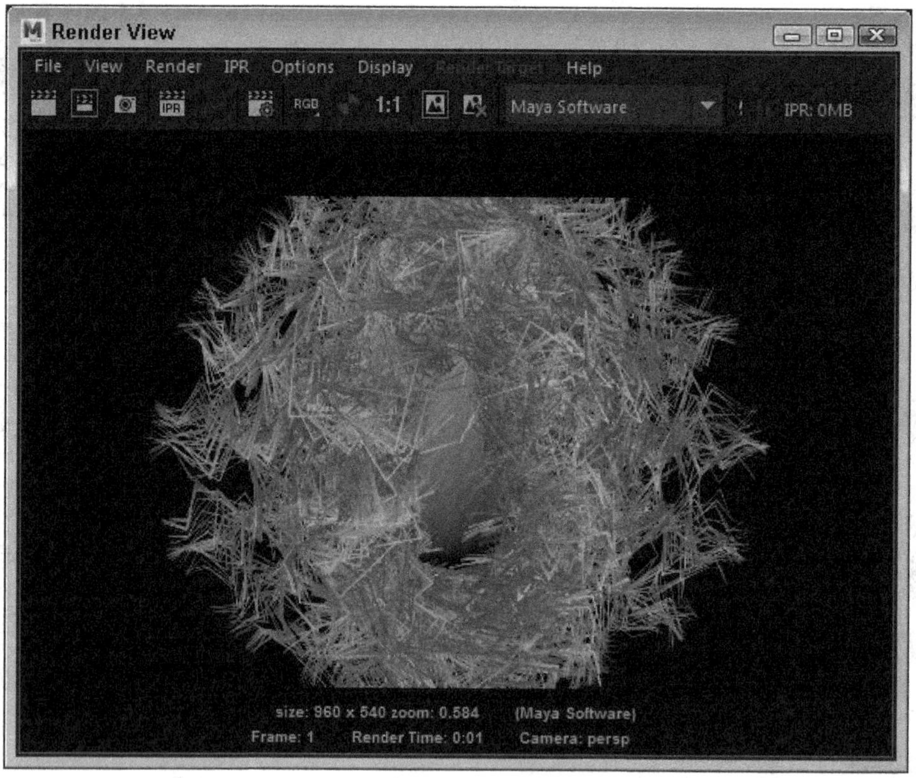

FIGURE 13-42

Rendered Duckling fur

Creating Hair with XGen

Maya has a second way to create hair and fur using the XGen system. The XGen menu commands are found under the Generate menu found in the Modeling menu set. The XGen system is quite robust and has a lot of features with hair and fur being only a small part.

Opening the XGen Editor

To create hair on an object, select the object and choose the Generate, Create Interactive Groom Splines menu command. This populates the object with hair particles extending straight up from the surface. It also adds several nodes to the Attribute Editor. You can access and control these groom splines in the XGen Editor, opened with the Generate, XGen Editor menu command, as shown in Figure 13-43. The XGen Editor shows three nodes: Sculpt, Scale and Base. If you select the Base node, then you can change the Density of the hair particles. The Scale node sets how big each spline is and the Sculpt node sets the hair style.

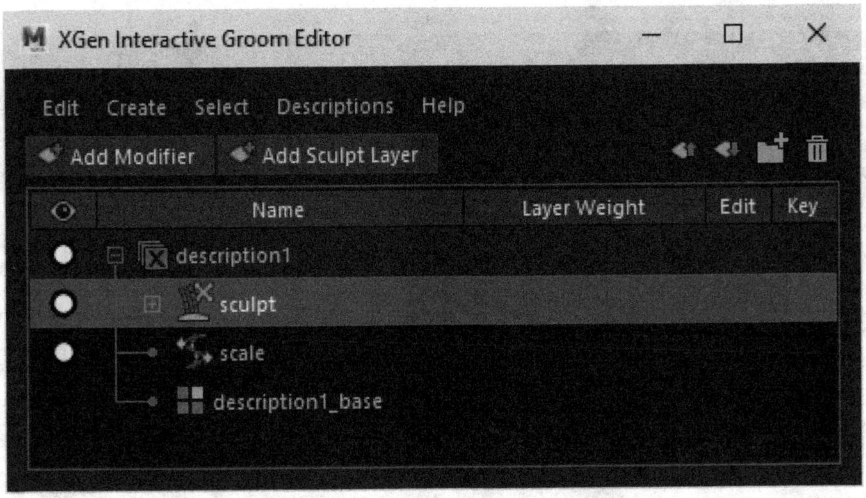

FIGURE 13-43

The XGen Editor

Sculpting Hair with Modifiers

At the top of the XGen Editor is an Add Modifier button. Using this button, you can add several unique looks to the hair. The Modifiers list includes Clump, Cut, Noise, etc. Each modifier adds a node to the Editor and has its own attributes. Figure 13-44 shows a simple sphere with the Clump modifier.

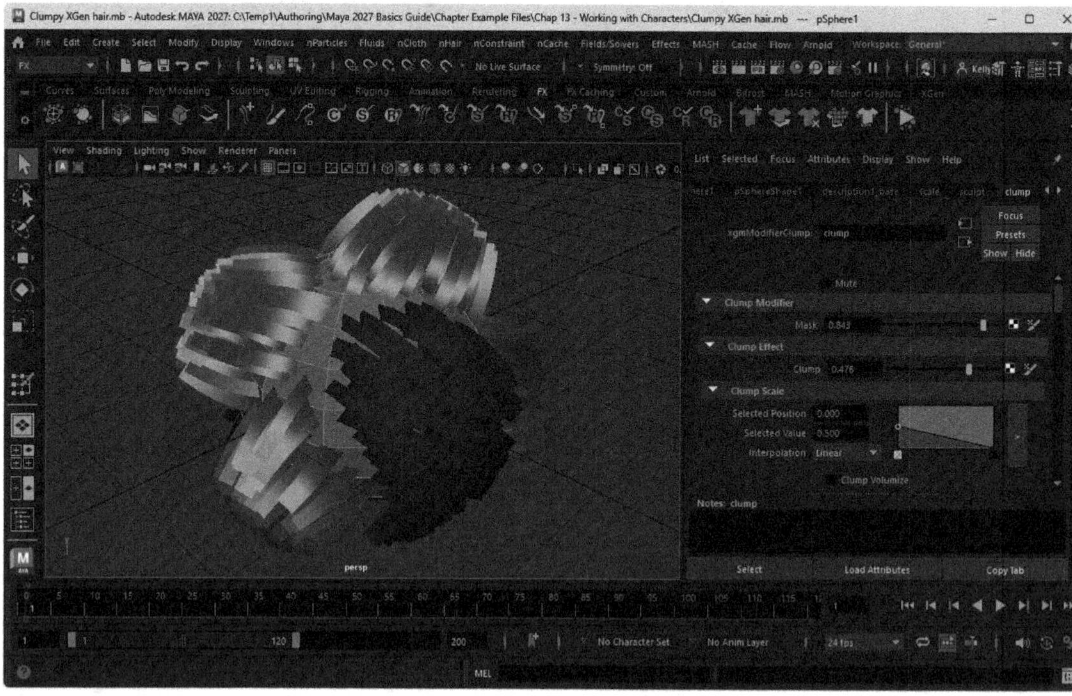

FIGURE 13-44

XGen hair with the Clump modifier added

Lesson 13.8-Tutorial 1: Add hair

1. Select the File, Open Scene menu command, and then locate and open the Simple face.mb file.
2. Select the back half of the head.

   The face object has been separated into a front part and the back half where the hair will be located.
3. Choose the FX menu set and choose the nHair, Create Hair, Options menu command. In the Create Hair Options dialog box, set the U and V Count values to 25 and the Randomization value to 1. Then click the Create Hairs button.

   Hair is added to the face object at regular intervals around the selected area.
4. Select the nHair, Scale Hair Tool menu command and drag in the view panel to reduce the length of the hair.
5. Select the nCache, Create Cache, nObjects menu command.

   All the hair is automatically set to be dynamic, so the Create Cache command causes the hair to fall about the head naturally.
6. Drag the Time Slider to frame 40 where the hair is relaxed.
7. Open the Attribute Editor and in the Clump and Hair Shape section, set the Hairs Per Clump value to 100.
8. Click the Render Current Frame button on the Status Line.

   The face is rendered with its dynamic hair, as shown in Figure 13-45.
9. Select File, Save Scene As, and save the file as **Simple face with hair.mb**.

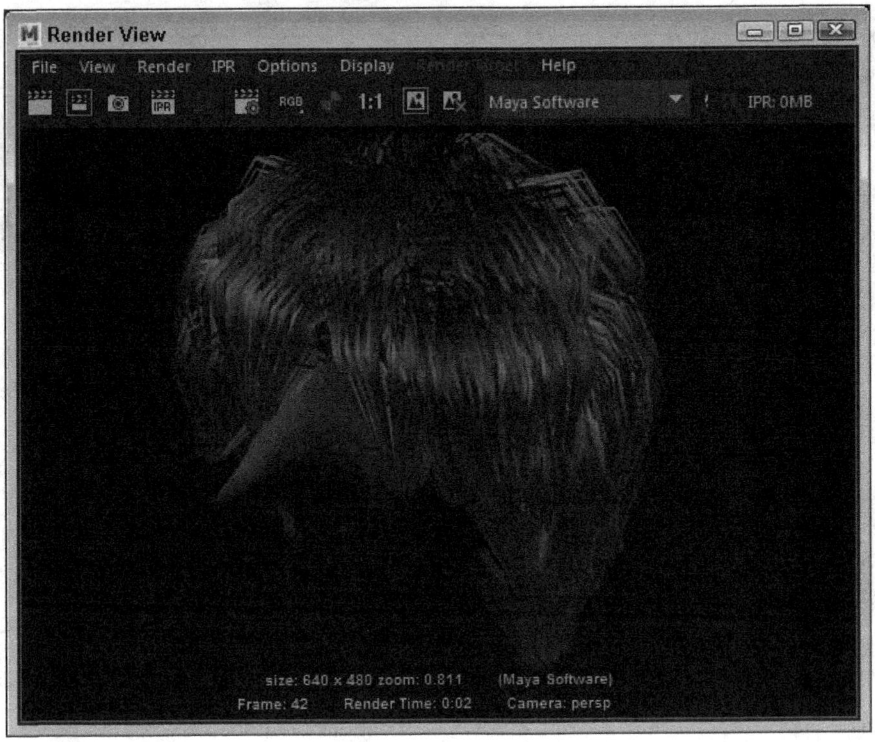

FIGURE 13-45

Simple face with hair

Lesson 13.8-Tutorial 2: Add XGen grass

1. Select the File, Open Scene menu command, and then locate and open the Rolling hills.mb file.
2. Select the hilly object and select the Generate, Create Interactive Groom Splines menu command.

   This adds groom splines to the entire Plane object.
3. Select the Generate, XGen Editor menu command to open the XGen Editor, then expand the Description node to reveal the other nodes. Select the Base node and set the Density Multiplier to 10.0.

   Hair is made thick enough to cover the entire mesh.
4. Select the Scale node in the XGen Editor and set the Scale value to 0.3, then click on the Add Modifier button in the XGen Editor and choose the Noise option.
5. Select the Description node in the XGen Editor and find the Hair Physical Shader node in the Attribute Editor. This node holds attributes for the hair's root and tip color. Select the Tip Color and change it to green.

   A dense green layer of grass is added to the hilly object, as shown in Figure 13-46.
6. Select File, Save Scene As, and save the file as **Grassy hills.mb**.

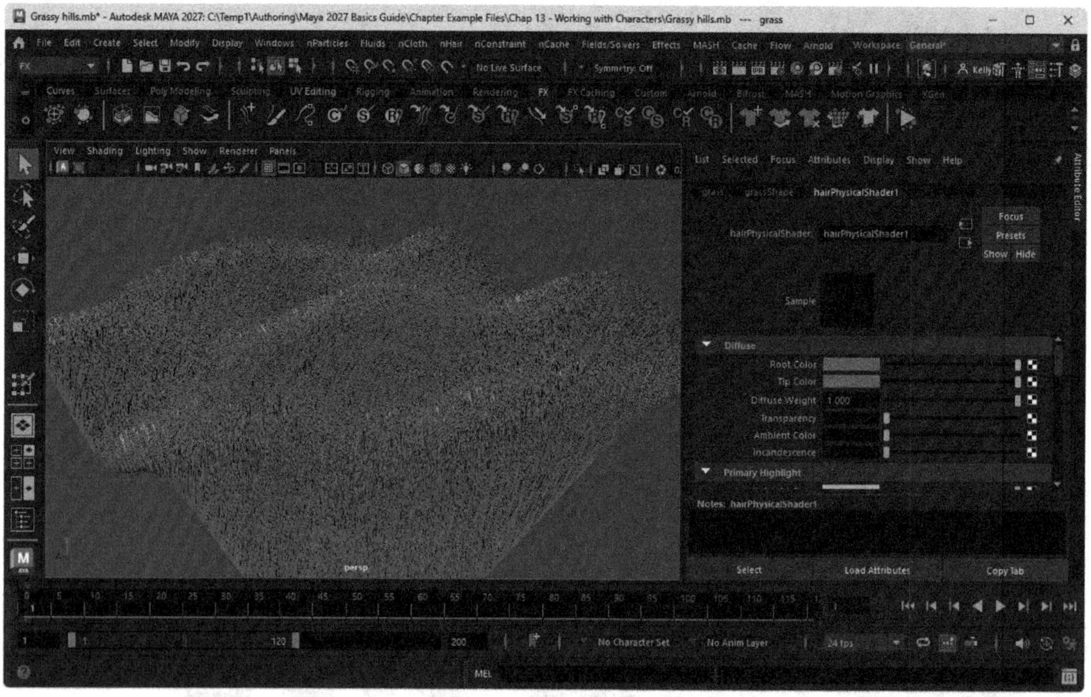

FIGURE 13-46

Hills with XGen created grass

Chapter Summary

This chapter covers creating and rigging characters, starting with building a character skeleton using bones and joints. Once you establish the skeleton, you can connect several joints together and edit the joints in different ways. Inverse Kinematics lets you control the skeleton by positioning the end joints, thus causing the rest of the joints to follow. The second part of creating a character involves adding a skin to the skeleton that is deformed as the skeleton underneath is moved. You can edit skin by painting its weights. Rigs can automatically be created for bipeds using the Quick Rig feature and animated using motion capture data and the MotionMaker Editor. Another way to add realism to characters is with hair using traditional hair or the XGen system.

What You Have Learned

In this chapter, you learned

* How to build a skeleton using joints.
* How to insert and connect a joint to an existing skeleton.
* How to remove and disconnect a joint.
* How to mirror a joint.
* How to name, orient, and label joints.
* How to show and hide joint labels.
* How to limit joint movement.

* How to add Inverse Kinematics using the IK Handle and IK Spline tools.
* How to use the IK manipulators.
* How to bind smooth and rigid skin.
* How to enable the X-Ray Joints display option.
* How to detach skin from a skeleton.
* How to add a skin influence object.
* How to paint skin weights.
* How to create a Quick Rig.
* How to animate a rig using motion capture data.
* How to generate automatic motion using the MotionMaker Editor.
* How to retarget motion to another rig.
* How to create and style hair.
* How to make hair dynamic.
* How to add fur to an object.
* How to render hair and fur.
* How to use the XGen system.
* How to open the XGen Editor.
* How to apply modifiers to a hair description.

Key Terms From This Chapter

* **Rigging.** The process of adding and configuring a skeleton to a character that is used to control its motion.
* **Joint.** An object connected to a bone used to rotate and move skeleton bones.
* **Bone.** An object that is connected between two joints and defines the rigid areas of a character.
* **Skeleton.** A hierarchical set of bones and joints used to define the underlying structure of a character.
* **Root joint.** The top joint in the skeleton hierarchy.

* **Inverse Kinematics.** A physics definition that allows objects at the end of a skeleton hierarchy to control the motion and position of the entire skeleton.

* **Forward Kinematics.** Physics that allows the position of child objects to be calculated when the parent object is moved.

* **IK Handle.** An IK solution that is used for parts such as arms and legs.

* **IK Spline.** An IK solution that is used for parts such as tails.

* **Skin.** The model that is placed over a skeleton that is bound to the skeleton and deformed by it.

* **Smooth skin.** A skin object that deforms as its bound skeleton is moved.

* **Default pose.** The skin's original position when it was first bound to the skeleton.

* **Influence object.** An object that controls the local deformation of a character skin.

* **Skin weight.** The amount of control each vertex has when an adjacent bone is moved.

* **Quick Rig.** The skeleton rig that is automatically created based on the skin geometry.

* **Motion Capture.** The motions of an actual actor captured using a suit that is saved as a file that can be used to animate a character rig.

* **MotionMaker Editor.** An editor window used to generate automatic biped, dog, or horse motion by positioning the Path Locator object.

* **Path Locator.** An object used to determine the position of a motion rig in the MotionMaker Editor.

* **Retarget.** The process of allowing a new rig to use the motion defined for another rig.

* **Hair splines**. A set of curves on an object that defines how the hair extends and its style.

* **XGen System**. An advanced system for adding hair and fur to objects.

Chapter 14
Animating with Dynamics

IN THIS CHAPTER

Dynamics is the physics of moving objects. Maya is smart enough to know all of the formulas for describing object motion and uses those to compute the position of objects that simulate real-world motions. For example, gravity is fairly easy to simulate by causing objects to fall downward. Likewise, you can simulate object collisions if you know the mass and velocity of the two colliding objects.

Particle objects are collections of small objects that act together to create dust, smoke, rain, and other effects. You can create **particles** using the Particle tool or using an **emitter,** which gives the particles speed and direction.

Another way to control particles is with **fields**. Fields, like Gravity, Turbulence, and Vortex, provide forces to the dynamic systems. These forces can control particles or objects.

The motion of rigid body objects can be automatically created by defining the properties of active and passive rigid bodies in the scene and subjecting them to the influence of a field. A second solution for rigid body dynamics is the MASH system.

In addition to particles, you can force objects to interact with each other using soft body dynamics. You can constrain dynamic objects using constraints. A system of several rigid and **soft body objects** can be solved to determine the physical motions of the object based on physical laws.

Maya also includes some additional dynamic features for working with flowing cloth objects and fluids. You can use fluids to create gaseous objects such as clouds, fire, and explosions. In many ways, fluids behave just like particle systems including the use of emitters. Fluids, however, are confined to a specific volume defined by a container.

Maya includes several effects that are scripted behaviors that use particles, glows, and dynamics to create fire, smoke, fireworks, and lightning.

Lesson 14.1: Use Particles

Particles are a collection of small objects that act together as a single unit. They are useful for creating effects like dust, smoke, and clouds. A particle system can include a few objects or millions of objects. The more objects, the more time it takes to render and even display them in the view panels.

Viewing Particle Examples

Within the Content Browser are several sample scenes that use particles. You can access these examples directly with the nParticles, Get nParticle Example menu command. This opens the examples in the Content Browser. Double click on one of the examples to load it into Maya and press the Play Forward button to see the results. Figure 14-1 shows the Curve Flow example.

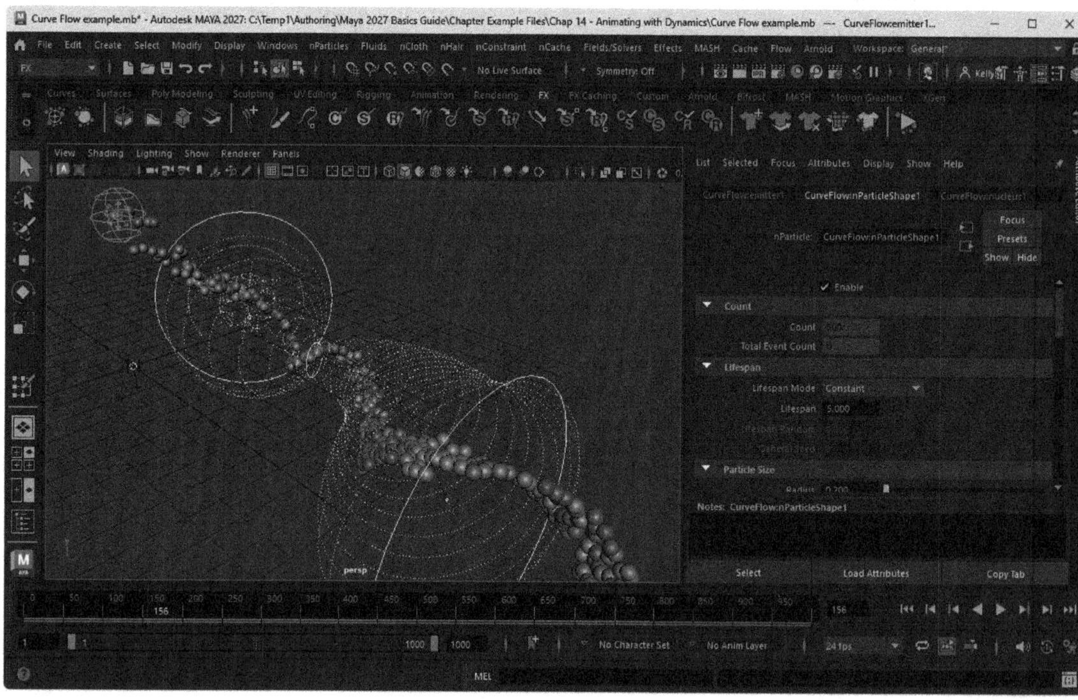

FIGURE 14-1

Particle examples

Creating Particles

You can begin creating particles by selecting the nParticles, nParticle Tool menu command. With the nParticle tool selected, just click at the location where you want to place particles and press Enter when done.

Note

The nParticles menu is found in the FX menu set.

The Tool Settings panel for the nParticle tool lets you name the particle collection, specify the number of particles to place with each click, and define the maximum radius within which the particles are placed. There is also a Sketch Particles option, which creates particles as you drag in the scene. The Sketch Interval value determines how close together the particles are. The Create Particle Grid option creates a grid of regularly spaced particles. The Particle Spacing value determines the spacing between each adjacent particle. The With Cursor option allows you to click on opposite corners to create a particle grid and the With Text Fields option lets you enter the corner dimensions. Figure 14-2 shows a particle system created using each of these methods.

Note

```
The 'n' in front of many of the menus stands for
the Nucleus simulation system.
```

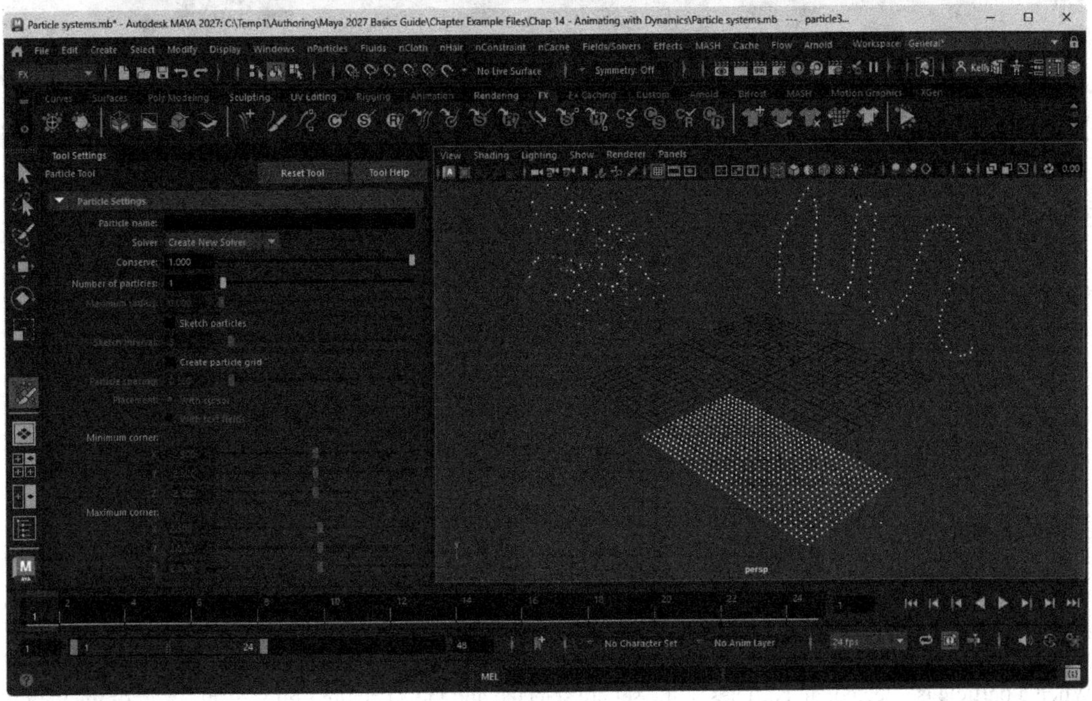

FIGURE 14-2

Particles options

Creating Surface Particles

If you select an object and choose the Modify, Make Live menu command, all of the particles that you create with the Particle tool are positioned on the surface of the object. Figure 14-3 shows a particle collection that is centered about a sphere.

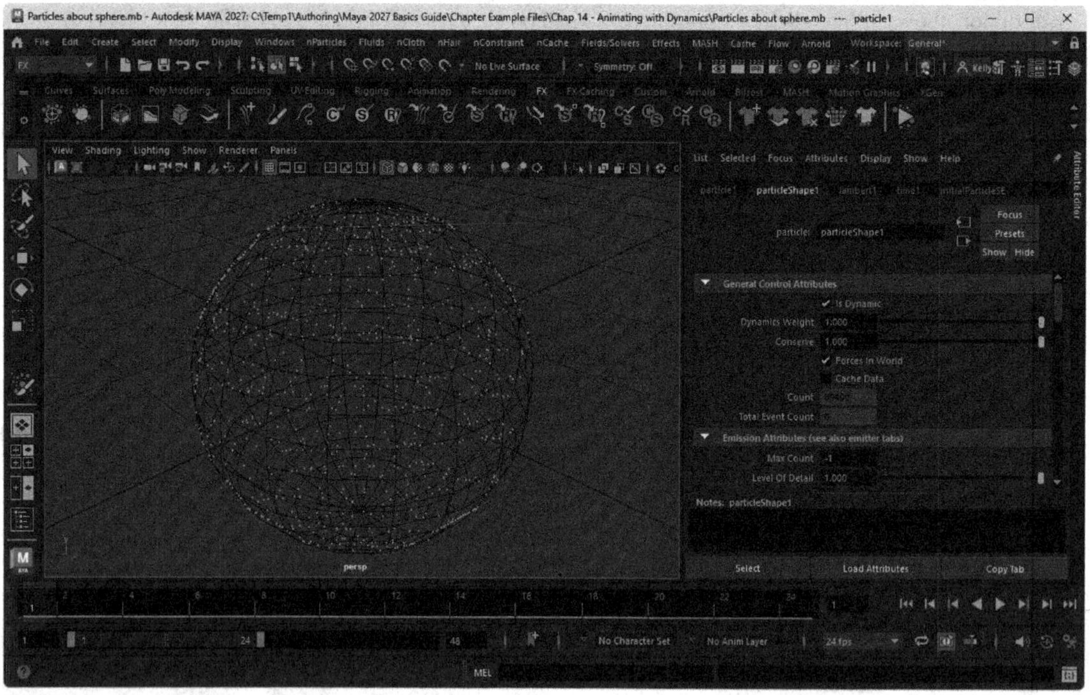

FIGURE 14-3

Particles about a sphere

Viewing Particle Attributes and Count

When a particle is selected, all particles in the set are selected and the Attribute Editor displays all of the various attributes for the particle collection. These attributes are split between a Transform node and a Shape node, just like other objects. In the Shape node for the selected particles set, the General Control Attributes section of the Attribute Editor includes a Count field that tells you how many particles make up the collection, as shown for a square array of particles in Figure 14-4.

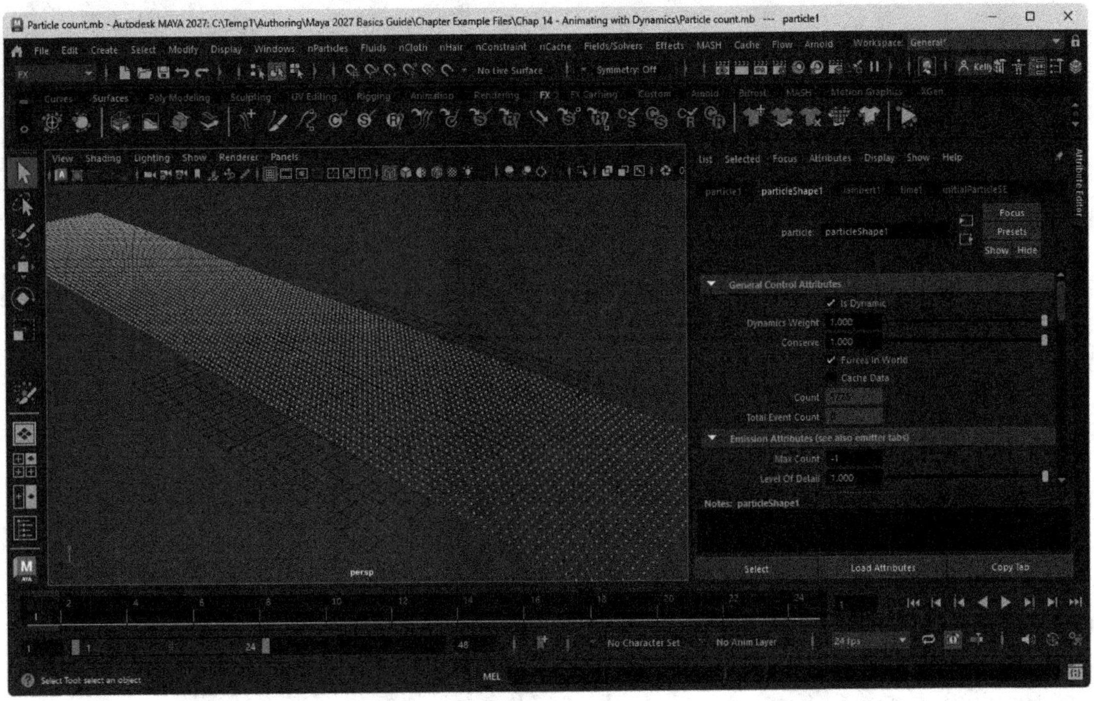

FIGURE 14-4

Particle's attributes

Setting Particle Lifespan

In the Lifespan Attributes section of the Attribute Editor, you can select a lifespan mode for the selected particle set. The options include Live Forever, Constant, and Random Range. If the Live Forever option is selected, the particles remain as long as the set is active. The Constant option lets you set a Lifespan value, which determines how many frames the particle stays around before disappearing; and the Random Range option randomly sets the lifespan of each particle in the set.

Changing Particle Render Type

Within the nParticles, Create Options submenu are several different particle types that you can select as the default particle. Whenever a new particle is created, it uses this display type. The options include Points, Balls, Cloud, Thick Cloud and Water.

In addition to the default options, there are many more particle types available in the Attribute Editor. In the Render Attributes section is a list of Render Types. Click the Render Type button to see additional attributes for the selected Render Type. The Render Types include the following:

* **MultiPoint.** Renders each particle as multiple points for a denser particle collection. Good for dust and smoke.
* **MultiStreak.** Combines each particle into several streaks for a denser particle collection.
* **Numeric.** Renders each particle using its particle number.

* **Points.** Makes each particle a simple point. You can set the Point size.

* **Spheres.** Renders each particle as a separate sphere.

* **Sprites.** Displays each particle as a rectangle that continually faces the camera. You can map images to these sprites.

* **Streak.** Renders each particle as a stretched point. The particle must be moving to be visible. The length of the streak depends on the speed of the particle. Good for rain and sleet.

* **Blobby Surface.** Renders each particle as a blobby sphere. When in close proximity, the blobby spheres run together like water drops.

* **Cloud.** Renders also as blobby spheres, except blurred to create the look of a cloud.

* **Tube.** Renders each particle as a tube.

Figure 14-5 shows a stream of particles rendered with the Blobby Surface and Cloud options selected.

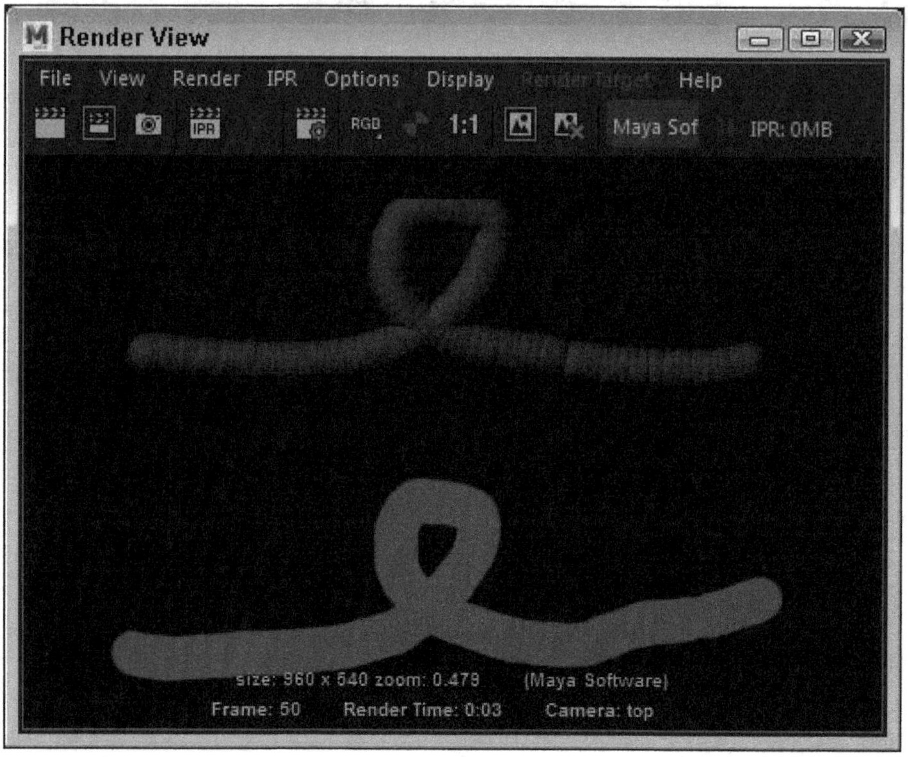

FIGURE 14-5

Particle shape rendered with Blobby Surface and Cloud

Using Instances

In addition to the default particle render types that you can set, you can also select any geometric object and use that as the particle's source object. To replace all of the particles with a geometric object, select the object, then select the particle set and choose the nParticles, Instancer menu command. This command replaces each particle with the geometric object. Changing the instanced geometry changes all of the particles also. Figure 14-6 shows a drawn path of particles that uses a cube object instance.

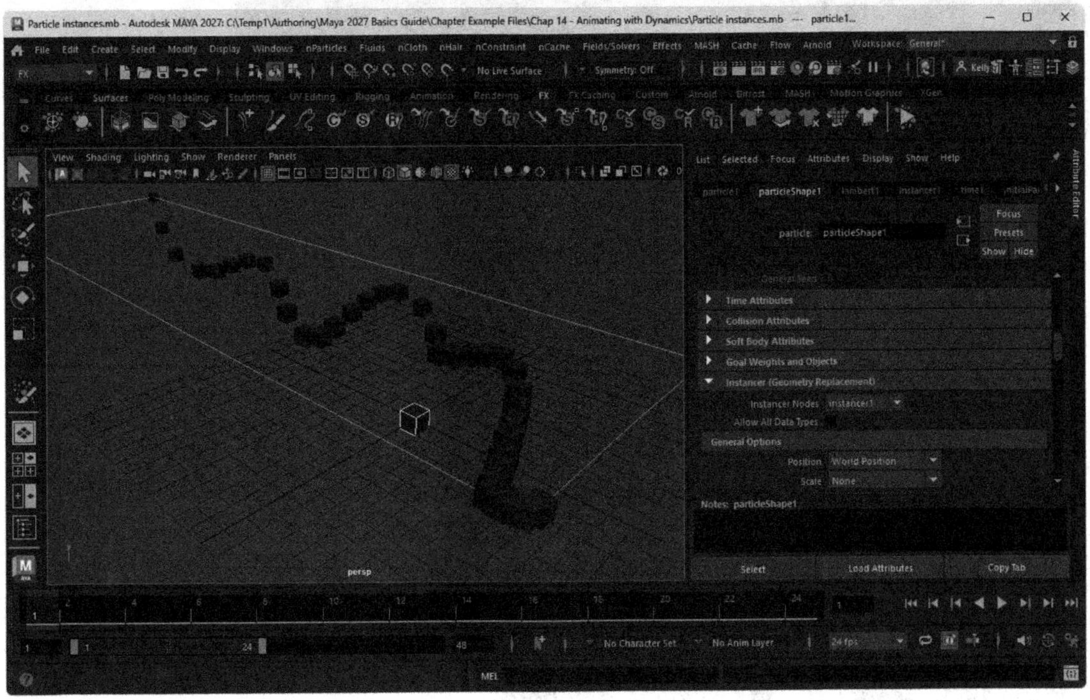

FIGURE 14-6

Particle instances

Cycling Instances

If you select the nParticles, Instancer, Options menu command, the Particle Instancer Options dialog box opens, as shown in Figure 14-7. This dialog box includes a list of instanced objects and several objects that you can add to the list by selecting an object and clicking the Add Selection button. You can set the particle system to cycle through the instanced objects in the list by selecting the Sequential option in the Cycle field. The Cycle Step Units can be set to Frames or Seconds, and the Cycle Step Size is the number of frames or seconds that must pass before the next object in the list replaces the current instances.

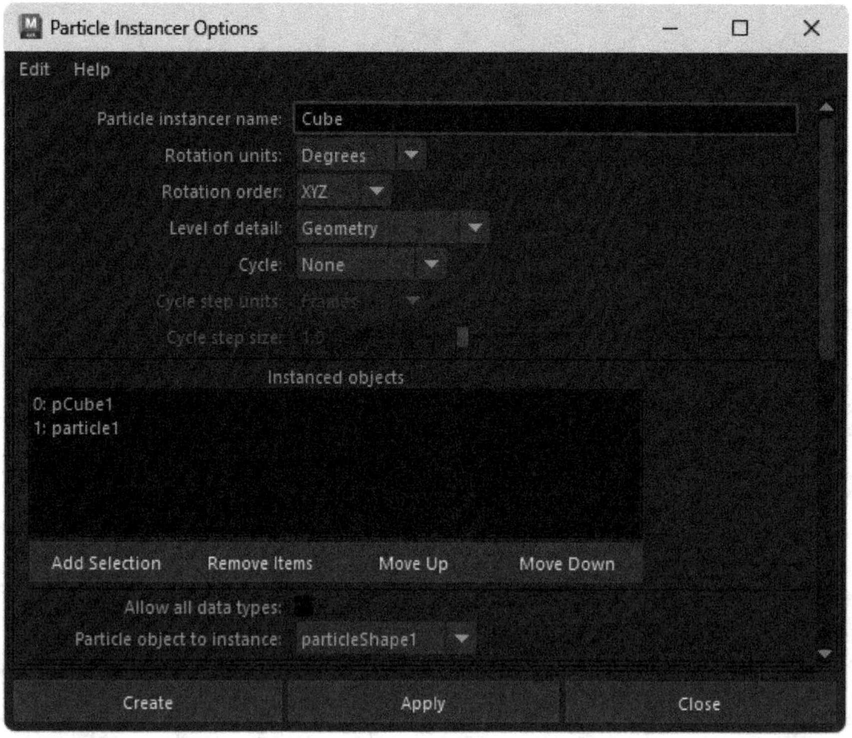

FIGURE 14-7

Particle Instancer Options dialog box

Lesson 14.1-Tutorial 1: Add Clouds to a Sphere

1. Create a NURBS sphere object with the Create, NURBS Primitives, Sphere menu command.
2. Select the Modify, Make Live menu command.

   The Make Live command causes all particles that are created to be positioned automatically on the surface of the live object.
3. Select the nParticles, nParticle Tool, Options menu command.
4. In the Particle Settings section of the Tool Settings panel, type the name **Clouds** then set the Number of Particles option to 5 with a Maximum Radius setting of 0.25.
5. Enable the Sketch Particles option and drag over the sphere to create the particles.
6. Press the Enter key when you're done creating particles.

   By setting the Maximum Radius value to 0.25, the particles are raised from the surface of the live object.
7. With the particle set selected, open the Attribute Editor.
8. Open the Render Attributes section of the Attribute Editor. In the Clouds Shape node, select the Cloud option for the Particle Render Type attribute.
9. Below the Particle Render Type attribute, click on the Current Render Type button.
10. Set the Radius value to 0.15.
11. Right-click on the Perspective view panel to select it and click the Render Current Frame button in the Status Line.

The sphere is rendered surrounded by wispy clouds, as shown in Figure 14-8.

12. Select File, Save Scene As and save the file as **Cloudy globe.mb**.

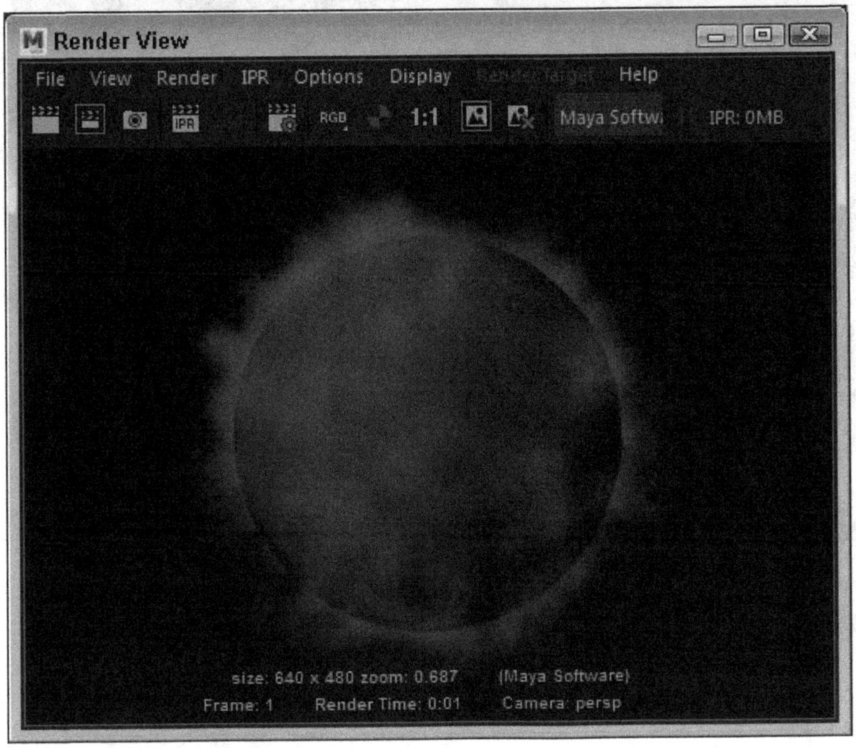

FIGURE 14-8

Cloudy globe

Lesson 14.1-Tutorial 2: Use an Instance

1. Select the File, Open Scene menu command, locate and open the Snowflake.mb file.
2. Select the nParticles, nParticle Tool, Options menu command.
3. In the Particle Settings section, type the name **Snowstorm** and set the Number of Particles option to 5 with a Maximum Radius setting of 10.0 and a Sketch Interval of 25.
4. Enable the Sketch Particles option and drag in the view panel.
5. Press the Enter key when you're done creating particles.
6. Select the Snowflake object, hold down the Shift key, and select the particles.
7. Select the nParticles, Instancer menu command.
8. Select the original snowflake object and scale it down with the Scale tool.

   Scaling the original snowflake scales all of the instanced particles also, as shown in Figure 14-9.
9. Select File, Save Scene As and save the file as **Snowstorm.mb**.

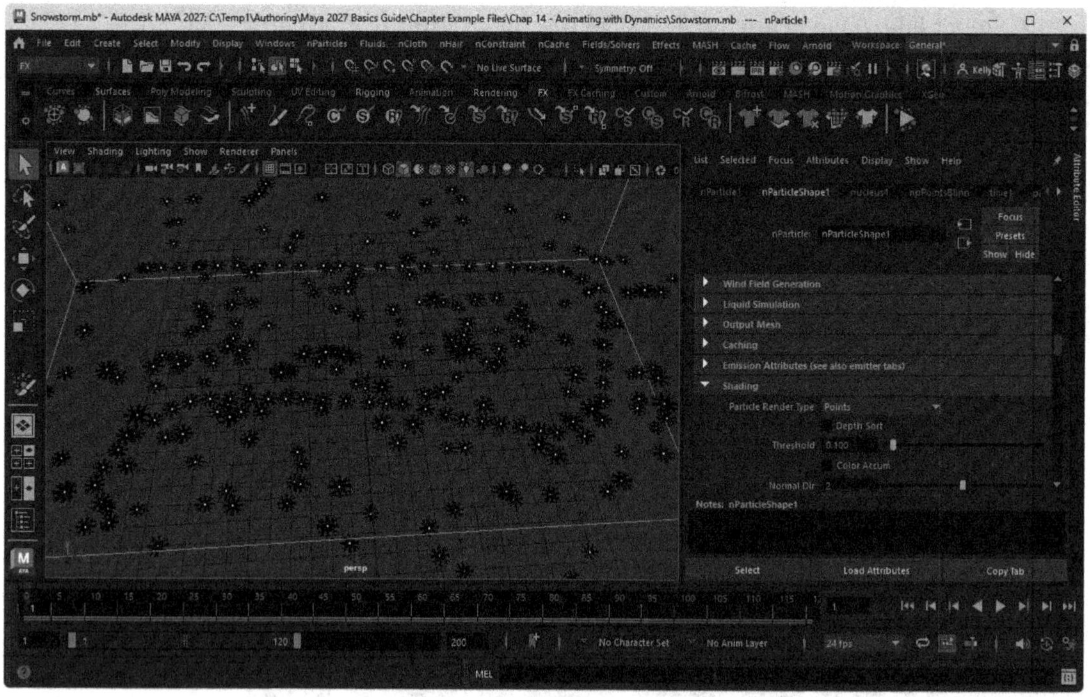

FIGURE 14-9

Instanced particles

Lesson 14.1-Tutorial 3: Cycle Instances

1. Select the Create, NURBS Primitives, Sphere menu command twice to create two sphere objects.
2. Click on the Select by Component Type button in the Status Line and stretch the end vertices of one of the spheres away from its center to create a football-shaped object.
3. Select the nParticles, nParticle Tool, Options menu command.
4. In the Particle Settings section, type the name **Sports ball storm** and set the Number of Particles option to 5 with a Maximum Radius setting of 5.0. Make sure that neither the Sketch Particles nor the Create Particle Grid options are enabled.
5. Click randomly in the view panel to create a particle set that covers the entire view panel. Press the Enter key when you're done creating particles.
6. Select both sphere objects and select the nParticles, Instancer, Options menu command.

   The names of each of the selected spheres appear in the Particle Instancer Options dialog box.
7. Set the Cycle attribute to Sequential and the Cycle Step Units to Frames.
8. Select the particle set in the view panel and click the Create button.
9. Drag the Time Slider.

   Clicking the Create button causes all the particles to use the football-shaped instance, as shown in Figure 14-10. As you drag the Time Slider, the particles switch back and forth between the football and the normal sphere objects for each frame.

10. Select File, Save Scene As, and save the file as **Sports ball storm.mb**.

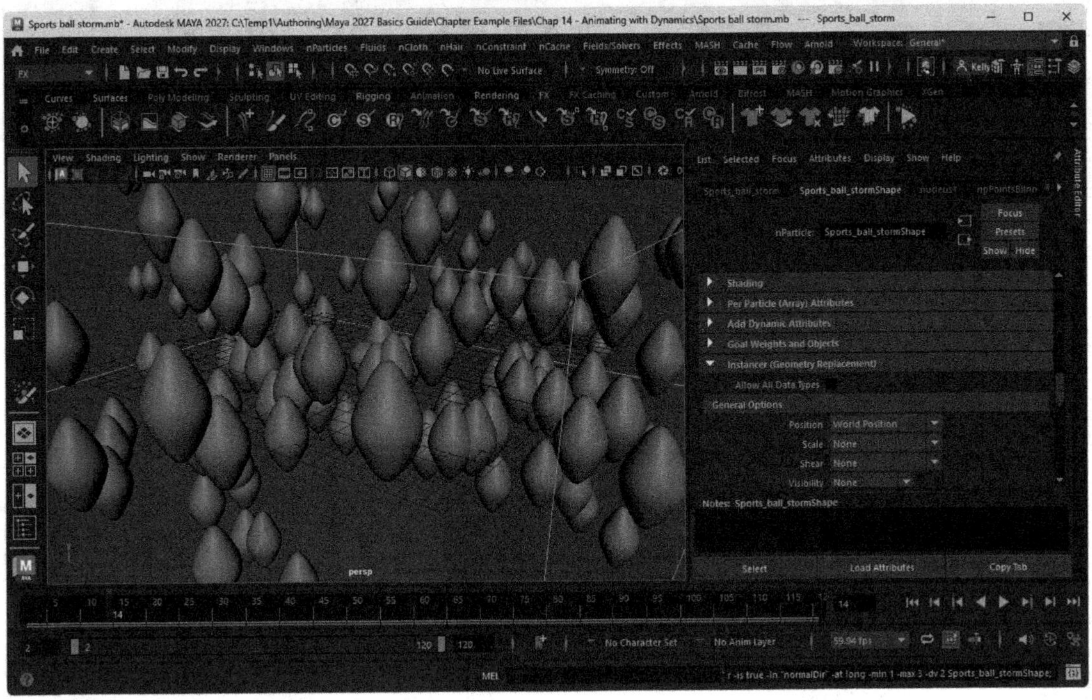

FIGURE 14-10

Raining footballs

Lesson 14.2: Create an Emitter

One of the key benefits of particles is that they can have motion. You can create this motion by moving the particle set with the Transform tools, but there are easier methods. An *emitter* is an object that creates and distributes particles at a regular rate.

Note

Although you can select individual particles, particles can only be transformed as an entire set.

Using an Emitter

An emitter sends particles into the scene. Emitters include attributes to define the number of particles created per second, as well as the particle's initial speed and direction. There are several types of particle emitters—Omni, Directional, Surface, Curve, and Volume. Dragging the Time Slider causes the particles to speed away from the emitter. Figure 14-11 shows three Omni emitters with different Rate values.

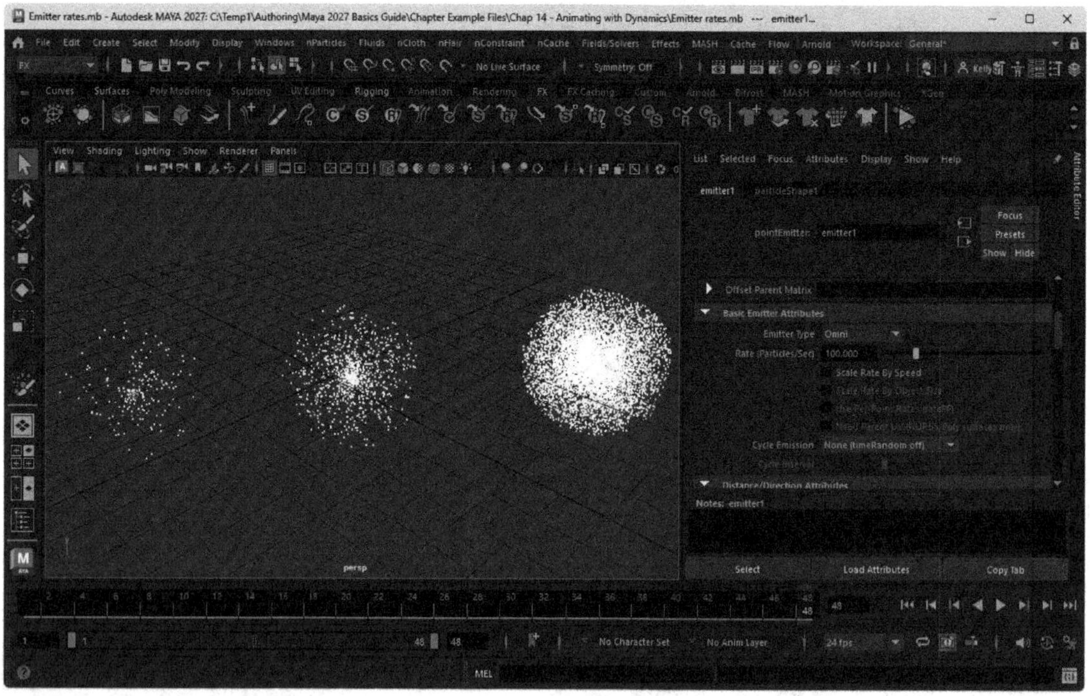

FIGURE 14-11

Emitters with different rates

Using a Directional Emitter

The Directional emitter type lets you set the direction that the particles move away from the emitter using the Direction X, Direction Y, and Direction Z attributes. Changing the Spread value causes the particles to spread randomly as they are emitted. A Spread value of 1.0 spreads the particles in the hemisphere. Figure 14-12 shows three directional emitters with increasing Spread values.

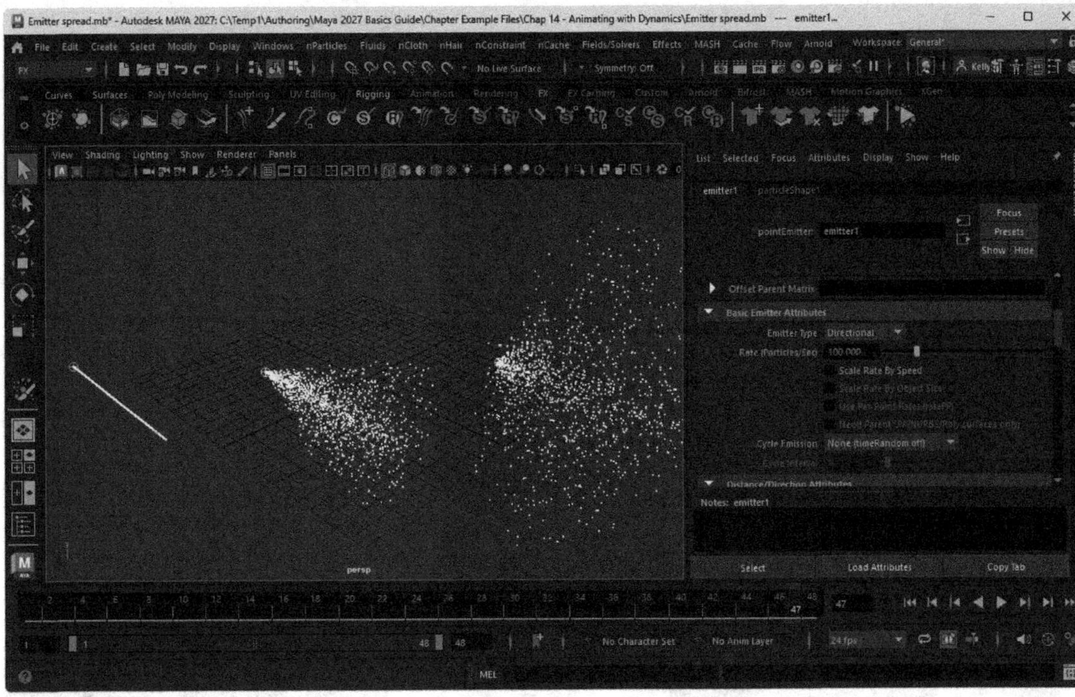

FIGURE 14-12

Directional emitters with different spreads

Using a Volume Emitter

The Volume emitter type can be cube, sphere, cylinder, cone, or torus shaped. For Volume emitters, you can set the particle's Sweep range and its speed Away From Center, Away From Axis, Along Axis, and Around Axis. Figure 14-13 shows cubic, spherical, and cylindrical Volume emitters.

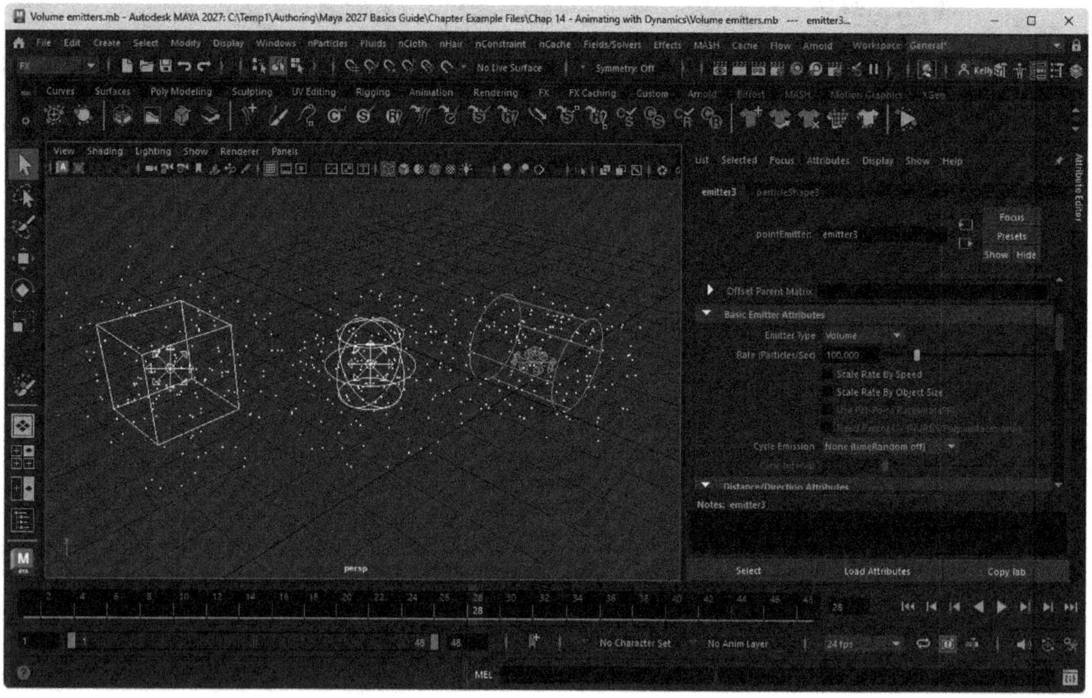

FIGURE 14-13
Volume emitters

Using an Object as an Emitter

In addition to the various emitter types, you can turn NURBS objects and curves into emitters using the nParticles, Emit from Object menu command. This causes particles to be spawned from the surface of the selected object or curve. Figure 14-14 shows a NURBS object acting as an emitter with the emitter type set to Surface.

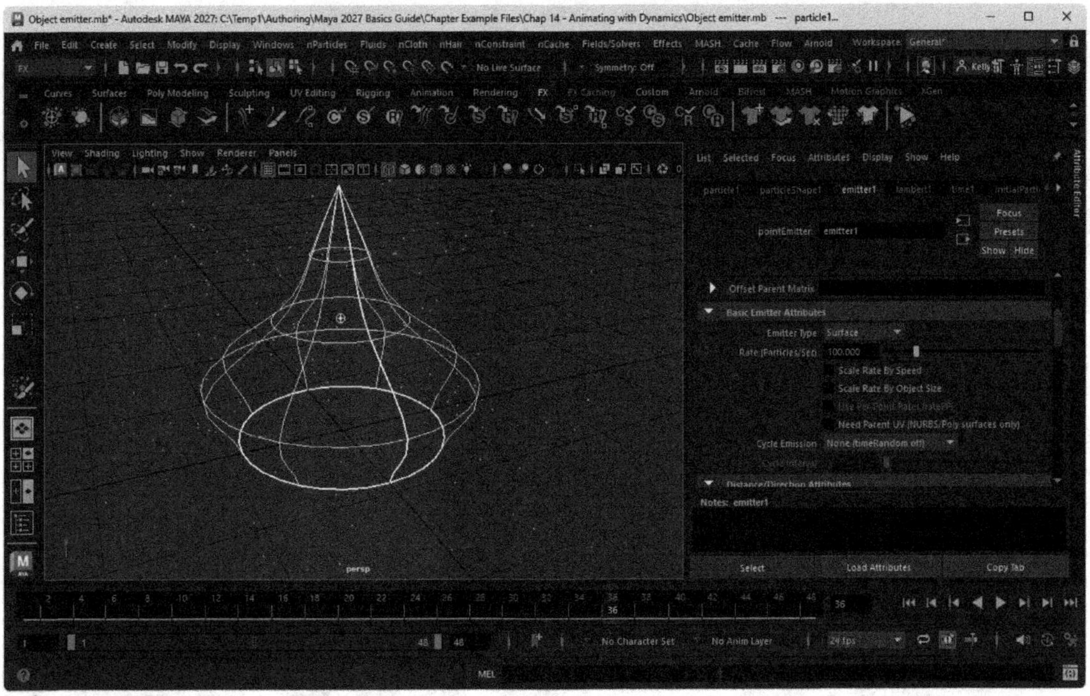

FIGURE 14-14

An object emitter

Changing Emitter Attributes

You can change the emitter's attributes in the Attribute Editor when the emitter is selected, but you can also change them using a manipulator, shown in Figure 14-15. With the emitter selected, click the Modify, Transformation Tools, Show Manipulator Tool menu, then drag with the middle mouse button to change the attribute's value.

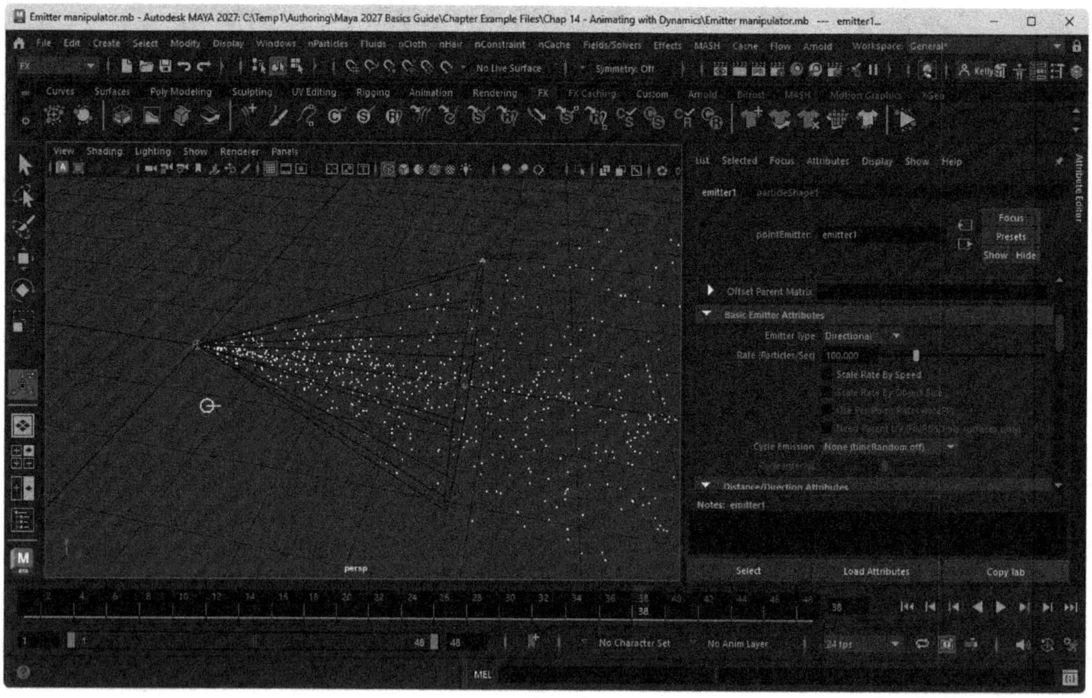

FIGURE 14-15

Emitter manipulator

Lesson 14.2-Tutorial 1: Create an Omni Emitter

1. Select the Create, Polygon Primitives, Cube menu command to create a cube object and move the cube away from the center of the view panel.
2. Select the nParticles, Create Emitter menu command.
3. In the Attribute Editor, select Omni from the Emitter Type drop-down list and set the Speed value to 10.
4. Drag the Time Slider to see the particles.
5. Select the cube object, and then hold down the Shift key and select the particle set. Be sure to select the individual particles being emitted and not the emitter icon.
6. Choose the nParticles, Instancer menu command.

   All the particles are replaced with cubes, as shown in Figure 14-16.
7. Select File, Save Scene As, and save the file as **Cube emitter.mb**.

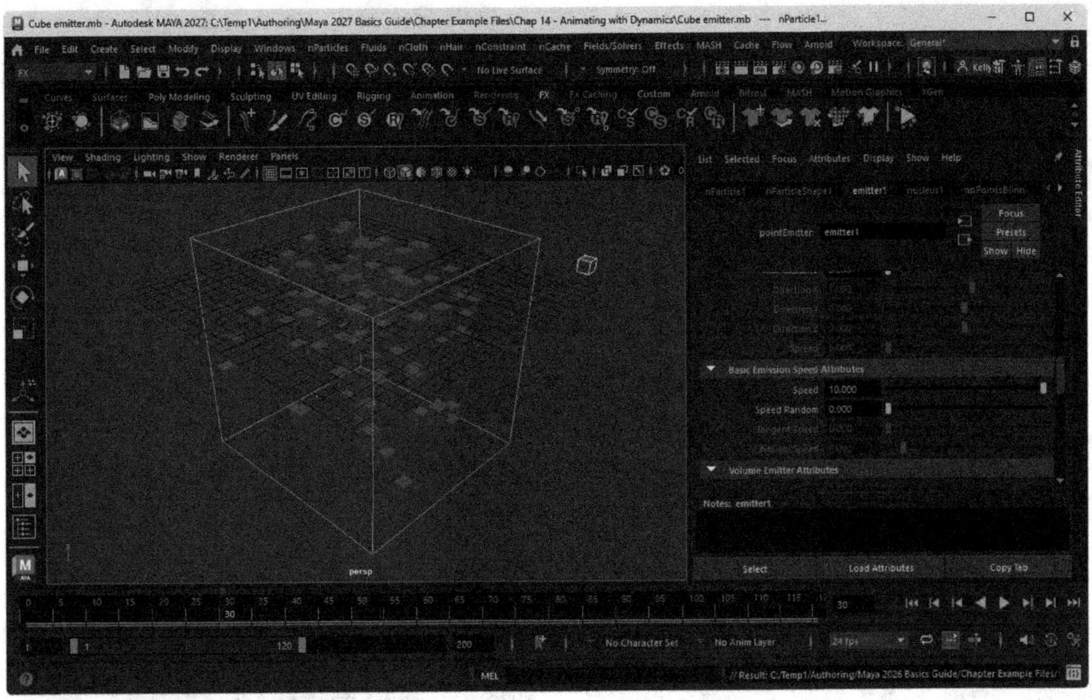

FIGURE 14-16

An Omni emitter

Lesson 14.2-Tutorial 2: Create a Directional Emitter

1. Select the File, Open Scene menu command and open the Simple tank.mb file.
2. Select the nParticles, Create Emitter menu command and move the emitter to the end of the tank's gun.
3. In the Attribute Editor, select Directional from the Emitter Type drop-down list.
4. In the Distance/Direction Attributes section, set the Direction X value to 1.0 and the Spread value to 0.25.
5. Select the Modify, Transformation Tools, Show Manipulator menu command.
6. Click and drag the manipulator with the middle mouse button until the Rate value is over 500.
7. Drag the Time Slider to see the particles.

   The particles all speed away from the emitter, as shown in Figure 14-17.
8. Select File, Save Scene As and save the file as **Directional emitter on tank.mb**.

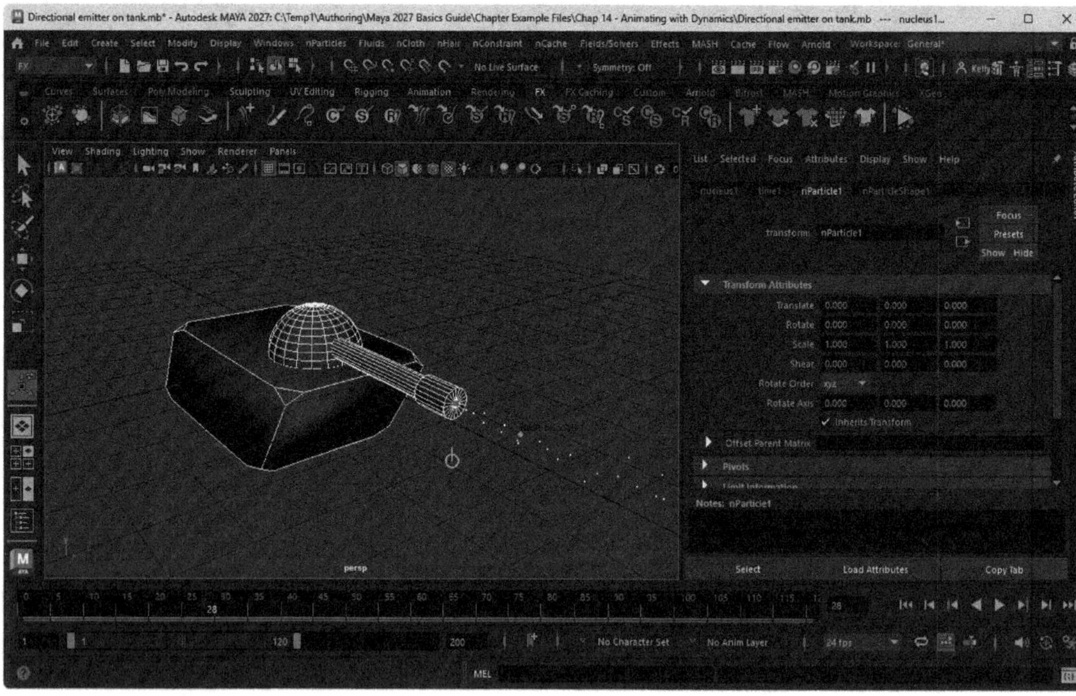

FIGURE 14-17

A Directional emitter on a tank gun

Lesson 14.2-Tutorial 3: Create an Object Emitter

1. Select the File, Open Scene menu command and open the Ceiling fan.mb file.
2. With the fan object selected, choose the nParticles, Emit from Object, Options menu command.
3. In the Emitter Options dialog box, select Surface from the Emitter Type drop-down list, enable the Scale Rate By Object Size option, and set the Speed value to 10. Then click the Create button.
4. Drag the Time Slider to see the particles.

    The particles all speed away from the surface of the fan object, as shown in Figure 14-18.
5. Select File, Save Scene As and save the file as **Ceiling fan emitter.mb**.

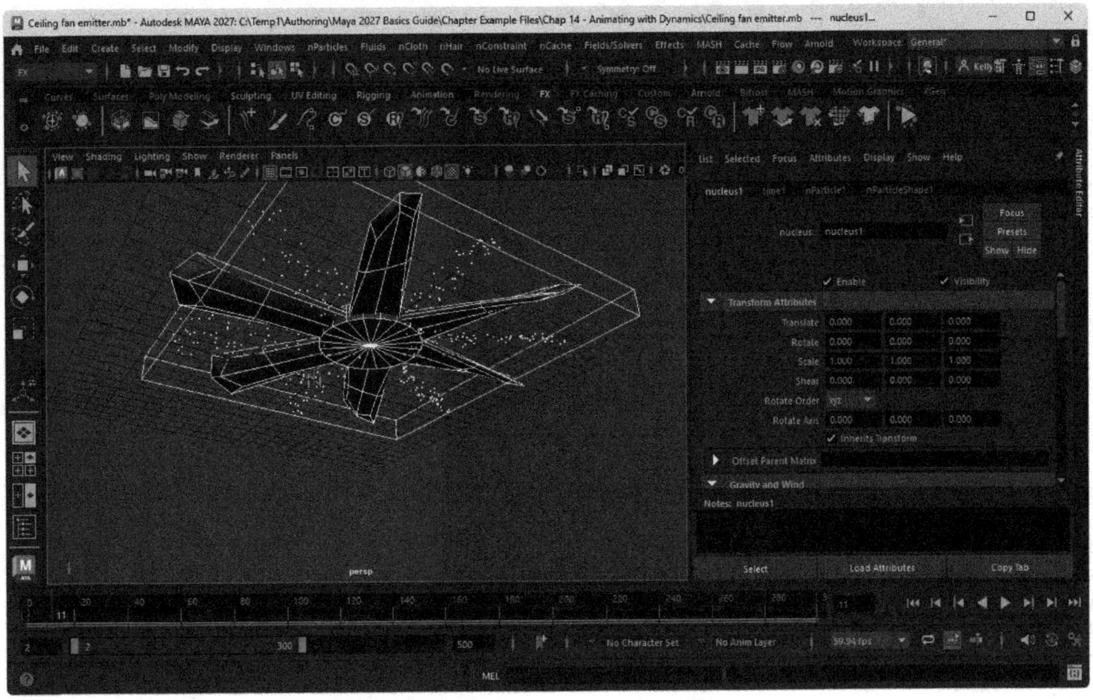

FIGURE 14-18

An emitter on the ceiling fan

Lesson 14.3: Create Fields and Goals

Fields define physical forces in the scene that objects and particles become subject to. You can also use **goals,** which are targets that the particles move towards.

Understanding Fields

Fields are a way of adding physical forces to the scene. All objects that are connected to a field are influenced by the field. Fields are created using the Fields/Solvers menu command. Maya includes the following default fields:

* **Air**. This field represents airflow, such as a fan blowing.
* **Drag**. This field applies friction to a moving object.
* **Gravity**. This field simulates the Earth's gravity field. It causes an object to accelerate in the direction of the field icon, which is typically downward in the negative Y-axis direction.
* **Newton**. This field pulls objects towards it.
* **Radial**. This field acts like a magnet repelling or attracting objects.

* **Turbulence**. This field randomly moves all particles within its influence.
* **Uniform**. This field pushes all objects in one direction with a consistent force.
* **Vortex**. This field pulls objects in a spiraling direction like a tornado or water down a drain.
* **Volume Axis**. This field moves all objects within a given volume a specified direction.

You can set the strength of a selected field in the Attribute Editor.

Connecting Objects to a Field

All objects that are selected when a field is created are connected to the field and are thereby affected by it. You can connect objects to a field at any time by first selecting the object or particles and then selecting the Field icon with the Shift key held down and using the Fields/Solvers, Assign to Selected menu command. The Fields/Solvers, Use Selected as Source menu command moves the field icon to the selected object and is useful for positioning fields.

Caution

When selecting particles to connect to a field or to a goal, be sure to select the actual particles and not the emitter.

Changing Field Attributes

When a Field is added to the scene, an icon is placed at the origin. You can move this icon using the Transform tools and modify the attributes for the field in the Attribute Editor. These attributes include Magnitude, Direction, and Distance. There is also a manipulator for these values that you can access using the Modify, Transformation Tools, Show Manipulator menu command, as shown in Figure 14-19.

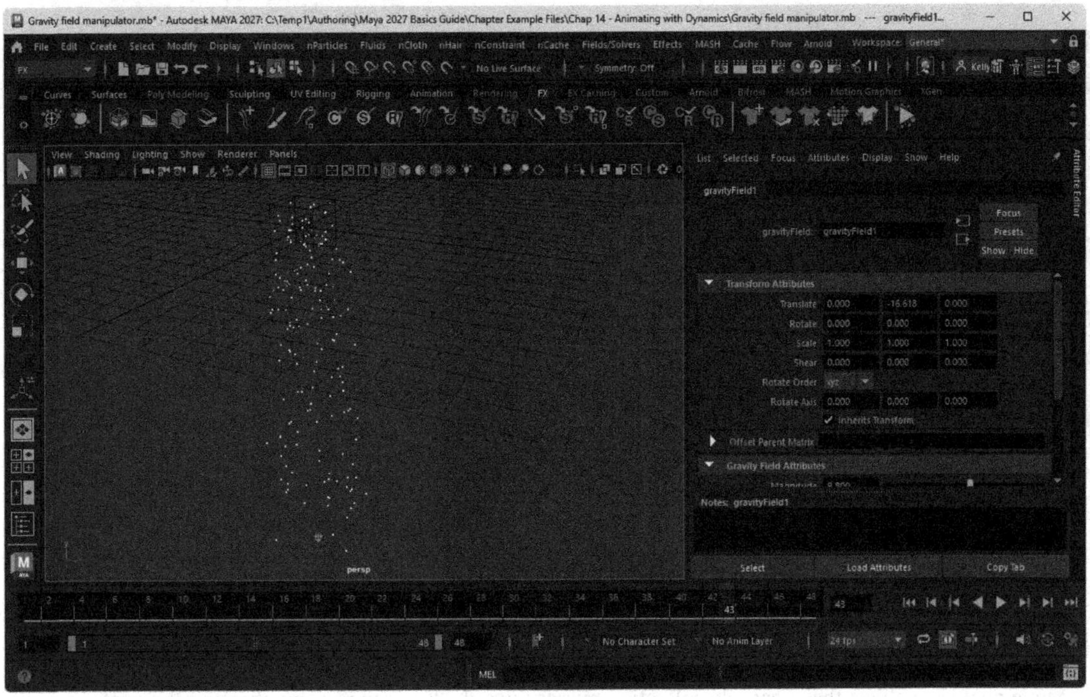

FIGURE 14-19

Gravity field and manipulator

Regulating Field Forces

When a field is applied to an object, it often takes a considerable force to get the object to first move, but if the force required to get the object moving continues to be applied, the object often accelerates out of the scene too quickly. If you enable the Use Max Distance attribute in the Distance section of the Attribute Editor for a field, a Falloff Curve section, shown in Figure 14-20, appears where you can define how the field's force diminishes as the object approaches its maximum distance.

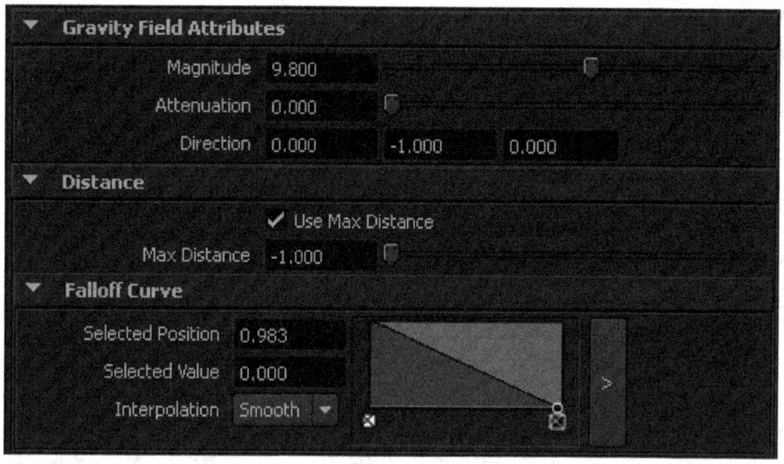

FIGURE 14-20

Falloff Curve section

Establishing Goals

A Maya goal is an object that a particle collection moves towards. You can use any object as the goal—it just needs to be connected to the particle object. To create a goal for a particle object, select the particle object then the object to be the goal, and then choose the nParticles, Goal menu command. Figure 14-21 shows two equal emitters, but the one on the right has the sphere as its goal and all its particles are directed towards the goal. To create multiple goal targets, deselect all objects and repeat the steps with another goal object.

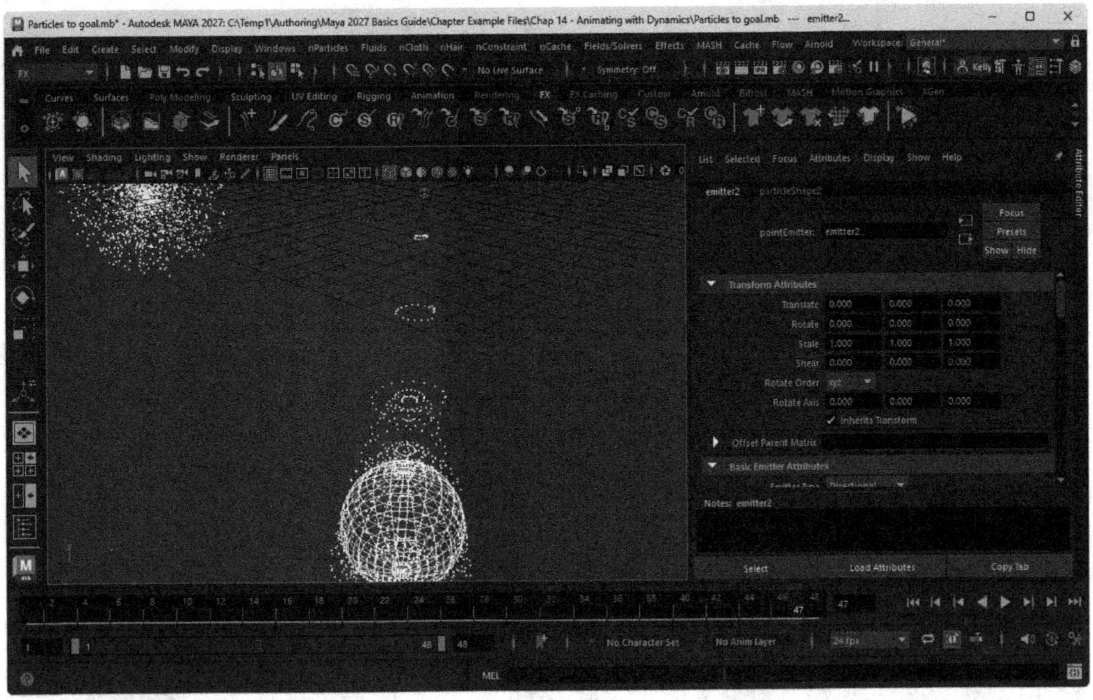

FIGURE 14-21

Particle goal

Lesson 14.3-Tutorial 1: Create a Vortex Field

1. Select the nParticles, Create Emitter menu command.
2. In the Attribute Editor, select Omni from the Emitter Type drop-down list and set the Rate to 1000.
3. Drag the Emitter icon upward using the Move tool.
4. Select the Fields/Solvers, Vortex menu command.
5. Drag the Time Slider to see the particles.
6. Select the particles, hold down the Shift key, and click on the Vortex field icon.
7. Select the Fields/Solvers, Assign to Selected menu command.
8. Set the Magnitude value to 50.
9. Drag the Time Slider to see the spiraling particles.

   The particles spiral around the Vortex field icon, as shown in Figure 14-22.
10. Select File, Save Scene As and save the file as **Spiral galaxy.mb**.

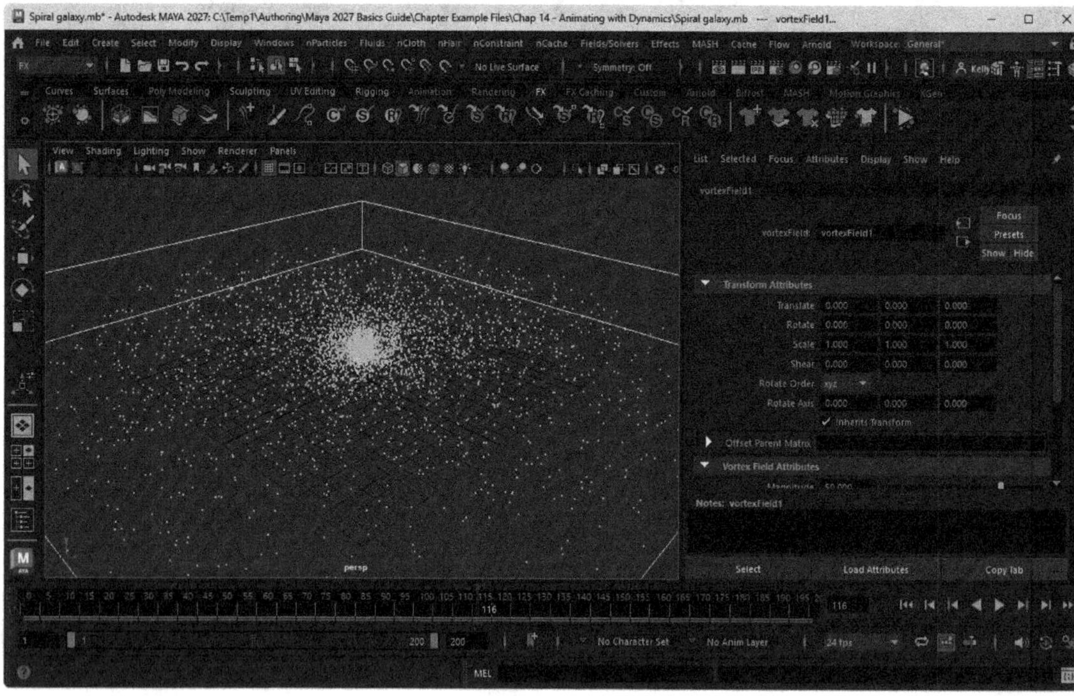

FIGURE 14-22

Vortex field

Lesson 14.3-Tutorial 2: Create a Goal

1. Select the File, Open Scene menu command and open the Bee and hive.mb file.
2. Select the nParticles, Create Emitter menu command and move the emitter away from the hive object.
3. With the emitter selected, set the Rate to 5 and the Speed Random value to 5 in the Attribute Editor.
4. Drag the Time Slider to see the particles.
5. Select the bee object, hold down the Shift key, select the particles, and then choose the nParticles, Instancer menu command.

   All the particles change to the bee object.
6. Select the particles, hold down the Shift key, select the hive object, and then choose the nParticles, Goal menu command.
7. Drag the Time Slider.

   The bee particles move towards the hive goal object, as shown in Figure 14-23.
8. Select File, Save Scene As and save the file as **Hive goal object.mb**.

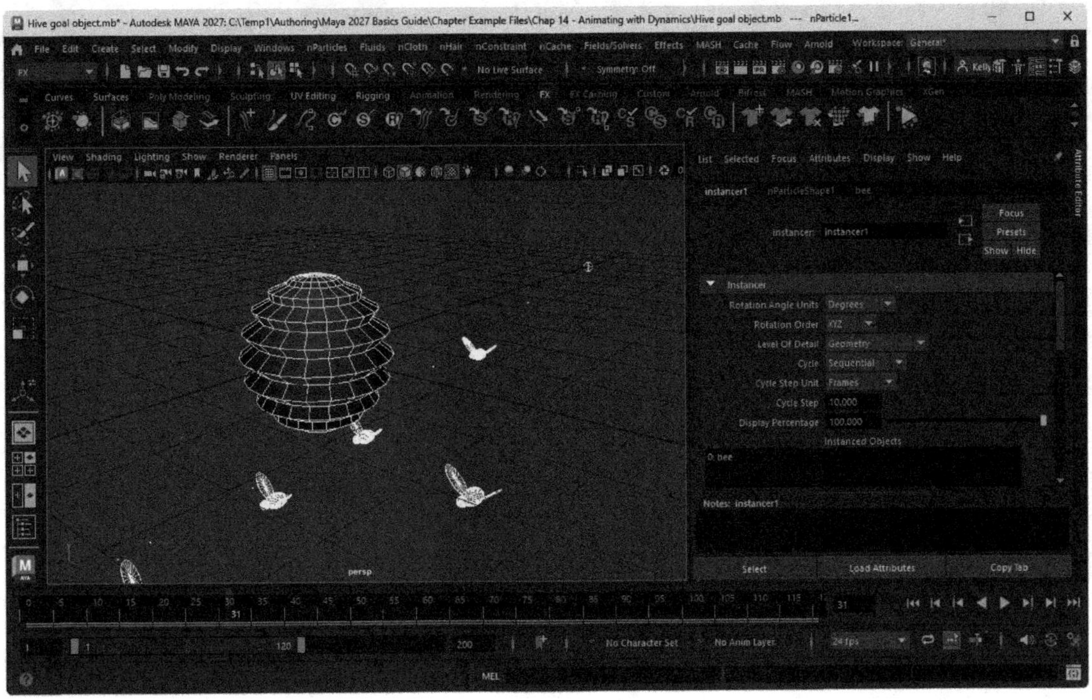

FIGURE 14-23

Goal object

Lesson 14.4: Animating Rigid Body Collisions

Now that you've learned about adding fields and forces to the scene, we will cover the animating of rigid body objects. Rigid body objects are objects that are solid and will not bend or break when colliding with other objects. To animate these objects, Maya includes two different solutions: a legacy system and a newer system called MASH. For the legacy system, you simply need to add the objects to the scene, define their properties, add a field to provide a force and play the animation. The MASH system is more complicated, but it can do a whole lot more.

Adding rigid body objects

For the legacy rigid body system, any mesh object can be used as a rigid body object. You simply need to select the object and choose the Fields/Solvers, Create Active Rigid Body menu command. The Rigid Options dialog box, shown in Figure 14-24, includes property values like Mass, Friction, Bounciness, and Damping. By changing these physical properties, you can impact how the object moves about the scene.

Caution

When placing objects in the scene, make sure that none of the objects overlap with one another. Doing so will confuse the solver and affect the results.

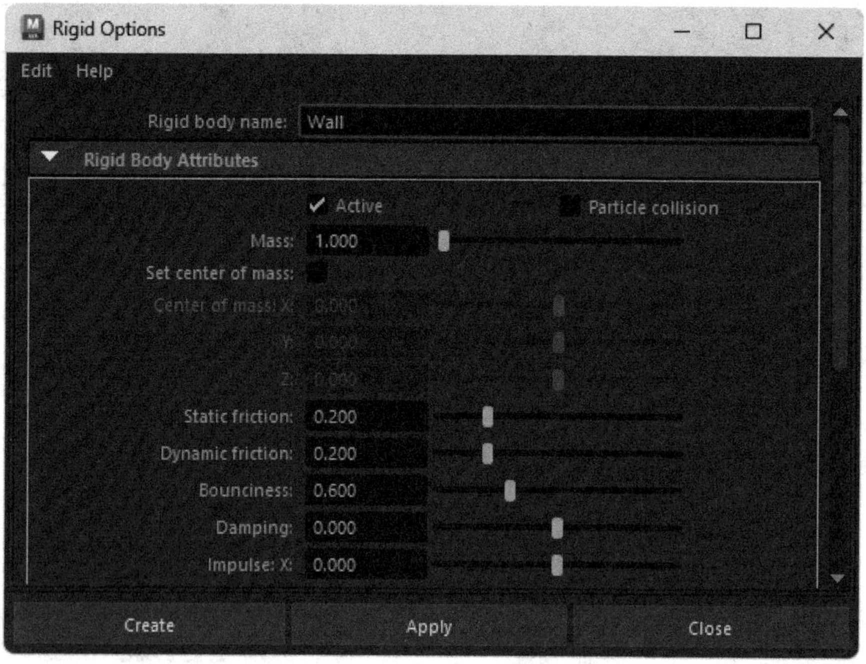

FIGURE 14-24

Rigid body object properties

Adding Passive body objects

In order to see collisions in the scene, the rigid body objects need to have something to collide against like the floor. These immovable objects are identified as passive objects. To make an object a passive object, just select it and choose the Fields/Solvers, Create Passive Rigid Body menu command.

Adding a force

Objects in the scene will not move unless they are subjected to some kind of force. To make all the objects, both active and passive, subject to a force, you need to select the object before choosing a field in the Fields/Solvers menu. This will automatically make them move according to the field force. If new objects are added to the scene after the field has been added, simply select the new object along with the field object and choose the Fields/Solvers Assign to Selected menu command.

Seeing the collisions

Once the scene is set up, press the Play Animation button to see the resulting collisions. Figure 14-25 shows a simple scene with four primitive objects falling under the effect of gravity and colliding with a passive sphere and floor.

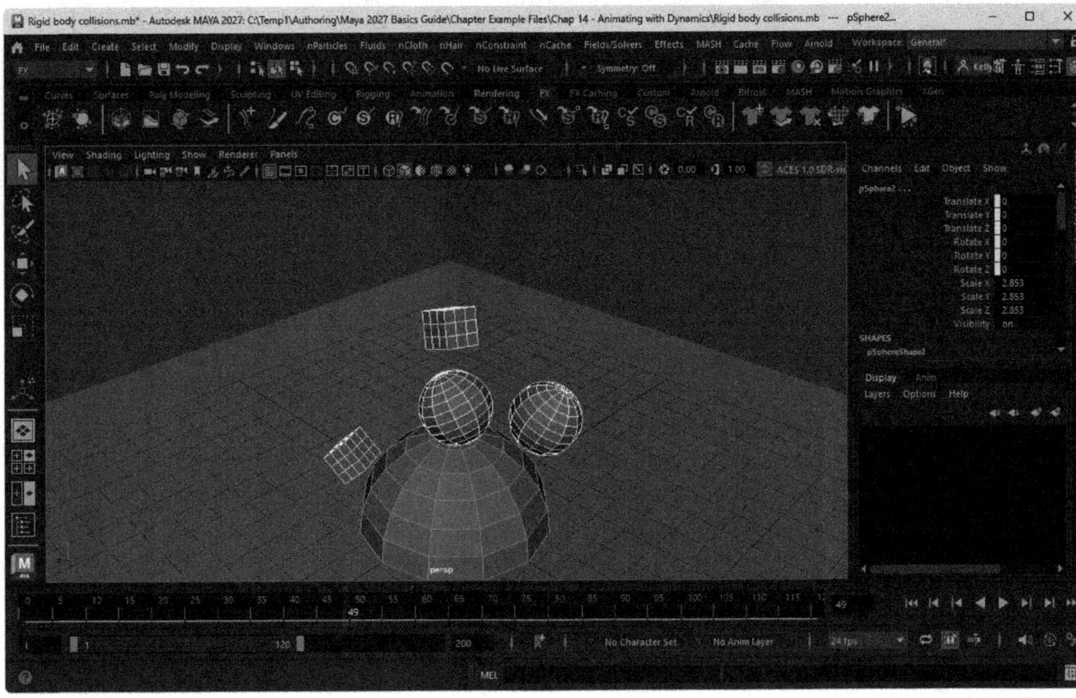

FIGURE 14-25

Rigid body collisions

Using MASH Dynamics

The **MASH** system in Maya has a wealth of features and rigid body dynamics is only part of this system. You can access the MASH commands in the MASH menu as part of the Animation and FX menu sets. There is also a MASH shelf. The first step is to create the objects that MASH works with, which it calls a MASH Network.

Creating a MASH Network

To create a MASH Network, add some objects to the scene and choose the MASH, Create MASH Network menu command. This duplicates the selected object with instances. Each instance of the original object is linked so that changing one of them changes all of them in the same way. If you open the MASH_Distribute node in the Attribute Editor, then you can change the number of instances, how they are distributed (Linear, Radial, Spherical, etc.), and the distance and rotation between each.

Opening the MASH Editor and enabling dynamics

Once you have a distribution of objects, you can use the MASH Editor, shown in Figure 14-26, to control how these objects move. To open the MASH Editor, choose the MASH, MASH Editor menu command. To enable dynamics, click on the Add Node (red plus icon) button in the MASH Editor toolbar and choose the Dynamics option. This node automatically adds a ground plane to the viewport and makes all the instances rigid body objects. If you hit the Play Animation button, the objects will fall and interact with the floor. Within the MASH_Dynamics node are all the physical properties for the instances including Mass, Bounce, and Friction, as shown in Figure 14-27.

Tip

You can also add nodes to the MASH system by clicking on its icon in the Add Node section of the MASH node.

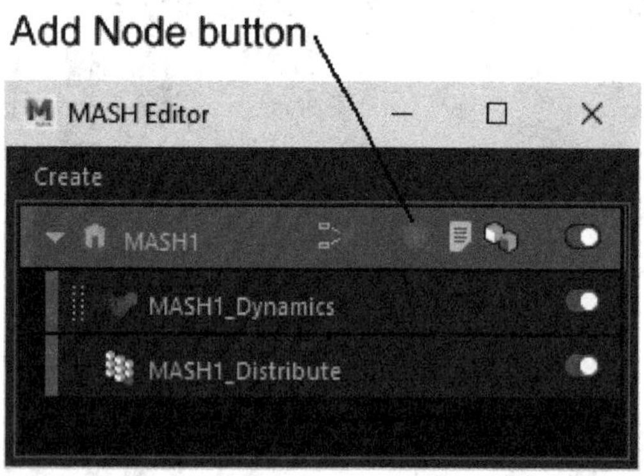

FIGURE 14-26

MASH Editor

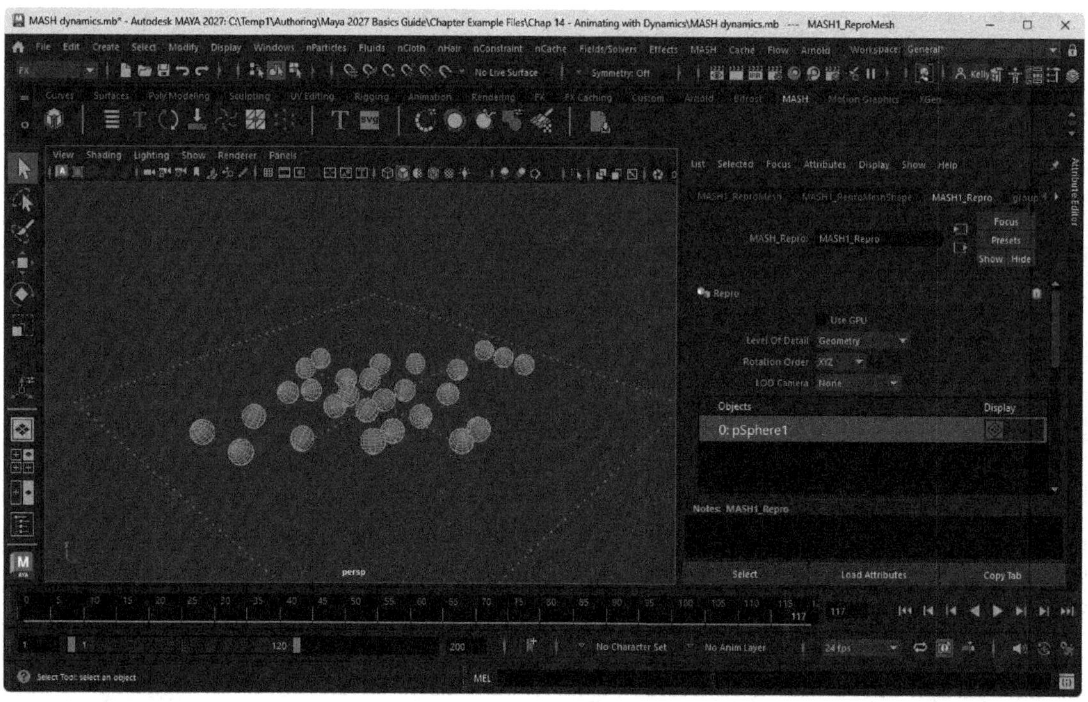

FIGURE 14-27

The MASH system makes rigid body animations possible

Adding collision objects and fields

When the Dynamics node is added to the MASH network, it appears in the Outliner named MASH_Bullet Solver. If this node is selected, two drag and drop panels appear in the Attribute Editor. One is for **Collider Objects** and the other is for Fields. Any new objects added to the scene can be selected in the Outliner with the middle mouse and dropped in this panel. This will add them to the scene as rigid body objects that will interact with the instance objects. You can also create field forces using the Fields/Solvers menu and drop them here to add forces to the scene.

Caution

```
The MASH system objects need to be polygon mesh
objects. They will not work with NURBS objects.
```

Lesson 14.4-Tutorial 1: Enable rigid body collisions

1. Select the File, Open Scene menu command and open the Billiards.mb file.
2. Select all objects that make up the table and choose the Fields/Solvers, Create Passive Rigid Body menu command.

   By making the table into a passive rigid body, the table becomes immovable, but objects can still be affected by it.
3. Select all of the balls in the scene and choose the Fields/Solvers, Create Active Rigid Body menu command.

   Selecting the Create Active Rigid Body menu command with the ball objects selected makes the balls into moveable rigid body objects.
4. Select just the cue ball and choose the Fields/Solvers, Uniform menu command. Then move the Uniform field just behind the cue ball and set its Direction attributes to 0,0,-1.
5. Drag the Time Slider to see how the rigid body objects interact.

   Since all the balls are active rigid bodies, the collisions make them bounce off one another and off the walls of the table, as shown in Figure 14-28.
6. Select File, Save Scene As, and save the file as **Rigid bodies on billiard table.mb**.

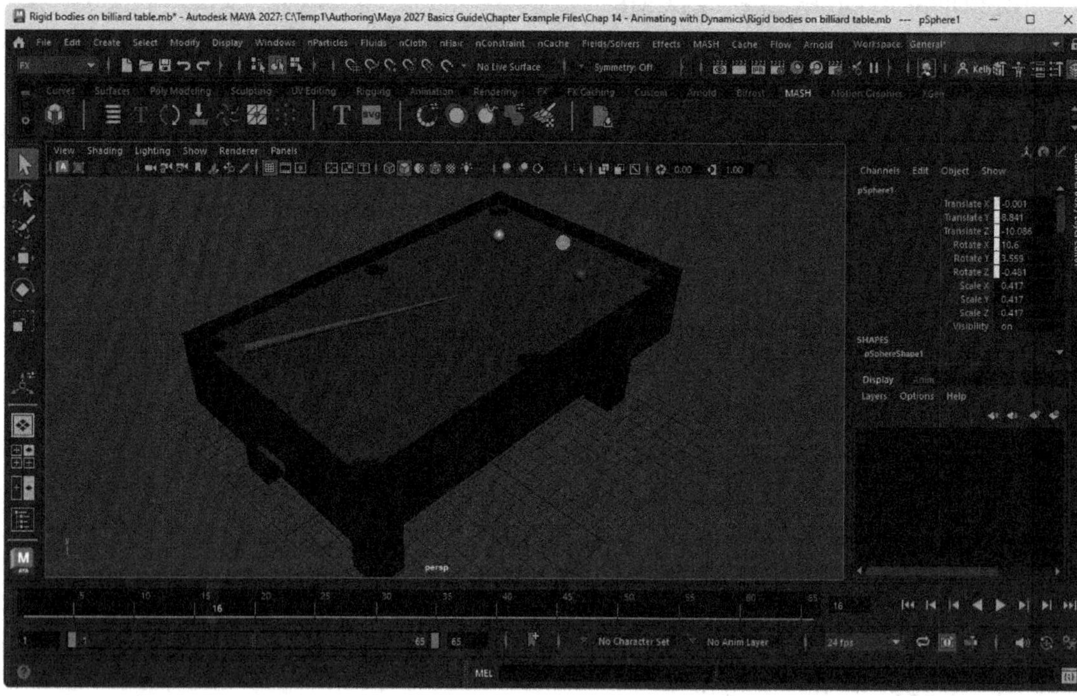

FIGURE 14-28

Rigid bodies on billiard table

Lesson 14.4-Tutorial 2: Using MASH dynamics

1. Select the File, Open Scene menu command and open the Skateboard.mb file.
2. Switch to the FX menu set, select the skateboard object and choose the MASH, Create MASH Network menu command.

   Ten instances of the skateboard are created and positioned next to each other.
3. Select the MASH1_Distribute node in the Attribute Editor and set the Number of Points to 1.
4. Select the MASH, MASH Editor menu command to open the MASH Editor, then click on the Add Node button in the MASH Editor toolbar and choose the Dynamics node.
5. Select the Create, Polygon Primitives, Plane menu command to create a Plane object, then scale, rotate and position the Plane object to be a ramp underneath the skateboard.
6. Open the Outliner and select the MASH1_BulletSolver node to open this node in the Attribute Editor, then drag the PPlane1 object from the Outliner with the middle mouse button and drop it in the Collider Objects pane in the Attribute Editor.

   The Plane's name is added to the Collider Objects pane and the ramp is now part of the MASH network, as shown in Figure 14-29.
7. Press the Play Animation button to see the skateboard move down the ramp.
8. Select File, Save Scene As, and save the file as **Skateboard on ramp.mb**.

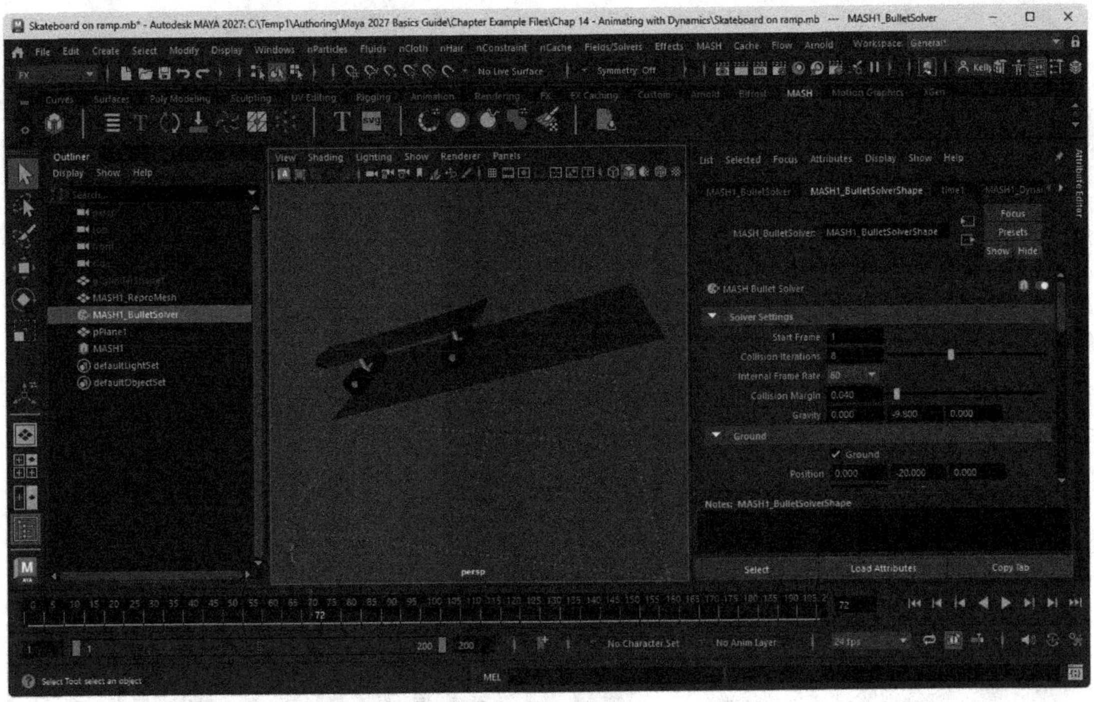

FIGURE 14-29

Rigid body skateboard moving down a ramp

Lesson 14.5: Manage Particle Collisions

Since Maya knows the position in 3D space of all objects, it is also aware of when two objects collide with one another. When a collision between objects is detected, it can cause the objects to rebound away from the collision according to physics formulas. It can further instruct the particles that collide to spawn new particles or tell an object how to respond to the collision.

Enabling Particle Collisions

You can enable collisions between a particle object and a passive object in the scene by selecting a passive object and choosing the nCloth, Create Passive Collider menu command. Figure 14-30 shows a simple directional emitter whose particles are colliding with passive sphere and plane objects. You also need to enable the Collisions option in the Collide section of the Attribute Editor for the Particle Shape node. The passive object also has a Collide option that is enabled by default.

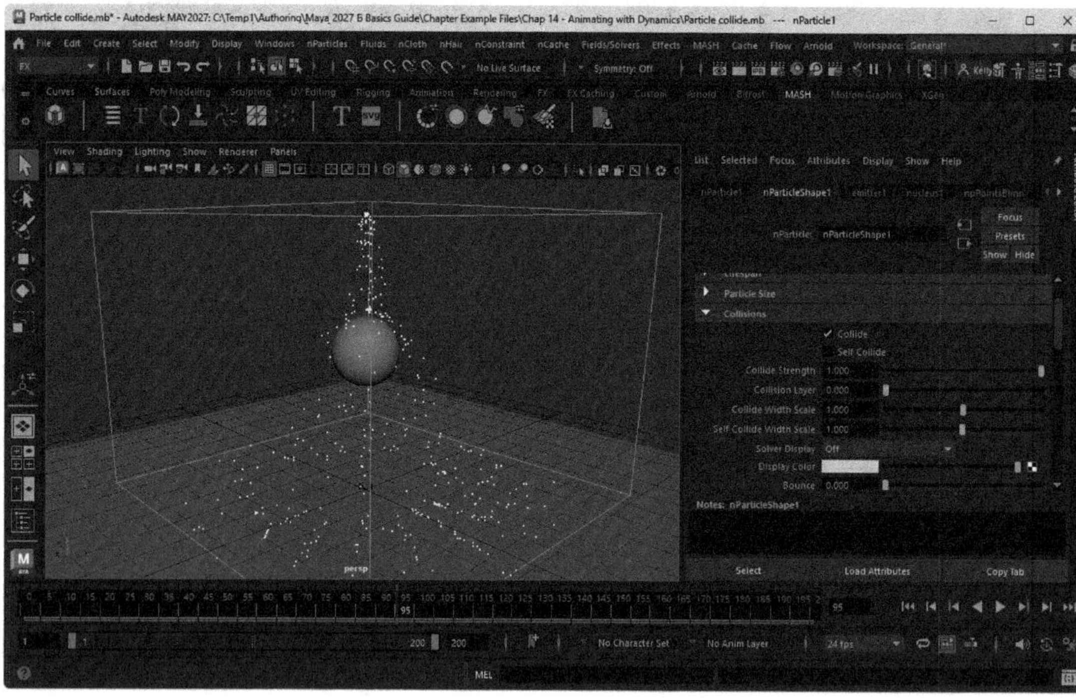

FIGURE 14-30

Particle collisions

Enabling Particle Collisions

Directly beneath the Collide option is the Self Collide option. If this option is enabled, then the system will detect collisions between particles. This adds a lot of realism to the particle system for balls, but it is unnecessary for cloud particles.

Setting Particle Attributes

The Collisions section also includes attributes for defining the physical properties of the colliding particles including Bounce, Friction and Stickiness. Increasing the Bounce value causes the particles to rebound off a colliding object, the Friction value opposes any motion, and the Stickiness value makes the particles stick to the surface when they stop moving. Figure 14-31 shows several particles bouncing off a passive plane object.

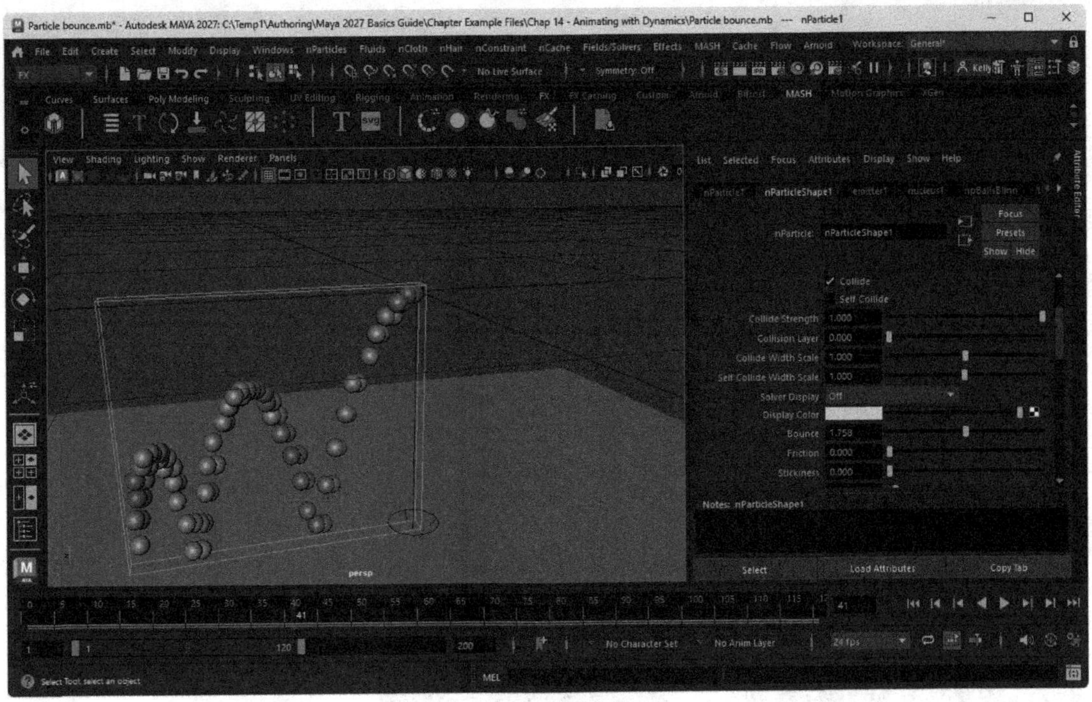

FIGURE 14-31

Particle bouncing

Defining New Events

When a particle collides with an object, you can cause a new **event**—such as making the particle split or emit new particles—to happen. To create a new event, open the Particle Collision Events dialog box (shown in Figure 14-32) with the nParticles, Particle Collision Event Editor menu command. With the options in this dialog box, you can cause the event to happen to all particles or to a given number of collisions.

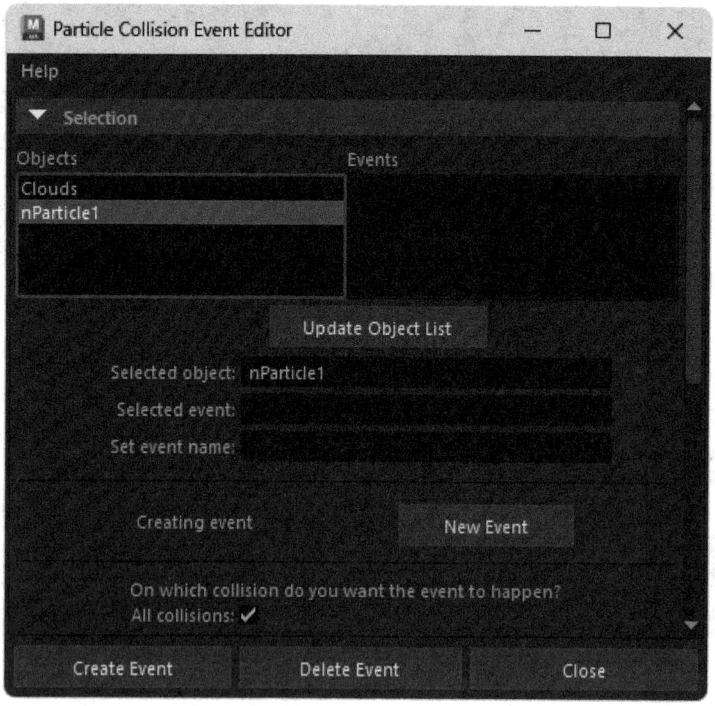

FIGURE 14-32

Particle collision Events dialog box

Assigning a Solver

In order for collisions to happen between objects, the colliding objects must be part of the same solver. You can assign a solver using the Fields/Solvers, Assign Solver menu command. By default all new nParticles and nCloth objects are added to a solver named nucleus1, but there is a New Solver option that lets you create a new independent set of colliding objects.

Creating Soft Body Objects

A soft body object is one that deforms as it comes in contact with forces, much like a pillow. The nParticles, Soft Body menu command causes a selected object to inherit the properties of a soft body object. Soft body objects can be affected by field forces.

Lesson 14.5-Tutorial 1: Enable Particle Collisions

1. Select the File, Open Scene menu command and open the Pinball.mb file.
2. Select the nParticles, Create Emitter menu command and move the emitter to the top of the pinball box.
3. In the Attribute Editor, set the Emitter Type to Directional, the Rate to 10, the Direction Y to –1, the Spread value to 0.25, and the Speed to 20.
4. Create a NURBS sphere with the Create, NURBS Primitives, Sphere menu command. Scale the sphere to fit within the pinball box.
5. Drag the Time Slider to see the particles.

6. Select the sphere object along with the particles and choose the nParticles, Instancer menu command.
7. Select the particles, hold down the Shift key and select the pinball box, and then select the nCloth, Create Passive Collider menu command.
8. Drag the Time Slider to see the particles.

    The particles bounce around the box as they collide with the walls of the pinball box, as shown in Figure 14-33.

9. Select File, Save Scene As and save the file as **Bouncing particles.mb**.

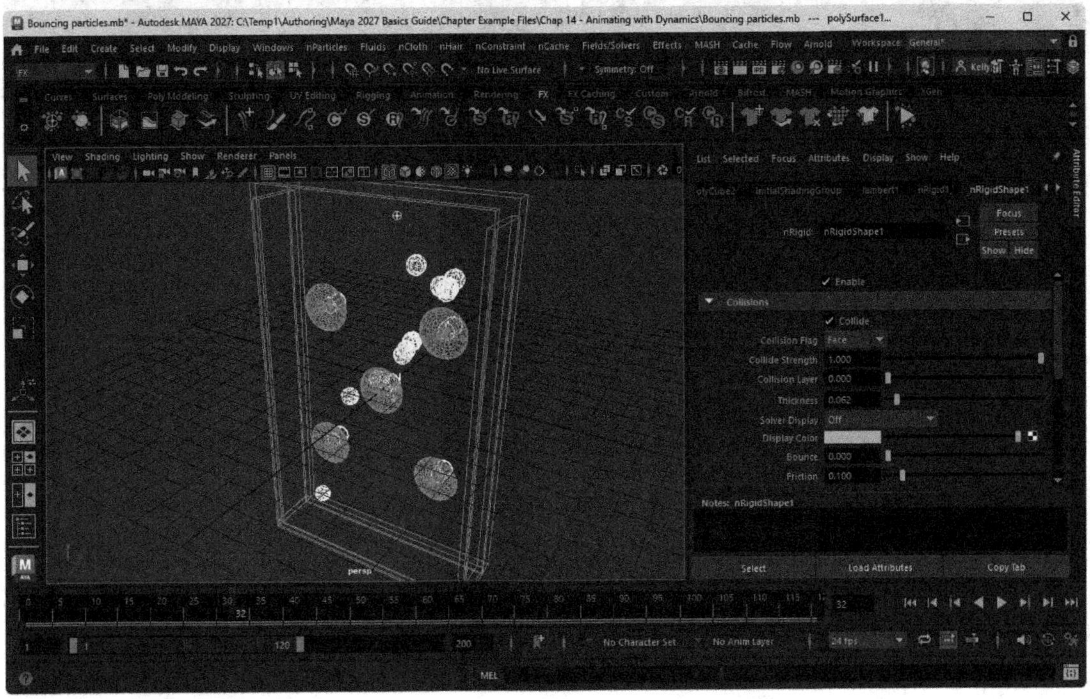

FIGURE 14-33

Colliding particles

Lesson 14.5-Tutorial 2: Add a Collision Event

1. Select the File, Open Scene menu command, and then locate and open the Bouncing particles.mb file.
2. Select the nParticles, Particle Collision Event Editor menu command.

    The Particle Collision Event Editor dialog box opens.

3. Click the New Event button, enable the Emit button, set the Number of Particles to 100 and click the Create Event button.

    The particles emit new particles when they collide with the pinball box object, as shown in Figure 14-34.

4. Select File, Save Scene As and save the file as **Emit on collision.mb**.

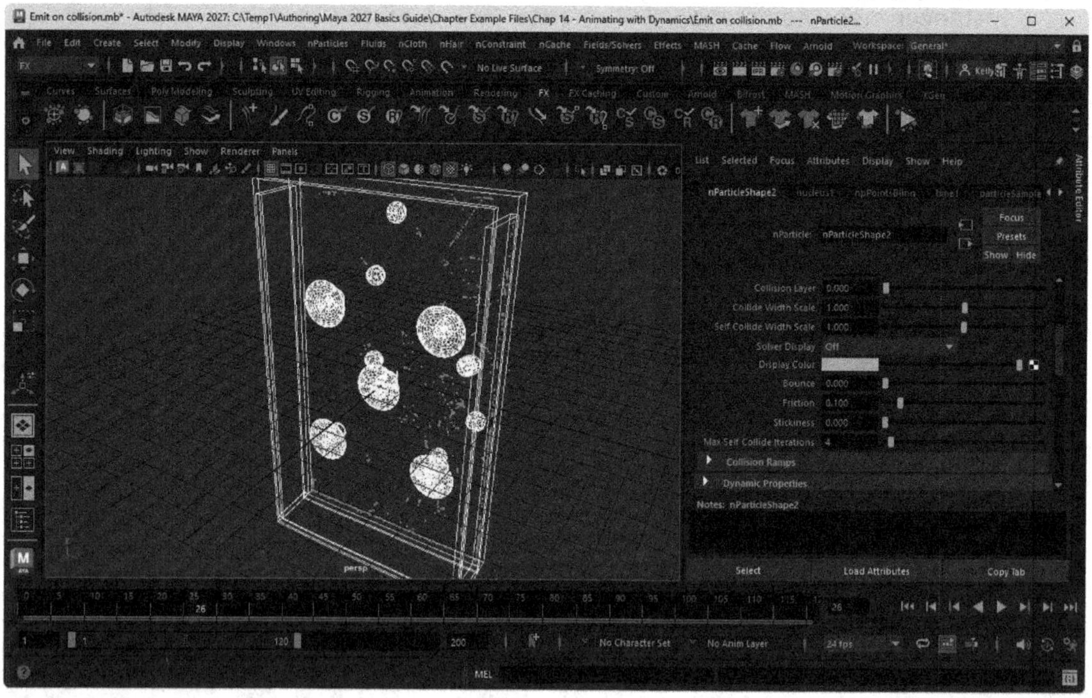

FIGURE 14-34

Emit on collisions

Lesson 14.5-Tutorial 3: Filling a Container with Particles

1. Select the File, Open Scene menu command and open the **Particle container.mb** file.

   This file includes a simple cylinder object with the top faces removed and a plane object.

2. Select both objects and choose the nCloth, Create Passive Collider menu command.
3. Select the nParticles, Create Options, Balls menu command, then choose the nParticles, Create Emitter menu command.
4. Select the nParticle Shape node in the Attribute Editor and set the Radius value in the Particle Size section to 0.035.
5. Open the Collisions section and enable both the Collide and Self Collide options.
6. Drag the Time Slider to see the balls fill the container, as shown in Figure 14-35.
7. Select File, Save Scene As, and save the file as **Filling a container with particles.mb**.

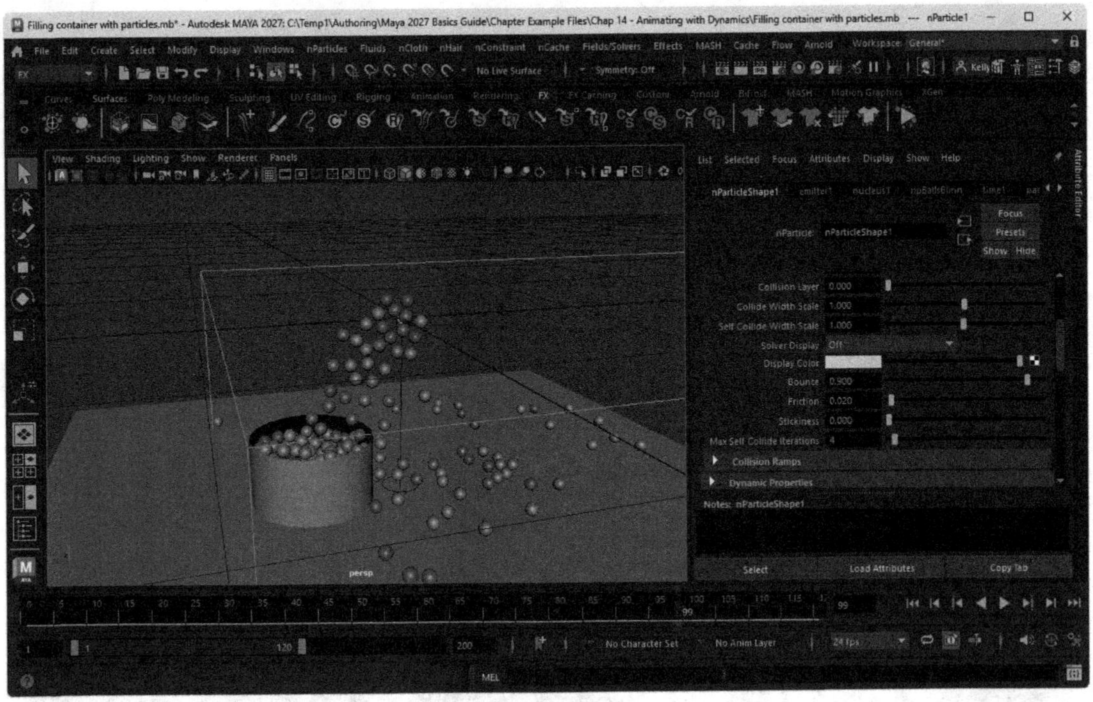

FIGURE 14-35

Filling a container with particles

Lesson 14.5-Tutorial 4: Create Soft Body Objects

1. Create a polygon plane object with the Create, Polygon Primitives, Plane menu command. Set the Width and Height Divisions in the Attribute Editor to 20.
2. Scale the plane object up with the Scale tool.
3. Select the nParticles, Soft Body menu command.
4. Select the plane object and choose the Fields/Solvers, Turbulence menu command.
5. Drag the Time Slider to see the rigid body objects interact.

   The plane object deforms under the Turbulence field, as shown in Figure 14-36.
6. Select File, Save Scene As and save the file as **Soft body.mb**.

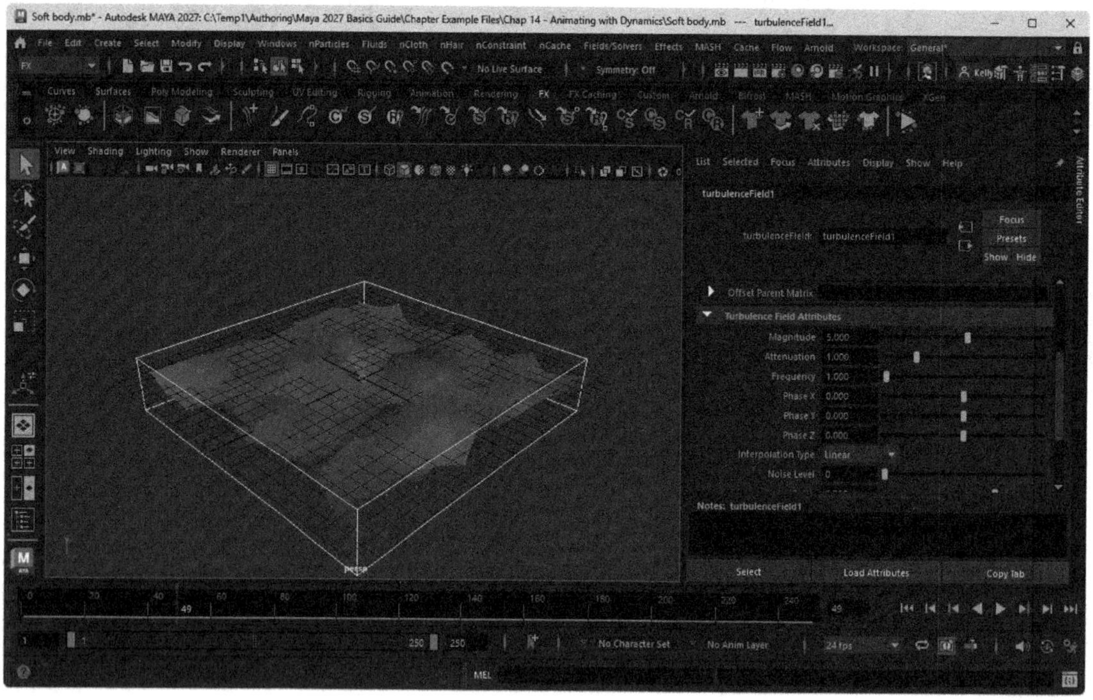

FIGURE 14-36

Soft body

Lesson 14.6: Use Cloth

Each nCloth object that is created automatically has all the controls and properties needed to dynamically simulate its motion. Cloth can require a significant amount of computing power and should be used with restraint. Cloth added to a scene is automatically draped over collision objects.

Viewing Cloth Examples

The nCloth, Get nCloth Example menu command opens a folder in the Content Browser with several nCloth examples. These examples show what is possible with nCloth. Figure 14-37 shows a simple tree with some nCloth leaves falling to the ground.

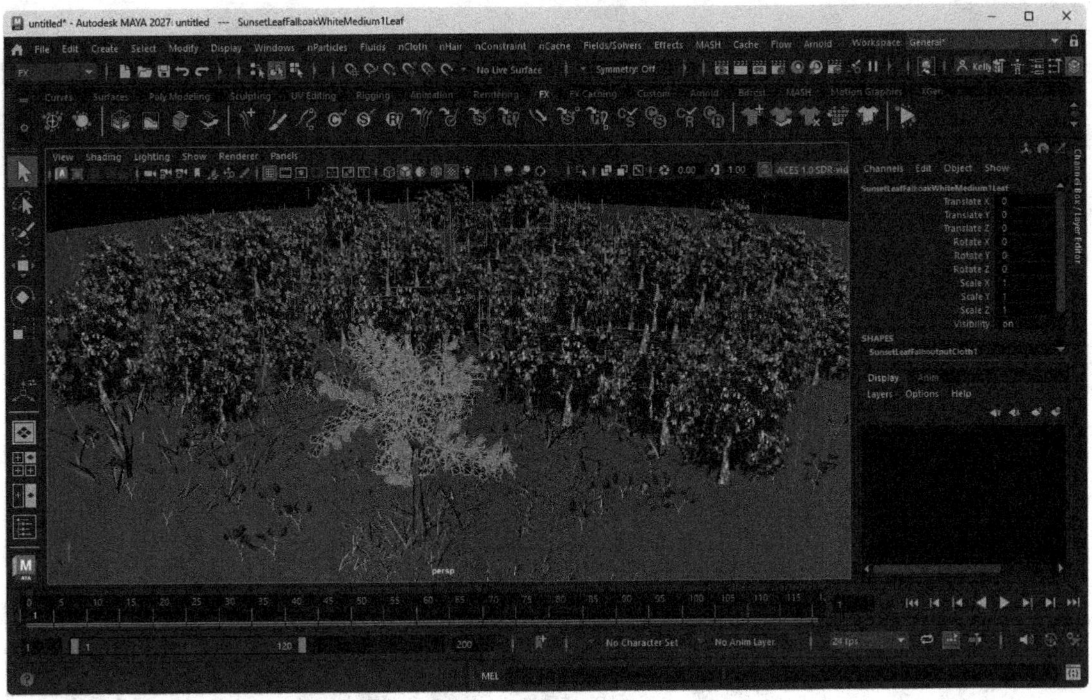

FIGURE 14-37

nCloth example

Creating Cloth

Any selected object can be made into a cloth object using the nCloth, Create nCloth menu command. This command converts the selected object into a cloth object. Cloth objects are automatically tessellated, as shown in Figure 14-38. You can create cloth objects, called *panels*, from a set of curves, and you can stitch several panels together to create a garment. Curves must be co-planar and closed in order to be used to make a panel. Cloth properties can be removed and returned to its original object using the nCloth, Remove nCloth menu command.

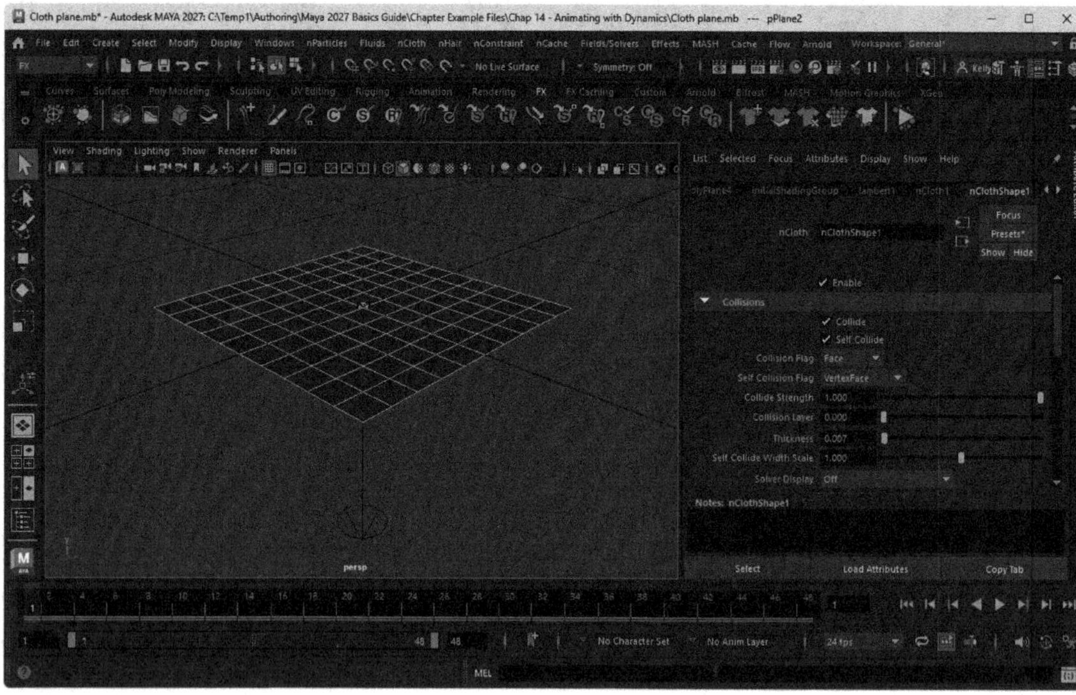

FIGURE 14-38

Cloth object and attributes

Creating a Cloth Collision Object

The dynamics of cloth aren't readily visible until the cloth object is draped over a passive object. To create a passive object to collide with, simply select the object or objects that the cloth will be draped over and choose the nCloth, Create Passive Collider menu command. Once a collision object has been defined, you'll want to create a cache of the draped cloth using the nCache, Create New Cache, nObject menu command. With the animation cached, you can drag the Time Slider and each frame of the cloth simulation is displayed. Figure 14-39 shows a simple cloth plane draped over a sphere passive object.

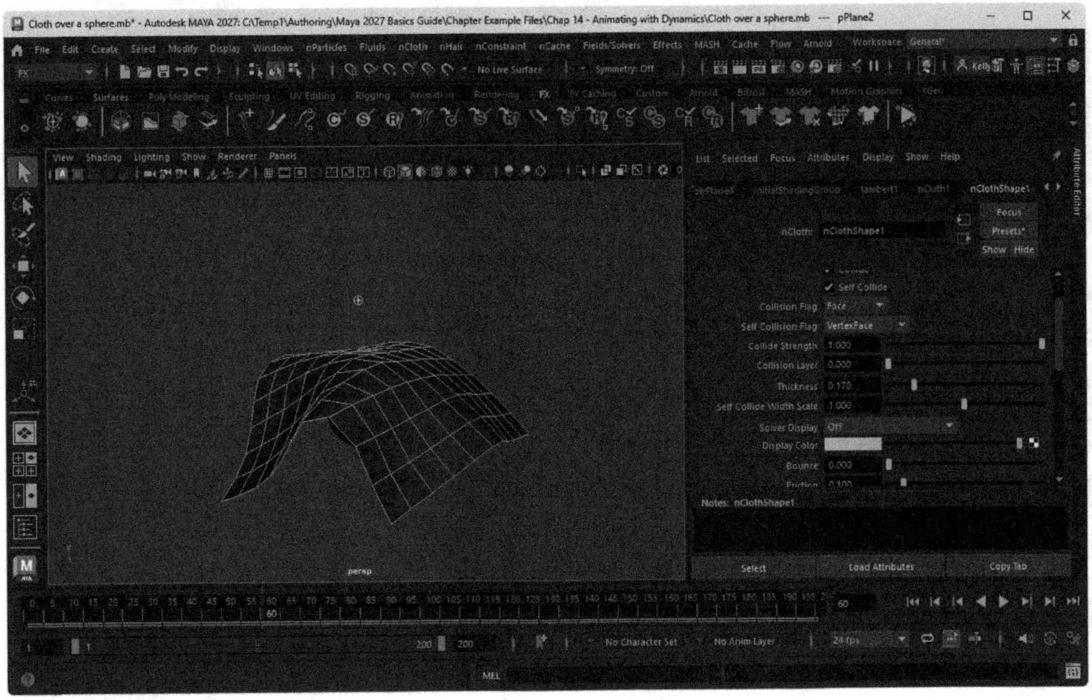

FIGURE 14-39

Cloth plane object draped over a collision sphere

Setting Cloth Object Properties

For the selected cloth object, you can set its physical properties using the nCloth Shape node in the Attribute Editor, as shown in Figure 14-40. The properties found here include Bend Resistance, Bend Rate, Stretch Resistance, Scale, Density, Thickness, Friction, and so on. You can paint cloth properties on the cloth object using the nCloth, Paint Texture Properties tool. Once a cloth property has been changed, you need to delete the current simulation cache before the new dynamic motion is displayed. You can delete the current cache using the nCache, Delete Cache menu command.

FIGURE 14-40

Cloth properties

Lesson 14.6-Tutorial 1: Drape a Tablecloth

1. Select the File, Open Scene menu command, locate and open the Table.mb file.
2. Select the Create, Polygon Primitives, Plane menu command to create a polygon plane object.
3. Move and scale the plane object so it is centered above the table. Be sure to position the plane object so it doesn't intersect with the table.
4. In the Channel Box, click on the polyPlane1 node and change the Subdivisions Width and Height values to 50 each.

   Increasing the resolution of the plane object enables the cloth simulation to better approximate its motion accurately.
5. Select the Cloth menu set from the drop-down list and, with the plane object selected, choose the nCloth, Create nCloth menu command.

   The cloth object is tessellated and divided into triangles.
6. Select the table top object and choose the nCloth, Create Passive Collider menu command.

   Only the table top object was selected in order to speed up the cloth calculations. The more polygons involved in the calculations, the slower it takes to compute a solution.
7. Select the nCache, Create New Cache, nObject menu command.

   The cloth animation of it falling under the effect of gravity is simulated and stored in a cache.
8. In the Animation Controls, click the Step Forward One Frame button several times.

   The plane object slowly descends and drapes over the table.

9. With the plane object selected, open the Attribute Editor and select the cpDefault Property node. Change the U and V Bend Resistance values to 1.0 and the U and V Bend Rate values to 2.0.

   The default cloth material is like a thick rubber, but changing these values makes the cloth act more like fabric.

10. Drag the Time Slider back to Frame 1 and select the nCache, Delete Cache menu command. Then select the nCache, Create New Cache, nObject menu command again.

    Because the default simulation is still saved in the cache, you need to delete the cache and rewind the frames before the updated simulation is displayed. Figure 14-41 shows the resulting tablecloth draped over a table.

11. Select File, Save Scene As and save the file as **Table with tablecloth.mb**.

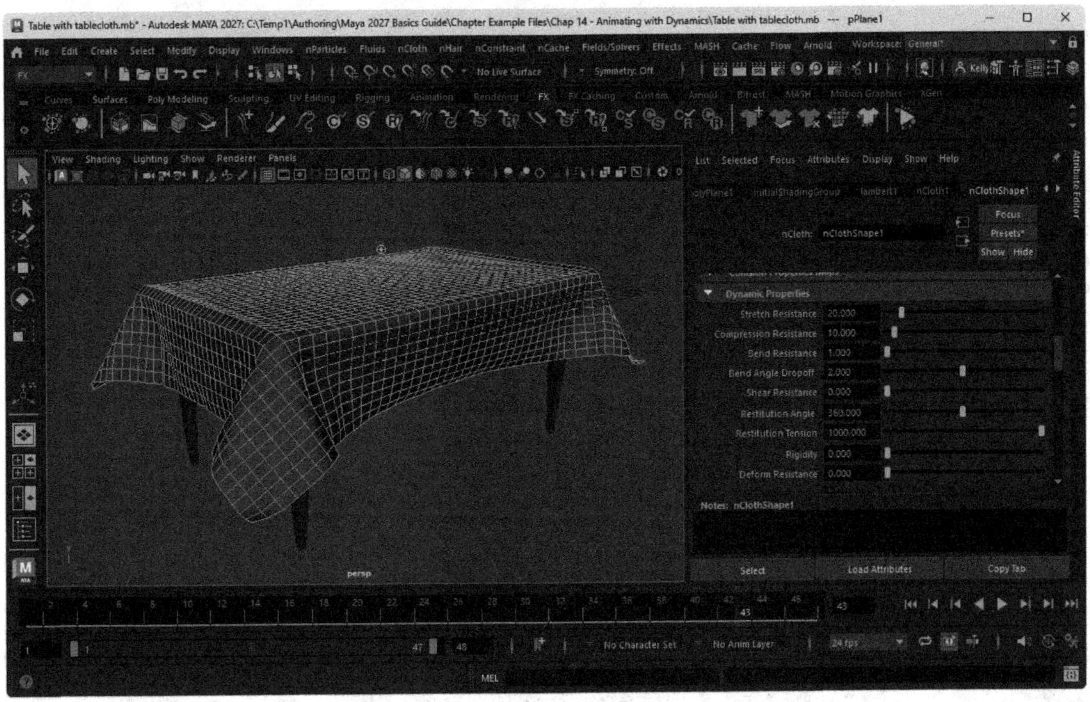

FIGURE 14-41

Table with tablecloth

Lesson 14.7: Constrain Motion

To control the simulations created from interactive objects, Maya includes several different constraint types that are useful for resisting motions. The constraint types include Component, Component to Component, Force Field, Point to Surface, Slide on Surface, Tearable Surface and Transform Constraint. They can all be selected from the nConstraint menu.

Adding Constraints

You can use **constraints** to limit the motion of dynamic objects. The nConstraint, Component menu command creates a constraint for the selected component. The Create Component nConstraints Options dialog box, shown in Figure 14-42, includes an option for selecting the Constraint Type. The options are Stretch or Bend.

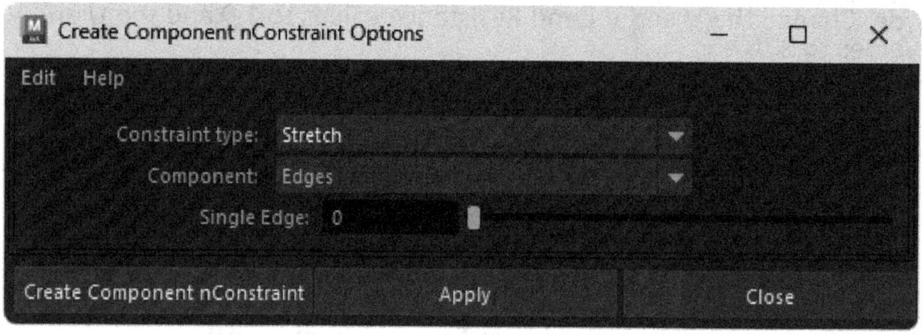

FIGURE 14-42

nConstraint Options dialog box

Creating Component Constraints

The nConstraint, Component to Component menu command connects the selected component of one dynamic object to a component of another dynamic object keeping them together. The dynamic objects can be either an nCloth object or a Passive Collider object. The object pivots around the connected components at a distance defined by the line between the two components. This is used to secure an end of a dynamic object from moving by linking it to a passive object, such as a flag to a flagpole. You can also use this constraint to connect several components together so they move together, as shown in Figure 14-43. To select components on two separate objects, select both objects and then click the Select by Component mode button on the Status Line and select components on both objects while holding down the Shift key.

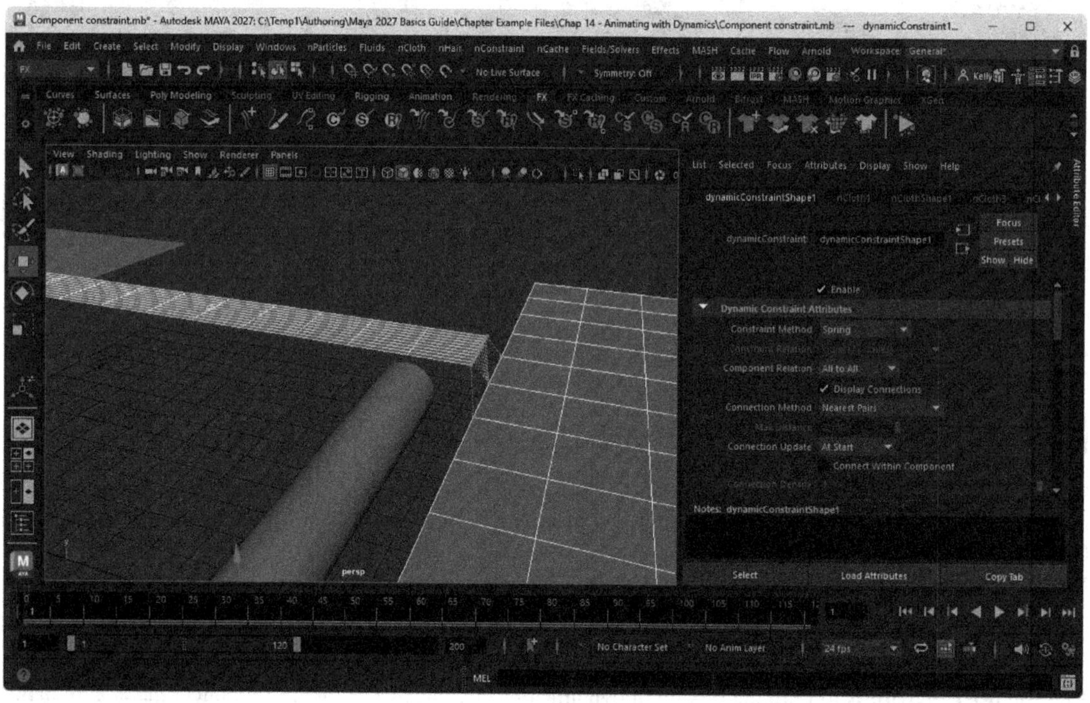

FIGURE 14-43

Component to component constraint

The nConstraint, Point to Component menu command connects the selected components of one dynamic object to the surface of a non-dynamic object. You can also use the Slide on Surface menu command which allows the connected components to move over the surface of the connected object.

Locking Components in Space

The nConstraint menu also includes an option to lock the selected components of a dynamic object to a location in space preventing them from moving with the Transform Constraint menu command. Within the dynamic Constraint Shape node are settings for the constraint Strength and Strength Dropoff.

Creating Springs

You can use the nParticles, Springs menu command on two selected objects to create springs between the two. This causes the two objects to move together and forces them toward each other as they are pulled apart. One of the objects must be a soft body object or a particle set. Springs are displayed as dashed lines between the two objects. Figure 14-44 shows the springs between two polygon objects. Springs act as a soft constraint between connected objects. They are useful to keep a particle set together.

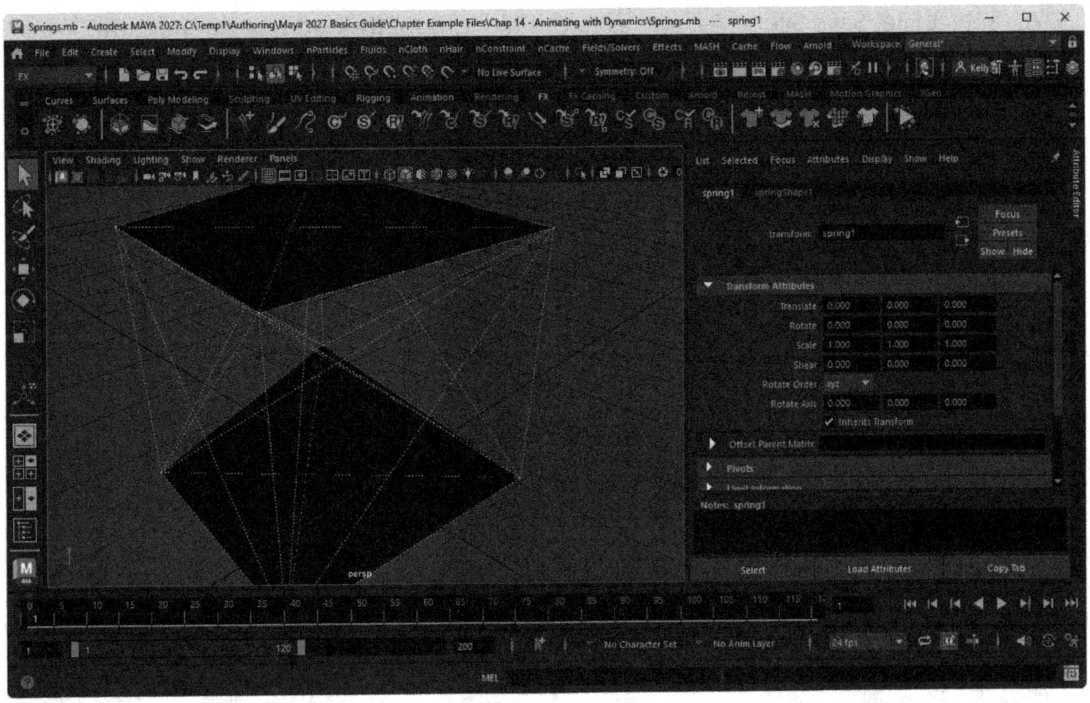

FIGURE 14-44

Springs between two plane objects

Lesson 14.7-Tutorial 1: Constrain a Flag to a Pole

1. Select the File, Open Scene menu command, locate and open the **Flag on a pole.mb** file.

   This file includes a simple polygon plane object with a flag texture next to a cylinder.

2. Select the flag object and choose the nCloth, Create nCloth menu command, then select the pole object and choose the nCloth, Create Passive Collider menu command.
3. Zoom in on the top corner of the flag near the pole. Drag over both the flag and the pole object to select them both, then click on the Select by Component button on the Status Line to enter component mode.
4. Select the top corner vertex on the flag, hold down the Shift key and select the nearest vertex on the pole, then choose the nConstraint, Component to Component menu command.
5. Pan the view downward to the lower left corner of the flag. Switch back to Object mode and select the flag and the pole, then choose the Select by Component option again and choose the flag's lower left corner vertex and its closest vertex on the pole and choose the nConstraint, Component to Component menu command.

   This creates constraints between the selected vertices tying the flag to the pole.
6. Drag the Timeline to see the flag flow under the effect of gravity, except where it is constrained to the pole, as shown in Figure 14-45.
7. Select File, Save Scene As, and save the file as **Constrained flag on pole.mb**.

FIGURE 14-45

Constrained flag on a pole

Lesson 14.8: Use Fluids

Each fluid object that is created automatically has all the controls and properties needed to dynamically simulate its motion. Fluids, like Cloth, require a significant amount of computing power and should be used with restraint. Fluids include all the characteristics to create waves, splashes, and settling. You can also use fluids to create gaseous phenomenon such as clouds, fire, and explosions.

Creating a Fluid Container

The first step to create a fluid effect is to create a container. This is the area where the fluids can exist and provides a boundary for the fluid. Each cell of the container is called a **voxel**. The number of voxels in a container determines the resolution of the fluid object. The Fluids menu (located in the FX menu set) includes commands for creating 2D and 3D containers. A 2D container has only one row of voxels. You can make a fluid collide with geometry objects by selecting both the fluid and the object and choosing the Fluids, Make Collide menu command.

Creating a Fluid Emitter

A **fluid emitter** is similar to a particle emitter, except it is the source of the fluid. It must be located within the container. Dragging the Time Slider causes the defined fluid to flow into the existing container. As the fluid collides with the walls of the container, it flows back and forth as the container is slowly filled. You can add an emitter to a selected container using the Fluids, Add/Edit Contents, Emitter menu command. There are also menu commands for creating a container and an emitter at once. Figure 14-46 shows a container being filled with fluid. Various emitter types are available including Omni, Surface, Curve, and Volume. Objects can also be used as emitters.

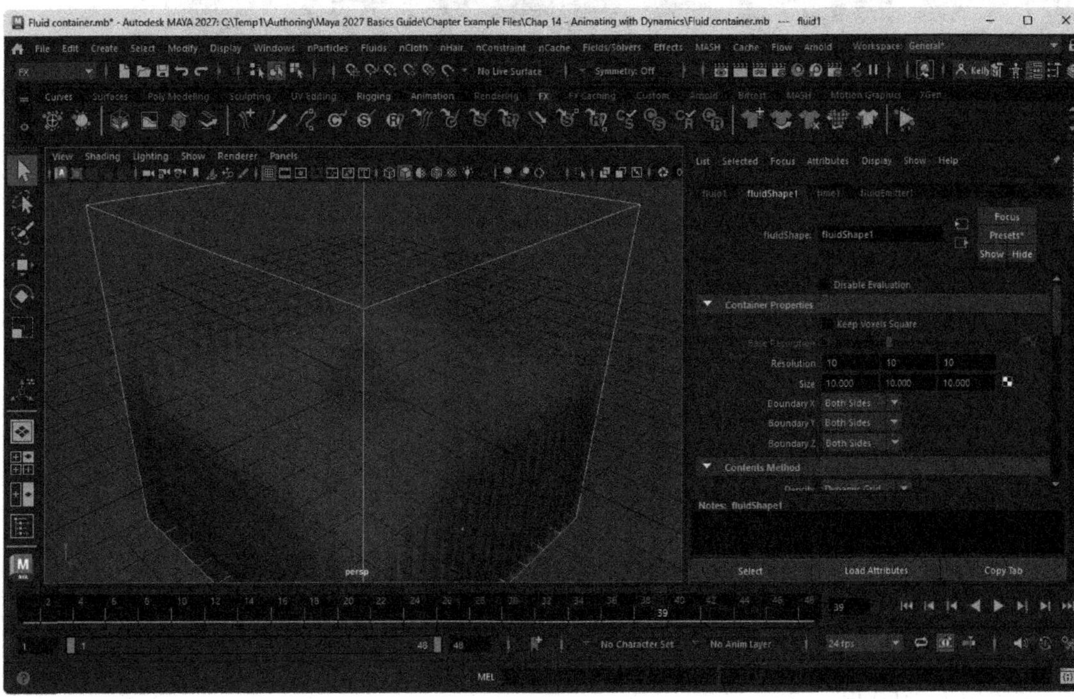

FIGURE 14-46

A 3D container being filled with fluid

Changing Fluid Properties

The type of fluid or gas that is created from a fluid emitter depends on the fluid's properties. The properties available for fluids are located in the Attribute Editor and include Density, Viscosity, Friction, Buoyancy, Dissipation, Turbulence, Temperature, Fuel, Color, Opacity, and so on. Once a property has changed, you can see the updated results immediately by dragging the Time Slider. You can also change the general shape of the fluid by scaling and sizing the container.

Creating Oceans and Ponds

The Fluids menu includes two specialized water objects for creating oceans and ponds. The ocean object is created using the Fluids, Ocean, Create Ocean menu command, and similar commands for a pond object. You can add a preview pane to an ocean object to see its effect in a local area. The Create Wake menu command adds waves, turbulence, and/or ripples to the ocean and pond objects. The menus can also add floating objects, buoys, and boats to the scene. Figure 14-47 shows an ocean object with a preview pane and a buoy object.

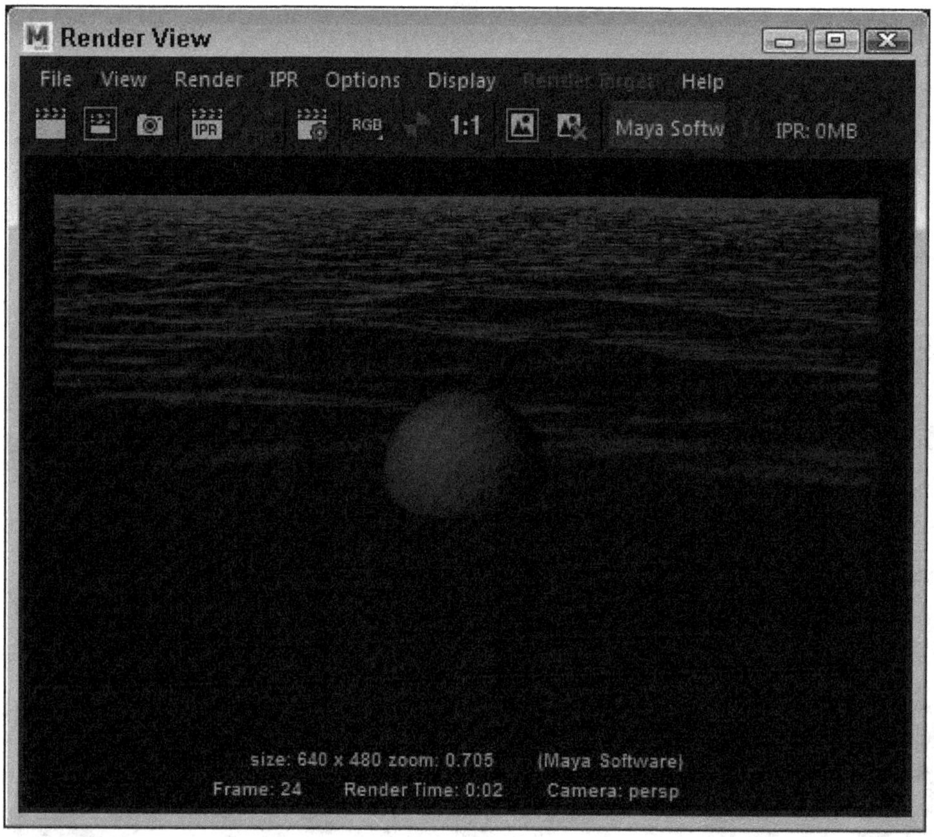

FIGURE 14-47

Ocean object with buoy

Lesson 14.8-Tutorial 1: Fill a Container

1. Select the FX menu set from the drop-down list.
2. Select the Fluids, 3D Container menu command, then select the Fluids, Add/Edit Contents, Emitter menu command and position the emitter inside the container.

   A cubic container with an emitter is added to the scene.
3. Open the Attribute Editor and select the fluidEmitter1 node. Change the Density/Voxel/Sec value to 2,000, and then enable the Emit Fluid Color option and set the Fluid Color to a dark red.

   When the Emit Fluid Color option is selected, a dialog box appears asking if you want to set the color of the dynamic grid. Press the Set to Dynamic button.

4. In the Attribute Editor, select the fluidShape1 node. In the Dynamic Simulation section, change the Gravity value to -9.8, and the Viscosity to 0.25.

   Making the Gravity value negative reverses the direction of gravity and the increased viscosity causes the fluid to move around less.

5. Drag the Time Slider to see the fluid move within the container.

   The fluid moves downward under the effect of gravity and then fills the container, as shown in Figure 14-48.

6. Select File, Save Scene As and save the file as **Fluid container and emitter.mb**.

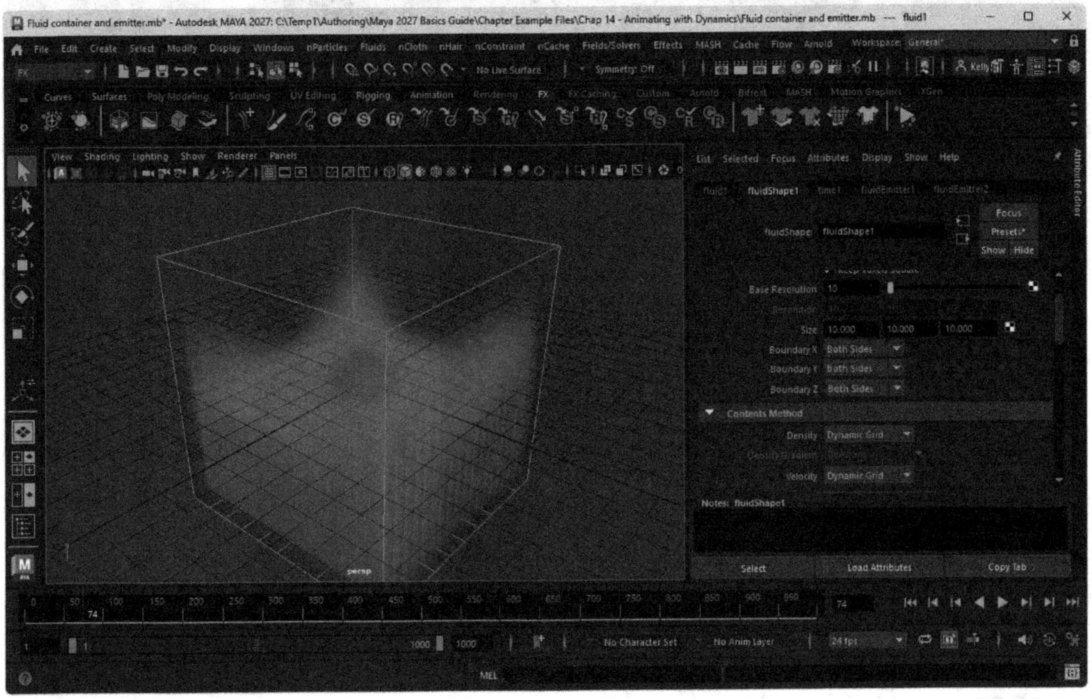

FIGURE 14-48

Fluid filling a container

Lesson 14.8-Tutorial 2: Create a Pond with Ripples

1. Select the FX menu set from the drop-down list.
2. Select the Fluids, Pond, Create Pond menu command.

   A pond object is added to the scene.

3. Select the Fluid Effects, Pond, Create Wake menu command.

   A spherical icon is added to the center of the pond object.

4. Drag the Time Slider to Frame 48.

   Ripples appear in the pond, as shown in Figure 14-49.

5. Select File, Save Scene As and save the file as **Pond with ripples.mb**.

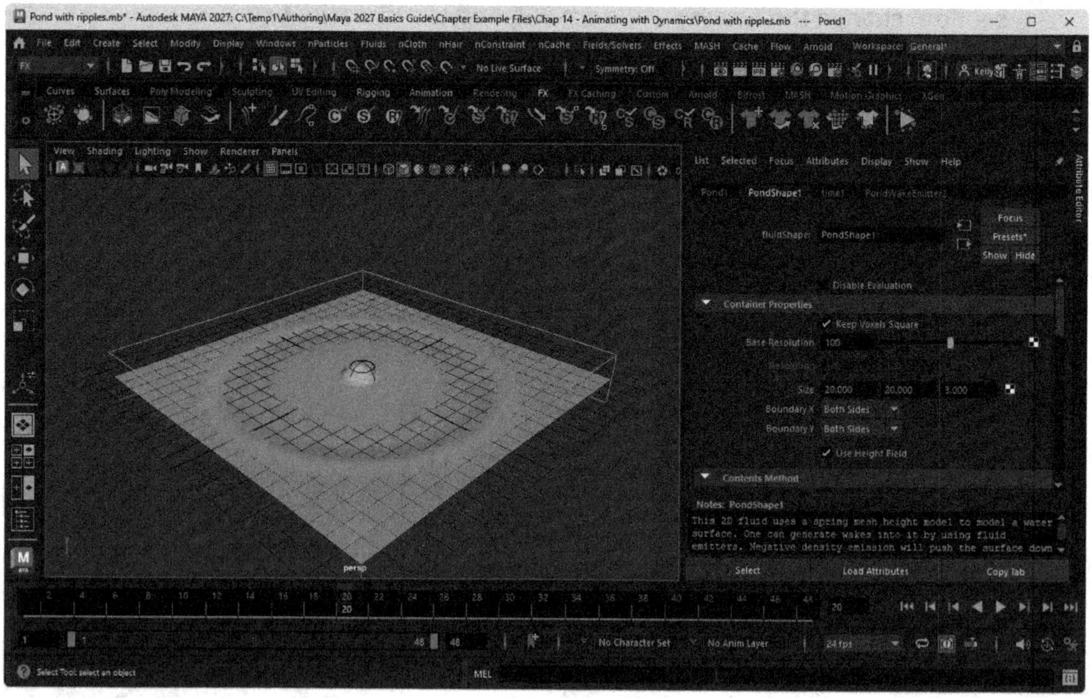

FIGURE 14-49

Pond with ripples

Lesson 14.9: Create Effects

Maya includes a number of special effects that you can apply directly to an object or a selection of components. These effects are all found in the Effects menu and include Fire, Smoke, Fireworks, Lightning, Shatter, Curve Flow, and Surface Flow.

Creating Fire and Smoke

You can add the Fire effect to the selected object using the Effects, Fire menu command. The Fire Options dialog box includes settings for Fire Density, Intensity, Fire Spread, and Turbulence, as shown in Figure 14-50. A plane object on fire is shown in Figure 14-51. Similar to the Fire effect is the Smoke effect, but it requires a sprite image to be rendered. Some sample sprite images appear in the Gifts/smoke directory.

Note

The Smoke effect requires a series of sprite images be loaded into the source images directory for the current project.

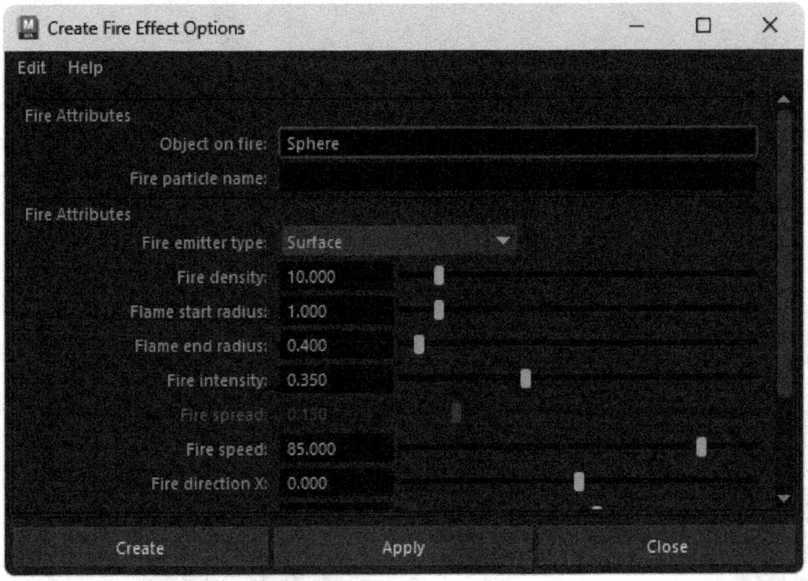

FIGURE 14-50

Fire effect options

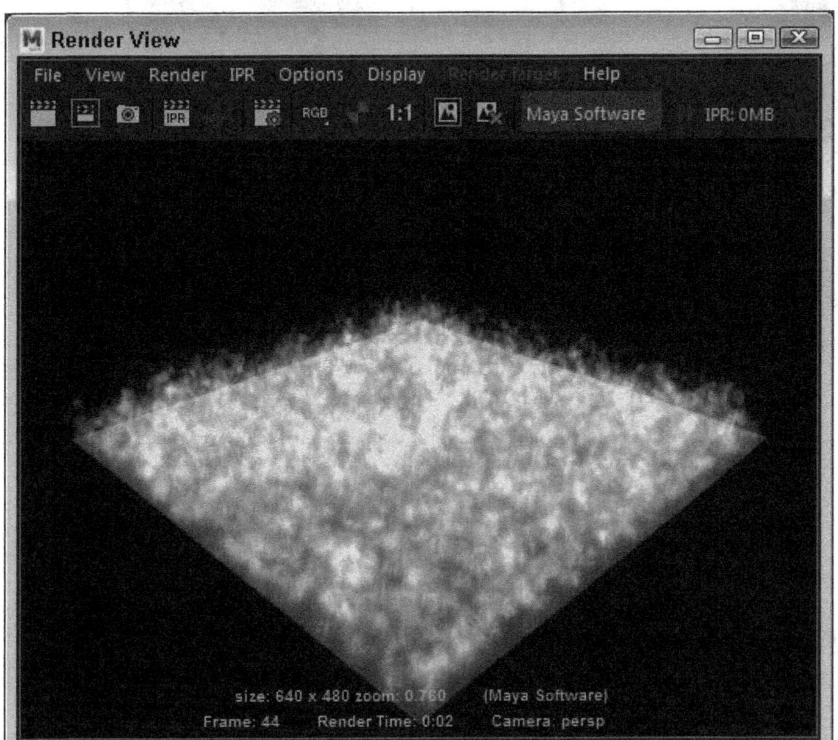

FIGURE 14-51

Rendered fire

Creating Fireworks

The Fireworks effect doesn't require an object be selected. The Effects, Create Fireworks adds a simple emitter to the scene. Dragging the Time Slider launches and displays the fireworks. Use the various attribute nodes to change the fireworks' colors and attributes. Figure 14-52 shows a rendered firework.

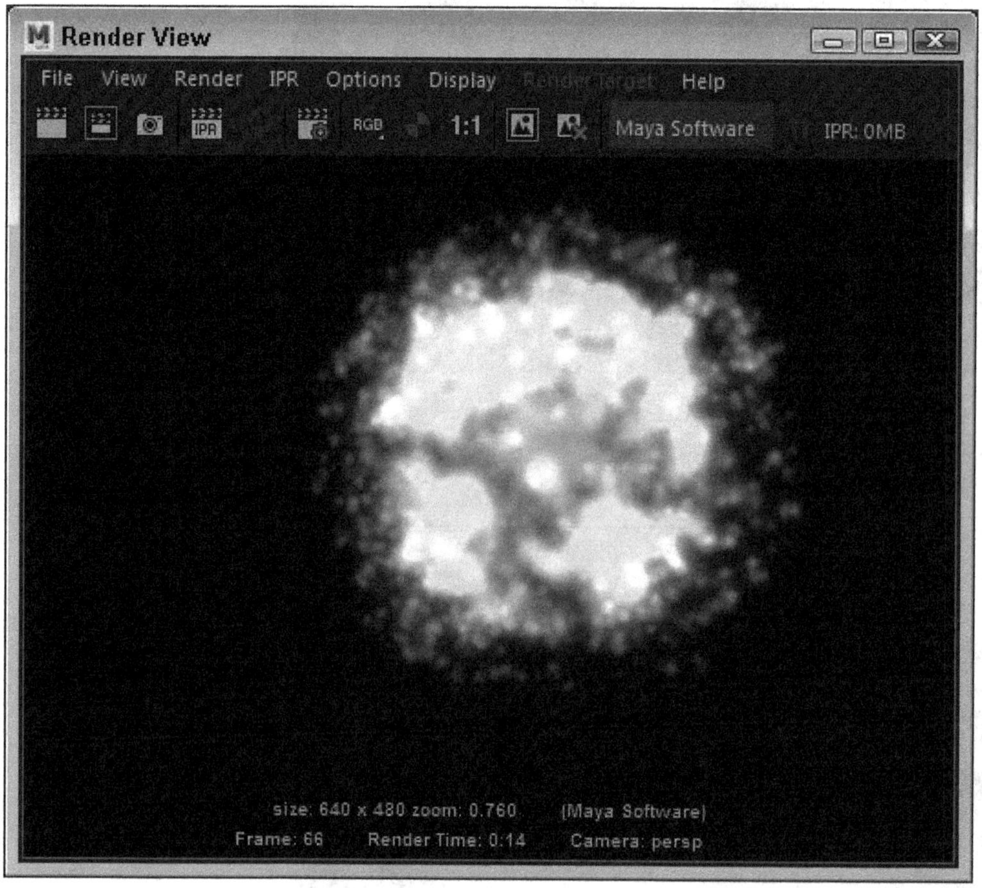

FIGURE 14-52

Fireworks

Creating Lightning

The Create Lightning effect can extend between several objects. The Lightning Options dialog box lets you specify whether the lightning spreads between all objects, in order, or from the first object. You can also specify the thickness, spread, and glow intensity of the lightning. Figure 14-53 shows a lightning arc between two cone objects.

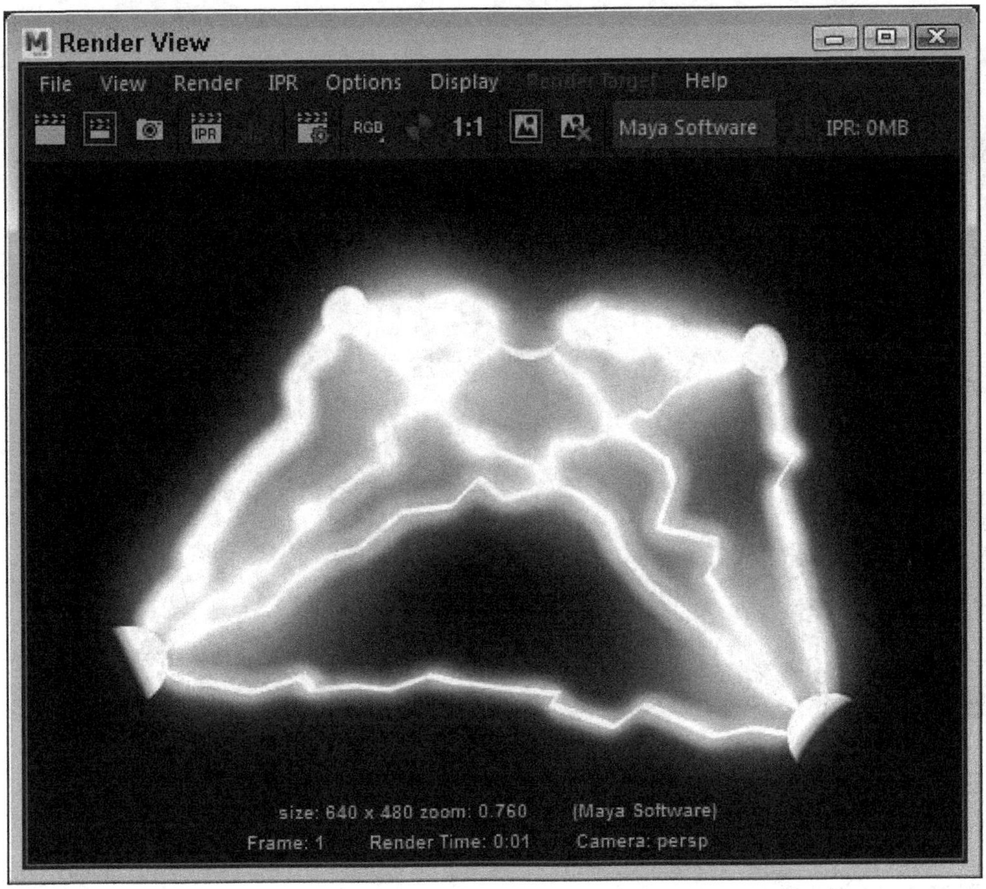

FIGURE 14-53

A lightning arc

Shattering Objects

The Create Shatter effect divides the selected objects into multiple separate objects, as shown in Figure 14-54. The Create Shatter Effect Options dialog box includes three tabs for Surface Shatter, Solid Shatter, and Crack Shatter. You can also specify the number of pieces that the object is broken into and the jaggedness of the shards.

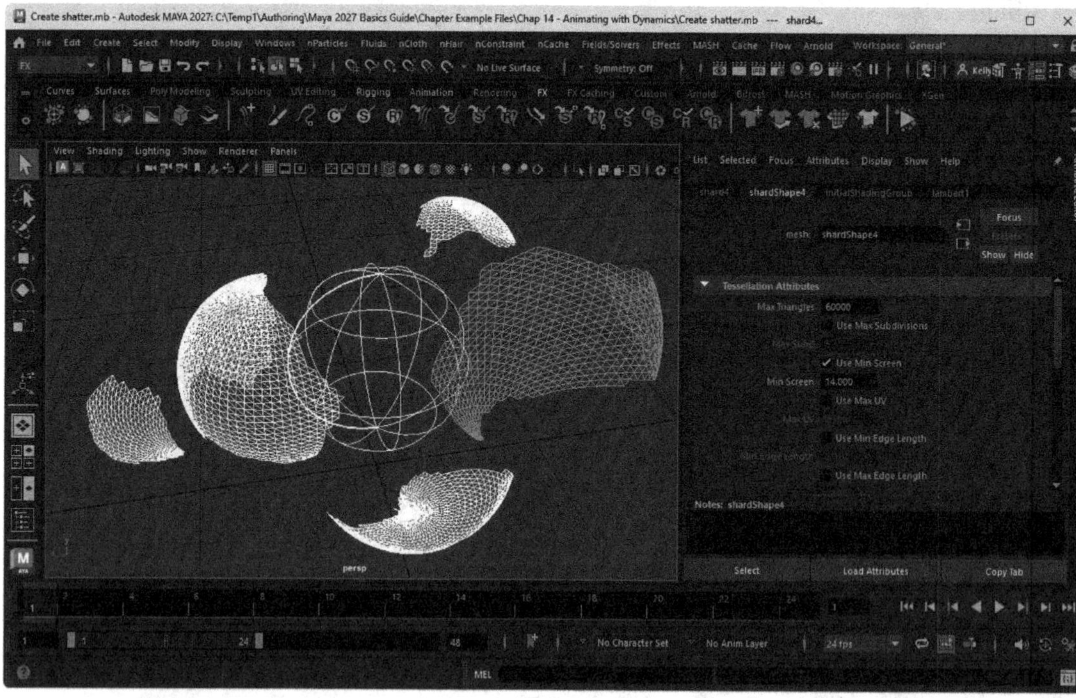

FIGURE 14-54

Shattered objects

Flowing Along a Curve

The Effects, Flow, Create Curve Flow effect lets you select a NURBS curve, and particle emitters are placed along the curve causing particles to follow the curve, as shown in Figure 14-55. Attributes for this effect include an Emission Rate, Particle Lifespan, and Speed. The Create Surface Flow effect allows particles to flow over a NURBS surface.

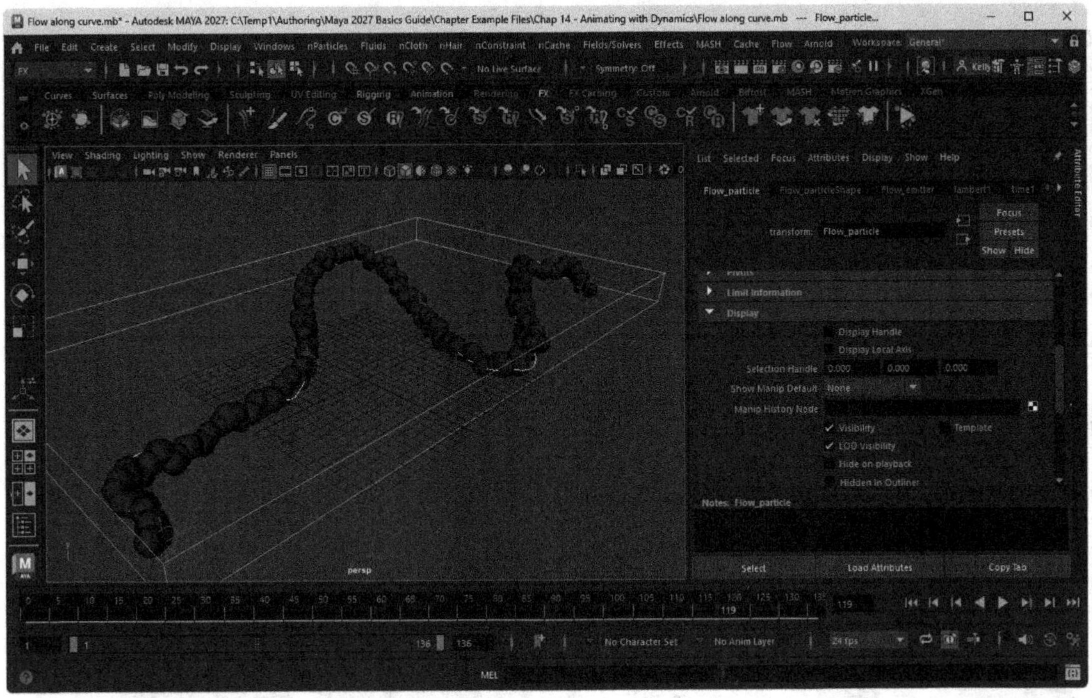

FIGURE 14-55

Particles flowing along a curve

Lesson 14.9-Tutorial 1: Create a Fire Effect

1. Create a polygon cylinder object with the Create, Polygon Primitives, Cylinder menu command.
2. Scale and rotate the cylinder object with the Scale tool to look like a log.
3. Select the Effects, Fire menu command.
4. Drag the Time Slider to see the flames rise.

   The cylinder object is engulfed in fire, as shown in Figure 14-56.
5. Select File, Save Scene As and save the file as **Log on fire.mb**.

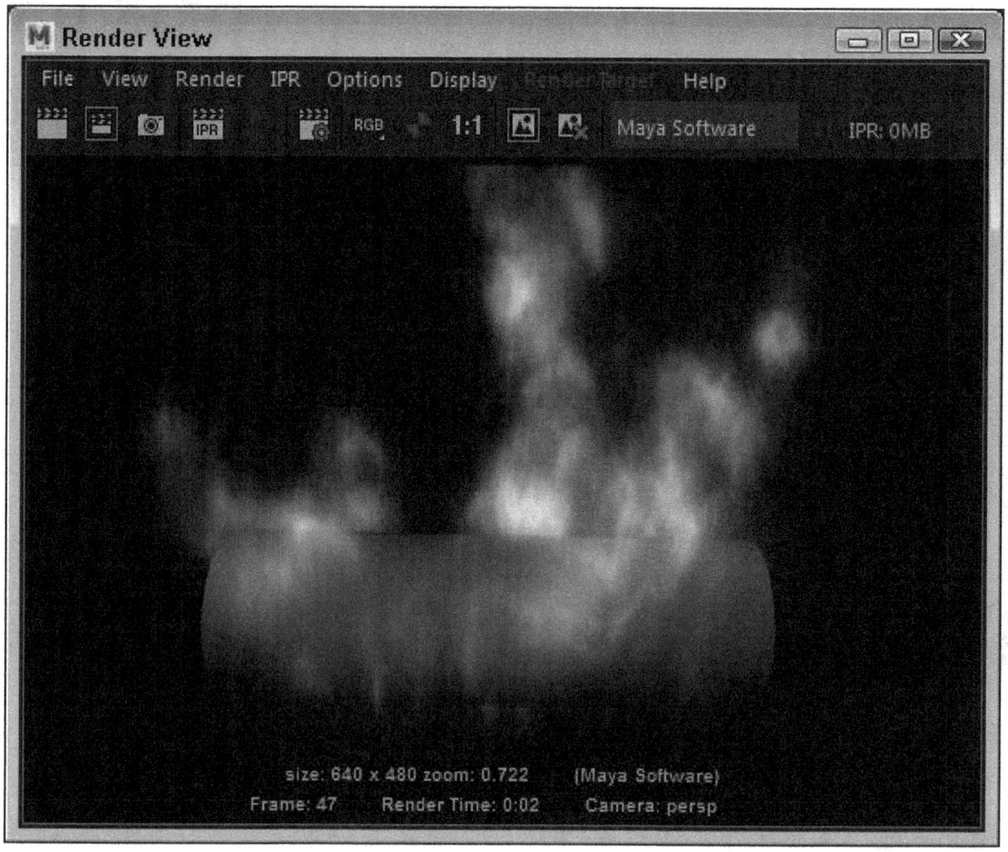

FIGURE 14-56
Fire effect

Lesson 14.9-Tutorial 2: Create Fireworks

1. Select the Effects, Fireworks menu command.
2. Enter a value of 200 in the End frame field for the Range Slider.
3. Drag the Range Slider to show the full 200 frames.
4. Click the Play Forwards button to see the fireworks.
   The fireworks explode on the view panel, as shown in Figure 14-57.
5. Select File, Save Scene As and save the file as **Fireworks.mb**.

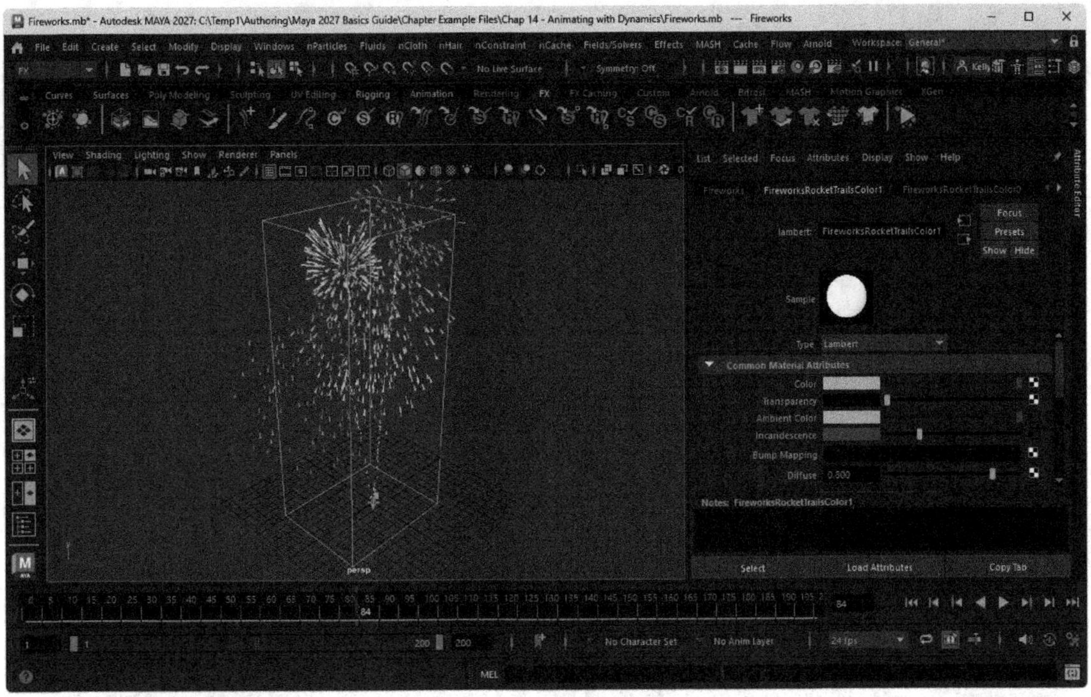

FIGURE 14-57

Fireworks

Lesson 14.9-Tutorial 3: Create Lightning

1. Create five NURBS sphere objects with the Create, NURBS Primitives, Sphere menu command.
2. Use the Move tool to move the five spheres away from each other and the center sphere above the rest.
3. Select all of the spheres and choose the Effects, Lightning menu command.

    Lightning objects and arcs connect each of the spheres, as shown in Figure 14-58.
4. Select File, Save Scene As and save the file as **Lightning.mb**.

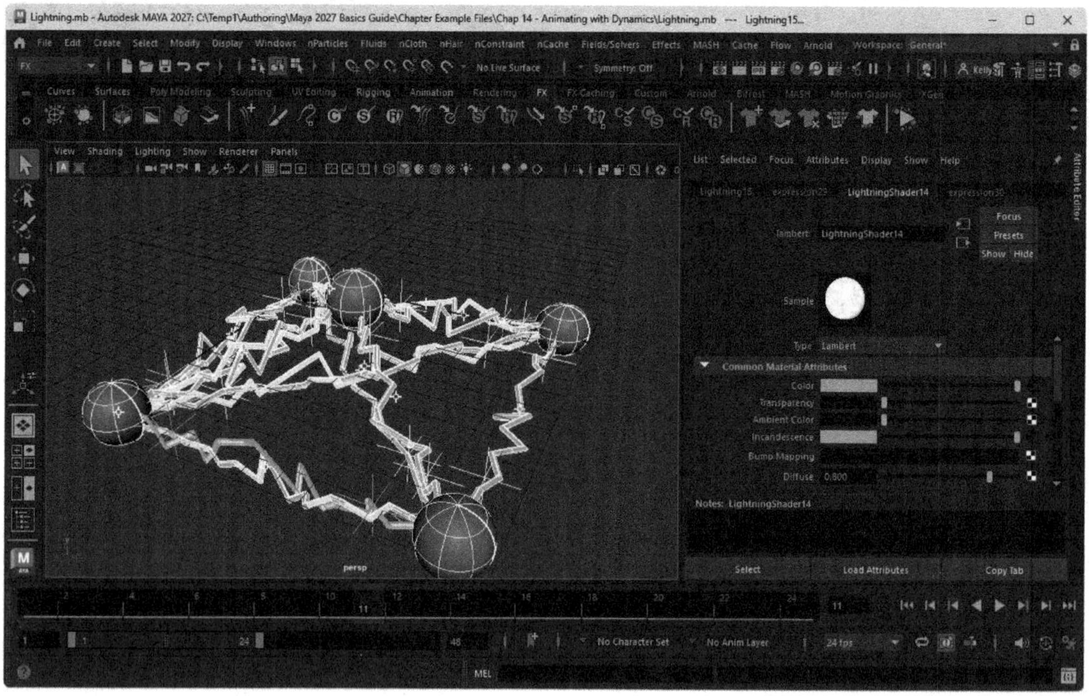

FIGURE 14-58

Lightning

Lesson 14.9-Tutorial 4: Create Curve Flow

1. Select the Create, Pencil Curve Tool menu command and draw in the view panel.
2. With the curve selected, choose the Effects, Create Curve Flow menu command.
3. In the Channel Box, set the Emission Rate to 1000.
4. Drag the Time Slider.

   The particles flow along the curve, as shown in Figure 14-59.
5. Select File, Save Scene As, and save the file as **Curve flow.mb**.

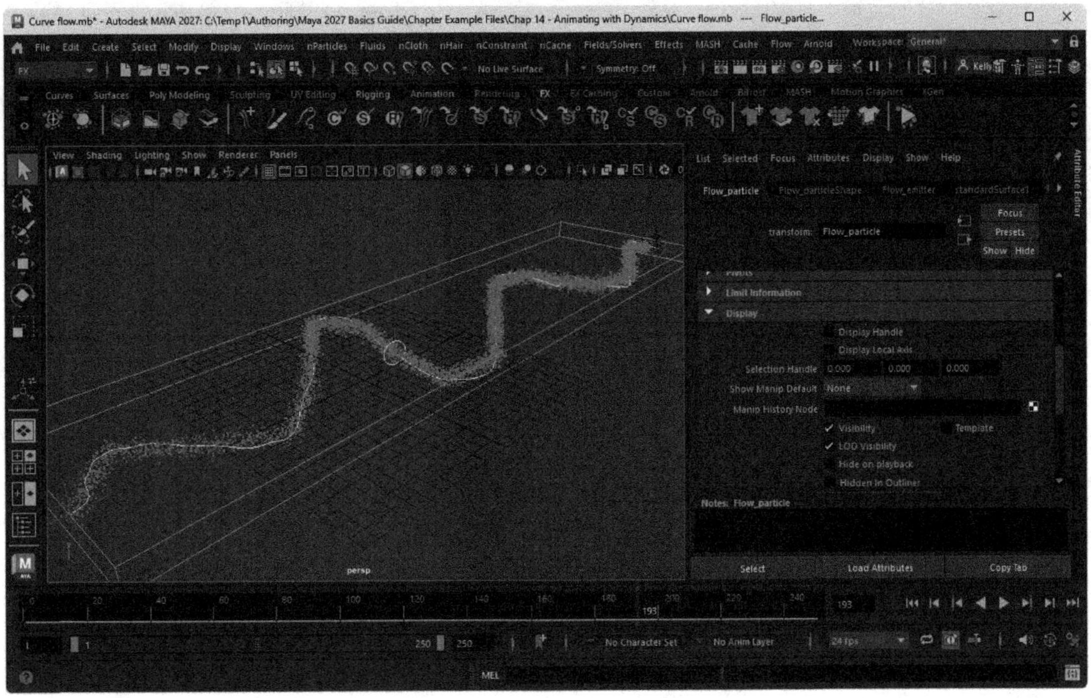

FIGURE 14-59

Curve flow

Chapter Summary

This chapter covers the basics of animating with dynamics. Creating and manipulating particles was discussed, including the various particle types, and particle attributes. You can use objects as particles with the Instancing feature. An emitter is a source that the particles start from. Several emitter types are available, and objects can also act as particle emitters. Once a particle system is added to the scene, its motion is controlled using fields and goals. Animating rigid body objects is possible by defining the active and passive rigid bodies in the scene. Rigid body animations can also be created using the MASH system. You can make particles collide with each other and with objects in the scene. Cloth is a specialized type of dynamic object that drapes over passive objects. Using constraints, you can link objects that are moving dynamically to one another or to constrained components and surfaces. Fluid objects are created using an emitter within a container. Ocean and pond objects are specialized fluid objects that you can create in Maya. The Effects features create special effects such as fire, lightning, and particle flow.

What You Have Learned

In this chapter, you learned

* How to create a set of particles.
* How to set the particle count.
* How to set the particle lifespan and render type.
* How to create particle instances.
* How to cycle through different particle instances.
* How to create an emitter.

* How to change the emitter type.
* How to use an object as an emitter.
* How to add a field to the scene and connect an object to it.
* How to change field attributes.
* How to create a goal.
* How to define active and passive rigid body objects.
* How to animate a scene of rigid bodies using fields.
* How to create a MASH Network.
* How to enable dynamics in a MASH Network.
* How to add Collider Objects and Fields to a MASH Network.
* How to enable particle collisions.
* How to respond to a collision event.
* How to create a soft body object.
* How to create and define cloth.
* How to specify a cloth collision object.
* How to constrain motion with constraints.
* How to use component and surface constraints.
* How to create fluid containers and emitters.
* How to change fluid properties.
* How to create ocean and pond objects.
* How to create fire and smoke.
* How to create fireworks and lightning.
* How to shatter objects.

Key Terms From This Chapter

* **Dynamics.** A type of animation where the keyframes are computed using physics calculations after assigning physical properties to the scene objects.
* **Particles.** A collection of small objects that act together as a single unit.
* **Lifespan.** The number of frames that a particle exists in the scene.
* **Instance.** An object that is used in place of a particle.
* **Emitter.** An icon of objects that is the source of the particles.

* **Field.** An icon in the scene that represents a physical force, such as gravity or drag.

* **Goal.** An object in the scene that a particle system is attracted towards.

* **MASH System.** A system that allows the creation of distributed objects and rigid body dynamics.

* **Collider Object.** An object that is allowed to collide with other objects in the scene during a simulation.

* **Event.** An action that occurs in the scene that spawns more particles, such as a collision.

* **Rigid body object.** A solid object that doesn't deform when it collides with other objects, such as a brick.

***Soft body object.** An object that deforms when it collides with other objects, such as a pillow.

* **Constraint.** An icon that binds objects to a physical force that limits their motion, such as a hinge.

* **Cloth.** A specialized object type that simulates the dynamic interactions of cloth.

* **Cloth collision object.** An object that a cloth object drapes over.

* **Fluid container.** A container that defines the boundaries of a fluid.

* **Voxel.** A single cell of a fluid; used to compute fluid dynamics.

* **Fluid emitter.** An icon that marks the source of the fluid.

Chapter 15

Rendering a Scene

IN THIS CHAPTER

- 15.1 Configure the render process.
- 15.2 Use special rendering features.
- 15.3 Use the Render View window.
- 15.4 Create a final render.
- 15.5 Render with Maya Vector.
- 15.6 Render with Arnold.
- 15.7 Use Arnold Materials.
- 15.8 Use Arnold Lights and Physical Sky.

After you've modeled and animated your scene, you're ready for the rendering process. **Rendering** is where the software computes all of the colors, highlights, shadows, and motions of all the objects in the scene to produce an image or a movie file.

You can render your scenes using several methods, including software, hardware, vector, and Arnold. The Render, Render Using menu command allows you to choose which render engine to use.

Before rendering, you'll need to configure the renderer. You can do this in the **Render Settings dialog box,** which you can open using Windows, Rendering Editors, Render Settings menu command or in the Render menu. The Render Settings dialog box includes settings for the path and name of the render file. You can also set the destination file format and the image resolution.

The Render Settings dialog box includes multiple panels with settings for the rendering engine that is selected. For the software rendering solution, you can enable special rendering features such as **raytracing, motion blur,** and environment **fog**.

You can preview your renders using the Render View window, which opens automatically when you use the Render, Render Current Frame menu command. The Render View window also includes an interactive mode known as **Interactive Photorealistic Rendering** (IPR). Using this mode, you can get automatic scene updates as the lighting and shading attributes are changed.

The Render, Batch Render menu command renders the selected view panel as a background task using the settings found in the Render Settings dialog box.

The **Maya Vector** rendering method strips all scene objects of their details and renders scenes using solid black lines and filled objects reminiscent of a cartoon. For images destined for the Web, this is a good choice. It can also export images and animations to the SWF format.

The **Arnold** renderer includes many additional features, such as sampling and ray tracing, which enables scenes to be rendered with much more detail. The Arnold renderer also supports many proprietary materials, textures, and lights that you can use within your scene. The Physical Sky feature adds a sky dome and a sun object that simulates real-world outdoor lighting.

Lesson 15.1: Configure the Render Process

Before rendering a scene, you should check the rendering settings found in the Render Settings dialog box, shown in Figure 15-1. You can open this dialog box using the Windows, Rendering Editors, Render Settings menu command or the Render, Render Settings menu command. The dialog box includes two tabbed panels—Common and another tab named after the selected renderer.

Note

The Render menu is made available when the Rendering menu set is selected.

Tip

You can also open the Render Settings dialog box by clicking on the Display Render Settings button in the Status Line.

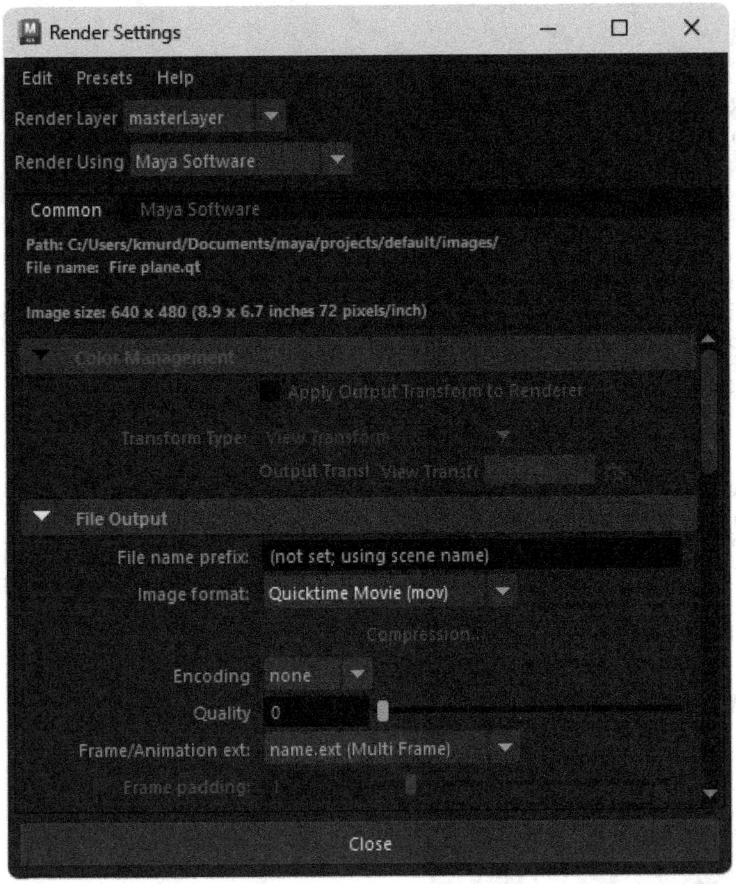

FIGURE 15-1

The Render Settings dialog box

Choosing a Renderer

You can render scenes using Maya Software, which uses the computer's CPU; using Maya Hardware, which uses the computer's video card; or by using a specialized plug-in renderer, such as Maya Vector or Arnold. The advantage of hardware rendering is that it typically is much faster than rendering with a software solution, but this is dependent on the power of your installed video card. You can switch between the hardware and software options using the Render, Render Using menu command or by selecting the renderer in the Render Using drop-down list at the top of the Render Settings dialog box. In the Preferences dialog box, you can set which renderer should be used by default.

Note

Actually, the Arnold renderer is the default rendering engine and you'll need to select the Maya Software option to use it.

Saving Render Presets

You can save all your changes to the Render Settings dialog box as a preset that can be easily reloaded. To save a preset, use the Presets, Export Render Settings menu command in the Render Settings dialog box. You can then reload your saved presets using the Presets, Import Render Settings menu command.

Changing a File Name

At the top of the Render Settings dialog box, the current path and file name for the current project are listed. This defines where the rendered image is saved and what its name is. You can change the project path using the File, Set Project menu command in the main interface or with the Edit, Change Project Image Directory in the Render Settings menu. The file name is the same name as the saved file unless you enter a new name in the File Name Prefix field.

Changing File Format

Maya can save rendered images to several different formats, including Maya IFF, Wavefront (RLA), Softimage (PIC), Alias (ALS), SGI, TIFF, GIF, JPEG, PNG, Targa (TGA), TIFF, Windows Bitmap (BMP), DDS, Photoshop (PSD), Encapsulated PostScript (EPS), Quantel, and more. You can select each of these formats in the Render Settings dialog box. You can also select which channels—including RGB, Alpha, and Depth—are saved with the image file. If the format doesn't support the various channels, the channels are saved as a separate file along with the RGB image file.

Changing Camera View and Resolution

The Renderable Cameras drop-down list lets you select which camera view is used to render the scene. The Image Size section, shown in Figure 15-2, includes a number of settings that define the resolution of the rendered image. You can select from a number of presets or specify custom dimensions.

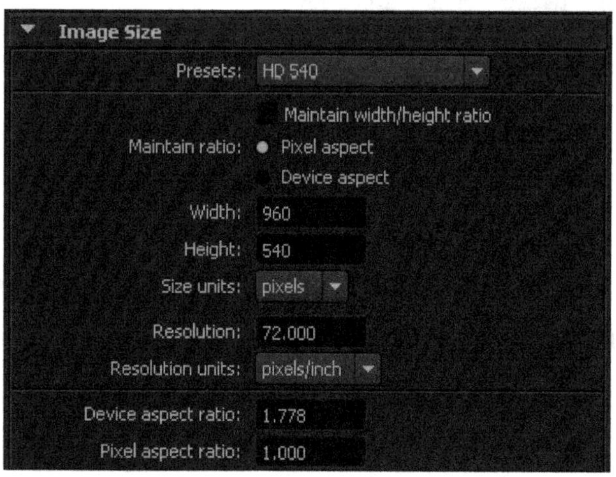

FIGURE 15-2

Image Size section

Using render layers

At the top of the Layer Editor (positioned below the Channel Box) are options for dividing the scene into Display layers and Render layers. Render layers allow you to specify different render settings for each layer. This approach lets you apply special render effects like motion blur to a single render layer that only includes those objects that render the render effect like birds flying through the scene. Each separate render layer can then be composited together to create the final image. The layer to render is specified from a drop-down list at the top of the Render Settings dialog box.

Lesson 15.1-Tutorial 1: Set Render Settings

1. Select the Windows, Rendering Editor, Render Settings menu command.

   The Render Settings dialog box opens.
2. In the Render Using drop-down list, select Maya Software.

   A tab labeled Maya Software appears in the Render Settings dialog box.
3. Select the Maya IFF image format.
4. Choose the Perspective Camera in the Camera drop-down list.
5. In the Image Size section, choose the Targa NTSC Resolution Preset.

   The Width and Height values are updated.
6. Click the Close button to close the Render Settings dialog box.

Lesson 15.1-Tutorial 2: Change the Rendering Path

1. Select the Windows, Rendering Editor, Render Settings menu command.
2. Select the File, Set Project menu command from the main interface.

   A Browse to Folder dialog box opens.
3. Locate the folder where you want to save the rendered scene to and click the OK button.

   The path in the Render Settings dialog box is updated to this new path.

Lesson 15.2: Use Special Rendering Features

On the Maya Software tab of the Render Settings dialog box are several sections that you can use to set the quality and special rendering features available in Maya, as shown in Figure 15-3. The Quality settings are for the overall anti-aliasing quality of the render to improve the smoothness of the edges and some of the special rendering features include Raytracing and Motion Blur.

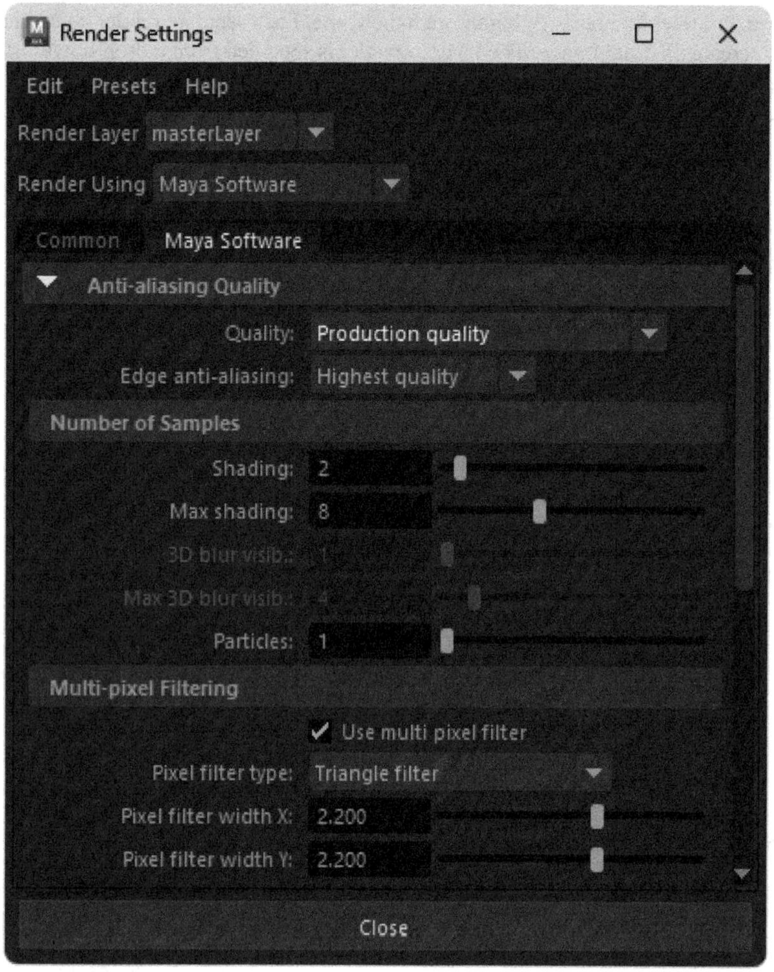

FIGURE 15-3

Maya software rendering settings

Adjusting Render Quality

At the top of the Maya Software tab in the Render Settings dialog box you can select one of several presets for the image quality and edge anti-aliasing. The Quality options include Custom, Preview, Intermediate, Production, Contrast Sensitive, and 3D Motion Blur. The Edge Anti-aliasing options include Low, Medium, High, and Highest. Higher-quality and anti-alias settings require more time to render. Figure 15-4 shows a simple scene rendered at the Preview Quality setting and Figure 15-5 shows the same scene rendered using the Production Quality setting. Notice how the edges appear jagged in the preview rendering because the anti-aliasing is set so low.

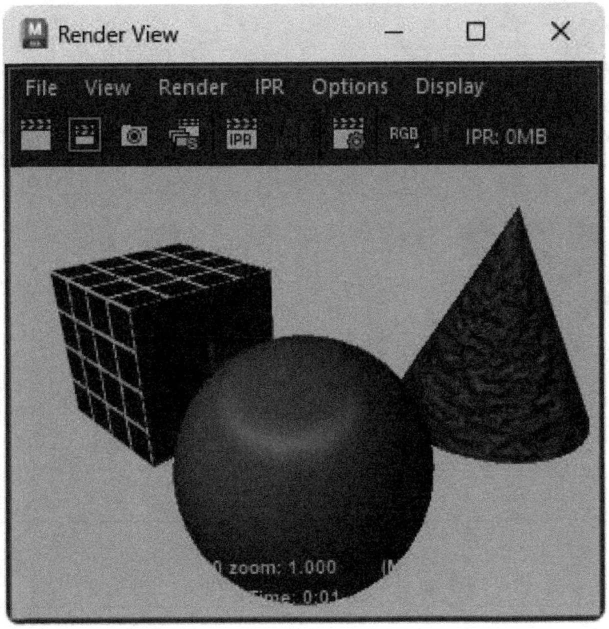

FIGURE 15-4

Scene rendered using the Preview Quality setting

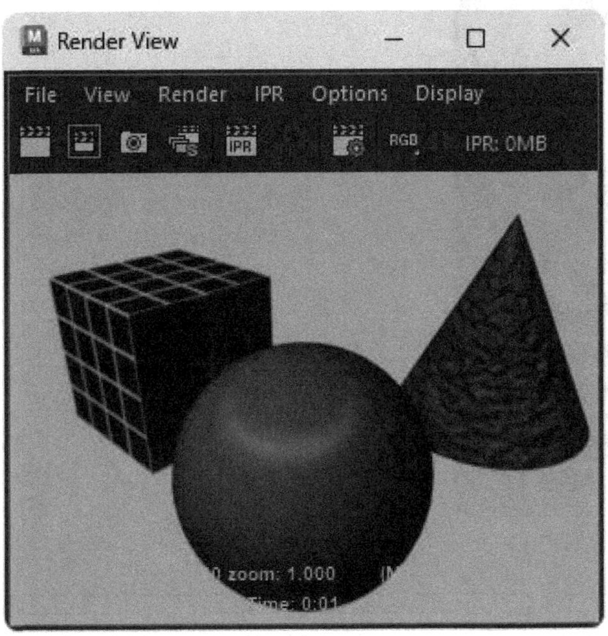

FIGURE 15-5

Scene rendered using the Production Quality setting

Enabling Raytracing

You can enable the Raytracing option in the Raytracing Quality section of the Render Settings dialog box, shown in Figure 15-6. Once raytracing is enabled, you can set the number of times a light ray is reflected, refracted, and able to cause a shadow. If you've enabled raytraced shadows for any of your lights, you'll need to enable raytracing here to see the shadows.

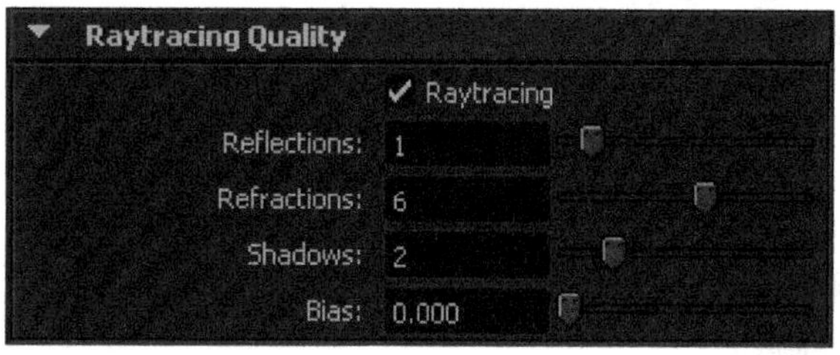

FIGURE 15-6

Raytracing settings

Enabling Motion Blur

Motion blur renders objects that move quickly through an animated scene blurred. This gives the illusion that the objects are moving fast. You can compute motion blur in 3D or in 2D (which is much quicker) and you can set the blur length and sharpness. Figure 15-7 shows the Motion Blur section of the Render Settings dialog box.

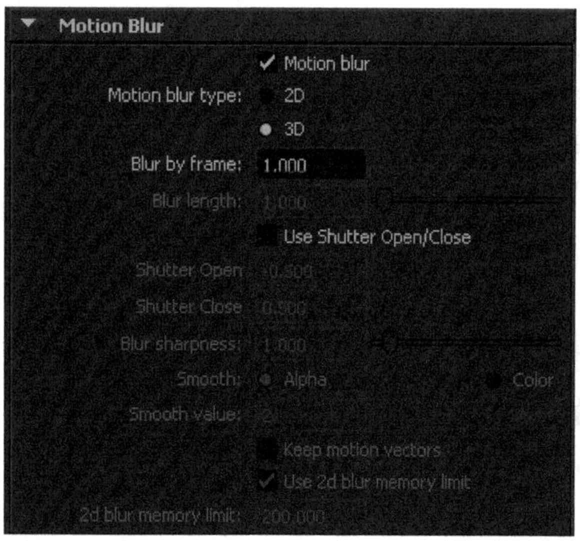

FIGURE 15-7

Motion Blur settings

Adding Environment Fog

Within the Render Options section of the Render Settings dialog box is a field where you can enable Environment Fog. Clicking on the Create Render Node button adds the Environment Fog node to the scene. Once added, you can change its attributes—including its color, saturation distance, and height—in the Attribute Editor.

Note

```
Environment Fog is different from Light Fog in
that it applies to the entire scene and Light Fog
is localized.
```

Lesson 15.2-Tutorial 1: Change the Render Quality

1. Select the Windows, Rendering Editor, Render Settings menu command.
2. Enable the Maya Software option in the Render Using drop-down list at the top of the dialog box.
3. Click on the Maya Software tab.

   Change the Quality setting to Production Quality.
4. The Edge Anti-aliasing setting is automatically changed to the Highest Quality setting.

Lesson 15.2-Tutorial 2: Enable Raytracing

1. Select the File, Open Scene menu command, locate and open the **Glass on table.mb** file.
2. Select the Point light in front of the glass object and open the Attribute Editor.
3. In the Shadows section, enable the Use Ray Trace Shadows option.
4. Select the Windows, Rendering Editor, Render Settings menu command.
5. Enable the Maya Software option in the Render Using drop-down list at the top of the dialog box.
6. Click on the Maya Software tab.
7. Open the Raytracing Quality section and enable the Raytracing option.
8. Right-click on the Perspective view panel to make it the active viewport and select the Render, Render Current Frame menu command.

   The scene is rendered in the Render View window with raytraced shadows, as shown in Figure 15-8.
9. Select File, Save Scene As, and save the file as **Raytraced glass.mb**.

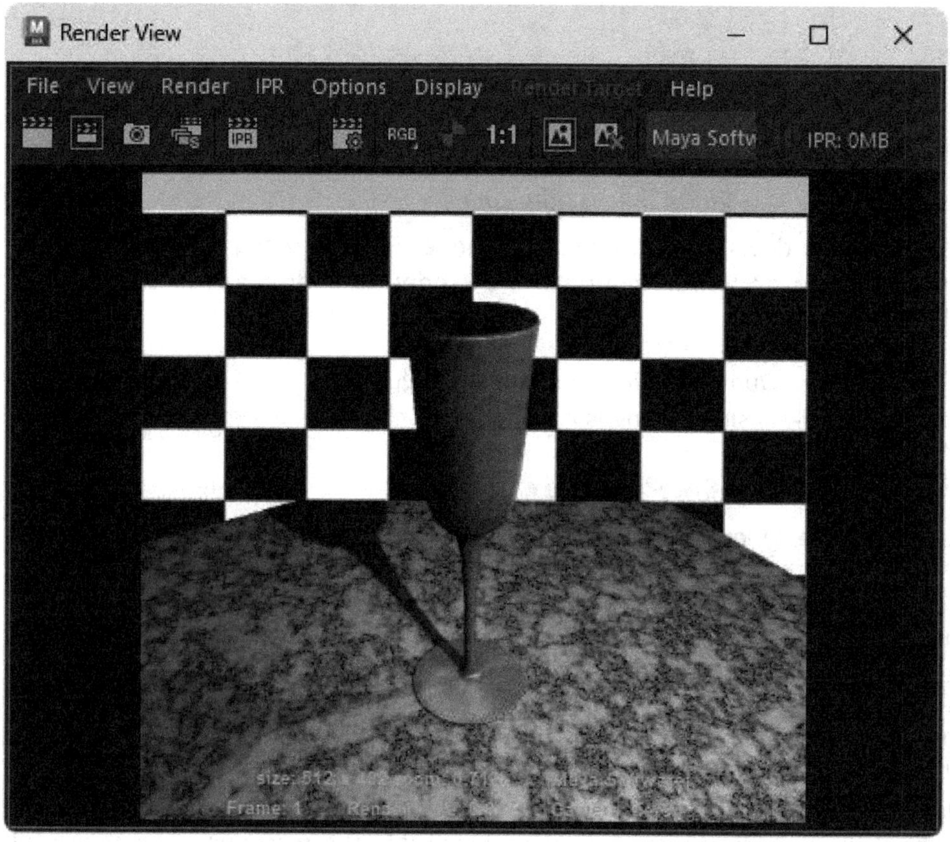

FIGURE 15-8

Raytraced glass

Lesson 15.2-Tutorial 3: Enable Motion Blur

1. Select the File, Open Scene menu command, locate and open the **Simple animated rocket.mb** file.
2. Drag the Frame Slider to Frame 10.
3. Select the Windows, Rendering Editor, Render Settings menu command.
4. Enable the Maya Software option in the Render Using drop-down list at the top of the dialog box.
5. Click on the Maya Software tab.
6. In the Anti-aliasing Quality section, select the 3D Motion Blur Production option in the Quality drop-down list.
7. Open the Motion Blur section and enable the Motion Blur and the 3D options. Set the Blur by Frame to 1.0.
8. Right-click on the Perspective view panel to select it and select the Render, Render Current Frame menu command.

   The scene is rendered in the Render View window. The rocket is blurred as it zooms past the camera, as shown in Figure 15-9.
9. Select File, Save Scene As and save the file as **Motion blur rocket.mb**.

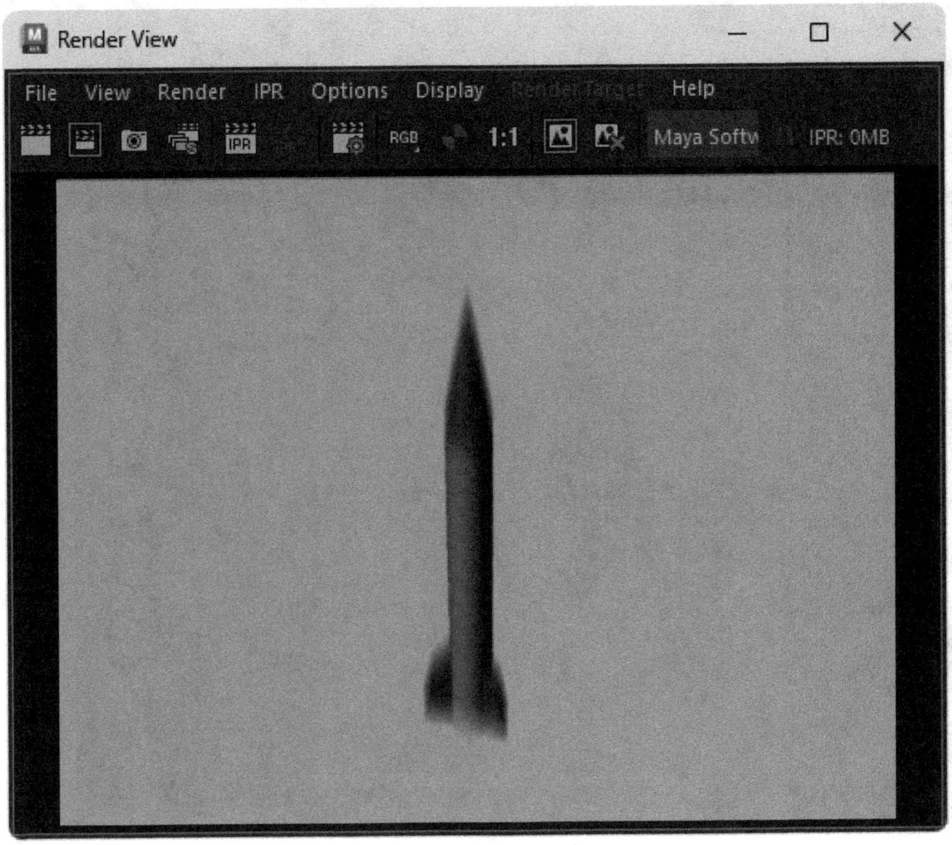

FIGURE 15-9

Motion blurred rocket

Lesson 15.2-Tutorial 4: Add Environment Fog

1. Select the File, Open Scene menu command, locate and open the **Hot air balloon.mb** file.
2. Select the Windows, Rendering Editor, Render Settings menu command.
3. Enable the Maya Software option in the Render Using drop-down list at the top of the dialog box.
4. Click on the Maya Software tab.
5. Open the Render Options section and click the Create Render Node button next to the Environment Fog field.

   An Environment Fog node is automatically added to the scene and its attributes are displayed in the Attribute Editor.
6. Right-click on the Perspective view panel and select the Render, Render Current Frame menu command.

   The scene is rendered in the Render View window with environment fog added to the scene, as shown in Figure 15-10.
7. Select File, Save Scene As and save the file as **Balloon in fog.mb**.

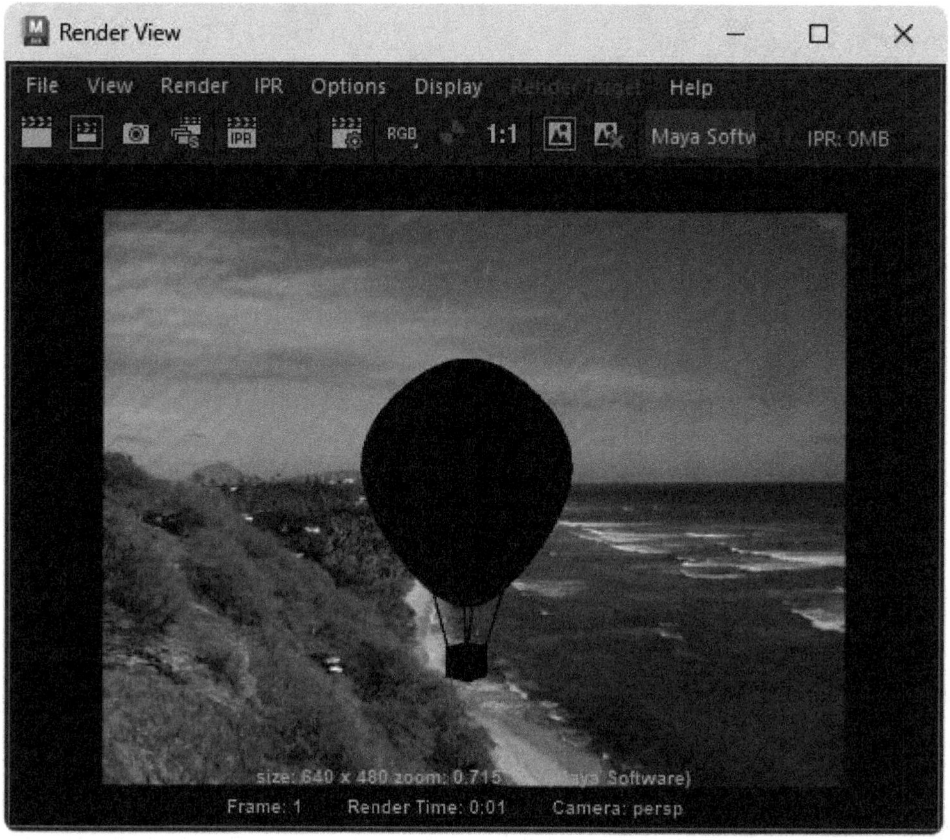

FIGURE 15-10

Balloon in the fog

Lesson 15.3: Use the Render View Window

When the Render, Render Current Frame menu command is used, the Render Frame window is opened automatically, but you can open this window at any time with the Windows, Rendering Editors, Render View menu command.

Opening the Render View

Selecting the Render, Render Current Frame menu command or the Render, Redo Previous Render menu command causes the Render View window, shown in Figure 15-11, to open and render the active view panel. The Render View window includes a menu and toolbar.

Note

If no view panel is active, a simple warning dialog box will ask you to select a view panel to render.

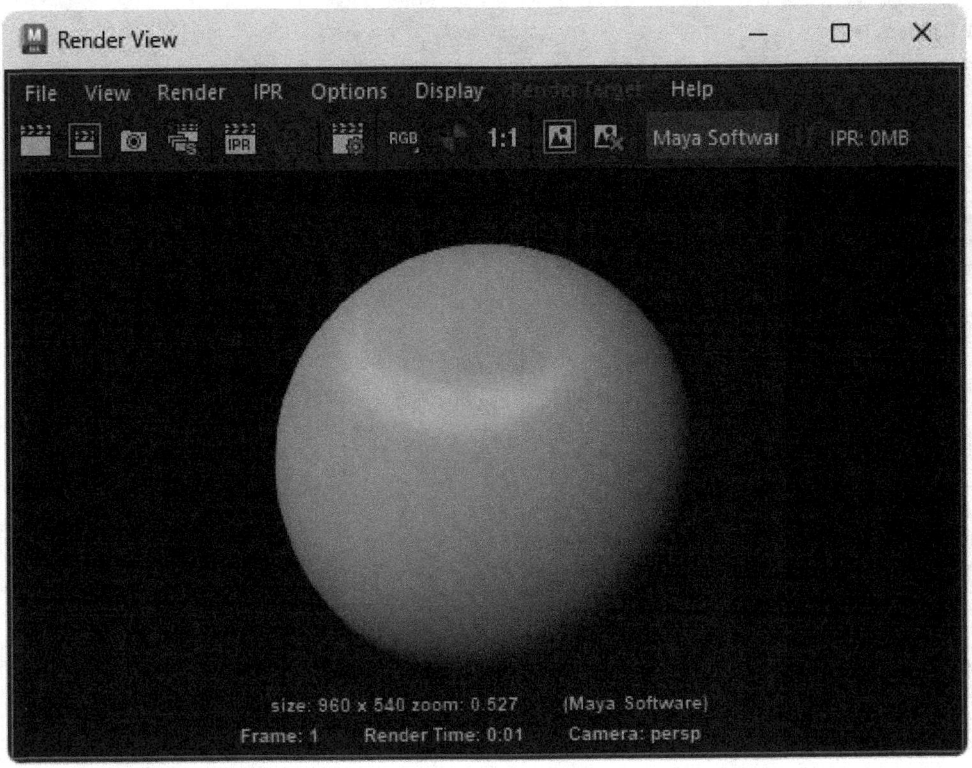

FIGURE 15-11

Render View window

Rendering a Region

With the Render View window open, you can drag within the window to define a region to be rendered. This region is outlined in red, as shown in Figure 15-12. Selecting the Render, Render Region menu command in the Render View window or clicking the Render Region button in the Render View window re-renders just the defined region. You can reset the region to the entire view using the View, Reset Region Marquee menu command.

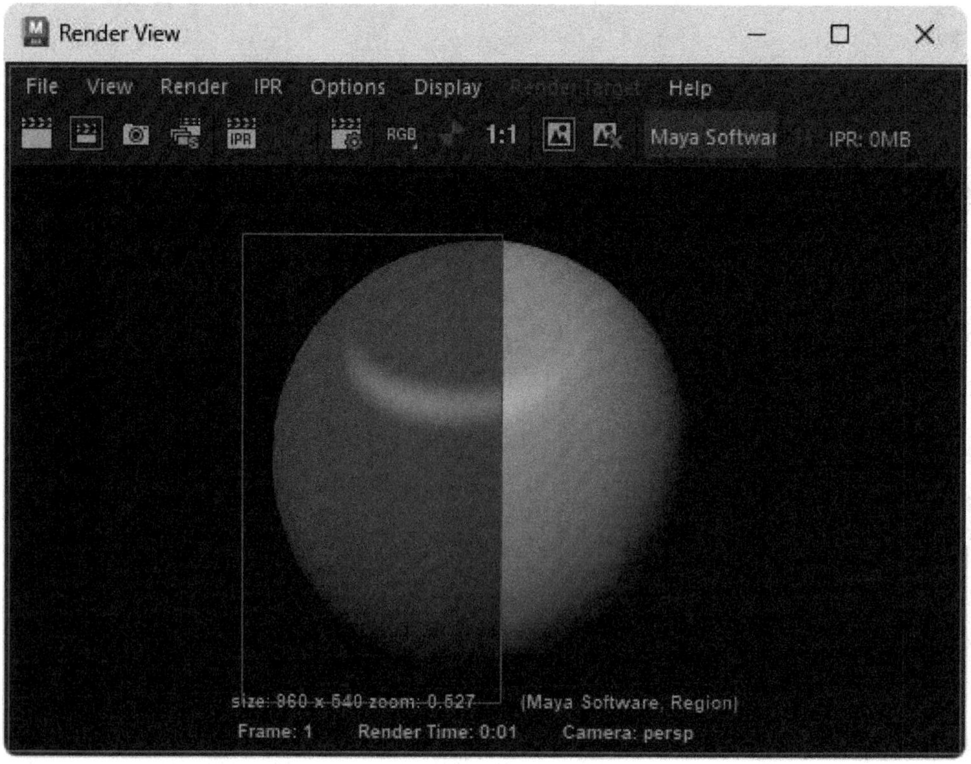

FIGURE 15-12

The Render region

Using Interactive Photorealistic Rendering (IPR)

The Render View window can render the current scene in an interactive mode called *Interactive Photorealistic Rendering* (IPR). In this mode, you can change object materials, textures, and scene lights, and the Render View window is updated. You can initialize this mode using the IPR, Redo Previous IPR Render menu command. Once in IPR mode, you can select a region that can be tuned (or updated). With a region selected, the IPR view automatically updates the region every time a light or shading attribute is changed. You can also update the entire image using the IPR, Refresh IPR Image menu command.

Note

The IPR render mode keeps render data in local memory, and the amount used is displayed at the left end of the toolbar.

Saving Rendered Images

You can save any image rendered to the Render View window using the File, Save Image window menu command. This command opens a file dialog box in which you can name the file and select the image format to use. You can also save and re-open IRP files.

Lesson 15.3-Tutorial 1: Render a Region

1. Select the File, Open Scene menu command to open the **Box of donuts.mb** file.

2. Right-click on the Perspective view panel to make it the active viewport and select the Render, Render Current Frame menu command.

   The scene is rendered in the Render View window.

3. Drag with the mouse inside the Render View window to define a tuning region.
4. Select the donut objects and choose the phong1 tab in the Attribute Editor, then change the Color swatch to bright orange.
5. Select the Render, Render Region menu command in the Render View window.

   As the Color attribute is changed, the region is updated, as shown in Figure 15-13.

6. Select File, Save Scene As and save the file as **Render region of donuts.mb**.

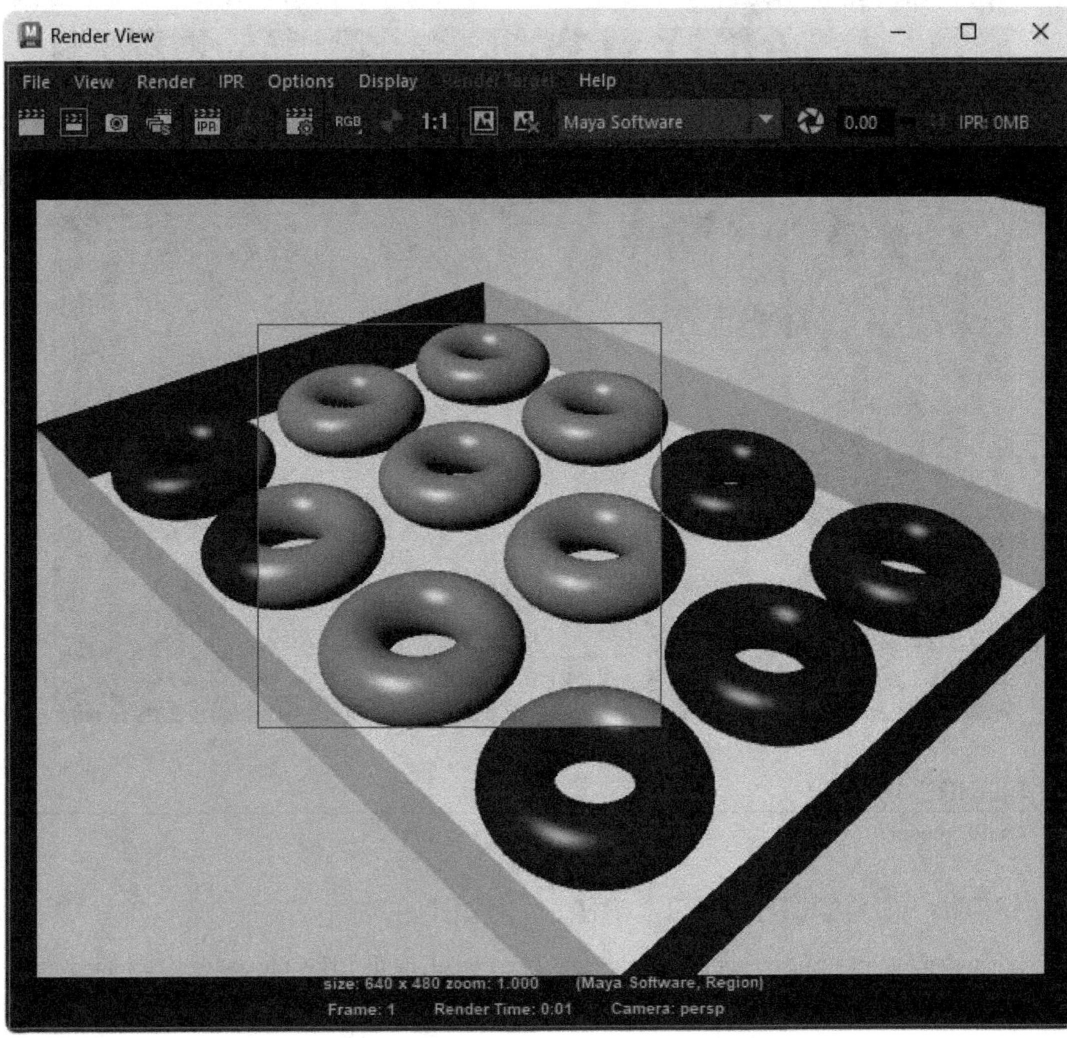

FIGURE 15-13

A Render region

Lesson 15.3-Tutorial 2: Use IPR Rendering

1. Select the File, Open Scene menu command to open the **Geometric flower.mb** file.

2. Right-click on the Perspective view panel and select the Render, IPR Render Current Frame menu command.

   The scene is rendered in the Render View window in IPR mode.

3. Drag with the mouse inside the Render View window to define a tuning region.
4. Select the object in the view panel, and then in the Attribute Editor, select the blinn1 node. In the Special Effects section, set the Glow Intensity to 0.5.

   As the Glow Intensity attribute is changed, the tuning region is updated, as shown in Figure 15-14.

5. Select File, Save Scene As and save the file as **IPR Render.mb**.

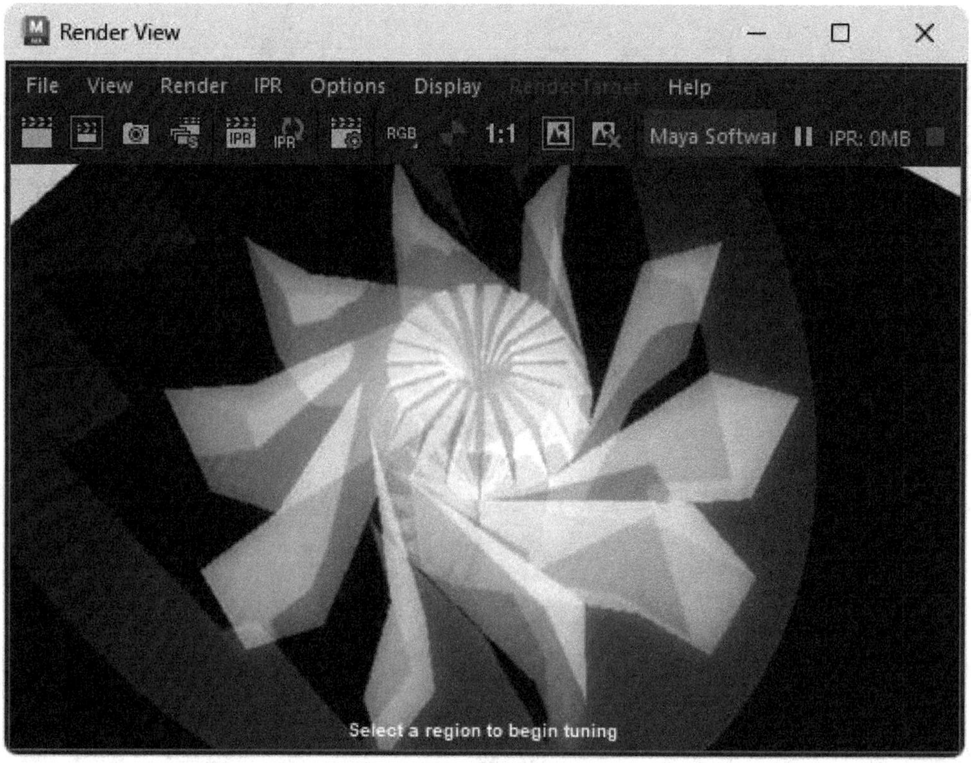

FIGURE 15-14

An IPR render

Lesson 15.4: Create a Final Render

The final step for producing output is to render a final version of the file. This file can then be composited with other images to create the final work. You typically do the compositing in another package.

Rendering a Single Frame

Whenever an image is rendered to the Render View window using the Render, Render Current Frame menu command, a copy of the image is also saved to the project folder using the settings found in the Render Settings dialog box. Within the Render Settings dialog box, you can set the destination folder (which is the project folder by default), the image format (with any compression settings), the Renderable Camera, and the image size and resolution. To render a single frame (which is the default), make sure that the Frame/Animation ext setting in the File Output rollout uses an option with (Single Frame), This causes only the current frame to be rendered and saved and not multiple frames.

Note

```
If you re-render the scene again, the saved render
on the hard drive is simply updated with the new
render unless the file format is changed.
```

Rendering an Animation Sequence

To render a sequence of frames, just select one of the available image formats in the Render Settings dialog box and set the Frame/Animation ext setting to one of the options where name is the filename, # is the frame number and ext is the extension. This renders each frame of the animation as a separate file designated by a frame number. Within the Frame Range rollout, set the Start and End Frame values, then select Render, Render Sequence and the resulting frames are rendered one by one in the Render View window and copies are also saved to the designated project folder. To compile the completed renders into a video file, load them into a video editing or compositing software.

Viewing Animations in the Render View Window

If you open the Options dialog box for the Render Sequence menu command, there is an option to Render to View. If you enable this option before rendering, then all the frames of the animation are kept in the Render View window and a scroll bar at the bottom of the window lets you scroll through the animated frames. Use the File, Remove All Images from Render View menu command to clear the animation frames.

Rendering to an Animation Format

Maya has only a few supported video formats. To render an animation as a video file, just select one of the available video formats in the Render Settings dialog box that is a video format, such as AVI for Quicktime (MOV). These formats automatically set the Frame/Animation ext setting to (Multi Frame) and it makes the Frame Range rollout active where you can specify the Start and End Frame values. Then choose the Render, Batch Render menu command. The frames are rendered in the background and a note on the Help Line at the bottom of the interface will inform you when the render is completed. The completed video file will be in the designated project folder.

Tip

```
The Batch Render feature can be used for any of
the rendering tasks and it frees up the interface
while rendering in the background.
```

Lesson 15.4-Tutorial 1: Render an Animation

1. Select the File, Open Scene menu command, locate and open the Newtons cradle.mb file.
2. Select the Windows, Rendering Editors, Render Settings menu command.
3. Enable the Arnold Renderer option in Render Using the drop-down list at the top of the dialog box.
4. Select the File, Set Project menu command. Choose the folder in which you want to save the rendered files and click the OK button.
5. Type the name **Newtons cradle** in the File Name Prefix field.
6. Choose the PNG option in the Image Format drop-down list.
7. Select the name#.ext option in the Frame/Animation Ext field.

8. Set the End Frame to 40.

   Selecting the name#.ext option causes each frame of the animation to be rendered and saved with the name followed by the frame number and the file extension. Figure 15-15 shows the Render Settings dialog box.

9. In the Image Size section, choose the 640*480 Preset and set the Renderable Camera to persp1.
10. Select the Arnold Renderer tab.
11. In the Sampling section, set the Camera (AA) samples to 5, the Diffuse and Specular samples to 3 and the other samples to 0.
12. Choose the Render, Render Sequence, Options menu command. Enable the Add to Render View option and click the Render Sequence button.

    The scene is rendered automatically and the rendered files are saved to the designated path. You can also view the animation frames in the Render View window, as shown in Figure 15-16.

13. Select File, Save Scene As and save the file as **Newtons cradle render.mb**.

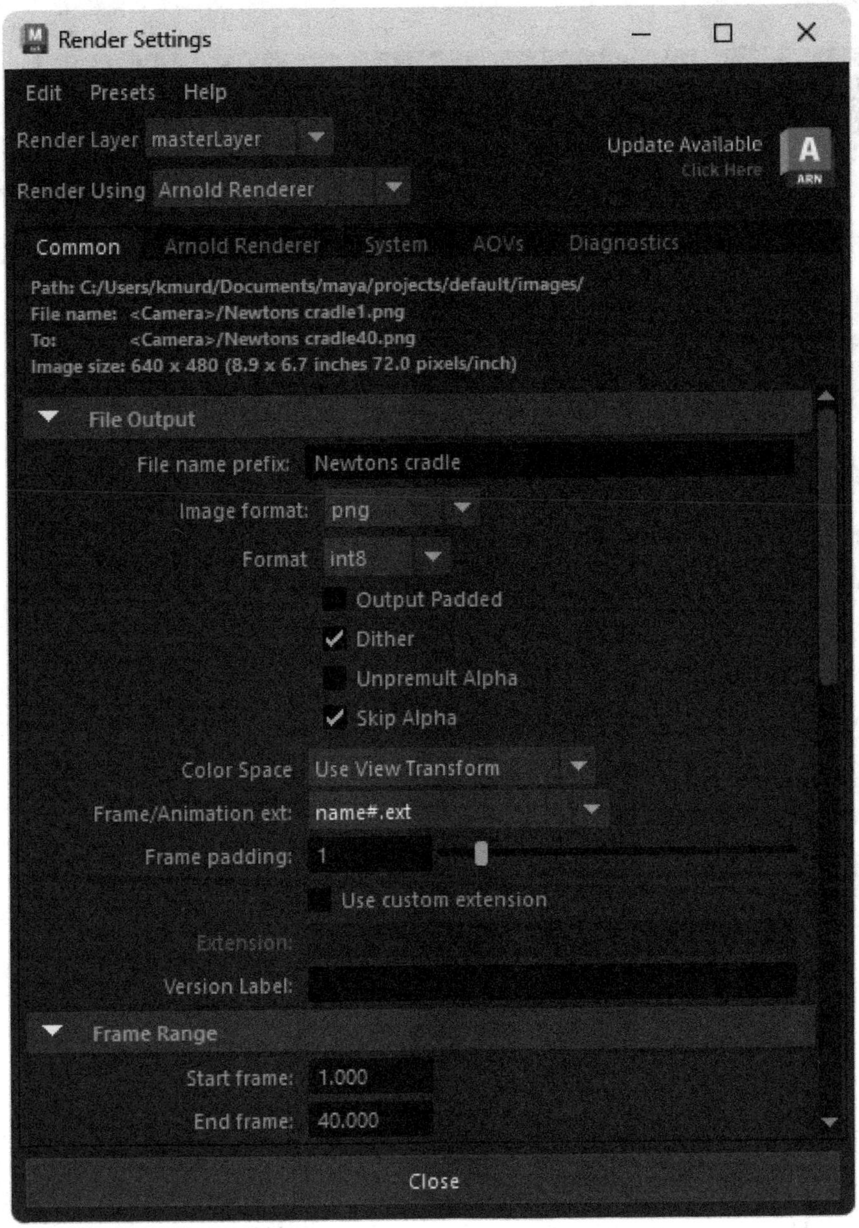

FIGURE 15-15

Rendering an animation

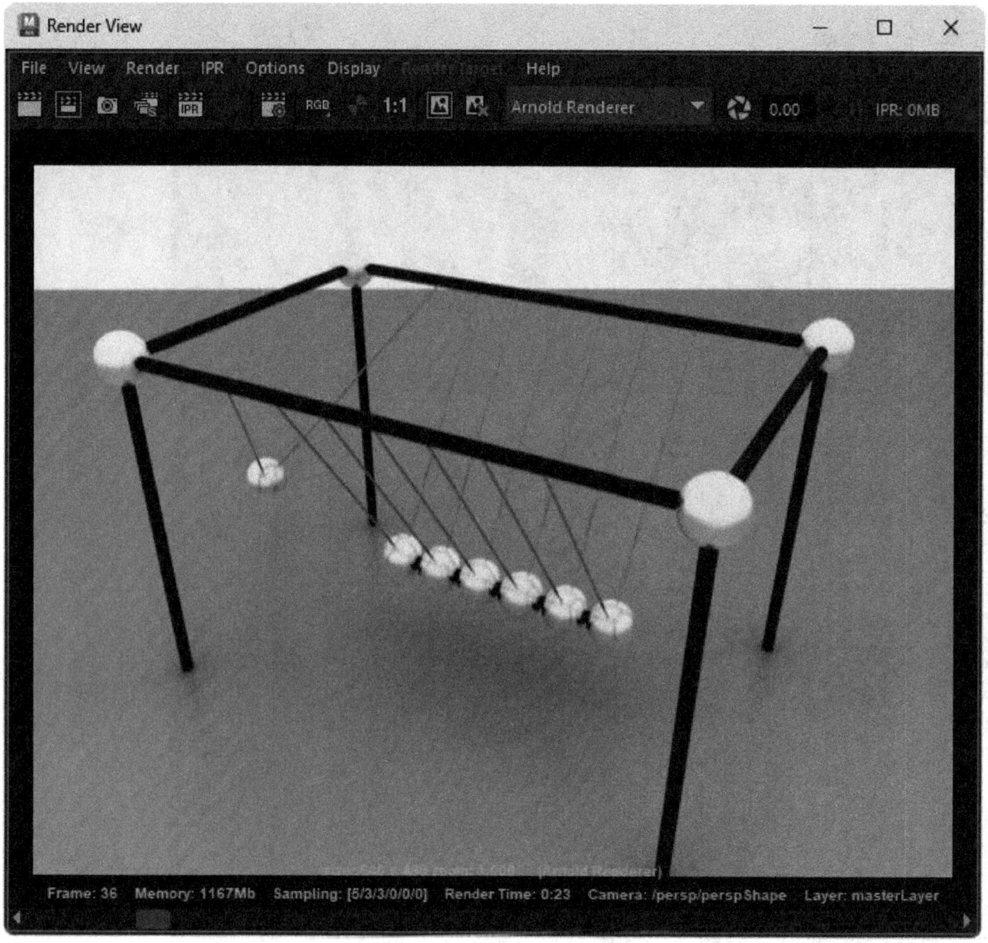

FIGURE 15-16

Frames viewed in the Render View window

Lesson 15.5: Render with Maya Vector

In addition to the Maya Software and Maya Hardware rendering methods, Maya also includes two other rendering methods—Maya Vector and Arnold. You can use the Maya Vector renderer to reduce a scene to simple vector-based lines like a cartoon, which is often called cel shading. Arnold is an advanced rendering engine that includes many additional settings, creating some amazing output. You can select each of these rendering methods by using the Render, Render Using menu.

Using Maya Vector

The Maya Vector rendering method lets you render and export scenes to several different vector-based formats including Macromedia's Flash (SWF), Swift 3D, EPS, Adobe Illustrator (AI), and SVG. The vector settings in the Render Settings dialog box include controls for determining how the edges and fills look. For fill objects, you can choose to use one, two, four, or full colors and choose whether shadows and highlights are included. For edges, you can set the edge weight, style, and color. Figure 15-17 shows the Maya Vector settings, and Figure 15-18 shows several objects rendered using the Maya Vector rendering method.

Note

If you don't see Maya Vector as an option in the Render Settings dialog box, then open the Plug-in Manager with the Windows, Settings/Preferences, Plug-in Manager menu. Then, locate and enable the Loaded and Auto Load options for the VectorRender.mll plug-in. This will cause Maya Vector to appear as an option in the Render Settings dialog box.

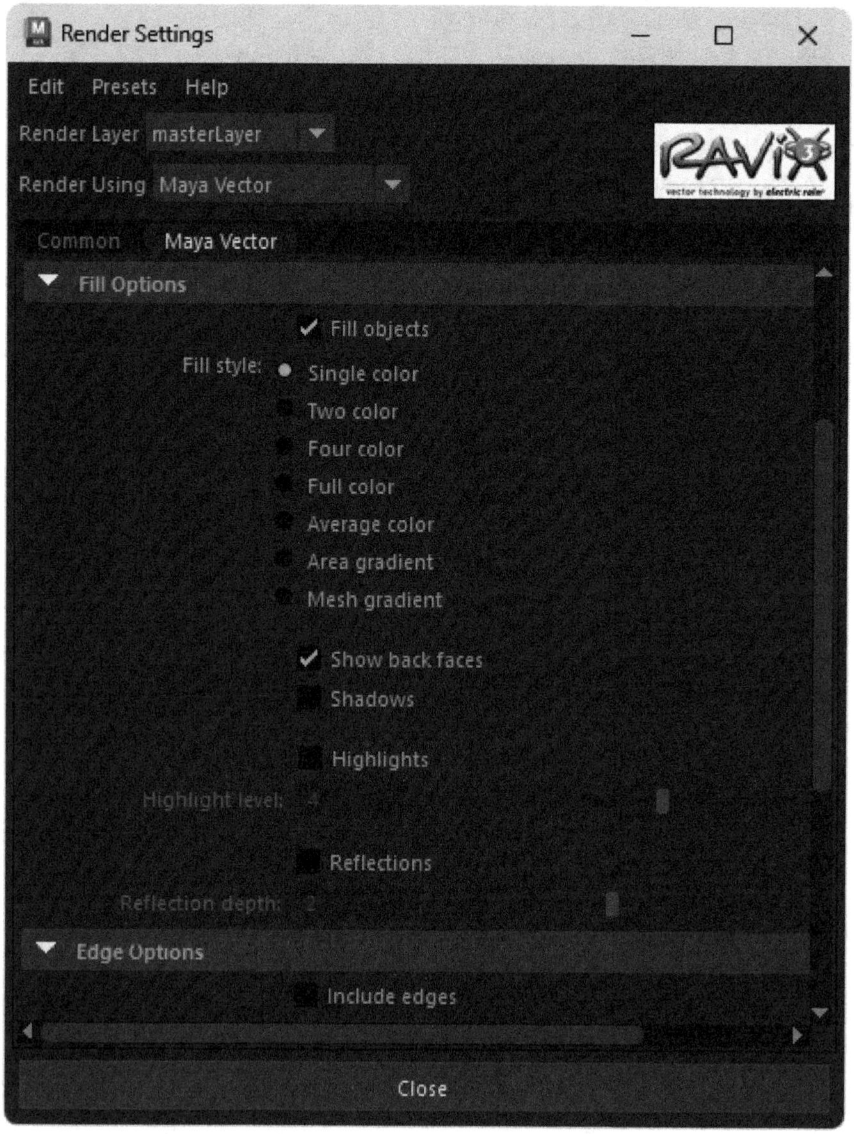

FIGURE 15-17

Maya Vector settings

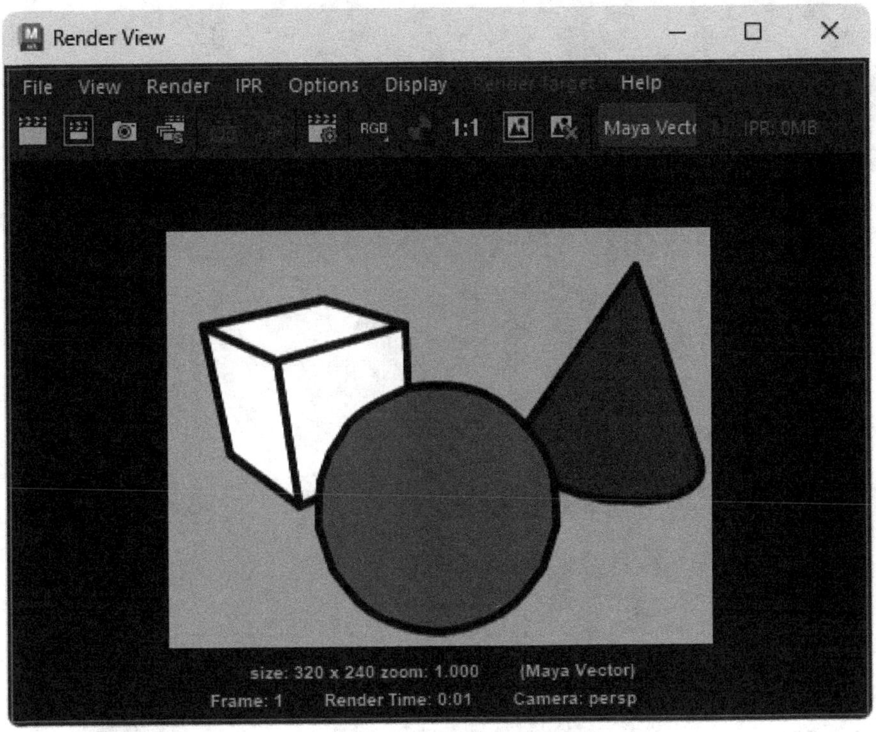

FIGURE 15-18

A Maya Vector rendered scene

Lesson 15.5-Tutorial 1: Render Using Vectors

1. Select the File, Open Scene menu command, and then locate and open the **Rose in crystal ball.mb** file.
2. Select the Windows, Rendering Editors, Render Settings menu command.
3. Enable the Maya Vector option in the Render Using drop-down list at the top of the dialog box.
4. Select the Maya Vector tab. In the Fill Options section, enable the Fill Objects, Full Color, and Shadows options; and in the Edge Options section enable the Include Edges option and set the Edge Weight to 3.0.
5. Right click on the Perspective view to select it and choose the Render, Render Current Frame menu command.

   The scene is rendered in the Render View window using the Maya Vector renderer, as shown in Figure 15-19.
6. Select File, Save Scene As and save the file as **Vector rose.mb**.

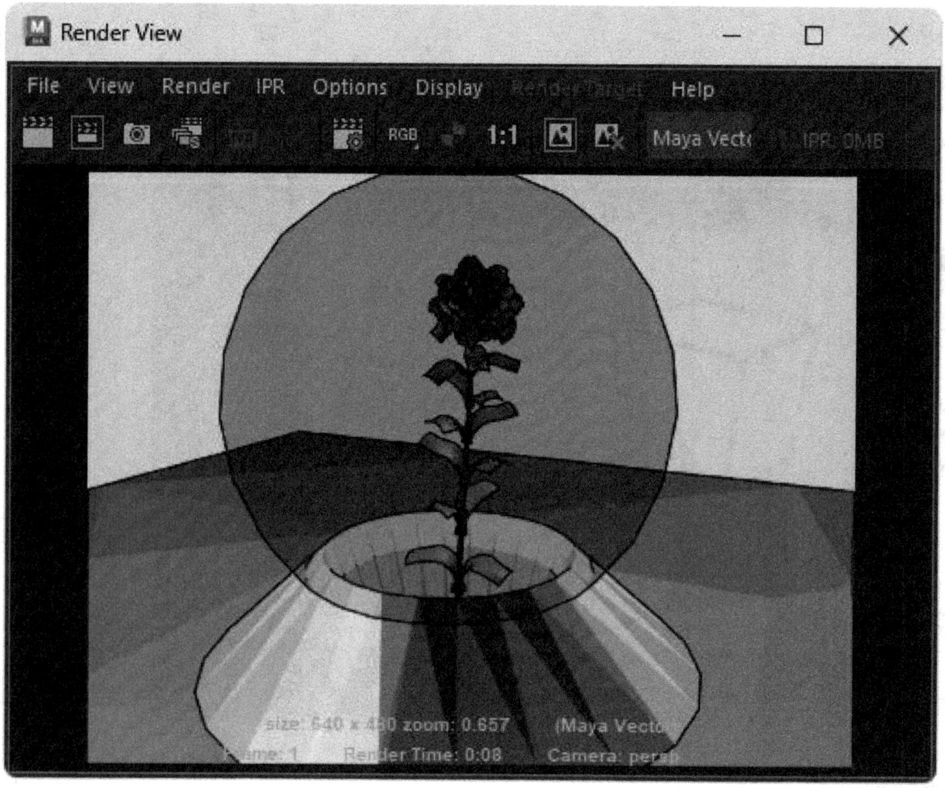

FIGURE 15-19

Vector rendered crystal ball on a table

Lesson 15.6: Render with Arnold

The Arnold renderer offers additional features such as Progressive Refinement, Sampling, Transmission, Ray Depth, and Sub-Surface Scattering. These feature different ways to compute how light moves around the scene between the objects. With many of these features enabled, rendering with Arnold can take a considerable amount of time even for the simplest scenes, but the results are stunning.

However, working with Arnold can be a little tricky. Arnold is a plug-in renderer and its best results come from using its own unique set of materials and lights. Arnold also uses its own Render View window. Some of the settings unique to Arnold, such as Arnold Lights, are found in the Arnold menu and others, like the Open PBR Surface shader, are built into other Maya interfaces. If you render a scene using Arnold and nothing shows up, it is probably because you are using the standard lights or materials that Arnold doesn't know how to use.

Selecting the Arnold Renderer

You can select to use the Arnold renderer by selecting it from the Render Using drop-down list in the Render Settings dialog box. Once the Arnold renderer is selected, you can render the scene using the Render, Render Current Frame menu command or by clicking on the Render buttons in the main toolbar. This causes the scene to be displayed in the Arnold Render View window, as shown in Figure 15-20.

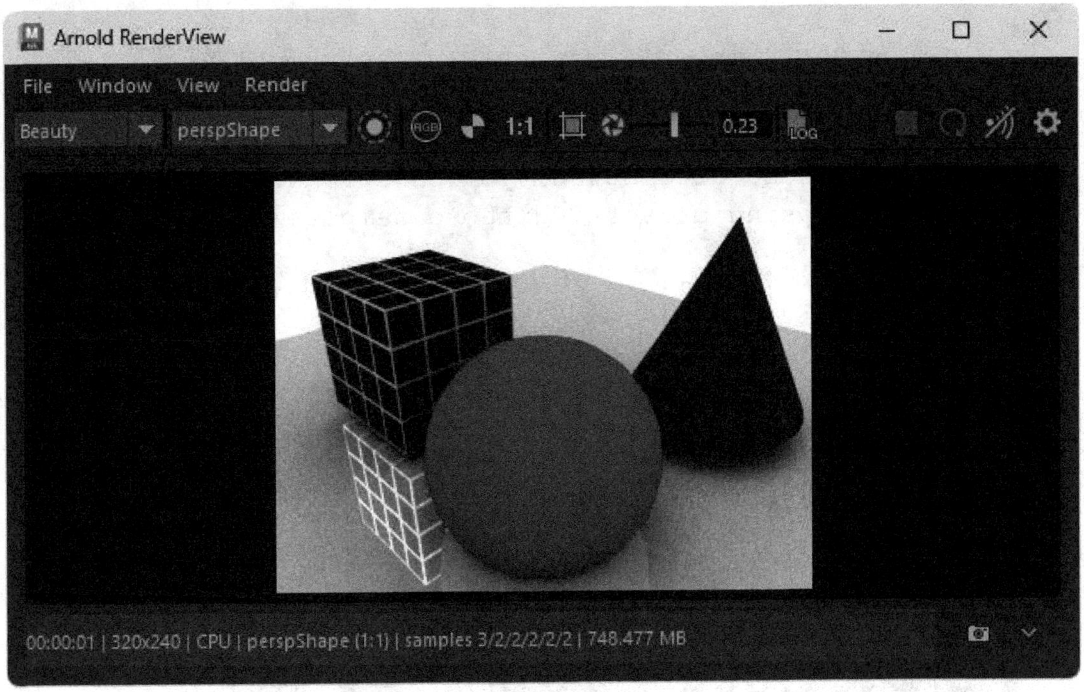

FIGURE 15-20

An Arnold rendered scene

Changing the Arnold Render Settings

The render settings for the Arnold renderer are located in the Render Settings dialog box. These settings are spread across several tabbed panels, as shown in Figure 15-21. The general settings are found in the Arnold Renderer panel. Within the Sampling rollout, you can set the number of samples that the Arnold renderer computes for each pixel in the scene. Each sample value is squared to get the total number of samples and the Camera (AA) is the global sample for anti-aliasing the render that gets multiplied by each subsequent sample, so a Camera (AA) sample of 3 yields 9 total Camera (AA) samples and a Diffuse setting of 2 yields 36 Diffuse samples (2 Diffuse square times 3 Camera (AA) squared). You can also set the samples for Diffuse surfaces, Specular highlights, Transmission, which includes reflections and refractions, Sub-Surface Scattering (SSS), and Volume Indirect.

Notice how the above image is a little grainy. You can remove this grain by increasing the Camera (AA) setting to 4 or 5 and increasing the Diffuse, Specular, and Transmission samples also in the Arnold Renderer panel. However, this will increase the render time because doing so increases the total number of samples that the renderer has to compute.

Caution

Because the Sample values are squared and also multiplied by the Camera (AA) global sample value squared, a small change in these values can have a huge impact and can greatly increase the render time. Change these values cautiously as needed.

Tip

Since the sample values only affect specific attributes such as specular highlights and sub-surface scattering. If the scene doesn't include any of these attributes, you save rendering time by decreasing or setting those samples to 0 if not needed.

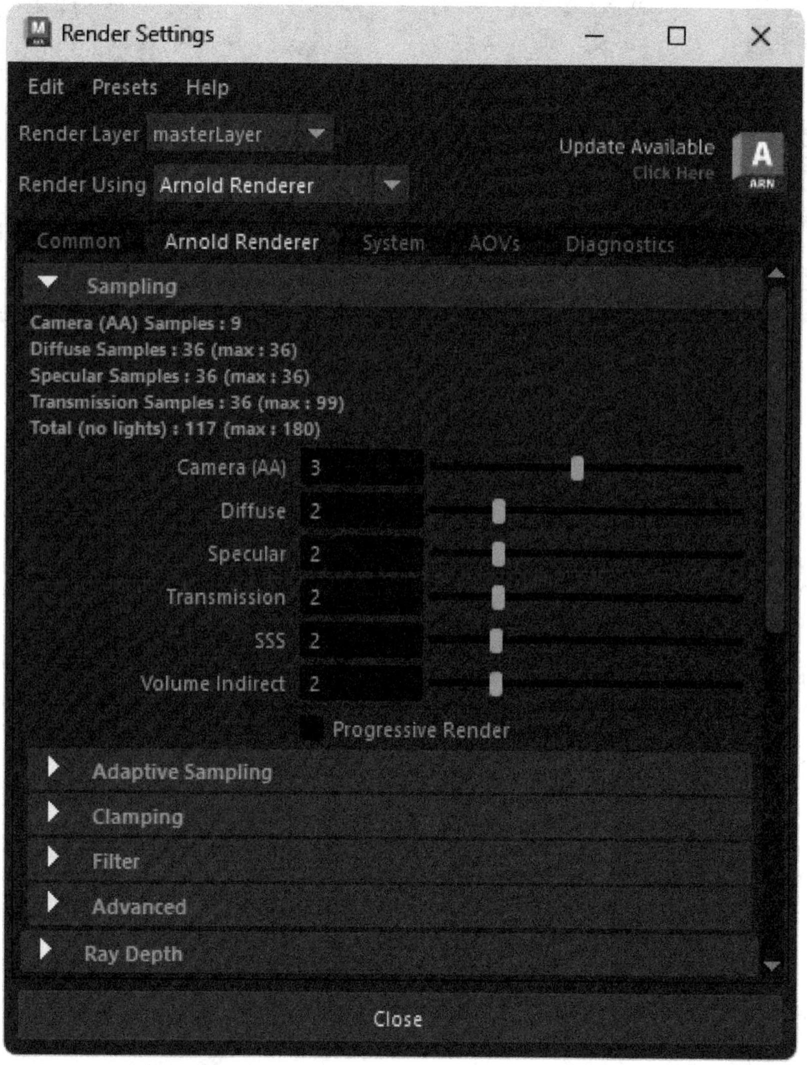

FIGURE 15-21

Arnold settings

The Systems panel includes a Render Device setting for causing the render to use the CPU or the GPU on your graphics card. If you have a graphics card that supports rendering, then switching to the GPU option can noticeably speed up your renders. The AOVs panel lets you select render passes for capturing specific render features such as shadows and highlights. These separate render passes are useful in a compositing package giving you more control over the final composition. The Diagnostics panel includes tools to help you identify problems with rendering the current scene.

Using the Arnold Render View window

When a scene is rendered with the Arnold renderer enabled, the scene is displayed in the Arnold Render View window. If you enable the IPR mode with the Render, Run IPR menu command or by clicking on the red Play button in the upper right corner of the window, then the scene is automatically updated as changes are made. The Render View window also lets you specify a render region with the Render, Crop Region menu command.

At the bottom right corner of the Render View window is a small Snapshot button. This button stores an image of the current render and displays it as a thumbnail in a shelf along the bottom edge, as shown in Figure 15-22. Right clicking on one of the thumbnails displays a menu where you can display the stored render in the Render View window. The right click menu also includes options to set one image as A and another as B. This displays both images (A and B) side by side with a handle that can move between the two loaded images. This provides an easy way to quickly compare different renders.

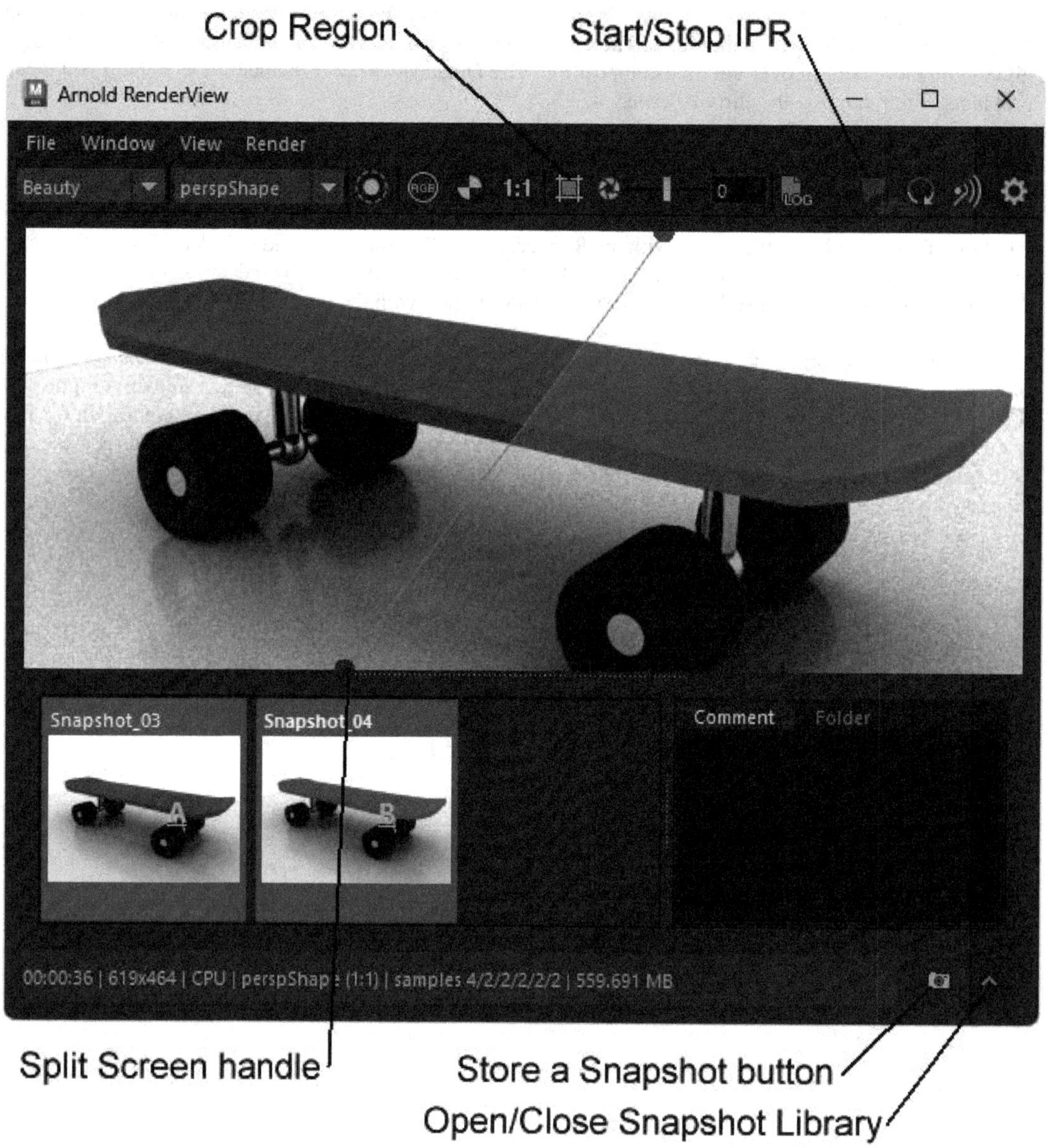

FIGURE 15-22

Arnold Render View window

Images rendered in the Render View window can be saved using the File, Save Image menu command. Although Render View images can be saved using multiple different image formats, the default format type (which is also the default in the Common panel of the Render Settings dialog box for Arnold) is the EXR image format. This format can save a wider dynamic range than other formats.

Lesson 15.6-Tutorial 1: Render with Arnold

1. Select the File, Open Scene menu command, and then locate and open the Billiard balls.mb file.

The scene includes a billiards table with Arnold compatible materials and an Arnold Skydome light.

Select the Windows, Rendering Editors, Render Settings menu command.

2. Enable the Arnold Renderer option in the Render Using drop-down list at the top of the dialog box.
3. Right-click on the Perspective view to select it and choose the Render, Render Current Frame menu command.

   The scene is rendered in the Render View window using the Arnold renderer.
4. Click on the Start IPR button in the upper right corner of the Render View window.
5. Select the Arnold Renderer tab in the Render Settings dialog box. In the Sampling section, set Camera (AA) to 5, Diffuse and Specular to 3, and Transmission, SSS and Volume Indirect to 0.

   As changes are made, the scene is updated in the Render View window. The completed render is shown in Figure 15-23.
6. Select File, Save Scene As and save the file as **Billiard balls render.mb**.

FIGURE 15-23

Arnold rendered billiard table

Lesson 15.7: Working with the Arnold Open PBR Surface Shader

The Arnold renderer can render most Maya materials without any problem, but most of the legacy materials don't include the features that Arnold needs to make it stand out. If you plan on rendering with Arnold, it is worth it to use Arnold compatible materials.

Using Arnold Materials

To get even more out of the Arnold renderer, you need to use Arnold specific materials and lights. These materials are listed as a separate Arnold category in the Create Render Node dialog box, shown in Figure 15-24, which is accessed using the Lighting/Shading, Assign New Material menu. Another way to identify Arnold compatible materials is that they all start with the 'ai' suffix. Most of these materials are for specific instances like skin and hair, but the Open PBR Surface material works well for most materials, and it also includes a decent number of presets that you can select. Within the Attribute Editor are settings for Color, Specular, Transmission, Subsurface, Fuzz, Coat, Emission, and Geometry (Bump Mapping).

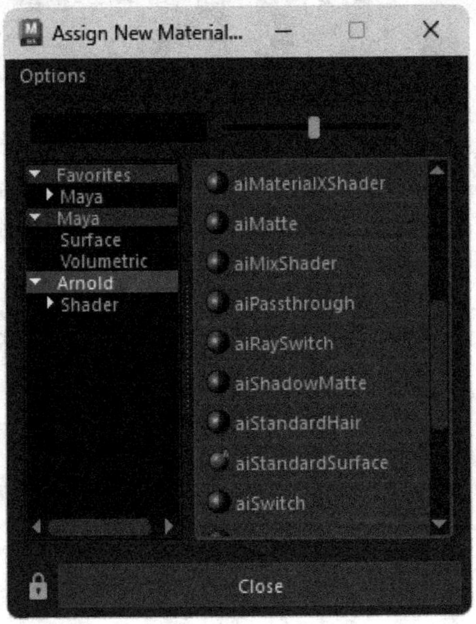

FIGURE 15-24

Arnold materials

Once an Open PBR Surface shader is applied to an object, you can click on the Presets button near the top of the Attribute Editor to choose one of many available material presets including Brushed Metal, Ceramic, Chrome, Copper, Diamond, Gold, Honey, Jade, Skin, Velvet, etc. Figure 15-25 shows the geometric flower example from earlier rendered in Arnold with several different presets applied.

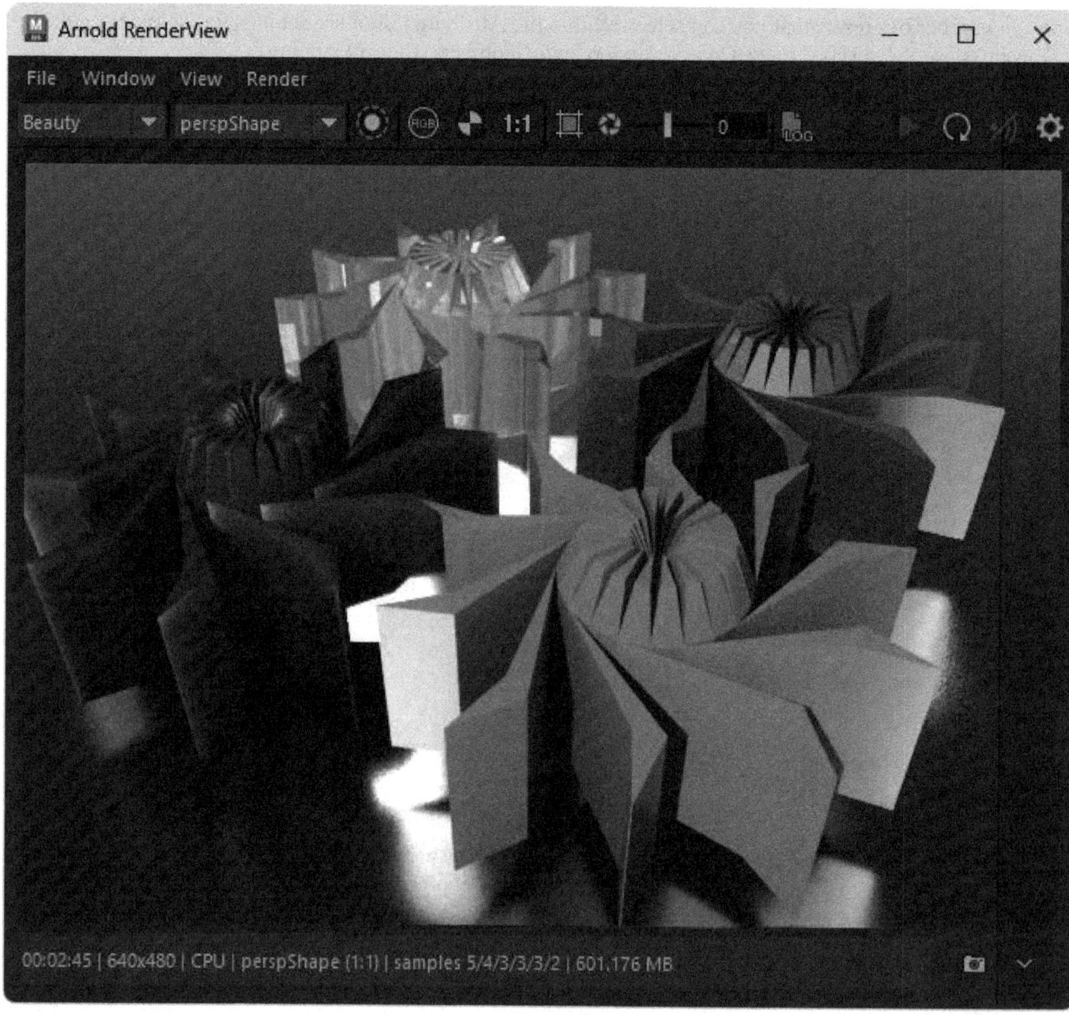

FIGURE 15-25

Arnold render with Arnold materials

Converting Legacy Materials to Arnold

If you have a legacy scene file with older materials that you want to render in Arnold, you can use the Arnold, Shaders, Convert Shaders to Arnold. This opens a dialog box that lets you convert all shaders in the scene or only those applied to the selected object. This command changes the material Type to use the AI Standard Surface material and tries its best to match the material settings. Note that even though you convert the materials for a legacy scene, they will not render until an Arnold light has been added to the scene.

Lesson 15.7-Tutorial 1: Use the Standard Surface Shader

1. Select the File, Open Scene menu command, and then locate and open the Shark in water.mb file.
2. Select the Windows, Rendering Editors, Render Settings menu command.
3. Enable the Arnold Renderer option in the Render Using drop-down list at the top of the dialog box.

4. Select the Arnold, Lights, Physical Sky menu command to add a light and a sky dome to the scene. In the Physical Sky node of the Attribute Editor, set the Elevation to 145 and the Intensity to 5.
5. Choose the Render, Render Current Frame menu command. In the upper right corner of the Render View window, press the Start IPR button.

   The scene is rendered in the Render View window using the Arnold renderer with auto updates using IPR enabled.
6. Select the Shark object and choose the Lighting/Shading, Assign New Material, then select the Arnold section and the ai Standard Surface material. In the ai Standard Surface tab of the Attribute Editor, click the Presets button and choose the Rubber, Replace menu command. Then, change the Color to a light gray.
7. Select the water surface plane object and choose the Lighting/Shading, Assign New Material, then select the Arnold section and the ai Standard Surface material. In the ai Standard Surface tab of the Attribute Editor, click the Presets button and choose the Plastic.
8. In the ai Standard Surface node in the Attribute Editor, set the Transmission Weight value to 0.65. In the Geometry rollout, click on the Create Render Node button to the right of the Bump Mapping setting and choose the Noise map. Set the Bump Depth to 0.4 and select the Noise tab in the Attribute Editor, change the Depth Max to 4, the Frequency to 30, and the Noise Type to Perlin Noise.

   The render is automatically updated as changes are made in the Render View window, Figure 15-26 shows the results when the render is complete.
9. Select File, Save Scene As and save the file as **Shark in water render.mb**.

FIGURE 15-26

Shark in water rendered in Arnold

Lesson 15.7-Tutorial 2: Convert Legacy Shaders to Arnold

1. Select the File, Open Scene menu command, and then locate and open the Geometric flower.mb file.

   This scene was rendered earlier in the chapter using the Maya Software renderer and includes legacy materials.
2. Select the Arnold, Shaders, Convert Shaders to Arnold menu command and choose All in the Convert Shaders dialog box that opens.
3. Select the Windows, Rendering Editors, Render Settings menu command.
4. Enable the Arnold Renderer option in the Render Using drop-down list at the top of the dialog box.
5. Select the Arnold, Lights, Skydome menu command to add a Skydome light to the scene. In the ai Sky Dome Light Shape node of the Attribute Editor, set the Intensity to 2.5.
6. Choose the Render, Render Current Frame menu command.

The scene is rendered in the Render View window using the Arnold renderer. Figure 15-27 shows the results when the render is complete, which you can compare to the earlier render.

7. Select File, Save Scene As and save the file as **Geometric flower converted.mb**.

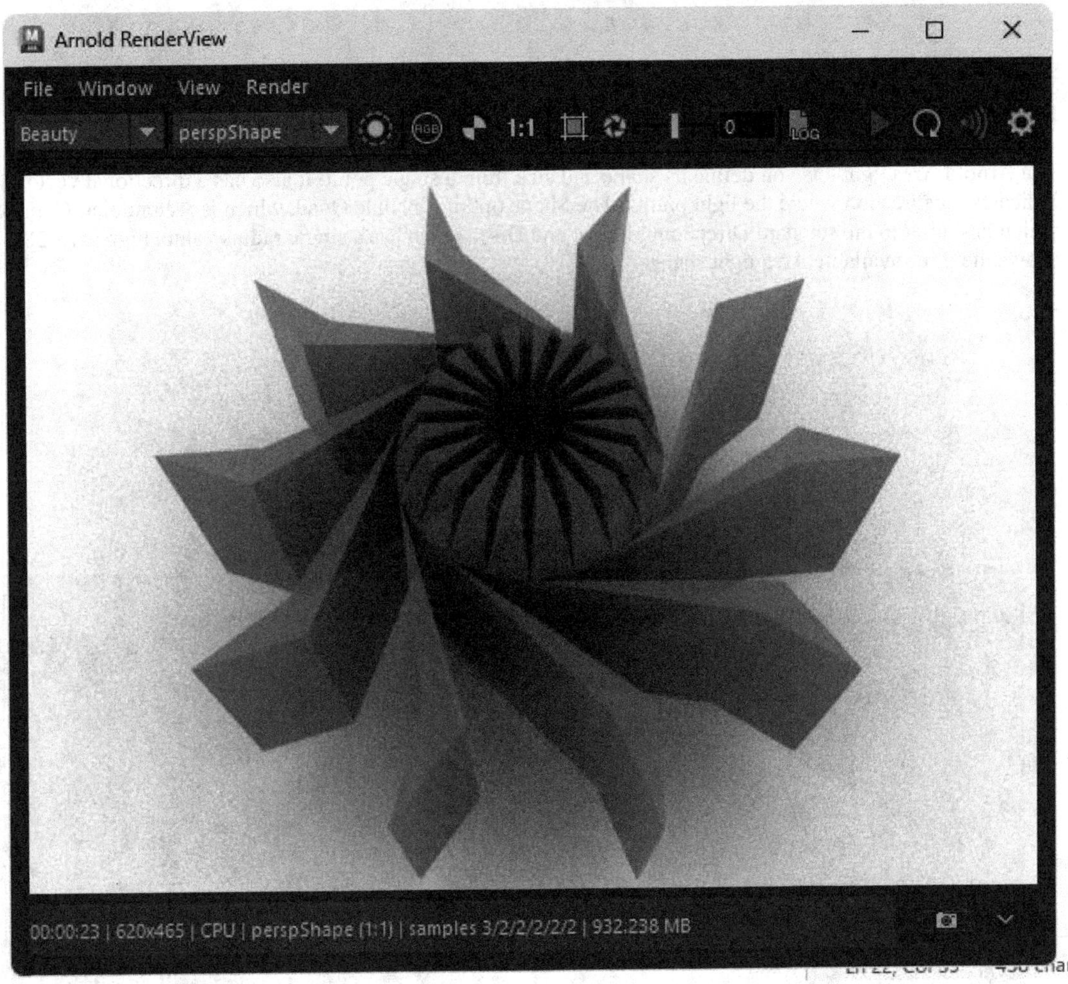

FIGURE 15-27

A geometric flower rendered in Arnold

Lesson 15.8: Using Arnold Lights and Physical Sky

Even though Arnold can render scenes using the standard lights, there is a marked improvement in scene quality and render speed if the scene is rendered using Arnold lights. You can find these lights in the Arnold menu, which is available when the Rendering menu set is selected. The available Arnold lights include several unique to Arnold such as Area, Skydome, Mesh, and Photometric. The Arnold, Lights menu also includes a Physical Sky option, which adds both a sun light object and a sky environment.

Note

The Arnold Renderer does not include any default lights, so if you render your scene and nothing shows up, either add an Arnold light to the scene or switch to the Software or Hardware rendering method.

Using Area Lights

The Arnold Area light lets you define its shape and size from a single point. It also has a directional vector that indicates the direction where the light points. The Shape options include Quad, which is rectangular, Cylinder, which is similar to the standard Directional lights, and Disc, which has a single radius value. Figure 15-28 shows the three available Area light shapes.

Tip

The default Intensity values for the Arnold Area light are really low and usually won't light the scene until the Intensity or the Exposure values are increased.

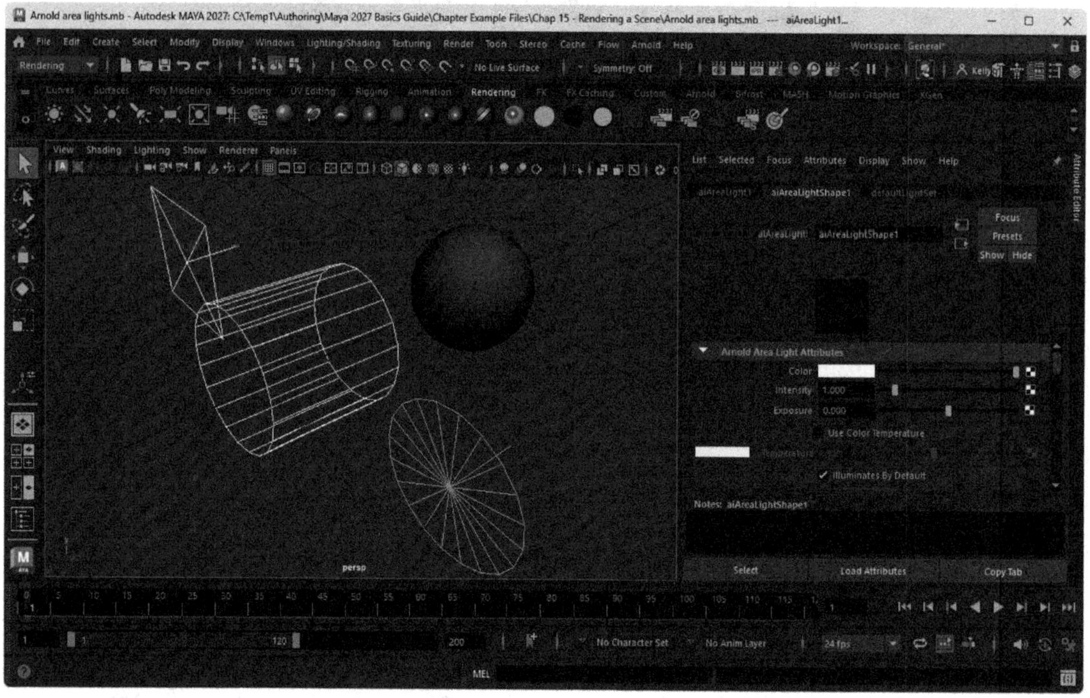

FIGURE 15-28

Arnold Area lights can be set to Quad, Cylinder, and Disc

Creating a Skydome Light

The Area lights typically require some work to get them in the right place with the right Intensity, but if you want to quickly add a light to your scene for a quick test render, then the Arnold, Lights, Skydome Light is a good choice. This command places a large sphere object in the scene that surrounds everything. This sphere has a simple color assigned to it along with a light source that simulates the sun.

Adding an HDRI Image to a Skydome

HDRI is an acronym for High Dynamic Range Image. These are a special image format that includes all lighting and environment information for the entire 360 degree around the current spot. When used in Maya and attached to a skydome object, Maya can treat any lighting sources in the image as a scene light. This provides a way to light the current scene with realistic indoor or outdoor lighting.

To attach an HDRI image to a Skydome object, locate and click on the mapping node at the right end of the Color attribute in the Attribute Editor. This opens the Create Render Node dialog where you need to select the File option. Then click on the file folder for the Image Name in the Attribute Editor and select the HDRI file to load. Figure 15-29 shows several sphere objects on a ground plane with an HDRI image attached to the Arnold Skydome. Once attached, you can rotate the Skydome to change the light source's orientation and background visuals.

Tip

You can also use EXR image files in place of HDRI images.

Tip

Although you can create your own HDRI images, there are several great repositories online including HDRI-Haven.com and PolyHaven.com.

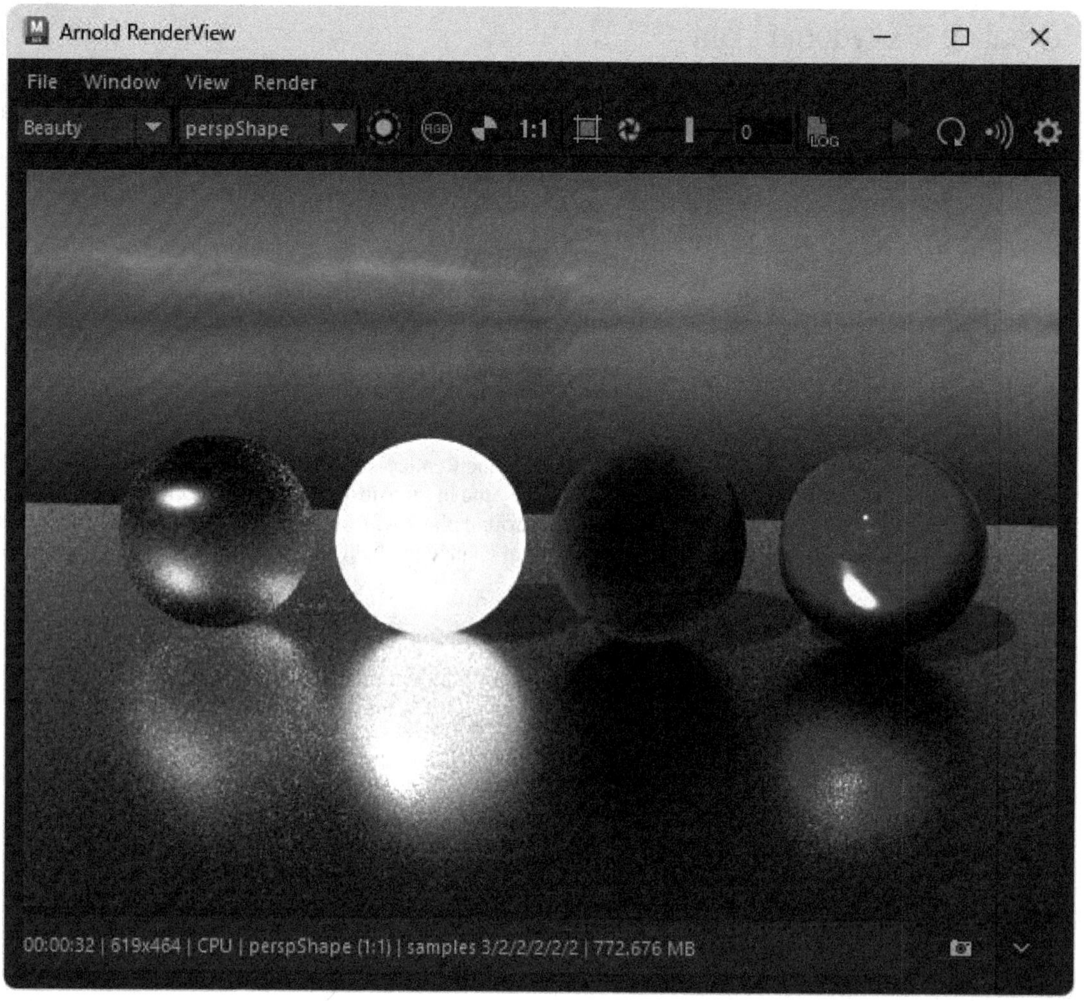

FIGURE 15-29

Environment images can be added to a Skydome

Adding Physical Sky

Another option to add a complete environment is to use the Arnold, Lights, Physical Sky menu command. This feature also adds a skydome object with a procedural texture and a sun light object that simulates real-world outdoor scenes. Figure 15-30 shows the toy duck mesh with the Arnold standard surface shade applied to all the various mesh parts and the Physical Sky feature added. Notice how it includes a background, shadows, and a light source.

FIGURE 15-30

Arnold Physical Sky

By selecting the Physical Sky node in the Attribute Editor, you can control the sun object's position in the sky. Figure 15-31 shows the available settings. Then changing the Elevation and Azimuth values, you can simulate the sun at sundown, as shown in Figure 15-32. Notice how the tint of the sky has changed also and the actual sun is also visible.

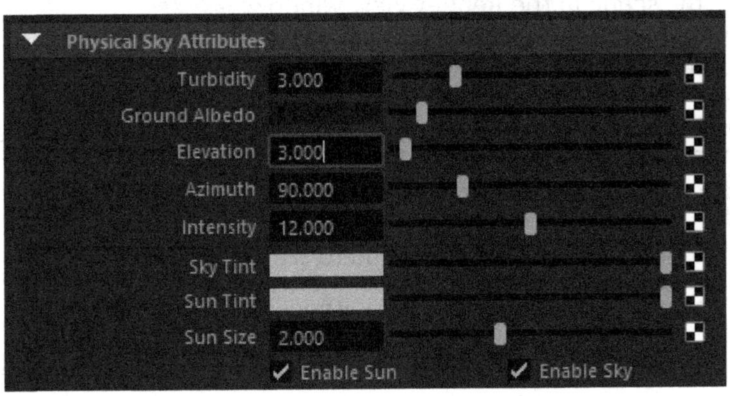

FIGURE 15-31

Arnold Physical Sky settings

FIGURE 15-32

Arnold Physical Sky at sundown

Lesson 15.8-Tutorial 1: Use Arnold Area Lights

1. Select the File, Open Scene menu command, and then locate and open the Gecko in grass.mb file.

   This scene already has the Arnold renderer enabled and an Arnold Skydome light applied so you can see the scene in the Render View window.
2. Select the View, Create Camera from View menu command from the active viewport menu. Select the Panels, Persp1 menu command to switch the current viewport to the new camera view.
3. Select the Render, Render Current Frame menu command to open the Render View window and click on the Start IPR button in the upper right corner.

   Since Arnold is already enabled and the scene includes an Arnold Skydome light, the gecko is rendered.
4. Select the Arnold, Lights, Area Light menu command to create a new light. In the viewport, move the light so it is close to the scene camera and rotate it so it is pointing at the gecko and name the light, 'key_light', then set the Intensity to 20 and the Exposure to 4.
5. Select the Windows, Outliner menu command and select and delete the Skydome Light object.

   By removing the skydome light, you can see the results of the Area light in the Render View window.
6. Select and clone the key light and position it so it is perpendicular to the key light when viewed from above and also pointing at the gecko. Name this light, 'fill_light'.
7. Select and clone the second light and position it so it is behind and pointing at the gecko opposite of the camera's position. Name this light, 'rim_light'. Reduce the Intensity of this light to 10.

8. Once the lighting is looking good, select the Render, Render Settings menu command, then select the Arnold Renderer tab. In the Sampling section, set Camera (AA) to 5 and Diffuse and Sub-Surface Scattering (SSS) to 4.

   The scene is rendered in the Render View window using the Arnold renderer, as shown in Figure 15-33.
9. Select File, Save Scene As and save the file as **Gecko in grass render.mb**.

FIGURE 15-33

Gecko in grass rendered using Arnold Area lights

Lesson 15.8-Tutorial 2: Render Skydome

1. Select the File, Open Scene menu command, and then locate and open the **Light bulbs.mb** file.

   This scene already has the Arnold renderer enabled with Arnold compatible materials applied to the scene objects.
2. Select the Arnold, Lights, Skydome Light menu command to create a new skydome light.

3. Select the Render, Render Current Frame menu command to open the Render View window and click on the Start IPR button in the upper right corner.

   The scene is displayed in the Render View window.

4. With the Skydome object selected, click on the Mapping button at the right end of the Color attribute in the Attribute Editor, select the File option and click on the File Folder button to the right of the Image Name attribute. Then, select and load the **partly_cloudy_ik.hdr** file.

   The environment HDRI file is loaded and mapped onto the skydome object.

5. Select the Skydome object again and set the Resolution to 2000 to match the size of the HDRI file.

   The scene is rendered in the Render View window using the Arnold renderer, as shown in Figure 15-34.

6. Select File, Save Scene As and save the file as **Light bulbs render.mb**.

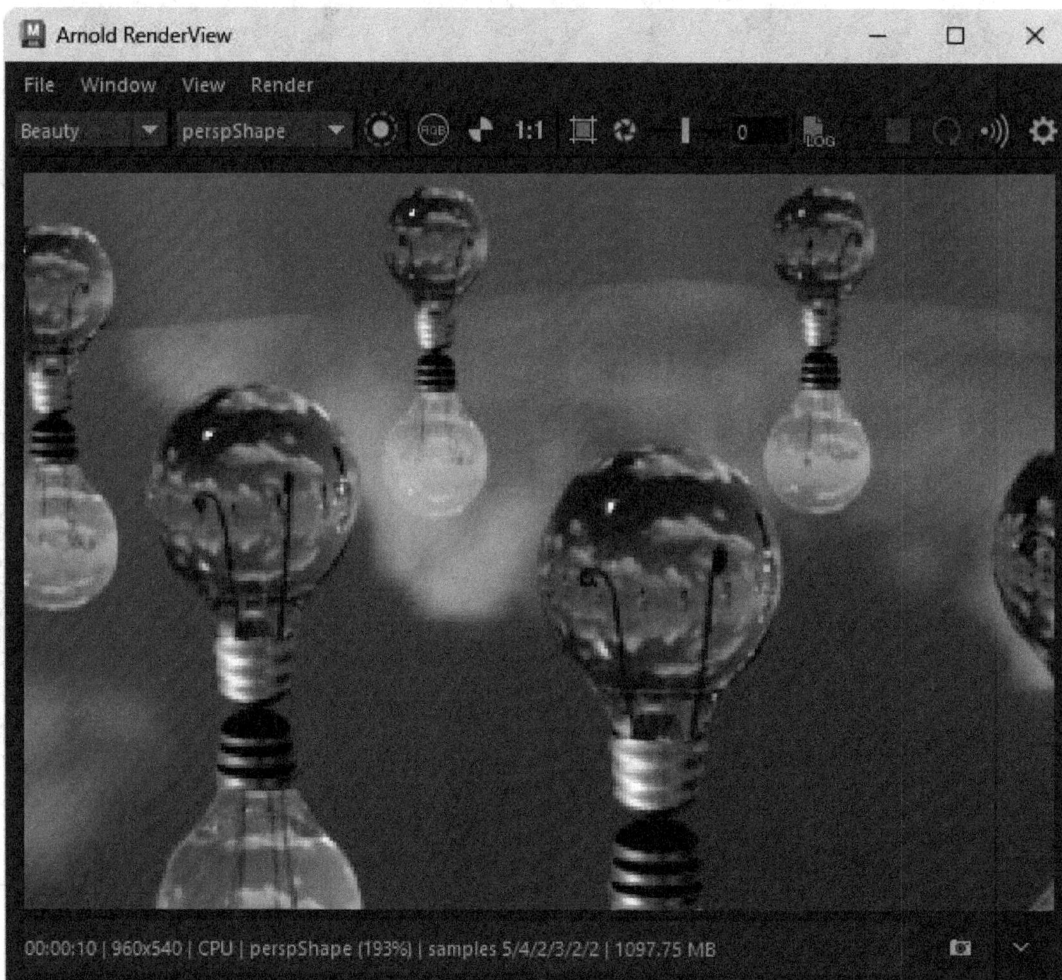

FIGURE 15-34

Light bulbs rendered with an Arnold Skydome

Lesson 15.8-Tutorial 3: Render Physical Sky

1. Select the File, Open Scene menu command, and then locate and open the Rose in crystal ball.mb file.
2. Select the Windows, Rendering Editors, Render Settings menu command.
3. Enable the Arnold Renderer option in the Render Using drop-down list at the top of the dialog box.
4. Select the Arnold Renderer tab. In the Sampling section, set Camera (AA) to 5 and Diffuse, Specular, and Transmission to 3. In the Ray Depth section, set the Total to 15.
5. Select the Rose object and choose the Lighting/Shading, Assign New Material, then select the Arnold section and the ai Standard Surface material and close the dialog box.
6. In the ai Standard Surface node in the Attribute Editor, set the Diffuse Color to red and the Specular Weight to 0.25. Then repeat this step for the other objects using the Presets button near the top of the Attribute Editor, setting the appropriate color and settings such as Gold for the base, Glass for the crystal ball and green Plastic for the leaves.
7. Select the Arnold, Lights, Physical Sky menu command to add a light and a sky dome to the scene. In the Physical Sky node of the Attribute Editor, set the Elevation to 143 and the Intensity to 3.5.
8. Right-click on the Perspective view to select it and choose the Render, Render Current Frame menu command.

   The scene is rendered in the Render View window using the Arnold renderer, as shown in Figure 15-35.
9. Select File, Save Scene As and save the file as **Arnold rose.mb**.

FIGURE 15-35

Arnold rendered crystal ball on a table

Chapter Summary

This chapter covers the rendering process. The Render Settings dialog box includes all the controls for configuring the renderer as well as several special render features including raytracing and motion blur. The Render View window lets you render to a window without having to save the image to a file. You can interactively render the Render View window using the IPR feature for quicker updates. You can render images at different settings, including preview, draft, and production qualities. You can specify that the render engine render uses the Vector or Arnold renderer. The Arnold renderer enables some advanced features such as sampling and ray tracing that improve the quality of the rendered results. Arnold lights include Skydomes and Physical Sky.

What You Have Learned

In this chapter, you learned

* How to configure a scene for rendering.
* How to choose a renderer and a render preset.
* How to change the render image file name and format.
* How to change a camera view and render resolution.
* How to adjust the render quality.
* How to enable raytracing, motion blur, and fog effects.
* How to use the Render View window.
* How to render a specific region.
* How to use IPR rendering.
* How to save rendered images.
* How to render a single frame, an animation, or batch render.
* How to render using Maya Vector.
* How to render using Arnold.
* How to add the Arnold Standard Surface shader to objects.
* How to use Arnold Area and Skydome lights.
* How to add an Arnold Physical Sky environment.

Key Terms From This Chapter

* **Rendering.** The process of computing all the lighting, object, and material effects for a scene into a final image.
* **Render Settings dialog box.** A dialog box of settings for configuring the rendering process.
* **Render preset.** A saved configuration of render settings that you can recall at any time.
* **Raytracing.** A rendering method that accurately traces the path of light rays traveling through the scene.
* **Motion blur.** A rendering effect that blurs objects in relation to their speed in the scene.
* **Fog.** A rendering effect that simulates fog being added to the scene.
* **Render region.** An option to render only a selected region in the Render View window.

* **Interactive Photorealistic Rendering.** A rendering mode that can display changes to the scene's materials, textures, and lights without having to re-render the entire scene.

* **Maya Vector.** A renderer option that renders the scene as an illustration with lines and fills.

* **Arnold.** A renderer option that provides accurate, high-detailed images.

* **HDRI.** High Dynamic Range Image. An image used to add a visual environment and a light source to the scene.

* **Skydome.** A spherical environment object that surrounds and provides light to the scene.

* **Physical Sky.** A lighting solution available in Arnold that adds a sun object and a sky dome where the sky and background simulate real-world settings.

Chapter 16
Using MEL Scripting

IN THIS CHAPTER

16.1 Use the command line.

16.2 Use the Script Editor.

MEL stands for *Maya Embedded Language*. It is the scripting language that lets you create scripts that can do anything that you can do using the interface. The effects covered in Chapter 14 like fire and lightning are great examples of what is possible with MEL Scripting.

MEL is a robust language that you can use to program actions and events in Maya, but you don't need to be a programmer to take advantage of MEL.

You can enter MEL commands directly into the **command line** found at the bottom of the interface. Once the command is entered, you can press the Enter key to execute it.

For a complete listing of the available MEL commands, select the Help, Scripting Reference, MEL Command Reference menu command.

In addition to MEL, Maya can also work with Python scripts. You can find more information about Python scripting in Maya using the reference accessible from the Help, Scripting Reference, Python Command Reference menu command.

You can also locate specific MEL and Python commands with the Search feature located under the Quick Layout Buttons. The hotkey of Command/Ctrl + F can also be used. From the drop-down menu at the top of the Search text field, select either MEL or Python, then type the command you wish to use, and a list of context appropriate scripting commands will be presented.

For larger scripts, you can use the **Script Editor,** which includes two expandable panes into which you can enter script commands and see the results. You can also use the Script Editor to view the script commands for interface commands. Scripts within the Script Editor can be saved, loaded, and moved to the Shelf as a button for quick access.

Lesson 16.1: Use the Command Line

You can enter MEL Script commands into the command line.

Using MEL in the Command Line

The command line includes two parts, shown in Figure 16-1. The left part is where you can enter MEL commands and the resulting answer appears in the grayed-out part on the right. If the command line isn't visible, you can make it appear using the Windows, UI Elements, Command Line menu command.

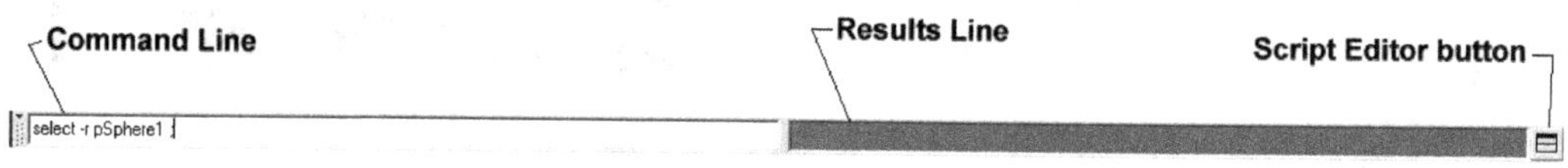

FIGURE 16-1

The command line

Repeating Command Line Commands

If the cursor is positioned within the command line, you can recall and execute commands that were previously entered into the command line using the Up and Down arrows. Pressing the Enter key executes the listed command.

Using the MEL Scripting Commands

MEL Scripting won't help you if you don't know any of the MEL commands. The following table provides a brief look at some of the more useful MEL commands. Table 16-1 only scratches the surface of the available commands, but it gives you some commands to try.

Each command line must have a semicolon (;) at the end of its line. This identifies the end of the command.

Table 16-1 MEL Commands

MEL Command	Description
help;	Lists helpful information on how to use a command, for example, help move.
rand(100);	Picks a random number between 0 and 100.
print "hello";	Prints the string listed in quotes.
sphere; nurbsCube; cylinder; cone; torus; circle; nurbsSquare;	Creates the listed NURBS primitive object.
polySphere; polyCube; polyCylinder; polyCone; polyTorus; polyPlane;	Creates the listed polygon primitive object.
move 5 0 0; rotate 90 0 0; scale 2 0 0;	Transforms the selected object the specified amount.
sphere -name "sp1" -radius 50;	Attributes have a dash (-) in front of them and their value after. This command creates a NURBS sphere with the name sp1 and a radius of 50.
polyEvaluate -f;	Counts the number of polygons in the selected object.
ls -sl;	Returns the name of the currently selected object.
select name;	Selects the object named name.

render; batchRender;	Renders the current view or begins the batch rendering process using the Render Global Settings.
convertUnit -fromUnit "in" -toUnit "cm" "11.5";	Returns the converted amount of 11.5 inches into centimeters.
curve -p 0 0 0 -p 1 1 1 -p 2 1 2 -p 8 5 3;	Creates a curve using the designated points.
delete;	Deletes the selected object.
duplicate;	Creates a copy of the selected object.
emitter;	Creates an Emitter object.
hide sp1; hide -all; showHidden -all;	Hides the specified object or, with -all, hides all objects. Shows all hidden objects.
play; playblast;	Starts playing the animation. Starts Playblast.
exit;	Exits the application.
undo; redo;	Undoes or redoes the last or next commands.
refresh;	Forces the view panel to be redrawn.
spotlight;	Creates a Spotlight object.
textCurves -t "hello";	Creates text curves using the specified string.
file -f -new;	Opens a new scene.
file -save;	Saves the current scene.
SaveSceneAs;	Opens the Save As dialog box.

Lesson 16.1-Tutorial 1: Enter MEL Commands in the Command Line

1. Click in the command line at the bottom of the interface and type **cylinder;** and then press Enter.

   A new polygon cylinder object appears in the view panel.
2. Click again on the command line and type **move 0 0 5;**.
3. Click on the command line and press the Up arrow key twice.
4. Press Enter again.

   Another cylinder object is created and displayed in the view panel, as shown in Figure 16-2.
5. Select File, Save Scene As and save the file as **Simple cylinders.mb**.

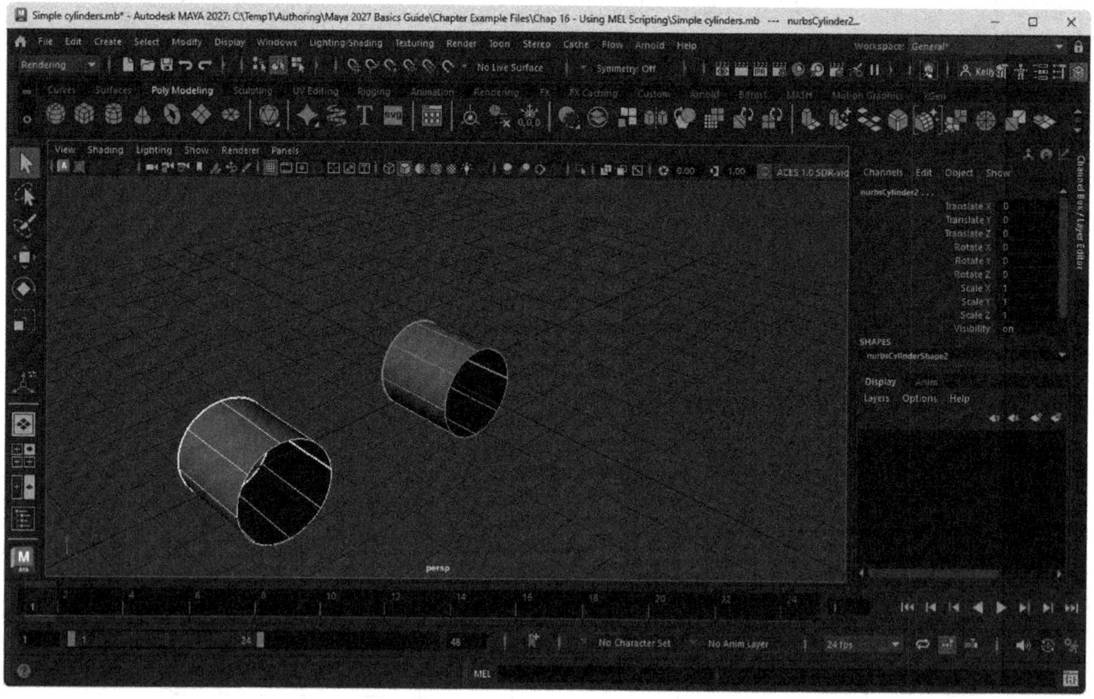

FIGURE 16-2

Cylinders created using the command line

Lesson 16.2: Use the Script Editor

You can create MEL Scripts in the Script Editor, shown in Figure 16-3. Clicking on the Script Editor button in the lower-right corner of the interface opens the Script Editor, or you can use the Windows, General Editors, Script Editor menu command. The Script Editor, like the command line, includes two panes. The lower pane is where you can type script commands and the upper pane displays the results.

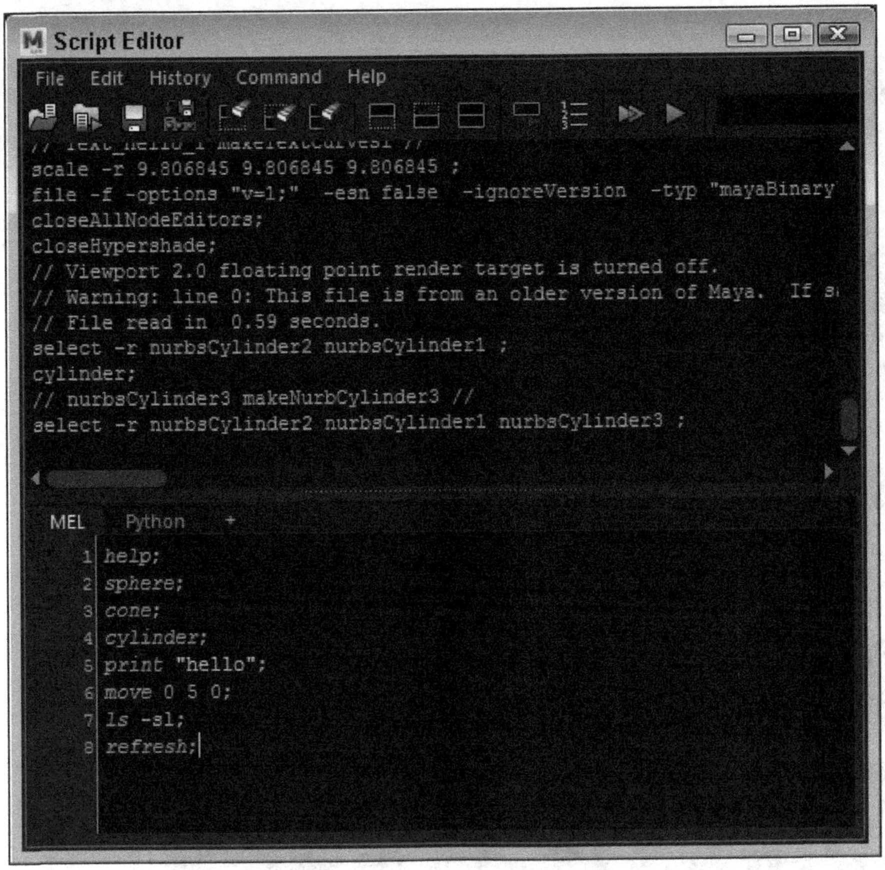

FIGURE 16-3

The Script Editor

Executing Script Commands

Select a command in the lower pane and press Ctrl/Command+Enter to execute the commands, or select the Script, Execute menu command in the Script Editor.

Viewing Interface Commands

The upper pane of the Script Editor displays the script command for every interface action. This is a great way to learn how to use new commands. To view the details of every interface action, you can enable the History, Echo All Commands menu option. The History menu also includes several options for limiting the amount of command details displayed in the upper pane. These options include Suppress Command Results, Suppress Info, Warning and Error Messages. To clear all the commands listed in the upper, lower, or both panes, choose the Edit, Clear History, Clear Input, or Clear All dialog menu commands.

Reusing Interface Commands

Any command that is listed in the upper pane of the Script Editor can be selected and moved to the lower pane using the Edit, Cut, Copy, and Paste menu commands. Once you move them to the lower pane, you can edit and execute the commands again. Figure 16-4 shows a series of commands that have been copied to the lower pane, where they have been edited.

Tip

> You also can move selected script commands in the upper pane to the lower pane by dragging and dropping them.

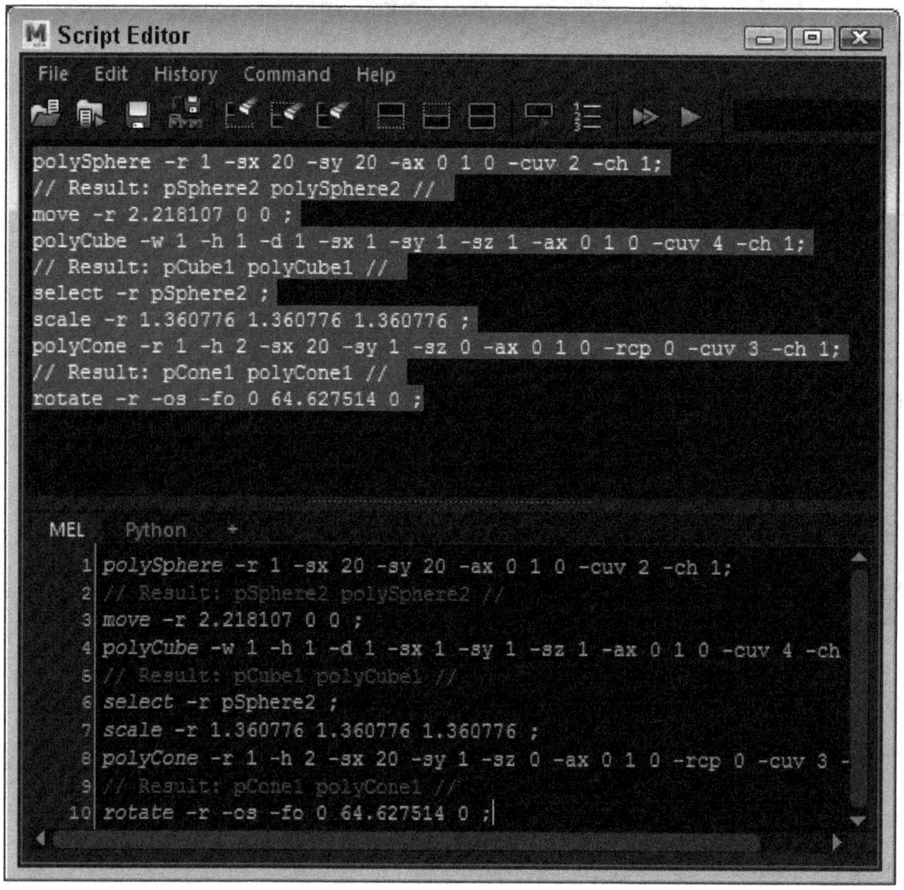

FIGURE 16-4

Commands copied to the lower pane

Saving Scripts

You can save commands that are listed in either pane as a text file for future loading and editing. To save the commands, select them in the Script Editor and choose the File, Save Selected menu command. This command opens a file dialog box where you can name the file. The File, Open Script menu command reopens a saved script file.

Adding Scripts to the Shelf

If you select script commands in the Script Editor and drag them with the middle mouse button to the Shelf, a button is created that allows you to execute the command by clicking it. Another way to do this is with the File, Save Selected to Shelf menu command.

Lesson 16.2-Tutorial 1: Use the Script Editor

1. Select the Windows, General Editors, Script Editor menu command.

   The Script Editor opens.

2. In the lower pane, type **sphere –radius 2;**.
3. Select the Script, Execute menu command.
4. With the sphere object selected, type **move 0 –1 0;** in the lower pane.
5. Select the Move command and choose the Script, Execute menu command (or press the Ctrl/Command+Enter hotkey).

   A sphere with a radius of 2 is created and moved downward in the negative Y-axis.

6. Select File, Save Scene As and save the file as **Simple script.mb**.

Lesson 16.2-Tutorial 2: View Interface Commands and Save a Script

1. Select the Windows, General Editors, Script Editor menu command.
2. Select the Create, Polygon Primitives, Cube menu command.
3. Click on the Select by Component Type button in the Status Line and drag over the top four vertices.
4. Select the Edit Mesh, Merge to Center menu command from the Polygons menu set.

   The top vertices are merged to form a pyramid object and all the commands to create this object are displayed in the top pane of the Script Editor, as shown in Figure 16-5.

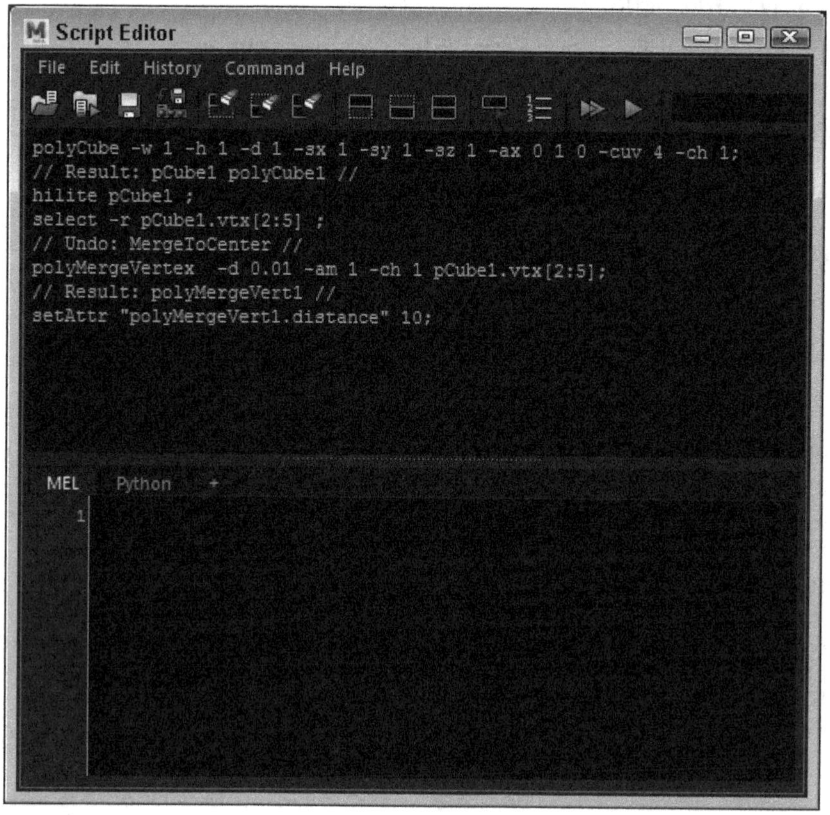

FIGURE 16-5

Interface commands

5. Drag over the commands in the upper pane of the Script Editor to select them and choose the File, Save Selected menu command.
6. In the dialog box that appears, save the file as **Pyramid.mel**.
7. Select the commands again and drag with the middle mouse button to the Shelf.

   A new button, named MEL, appears on the Shelf, as shown in Figure 16-6.
8. Select File, Save Scene As and save the file as **Pyramid.mb**.

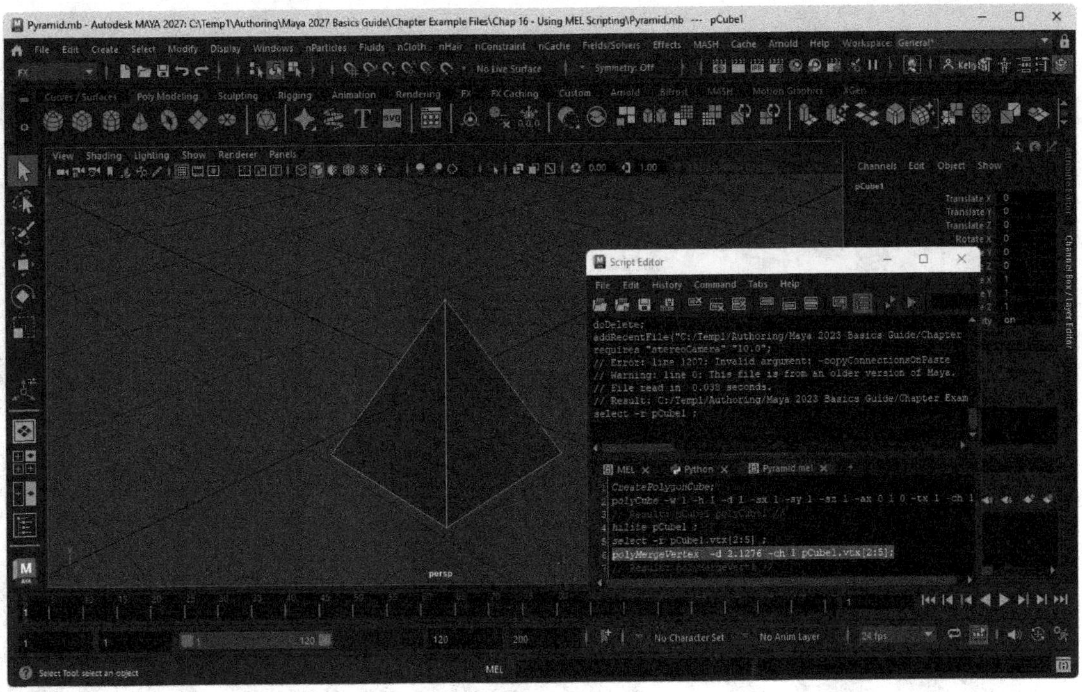

FIGURE 16-6

Pyramid

Lesson 16.2-Tutorial 3: Execute a Custom Script

1. Type **polySphere;** into the command line and press Enter.
2. Select the Windows, General Editors, Script Editor menu command. Select the Edit, Clear All menu command in the Script Editor.

   The Script Editor opens and all existing text is removed.
3. Select the sphere and click the Select by Component Type button in the Status Line. Drag over the sphere to select all vertices. Select the Edit Mesh, Extrude menu command.

   The vertices of the sphere are extruded outward.
4. Select the commands in the top pane of the Script Editor. Select the File, Save Selected menu command. Save the file as **Extrude vertices.mel**.
5. Select all the commands in the upper pane of the Script Editor. Drag and drop the selected commands to lower pane. Select the Command, Execute menu command.

   The script commands are executed and another sphere with extruded vertices is created, as shown in Figure 16-7.

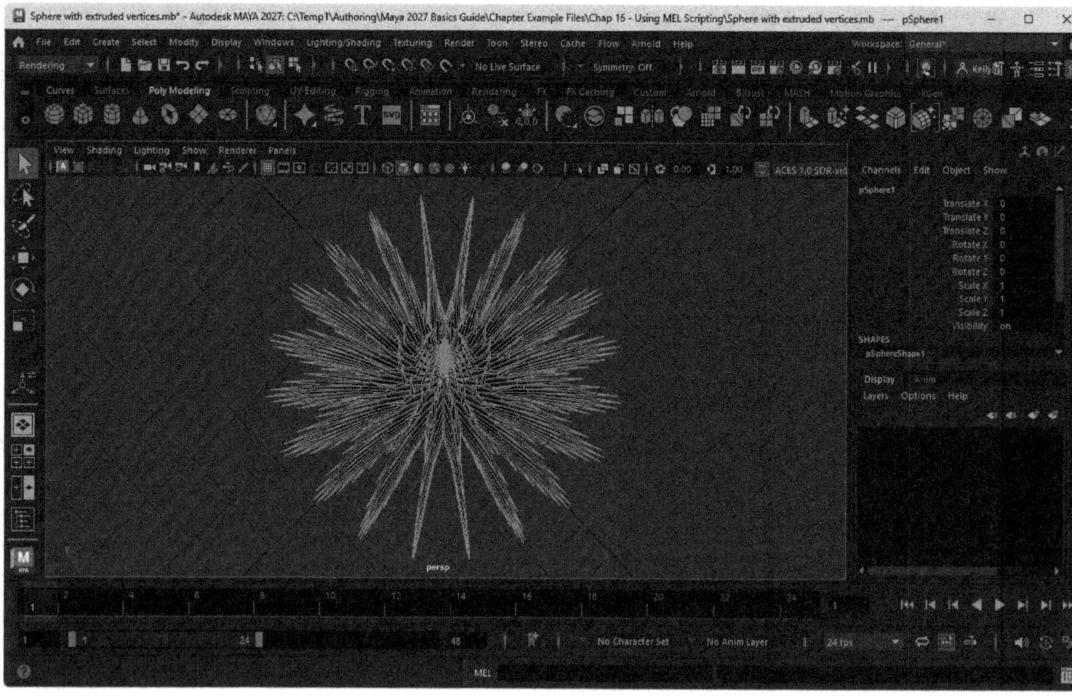

FIGURE 16-7

Sphere with extruded vertices

Chapter Summary

This chapter introduces MEL Scripting. You can enter and execute script commands using the command line and also using the Script Editor. Using the Script Editor lets you create and record new scripts and also load and save scripts.

What You Have Learned

In this chapter, you learned

* How to enter a MEL Script command into the command line.
* How to repeat commands entered into the command line.
* How to use several MEL Script commands.
* How to use the Script Editor.
* How to view interface commands.
* How to save scripts.
* How to add scripts to the Shelf.

Key Terms From This Chapter

* **MEL.** (Maya Embedded Language) A scripting language used to create scripts.
* **Command line.** An interface field where you execute script commands.
* **Script Editor.** An editor interface where you compile, save, and execute multi-line scripts.

Glossary

* **Aligning.** The process of moving objects so that certain components have the same position.
* **Alpha channel.** An image that shows the transparency values of the scene as a grayscale image.
* **Angle of View.** A camera's angle value used to set the width of the scene viewed through the camera. Sets the width of the view area.
* **Animation controls.** A set of buttons used to control animation frames.
* **Anisotropic.** A material noted for its elliptical specular highlights.
* **Appending.** The process of attaching a polygon to an existing polygon.
* **Arc.** A curve made up of part of a circle.
* **Arnold.** A renderer option that provides accurate, high-detailed images.
* **Attributes.** Values that determine the properties of the node.
* **Auto Key.** The mode that automatically creates keys whenever an object moves or a parameter changes.
* **Auto Paint.** A painting mode that automatically applies strokes to the selected object.
* **Backface Culling.** A display option that makes object elements located on the backside invisible.
* **Bevel.** An operation that replaces an edge with a polygon face.
* **Beveling.** The process of smoothing a surface by adding a face to the surface edges.
* **Blinn.** A material with soft circular highlights; good for metallic surfaces.
* **Bone.** An object that is connected between two joints and defines the rigid areas of a character.
* **Boolean.** Operations used to combine surfaces by adding, subtracting, or intersecting two or more objects.
* **Boolean Stack.** A list in the Attribute Editor of all the objects used in a boolean operation.
* **Border.** A series of edges that line a polygon hole.
* **Brush.** An interface element used to create Paint Effects within a scene.

* **Bump map.** A texture that is used to set the relief of a material where dark areas are raised and lighter areas are indented.

* **Canvas.** A 2D interface where you can paint and save objects.

* **Chamfer.** An operation that replaces the selected vertices with polygon faces.

* **Channel Box.** A panel of editable parameters that relate to the current selection.

* **Cleanup.** An operation that removes potential trouble parts of a polygon model such as unattached vertices.

* **Cloth collision object.** An object that a cloth object drapes over.

* **Cloth.** A specialized object type that simulates the dynamic interactions of cloth.

* **Cluster.** A group of vertices that moves together.

* **Collider Object.** An object that is allowed to collide with other objects in the scene during a simulation.

* **Command line.** An interface field where you execute script commands.

* **Components.** The subobjects that make up an entire object. Can include faces, vertices, CVs, and so on.

* **Component Tag.** A named and marked set of selected components for easy recall.

* **Connection Editor.** An interface for defining the connections between various nodes.

* **Constraint.** An icon that binds objects to a physical force that limits their motion, such as a hinge.

* **Construction history.** A list of commands executed to build a scene.

* **Construction Plane.** A plane that shows where each axis plane is located.

* **Content Browser.** A dialog box that holds presets that can be quickly selected, such as Paint Effects.

* **Convert.** A series of commands that lets you change one modeling type such as NURBS to another modeling type such as a subdivision surface.

* **Create Bar.** A selection list in the Hypershade where you can choose from default materials, textures and nodes.

* **Curve degree.** The amount of curve applied to a line.

* **CV curve.** A curve created by placing CV points.

* **CV.** Control Vertex. A curve component that defines the curvature of the curve.

* **Default grid.** An invisible array of points that mark the origin of the scene.

* **Default lights.** A set of lights that are available by default as part of a new scene.

* **Default pose.** The skin's original position when it was first bound to the skeleton.

* **Depth map shadow**. A shadowing method created by saving the shadows into a bitmap that is projected onto the scene.

* **Depth of Field.** A camera effect where objects farther away from the focus point become gradually blurrier.

* **Deformer.** A command that adds a manipulator to an object with attributes that can deform its surface.

* **Deformer Weights.** A weight value that is applied to each vertex in an object to set its influence by a specific attribute. These are applied using a paint brush interface.

* **Delta Mush deformer.** A deformer that smoothes out wild distortions.

* **Dolly.** The act of zooming the camera to change the view's focus width.

* **Dope sheet.** An interface used to display and edit the timing of an animation.

* **Dynamics.** A type of animation where the keyframes are computed using physics calculations after assigning physical properties to the scene objects.

* **Edge loop.** A series of edges that run end to end across the surface of a polygon object.

* **Edge ring.** A series of parallel edges that run across the surface of a polygon object.

* **Edit Curve tool.** A tool used to edit the curvature of a curve using handles attached to the curve.

* **Emitter.** An icon of objects that is the source of the particles.

* **EP curve.** A curve created by placing points that the curve passes through.

* **Event.** An action that occurs in the scene that spawns more particles, such as a collision.

* **Extruding.** The process of creating a surface by moving the curve perpendicular to itself.

* **Field.** An icon in the scene that represents a physical force, such as gravity or drag.

* **Filleting.** The process of smoothing the corner between two adjacent faces.

* **Fluid container.** A container that defines the boundaries of a fluid.

* **Fluid emitter.** An icon that marks the source of the fluid.

* **Focal Length.** A camera setting used to determine where the camera's focus is located.

* **Fog.** A rendering effect that simulates fog being added to the scene.

* **Forward Kinematics.** Physics that allows the position of child objects to be calculated when the parent object is moved.

* **Framing.** The process of zooming and panning the camera to focus on the selected object.

* **Ghosting.** A setting that makes multiple copies of the animated objects appear at regular intervals along a motion path.

* **Goal.** An object in the scene that a particle system is attracted towards.

* **Graph Editor.** An interface that displays all animation actions as graphed curves allowing editing and modification.

* **Grouping.** The process of collecting multiple objects together into a named group.

* **Hair splines**. A set of curves on an object that define how the hair extends and its style.

* **Handles.** A manipulator part that lets you change attributes by dragging in the viewport.

* **Heads-Up Display.** A menu command for adding informative text to the view panel.

* **Help Line.** A text field that presents the next action that is expected.

* **Hotbox.** A comprehensive set of menu options accessible by pressing the Spacebar.

* **Hotkey.** A keyboard shortcut that executes a command when pressed.

* **Hull.** A set of straight lines that connects a curve's CV points.

* **Hypershade.** An interface where materials and shaders are created.

* **IK Handle.** An IK solution that is used for parts such as arms and legs.

* **IK Spline.** An IK solution that is used for parts such as tails.

* **Image plane.** A background plane where a background texture or image can be loaded.

* **In-View Editor.** A small dialog box of attributes that appears next to the object being edited in lieu of the Channel Box.

* **Infinity conditions.** A setting that enables an animated sequence to repeat indefinitely.

* **Influence object.** An object that controls the local deformation of a character skin.

* **Instance.** An object that is used in place of a particle.

* **Interactive Photorealistic Rendering.** A rendering mode that can display changes to the scene's materials, textures, and lights without having to re-render the entire scene.

* **Inverse Kinematics.** A physics definition that allows objects at the end of a skeleton hierarchy to control the motion and position of the entire skeleton.

* **Isoparametric curve.** Representative lines that show the object's surface. Called isoparms for short.

* **Joint.** An object connected to a bone used to rotate and move skeleton bones.

* **Key object.** The last object that is selected. The key object is the base object for certain commands.

* **Keyframe.** An animation setting that records the state of an object for a given frame.

* **Lambert.** A material with no highlights; useful for cloth and non-reflective surfaces.

* **Lattice.** A deformer that surrounds the object with a grid of points that influences the shape of the object contained within it.

* **Layer.** A selection of objects grouped together into a set that can be easily selected.

* **Lens flare**. A lighting effect that simulates the effect of pointing a camera at a light source.

* **Lifespan.** The number of frames that a particle exists in the scene.

* **Light decay**. A light property that causes light intensity to gradually diminish.

* **Light intensity**. A value that denotes the power of a light source.

* **Linear curve.** A curve with a degree of 1, resulting in straight lines.

* **Locator.** A non-rendered marker that identifies a point in space.

* **Lofting.** The process of creating a surface by connecting several cross sections together.

* **Looping.** A setting that causes an animation to repeatedly play.

* **Mapping.** The method used to wrap a texture around an object.

* **Marking menu.** A dynamic set of menus accessible by right-clicking on an object.

* **MASH System.** A system that allows the creation of distributed objects and rigid body dynamics.

* **Material.** A set of surface properties that are assigned to an object to simulate various object materials.

* **Maya Vector.** A renderer option that renders the scene as an illustration with lines and fills.

* **MEL.** (Maya Embedded Language.) A scripting language used to create scripts.

* **Menu set.** A dynamic set of menu options selected from a drop-down list at the top left of the interface.

* **Modeling Toolkit.** A panel of commands placed together for working with polygon objects.

* **Motion blur.** A rendering effect that blurs objects in relation to their speed in the scene.

* **Motion Capture.** The motions of an actual actor captured using a suit that is saved as a file that can be used to animate a character rig.

* **Motion path.** A created curve that defines the animation path that an object follows.

* **Motion trail.** A curve that shows the path of the animated object.

* **Near and Far Clipping planes.** Near and Far camera planes that define where objects are not visible.

* **Node Editor.** An interface that shows all scene objects as nodes in a hierarchical display.

* **Node.** A selectable scene container that holds specific attributes.

* **Non-Uniform Scaling.** Scaling an object along only one or two axes to change the overall shape of the object.

* **Normal.** A vector extending perpendicular from the surface of a polygon used to determine the polygon's inner and outer faces.

* **NURBS patch.** The surface area that lies in between isoparms.

* **NURBS Primitives.** A collection of pre-built NURBS-based objects.

* **NURBS.** A 3D surface created from curves that define its area. An acronym that stands for Non-Uniform Rational B-Spline.

* **Object density.** The total number of divisions that make up an object.

* **Offset curve.** A duplicated curve that is moved parallel to the selected curve.

* **Option dialog box.** A dialog box with additional options opened using the icon found to the right of specific menu options.

* **Outliner.** An interface that displays all scene objects as simple nodes.

* **Paint Effects.** An innovative Maya feature that lets you paint objects in the scene using brushes.

* **Particles.** A collection of small objects that act together as a single unit.

* **Phong.** A material with a hard circular highlight; good for glass surfaces.

* **Pivot point.** The point about which the object or objects are rotated.

* **Playblast.** A feature that plays the current animation in a separate media player.

* **Poking.** An operation that adds a vertex to the center of the selected face and attaches edges to the new vertex.

* **Polygon.** A co-planar surface created from three or more linear edges.

* **Polygon Primitives.** A collection of pre-built polygon-based objects.

* **Pop-up help.** A small text title that appears when the cursor is held over the top of an icon.

* **Quad Draw tool.** A tool found in the Modeling Toolkit that lets you move and work with all components at once.

* **Quick Layout buttons.** A set of buttons for changing the interface layout.

* **Quick Rig.** The skeleton rig that is automatically created based on the skin geometry.

* **Ray trace shadows**. A shadowing method that computes shadows by following light rays as they move around the scene.

* **Raytracing.** A rendering method that accurately traces the path of light rays traveling through the scene.

* **Reduce.** An operation that reduces the total number of polygons in a model.

* **Render preset.** A saved configuration of render settings that you can recall at any time.

* **Render region.** An option to render only a selected region in the Render View window.

* **Render Settings dialog box.** A dialog box of settings for configuring the rendering process.

* **Rendering.** The process of computing all the lighting, object, and material effects for a scene into a final image.

* **Resolution.** A measure of the detail (or number of elements) used to display scene objects.

* **Retopology.** The process of simplifying the topology (or surface) of an object resulting in fewer and more regularly aligned polygons.

* **Revolving.** The process of creating a surface by rotating a curve about an axis.

* **Rigging.** The process of adding and configuring a skeleton to a character that is used to control its motion.

* **Rigid body object.** A solid object that doesn't deform when it collides with other objects, such as a brick.

* **Root joint.** The top joint in the skeleton hierarchy.

* **Safe area.** A set of camera markings that denote where title and action areas are definitely visible.

* **Script Editor.** An editor interface where you compile, save, and execute multi-line scripts.

* **Sculpt Geometry tool.** A tool used to push and pull on an object's surface.

* **Seamless texture.** An image that allows strokes drawn on one edge of the canvas to be wrapped to the opposite edge.

* **Selection mask.** A filter that limits the types of objects that can be selected.

* **Selection set.** A selection of objects that are named for quick recall.

* **Shader.** A complex set of connected material nodes that define a specific material.

* **Shading.** A display method used to show scene objects as solid objects.

* **Shelf.** A customizable set of buttons organized into separate groups.

* **ShrinkWrap deformer.** A deformer that wraps one object onto the surface of another.

* **Skeleton.** A hierarchical set of bones and joints used to define the underlying structure of a character.

* **Skin weight.** The amount of control each vertex has when an adjacent bone is moved.

* **Skin.** The model that is placed over a skeleton that is bound to the skeleton and deformed by it.

* **Smooth proxy.** A smoothed copy of an original polygon object.

* **Smooth skin.** A skin object that deforms as its bound skeleton is moved.

* **Snapping.** The process of automatically moving an object to precisely align with a specific component.

* **Soft body object.** An object that deforms when it collides with other objects, such as a pillow.

* **Solidify.** A deformer that removes a set of components from the influence of other deformers.

* **Status Line.** A set of toolbar icons located at the top of the interface.

* **Stitching.** The process of attaching adjacent patches together so they move without creating holes.

* **Stroke.** The resulting lines produced by dragging a brush in the scene.

* **Subdividing.** An operation for splitting all polygon faces into two or more faces.

* **Surface Editing tool.** A tool that uses a manipulator to edit the surface curvature.

* **Super Shapes.** A collection of abstract primitive objects.

* **Sweep Mesh**. An object created by sweeping a given cross-section along the length of a curve.

* **Tangents.** Handles that control the curvature of a curve near each key point.

* **Taper**. When an object changes its cross-section diameter over the length of the object.

* **Tear-off menu.** A panel of menu options that is removed to float freely from the interface.

* **Tension deformer.** A deformer that makes objects act like softbody objects.

* **Texture deformer.** A deformer that deforms the surface based on the texture's luminance.

* **Texture.** A bitmap file that is wrapped around an object.

* **Time Slider.** An interface element that displays all the frames and keys for the current animation.

* **Toolbox.** A set of selection and transformation icons located to the left of the interface.

* **Torus.** A circular primitive object with a circular cross section, shaped like a doughnut.

* **Track.** The act of panning the camera to change the view's focal point.

* **Trimming.** The process of cutting holes into a NURBS surface.

* **Tumble.** The act of rotating a camera to change the view's orientation.

* **Twist**. When an object twists about itself over the length of the object.

* **Uniform Scaling.** Changing the entire size of an object without changing its shape.

* **View panel.** The central scene window where objects are displayed.

* **ViewCube.** A manipulator icon in the upper-right corner of the view panel for quickly changing the current view.

* **Voxel.** A single cell of a fluid; used to compute fluid dynamics.

* **Wedge.** A model structure created by rotating a face about an edge and connecting it to the original face's position.

* **Wire deformer.** A curve that is attached to a selected set of components under its influence.

* **Wireframe.** A display method that shows scene objects using contour lines.

* **XGen System**. An advanced system for adding hair and fur to objects.

Index

F

G

H

I

J

K

L

M

N

O

P

Q

R

S

T

U

V

W

X

Y

Z

9781630578084